Lecture Notes in Computer Science   13992

Advanced Research in Computing and Software Science
Subline of Lecture Notes in Computer Science

More information about this series at https://link.springer.com/bookseries/558

Orna Kupferman · Pawel Sobocinski
Editors

Foundations of Software Science and Computation Structures

26th International Conference, FoSSaCS 2023
Held as Part of the European Joint Conferences
on Theory and Practice of Software, ETAPS 2023
Paris, France, April 22–27, 2023
Proceedings

Editors
Orna Kupferman
The Hebrew University of Jerusalem
Jerusalem, Israel

Pawel Sobocinski
Tallinn University of Technology
Tallinn, Estonia

ISSN 0302-9743   ISSN 1611-3349   (electronic)
Lecture Notes in Computer Science
ISBN 978-3-031-30828-4   ISBN 978-3-031-30829-1   (eBook)
https://doi.org/10.1007/978-3-031-30829-1

ETAPS Foreword

Welcome to the 26th ETAPS! ETAPS 2023 took place in Paris, the beautiful capital of France. ETAPS 2023 was the 26th instance of the European Joint Conferences on Theory and Practice of Software. ETAPS is an annual federated conference established in 1998, and consists of four conferences: ESOP, FASE, FoSSaCS, and TACAS. Each conference has its own Program Committee (PC) and its own Steering Committee (SC). The conferences cover various aspects of software systems, ranging from theoretical computer science to foundations of programming languages, analysis tools, and formal approaches to software engineering. Organising these conferences in a coherent, highly synchronized conference programme enables researchers to participate in an exciting event, having the possibility to meet many colleagues working in different directions in the field, and to easily attend talks of different conferences. On the weekend before the main conference, numerous satellite workshops took place that attracted many researchers from all over the globe.

ETAPS 2023 received 361 submissions in total, 124 of which were accepted, yielding an overall acceptance rate of 34.3%. I thank all the authors for their interest in ETAPS, all the reviewers for their reviewing efforts, the PC members for their contributions, and in particular the PC (co-)chairs for their hard work in running this entire intensive process. Last but not least, my congratulations to all authors of the accepted papers!

ETAPS 2023 featured the unifying invited speakers Véronique Cortier (CNRS, LORIA laboratory, France) and Thomas A. Henzinger (Institute of Science and Technology, Austria) and the conference-specific invited speakers Mooly Sagiv (Tel Aviv University, Israel) for ESOP and Sven Apel (Saarland University, Germany) for FASE. Invited tutorials were provided by Ana-Lucia Varbanescu (University of Twente and University of Amsterdam, The Netherlands) on heterogeneous computing and Joost-Pieter Katoen (RWTH Aachen, Germany and University of Twente, The Netherlands) on probabilistic programming.

As part of the programme we had the second edition of TOOLympics, an event to celebrate the achievements of the various competitions or comparative evaluations in the field of ETAPS.

ETAPS 2023 was organized jointly by Sorbonne Université and Université Sorbonne Paris Nord. Sorbonne Université (SU) is a multidisciplinary, research-intensive and worldclass academic institution. It was created in 2018 as the merge of two first-class research-intensive universities, UPMC (Université Pierre and Marie Curie) and Paris-Sorbonne. SU has three faculties: humanities, medicine, and 55,600 students (4,700 PhD students; 10,200 international students), 6,400 teachers, professor-researchers and 3,600 administrative and technical staff members. Université Sorbonne Paris Nord is one of the thirteen universities that succeeded the University of Paris in 1968. It is a major teaching and research center located in the north of Paris. It has five campuses, spread over the two departments of Seine-Saint-Denis and Val d'Oise: Villetaneuse, Bobigny, Saint-Denis, the Plaine Saint-Denis and Argenteuil. The university has more than 25,000 students in different fields, such as health, medicine, languages, humanities, and science. The local organization team consisted of Fabrice Kordon (general co-chair), Laure Petrucci (general co-chair), Benedikt Bollig (workshops), Stefan Haar (workshops), Étienne André (proceedings and tutorials), Céline Ghibaudo (sponsoring), Denis Poitrenaud (web), Stefan Schwoon (web), Benoît Barbot (publicity), Nathalie Sznajder (publicity), Anne-Marie Reytier (communication), Hélène Pétridis (finance) and Véronique Criart (finance).

ETAPS 2023 is further supported by the following associations and societies: ETAPS e.V., EATCS (European Association for Theoretical Computer Science), EAPLS (European Association for Programming Languages and Systems), EASST (European Association of Software Science and Technology), Lip6 (Laboratoire d'Informatique de Paris 6), LIPN (Laboratoire d'informatique de Paris Nord), Sorbonne Université, Université Sorbonne Paris Nord, CNRS (Centre national de la recherche scientifique), CEA (Commissariat à l'énergie atomique et aux énergies alternatives), LMF (Laboratoire méthodes formelles), and Inria (Institut national de recherche en informatique et en automatique).

The ETAPS Steering Committee consists of an Executive Board, and representatives of the individual ETAPS conferences, as well as representatives of EATCS, EAPLS, and EASST. The Executive Board consists of Holger Hermanns (Saarbrücken), Marieke Huisman (Twente, chair), Jan Kofroň (Prague), Barbara König (Duisburg), Thomas Noll (Aachen), Caterina Urban (Inria), Jan Křetínský (Munich), and Lenore Zuck (Chicago).

Other members of the steering committee are: Dirk Beyer (Munich), Luís Caires (Lisboa), Ana Cavalcanti (York), Bernd Finkbeiner (Saarland), Reiko Heckel (Leicester), Joost-Pieter Katoen (Aachen and Twente), Naoki Kobayashi (Tokyo), Fabrice Kordon (Paris), Laura Kovács (Vienna), Orna Kupferman (Jerusalem), Leen Lambers (Cottbus), Tiziana Margaria (Limerick), Andrzej Murawski (Oxford), Laure Petrucci (Paris), Elizabeth Polgreen (Edinburgh), Peter Ryan (Luxembourg), Sriram Sankaranarayanan (Boulder), Don Sannella (Edinburgh), Natasha Sharygina (Lugano), Pawel Sobocinski (Tallinn), Sebastián Uchitel (London and Buenos Aires), Andrzej Wasowski (Copenhagen), Stephanie Weirich (Pennsylvania), Thomas Wies (New York), Anton Wijs (Eindhoven), and James Worrell (Oxford).

I would like to take this opportunity to thank all authors, keynote speakers, attendees, organizers of the satellite workshops, and Springer-Verlag GmbH for their support. I hope you all enjoyed ETAPS 2023.

Finally, a big thanks to Laure and Fabrice and their local organization team for all their enormous efforts to make ETAPS a fantastic event.

April 2023

Marieke Huisman
ETAPS SC Chair
ETAPS e.V. President

Preface

This volume contains the papers presented at the 26th International Conference on Foundations of Software Science and Computation Structures (FoSSaCS 2023), which was held 24–27 April, 2023, in Paris, France. The conference is dedicated to foundational research with a clear significance for software science and brings together research on theories and methods to support the analysis, integration, synthesis, transformation, and verification of programs and software systems.

The program consisted of 26 contributed papers, selected from among 85 submissions. Each submission was assessed by three or more Program Committee members. The conference management system EasyChair was used to handle the submissions, to conduct the electronic Program Committee discussions, and to assist with the assembly of the proceedings.

We wish to thank all the authors who submitted papers for consideration, the members of the Program Committee for their conscientious work, and all additional reviewers who assisted the Program Committee in the evaluation process. Finally, we would like to thank the ETAPS organization for providing an excellent environment for FoSSaCS, other conferences, and workshops.

February 2023

Orna Kupferman
Pawel Sobocinski

Organization

Program Committee

Parosh Aziz Abdulla	Uppsala University, Sweden
Giovanni Bacci	Aalborg University, Denmark
Patrick Baillot	CNRS and Université de Lille, France
Nathalie Bertrand	Inria, France
Lars Birkedal	Aarhus University, Denmark
Véronique Bruyère	University of Mons, Belgium
Marco Carbone	IT University of Copenhagen, Denmark
Thomas Colcombet	CNRS, France
Ugo Dal Lago	Università di Bologna, Italy and Inria Sophia Antipolis, France
Emmanuel Filiot	Université libre de Bruxelles, Belgium
Marco Gaboardi	Boston University, USA
Bart Jacobs	Radboud University, The Netherlands
Bartek Klin	University of Oxford, UK
Orna Kupferman	Hebrew University of Jerusalem, Israel
Barbara König	University of Duisburg-Essen, Germany
Assia Mahboubi	Inria, France
Shahar Maoz	Tel Aviv University, Israel
Kuldeep S. Meel	National University of Singapore, Singapore
Stefan Milius	FAU Erlangen, Germany
Filip Murlak	University of Warsaw, Poland
Koko Muroya	RIMS, Kyoto University, Japan
Joel Ouaknine	Max Planck Institute for Software Systems, Germany
Alexandra Silva	University College London, UK
Pawel Sobocinski	Tallinn University of Technology, Estonia
Sam Staton	University of Oxford, UK
Alwen Tiu	Australian National University, Australia
Frank Valencia	LIX, Ecole Polytechnique, France
Daniele Varacca	LACL - Université Paris Est Créteil, France

Additional Reviewers

Aguirre, Alejandro
Akshay, S.
Aranda, Jesus
Arsiwalla, Xerxes
Asada, Kazuyuki
Aubert, Clément
Bacci, Giorgio
Bahr, Patrick
Balachander, Mrudula
Balaji, Nikhil
Balasubramanian, A. R.
Baldan, Paolo
Bansal, Suguman
Barbarossa, Davide
Basold, Henning
Benerecetti, Massimo
Bengtson, Jesper
Bernardi, Giovanni
Boker, Udi
Bonchi, Filippo
Brice, Léonard
Béal, Marie-Pierre
Casares, Antonio
Castiglioni, Valentina
Chockler, Hana
Chroboczek, Juliusz
Clairambault, Pierre
Clemente, Lorenzo
Clouston, Ranald
Cohen, Liron
Corbyn, Nathan
Corradini, Andrea
Danielsson, Nils Anders
Dantchev, Stefan
de Groot, Jim
de Vilhena, Paulo
Dell'Erba, Daniele
Demangeon, Romain
Dima, Catalin
Dragoi, Cezara
Dubut, Jérémy
Fahrenberg, Uli
Feier, Cristina

Fijalkow, Nathanaël
Finster, Eric
Fiterau-Brostean, Paul
Freund, Anton
Ganty, Pierre
Gavazzo, Francesco
Geeraerts, Gilles
Ghyselen, Alexis
Goy, Alexandre
Gratzer, Daniel
Guilmant, Quentin
Gurke, Sebastian
Gutierrez, Julian
Hadzihasanovic, Amar
Hamel-de Le Court, Edwin
Hansen, Helle Hvid
Helouet, Loic
Henry, Léo
Hirschowitz, Tom
Hofman, Piotr
Hou, Zhe
Jaber, Guilhem
Jaquard, Arthur
Jindal, Gorav
Jonsson, Bengt
Kappé, Tobias
Karimov, Toghrul
Kavvos, Alex
Kelmendi, Edon
Kerjean, Marie
Kopczynski, Eryk
Kruckman, Alex
Lebeda, Christian Janos
Li, Yong
Lucyshyn-Wright, Rory
Luttik, Bas
Main, James C. A.
Marin, Sonia
Markey, Nicolas
Mascle, Corto
Mathur, Umang
Mazza, Damiano
McKenzie, Pierre

Michaliszyn, Jakub
Michaux, Christian
Mimram, Samuel
Morales Elena, Marianela
Nieuwveld, Joris
Niewerth, Matthias
Niwinski, Damian
Norrish, Michael
Nuyts, Andreas
Olarte, Carlos
Oliva, Paulo
Pagani, Michele
Patterson, Evan
Perez, Guillermo
Piedeleu, Robin
Pinzón, Carlos
Pommellet, Adrien
Pous, Damien
Pradic, Pierre
Praveen, M.
Purser, David
Ramírez, Sergio
Raskin, Jean-Francois
Reynouard, Raphaël
Riba, Colin
Román, Mario
Rossberg, Andreas
Rot, Jurriaan
Saivasan, Prakash
Sakayori, Ken
Sanan, David
Sangnier, Arnaud
Sankur, Ocan
Schmid, Todd
Schmitz, Sylvain

Shevrin, Ilia
Shillito, Ian
Shirmohammadi, Mahsa
Skrzypczak, Michał
Sokolova, Ana
Spies, Simon
Stefanesco, Leo
Stefański, Rafał
Stein, Dario
Sterling, Jonathan
Totzke, Patrick
Traytel, Dmitriy
Tsampas, Stelios
Tsukada, Takeshi
Ulrik, Nikolaj Jensen
Urbat, Henning
Vahanwala, Mihir
van der Weide, Niels
van Dijk, Tom
van Glabbeek, Rob
van Gool, Sam
Vandenhove, Pierre
Vignudelli, Valeria
Vilmart, Renaud
Vákár, Matthijs
Wagemaker, Jana
Wang, Di
Weininger, Maximilian
Winskel, Glynn
Winter, Sarah
Wißmann, Thorsten
Worrell, James
Yamakami, Tomoyuki
Yatapanage, Nisansala

Contents

When Programs Have to Watch Paint Dry

Danel Ahman[✉]

Faculty of Mathematics and Physics, University of Ljubljana, Ljubljana, Slovenia
danel.ahman@fmf.uni-lj.si

Abstract. We explore type systems and programming abstractions for
the safe usage of resources. In particular, we investigate how to use types
to modularly specify and check *when* programs are allowed to use their
resources, e.g., when programming a robot arm on a production line, it
is crucial that painted parts are given enough time to dry before assembly. We capture such *temporal resources* using a time-graded variant of
Fitch-style modal type systems, develop a corresponding modally typed,
effectful core calculus, and equip it with a graded-monadic denotational
semantics illustrated by a concrete presheaf model. Our calculus also includes graded algebraic effects and effect handlers. They are given a novel
temporally aware treatment in which operations' specifications include
their execution times and their continuations know that an operation's
worth of additional time has passed before they start executing, making
it possible to safely access further temporal resources in them.

Keywords: Temporal resources · Modal types · Graded monads ·
Algebraic effects · Effect handlers.

1 Introduction

The correct usage of resources is at the heart of many programs, especially if
they control safety-critical machinery. Such resources can take many different
forms: ensuring that file handles are not arbitrarily duplicated or discarded (as
captured by linear and uniqueness types) [11,25,40], or guaranteeing that communication happens according to protocols (as specified by session types) [30,70],
or controlling how data is laid out in memory (as in Hoare and separation logics) [2,34,56,64], or assuring that resources are correctly finalised [1,43].

In contrast to the above approaches that predominantly focus on *how* resources are used, we study how to modularly specify and verify *when* programs
can use their resources—we call such resources *temporal*. For instance, consider
the following code snippet controlling a robot arm on a (car) production line:

```
let (body', left-door', right-door') = paint (body, left-door, right-door) in
assemble (body', left-door', right-door')
```

Here, the correct execution of the program (and thus operation of the robot
arm it is controlling) relies on the car parts given enough time to dry between
painting and assembly. Therefore, in its current form, the above code is correct

© The Author(s) 2023
O. Kupferman and P. Sobocinski (Eds.): FoSSaCS 2023, LNCS 13992, pp. 1–23, 2023.
https://doi.org/10.1007/978-3-031-30829-1_1

only if a compiler (or a scheduler) inserts enough of a time delay at compile time (resp. dynamically blocks program's execution for enough time) between the calls to paint and assemble. However, in either case, one still faces the question of how to reason about the correctness of the compiled code (resp. dynamic checks).

In this paper, we focus on developing a type system based means for reasoning about the temporal correctness of the code that the above-mentioned compiler might produce, or that a programmer might write directly when full control of the code is important. In particular, we had *three desiderata* we set out to fulfil:

1. We did not want the delay between paint and assemble to be limited to just *blocking execution*, with the robot sitting idly while watching paint dry. Instead, we wanted a flexible formalism that would allow the robot to spend that time *doing other useful work*, while ensuring that enough time passes.

2. We wanted the *passage of time of program execution to be modelled within the type system*, rather than being left to some unspecified meta-level run-time.

3. We wanted the resulting language to give programmers the freedom to *redefine the behaviour of operations* such as paint and assemble, say, via *effect handling* [61], while respecting the operations' temporal specifications.

Paper Structure We achieve these goals by designing a *mathematically natural core programming language* for safe and correct programming with temporal resources: on the one hand, based on a time-graded, temporal variant of *Fitch-style modal type systems* [19,27], and on the other hand, on *graded monads* [35,51,67].

We review modal types and discuss how we use them to capture temporal resources in §2. In §3, we present $\lambda_{[\tau]}$—our modally typed, effectful, equationally presented core calculus for safe programming with temporal resources. We justify the design of $\lambda_{[\tau]}$ by giving it a mathematically natural sound denotational semantics in §4, based on graded monads and adjunctions between strong monoidal functors, including a concrete presheaf example. In §5, we briefly discuss a specialisation of $\lambda_{[\tau]}$ with equations for time delays. We review related work and remark on future work in §6, and conclude in §7. This paper is also accompanied by an online appendix (https://arxiv.org/abs/2210.07738) that presents further details of renamings and denotational semantics that we omit in §3 and §4.

For supplementary rigour, we have formalised the main results of §3 and §4 also in Agda [68], available at https://github.com/danelahman/temporal-resources/releases/tag/fossacs2023. Regrettably, it currently lacks (i) proofs of some auxiliary lemmas noted in Prop. 4 due to a bug in Agda where WITH-abstractions produce ill-typed terms,[1] and (ii) two laws of the presheaf model because unfolding of definitions produces unmanageably large terms for Agda.

2   Modal Types for Temporal Resources

We begin with an overview of (Fitch-style) modal type systems and how a time-graded variant of them naturally captures temporal aspects of resources.

---

[1] Eta-contraction is not type-preserving: https://github.com/agda/agda/issues/2732

2.1   (Fitch-Style) Modal Types

A *modal type system* extends the types of an underlying type system with new *modal type formers*,[2] e.g., $\Box X$, which states that the type is to be considered and reasoned about in a *different mode* compared to X, which can take many forms. For instance, in Kripke's possible worlds semantics, $\Box X$ means that values of type X are *available in all future worlds* [41]; in run-time code generation, the type $\Box X$ captures *generators of X-typed code* [72]; and in asynchronous and distributed programming, the type $\Box X$ specifies *mobile X-typed values* [3,54,63].

Many different approaches to presenting modal type systems have been developed, with one of the main culprits being the difficulty of getting the *introduction rule* for $\Box X$ correct. Namely, bearing in mind Kripke's possible worlds semantics, the introduction rule for $\Box X$ must allow one to use only those hypotheses that also hold in all future worlds, while at the same time ensuring that the system still enjoys expected structural properties. Solutions to this problem have involved proving $\Box X$ in a context containing only $\Box$-types [62] (with a failure of structural properties in the naive approaches), or building a form of explicit substitutions into the introduction rule for $\Box X$ to give the rule premise access to only $\Box$-types [12], or incorporating the Kripke semantics in the type system by explicitly indexing types with worlds [66]—see [37] for an in-depth survey.

In this paper, we build on *Fitch-style modal type systems* [15,19,27,48], where the typing rules for $\Box X$ are given with respect to another modality, $\blacksquare$, that acts on contexts, resulting in a particularly pleasant type-theoretic presentation.

As an illustrative example, in a Fitch-style modal type system corresponding to the modal logic S4 (whose Kripke models require the order on worlds to be reflexive and transitive, thus also corresponding to natural properties of time), the typing rules for variables and the $\Box X$ type have the following form:[3]

$$\frac{\blacksquare \notin \Gamma'}{\Gamma, x : X, \Gamma' \vdash x : X} \text{ Var} \qquad \frac{\Gamma, \blacksquare \vdash t : X}{\Gamma \vdash \text{shut } t : \Box X} \text{ Shut} \qquad \frac{\Gamma \vdash t : \Box X}{\Gamma, \Gamma' \vdash \text{open } t : X} \text{ Open}$$

Intuitively, the *context modality* $\blacksquare$ creates a barrier in the premise of Shut so that only $\Box$-typed variables can be used from Γ in t, achieving the above-mentioned correctness goal for the introduction rule of $\Box X$. Alternatively, in the context of Kripke's possible worlds semantics, one can also read the occurrences of the $\blacksquare$ modality as advancing the underlying world—in Shut, t in the premise is typed in some future world compared to where shut t is typed at. This intuition will be useful to how we use a similar modality to capture the passage of time in $\lambda_{[\tau]}$. The context weakening Γ, Γ' in Open ensures the admissibility of structural rules, and in the possible worlds reading, it intuitively expresses that if $\Box X$ is available in some world, then X will be available in all possible future worlds.

---

[2] For brevity, we use the term *modal type system* to interchangeably refer to both modal type systems and natural deduction systems of (intuitionistic) modal logics.

[3] Depending on which exact modal logic one is trying to capture, the form of contexts used in the introduction/elimination rules can differ, see [19] for a detailed overview.

2.2   Modal Types for Temporal Resources

Next, we give a high-level overview of how we use a time-graded variant of Fitch-style modal type systems to capture temporal properties of resources in $\lambda_{[\tau]}$. For this, we use the production line code snippet from §1 as a working example.

A Naive Approach Before turning to modal types, a naive solution to achieve the desired time delay would be for paint to return the required drying time and for the program to delay execution for that time duration, e.g., as expressed in

```
let (τ_dry, body', left-door', right-door') = paint (body, left-door, right-door) in
delay τ_dry;
assemble (body', left-door', right-door')
```

It is not difficult to see that we could generalise this solution to allow performing other useful activities while waiting for τ_{dry} time to pass. So are we done and can we conclude the paper here? Well, no, because this solution puts all the burden for writing correct code on the shoulders of the programmer, with successful typechecking giving no additional guarantees that τ_{dry} indeed will have passed.

A Temporal Resource Type Instead, inspired by Fitch-style modal type systems and Kripke's possible worlds semantics of the $\Box$-modality, we propose a *temporal resource type*, written $[\tau] X$, to specify that a value of type X will become available for use in *at most* τ time units, or to put it differently, the boxed value of type X can be explicitly unboxed only when *at least* τ time units have passed. Concretely, $[\tau] X$ is presented by the following two typing rules:

$$\frac{\text{Box}}{\Gamma, \langle \tau \rangle \vdash V : X}{\Gamma \vdash \text{box}_\tau V : [\tau] X} \qquad \frac{\text{Unbox}}{\tau \leqslant \text{time } \Gamma \quad \Gamma - \tau \vdash V : [\tau] X \quad \Gamma, x : X \vdash N : Y \,!\, \tau'}{\Gamma \vdash \text{unbox}_\tau V \text{ as } x \text{ in } N : Y \,!\, \tau'}$$

Above, τs are natural numbers that count discrete time moments, and $Y \,!\, \tau'$ is a type of computations returning Y-typed values and executing in τ' time units.

Analogously to the context modality $\blacklozenge$ of Fitch-style modal type systems, we introduce a similar *modality on contexts*, written $\langle \tau \rangle$, to express that when typechecking a term of the form $\Gamma, \langle \tau \rangle \vdash V : X$, we can safely assume that *at least* τ time will have passed before V is accessed or executed, as in the premise of the Box rule. Accordingly, in Unbox, we require that at least τ time units have passed since the resource V of type $[\tau] X$ was created or brought into scope, by typing V in the "earlier" context $\Gamma - \tau$ (we define this operation in §3.3).

Encapsulating temporal resources as a type gives us flexible first-class access to them, and allows to pack them in data structures and pass them to functions.

Modelling Passage of Time As we see in the Unbox rule, we can unbox a temporal resource only when enough time has passed since its creation. This begs the question: How can the passage of time be modelled within the type system?

For this, we propose a new notion of *temporally aware graded algebraic effects*, where each operation op is specified not only by its parameter and result types, but also by its prescribed execution time, and with op's continuation knowing that op's worth of additional time has passed before it begins executing. We refer the reader to [8,31,35,60] for background on ordinary (graded) algebraic effects.

For instance, the paint operation, taking τ_{paint} time, is typed in $\lambda_{[\tau]}$ as[4]

$$\frac{\Gamma \vdash V : \text{Body} \times \text{Door} \times \text{Door} \qquad \Gamma, \langle \tau_{\text{paint}} \rangle, x : [\tau_{\text{dry}}] \text{ Body} \times [\tau_{\text{dry}}] \text{ Door} \times [\tau_{\text{dry}}] \text{ Door} \vdash M : X \mathbin{!} \tau}{\Gamma \vdash \text{paint } V \ (x \,.\, M) : X \mathbin{!} \tau_{\text{paint}} + \tau}$$

Here, $\langle \tau_{\text{paint}} \rangle$ expresses that from the perspective of any unboxes in M, an *additional* τ_{paint} *time* will have passed compared to the beginning of the execution of paint $V \ (x \,.\, M)$, which is typed in the "earlier" context Γ. Also, observe that paint's result x is available *after* τ_{paint} time has passed (i.e., after paint finishes), and its type has the car part types wrapped as temporal resources, ensuring that any further operations (e.g., assemble) can access them only after *at least* τ_{dry} time has passed *after* paint finishes. The delay τ operation is typed analogously.

Finally, similarly to algebraic operations, we also use the context modality $\langle \tau \rangle$ to model the passage of time in sequential composition, as specified in

$$\frac{\Gamma \vdash M : X \mathbin{!} \tau \qquad \Gamma, \langle \tau \rangle, x : X \vdash N : Y \mathbin{!} \tau'}{\Gamma \vdash \text{let } x = M \text{ in } N : Y \mathbin{!} \tau + \tau'}$$

The type $X \mathbin{!} \tau$ (for specifying the execution time of computations) is standard from graded monads style effect systems [35]. The novelty of our work is to use this effect information to inform continuations that they can safely assume that the given amount of additional time has passed before they start executing.

Putting It All Together We conclude this overview by revisiting the production line code snippet and note that in the $\lambda_{[\tau]}$-calculus we can write it as

```
let (body', left-door', right-door') = paint (body, left-door, right-door) in
delay τ_dry;
unbox body' as body" in
unbox left-door' as left-door" in
unbox right-door' as right-door" in
assemble (body", left-door", right-door")
```

Observe that apart from the unbox operations, the code looks identical to the naive, unsafe solution discussed earlier. However, crucially, now any code that wants to use the outputs of paint will typecheck only if these resources are accessed after at least τ_{dry} time units have passed after paint finishes. In the code snippet, this is achieved by blocking execution with delay τ_{dry} for τ_{dry} time units, but this could have been equally well achieved by executing other useful operations $\text{op}_1; \ldots; \text{op}_n$, as long as they collectively take at least τ_{dry} time.

---

[4] We present $\lambda_{[\tau]}$ formally using algebraic operations with explicit continuations, while in code snippets we use so-called *generic effects* [59] without explicit continuations.

$$\begin{aligned}
\text{Time grade:} \quad & \tau \in \mathbb{N} \\
\text{Ground type } A, B, C \; ::= \; & \mathsf{b} \mid \mathsf{unit} \mid A \times B \mid [\tau]\, A \\
\text{Value type } X, Y, Z \; ::= \; & A \mid X \times Y \mid X \to Y\,!\,\tau \mid [\tau]\, X \\
\text{Computation type:} \quad & X\,!\,\tau
\end{aligned}$$

Fig. 1. Types of $\lambda_{[\tau]}$.

3   A Calculus for Programming with Temporal Resources

We now recast the ideas explained above as a formal, modally typed, effectful core calculus, called $\lambda_{[\tau]}$. We base it on the fine-grain call-by-value λ-calculus [44].

3.1   Types

The types of $\lambda_{[\tau]}$ are given in Fig. 1. *Ground types* include base types b, and are closed under finite products and the modal *temporal resource type* $[\tau]\, A$. The latter denotes that an A-typed value will become available in *at most* τ time units, where $\tau \in \mathbb{N}$ counts discrete time moments.[5] The ground types can also come with *constants* f with associated *constant signatures* $\mathsf{f} : (A_1, \ldots, A_n) \to B$.

To model operations such as paint and $\mathsf{assemble}$ discussed in §2.2, we assume a set of *operations symbols* $\mathcal{O}$, with each $\mathsf{op} \in \mathcal{O}$ assigned an *operation signature* $\mathsf{op} : A_{\mathsf{op}} \rightsquigarrow B_{\mathsf{op}}\,!\,\tau_{\mathsf{op}}$, which specifies that op accepts inputs of type A_{op}, returns values of type B_{op}, and its execution takes τ_{op} time units. Observe that by typing operations with ground types, as opposed to simply with base types, we can specify operations such as $\mathsf{paint} : \mathsf{Part} \rightsquigarrow ([\tau_{\mathrm{dry}}]\,\mathsf{Part})\,!\,\tau_{\mathrm{paint}}$, returning values that can be accessed only after a certain amount of time, here, after τ_{dry}.

Value types extend ground types with *function type* $X \to Y\,!\,\tau$ that specifies functions taking X-typed arguments to computations that return Y-typed values and take τ time to execute, as expressed by the *computation type* $Y\,!\,\tau$.

3.2   Terms

The syntax of terms is given in Fig. 2, separated into values and computations.

Values include variables, constants, finite tuples, functions, and the *boxing up of temporal resources*, $\mathsf{box}_\tau\, V$, which allows us to consider an arbitrary value V as a temporal resource as long as it is safe to access V after τ time units.

Computations include returning values, sequential composition, function application, pattern-matching[6], algebraic operation calls, effect handling, and the *unboxing of temporal resources*, where given a temporal resource V of type $[\tau]\, X$,

---

[5] For concreteness, we work with $(\mathbb{N}, 0, +, \dot{-}, \leqslant)$ for time grades, but we do not foresee problems generalising these to come from other analogous algebraic structures.

[6] The form $\mathsf{let}\ (x, y, z) = M\ \mathsf{in}\ N$ in §1,2 is the natural combination of let and match.

Values

$$V, W ::= x \qquad\qquad\qquad\qquad\qquad\text{variable}$$

$$| \quad f(V_1, \ldots, V_n) \qquad\qquad\qquad \text{constant}$$

$$| \quad () \mid (V, W) \qquad\qquad\qquad\quad \text{unit and pairing}$$

$$| \quad \text{fun } (x : X) \mapsto M \qquad\qquad \text{function}$$

$$| \quad \text{box}_\tau V \qquad\qquad\qquad\qquad \text{boxing up a temporal resource}$$

Computations

$$M, N ::= \text{return } V \qquad\qquad\qquad\qquad \text{returning a value}$$

$$| \quad \text{let } x = M \text{ in } N \qquad\qquad \text{sequential composition}$$

$$| \quad V\, W \qquad\qquad\qquad\qquad\quad \text{function application}$$

$$| \quad \text{match } V \text{ with } \{(x, y) \mapsto N\} \qquad \text{pattern-matching}$$

$$| \quad \text{op } V\, (x . M) \qquad\qquad\qquad \text{operation call}$$

$$| \quad \text{delay } \tau\, M \qquad\qquad\qquad\quad \text{time delay}$$

$$| \quad \text{handle } M \text{ with } H \text{ to } x \text{ in } N \qquad \text{effect handling}$$

$$| \quad \text{unbox}_\tau V \text{ as } x \text{ in } N \qquad\quad \text{unboxing a temporal resource}$$

Effect handlers

$$H ::= (x . k . M_{\text{op}})_{\text{op} \in \mathcal{O}} \qquad\qquad \text{operation clauses}$$

Fig. 2. Values, computations, and effect handlers of $\lambda_{[\tau]}$.

the computation $\text{unbox}_\tau V$ as x in N is used to access the underlying value of type X if at least τ time units have passed since the creation of the resource V.

In addition to user-specifiable operation calls (via operation signatures and effect handling), we include a separate $\text{delay } \tau\, M$ operation that blocks the execution of its continuation for the given amount of time. For simplicity, we require effect handlers to have *operation clauses* M_{op} for all op $\in \mathcal{O}$, but we do not allow delays to be handled in light of the equations we want of them in §5, where all consecutive delays are collapsed and all zero-delays are removed.

3.3 Type System

We now equip $\lambda_{[\tau]}$ with a modal type-and-effect system. On the one hand, for modelling temporal resources, we build on Fitch-style modal type systems [19]. On the other hand, for modelling effectful computations and their specifications, we build on type-and-effect systems for calculi based on graded monads [35].

The *typing judgements* are written as $\Gamma \vdash V : X$ and $\Gamma \vdash M : X \,!\, \tau$, where τ specifies M's execution time and Γ is a *temporal typing context*, given by

$$\Gamma ::= \cdot \mid \Gamma, x : X \mid \Gamma, \langle \tau \rangle$$

Here, $\langle \tau \rangle$ is a *temporal context modality*, akin to $\blacksquare^\curvearrowright$ in Fitch-style systems. We use it to express that when typechecking a term of the form $\Gamma, \langle \tau \rangle \vdash V : X$, we

Values

$$
\text{VAR} \quad \frac{}{\Gamma, x:X, \Gamma' \vdash x:X}
$$

$$
\text{CONST} \quad \frac{(\Gamma \vdash V_i : A_i)_{1 \leqslant i \leqslant n}}{\Gamma \vdash \mathsf{f}(V_1, \ldots, V_n) : B}
$$

$$
\text{PAIR} \quad \frac{\Gamma \vdash V:X \qquad \Gamma \vdash W:Y}{\Gamma \vdash (V,W):X \times Y}
$$

$$
\text{UNIT} \quad \frac{}{\Gamma \vdash ():\mathsf{unit}}
$$

$$
\text{FUN} \quad \frac{\Gamma, x:X \vdash M:Y\,!\,\tau}{\Gamma \vdash \mathsf{fun}\,(x:X) \mapsto M : X \to Y\,!\,\tau}
$$

$$
\text{BOX} \quad \frac{\Gamma, \langle \tau \rangle \vdash V:X}{\Gamma \vdash \mathsf{box}_\tau\, V : [\tau]\,X}
$$

Computations

$$
\text{RETURN} \quad \frac{\Gamma \vdash V:X}{\Gamma \vdash \mathsf{return}\,V : X\,!\,0}
$$

$$
\text{LET} \quad \frac{\Gamma \vdash M:X\,!\,\tau \qquad \Gamma, \langle \tau \rangle, x:X \vdash N:Y\,!\,\tau'}{\Gamma \vdash \mathsf{let}\,x = M\,\mathsf{in}\,N : Y\,!\,\tau + \tau'}
$$

$$
\text{APPLY} \quad \frac{\Gamma \vdash V:X \to Y\,!\,\tau \qquad \Gamma \vdash W:X}{\Gamma \vdash VW : Y\,!\,\tau}
$$

$$
\text{MATCH} \quad \frac{\Gamma \vdash V:X \times Y \qquad \Gamma, x:X, y:Y \vdash N:Z\,!\,\tau}{\Gamma \vdash \mathsf{match}\,V\,\mathsf{with}\,\{(x,y) \mapsto N\} : Z\,!\,\tau}
$$

$$
\text{OP} \quad \frac{\Gamma \vdash V:A_{\mathsf{op}} \qquad \Gamma, \langle \tau_{\mathsf{op}} \rangle, x:B_{\mathsf{op}} \vdash M:X\,!\,\tau}{\Gamma \vdash \mathsf{op}\,V\,(x.M) : X\,!\,\tau_{\mathsf{op}} + \tau}
$$

$$
\text{DELAY} \quad \frac{\Gamma, \langle \tau \rangle \vdash M:X\,!\,\tau'}{\Gamma \vdash \mathsf{delay}\,\tau\,M : X\,!\,\tau + \tau'}
$$

$$
\text{HANDLE} \quad \frac{\Gamma \vdash M:X\,!\,\tau \qquad \Gamma, \langle \tau \rangle, x:X \vdash N:Y\,!\,\tau' \qquad H = (x\,.\,k\,.\,M_{\mathsf{op}})_{\mathsf{op} \in \mathcal{O}} \qquad \left(\forall \tau''\,.\,\Gamma, x:A_{\mathsf{op}}, k:[\tau_{\mathsf{op}}]\,(B_{\mathsf{op}} \to Y\,!\,\tau'') \vdash M_{\mathsf{op}} : Y\,!\,\tau_{\mathsf{op}} + \tau''\right)_{\mathsf{op} \in \mathcal{O}}}{\Gamma \vdash \mathsf{handle}\,M\,\mathsf{with}\,H\,\mathsf{to}\,x\,\mathsf{in}\,N : Y\,!\,\tau + \tau'}
$$

$$
\text{UNBOX} \quad \frac{\tau \leqslant \mathsf{time}\,\Gamma \qquad \Gamma - \tau \vdash V:[\tau]\,X \qquad \Gamma, x:X \vdash N:Y\,!\,\tau'}{\Gamma \vdash \mathsf{unbox}_\tau\,V\,\mathsf{as}\,x\,\mathsf{in}\,N : Y\,!\,\tau'}
$$

Fig. 3. Typing rules of $\lambda_{[\tau]}$.

can safely assume that *at least* τ time will have passed before the resource V is accessed or executed. The *rules* defining these judgements are given in Fig. 3.

In contrast to Fitch-style modal type systems discussed in §2.1, VAR does not restrict the Γ' right of x to not include any context modalities. This is so because in the possible worlds reading of $\lambda_{[\tau]}$ (see §4) we treat all types as being monotone for time—this is not usually the case for formulae in modal logics such as S4, but in $\lambda_{[\tau]}$ this models that once any value is available it will remain so.

As in systems based on graded monads, RETURN specifies that returning a value takes zero time, and LET that the execution time of sequentially composed computations is the sum of the individual ones. Novel to $\lambda_{[\tau]}$, LET, OP, DELAY, and HANDLE state that the continuations can safely assume that relevant amount of additional time has passed before they start executing, as discussed in §2.2.

When typing the operation clauses M_{op} in HANDLE, we universally quantify (at the meta-level) over the execution time τ'' of the continuation k of M_{op}. We do so as the operation clauses M_{op} must be able to execute at any point when effect handling recursively traverses M. Further, observe that k is wrapped inside a resource type. This ensures that k is invoked only after τ_{op} amount of time has been spent in M_{op}, thus guaranteeing that the temporal discipline is respected. Note that this enforces a *linear* discipline for our effect handlers: for $\tau_{op} > 0$, k must be executed exactly once for M_{op}'s execution time to match $\tau_{op} + \tau''$.

Finally, BOX specifies that in order to box up a value V of type X as a temporal resource of type $[\tau] X$, we must be able to type V when assuming that τ additional time units will have passed before V is accessed. At the same time, UNBOX specifies that we can unbox a temporal resource V of type $[\tau] X$ only if at least τ time units have passed since its creation: the time captured by Γ must be at least τ, and we must be able to type V in a τ time units "earlier" context $\Gamma - \tau$. The *time captured by a context*, time Γ, is calculated recursively as

$$\text{time} \cdot \overset{\text{def}}{=} 0 \qquad \text{time}\,(\Gamma, x : X) \overset{\text{def}}{=} \text{time}\,\Gamma \qquad \text{time}\,(\Gamma, \langle\tau\rangle) \overset{\text{def}}{=} \text{time}\,\Gamma + \tau$$

and the *"time travelling"* operation $\Gamma - \tau$ as (where $\tau_+ \equiv 1 + \tau''$ for some τ'')

$$\Gamma - 0 \overset{\text{def}}{=} \Gamma \qquad \cdot - \tau_+ \overset{\text{def}}{=} \cdot \qquad (\Gamma, x : X) - \tau_+ \overset{\text{def}}{=} \Gamma - \tau_+$$

$$(\Gamma, \langle\tau'\rangle) - \tau_+ \overset{\text{def}}{=} \text{if } \tau_+ \leqslant \tau' \text{ then } \Gamma, \langle\tau' \dot- \tau_+\rangle \text{ else } \Gamma - (\tau_+ \dot- \tau')$$

taking Γ to an "earlier" state by removing τ worth of modalities and variables.

3.4 Admissibility of Renamings and Substitutions

We now show that expected *structural* and *substitution rules* [7] are admissible.

Theorem 1. *The typing relations $\Gamma \vdash V : X$ and $\Gamma \vdash M : X\,!\,\tau$ are closed under standard structural rules of weakening, exchange of consecutive variables, and contraction (omitted here). Furthermore, both typing relations are also closed under rules making $\langle-\rangle$ into a strong monoidal functor (with a co-strength) [45]:*

$$\frac{\Gamma, \langle 0 \rangle \vdash J}{\Gamma \vdash J} \qquad \frac{\Gamma, \langle \tau_1 + \tau_2 \rangle \vdash J}{\Gamma, \langle \tau_1 \rangle, \langle \tau_2 \rangle \vdash J} \qquad \frac{\Gamma, \langle \tau \rangle \vdash J \quad \tau \leqslant \tau'}{\Gamma, \langle \tau' \rangle \vdash J} \qquad \frac{\Gamma, \langle \tau \rangle, x : X \vdash J}{\Gamma, x : X, \langle \tau \rangle \vdash J}$$

where $\Gamma \vdash J$ ranges over both typing relations, where the first two rules hold in both directions, and the last rule expresses that if we can type J using a variable "now", we can also type J if that variable was brought into scope "earlier".

Proof. First, we define a *renaming relation* $\rho : \Gamma \rightsquigarrow \Gamma'$, and then prove by induction that if $\Gamma \vdash J$ and $\rho : \Gamma \rightsquigarrow \Gamma'$ then $\Gamma' \vdash J[\rho]$, where $J[\rho]$ is J renamed with ρ. The $\rightsquigarrow$ relation is defined as the reflexive-transitive-congruent closure of rules corresponding to the desired structural rules, e.g., $\text{var}^r_{x : X \in \Gamma} : \Gamma, y : X \rightsquigarrow \Gamma$ and $\mu^r : \Gamma, \langle \tau_1 + \tau_2 \rangle \rightsquigarrow \Gamma, \langle \tau_1 \rangle, \langle \tau_2 \rangle$. The full list is given in the online appendix.

For the VAR and UNBOX cases of the proof, we show that if $\rho : \Gamma \rightsquigarrow \Gamma'$ and $x \in_\tau \Gamma$, then $\rho x \in_{\tau'} \Gamma'$ for some τ' with $\tau \leqslant \tau'$, where $x \in_\tau \Gamma$ means that $x \in \Gamma$ and there is τ worth of modalities right of x in Γ, and ρx is the variable that ρ maps x to. For UNBOX, we further prove that if $\rho : \Gamma \rightsquigarrow \Gamma'$, then for any τ

we can build $\rho - \tau : \Gamma - \tau \rightsquigarrow \Gamma' - \tau$, using the result about ϵ_τ to ensure that ρ does not map any $x \in \Gamma - \tau$ outside of $\Gamma' - \tau$. We also establish that if $\Gamma \rightsquigarrow \Gamma'$, then time $\Gamma \leqslant$ time Γ', allowing us to deduce $\tau \leqslant$ time Γ' from $\tau \leqslant$ time Γ.

The admissibility of the rules corresponding to μ^r (and its inverse) relies on us having defined context splitting in UNBOX using $\Gamma - \tau$, as opposed to more rigidly as Γ, Γ', as in [19], as then it would be problematic if the split happens between $\langle \tau_1 \rangle, \langle \tau_2 \rangle$. Inverses of the last two rules in Thm. 1 are not valid—they would allow unboxing temporal resources without enough time having passed.

Theorem 2. *The typing relations $\Gamma \vdash V : X$ and $\Gamma \vdash M : X \, ! \, \tau$ are closed under substitution, i.e., if $\Gamma, x : X, \Gamma' \vdash J$ and $\Gamma \vdash W : X$, then $\Gamma, \Gamma' \vdash J[W/x]$, where $J[W/x]$ is standard recursively defined capture-avoiding substitution [7].*

Proof. The proof proceeds by induction on the derivation of $\Gamma, x : X, \Gamma' \vdash J$. The most involved case is UNBOX, where we construct the derivation of $\Gamma, \Gamma' \vdash$ unbox$_\tau$ $V[W/x]$ as y in $N[W/x] : Y \, ! \, \tau'$ by first analysing whether $\tau \leqslant$ time Γ', which tells us whether x is in the context $(\Gamma, x : X, \Gamma') - \tau$ of V, based on which we learn whether W continues to be substituted for x in V or whether $V[W/x] = V$.

3.5   Equational Theory

We conclude the definition of $\lambda_{[\tau]}$ by equipping it with an *equational theory* to reason about program equivalence, defined using judgements $\Gamma \vdash V \equiv W : X$ and $\Gamma \vdash M \equiv N : X \, ! \, \tau$, where we presuppose that the terms are well-typed for the given contexts and types. The rules defining these relations are given in Fig. 4. We omit standard equivalence, congruence, and substitutivity rules [7].

The equational theory consists of standard β/η-equations for the unit, product, and function types. We also include monadic equations for return and let [52]. For op and delay, we include algebraicity equations, allowing us to pull them out of let [8]. For handle, we include equations expressing that effect handling recursively traverses a term, replacing each op-occurrence with the operation clause M_{op}, leaving delays untouched, and finally executes the continuation N when reaching return values [61]. Finally, we include β/η-equations for box and unbox, expressing that unbox behaves as a pattern-matching elimination form for box.

4   Denotational Semantics

We justify the design of $\lambda_{[\tau]}$ by giving it a mathematically natural semantics based on *adjunctions between strong monoidal functors* [45] (modelling modalities) and a *strong[7] graded monad* [35] (modelling computations). We assume general knowledge of category theory, only spelling out details specific to $\lambda_{[\tau]}$. To optimise for space, we discuss the abstract model structure simultaneously with a concrete example using presheaves [46], but note that the interpretation is defined, and its soundness proved, with respect to the abstract structure.

---

[7] To be more specific, we use a modal notion of $[-]$-*strength* that we define below.

$$() \equiv V : \mathsf{unit} \qquad (\eta)$$

$$\mathsf{fun}\ (x : X) \mapsto V\, x \equiv V : X \to Y\,!\,\tau \qquad (\eta)$$

$$(\mathsf{fun}\ (x : X) \mapsto M)\, V \equiv M[V/x] \qquad (\beta)$$

$$\mathsf{match}\ (V, W)\ \mathsf{with}\ \{(x, y) \mapsto N\} \equiv N[V/x, W/y] \qquad (\beta)$$

$$\mathsf{match}\ V\ \mathsf{with}\ \{(x, y) \mapsto N[(x, y)/z]\} \equiv N[V/z] \qquad (\eta)$$

$$\mathsf{let}\ x = (\mathsf{return}\ V)\ \mathsf{in}\ N \equiv N[V/x] \qquad (\beta)$$

$$\mathsf{let}\ y = (\mathsf{let}\ x = M\ \mathsf{in}\ N)\ \mathsf{in}\ P \equiv \mathsf{let}\ x = M\ \mathsf{in}\ (\mathsf{let}\ y = N\ \mathsf{in}\ P) \qquad (\beta)$$

$$\mathsf{let}\ x = M\ \mathsf{in}\ \mathsf{return}\ x \equiv M \qquad (\eta)$$

$$\mathsf{let}\ x = (\mathsf{op}\ V\ (y.\,M))\ \mathsf{in}\ N \equiv \mathsf{op}\ V\ (y.\,\mathsf{let}\ x = M\ \mathsf{in}\ N) \qquad (\beta)$$

$$\mathsf{let}\ x = (\mathsf{delay}\ \tau\ M)\ \mathsf{in}\ N \equiv \mathsf{delay}\ \tau\ (\mathsf{let}\ x = M\ \mathsf{in}\ N) \qquad (\beta)$$

$$\mathsf{handle}\ (\mathsf{return}\ V)\ \mathsf{with}\ H\ \mathsf{to}\ x\ \mathsf{in}\ N \equiv N[V/x] \qquad (\beta)$$

$$\mathsf{handle}\ (\mathsf{op}\ V\ (y.\,M))\ \mathsf{with}\ H\ \mathsf{to}\ x\ \mathsf{in}\ N \equiv$$
$$M_{\mathsf{op}}[V/x, \mathsf{box}_{\tau_{\mathsf{op}}}\ (\mathsf{fun}\ (y : B_{\mathsf{op}}) \mapsto \mathsf{handle}\ M\ \mathsf{with}\ H\ \mathsf{to}\ x\ \mathsf{in}\ N)/k] \qquad (\beta)$$

$$\mathsf{handle}\ (\mathsf{delay}\ \tau\ M)\ \mathsf{with}\ H\ \mathsf{to}\ x\ \mathsf{in}\ N \equiv \mathsf{delay}\ \tau\ (\mathsf{handle}\ M\ \mathsf{with}\ H\ \mathsf{to}\ x\ \mathsf{in}\ N) \qquad (\beta)$$

$$\mathsf{unbox}_\tau\ (\mathsf{box}_\tau\ V)\ \mathsf{as}\ x\ \mathsf{in}\ N \equiv N[V/x] \qquad (\beta)$$

$$\mathsf{unbox}_\tau\ V\ \mathsf{as}\ x\ \mathsf{in}\ N[\mathsf{box}_\tau\ x/y] \equiv N[V/y] \qquad (\eta)$$

Fig. 4. Equational theory of $\lambda_{[\tau]}$.

When referring to the *abstract model structure*, we denote the underlying category with $\mathbb{C}$. Meanwhile, the *concrete presheaf example* is given in $\mathsf{Set}^{(\mathbb{N}, \leqslant)}$, consisting of functors from $(\mathbb{N}, \leqslant)$ to the category Set of sets and functions.

The model in $\mathsf{Set}^{(\mathbb{N}, \leqslant)}$ is similar to Kripke's possible worlds semantics, except that in $\mathsf{Set}^{(\mathbb{N}, \leqslant)}$ all objects are *monotone* for $\leqslant$, i.e., for any $A \in \mathsf{Set}^{(\mathbb{N}, \leqslant)}$ we have functions $A(t_1 \leqslant t_2) : A(t_1) \to A(t_2)$ respecting reflexivity and transitivity, whereas Kripke models are commonly given by discretely indexed presheaves and only modalities change worlds. For $\lambda_{[\tau]}$, working in $\mathsf{Set}^{(\mathbb{N}, \leqslant)}$ gives us that when a resource becomes available, it will remain so without need for reboxing, leading to a more natural system for temporal resources and a simpler VAR rule.

4.1 Interpretation of Types

Value Types and Contexts To interpret value types, we require the category $\mathbb{C}$ to have *finite products* $(\mathbb{1}, A \times B)$ and *exponentials* $A \Rightarrow B$, so as to model the unit, product, and function types. In $\mathsf{Set}^{(\mathbb{N}, \leqslant)}$, the former are given pointwise using the finite products in Set, and the latter are given as $(A \Rightarrow B)(t) \stackrel{\mathrm{def}}{=} \mathsf{Set}^{(\mathbb{N}, \leqslant)}(\mathrm{hom}\, t \times A, B)$, where $\mathrm{hom}\, t : (\mathbb{N}, \leqslant) \to \mathsf{Set}$ is the covariant *hom-functor* for $(\mathbb{N}, \leqslant)$, given by $\hom t \overset{\text{def}}{=} t \leqslant (-)$ [46]. When unfolding it further, the above means that $(A \Rightarrow B)(t)$ is the set of functions $(f_{t'} : A(t') \to B(t'))_{t' \in \{t' \in \mathbb{N} | t \leqslant t'\}}$ that are natural in t', capturing the intuition that in $\lambda_{[\tau]}$ functions can be applied in any future context. For base types, we require an object $[\![b]\!]$ of $\mathbb{C}$ for each b.

To interpret the temporal resource type, we require a *strong monoidal functor* $[-] : (\mathbb{N}, \leqslant) \to [\mathbb{C}, \mathbb{C}]$, where $[\mathbb{C}, \mathbb{C}]$ is the category of endofunctors on $\mathbb{C}$. This means that we have functors $[\tau] : \mathbb{C} \to \mathbb{C}$, for all $\tau \in \mathbb{N}$, together with morphisms $[\tau_1 \leqslant \tau_2]_A : [\tau_1]A \to [\tau_2]A$, natural in A and respecting $\leqslant$. Strong monoidality of $[-]$ means that we have natural isomorphisms $\varepsilon_A : [0]A \overset{\cong}{\to} A$ and $\delta_{A,\tau_1,\tau_2} : [\tau_1 + \tau_2]A \overset{\cong}{\to} [\tau_1]([\tau_2]A)$, satisfying time-graded variants of comonad laws [10]:

$$\varepsilon \circ \delta_{A,0,\tau} \equiv \text{id} \qquad [\tau](\varepsilon) \circ \delta_{A,\tau,0} \equiv \text{id} \qquad \delta_{[\tau_3]A,\tau_1,\tau_2} \circ \delta_{A,\tau_1+\tau_2,\tau_3} \equiv [\tau_1](\delta) \circ \delta$$

We also require $(\delta_{A,\tau_1,\tau_2}, \delta^{-1}_{A,\tau_1,\tau_2})$ to be monotone in τ_1, τ_2, i.e., if $\tau_1 \leqslant \tau_1'$ and $\tau_2 \leqslant \tau_2'$, then $[\tau_1']([\tau_2 \leqslant \tau_2']) \circ [\tau_1 \leqslant \tau_1'] \circ \delta \equiv \delta \circ [\tau_1 + \tau_2 \leqslant \tau_1' + \tau_2']_A$. We omit the indices of the components of natural transformations when convenient.

In $\mathbf{Set}^{(\mathbb{N}, \leqslant)}$, we define $([\tau]A)(t) \overset{\text{def}}{=} A(t + \tau)$, with $[\tau]A$-values given by future A-values, and with $(\varepsilon_A, \varepsilon_A^{-1}, \delta_A, \delta_A^{-1})$ given by identities on A-values, combined with the laws of $(0, +)$, e.g., as $(\varepsilon_A)_t (a \in ([0]A)(t) \equiv A(t + 0)) \overset{\text{def}}{=} a \in A(t)$.

Using the above, we interpret a value type X as an object $[\![X]\!]$ of $\mathbb{C}$, as

$$[\![A]\!] \overset{\text{def}}{=} [\![A]\!]^g \qquad [\![\text{unit}]\!] \overset{\text{def}}{=} \mathbb{1} \qquad [\![X \times Y]\!] \overset{\text{def}}{=} [\![X]\!] \times [\![Y]\!]$$

$$[\![X \to Y\,!\,\tau]\!] \overset{\text{def}}{=} [\![X]\!] \Rightarrow T\,\tau\,[\![Y]\!] \qquad [\![[\tau]\,X]\!] \overset{\text{def}}{=} [\tau][\![X]\!]$$

where T is a graded monad for modelling computations—we return to it below. The interpretation of ground types $[\![A]\!]^g$ is defined similarly, so we omit it here.

Next, we define the interpretation of contexts, for which we require another *strong monoidal functor*, $\langle - \rangle : (\mathbb{N}, \leqslant)^{\text{op}} \to [\mathbb{C}, \mathbb{C}]$. Note that $\langle - \rangle$ is *contravariant*—this enables us to model the structural rules that allow terms typed in an earlier context to be used in future ones (see Thm. 1). We denote the strong monoidal structure of $\langle - \rangle$ with $\eta_A : A \overset{\cong}{\to} \langle 0 \rangle A$ and $\mu_{A,\tau_1,\tau_2} : \langle \tau_1 \rangle (\langle \tau_2 \rangle A) \overset{\cong}{\to} \langle \tau_1 + \tau_2 \rangle A$, required to satisfy time-graded variants of monad laws [45], given by

$$\mu_{A,0,\tau} \circ \eta \equiv \text{id} \qquad \mu_{A,\tau,0} \circ \langle \tau \rangle(\eta) \equiv \text{id} \qquad \mu_{A,\tau_1+\tau_2,\tau_3} \circ \mu_{\langle \tau_3 \rangle A,\tau_1,\tau_2} \equiv \mu \circ \langle \tau_1 \rangle(\mu)$$

and $(\mu_{A,\tau_1,\tau_2}, \mu^{-1}_{A,\tau_1,\tau_2})$ have to be monotone in τ_1, τ_2, similarly to (δ, δ^{-1}) above.

In $\mathbf{Set}^{(\mathbb{N}, \leqslant)}$, we define $(\langle \tau \rangle A)(t) \overset{\text{def}}{=} (\tau \leqslant t) \times A(t \,\dot{-}\, \tau)$, as past A-values, with the *side-condition* $\tau \leqslant t$ crucial for the existence of the adjunctions $\langle \tau \rangle \dashv [\tau]$ we require below. We define $(\eta_A, \eta_A^{-1}, \mu_A, \mu_A^{-1})$ similarly to earlier, as identities on A-values, combined with the laws of $(0, +, \dot{-})$, so as to satisfy the side-conditions.

With this, we can interpret *contexts* Γ as *functors* $[\![\Gamma]\!] : \mathbb{C} \to \mathbb{C}$, given by:

$$[\![\cdot]\!]A \overset{\text{def}}{=} A \qquad [\![\Gamma, x : X]\!]A \overset{\text{def}}{=} [\![\Gamma]\!]A \times [\![X]\!] \qquad [\![\Gamma, \langle \tau \rangle]\!]A \overset{\text{def}}{=} \langle \tau \rangle([\![\Gamma]\!]A)$$

We interpret contexts as functors to easily manipulate denotations of composite contexts, e.g., we then have $\iota_{\Gamma;\Gamma';A} : [\![\Gamma, \Gamma']\!]A \overset{\cong}{\to} [\![\Gamma']\!]([\![\Gamma]\!]A)$, natural in A.

Finally, to formulate the semantics of computation types and terms, we require there to be a family of *adjunctions* $\langle\tau\rangle \dashv [\tau]$, i.e., natural transformations $\eta^{\dashv}_{A,\tau} : A \to [\tau](\langle\tau\rangle A)$ (the *unit*) and $\varepsilon^{\dashv}_{A,\tau} : \langle\tau\rangle([\tau]A) \to A$ (the *counit*), for all $\tau \in \mathbb{N}$, satisfying time-graded variants of standard adjunction laws [45], given by

$$\varepsilon^{\dashv}_{\langle\tau\rangle A,\tau} \circ \langle\tau\rangle(\eta^{\dashv}_{A,\tau}) \equiv \mathsf{id} \qquad [\tau](\varepsilon^{\dashv}_{A,\tau}) \circ \eta^{\dashv}_{[\tau]A,\tau} \equiv \mathsf{id}$$

We also require $(\eta^{\dashv}, \varepsilon^{\dashv})$ to interact well with the strong monoidal structures:

$$[\tau](\langle 0 \leqslant \tau\rangle) \circ \eta^{\dashv}_{A,\tau} \circ \eta^{-1} \circ \varepsilon \equiv [0 \leqslant \tau] \qquad [\tau_1](\,[\tau_2](\mu)) \circ [\tau_1](\eta^{\dashv}_{\langle\tau_1\rangle A,\tau_2}) \circ \eta^{\dashv}_{A,\tau_1} \equiv \delta \circ \eta^{\dashv}$$

$$\langle 0\rangle([0 \leqslant \tau]) \circ \eta \circ \varepsilon^{-1} \circ \varepsilon^{\dashv}_{A,\tau} \equiv \langle 0 \leqslant \tau\rangle \quad \varepsilon^{\dashv}_{A,\tau_1} \circ \langle\tau_1\rangle(\varepsilon^{\dashv}_{[\tau_1]A,\tau_2}) \circ \langle\tau_1\rangle(\langle\tau_2\rangle(\delta)) \equiv \varepsilon^{\dashv} \circ \mu$$

Proposition 1. *It then follows that* $\eta^{\dashv}_{A,0} \equiv \varepsilon^{-1}_{\langle 0\rangle A} \circ \eta_A$ *and* $\varepsilon^{\dashv}_{A,0} \equiv \varepsilon_A \circ \eta^{-1}_{[0]A}$.

In $\mathsf{Set}^{(\mathbb{N},\leqslant)}$, $\eta^{\dashv}_{A,\tau}$ and $\varepsilon^{\dashv}_{A,\tau}$ are given by identities on A-values, respectively combined with $\tau \leqslant t + \tau$ and monotonicity for $(t \mathbin{\dot-} \tau) + \tau \equiv t$. For the latter, we crucially know $\tau \leqslant t$ due to the side-condition included in the definition of $\langle-\rangle$.

We note that modulo the time grades τ, the above structure is analogous to the models of the Fitch-style presentation of S4 [19], where $\square$ is modelled by an idempotent comonad, $\blacklozenge$ by an idempotent monad, and boxing/unboxing by $\blacklozenge \dashv \square$. This is also why we present $[-]$ and $\langle-\rangle$ as comonad- and monad-like.

Computation Types For computation types, we require a $[-]$-*strong graded monad* $(T, \eta^T, \mu^T, \mathsf{str}^T)$ on $\mathbb{C}$, with grades in $\mathbb{N}$.[8] In detail, this means a functor $T : \mathbb{N} \to [\mathbb{C}, \mathbb{C}]$, together with natural transformations $\eta^T_A : A \to T\,0\,A$ (the *unit*), $\mu^T_{A,\tau_1,\tau_2} : T\,\tau_1(T\,\tau_2\,A) \to T\,(\tau_1 + \tau_2)\,A$ (the *multiplication*), and $\mathsf{str}^T_{A,B,\tau} : [\tau]A \times T\,B\,\tau \to T\,(A \times B)\,\tau$ (the *strength*), with the first two satisfying standard graded monad laws (see [35] or (η, μ) of $\langle-\rangle$). Below we only present the laws for str^T because it has a novel temporal aspect to it—its first argument appears under $[\tau]$. As such, str^T expresses that if we know an A-value will be available after τ time units, we can push it into computations taking τ-time to execute.

We say that T is a $[-]$-strong graded monad following the parlance of Bierman and de Paiva [12]—in their work they model the possibility modality $\Diamond A$ as a $\square$-strong monad. While the laws governing str^T are not overly different from standard graded strength laws [35], we have to correctly account for $[-]$ in them

$$\mathsf{str}^T_{A,B,0} \circ (\varepsilon^{-1}_A \times \eta^T_A) \equiv \eta^T_{A \times B} \quad \mu^T_{A \times B,\tau_1,\tau_2} \circ T\,(\mathsf{str}^T) \circ \mathsf{str}^T \equiv \mathsf{str}^T \circ (\delta^{-1} \times \mu^T)$$

$$T\,(\mathsf{snd}) \circ \mathsf{str}^T_{A,B,\tau} \equiv \mathsf{snd} \quad T\,(\alpha) \circ \mathsf{str}^T \circ (\mathsf{m} \times \mathsf{id}) \circ \alpha^{-1} \equiv \mathsf{str}^T_{A,B \times C,\tau} \circ (\mathsf{id} \times \mathsf{str}^T)$$

where $\alpha_{A,B,C} : (A \times B) \times C \xrightarrow{\cong} A \times (B \times C)$, and $\mathsf{m}_{A,B,\tau} : [\tau]A \times [\tau]B \to [\tau](A \times B)$ witnesses that $[\tau]$ is monoidal for $\times$, which follows from $[\tau]$ being a right adjoint [45]. Observe that it is the $[-]$-strength that naturally gives T a temporal flavour—the rest of it is standard [35]. Below we show that str^T is also mathematically natural, admitting an analogous characterisation to ordinary strength.

---

[8] As $\lambda_{[\tau]}$ does not include sub-effecting (see §6.2), a discretely graded monad T suffices.

Proposition 2. *Analogously to ordinary strong and enriched monads [39], T having $[-]$-strength is equivalent to $[-]$-enrichment of T, given by morphisms $[\tau](A \Rightarrow B) \to (T\tau A \Rightarrow T\tau B)$ respecting $\mathbb{C}$'s self-enrichment [38] and (η^T, μ^T).*

In order to model operations op and delay in §4.2, we require T to be equipped with *algebraic operations*: we ask there to be families of natural transformations $\mathsf{op}^T_{A,\tau} : [\![A_{\mathsf{op}}]\!]^g \times [\tau_{\mathsf{op}}]([\![B_{\mathsf{op}}]\!]^g \Rightarrow T\tau A) \to T(\tau_{\mathsf{op}} + \tau) A$, for all op $: A_{\mathsf{op}} \rightsquigarrow B_{\mathsf{op}} ! \tau_{\mathsf{op}} \in \mathcal{O}$, and $\mathsf{delay}^T_{A,\tau'} \tau : [\tau](T\tau' A) \to T(\tau + \tau') A$, for all $\tau \in \mathbb{N}$, satisfying algebraicity laws [61], which state that both commute with μ^T and str^T, e.g.,

$$\mathsf{str}^T_{A,B,\tau+\tau'} \circ (\mathsf{id} \times \mathsf{delay}^T \tau) \equiv \mathsf{delay}^T_{A \times B, \tau'} \tau \circ [\tau](\mathsf{str}^T) \circ \mathsf{m} \circ (\delta_{A,\tau,\tau'} \times \mathsf{id})$$

In $\mathsf{Set}^{(\mathbb{N}, \leqslant)}$, we can define T as the initial algebra of a corresponding signature functor for operations op and delay, analogously to the usual treatment of algebraic effects [8]. Concretely, such T is determined inductively by three cases

$$\frac{a \in A(t)}{\mathsf{ret}\, a \in (T\, 0\, A)(t)} \qquad \frac{\substack{a \in [\![A_{\mathsf{op}}]\!]^g(t)\\ k \in ([\tau_{\mathsf{op}}]([\![B_{\mathsf{op}}]\!]^g \Rightarrow T\tau A))(t)}}{\mathsf{op}\, a\, k \in (T(\tau_{\mathsf{op}} + \tau) A)(t)} \qquad \frac{k \in [\tau](T\tau' A)(t)}{\mathsf{delay}\, \tau\, k \in (T(\tau + \tau') A)(t)}$$

with $(\eta^T, \mu^T, \mathsf{str}^T, \mathsf{op}^T, \mathsf{delay}^T)$ defined in the expected way, e.g., str^T is given by recursively traversing a computation of type $T\tau B$ and moving the argument of type $[\tau]A$ under ret cases, modifying τ when going under the op and delay cases.

4.2 Interpretation of Value and Computation Terms

The interpretation of values and computations is defined simultaneously. We only present the temporally interesting cases—full details are in the online appendix.

As $\lambda_{[\tau]}$ does not have sub-effecting and includes enough type annotations for typing derivations to be unique, this interpretation is *coherent* by construction.

Values We assume a morphism $[\![\mathsf{f}]\!] : [\![A_1]\!]^g \times \ldots \times [\![A_n]\!]^g \to [\![B]\!]^g$ for every $\mathsf{f} : (A_1, \ldots, A_n) \to B$. We interpret a well-typed value $\Gamma \vdash V : X$ as a morphism $[\![\Gamma \vdash V : X]\!] : [\![\Gamma]\!]1 \to [\![X]\!]$ in $\mathbb{C}$ by induction on the given typing derivation.

Most of the value cases are standard, and analogous to other calculi based on fine-grain call-by-value [44] and graded monads [35], using the Cartesian-closed structure of $\mathbb{C}$. The temporally interesting cases are VAR and BOX, given by

$$[\![\Gamma, x : X, \Gamma' \vdash x : X]\!] \stackrel{\mathsf{def}}{=} [\![\Gamma, x : X, \Gamma']\!]1 \stackrel{\iota}{\longrightarrow} [\![\Gamma']\!]([\![\Gamma]\!]1 \times [\![X]\!])$$

$$\stackrel{e}{\longrightarrow} \langle \mathsf{time}\, \Gamma' \rangle([\![\Gamma]\!]1 \times [\![X]\!]) \stackrel{\varepsilon^{\Diamond}}{\longrightarrow} [\![\Gamma]\!]1 \times [\![X]\!] \stackrel{\mathsf{snd}}{\longrightarrow} [\![X]\!]$$

$$[\![\Gamma \vdash \mathsf{box}_\tau\, V : [\tau]\, X]\!] \stackrel{\mathsf{def}}{=} [\![\Gamma]\!]1 \stackrel{\eta^{-1}}{\longrightarrow} [\tau](\langle \tau \rangle([\![\Gamma]\!]1)) \stackrel{[\tau]([\![V]\!])}{\longrightarrow} [\tau][\![X]\!]$$

where $\mathsf{e}_{A,\Gamma} : [\![\Gamma]\!]A \to \langle \mathsf{time}\, \Gamma \rangle A$ extracts and collapses all temporal modalities in Γ, and the counit-like $\varepsilon^{\Diamond}_{A,\tau}$ is given by the composite $\langle \tau \rangle A \stackrel{\langle 0 \leqslant \tau \rangle A}{\longrightarrow} \langle 0 \rangle A \stackrel{\eta^{-1}_A}{\longrightarrow} A$.

Computations We interpret a well-typed computation $\Gamma \vdash M : X \,!\, \tau$ as a morphism $[\![\Gamma \vdash M : X \,!\, \tau]\!] : [\![\Gamma]\!]1 \to T\,\tau\,[\![X]\!]$ in $\mathbb{C}$ by induction on the typing derivation. The definition is largely unsurprising and follows a pattern similar to [35,44]—the novelty lies in controlling the occurrences of $\langle - \rangle$ and $[-]$.

In LET, we use $\langle \tau \rangle \dashv [\tau]$ to push the environment "into the future", and then follow the standard monadic strength-followed-by-multiplication pattern [35,52]:

$$[\![\Gamma \vdash \mathsf{let}\ x = M\ \mathsf{in}\ N : Y \,!\, \tau + \tau']\!] \overset{\text{def}}{=} [\![\Gamma]\!]1 \xrightarrow{\langle \eta^{\dashv}, [\![M]\!] \rangle} [\tau](\langle \tau \rangle([\![\Gamma]\!]1)) \times T\,\tau\,[\![X]\!]$$
$$\xrightarrow{\mathsf{str}^T} T\,\tau\,(\langle \tau \rangle([\![\Gamma]\!]1) \times [\![X]\!]) \xrightarrow{T\,([\![N]\!])} T\,\tau\,(T\,\tau'\,[\![Y]\!]) \xrightarrow{\mu^T} T\,(\tau + \tau')\,[\![Y]\!]$$

An analogous use of $\langle \tau \rangle \dashv [\tau]$ also appears in the cases for operations, e.g., in

$$[\![\Gamma \vdash \mathsf{op}\ V\ (x\,.\,M) : X \,!\, \tau_{\mathsf{op}} + \tau]\!] \overset{\text{def}}{=} [\![\Gamma]\!]1 \xrightarrow{\langle [\![V]\!], \eta^{\dashv} \rangle} [\![A_{\mathsf{op}}]\!]^g \times [\tau_{\mathsf{op}}](\langle \tau_{\mathsf{op}} \rangle([\![\Gamma]\!]1))$$
$$\xrightarrow{\mathsf{id} \times [\tau_{\mathsf{op}}](\mathsf{curry}([\![M]\!]))} [\![A_{\mathsf{op}}]\!]^g \times [\tau_{\mathsf{op}}]([\![B_{\mathsf{op}}]\!]^g \Rightarrow T\,\tau\,[\![X]\!]) \xrightarrow{\mathsf{op}^T} T\,(\tau_{\mathsf{op}} + \tau)\,[\![X]\!]$$

Next, the UNBOX case of the interpretation is defined as

$$[\![\Gamma \vdash \mathsf{unbox}_\tau\ V\ \mathsf{as}\ x\ \mathsf{in}\ N : Y \,!\, \tau']\!] \overset{\text{def}}{=} [\![\Gamma]\!]1 \xrightarrow{\langle \mathsf{id}, \eta^{\mathrm{PRA}} \rangle} [\![\Gamma]\!]1 \times \langle \tau \rangle([\![\Gamma - \tau]\!]1)$$
$$\xrightarrow{\mathsf{id} \times \langle \tau \rangle([\![V]\!])} [\![\Gamma]\!]1 \times \langle \tau \rangle([\tau][\![X]\!]) \xrightarrow{\mathsf{id} \times \varepsilon^{\dashv}} [\![\Gamma]\!]1 \times [\![X]\!] \xrightarrow{[\![N]\!]} T\,\tau'\,[\![Y]\!]$$

showing that temporal resources follow the common pattern in which elimination forms are modelled by counits of adjunctions, whereas units model introduction forms (akin to functions). The morphism $\eta^{\mathrm{PRA}}_{\Gamma,A,\tau} : [\![\Gamma]\!]A \to \langle \tau \rangle([\![\Gamma - \tau]\!]A)$ extracts and collapses τ worth of context modalities in Γ, as long as $\tau \leqslant \mathsf{time}\ \Gamma$. It is a semantic counterpart to an observation that the context modality $\Gamma, \langle \tau \rangle$ is a *parametric right adjoint* to the $\Gamma - \tau$ operation, as in recent dependently typed presentations of Fitch-style modal types [27], see §6.1 for further discussion.

Finally, we discuss the interpretation of effect handling. For this, we additionally require $\mathbb{C}$ to have *set-indexed products* $\Pi_{i \in I} A_i$ and *handling morphisms*

$$\chi_{A,\tau,\tau'} : \Pi_{\mathsf{op} \in \mathcal{O}} \Pi_{\tau'' \in \mathbb{N}}\big(([\![A_{\mathsf{op}}]\!]^g \times [\tau_{\mathsf{op}}]([\![B_{\mathsf{op}}]\!]^g \Rightarrow T\,\tau''\,A)) \Rightarrow T\,(\tau_{\mathsf{op}} + \tau'')\,A\big)$$
$$\to T\,\tau\,(T\,\tau'\,A) \Rightarrow T\,(\tau + \tau')\,A$$

satisfying laws which state that χ_A returns a graded T-algebra [22,50], e.g., we require $\mathsf{uncurry}(\chi_{A,0,\tau'}) \circ (\mathsf{id} \times \eta^T) \equiv \mathsf{snd}$, where $\mathsf{uncurry}$ (and curry earlier) is part of the universal property of $A \Rightarrow B$. We also require similar laws for χ's interaction with op^T and delay^T. In $\mathsf{Set}^{(\mathbb{N}, \leqslant)}$, χ is defined by recursively traversing a given tree, replacing all occurrences of $\mathsf{op}\ a\ k$ with respective operation clauses. Writing $\mathcal{H}$ for the domain of $\chi_{[\![Y]\!], \tau, \tau'}$, the HANDLE case is then defined as

$$[\![\Gamma \vdash \mathsf{handle}\ M\ \mathsf{with}\ H\ \mathsf{to}\ x\ \mathsf{in}\ N : Y \,!\, \tau + \tau']\!] \overset{\text{def}}{=}$$

$$[\![\Gamma]\!]1 \xrightarrow{\langle \mathsf{id}, \langle \eta^{\dashv}, [\![M]\!] \rangle \rangle} [\![\Gamma]\!]1 \times \big([\tau](\langle \tau \rangle([\![\Gamma]\!]1)) \times T\,\tau\,[\![X]\!]\big)$$
$$\xrightarrow{\mathsf{id} \times \mathsf{str}^T} [\![\Gamma]\!]1 \times T\,\tau\,(\langle \tau \rangle([\![\Gamma]\!]1) \times [\![X]\!]) \xrightarrow{\mathsf{id} \times T\,\tau\,([\![N]\!])} [\![\Gamma]\!]1 \times T\,\tau\,(T\,\tau'\,[\![Y]\!])$$
$$\xrightarrow{[\![H]\!] \times \mathsf{id}} \mathcal{H} \times T\,\tau\,(T\,\tau'\,[\![Y]\!]) \xrightarrow{\mathsf{uncurry}(\chi_{[\![Y]\!], \tau, \tau'})} T\,(\tau + \tau')\,[\![Y]\!]$$

where we write $[\![H]\!]$ for the point-wise interpretation of operation clauses

$$[\![\Gamma]\!]\mathbb{1} \xrightarrow{\langle\langle\mathrm{id}\rangle_{\tau''\in\mathbb{N}}\rangle_{\mathrm{op}\in\mathcal{O}}} \Pi_{\mathrm{op}\in\mathcal{O}}\Pi_{\tau''\in\mathbb{N}}\big([\![\Gamma]\!]\mathbb{1}\big) \xrightarrow{\Pi_{\mathrm{op}\in\mathcal{O}}\Pi_{\tau''\in\mathbb{N}}\big(\mathrm{curry}([\![M_{\mathrm{op}}\,\tau'']\!]\circ\alpha^{-1})\big)} \mathcal{H}$$

4.3   Renamings, Substitutions, and Soundness

We now show how syntactic renamings and substitutions relate to semantic morphism composition, using which we then prove the interpretation to be *sound*.

Proposition 3. *Given $\rho : \Gamma \rightsquigarrow \Gamma'$ and $\Gamma \vdash J$, then $[\![J[\rho]]\!] \equiv [\![J]\!]\circ[\![\rho]\!]_\mathbb{1}$, where the interpretation of renamings $[\![\rho]\!]_A : [\![\Gamma']\!]A \to [\![\Gamma]\!]A$ is defined by induction on the derivation of $\rho : \Gamma \rightsquigarrow \Gamma'$, with the morphism $[\![\rho]\!]_A$ also natural in A.*

Proposition 4. *Given $\Gamma, x : X, \Gamma' \vdash J$ and $\Gamma \vdash W : X$, we have $[\![J[W/x]]\!] \equiv [\![J]\!] \circ \iota^{-1}_{\Gamma,x:X;\Gamma';\mathbb{1}} \circ [\![\Gamma']\!](\langle\mathrm{id}, [\![W]\!]\rangle) \circ \iota_{\Gamma;\Gamma';\mathbb{1}}$, where (ι, ι^{-1}) are discussed in §4.1.*

Proof. We prove both results by induction on the derivation of $\Gamma \vdash J$. The proofs are unsurprising but require us to prove auxiliary lemmas about recursively defined renamings and semantic morphisms. For example, for Prop. 3, we show $\eta^{\mathrm{PRA}}\circ[\![\rho]\!] \equiv \langle\tau\rangle([\![\rho-\tau]\!])\circ\eta^{\mathrm{PRA}} : [\![\Gamma']\!]A \to \langle\tau\rangle([\![\Gamma-\tau]\!]A)$, and for Prop. 4, that $\eta^{\mathrm{PRA}}\circ\iota \equiv \langle\tau\rangle(\iota)\circ\eta^{\mathrm{PRA}} : [\![\Gamma, \Gamma']\!]A \to \langle\tau\rangle([\![\Gamma'-\tau]\!]([\![\Gamma]\!]A))$, when $\tau \leqslant \mathrm{time}\ \Gamma'$. $\square$

Theorem 3. *Given $\Gamma \vdash I \equiv J$ derived using the rules in §3.5, then $[\![I]\!] \equiv [\![J]\!]$.*

Proof. The proof proceeds by induction on the derivation of $\Gamma \vdash I \equiv J$, using Prop. 3 and Prop. 4 to unfold the renamings and substitutions in the equations of §3.5, and using the properties of the abstract structure we required $\mathbb{C}$ to have. $\square$

5   Quotienting Delays

Observe that in $\lambda_{[\tau]}$ the computations delay τ (delay $\tau'\ M$) and delay $(\tau + \tau')\ M$ cannot be proved equivalent, though in some situations this might be desired.

In order to deem the above two programs (and others alike) equivalent, we extend $\lambda_{[\tau]}$'s equational theory with the following natural equations for delays:

$$\mathrm{delay}\ 0\ M \equiv M \qquad \mathrm{delay}\ \tau\ (\mathrm{delay}\ \tau'\ M) \equiv \mathrm{delay}\ (\tau + \tau')\ M$$

Theorem 4. *If the algebraic operations delay^T of T satisfy analogous two equations, the interpretation of §4 is sound for this extended equational theory.*

For the concrete model in $\mathrm{Set}^{(\mathbb{N}, \leqslant)}$, we have to *quotient* T [36] by these two equations—the resulting graded monad is determined inductively by the cases

$$\frac{k \in (S\,\tau\,A)(t)}{\mathrm{comp}\ k \in (T\,\tau\,A)(t)} \qquad \frac{\tau > 0 \qquad k \in [\tau](S\,\tau'\,A)(t)}{\mathrm{delay}\,\tau\,k \in (T\,(\tau + \tau')\,A)(t)}$$

$$\frac{a \in A(t)}{\mathrm{ret}\ a \in (S\,0\,A)(t)} \qquad \frac{a \in [\![A_{\mathrm{op}}]\!]^g(t) \qquad k \in ([\tau_{\mathrm{op}}]([\![B_{\mathrm{op}}]\!]^g \Rightarrow T\,\tau\,A))(t)}{\mathrm{op}\,a\,k \in (S\,(\tau_{\mathrm{op}} + \tau)\,A)(t)}$$

where $(T\,\tau\,A)(t)$ and $(S\,\tau\,A)(t)$ are defined simultaneously in such a way that only non-zero, non-consecutive delays can appear in the tree structure.

6   Related and Future Work

6.1   Related Work

We contribute to two prominent areas: (i) modal types and (ii) graded monads.

As noted in §2.1, *modal types* provide a mathematically natural means for capturing many aspects of programming. Adding to §2.1, types corresponding to the *eventually* and *always modalities* of temporal logics capture *functional reactive programming (FRP)* [18,32,42], including a combination with linearity and time-annotations to model resources [33], where *all* values are annotated with inhabitation times. Recently, FRP has also been studied in Fitch-style [6]. Starting with Nakano [55], modal types have also been used for *guarded recursion*, even in the dependently typed setting [5,14,47], including in Fitch-style [13].

We also note that $\lambda_{[\tau]}$'s time grades τ and the $\Gamma - \tau$ operation are closely related to recent dependently typed Fitch-style frameworks. Namely, [28] develops a *multimodal type theory* (MTT) where types $[\mu]X$ are indexed by 1-cells μ of a strict 2-category (a mode theory). The time grades τ of $\lambda_{[\tau]}$ are an example of such mode theories, given by the delooping of $\mathbb{N}$, i.e., by a single 0-cell, τs as 1-cells, and $\tau \leqslant \tau'$s as 2-cells. While ensuring the admissibility of and naturality under substitutions, MTT with its indirect elimination rule for $[\mu]X$ is weaker than earlier systems (such as [13]). The direct-style elimination rule is recovered in [27] by observing that in addition to $\Gamma, \langle \mu \rangle$ being a left adjoint to $[\mu]X$, it should further form a *parametric right adjoint (PRA)* [17,71] to contexts of the form $\Gamma/(r : \mu)$, where r is a substitution $\cdot, \langle \mu \rangle \rightsquigarrow \Gamma$. The operation $\Gamma - \tau$ in $\lambda_{[\tau]}$ is an instance of this: μ is a τ, r corresponds to the condition $\tau \leqslant$ time Γ in UN-BOX, contexts $\Gamma/(r : \mu)$ are given by $\Gamma - \tau$, and the PRA situation is witnessed by renamings $((\Gamma - \tau), \langle \tau \rangle) \rightsquigarrow \Gamma$, when $\tau \leqslant$ time Γ, and $\Gamma \rightsquigarrow ((\Gamma, \langle \tau \rangle) - \tau)$.

Graded monads provide a uniform framework for different effect systems and effect-based analyses [22,35,36,50,51]. A major contribution of ours is showing that context modalities can inform continuations of preceding computations' effects. While the theory of graded monads can be instantiated with any ordered monoid, we focus on natural numbers to model time, but do not expect complications generalising $\lambda_{[\tau]}$ to other structures with same properties as $(\mathbb{N}, 0, +, \dot{-}, \leqslant)$, and perhaps even to grading T and $\langle - \rangle, [-]$ with different structures, akin to [23].

Our use of $[\tau] X$ to restrict when resources are available is somewhat reminiscent of *coeffects* [16,24,57,58] and *quantitative type systems* [4,49,53]. In these works, variables are graded by (semi)ring-valued rs, as $x :_r X$, counting how many times and in which ways x is used, enabling applications such as liveness and dataflow analyses [57]. Semantically, these systems often interpret $x :_r X$ using a graded comonad, as $\Box_r X$, where one can access X only if $r \equiv 1$. Of such works, the closest to ours is that of Gaboardi et al. [23], who combine coeffects with effectful programs via distributive laws between the grades of coeffects and effects, allowing coeffectful analyses to be propagated through effectful computations.

We also note that the type $[\tau] X$ can be intuitively also viewed as a temporally-graded variant of *promise types* [29,65], in that it expresses that a value of type X will be available in the future, but with additional time guarantees.

6.2   Future Work

Currently, $\lambda_{[\tau]}$ does not support *sub-effecting*: we cannot deduce from $\tau \leqslant \tau'$ and $\Gamma \vdash M : X \,!\, \tau$ that $\Gamma \vdash M : X \,!\, \tau'$. Of course, we can simulate this by inserting $\tau' \dot{-} \tau$ worth of explicit delays into M, but this is extremely intensional, fixing where delays happen. In particular, we cannot type equations such as let $x =$ (return V) in $N \equiv N[V/x]$ if return V was sub-effected to $\tau > 0$, with the $\langle \tau \rangle$ in N's context the culprit. However, when considering sub-effecting as a *coercion* coerce$_{\tau \leqslant \tau'} M$, we believe we can add it by considering equations stating that it will produce *all the possible ways* how $\tau' \dot{-} \tau$ worth of delays could be inserted into M. Of course, this will require a more complex non-deterministic semantics.

It would be neat if $\lambda_{[\tau]}$ also included *recursion* in a way that programs could make use of the temporal discipline. This is likely unattainable for general recursion, but we hope that *primitive recursion* (say, on natural numbers) can be added via *type-dependency* of time grades τ on the values being recursed on.

It would be interesting to combine $\lambda_{[\tau]}$ with linear [25] and separation logics [34,64] to model *linear* and *spatial properties* of temporal resources. Another goal would be to add *concurrency*, e.g., using (multi)handlers [9,20,21]. We also plan to look into capturing *expiring* and *available-for-an-interval* style resources.

Further, we plan to study $\lambda_{[\tau]}$'s *operational semantics*, namely, one that takes time seriously and does not model delays simply as uninterpreted operations [9], together with developing a *prototype*, and proving *normalisation* akin to [26,69].

We also plan to study the *completeness* of the denotational semantics of $\lambda_{[\tau]}$. For such semantic investigations, it could be beneficial to also study the general theory of the kinds of temporally aware graded algebraic effects used in this paper, by investigating their *algebras* and *equational presentations* [36,50].

7   Conclusion

We have shown how a temporal, time-graded variant of Fitch-style modal type systems, when combined with an effect system based on graded monads, provides a natural framework for safe programming with temporal resources. To this end, we developed a modally typed, effectful, equationally-presented core calculus, and equipped it with a sound denotational semantics based on strong monoidal functors (for modelling modalities) and graded monads (for modelling effects). The calculus also includes temporally aware graded algebraic effects and effect handlers, with the continuations of the former knowing that an operation's worth of additional time has passed before they start executing, and where the user-defined effect handlers are guaranteed to respect this temporal discipline.

Acknowledgements We thank Andrej Bauer, Juhan-Peep Ernits, Niccolò Veltri, and Niels Voorneveld for useful discussions. We also thank one of the reviewers for drawing our attention to the recent work on presenting Fitch-style modal types in terms of parametric right adjoints, and its relationship to the work presented in this paper. This material is based upon work supported by the Air Force Office of Scientific Research under award number FA9550-21-1-0024.

References

1. Ahman, D., Bauer, A.: Runners in Action. In: Proc. of 29th European Symp. on Programming, ESOP 2020. Lect. Notes Comput. Sci., vol. 12075, pp. 29–55. Springer (2020)
2. Ahman, D., Fournet, C., Hritcu, C., Maillard, K., Rastogi, A., Swamy, N.: Recalling a witness: foundations and applications of monotonic state. Proc. ACM Program. Lang. **2**(POPL), 65:1–65:30 (2018)
3. Ahman, D., Pretnar, M., Radešček, J.: Higher-Order Asynchronous Effects (2021), extended abstract presented at the 9th ACM-SIGPLAN Wksh. on Higher-Order Programming with Effects, HOPE 2021
4. Atkey, R.: Syntax and Semantics of Quantitative Type Theory. In: Proc. of 33rd Annual ACM/IEEE Symp. on Logic in Computer Science, LICS 2018. pp. 56–65. ACM (2018)
5. Bahr, P., Grathwohl, H.B., Møgelberg, R.E.: The clocks are ticking: No more delays! In: Proc. of 32nd Annual ACM/IEEE Symp. on Logic in Computer Science, LICS 2017. pp. 1–12. IEEE Computer Society (2017)
6. Bahr, P., Graulund, C., Møgelberg, R.E.: Simply RaTT: a fitch-style modal calculus for reactive programming without space leaks. Proc. ACM Program. Lang. **3**(ICFP), 109:1–109:27 (2019)
7. Barendregt, H., Dekkers, W., Statman, R.: Lambda Calculus with Types. Cambridge University Press (2013)
8. Bauer, A.: What is algebraic about algebraic effects and handlers? CoRR **abs/1807.05923** (2018)
9. Bauer, A., Pretnar, M.: Programming with algebraic effects and handlers. J. Log. Algebr. Meth. Program. **84**(1), 108–123 (2015)
10. Beck, J.M.: Triples, algebras and cohomology. Reprints in Theory and Applications of Categories (2), 1–59 (2003), Note: Originally published as: Ph.D. thesis, Columbia University, 1967
11. Benton, N., Bierman, G.M., de Paiva, V., Hyland, M.: Linear lambda-calculus and categorial models revisited. In: Selected Papers from Computer Science Logic, CSL '92. Lect. Notes Comput. Sci., vol. 702, pp. 61–84. Springer (1992)
12. Bierman, G.M., de Paiva, V.: On an Intuitionistic Modal Logic. Studia Logica **65**(3), 383–416 (2000)
13. Birkedal, L., Clouston, R., Mannaa, B., Møgelberg, R.E., Pitts, A.M., Spitters, B.: Modal dependent type theory and dependent right adjoints. Math. Struct. Comput. Sci. **30**(2), 118–138 (2020)
14. Bizjak, A., Grathwohl, H.B., Clouston, R., Møgelberg, R.E., Birkedal, L.: Guarded Dependent Type Theory with Coinductive Types. In: Proc. of 19th Int. Conf. on Foundations of Software Science and Computation Structures, FoSSaCS 2016. Lect. Notes Comput. Sci., vol. 9634, pp. 20–35. Springer (2016)
15. Borghuis, V.: Coming to terms with modal logic: on the interpretation of modalities in typed lambda-calculus. Ph.D. thesis, Mathematics and Computer Science, Technische Universiteit Eindhoven (1994)
16. Brunel, A., Gaboardi, M., Mazza, D., Zdancewic, S.: A Core Quantitative Coeffect Calculus. In: Proc. of 23rd European Symp. on Programming, ESOP 2014. Lect. Notes Comput. Sci., vol. 8410, pp. 351–370. Springer (2014)
17. Carboni, A., Johnstone, P.: Connected limits, familial representability and artin glueing. Math. Struct. Comput. Sci. **5**(4), 441–459 (1995)

18. Cave, A., Ferreira, F., Panangaden, P., Pientka, B.: Fair reactive programming. In: Proc. of 41st Annual ACM SIGPLAN-SIGACT Symp. on Principles of Programming Languages, POPL 2014. pp. 361–372. ACM (2014)
19. Clouston, R.: Fitch-Style Modal Lambda Calculi. In: Proc. of 21st Int. Conf. on Foundations of Software Science and Computation Structures, FoSSaCS 2018. Lect. Notes Comput. Sci., vol. 10803, pp. 258–275. Springer (2018)
20. Convent, L., Lindley, S., McBride, C., McLaughlin, C.: Doo bee doo bee doo. J. Funct. Program. **30**, e9 (2020)
21. Dolan, S., Eliopoulos, S., Hillerström, D., Madhavapeddy, A., Sivaramakrishnan, K.C., White, L.: Concurrent System Programming with Effect Handlers. In: Trends in Functional Programming. pp. 98–117. Springer (2018)
22. Fujii, S., Katsumata, S., Melliès, P.: Towards a Formal Theory of Graded Monads. In: Proc. of 19th Int. Conf. on Foundations of Software Science and Computation Structures, FoSSaCS 2016. Lect. Notes Comput. Sci., vol. 9634, pp. 513–530. Springer (2016)
23. Gaboardi, M., Katsumata, S., Orchard, D.A., Breuvart, F., Uustalu, T.: Combining effects and coeffects via grading. In: Proc. of 21st ACM SIGPLAN Int. Conf. on Functional Programming, ICFP 2016. pp. 476–489. ACM (2016)
24. Ghica, D.R., Smith, A.I.: Bounded Linear Types in a Resource Semiring. In: Proc. of 23rd European Symp. on Programming, ESOP 2014. Lect. Notes Comput. Sci., vol. 8410, pp. 331–350. Springer (2014)
25. Girard, J.Y.: Linear logic. Theor. Comput. Sci. **50**(1), 1–101 (1987)
26. Gratzer, D.: Normalization for multimodal type theory. In: Proc. of 37th Annual ACM/IEEE Symp. on Logic in Comp. Sci., LICS 2022. pp. 2:1–2:13. ACM (2022)
27. Gratzer, D., Cavallo, E., Kavvos, G.A., Guatto, A., Birkedal, L.: Modalities and parametric adjoints. ACM Trans. Comput. Logic **23**(3) (2022)
28. Gratzer, D., Kavvos, G.A., Nuyts, A., Birkedal, L.: Multimodal dependent type theory. Log. Methods Comput. Sci. **17**(3) (2021)
29. Haller, P., Prokopec, A., Miller, H., Klang, V., Kuhn, R., Jovanovic, V.: SCALA documentation: Futures and promises (October 2022), available online at `https://docs.scala-lang.org/overviews/core/futures.html`
30. Honda, K., Vasconcelos, V., Kubo, M.: Language Primitives and Type Discipline for Structured Communication-Based Programming. In: Proc. of 7th European Symp. on Programming, ESOP 1998. Lect. Notes Comput. Sci., vol. 1381, pp. 122–138. Springer (1998)
31. Hyland, M., Plotkin, G., Power, J.: Combining effects: Sum and tensor. Theor. Comput. Sci. **357**(1–3), 70–99 (2006)
32. Jeltsch, W.: Towards a Common Categorical Semantics for Linear-Time Temporal Logic and Functional Reactive Programming. In: Proc. of the 28th Conf. on the Mathematical Foundations of Programming Semantics, MFPS 2012. ENTCS, vol. 286, pp. 229–242. Elsevier (2012)
33. Jeltsch, W.: Abstract categorical semantics for resourceful functional reactive programming. J. Log. Algebraic Methods Program. **85**(6), 1177–1200 (2016)
34. Jung, R., Krebbers, R., Jourdan, J., Bizjak, A., Birkedal, L., Dreyer, D.: Iris from the ground up: A modular foundation for higher-order concurrent separation logic. J. Funct. Program. **28**, e20 (2018)
35. Katsumata, S.: Parametric effect monads and semantics of effect systems. In: Proc. of 41st Annual ACM SIGPLAN-SIGACT Symp. on Principles of Programming Languages, POPL 2014. pp. 633–646. ACM (2014)
36. Katsumata, S., McDermott, D., Uustalu, T., Wu, N.: Flexible presentations of graded monads. Proc. ACM Program. Lang. **6**(ICFP), 902–930 (2022)

37. Kavvos, G.A.: The Many Worlds of Modal λ-calculi: I. Curry-Howard for Necessity, Possibility and Time. CoRR **abs/1605.08106** (2016)
38. Kelly, G.: Basic Concepts of Enriched Category Theory. No. 64 in Lecture Notes in Mathematics, Cambridge University Press (1982)
39. Kock, A.: Strong functors and monoidal monads. Archiv der Mathematik **23**(1), 113–120 (1972)
40. Koopman, P., Fokker, J., Smetsers, S., van Eekelen, M., Plasmeijer, R.: Functional Programming in Clean. University of Nijmegen (1998), draft
41. Kripke, S.A.: Semantical Analysis of Modal Logic I. Normal Propositional Calculi. Zeitschrift fur mathematische Logik und Grundlagen der Mathematik **9**(5-6), 67–96 (1963)
42. Krishnaswami, N.R.: Higher-order functional reactive programming without space-time leaks. In: Proc. of 18th ACM SIGPLAN Int. Conf. on Functional Programming, ICFP 2013. pp. 221–232. ACM (2013)
43. Leijen, D.: Algebraic Effect Handlers with Resources and Deep Finalization. Tech. Rep. MSR-TR-2018-10, Microsoft Research (April 2018)
44. Levy, P.B., Power, J., Thielecke, H.: Modelling environments in call-by-value programming languages. Inf. Comput. **185**(2), 182–210 (2003)
45. Mac Lane, S.: Categories for the Working Mathematician. No. 5 in Graduate Texts in Mathematics, Springer-Verlag (1971)
46. Mac Lane, S., Moerdijk, I.: Sheaves in Geometry and Logic: A First Introduction to Topos Theory. Universitext, Springer (1992)
47. Mannaa, B., Møgelberg, R.E.: The Clocks They Are Adjunctions Denotational Semantics for Clocked Type Theory. In: Proc. of 3rd Int. Conf. on Formal Structures for Computation and Deduction, FSCD 2018. LIPIcs, vol. 108, pp. 23:1–23:17. Schloss Dagstuhl - Leibniz-Zentrum für Informatik (2018)
48. Martini, S., Masini, A.: A Computational Interpretation of Modal Proofs, pp. 213–241. Springer Netherlands (1996)
49. McBride, C.: I Got Plenty o' Nuttin'. In: A List of Successes That Can Change the World - Essays Dedicated to Philip Wadler on the Occasion of His 60th Birthday. Lect. Notes Comput. Sci., vol. 9600, pp. 207–233. Springer (2016)
50. McDermott, D., Uustalu, T.: Flexibly Graded Monads and Graded Algebras. In: Proc. of 14th Int. Conf. on Mathematics of Program Construction, MPC 2022. Lect. Notes Comput. Sci., vol. 13544, pp. 102–128. Springer (2022)
51. Melliès, P.A.: Parametric Monads and Enriched Adjunctions (2012), manuscript. https://www.irif.fr/~mellies/tensorial-logic/8-parametric-monads-and-enriched-adjunctions.pdf
52. Moggi, E.: Computational Lambda-Calculus and Monads. In: Proc. of 4th Ann. Symp. on Logic in Computer Science, LICS 1989. pp. 14–23. IEEE (1989)
53. Moon, B., Eades III, H., Orchard, D.: Graded Modal Dependent Type Theory. In: Proc. of 30th European Symp. on Programming, ESOP 2021. Lect. Notes Comput. Sci., vol. 12648, pp. 462–490. Springer (2021)
54. Murphy VII, T.: Modal Types for Mobile Code. Ph.D. thesis, School of Computer Science, Carnegie Mellon University (2008)
55. Nakano, H.: A Modality for Recursion. In: Proc. of 15th Annual IEEE Symp. on Logic in Computer Science, LICS 2000. pp. 255–266. IEEE Computer Society (2000)
56. Nanevski, A., Morrisett, G., Birkedal, L.: Hoare type theory, polymorphism and separation. J. Funct. Program. **18**(5-6), 865–911 (2008)

57. Petricek, T., Orchard, D.A., Mycroft, A.: Coeffects: Unified Static Analysis of Context-Dependence. In: Proc. of 40th International Colloquium on Automata, Languages, and Programming, ICALP 2013. Lect. Notes Comput. Sci., vol. 7966, pp. 385–397. Springer (2013)

58. Petricek, T., Orchard, D.A., Mycroft, A.: Coeffects: a calculus of context-dependent computation. In: Proc. of 19th ACM SIGPLAN Int. Conf. on Functional Programming, ICFP 2014. pp. 123–135. ACM (2014)

59. Plotkin, G., Power, J.: Algebraic Operations and Generic Effects. Appl. Categor. Struct. (1), 69–94 (2003)

60. Plotkin, G.D., Power, J.: Notions of Computation Determine Monads. In: Proc. of 5th Int. Conf. on Foundations of Software Science and Computation Structures, FoSSaCS 2002. Lect. Notes Comput. Sci., vol. 2303, pp. 342–356. Springer (2002)

61. Plotkin, G.D., Pretnar, M.: Handling Algebraic Effects. Log. Methods Comput. Sci. 9(4:23) (2013)

62. Prawitz, D.: Natural Deduction: A Proof-Theoretical Study. Almquist and Wiksell (1965)

63. Radešček, J.: Asinhroni algebrajski učinki. Master's thesis, Faculty of Mathematics and Physics, University of Ljubljana (2021)

64. Reynolds, J.C.: Separation Logic: A Logic for Shared Mutable Data Structures. In: Proc. of 17th IEEE Symp. on Logic in Computer Science, LICS 2002. pp. 55–74. IEEE Computer Society (2002)

65. Schwinghammer, J.: A Concurrent Lambda-Calculus with Promises and Futures. Master's thesis, Programming Systems Lab, Universität des Saarlandes (2002)

66. Simpson, A.: The Proof Theory and Semantics of Intuitionistic Modal Logic. Ph.D. thesis, University of Edinburgh (1994)

67. Smirnov, A.L.: Graded monads and rings of polynomials. J. Math. Sci. 151(3), 3032–3051 (2008)

68. The Agda Team: The Agda Wiki. Available at https://wiki.portal.chalmers.se/agda/pmwiki.php (2022)

69. Valliappan, N., Ruch, F., Cortiñas, C.T.: Normalization for Fitch-style modal calculi. Proc. ACM Program. Lang. 6(ICFP), 772–798 (2022)

70. Wadler, P.: Propositions as sessions. J. Funct. Program. 24(2-3), 384–418 (2014)

71. Weber, M.: Familial 2-functors and parametric right adjoints. Theory Appl. Categories 18(22), 665–732 (2007)

72. Wickline, P., Lee, P., Pfenning, F., Davies, R.: Modal Types as Staging Specifications for Run-Time Code Generation. ACM Comput. Surv. 30(3es), 8 (1998)

Deciding Contextual Equivalence of ν-Calculus with Effectful Contexts

Daniel Hirschkoff[1], Guilhem Jaber[2]([⊠]), and Enguerrand Prebet[1]

[1] Université de Lyon, ENS de Lyon, UCB Lyon 1, CNRS, INRIA, LIP, France
[2] Nantes Université, LS2N, Inria, France
guilhem.jaber@univ-nantes.fr

Abstract. We prove decidability for contextual equivalence of the $\lambda\mu\nu$-calculus, that is the simply-typed call-by-value $\lambda\mu$-calculus equipped with booleans and fresh name creation, with contexts taken in $\lambda\mu_{\mathtt{ref}}$, that is $\lambda\mu\nu$-calculus extended with higher-order references.

The proof exploits a labelled transition system capturing the interactions between $\lambda\mu\nu$ programs and $\lambda\mu_{\mathtt{ref}}$ contexts. The induced bisimulation equivalence is characterized as equality of certain trees, inspired by the work of Lassen. Since these trees are computable and finite, decidability follows. Bisimulation coincides also with trace equivalence, which in turn coincides with contextual equivalence .

1 Introduction

Dynamic allocation is central to many programming constructions. Many languages provide built-in support for dynamically-allocated resources, for example, objects in Java or references in ML. The creation of these resources is *local*, meaning that resources can be accessed only within their scope. They can also be passed around via function applications, in which case their scope is not static but evolves dynamically. When building semantics for such languages, one represents dynamic allocation as the creation of fresh locations, that can be seen as atoms or names.

In this paper, we study a paradigmatic language with dynamic allocation, namely the ν-calculus, a simply-typed call-by-value λ-calculus with fresh atom creation and equality test of atoms, as introduced by Pitts and Stark in [24]. For instance, the ν-calculus program new n in $\lambda x.(x = n)$ allocates a new atom n, receives an atom x and returns the result of the comparison between x and n.

A central question while studying this language is to determine when two programs can be considered to be equivalent. The most studied approach to express behavioral equivalence between programs is contextual equivalence. Intuitively, two programs are deemed equivalent if and only if whenever they are run as part of an enclosing program called the *context*, it is not possible to distinguish one from the other. For instance, because the context has no way to guess the atom n, we expect the program above to be equivalent to $\lambda x.\mathtt{false}$.

Reasoning on contextual equivalence for the ν-calculus has shown to be challenging, due to the interplay between the higher-order control flow and the scope

O. Kupferman and P. Sobocinski (Eds.): FoSSaCS 2023, LNCS 13992, pp. 24–45, 2023.
https://doi.org/10.1007/978-3-031-30829-1_2

extrusion of atoms. A variety of frameworks has been introduced to do so, based on logical relations [24], environmental bisimulations [5], and game semantics [1].

However, the question of whether this equivalence is *decidable* remains open since the introduction of this language 30 years ago.

In this paper, we address this question by working in an asymmetric setting, giving contexts more discriminating power than just the mere creation of atoms. Indeed, contextual equivalence depends on two languages: the language for programs, and the language for contexts interacting with these programs. We take contexts in the $\lambda\mu_{\mathtt{ref}}$-calculus, an extension of the ν-calculus with both higher-order references and continuations. In this setting, atoms are simply references where only the unit value can be stored. Contextual equivalence is then coarser than for the symmetric setting when the contexts are also taken in the ν-calculus. For example, one of the standard examples of equivalence of the literature

$$\mathtt{new}\ n\ \mathtt{in}\ \mathtt{new}\ n'\ \mathtt{in}\ \lambda f.(f\ n = f\ n')\ \simeq_{ctx}\ \lambda f.\mathtt{true}$$

is not an equivalence anymore, since a $\lambda\mu_{\mathtt{ref}}$ context can provide a function that stores its argument in a reference and use it to discriminate these programs.

The main result we establish in this paper is the decidability of contextual equivalence for terms of ν-calculus with contexts in the $\lambda\mu_{\mathtt{ref}}$-calculus. More generally, we establish this result for terms of the $\lambda\mu\nu$-calculus, which corresponds to terms of the $\lambda\mu_{\mathtt{ref}}$-calculus that only use references storing the unit value.

To establish this result, we provide a Böhm-like tree representation [6,3] for the terms of the $\lambda\mu\nu$-calculus. Being in call-by-value, equality of such trees coincides with Lassen's eager normal form bisimulations [16]. Moreover, since programs in the $\lambda\mu\nu$-calculus are terminating, these trees, which we call *Lassen trees*, are finite. It is thus straightforward to check their equality. Then, we prove that Lassen trees equality is fully-abstract, that is it coincides with contextual equivalence with contexts in the $\lambda\mu_{\mathtt{ref}}$-calculus.

Proving this full-abstraction result is done through the introduction of an *operational game semantics* (OGS) for $\lambda\mu_{\mathtt{ref}}$ by defining a Labelled Transition System (LTS) that distinguishes between internal operations, Proponent moves (originating in the program) and Opponent moves (originating in the context). Trace equivalence based on these labelled transitions is shown to coincide with the contextual equivalence of $\lambda\mu_{\mathtt{ref}}$.

The OGS also gives rise to a notion of *bipartite bisimulation*, describing a game between Proponent (the program in $\lambda\mu_{\mathtt{ref}}$) and Opponent (a context in $\lambda\mu_{\mathtt{ref}}$). Proponent reduces the program until it reaches a normal form, that triggers an interaction with the context. Along the game, knowledge is accumulated in configurations. When it is Opponent's turn to play, it chooses between answering a previous function call from Proponent, or generating a new function call, to which Proponent shall answer. Among this knowledge, we accumulate the atoms that have been disclosed by the two players, so that Opponent cannot use an atom private to Proponent.

The OGS LTS generates infinite trees since Opponent can interrogate an arbitrary number of times each value provided by Proponent. The Lassen trees used to decide contextual equivalence are generated using a *linearized* variant of the OGS LTS, called the *Prime Operational Game Semantics* (POGS) LTS. The POGS LTS enforces that Opponent interrogates only once each value provided by Proponent. For this linearization to be sound, one has to guess the disclosed status of atoms as soon as they are created. This can be illustrated by considering the following example of inequivalence

$$\text{new } n \text{ in } \lambda x.n \not\approx_{ctx} \lambda x.\text{new } n \text{ in } n.$$

Opponent must be able to interrogate at least twice each of these two programs to discriminate them. The first program would then return the same atom at each call, while the second program would return two different atoms. The Lassen tree of the first program would declare n to be disclosed when giving back the control to Opponent by providing the λ-abstraction, but this could not be matched by the second program, since n would not exist yet at that point of the interaction.

The main technical challenge at this point is to prove that this forecasting of the disclosure process is sound and complete. This is done by proving that the bipartite bisimilarities defined over the OGS LTS and the POGS LTS coincide. One direction is proven by lifting POGS bisimulations into OGS bisimulations via an *up-to* technique. The other direction is done by introducing a new *limit* construction of the disclosed set of atoms appearing in the OGS bisimulations, to transform it into a POGS bisimulation.

Paper outline. After introducing the $\lambda\mu_{\texttt{ref}}$-calculus and the $\lambda\mu\nu$-calculus in Section 2, we define the LTS for the OGS in Section 3. The induced trace equivalence coincides with contextual equivalence. We then move to Lassen trees in Section 4, and show that they yield an equivalence that coincides with bipartite bisimilarity in the OGS in Section 5. We discuss related work in Section 6, and present concluding remarks in Section 7. For lack of space, several technical developments are given in [9].

2 The $\lambda\mu_{\texttt{ref}}$-calculus and the $\lambda\mu\nu$-calculus

The syntax of the $\lambda\mu_{\texttt{ref}}$-calculus is given by the following grammar:

Values $V, W \triangleq x \mid () \mid \lambda x.M \mid \texttt{true} \mid \texttt{false} \mid \ell$

Terms $M, N \triangleq V \mid \texttt{let } x = M \texttt{ in } N \mid VW \mid \texttt{if } V \texttt{ then } N_1 \texttt{ else } N_2$
$\mid V = W \mid \texttt{new } x = V \texttt{ in } M \mid V := W \mid !V \mid \mu c.M \mid [c]M$

Contexts $C, C' \triangleq \bullet \mid [c]C \mid \texttt{let } x = C \texttt{ in } M \mid \texttt{let } x = M \texttt{ in } C \mid \lambda x.C \mid \mu c.C$
$\mid \texttt{if } V \texttt{ then } C \texttt{ else } M \mid \texttt{if } V \texttt{ then } M \texttt{ else } C \mid \texttt{new } x = V \texttt{ in } C$

Evaluation Contexts $E, E' \triangleq [c]\bullet \mid E[\texttt{let } x = \bullet \texttt{ in } M]$

Types $\sigma, \tau \triangleq \texttt{Unit} \mid \texttt{Bool} \mid \sigma \to \tau \mid \texttt{ref}_\sigma \mid \bot$

with $x \in$ Vars (variables), $c \in$ Covars (continuation variables), $\ell \in$ Locs (locations). We write supp(M) for the set of locations appearing in M, and **FV**(M) for

$$\frac{\Gamma(x) = \sigma}{\Sigma; \Gamma \vdash x : \sigma} \qquad \frac{\Gamma(c) = \neg\sigma}{\Sigma; \Gamma \vdash c : \neg\sigma} \qquad \frac{\Sigma(\ell) = \mathsf{ref}_\sigma}{\Sigma; \Gamma \vdash \ell : \mathsf{ref}_\sigma} \qquad \frac{}{\Sigma; \Gamma \vdash () : \mathsf{Unit}}$$

$$\frac{b \in \{\mathsf{true}, \mathsf{false}\}}{\Sigma; \Gamma \vdash b : \mathsf{Bool}} \qquad \frac{\Sigma; \Gamma, x : \sigma \vdash M : \tau}{\Sigma; \Gamma \vdash \lambda x.M : \sigma \to \tau} \qquad \frac{\Sigma; \Gamma \vdash V : \sigma \to \tau \quad \Sigma; \Gamma \vdash W : \sigma}{\Sigma; \Gamma \vdash VW : \tau}$$

$$\frac{\Sigma; \Gamma \vdash N : \sigma \quad \Sigma; \Gamma, x : \sigma \vdash M : \tau}{\Sigma; \Gamma \vdash \mathsf{let}\ x = N\ \mathsf{in}\ M : \tau} \qquad \frac{\Sigma; \Gamma \vdash V : \mathsf{Bool} \quad \Sigma; \Gamma \vdash M_1 : \sigma \quad \Sigma; \Gamma \vdash M_2 : \sigma}{\Sigma; \Gamma \vdash \mathsf{if}\ V\ \mathsf{then}\ M_1\ \mathsf{else}\ M_2 : \sigma}$$

$$\frac{\Sigma; \Gamma \vdash V : \tau \quad \Sigma; \Gamma, x : \mathsf{ref}_\tau \vdash M : \sigma}{\Sigma; \Gamma \vdash \mathsf{new}\ x = V\ \mathsf{in}\ M : \sigma} \qquad \frac{\Sigma; \Gamma \vdash V : \mathsf{ref}_\sigma \quad \Sigma; \Gamma \vdash W : \sigma}{\Sigma; \Gamma \vdash V := W : \mathsf{Unit}}$$

$$\frac{\Sigma; \Gamma \vdash V : \mathsf{ref}_\sigma}{\Sigma; \Gamma \vdash !V : \sigma} \qquad \frac{\Sigma; \Gamma \vdash V : \mathsf{ref}_\sigma \quad \Sigma; \Gamma \vdash W : \mathsf{ref}_\sigma}{\Sigma; \Gamma \vdash V = W : \mathsf{Bool}} \qquad \frac{\Sigma; \Gamma, c : \neg\sigma \vdash M : \bot}{\Sigma; \Gamma \vdash \mu c.M : \sigma}$$

$$\frac{\Sigma; \Gamma \vdash M : \sigma \quad \Gamma(c) = \neg\sigma}{\Sigma; \Gamma \vdash [c]M : \bot} \qquad \frac{\Gamma(c) = \neg\sigma}{\Sigma; \Gamma \vdash [c]\bullet : \neg\sigma} \qquad \frac{\Sigma; \Gamma, x : \sigma \vdash M : \tau \quad \Sigma; \Gamma \vdash E : \neg\tau}{\Sigma; \Gamma \vdash E[\mathsf{let}\ x = \bullet\ \mathsf{in}\ M] : \neg\sigma}$$

Fig. 1. $\lambda\mu_{\mathsf{ref}}$: typing rules for terms and evaluation contexts

the *free variables* of M. This language has two binders, the standard λ-abstraction, and the μ binder for *continuation variables* c, d [22].

A store, ranged over by S, T, is a finite mapping from locations to values. $S(\ell)$ stands for the value associated to ℓ in S. We use notation $S \cdot [\ell \mapsto V]$ for the extension of S with a mapping for ℓ, which is only defined if ℓ is not defined in S. $S[\ell \mapsto V]$ denotes the store S in which the value associated to ℓ is updated.

The operational semantics $\mapsto_{\mathsf{op}}$ of the $\lambda\mu_{\mathsf{ref}}$-calculus is defined over *configurations*, which are pairs (M, S) formed by a term and a store. It is given by the following rules:

$$
\begin{aligned}
(E[(\lambda x.M)V], S) &\mapsto_{\mathsf{op}} (E[M\{x := V\}], S) \\
(E[\mathsf{let}\ x = V\ \mathsf{in}\ M], S) &\mapsto_{\mathsf{op}} (E[M\{x := V\}], S) \\
(E[\mathsf{if\ true\ then}\ N_1\ \mathsf{else}\ N_2], S) &\mapsto_{\mathsf{op}} (E[N_1], S) \\
(E[\mathsf{if\ false\ then}\ N_1\ \mathsf{else}\ N_2], S) &\mapsto_{\mathsf{op}} (E[N_2], S) \\
(E[\mathsf{new}\ x = V\ \mathsf{in}\ M], S) &\mapsto_{\mathsf{op}} (E[M\{x := \ell\}], S \cdot [\ell \mapsto V]) \\
(E[\ell := V], S) &\mapsto_{\mathsf{op}} (E[()], S[\ell \mapsto V]) \\
(E[!\ell], S) &\mapsto_{\mathsf{op}} (E[S(\ell)], S) \\
(E[\ell = \ell], S) &\mapsto_{\mathsf{op}} (E[\mathsf{true}], S) \\
(E[\ell = \ell'], S) &\mapsto_{\mathsf{op}} (E[\mathsf{false}], S) \\
(E[\mu c.M], S) &\mapsto_{\mathsf{op}} (M\{c := E\})
\end{aligned}
$$

The typing system for terms is given by the rules in Figure 1. We chose here a typing judgement with a single typing context Γ, so that continuation variables are given types of the shape $\neg\sigma$. Such negated types are also used to type evaluation contexts, as specified by the two last rules in Figure 1. While we cannot store a continuation variable c in a reference, we can always store its associated function $\lambda x.[c]x$. Typing rules force terms of type $\bot$ to be of the shape $[d]M$, following Parigot's original presentation of the $\lambda\mu$-calculus [22].

We also consider a typing judgement of the shape $\Sigma \vdash C : (\Gamma; \sigma) \rightsquigarrow (\Delta; \tau)$, for contexts C that take terms M of type $\Sigma; \Gamma \vdash M : \sigma$ and produce terms of type $\Sigma; \Delta \vdash C[M] : \tau$. The typing rules defining this judgement are standard and not recalled here.

In the following, we consider the $\lambda\mu\nu$-calculus, the fragment of the $\lambda\mu_{\text{ref}}$-calculus that only handles references of type $\textbf{ref}_{\text{Unit}}$. That is, for any reference type $\textbf{ref}_\sigma$ appearing in the typing derivation, we have $\sigma = \texttt{Unit}$.

We use $a, b, \ldots$ to range over locations of type $\textbf{ref}_{\text{Unit}}$, also called atoms, and introduce the slightly shorter notation $\textbf{new } n \textbf{ in } M$ to stand for $\textbf{new } n = () \textbf{ in } M$ in $\lambda\mu$. The syntax for values and terms of the $\lambda\mu\nu$-calculus is thus:

Values $V, W \triangleq x \mid () \mid \lambda x.N \mid \texttt{true} \mid \texttt{false} \mid a$
Terms $M, N \triangleq V \mid \texttt{let } x = M \texttt{ in } N \mid VW \mid \texttt{if } V \texttt{ then } N_1 \texttt{ else } N_2 \mid V = W \mid \textbf{new } n \textbf{ in } M$
$\qquad\qquad \mid \mu c.M$

In this setting, we see stores S directly as sets of atoms, all mapping to the unit value (). For L a set of atoms. we write $\widehat{L}$ for the store that maps atoms in L to the unit value ().

We consider the following extension of the typing judgement respectively to stores S and value-mapping substitutions γ:

$$\frac{\forall \ell \in \text{dom}(S), \Sigma; \varnothing \vdash S(\ell) : \Sigma(\ell) \qquad \text{dom}(S) = \text{dom}(\Sigma)}{\vdash S : \Sigma}$$

$$\frac{\forall x \in \text{dom}(\Gamma), \Sigma; \Delta \vdash \gamma(x) : \Gamma(x) \qquad \text{dom}(\gamma) = \text{dom}(\Gamma)}{\Sigma; \Delta \vdash \gamma : \Gamma}$$

Definition 1. *A normal form* (M, S) *is a configuration that is irreducible for the reduction relation* $\mapsto_{\text{op}}$. *We write* (M, S)$\Downarrow$ N *when there exists a store* T *such that* $(M; S) \mapsto^*_{\text{op}} (N; T)$ *and that* (N; T) *is a normal form.*

We call the types $\texttt{Bool}, \texttt{Unit}$ and $\textbf{ref}_\sigma$ *positive* types, while $\sigma \to \tau$ and $\neg\sigma$ are called *negative* types. By only allowing free variables of negative types, we can provide a sharp characterization of normal forms.

Theorem 2. *Taking a term* M *such that* $\Sigma; \Gamma \vdash M : \bot$ *with* Γ *a typing context mapping variables to negative types, if* (M, S) *is in normal form with respect to* $\mapsto_{\text{op}}$, *then* M *is either a named value* [c]V *or a neutral term* E[xV].

Moreover, for any configuration (M, S) *such that* M *is in* $\lambda\mu\nu$, $\Sigma; \Gamma \vdash M : \bot$ *and* $\vdash S : \Sigma$, *there exists* N *such that* (M, S)$\Downarrow$ N.

Definition 3. *Taking two terms* M, N *such that* $\Sigma; \Gamma \vdash M : \sigma$ *and* $\Sigma; \Gamma \vdash N : \sigma$, *we say that they are* contextually equivalent, *written* $\Sigma; \Gamma \vdash M \simeq_{ctx} N : \sigma$, *when for all* *continuation variable* c *and context* C *such that* $\Sigma \vdash C : (\Gamma; \sigma) \rightsquigarrow (c : \neg\texttt{Unit}; \bot)$, *and for all store* S *such that* $\vdash S : \Sigma'$, *we have* $(C[M], S) \Downarrow [c]()$ *if and only if* $(C[N], S) \Downarrow [c]()$.

In the definition above, we use $\lambda\mu_{\texttt{ref}}$ contexts to observe $\lambda\mu\nu$ terms. Such contexts can use higher-order references, and lead to divergent computations. For this reason, testing for convergence to () is enough when defining $\approx_{ctx}$.

3   Operational Game Semantics

We now introduce a fully-abstract trace semantics for $\lambda\mu_{\texttt{ref}}$ programs. We follow a modular presentation, inspired by the one provided by Laird in [15], where the semantics is built from a synchronization product of three LTS:

- the Interactive LTS $\mathcal{L}_\mathsf{I}$, that represents the raw interactions of programs with their environment.
- the Typing LTS $\mathcal{L}_\mathsf{Ty}$, that keeps track of the polarization and types of names exchanged, to preserve well-typedness.
- the Disclosing LTS $\mathcal{L}_\mathsf{Di}$, that prevents the environment from using private resources that have not been disclosed by Proponent.

3.1   Abstract values

To represent the interaction between the program and its environment, we distinguish between values that we can observe and values that we can interact with. The two players only exchange observable values, called *abstract values* in this paper. They are defined by the following grammar:

$$A, B \triangleq f \mid a \mid \texttt{true} \mid \texttt{false} \mid ()$$

with f a *function name*, that is a variable used to represent functions exchanged between the two players. These correspond to the positive part of values, and are also called *ultimate patterns* in [17]. Like for terms, supp(A) stands for the set of atoms occurring in A. We consider the typing judgement $\Delta \Vdash A : \sigma$ for abstract values, with σ a positive type, that is defined similarly as done for terms.

Then we introduce the abstraction relation $\nearrow\!\!\!\!/$ that transforms a value V into a pair (A, γ) formed by an abstract value and a substitution, such that $A\{\gamma\} = V$:

$$\frac{\text{f, g function names}}{\text{f} \nearrow\!\!\!\!/ (\text{g}, [\text{g} \mapsto \text{f}])} \qquad \frac{}{() \nearrow\!\!\!\!/ ((), \varepsilon)} \qquad \frac{\text{b} \in \{\texttt{true, false}\}}{\text{b} \nearrow\!\!\!\!/ (\text{b}, \varepsilon)} \qquad \frac{\text{a an atom}}{\text{a} \nearrow\!\!\!\!/ (\text{a}, \varepsilon)}$$

$$\frac{}{\lambda x.M \nearrow\!\!\!\!/ (\text{f}, [\text{f} \mapsto \lambda x.M])}$$

3.2 Labelled Transition Systems

The two players, Opponent and Proponent, exchange *moves*, which are in one of six forms:

P-question	P-answer	O-question	O-answer	P-init question	O-init question
$\overline{f}(A, c)$	$\overline{c}(A)$	$f(A, c)$	$c(A)$	$\overline{?(\vec{A_i})}$	$?(\vec{A_i})$

We use **m** to range over moves, and **p** (resp. **o**) to range over Proponent (resp. Opponent) moves. Initial questions are the introductory moves. In contrast with other moves, they can introduce multiple abstract values in a row, which is useful to instantiate all the variables of a typing context Γ. They use a distinguished function name ?.

Traces **t** are sequences of moves. We write $\overline{m}$ for the corresponding move with reversed polarity (input switched to output, and vice-versa). We extend this definition to switch traces, written $\overline{t}$.

The three labelled transition systems we define are instances of the following definition:

Definition 4. *A labelled transition system (LTS) $\mathcal{L}$ is a triple of the form* (Confs, Actions, →). *Confs is a set of configurations* $\mathbb{C}, \mathbb{D}$. *Actions is a set of actions* **a**, *formed by the* moves **m**, *together with a silent action* op, *corresponding to internal computations. Relation* → ⊆ Confs × Actions × Confs *is the labelled transition relation. We write* $\mathbb{C} \xrightarrow{a} \mathbb{D}$ *for* $(\mathbb{C}, \mathbf{a}, \mathbb{D}) \in \rightarrow$.

Taking $\mathbb{C}$ a configuration of an LTS $\mathcal{L}$, we write $\mathbf{Tr}_{\mathcal{L}}(\mathbb{C})$ for the set of traces, as sequences of moves generated by this LTS over $\mathbb{C}$ (so with op actions removed). We write $\mathbb{C} \simeq_{tr} \mathbb{D}$ for the trace equivalence relation, which equates configurations $\mathbb{C}, \mathbb{D}$ when both have the same set of traces.

3.3 Interactive LTS

We consider *interactive configurations* $\mathbb{I}; \mathbb{J} \in$ IConfs which are either passive of the shape $\langle S; \gamma \rangle$, or active of the shape $\langle M; S; \gamma \rangle$ with M a term, S a store, and γ a substitution. The Interactive LTS $\mathcal{L}_\mathsf{I}$ is then defined as the triple (IConfs, Actions, →$_\mathsf{I}$) with relation →$_\mathsf{I}$ defined in Figure 2.

The two rules for Proponent moves describe transitions performed by normal forms and make use of the abstraction relation. In the two rules for Opponent, the notation $S \odot [\overline{\mathsf{supp}(A)}]$ stands for S extended with a binding $\mathbf{a} \mapsto ()$ in the case when $A = \mathbf{a}$ and $\mathbf{a}$ is fresh for Proponent, and simply S otherwise: Proponent extends its store when a new atom is received.

3.4 Typing LTS

We consider *type-context configurations* $\mathbb{S}, \mathbb{T} \in$ Confs$_{\mathsf{Ty}}$ which are either active of the shape $\langle \Delta_\mathsf{O} \mid \bot; \Delta_\mathsf{P} \rangle$ or passive of the shape $\langle \Delta_\mathsf{O} \mid \Delta_\mathsf{P} \rangle$, with $\Delta_\mathsf{O}, \Delta_\mathsf{P}$ two disjoint typing contexts that map variables to *negative* types.

$$\text{op} \ \frac{(M; S) \mapsto_{op} (N; T)}{\langle M; S; \gamma \rangle \xrightarrow{op}_I \langle N; T; \gamma \rangle}$$

$$\text{PQ} \ \frac{V \not\!\!/ (A; \gamma')}{\langle E[fV]; S; \gamma \rangle \xrightarrow{\bar{f}(A,c)}_I \langle S; \gamma \cdot \gamma' \cdot [c \mapsto E] \rangle} \qquad\qquad \frac{V \not\!\!/ (A; \gamma')}{\langle [c]V; S; \gamma \rangle \xrightarrow{\bar{c}(A)}_I \langle S; \gamma \cdot \gamma' \rangle} \ \text{PA}$$

$$\text{OQ} \ \frac{}{\langle S; \gamma \rangle \xrightarrow{f(A,c)}_I \langle [c]\gamma(f)A; S \odot \widehat{[\mathsf{supp}(A)]}; \gamma \rangle} \qquad\qquad \frac{}{\langle S; \gamma \rangle \xrightarrow{c(A)}_I \langle \gamma(c)[A]; S \odot \widehat{[\mathsf{supp}(A)]}; \gamma \rangle} \ \text{OA}$$

Fig. 2. Definition of $\mathcal{L}_I$, the Interactive LTS: transitions of interactive configurations

$$\text{PQ} \ \frac{\Delta_O(f) = \sigma \to \tau \qquad \Delta \Vdash A : \sigma}{\langle \Delta_O \mid \perp; \Delta_P \rangle \xrightarrow{\bar{f}(A,c)}_{\mathsf{Ty}} \langle \Delta_O \mid \Delta_P, \Delta, c : \neg\tau \rangle} \qquad \frac{\Delta_O(c) = \neg\sigma \qquad \Delta \Vdash A : \sigma}{\langle \Delta_O \mid \perp; \Delta_P \rangle \xrightarrow{\bar{c}(A)}_{\mathsf{Ty}} \langle \Delta_O \mid \Delta_P, \Delta \rangle} \ \text{PA}$$

$$\text{OQ} \ \frac{\Delta_P(f) = \sigma \to \tau \qquad \Delta \Vdash A : \sigma}{\langle \Delta_O \mid \Delta_P \rangle \xrightarrow{f(A,c)}_{\mathsf{Ty}} \langle \Delta_O, \Delta, c : \neg\tau \mid \perp; \Delta_P \rangle} \qquad \frac{\Delta_P(c) = \neg\sigma \qquad \Delta \Vdash A : \sigma}{\langle \Delta_O \mid \Delta_P \rangle \xrightarrow{c(A)}_{\mathsf{Ty}} \langle \Delta_O, \Delta \mid \perp; \Delta_P \rangle} \ \text{OA}$$

Fig. 3. Definition of $\mathcal{L}_{\mathsf{Ty}}$, the typing LTS: transitions of type-context configurations

The Interactive LTS $\mathcal{L}_I$ is then defined as the triple $(\mathsf{Confs}_{\mathsf{Ty}}, \mathsf{Actions}, \to_{\mathsf{Ty}})$ with relation $\to_{\mathsf{Ty}}$ defined in Figure 3. Notice that the type of the active term is $\perp$ since the reduction relation $\mapsto_{op}$ is well-defined only on terms of this type.

Typing configurations can be used to specify interactive configurations, via the following validity judgement.

Definition 5. *An interactive configuration* $\mathbb{I}$ *is said to be validated by a typing configuration* $\mathbb{S}$*, written* $\mathbb{I} \triangleright \mathbb{S}$*, when:*

- *either* $\mathbb{I} = \langle S; \gamma \rangle$, $\mathbb{S} = \langle \Delta_O \mid \Delta_P \rangle$, *and there exists a store typing context* Σ *such that* $\Sigma; \Delta_O \vdash \gamma : \Delta_P$ *and* $\vdash S : \Sigma$,
- *or* $\mathbb{I} = \langle M; S; \gamma \rangle$, $\mathbb{S} = \langle \Delta_O \mid \perp; \Delta_P \rangle$, *and there exists a store typing context* Σ *such that* $\Sigma; \Delta_O \vdash M : \perp$, $\Sigma; \Delta_O \vdash \gamma : \Delta_P$ *and* $\vdash S : \Sigma$.

3.5 Disclosing LTS

In order to enforce a *non-omniscient* condition on Opponent transitions, we introduce a Disclosing LTS $\mathcal{L}_{\mathsf{Di}} \triangleq (\mathsf{DConfs}, \mathsf{Actions}, \to_{\mathsf{Di}})$ whose configurations DConfs are pairs of sets of locations $\langle L; D \rangle$ with D a set of atoms contained in L. The transition relation $\to_{\mathsf{Di}}$ is defined in Figure 4. The condition $L \cap \mathsf{supp}(o) \subseteq D$ corresponds to the fact that Opponent cannot play Proponent atoms that have not been disclosed yet, i.e. not in D.

$$\text{op} \; \frac{}{\langle L; D \rangle \xrightarrow{\text{op}}_{\text{Di}} \langle L \cup L'; D \rangle}$$

$$\text{PQ/PA} \; \frac{}{\langle L; D \rangle \xrightarrow{p}_{\text{Di}} \langle L; D \cup \text{supp}(p) \rangle} \qquad \frac{L \cap \text{supp}(o) \subseteq D}{\langle L; D \rangle \xrightarrow{o}_{\text{Di}} \langle L \cup \text{supp}(o); D \cup \text{supp}(o) \rangle} \; \text{OQ/OA}$$

Fig. 4. Definition of $\mathcal{L}_{\text{Di}}$, the Disclosing LTS

Definition 6. *An interactive configuration* $\mathbb{I}$ *is said to be validated by a disclosing configuration* $\mathbb{D} = \langle L; D \rangle$, *written* $\mathbb{I} \triangleright \mathbb{D}$, *if when writing* S *for the store component of* $\mathbb{I}$, *we have* $\text{dom}(S) = L$.

3.6   Operational Game Semantics: LTS and Trace Equivalence

The *Operational Game Semantics* (OGS) LTS $\mathcal{L}_{\text{OGS}} \triangleq (\text{Confs}_{\text{ogs}}, \text{Actions}, \xrightarrow{a}_{\text{ogs}})$ is defined over configurations $\mathbb{G}, \mathbb{H} \in \text{Confs}_{\text{ogs}}$ of the shape $(\mathbb{I}, \mathbb{S}, \mathbb{D})$, with $\mathbb{I} \triangleright \mathbb{S}$ and $\mathbb{I} \triangleright \mathbb{D}$, or over initial configurations $\langle \Sigma; \Gamma \vdash M : \sigma \rangle$ for Proponent and $\langle c : \neg\text{Unit} \vdash (S; \delta) : (\Sigma; \Gamma) \rangle$ for Opponent. Its transition relation is defined by the following rules:

$$\frac{\mathbb{I} \xrightarrow{a}_{\text{I}} \mathbb{J} \qquad \mathbb{S} \xrightarrow{a}_{\text{Ty}} \mathbb{T} \qquad \mathbb{D} \xrightarrow{a}_{\text{Di}} \mathbb{E} \qquad \mathbb{J} \triangleright \mathbb{T} \qquad \mathbb{J} \triangleright \mathbb{E}}{(\mathbb{I}, \mathbb{S}, \mathbb{D}) \xrightarrow{a}_{\text{ogs}} (\mathbb{J}, \mathbb{T}, \mathbb{E})}$$

$$\frac{\Gamma = \overrightarrow{(x_i : \sigma_i)} \qquad \overrightarrow{\Delta_i \Vdash A_i : \sigma_i} \qquad L = (\cup_i \text{supp}(A_i)) \cup \text{dom}(\Sigma)}{\langle \Sigma; \Gamma \vdash M : \bot \rangle \xrightarrow{?\overrightarrow{(A_i)}}_{\text{ogs}} \left(\langle M\{x_i := A_i\}; \widehat{L}; \varepsilon \rangle, \langle \overrightarrow{\Delta_i} | \bot; \varnothing \rangle, \langle L; L \rangle \right)}$$

$$\frac{\Gamma = \overrightarrow{(x_i : \sigma_i)} \qquad \delta(x_i) \not\!\!\nearrow (A_i; \gamma_i) \qquad \overrightarrow{\Delta_i \Vdash A : \sigma_i} \qquad L = \Sigma^{-1}(\text{ref}_{\text{Unit}})}{\langle c : \neg\text{Unit} \vdash (S; \delta) : (\Sigma; \Gamma) \rangle \xrightarrow{\overline{?\overrightarrow{(A_i)}}}_{\text{ogs}} \left(\langle S; \overrightarrow{\gamma_i} \rangle, \langle c : \neg\text{Unit} | \overrightarrow{\Delta_i} \rangle, \langle L; L \rangle \right)}$$

The initial question generated by $\langle \Sigma; \Gamma \vdash M : \sigma \rangle$ provides a way for Opponent to instantiate variables of Γ with abstract values. In this setting Σ only contains atoms since M is a term of $\lambda\mu v$. The transition for $\langle c : \neg\text{Unit} \vdash (S; \delta) : (\Sigma; \Gamma) \rangle$ represents this behavior from the point of view of Opponent. Since contexts belong to $\lambda\mu_{\text{ref}}$, these initial configurations come equipped with an initial store S of type Σ, but only the locations of type ref_{Unit} are considered to be disclosed, since the other ones cannot be used by Proponent. The continuation name c is used for Opponent to provide its final answer, which is of type Unit, following the notion of observation used to define contextual equivalence.

We use notation $\xRightarrow{p}_{\text{ogs}}$ to denote a p transition preceded by a possibly empty sequence of op transitions. Trace equivalence according to $\mathcal{L}_{\text{OGS}}$ and contextual equivalence coincide.

$$\text{op} \; \frac{(M;\widehat{L}) \mapsto_{op} (N;\widehat{L'})}{\langle M;L \rangle \xrightarrow{op}_{\text{PI}} \langle N;L' \rangle} \qquad \text{PQ} \; \frac{V \mathbin{/\!\!/} (A;\gamma)}{\langle E[fV];L \rangle \xrightarrow{\bar{f}(A,c)}_{\text{PI}} \langle L; \gamma \cdot [c \mapsto E] \rangle} \qquad \frac{V \mathbin{/\!\!/} (A;\gamma)}{\langle [c]V;L \rangle \xrightarrow{\bar{c}(A)}_{\text{PI}} \langle L; \gamma \rangle} \; \text{PA}$$

$$\text{OQ} \; \frac{}{\langle L; \gamma \rangle \xrightarrow{f(A,c)}_{\text{PI}} \langle [c]\gamma(f)A; L \cup \operatorname{supp}(A) \rangle} \qquad \frac{}{\langle L; \gamma \rangle \xrightarrow{c(A)}_{\text{PI}} \langle \gamma(c)[A]; L \cup \operatorname{supp}(A) \rangle} \; \text{OA}$$

Fig. 5. Definition of $\mathcal{L}_{\text{PI}}$: transitions of prime interactive configurations

Theorem 7. *Consider two terms* M, N *such that* $\Sigma; \Gamma \vdash M, N : \sigma$.
We have $\langle \Sigma; \Gamma \vdash M : \sigma \rangle \approx_{tr} \langle \Sigma; \Gamma \vdash N : \sigma \rangle$ *if and only if* $\Sigma; \Gamma \vdash M \simeq_{ctx} N : \sigma$.

Such a full-abstraction theorem was proven in [13] for *RefML*, that is the intuitionistic fragment of $\lambda\mu_{\text{ref}}$-calculus, without control operators. It was also proven in [10] for *HOSC*, a variant of the $\lambda\mu_{\text{ref}}$-calculus, with the call/cc operator, but without atom disclosure. Such a full-abstraction result being rather standard, we have chosen to present its proof in [9].

In the remainder of the paper, we focus on the $\lambda\mu\nu$-calculus. In particular, we only consider OGS configurations corresponding to $\lambda\mu\nu$ from now on.

4   Lassen Trees for the $\lambda\mu\nu$-calculus

4.1   POGS and POGS bipartite bisimulation

We introduce Lassen trees for terms of the $\lambda\mu\nu$-calculus, as a form of *linearized* version of $\mathcal{L}_{\text{OGS}}$, where Opponent can interrogate a name provided by Proponent only once, immediately after it has been introduced. So we consider *prime interactive configurations* which are either passive of the shape $\langle L; \gamma \rangle$, or active of the shape $\langle M; L \rangle$ with M a term, L a set of atoms, and γ a substitution. Compared to interactive configurations, the active configurations do not carry an environment γ. Furthermore, we have a set of atoms rather than a full store, since this LTS is defined only for the $\lambda\mu\nu$-calculus and not for the whole $\lambda\mu_{\text{ref}}$-calculus.

The Prime Interactive LTS, $\mathcal{L}_{\text{PI}}$, is then defined as $(\text{Confs}_{\text{PI}}, \text{Actions}, \rightarrow_{\text{PI}})$, with $\rightarrow_{\text{PI}}$ defined in Figure 5.

The corresponding Typing LTS is defined using the transitions given in Figure 6, which are very close in spirit to the transitions in Figure 3.

The transitions for the Disclosing LTS for POGS are presented on Figure 7. We compare these with the Disclosing LTS for OGS (Figure 4) below.

The Prime Operational Game Semantics LTS is introduced as a synchronization product, together with initial transitions, like for OGS. More precisely, the synchronization between the interactive and typing LTSs requires that active configurations $\langle M; L \rangle$ correspond to type-contexts of the shape $\langle \Delta_O \mid \bot \rangle$, with $\Sigma; \Delta_O \vdash M : \bot$ and $\vdash \widehat{L} : \Sigma$, for some store typing context Σ. Accordingly, for passive configurations $\langle L; \gamma \rangle$, we synchronize with $\langle \Delta_O \mid \Delta_P \rangle$, and check that $\Sigma; \Delta_O \vdash \gamma : \Delta_P$ and $\vdash \widehat{L} : \Sigma$, for some store typing context Σ.

$$PQ \quad \frac{\Delta_O(f) = \sigma \to \tau \qquad \Delta \Vdash A : \sigma}{\langle \Delta_O \mid \perp \rangle \xrightarrow{\bar{f}(A,c)}_{PTy} \langle \Delta_O \mid \Delta, c : \neg\tau \rangle}$$

$$PA \quad \frac{\Delta_O(c) = \neg\sigma \qquad \Delta \Vdash A : \sigma}{\langle \Delta_O \mid \perp \rangle \xrightarrow{\bar{c}(A)}_{PTy} \langle \Delta_O \mid \Delta \rangle}$$

$$OQ \quad \frac{\Delta_P(f) = \sigma \to \tau \qquad \Delta \Vdash A : \sigma}{\langle \Delta_O \mid \Delta_P \rangle \xrightarrow{f(A,c)}_{PTy} \langle \Delta_O, \Delta, c : \neg\tau \mid \perp \rangle}$$

$$OA \quad \frac{\Delta_P(c) = \neg\sigma \qquad \Delta \Vdash A : \sigma}{\langle \Delta_O \mid \Delta_P \rangle \xrightarrow{c(A)}_{PTy} \langle \Delta_O, \Delta \mid \perp \rangle}$$

Fig. 6. Definition of $\mathcal{L}_{PTy}$: transitions of prime type-context configurations

$$op \quad \frac{D' \subseteq L'}{\langle L; D \rangle \xrightarrow{op}_{pd} \langle L \uplus L'; D \uplus D' \rangle}$$

$$PQ/PA \quad \frac{supp(p) \subseteq D}{\langle L; D \rangle \xrightarrow{p}_{pd} \langle L; D \rangle}$$

$$OQ/OA \quad \frac{L \cap supp(o) \subseteq D}{\langle L; D \rangle \xrightarrow{o}_{pd} \langle L \cup supp(o); D \cup supp(o) \rangle}$$

Fig. 7. Definition of $\mathcal{L}_{PDi}$: Disclosing LTS for POGS

To synchronize with the Disclosing LTS, whose states are of the form $\langle L; D \rangle$, we simply impose that the L component is the same in the state of $\mathcal{L}_{PI}$, both for active and passive configurations.

We call $\mathcal{L}_{POGS}$ the LTS obtained by synchronizing $\mathcal{L}_{PI}$, $\mathcal{L}_{PTy}$ and $\mathcal{L}_{PDi}$. We write $P, Q \in Confs_{POGS}$ the configurations of $\mathcal{L}_{POGS}$. The *Lassen tree* of a term is then defined as the unfolding of the $\mathcal{L}_{POGS}$ on the initial active configuration associated with this term.

Example 8. The Lassen trees (omitting the typing configurations) for [c]new n in $\lambda\_.n$ and [c]$\lambda\_.$new n in n are given by:

Due to the condition $supp(p) \subseteq D$ in $\xrightarrow{p}_{pd}$, some configurations with terms in normal form do not have a corresponding Proponent transition. The dashed arrows correspond to op transitions that lead to such stuck configurations.

4.2 Bipartite Bisimulations for OGS and POGS

We consider typed relations on passive and active configurations, that is, we require related configurations to have the same type. This means in particular that the environment components γ of the two configurations have the same domain. In addition to the typing, we also enforce that both sets of disclosed atoms are identical.

Definition 9. *A* bipartite bisimulation *is a pair of relations* $(\mathcal{R}_{Act}, \mathcal{R}_{Pas})$ *respectively on active and passive configurations, such that:*

- *If* $(\mathbb{G}_1, \mathbb{G}_2) \in \mathcal{R}_{Pas}$ *then for all Opponent moves* $\mathbf{o}$ *and* $\mathbb{H}_1, \mathbb{H}_2$ *such that* $\mathbb{G}_1 \xrightarrow{\mathbf{o}} \mathbb{H}_1$ *and* $\mathbb{G}_2 \xrightarrow{\mathbf{o}} \mathbb{H}_2$, *we have* $(\mathbb{H}_1, \mathbb{H}_2) \in \mathcal{R}_{Act}$.
- *If* $(\mathbb{G}_1, \mathbb{G}_2) \in \mathcal{R}_{Act}$ *then there exists a Proponent move* $\mathbf{p}$ *and* $(\mathbb{H}_1, \mathbb{H}_2) \in \mathcal{R}_{Pas}$ *such that* $\mathbb{G}_1 \xRightarrow{\mathbf{p}} \mathbb{H}_1$ *and* $\mathbb{G}_2 \xRightarrow{\mathbf{p}} \mathbb{H}_2$.

An OGS-*bipartite bisimulation is a bipartite bisimulation defined over* $\mathcal{L}_{OGS}$, *and a* POGS-*bipartite bisimulation is a bipartite bisimulation defined over* $\mathcal{L}_{POGS}$. *We write* $\simeq_{ogs}$ *and* $\simeq_{pogs}$ *respectively for the greatest bipartite bisimulation respectively over* $\mathcal{L}_{OGS}$ *and* $\mathcal{L}_{POGS}$.

The following property follows from the fact that the transition relation is deterministic (up to the choice of fresh names).

Lemma 10. $\simeq_{ogs}$ *coincides with trace equivalence on* OGS *configurations.*

For op transitions, the difference between OGS and POGS shows up in the disclosing LTS: in $\xrightarrow{\text{op}}_{pd}$, a D' component can be chosen non-deterministically. This observation is related to the existential quantification in the second clause of Definition 13. Both in $\mathcal{L}_{OGS}$ and $\mathcal{L}_{POGS}$, there is only one possible next visible (Proponent) move. However, in $\simeq_{pogs}$, the game involves choosing an appropriate set of atoms to be disclosed along $\xrightarrow{\text{op}}_{pd}$ transitions. For instance, when constructing a POGS bipartite bisimulation between terms $\mathsf{new}\ n\ \mathsf{in}\ \lambda\_.n$ and $\lambda\_.\mathsf{new}\ n\ \mathsf{in}\ n$ from Example 8, we have two choices for the second step:

$$((\langle\{a\}; [f \mapsto \lambda\_.a]\rangle, \langle\{a\}, \emptyset\rangle), \quad (\langle\emptyset; [f \mapsto \lambda\_.\mathsf{new}\ n\ \mathsf{in}\ n]\rangle, \langle\emptyset, \emptyset\rangle))$$
$$((\langle\{a\}; [f \mapsto \lambda\_.a]\rangle, \langle\{a\}, \{a\}\rangle), \quad (\langle\emptyset; [f \mapsto \lambda\_.\mathsf{new}\ n\ \mathsf{in}\ n]\rangle, \langle\emptyset, \emptyset\rangle))$$

The latter does not satisfy the constraint on the disclosed set, since the sets are not the same in the two configurations. The former leads to a stuck configuration: $(\langle[c'](\lambda\_.a)(), \{a\}\rangle, \langle\{a\}, \emptyset\rangle)$ cannot perform any Proponent move. Thus the two programs are not equivalent.

4.3 Deciding $\simeq_{pogs}$

We now study how to decide when two POGS configurations are bisimilar. First, trees generated by $\mathcal{L}_{POGS}$ are of finite depth.

Lemma 11. *Taking a POGS configuration* $\mathbb{G}$, *any trace in* $\mathbf{Tr}_{\mathsf{POGS}}(\mathbb{G})$ *is finite.*

This lemma is proven using a biorthogonal logical predicate, following the use of biorthogonality to prove strong normalization of $\lambda\mu$-calculus [23], the computational metalanguage [18], and cut elimination for linear logic [8]. The proof can be found in [9].

Due to the non-determinism of atom generation in $\mapsto_{\mathsf{op}}$, of function name generation in $\nearrow\!\!\nearrow$, and of name picking in Opponent transitions, the trees generated by $\mathcal{L}_{\mathsf{POGS}}$ are infinitely branching. To tame this infinite branching, we see the set of moves Moves and the set of configurations Confs$_{\mathsf{POGS}}$ of $\mathcal{L}_{\mathsf{POGS}}$ as *nominal sets* [7] over atoms, function and continuation variables. So taking π a finite permutation over these sets, we write $\pi * X$ for the action of permutation π over elements of nominal set X. The transition relation $\rightarrow_{\mathsf{pogs}}$ of $\mathcal{L}_{\mathsf{POGS}}$ preserves this action of permutation, i.e., it is *equivariant*: if $\mathbb{P} \xrightarrow{m}_{\mathsf{pogs}} \mathbb{Q}$ then for all finite permutation π, we have $\pi * \mathbb{P} \xrightarrow{\pi * m}_{\mathsf{pogs}} \pi * \mathbb{Q}$.

One can then consider a variant $\mathcal{L}_{\mathsf{DPOGS}}$ of the POGS LTS which uses the same set of configurations as $\mathcal{L}_{\mathsf{POGS}}$, but whose transition relation $\rightarrow_{\mathsf{dpogs}}$ chooses fresh atoms and names deterministically. So $\rightarrow_{\mathsf{dpogs}}$ is then deterministic on op and Proponent actions, and finitely branching on Opponent actions.

We remark at this point that the notion of bipartite bisimulation $\approx_{\mathsf{pogs}}$ introduced in Definition 13 is not suited for $\mathcal{L}_{\mathsf{DPOGS}}$. Indeed, it requires equality of actions in the bisimulation game, and also that configurations related by bisimulation have the same type. So we relax the definition of $\approx_{\mathsf{pogs}}$ and work with ternary relations, adding a finite permutation of names and atoms in order to match the actions, rather than enforcing syntactic equality.

Definition 12. *A relation* $\mathcal{R} \subseteq \mathsf{Confs}_{\mathsf{POGS}} \times \mathsf{Confs}_{\mathsf{POGS}} \times \mathsf{Perm}$ *is said to be* valid *when, for all* $((\mathbb{I}, \mathbb{S}, \langle\_, \mathsf{D}\rangle), (\mathbb{J}, \mathbb{T}, \langle\_, \mathsf{D}'\rangle), \pi) \in \mathcal{R}$, *we have* $\mathbb{T} = \pi * \mathbb{S}$ *and* $\mathsf{D}' = \pi * \mathsf{D}$.

Definition 13. *A* relaxed bipartite bisimulation *is a pair of valid relations* $(\mathcal{R}_{Act}, \mathcal{R}_{Pas})$ *respectively on active and passive configurations such that:*

- *If* $(\mathbb{P}_1, \mathbb{P}_2, \pi) \in \mathcal{R}_{Pas}$ *then for all Opponent moves* $\mathbf{o}_1, \mathbf{o}_2$, *permutation* π' *extending* π, *and active POGS configurations* $\mathbb{Q}_1, \mathbb{Q}_2$ *satisfying* $\mathbf{o}_2 = \pi' * \mathbf{o}_1$, $\mathbb{P}_1 \xrightarrow{\mathbf{o}_1} \mathbb{Q}_1$ *and* $\mathbb{P}_2 \xrightarrow{\mathbf{o}_2} \mathbb{Q}_2$, *we have* $(\mathbb{Q}_1, \mathbb{Q}_2, \pi') \in \mathcal{R}_{Act}$.
- *If* $(\mathbb{P}_1, \mathbb{P}_2, \pi) \in \mathcal{R}_{Act}$ *then there exists a permutation* π' *extending* π, *two Proponent moves* $\mathbf{p}_1, \mathbf{p}_2$ *s.t.* $\mathbf{p}_2 = \pi' * \mathbf{p}_1$, *and two passive POGS configurations* $\mathbb{Q}_1, \mathbb{Q}_2$ *such that* $(\mathbb{Q}_1, \mathbb{Q}_2, \pi') \in \mathcal{R}_{Pas}$, $\mathbb{P}_1 \xRightarrow{\mathbf{p}_1} \mathbb{Q}_1$ *and* $\mathbb{P}_2 \xRightarrow{\mathbf{p}_2} \mathbb{Q}_2$.

We write $\approx^r_{\mathsf{pogs}}$ for the greatest relaxed bipartite bisimulation over $\mathcal{L}_{\mathsf{POGS}}$. From the fact that $\rightarrow_{\mathsf{pogs}}$ is equivariant, we deduce that $\approx^r_{\mathsf{pogs}}$ and $\approx_{\mathsf{ogs}}$ coincide. Since $\mathcal{L}_{\mathsf{DPOGS}}$ generates finite Lassen trees, we deduce that the bisimulation game can be decided.

Theorem 14. *Taking two POGS configurations* $\mathbb{P}, \mathbb{Q}$, *we can decide if* $\mathbb{P} \approx_{\mathsf{pogs}} \mathbb{Q}$.

4.4   Relating the Transitions in OGS and POGS

To relate the transitions in the OGS and in the POGS, we need to introduce some relations and operations on OGS configurations.

Definition 15. *Let* $\mathbb{G} = (\mathbb{I}, \mathbb{S}, \langle L; D \rangle)$ *and* $\mathbb{H} = (\mathbb{I}, \mathbb{S}, \langle L; D' \rangle)$ *be two OGS configurations. We write* $\mathbb{G} \subseteq_{Di} \mathbb{H}$ *when* $D \subseteq D'$.

When $\mathbb{G} \subseteq_{Di} \mathbb{H}$, the configurations only differ by their set of disclosed atoms.

Lemma 16. *If* $\mathbb{G} \subseteq_{Di} \mathbb{H}$ *and* $\mathbb{G} \xrightarrow{a}_{ogs} \mathbb{G}'$ *then* $\mathbb{H} \xrightarrow{a}_{ogs} \mathbb{H}'$ *and* $\mathbb{G}' \subseteq_{Di} \mathbb{H}'$.

Lemma 17. *Let* $\mathbb{P}$ *be an active prime configuration. We have the following:*

- *if* $\mathbb{P} \xrightarrow{op}_{ogs} \mathbb{P}'$, *then* $\mathbb{P} \xrightarrow{op}_{pogs} \mathbb{P}'$,
- *if* $\mathbb{P} \xrightarrow{op}_{pogs} \mathbb{P}'$, *then* $\mathbb{P} \xrightarrow{op}_{ogs} \subseteq_{Di} \mathbb{P}'$.

In POGS, the disclosed set increases in op transitions as seen above, but not in p transitions. In a sense, disclosing in OGS is done only when needed, whereas in POGS, disclosing must be declared as soon as the atom is created. This is ensured by the additional condition $\mathsf{supp}(p) \subseteq D$ in the rule for $\xrightarrow{p}_{pd}$.

Lemma 18. *When* $\mathbb{P} \xrightarrow{p}_{pogs} \mathbb{P}'$ *with* $\mathbb{P}$ *active, we also have* $\mathbb{P} \xrightarrow{p}_{ogs} \mathbb{P}'$.

However, the converse does not always hold, specifically if an atom has been declared non-disclosed but still appears in the action p. Indeed, the transition $(\langle [c]a; \widehat{L}; \emptyset \rangle, \mathbb{S}, \langle L; \emptyset \rangle) \xrightarrow{\bar{c}(a)}_{ogs} (\langle \widehat{L}; \emptyset \rangle, \mathbb{S}, \langle L; \{a\} \rangle)$ is valid for OGS, but has no counterpart in POGS, since $\langle L; \emptyset \rangle$ cannot make the transition $\xrightarrow{\bar{c}(a)}_{pd}$.

Using the following notion of limit (on OGS configurations), we can intuitively replace D by its minimal extension, preventing this phenomenon from happening.

Definition 19. *Given a configuration* $\mathbb{G} = (\mathbb{I}, \mathbb{S}, \langle L; D \rangle)$, *we define its* limit *as:*

$$\mathsf{lim}(\mathbb{G}) \triangleq (\mathbb{I}, \mathbb{S}, \langle L; \bigcup_{t \in \mathrm{Traces}} (L \cap D') \rangle) \text{ with } \mathbb{G} \xrightarrow{t}_{ogs} (\_, \_, \langle \_, D' \rangle).$$

We have that $\mathbb{G} \subseteq_{Di} \mathsf{lim}(\mathbb{G})$ and lim is idempotent. We call *limit configurations* those configurations that are a limit (or alternatively, that are their own limit). Being a limit configuration is preserved by moves but not necessarily by op.

Lemma 20. *Let* $\mathbb{P}$ *be a limit configuration. If* $\mathbb{P} \xrightarrow{p}_{ogs} \mathbb{P}'$, *then* $\mathbb{P} \xrightarrow{p}_{pogs} \mathbb{P}'$.

For Opponent transitions, the situation is less simple since not all active OGS configurations are active POGS configurations. To circumvent that issue, we reuse the tensor product from [12]. For two OGS configurations where at least one is passive, we define the tensor product, written $\otimes$, as follows:

$$(\mathbb{I}, S, D) \otimes (\mathbb{J}, T, E) = (\mathbb{I} \otimes \mathbb{J}, S \otimes T, D \otimes E)$$

$$\langle S; \gamma \rangle \otimes \langle S'; \gamma' \rangle = \langle S \cup S'; \gamma \cdot \gamma' \rangle \qquad \langle M; S; \gamma \rangle \otimes \langle S'; \gamma' \rangle = \langle M; S \cup S'; \gamma \cdot \gamma' \rangle$$

$$\langle L; D \rangle \otimes \langle L'; D' \rangle = \langle L \cup L'; D \cup D' \rangle \text{ when } \begin{array}{l} D' \cap L \subseteq D \\ D \cap L' \subseteq D' \end{array}$$

The side conditions for the L and D components ensure that no shared atom is disclosed on one configuration but not the other.

We can then describe an active OGS configuration as the tensor of two POGS configurations (where $S = \widehat{L}$):

$$((\langle M; S; \gamma \rangle, \langle \Delta_O \vdash \bot; \Delta_P \rangle, \langle L, D \rangle) = ((\langle M; L \rangle, \langle \Delta_O \vdash \bot \rangle, \langle L, D \rangle) \otimes (\langle L; \gamma \rangle, \langle \Delta_O \vdash \Delta_P \rangle, \langle L, D \rangle)$$

Finally, we have the following property for opponent transitions:

Lemma 21. *When* $\mathbb{P} \xrightarrow{o}_{\text{pogs}} \mathbb{Q}$, *we have* $\mathbb{P} \xrightarrow{o}_{\text{ogs}} \mathbb{Q} \otimes \mathbb{P}$.
When $\mathbb{P} \xrightarrow{o}_{\text{ogs}} \mathbb{G}$, *we have* $\mathbb{P} \xrightarrow{o}_{\text{pogs}} \mathbb{Q}$ *with* $\mathbb{G} = \mathbb{Q} \otimes \mathbb{P}$.

5   Relating Bisimilarities in OGS and POGS

In this section, we show that $\simeq_{\text{pogs}}$ can be used to characterize $\simeq_{\text{ogs}}$ for the limit configurations introduced above. We rely for that on up-to techniques for bipartite bisimulation in OGS, which we introduce first.

5.1   Up-to techniques for $\simeq_{\text{ogs}}$

The proofs in this section use the theory of compatible functions [27,25]. More details can be found in [9].

Definition 22 (Bipartite bisimulation up-to). *Given a function* f, *a bipartite bisimulation up to* f *is a pair* $(\mathcal{R}_{Act}, \mathcal{R}_{Pas})$ *such that:*

- *If* $(\mathbb{G}_1, \mathbb{G}_2) \in \mathcal{R}_{Pas}$ *then for all Opponent moves* o *and* $\mathbb{H}_1, \mathbb{H}_2$ *such that* $\mathbb{G}_1 \xrightarrow{o}_{\text{ogs}} \mathbb{H}_1$ *and* $\mathbb{G}_2 \xrightarrow{o}_{\text{ogs}} \mathbb{H}_2$, *we have* $(\mathbb{H}_1, \mathbb{H}_2) \in f(\mathcal{R}_{Act})$.
- *If* $(\mathbb{G}_1, \mathbb{G}_2) \in \mathcal{R}_{Act}$ *then there exists a Proponent move* p *and* $(\mathbb{H}_1, \mathbb{H}_2) \in f(\mathcal{R}_{Pas})$ *such that* $\mathbb{G}_1 \overset{p}{\Rightarrow}_{\text{ogs}} \mathbb{H}_1$ *and* $\mathbb{G}_2 \overset{p}{\Rightarrow}_{\text{ogs}} \mathbb{H}_2$.

We then define $\text{hide}(\mathcal{R}_{Act}, \mathcal{R}_{Pas}) \triangleq (\subseteq_{\text{Di}} \mathcal{R}_{Act} \supseteq_{\text{Di}}, \subseteq_{\text{Di}} \mathcal{R}_{Pas} \supseteq_{\text{Di}})$. Recall that we still require that $\text{hide}(\mathcal{R}_{Act}, \mathcal{R}_{Pas})$ only contains pairs of configurations with the same disclosed set. The soundness of hide can be proved using Lemma 16.

Lemma 23. hide *is a sound up-to technique, i.e. if* $(\mathcal{R}_{Act}, \mathcal{R}_{Pas})$ *is a bisimulation up to* hide, *then* $(\mathcal{R}_{Act}, \mathcal{R}_{Pas}) \subseteq \simeq_{\text{ogs}}$.

Given a pair of relations $(\mathcal{R}_{Act}, \mathcal{R}_{Pas})$ on active and passive OGS configurations respectively, we define the following functions:

$$
\begin{aligned}
\texttt{tensor}(\mathcal{R}_{Act}, \mathcal{R}_{Pas}) &\triangleq \big(\; \{(\mathbb{G}_1 \otimes \mathbb{G}_2, \mathbb{H}_1 \otimes \mathbb{H}_2) \text{ s.t. } (\mathbb{G}_1, \mathbb{H}_1) \in \mathcal{R}_{Act}, (\mathbb{G}_2, \mathbb{H}_2) \in \mathcal{R}_{Pas}\}, \\
&\quad\;\; \{(\mathbb{G}_1 \otimes \mathbb{G}_2, \mathbb{H}_1 \otimes \mathbb{H}_2) \text{ s.t. } (\mathbb{G}_1, \mathbb{H}_1), (\mathbb{G}_2, \mathbb{H}_2) \in \mathcal{R}_{Pas}\} \;\big) \\
\texttt{split}(\mathcal{R}_{Act}, \mathcal{R}_{Pas}) &\triangleq \big(\; \{(\mathbb{G}_1, \mathbb{H}_1) \qquad\qquad\;\; \text{s.t. } (\mathbb{G}_1 \otimes \mathbb{G}_2, \mathbb{H}_1 \otimes \mathbb{H}_2) \in \mathcal{R}_{Act}\}, \\
&\quad\;\; \{(\mathbb{G}_1, \mathbb{H}_1) \qquad\qquad\;\; \text{s.t. } (\mathbb{G}_1 \otimes \mathbb{G}_2, \mathbb{H}_1 \otimes \mathbb{H}_2) \in \mathcal{R}_{Pas}\} \;\big)
\end{aligned}
$$

Lemma 24. $\texttt{split}(\approx_{\text{ogs}}) \subseteq \approx_{\text{ogs}}$.

$\texttt{tensor}$ is not a sound up-to technique. It is nevertheless useful to reason about POGS bipartite bisimilar configurations; see Theorem 30 below.

5.2 Properties of the Limit (in OGS)

Lemma 25 (Monotonicity). *If $\mathbb{G}$ is passive and $\mathbb{G} \xrightarrow{t}_{\text{ogs}} \mathbb{H}$, then there exists $\mathbb{G}'$ such that $\mathbb{G} \otimes \mathbb{G}' \subseteq_{\text{Di}} \mathbb{H}$.*

Lemma 25 shows that transitions can only increase the substitution and the store (corresponding to the $\mathbb{G}'$ component), and the set of disclosed atoms (represented by the use of $\subseteq_{\text{Di}}$). More precisely, $\subseteq_{\text{Di}}$ is required if some atoms from $\mathbb{G}$ are disclosed along the trace t, in which case new ones can appear in $\mathbb{G}'$.

Lemma 25 is language specific. It does not hold when the language allows the content of the store to be modified (like, e.g. in $\lambda\mu_{\text{ref}}$). Additionally, LTSs enforcing some local restriction on the usage of function or continuation names usually have extra components that are modified along the transitions; we return to this point in Section 7.

In a limit configuration (Definition 19), all atoms that may be disclosed at some point are disclosed. By Lemma 25, these atoms can be disclosed using a single trace.

Lemma 26. *Given a passive configuration $\mathbb{G}$, there exists a trace t and a configuration $\mathbb{H}$ such that $\mathbb{G} \xrightarrow{t}_{\text{ogs}} \textbf{lim}(\mathbb{G}) \otimes \mathbb{H}$.*

The limit is also useful to relate transitions in OGS and in POGS as follows.

Lemma 27. *Take a POGS configuration $\mathbb{P}$.*
If $\mathbb{P}$ is active and $\mathbb{P} \xrightarrow{a}_{\text{ogs}} \mathbb{Q}$, then $\textbf{lim}(\mathbb{P}) \xrightarrow{a}_{\text{pogs}} \textbf{lim}(\mathbb{Q})$.
If $\mathbb{P}$ is passive and $\mathbb{P} \xrightarrow{o}_{\text{ogs}} \mathbb{Q} \otimes \mathbb{P}$, then $\textbf{lim}(\mathbb{P}) \xrightarrow{o}_{\text{pogs}} \textbf{lim}(\mathbb{Q})$.

All in all, we obtain that $\approx_{\text{ogs}}$ is a congruence for $\textbf{lim}$. For $\mathcal{R}$ a relation over configurations, we write $\textbf{lim}(\mathcal{R})$ for the set $\{(\textbf{lim}(\mathbb{G}), \textbf{lim}(\mathbb{H})) \mid (\mathbb{G}, \mathbb{H}) \in \mathcal{R}\}$.

Lemma 28. $\approx_{\text{ogs}}$ *is closed by computing the limit:* $\textbf{lim}(\approx_{\text{ogs}}) \subseteq \approx_{\text{ogs}}$.

The case for passive configurations follows immediately from Lemmas 26 and 24.

The property of the limit might make us think that the disclosure process of an atom could be decided statically, by annotating new syntactically. The following example shows that it is not the case:

$$\lambda b.\text{new } n, m \text{ in } \lambda\_.\text{if } b \text{ then } n \text{ else } m$$

Either n or m will be disclosed depending on the boolean b given by Opponent, but never both. So this term is indeed contextually equivalent to $\lambda b.\text{new } n \text{ in } \lambda\_.n$.

5.3 Correspondence Between $\approx_{\text{ogs}}$ and $\approx_{\text{pogs}}$

Theorem 29 (From $\approx_{\text{ogs}}$ to $\approx_{\text{pogs}}$). *Consider two POGS configurations $\mathbb{P}$ and $\mathbb{Q}$. If $\mathbb{P} \approx_{\text{ogs}} \mathbb{Q}$ are both limit configurations, then $\mathbb{P} \approx_{\text{pogs}} \mathbb{Q}$.*

To reason about bisimilar POGS configurations, we use the closure of tensor, written $\overline{\text{tensor}}$. Intuitively, $\overline{\text{tensor}}(\mathcal{R}_{Act})$ contains the pairs $(\mathbb{G}_1 \otimes \mathbb{G}_2, \mathbb{H}_1 \otimes \mathbb{H}_2)$ with $(\mathbb{G}_1, \mathbb{H}_1) \in \mathcal{R}_{Act}$, $(\mathbb{G}_2, \mathbb{H}_2) \in \overline{\text{tensor}}(\mathcal{R}_{Pas})$, and $\overline{\text{tensor}}(\mathcal{R}_{Pas})$ contains the pairs $(\mathbb{G}_1 \otimes \mathbb{G}_2, \mathbb{H}_1 \otimes \mathbb{H}_2)$ with $(\mathbb{G}_1, \mathbb{H}_1) \in \mathcal{R}_{Pas}$, $(\mathbb{G}_2, \mathbb{H}_2) \in \overline{\text{tensor}}(\mathcal{R}_{Pas})$.

Theorem 30 (From $\approx_{\text{pogs}}$ to $\approx_{\text{ogs}}$). *Suppose $\mathcal{R}$ is a POGS bipartite bisimulation. Then $\overline{\text{tensor}}(\mathcal{R})$ is a OGS bipartite bisimulation up-to hiding.*

By Lemma 23, Theorem 30 means that if $\mathbb{P} \approx_{\text{pogs}} \mathbb{Q}$, then $\mathbb{P} \approx_{\text{ogs}} \mathbb{Q}$.

The correspondence between $\approx_{\text{ogs}}$ and $\approx_{\text{pogs}}$ is restricted to prime configurations as $\approx_{\text{pogs}}$ can only relate those. Having the additional conditions of configurations being limits is enough for our decidability result.

6 Related Work

The ν-calculus was introduced in [24], together with logical relations to reason over contextual equivalence for this language. These logical relations use a Kripke-style definition, worlds being defined as spans of atoms to keep track of the disclosed atoms, similar to the permutation we use in our relaxed bipartite bisimulations. They capture contextual equivalence for programs of *first order* type, but are an incomplete technique for higher-order programs. This entails a decidability result for the first-order fragment of the ν-calculus, since logical relations only quantify over finite objects at first-order types.

Categorical models of the ν-calculus were provided in [29,30], using a representation of name creation via a strong monad. Two examples of such models were given: (i) the functor category Set^I with I the category of finite sets and injection; (ii) the category $\mathbf{B}G$ of continuous G-sets, with G the topological group of automorphisms over $\mathbb{N}$. None of these models are fully-abstract, since they distinguish new n in $\lambda x.x = n$ from $\lambda x.\text{false}$.

These models were later refined using nominal sets [7], so that types are interpreted via *Fraenkel-Mostowski* sets [28] or domains [14]. Both of these works are continuation models; they might be used to provide a semantics for the $\lambda\mu\nu$-calculus studied in this paper, a direction we wish to explore in future work. Such use of continuations was justified in [28] to provide a model for an extension of the ν-calculus with recursion. More recently, *proof-relevant* logical relations were introduced to deal with recursion in the presence of name generation [4].

In [26], a model of the ν-calculus is given in quasi-Borel spaces, showing a correspondence between random sampling and fresh name generation. This model is shown to be fully-abstract for terms of first-order types.

In [5], environmental bisimulations for the ν-calculus are defined and shown to be fully abstract. Nevertheless, it does not seem possible to extract a decision procedure from that result, since environmental bisimulations are played over a higher-order LTS, that is, an LTS whose actions contain λ-terms. So this LTS is infinitely branching at higher-order types.

Eager normal-form bisimulations have been introduced by Lassen for the call-by-value λ-calculus [16] and λμ-calculus. In [31], a notion of bisimulation similar to $\simeq_{\mathsf{ogs}}$ is introduced and shown to be fully abstract for an untyped version of $\lambda\mu_{\mathsf{ref}}$. Compared to the standard notion of eager normal form bisimulations, the configurations in the bisimulations in [31] contain an environment similar to the environment component γ of the OGS LTS in Section 3.

In [1], a fully-abstract game model is provided for the ν-calculus. However, this model requires an extensional collapse, that is not directly computable at higher-order type. So that model could only be used to prove the decidability of contextual equivalence for terms of first-order types. Enforcing a well-bracketed and visible behavior for Opponent in the OGS model, we believe that our trace model would coincide with the intentional game model of [1]. Nominal game semantics was developed for languages with nominal references and exceptions in [32]. In that setting, algorithmic presentations of game semantics make it possible to provide a classification of decidability of call-by-value languages with (bounded) integer references [19], and ground references [21]. In this setting, the undecidability of contextual equivalence originates from the use of integer references by Proponent. A detailed survey on the literature on contextual equivalence for the ν-calculus is available in [33].

7   Conclusion

To decide the contextual equivalence between two λμν typed terms M and N with contexts in the $\lambda\mu_{\mathsf{ref}}$-calculus, we first construct the corresponding initial configurations, and we can decide by Thm. 14 if they are POGS-bisimilar. This decidability result comes from the fact that the POGS LTS generates finite trees.

Then, we prove in Thm. 29 and Thm. 30 that two initial active configurations are POGS-bisimilar iff they are OGS-bisimilar. This is possible because initial configurations are prime (they are active and γ is empty) and are also limit configurations (their disclosed sets contain all the atoms of the store). In Thm. 7 and Lemma 10, we prove that M and N are contextually equivalent iff the corresponding initial configurations are OGS-bisimilar, which yields decidability.

We now examine the obstacles that remain to prove the decidability of contextual equivalence with contexts in the ν-calculus.

First of all, in that setting, trace equivalence would not be fully-abstract anymore (Thm. 7). Indeed, without integer references, one cannot observe the sequentiality of calls and returns. So an extensional collapse would be necessary.

Another obstacle is that in the absence of higher-order references, Opponent must satisfy a condition of *O-visibility* [2], that corresponds to a local well-scoping discipline, for the function names it is allowed to call. Working in an intuitionistic type system, corresponding to the standard λ-calculus without control operators, the call-and-return discipline of the interaction between Proponent and Opponent has to be *well-bracketed*. These two conditions, namely O-visibility and well-bracketing, can be enforced operationally [13] in the LTS, by keeping track of part of the history of the interaction. However the reduction of $\simeq_{\mathsf{ogs}}$ to $\simeq_{\mathsf{pogs}}$ is not possible anymore in that setting. Indeed, the limit over-approximates the set of atoms that can be tested. This can be seen when comparing the programs

$$\mathtt{new}\ n\ \mathtt{in}\ \mathsf{let}\ \_ = y(\lambda z.z = a)\,\mathsf{in}\,n \quad \text{and} \quad \mathtt{new}\ n\ \mathtt{in}\ \mathsf{let}\ \_ = y(\lambda z.\mathtt{false})\,\mathsf{in}\,n$$

Assuming n is immediately disclosed makes it possible to distinguish the two programs. Because the local conditions of well-bracketing or visibility would prevent Opponent from playing some actions, Opponent could perform irreversible changes that would invalidate Lemma 25. This would make $\simeq_{\mathsf{pogs}}$ incomplete.

To handle this difficulty, we could try and use Kripke eager normal-form bisimulation [11], using a structure for worlds richer than just a set of atoms.

Finally, in absence of *full ground references*, that can store locations, atoms played by Opponent would also follow a local well-scoping discipline, but the discriminatory power over Player atoms would also be restricted [20]. In such a setting, the same difficulties as with well-bracketing and O-visibility would arise, and a more complex extensional collapse would be needed.

References

1. Samson Abramsky, Dan R. Ghica, Andrzej S. Murawski, C.-H. Luke Ong, and Ian David Bede Stark. Nominal games and full abstraction for the nu-calculus. In *19th IEEE Symposium on Logic in Computer Science (LICS 2004), 14-17 July 2004, Turku, Finland, Proceedings*, pages 150–159. IEEE Computer Society, 2004.
2. Samson Abramsky, Kohei Honda, and Guy McCusker. A fully abstract game semantics for general references. In *Thirteenth Annual IEEE Symposium on Logic in Computer Science, Indianapolis, Indiana, USA, June 21-24, 1998*, pages 334–344. IEEE Computer Society, 1998.
3. Hendrik Pieter Barendregt. *The lambda calculus - its syntax and semantics*, volume 103 of *Studies in logic and the foundations of mathematics*. North-Holland, 1985.
4. Nick Benton, Martin Hofmann, and Vivek Nigam. Proof-relevant logical relations for name generation. *Log. Methods Comput. Sci.*, 14(1), 2018.
5. Nick Benton and Vasileios Koutavas. A mechanized bisimulation for the nu-calculus. *Higher Order and Symbolic Computation - Special Issue in Honor of Mitchell Wand*, sep 2012. In Press.

6. Corrado Böhm. Alcune proprieta delle forme β-η-normali nel λ-k-calcolo. *Pubblicazioni dell'Istituto per le Applicazioni del Calcolo*, 696:19, 1968.

7. Murdoch Gabbay and Andrew M. Pitts. A new approach to abstract syntax with variable binding. *Formal Aspects Comput.*, 13(3-5):341–363, 2002.

8. Jean-Yves Girard. Linear logic. *Theor. Comput. Sci.*, 50:1–102, 1987.

9. Daniel Hirschkoff, Guilhem Jaber, and Enguerrand Prebet. Deciding contextual equivalence of ν-calculus with effectful contexts (full version). https://hal.science/hal-03955303.

10. Guilhem Jaber and Andrzej S. Murawski. Complete trace models of state and control. In Nobuko Yoshida, editor, *Programming Languages and Systems - 30th European Symposium on Programming, ESOP 2021, Held as Part of the European Joint Conferences on Theory and Practice of Software, ETAPS 2021, Luxembourg City, Luxembourg, March 27 - April 1, 2021, Proceedings*, volume 12648 of *Lecture Notes in Computer Science*, pages 348–374. Springer, 2021.

11. Guilhem Jaber and Andrzej S. Murawski. Compositional relational reasoning via operational game semantics. In *36th Annual ACM/IEEE Symposium on Logic in Computer Science, LICS 2021, Rome, Italy, June 29 - July 2, 2021*, pages 1–13. IEEE, 2021.

12. Guilhem Jaber and Davide Sangiorgi. Games, mobile processes, and functions. In Florin Manea and Alex Simpson, editors, *30th EACSL Annual Conference on Computer Science Logic, CSL 2022, February 14-19, 2022, Göttingen, Germany (Virtual Conference)*, volume 216 of *LIPIcs*, pages 25:1–25:18. Schloss Dagstuhl - Leibniz-Zentrum für Informatik, 2022.

13. James Laird. A fully abstract trace semantics for general references. In Lars Arge, Christian Cachin, Tomasz Jurdzinski, and Andrzej Tarlecki, editors, *Automata, Languages and Programming, 34th International Colloquium, ICALP 2007, Wroclaw, Poland, July 9-13, 2007, Proceedings*, volume 4596 of *Lecture Notes in Computer Science*, pages 667–679. Springer, 2007.

14. James Laird. Sequentiality and the CPS semantics of fresh names. In Marcelo Fiore, editor, *Proceedings of the 23rd Conference on the Mathematical Foundations of Programming Semantics, MFPS 2007, New Orleans, LA, USA, April 11-14, 2007*, volume 173 of *Electronic Notes in Theoretical Computer Science*, pages 203–219. Elsevier, 2007.

15. James Laird. A Curry-style semantics of interaction: From untyped to second-order lazy λ μ-calculus. In Jean Goubault-Larrecq and Barbara König, editors, *Foundations of Software Science and Computation Structures - 23rd International Conference, FOSSACS 2020, Held as Part of the European Joint Conferences on Theory and Practice of Software, ETAPS 2020, Dublin, Ireland, April 25-30, 2020, Proceedings*, volume 12077 of *Lecture Notes in Computer Science*, pages 422–441. Springer, 2020.

16. Søren B. Lassen. Eager normal form bisimulation. In *20th IEEE Symposium on Logic in Computer Science (LICS 2005), 26-29 June 2005, Chicago, IL, USA, Proceedings*, pages 345–354. IEEE Computer Society, 2005.

17. Søren B. Lassen and Paul Blain Levy. Typed normal form bisimulation. In Jacques Duparc and Thomas A. Henzinger, editors, *Computer Science Logic, 21st International Workshop, CSL 2007, 16th Annual Conference of the EACSL, Lausanne, Switzerland, September 11-15, 2007, Proceedings*, volume 4646 of *Lecture Notes in Computer Science*, pages 283–297. Springer, 2007.

18. Sam Lindley and Ian Stark. Reducibility and tt-lifting for computation types. In Pawel Urzyczyn, editor, *Typed Lambda Calculi and Applications, 7th International*

Conference, *TLCA 2005, Nara, Japan, April 21-23, 2005, Proceedings*, volume 3461 of *Lecture Notes in Computer Science*, pages 262–277. Springer, 2005.

19. Andrzej S. Murawski and Nikos Tzevelekos. Algorithmic nominal game semantics. In Gilles Barthe, editor, *Programming Languages and Systems - 20th European Symposium on Programming, ESOP 2011, Held as Part of the Joint European Conferences on Theory and Practice of Software, ETAPS 2011, Saarbrücken, Germany, March 26-April 3, 2011. Proceedings*, volume 6602 of *Lecture Notes in Computer Science*, pages 419–438. Springer, 2011.

20. Andrzej S. Murawski and Nikos Tzevelekos. Full abstraction for reduced ML. *Ann. Pure Appl. Log.*, 164(11):1118–1143, 2013.

21. Andrzej S. Murawski and Nikos Tzevelekos. Algorithmic games for full ground references. *Formal Methods Syst. Des.*, 52(3):277–314, 2018.

22. Michel Parigot. Lambda-mu-calculus: An algorithmic interpretation of classical natural deduction. In Andrei Voronkov, editor, *Logic Programming and Automated Reasoning,International Conference LPAR'92, St. Petersburg, Russia, July 15-20, 1992, Proceedings*, volume 624 of *Lecture Notes in Computer Science*, pages 190–201. Springer, 1992.

23. Michel Parigot. Strong normalization for second order classical natural deduction. In *Proceedings of the Eighth Annual Symposium on Logic in Computer Science (LICS '93), Montreal, Canada, June 19-23, 1993*, pages 39–46. IEEE Computer Society, 1993.

24. Andrew M. Pitts and Ian David Bede Stark. Observable properties of higher order functions that dynamically create local names, or what's new? In Andrzej M. Borzyszkowski and Stefan Sokolowski, editors, *Mathematical Foundations of Computer Science 1993, 18th International Symposium, MFCS'93, Gdansk, Poland, August 30 - September 3, 1993, Proceedings*, volume 711 of *Lecture Notes in Computer Science*, pages 122–141. Springer, 1993.

25. D. Pous and D. Sangiorgi. *Advanced Topics in Bisimulation and Coinduction (D. Sangiorgi and J. Rutten editors)*, chapter Enhancements of the coinductive proof method. Cambridge University Press, 2011.

26. Marcin Sabok, Sam Staton, Dario Stein, and Michael Wolman. Probabilistic programming semantics for name generation. *Proc. ACM Program. Lang.*, 5(POPL):1–29, 2021.

27. Davide Sangiorgi. On the bisimulation proof method. *Mathematical Structures in Computer Science*, 8(5):447–479, 1998.

28. Mark R. Shinwell and Andrew M. Pitts. On a monadic semantics for freshness. *Theor. Comput. Sci.*, 342(1):28–55, 2005.

29. Ian Stark. *Names and Higher-Order Functions*. PhD thesis, University of Cambridge, December 1994. Also available as Technical Report 363, University of Cambridge Computer Laboratory.

30. Ian Stark. Categorical models for local names. *LISP Symb. Comput.*, 9(1):77–107, 1996.

31. Kristian Støvring and Søren B. Lassen. A complete, co-inductive syntactic theory of sequential control and state. In Jens Palsberg, editor, *Semantics and Algebraic Specification, Essays Dedicated to Peter D. Mosses on the Occasion of His 60th Birthday*, volume 5700 of *Lecture Notes in Computer Science*, pages 329–375. Springer, 2009.

32. Nikos Tzevelekos. *Nominal Game Semantics*. PhD thesis, University of Oxford, 2009.

33. Nikos Tzevelekos. Program equivalence with names. In Amal Ahmed, Nick Benton, Lars Birkedal, and Martin Hofmann, editors, *Modelling, Controlling and Reasoning About State, 29.08. - 03.09.2010*, volume 10351 of *Dagstuhl Seminar Proceedings*. Schloss Dagstuhl - Leibniz-Zentrum für Informatik, Germany, 2010.

Kantorovich Functors and Characteristic Logics for Behavioural Distances

Sergey Goncharov[1] [ID]*, Dirk Hofmann[2] [ID]**, Pedro Nora[1(✉)] [ID]***,
Lutz Schröder[1] [ID]† and Paul Wild[1] [ID]

[1] Friedrich-Alexander-Universität Erlangen-Nürnberg, Erlangen, Germany
sergey.goncharov@fau.de, pedro.nora@fau.de, lutz.schroeder@fau.de,
paul.wild@fau.de
[2] Center for Research and Development in Mathematics and Applications, University
of Aveiro, Aveiro, Portugal
dirk@ua.pt

Abstract. Behavioural distances measure the deviation between states
in quantitative systems, such as probabilistic or weighted systems. There
is growing interest in generic approaches to behavioural distances. In
particular, coalgebraic methods capture variations in the system type (non-
deterministic, probabilistic, game-based etc.), and the notion of *quantale*
abstracts over the actual values distances take, thus covering, e.g., two-
valued equivalences, (pseudo)metrics, and probabilistic (pseudo)metrics.
Coalgebraic behavioural distances have been based either on *liftings*
of Set-functors to categories of metric spaces, or on *lax extensions* of
Set-functors to categories of quantitative relations. Every lax extension
induces a functor lifting but not every lifting comes from a lax extension.
It was shown recently that every lax extension is Kantorovich, i.e. induced
by a suitable choice of monotone predicate liftings, implying via a quantitative coalgebraic Hennessy-Milner theorem that behavioural distances
induced by lax extensions can be characterized by quantitative modal
logics. Here, we essentially show the same in the more general setting of
behavioural distances induced by functor liftings. In particular, we show
that every functor lifting, and indeed every functor on (quantale-valued)
metric spaces, that preserves isometries is Kantorovich, so that the induced behavioural distance (on systems of suitably restricted branching
degree) can be characterized by a quantitative modal logic.

1 Introduction

Qualitative transition systems, such as standard labelled transition systems,
are typically compared under two-valued notions of behavioural equivalence,

* Funded by the Deutsche Forschungsgemeinschaft (DFG, German Research Foundation) – project number 501369690.
** Funded by The Center for Research and Development in Mathematics and Applications (CIDMA) through the Portuguese Foundation for Science and Technology
(FCT) – project numbers UIDB/04106/2020 and UIDP/04106/2020.
*** Funded by the Deutsche Forschungsgemeinschaft (DFG, German Research Foundation) – project number 259234802.
† Funded by the Deutsche Forschungsgemeinschaft (DFG, German Research Foundation) – project number 434050016.

O. Kupferman and P. Sobocinski (Eds.): FoSSaCS 2023, LNCS 13992, pp. 46–67, 2023.
https://doi.org/10.1007/978-3-031-30829-1_3

such as Park-Milner bisimilarity. For quantitative systems, such as probabilistic, weighted, or metric transition systems, notions of *behavioural distance* allow for a more fine-grained comparison, in particular give a numerical measure of the deviation between inequivalent states, instead of just flagging them as inequivalent [14,6,2,24].

The variation found in the mentioned system types calls for unifying methods, and correspondingly has given rise to generic notions of behavioural distance based on *universal coalgebra* [33], a framework for state-based systems in which the transition type of systems is encapsulated as an (endo-)functor on a suitable base category. Coalgebraic behavioural distances have been defined on the one hand using *liftings* of given set functors to the category of metric spaces [5], and on the other hand using *lax extensions*, i.e. extensions of set functors to categories of quantitative relations [13,38]. Since every lax extension induces a functor lifting in a straightforward way [38] but on the other hand not every functor lifting is induced by a lax extension, the approach via liftings is more widely applicable. On the other hand, it has been shown that every lax extension is *Kantorovich*, i.e. induced by a suitable choice of modalities, modelled as predicate liftings in the spirit of coalgebraic logic [28,34]. Using quantitative coalgebraic Hennessy-Milner theorems, it follows that under expected conditions on the functor and the lax extension, behavioural distance coincides with logical distance.

Roughly speaking, our main contribution in the present paper is to show that the same holds for functor liftings and their induced behavioural distances. In more detail, we have the following (cf. Figure 1 for a graphical summary):

- *Every* lifting of a set functor is *topological*, i.e. induced by a generalized form of predicate liftings in which one may need to switch to non-standard spaces of truth values for the predicates involved (Theorem 3.1).
- Functor liftings that preserve isometries are *Kantorovich*, i.e. induced by (possibly polyadic) predicate liftings. (Here, we understand predicate liftings as involving only the standard space of truth values – that is, the unit interval, in the case of 1-bounded metric spaces). In fact, preservation of isometries is also necessary (Theorem 3.9).
- Lastly, we detach the technical development from set functors, and show that a functor on (pseudo)metric spaces is *Kantorovich*, in the sense that the distance of its elements can be characterized by predicate liftings, iff it preserves isometries (Theorem 5.3).

By a recent coalgebraic quantitative Hennessy-Milner theorem that fits this level of generality [12], it follows that given a functor F on (pseudo<)metric spaces that preserves isometries, acts non-expansively on morphisms, and admits a dense finitary subfunctor, behavioural distance can be characterized by quantitative modal logic (Corollary 5.10). In additional results, we further clarify the relationship between functor liftings and lax extensions, and in particular characterize the functor liftings that are induced by lax extensions (Theorem 3.18).

Indeed, we conduct the main technical development not only in coalgebraic generality, but also parametric in a quantale, hence abstracting both over distances and over truth values. One benefit of this generality is that our results cover the two-valued case, captured by the two-element quantale. In particular, one instance of our results is the fact that every finitary set functor has a separating set of finitary predicate liftings, and hence admits a modal logic having the Hennessy-Milner property [34]. Moreover, we do not restrict to symmetric distances, and hence cover also simulation preorders and simulation distances [24].

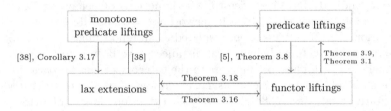

Fig. 1. Summary of connections (a rigorous categorical interpretation of these connections involves a square of adjunctions (3)).

Related Work Quantale-valued quantitative notions of bisimulation for functors that already live on generalized metric spaces (rather than being lifted from functors on sets) have been considered early on [40]. We have already mentioned previous work on coalgebraic behavioural metrics, for functors originally living on sets, via metric liftings [5] and via lax extensions [13,38]. Existing work that combines coalgebraic and quantalic generality and accommodates asymmetric distances, like the present work, has so far concentrated on establishing so-called van Benthem theorems, concerned with characterizing (coalgebraic) quantitative modal logics by bisimulation invariance [39]. There is a line of work on Kantorovich-type coinductive predicates at the level of generality of topological categories [21,22] (phrased in fibrational terminology), with results including a game characterization and expressive logics for coinductive predicates already assumed to be Kantorovich in a general sense, i.e. induced by variants of predicate liftings. In this work, the condition of preserving isometries already shows up as *fiberedness*, and indeed the condition already appears in work on metric liftings [5]. As mentioned in the above discussion, we complement existing work on quantitative coalgebraic Hennessy-Milner theorems [23,38,12] by establishing the Kantorovich property they assume.

2   Preliminaries

We will need a fair amount of material on coalgebra, quantales and quantale-enriched categories (generalizing metric spaces), predicate liftings, and lax extension, which we recall in the sequel. New material starts in Section 3.

2.1   Categories and Coalgebras

We assume basic familiarity with category theory [1,4]. More specifically, we make extensive use of topological categories [1] and quantale-enriched categories

[26,20,36]. Recall that a *coalgebra* for a functor $F\colon C \to C$ consists of an object X of C, thought of as an object of *states*, and a morphism $\alpha\colon X \to FX$, thought of as assigning structured collections (sets, distributions, etc.) of successors to states. A *coalgebra morphism* from (X, α) to (Y, β) is a morphism $f \in C(X, Y)$ such that $\beta \cdot f = Ff \cdot \alpha$. We will focus on *concrete categories* over Set, that is categories that come equipped with a faithful functor $|-|\colon C \to$ Set, which allows speaking about individual *states* as elements of $|X|$. A *lifting* of an endofunctor $F\colon$ Set $\to$ Set to C is an endofunctor $\overline{F}\colon C \to C$ such that $|-| \cdot \overline{F} = F \cdot |-|$.

Example 2.1. Some functors of interest for coalgebraic modelling are as follows.

1. The *finite powerset functor* $P_\omega\colon$ Set $\to$ Set maps each set to its finite powerset, and for a map g, $P_\omega(g)$ takes direct images under g. Given a set A (of *labels*), coalgebras for the the functor $P_\omega(A \times -)$ are finitely branching A-labelled transition systems.

2. The *finite distribution functor* $D_\omega\colon$ Set $\to$ Set maps a set X to the set $D_\omega X$ of finitely supported probability distributions on X. Given a finite set A, coalgebras for the functor $(1 + D_\omega)^A$, are probabilistic transition systems [25,10].

Finitary functors are those which are determined by their action on finite sets. More precisely, a functor is finitary if for every set X and every $\mathfrak{x} \in FX$, there is a finite subset inclusion $m\colon A \to X$ such that $\mathfrak{x}$ is in the image of Fm.

Standard examples of non-finitary functors are as follows.

3. The (unbounded) powerset functor $P\colon$ Set $\to$ Set.
4. The neighbourhood functor $N\colon$ Set $\to$ Set sends a set X to the set PPX, and a function $f\colon X \to Y$ to the function $Nf\colon NX \to NY$ that assigns to every element $\mathfrak{x} \in NX$ the set $\{B \subseteq Y \mid f^{-1}B \in \mathfrak{x}\}$.

2.2 Quantales and Quantale-Enriched Categories

A central notion of our development is that of a quantale, which will serve as a parameter determining the range of truth values and distances. A *quantale* $(\mathcal{V}, \otimes, k)$, more precisely a commutative and unital quantale, is a complete lattice $\mathcal{V}$ – with joins and meets denoted by $\bigvee$ and $\bigwedge$, respectively – that carries the structure of a commutative monoid with *tensor* $\otimes$ and *unit* k, such that for every $u \in \mathcal{V}$, the map $u \otimes -\colon \mathcal{V} \to \mathcal{V}$ preserves suprema. This entails that every $u \otimes -$ has a right adjoint $\hom(u, -)\colon \mathcal{V} \to \mathcal{V}$, characterized by the property $u \otimes v \le w \iff v \le \hom(u, w)$. We denote by $\top$ and $\bot$ the greatest and the least element of a quantale, respectively. A quantale is *non-trivial* if $\bot \neq \top$, and *integral* if $\top = k$.

Example 2.2.   1. Every frame (i.e. a complete lattice in which binary meets distribute over infinite joins) is a quantale with $\otimes = \wedge$ and $k = \top$. In particular, every finite distributive lattice is a quantale, prominently 2, the two-element lattice $\{\bot, \top\}$ and 1, the trivial quantale.

2. Every left continuous t-norm [3] defines a quantale on the unit interval equipped with its natural order.

3. The previous clause (up to isomorphism) further specializes as follows:
   (a) The quantale $[0, \infty]_+ = ([0, \infty], \inf, +, 0)$ of non-negative real numbers with infinity, ordered by the greater or equal relation, and with tensor given by addition.
   (b) The quantale $[0, \infty]_{\max} = ([0, \infty], \inf, \max, 0)$ of non-negative real numbers with infinity, ordered by the greater or equal relation, and with tensor given by maximum.
   (c) The quantale $[0, 1]_\oplus = ([0, 1], \inf, \oplus, 0)$ of the unit interval, ordered by the greater or equal order, and with tensor given by truncated addition.

(Note that the quantalic order here is dual to the standard numeric order).

4. Every commutative monoid $(M, \cdot, e)$ generates a quantale on PM (the free quantale over M) w.r.t. set inclusion and with the tensor $A \otimes B = \{a \cdot b \mid a \in A \text{ and } b \in B\}$, for all $A, B \subseteq M$. The unit of this multiplication is the set $\{e\}$.

A $\mathcal{V}$-***category*** is pair (X, a) consisting of a set X and a map $a: X \times X \to \mathcal{V}$ such that $k \leq a(x, x)$ and $a(x, y) \otimes a(y, z) \leq a(x, z)$ for all $x, y, z \in X$. We view a as a (not necessarily symmetric) *distance* function, noting however that objects with 'greater' distance should be seen as being closer together. A $\mathcal{V}$-category (X, a) is ***symmetric*** if $a(x, y) = a(y, x)$ for all $x, y \in X$. Every $\mathcal{V}$-category (X, a) carries a ***natural order*** defined by $x \leq y$ whenever $k \leq a(x, y)$, which induces a faithful functor $\mathcal{V}$-Cat $\to$ Ord. A $\mathcal{V}$-category is ***separated*** if its natural order is antisymmetric. A $\mathcal{V}$-***functor*** $f: (X, a) \to (Y, b)$ is a map $f: X \to Y$ such that, for all $x, y \in X$, $a(x, y) \leq b(f(x), f(y))$. $\mathcal{V}$-categories and $\mathcal{V}$-functors form the category $\mathcal{V}$-Cat, and we denote by $\mathcal{V}$-Cat$_{\mathrm{sym}}$ the full subcategory of $\mathcal{V}$-Cat determined by the symmetric $\mathcal{V}$-categories and by $\mathcal{V}$-Cat$_{\mathrm{sym,sep}}$ the full subcategory of $\mathcal{V}$-Cat$_{\mathrm{sym}}$ determined by the separated symmetric $\mathcal{V}$-categories.

Example 2.3.   1. The Category 1-Cat is equivalent to the category Set of ***sets*** and functions.

2. The category 2-Cat is equivalent to the category Ord of ***preordered sets*** and monotone maps.

3. Metric, ultrametric and bounded metric spaces à la Lawvere [26] can be seen as quantale-enriched categories:
   (a) The category $[0, \infty]_+$-Cat is equivalent to the category GMet of generalized ***metric spaces*** and non-expansive maps.
   (b) The category $[0, \infty]_{\max}$-Cat is equivalent to the category GUMet of generalized ***ultrametric spaces*** and non-expansive maps.
   (c) The category $[0, 1]_\oplus$-Cat is equivalent to the category BHMet of ***bounded-by-1 hemimetric spaces*** and non-expansive maps.

4. Categories enriched in a free quantale PM on a monoid M can be interpreted as sets equipped with a non-deterministic M-valued structure.

We focus on $\mathcal{V} = 2$ and $\mathcal{V} = [0, 1]_\oplus$, which we will use to capture classical (qualitative) and metric (quantitative) aspects of system behaviour, respectively.. Table 1 provides some instances of generic quantale-based concepts (either introduced above or to be introduced presently) in these two cases, for further reference.

General $\mathcal{V}$	Qualitative ($\mathcal{V} = 2$)	Quantitative ($\mathcal{V} = [0,1]_\oplus$)
$\mathcal{V}$-category	preorder	bounded-by-1 hemimetric space
symmetric $\mathcal{V}$-category	equivalence	bounded-by-1 pseudometric space
$\mathcal{V}$-functor	monotone map	non-expansive map
initial $\mathcal{V}$-functor	order-reflecting monotone map	isometry

Table 1. $\mathcal{V}$-categorical notions in the qualitative and the quantitative setting. The prefix 'pseudo' refers to absence of separatedness, and the prefix 'hemi' additionally indicates absence of symmetry.

A $\mathcal{V}$-category (X, a) is **discrete** if $a = 1_X$, and **indiscrete** if $a(x, y) = \top$ for all $x, y \in X$. The **dual** of (X, a) is the $\mathcal{V}$-category $(X, a)^{\mathrm{op}} = (X, a^\circ)$ given by $a^\circ(x, y) = a(y, x)$. Given a set X and a **structured cone**, i.e. a family $(f_i \colon X \to |(X_i, a_i)|)_{i \in I}$ of maps into $\mathcal{V}$-categories (X_i, a_i), the **initial structure** $a \colon X \times X \to \mathcal{V}$ on X is defined by $a(x, y) = \bigwedge_{i \in I} a_i(f_i(x), f_i(y))$, for all $x, y \in X$. A cone $((X, a) \to (X_i, a_i))_{i \in I}$ is said to be **initial** (w.r.t. the forgetful functor $|-| \colon \mathcal{V}\text{-Cat} \to \text{Set}$) if a is the initial structure w.r.t. the structured cone $(X \to |(X_i, a_i)|)_{i \in I}$; a $\mathcal{V}$-functor is **initial** if it forms a singleton initial cone. For every $\mathcal{V}$-category (X, a) and every set S, the S-**power** $(X, a)^S$ is the $\mathcal{V}$-category consisting of the set of all functions from S to X, equipped with the $\mathcal{V}$-category structure $[-, -]$ given by $[f, g] = \bigwedge_{x \in X} a(f(x), g(x))$, for all $f, g \colon S \to X$. By equipping its hom-sets with the substructure of the appropriate power, the category $\mathcal{V}$-Cat becames $\mathcal{V}$-Cat-enriched and, hence, also Ord-enriched w.r.t to the corresponding natural order of $\mathcal{V}$-categories. We say that an endofunctor on $\mathcal{V}$-Cat is **locally monotone** if it preserves this preorder.

Remark 2.4. Let us briefly outline the connections between $\mathcal{V}$-Cat and $\mathcal{V}$-Cat$_{\mathrm{sym}}$, which for real-valued $\mathcal{V}$ correspond to hemimetric and pseudometric spaces, respectively. By virtue of the above construction of initial structures, the categories $\mathcal{V}$-Cat and $\mathcal{V}$-Cat$_{\mathrm{sym}}$ are topological over Set [1]; in particular, both categories are complete and cocomplete. Moreover, $\mathcal{V}$-Cat$_{\mathrm{sym}}$ is a (reflective and) coreflective full subcategory of $\mathcal{V}$-Cat. The coreflector $(-)_s \colon \mathcal{V}$-Cat $\to \mathcal{V}$-Cat$_{\mathrm{sym}}$ is identity on morphisms and sends every (X, a) to its symmetrization, the $\mathcal{V}$-category (X, a_s) where $a_s(x, y) = a(x, y) \wedge a(y, x)$ (keep in mind that in Example 2.2.3, the order is the dual of the numeric order).

Finally, we note that for every quantale $\mathcal{V}$, $(\mathcal{V}, \mathrm{hom})$ is a $\mathcal{V}$-category, which for simplicity we also denote by $\mathcal{V}$. The following result records two fundamental properties of the $\mathcal{V}$-category $\mathcal{V}$.

Proposition 2.5. *The $\mathcal{V}$-category $\mathcal{V} = (\mathcal{V}, \mathrm{hom})$ is injective w.r.t. initial morphisms, and for every $\mathcal{V}$-category X, the cone $(f \colon X \to \mathcal{V})_f$ is initial.*

2.3   Predicate Liftings

Given a cardinal κ and a $\mathcal{V}$-category X, a κ-ary X-**valued predicate lifting** for a functor $\mathsf{F} \colon \mathcal{V}$-Cat $\to \mathcal{V}$-Cat is a natural transformation $\lambda \colon \mathcal{V}$-Cat$(-, X^\kappa) \to$

$\mathcal{V}$-Cat(F−, X). When $\mathcal{V}$ is the trivial quantale, we identify an X-valued predicate lifting with a natural transformation λ: Set(−, X^κ) → Set(F−, X) via the isomorphism Set $\cong$ 1-Cat. In this case, we are primarily interested in predicate liftings valued in the underlying set of another quantale, and we say that such predicate liftings are **monotone** if each of its components is a monotone map w.r.t. the pointwise order induced by that quantale.

Remark 2.6. By the Yoneda lemma, every κ-ary X-valued predicate lifting for a functor F: $\mathcal{V}$-Cat → $\mathcal{V}$-Cat is determined by a $\mathcal{V}$-functor FX^κ → X. In particular, the collection of all X-valued κ-ary predicate liftings for a functor is a set.

Example 2.7.   1. The Kripke semantics of the standard diamond modality $\Diamond$ of the modal logic K is induced (in a way recalled in Section 5) by the unary predicate lifting $\Diamond_X(A) = \{B \subseteq X \mid A \cap B \neq \varnothing\}$ for the (finite) powerset functor (modulo the isomorphism $\mathcal{P}X \cong$ Set(X, 2)).

2. Computing the expected value for a given [0, 1]-valued function with respect to each probability distribution defines a unary [0, 1]-valued predicate lifting for the functor D_ω: Set → Set, which we denote by $\mathbb{E}$.

2.4   Quantale-Enriched Relations and Lax Extensions

The structure of a quantale-enriched category is a particular kind of "enriched relation". For a quantale $\mathcal{V}$ and sets X and Y, a $\mathcal{V}$-**relation** from X to Y is a map r: $X \times Y \to \mathcal{V}$; we then write r: $X \nrightarrow Y$. As for ordinary relations, a pair of $\mathcal{V}$-relations r: $X \nrightarrow Y$ and s: $Y \nrightarrow Z$ can be composed via "matrix multiplication": $(s \cdot r)(x, z) = \bigvee_{y \in Y} r(x, y) \otimes s(y, z)$ for $x \in X$, $z \in Z$. With this composition, the collection of all sets and $\mathcal{V}$-relations between them form a category, denoted $\mathcal{V}$-Rel. The identity morphism on a set X is the $\mathcal{V}$-relation 1_X: $X \nrightarrow X$ that sends every diagonal element to k and all the others to $\perp$.

Example 2.8. The category of 2-relations is the usual category Rel of sets and relations. Quantitative or "fuzzy" relations are usually defined as $[0, 1]_\oplus$-relations (e.g. [38,5]).

The category $\mathcal{V}$-Rel comes with an involution $(−)^\circ$: $\mathcal{V}$-Rel^{op} → $\mathcal{V}$-Rel that maps objects identically and sends a $\mathcal{V}$-relation r: $X \nrightarrow Y$ to the $\mathcal{V}$-relation r°: $Y \nrightarrow X$ given by $r^\circ(y, x) = r(x, y)$, the **converse** of r. Moreover, by equipping its hom-sets with the pointwise order induced by $\mathcal{V}$, $\mathcal{V}$-Rel is made into a quantaloid (e.g. [31]), i.e. enriched over complete join semilattices. This entails that there is an optimal way of extending a $\mathcal{V}$-relation r: $X \nrightarrow Y$ along a $\mathcal{V}$-relation s: $X \nrightarrow Z$: the (Kan) **extension** of r along s is the $\mathcal{V}$-relation $r \bullet\!\!- s$: $Z \nrightarrow Y$ defined by the property $t \cdot s \leq r \iff t \leq r \bullet\!\!- s$, for all t: $Z \nrightarrow Y$.

A **lax extension** [1] of a functor F: Set → Set to $\mathcal{V}$-Rel is a lax functor $\widehat{F}$: $\mathcal{V}$-Rel → $\mathcal{V}$-Rel that agrees with F on sets and whose action on functions

---

[1] Extensions of Set-functors to Rel are also commonly referred to as "relators", "relational liftings" or "lax relational liftings".

is compatible with F. To make the latter requirement precise, we note that a function is interpreted as the $\mathcal{V}$-relation that sends every element of its graph to k and all the others to $\bot$; then, a lax extension of F to $\mathcal{V}$-Rel, or simply a lax extension, is a map $(r\colon X \nrightarrow Y) \longmapsto (\widehat{\mathsf{F}}r\colon \mathsf{F}X \nrightarrow \mathsf{F}Y)$ such that:

(L1) $\quad r \le r' \implies \widehat{\mathsf{F}}r \le \widehat{\mathsf{F}}r'$,

(L2) $\quad \widehat{\mathsf{F}}s \cdot \widehat{\mathsf{F}}r \le \widehat{\mathsf{F}}(s \cdot r)$,

(L3) $\quad \mathsf{F}f \le \widehat{\mathsf{F}}f$ and $(\mathsf{F}f)^{\circ} \le \widehat{\mathsf{F}}(f^{\circ})$,

for all $r\colon X \nrightarrow Y$, $s\colon Y \nrightarrow Z$ and $f\colon X \to Y$.

Example 2.9. The generalized "lower-half" Egli-Milner order between powersets, which for a relation $r\colon X \nrightarrow Y$ is defined as the relation $\widehat{\mathsf{P}}r\colon \mathsf{P}X \nrightarrow \mathsf{P}Y$ given by

$$A(\widehat{\mathsf{P}}r)B \iff \forall a \in A.\, \exists b \in B.\, a\, r\, b,$$

defines a lax extension of the powerset functor $\mathsf{P}\colon \mathsf{Set} \to \mathsf{Set}$ to Rel. Similarly, the generalized "upper-half" and the generalized Egli-Milner order define lax extensions of the powerset functor to Rel.

Lax extensions are deeply connected with monotone predicate liftings. To realize this, it is convenient to think of the X-component of a κ-ary predicate lifting as a map of type $\mathcal{V}\text{-Rel}(\kappa, X) \to \mathcal{V}\text{-Rel}(1, \mathsf{F}X)$ [16]. [2]

Definition 2.10. A κ-ary predicate lifting λ for a functor $\mathsf{F}\colon \mathsf{Set} \to \mathsf{Set}$ is **induced** by a lax extension $\widehat{\mathsf{F}}\colon \mathcal{V}\text{-Rel} \to \mathcal{V}\text{-Rel}$ if there is a $\mathcal{V}$-relation $\mathfrak{r}\colon 1 \nrightarrow \mathsf{F}\kappa$ such that $\lambda(f) = \widehat{\mathsf{F}}f \cdot \mathfrak{r}$, for every $\mathcal{V}$-relation $f\colon \kappa \nrightarrow X$.

Example 2.11. By interpreting a subset of a set X as a relation from 1 to X, the unary predicate lifting $\Diamond$ (see Example 2.7) for the powerset functor $\mathsf{P}\colon \mathsf{Set} \to \mathsf{Set}$ is induced by the lax extension of Example 2.9; indeed, it is determined by the map $1 \to \mathsf{P}1$ that selects the set 1.

Remark 2.12. Every predicate lifting induced by a lax extension is monotone.

Lax extensions have been instrumental in coalgebraic notions of *behavioural distance* (e.g. [13,38,39]), and the notion of Kantorovich extension has been crucial to connect such notions with coalgebraic modal logic [7].

Definition 2.13. Let $\mathsf{F}\colon \mathsf{Set} \to \mathsf{Set}$ be a functor, and Λ a *class* of monotone predicate liftings for F. The **Kantorovich** lax extension of F w.r.t. Λ is the lax extension $\widehat{\mathsf{F}}^{\Lambda} = \bigwedge_{\lambda \in \Lambda} \widehat{\mathsf{F}}^{\lambda}$, where for every $\mathcal{V}$-relation $r\colon X \nrightarrow Y$, the $\mathcal{V}$-relation $\widehat{\mathsf{F}}^{\lambda}r\colon \mathsf{F}X \nrightarrow \mathsf{F}Y$ given by $\widehat{\mathsf{F}}^{\lambda}r = \bigwedge_{g\colon \kappa \nrightarrow X} \lambda(r \cdot g) \bullet\!\!- \lambda(g)$.

---

[2] Note that Goncharov et. al. consider as their main point of view the dual of the one considered here [16, Proposition 4.2]. Our choice prevents a harmless mismatch between the Kantorovich liftings and Kantorovich extensions in Theorem 3.9.

Example 2.14. The Kantorovich extension of the powerset functor $\mathsf{P}\colon \mathsf{Set} \to \mathsf{Set}$ to Rel w.r.t the $\Diamond$ predicate lifting coincides with the extension given by the "lower-half" of the Egli-Milner order (Example 2.9).

As suggested by the previous example, the Kantorovich extension leads to a representation theorem that plays an important role in Section 3.2.

Theorem 2.15 ([16]). *Let* $\widehat{\mathsf{F}}\colon \mathcal{V}\text{-Rel} \to \mathcal{V}\text{-Rel}$ *be a lax extension, and let* Λ *be the class of all predicate liftings induced by* $\widehat{\mathsf{F}}$. *Then,* $\widehat{\mathsf{F}} = \widehat{\mathsf{F}}^{\Lambda}$.

3   Topological Liftings

It is well-known that every lax extension $\widehat{\mathsf{F}}\colon \mathcal{V}\text{-Rel} \to \mathcal{V}\text{-Rel}$ of a functor $\mathsf{F}\colon \mathsf{Set} \to \mathsf{Set}$ gives rise to a lifting (which we denote by the same symbol) of F to $\mathcal{V}\text{-Cat}$ (for instance, see [37]). By definition, liftings are completely determined by their action on objects. In particular, the **lifting induced by a lax extension** $\widehat{\mathsf{F}}\colon \mathcal{V}\text{-Cat} \to \mathcal{V}\text{-Cat}$ sends a $\mathcal{V}$-category (X, a) to the $\mathcal{V}$-category $(\mathsf{F}X, \widehat{\mathsf{F}}a)$. Of course, it does not make sense to talk about functor liftings to the category $\mathcal{V}\text{-Cat}$ when $\mathcal{V}$ is trivial, hence we assume from now on that $\mathcal{V}$ *is non-trivial*.

Predicate liftings also induce functor liftings, via a simple construction available on all topological categories that goes back, at least, to work in categorical duality theory [11,29]: To lift a functor $\mathsf{G}\colon \mathsf{A} \to \mathsf{Y}$ along a topological functor $|-|\colon \mathsf{B} \to \mathsf{Y}$, it is enough to give, for every object A in A, a structured cone

$$\mathcal{C}(A) = (\mathsf{G}A \xrightarrow{h} |B|)_{h,B} \tag{1}$$

so that, for every h in $\mathcal{C}(A)$ and every $f\colon A' \to A$, the composite $h \cdot \mathsf{G}f$ belongs to the cone $\mathcal{C}(A')$. Then, for an object A in A, one defines $\mathsf{G}^I A$ by equipping $\mathsf{G}A$ with the initial structure w.r.t. the structured cone (1). It is easy to see that the assignment $X \mapsto \mathsf{G}^I X$ indeed defines a functor $\mathsf{G}^I\colon \mathsf{A} \to \mathsf{B}$ such that $|-| \cdot \mathsf{G}^I = \mathsf{G}$. This technique has been previously applied in the context of *codensity liftings* [21,22,35,19] and *Kantorovich liftings* [5]. We apply this to our situation as follows. Given a functor $\mathsf{F}\colon \mathsf{Set} \to \mathsf{Set}$, take $\mathsf{G} = \mathsf{F} \cdot |-|$; then a lifting of F to $\mathcal{V}\text{-Cat}$ can be specified by a *class* of natural transformations

$$\lambda\colon \mathcal{V}\text{-Cat}(-, A_\lambda) \longrightarrow \mathsf{Set}(\mathsf{F}|-|, |B_\lambda|), \tag{2}$$

(which may be thought of as generalized predicate liftings, in that they lift A_λ-valued predicates to B_λ-valued ones). Namely, given a $\mathcal{V}$-category X, we consider the structured cone consisting of all maps

$$\lambda(f)\colon \mathsf{F}|X| \longrightarrow |B_\lambda|$$

where λ ranges over the given natural transformations and f over all $\mathcal{V}$-functors $X \to A_\lambda$. As described above, we obtain a $\mathcal{V}$-category $\mathsf{F}^I X$ by equipping $\mathsf{F}|X|$ with the initial structure w.r.t. this cone. We call functor liftings constructed in this way **topological**. Indeed, it turns out that *every* functor lifting is topological, even when one restricts B_λ in (2) to be the $\mathcal{V}$-category $(\mathcal{V}, \mathrm{hom})$:

Theorem 3.1. *Every lifting of a* Set-*functor to* $\mathcal{V}$-Cat *is topological w.r.t. a* class *of natural transformations* $\lambda\colon \mathcal{V}\text{-Cat}(-, A_\lambda) \longrightarrow \text{Set}(\text{F}|-|, |\mathcal{V}|)$.

In examples, we usually construct a generalized predicate lifting (2) from a κ-ary predicate lifting λ for the set functor F: Choose a pair (A, B) of $\mathcal{V}$-categories over the sets $\mathcal{V}^\kappa$ and $\mathcal{V}$, respectively (the above theorem allows restricting to $B = \mathcal{V}$, and the examples we present are of this kind). We can then precompose λ with the inclusion natural transformation $\mathcal{V}\text{-Cat}(-, A) \longrightarrow \text{Set}(|-|, |A|)$, obtaining a natural transformation $\lambda^{(A,B)}\colon \mathcal{V}\text{-Cat}(-, A) \to \text{Set}(\text{F}|-|, |B|)$ that applies λ to maps underlying $\mathcal{V}$-functors with codomain A.

Example 3.2.   1. The discrete lifting of the identity functor Id: Set $\to$ Set, which sends every $\mathcal{V}$-category to the discrete $\mathcal{V}$-category with the same underlying set, can be obtained as a topological lifting constructed from the identity $\mathcal{V}$-valued predicate lifting for Id by choosing A to be the $\mathcal{V}$-category consisting of the set $\mathcal{V}$ equipped with the indiscrete structure.

2. The lifting of the identity functor Id: Set $\to$ Set to Ord that computes the smallest equivalence relation that contains a given preorder can be obtained as a topological lifting constructed from the 2-valued identity predicate lifting for Id by choosing A to be the discrete preordered set with two elements.

3. It is well-known that the total variation distance between finite distributions μ, v on a set X coincides with the Kantorovich distance on the discrete bounded-by-1 metric space X (e.g. [15]); that is, $d^{TV}(\mu, v) = \bigvee_{f\colon X \to [0,1]} \mathbb{E}_X(f)(v) \ominus \mathbb{E}_X(f)(\mu)$ (see Example 2.7(2)). Therefore, the total variation distance defines a lifting of the finite distribution functor to BHMet that can be obtained as the topological lifting constructed from the predicate lifting $\mathbb{E}$ by choosing A to be the indiscrete space $[0, 1]$. This example is closely related to the first one. Indeed, this lifting is the composite of the Kantorovich lifting of the finite distribution functor to BHMet (see Example 3.5) and the discrete lifting of the identity functor to BHMet. By Theorem 3.9 below, precomposing functor liftings with the discrete lifting of the identity functor can be used to derive non-Kantorovich liftings.

Remark 3.3. Theorem 3.1 can be fine-tuned to show that the discrete lifting $\text{F}^d\colon \text{Ord} \to \text{Ord}$ of a finitary functor F: Set $\to$ Set is a topological lifting constructed from a set Λ of finitary 2-valued predicate liftings for F. Hence, for every set X, considered as a discrete preordered set, we have that the cone of all maps $\lambda(f)\colon \text{F}^d(X, 1_X) \to 2$, for κ-ary predicate liftings $\lambda \in \Lambda$ and maps $X \to 2^\kappa$, is initial. Thus, as $\text{F}^d(X, 1_X)$ is antisymmetric, this cone is mono. In this sense, our results subsume the result that every finitary Set-functor admits a separating set of finitary predicate liftings [34].

3.1   Kantorovich Liftings

For our present purposes, we are primarily interested in topological liftings induced by predicate liftings in the standard sense, i.e. the natural transformations (2) are of the shape $\lambda\colon \mathcal{V}\text{-Cat}(-, \mathcal{V}^\kappa) \longrightarrow \text{Set}(\text{F}|-|, |\mathcal{V}|)$, and thus employ $\mathcal{V}$, equipped with its standard $\mathcal{V}$-category structure, as the object of truth values throughout.

In particular, this format is needed to use predicate liftings as modalities in existing frameworks for quantitative coalgebraic logic (Section 5). Many functor liftings considered in work on coalgebraic behavioural distance can be understood as topological liftings constructed in this way (e.g. [5,22,38,39,12]). To simplify notation, in the sequel we often omit the forgetful functor to Set.

Definition 3.4. Let $\mathsf{F}\colon \mathsf{Set} \to \mathsf{Set}$ be a functor and Λ a class of $\mathcal{V}$-valued predicate liftings for F. The ***Kantorovich lifting*** of F w.r.t. Λ is the topological lifting $\mathsf{F}^\Lambda \colon \mathcal{V}\text{-}\mathsf{Cat} \to \mathcal{V}\text{-}\mathsf{Cat}$ that sends a $\mathcal{V}$-category X to the $\mathcal{V}$-category $(\mathsf{F}X, \mathsf{F}^\Lambda a)$, where $\mathsf{F}^\Lambda a$ denotes the initial structure on $\mathsf{F}X$ w.r.t. the structured cone of all functions

$$\lambda(f)\colon \mathsf{F}|X| \longrightarrow |\mathcal{V}|$$

where $\lambda \in \Lambda$ is κ-ary and $f\colon (X,a) \to \mathcal{V}^\kappa$ is a $\mathcal{V}$-functor. Generally, a lifting $\bar{\mathsf{F}}\colon \mathcal{V}\text{-}\mathsf{Cat} \to \mathcal{V}\text{-}\mathsf{Cat}$ of F is ***Kantorovich*** if $\bar{\mathsf{F}} = \mathsf{F}^\Lambda$ some class Λ of predicate liftings for F.

Example 3.5. As the name suggests, the prototypical example of a Kantorovich lifting is given by the (non-symmetric) Kantorovich distance between finite distributions, which arises as the Kantorovich lifting of the finite distribution functor on Set to the category BHMet w.r.t the predicate lifting $\mathbb{E}$ that computes expected values, i.e. $\mathsf{D}_\omega^{\mathbb{E}}(X,a)(\mu,\upsilon) = \bigvee_{f\colon (X,a)\to[0,1]} \mathbb{E}_X(f)(\upsilon) \ominus \mathbb{E}_X(f)(\mu)$.

We go on to exploit the universal property of initial lifts of cones to characterize the liftings that are Kantorovich. In the following, fix a functor $\mathsf{F}\colon \mathsf{Set} \to \mathsf{Set}$ and a quantale $\mathcal{V}$. Consider the partially ordered conglomerate $\mathsf{Pred}(\mathsf{F})$ of *classes* of $\mathcal{V}$-valued predicate liftings for F ordered by containment, i.e. $\Lambda \leq \Lambda' \iff \Lambda \supseteq \Lambda'$; and the partially ordered class $\mathsf{Lift}(\mathsf{F})$ of liftings of F to $\mathcal{V}\text{-}\mathsf{Cat}$ ordered pointwise, i.e. $\bar{\mathsf{F}} \leq \bar{\mathsf{F}}' \iff \bar{\mathsf{F}}a \leq \bar{\mathsf{F}}'a$, for every $\mathcal{V}$-category (X,a).

Definition 3.6. Let $\bar{\mathsf{F}}\colon \mathcal{V}\text{-}\mathsf{Cat} \to \mathcal{V}\text{-}\mathsf{Cat}$ be a lifting of F. A κ-ary $\mathcal{V}$-valued ***predicate lifting*** λ for F is ***compatible with*** $\bar{\mathsf{F}}$ if it restricts to a predicate lifting for $\bar{\mathsf{F}}$:

$$
\begin{array}{ccc}
\mathcal{V}\text{-}\mathsf{Cat}(-,\mathcal{V}^\kappa) & \xdashrightarrow{\ \lambda\ } & \mathcal{V}\text{-}\mathsf{Cat}(\bar{\mathsf{F}}-,\mathcal{V}) \\
\downarrow & = & \downarrow \\
\mathsf{Set}(-,|\mathcal{V}^\kappa|) & \xrightarrow{\ \lambda\ } & \mathsf{Set}(\mathsf{F}|-|,|\mathcal{V}|)
\end{array}
$$

where the vertical arrows denote set inclusions – that is, if λ lifts $\mathcal{V}$-functorial predicates on X to $\mathcal{V}$-functorial predicates on $\bar{\mathsf{F}}X$. The class of all predicate liftings compatible with $\bar{\mathsf{F}}$ is denoted by $\mathsf{P}(\bar{\mathsf{F}})$.

Proposition 3.7. *A κ-ary $\mathcal{V}$-valued predicate lifting λ for F is compatible with $\bar{\mathsf{F}}$ iff the map $\lambda(1_{|\mathcal{V}^\kappa|})\colon \mathsf{F}(|\mathcal{V}^\kappa|) \to |\mathcal{V}|$ is a $\mathcal{V}$-functor of type $\bar{\mathsf{F}}\mathcal{V}^\kappa \to \mathcal{V}$.*

The Kantorovich lifting defines a universal construction:

Theorem 3.8. *Let $\mathsf{F}\colon \mathsf{Set} \to \mathsf{Set}$ be a functor. Assigning to a class of predicate liftings for F the corresponding Kantorovich lifting yields a right adjoint*

$F^{(-)}$: Pred(F) → Lift(F) *whose left adjoint* P: Lift(F) → Pred(F) *maps a lifting of* F *to the class* $P(\overline{F})$ *of all $\mathcal{V}$-valued predicate liftings for* F *that are compatible with the lifting.*

The following result shows that Kantorovich liftings are characterized by a pleasant property that is required in multiple results in the context of coalgebraic approaches to *behavioural distance* (e.g. [5,22,12,40]).

Theorem 3.9. *A lifting of a Set-functor to $\mathcal{V}$-Cat is Kantorovich iff it preserves initial morphisms.*

Corollary 3.10. *Every topological lifting of a functor F: Set → Set w.r.t. a class of natural transformations λ: $\mathcal{V}$-Cat$(-, A_\lambda)$ → Set(F$-, |B_\lambda|$) where each A_λ is injective in $\mathcal{V}$-Cat w.r.t. initial morphisms is Kantorovich.*

Corollary 3.11. *The composite of Kantorovich liftings is Kantorovich.*

Example 3.12. The characterization of Theorem 3.9 makes it easy to distinguish Kantorovich liftings.

1. It is an elementary fact that every lifting induced by a lax extension preserves initial morphisms (e.g. [18, Proposition 2.16]). In particular, the Wasserstein lifting [5] is Kantorovich.

2. The identity functor on Set has a lifting $(-)^\circ$: $\mathcal{V}$-Cat → $\mathcal{V}$-Cat that sends every $\mathcal{V}$-category to its dual. Clearly, this lifting preserves initial morphisms, and hence it is Kantorovich. Indeed, one can show that it is the Kantorovich lifting of the identity functor w.r.t. the set of $\mathcal{V}$-valued predicate liftings determined by the representable $\mathcal{V}$-functors $\mathcal{V}^{op} \to \mathcal{V}$.

3. The functor $(-)_s$: $\mathcal{V}$-Cat → $\mathcal{V}$-Cat$_{sym}$ that symmetrizes $\mathcal{V}$-categories gives rise to a lifting $(-)_s$: $\mathcal{V}$-Cat → $\mathcal{V}$-Cat of the identity functor on Set. Clearly, this functor preserves initial morphisms, and hence it is Kantorovich. Indeed, one can show that it is the Kantorovich lifting of the identity functor w.r.t. the set of all $\mathcal{V}$-valued predicate liftings determined by the representable $\mathcal{V}$-functors $\mathcal{V}_s \to \mathcal{V}$.

4. The discrete lifting of the identity functor on Set to $\mathcal{V}$-Cat is *not* Kantorovich, as it fails to preserve initial morphisms.

5. The lifting of the identity functor on Set to $\mathcal{V}$-Cat that sends a $\mathcal{V}$-category (X, a) to the $\mathcal{V}$-category given by the final structure w.r.t. the structured cospan of identity maps $|(X, a)| \to X \leftarrow |(X, a^\circ)|$ is *not* Kantorovich. This lifting generalizes Example 3.2(2).

6. The lifting of the finite distribution functor on Set to BHMet given by the Kantorovich distance is Kantorovich, while the lifting given by the total variation distance is *not* Kantorovich.

3.2 Liftings Induced by Lax Extensions

We show next that lax extensions, functor liftings, and predicate liftings are linked by adjunctions, and characterize the liftings induced by lax extensions. We begin by showing that the Kantorovich extension and the Kantorovich lifting are compatible.

Theorem 3.13. *Let* $\widehat{\mathsf{F}}\colon \mathcal{V}\text{-}\mathsf{Cat} \to \mathcal{V}\text{-}\mathsf{Cat}$ *be a lifting of a functor* $\mathsf{F}\colon \mathsf{Set} \to \mathsf{Set}$ *induced by a lax extension* $\widehat{\mathsf{F}}\colon \mathcal{V}\text{-}\mathsf{Rel} \to \mathcal{V}\text{-}\mathsf{Rel}$. *If* $\widehat{\mathsf{F}}\colon \mathcal{V}\text{-}\mathsf{Rel} \to \mathcal{V}\text{-}\mathsf{Rel}$ *is the Kantorovich extension w.r.t. a class* Λ *of predicate liftings, then the functor* $\widehat{\mathsf{F}}\colon \mathcal{V}\text{-}\mathsf{Cat} \to \mathcal{V}\text{-}\mathsf{Cat}$ *is the Kantorovich lifting of* $\mathsf{F}\colon \mathsf{Set} \to \mathsf{Set}$ *w.r.t.* Λ.

Let $\mathsf{Lax}(\mathsf{F})$ denote the partially ordered class of lax extensions of a functor $\mathsf{F}\colon \mathsf{Set} \to \mathsf{Set}$ to $\mathcal{V}\text{-}\mathsf{Rel}$ ordered pointwise:

$$\widehat{\mathsf{F}} \le \widehat{\mathsf{F}}' \iff \forall r \in \mathcal{V}\text{-}\mathsf{Rel}.\ \widehat{\mathsf{F}}r \le \widehat{\mathsf{F}}'r;$$

let $\mathsf{Lift}(\mathsf{F})_\mathsf{I}$ denote the partially ordered *subclass* of $\mathsf{Lift}(\mathsf{F})$ consisting of the liftings that preserve initial morphisms, and let $\mathsf{Pred}(\mathsf{F})_\mathsf{M}$ denote the partially ordered *subconglomerate* of $\mathsf{Pred}(\mathsf{F})$ of monotone predicate liftings. Clearly, the operations of taking Kantorovich extensions $\widehat{\mathsf{F}}^{(-)}\colon \mathsf{Pred}(\mathsf{F})_\mathsf{M} \to \mathsf{Lax}(\mathsf{F})$, and inducing liftings from lax extensions $\mathsf{I}\colon \mathsf{Lax}(\mathsf{F}) \to \mathsf{Lift}(\mathsf{F})_\mathsf{I}$ define monotone maps. Moreover, as we have seen in Theorem 3.9, the monotone map $\mathsf{F}^{(-)}\colon \mathsf{Pred}(\mathsf{F}) \to \mathsf{Lift}(\mathsf{F})$ corestricts to $\mathsf{Lift}(\mathsf{F})_\mathsf{I}$. Therefore, our results so far tell us that lax extensions, liftings and predicate liftings are connected through a diagram of monotone maps

$$
\begin{array}{ccc}
\mathsf{Lax}(\mathsf{F}) & \xrightarrow{\ \mathsf{I}\ } & \mathsf{Lift}(\mathsf{F})_\mathsf{I} \\
{\scriptstyle \widehat{\mathsf{F}}^{(-)}}\uparrow & {\scriptstyle \mathsf{F}^{(-)}}\left(\ \vdash\ \right){\scriptstyle \mathsf{P}} & \\
\mathsf{Pred}(\mathsf{F})_\mathsf{M} & \lhook\joinrel\longrightarrow & \mathsf{Pred}(\mathsf{F})
\end{array}
$$

which commutes if the left adjoint is ignored. In the sequel, we will see that every monotone map in this diagram is an adjoint. In particular, it might not be immediately obvious that the monotone map $\widehat{\mathsf{F}}^{(-)}\colon \mathsf{Pred}(\mathsf{F})_\mathsf{M} \to \mathsf{Lax}(\mathsf{F})$ is a right adjoint without first thinking in terms of functor liftings induced by lax extensions, because the obvious guess – taking the predicate liftings induced by a lax extension (Definition 2.10) – in general does not define a monotone map $\mathsf{Lax}(\mathsf{F}) \to \mathsf{Pred}(\mathsf{F})_\mathsf{M}$. The next example illustrates this as well as the fact that there are predicate liftings compatible with a functor lifting induced by a lax extension that are not induced by the lax extension.

Example 3.14. The identity functor on Ord is the lifting induced by the identity functor on Rel as a lax extension of the identity functor on Set. The constant map into $\top$ is a monotone map $2 \to 2$ and, hence, determines a predicate lifting that is compatible with the identity functor on Ord. It is easy to see that this predicate lifting is induced by the largest extension of the identity functor, however, it is not induced by the identity functor on Rel [16, Example 3.12].

It should also be noted that the predicate liftings compatible with a functor lifting that preserves initial morphisms are not necessarily monotone. That is, the map $\mathsf{P}\colon \mathsf{Lift}(\mathsf{F})_\mathsf{I} \to \mathsf{Pred}(\mathsf{F})$ does not necessarily corestrict to $\mathsf{Pred}(\mathsf{F})_\mathsf{M}$.

Example 3.15. Consider the lifting $(-)^\circ\colon \mathsf{Ord} \to \mathsf{Ord}$ of the identity functor on Set that sends each preordered set to its dual. Then, the predicate lifting for $(-)^\circ$ determined by the $\mathcal{V}$-functor $\hom(-, 0)\colon (2, \hom)^{\mathrm{op}} \to (2, \hom)$ is not monotone since it sends the constant map $0\colon 1 \to 2$ to the constant map $1\colon 1 \to 2$.

Accordingly, we need to "filter the monotone predicate liftings" first. This operation trivially defines the left adjoint $M: Pred(F) \to Pred(F)_M$ of the inclusion map $Pred(F)_M \hookrightarrow Pred(F)$.

Theorem 3.16. *Let* $F: Set \to Set$ *be a functor. The monotone map* $I: Lax(F) \to Lift(F)_I$ *is order-reflecting and right adjoint to the monotone map* $\widehat{F}^{MP}(-): Lift(F)_I \to Lax(F)$.

Corollary 3.17. *Let* $F: Set \to Set$ *be a functor. The monotone map* $\widehat{F}^{(-)}: Pred(F)_M \to Lax(F)$ *is right adjoint to the order-reflecting monotone map* $MPI: Lax(F) \to Pred(F)_M$.

Therefore, the interplay between lax extensions, liftings and predicate liftings is captured by the diagram

$$
\begin{array}{ccc}
 & \xleftarrow{\widehat{F}^{MP}(-)} & \\
Lax(F) & \xrightarrow[I]{\;\;\perp\;\;} & Lift(F)_I \\
MPI \left(\dashv \right) \widehat{F}^{(-)} & & F^{(-)} \left(\vdash \right) P \\
Pred(F)_M & \xleftarrow[\quad\top\quad]{\hookrightarrow} & Pred(F) \\
 & \xleftarrow{M} &
\end{array}
\tag{3}
$$

which commutes when only the right adjoints or only the left adjoints are considered. Finally, we characterize the liftings induced by lax extensions.

Theorem 3.18. *A lifting $\widehat{F}$ of a* Set*-functor* F *to* $\mathcal{V}$-Cat *is induced by a lax extension of* F *to* $\mathcal{V}$-Rel *iff* $\widehat{F}$ *preserves initial morphisms and is locally monotone.*

$\mathcal{V}$-enriched lax extensions have proved to be crucial to deduce quantitative van Benthem and Hennessy-Milner theorems [38,39]. We recall that a lax extension of a functor $F: Set \to Set$ to $\mathcal{V}$-Rel is $\mathcal{V}$-***enriched*** [39,16] if, for all $u \in \mathcal{V}$, $u \otimes 1_{FX} \le \widehat{F}(u \otimes 1_X)$; where $u \otimes r$ denotes the $\mathcal{V}$-relation "r scaled by u", that is, $(u \otimes r)(x, y) = u \otimes r(x, y)$.

Theorem 3.19. *A lifting $\widehat{F}$ of a* Set*-functor* F *to* $\mathcal{V}$-Cat *is induced by a* $\mathcal{V}$*-enriched lax extension of* F *to* $\mathcal{V}$-Rel *iff* $\widehat{F}$ *preserves initial morphisms and is* $\mathcal{V}$-Cat*-enriched.*

Our characterization of lax extensions makes it clear that there is a large collection of Kantorovich liftings that are not induced by lax extensions. For instance, it follows from Theorem 3.18 that the liftings $(-)^\circ: \mathcal{V}$-Cat $\to \mathcal{V}$-Cat and $(-)_s: \mathcal{V}$-Cat $\to \mathcal{V}$-Cat (see Example 3.12) of the identity functor on Set to $\mathcal{V}$-Cat are Kantorovich but are not induced by lax extensions. Furthermore, as the composite of Kantorovich liftings is Kantorovich, in many situations it is possible to compose these functors with other Kantorovich liftings to generate liftings that are not induced by lax extensions.

4   Behavioural Distance

One main motivation for lifting functors to metric spaces was to obtain coalgebraic notions of behavioural distance [5,38]. Indeed, *every* functor $F: \mathcal{V}\text{-Cat} \to \mathcal{V}\text{-Cat}$ gives rise to a notion of distance on a F-coalgebras:

Definition 4.1. [12] Let (X, a, α) be a coalgebra for a functor $F: \mathcal{V}\text{-Cat} \to \mathcal{V}\text{-Cat}$. The *behavioural distance* $\mathrm{bd}_\alpha^F(x, y)$ of $x, y \in X$ is

$$\mathrm{bd}_\alpha^F(x, y) = \bigvee \{b(f(x), f(y)) \mid f: (X, a, \alpha) \to (Y, b, \beta) \in \mathsf{CoAlg}(F)\}. \quad (4)$$

Notice the analogy with the standard notion of behavioural equivalence: Two states are behaviourally equivalent if they can be made equal under some coalgebra morphism; and according to the above definition, two states in a metric coalgebra have low behavioural distance if they can be made to have low distance under some coalgebra morphism.

Kantorovich liftings and lax extensions are key ingredients in mentioned alternative coalgebraic approaches to behavioural distance on Set-based coalgebras. Let $F: \mathsf{Set} \to \mathsf{Set}$ be a functor. A Kantorovich lifting $F^\Lambda: \mathcal{V}\text{-Cat} \to \mathcal{V}\text{-Cat}$ induces a notion of *behavioural distance* on an F-coalgebra $\alpha: X \to FX$ as the greatest $\mathcal{V}$-categorical structure (X, a) that makes α a $\mathcal{V}$-functor of type $(X, a) \to F^\Lambda(X, a)$ [5,22]. From Theorem 3.9 and [12, Proposition 12] (generalized to $\mathcal{V}$-Cat, with the same proof), we obtain that this distance coincides with behavioural distance as defined above. On the other hand, every lax extension $\widehat{F}: \mathcal{V}\text{-Rel} \to \mathcal{V}\text{-Rel}$ of F also induces a *behavioural distance* on an F-coalgebra $\alpha: X \to FX$ as the greatest *simulation* on α [32,40,13,38], i.e. the greatest $\mathcal{V}$-relation $s: X \nrightarrow X$ such that $\alpha \cdot s \leq \widehat{F}s \cdot \alpha$. It follows by routine calculation that this distance coincides with the distance defined via the lifting induced by the lax extension and, hence, Theorem 3.13 ensures that, if we start with a collection of monotone predicate liftings, then the corresponding Kantorovich extension and Kantorovich lifting yield the same notion of behavioural distance. This allows including the approach to behavioural distance via lax extensions in the categorical framework for *indistinguishability* introduced recently by Komorida et al. [22]. On the other hand, there are notions of behavioural distance defined via Kantorovich liftings that do not arise via lax extensions. Indeed, it has been shown that the neighbourhood functor $N: \mathsf{Set} \to \mathsf{Set}$ does not admit a lax extension to Rel that preserves converses $(\widehat{F}(r^\circ) = (\widehat{F}r)^\circ)$ whose (2-valued) notion of behavioural distance coincides with behavioural equivalence [27, Theorem 12]. However, from [12, Theorem 34, Proposition A.6] (see also [17]), we can conclude that the (2-valued) notion of behavioural distance defined by the canonical Kantorovich lifting of N to Equ w.r.t. to the predicate lifting induced by the identity natural transformation $N \to N$ coincides with behavioural equivalence. (It is easy to see that Marti and Venema's result holds even if one allows lax extensions of N that do not preserve converses, and that the situation remains the same in the asymmetric case.)

5   Expressivity of Quantitative Coalgebraic Logics

We proceed to connect the characterization of Kantorovich functors with existing expressivity results for quantitative coalgebraic logic, focusing from now on on symmetric $\mathcal{V}$-categories. Therefore, we interpret the $\mathcal{V}$-categorical notions and results also with $\mathcal{V}$-Cat$_{\mathrm{sym}}$ instead of $\mathcal{V}$-Cat and $\mathcal{V}_s$ instead of $\mathcal{V}$.

We recall a variant [12] of (quantitative) coalgebraic logic [28,34,7,23,38] that follows the paradigm of interpreting modalities via predicate liftings, in this case of $\mathcal{V}$-valued predicates for a $\mathcal{V}$-Cat-functor (Section 2.3). Let Λ be a *set* of finitary predicate liftings for a functor $\mathsf{F}\colon \mathcal{V}$-Cat$_{\mathrm{sym}} \to \mathcal{V}$-Cat$_{\mathrm{sym}}$. The syntax of *quantitative coalgebraic modal logic* is then defined by the grammar

$$\phi ::= \top \mid \phi_1 \vee \phi_2 \mid \phi_1 \wedge \phi_2 \mid u \otimes \phi \mid \hom_s(u, \phi) \mid \lambda(\phi_1, \ldots, \phi_n) \quad (u \in \mathcal{V}, \lambda \in \Lambda)$$

where Λ is a set of *modalities* of finite arity, which we identify, by abuse of notation, with the given set Λ of predicate liftings. We view all other connectives as propositional operators. Let $\mathcal{L}(\Lambda)$ be the set of modal formulas thus defined.

The semantics is given by assigning to each formula $\phi \in \mathcal{L}(\Lambda)$ and each coalgebra $\alpha\colon X \to \mathsf{F}X$ the *interpretation* of ϕ over α, i.e. the $\mathcal{V}$-functor $[\![\phi]\!]_\alpha\colon X \to \mathcal{V}$ recursively defined as follows:

– for $\phi = \top$, we take $[\![\top]\!]_\alpha$ to be the $\mathcal{V}$-functor given by the constant map into $\top$;

– for an n-ary propositional operator p, we put $[\![p(\phi_1, \ldots, \phi_n)]\!]_\alpha = p([\![\phi_1]\!]_\alpha, \ldots, [\![\phi_n]\!]_\alpha)$, with p interpreted using the lattice structure of $\mathcal{V}$ and the $\mathcal{V}$-categorical structure $\hom_s$ of $\mathcal{V}_s$, respectively, on the right-hand side;

– for n-ary $\lambda \in \Lambda$, we put $[\![\lambda(\phi_1, \ldots, \phi_n)]\!]_\alpha = \lambda(\langle [\![\phi_1]\!]_\alpha, \ldots, [\![\phi_n]\!]_\alpha \rangle) \cdot \alpha$, where $\langle [\![\phi_1]\!]_\alpha, \ldots, [\![\phi_n]\!]_\alpha \rangle$ denotes the $\mathcal{V}$-functor $(X, a) \to \mathcal{V}^n$ canonically determined by $[\![\phi_1]\!]_\alpha, \ldots, [\![\phi_n]\!]_\alpha$.

We then obtain a notion of logical distance:

Definition 5.1. Let Λ be a set of predicate liftings for a functor $\mathsf{F}\colon \mathcal{V}$-Cat $\to$ $\mathcal{V}$-Cat. The **logical distance** ld_α^Λ on an F-coalgebra (X, a, α) is the initial structure on X w.r.t. the structured cone of all maps $[\![\phi]\!]_\alpha\colon X \to |(\mathcal{V}, \hom_s)|$ with $\phi \in \mathcal{L}(\Lambda)$. More explicitly, for all $x, y \in X$,

$$ld_\alpha^\Lambda(x, y) = \bigwedge \{\hom_s([\![\phi]\!]_\alpha(x), [\![\phi]\!]_\alpha(y)) \mid \phi \in \mathcal{L}(\Lambda)\}.$$

In the remainder of the paper, we establish criteria under which a $\mathcal{V}$-Cat$_{\mathrm{sym}}$-functor admits a set of predicate liftings for which logical and behavioural distances coincide. Recall that a (quantitative) coalgebraic logic is **expressive** if $ld_\alpha^\Lambda \leq \mathsf{bd}_\alpha^\mathsf{F}$, for every F-coalgebra (X, α). (It is easy to show that the reverse inequality holds universally [12, Theorem 16]).

Existing expressivity results for quantitative coalgebraic logics for Set-functors depend crucially on Kantorovich liftings (e.g. [38,39,22,12]). However, it has been shown [12] that the Kantorovich property can be usefully detached from the notion of functor lifting.

Definition 5.2. Let Λ be a class of predicate liftings for a functor $\mathsf{F} \colon \mathcal{V}\text{-Cat} \to \mathcal{V}\text{-Cat}$. The functor F is Λ-***Kantorovich*** if for every $\mathcal{V}$-category X, the cone of all $\mathcal{V}$-functors $\lambda(f) \colon \mathsf{F}X \to \mathcal{V}$, with $\lambda \in \Lambda$ κ-ary and $f \in \mathcal{V}\text{-Cat}(X, \mathcal{V}^\kappa)$, is initial. A functor $\mathsf{F} \colon \mathcal{V}\text{-Cat} \to \mathcal{V}\text{-Cat}$ is said to be ***Kantorovich*** if it is Λ-Kantorovich for some class Λ of predicate liftings for F.

Clearly, every Kantorovich lifting of a Set-functor to $\mathcal{V}\text{-Cat}$ w.r.t. a class Λ of predicate liftings is Λ-Kantorovich. Moreover, Theorem 3.9 is easily generalized to Kantorovich functors.

Theorem 5.3. *A $\mathcal{V}$-Cat-functor is Kantorovich iff it preserves initial morphisms.*

Theorem 5.4. *A $\mathcal{V}\text{-Cat}_{\mathrm{sym}}$-functor is Kantorovich iff it preserves initial morphisms.*

Example 5.5.   1. The inclusion functor $\mathcal{V}\text{-Cat}_{\mathrm{sym,sep}} \hookrightarrow \mathcal{V}\text{-Cat}_{\mathrm{sym}}$ has a left adjoint $(-)_q \colon \mathcal{V}\text{-Cat}_{\mathrm{sym}} \to \mathcal{V}\text{-Cat}_{\mathrm{sym,sep}}$ that quotients every X by its natural preorder, which for symmetric X is an equivalence, and gives rise to a Kantorovich functor on $\mathcal{V}\text{-Cat}_{\mathrm{sym}}$.

2. Given a bounded-by-1 pseudometric space (X, d), i.e. an object of $[0, 1]_\oplus\text{-Cat}_{\mathrm{sym}} \simeq \mathsf{BPMet}$, the ***Prokhorov distance*** [30] for probability measures on the measurable space of Borel sets of (X, d) is defined by $d^P(\mu, v) = \inf\{\epsilon > 0 \mid \mu(A) \leq v(A^\epsilon) + \epsilon \text{ for all Borel sets } A \subseteq X\}$, where $A^\epsilon = \{x \in X \mid \inf_{y \in A} d(x, y) \leq \epsilon\}$. It is straightforward to verify that this distance defines a BPMet-functor (which acts on morphisms by measuring preimages) that preserves isometries and, therefore, it is Kantorovich.

3. For every $\mathcal{V}$-category (X, a), the functor $(X, a) \times - \colon \mathcal{V}\text{-Cat} \to \mathcal{V}\text{-Cat}$ is Kantorovich. If the underlying lattice of $\mathcal{V}$ is Heyting, then under certain conditions this functor has a right adjoint [8,9] which is Kantorovich as well. Here, for $X = (X, a)$ exponentiable, the right adjoint $(-)^X$ of $X \times -$ sends a $\mathcal{V}$-category $Y = (Y, b)$ to the $\mathcal{V}$-category $Y^X = (Y^X, c)$ with underlying set $\{$all $\mathcal{V}$-functors $(1, k) \times (X, a) \to (Y, b)\}$ and, for $h, k \in Y^X$,

$$c(h, k) = \bigwedge\nolimits_{x_1, x_2 \in X} b(h(x_1), k(x_2))^{a(x_1, x_2)},$$

where $(-)^u \colon \mathcal{V} \to \mathcal{V}$ denotes the right adjoint of $u \wedge - \colon \mathcal{V} \to \mathcal{V}$. For a $\mathcal{V}$-functor $f \colon (Y_1, b_1) \to (Y_2, b_2)$, the $\mathcal{V}$-functor $f^X \colon (Y_1^X, c_1) \to (Y_2^X, c_2)$ sends $h \in Y_1^X$ to $f \cdot h$.

To ensure that a Kantorovich functor is represented by finitary predicate liftings, we need to impose a size constraint:

Definition 5.6. A functor $\mathsf{F} \colon \mathcal{V}\text{-Cat}_{\mathrm{sym}} \to \mathcal{V}\text{-Cat}_{\mathrm{sym}}$ is ω-***bounded*** if for every symmetric $\mathcal{V}$-category X and every $t \in \mathsf{F}X$, there exists a finite subcategory $X_0 \subseteq X$ and $t' \in \mathsf{F}X_0$ such that $t = \mathsf{F}i(t')$ where i is the inclusion $X_0 \to X$.

Example 5.7. Every lifting of a finitary Set-functor to $\mathcal{V}\text{-Cat}_{\mathrm{sym}}$ is ω-bounded.

Proposition 5.8. *Let $\mathsf{F} \colon \mathcal{V}\text{-Cat}_{\mathrm{sym}} \to \mathcal{V}\text{-Cat}_{\mathrm{sym}}$ be a Kantorovich functor. If F is ω-bounded, then F is Kantorovich w.r.t. a set of finitary predicate liftings.*

Finally, from [12, Theorem 31] we obtain:

Corollary 5.9. *Let $\mathcal{V}$ be a finite quantale, and let* $\mathsf{F}\colon \mathcal{V}\text{-}\mathsf{Cat}_{\mathrm{sym}} \to \mathcal{V}\text{-}\mathsf{Cat}_{\mathrm{sym}}$ *be a lifting of a finitary functor that preserves initial morphisms. Then there is a set Λ of predicate liftings for* F *of finite arity such that the coalgebraic logic $\mathcal{L}(\Lambda)$ is expressive.*

Corollary 5.10. *Let* $\mathsf{F}\colon \mathsf{BPMet} \to \mathsf{BPMet}$ *be a functor that preserves isometries, is locally non-expansive, and admits a dense ω-bounded subfunctor. Then there is a set Λ of predicate liftings for* F *of finite arity such that the coalgebraic logic $\mathcal{L}(\Lambda)$ is expressive.*

These instantiate to results on concrete system types, e.g. ones induced by (sub)functors listed in Example 5.5, such as probabilistic transition systems equipped with a behavioural distance induced by the functor that sends a bounded metric space X to the subspace of the space of all probability measures on X equipped with the Prokhorov distance (see Example 5.5(2)) determined by the closure of the set of finitely supported probability measures.

6   Conclusions and Future Work

Quantitative coalgebraic Hennessy-Milner theorems [23,38,12] assume that the functor (on metric spaces) describing the system type is *Kantorovich*, i.e. canonically induced by a suitable choice of – not necessarily monotone – predicate liftings, which then serve as the modalities of a logic that characterizes behavioural distance. We have shown as one of our main results that a functor on (quantale-valued) metric spaces is Kantorovich iff it preserves initial morphisms (i.e. isometries). As soon as such a functor additionally adheres to the expected size and continuity constraints (which replace the condition of finite branching found in the classical Hennessy-Milner theorem for labelled transition systems), one thus has a logical characterization of behavioural distance in coalgebras for the functor, in the sense that behavioural distance equals logical distance.

In fact we have shown that *every* functor on metric spaces can be captured by a generalized form of predicate liftings where the object of truth values may change along the lifting. A simple example is the discretization functor, which is characterized by a predicate lifting in which the truth value object for the input predicates is equipped with the indiscrete pseudometric, so that the lifting accepts *all* predicates instead of only non-expansive ones. This hints at a perspective to design heterogeneous modal logics that characterize behavioural distance for such functors, with modalities connecting different types of formulas (e.g. non-expansive vs. unrestricted), which we will pursue in future work. One application scenario for such a logic are behavioural distances on probabilistic systems involving total variation distance, which may be seen as a composite of the usual probabilistic Kantorovich functor and the discretization functor.

References

1. Adámek, J., Herrlich, H., Strecker, G.E.: Abstract and concrete categories: The joy of cats. Pure and Applied Mathematics (New York), John Wiley & Sons Inc., New York (1990), http://tac.mta.ca/tac/reprints/articles/17/tr17abs.html, republished in: Reprints in Theory and Applications of Categories, No. 17 (2006) pp. 1–507
2. de Alfaro, L., Faella, M., Stoelinga, M.: Linear and Branching System Metrics. IEEE Transactions on Software Engineering 35(2), 258–273 (mar 2009). https://doi.org/10.1109/TSE.2008.106
3. Alsina, C., Frank, M.J., Schweizer, B.: Associative functions. Triangular norms and copulas. Hackensack, NJ: World Scientific (2006). https://doi.org/10.1142/9789812774200
4. Awodey, S.: Category Theory. Oxford University Press, 2nd edn. (2010)
5. Baldan, P., Bonchi, F., Kerstan, H., König, B.: Coalgebraic Behavioral Metrics. Log. Methods Comput. Sci. 14(3), 1860–5974 (2018). https://doi.org/10.23638/lmcs-14(3:20)2018
6. van Breugel, F., Worrell, J.: A behavioural pseudometric for probabilistic transition systems. Theoretical Computer Science 331(1), 115–142 (feb 2005). https://doi.org/10.1016/j.tcs.2004.09.035
7. Cîrstea, C., Kurz, A., Pattinson, D., Schröder, L., Venema, Y.: Modal Logics are Coalgebraic. Computer Journal 54(1), 31–41 (2011). https://doi.org/10.1093/comjnl/bxp004
8. Clementino, M.M., Hofmann, D.: Exponentiation in V-categories. Topology and its Applications 153(16), 3113–3128 (Oct 2006). https://doi.org/10.1016/j.topol.2005.01.038
9. Clementino, M.M., Hofmann, D., Stubbe, I.: Exponentiable functors between quantaloid-enriched categories. Applied Categorical Structures 17(1), 91–101 (Sep 2009). https://doi.org/10.1007/s10485-007-9104-5
10. Desharnais, J., Edalat, A., Panangaden, P.: Bisimulation for labelled markov processes. Inf. Comput. 179(2), 163–193 (2002). https://doi.org/10.1006/inco.2001.2962
11. Dimov, G.D., Tholen, W.: A characterization of representable dualities. In: Adámek, J., MacLane, S. (eds.) Categorical topology and its relation to analysis, algebra and combinatorics: Prague, Czechoslovakia, 22-27 August 1988, pp. 336–357. World Scientific (1989)
12. Forster, J., Goncharov, S., Hofmann, D., Nora, P., Schröder, L., Wild, P.: Quantitative Hennessy-Milner theorems via notions of density. In: Klin, B., Pimentel, E. (eds.) Computer Science Logic, CSL 2023. LIPIcs, Schloss Dagstuhl – Leibniz-Zentrum für Informatik (2023), to appear. Preprint avaible on arXiv under https://doi.org/10.48550/arXiv.2207.09187
13. Gavazzo, F.: Quantitative behavioural reasoning for higher-order effectful programs: Applicative distances. In: Dawar, A., Grädel, E. (eds.) Logic in Computer Science, LICS 2018. pp. 452–461. ACM (2018). https://doi.org/10.1145/3209108.3209149
14. Giacalone, A., Jou, C., Smolka, S.A.: Algebraic Reasoning for Probabilistic Concurrent Systems. In: Broy, M., Jones, C.B. (eds.) Programming concepts and methods: Proceedings of the IFIP Working Group 2.2, 2.3 Working Conference on Programming Concepts and Methods, Sea of Galilee, Israel, 2-5 April, 1990. pp. 443–458. North-Holland (1990)

15. Gibbs, A.L., Su, F.E.: On choosing and bounding probability metrics. International statistical review **70**(3), 419–435 (2002)
16. Goncharov, S., Hofmann, D., Nora, P., Schröder, L., Wild, P.: A point-free perspective on lax extensions and predicate liftings. CoRR **abs/2112.12681** (2021), https://arxiv.org/abs/2112.12681
17. Hansen, H.H., Kupke, C., Pacuit, E.: Neighbourhood structures: Bisimilarity and basic model theory. Log. Methods Comput. Sci. **5**(2) (2009), http://arxiv.org/abs/0901.4430
18. Hofmann, D., Nora, P.: Hausdorff Coalgebras. Applied Categorical Structures **28**(5), 773–806 (Apr 2020). https://doi.org/10.1007/s10485-020-09597-8
19. Katsumata, S.: A semantic formulation of tt-lifting and logical predicates for computational metalanguage. In: Ong, C.L. (ed.) Computer Science Logic, 19th International Workshop, CSL 2005, 14th Annual Conference of the EACSL, Oxford, UK, August 22-25, 2005, Proceedings. Lecture Notes in Computer Science, vol. 3634, pp. 87–102. Springer (2005). https://doi.org/10.1007/11538363_8, https://doi.org/10.1007/11538363_8
20. Kelly, G.M.: Basic concepts of enriched category theory, London Mathematical Society Lecture Note Series, vol. 64. Cambridge University Press, Cambridge (1982), Republished in: Reprints in Theory and Applications of Categories. No. 10 (2005), 1–136
21. Komorida, Y., Katsumata, S., Hu, N., Klin, B., Hasuo, I.: Codensity Games for Bisimilarity. In: 34th Annual ACM/IEEE Symposium on Logic in Computer Science, LICS 2019, Vancouver, BC, Canada, June 24-27, 2019. pp. 1–13. IEEE (2019). https://doi.org/10.1109/LICS.2019.8785691
22. Komorida, Y., Katsumata, S., Kupke, C., Rot, J., Hasuo, I.: Expressivity of Quantitative Modal Logics : Categorical Foundations via Codensity and Approximation. In: 36th Annual ACM/IEEE Symposium on Logic in Computer Science, LICS 2021, Rome, Italy, June 29 - July 2, 2021. pp. 1–14. IEEE (2021). https://doi.org/10.1109/LICS52264.2021.9470656
23. König, B., Mika-Michalski, C.: (metric) bisimulation games and real-valued modal logics for coalgebras. In: Schewe, S., Zhang, L. (eds.) 29th International Conference on Concurrency Theory, CONCUR 2018, September 4-7, 2018, Beijing, China. LIPIcs, vol. 118, pp. 37:1–37:17. Schloss Dagstuhl - Leibniz-Zentrum für Informatik (2018). https://doi.org/10.4230/LIPIcs.CONCUR.2018.37
24. Larsen, K.G., Fahrenberg, U., Thrane, C.R.: Metrics for weighted transition systems: Axiomatization and complexity. Theor. Comput. Sci. **412**(28), 3358–3369 (2011). https://doi.org/10.1016/j.tcs.2011.04.003
25. Larsen, K.G., Skou, A.: Bisimulation through probabilistic testing. Inf. Comput. **94**(1), 1–28 (1991). https://doi.org/10.1016/0890-5401(91)90030-6
26. Lawvere, F.W.: Metric spaces, generalized logic, and closed categories. Rendiconti del Seminario Matemàtico e Fisico di Milano **43**(1), 135–166 (Dec 1973). https://doi.org/10.1007/bf02924844, Republished in: Reprints in Theory and Applications of Categories, No. 1 (2002), 1–37
27. Marti, J., Venema, Y.: Lax extensions of coalgebra functors and their logic. Journal of Computer and System Sciences **81**(5), 880–900 (2015). https://doi.org/10.1016/j.jcss.2014.12.006
28. Pattinson, D.: Expressive logics for coalgebras via terminal sequence induction. Notre Dame J. Formal Log. **45**(1), 19–33 (jan 2004). https://doi.org/10.1305/ndjfl/1094155277

29. Porst, H.E., Tholen, W.: Concrete dualities. In: Herrlich, H., Porst, H.E. (eds.) Category theory at work, Research and Exposition in Mathematics, vol. 18, pp. 111–136. Heldermann Verlag, Berlin (1991), http://www.heldermann.de/R&E/RAE18/ctw07.pdf, with Cartoons by Marcel Erné

30. Prokhorov, Y.V.: Convergence of random processes and limit theorems in probability theory. Theory of Probability & Its Applications **1**(2), 157–214 (1956). https://doi.org/10.1137/1101016, https://doi.org/10.1137/1101016

31. Rosenthal, K.: Quantaloids, enriched categories and automata theory. Appl. Cat. Struct. **3**, 279-301 (1995). https://doi.org/10.1007/BF00878445

32. Rutten, J.: Relators and Metric Bisimulations. Electronic Notes in Theoretical Computer Science **11**, 252–258 (1998). https://doi.org/10.1016/S1571-0661(04)00063-5

33. Rutten, J.: Universal coalgebra: a theory of systems. Theoretical Computer Science **249**(1), 3–80 (Oct 2000). https://doi.org/10.1016/s0304-3975(00)00056-6

34. Schröder, L.: Expressivity of coalgebraic modal logic: The limits and beyond. Theor. Comput. Sci. **390**(2-3), 230–247 (jan 2008). https://doi.org/10.1016/j.tcs.2007.09.023

35. Sprunger, D., Katsumata, S., Dubut, J., Hasuo, I.: Fibrational bisimulations and quantitative reasoning: Extended version. J. Log. Comput. **31**(6), 1526–1559 (2021). https://doi.org/10.1093/logcom/exab051, https://doi.org/10.1093/logcom/exab051

36. Stubbe, I.: An introduction to quantaloid-enriched categories. Fuzzy Sets and Systems **256**, 95–116 (Dec 2014). https://doi.org/10.1016/j.fss.2013.08.009, special Issue on Enriched Category Theory and Related Topics (Selected papers from the 33rd Linz Seminar on Fuzzy Set Theory, 2012)

37. Tholen, W.: Ordered topological structures. Topology and its Applications **156**(12), 2148–2157 (Jul 2009). https://doi.org/10.1016/j.topol.2009.03.038

38. Wild, P., Schröder, L.: Characteristic logics for behavioural metrics via fuzzy lax extensions. In: Konnov, I., Kovács, L. (eds.) Concurrency Theory, CONCUR 2020. LIPIcs, vol. 171, pp. 27:1–27:23. Schloss Dagstuhl - Leibniz-Zentrum für Informatik (2020). https://doi.org/10.4230/LIPIcs.CONCUR.2020.27, extended version in *Log. Methods Comput. Sci.* 18(2), 2022

39. Wild, P., Schröder, L.: A Quantified Coalgebraic van Benthem Theorem. In: Kiefer, S., Tasson, C. (eds.) Foundations of Software Science and Computation Structures, FOSSACS 2021. LNCS, vol. 12650, pp. 551–571. Springer (2021). https://doi.org/10.1007/978-3-030-71995-1_28

40. Worrell, J.: Coinduction for recursive data types: partial orders, metric spaces and Ω-categories. In: Reichel, H. (ed.) Coalgebraic Methods in Computer Science, CMCS 2000, Berlin, Germany, March 25-26, 2000. Electronic Notes in Theoretical Computer Science, vol. 33, pp. 337–356. Elsevier (2000). https://doi.org/10.1016/S1571-0661(05)80356-1

A Logical Framework with
Higher-Order Rational (Circular) Terms

Zhibo Chen$^{(\boxtimes)}$ ⓘ and Frank Pfenning ⓘ

Carnegie Mellon University, Pittsburgh, PA, USA
`zhiboc@andrew.cmu.edu, fp@cs.cmu.edu`

Abstract. Logical frameworks provide natural and direct ways of specifying and reasoning within deductive systems. The logical framework LF and subsequent developments focus on finitary proof systems, making the formalization of circular proof systems in such logical frameworks a cumbersome and awkward task. To address this issue, we propose CoLF, a conservative extension of LF with higher-order rational terms and mixed inductive and coinductive definitions. In this framework, two terms are equal if they unfold to the same infinite regular Böhm tree. Both term equality and type checking are decidable in CoLF. We illustrate the elegance and expressive power of the framework with several small case studies.

Keywords: Logical Frameworks, Circular Proofs, Regular Böhm Trees

1 Introduction

A logical framework provides a uniform way of formalizing and mechanically checking derivations for a variety of deductive systems common in the definitions of logics and programming languages. In this paper we propose a conservative extension of the logical framework LF [18] to support direct representations of rational (circular) terms and deductions.

The main methodology of a logical framework is to establish a bijective correspondence between derivations of a judgment in the object logic and canonical terms of a type in the framework. In this way, proof checking in the object logic is reduced to type checking in the framework. One notable feature of LF is the use of abstract binding trees, where substitution in the object logic can be encoded as substitution in the framework, leading to elegant encodings. On the other hand, encodings of rational terms, circular derivations, and their equality relations are rather cumbersome. We therefore propose the logical framework CoLF as a conservative extension of LF in which both circular syntactic objects and derivations in an object logic can be elegantly represented as higher-order rational dependently typed terms. This makes CoLF a uniform framework for formalizing proof systems on cyclic structures. We prove the decidability of type checking and soundness of equality checking of higher-order rational terms.

ⓒ The Author(s) 2023
O. Kupferman and P. Sobocinski (Eds.): FoSSaCS 2023, LNCS 13992, pp. 68–88, 2023.
https://doi.org/10.1007/978-3-031-30829-1_4

While CoLF allows formalization of circular derivations, proofs by coinduction *about* such circular encodings can only be represented as relations in CoLF, mirroring a similar limitation of LF regarding induction. In future work, we plan to extend CoLF to support checking of meta-theoretic properties of encodings analogous to the way Twelf [27] can check properties of encodings in LF.

The main contributions of this paper are:

- The type theory of a logical framework with higher-order rational terms. The theory allows natural and adequate representations of circular objects and circular derivations (Section 3).
- A decidable trace condition for ensuring the validity of circular terms and derivations arising from mixed inductive and coinductive definitions (Section 3.3).
- A sound and complete algorithm to decide the equality of two higher-order rational terms (Section 3.5).
- A proof of decidability of type-checking in the framework (Section 3.7).
- Case studies of encoding subtyping derivations of recursive types (Section 4).

An extended version of this paper, available at https://arxiv.org/abs/2210.06663, has an appendix that contains additional materials. We have implemented CoLF in OCaml and the implementation can be accessed at https://www.andrew.cmu.edu/user/zhiboc/colf.html. An additional case study of the meta-encoding the term model of CoLF in CoLF is presented in Appendix J of the extended version.

2   Mixed Inductive and Coinductive Definitions

We motivate our design through simple examples of natural numbers, conatural numbers, and finitely padded streams. The examples serve to illustrate the idea of coinductive interpretations, and they do not involve dependent types or higher-order terms. More complex examples will be introduced later in the case studies (Section 4).

Natural Numbers. The set of natural numbers is inductively generated by zero and successor. In a logical framework such as LF, one would encode natural numbers as the signature consisting of the first three lines in the top left part of Fig. 1.

The type theory ensures that canonical terms of the type nat are in one-to-one correspondence with the natural numbers. Specifically the *infinite* stack of successors succ (succ (succ ...)) is not a valid term of type nat. Therefore, the circular term w1 is not a valid term.

Conatural Numbers. We may naturally specify that a type admits a coinductive interpretation by introducing a new syntactic kind cotype. The kind cotype behaves just like the kind type except that now the terms under cotype

```
nat : type.                      padding : type.
zero : nat.                      pstream : cotype.
succ : nat -> nat.               cocons : nat -> padding -> pstream.
                                 pad : padding -> padding.
w1 : nat = succ w1. (not valid)  next : pstream -> padding.
conat : cotype.
cozero : conat.                  s1 : pstream = cocons (succ zero)
cosucc : conat -> conat.                    (pad (pad (next s1))).

w2 : conat = cosucc w2.          p2 : padding = pad p2. (not valid)
w3 : conat = cosucc (cosucc w3). s3 : pstream = cocons zero (next s3).
                                 s4 : pstream = cocons zero p5.
eq : conat -> conat -> type.     p5 : padding = next s4.
eq/refl : eq N N.                p6 : padding = pad p7. (not valid)
eqw2w3 : eq w2 w3 = eq/refl.     p7 : padding = pad p6. (not valid)
```

Fig. 1. Signatures and Examples for Section 2

are allowed to be circular. A slightly adapted signature would encode the set of conatural numbers, shown as the first three lines in the bottom left part of Fig. 1.

Because conat is a coinductive type, the canonical forms of type conat includes $cosucc^n$ cozero for all n and the infinite stack of cosucc, which is in one to one correspondence with the set of conatural numbers. Specifically, the infinite stack of cosucc, may be represented by the valid circular term w2 as in Fig. 1. The equality of terms in CoLF is the equality of the infinite trees generated by unfolding the terms, which corresponds to a bisimulation between circular terms. For example, an alternative representation of the infinite stack of cosucc is the term w3, and CoLF will treat w2 and w3 as equal terms, as shown by the last three lines in the bottom left part of Fig. 1. The terms w2 and w3 are proved equal by reflexivity. On the other hand, a formulation of conats in LF would involve an explicit constructor, e.g. mu : (conat -> conat) -> conat. The encoding of equality is now complicated and one needs to work with an explicit equality judgment whenever a conat is used. Functions defined by coinduction (e.g., bisimulation in Appendix K of the extended version) need to be encoded as relations in CoLF.

2.1 Finitely Padded Rational Streams

As an example of mixed inductive and coinductive definition, we consider rational streams of natural numbers with finite paddings in between. These streams are special instances of left-fair streams [5]. We define streams coinductively and define paddings inductively, such that there are infinitely many numbers in the stream but only finitely many paddings between numbers, shown in the signature consisting of first five lines in the right column of Fig. 1. For example, the term s1 in Fig. 1 represents a stream of natural number 1's with two paddings in between. Because padding is a type, the term p2 is not valid, as it is essentially an infinite stack of **pad** constructors. Definitions in a CoLF signature can refer to each other. Thus, the terms s3 and s4 denote the same padded stream, and the terms p6, p7 and p2 denote the same invalid stream consisting of purely paddings.

Priorities. To ensure the adequacy of representation, types of kind cotype admit circular terms while types of kind type admit only finitary terms. It is obvious that the circular term w1 is *not* a valid term of type nat due to the presence of an infinite stack of inductive constructors, and the circular term w2 is a valid term of type conat because it is a stack of coinductive constructors. However, when we have both inductive and coinductive types, it is unclear whether a circular term (e.g. s1) is valid. Historically, priorities are used to resolve this ambiguity [11]. A priority is assigned to each inductive or coinductive type, and constructors inherit priorities from their types. Constructors with the highest priority types are then viewed as primary. In CoLF, priorities are determined by the order of their declarations. Type families declared later have higher priorities than those declared earlier. In this way, the type pstream has higher priority than the type padding. Constructor cocons inherits the priority of pstream, and the term s1 is viewed as an infinite stack of cocons and is thus valid. Similarly, terms s3 and s4 are also valid. If we switch the order of declaration of padding and pstream (thereby switching their priorities), then terms s1, s3, and s4 are no longer valid.

3   The Type Theory

We formulate the type theory of CoLF, a dependent type theory with higher-order rational terms and decidable type checking. The higher-order rational terms correspond to $\bot$-free regular Böhm trees [21] and have decidable equality.

3.1   Higher-Order Rational Terms

When we consider first order terms (terms without λ-binders), the rational terms are terms with only finitely many distinct subterms, and thus their equality is decidable. We translate this intuition to the higher-order setting. The higher-order rational terms are those with finitely many subterms up to renaming of free and bound variables. We give several examples of rational and non-rational terms using the signatures in Section 2.

1. The term w2 in Fig. 1 is a first-order rational term.
2. A stream counting up from zero $\mathbf{up_0}$ = cocons zero (next (cocons (succ zero) (next (...)))) is a first-order term that is not rational.
3. A stream that repeats its argument $\mathbf{R_2} = \lambda x.$ cocons x (next ($\mathbf{R_2}\ x$)) is a higher-order rational term.
4. A stream that counts up from a given number $\mathbf{up} = \lambda x.$ cocons x (next (**up** (succ x))) is *not* a rational higher-order term.

In the definitions above, bolded symbols on the left of the equality signs are called recursion constants. It is crucial that in higher-order rational terms, all arguments to recursion constants are bound variables and not other kinds of terms. We call this restriction the *prepattern restriction* as it is similar to Miller's pattern restriction [24] except that we allow repetition of arguments. The prepattern restriction marks the key difference between the higher-order rational term $\mathbf{R_2}$ and the infinitary term $\mathbf{up}$. The term $\mathbf{up}$ is not rational because the argument to $\mathbf{up}$ is succ x, which is not a bound variable.

3.2 Syntax

We build subsequent developments on canonical LF [19], a formulation of the LF type theory where terms are always in their canonical form. Canonical forms do not contain β-redexes and are fully η-expanded with respect to their typing, supporting bijective correspondences between object logic derivations and the terms of the framework. One drawback of this presentation is that canonical terms are not closed under syntactic substitutions, and the technique of hereditary substitution addresses this problem [29].

The syntax of the theory follows the grammar shown in Fig. 2. We use the standard notion of spines. For example, a term $x\, M_1\, M_2\, M_3$ will be written as $x \cdot (M_1; M_2; M_3)$ where x is the head and $M_1; M_2; M_3$ is the spine. To express rational terms, we add recursive definitions of the form $r : A = M$ to the signature, where M must be contractive (judgment M contra) in that the head of M must be a constant or a variable. Recursive definitions look like notational definitions [26], but their semantics are very different. Recursive definitions are interpreted recursively in that the definition M may mention the recursion constant r, and other recursion constants including those defined later in the signature, while notational definitions in LF [26] cannot be recursive. Recursion constants are treated specially as a syntactic entity that is different from variables or constructors (nonrecursive constants). To ensure the conservativity over LF, we further require all definitions in Σ to be linearly ordered. That is, only in the body of a recursive definition can we "forward reference", and we can only forward reference other recursion constants. All other declarations must strictly refer to names that have been defined previously. We write $\lambda\overline{x}$ and $\overline{M}$ to mean a sequence of λ-abstractions and a sequence of terms respectively. We write x, y, z for variables, c, d for term constants (also called constructors), a for type family constants, and r, r', r'' for recursion constants.

To enforce the prepattern restriction, we use a technical device called *prepattern Π-abstractions*, and associated notion of *prepattern variables* and *prepattern spines*. Prepattern Π-abstractions are written as $\Pi x \mathbin{\overset{\cdot}{\cdot}} A_2.\, A_1$, and x will be a prepattern variable (written $x \mathbin{\overset{\cdot}{\cdot}} A_2$) in A_1. Moreover, in A_1, if y is a variable of a prepattern type $\Pi w \mathbin{\overset{\cdot}{\cdot}} A_2.B$, then the prepattern application of y to x will be realized as the head y followed by a prepattern spine $([x])$, written $y \cdot ([x])$. The semantics is that prepattern variables may only be substituted by other prepattern variables, while ordinary variables can be substituted by arbitrary terms (which include other prepattern variables). In a well-typed signature, if

Signatures	$\Sigma ::= \cdot \mid \Sigma, a : K \mid \Sigma, c : A \mid \Sigma, r : A = M$
Contexts	$\Gamma ::= \cdot \mid \Gamma, x : A \mid \Gamma, x \overset{\circ}{:} A$
Kinds	$K ::= \textsf{type} \mid \textsf{cotype} \mid \Pi x : A.\ K \mid \Pi x \overset{\circ}{:} A.\ K$
Canonical types	$A, B ::= P \mid \Pi x : A_2.\ A_1 \mid \Pi x \overset{\circ}{:} A_2.\ A_1$
Atomic types	$P ::= a \cdot S$
Canonical terms	$M ::= R \mid \lambda x.\ M$
Neutral terms	$R ::= H \cdot S$
Heads	$H ::= x \mid c \mid r$
Spines	$S ::= M; S \mid [x]; S \mid ()$

Fig. 2. The Syntax for CoLF

$r : A = M$ is a recursion declaration, then A consists of purely prepattern Π-abstractions (judgment $A\,\textsf{prepat}$) and for all $r \cdot S$ in the signature, S consists of purely prepattern applications and is thus called a prepattern spine (judgment $S\,\textsf{prepat}$). The prepattern variables are similar to those introduced by the ∇-operator [25], which models the concept of fresh names, but here in a dependently typed setting, types may depend on prepattern variables.

In an actual implementation, the usages of prepattern types may impose additional burdens on the programmer. As a remedy, the implementation could infer which variables are prepattern variables based on whether they appear as arguments to recursion constants and propagate such information.

3.3 Trace Condition

In a signature Σ, we say that a type A is inductive if $A = \Pi x_1 \ldots \Pi x_n : A_n.a \cdot S$ and $a : \Pi y_1 \ldots \Pi y_m : B_m.\ \textsf{type}$, and a type A coinductive if $A = \Pi x_1 \ldots \Pi x_n : A_n.a \cdot S$ and $a : \Pi y_1 \ldots \Pi y_m : B_m.\ \textsf{cotype}$. A constructor c is inductive if $c : A \in \Sigma$ and A is inductive, and c is coinductive if $c : A \in \Sigma$ and A is coinductive.

The validity of the terms is enforced through a trace condition [17,8] on cycles. A trace is a sequence of constructor constants or variables, where each constructor or variable is a child of the previous one. A trace from a recursion constant r to itself is a sequence starting with the head of the definition of r and ending with the parent of an occurrence of r. In Fig. 1, a trace from p2 to itself is [pad], and a trace from s1 to itself is [cocons, pad, pad, next]. Traces cross into definitions of recursion constants. Thus, a trace from p6 to itself is [pad, pad], which is also a trace from p7 to itself. A trace from s4 to itself is [cocons, next], and a trace from p5 to itself is [next, cocons]. If $r = \lambda x.f\,(r\,x)\,(g\,(r\,x))$ (more precisely $r = \lambda x.\ f \cdot (r \cdot ([x]); g \cdot (r \cdot ([x])))$), then there are two traces from r to itself, i.e., $[f]$ and $[f, g]$.

A higher-order rational term M is *trace-valid* if for all recursion constants r in M, each trace from r to itself contains a coinductive constructor, and that coinductive constructor has the highest priority among all constructors on that trace. To ensure trace validity, it is sufficient to check in a recursive definition, all occurrences of recursion constants are *guarded by* some coinductive constructor of the highest priority. The guardedness condition (judgment $\vdash_\Sigma r \bowtie M$) means that occurrences of r in M are guarded by some coinductive constructor of the highest priority, and the condition is decidable. In a well-typed signature Σ, if $r : A = M \in \Sigma$, then $\vdash_\Sigma r \bowtie M$. A detailed algorithm for checking trace-validity is presented in Appendix B.2 of the extended version. The reader may check guardedness for all valid terms in Fig. 1.

3.4   Hereditary Substitution

Hereditary substitution [29,19] provides a method of substituting one canonical term into another and still get a canonical term as the output by performing type-based normalization. This technique simplifies the definition of the term equality in the original LF [18,20] by separating the term equality and normalization from type checking. We extend the definition of hereditary substitution to account for recursion constants. Hereditary substitution is a partial operation on terms. When input term is not well-typed or prepattern restriction is not respected, the output may be undefined.

Hereditary substitution takes as an extra argument the simple type of the term being substituted by. The simple type τ is inductively generated by the following grammar.

$$\tau ::= * \mid \tau_1 \to \tau_2$$

We write A° for the simple type that results from erasing dependencies in A. We write $[N/x]^\tau M$ for hereditarily substituting N for free ordinary variable x in M. The definition proceeds by induction on τ and the structure of M. For prepattern variables, since they may only stand for other prepattern variables, we use a notion of renaming substitution. The renaming substitution $[y/x]M$ renames a prepattern variable or an ordinary variable x to prepattern variable y in M. Both substitutions naturally extend to other syntactic kinds. Hereditary substitution relies on renaming substitution when reducing prepattern applications. Because of the prepattern restriction, recursion constants are only applied to prepattern variables in a well-formed signature, and we never substitute into a recursive definition. Let σ be a simultaneous renaming substitution, a notion generalized from renaming substitutions, we write $[\sigma]M$ for carrying out substitution σ on M.

The definition for hereditary substitution is shown in Fig. 3. Appendix A of the extended version contains other straightforward cases of the definition. We note that prepattern Π-types erase to a base type $*$ because we may only apply terms of prepattern Π-types to prepattern variables, and thus the structure of the argument term does not matter.

3.5   Term Equality

The equality checking of circular terms is carried out by iteratively unfolding recursive definitions [1,6,14,23]. The algorithm here is a slight adaptation of the equality algorithm for regular Böhm trees by Huet [21], tailored to the specific

$$\boxed{A^\circ = \tau}$$
$$(\Pi x : A_2.\, A_1)^\circ = (A_2^\circ) \to (A_1^\circ)$$
$$(\Pi x \overset{?}{:} A_2.\, A_1)^\circ = * \to (A_1^\circ)$$
$$(P)^\circ = *$$

$$\boxed{[N/x]^\tau M = M'}$$
$$[N/x]^\tau R = [N/x]^\tau R$$
$$[N/x]^\tau (\lambda y. M) = \lambda y. [N/x]^\tau M,\ y \neq x$$

$$\boxed{[N/x]^\tau R = R'}$$
$$[N/x]^\tau (x \cdot S) = ([N/x]^\tau S) \rhd^\tau N$$
$$[N/x]^\tau (y \cdot S) = y \cdot ([N/x]^\tau S),\ y \neq x$$

$$[N/x]^\tau (c \cdot S) = c \cdot ([N/x]^\tau S)$$
$$[N/x]^\tau (r \cdot S) = r \cdot ([N/x]^\tau S)$$

$$\boxed{[N/x]^\tau S = S'}$$
$$[N/x]^\tau () = ()$$
$$[N/x]^\tau (M; S) = ([N/x]^\tau M); ([N/x]^\tau S)$$
$$[N/x]^\tau ([x]; S) = \mathsf{undefined}$$
$$[N/x]^\tau ([z]; S) = [z]; ([N/x]^\tau S),\ x \neq z$$

$$\boxed{S \rhd^\tau N = R'}$$
$$() \rhd^* R = R$$
$$(N; S) \rhd^{\tau_2 \to \tau_1} (\lambda x. M) = S \rhd^{\tau_1} ([N/x]^{\tau_2} M)$$
$$([y]; S) \rhd^{* \to \tau_1} (\lambda x. M) = S \rhd^{\tau_1} ([\![y/x]\!] M)$$

Fig. 3. Hereditary Substitutions

case of CoLF's canonical term syntax. We emphasize that the equality algorithm can treat terms that are not trace-valid or well-typed, and is thus decoupled from validity checking and type checking. The algorithm itself checks for the prepattern restriction on recursion constants and contractiveness condition on recursive definitions. These checks are essential to ensure termination in the presence of forward referencing inside recursive definitions.

We define the judgment $\Delta; \Theta \vdash_\Sigma M = M'$ to mean M and M', with free variables from Θ, are equal under the assumptions Δ, with consideration of recursive definitions in Σ. The variable list Θ is similar to Γ except it doesn't have the types for the variables. It is merely a list of pairwise distinct variables. Similarly, we define the judgment $\Delta; \Theta \vdash_\Sigma S = S'$ to mean spines S and S' are element-wise equal. Equalities in Δ will be of the form $(\Theta \vdash M = M')$ where Θ holds free variables of M and M'. We write $\Theta \vdash M$ to mean that $FV(M) \subseteq \Theta$. We define simultaneous variable renaming, that σ is a variable renaming from Θ' to Θ, written $\Theta \vdash \sigma : \Theta'$ to mean that if $\Theta' \vdash M$, then $\Theta \vdash [\![\sigma]\!]M$. For instance, if we have $x \vdash [\![x/y, x/z]\!] : y, z$ and $y, z \vdash y \cdot [z]$, then $x \vdash [\![x/y, x/z]\!](y \cdot [z])$, i.e., $x \vdash x \cdot [x]$. The rules for the judgments are presented in Fig. 4. Recall that M is contractive (M contra) if the head of M is not a recursion constant.

An Example. Assume the signature in Section 2.1, and consider a stream generator that repeats its arguments. The stream may be represented by terms r1 and r2 below. Note that in the concrete syntax, square brackets represent λ-abstractions.

```
r1 : nat -> pstream = [x] cocons x (next (r1 x)).
r2 : nat -> pstream = [x] cocons x (next (cocons x (next (r2 x)))).
```

Because r1 is a recursion constant, its type is a prepattern-Π type, and this restriction is respected in the body as x is a prepattern variable.

We want to show that r1 and r2 are equal in the framework. Let Σ be the signature of Section 2.1 plus the definitions for r1 and r2. We illustrate the

$\boxed{\Delta; \Theta \vdash_\Sigma M = M'}$

$$\frac{\Theta \vdash \sigma : \Theta'}{\Delta, (\Theta' \vdash H \cdot S_1 = H' \cdot S_2); \Theta \vdash_\Sigma [\![\sigma]\!](H \cdot S_1) = [\![\sigma]\!](H' \cdot S_2)}(1)$$

$$\frac{S_1 \ \mathsf{prepat} \qquad M \ \mathsf{contra} \qquad \begin{array}{c} r : A = M \in \Sigma \\ \Delta, (\Theta \vdash r \cdot S_1 = H \cdot S_2); \Theta \vdash_\Sigma S_1 \rhd^{A^o} M = H \cdot S_2 \end{array}}{\Delta; \Theta \vdash_\Sigma r \cdot S_1 = H \cdot S_2}(2)$$

$$\frac{M \ \mathsf{contra} \qquad H \neq r' \qquad \begin{array}{c} r : A = M \in \Sigma \qquad S_2 \ \mathsf{prepat} \\ \Delta, (\Theta \vdash H \cdot S_1 = r \cdot S_2); \Theta \vdash_\Sigma H \cdot S_1 = S_2 \rhd^{A^o} M \end{array}}{\Delta; \Theta \vdash_\Sigma H \cdot S_1 = r \cdot S_2}(3)$$

$$\frac{\Delta; \Theta \vdash_\Sigma S = S'}{\Delta; \Theta \vdash_\Sigma c \cdot S = c \cdot S'}(4) \qquad \frac{\Delta; \Theta \vdash_\Sigma S = S'}{\Delta; \Theta \vdash_\Sigma y \cdot S = y \cdot S'}(5) \qquad \frac{\Delta; \Theta, x \vdash_\Sigma M = M'}{\Delta; \Theta \vdash_\Sigma \lambda x. M = \lambda x. M'}(6)$$

$\boxed{\Delta; \Theta \vdash_\Sigma S = S'}$

$$\frac{}{\Delta; \Theta \vdash_\Sigma () = ()} \qquad \frac{\Delta; \Theta \vdash_\Sigma M = M' \qquad \Delta; \Theta \vdash_\Sigma S = S'}{\Delta; \Theta \vdash_\Sigma M; S = M'; S'} \qquad \frac{\Delta; \Theta \vdash_\Sigma S = S'}{\Delta; \Theta \vdash_\Sigma [x]; S = [x]; S'}$$

Fig. 4. Equality Checking

process of checking that $; \vdash_\Sigma \lambda x.\ \mathtt{r1} \cdot ([x]) = \lambda x.\ \mathtt{r2} \cdot ([x])$ as a search procedure for a derivation of this judgment, where initially both Δ and Θ are empty.

Immediately after rule (6) we encounter $; x \vdash_\Sigma \mathtt{r1} \cdot ([x]) = \mathtt{r2} \cdot ([x])$, we memoize this equality by storing $(x \vdash \mathtt{r1} \cdot ([x]) = \mathtt{r2} \cdot ([x]))$ in Δ as in rule (2), and unfold the left-hand side. Then we proceed with the judgment.

$$(x \vdash \mathtt{r1} \cdot ([x]) = \mathtt{r2} \cdot ([x])); x \vdash_\Sigma \mathtt{cocons} \cdot (x; \mathtt{next} \cdot (\mathtt{r1} \cdot ([x]))) = \mathtt{r2} \cdot ([x])$$

We then use rule (3) to unfold the right-hand side and store then current equation in the context. Then after several structural rules, we have

$$(x \vdash \mathtt{r1} \cdot ([x]) = \mathtt{r2} \cdot ([x])), \ldots; x \vdash_\Sigma \mathtt{r1} \cdot ([x]) = \mathtt{cocons} \cdot (x; \mathtt{next} \cdot (\mathtt{r2} \cdot ([x])))$$

At this point, rule (2) applies. We add the current equation to the context and unfold the left recursive definition. Then after several structural rules, we encounter the following judgment.

$$(x \vdash \mathtt{r1} \cdot ([x]) = \mathtt{r2} \cdot ([x])), \ldots; x \vdash_\Sigma \mathtt{r1} \cdot ([x]) = \mathtt{r2} \cdot ([x])$$

Now we can close the derivation with rule (1) using identity substitution.

Decidability. Huet [21] has proved the termination, soundness, and completeness in the case of untyped regular Böhm trees. Our proof shares the essential idea with their proof. The termination relies on the fact that terms only admit finitely many subterms modulo renaming of both free and bound variables, and only subterms will appear in Δ. The soundness and completeness are proved with respect to the infinite Böhm tree [4] generated by unfolding the terms indefinitely, which again corresponds to a bisimulation between terms.

Theorem 1 (Decidability of Term Equality). *It is decidable whether* $\Delta; \Theta \vdash_\Sigma M = M'$ *for any rational term* M *and* M'.

Proof. We first show that there is a limit on the number of equations in Δ. Then the termination follows the lexicographic order of the assumption capacity (difference between current number of assumptions in Δ and the maximum), and the structure of the terms under comparison. It is obvious that rules (4)(5)(6) decompose the structure of the terms and rules (2)(3) reduce assumption capacity. It remains to show that the size of Δ has a limit.

The prepattern conditions on rules (2)(3) ensure that the expansion of recursive definitions will only involve renaming substitutions, and thus the resulting term will be an α-renaming of the underlying definition. No structurally new terms will be produced as a result of renaming substitution in rules (2)(3). We construct a finite set of all possible terms that could be added to the context. Each term is of finite depth and breadth limited by the existing constructs in the signature, and consists of finitely many constants, variables, and recursion constants. The constants and recursion constants are limited to those already presented in the signature. Although there are infinitely many variables, there are finitely many terms of bounded depth and width that are distinct modulo renaming of both bound and free variables. Thus, the set of terms that can appear as an element of Δ is finite, modulo renaming of free variables. The estimate of a rough upper bound can be found in Appendix D of the extended version.

We specify the infinite unfolding by specifying its unfolding to a Böhm tree of depth k, which is a finite approximation to the infinite Böhm tree, for each $k \in \mathbb{N}$. Then the infinite Böhm tree is limit of all its finite approximations. We use the judgment $\exp_{(k)}(M) =_{(k)} M'$ to denote the expansion of a higher-order rational term M to a Böhm tree M' of depth k, and use the judgment $\exp(N) = N'$ to express that the higher-order rational term M expands to infinite Böhm tree N'. We also enrich the syntax of Böhm trees with prepattern variables. The full set of expansion rules can be found in Appendix E of the extended version. All cases are structural except for the following case when we expand a recursion constant, where we look up the definition of the recursion constant and plug in the arguments.

$$\exp_{(k+1)}(r \cdot S) =_{(k+1)} \exp_{(k+1)}(S \rhd^{A^\circ} M) \text{ if } r : A = M \in \Sigma \text{ and } S \text{ prepat}$$

Lemma 1 (Expansion Commutes with Hereditary Substitution). *For all* k, τ, M *and* N, $\exp_{(k)}([N/x]^\tau M) =_{(k)} [\exp_{(k)}(N)/x]^\tau (\exp_{(k)}(M))$ *if defined.*

Proof. Directly by lexicographic induction on k and the structure of M.

Theorem 2 (Soundness of Term Equality).

  If $\cdot; \Theta \vdash M = M'$, *then* $\exp_{(k)}(M) =_{(k)} \exp_{(k)}(M')$ *for all* k.

Proof. By lexicographic induction on the depth k and the derivation $\Delta; \Theta \vdash M = M'$. The case for the rule (1) is immediate by applying renaming substitutions at the closure rule. The cases for rules (2)(3) follow from the commutation lemma. The cases for rules (4)(5)(6) follow from the definition of exp.

Theorem 3 (Completeness of Term Equality).

  For rational terms M *and* M', *with free variables from* Θ, *if* $\exp(M) = \exp(M')$, *then* $\cdot; \Theta \vdash M = M'$.

Proof. The equality algorithm is syntax-directed. We construct the derivation of $\cdot; \Theta \vdash M = M'$ by syntax-directed proof search following the structure of M. Every trace of $\exp(M)$ and $\exp(M')$ corresponds to a trace in the derivation of $\cdot; \Theta \vdash M = M'$. If $\exp(M) = \exp(M')$, then two terms are equal on every trace, and there will be exactly one rule that applies at every point in the construction of the equality derivation. Termination is assured by Theorem 1.

3.6   Type Checking Rules

For type checking, we define the judgments in Fig. 5 by simultaneous induction. Because recursion constants may be forward referenced, we need to have access to later declarations that have not been checked during the checking of earlier declarations. In order to ensure the otherwise linear order of the declarations, the type checking judgments are parametrized by a pair of signatures $\Xi; \Sigma$, where Ξ is the local signature that contains type-checked declarations before the current declaration and Σ is the global signature that contains full signatures, including declarations that have not been checked. In particular, recursion constants available for forward-referencing will be in Σ but not Ξ. The type equality judgments $\Gamma \vdash_\Sigma A_1 = A_2$, $\Gamma \vdash_\Sigma P_1 = P_2$ only need to read recursive definitions from the global signature, and do not need to access the local signature.

  A selection of type checking rules that are essential are presented in Fig. 6. The rest of the rules can be found in Appendix F of the extended version. To ensure the correct type checking order, i.e., the body of a recursive definition is checked after the types of all recursion constants within are checked, we defer checking the body of all recursive definitions to the end. This approach is viable because the term equality algorithm soundly terminates even when the recursive definition is not well-typed. For instance, if the signature $\Sigma = c_1 : A_1, c_2 : A_2, r_1 : A_3 = M_1, c_3 : A_4, r_2 : A_5 = M_2$, then the order of checking is $A_1, A_2, A_3, A_4, A_5, M_1, M_2$. This order is expressed in the type checking rules by an annotation on specific premise of the rules. The annotation $[\vdash_{\Xi; \Sigma} M \Leftarrow A]^{1:\text{deferred}}$ means that this judgment is to be checked after all the typing judgments have been checked. That is, when we check this premise, we have checked that $\vdash_\Sigma \Sigma$ sig. Because of the deferred checking of recursive

Σ sig	Signature Σ is type correct categorically
$\vdash_\Sigma \Xi$ sig	Local signature Ξ is type correct with global signature Σ
$\vdash_{\Xi;\Sigma} \Gamma$ ctx	Context Γ is well-formed
$\Gamma \vdash_{\Xi;\Sigma} K \Leftarrow$ kind	Kind K is a valid kind
$\Gamma \vdash_{\Xi;\Sigma} A \Leftarrow$ (co)type	Type A is a canonical type
$\Gamma \vdash_{\Xi;\Sigma} P \Rightarrow K$	Atomic type P synthesizes kind K
$\Gamma \vdash_{\Xi;\Sigma} S \triangleright K \Rightarrow K'$	Spine S applied to kind K produces kind K'
$\Gamma \vdash_{\Xi;\Sigma} M \Leftarrow A$	Term M checks against type A
$\Gamma \vdash_{\Xi;\Sigma} R \Rightarrow P$	Neutral term R synthesizes type P
$\Gamma \vdash_{\Xi;\Sigma} S \triangleright A \Rightarrow P$	Spine S applied to canonical type A produces atomic type P
$\Gamma \vdash_\Sigma A_1 = A_2$	Types A_1 and A_2 are equal canonical types
$\Gamma \vdash_\Sigma P_1 = P_2$	Types P_1 and P_2 are equal atomic types

Fig. 5. Type Checking Judgments

definitions, the judgment $\vdash_\Sigma \Xi$ sig does not require the body of recursion declarations in Ξ to be well-typed. However, the categorical judgment Σ sig requires the body of every recursion declaration to be well-typed.

To enforce the restriction that forward references only happen in a recursive definition, the annotation [or $r : A = M \in \Sigma]^{2:\text{definitions}}$ means that forward reference only occurs during the checking of recursive definitions (which are deferred) and nowhere else.

3.7 Metatheorems

We state some properties about hereditary substitution and type checking.

Theorem 4 (Hereditary Substitution Respects Typing).

Given a checked signature Σ where Σ sig, if $\Gamma \vdash_{\Xi;\Sigma} N \Leftarrow A$ and $\Gamma, x : A, \Gamma' \vdash M \Leftarrow B$, then $\Gamma, [N/x]^{A^\circ}\Gamma' \vdash_{\Xi;\Sigma} [N/x]^{A^\circ} M \Leftarrow [N/x]^{A^\circ} B$.

Proof. By induction on the second derivation, with similar theorems for other judgment forms. This proof is similar to those in [29,19]. Because of the prepattern restriction, hereditary substitutions do not occur inside recursive definitions and is thus similar to hereditary substitutions in LF.

Theorem 5 (Decidability of Type Checking).

All typing judgments are algorithmically decidable.

Proof. The type checking judgment is syntax directed. Hereditary substitutions are defined by induction on the erased simple types and always terminate. Equality of types ultimately reduces to equality of terms, and we have proved its termination in Section 3.5.

$\boxed{\Sigma \text{ sig}}$

$$\frac{\vdash_\Sigma \Sigma \text{ sig}}{\Sigma \text{ sig}}$$

$\boxed{\vdash_\Sigma \Xi \text{ sig}}$

$$\frac{}{\vdash_\Sigma \cdot \text{ sig}} \qquad \frac{\vdash_\Sigma \Xi \text{ sig} \quad \vdash_{\Xi;\Sigma} K \Leftarrow \text{kind}}{\vdash_\Sigma \Xi, a : K \text{ sig}}$$

$$\frac{\vdash_\Sigma \Xi \text{ sig} \quad \vdash_{\Xi;\Sigma} A \Leftarrow \text{(co)type}}{\vdash_\Sigma \Xi, c : A \text{ sig}}$$

$$\frac{\vdash_\Sigma \Xi \text{ sig} \quad \vdash_{\Xi;\Sigma} A \Leftarrow \text{(co)type} \quad [\vdash_{\Xi;\Sigma} M \Leftarrow A]^{1:\text{deferred}} \quad A \text{ prepat} \quad M \text{ contra} \quad \vdash_\Sigma r \bowtie M}{\vdash_\Sigma \Xi, r : A = M \text{ sig}}$$

$\boxed{\Gamma \vdash_{\Xi;\Sigma} K \Leftarrow \text{kind}}$

$$\frac{}{\Gamma \vdash_{\Xi;\Sigma} \text{type} \Leftarrow \text{kind}}$$

$$\frac{}{\Gamma \vdash_{\Xi;\Sigma} \text{cotype} \Leftarrow \text{kind}}$$

$$\frac{\Gamma \vdash_{\Xi;\Sigma} A \Leftarrow \text{(co)type} \quad \Gamma, x \overset{(\cdot)}{:} A \vdash_{\Xi;\Sigma} K \Leftarrow \text{kind}}{\Gamma \vdash_{\Xi;\Sigma} \Pi x \overset{(\cdot)}{:} A.\, K \Leftarrow \text{kind}}$$

$\boxed{\Gamma \vdash_{\Xi;\Sigma} A \Leftarrow \text{(co)type}}$

$$\frac{\Gamma \vdash_{\Xi;\Sigma} A_2 \Leftarrow \text{(co)type} \quad \Gamma, x \overset{(\cdot)}{:} A_2 \vdash_{\Xi;\Sigma} A_1 \Leftarrow \text{(co)type}}{\Gamma \vdash_{\Xi;\Sigma} \Pi x \overset{(\cdot)}{:} A_2.\, A_1 \Leftarrow \text{(co)type}}$$

$$\frac{\Gamma \vdash_{\Xi;\Sigma} P \Rightarrow K \quad K = \text{type} / \text{cotype}}{\Gamma \vdash_{\Xi;\Sigma} P \Leftarrow \text{(co)type}}$$

$\boxed{\Gamma \vdash_{\Xi;\Sigma} P \Rightarrow K}$

$$\frac{a : K \in \Xi \quad \Gamma \vdash_{\Xi;\Sigma} S \triangleright K \Rightarrow K'}{\Gamma \vdash_{\Xi;\Sigma} a \cdot S \Rightarrow K'}$$

$\boxed{\Gamma \vdash_{\Xi;\Sigma} S \triangleright K \Rightarrow K'}$

$$\frac{}{\Gamma \vdash_{\Xi;\Sigma} () \triangleright K \Rightarrow K}$$

$$\frac{\Gamma \vdash_{\Xi;\Sigma} M \Leftarrow A_2 \quad [M/x]^{A_2^o} K = K' \quad \Gamma \vdash_{\Xi;\Sigma} S \triangleright K' \Rightarrow K''}{\Gamma \vdash_{\Xi;\Sigma} M; S \triangleright \Pi x : A_2.\, K \Rightarrow K''}$$

$$\frac{y \overset{?}{:} A_2' \in \Gamma \quad \Gamma \vdash_{\Xi;\Sigma} A_2' = A_2 \quad [\![y/x]\!] K = K' \quad \Gamma \vdash_{\Xi;\Sigma} S \triangleright K' \Rightarrow K''}{\Gamma \vdash_{\Xi;\Sigma} [y]; S \triangleright \Pi x \overset{?}{:} A_2.\, K \Rightarrow K''}$$

$\boxed{\Gamma \vdash_{\Xi;\Sigma} M \Leftarrow A}$

$$\frac{\Gamma \vdash_{\Xi;\Sigma} R \Rightarrow P' \quad \Gamma \vdash_\Sigma P' = P}{\Gamma \vdash_{\Xi;\Sigma} R \Leftarrow P}$$

$$\frac{\Gamma, x \overset{(\cdot)}{:} A_2 \vdash_{\Xi;\Sigma} M \Leftarrow A_1}{\Gamma \vdash_{\Xi;\Sigma} \lambda x.\, M \Leftarrow \Pi x \overset{(\cdot)}{:} A_2.\, A_1}$$

$\boxed{\Gamma \vdash_{\Xi;\Sigma} R \Rightarrow P}$

$$\frac{(c/x : A \in \Gamma \text{ or } x \overset{?}{:} A \in \Gamma) \quad \Gamma \vdash_{\Xi;\Sigma} S \triangleright A \Rightarrow P}{\Gamma \vdash_{\Xi;\Sigma} c/x \cdot S \Rightarrow P}$$

$$\frac{r : A = M \in \Xi \quad [\text{or } r : A = M \in \Sigma]^{2:\text{definitions}} \quad \Gamma \vdash_{\Xi;\Sigma} S \triangleright A \Rightarrow P}{\Gamma \vdash_{\Xi;\Sigma} r \cdot S \Rightarrow P}$$

$\boxed{\Gamma \vdash_{\Xi;\Sigma} S \triangleright A \Rightarrow P}$

$$\frac{}{\Gamma \vdash_{\Xi;\Sigma} () \triangleright P \Rightarrow P}$$

$$\frac{\Gamma \vdash_{\Xi;\Sigma} M \Leftarrow A_2 \quad [M/x]^{A_2^o} A_1 = A_1' \quad \Gamma \vdash_{\Xi;\Sigma} S \triangleright A_1' \Rightarrow P}{\Gamma \vdash_{\Xi;\Sigma} M; S \triangleright \Pi x : A_2.\, A_1 \Rightarrow P}$$

$$\frac{y \overset{?}{:} A_2' \in \Gamma \quad \Gamma \vdash_{\Xi;\Sigma} A_2' = A_2 \quad [\![y/x]\!] A_1 = A_1' \quad \Gamma \vdash_{\Xi;\Sigma} S \triangleright A_1' \Rightarrow P}{\Gamma \vdash_{\Xi;\Sigma} [y]; S \triangleright \Pi x \overset{?}{:} A_2.\, A_1 \Rightarrow P}$$

Fig. 6. Type Checking Rules (Condensed Selection)

4 Encoding Subtyping Systems for Recursive Types

In the presentation of case studies, we use the concrete syntax of our implementation, following Twelf [27]. The prepattern annotations are omitted. The full convention can be found in Appendix G of the extended version. Representations of circular derivations involve dependent usages of cotype's.

4.1 Encoding a Classical Subtyping System

We present a mixed inductive and coinductive definition of subtyping using Danielsson and Altenkirch's [14] subtyping system. The systems concern the subtyping of types given by the following grammar.

$$\tau ::= \bot \mid \top \mid \tau_1 \to \tau_2 \mid \mu X.\tau_1 \to \tau_2 \mid X$$

The subtyping judgment is defined by five axioms and two rules, The axioms are

1. $\bot \le \tau$ (bot)
2. $\tau \le \top$ (top)
3. $\mu X.\tau_1 \to \tau_2 \le [\mu X.\tau_1 \to \tau_2/X](\tau_1 \to \tau_2)$ (unfold)
4. $[\mu X.\tau_1 \to \tau_2/X](\tau_1 \to \tau_2) \le \mu X.\tau_1 \to \tau_2$ (fold)
5. $\tau \le \tau$ (refl)

And the rules are shown below, where arr is coinductive and is written using a double horizontal line, and trans is inductive. The validity condition of mixed induction and coinduction entails that a derivation consisting purely of trans rules is not valid.

$$\frac{\tau_1 \le \sigma_1 \quad \sigma_2 \le \tau_2}{\sigma_1 \to \sigma_2 \le \tau_1 \to \tau_2}\text{(arr)} \qquad \frac{\tau_1 \le \tau_2 \quad \tau_2 \le \tau_3}{\tau_1 \le \tau_3}\text{(trans)}$$

Danielsson and Altenkirch defined the rules using Agda's mixed inductive and coinductive datatype (shown in Appendix H of the extended version) and the encoding in CoLF is shown in Fig. 7. The curly brackets indicate explicit Π-abstractions and the free capitalized variables are implicit Π-abstracted. We note that the mixed inductive and coinductive nature of the subtyping rules reflected in CoLF as two predicates, the inductive subtp and the coinductive subtpinf, and the latter has a higher priority. Clauses defining one predicate refer to the other predicate as a premise, e.g. subtp/arr and inf/arr. Let $\ulcorner-\urcorner$ denote the encoding relation, and we have $\ulcorner\mu X.\sigma \to \tau\urcorner = \text{mu} \ulcorner X.\sigma\urcorner\ulcorner X.\tau\urcorner$.

Theorem 6 (Adequacy of Encoding).

1. *There is a compositional bijection between recursive types and valid canonical terms of type* tp
2. *For types σ and τ, there is a compositional bijection between valid cyclic subtyping derivations of $\sigma \le \tau$, and valid canonical terms of type* subtp $\ulcorner\sigma\urcorner\ulcorner\tau\urcorner$.

```
tp : type.                          subtp : tp -> tp -> type.
bot : tp.                           subtpinf : tp -> tp -> cotype.
top : tp.                           subtp/top : subtp T top.
arr : tp -> tp -> tp.               subtp/bot : subtp bot T.
mu : (tp -> tp) -> (tp -> tp) -> tp.  refl : subtp T T.
trans : subtp T1 T2 -> subtp T2 T3 -> subtp T1 T3.
subtp/arr : subtpinf T1 T2 -> subtp T1 T2.
unfold : {T1}{T2} subtp (mu T1 T2) (arr (T1 (mu T1 T2)) (T2 (mu T1 T2))).
fold : {T1}{T2} subtp (arr (T1 (mu T1 T2)) (T2 (mu T1 T2))) (mu T1 T2).
inf/arr : subtp T1 S1 -> subtp S2 T2 -> subtpinf (arr S1 S2) (arr T1 T2).
```

Fig. 7. An Encoding of Subtyping in CoLF

Proof. 1. Directly by induction on the structure of recursive types in the forward direction, and by induction on the structure of the typing derivation in the reverse direction.

2. By induction on the syntax of the circular derivations in the forward direction, and by induction on the syntax of the higher-order rational terms in the reverse direction. Note that cycles in the circular derivations correspond directly to occurrences of recursion constants. The validity condition of mixed induction and coinduction coincides with CoLF validity.

We give an example of the subtyping derivation of $\mu X.X \to X \leq \mu X.(X \to \bot) \to \top$. Let $S = \mu X.X \to X$ and $T = \mu X.(X \to \bot) \to \top$.

$$
\dfrac{
\dfrac{
\dfrac{
\dfrac{\dfrac{(\text{s\_sub\_t})}{S \leq T} \quad \dfrac{\bot \leq S \; \bot}{T \to \bot \leq S \to S} \to \; \dfrac{}{S \to S \leq S} \text{fold}}{T \to \bot \leq S} \text{trans}
}{\dfrac{S \leq S \to S}{\quad} \text{unfold} \quad \dfrac{S \to S \leq (T \to \bot) \to \top}{\quad}}
\quad
\dfrac{\dfrac{S \leq T \; \top}{(T \to \bot) \to \top \leq T} \to \text{fold}}{}
}{S \to S \leq T} \text{trans}
}{(\text{s\_sub\_t}) \; S \leq T}
$$

Here is the encoding in CoLF:

```
s : tp = mu ([x] x) ([x] x).
t : tp = mu ([x] arr x bot) ([x] top).
s_sub_t : subtp s t =
    trans (unfold ([x] x) ([x] x)) (trans (subtp/arr (inf/arr
                        (trans (subtp/arr (inf/arr s_sub_t subtp/bot))
                            (fold ([x] x) ([x] x))) subtp/top))
                            (fold ([x] arr x bot) ([x] top))).
```

We note that the circular definition is valid by the presence of the constructor inf/arr along the trace from s_sub_t to itself. The presence of the coinductive arr rule is the validity condition of mixed inductive and coinductive definitions.

There are two key differences between a CoLF encoding and an Agda encoding. First, in Agda one needs to use explicit names for μ-bound variables or de Bruijn indices, while in CoLF one uses abstract binding trees. Second, Agda does not have built-in coinductive equality but CoLF has built-in equality. In Agda, the one step of unfolding `s_sub_t` is not equal to `s_sub_t`, but in CoLF, they are equal.

4.2 Encoding a Polarized Circular Subtyping System for Equirecursive Types

We present an encoding of a variant Lakhani et al.'s polarized subtyping system [22] into CoLF. The system is circular. Due to space constraints, we only present the encoding for the positive types fragment and their emptiness derivations. This is an important part in the subtyping system because an empty type is a subtype of any other type. The full encoding of the polarized subtyping system can be found in Appendix I of the extended version.

Encoding of Positive Equirecursive Types. The equirecursive nature is captured by a signature Σ providing recursive definitions for type names t^+.

$$\tau^+, \sigma^+ ::= t_1^+ \otimes t_2^+ \mid 1 \mid t_1^+ \oplus t_2^+ \mid 0$$
$$\Sigma \quad ::= \cdot \mid \Sigma, t^+ = \tau^+$$

Equirecursive types are directly encoded as recursion constants in the system, and the framework automatically provides equirecursive type equality checking. Because equirecursive types are circular, positive types are encoded as cotype.

```
postp : cotype.                        one : postp.
                                       plus : postp -> postp -> postp.
times : postp -> postp -> postp.       zero : postp.
```

Theorem 7 (Adequacy of Type Encoding). *There is a bijection between circular types defined in an object signature for the positive types fragment and canonical forms of the postp in CoLF.*

Proof. By induction on the syntax in both directions.

Encoding of the Emptiness Judgment. The emptiness judgment t empty is defined by the following rules. We stress that these rules are to be interpreted coinductively.

$$\frac{}{0 \text{ empty}}(0\,\mathsf{EMP}) \qquad \frac{t = t_1 \oplus t_2 \in \Sigma \quad t_1 \text{ empty} \quad t_2 \text{ empty}}{t \text{ empty}}(\oplus\mathsf{EMP})$$

$$\frac{t = t_1 \otimes t_2 \in \Sigma \quad t_1 \text{ empty}}{t \text{ empty}}(\otimes\mathsf{EMP}_1) \qquad \frac{t = t_1 \otimes t_2 \in \Sigma \quad t_2 \text{ empty}}{t \text{ empty}}(\otimes\mathsf{EMP}_2)$$

In CoLF, the rules are encoded as follows. The coinductive nature is reflected by the typing of `empty` : `postp -> cotype`, which postulates that the predicate `empty` is to be interpreted coinductively.

```
empty : postp -> cotype.
zero_emp : empty zero.
plus_emp : empty T1 -> empty T2 -> empty (plus T1 T2).
times_emp_1 : empty T1 -> empty (times T1 T2).
times_emp_2 : empty T2 -> empty (times T1 T2).
```

Theorem 8 (Adequacy of Encoding). *There is a bijection between the circular derivations of t* empty *and the canonical forms of the type* empty⌜t⌝.

Proof. By induction on the syntax of the circular derivation in both directions.

As an example, we may show that the type t, where $t = \mathbf{1} \otimes t$, is empty by the following circular derivation.

$$\frac{(\mathsf{t\_empty})\ t\,\mathsf{empty}}{(\mathsf{t\_empty})\ \mathbf{1} \otimes t\,\mathsf{empty}}\ \otimes\mathsf{EMP}_2$$

This derivation can be encoded as follows.

```
t : postp = times one t.
t_empty : empty t = times_emp_2 t_empty.
```

The reader is advised to take a look at Appendix I.3 of the extended version for two simple yet elegant examples of subtyping derivations.

5   Related Work

Cyclic λ-Calculus and Circular Terms. Ariola and Blom [2], and Ariola and Klop [3] studied the confluence property of reduction of cyclic λ-calculus. Their calculus differs from CoLF in several aspects. Their calculus is designed to capture reasoning principles of recursive functions and thus has a general recursive let structure that can be attached to terms at any levels. Terms are equated up to infinite Lévy-Longo trees (with decidable equality), but equality as Böhm trees is not decidable. CoLF is designed for circular terms and circular derivations, and all recursive definitions occur at the top level. Terms are equated up to infinite Böhm trees and the equality is decidable. Our equality algorithm is adapted from Huet'algorithm for the regular Böhm trees [21]. Equality on first-order terms has been studied both in its own respect [16] and in the context of subtyping for recursive types [1,6,14,23]. Our algorithm when applied to first-order terms is "the same". Courcelle [13] and Djelloul et al. [15] have studied the properties of first-order circular terms. Simon [28] designed a coinductive logic programming language based on the first-order circular terms. Contrary to CoLF, there are no mutual dependencies between inductive and coinductive predicates in Simon's language.

Logical Frameworks. Harper et al. [18] designed the logical framework LF, which this work extends upon. Pfenning et al. later adds notational definitions [26]. The method of hereditary substitution was developed as part of the research on linear and concurrent logical frameworks [9,29,10]. Harper and Licata demonstrated the method in formalizing the metatheory of simply typed λ-calculus [19]. In his master's thesis, Chen has investigated a mixed inductive and coinductive logical framework with an infinite stack of priorities but only in the context of a first-order type theory [12].

Mixed Induction and Coinduction and Circular Proof Systems. The equality and subtyping systems of recursive types [1,6,14,23,22] have traditionally recognized coinduction and more recently mixed induction and coinduction as an underlying framework. Fortier and Santocanale [17] devised a circular proof system for propositional linear sequent calculus with mixed inductive and coinductive predicates. This system together with Charatonik et al.'s Horn μ-calculus [11] motivated the validity condition of CoLF. Brotherston and Simpson devised an infinitary and a circular proof system as methods of carrying out induction [7,8]. Due to the complexity of their validity condition, the encoding of Brotherston and Simpson's system in full generality and Fortier and Santocanale's system is currently not immediate and is considered in ongoing work.

6   Conclusion

We have presented the type theory of a novel logical framework with higher-order rational terms, that admit coinductive and mixed inductive and coinductive interpretations. We have proposed the prepattern variables and prepattern Π-types to give a type-theoretic formulation of regular Böhm trees. Circular objects and derivations are represented as higher-order rational terms, as demonstrated in the case study of the subtyping deductive systems for recursive types.

We once again highlight the methodology of logical frameworks and what CoLF accomplishes. Logical frameworks internalize equalities that are present in the term model for an object logic. LF [18] internalizes $\alpha\beta\eta$-equivalence of the dependently typed λ-calculus. Within LF, one is not able to write a specification that distinguishes two terms that are α or β-equivalent, because those two corresponding derivations are identical in the object logic. Similarly, the concurrent logical framework CLF [29] internalizes equalities of concurrent processes that only differ in the order of independent events. The logical framework CoLF internalizes the equality of circular derivations. Using CoLF, one cannot write a specification that distinguishes between two different finitary representations of the same circular proof. It is this property that makes CoLF a more suitable framework for encoding circular derivations than existing finitary frameworks.

Acknowledgments. We would like to thank Robert Harper and Brigitte Pientka for insightful discussion on the research presented here and the anonymous reviewers for their helpful comments and suggestions.

References

1. Amadio, R.M., Cardelli, L.: Subtyping recursive types. ACM Transactions on Programming Languages and Systems **15**(4), 575–631 (1993)
2. Ariola, Z.M., Blom, S.: Cyclic lambda calculi. In: Abadi, M., Ito, T. (eds.) Theoretical Aspects of Computer Software, Third International Symposium, TACS '97, Sendai, Japan, September 23-26, 1997, Proceedings. Lecture Notes in Computer Science, vol. 1281, pp. 77–106. Springer, Sendai, Japan (1997). https://doi.org/10.1007/BFb0014548
3. Ariola, Z.M., Klop, J.W.: Lambda calculus with explicit recursion. Information and Computation **139**(2), 154–233 (1997). https://doi.org/10.1006/inco.1997.2651
4. Barendregt, H.P.: The lambda calculus - its syntax and semantics, Studies in logic and the foundations of mathematics, vol. 103. North-Holland (1985)
5. Basold, H.: Mixed Inductive-Coinductive Reasoning Types, Programs and Logic. Ph.D. thesis, Radboud University (Apr 2018), https://hdl.handle.net/2066/190323
6. Brandt, M., Henglein, F.: Coinductive axiomatization of recursive type equality and subtyping. Fundamenta Informaticae **33**(4), 309–338 (1998)
7. Brotherston, J.: Cyclic proofs for first-order logic with inductive definitions. In: Beckert, B. (ed.) International Conference on Automated Reasoning with Analytic Tableaux and Related Methods (TABLEAUX 2005). pp. 78–92. Springer LNCS 3702, Koblenz, Germany (Sep 2005)
8. Brotherston, J., Simpson, A.: Sequent calculi for induction and infinite descent. Journal of Logic and Computation **21**(6), 1177–1216 (2011)
9. Cervesato, I., Pfenning, F.: A linear logical framework. In: Clarke, E. (ed.) Proceedings of the Eleventh Annual Symposium on Logic in Computer Science. pp. 264–275. IEEE Computer Society Press, New Brunswick, New Jersey (Jul 1996)
10. Cervesato, I., Pfenning, F., Walker, D., Watkins, K.: A concurrent logical framework II: Examples and applications. Tech. Rep. CMU-CS-02-102, Department of Computer Science, Carnegie Mellon University (2002), revised May 2003
11. Charatonik, W., McAllester, D.A., Niwinski, D., Podelski, A., Walukiewicz, I.: The Horn mu-calculus. In: Proceedings of the Thirteenth Annual IEEE Symposium on Logic in Computer Science (LICS 1998). pp. 58–69. IEEE Computer Society Press (June 1998)
12. Chen, Z.: Towards a mixed inductive and coinductive logical framework. Tech. Rep. CMU-CS-21-144, Department of Computer Science, Carnegie Mellon University (2021)
13. Courcelle, B.: Fundamental properties of infinite trees. Theoretical Computer Science **25**, 95–169 (1983)
14. Danielsson, N.A., Altenkirch, T.: Subtyping, declaratively. In: 10th International Conference on Mathematics of Program Construction (MPC 2010). pp. 100–118. Springer LNCS 6120, Québec City, Canada (Jun 2010)
15. Djelloul, K., Dao, T., Frühwirth, T.W.: Theory of finite or infinite trees revisited. Theory and Practice of Logic Programming **8**(4), 431–489 (2008)
16. Endrullis, J., Grabmayer, C., Klop, J.W., van Oostrom, V.: On equal μ-terms. Theoretical Computer Science **412**(28), 3175–3202 (2011). https://doi.org/10.1016/j.tcs.2011.04.011
17. Fortier, J., Santocanale, L.: Cuts for circular proofs: Semantics and cut-elimination. In: Rocca, S.R.D. (ed.) 22nd Annual Conference on Computer Science Logic (CSL 2013). pp. 248–262. LIPIcs 23, Torino, Italy (Sep 2013)

18. Harper, R., Honsell, F., Plotkin, G.: A framework for defining logics. Journal of the Association for Computing Machinery **40**(1), 143–184 (Jan 1993)
19. Harper, R., Licata, D.R.: Mechanizing metatheory in a logical framework. Journal of Functional Programming **17**(4-5), 613–673 (2007)
20. Harper, R., Pfenning, F.: On equivalence and canonical forms in the LF type theory. Transactions on Computational Logic **6**, 61–101 (Jan 2005)
21. Huet, G.P.: Regular Böhm trees. Mathematical Structures in Computer Science **8**(6), 671–680 (1998), `http://journals.cambridge.org/action/displayAbstract?aid=44783`
22. Lakhani, Z., Das, A., DeYoung, H., Mordido, A., Pfenning, F.: Polarized subtyping. In: Sergey, I. (ed.) Programming Languages and Systems - 31st European Symposium on Programming, ESOP 2022, Munich, Germany, April 2-7, 2022, Proceedings. Lecture Notes in Computer Science, vol. 13240, pp. 431–461. Springer (2022). `https://doi.org/10.1007/978-3-030-99336-8_16`
23. Ligatti, J., Blackburn, J., Nachtigal, M.: On subtyping-relation completeness, with an application to iso-recursive types. ACM Transactions on Programming Languages and Systems **39**(4), 4:1–4:36 (Mar 2017)
24. Miller, D.: A logic programming language with lambda-abstraction, function variables, and simple unification. Journal of Logic and Computation **1**(4), 497–536 (1991). `https://doi.org/10.1093/logcom/1.4.497`
25. Miller, D., Tiu, A.: A proof theory for generic judgments. ACM Transactions on Computational Logic **6**(4), 749–783 (2005). `https://doi.org/10.1145/1094622.1094628`
26. Pfenning, F., Schürmann, C.: Algorithms for equality and unification in the presence of notational definitions. In: Galmiche, D. (ed.) Proceedings of the CADE Workshop on Proof Search in Type-Theoretic Languages. Electronic Notes in Theoretical Computer Science (Jul 1998)
27. Pfenning, F., Schürmann, C.: Twelf User's Guide, 1.2 edn. (Sep 1998), available as Technical Report CMU-CS-98-173, Carnegie Mellon University
28. Simon, L.E.: Extending logic programming with coinduction. Ph.D. thesis, University of Texas at Dallas (2006)
29. Watkins, K., Cervesato, I., Pfenning, F., Walker, D.: A concurrent logical framework I: Judgments and properties. Tech. Rep. CMU-CS-02-101, Department of Computer Science, Carnegie Mellon University (2002), revised May 2003

A Higher-Order Language for Markov Kernels and Linear Operators

Pedro H. Azevedo de Amorim$^{(\boxtimes)}$

Cornell University, Ithaca, NY, USA
pamorim@cs.cornell.edu

Abstract. Much work has been done to give semantics to probabilistic programming languages. In recent years, most of the semantics used to reason about probabilistic programs fall in two categories: semantics based on Markov kernels and semantics based on linear operators.
Both styles of semantics have found numerous applications in reasoning about probabilistic programs, but they each have their strengths and weaknesses. Though it is believed that there is a connection between them there are no languages that can handle both styles of programming. In this work we address these questions by defining a two-level calculus and its categorical semantics which makes it possible to program with both kinds of semantics. From the logical side of things we see this language as an alternative resource interpretation of linear logic, where the resource being kept track of is sampling instead of variable use.

Keywords: Linear Logic, Probabilistic Programming, Categorical Semantics.

1 Introduction

Probabilistic primitives have been a standard feature of programming languages since the 70s. At first, randomness was mostly used to program so called random algorithms, i.e. algorithms that require access to a source of randomness. Recently, however, with the rise of computational statistics and machine learning, randomness is also used to program statistical models and inference algorithms.

Programming languages researchers have seen this rise in interest as an opportunity to further study the interaction of probability and programming languages, establishing it as an active subfield within the PL community.

One of the main goals of this subfield is giving semantics to programming languages that are both expressive in the regular PL sense as well as in its abilities to program with randomness. One particular difficulty is that the mathematical machinery used for probability theory, i.e. measure theory, does not interact well with higher-order functions [2].

Currently, there are two classes of models of probabilistic programming — in its broad sense — that have found numerous applications: models based on linear logic and models based on Markov kernels. Since each kind of semantics has peculiarities that make them more or less adequate to give semantics to expressive programming languages, it is an important theoretical question to understand how these classes of models are related.

© The Author(s) 2023
O. Kupferman and P. Sobocinski (Eds.): FoSSaCS 2023, LNCS 13992, pp. 89–112, 2023.
https://doi.org/10.1007/978-3-031-30829-1_5

Linear Logic for Probabilistic Semantics The models of linear logic that have been used to give semantics to probabilistic languages are usually based on categories of vector spaces where programs are denoted by linear operators. We highlight two of them:

- Ehrhard et. al [11,10,9] have defined models of linear logic with probabilistic primitives and have used the translation of intuitionistic logic into linear logic $A \to B = !A \multimap B$, where $!A$ is the exponential modality, to give semantics to a stochastic λ-calculus.
- Dahlqvist and Kozen [8] have defined an imperative, higher-order, linear probabilistic language and added a type constructor ! to accommodate non-linear programs.

The main advantage of models based on linear logic is that programs are denoted by linear operators between spaces of distributions, a formalism that has been extensively used to reason about stochastic processes, as illustrated by Dahlqvist and Kozen who have used results from ergodic theory to reason about a Gibbs sampling algorithm written in their language, and by Clerc et al. who have shown how Bayesian inference can be given semantics using adjoint of linear operators [7].

Unfortunately, these insights are hard to realize in practice, since languages based on linear logic enforce that variables must be used exactly once, making it hard to use it as a programming language. The usual way linear logic deals with this limitation is through the ! modality which allows variables to be reused.

The problem with the exponential modality, when it comes to probabilistic programming, is that they are usually difficult to construct, do not have any clear interpretation in terms of probability, making the linear operator formalism not applicable anymore and, more operationally, through its connections with call-by-name (CBN) semantics [18], makes it mathematically hard to reuse sampled values.

Ehrhard et al. have found a way around this problem by introducing a call-by-value (CBV) let operator that allows samples to be reused [11,24]. In the discrete case this operator is elegantly defined by a categorical argument which is unknown to scale to the continuous case, which they deal with by making use of an ad-hoc construction that is unclear if it can be generalized to other models of linear logic. Therefore, our current understanding of models of linear logic does not provide a uniform way of reusing samples.

The difference between CBV and CBN can be illustrated by the program let $x = $ coin in $x + x$, where coin is a primitive that outputs 0 or 1 with equal probability. In the CBN semantics each use of x corresponds to a new sample from coin, whereas in the CBV semantics the coin is only sampled once.

A subtler problem of probabilistic models based on linear logic is that they are ill-equipped to program with joint distributions. For instance, the language proposed by Ehrhard et. al can be easily extended with product types which, under their semantics, would make the type $\mathbb{R} \times \mathbb{R}$ be interpreted as $\mathcal{M}\mathbb{R} \times \mathcal{M}\mathbb{R}$, where $\mathcal{M}\mathbb{R}$ is the set of distributions over $\mathbb{R}$ – which is isomorphic to the set of independent distributions over $\mathbb{R}^2$. Dahlqvist and Kozen deal with this issue by adding primitive types $\mathbb{R}^n$ to their language which are interpreted as the set of joint distributions over $\mathbb{R}^n$. However, since they are not defined using the type constructors provided by the semantic domain, programs of type $\mathbb{R}^n$ can only be manipulated by primitives defined outside the language.

Markov Kernel Semantics Markov kernels are a generalization of transition matrices, i.e. functions that map states to probability distributions over them. They are appealing from a programming languages perspective because their programming model is usually captured by monads and Kleisli arrows, a common abstraction in programming languages semantics, and have been extensively used to reason about probabilistic programs [1,22,3]. By being related to monadic programming they differ from their linear operator counterpart by being able to naturally capture a call-by-value semantics which, as we argued above, is the most natural one for probabilistic programming.

Unfortunately, even though these semantics can be generalized to continuous distributions, they are notoriously brittle when it comes to higher-order programming. Only recently, with the introduction of quasi Borel spaces [15] and its probability monad, it is possible to give a kernel-centric semantics to higher-order probabilistic programming with continuous distributions.

However, due to quasi Borel spaces being a different foundation to probability theory, it is unclear which theorems and theories can be generalized to higher-order. For instance, martingale theory has been used in Computer Science to reason about termination of probabilistic programs [6,20,16]. In order to generalize these ideas to higher-order functions it would be necessary to define a quasi Borel version of martingales and prove appropriate versions of the main theorems from martingale theory, a non-trivial task.

Our Work: Combining both Kinds of Semantics Though both styles of semantics provide insights into how to interpret probabilistic programming languages (PPL), it is still too early to claim that we have a "correct" semantics which subsumes all of the existing ones. Both approaches mentioned above have their advantages and drawbacks.

In this work we shed some light into how both semantics relate to one another by showing that it is possible to use both styles of semantics to interpret a linear calculus that has higher-order functions, looser linearity restrictions, a uniform way of dealing with sample reuse and better syntax for programming joint distributions while still being close to their kernel and linear operator counterparts. Interestingly, we identify the joint distribution problem described above to be a consequence of linear logic requiring the non-linear product to be cartesian. In order to tackle this problem we build on categorical semantics of linear logic and on recent work on Markov categories, a suitable categorical generalization of Markov kernels defined using semicartesian products.

We bridge the gap between these semantics by noting that the regular resource interpretation of linear logic, i.e. $A \multimap B$ being equivalent to "by using one copy of A I get one copy of B" is too restrictive an interpretation for probabilistic programming. Instead, we should think of usage as being equivalent to sampling. Therefore the linear arrow $A \multimap B$ should be thought of as "by sampling from A once I get B", which is the computational interpretation of Markov kernels.

We realize this interpretation through a multilanguage approach: we have one language that programs Markov kernels, a second language that programs linear operators and add syntax that transports programs from the former language into the latter one. To justify the viability of our categorical framework we show how existing probabilistic semantics are models to our language and show how, under mild conditions, this semantics can be generalized to commutative effects.

Our contributions are:

- We define a multi-language syntax that can program both Markov kernels as well as linear operators.(§3)
- We define its categorical semantics and prove certain interesting equations satisfied by it. (§4)
- We show that our semantics is already present in existing models for discrete and continuous probabilistic programming. (§5)
- We show how our semantics can be generalized to commutative effects. (§6)

2   Mathematical Preliminaries

We are assuming that the reader is familiar with basic notions from category theory such as categories, functors and monads.

Probability Theory

Transition matrices are one of the simplest abstractions used to model stochastic processes. Given two countable sets A and B, the entry (a, b) of a transition matrix is the probability of ending up in state $b \in B$ whenever you start from the initial state $a \in A$ and every row adds up to 1.

Definition 1. *The category* **CountStoch** *has countable sets as objects and transition matrices as morphisms. The identity morphism is the identity matrix and composition is given by matrix multiplication.*

Though transition matrices are conceptually simple, they can only model discrete probabilistic processes and, in order to generalize them to continuous probability we must use measurable sets and Markov kernels.

Definition 2. *A measurable set is a pair* (A, Σ_A), *where A is a set and $\Sigma_A \subseteq \mathcal{P}(A)$ is a σ-algebra, i.e. it contains the empty set and it is closed under complements and countable unions.*

Definition 3. *A function* $f : (A, \Sigma_A) \to (B, \Sigma_B)$ *is called measurable if for every* $\mathcal{B} \in \Sigma_B$, $f^{-1}(\mathcal{B}) \in \Sigma_A$.

Definition 4. *Let* (A, Σ_A) *be a measurable space. A probability distribution* (A, Σ_A) *is a function* $\mu : \Sigma_A \to [0,1]$ *such that* $\mu(\emptyset) = 0$, $\mu(A) = 1$ *and* $\mu(\uplus_{i \in \mathbb{N}} A_i) = \sum_{i \in \mathbb{N}} \mu(A_i)$.

Given two measurable sets (A, Σ_A) and (B, Σ_B) it is possible to define a σ-algebra over $A \times B$ generated by the sets $X \times Y$ which we denote by $\Sigma_A \otimes \Sigma_B$, where $X \in \Sigma_A$ and $Y \in \Sigma_B$. Furthermore, every pair of distributions μ_A and μ_B over A and B respectively, can be lifted to a distribution $\mu_A \otimes \mu_B$ over $A \times B$ such that $(\mu_A \otimes \mu_B)(X \times Y) = \mu_A(X)\mu_B(Y)$, for $X \in \Sigma_A$ and $Y \in \Sigma_B$.

Definition 5. *Let* (A, Σ_A) *and* (B, Σ_B) *be two measurable spaces. A Markov kernel is a function* $f : A \times \Sigma_B \to [0,1]$ *such that*

- *For every* $a \in A$, $f(a, -)$ *is a probability distribution.*
- *For every* $\mathcal{B} \in \Sigma_B$, $f(-, \mathcal{B})$ *is a measurable function.*

Definition 6. *The category* **Kern** *has measurable sets as objects and Markov kernels as morphisms. The identity arrow is the function* $id_A(a, \mathcal{A}) = 1$ *if* $a \in \mathcal{A}$ *and* 0 *otherwise and Composition is given by* $(f \circ g)(a, \mathcal{C}) = \int f(-, \mathcal{C})d(g(a, -))$.

Markov Categories

The field of categorical probability was developed in order to get a more conceptual understanding of Markov kernels. One of its cornerstone definitions is that of a Markov category which are categories where objects are abstract sample spaces, morphisms are abstract Markov kernels and every object has "contraction" and "weakening" morphisms which correspond to duplicating and discarding a sample, respectively, without adding any new randomness.

Definition 7 (Markov category [12]). *A Markov category is a semicartesian symmetric monoidal category* $(\mathbf{C}, \otimes, 1)$ *in which every object A comes equipped with a commutative comonoid structure, denoted by* $\mathsf{copy}_X : X \to X \otimes X$ *and* $\mathsf{delete}_X : X \to 1$, *where* copy *satisfies*

$$\mathsf{copy}_{X \otimes Y} = (id_X \otimes b_{Y,X} \otimes id_Y) \circ (\mathsf{copy}_X \otimes \mathsf{copy}_Y),$$

where $b_{Y,X}$ is the natural isomorphism $Y \otimes X \cong X \otimes Y$. The category being semicartesian means that the monoidal product comes equipped with projection morphisms $\pi_1 : A \otimes B \to A$ and $\pi_2 : A \otimes B \to B$, but it is not Cartesian because the equation $(\pi_1 \circ f, \pi_2 \circ f) = f$ does not hold in general which, intuitively, corresponds to the fact that joint distributions might be correlated.

Theorem 1 ([12]). **CountStoch** *is a Markov category.*

The monoidal product is given by the Cartesian product and the monoidal unit is the singleton set. The copy_X morphism is the matrix $X \times X \times X \to [0,1]$ which is 1 in the positions (x, x, x) and 0 elsewhere, and the delete_X morphism is the constant 1 matrix indexed by X.

Theorem 2 ([12]). Kern *is a Markov category.*

  This category is the continuous generalization of **CountStoch** and the monoidal product is the Cartesian product with the *product* σ-algebra and the monoidal unit is the singleton set $\{*\}$. The copy_X morphism is the Markov kernel $\text{copy}_X :$ $X \times \Sigma_X \otimes \Sigma_X \to [0,1]$ such that $\text{copy}_X(x, S \times T) = 1$ if $x \in S \cap T$ and 0 otherwise. Its delete morphism is simply the function that given any element in X, returns the function which is 1 on the measurable set $\{*\}$ and 0 on the empty measurable set.

Linear Logic and Monoidal Categories

We recall the categorical semantics of the multiplicative fragment of linear logic (MLL):

Definition 8 ([21]). *A category* **C** *is an MLL model if it is symmetric monoidal closed (SMCC), i.e. the functors* $A \otimes -$ *have a right adjoint* $A \multimap -$.

  We denote the monoidal product as $\otimes$ and the space of linear maps between objects X and Y as $X \multimap Y$, $\text{ev} : ((X \multimap Y) \otimes X) \to Y$ is the counit of the monoidal closed adjunction and $\text{cur} : \mathbf{C}(X \otimes Y, Z) \to \mathbf{C}(X, Y \multimap Z)$ is the linear curryfication map. We use the triple $(\mathcal{C}, \otimes, \multimap)$ to denote such models.

Definition 9. *Let* $(\mathbf{C}, \otimes_\mathbf{C}, 1_\mathbf{C})$ *and* $(\mathbf{D}, \otimes_\mathbf{D}, 1_\mathbf{D})$ *be two monoidal categories. We say that a functor* $F : \mathbf{C} \to \mathbf{D}$ *is* lax monoidal *if there is a morphism* $\epsilon : 1_\mathbf{D} \to F(1_\mathbf{C})$ *and a natural transformation* $\mu_{X,Y} : F(X) \otimes_\mathbf{D} F(Y) \to F(X \otimes_\mathbf{C} Y)$ *making the diagrams in Figure 8 (in Appendix B) commute.*

  If ϵ and $\mu_{X,Y}$ are isomorphisms we say that F is *strong* monoidal.

  One key observation of this paper is that there are many lax monoidal functors between Markov categories and models of linear logic that can interpret probabilistic processes.

3   Syntax

In this section we will design a syntax that reflects the fact that linearity corresponds to sampling, not variable usage. We achieve this by making use of a multi-language semantics that enables the programmer to transport programs defined in a Markov kernel-centric language (MK) to a linear, higher-order, language (LL).

  Our thesis is that in the context of probabilistic programming, linear logic, through its connection with linear algebra, departs from its usual Computer Science applications of enforcing syntactic invariants and, instead, provides a natural mathematical formalism to express ideas from probability theory, as shown by Dahlqvist and Kozen [8].

  Therefore, since many probabilistic programming constructs, such as Bayesian inference and Markov kernels, can be naturally interpreted in linear logic terms,

$$\tau := 1 \mid \tau \times \tau$$

$$M, N := x \mid \mathsf{unit} \mid \mathsf{let}\ x = M\ \mathsf{in}\ N \mid (M, N) \mid \pi_1 M \mid \pi_2 N \mid f(M)$$

$$\Gamma := \cdot \mid x : \tau, \Gamma$$

Fig. 1: Syntax MK

we believe that our calculus allows the user to benefit from the insights linearity provides to PPL while unburdening them from worrying about syntactic restrictions by making it possible to also program using kernels.

We use standard notation from the literature: $\Gamma \vdash t : \tau$ means that the program t has type τ under context Γ, $t\{x/u\}$ means substitution of u for x in t and $t\{\vec{x}/\vec{u}\}$ is the simultaneous substitution of the term list $\vec{u}$ for a variable list $\vec{x}$ in t.

Both languages will be defined in this section and, for presentation's sake, we are going to use orange to represent MK programs and purple to represent LL programs.

3.1   A Markov Kernel Language

We need a language to program Markov kernels. Since we are aiming at generality, we are assuming the least amount of structure possible. As such we will be working with the internal language of Markov categories, as presented in Figure 1 and Figure 4[1]. Note that we are implicitly assuming a set of primitives for the functions f.

By construction, every Markov category can interpret this language, as we show in Figure 6, with types being interpreted as

$$[\![1]\!] = 1$$
$$[\![\tau_1 \times \tau_2]\!] = [\![\tau_1]\!] \times [\![\tau_2]\!]$$

and the contexts are interpreted using $\times$ over the interpretation of the types. However, as it stands, it is not very expressive, since it does not have any probabilistic primitives nor does it have any interesting types since $1 \times 1 \cong 1$.

When working with concrete models (c.f. Section 5) we can extend the language with more expressive types as well as with concrete probabilistic primitives. For instance, in the context of continuous probabilities we could add a $\mathbb{R}$ datatype and a $\cdot \vdash \mathsf{uniform} : \mathbb{R}$ uniform distribution primitive.

Note that even though this language does not have any explicit sampling operators, this is implicitly achieved by the let operator. For instance, the program

---

[1] c.f. Appendix A.

$$\tau := 1 \mid \tau \multimap \tau \mid \tau \otimes \tau$$

$$t, u := x \mid \mathsf{unit} \mid \lambda x. \, t \mid t \, u \mid t \otimes u \mid \mathsf{let} \, x \otimes y = t \, \mathsf{in} \, u$$

$$\Gamma := \cdot \mid x : \tau, \Gamma$$

Fig. 2: Syntax LL

let x = uniform in $x + x$ samples from a uniform distribution, binds the result to the variable x and adds the sample to itself (Fig. 2).

3.2   A Linear Language

Our second language is a linear simply-typed λ-calculus, with the usual typing rules shown in Figure 5 in Appendix A, which can be interpreted in every symmetric monoidal closed category as shown in Figure 7, also in Appendix A, with types interpreted by

$$[\![1]\!] = 1$$
$$[\![\tau_1 \otimes \tau_2]\!] = [\![\tau_1]\!] \otimes [\![\tau_2]\!]$$
$$[\![\tau_1 \multimap \tau_2]\!] = [\![\tau_1]\!] \multimap [\![\tau_2]\!]$$

and the contexts are interpreted using $\otimes$ over the interpretation of the types. Once again, we are aiming at generality instead of expressivity. In a concrete setting it would be fairly easy to extend the calculus with a datatype $\mathbb{N}$ for natural numbers and probabilistic primitives such as $\cdot \vdash \mathsf{coin} : \mathbb{N}$ that flips a fair coin.

The idea behind the particular linear logic models that we are interested in is that, by integration, Markov kernels can be seen as linear operators between vector spaces of probability distributions. As such, an LL program $x : \mathbb{N} \vdash_{LL} t : \mathbb{N}$ will be denoted by a linear function between distributions over the natural numbers. Therefore, from a programming point of view, variables are placeholders for probability distributions, i.e. computations, not values, and sampling occurs when variables are used.

3.3   Combining Languages

The main drawback of the linear calculus above is that the syntactic linearity restriction makes it hard to program with it, while the main drawback of the Markov language is that it does not have higher-order functions. In this section we will show how we can combine both language so that we get a calculus with looser linearity restrictions while still being higher-order.

$$\tau := 1 \mid \tau \times \tau$$
$$\underline{\tau} := 1 \mid \mathcal{M}\tau \mid \underline{\tau} \multimap \underline{\tau} \mid \underline{\tau} \otimes \underline{\tau}$$

$$M, N := x \mid \mathsf{unit} \mid \mathsf{let}\ x = M\ \mathsf{in}\ N \mid f(M)$$
$$\mid (M, N) \mid \pi_1 M \mid \pi_2 M$$
$$t, u := x \mid \mathit{unit} \mid \lambda x.\, t \mid t\, u \mid t \otimes u \mid \mathsf{let}\ x \otimes y = t\ \mathsf{in}\ u$$
$$\mid \mathsf{sample}\ t_i\ \mathsf{as}\ x_i\ \mathsf{in}\ M$$

Fig. 3: Syntax LL+MK

As we will show in Section 5, when looking at concrete models for these languages we can see that the semantic interpretations of variables in both languages are completely different: in the MK language variables should be thought of as values, i.e. the values that were sampled from a distribution, whereas in the LL language, variables of ground type are distributions. In order to bridge these languages we must use the observation that Markov kernels — i.e. open MK terms — have a natural resource-aware interpretation of being "sample-once" stochastic processes and, by integration, can be seen as linear maps between measure spaces — i.e. open LL terms. The combined syntax for the language is depicted in Figure 3.

We now have a language design problem: we want to capture the fact that every open MK program is, semantically, also an open LL term. The naive typing rule is:

$$\frac{x_1 : \tau_1, \cdots, x_n : \tau_n \vdash_{MK} M : \tau}{x_1 : \mathcal{M}\tau_1, \cdots, x_n : \mathcal{M}\tau_n \vdash_{LL} \mathsf{MK}(M) : \mathcal{M}\tau}$$

The problem with this rule is that it breaks substitution: the variables in the premise are MK variables whereas the ones in the conclusion are LL variables.

We solve this problem by making the syntax reflect a common idiom of PPLs: compute distributions (elements of $\mathcal{M}\tau$), sample from it and then use the result in a non-linear continuation. This is captured by the following syntax:

$$\mathsf{sample}\ t_1, \cdots, t_n\ \mathsf{as}\ x_1, \cdots, x_n\ \mathsf{in}\ M$$

Note that we are sampling from LL programs t_i (possibly an empty list), outputting the results to MK variables x_i and binding them to an MK program M. When clear from the context we simply use sample t_i as x_i in M. Its corresponding typing rule is:

SAMPLE
$$\frac{x_1 : \tau_1 \cdots x_n : \tau_n \vdash_{MK} M : \tau \quad \Gamma_i \vdash_{LL} t_i : \mathcal{M}\tau_i \quad 0 \leq i < n}{\Gamma_1, \cdots, \Gamma_n \vdash_{LL} \mathsf{sample}\ t_i\ \mathsf{as}\ x_i\ \mathsf{in}\ M : \mathcal{M}\tau}$$

As the typing rule suggests, its semantics should be some sort of composition. However, since we are composing programs that are interpreted in different categories, we must have a way of translating MK programs into LL programs — as we will see in Section 4 this translation will be functorial. The operational interpretation of this rule is that we have a set of distributions $\{t_i\}$ defined using the linear language — possibly using higher-order programs — we sample from them, bind the samples to the variables $\{x_i\}$ in the MK program M where there are no linearity restrictions. Note that the rule above looks very similar to a monadic composition, though they are semantically different (cf. Section 4).

With this new syntax we can finally program in accordance with our new resource interpretation of linear logic, allowing us to write the program

$$\textsf{sample coin as } x \textsf{ in } (x = x),$$

which flips a coin once and tests the result for equality with itself, making it equivalent to true.

This combined calculus enjoys the expected syntactic properties[2].

Theorem 3. *Let* $\Gamma, x : \tau_1 \vdash_{LL} t : \tau$ *and* $\Delta \vdash_{LL} u : \tau_1$ *be well-typed terms, then* $\Gamma, \Delta \vdash_{LL} t\{x/u\} : \tau$

Proof. The proof can be found in Appendix D.

The following example illustrates how we can use the MK language to duplicate and discard linear variables.

Example 1. The program which samples from a distribution t and then returns a perfectly correlated pair is given by:

$$\cdot \vdash_{LL} \textsf{sample } t \textsf{ as } x \textsf{ in } (x, x) : \mathcal{M}(\tau \times \tau)$$

Similarly, the program that samples from a distribution t and does not use its sampled value is represented by the term

$$\cdot \vdash_{LL} \textsf{sample } t \textsf{ as } x \textsf{ in unit} : \mathcal{M}1$$

Example 2. Suppose that we have a Markov kernel given by an open MK term $x : \mathsf{N} \vdash M : \mathsf{N}$. If we want to encapsulate it as a linear program of type $\mathcal{M}\mathsf{N} \multimap \mathcal{M}\mathsf{N}$ we can write:

$$\cdot \vdash_{LL} \lambda \mathit{meas}.(\textsf{sample } \mathit{meas} \textsf{ as } x \textsf{ in } M) : \mathcal{M}\mathsf{N} \multimap \mathcal{M}\mathsf{N}$$

Example 3. As we explain in the introduction, Dahlqvist and Kozen must add many primitives to their language to work around their linearity restrictions. For instance, in order to write projection functions $\mathbb{R}^n \to \mathbb{R}^m$, $n > m$ they must add projection primitives to the language.

---

[2] To avoid visually polluting the proofs we will drop the color code in Theorem 3 and Theorem 7

By having compositional type constructors that can represent joint distributions , i.e. $\mathcal{M}(\tau \times \tau)$, it is possible to write the program sample t as x in $(\pi_1 \, x, \pi_3 \, x)$ which samples from a distribution over triples and returns only the first and third components by only using the syntax of products in MK.

Unfortunately there are some aspects of this language that still are restrictive. For instance, imagine that we want to write an LL program that receives two "Markov kernels" $\mathcal{M}\mathbb{N}\multimap\mathcal{M}\mathbb{N}$ and a distribution over $\mathbb{N}$ as inputs, samples from the input distribution, feeds the result to the Markov kernels, samples from them and adds the results. Its type would be

$$(\mathcal{M}\mathbb{N}\multimap\mathcal{M}\mathbb{N})\multimap(\mathcal{M}\mathbb{N}\multimap\mathcal{M}\mathbb{N})\multimap\mathcal{M}\mathbb{N}\multimap\mathcal{M}\mathbb{N}$$

Even though the program only requires you to sample once from each distribution, it is still not possible to write it in the linear language.

We will show in Section 4 how the type constructor $\mathcal{M}$ actually corresponds to an applicative functor [19], and the limitation above is actually a particular case of a fundamental difference between programming with applicative functors compared to programming with monads.

Remark 1. We now have two languages that can interpret probabilistic primitives such as coin. However, every primitive M in the MK language can be easily transported to an LL program by using an empty list of LL programs: sample _ as _ in M. Therefore it makes sense to only add these primitives to the MK language.

4   Categorical Semantics

As it is the case with categorical interpretations of languages/logics, types and contexts are interpreted as objects in a category and every well-typed program/proof gives rise to a morphism.

In our case, MK types τ are interpreted as objects $[\![\tau]\!]$ in a Markov category $(\mathbf{M}, \times)$ and well-typed programs $\Gamma \vdash_{MK} M : \tau$ are interpreted as an $\mathbf{M}$ morphism $[\![\Gamma]\!] \to [\![\tau]\!]$, as shown in Figure 6. Similarly, LL types $\underline{\tau}$ are interpreted as objects $[\![\underline{\tau}]\!]$ in a model of linear logic $(\mathbf{C}, \otimes, \multimap)$ and well-typed programs $\Gamma \vdash_{LL} t : \underline{\tau}$ are interpreted as a $\mathbf{C}$ morphism $[\![\Gamma]\!] \to [\![\underline{\tau}]\!]$, as shown in Figure 7.

To give semantics to the combined language is not as straightforward. The sample rule allows the programmer to run LL programs, bind the results to MK variables and use said variables in an MK continuation. The implication of this rule in our formalism is that our semantics should provide a way of translating MK programs into LL programs. In category theory this is usually achieved by a functor $\mathcal{M} : \mathbf{M} \to \mathbf{C}$.

However, we can easily see that functors are not enough to interpret the sample rule. Consider what happens when you apply $\mathcal{M}$ to an MK program $x : \tau_1, y : \tau_2 \vdash_{MK} N : \tau$:

$$\mathcal{M} [\![N]\!] : \mathcal{M}(\tau_1 \otimes \tau_2) \to \mathcal{M}\tau$$

To precompose it with two LL programs outputting $\mathcal{M}\tau_1$ and $\mathcal{M}\tau_2$ we need a mediating morphism $\mu_{\tau_1,\tau_2} : \mathcal{M}\tau_1 \otimes \mathcal{M}\tau_2 \to \mathcal{M}(\tau_1 \times \tau_2)$. Furthermore, if N has three or more free variables, there would be several ways of applying μ. Since from a programming standpoint it should not matter how the LL programs are associated, we require that μ_{τ_1,τ_2} makes the lax monoidality diagrams to commute. Therefore, assuming lax monoidality of μ we can interpret the sample rule:

SAMPLE
$$\frac{\tau_1 \times \cdots \times \tau_n \xrightarrow{N} \tau \qquad \Gamma_i \xrightarrow{t_i} \mathcal{M}\tau_i}{\Gamma \xrightarrow{t_1 \otimes \cdots \otimes t_n} \mathcal{M}\tau_1 \otimes \cdots \otimes \mathcal{M}\tau_n \xrightarrow{\mu} \mathcal{M}(\tau_1 \times \cdots \times \tau_n) \xrightarrow{\mathcal{M}N} \mathcal{M}\tau}$$

In case it only has one MK variable, the semantics is given by $[\![t]\!]; \mathcal{M}[\![N]\!]$ and in case it does not have any free variables the semantics is $\epsilon; \mathcal{M}[\![N]\!]$.

The equational theory of the LL languages is the well-known theory of the simply-typed λ-calculus and the MK equational theory has been described, in graphical notation, by Fritz [12]. Something which is not obvious is understanding how they interact at their boundary. This is where $\mathcal{M}$ being a functor becomes relevant, since from functoriality it follows the two program equivalences:

Theorem 4. *Let t, M and N be well-typed programs,*

$$[\![(\lambda y. \text{ sample } y \text{ as } z \text{ in } N) \text{ (sample } t \text{ as } x \text{ in } M)]\!] =$$
$$[\![\text{sample } t \text{ as } x \text{ in } (\text{let } y = M \text{ in } N)]\!]$$

Proof.

$$[\![(\lambda y. \text{ sample } y \text{ as } z \text{ in } N) \text{ (sample } t \text{ as } x \text{ in } M)]\!] =$$
$$[\![t]\!]; \mathcal{M}[\![M]\!]; \mathcal{M}[\![N]\!] = [\![t]\!]; \mathcal{M}([\![M]\!]; [\![N]\!]) =$$
$$[\![\text{sample } t \text{ as } x \text{ in } (\text{let } y = M \text{ in } N)]\!]$$

Theorem 5. *Let t be a well-typed program,*

$$[\![\text{sample } t \text{ as } x \text{ in } x]\!] = [\![t]\!]$$

Proof. $[\![\text{sample } t \text{ as } x \text{ in } x]\!] = [\![t]\!]; \mathcal{M}([\![x]\!]) = [\![t]\!]; \mathcal{M}(id) = [\![t]\!]; id = [\![t]\!]$

Furthermore, we also have a modularity property that can be easily proven:

Theorem 6. *Let t, M and N be well-typed programs. If $[\![M]\!] = [\![N]\!]$ then*

$$[\![\text{sample } t \text{ as } x \text{ in } M]\!] = [\![\text{sample } t \text{ as } x \text{ in } N]\!]$$

The expected compositionality of the semantics also holds:

Theorem 7. *Let $x_1 : \tau_1, \cdots, x_n : \tau_n \vdash t : \tau$ and $\Gamma_i \vdash t_i : \tau_i$ be well-typed terms.*
$$\left[\!\left[\Gamma_1, \cdots, \Gamma_n \vdash t\{\overrightarrow{x_i}/\overrightarrow{t_i}\} : \underline{\tau}\right]\!\right] = ([\![\Gamma_1 \vdash t_1 : \underline{\tau_1}]\!] \otimes \cdots \otimes [\![\Gamma_n \vdash t_n : \underline{\tau_n}]\!]); [\![\Gamma_1, \cdots, \Gamma_n]\!] \vdash t : \underline{\tau}.$$

Proof. The proof can be found in Appendix D.

SUBST

$$\frac{\Gamma \vdash u_1 : \tau' \qquad \Gamma \vdash u_2 : \tau' \qquad \Gamma, x : \tau' \vdash t : \tau \qquad \Gamma \vdash u_1 \equiv u_2 : \tau'}{\Gamma \vdash t\{x/u_1\} \equiv t\{x/u_2\} : \tau}$$

From this theorem we can conclude:

Corollary 1. *The Subst rule shown above is sound with respect to the categorical semantics.*

Lax monoidal functors, under the name *applicative functors*, are widely used in programming languages research[19]. They are often used to define embedded domain-specific languages (eDSL) within a host language. This suggests that from a design perspective the Markov kernel language can be thought of as an eDSL inside a linear language.

We have just shown that $\mathcal{M}$ being lax monoidal is sufficient to give semantics to our combined language, but what would happen if it had even more structure? If it were also full it would be possible to add a reification command[3]:

$$\frac{\mathcal{M}\Gamma \vdash_{LL} t : \mathcal{M}\tau}{\Gamma \vdash_{MK} \mathsf{reify}(t) : \tau}$$

where $\mathcal{M}\Gamma$ is notation for every variable in Γ being of the form $\mathcal{M}\tau'$, for some τ'. The semantics for the rule would be taking the inverse image of $\mathcal{M}$. As we will show in the next section, there are some concrete models where $\mathcal{M}$ is full and some other models where it is not. Computationally, fullness of $\mathcal{M}$ can be interpreted as every program of type $\mathcal{M}\tau \multimap \mathcal{M}\tau'$ being equal to a Markov kernel.

A property which is easier to satisfy is faithfulness, which is verified by both models in the next section. In this case the translation of the MK language into the LL language would be fully-abstract in the following sense:

Theorem 8. *Let* $x : \tau_1 \vdash M : \tau_2$ *and* $x : \tau_1 \vdash N : \tau_2$ *be two well-typed MK programs. If* $\mathcal{M}$ *is faithful then* $[\![\mathsf{sample}\ y\ \mathsf{as}\ x\ \mathsf{in}\ M]\!] = [\![\mathsf{sample}\ y\ \mathsf{as}\ x\ \mathsf{in}\ N]\!]$ *implies* $[\![M]\!] = [\![N]\!]$.

Proof. $[\![\mathsf{sample}\ y\ \mathsf{as}\ x\ \mathsf{in}\ M]\!] = [\![\mathsf{sample}\ y\ \mathsf{as}\ x\ \mathsf{in}\ N]\!] \implies id_{\mathcal{M}\tau_1} ; \mathcal{M}[\![M]\!] = id_{\mathcal{M}\tau_1} ; \mathcal{M}[\![N]\!] \implies [\![M]\!] = [\![N]\!]$.

5   Concrete Models

In this section we show how existing models for both discrete as well as continuous probabilities fit within our formalism.

---

[3] The proposed rule breaks the substitution theorem, but it is possible to define a variant for it where this is not the case.

5.1 Discrete Probability

For the sake of simplicity we will denote the monoidal product of **CountStoch** as $\times$.

The probabilistic coherence space model of linear logic has been extensively studied in the context of semantics of discrete probabilistic languages[9].

Definition 10 (Probabilistic Coherence Spaces [9]). *A probabilistic coherence space (PCS) is a pair $(|X|, \mathcal{P}(X))$ where $|X|$ is a countable set and $\mathcal{P}(X) \subseteq |X| \to \mathbb{R}^+$ is a set, called the* web, *such that:*

- *$\forall a \in X\ \exists \varepsilon_a > 0\ \varepsilon_a \cdot \delta_a \in \mathcal{P}(X)$, where $\delta_a(a') = 1$ iff $a = a'$ and 0 otherwise, and we use the notation $\varepsilon_a = \varepsilon(a)$;*
- *$\forall a \in X\ \exists \lambda_a\ \forall x \in \mathcal{P}(X)\ x_a \leq \lambda_a$;*
- *$\mathcal{P}(X)^{\perp\perp} = \mathcal{P}(X)$, where $\mathcal{P}(X)^{\perp} = \{x \in X \to \mathbb{R}^+ \mid \forall v \in \mathcal{P}(X)\ \sum_{a \in X} x_a v_a \leq 1\}$.*

We can define a category **PCoh** where objects are probabilistic coherence spaces and morphisms $X \multimap Y$ are matrices $f : |X| \times |Y| \to \mathbb{R}^+$ such that for every $v \in \mathcal{P}(X)$, $(f\,v) \in \mathcal{P}(Y)$, where $(f\,v)_b = \sum_{a \in |A|} f_{(a,b)} v_a$.

Definition 11. *Let $(|X|, \mathcal{P}(X))$ and $(|Y|, \mathcal{P}(Y))$ be PCS, we define $X \otimes Y = (|X| \times |Y|, \{x \otimes y \mid x \in \mathcal{P}(X), y \in \mathcal{P}(Y)\}^{\perp\perp})$, where $(x \otimes y)(a, b) = x(a)y(b)$*

Lemma 1. *Let X be a countable set, the pair $(X, \{\mu : X \to \mathbb{R}^+ \mid \sum_{x \in X} \mu(x) \leq 1\})$ is a PCS.*

Proof. The first two points are obvious, as the Dirac measure is a subprobability measure and every subprobability measure is bounded above by the constant function $\mu_1(x) = 1$.

To prove the last point we use the — easy to prove — fact that $\mathcal{P}X \subseteq \mathcal{P}X^{\perp\perp}$. Therefore we must only prove the other direction. First, observe that, if $\mu \in \{\mu : X \to \mathbb{R}^+ \mid \sum_{x \in X} \mu(x) \leq 1\}$, then we have $\sum \mu(x)\mu_1(x) = \sum 1\mu(x) = \sum \mu(x) \leq 1$, $\mu_1 \in \{\mu : X \to \mathbb{R}^+ \mid \sum_{x \in X} \mu(x) \leq 1\}^{\perp}$.

Let $\tilde{\mu} \in \{\mu : X \to \mathbb{R}^+ \mid \sum_{x \in X} \mu(x) \leq 1\}^{\perp\perp}$. By definition, $\sum \tilde{\mu}(x) = \sum \tilde{\mu}(x)\mu_1(x) \leq 1$ and, therefore, the third point holds.

This lemma can be used to give semantics to probabilistic primitives. For instance, a fair coin is interpreted as a function coin : $\mathbb{N} \to [0, 1]$ which is .5 at 0 and 1 and 0 elsewhere and is an element of $\mathcal{P}(\mathbb{N})$.

Lemma 2. *Let $X \to Y$ be a **CountStoch** morphism. It is also a **PCoh** morphism.*

Theorem 9. *There is a lax monoidal functor $\mathcal{M} : \textbf{CountStoch} \to \textbf{PCoh}$.*

Proof. The functor is defined using the lemmas above. Functoriality holds due to the functor being the identity on arrows. The lax monoidal structure is given by $\epsilon = id_1$ and $\mu_{X,Y} = id_{X \times Y}$

Lemma 3. *If $\mu \in \{x \otimes y \mid x \in \mathcal{M}(X), y \in \mathcal{M}(Y)\}^{\perp}$ then for every $x \in X$ and $y \in Y$, $\mu(x, y) \leq 1$.*

Proof. If there were such indices such that $\mu(x_1, y_1) > 1$ then $\sum \sum \mu(x, y)(\delta_{x_1} \otimes \delta_{y_1})(x, y) > \mu(x_1, y_1)(\delta_{x_1} \otimes \delta_{y_1})(x_1, y_1) = \mu(x_1, y_1) > 1$, which is a contradiction.

Lemma 4. *Let X and Y be two countable sets, then*

$$\mathcal{M}X \otimes \mathcal{M}Y = \left(X \times Y, \{\mu : X \times Y \to \mathbb{R}^+ \mid \sum_{x \in X} \sum_{y \in Y} \mu(x, y) \leq 1\} \right) = \mathcal{M}(X \times Y).$$

Proof. By the lemma above it follows that if we have a joint probability distribution $\tilde{\mu}$ over $X \times Y$ and an element $\mu \in \{x \otimes y \mid x \in \mathcal{M}(X), y \in \mathcal{M}(Y)\}^{\perp}$ then $\sum \sum \mu(x, y)\tilde{\mu}(x, y) \leq \sum \sum \tilde{\mu}(x, y) \leq 1$.

Theorem 10. *Both ϵ and $\mu_{X,Y}$ are isomorphisms.*

Proof. Since ϵ is the identity morphism, it is trivially an isomorphim. The morphisms $\mu_{X,Y}$ being an isomorphism is a direct consequence of the lemmas above.

Theorem 11. *The functor $\mathcal{M}$ is full.*

Both results above can be directly used to enhance the syntax of the combined language. From Theorem 10 we can conclude that elements of type $\mathcal{M}(\tau_1 \times \tau_2)$, by projecting their marginal distributions, can be manipulated as if they had type $\mathcal{M}\tau_1 \otimes \mathcal{M}\tau_2$. Something to note is that when we do this marginalization process we lose potential correlations between the elements of the pair.

5.2 Continuous Probability

In order to accommodate continuous distributions we can use regularly ordered Banach spaces, whose detailed definition goes beyond the scope of this paper.

Definition 12 ([8]). *The category $\mathbf{RoBan}$ has regularly ordered Banach spaces as objects and regular linear functions as morphisms.*

Theorem 12. *There is a lax monoidal functor $\mathcal{M} : \mathbf{Kern} \to \mathbf{RoBan}$.*

Proof. The functor acts on objects by sending a measurable space to the set of signed measures over it, which can be equipped with a $\mathbf{RoBan}$ structure. On morphisms it sends a Markov kernel f to the linear function $\mathcal{M}(f)(\mu) = \int f d\mu$.

The monoidal structure of $\mathbf{RoBan}$ satisfies the universal property of tensor products and, therefore, we can define the natural transformation $\mu_{X,Y} : \mathcal{M}(X) \otimes \mathcal{M}(Y) \to \mathcal{M}(X \times Y)$ as the function generated by the bilinear function $\mathcal{M}(X); \mathcal{M}(Y) \multimap \mathcal{M}(X \times Y)$ which maps a pair of distributions to its product measure. The map ϵ is, once again, equal to the identity function.

The commutativity of the lax monoidality diagrams follows from the universal property of the tensor product: it suffices to verify it for elements $\mu_A \otimes \mu_B \otimes \mu_C$.

In **RoBan** the uniform distribution over the interval $[0,1]$ is an element of $\mathcal{M}\mathbb{R}$, meaning that it can soundly interpret a $\cdot \vdash_{LL}$ uniform : $\mathcal{M}\mathbb{R}$ primitive.

Even though $\mathcal{M}$ looks very similar to the discrete case, it follows from a well-known theorem from functional analysis that the functor is *not* strong monoidal, meaning that there are joint probability distributions (elements of $\mathcal{M}(A \times B)$) that cannot be represented as an element of the tensor product $\mathcal{M}(A) \otimes \mathcal{M}(B)$ and, as such, programs of type $M(A \times B)$ must be manipulated in MK language, as shown in Example 3.

6   Beyond Probability

We have seen that this new resource interpretation is present in different models of linear logic models for probabilistic programming. In this section we show that this model can be generalized to commutative effects, i.e. effects where the program equation Commutativity below holds. Categorically, these effects are captured by monoidal monads[4]. Due to length issues, we will not fully detail the definition of monoidal monads, but we suggest the interested reader to read Seal [23].

COMMUTATIVITY

$$\frac{\Gamma \vdash t_1 : \tau_1 \qquad \Gamma \vdash t_2 : \tau_2 \qquad \Gamma, x : \tau_1, y : \tau_2 \vdash u : \tau}{\text{let } x_1 = t_1 \text{ in (let } x_2 = t_2 \text{ in } u) \equiv \text{let } x_2 = t_2 \text{ in (let } x_1 = t_1 \text{ in } u) : \tau}$$

Definition 13 ([23]). *Let* $(\mathbf{C}, \otimes, I)$ *be a monoidal category and* (T, η, μ) *a monad over it. The monad* T *is called monoidal if it comes equipped with a natural transformation* $\kappa_{X,Y} : TX \otimes TY \to T(X \otimes Y)$ *making certain diagrams commute*

For probability monads the transformation κ corresponds to forming the product probability distribution and, more generally, this can be thought of a program that runs both of its (effectful) inputs and pairs the outputs.

Every monad give rise to the interesting categories $\mathbf{C}_T$ and $\mathbf{C}^T$ which are, respectively, the Kleisli category and Eilenberg-Moore category. The objects of $\mathbf{C}_T$ are the same as $\mathbf{C}$ and morphisms between A and B are $\mathbf{C}$ morphisms $A \to TB$, with the identity morphism being equal to the unit η of the monad and composition is given by $f; g = f; Tg; \mu$.

The objects of the category $\mathbf{C}^T$ are pairs (X, x), where X is a $\mathbf{C}$ object and $x : TX \to X$ is a $\mathbf{C}$ morphism such that $\mu; x = Tx; x$ and $\eta; x = id_X$, and morphisms between objects (X, x) and (Y, y) are $\mathbf{C}$ morphisms $f : X \to Y$ such that $x; f = Tf; y$.

For every monad T there is a canonical inclusion functor $\iota : \mathbf{C}_T \to \mathbf{C}^T$ which maps X to (TX, μ) and $f : X \to Y$ to $Tf; \mu_Y$.

Theorem 13 ([5]). *The functor* ι *is full and faithful.*

---

[4] Monoidal monads are equivalent to commutative monads, which is the nomenclature usually used in the context of programming languages semantics.

As we explain in Appendix C, assuming enough structure on the category $\mathbf{C}$ we can show that the triple $(\mathbf{C}_T, \mathbf{C}^T, \iota)$ is a model to the MK+LL language and we can bring our new resource interpretation of linear logic to other commmutative effects.

An illustrative example is the powerset monad $\mathcal{P} : \mathbf{Set} \to \mathbf{Set}$ which is monoidal and since $\mathbf{Set}$ has the necessary structure, the triple $(\mathbf{C}_{\mathcal{P}}, \mathbf{C}^{\mathcal{P}}, \mathcal{P})$ is a model to our language and can be used to give semantics to non-deterministic computation.

In the context of commutative effects other than randomness, the syntax sample t as x in M does not make as much sense, in which case we can use the syntax observe t_i as x_i in M instead. Once again, operationally, the programs t_i are fully executed, the values are bound to x_i in M which is then executed.

Furthermore, other effects have other relevant effectful operations and, therefore, we can assume that there is a set of operations in the MK language that are interpreted in the Kleisli category and can be transported to LL using observe, similar to how it was done in the probabilistic case.

For the non-deterministic case we can assume the existence of typing rules for non-deterministic choice and failure:

$$
\begin{array}{cc}
\text{CHOICE} & \text{NULL} \\[4pt]
\dfrac{\Gamma \vdash_{MK} t_1 : \tau \qquad \Gamma \vdash_{MK} t_2 : \tau}{\Gamma \vdash_{MK} t_1 \oplus t_2 : \tau} & \dfrac{}{\Gamma \vdash_{MK} 0_\tau : \tau}
\end{array}
$$

satisfying the expected equations and interpreted using set-theoretic union and the empty set, respectively.

A similar connection between linear logic and monoidal monads has been made by Benton and Wadler[4], where they want to relate Moggi's monadic λ-calculus with linear logic by showing that if a monad is monoidal and the category has equalizers and coequalizers, then the Eillenberg-Moore category is a model of linear logic.

7   Related Work

Semantics of Probabilistic Programming Ehrhard et al. [11,10] have defined a model of linear logic $\mathbf{CLin}$ which can be used to interpret a higher-order probabilistic programming language. They have used the call-by-name translation of intuitionistic logic into linear logic $A \to B = !A \multimap B$ to give semantics to their language. The authors extend their language with a call-by-value let syntax which makes it possible to reuse sampled values. In order to give semantics to this new language they introduce a new category $\mathbf{CLin_m}$ which can interpret this new operator, at the cost of complicating their model.

Because there is an analogous proof of Theorem 12 with the category $\mathbf{CLin}$ replacing $\mathbf{RoBan}$, we can use their original, simpler, model to interpret our language, while not needing to use the linear logic exponential to interpret non-linear programs.

Dahlqvist and Kozen [8] have defined a category of partially ordered Banach spaces and shown that it is a model of intuitionistic linear logic. An important difference from their approach and the one mentioned above is that they embrace variable linearity as part of their syntax. As we argued in this paper, we believe that the syntactic restriction of linearity they have used is not adequate for the purposes of probabilistic programming. They deal with this limitation by adding primitives to their languages which, by using the results of Section 5, could be programmed using the MK language.

Quasi Borel spaces [15] are a conservative extension of **Meas** that are Cartesian closed and have a commutative probability monad. The drawback of this model is that it is still not as well understood as its measure-theoretic counterpart, and there are theorems from probability theory used to reason about programs that may not hold in the category of quasi Borel spaces **QBS**.

Recently, Geoffroy [13] has made progress in connecting linear logic and quasi Borel Spaces by showing that a certain subcategory of the Eillenberg-Moore category for the probability monad in **QBS** is a model of classical linear logic, which we see as an instance of our model where the MK language can have higher-order functions as well.

Call-by-Push-Value The idea of having two distinct type systems that are connected by a functorial layer is reminiscent of Call-by-Push-Value (CBPV) [17], which has a type system for values and a type system for computations that are connected by an adjunction. In recent work, Ehrhard and Tasson [24] use the Eilenberg-Moore adjunction of the linear logic exponential ! to give semantics to a calculus that can interpret lazy and eager probabilistic computation, allowing for the interpretation of an eager let operator which is operationally similar to our sample construct. However, the existence of the let operator depends on properties of the ! that are unknown to hold for continuous distributions, while our semantics can naturally deal with continuous distributions as we have shown in Section 5.

Furthermore, the exponential which lies at the center of their approach is, semantically, hard to work with and does not have any clear connections to probability theory, making it unlikely that their semantics can be seen as a bridge between the Markov and linear semantics, which is the case for the models presented in Section 5.

Goubault-Larrecq [14] has defined a CBPV domain semantics to a language that mixes probability and non-determinism, a long-standing challenge in the theory of programming languages. His focus is in understanding how to make probability interact with non-determinism in a sound way. He studies the full-abstraction of his semantics but does not deal with connections to linear logic.

Acknowledgements The support of the National Science Foundation under grant CCF-2008083 is gratefully acknowledged. I would also like to thank Arthur Azevedo de Amorim, Justin Hsu, Michael Roberts, Christopher Lam and Deepak Garg for their useful comments on earlier versions of this paper.

A Typing Rules and Denotational Semantics LL and MK

$$\frac{}{\Gamma, x : \tau \vdash x : \tau} \text{ Var}$$

$$\frac{}{\Gamma \vdash \text{unit} : 1} \text{ Unit}$$

Let
$$\frac{\Gamma \vdash M : \tau_1 \qquad \Gamma, x : \tau_1 \vdash N : \tau}{\Gamma \vdash \text{let } x = M \text{ in } N : \tau}$$

Primitive
$$\frac{\Gamma \vdash M : \tau_1 \qquad f : \tau_1 \to \tau_2}{\Gamma \vdash f(M) : \tau_2}$$

Pair
$$\frac{\Gamma \vdash M : \tau_1 \qquad \Gamma \vdash N : \tau_2}{\Gamma \vdash (M, N) : \tau_1 \times \tau_2}$$

Proj1
$$\frac{\Gamma \vdash M : \tau_1 \times \tau_2}{\Gamma \vdash \pi_1 M : \tau_1}$$

Proj2
$$\frac{\Gamma \vdash M : \tau_1 \times \tau_2}{\Gamma \vdash \pi_2 M : \tau_2}$$

Fig. 4: Typing rules MK

Axiom
$$\frac{}{x : \tau \vdash x : \tau}$$

Unit
$$\frac{}{\cdot \vdash \text{unit} : 1}$$

Abstraction
$$\frac{\Gamma, x : \tau_1 \vdash t : \tau_2}{\Gamma \vdash \lambda x.\, t : \tau_1 \multimap \tau_2}$$

Application
$$\frac{\Gamma_1 \vdash t : \tau_1 \multimap \tau_2 \qquad \Gamma_2 \vdash u : \tau_1}{\Gamma_1, \Gamma_2 \vdash t\, u : \tau_2}$$

Tensor
$$\frac{\Gamma_1 \vdash t : \tau_1 \qquad \Gamma_2 \vdash u : \tau_2}{\Gamma_1, \Gamma_2 \vdash t \otimes u : \tau_1 \otimes \tau_2}$$

LetTensor
$$\frac{\Gamma_1 \vdash t : \tau_1 \otimes \tau_2 \qquad \Gamma_2, x : \tau_1, y : \tau_2 \vdash u : \tau}{\Gamma_1, \Gamma_2 \vdash \text{let } x \otimes y = t \text{ in } u : \tau}$$

Fig. 5: Typing rules LL

Var
$$\frac{}{\Gamma \times \tau \xrightarrow{\text{delete} \times id_\tau} 1 \times \tau \cong \tau}$$

Pair
$$\frac{\Gamma \xrightarrow{M} \tau_1 \qquad \Gamma \xrightarrow{N} \tau_2}{\Gamma \xrightarrow{\text{copy}} \Gamma \times \Gamma \xrightarrow{M \times N} \tau_1 \times \tau_2}$$

Proj
$$\frac{\Gamma \xrightarrow{M} \tau_1 \times \tau_2}{\Gamma \xrightarrow{M;(id_{\tau_1} \times \text{delete})} \tau_1 \times 1 \cong \tau_1}$$

Let
$$\frac{\Gamma \xrightarrow{M} \tau_1 \qquad \Gamma \times \tau_1 \xrightarrow{N} \tau}{\Gamma \xrightarrow{\text{copy}} \Gamma \times \Gamma \xrightarrow{(id_\Gamma \times M);N} \tau}$$

Primitive
$$\frac{\Gamma \xrightarrow{M} \tau_1 \qquad \tau_1 \xrightarrow{f} \tau_2}{\Gamma \xrightarrow{M} \tau_1 \xrightarrow{f} \tau_2}$$

Fig. 6: Denotational semantics for MK

Axiom

$$\frac{}{\tau \xrightarrow{id_\tau} \tau}$$

Tensor

$$\frac{\Gamma_1 \xrightarrow{t_1} \underline{\tau_1} \quad \Gamma_2 \xrightarrow{t_2} \underline{\tau_2}}{\Gamma_1, \Gamma_2 \xrightarrow{t_1 \otimes t_2} \underline{\tau_1} \otimes \underline{\tau_2}}$$

LetTensor

$$\frac{\Gamma_1 \xrightarrow{t} \underline{\tau_1} \otimes \underline{\tau_2} \quad \Gamma_2 \otimes \underline{\tau_1} \otimes \underline{\tau_2} \xrightarrow{u} \underline{\tau}}{\Gamma_1 \otimes \Gamma_2 \xrightarrow{(id \otimes t);u} \underline{\tau}}$$

Abstraction

$$\frac{\Gamma \otimes \underline{\tau_1} \xrightarrow{t} \underline{\tau_2}}{\Gamma \xrightarrow{\mathrm{cur}(\llbracket t \rrbracket)} \underline{\tau_1} \multimap \underline{\tau_2}}$$

Application

$$\frac{\Gamma_1 \xrightarrow{t} \underline{\tau_1} \multimap \tau 2 \quad \Gamma_2 \xrightarrow{u} \underline{\tau_1}}{\Gamma_1 \otimes \Gamma_2 \xrightarrow{(t \otimes u);\mathrm{ev}} \underline{\tau_2}}$$

Fig. 7: Denotational semantics for LL

B   Commutative Diagrams

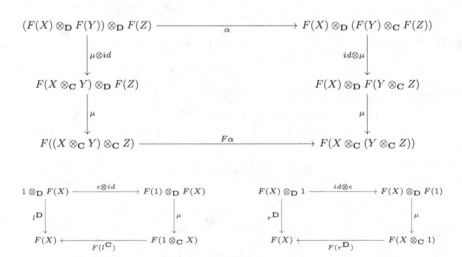

Fig. 8: Lax monoidal diagrams

C   Monoidal Monads and Their Algebras

An important theorem from the categorical probability literature is that Markov categories are an abstraction of programming in the Kleisli category of monoidal affine monads, where affinity means that $T1 \cong 1$.

Theorem 14 ([12]). *Let* $(\mathbf{C}, \times, 1)$ *be a cartesian category and* $T : \mathbf{C} \to \mathbf{C}$ *a monoidal (affine) monad. The Kleisli category* $\mathbf{C}_T$ *is a Markov category.*

The monoidal product of $\mathbf{C}_T$ is $\times$ with unit 1, the copy operation is given by $\Delta_X; \eta_X : X \to T(X \times X)$ and the deletion operation is given by $T1 \cong 1$ and 1 being terminal.

Furthermore, under certain conditions, the Eilenberg-Moore category $\mathbf{C}^T$ for monoidal monads is symmetric monoidal closed. The monoidal unit is given by TI, the monoidal product is given by the coequalizer depicted in Figure 9 and the closed struture is given by the equalizer depicted in Figure 10.

Theorem 15. *Let $\mathbf{C}$ be a symmetric monoidal closed category with equalizers, reflexive co-equalizers and $T : \mathbf{C} \to \mathbf{C}$ a monoidal monad. The category $\mathbf{C}^T$ is also symmetric monoidal closed.*

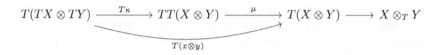

$$T(TX \otimes TY) \xrightarrow{\;T\kappa\;} TT(X \otimes Y) \xrightarrow{\;\mu\;} T(X \otimes Y) \longrightarrow X \otimes_T Y$$

$$T(x \otimes y)$$

Fig. 9: Symmetric Monoidal Structure in $\mathbf{C}^T$

$$X \multimap_T Y \longrightarrow X \multimap Y \xrightarrow{\;s\;} TX \multimap TY \xrightarrow{id_{TX} \multimap y} TX \multimap Y$$

$$x \multimap id_Y$$

Fig. 10: Closed Structure in $\mathbf{C}^T$

Even though, in general, in order to define the monoidal product one requires a coequalizer, for our purposes we are only interested in products of the form $TA \otimes_T TB$ which, luckily, are easier to characterize, since the equality $TX \otimes_T TY = T(X \otimes Y)$ holds [23].

In this case the lax monoidal transformations $\mu_{X,Y} : TX \otimes_T TY \to T(X \otimes Y)$ and $\epsilon : FI \to FI$ are simply the identity morphisms. Besides, by using the universal properties of coequalizers it is possible to show the equality $\tilde{\alpha}_{TX,TY,TZ} = \alpha_{X,Y,Z}$, where $\tilde{\alpha}$ is the associator for the monoidal product $\otimes_T$.

Theorem 16. *Let $\mathbf{C}$ be a symmetric monoidal category with reflexive co-equalizers and $T : \mathbf{C} \to \mathbf{C}$ a monoidal monad. The triple (ι, μ, ϵ) is a lax monoidal functor.*

Proof. The proof follows by unfolding the definitions.

D   Proofs

Theorem 3. Let $\Gamma, x : \underline{\tau_1} \vdash t : \underline{\tau}$ and $\Delta \vdash u : \underline{\tau_1}$ be well-typed terms, then $\Gamma, \Delta \vdash t\{x/u\} : \underline{\tau}$

Proof. The proof follows by structural induction on the typing derivation $\Gamma, x : \underline{\tau_1} \vdash t : \underline{\tau}$:

- Axiom: Since $t = x$ then $t\{x/u\} = u$ and $\underline{\tau_1} = \underline{\tau}$.
- Abstraction: By hypothesis, $\Gamma, x : \underline{\tau_1}, y : \underline{\tau_2} \vdash t : \tau_3$. Since we can assume wlog that $x \neq y$ and that $y \notin \Delta$, $\lambda y. \, t\{x/u\} = \lambda y. \, t\{x/u\}$. Therefore we can show that $\Gamma, \Delta \vdash \lambda y. \, t\{x/u\} : \tau_2 \multimap \tau_3$ by applying the rule Abstraction and by the induction hypothesis.
- Application: $t_1 \, t_2\{x/u\} = t_1\{x/u\} \, t_2\{x/u\}$. Since the language LL is linear, only one of t_1 or t_2 will have x as a free variable. By symmetry we can assume that t_1 has x as a free variable and we can prove $\Gamma, \Delta \vdash t_1\{x/u\} \, t_2 : \underline{\tau}$ by applying the rule Application and by the induction hypothesis.
- Sample: It is easy to prove that $(\text{sample } t \text{ as } y \text{ in } M)\{x/u\} = \text{sample } (t\{x/u\}) \text{ as } y \text{ in } M$

Theorem 7. Let $x_1 : \tau_1, \cdots, x_n : \tau_n \vdash t : \tau$ and $\Gamma_i \vdash t_i : \tau_i$ be well-typed terms. $\left[\!\left[\Gamma_1, \cdots, \Gamma_n \vdash t\{\overrightarrow{x_i}/\overrightarrow{t_i}\} : \underline{\tau} \right]\!\right] = (\left[\!\left[\Gamma_1 \vdash t_1 : \underline{\tau_1} \right]\!\right] \otimes \cdots \otimes \left[\!\left[\Gamma_n \vdash t_n : \underline{\tau_n} \right]\!\right]); \left[\!\left[\Gamma_1, \cdots, \Gamma_n \right]\!\right] \vdash t : \underline{\tau}$.

Proof. The proof follows by induction on the typing derivation of t.

- Axiom: Since $t = x$ then $t\{x/t_0\} = t_0$ and $[\![t\{x/t_0\}]\!] = [\![t_0]\!] = [\![t_0]\!]; id = [\![t_0]\!]; [\![x]\!]$.
- Unit: Since $t = x$ then $t\{x/t_0\} = t_0$ and $[\![t\{x/t_0\}]\!] = [\![t_0]\!] = [\![t_0]\!]; id = [\![t_0]\!]; [\![x]\!]$.
- Tensor: We know that $t = t_1 \otimes t_2$. Furthermore, from linearity we know that each free variable appears either in t_1 or in t_2. Without loss of generality we can assume that $(t_1 \otimes t_2)\{x_1, \cdots, x_n/u_1, \cdots, u_n\} = (t_1\{x_1, \cdots, x_k/u_1, \cdots, u_k\}) \otimes (t_2\{x_{k+1}, \cdots, x_n/u_{k+1}, \cdots, u_n\})$. We can conclude this case from the induction hypothesis and functoriality of $\otimes$.
- LetTensor: This case follows from the functoriality of $\otimes$ and the induction hypothesis.
- Abstraction: This case follows from unfolding the definitions, using the induction hypothesis and by naturality of cur.
- Application: Analogous to the Tensor case
- Sample: This case is analogous to the Tensor case.

References

1. de Amorim, A.A., Gaboardi, M., Hsu, J., Katsumata, S.y.: Probabilistic relational reasoning via metrics. In: Symposium on Logic in Computer Science (LICS) (2019)

2. Aumann, R.J.: Borel structures for function spaces. Illinois Journal of Mathematics (1961)
3. Barthe, G., Fournet, C., Grégoire, B., Strub, P.Y., Swamy, N., Zanella-Béguelin, S.: Probabilistic relational verification for cryptographic implementations. In: Principles of Programming Languages (POPL) (2014)
4. Benton, N., Wadler, P.: Linear logic, monads and the lambda calculus. In: Symposium on Logic in Computer Science (LICS) (1996)
5. Borceux, F.: Handbook of Categorical Algebra: Volume 2, Categories and Structures, vol. 2. Cambridge University Press (1994)
6. Chakarov, A., Sankaranarayanan, S.: Probabilistic program analysis with martingales. In: International Conference on Computer Aided Verification (CAV) (2013)
7. Clerc, F., Danos, V., Dahlqvist, F., Garnier, I.: Pointless learning. In: International Conference on Foundations of Software Science and Computation Structures (FoSSaCS) (2017)
8. Dahlqvist, F., Kozen, D.: Semantics of higher-order probabilistic programs with conditioning. In: Principles of Programming Languages (POPL) (2019)
9. Danos, V., Ehrhard, T.: Probabilistic coherence spaces as a model of higher-order probabilistic computation. Information and Computation **209**(6), 966–991 (2011)
10. Ehrhard, T.: On the linear structure of cones. In: Logic in Computer Science (LICS) (2020)
11. Ehrhard, T., Pagani, M., Tasson, C.: Measurable cones and stable, measurable functions: a model for probabilistic higher-order programming. In: Principles of Programming Languages (POPL) (2017)
12. Fritz, T.: A synthetic approach to markov kernels, conditional independence and theorems on sufficient statistics. Advances in Mathematics **370**, 107239 (2020)
13. Geoffroy, G.: Extensional denotational semantics of higher-order probabilistic programs, beyond the discrete case (unpublished) (2021)
14. Goubault-Larrecq, J.: A probabilistic and non-deterministic call-by-push-value language. In: Logic in Computer Science (LICS) (2019)
15. Heunen, C., Kammar, O., Staton, S., Yang, H.: A convenient category for higher-order probability theory. In: Logic in Computer Science (LICS) (2017)
16. Huang, M., Fu, H., Chatterjee, K., Goharshady, A.K.: Modular verification for almost-sure termination of probabilistic programs. Proceedings of the ACM on Programming Languages (OOPSLA) (2019)
17. Levy, P.B.: Call-by-push-value. Ph.D. thesis (2001)
18. Maraist, J., Odersky, M., Turner, D.N., Wadler, P.: Call-by-name, call-by-value, call-by-need and the linear lambda calculus. Theoretical Computer Science (1999)
19. McBride, C., Paterson, R.: Applicative programming with effects. Journal of functional programming **18**(1), 1–13 (2008)
20. McIver, A., Morgan, C., Kaminski, B.L., Katoen, J.P.: A new proof rule for almost-sure termination. Proceedings of the ACM on Programming Languages (POPL) (2017)
21. Mellies, P.A.: Categorical semantics of linear logic. Panoramas et syntheses **27**, 15–215 (2009)
22. Scibior, A., Kammar, O., Vakar, M., Staton, S., Yang, H., Cai, Y., Ostermann, K., Moss, S., Heunen, C., Ghahramani, Z.: Denotational validation of higher-order bayesian inference. Proceedings of the ACM on Programming Languages (2018)
23. Seal, G.J.: Tensors, monads and actions. arXiv preprint arXiv:1205.0101 (2012)
24. Tasson, C., Ehrhard, T.: Probabilistic call by push value. Logical Methods in Computer Science (2019)

A Formal Logic for Formal Category Theory

Max S. New[1,2] (✉) ⓘ and Daniel R. Licata[2]

[1] University of Michigan, Ann Arbor, USA
`maxsnew@umich.edu`
[2] Wesleyan University, Middletown, USA
`dlicata@wesleyan.edu`

Abstract. We present a domain-specific type theory for constructions and proofs in category theory. The type theory axiomatizes notions of category, functor, profunctor and a generalized form of natural transformations. The type theory imposes an ordered linear restriction on standard predicate logic, which guarantees that all functions between categories are functorial, all relations are profunctorial, and all transformations are natural by construction, with no separate proofs necessary. Important category-theoretic proofs such as the Yoneda lemma and Co-yoneda lemma become simple type-theoretic proofs about the relationship between unit, tensor and (ordered) function types, and can be seen to be ordered refinements of theorems in predicate logic. The type theory is sound and complete for a categorical model in *virtual equipments*, which model both internal and enriched category theory. While the proofs in our type theory look like standard set-based arguments, the syntactic discipline ensure that all proofs and constructions carry over to enriched and internal settings as well.

1 Introduction

Category theory is a branch of mathematics that studies higher-dimensional typed algebraic structures. Originally developed for applications to homological algebra, it was quickly discovered that categorical structures were common in logic and computer science. Formal systems like logics, type theories and programming languages typically have sound and complete models given by notions of structured categories [31,30,34]. This Curry-Howard-Lambek correspondence applies to simply typed lambda calculus [30], computational lambda calculus [34], linear logic [24] dependent type theory [14,45], and many other type theories designed based on category-theoretic semantics. The syntax of a type theory should present an initial object in its category of models, a category-theoretic reformulation of logical soundness and completeness.

While this research program has been quite successful, category-theoretic notions can be overwhelming for beginners. In a traditional set-theoretic formulation, notions such as adjoint functors and limits produce a proliferation of "naturality" and "functoriality" side-conditions that must be discharged. For example, when constructing an adjoint pair of functors between two categories, a naïve approach would define all of the data of the action on objects, action on arrows, prove the functoriality of such actions, as well as construct two families

© The Author(s) 2023
O. Kupferman and P. Sobocinski (Eds.): FoSSaCS 2023, LNCS 13992, pp. 113–134, 2023.
https://doi.org/10.1007/978-3-031-30829-1_6

of transformations, prove they are natural and then finally proving a pair of equalities relating compositions of natural transformations. Carrying out these proofs explicitly is quite tedious and many newcomers are left with the impression that category theory is full of long, but ultimately trivial constructions. This complexity is compounded when moving from ordinary category theory to enriched and internal category theory, where constructions must be additionally proven continuous, monotone, etc, in addition to natural or functorial. However, these generalizations are often exactly what is needed for programming language applications; for example, domain-, metric- and step-index-enriched categories have been used to model recursive programming languages and internal categories have been used to model parametricity and gradual typing [53,9,44,36].

Fortunately, the tools of category theory itself can be employed to simplify this complexity, specifically the tools of *higher* category theory. As an analogy in differential calculus, when an adept analyst writes down a function, they do not expand out the $\epsilon-\delta$ definition of continuity for a function and proceed from first principles, but rather use certain *syntactic principles* for defining functions that are continuous by construction — e.g. that composition of continuous functions is continuous. Similar principles apply to category theory itself: functors and natural transformations are closed under composition and whiskering operations, and experienced category theorists rely on these syntactic principles to eliminate the tedium of explicit proofs. In the case of category theory, these principles can be formalized using algebraic structures such as 2-categories, bicategories, Yoneda structures, (virtual) double categories, pro-arrow equipments [6,56,49,32,17], an approach known as *formal category theory*. In these structures, rather than defining notions of category, functor and natural transformation from first principles, they are axiomatized in a manner similar to how a category axiomatizes a notion of space and homomorphism. Proofs in formal category theory apply to enriched and internal settings, which are instances of the formal axioms. A downside is that these algebraic structures are quite complicated, and practitioners typically employ either an algebraic combinator syntax (formalized in [18]) or a 2-dimensional diagrammatic language that can be quite beautiful and elegant, but is also somewhat removed from the traditional formulation of category theory in terms of sets and functions.

In this work, we apply the techniques of categorical logic to define a more familiar logical syntax for carrying out constructions and proofs in formal category theory. We call the resulting theory *virtual equipment type theory* (VETT) as (hyperdoctrines of) *virtual equipments* [32,17], a particular semantic model of formal category theory, provide a sound and complete notion of model for the theory. VETT provides syntax for categories, functors, profunctors, and natural transformations, which are defined using familiar term syntax and $\beta\eta$ reasoning principles for λ-functions, bound variables, tuples, etc. By adhering to a *syntactic discipline*, the logic guarantees that all functor terms are automatically functorial, and all natural transformation terms are natural. More specifically, the syntax for transformations is a kind of *indexed, ordered linear lambda* calculus, where the indexing ensures that transformations are correctly natural and the ordering and linearity ensure that the proofs are valid in a large class of enriched and internal categories, such as enrichment in a non-symmetric monoidal category. VETT provides an alternative to algebraic and string-diagram syntaxes for working with virtual equipments, similar to how the lambda calculus provides an alternative to categorical combinators and string diagram calculi for cartesian closed categories.

The syntax of VETT is an indexed, ordered linear, proof-relevant variant of predicate logic over a unary type theory. Just as a predicate logic has a notion of type, term, relation and implication, VETT is based on four analogous category-theoretic concepts: categories, functors, profunctors and natural transformations of profunctors. Categories are treated like types, and the unary functors we consider in this paper are each represented by a term whose type is a category and whose one free variable ranges over a category. The analog of a relation is a *profunctor* (defined below), which is written like a set with free category variables. Like the restriction to unary functors, we restrict to profunctors with two free variables. The logic is proof-relevant in that the implications of relations are generalized to natural transformations of profunctors, and we use a λ-calculus notation to describe these "proof terms". This analogy to predicate logic can be made formal: any construction in VETT can be erased to a corresponding construction or proof in predicate logic, as sets, functions, relations, and implication of relations define a (somewhat degenerate) virtual equipment.

While the restricted syntax developed in this paper does not express some important concepts such as functor categories or opposite categories, the restriction is natural in that it corresponds exactly to virtual equipments, a well-understood notion of model that can express a great deal of fundamental results and constructions in category theory [43,47]. Moreover, we can work around these unary/binary restrictions to some extent by viewing the type theory as a domain-specific language embedded in a metalanguage. For example, while we cannot talk about functor categories, we can state a theorem that quantifies over functors using the meta-language's "external" universal quantifier (which does not have automatic functoriality/naturality properties). To support this, VETT includes a third layer, an extensional dependent type theory in the style of Martin-Löf type theory. All of our ordered predicate logic judgments are also indexed by a context from this dependent type theory, and the type theory includes universe types for categories, functors, profunctors and natural transformations. This allow us to formalize theorems the object logic is too restrictive to encode, analogous to 2-level [51,2,39] or indexed type theories [27,15,52,29].

While we emphasize the applications to enriched and internal category theory in this work, there is potential for more direct application to programming language semantics. Ordinary predicate logic is the foundation for proof-theoretic presentations of logical relations, such as Abadi-Plotkin logic for parametricity and LSLR and Iris for step-indexed logical relations proofs [40,20,28]. We conjecture that VETT might similarly serve as the foundation for a logic of *ordered* structures, which abound in applications: rewriting and approximation relations can both be modeled as orderings and logical relations involving these structures are proven to respect orderings; operational logical relations must be downward-closed and approximation relations should satisfy transitivity. Just as LSLR and Iris release the user from the syntactic burden of explicit step-indexing, VETT may be used to release the user from the syntactic burden of proving downward-closure or transitivity side-conditions. Additionally, VETT may serve as the basis of a future domain specific proof assistant for category-theoretic proofs. To pilot-test this, we have formalized the syntax of VETT in Agda 2.6.2.2, using the rewrite mechanism to make VETT's substitution and β-reduction rules definitional equalities.[1] We have used this lightweight implementation to check a number of examples.

Basics of Profunctors. While we assume the reader has some background knowledge of category theory, we briefly define profunctors, which are not included in many introductory texts. Recall that a category $\mathbb{C}$ has a collection of objects and morphisms with identity and composition, and a functor $F : \mathbb{C} \to \mathbb{D}$ is a function on objects and a function on morphisms that preserves identity and composition. A category can be thought of as a generalization of a preordered set, which has a set of elements and a binary *relation* on its objects satisfying reflexivity and transitivity. A category is then a *proof-relevant preorder*, where morphisms are the proofs of ordering, and the reflexivity and transitivity proofs must satisfy identity and unit equations. A functor is then a *proof-relevant monotone function*. Given categories $\mathcal{C}$ and $\mathcal{D}$, a profunctor R from $\mathcal{C}$ to $\mathcal{D}$, written $R : \mathbb{C} \nrightarrow \mathbb{D}$ is a functor $R : \mathbb{C}^o \times \mathbb{D} \to \text{Set}$.[2] Because a profunctor outputs a Set rather than a proposition, it is itself a *proof-relevant relation*. Thinking of categories as proof-relevant preorders, functoriality says that the profunctor is downward-closed in $\mathbb{C}$ and upward-closed in $\mathbb{D}$. Given profunctors $R, S : \mathbb{C} \nrightarrow \mathbb{D}$, a homomorphism from R to S is a natural transformation, which in the preordered setting is simply an implication of relations.

Profunctors are very useful for formalizing category theory, but an additional reason we make them a basic concept of VETT is that they allow us to give a *universal property* for the type of "morphisms in a category $\mathbb{C}$". This is analogous to how the J elimination rule for the identity type in Martin-Löf type theory gives a universal property for morphisms in a groupoid (the special case of a category where all morphisms are invertible) [26,5,50]. The reason profunctors are useful for this purpose is that, for any category $\mathbb{C}$, $\text{Hom}_{\mathbb{C}} : \mathbb{C} \nrightarrow \mathbb{C}$ is a profunctor. On preorders this is just the preorder's ordering relation itself. Moreover, the hom profunctor is the unit for a composition of profunctors $R \odot S$ which is defined as a *co-end*. The composition of profunctors is a generalization of the composition of relations, and just as the equality relation is the identity for the composition of relations, the hom profunctor is the identity for this composition. The unit law for the hom profunctor can be seen as a "morphism induction" principle, analogous to the "path induction" used in homotopy type theory (though in this paper we consider only ordinary 1-dimensional categories, not higher generalizations).

---

[1] https://github.com/maxsnew/virtual-equipments/blob/master/agda/STC.agda
[2] $\mathbb{C}^o$ is the notation we use for the opposite category of $\mathbb{C}$

Outline. In Section 2 we introduce the syntax of VETT. In Section 3 we demonstrate how to use our syntax for formal category theory. In Section 4, we develop some model theory for VETT, including a sound and complete notion of categorical model and sound interpretation in virtual equipments modeling ordinary, enriched and internal category theory. In Section 5, we discuss related type theories and potential extensions.

2   Syntax of VETT

In Figure 1 we give a table summarizing the relationship between the judgments and connectives of higher-order predicate logic with our ordered variant. Due to the incorporation of variance, some unordered concepts generalize to multiple different ordered notions. For instance, covariant and contravariant presheaf categories generalize the power set. Further, because we only have binary relations rather than relations of arbitrary arity, we have only restricted forms of universal and existential quantification which come combined with implications and conjunctions.

Higher-Order Logic	Virtual Equipment Type Theory
Set X	Category $\mathbb{C}$
$X \times Y$	$\mathbb{C} \times \mathbb{D}$
1	1
$\mathcal{P}X$	$\mathcal{P}^+X$ and $\mathcal{P}^-X$
$\{(x,y) \in X \times Y \mid R(x,y)\}$	$\sum_{\alpha:C;\beta:D} R$
Function $f(x : X) : Y$	Functor/Object $\alpha : \mathbb{C} \vdash A : \mathbb{D}$
Relation $R(x,y)$	Profunctor/Set $\alpha : \mathbb{C}; \beta : \mathbb{D} \vdash R$
$R \wedge Q$	$R \times Q$
$\top$	1
$\forall x.P \Rightarrow Q$	$P \rhd^{\forall \alpha:\mathbb{C}} Q$ and $Q^{\forall \alpha:\mathbb{C}} \lhd P$
$\exists x.P \wedge Q$	$P \overset{\exists \alpha:\mathbb{C}}{\odot} Q$
$x =_X y$	$\alpha \to_{\mathbb{C}} \beta$
Proof $\forall \vec{\alpha}.R_1 \wedge \cdots \Rightarrow Q$	Nat. Trans./Element $\alpha_1, x_1 : R_1(\alpha_1, \alpha_2), \ldots \vdash t : Q$

Fig. 1. Analogy between Higher-Order Logic and VETT Judgments and Connectives

The syntactic forms of VETT are given in Figure 2. First, we have categories, which are analogous to sorts in a first-order theory. We have M a base sort, product and unit sorts, as well as the graph of a profunctor and the negative and positive presheaf categories. Next, objects a, b, c are the syntax for the *functors* between categories. We call them objects rather than functors, because in type-theoretic style, a functor is viewed as a "generalized object" parameterized by an input variable $\alpha : \mathbb{C}$. Next, sets P, Q, R are the syntax for *sets*. These sets denote *profunctors*, i.e., a categorification of relations. Similar to functors, rather than writing profunctors as functions $\mathbb{C}^o \times \mathbb{D} \to$ Set, we write them as sets with a contravariant variable $\alpha : \mathbb{C}$ and a covariant variable $\beta : \mathbb{D}$. The sets we can define are the Hom-set, the tensor and internal hom, as well as products of sets, profunctors applied to two objects and elements of positive and negative presheaves. Finally we have elements of sets, which correspond to natural transformations of multiple inputs, where again we view natural transformations valued in a profunctor as generalized elements of profunctors.

After these forms we have types and terms, which represent the meta-language that we use to talk about categories/profunctors/natural transformations. In addition to standard dependent type theory with Π and Σ and identity types, we have universes of categories, functors, profunctors and natural transformations.

Finally we have several forms of context which are used in the theory. The contexts Γ of term variables with their types are as usual; we write "Γ type context" to indicate that a context is well-formed. We name the remaining contexts after the judgements that they are used by. The set contexts Ξ, which will be used to type-check sets, contain object variables with their categories. The two forms of set context are $\alpha : \mathbb{C}$, containing one variable that can be used both contravariantly and covariantly, and $\alpha : \mathbb{C}; \beta : \mathbb{D}$, containing a contravariant variable α and covariant variable β. Finally, the transformation contexts Φ contain element variables with their sets, alternating with those sets' object variables with their categories. A typical Φ has the shape

$$\alpha_1 : \mathbb{C}_1, x_1 : R_1(\alpha_1, \alpha_2), \alpha_2 : \mathbb{C}_2, x_2 : R_2(\alpha_2, \alpha_3), \ldots, R_n(\alpha_n, \alpha_{n+1}), \alpha_{n+1} : \mathbb{C}_{n+1}$$

and represents the composition of the "relations" $R_1, R_2, R_3, \ldots, R_n$. We write $d^-(\Phi)$ for the first category variable in Φ (which we regard as the negative or contravariant position), $d^+(\Phi)$ for the last category variable in Φ (which we regard as the positive or covariant position) and use the notation $d^{\pm}\Xi$ with the same meaning. We write $\Phi_1 \curlyvee \Phi_2$ for the append of two transformation contexts, which is only well-formed when the last variable in Φ_1 is equal to the first variable in Φ_2. Formal inductive definitions are in the appendix, but intuitively:

$$d^-(\alpha_1 : \mathbb{C}_1, x_1 : R_1(\alpha_1, \alpha_2), \ldots, x_n : R_n(\alpha_n, \alpha_n), \alpha_{n+1} : \mathbb{C}_{n+1}) = \alpha_1 : \mathbb{C}_1$$
$$d^+(\alpha_1 : \mathbb{C}_1, x_1 : R_1(\alpha_1, \alpha_2), \ldots, x_n : R_n(\alpha_n, \alpha_n), \alpha_{n+1} : \mathbb{C}_{n+1}) = \alpha_{n+1} : \mathbb{C}_{n+1}$$
$$(\Phi_1, \beta : \mathbb{D}) \curlyvee (\beta : \mathbb{D}, \Phi_2) \qquad\qquad = \Phi_1, \beta : \mathbb{D}, \Phi_2$$

Next, we overview our basic judgement forms. We have

- Categories: $\Gamma \vdash \mathbb{C}$ Cat, where Γ type context.
- Objects/functors: $\Gamma \mid \alpha : \mathbb{C} \vdash a : \mathbb{D}$, where $\Gamma \vdash \mathbb{C}$ Cat and $\Gamma \vdash \mathbb{D}$ Cat. Objects are typed with an input object variable $\alpha : \mathbb{C}$ and an output category $\mathbb{D}$; in the semantics, objects are modeled as functors $\mathbb{C} \to \mathbb{D}$.
- Sets/profunctors: $\Gamma \mid \Xi \vdash S$ Set, where $\Gamma \vdash \Xi$ set context. A set S is typed with respect to a set context Ξ to describe its covariant/contravariant dependence on some input objects. Sets are semantically modeled as profunctors.
- Elements/natural transformations: $\Gamma \mid \Phi \vdash s : R$, where $\Gamma \vdash \Phi$ trans. context and $\Gamma \mid \underline{\Phi} \vdash R$ Set. A transformation s has a context Φ of transformation variables and a single output set R. To be well-formed, the context and set

$$\begin{aligned}
\text{Categories} \quad \mathbb{C}, \mathbb{D}, \mathbb{E} &::= \lfloor M \rfloor \mid \mathbb{C} \times \mathbb{D} \mid \mathbb{1} \mid \sum_{\alpha;\beta} P \mid \mathcal{P}^- \mathbb{C} \mid \mathcal{P}^+ \mathbb{C} \\
\text{Objects} \quad a, b, c &::= \alpha \mid Ma \mid (a, b) \mid () \mid \pi_i a \mid (a_-, a_+, s) \mid \pi_- a \mid \pi_+ a \mid \lambda\alpha : \mathbb{C}.R \\
\text{Sets} \quad P, Q, R &::= a \to_{\mathbb{C}} b \mid P \overset{\exists\beta}{\odot} Q \mid P \rhd^{\forall\beta} Q \mid S^{\forall\alpha} \lhd R \mid 1 \mid P \times Q \\
&\quad \mid M(a; b) \mid b \in a \mid a \ni b \\
\text{Elements} \quad s, t, u &::= x \mid \operatorname{ind}_\to(\alpha.t, b_1, s, b_2) \mid \operatorname{id}_b \mid \operatorname{ind}_\odot(x, \beta, y.r; s) \mid (s, b, t) \mid s \rhd^a t \\
&\quad \mid \lambda^\rhd(x, \alpha).s \mid s^{\,a}\lhd t \mid \lambda^\lhd(\alpha, x).s \mid \pi_i s \mid (s_1, s_2) \mid () \mid \pi_e a \mid M^b \\
\text{Type} \quad A, B, C &::= \ldots \mid \mathsf{SmallCat} \mid \mathsf{Cat} \mid \mathsf{Fun}\,\mathbb{C}\,\mathbb{D} \mid \mathsf{Prof}\,\mathbb{C}\,\mathbb{D} \mid \forall\alpha : \mathbb{C}.R \\
\text{Term} \quad L, M, N &::= \ldots \mid \lceil \mathbb{C} \rceil \mid \lambda\alpha : \mathbb{C}.a \mid \lambda(\alpha : \mathbb{C}; \beta : \mathbb{D}).R \mid \lambda\alpha.t \\
\text{Type Context} \quad \Gamma, \Delta &::= \cdot \mid \Gamma, X : A \\
\text{Set Context} \quad \Xi, Z &::= \alpha : \mathbb{C} \mid \alpha : \mathbb{C}; \beta : \mathbb{D} \\
\text{Trans. Context} \quad \Phi, \Psi &::= \alpha : \mathbb{C} \mid \Phi, x : P, \beta : \mathbb{D}
\end{aligned}$$

Fig. 2. VETT Syntactic Forms

must be parameterized by the same contravariant and covariant object variables. To ensure this, we use a coercion operation $\underline{\Phi}$ from transformation contexts to set contexts that erases everything in the context but the leftmost and right-most object variables ($\underline{\alpha : \mathbb{C}} = \alpha : \mathbb{C}$ and $\underline{\Phi} = d^-(\Phi); d^+(\Phi)$).

– Meta-language types and terms: $\Gamma \vdash A$ Type and $\Gamma \vdash M : A$ as in standard dependent type theory.

The variable rules for objects and elements are

$$\frac{}{\Gamma \mid \alpha : \mathbb{C} \vdash \alpha : \mathbb{C}} \qquad \frac{}{\Gamma \mid \alpha : \mathbb{C}, x : R, \beta : \mathbb{D} \vdash x : R}$$

As when using variables in linear logic, the latter rule applies only when the context contains a single set R. All syntactic forms typed in context admit an action of substitution. For types and terms, this is as usual. Objects $\alpha : \mathbb{C} \vdash a : \mathbb{D}$ can be substituted for object variables $\beta : \mathbb{D}$ in other objects. We can also substitute objects into *sets*, that is, if we have a set P parameterized by a contravariant variable $\alpha : \mathbb{C}$ and a covariant variable $\beta : \mathbb{D}$, then we can substitute objects $a : \mathbb{C}$ and $b : \mathbb{D}$ for these variables $P[a/\alpha; b/\beta]$. This generalizes the ordinary precomposition of a relation by a function. Semantically this is the "restriction" of a profunctor along two functors, which is just composition of functors if a profunctor is viewed as a functor to Set. Modeling this operation as a substitution considerably simplifies reasoning using profunctors. Finally we have the action of substitution on elements/natural transformations. First, we can substitute elements/natural transformations for the set variables in elements, denoting the composition of natural transformations. Second, an element is also parameterized by a contravariant and a covariant category variable $\alpha; \beta$. We can think of natural transformations as *polymorphic* in the categories involved, and so when we make a transformation substitution, we also *instantiate* the polymorphic category variables with objects. The full syntactic details of substitution are included in the appendix.

2.1   Category Connectives

In this section we discuss some connectives for constructing categories, which are specified by introduction and elimination rules in Figure 3 (the $\beta\eta$ equality and substitution rules are included in the appendix). The introduction and elimination rules make use of functors, profunctors, and natural transformations. First we introduce the additive connectives: the unit category 1 and product category $\mathbb{C} \times \mathbb{D}$ have the usual introduction and elimination rules defining functors to/from them. Next, we introduce the *graph of a profunctor* $\sum_{\alpha;\beta} P$. Just as a relation $R : A \times B \to$ Set can be viewed as a subset $\{(a, b) \in A \times B | R(a, b)\}$, any profunctor $P : \mathbb{C}^o_- \times \mathbb{D}_+ \to$ Set can be viewed as a category with a functor to $\mathbb{C}_- \times \mathbb{D}_+$ (no op), specifically a two-sided discrete fibration. In set-based category theory, the objects of $\sum_{\alpha;\beta} P$ are triples $(a_-, a_+, s : P(a_-, a_+))$ and morphisms from (a_-, a_+, s) to (a'_-, a'_+, s') are pairs of morphisms $f_- : a_- \to a'_-$ and $f_+ : a_+ \to a'_+$ such that $P(\mathrm{id}, f_+)(s) = P(f_-, \mathrm{id})(s')$. With various choices of P, this connective can be used to define the arrow category, slice category, comma category and category of elements. In our syntax we define it as the universal category $\mathbb{C}$ equipped with functors to $\mathbb{C}_-$ and $\mathbb{C}_+$ and a natural transformation to P.

Lastly, we define the *negative* and *positive* presheaf categories $\mathcal{P}^-\mathbb{C}$ and $\mathcal{P}^+\mathbb{D}$. These are given a syntax suggestive of the fact that they generalize the notion of a powerset, and so can be thought of as "power categories". Note that we include a restriction that the input category is *small*, which is an inductively defined by saying all base categories are small, the unit is small, product of small categories is small and the graph of a profunctor over small categories is small. Notably, the presheaf categories themselves are not small. The negative presheaf category is defined by its universal property that a functor into it $\mathbb{D} \to \mathcal{P}^-\mathbb{C}$ is equivalent to a profunctor $\mathbb{C}^o \times \mathbb{D} \to$ Set. The introduction rule constructs an object of the negative presheaf category from such a profunctor and the elimination rule inverts it. We use the notation $p \in a$ for the elements of the induced profunctor. Since a occurs in a negative position, it must depend only on the contravariant variable $d^- \Xi$ and vice-versa for p. The positive presheaf category is then the dual. In ordinary set-theoretic category theory the negative presheaf category is the usual presheaf category $\mathrm{Set}^{\mathbb{C}^o}$, and the positive presheaf category is the opposite of the dual presheaf category $(\mathrm{Set}^{\mathbb{D}})^o$.

2.2   Set Connectives

Next, in Figure 4, we cover the connectives for the sets/profunctors, which classify elements/natural transformations (the β/η-rules are in the appendix). First, the unit set $a \to_\mathbb{C} b$ is our syntax for the profunctor of morphisms in $\mathbb{C}$ instantiated at generalized objects a and b. Its introduction and elimination rules are analogous to the usual rules for equality in intensional Martin-Löf type theory. The introduction rule is the identity morphism (reflexivity) and the elimination rule is an induction principle: we can use a term of $s : a \to_\mathbb{C} b$ by specifying the behavior when s is of the form id_α in the form of a continuation $\alpha.t$. Like

Unit:
$$\frac{}{\Gamma \vdash 1 \; \text{Cat}} \qquad \frac{}{\Gamma \mid \alpha : C \vdash () : 1}$$

Product:
$$\frac{\Gamma \vdash \mathbb{C}_1 \; \text{Cat} \quad \mathbb{C}_2 \; \text{Cat}}{\Gamma \vdash \mathbb{C}_1 \times \mathbb{C}_2 \; \text{Cat}} \quad \frac{\Gamma \mid \alpha : \mathbb{C} \vdash a_1 : \mathbb{C}_1 \quad \Gamma \mid \alpha : \mathbb{C} \vdash a_2 : \mathbb{C}_2}{\Gamma \mid \alpha : \mathbb{C} \vdash (a_1, a_2) : \mathbb{C}_1 \times \mathbb{C}_2} \quad \frac{\Gamma \mid \alpha : \mathbb{C} \vdash a : \mathbb{C}_1 \times \mathbb{C}_2}{\Gamma \mid \alpha : \mathbb{C} \vdash \pi_i a : \mathbb{C}_i}$$

Graph of a profunctor:
$$\frac{\Gamma \mid \alpha : \mathbb{C}; \beta : \mathbb{D} \vdash P \; \text{Set}}{\Gamma \vdash \sum_{\alpha;\beta} P \; \text{Cat}} \quad \frac{\Gamma \mid \alpha : \mathbb{C} \vdash a_- : \mathbb{C}_- \quad \Gamma \mid \alpha : \mathbb{C} \vdash a_+ : \mathbb{C}_+ \quad \Gamma \mid \alpha : \mathbb{C} \vdash s : P[a_-/\alpha; a_+/\beta]}{\Gamma \mid \alpha : \mathbb{C} \vdash (a_-, a_+, s) : \sum_{\alpha: \mathbb{C}_-; \beta: \mathbb{C}_+} P}$$

$$\frac{\Gamma \mid \alpha : \mathbb{C} \vdash a : \sum_{\alpha: \mathbb{C}_-; \beta} P}{\Gamma \mid \alpha : \mathbb{C} \vdash \pi_- a : \mathbb{C}_-} \quad \frac{\Gamma \mid \alpha : \mathbb{C} \vdash a : \sum_{\alpha;\beta: \mathbb{C}_+} P}{\Gamma \mid \alpha : \mathbb{C} \vdash \pi_+ a : \mathbb{C}_+} \quad \frac{\Gamma \mid \alpha : \mathbb{C} \vdash a : \sum_{\alpha;\beta} P}{\Gamma \mid \alpha : \mathbb{C} \vdash \pi_e a : P[\pi_- a/\alpha; \pi_+ a/\beta]}$$

Negative Presheaf:
$$\frac{\Gamma \vdash \mathbb{C} \; \text{Cat} \quad \mathbb{C} \; \text{Small}}{\Gamma \vdash \mathcal{P}^- \mathbb{C} \; \text{Cat}} \quad \frac{\Gamma \mid d^- \Xi \vdash a : \mathbb{C} \quad \Gamma \mid d^+ \Xi \vdash p : \mathcal{P}^- \mathbb{C}}{\Gamma \mid \Xi \vdash a \in p \; \text{Set}} \quad \frac{\Gamma \mid \alpha : \mathbb{C}; \beta : \mathbb{D} \vdash R : \; \text{Set}}{\Gamma \mid \beta : \mathbb{D} \vdash \lambda \alpha : \mathbb{C}.R : \mathcal{P}^- \mathbb{C}}$$

Positive Preshaf:
$$\frac{\Gamma \vdash \mathbb{D} \; \text{Cat} \quad \mathbb{D} \; \text{Small}}{\Gamma \vdash \mathcal{P}^+ \mathbb{D} \; \text{Cat}} \quad \frac{\Gamma \mid d^- \Xi \vdash p : \mathcal{P}^+ \mathbb{D} \quad \Gamma \mid d^+ \Xi \vdash a : \mathbb{D}}{\Gamma \mid \Xi \vdash p \ni a \; \text{Set}} \quad \frac{\Gamma \mid \alpha : \mathbb{C}; \beta : \mathbb{D} \vdash R : \; \text{Set}}{\Gamma \mid \alpha : \mathbb{C} \vdash \lambda \beta : \mathbb{D}.R : \mathcal{P}^+ \mathbb{D}}$$

Fig. 3. Category Conectives

the J elimination rule for equality in Martin-Löf type theory, P must be "fully general", i.e. well-typed for variables α and β. This is because for distinct variables α and β, $\alpha \to_{\mathbb{C}} \beta$ denotes the unit in a virtual double category, which has a universal property, but $a \to_{\mathbb{C}} b$ denotes a restriction of the unit, which in general does not. Those familiar with linear logic as in e.g. [41] might expect a more general rule, where the continuation t is allowed to use variables that are not used in s, i.e., have a context $\Phi_l \curlyvee \Phi_r$ and the conclusion of the rule to have a context $\Phi_l \curlyvee \Phi \curlyvee \Phi_r$. Because of dependency, this is not necessarily well-formed in cases where the endpoints a and b of $a \to_{\mathbb{C}} b$ are not distinct variables. However, the instances of this more general rule that do type check are derivable from our more restricted rule using right/left-hom types.

The tensor product of sets is a kind of combined existential quantifier and monoidal product, which we combine into a single notation $P \overset{\exists \beta}{\odot} Q$, where β is the covariant variable of P and the contravariant variable of Q. Then the covariant variable of the tensor product is the covariant variable of Q and the contravariant variable similarly comes from P. In ordinary category theory, this is the *composition* of profunctors, and is defined by a coend of a product. We require that the variable β quantifies over a small category $\mathbb{D}$, as in general this composite doesn't exist for large categories. The introduction and elimination are like those for a combined tensor product and existential type: the introduction rule is a pair of terms, with an appropriate instantiation of β, and the elimination rule says to use a term of a tensor product, it is sufficient to specify the behavior on two elements typed with an arbitrary middle object β.

Next, we introduce the contravariant $(P^{\forall\alpha} \lhd R)$ and covariant $(R \rhd^{\forall\alpha} P)$ homs of sets, which are different from each other because we are in an ordered logic. These are a kind of universally quantified function type, where the universally quantified variable must occur with the same variance in domain and codomain. In the contravariant case, it occurs as the contravariant variable in both, and vice-versa for the covariant case. To highlight this, the notation for the contravariant dependence puts the quantified variable on the *left* of the triangle, as contravariant variables occur to the left of the covariant variable, and similarly the covariant hom has the quantified variable on the right. Similar to ordered lambda calculus, the covariant hom is right-associative while the contravariant hom is left-associative. Then the covariant variable of the contravariant hom set is the covariant variable of the codomain and, and the contravariant variable of the hom set is the *covariant* variable of the domain, as the two contravariances cancel. The covariant hom is dual. Semantically, in ordinary category theory these are known as the *hom* of profunctors and are adjoint to the composition of profunctors [7]. The two connectives have similar introduction and elimination rules in the form of λ terms abstracting over both the object of the category and the element of the set, and appropriate application forms. To keep with our invariant that the variable occurrences occur left to right in the term syntax in a manner matching the context, we write the covariant application in the usual order $s \rhd^a t$ where the function is on the left and the argument is on the right, and the contravariant application in the flipped order. We also write the instantiating object as a superscript to de-emphasize it, as in practice it can often be inferred.

Finally, we have the cartesian unit and product sets, which are analogous to the normal unit and product of types. The most notable point to emphasize is that in the formation rule for the product, the two subformulae should have the same covariant and contravariant dependence (as with linear logic, some constructions can syntactically use a variable more than once and still be "linear").

2.3   Type Connectives

Finally, we briefly describe the connectives for the "meta-logic", which extends Martin-Löf type theory with Π/Σ and extensional identity types (with their standard rules) (Fig. 5). We use extensional identity types so that the description of models is simpler, but intensional identity types could be used instead. The types we include are *universes* for the object categorical logic: types of small categories and locally small categories, functors, profunctors and natural transformations. The rule for the types of small categories and (large) categories are very similar: any definable category defines an element of type Cat, and any element of that type can be reflected back into a category. The only difference for SmallCat is that the categories involved additionally satisfy $\mathbb{C}$ Small. Again we elide the $\beta\eta$ principles, which state that $\lceil - \rceil$ and $\lfloor - \rfloor$ are mutually inverse. Since every small category $\mathbb{C}$ Small is a category $\mathbb{C}$ Cat, there is a definable inclusion function from SmallCat to Cat and the $\beta\eta$ properties ensure that this is a monomorphism.

Unit/morphism set:

$$\frac{\Gamma \mid d^- \Xi \vdash a_1 : \mathbb{C} \quad \Gamma \mid d^+ \Xi \vdash a_2 : \mathbb{C}}{\Gamma \mid \Xi \vdash a_1 \to_{\mathbb{C}} a_2 \text{ Set}}$$

$$\frac{\Gamma \mid \beta : \mathbb{D} \vdash a : \mathbb{C}}{\Gamma \mid \beta : \mathbb{D} \vdash \mathrm{id}_a : a \to_{\mathbb{C}} a}$$

$$\frac{\Gamma \mid \alpha : \mathbb{C}; \beta : \mathbb{C} \vdash P \text{ Set} \quad \Gamma \mid \alpha : \mathbb{C} \vdash t : P[\alpha/\alpha; \alpha/\beta] \quad \Gamma \mid \Phi \vdash s : a \to_{\mathbb{C}} b}{\Gamma \mid \Phi \vdash \mathrm{ind}_{\to}(\alpha.t, A, s, B) : P[a/\alpha; b/\beta]}$$

Tensor product:

$$\frac{\mathbb{D} \text{ Small} \quad \Gamma \mid d^- \Xi; \beta : \mathbb{D} \vdash P \text{ Set} \quad \Gamma \mid \beta : \mathbb{D}; d^+ \Xi \vdash Q \text{ Set}}{\Gamma \mid \Xi \vdash P \overset{\exists \beta : \mathbb{D}}{\odot} Q \text{ Set}}$$

$$\frac{\Gamma \mid d^+ \Psi_s \vdash b : \mathbb{D} \quad \Gamma \mid \Psi_s \vdash s : P[b/\beta] \quad \Gamma \mid \Psi_t \vdash t : Q[b/\beta]}{\Gamma \mid \Psi_s \curlyvee \Psi_t \vdash (s, b, t) : P \overset{\exists \beta : \mathbb{D}}{\odot} Q}$$

$$\frac{\Gamma \mid \Phi_l \curlyvee x : P, \beta : \mathbb{D}, y : Q \curlyvee \Phi_r \vdash t : R}{\Gamma \mid \Phi_m \vdash s : P \overset{\exists \beta : \mathbb{D}}{\odot} Q} \quad \frac{}{\Gamma \mid \Phi_l \curlyvee \Phi_m \curlyvee \Phi_r \vdash \mathrm{ind}_{\odot}(x, \beta, y.t; s) : R}$$

Right hom:

$$\frac{d^+ \Xi \text{ Small} \quad \Gamma \mid d^+ \Xi; \alpha : \mathbb{C} \vdash R \text{ Set} \quad \Gamma \mid d^- \Xi; \alpha : \mathbb{C} \vdash P \text{ Set}}{\Gamma \mid \Xi \vdash R \triangleright^{\forall \alpha : \mathbb{C}} P \text{ Set}}$$

$$\frac{\Gamma \mid \Phi, x : R, \alpha : \mathbb{C} \vdash t : P}{\Gamma \mid \Phi \vdash \lambda^{\triangleright}(x : R, \alpha : \mathbb{C}).t : R \triangleright^{\forall \alpha : \mathbb{C}} P}$$

$$\frac{\Gamma \mid \Phi_f \vdash s : R \triangleright^{\forall \alpha : \mathbb{C}} P \quad d^+ \Phi_a \vdash a : \mathbb{C} \quad \Phi_a \vdash t : R[a/\alpha]}{\Gamma \mid \Phi_f \curlyvee \Phi_a \vdash s \triangleright^a t : P[a/\alpha]}$$

Left hom:

$$\frac{d^- \Xi \text{ Small} \quad \Gamma \mid \alpha : \mathbb{C}; d^- \Xi \vdash R \text{ Set} \quad \Gamma \mid \alpha : \mathbb{C}; d^+ \Xi \vdash P \text{ Set}}{\Gamma \mid \Xi \vdash P^{\forall \alpha : \mathbb{C}} \triangleleft R \text{ Set}}$$

$$\frac{\Gamma \mid \alpha : \mathbb{C}, x : R, \Phi \vdash t : P}{\Gamma \mid \Phi \vdash \lambda^{\triangleleft}(\alpha : \mathbb{C}, x : R).t : P^{\forall \alpha : \mathbb{C}} \triangleleft R}$$

$$\frac{\Gamma \mid d^- \Phi_a \vdash a : \mathbb{C} \quad \Gamma \mid \Phi_a \vdash s : R[a/\alpha] \quad \Gamma \mid \Phi_f \vdash t : P^{\forall \alpha : \mathbb{C}} \triangleleft R}{\Gamma \mid \Phi_a \curlyvee \Phi_f \vdash s^a \triangleleft t : P[a/\alpha]}$$

Cartesian unit and products:

$$\frac{}{\Gamma \mid \Xi \vdash 1 \text{ Set}} \quad \frac{}{\Gamma \mid \Phi \vdash () : 1}$$

$$\frac{\Gamma \mid \Xi \vdash R \text{ Set} \quad \Gamma \mid \Xi \vdash S \text{ Set}}{\Gamma \mid \Xi \vdash R \times S \text{ Set}} \quad \frac{\forall i \in \{1,2\}. \ \Gamma \mid \Phi \vdash s_i : R_i}{\Gamma \mid \Phi \vdash (s_1, s_2) : R_1 \times R_2} \quad \frac{\Gamma \mid \Phi \vdash s : R_1 \times R_2}{\Gamma \mid \Phi \vdash \pi_i s : R_i}$$

Fig. 4. Set Connectives

Next, we have the types of all functors and profunctors between any two fixed categories. The introduction and elimination forms are those for unary and binary function types respectively, where metalanguage terms of type $\mathrm{Fun}\,\mathbb{C}\,\mathbb{D}$ can be used to construct an object/functor, while metalanguage terms of type $\mathrm{Prof}\,\mathbb{C}\,\mathbb{D}$ can be used to construct a set/profunctor.

Finally we include a type $\forall \alpha : \mathbb{C}.P$ which we call the set of "natural elements" of P. The name comes from the case that P is of the form $F(\alpha) \to G(\alpha)$ in which case the type $\forall \alpha : \mathbb{C}.F(\alpha) \to G(\alpha)$ can be interpreted as the set of all natural transformations from F to G. More generally this is modeled as an end, and we notate it with a universal quantifier (just as we do for the quantifiers in left/right hom types). Syntactically, $\forall \alpha.P$ is a meta-language type that represents elements/natural transformations with exactly one free variable.

3   Formal Category Theory in VETT

To demonstrate what formal category theory in VETT looks like, we demonstrate some basic definitions and theorems. While it is well known that much category theory can be formalized in virtual equipments, we show these examples to demonstrate how the VETT syntax gives a more familiar syntax to these constructions, while still avoiding the need for explicit naturality and functorial-

$$\frac{\Gamma \vdash \mathbb{C} \text{ Small}}{\Gamma \vdash \text{SmallCat}} \qquad \frac{\Gamma \vdash M : \text{SmallCat}}{\Gamma \vdash \lceil \mathbb{C} \rceil : \text{SmallCat}} \qquad \frac{\Gamma \vdash M : \text{SmallCat}}{\Gamma \vdash \lfloor M \rfloor \text{ Small}} \qquad \frac{\Gamma \vdash \mathbb{C} \text{ Cat}}{\Gamma \vdash \text{Cat}} \qquad \frac{\Gamma \vdash \mathbb{C} \text{ Cat}}{\Gamma \vdash \lceil \mathbb{C} \rceil : \text{Cat}} \qquad \frac{\Gamma \vdash M : \text{Cat}}{\Gamma \vdash \lfloor M \rfloor \text{ Cat}}$$

$$\frac{\Gamma \vdash \mathbb{C} \text{ Cat} \qquad \Gamma \vdash \mathbb{D} \text{ Cat}}{\Gamma \vdash \text{Fun } \mathbb{C} \, \mathbb{D} \text{ Type}} \qquad \frac{\Gamma \mid \alpha : \mathbb{C} \vdash A : \mathbb{D}}{\Gamma \vdash \lambda\alpha : \mathbb{C}.A : \text{Fun } \mathbb{C} \, \mathbb{D}} \qquad \frac{\Gamma \mid \alpha : \mathbb{C} \vdash A : \mathbb{D} \qquad \Gamma \vdash M : \text{Fun } \mathbb{D} \, \mathbb{E}}{\Gamma \mid \alpha : \mathbb{C} \vdash MA : \mathbb{E}}$$

$$\frac{\Gamma \vdash \mathbb{C} \text{ Cat} \qquad \Gamma \vdash \mathbb{D} \text{ Cat}}{\Gamma \vdash \text{Prof } \mathbb{C} \, \mathbb{D} \text{ Type}} \qquad \frac{\Gamma \mid \alpha : \mathbb{C}; \beta : \mathbb{D} \vdash R \text{ Set}}{\Gamma \vdash \lambda\alpha : \mathbb{C}; \beta : \mathbb{D}.R : \text{Prof } \mathbb{C} \, \mathbb{D}} \qquad \frac{\Gamma \vdash M : \text{Prof } \mathbb{C} \, \mathbb{D} \quad \Gamma \mid d^- \, \varXi \vdash A : \mathbb{C} \quad \Gamma \mid d^+ \, \varXi \vdash B : \mathbb{C}}{\Gamma \mid \varXi \vdash MAB \text{ Set}}$$

$$\frac{\Gamma \mid \alpha : \mathbb{C} \vdash P \text{ Set}}{\Gamma \vdash \forall\alpha : \mathbb{C}.P \text{ Type}} \qquad \frac{\Gamma \mid \alpha : \mathbb{C} \vdash t : P}{\Gamma \vdash \lambda\alpha.t : \forall\alpha.P} \qquad \frac{\Gamma \vdash M : \forall\alpha.P \qquad \Gamma \mid \beta : \mathbb{D} \vdash a : \mathbb{C}}{\Gamma \mid \beta : \mathbb{D} \vdash M^a : P[a/\alpha]}$$

Fig. 5. Type Connectives

ity side conditions. We have mechanized some of the results in this section (e.g. Lemma 2 and Lemma 3 and the maps in Lemma 4) in Agda.[3]

First, we using the elimination for the unit set, we can see that all constructions are (pro-)functorial:

Construction 1 *For any small category* $\mathbb{C}$, *we can construct natural elements*

1. *Identity:* $\forall\alpha : \mathbb{C}.\alpha \to_{\mathbb{C}} \alpha$
2. *Composition:* $\forall\alpha_1 : \mathbb{C}.(\alpha_1 \to_{\mathbb{C}} \alpha_2) \triangleright^{\forall\alpha_2:\mathbb{C}} (\alpha_2 \to_{\mathbb{C}} \alpha_3) \triangleright^{\forall\alpha_3:\mathbb{C}} (\alpha_1 \to_{\mathbb{C}} \alpha_3)$
3. *Functoriality: for any* $F : \text{Fun } \mathbb{C} \, \mathbb{D}$, $\forall\alpha_1 : \mathbb{C}.(\alpha_1 \to_{\mathbb{C}} \alpha_2) \triangleright^{\forall\alpha_2:\mathbb{C}} (F(\alpha_1) \to_{\mathbb{D}} F(\alpha_2))$.
4. *Profunctoriality: for any* $R : \text{Prof } \mathbb{C} \, \mathbb{D}$ *if* $\mathbb{D}$ *is small then*
   $\forall\alpha_1 : \mathbb{C}.(\alpha_1 \to_{\mathbb{C}} \alpha_2) \triangleright^{\forall\alpha_2:\mathbb{C}} R\alpha_2\beta_2 \triangleright^{\forall\beta_2:\mathbb{D}} (\beta_2 \to_{\mathbb{D}} \beta_1) \triangleright^{\forall\beta_1:\mathbb{D}} R\alpha_1\beta_1$

Identity and Composition generalize the reflexivity and transitivity properties of equality, respectively, with the lack of symmetry being a key feature of the generalization. In addition, we can prove that the (pro)-functoriality axioms commute with the composition proof by the η principle for the unit. (Pro-)Functoriality generalizes the statement that all functions and relations respect equality. Naturality is more complex to state, and it is a statement about the *proofs* so it has no analog in ordinary higher-order logic. The following version is stated for any *profunctor*, with the usual case of naturality arising when $R\alpha\beta = F\alpha \to_{\mathbb{C}} G\beta$.

Lemma 1 (Naturality). *For any* $t : \forall\alpha : \mathbb{C}.R(\alpha; \alpha)$, *by composing with profunctoriality, we can construct terms* $\alpha_1 : \mathbb{C}, f : \alpha_1 \to_{\mathbb{C}} \alpha_2, \alpha_2 : \mathbb{C} \vdash lcomp(f, t^{\alpha_2})$ *and* $rcomp(t^{\alpha_1}, f) : R(\alpha_1; \alpha_2)$ *that are both equal to* $ind_\to(f, t)$.

Next, we turn to some of the central theorems of category theory, the Yoneda and Co-Yoneda lemmas. Despite being ultimately quite elementary, these are notoriously abstract. In VETT, we view these as ordered generalizations of some very simple tautologies about equality. For instance, the Yoneda lemma generalizes the equivalence between the formulae $\forall y.x = y \Rightarrow Py$ and Px for any x.

---

[3] https://github.com/maxsnew/virtual-equipments/blob/master/agda/
Examples.agda

Lemma 2. *Let* $\alpha : \mathbb{C}$ *and* $\pi : \mathcal{P}^+\mathbb{C}$. *Then*

1. *(Yoneda) The profunctor* $(\alpha \to_{\mathbb{C}} \alpha') \triangleright^{\forall \alpha'} (\pi \ni \alpha')$ *is isomorphic to* $\pi \ni \alpha$
2. *(Co-Yoneda) The profunctor* $(\pi \ni \alpha') \overset{\exists \alpha'}{\odot} (\alpha' \to \alpha)$ *is isomorphic to* $\pi \ni \alpha$

The proofs both follow from the unit elimination rule, which is essentially the Yoneda lemma—the two cases of showing (1) is an isomorphism are precisely the β and η rules for the unit.

Next, we have the "Fubini" theorems, which relate the tensor and hom types. The statement and proofs for these theorems are analogous to proofs relating tensor and hom in ordered logic. For instance, the second isomorphism below is analogous to the equivalence $(P \odot Q) \multimap R \cong P \multimap Q \multimap R$ in ordered logic.

Lemma 3 (Fubini). *The following isomorphisms hold when the corresponding profunctors are well typed.*

1. $P(\alpha; \beta) \overset{\exists \beta}{\odot} (Q(\beta; \gamma) \overset{\exists \gamma}{\odot} R(\gamma; \delta)) \cong (P(\alpha; \beta) \overset{\exists \beta}{\odot} Q(\beta; \gamma)) \overset{\exists \gamma}{\odot} R(\gamma; \delta)$
2. $(P(\delta; \beta) \overset{\exists \beta}{\odot} Q(\beta; \gamma)) \triangleright^{\forall \gamma} S(\alpha; \gamma) \cong P(\delta; \beta) \triangleright^{\forall \beta} Q(\beta; \gamma) \triangleright^{\forall \gamma} S(\alpha; \gamma)$
3. $S(\gamma; \delta) \overset{\forall \gamma}{\triangleleft} (P(\gamma; \beta) \overset{\exists \beta}{\odot} Q(\beta; \alpha)) \cong S(\gamma; \delta) \overset{\forall \gamma}{\triangleleft} P(\gamma; \beta) \overset{\forall \beta}{\triangleleft} Q(\beta; \alpha)$
4. $Q(\delta; \gamma) \triangleright^{\forall \gamma} (S(\beta; \gamma) \overset{\forall \beta}{\triangleleft} P(\beta; \alpha)) \cong (Q(\delta; \gamma) \triangleright^{\forall \gamma} S(\beta; \gamma)) \overset{\forall \beta}{\triangleleft} P(\beta; \alpha)$
5. $\forall \alpha.P(\alpha; \beta) \triangleright^{\forall \beta} Q(\alpha; \beta) \cong \forall \beta.Q(\alpha; \beta) \overset{\forall \alpha}{\triangleleft} P(\alpha; \beta)$

Proof. We show one case as an example, the forward direction of (1) is given by $\lambda \alpha.\lambda^{\triangleright}(x, \delta).\text{ind}_{\odot}(p, \beta, y.\text{ind}_{\odot}(q, \gamma, r.((p, \beta, q), \gamma, r); y); x)$

Next, we can prove that two definitions of an adjunction are equivalent:

Lemma 4. *For* $R : \text{Fun}\,\mathbb{D}\,\mathbb{C}$ *and* $L : \text{Fun}\,\mathbb{C}\,\mathbb{D}$, *the following are in bijection:*

1. *An isomorphism of profunctors* $(L\alpha \to_{\mathbb{D}} \beta) \cong (\alpha \to_{\mathbb{C}} R\beta)$
2. *A unit* $\eta : \forall \alpha.\alpha \to_{\mathbb{C}} R(L\alpha)$ *and co-unit* $\varepsilon : \forall \beta.L(R(\beta)) \to_{\mathbb{D}} \beta$ *satisfying triangle identities.*

Proof. Given the forward homomorphism lr, we can construct $\eta = \lambda \alpha.\text{lr}^{\alpha} \triangleright^{L\alpha} \text{id}_{\alpha}$. Given the unit we can reconstruct the forward homomorphism using comp (composition) and fctor (functoriality) from Construction 1 as $\text{comp}^{\alpha} \triangleright^{R(L\alpha)} \eta^{\alpha} \triangleright^{R\beta} (\text{fctor}(R)^{L\alpha} \triangleright^{\beta} f)$.

We can define weighted limits, which as special cases include ordinary limits and Kan extensions.

Definition 1. *For a functor* $D : \text{Fun}\,\mathbb{J}\,\mathbb{C}$ *and a profunctor* $W : \text{Prof}\,\mathbb{K}\,\mathbb{J}$, *the limit of* D *weighted by* W *is (if it exists) a functor* $\lim^{W} D : \text{Fun}\,\mathbb{K}\,\mathbb{C}$ *with an isomorphism* $\alpha \to_{\mathbb{C}} (\lim^{W} D)k \cong W kj \triangleright^{\forall j} (\alpha \to_{\mathbb{C}} Dj)$

This generalizes the usual definition that a morphism into a limit is a cone over the diagram $(\alpha \to_{\mathbb{C}} Dj)$ to be parameterized by a weight $W kj$. Then we can prove the well-known theorem that right adjoints preserve (weighted) limits:

Theorem 1. *If $\lim^W D$ exists and is a limit and $R : Fun\,\mathbb{C}\,\mathbb{C}'$ has a left adjoint L, then $\lambda\kappa.R((\lim^W D)\kappa)$ is the limit of $\lambda j.R(Dj)$ weighted by W.*

Proof.

$$\gamma \to R((\lim^W D)\kappa) \cong L\gamma \to (\lim^W D)\kappa \cong Wkj \vartriangleright^{\forall j} L\gamma \to Dj \cong Wkj \vartriangleright^{\forall j} \gamma \to R(Dj)$$

This is a high level proof in terms of isomorphisms that may be written in VETT. The first two steps are the instantiation of assumptions (adjointness, weighted limits). The last step uses the fact that a natural isomorphisms lift to natural isomorphism of homs of profunctors. The construction of this isomorphism illustrates how naturality need not be proved explicitly in VETT. For any $\phi : \forall\alpha.R'\alpha\beta \vartriangleright^{\forall\beta} R\alpha\beta$ and $\psi : \forall\gamma.S\gamma\beta \vartriangleright^{\forall\beta} S'\gamma\beta$ we can construct a natural transformation $\phi \vartriangleright \psi : \forall\gamma.(R\alpha\beta \vartriangleright^{\forall\beta} S\gamma\beta) \vartriangleright^{\forall\alpha} R'\alpha\beta \vartriangleright^{\forall\beta} S'\gamma\beta$ as $\lambda\gamma.\lambda^\vartriangleright(f,\alpha).\lambda^\vartriangleright(r,\beta).\psi^\gamma \vartriangleright^\beta (f \vartriangleright^\beta (\phi^\alpha \vartriangleright^\beta r))$. Furthermore if ϕ and ψ have inverses, then $\phi^{-1} \vartriangleright \psi^{-1}$ is the inverse of $\phi \vartriangleright \psi$.

4   Semantics

Next, we develop the basics of the model theory for VETT. First, we define a sound and complete notion of categorical model based on hyperdoctrines of virtual equipments. Then we instantiate this general notion of model to show that the VETT can be interpreted in ordinary category theory as well as enriched, internal and indexed notions.

First, we can model the judgmental structure of the unary type theory and predicate logic in *virtual double categories* that are *split fibrant* and have a notion of *small object* [32,17]. We briefly recount the structure present in a virtual double category, but see [17] for a precise definition of the composition rules for 2-cells and functor of virtual double categories.

Definition 2. *A virtual double category V consists of*

1. *A category V_o of "objects and vertical arrows"*
2. *A set V_h of "horizontal arrows" with source and target functions $s, t : V_h \to V_o{}^2$*
3. *Sets of 2-cells of the following form, with appropriate "multi-categorical" notions of identity and composition:*

$$
\begin{array}{ccc}
C_0 & \xrightarrow{R_0} \cdots \xrightarrow{R_n} & C_n \\
f \downarrow & \phi & \downarrow g \\
D_0 & \xrightarrow[s]{} & D_1
\end{array}
$$

We say that the 2-cell ϕ has S as codomain, the sequence $R_0 \ldots R_n$ as domain and call f and g the left and right "frames", or that ϕ is framed by f and g.

We say a virtual double category is split fibrant *when it has a choice of re-strictions, that is, for any horizontal arrow* $R : C \nrightarrow D$ *and vertical arrows* $f : C' \to C$ *and* $g : D' \to D$ *there is a chosen horizontal arrow* $R(f,g) : C' \nrightarrow D'$ *with a cartesian 2-cell to* R *framed by* f,g *and these chosen cartesian lifts are functorial in* f,g *([46]).* A choice of small objects *is a subset of the objects* $V_s \subseteq V_o$. A morphism *of split fibrant virtual double categories with small objects is a functor of the virtual double categories that additionally preserves the restrictions and smallness of objects. This defines a category fVDCs.*

In the presence of restrictions, every 2-cell can be represented as a "globular" 2-cell where the left and right frame are identities [46]. For example the 2-cell ϕ above can be represented as one with the same domain but whose codomain is $S(f,g)$. This property is crucial for the completeness of our semantics as we only include a syntax for these globular terms (proof of Construction 2). Each component of this definition has a direct correspondence to a syntactic structure in VETT. The objects of V_o models the category judgment and the morphisms model the functor judgment. The set V_h models the profunctor judgment. A composable string $R_0 \cdots R_n$ models the profunctor contexts. The 2-cells correspond to the natural transformation judgment where we have taken the restriction $S(F,G)$ of the codomain. Note that Cruttwell and Shulman define a *virtual equipment* to be a virtual double category with all restrictions and all units. The units are the model of the unit of profunctors connective and so all of our models with the unit will be virtual equipments, hence the name VETT.

To model the dependent type theory and indexing of category-theoretic judgments by a Γ with an action of substitution, we use a variation on Lawvere's notion of *hyperdoctrine* for modeling predicate logic[31][4]:

Definition 3 (VETT Judgmental model). *A VETT judgmental model (VM$_J$) is a pair of a category with families $\mathcal{C}$ and a functor $V^{(-)} : \mathcal{C}^o \to fVDCs$.*

Categories with families $\mathcal{C}$ model dependent type theory [22] and for each semantic context Γ, V^{Γ} models the VETT judgments in context Γ, with the functoriality modeling the fact that all of these judgments admit a well-behaved action of substitution. A VM$_J$ is then precisely the structure corresponding to the judgments and actions of substitution in VETT.

Construction 2 (Syntactic Model) *The syntax of VETT with with any subset of connectives are included presents a VM$_J$.*

Proof. Define the category of families using the dependent type structure and the virtual equipment structure having (α-equivalence classes of) syntactic categories as objects, functors/sets as vertical/horizontal arrows and interpreting compositions/restrictions as substitutions. The biggest gap between syntax and semantics is in the definition of the 2-cells. A 2-cell from
$(\alpha_1 : \mathbb{C}_1; \alpha_2 : \mathbb{C}_2 \vdash R_1), (\alpha_2 : \mathbb{C}_2; \alpha_3 : \mathbb{C}_3 \vdash R_2), \ldots$ to $(\beta_1 : \mathbb{D}_1; \beta_2 : \mathbb{D}_2 \vdash S)$

---

[4] note that unlike in hyperdoctrines, we do not require *quantifiers* adjoint to substitution

with frames $\alpha_1 : \mathbb{C}_1 \vdash b_1 : \mathbb{D}_1$ and $\alpha_n : \mathbb{C}_n \vdash b_2 : \mathbb{D}_2$ is given by a term $x_1 : R_1, x_2 : R_2 \ldots \vdash s : S[b_1/\beta_1; b_2/\beta_2]$. Composition is defined by substitution.

Then the *connectives* of VETT each precisely correspond to a universal construction in a VM_J. The Π, Σ, Id types correspond to their standard semantics in a CwF and the connectives for categories and profunctors correspond to universal constructions in the virtual double categories. Products of categories are interpreted as products in the vertical category, and products of sets as products in the category of pro-arrows and 2-cells. The units, tensor and covariant and contravariant homs are modeled by the universal properties of the same names, as described in [46]. The graph of a profunctor is modeled by *tabulators* [25]. Finally, the covariant and contravariant presheaf categories can be described as a weakening of the definition of a Yoneda equipment from [19] to virtual double categories. More detailed descriptions of these universal properties are included in the extended version [37]. Then the soundness and completeness of this notion of categorical model is formalized by the following initiality theorem.

Theorem 2 (Initiality). *The syntax of VETT with any subset of connectives that includes the hom types presents a VM_J that is initial in the category of VM_J with the chosen instances of the universal properties and functors that preserve such chosen instances.*

Proof. The construction 2 can be extended for any connective modularly, with the exception that the unit relies on the presence of hom sets in order to satisfy the "distributivity" requirement that its elimination can occur in any context. Then we can construct the unique morphism to any HVE induction on syntax.

Now that we have a category-theoretic notion of model, we give some model construction theorems that can be used to justify our intuitive notion of semantics in (enriched, internal, indexed) category theory. First, we can extend any set-theoretic model of the category theoretic judgments to a hyperdoctrine of models where the category of families is the category of sets:

Construction 3 *Given a $\mathcal{V} \in fVDCs$, we can construct a VM_J $\mathcal{V}^- : Set \to vDbl_r$ by defining of $(\mathcal{V}^\Gamma)_o$ to be functions $\mathcal{V}_o^\Gamma$, and similarly for morphisms and 2-cells with all operations given pointwise.*

Then to define a model of VETT with a collection of connectives it is sufficient to construct a virtual equipment with the corresponding universal properties. The "standard model" is the virtual double category of locally small categories where the small objects are the small categories.

Construction 4 *Fix a cardinal κ. The virtual double category Cat_κ is defined to have as objects locally κ-small categories, small objects as κ-small categories, vertical morphisms as functors, horizontal arrows as functors $\mathbb{C}^o \times \mathbb{D} \to \kappa Set$ and 2-cells as morphisms of profunctors. Restriction of profunctors is given by composition, which is strictly associative and unital. Cat_U has objects satisfying the universal properties of all connectives in VETT.*

More generally, categories internal to, enriched in and/or indexed by sufficiently nice categories define a virtual equipment that model the connectives of VETT. We highlight one example from the literature that is highly general: Shulman's enriched indexed categories [47]. Shulman's construction defines a virtual double category of large and small $\mathcal{V}$-categories for any pseudofunctor $\mathcal{V} : S^o \to \mathrm{MonCat}$ where S is a category with finite products. He gives examples that show that this subsumes ordinary internal, enriched and indexed categories for suitable choices of $\mathcal{V}$, as well as more general categories that can be thought of as both indexed and enriched. This is slightly weaker then what we require: to have *split* restrictions, we need that $\mathcal{V}$ be a *strict* functor, not merely a pseudo-functor. This is analogous to the situation for dependent type theory, where syntactic substitution is strictly associative, but semantic substitution is typically given by pullback, which is only associative up to unique isomorphism. Shulman's construction carries over when the functor is strict but some of their example instances would require a strictification theorem.

Construction 5 (Shulman [47]) *Given any functor $\mathcal{V} : S^o \to SymMonCat$ such that S and $\mathcal{V}$ have sufficiently well-behaved (indexed) κ-products, then there is a virtual equipment $\mathcal{V} - Cat$ whose objects are locally κ-small $\mathcal{V}$-categories, small objects are κ-small $\mathcal{V}$-categories etc. This virtual equipment has objects satisfying all of the universal properties needed for a model of VETT.*

A final model that uses a CwF that is not Set would be given by taking extensional dependent type theory as the CwF and interpreting the category-theoretic constructions by their definitions inside type theory.

5 Related and Future Work

We now compare VETT with other calculi for formal category theory.

Cáccamo and Winskel [12] develop a formal language for defining categories, functors (of many variables) and proving existence of natural equivalences between them. Their system can encode profunctors as functors into Set. Their natural equivalence judgment does not have proof terms or equality between equivalences and they do not support natural transformations. Additionally, they only consider ordinary categories as the intended model and do not develop a more general semantics. Riehl and Verity [43] use a formal language of virtual equipments to prove results valid for ∞-categories without concrete manipulation of model categories. They formalize this language as a theory in Makkai's framework of first-order logic with dependent sorts (FOLDS). While this previous work has the same models as VETT, we believe that the syntax we propose in this paper formalizes informal arguments more directly, as shown in Section 3. This is because FOLDS approach approach is entirely relational, whereas we formalize concepts like restriction of a profunctor or composition of natural transformations as functional operations (substitution). In particular, this means that our calculus requires only vertically degenerate squares (elements/natural transformations) as a "user-facing" notion, with general squares occurring only in the admissible substitution operations.

The coend calculus [33] is an informal syntax for manipulating profunctors involving ends and coends; an extension of VETT to treat profunctors of many variables of different variances may provide a formal treatment of it.

Myers [35] provides a string diagram calculus for double categories and pro-arrow equipments, generalizing string diagrams for monoidal categories. These are an alternative approach to type-theoretic calculi, with the string diagrams typically making tensor products simpler to work with, while a type-theoretic calculus like VETT makes the closed structure $P \triangleright^{\forall \alpha} Q$ simpler to work with by using bound variables.

Cartesian bicategories are similar to equipments but they axiomatize the bicategory of profunctors rather than the full double category of functors and profunctors [13]. Frey [23] describes preliminary work on a proof system for Cartesian bicateogires. Their profunctors are more general than in VETT in as they may have 0, 1 or more covariant or contravariant variables. But they do not have a term syntax for functors or natural transformations.

Our work in this paper fits broadly into a line of work on *directed dependent type theories*, a type theory where the identity type is interpreted as morphisms in a (possibly ∞-)category. In directed type theories based on a bisimplicial model [42,11,55,54], morphism types are defined using an interval object, like in cubical type theory [8,16,4,3], and universal properties like "morphism induction" are an internally definable property of certain types. Other type theories [38,1] define morphism types via an induction principle, corresponding to the lifting properties of certain kinds of fibrations of categories. While these previous works can express some constructions on Cat that are not expressible in VETT, because VETT is more restricted, VETT contrariwise has more models, for instance categories enriched in non-cartesian monoidal categories, so the theorems that are provable in VETT apply in more settings.

Finally, some variations on double categories have been used to model the structure of certain program logics. GTT [36] is a logic for *vertically thin* pro-arrow equipments, where there is at most one vertical arrow or 2-cell of any tyepe, so their calculus does not include functor or transformation judgments. Another similar calculus is System P [21] which is an internal language of *reflexive graph categories*, which are like double categories without horizontal composition.

In future work, VETT could incorporate functor categories by generalizing the unary type theory of functors to functors of many variables, in which case ordinary λ calculus can be used to define functor categories as function types, and incorporate multi-variable profunctors as in [23]. This would require to the models to have a monoidal structure. Ideas from coeffects and enriched category theory may be useful for defining opposite categories [48,10].

Acknowledgments. This material is based on research sponsored by the National Science Foundation under agreement number CCF-1909517 and the United States Air Force Research Laboratory under agreement number FA9550-21-0009 (Tristan Nguyen, program manager). The authors would like to thank David Jaz Myers, Emily Riehl, Mike Shulman, Dominic Verity for helpful feedback on this work.

References

1. Ahrens, B., North, P., van der Weide, N.: Semantics for two-dimensional type theory. In: ACM/IEEE Symposium on Logic in Computer Science (LICS) (2022)
2. Altenkirch, T., Capriotti, P., Kraus, N.: Extending homotopy type theory with strict equality. In: EACSL Annual Conference on Computer Science Logic (CSL) (2016)
3. Angiuli, C., Brunerie, G., Coquand, T., Hou (Favonia), K.B., Harper, R., Licata, D.R.: Syntax and models of cartesian cubical type theory. Mathematical Structures in Computer Science (2021)
4. Angiuli, C., Hou (Favonia), K.B., Harper, R.: Cartesian cubical computational type theory: Constructive reasoning with paths and equalities. In: Computer Science Logic (CSL) (2018)
5. Awodey, S., Warren, M.: Homotopy theoretic models of identity types. Mathematical Proceedings of the Cambridge Philosophical Society (2009)
6. Bénabou, J.: Introduction to bicategories. In: Reports of the Midwest Category Seminar. pp. 1–77. Springer Berlin Heidelberg, Berlin, Heidelberg (1967)
7. Bénabou, J.: Distributors at work. Lecture notes written by Thomas Streicher **11** (2000)
8. Bezem, M., Coquand, T., Huber, S.: The univalence axiom in cubical sets. Journal of Automated Reasoning (June 2018). https://doi.org/10.1007/s10817-018-9472-6
9. Birkedal, L., Møgelberg, R.E., Schwinghammer, J., Støvring, K.: First steps in synthetic guarded domain theory: step-indexing in the topos of trees. Logical Methods in Computer Science **Volume 8, Issue 4** (Oct 2012). https://doi.org/10.2168/LMCS-8(4:1)2012
10. Brunel, A., Gaboardi, M., Mazza, D., Zdancewic, S.: A core quantitative coeffect calculus. In: Proceedings of the 23rd European Symposium on Programming Languages and Systems - Volume 8410. p. 351–370 (2014). https://doi.org/10.1007/978-3-642-54833-8_19
11. Buchholtz, U., Weinberger, J.: Synthetic fibered $(\infty,1)$-category theory, higher Structures, to appear. arXiv:2105.01724
12. Cáccamo, M., Winskel, G.: A higher-order calculus for categories. In: Boulton, R.J., Jackson, P.B. (eds.) Theorem Proving in Higher Order Logics. pp. 136–153. Springer Berlin Heidelberg, Berlin, Heidelberg (2001)
13. Carboni, A., Walters, R.: Cartesian bicategories i. Journal of Pure and Applied Algebra **49**(1), 11–32 (1987). https://doi.org/https://doi.org/10.1016/0022-4049(87)90121-6
14. Cartmell, J.: Generalised algebraic theories and contextual categories. Annals of Pure and Applied Logic **32**, 209–243 (1986). https://doi.org/https://doi.org/10.1016/0168-0072(86)90053-9
15. Cervesato, I., Pfenning, F.: A linear logical framework. Information and Computation **179**(1), 19–75 (2002)
16. Cohen, C., Coquand, T., Huber, S., Mörtberg, A.: Cubical type theory: A constructive interpretation of the univalence axiom. In: Uustalu, T. (ed.) 21st International Conference on Types for Proofs and Programs (TYPES 2015). pp. 5:1–5:34 (2018). https://doi.org/10.4230/LIPIcs.TYPES.2015.5
17. Crutwell, G., Shulman, M.A.: A unified framework for generalized multicategories. Theory and Applications of Categories **24**, 580–655 (2010)
18. Curien, P.L.: Categorical combinators. Information and Control **69**(1), 188–254 (1986). https://doi.org/https://doi.org/10.1016/S0019-9958(86)80047-X

19. Di Liberti, I., Loregian, F.: On the unicity of formal category theories (2019). https://doi.org/10.48550/ARXIV.1901.01594
20. Dreyer, D., Ahmed, A., Birkedal, L.: Logical step-indexed logical relations. In: 2009 24th Annual IEEE Symposium on Logic In Computer Science. pp. 71–80 (2009). https://doi.org/10.1109/LICS.2009.34
21. Dunphy, B.P., Reddy, U.S.: Parametric limits. In: 19th IEEE Symposium on Logic in Computer Science (LICS 2004), 14-17 July 2004, Turku, Finland, Proceedings. pp. 242–251 (2004). https://doi.org/10.1109/LICS.2004.1319618
22. Dybjer, P.: Internal type theory. In: Berardi, S., Coppo, M. (eds.) Types for Proofs and Programs. pp. 120–134. Springer Berlin Heidelberg (1996)
23. Frey, J.: A language for closed cartesian bicategories (2019), category Theory 2019
24. Girard, J.Y.: Linear logic. Theoretical Computer Science **50**(1), 1–101 (1987). https://doi.org/https://doi.org/10.1016/0304-3975(87)90045-4
25. Grandis, M., Pare, R.: Limits in double categories. Cahiers de Topologie et Géométrie Différentielle Catégoriques **40**(3), 162–220 (1999)
26. Hofmann, M., Streicher, T.: The groupoid interpretation of type theory. In: Twenty-five years of constructive type theory. Oxford University Press (1998)
27. Isaev, V.: Indexed type theories. Mathematical Structures in Computer Science **31**(1), 3–63 (2021). https://doi.org/10.1017/S0960129520000092
28. Jung, R., Swasey, D., Sieczkowski, F., Svendsen, K., Turon, A., Birkedal, L., Dreyer, D.: Iris: Monoids and invariants as an orthogonal basis for concurrent reasoning. In: Proceedings of the 42nd Annual ACM SIGPLAN-SIGACT Symposium on Principles of Programming Languages. p. 637–650. POPL '15, Association for Computing Machinery (2015). https://doi.org/10.1145/2676726.2676980
29. Krishnaswami, N.R., Pradic, P., Benton, N.: Integrating dependent and linear types. In: ACM Symposium on Principles of Programming Languages (2015)
30. Lambek, J., Scott, P.: Introduction to Higher-Order Categorical Logic. Cambridge University Press (1988)
31. Lawvere, F.W.: Adjointness in foundations. Dialectica **23** (1969)
32. Leinster, T.: Generalized enrichment of categories. Journal of Pure and Applied Algebra **168**(2), 391–406 (2002). https://doi.org/https://doi.org/10.1016/S0022-4049(01)00105-0, category Theory 1999: selected papers, conference held in Coimbra in honour of the 90th birthday of Saunders Mac Lane
33. Loregian, F.: (Co)end Calculus. London Mathematical Society Lecture Note Series, Cambridge University Press (2021). https://doi.org/10.1017/9781108778657
34. Moggi, E.: Notions of computation and monads. Information and Computation **93**(1), 55–92 (1991). https://doi.org/https://doi.org/10.1016/0890-5401(91)90052-4, selections from 1989 IEEE Symposium on Logic in Computer Science
35. Myers, D.J.: String diagrams for double categories and equipments (2016). https://doi.org/10.48550/ARXIV.1612.02762
36. New, M.S., Licata, D.R.: Call-by-Name Gradual Type Theory. In: Kirchner, H. (ed.) 3rd International Conference on Formal Structures for Computation and Deduction (FSCD 2018). Leibniz International Proceedings in Informatics (LIPIcs), vol. 108, pp. 24:1–24:17. Schloss Dagstuhl–Leibniz-Zentrum fuer Informatik, Dagstuhl, Germany (2018). https://doi.org/10.4230/LIPIcs.FSCD.2018.24
37. New, M.S., Licata, D.R.: A formal logic for formal category theory (extended version) (2022). https://doi.org/10.48550/ARXIV.2210.08663, https://arxiv.org/abs/2210.08663
38. North, P.R.: Towards a directed homotopy type theory. In: Mathematical Foundations of Programming Semantics (MFPS) (2019)

39. Palmgren, E.: Categories with families and first-order logic with dependent sorts. Annals of Pure and Applied Logic **170**(12), 102715 (2019). https://doi.org/https://doi.org/10.1016/j.apal.2019.102715, `https://www.sciencedirect.com/science/article/pii/S0168007219300727`

40. Plotkin, G., Abadi, M.: A logic for parametric polymorphism. In: Bezem, M., Groote, J.F. (eds.) Typed Lambda Calculi and Applications. pp. 361–375. Springer Berlin Heidelberg, Berlin, Heidelberg (1993)

41. Polakow, J., Pfenning, F.: Natural deduction for intuitionistic non-communicative linear logic. In: Girard, J. (ed.) Typed Lambda Calculi and Applications, 4th International Conference, TLCA'99, L'Aquila, Italy, April 7-9, 1999, Proceedings. Lecture Notes in Computer Science, vol. 1581, pp. 295–309. Springer (1999). https://doi.org/10.1007/3-540-48959-2_21

42. Riehl, E., Shulman, M.: A type theory for synthetic ∞-categories. Higher Structures **1**(1) (2018)

43. Riehl, E., Verity, D.: Elements of ∞-Category Theory. Cambridge Studies in Advanced Mathematics, Cambridge University Press (2022). https://doi.org/10.1017/9781108936880

44. Robinson, E., Rosolini, G.: Reflexive graphs and parametric polymorphism. In: Proceedings Ninth Annual IEEE Symposium on Logic in Computer Science. pp. 364–371 (1994). https://doi.org/10.1109/LICS.1994.316053

45. Seely, R.A.G.: Locally cartesian closed categories and type theory. Mathematical Proceedings of the Cambridge Philosophical Society **95**(1), 33–48 (1984). https://doi.org/10.1017/S0305004100061284

46. Shulman, M.: Framed bicategories and monoidal fibrations. Theory and Applications of Categories **20**, 650–738 (2008), `http://www.tac.mta.ca/tac/volumes/20/18/20-18abs.html`

47. Shulman, M.: Enriched indexed categories. Theory and Applications of Categories **28**, 616–695 (2013), `http://www.tac.mta.ca/tac/volumes/28/21/28-21abs.html`

48. Shulman, M.: Contravariance through enrichment. Theory and Applications of Categories **33**, 95–130 (2018), `http://tac.mta.ca/tac/volumes/33/5/33-05abs.html`

49. Street, R., Walters, R.: Yoneda structures on 2-categories. Journal of Algebra **50**(2), 350–379 (1978). https://doi.org/https://doi.org/10.1016/0021-8693(78)90160-6, `https://www.sciencedirect.com/science/article/pii/0021869378901606`

50. Voevodsky, V.: A very short note on homotopy λ-calculus (September 2006), unpublished.

51. Voevodsky, V.: A type system with two kinds of identity types (2013), talk at Andre Joyal's 70th birthday conference (IAS)

52. Vákár, M.: A categorical semantics for linear logical frameworks. In: Foundations of Software Science and Computation Structures (FoSSaCS) (2015)

53. Wand, M.: Fixed-point constructions in order-enriched categories. Theoretical Computer Science **8**(1), 13–30 (1979). https://doi.org/https://doi.org/10.1016/0304-3975(79)90053-7

54. Weaver, M.Z., Licata, D.R.: A constructive model of directed univalence in bicubical sets. In: Proceedings of the 35th Annual ACM/IEEE Symposium on Logic in Computer Science. pp. 915–928. LICS '20, Association for Computing Machinery, New York, NY, USA (2020). https://doi.org/10.1145/3373718.3394794

55. Weinberger, J.: A Synthetic Perspective on $(\infty,1)$-Category Theory: Fibrational and Semantic Aspects. Ph.D. thesis, TU Darmstadt (2022), arXiv:2202.13132

56. Wood, R.J.: Abstract pro arrows I. Cahiers de Topologie et Géométrie Différentielle Catégoriques **23**(3), 279–290 (1982)

A Strict Constrained Superposition Calculus for Graphs

Rachid Echahed, Mnacho Echenim, Mehdi Mhalla, and Nicolas Peltier[✉]

Université Grenoble Alpes, LIG, CNRS, Inria, Grenoble INP,
38000 Grenoble, France
nicolas.peltier@imag.fr

Abstract. We propose a superposition-based proof procedure to reason on equational first order formulas defined over graphs. First, we introduce the considered graphs that are directed labeled graphs with lists of roots standing for pins or interfaces for replacements. Then the syntax and semantics of the considered logic are defined. The formulas at hand are clause sets built on equations and disequations on graphs. Afterwards, a sound and complete proof procedure is provided, and redundancy criteria are introduced to dismiss useless clauses and improve the efficiency of the procedure. In a first step, a set of inferences rules is provided in the case of uninterpreted labels. In a second step, the proposed rules are lifted to take into account labels defined as terms interpreted in some arbitrary theory. Particular formulas of interest are Horn clauses, for which stronger redundancy criteria can be devised. Essential differences with the usual term superposition calculus are emphasized.

1 Introduction

Graphs are ubiquitous structures in computer science. They are used to model several notions such as data, program runs (transition systems), networks, software and hardware architectures. They are also often used as foundational structures to model knowledge or data bases, cognitive or intelligent systems as well as physical, chemical or biological phenomena. They constitute, in addition, the basis of operational research or combinatorics. Graphs are, definitely, fundamental structures for modelling, computing and reasoning. Graph transformations have been studied since the early 70's [29]. Some of their applications can be found in [16,18]. In the literature, one can distinguish two main streams of approaches for graph transformation, namely the algebraic approaches [15,12] where category theory is used to define structure transformations in a very abstract and elegant way and the algorithmic approaches where graph transformations are defined by means of the actual algorithms involved in the transformations [20,13].

During the last decade, a very interesting application of graph transformations has emerged in the area of quantum models of computation, see e.g., the calculi ZX [11], ZH [3], ZW [24] or PBS [10]. In these calculi, one can specify quantum algorithms using particular graphs and can make some equational reasoning on them to verify correctness of quantum algorithms, see e.g. the

© The Author(s) 2023
O. Kupferman and P. Sobocinski (Eds.): FoSSaCS 2023, LNCS 13992, pp. 135–155, 2023.
https://doi.org/10.1007/978-3-031-30829-1_7

Quantomatic tool [25]. In such situations, making automated equational reasoning over graphs is very desirable even though equational theories over graphs are not recursively enumerable in general (see e.g. [7]).

The *superposition calculus* [1] is one of the most successful automated proof procedures which handles equational theories (on terms) which is being actually implemented in various theorem provers such as Vampire [28], Spass [32], or E [30]. The calculus operates on finite sets of equational clauses. It is defined as a set of *inference rules*, which deduce new clauses from previous ones. To prune the search space, strong restrictions (based on term orderings and literal selection functions) are imposed on the inferences, and redundancy criteria are provided to detect and dismiss useless clauses. The rules are applied until a contradiction (i.e., the empty clause) is derived or until the set is *saturated*, i.e., no further non-redundant clause may be deduced. The calculus is *refutationally complete*, in the sense that it is able to derive a contradiction from any unsatisfiable clause set. In a recent work [14], we proposed a superposition calculus for testing the unsatisfiability of sets of equations and disequations between graphs whose shapes are inspired by those used in the ZX calculus, where nodes are labeled by first-order (uninterpreted) terms. In the present paper we extend this work in several directions: (i) We tackle full clauses, i.e., disjunctions of equations and disequations. This extension turned out to be much more difficult than we initially expected, due to the fact that no reduction order exists on the considered graphs (see Examples 19 and 22), which complicates the completeness proof. We introduce redundancy criteria that cover some usual deletion and simplification rules. (ii) We lift the obtained calculus into a constrained calculus operating on graphs labeled by terms interpreted in some base theory. The procedure is a semi-decision procedure for unsatisfiability if the underlying theory is (semi) decidable and compact. (iii) We consider a slightly different class of graphs, where multi-edges are allowed. The new framework has the advantage of being both more general and simpler, and it also improves the efficiency of the calculus (more precisely for the computation of "merges" between graphs, see Remark 9).

Why defining a graph superposition calculus is difficult. We wish to emphasize some important differences between term and graph superposition. (i) It is well-known that term rewrite systems that are terminating and in which all critical pairs are joinable are confluent. This property plays a key rôle in the completeness proof of the superposition calculus. However, such a property does *not* hold for graph rewrite systems, and, worse, confluence is undecidable for terminating graph rewrite rules (if confluence is meant modulo isomorphism). As it is done in [14] we overcome this issue by considering a special class of graphs, for which the above property holds. This class is obtained by restricting the way graphs can be composed and replaced, using a sequence of distinguished nodes in the graphs, called roots. (ii) The usual superposition calculus is based on the use of a *reduction order*, i.e., a well-founded order on terms that is total on ground terms and closed under instantiation and embedding. Unfortunately no such order exists for graphs in general (see Example 19). Thus the model construction algorithm used to establish refutational completeness must cope with non terminating systems (indeed, since a ground equation $\mathfrak{g} \approx \mathfrak{h}$ cannot always be oriented, one must consider both rules: $\mathfrak{g} \to \mathfrak{h}$ and $\mathfrak{h} \to \mathfrak{g}$, which entails that the system does not terminate). Confluence is harder to establish for non terminating systems and we need to devise a new confluence criterion. (iii) The usual redundancy criterion of [1] (where a clause is considered redundant if it is implied by smaller clauses) does not apply to graphs. For instance the conclusion of an inference may be strictly bigger than all the premises (see Example 21). This is due to the fact that two graphs may overlap without one of them being included in the other. Such a behavior cannot be avoided, since, as proven in [14, Theorem 45], satisfiability is undecidable for sets of ground equational clauses defined on graphs (whereas it is well known to be decidable for standard ground clauses based on terms), thus superposition cannot terminate on ground graphs. Furthermore, we show (see Example 22) that the calculus is – rather surprisingly – not compatible with tautology deletion in general (tautology deletion is possible for Horn clauses).

Related work. The graphs we are considering are intended to capture (possibly cyclic) circuit shaped structures such as those used in the ZX or related calculi. They are close to hypergraphs with interfaces as used in some papers (see, e.g. [5]) where the roots or interfaces are used in the gluing process while transforming a graph. We follow an algorithmic approach when transforming the graphs. This approach eases the completeness proofs of the proposed superposition calculus. However, the performed graph transformations used in the present paper can be encoded as simple double pushout (DPO) [19] steps of the form $L \longleftarrow Roots \longrightarrow R$ with some additional constraints on matched subgraphs. It is also a particular case of DPOI steps (DPO with interfaces) where the roots play the rôle of the interfaces [5]. Automated reasoning in presence of graph structures is not an easy task in general. Several authors did tackle this problem and one can distinguish different approaches in the literature. Variants of Hoare-like calculi have been proposed for the verification of graph transformation systems see, e.g., [23,26,6,8]. Likewise, model checking procedures have also been devised in presence of graph structures see, e.g. [27,31]. In these works, a dynamic logic underlying program execution is assumed. In addition, a dedicated logic is used to express graph properties to be proven. Other techniques have been used to prove graph equivalences such as bisimulation [17] or normalization using terminating and confluent graph rewriting systems [9]. In the paper at hand, we are rather concerned by a refutational proof technique based on superposition dedicated to a class of graphs. Thus our proof procedure departs from all the aforementioned works. To our knowledge, only the report [22] presents a refutational procedure dedicated to ZX diagrams which is close to ours. However, the authors use the classical superposition calculus [1] over first-order terms and provide a translation from the considered graphs to first-order terms. Such translation needs the use of additional axioms encoding some graph properties such as associativity and commutativity of graph constructor operations. Such additional axioms are useless in our framework. The class of graph rewriting systems handled in our proof procedure are not necessarily terminating and thus we had to devise new criteria to ensure their (ground) confluence instead of using joinability of pre-critical pairs as done in [4].

The paper is organized as follows. Section 2 introduces some basic notations and defines the considered graphs and the operations used over them. In Section 3 the syntax and semantics of the formulas are introduced. In Section 4, a first set of inference rules is defined to test the satisfiability of sets of clauses where graphs are endowed with uninterpreted labels and its completeness is established modulo a redundancy criterion that captures usual deletion or simplification rules (such as subsumption). In Section 5 the obtained calculus is lifted to graphs labeled with terms that can be interpreted in some arbitrary theory and possibly containing variables. Completeness is guaranteed if the theory is semi-decidable and compact. This last calculus is proven complete and an enhanced redundancy test is proposed. Concluding remarks are given in Section 6. Due to lack of space, proofs are omitted.

2   Graphs and Graph Operations

We briefly review some usual definitions and notations. For any partial function f, we denote by $dom(f)$ the domain of f. If f and g are partial functions, we write $f(x) = g(x)$ to state that either $x \notin dom(f) \cup dom(g)$ or that $x \in dom(f) \cap dom(g)$ and the images of x by f and g are identical. Given a multiset $\mathfrak{m}$ and an element e, $\mathfrak{m}(e)$ denotes the multiplicity of e in $\mathfrak{m}$. For all multisets $\mathfrak{m}_1$ and $\mathfrak{m}_2$, we denote by $\mathfrak{m}_1 + \mathfrak{m}_2$ and $\mathfrak{m}_1 - \mathfrak{m}_2$ the sum and difference of $\mathfrak{m}_1$ and $\mathfrak{m}_2$, respectively. We write $\mathfrak{m}_1 \sqsubseteq \mathfrak{m}_2$ to state that $\mathfrak{m}_1$ is included in $\mathfrak{m}_2$. A multiset containing exactly the elements $e_1, \ldots, e_n$ is written $\{e_1, \ldots, e_n\}$. We denote by $\mathfrak{m}_1 \sqcup \mathfrak{m}_2$ the union of $\mathfrak{m}_1$ and $\mathfrak{m}_2$ (i.e., the minimal multiset containing $\mathfrak{m}_1$ and $\mathfrak{m}_2$) defined as follows: for all elements e, $(\mathfrak{m}_1 \sqcup \mathfrak{m}_2)(e) = \max(\mathfrak{m}_1(e), \mathfrak{m}_2(e))$. Finite sequences may sometimes be identified with sets if the order is not important, e.g., if $y = (y_1, \ldots, y_n)$, we may write $x \in y$ to state that $x = y_i$, for some $i = 1, \ldots, n$. We recall that a preorder is a binary relation that is reflexive and transitive. Any preorder $\leq$ may be associated with a strict order $<$ defined as follows: $x < y \iff (x \leq y \wedge y \nleq x)$.

The graphs we consider are directed, labeled graphs enriched with a sequence of distinguished nodes, called *roots*:

Definition 1. *Let $\mathcal{N}$ be a countably infinite set of nodes and let $\mathcal{L}$ be a set of labels, disjoint from $\mathcal{N}$. An $\mathcal{L}$-graph $\mathfrak{g}$ is a tuple $\langle N, E, R, L \rangle$, where:*
- *$N \subseteq \mathcal{N}$ is a finite set of nodes in $\mathcal{N}$, called vertices or nodes;*
- *E is a finite multiset of pairs in $N \times N$, called edges;*
- *R is a sequence of nodes in N, with no repetition, called the roots of $\mathfrak{g}$;*
- *L is a function mapping every node in $N \setminus R$ to a label in $\mathcal{L}$.*

The components N, E, R and L of a graph $\mathfrak{g}$ are denoted by $N_\mathfrak{g}$, $E_\mathfrak{g}$, $R_\mathfrak{g}$ and $L_\mathfrak{g}$, respectively. We denote by $\widehat{N}_\mathfrak{g}$ the set of nodes $\alpha \in N_\mathfrak{g}$ that do not occur in $R_\mathfrak{g}$. The profile *of a graph $\mathfrak{g}$, written $pr(\mathfrak{g})$, is the length of $R_\mathfrak{g}$.*

Example 2. The $\mathcal{L}$-graph $\mathfrak{g}$ with $N_\mathfrak{g} = \{\rho_1, \alpha, \beta\}$, $E_\mathfrak{g} = \{(\rho_1, \alpha), (\rho_1, \beta), (\alpha, \beta)\}$, $R_\mathfrak{g} = (\rho_1)$, $dom(L_\mathfrak{g}) = \{\alpha, \beta\}$, $L_\mathfrak{g}(\alpha) = 0$ and $L_\mathfrak{g}(\beta) = 1$ is depicted graphically as follows:

We write $\alpha : \ell$ to state that a node named α is labeled by ℓ. In many cases, the names of the non-root nodes will be irrelevant, and will thus be omitted. When possible, root nodes will be named $\rho_1, \rho_2, \rho_3, \ldots$ in this order.

In the following, $\mathcal{L}$-graphs will be considered up to a renaming of nodes. More precisely, the isomorphism relation on $\mathcal{L}$-graphs is defined as follows.

Definition 3. *An $\mathcal{N}$-renaming μ is an injective mapping from $\mathcal{N}$ to $\mathcal{N}$. It is extended to any $\mathcal{L}$-graph $\mathfrak{g}$ by replacing every occurrence of a node α by $\mu(\alpha)$. In particular, the function $L_{\mu(\mathfrak{g})}$ is defined as follows: $L_{\mu(\mathfrak{g})}(\alpha) = \ell$ iff $L_\mathfrak{g}(\beta) = \ell$ for some $\beta \in N_\mathfrak{g}$ such that $\mu(\beta) = \alpha$ ($L_{\mu(\mathfrak{g})}$ is well-defined since μ is injective). We write $\mathfrak{g} \equiv \mathfrak{h}$ if $\mathfrak{h} = \mu(\mathfrak{g})$, for some $\mathcal{N}$-renaming μ. It is easy to check that $\equiv$ is an equivalence relation. Two $\mathcal{L}$-graphs $\mathfrak{g}, \mathfrak{h}$ such that $\mathfrak{g} \equiv \mathfrak{h}$ are* isomorphic.

2.1 Subgraphs and Replacement

We define the notion of a subgraph. The definition is slightly stronger than the usual one in graph theory because it imposes that only nodes that are roots in the subgraph can be connected to a node outside the subgraph. These roots can be viewed as an "interface" which restricts the way graphs may be connected and composed.

Definition 4 (Subgraph). *A graph $\mathfrak{h}$ is a subgraph of $\mathfrak{g}$ (written $\mathfrak{h} \leq^g \mathfrak{g}$) if $N_\mathfrak{h} \subseteq N_\mathfrak{g}$, $E_\mathfrak{h} \sqsubseteq E_\mathfrak{g}$, $\widehat{N}_\mathfrak{h} \subseteq \widehat{N}_\mathfrak{g}$, $L_\mathfrak{h}(\alpha) = L_\mathfrak{g}(\alpha)$ for all $\alpha \in \widehat{N}_\mathfrak{h}$ and if a node α occurs in an edge in $E_\mathfrak{g} - E_\mathfrak{h}$ then $\alpha \notin \widehat{N}_\mathfrak{h}$.*

Example 5. Consider the $\mathcal{L}$-graphs $\mathfrak{h}$, $\mathfrak{i}$, $\mathfrak{j}$ and $\mathfrak{k}$ with respective roots (α, β), (β), (α) and (ρ_1), defined as follows:

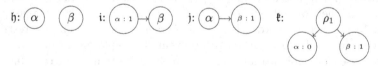

The $\mathcal{L}$-graph $\mathfrak{h}$ is a subgraph of the $\mathcal{L}$-graph $\mathfrak{g}$ from Example 2, but $\mathfrak{i}$, $\mathfrak{j}$ and $\mathfrak{k}$ are not. Indeed, α has different labels in $\mathfrak{g}$ and $\mathfrak{i}$; $\mathfrak{g}$ contains an edge between ρ_1 and β that does not occur in $\mathfrak{j}$ and β is not a root node in $\mathfrak{j}$; and $E_\mathfrak{g} - E_\mathfrak{k}$ contains the edge (α, β) between nodes that are not roots in $\mathfrak{k}$.

The replacement operation is defined in a natural way: all vertices and edges occurring from the replaced subgraph are deleted and replaced by those in the replacing graph (we assume that the considered graphs share the same roots).

Definition 6 (Subgraph replacement). *Let* $\mathfrak{g}$ *be an* $\mathcal{L}$-*graph and let* $\mathfrak{h}$ *be a subgraph of* $\mathfrak{g}$. *An* $\mathcal{L}$-*graph* $\mathfrak{i}$ *is substitutable for* $\mathfrak{h}$ *in* $\mathfrak{g}$ *if* $R_{\mathfrak{i}} = R_{\mathfrak{h}}$ *and* $N_{\mathfrak{g}} \cap \widehat{N}_{\mathfrak{i}} = \emptyset$. *If* $\mathfrak{i}$ *is substitutable for* $\mathfrak{h}$ *in* $\mathfrak{g}$, *then we denote by* $\mathfrak{g}\{\mathfrak{h} \leftarrow \mathfrak{i}\}$ *(the* $\mathcal{L}$-*graph obtained by replacing* $\mathfrak{h}$ *by* $\mathfrak{i}$ *in* $\mathfrak{g}$) *the tuple* $\langle N', E', R', L' \rangle$, *where:*

- $N' \overset{def}{=} (N_{\mathfrak{g}} \setminus N_{\mathfrak{h}}) \cup N_{\mathfrak{i}}$. *Note that since* $R_{\mathfrak{i}} = R_{\mathfrak{h}}$ *we have* $N' = (N_{\mathfrak{g}} \setminus \widehat{N}_{\mathfrak{h}}) \cup \widehat{N}_{\mathfrak{i}}$.
- $E' \overset{def}{=} (E_{\mathfrak{g}} - E_{\mathfrak{h}}) + E_{\mathfrak{i}}$.
- $R' \overset{def}{=} R_{\mathfrak{g}}$.
- $L'(\alpha) \overset{def}{=} \begin{cases} L_{\mathfrak{g}}(\alpha) & \text{if } \alpha \in N_{\mathfrak{g}} \setminus \widehat{N}_{\mathfrak{i}} \\ L_{\mathfrak{i}}(\alpha) & \text{if } \alpha \in \widehat{N}_{\mathfrak{i}} \end{cases}$ *for all* $\alpha \in N' \setminus R'$.

Example 7. Let $\mathfrak{i}'$ be the $\mathcal{L}$-graph with root (α, β) defined below. Using the $\mathcal{L}$-graphs $\mathfrak{g}$ and $\mathfrak{h}$ from Examples 2 and 5, we get the following $\mathcal{L}$-graph $\mathfrak{g}\{\mathfrak{h} \leftarrow \mathfrak{i}'\}$ (the edge (α, β) occurs twice because it occurs both in $E_{\mathfrak{i}'}$ and in $E_{\mathfrak{g}} - E_{\mathfrak{h}}$):

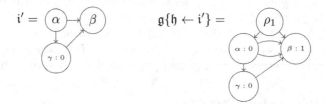

The notation $\mathfrak{g}\{\mathfrak{h} \leftarrow \mathfrak{i}\}$ is extended to the case where $pr(\mathfrak{i}) = pr(\mathfrak{h})$ as follows: $\mathfrak{g}\{\mathfrak{h} \leftarrow \mathfrak{i}\} \overset{def}{=} \mathfrak{g}\{\mathfrak{h} \leftarrow \mathfrak{i}'\}$, where $\mathfrak{i}'$ is any $\mathcal{L}$-graph substitutable for $\mathfrak{h}$ in $\mathfrak{g}$ such that $\mathfrak{i} \equiv \mathfrak{i}'$. Thus the replacement operation possibly involves a renaming step, to avoid conflicts on the names of the nodes. The next proposition states a straightforward property of subgraph replacement:

Proposition 8. *Let* $\mathfrak{g}, \mathfrak{h}, \mathfrak{i}, \mathfrak{j}$ *be* $\mathcal{L}$-*graphs, where* $\mathfrak{i} \leq^g \mathfrak{h} \leq^g \mathfrak{g}$ *and* $pr(\mathfrak{i}) = pr(\mathfrak{j})$. *Then* $\mathfrak{g}\{\mathfrak{h} \leftarrow \mathfrak{h}\{\mathfrak{i} \leftarrow \mathfrak{j}\}\} \equiv \mathfrak{g}\{\mathfrak{i} \leftarrow \mathfrak{j}\}$.

Remark 9. Note that Proposition 8 would not hold if edges were defined as sets and not as multisets. For instance, consider $\mathcal{L}$-graphs $\mathfrak{g}, \mathfrak{h}$ with two root nodes ρ_1, ρ_2, where $\mathfrak{g}$ contains an edge (ρ_1, ρ_2) and $\mathfrak{h}$ contains no edges. If edges are taken as sets then we get $\mathfrak{g}\{\mathfrak{h} \leftarrow \mathfrak{g}\} = \mathfrak{g}$ and $\mathfrak{g}\{\mathfrak{g} \leftarrow \mathfrak{h}\} = \mathfrak{h}$, whereas $\mathfrak{g}\{\mathfrak{h} \leftarrow \mathfrak{h}\} = \mathfrak{g}$. In our previous work [14], this problem was overcome by restricting ourselves to induced subgraphs (which prevents the replacement of $\mathfrak{h}$ by $\mathfrak{g}$ in $\mathfrak{g}$), but this causes a combinatorial explosion in the definition of the calculus: when one "merges" two subgraphs, it is necessary to add every possible combination of edges connecting a root of the first $\mathcal{L}$-graph to a root of the second one, yielding exponentially many solutions w.r.t. the number of roots (see [14, Definition 30]). Such a behavior is avoided in the new framework.

We now introduce a notion of orthogonality between graphs. The intuition is that two $\mathcal{L}$-graphs will be considered orthogonal if they share no edges and no nodes other than roots.

Definition 10 (Orthogonal graphs). *Let* $\mathfrak{g}$ *be an* $\mathcal{L}$*-graph. Two subgraphs* $\mathfrak{h}$ *and* $\mathfrak{i}$ *of* $\mathfrak{g}$ *are orthogonal in* $\mathfrak{g}$, *or simply orthogonal, if* $\widehat{N}_{\mathfrak{h}} \cap \widehat{N}_{\mathfrak{i}} = \emptyset$ *and* $E_{\mathfrak{h}} + E_{\mathfrak{i}} \sqsubseteq E_{\mathfrak{g}}$.

Note that $\mathfrak{h}$ and $\mathfrak{i}$ may share root nodes. Proposition 11 states that the result of the replacement of two orthogonal subgraphs does not depend on the order in which the $\mathcal{L}$-graphs are considered.

Proposition 11. *Let* $\mathfrak{g}$ *be an* $\mathcal{L}$*-graph, and let* $\mathfrak{h}_1, \mathfrak{h}_2$ *be orthogonal subgraphs of* $\mathfrak{g}$. *For all* $\mathcal{L}$*-graphs* $\mathfrak{i}_1, \mathfrak{i}_2$ *of respective profiles* $pr(\mathfrak{h}_1)$ *and* $pr(\mathfrak{h}_2)$, $\mathfrak{h}_2$ *and* $\mathfrak{h}_1$ *are subgraphs of* $\mathfrak{g}\{\mathfrak{h}_1 \leftarrow \mathfrak{i}_1\}$ *and* $\mathfrak{g}\{\mathfrak{h}_2 \leftarrow \mathfrak{i}_2\}$, *respectively, and* $\mathfrak{g}\{\mathfrak{h}_1 \leftarrow \mathfrak{i}_1\}\{\mathfrak{h}_2 \leftarrow \mathfrak{i}_2\} \equiv \mathfrak{g}\{\mathfrak{h}_2 \leftarrow \mathfrak{i}_2\}\{\mathfrak{h}_1 \leftarrow \mathfrak{i}_1\}$.

2.2 Graph Merging

Intuitively, a merge of two $\mathcal{L}$-graphs $\mathfrak{g}_1$ and $\mathfrak{g}_2$ denotes any minimal $\mathcal{L}$-graph containing all vertices, labels and edges in $\mathfrak{g}_1$ and $\mathfrak{g}_2$. More formally:

Definition 12. *A merge of two* $\mathcal{L}$*-graphs* $\mathfrak{g}_1$ *and* $\mathfrak{g}_2$ *is an* $\mathcal{L}$*-graph* $\mathfrak{h}$ *such that:* *(i)* $\mathfrak{g}_i \leq^g \mathfrak{h}$, *for all* $i = 1, 2$; *(ii)* $N_{\mathfrak{h}} = N_{\mathfrak{g}_1} \cup N_{\mathfrak{g}_2}$, $E_{\mathfrak{h}} = E_{\mathfrak{g}_1} \sqcup E_{\mathfrak{g}_2}$ *and* $\widehat{N}_{\mathfrak{h}} = \widehat{N}_{\mathfrak{g}_1} \cup \widehat{N}_{\mathfrak{g}_2}$; *(iii) for all* $i = 1, 2$ *and for all* $\alpha \in \widehat{N}_{\mathfrak{g}_i}$, $L_{\mathfrak{h}}(\alpha) = L_{\mathfrak{g}_i}(\alpha)$.

Note that in contrast to [14, Definition 30], the merge contains no node and edge other than those occurring in $\mathfrak{g}_1$ or $\mathfrak{g}_2$. Moreover, the multiplicity of edges is minimal ($E_{\mathfrak{h}}$ is defined as $E_{\mathfrak{g}_1} \sqcup E_{\mathfrak{g}_2}$ instead of $E_{\mathfrak{g}_1} + E_{\mathfrak{g}_2}$). It is easy to check that a merge of $\mathfrak{g}_1, \mathfrak{g}_2$ exists iff $L_{\mathfrak{g}_1}(\alpha) = L_{\mathfrak{g}_2}(\alpha)$ holds for all $\alpha \in \widehat{N}_{\mathfrak{g}_1} \cap \widehat{N}_{\mathfrak{g}_2}$. Moreover, all the merges are equal up to a permutation of their roots.

Example 13. Consider the following $\mathcal{L}$-graphs $\mathfrak{g}$ and $\mathfrak{h}$ below of respective roots (ρ_1, ρ_2) and (ρ_2, ρ_3), where the nodes α, β, γ are labeled by 0, 1 and 2, respectively. These $\mathcal{L}$-graphs admit the following merge $\mathfrak{i}$, of root (ρ_1, ρ_2, ρ_3):

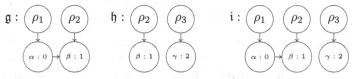

Example 14. Let $\mathfrak{g}, \mathfrak{h}, \mathfrak{i}$ and $\mathfrak{j}$ be the $\mathcal{L}$-graphs, defined as follows:

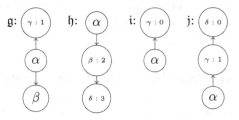

The $\mathcal{L}$-graph $\mathfrak{g}$ has roots (α, β) and $\mathfrak{h}, \mathfrak{i}, \mathfrak{j}$ have roots (α). Then $\mathfrak{g}$ and $\mathfrak{h}$ admit the following merge, of root (α):

In contrast, $\mathfrak{g}$ and $\mathfrak{i}$ admit no merge (since γ has different labels in the two graphs), and neither do $\mathfrak{g}$ and $\mathfrak{j}$ (due to the edge connecting the non-root node γ to δ, that is outside of $\mathfrak{g}$).

Lemma 15. *Let $\mathfrak{g}$ be an $\mathcal{L}$-graph and let $\mathfrak{h}, \mathfrak{i}$ be subgraphs of $\mathfrak{g}$. Then $\mathfrak{h}$ and $\mathfrak{i}$ admit a merge $\mathfrak{j}$, and for all merges $\mathfrak{j}$ of $\mathfrak{h}$ and $\mathfrak{i}$ we have $\mathfrak{j} \leq^{g} \mathfrak{g}$.*

3   An Equational Logic on Graphs

We now define equational clauses built on $\mathcal{L}$-graphs and their semantics.

Definition 16. *An* equation *is an unordered pair written $\mathfrak{g} \approx \mathfrak{h}$, where $\mathfrak{g}, \mathfrak{h}$ are $\mathcal{L}$-graphs such that $R_{\mathfrak{g}} = R_{\mathfrak{h}}$. A* literal *is either an equation (positive literal) or the negation of an equation, written $\mathfrak{g} \not\approx \mathfrak{h}$ (negative literal). A* clause *is a disjunction of literals. The disjunction may be empty, in which case the clause is written $\square$. A clause is* Horn *if it contains at most one positive literal. A set of clauses is* Horn *if it contains only Horn clauses.*

Note that we assume for technical convenience that the two members of an equation share the same roots. $\mathcal{N}$-renamings μ are extended to equations, literals and clauses in a straightforward way: $\mu(\mathfrak{g} \approx \mathfrak{h}) \overset{def}{=} \mu(\mathfrak{g}) \approx \mu(\mathfrak{h})$, $\mu(\mathfrak{g} \not\approx \mathfrak{h}) \overset{def}{=} \mu(\mathfrak{g}) \not\approx \mu(\mathfrak{h})$ and $\mu(C \vee D) \overset{def}{=} \mu(C) \vee \mu(D)$. The relation $\equiv$ is extended accordingly.

Sets of clauses built on $\mathcal{L}$-graphs will be interpreted w.r.t. a congruence on $\mathcal{L}$-graphs. Graph congruences are defined in same way as for terms, except that we also assume that they are closed under isomorphism.

Definition 17 (Graph Congruence). *A binary relation $\bowtie$ on $\mathcal{L}$-graphs is* closed under isomorphisms *if $\mathfrak{i} \bowtie \mathfrak{h}$ when $\mathfrak{g} \bowtie \mathfrak{h}$ and $\mathfrak{g} \equiv \mathfrak{i}$. It is* closed under embeddings *if $\mathfrak{h} \bowtie \mathfrak{i}$ entails $\mathfrak{g}\{\mathfrak{h} \leftarrow \mathfrak{i}\} \bowtie \mathfrak{g}$. A* congruence *is an equivalence relation on $\mathcal{L}$-graphs that is closed under isomorphisms and embeddings.*

Definition 18. *A congruence $\sim$* validates *an expression E (written $\sim\models E$) iff one of the following conditions holds: (i) E is an equation $\mathfrak{g} \approx \mathfrak{h}$ and $\mathfrak{g} \sim \mathfrak{h}$; (ii) E is a literal $\mathfrak{g} \not\approx \mathfrak{h}$ and $\mathfrak{g} \not\sim \mathfrak{h}$; (iii) E is a clause C and $\sim$ validates at least one literal in C; (iv) E is a set of clauses Γ and $\sim$ validates all the clauses in Γ. A congruence $\sim$ is a* model *of E if $\sim\models E$. An expression is* satisfiable *if it admits a model and* unsatisfiable *otherwise. A* tautology *is a clause that is true in all congruences.*

4   Superposition Calculus with Uninterpreted Labels

We define a superposition calculus for testing the satisfiability of sets of clauses. This calculus is *strict* (see, e.g., [2]) in the sense that it does not use the equational factorization rule (as defined in [1]), but uses instead the standard factorization rule that unifies both members of two equations. This choice is motivated by the fact that, as shown in Example 22, graph superposition is not compatible with tautology deletion (except when the clauses are Horn). Since tautology deletion is disabled for non-Horn clauses, equational factorization is not needed anyway. Selection functions are not considered, since they are not compatible with the redundancy criterion.

The usual superposition calculus [1] is parameterized by a *reduction order*, i.e., an order on terms that is well-founded, total on ground terms, and closed under substitutions and embeddings. In the case of $\mathcal{L}$-graphs, no such order possibly exists, if we also add the natural requirement that the order must be closed under renamings, as evidenced by the following example:

Example 19. Assume that an order $<$ exists, satisfying the following properties: $<$ is well-founded, closed under isomorphisms and embeddings, and total up to isomorphism (i.e., if $\mathfrak{g} \not\equiv \mathfrak{h}$ then either $\mathfrak{g} < \mathfrak{h}$ or $\mathfrak{h} < \mathfrak{g}$). Consider the $\mathcal{L}$-graphs $\mathfrak{g}$ and $\mathfrak{h}$ with roots $(\rho_1, \rho_2, \rho_3, \rho_4)$ and containing no labels, as well as the $\mathcal{L}$-graphs $\mathfrak{i}, \mathfrak{j}$ with an empty sequence of roots, where all nodes are labeled by 0:

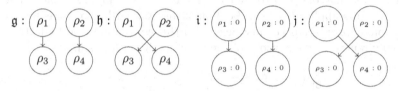

It is clear that $\mathfrak{g} \not\equiv \mathfrak{h}$. Indeed, if $\mu(\mathfrak{g}) = \mathfrak{h}$ holds for some $\mathcal{N}$-renaming μ, then $\mu(R_{\mathfrak{g}}) = R_{\mathfrak{h}}$, i.e., $\mu((\rho_1, \rho_2, \rho_3, \rho_4)) = (\rho_1, \rho_2, \rho_3, \rho_4)$, which entails that μ is the identity on these nodes. Thus we cannot have $\mu(E_{\mathfrak{g}}) = E_{\mathfrak{h}}$, as the first root (ρ_1) is connected to the third root (ρ_3) in $\mathfrak{g}$ and to the fourth one (ρ_4) in $\mathfrak{h}$. Consequently, we have either $\mathfrak{g} < \mathfrak{h}$ or $\mathfrak{h} < \mathfrak{g}$. Now we also have $\mathfrak{g} \leq^g \mathfrak{i}$ and $\mathfrak{h} \leq^g \mathfrak{j}$, and it is easy to check that $\mathfrak{i}\{\mathfrak{g} \leftarrow \mathfrak{h}\} = \mathfrak{j}$ and $\mathfrak{j}\{\mathfrak{h} \leftarrow \mathfrak{g}\} = \mathfrak{i}$. Thus we have either $\mathfrak{i} < \mathfrak{j}$ or $\mathfrak{j} < \mathfrak{i}$. But since $R_{\mathfrak{i}} = R_{\mathfrak{j}} = ()$ we have $\mathfrak{i} \equiv \mathfrak{j}$: indeed, if $\mu(\rho_1) = \rho_1$, $\mu(\rho_2) = \rho_2$, $\mu(\rho_3) = \rho_4$ and $\mu(\rho_4) = \rho_3$, then $\mu(\mathfrak{i}) = \mathfrak{j}$.

We thus slightly relax the requirement of having a reduction order, and consider instead a pre-order $<$ on $\mathcal{L}$-graphs, that is well-founded, closed under isomorphisms and embeddings, and contains $\leq^g$. We write $\mathfrak{g} < \mathfrak{h}$ if $\mathfrak{g} \leq \mathfrak{h}$ and $\mathfrak{h} \not\leq \mathfrak{g}$, and we write $\mathfrak{g} \simeq \mathfrak{h}$ if $\mathfrak{g} \leq \mathfrak{h}$ and $\mathfrak{h} \leq \mathfrak{g}$. We also assume that the equivalence classes of $\simeq$ are finite, up to isomorphism. It is clear that such pre-orders exist, for instance, the pre-order: $\mathfrak{g} \leq \mathfrak{h} \iff card(N_{\mathfrak{g}}) \leq card(N_{\mathfrak{h}})$ fulfills the above properties.

Similarly to the usual superposition calculus, we associate every literal L with a multiset defined as follows: $mset(\mathfrak{g} \not\approx \mathfrak{h}) \overset{def}{=} \{\{\mathfrak{g}, \mathfrak{h}\}\}$ and $mset(\mathfrak{g} \approx \mathfrak{h}) \overset{def}{=} \{\{\mathfrak{g}\}, \{\mathfrak{h}\}\}$. For every clause $C = L_1 \vee \cdots \vee L_n$, we define: $mset(C) \overset{def}{=} \{mset(L_i) \mid i = 1, \ldots, n\}$. Any order or preorder $\rhd$ on $\mathcal{L}$-graphs may then be extended into an order on clauses as follows: $C \rhd D \iff mset(C) \rhd_m mset(D)$, where $\rhd_m$ denotes the multiset extension of $\rhd$ (note that $\rhd_m$ is also a (pre)order). A literal L is $<$-*maximal* in a clause C if there is no literal $L' \in C$ such that $L' > L$. An $\mathcal{L}$-graph $\mathfrak{g}$ is $<$-*maximal* in a literal L if L contains no $\mathcal{L}$-graph $\mathfrak{g}'$ such that $\mathfrak{g}' > \mathfrak{g}$.

A literal L is *eligible* in a clause C if L is a $<$-maximal literal in C. Intuitively, eligible literals are those that may be considered for performing inferences. For instance, given a clause $(\mathfrak{g} \approx \mathfrak{h}) \vee (\mathfrak{i} \approx \mathfrak{j})$, if $(\mathfrak{g} \approx \mathfrak{h}) > (\mathfrak{i} \approx \mathfrak{j})$, then $\mathfrak{g} \approx \mathfrak{h}$ is eligible but not $\mathfrak{i} \approx \mathfrak{j}$. Consequently the inference rules (as defined in Section 4.1) will be allowed to replace $\mathfrak{g}$ by $\mathfrak{h}$ using the equation $\mathfrak{g} \approx \mathfrak{h}$ (provided $\mathfrak{g} \not< \mathfrak{h}$) but not, e.g., $\mathfrak{i}$ by $\mathfrak{j}$ (this restricts the number of inferences and prune the search space). Non eligible literals are simply attached to the conclusion of the inference but they play no active role until they (eventually) become eligible.

4.1   Inference Rules

The Superposition calculus $\mathtt{SC}$ is defined by the following rules: $\mathtt{Sp}^+$ (positive superposition), $\mathtt{Sp}^-$ (negative superposition), $\mathtt{R}$ (Reflection) and $\mathtt{F}$ (Factoring). The rules and their side conditions are very similar to those of the usual (ground) superposition calculus, except for the use of the merging operation for positive superposition. To simplify notations, the rules are defined modulo isomorphims, which means that one has to find a renaming of the premises such that the considered rule applies (this can be done using standard algorithms for finding graph homomorphisms). For instance, with this convention, the Reflection rule $\mathtt{R}$ actually removes all equations of the form $\mathfrak{g} \not\approx \mathfrak{h}$, with $\mathfrak{g} \equiv \mathfrak{h}$.

$$\mathtt{Sp}^+ : \frac{\mathfrak{g}_1 \approx \mathfrak{h}_1 \vee C_1 \quad \mathfrak{g}_2 \approx \mathfrak{h}_2 \vee C_2}{\mathfrak{i}\{\mathfrak{g}_1 \leftarrow \mathfrak{h}_1\} \approx \mathfrak{i}\{\mathfrak{g}_2 \leftarrow \mathfrak{h}_2\} \vee C_1 \vee C_2}$$

where:

1. $\mathfrak{i}$ is a merge of $\mathfrak{g}_1$ and $\mathfrak{g}_2$, and $\mathfrak{g}_1, \mathfrak{g}_2$ are not orthogonal;
2. $\mathfrak{g}_i \approx \mathfrak{h}_i$ is eligible in $\mathfrak{g}_i \approx \mathfrak{h}_i \vee C_i$ for $i = 1, 2$.
3. $\mathfrak{g}_i \not< \mathfrak{h}_i$ for $i = 1, 2$.

The non-orthogonality condition is the analogous of the non-variable condition of the usual calculus, it dismisses trivial replacements.

$$\mathtt{Sp}^- : \frac{\mathfrak{g} \approx \mathfrak{h} \vee C \quad \mathfrak{i} \not\approx \mathfrak{j} \vee D}{\mathfrak{i}\{\mathfrak{g} \leftarrow \mathfrak{h}\} \not\approx \mathfrak{j} \vee C \vee D}$$

where:

1. $\mathfrak{g} \leq^g \mathfrak{i}$;
2. $\mathfrak{g} \approx \mathfrak{h}$ and $\mathfrak{i} \not\approx \mathfrak{j}$ are eligible in $\mathfrak{g} \approx \mathfrak{h} \vee C$ and $\mathfrak{i} \not\approx \mathfrak{j} \vee D$, respectively.
3. $\mathfrak{g} \not< \mathfrak{h}$ and $\mathfrak{i} \not< \mathfrak{j}$.

$$\mathtt{F} : \frac{\mathfrak{g} \approx \mathfrak{h} \vee \mathfrak{g} \approx \mathfrak{h} \vee C}{\mathfrak{g} \approx \mathfrak{h} \vee C} \qquad \text{if } \mathfrak{g} \approx \mathfrak{h} \text{ is eligible in } \mathfrak{g} \approx \mathfrak{h} \vee \mathfrak{g} \approx \mathfrak{h} \vee C.$$

$$\mathtt{R} : \frac{\mathfrak{g} \not\approx \mathfrak{g} \vee C}{C} \qquad \text{if } \mathfrak{g} \not\approx \mathfrak{g} \text{ is eligible in } \mathfrak{g} \not\approx \mathfrak{g} \vee C.$$

Lemma 20. *The rules* $\mathtt{Sp}^+$, $\mathtt{Sp}^-$, $\mathtt{F}$ *and* $\mathtt{R}$ *are sound, i.e., for all congruences* $\sim$ *and for all clauses* C *deducible from a set of premises* Γ, *we have* $\sim \models \Gamma \implies \sim \models C$.

4.2   Redundancy

In the usual superposition calculus [1], a clause is redundant if all its ground instances are entailed by smaller clauses (w.r.t. the considered order). Such clauses can be deleted without threatening refutational completeness, which reduces the search space. In our context, such a definition cannot be used, because one of the inference rules –namely Sp^+– may generate clauses that are strictly larger than the premises (hence such clauses would be considered as redundant if the usual criterion were to be used).

Example 21. Consider the clauses: $\mathfrak{g} \approx \mathfrak{h}$ and $\mathfrak{i} \approx \mathfrak{j}$, where $\mathfrak{g}, \mathfrak{h}, \mathfrak{i}, \mathfrak{j}$ are $\mathcal{L}$-graphs with root (ρ_1) that are defined as follows:

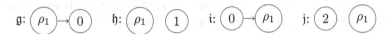

The $\mathcal{L}$-graphs $\mathfrak{g}$ and $\mathfrak{i}$ admit the following merge (of root (ρ_1)): (0)→(ρ_1)→(0)
Therefore, rule Sp^+ applies, yielding $\mathfrak{g}' \approx \mathfrak{g}''$, where:

$$\mathfrak{g}': (0) \to (\rho_1) \quad (1) \qquad \mathfrak{g}'': (2) \quad (\rho_1) \to (0)$$

If $\mathcal{L}$-graphs are ordered according to their number of nodes, then we have $(\mathfrak{g}' \approx \mathfrak{g}'') > (\mathfrak{g} \approx \mathfrak{h})$ and $(\mathfrak{g}' \approx \mathfrak{g}'') > (\mathfrak{i} \approx \mathfrak{j})$.

Worse, the calculus is actually incomplete if tautologies are deleted, as shown in the following example.

Example 22. Consider the $\mathcal{L}$-graphs $\mathfrak{g}_1, \mathfrak{g}_2$ and $\mathfrak{g}_3$ with roots (ρ_1, ρ_2, ρ_3):

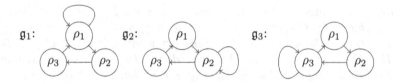

Let $\dot{\mathfrak{g}}_i$ denote the graph obtained from $\mathfrak{g}_i$ by adding one additional non root node α distinct from ρ_1, ρ_2, ρ_3, with some arbitrary (but fixed) label, e.g., 0. Assume that the graphs are ordered by the number of nodes, so that $\dot{\mathfrak{g}}_i > \mathfrak{g}_j$, $\dot{\mathfrak{g}}_i \simeq \dot{\mathfrak{g}}_j$ and $\mathfrak{g}_i \simeq \mathfrak{g}_j$ (for all $i, j \in \{1, 2, 3\}$). Let $\Gamma = \{\dot{\mathfrak{g}}_1 \approx \mathfrak{g}_2 \lor \dot{\mathfrak{g}}_2 \approx \mathfrak{g}_3 \lor \dot{\mathfrak{g}}_3 \approx \mathfrak{g}_1, \dot{\mathfrak{g}}_1 \not\approx \mathfrak{g}_2 \lor \dot{\mathfrak{g}}_2 \not\approx \mathfrak{g}_3 \lor \dot{\mathfrak{g}}_3 \not\approx \mathfrak{g}_1\}$. Intuitively, every equation $\dot{\mathfrak{g}}_i \approx \mathfrak{g}_j$ where $(i, j) \in \{(1, 2), (2, 3), (3, 1)\}$ states that the semantics of the graph is preserved when the isolated node is deleted and the graph is rotated by 90 degrees clockwise, for each possible position of the loop. Since the graphs are invariant by rotation, all these transformations are actually equivalent. It is easy to check that every clause that can be generated from Γ by applying the negative superposition rule from the first clause into the second clause contains two complementary literals (i.e. two literals of the form $\dot{g}_i \approx g_j$ and $\dot{g}_i \not\approx g_j$) hence is a tautology. Moreover, the clauses obtained by superposition using the first clause only either are subsumed by the first clause (if the superposition rule is applied on two different literals) or contains a literal $g_i \approx g_i$ (hence is a tautology). The equational factorization rule (as defined in [1]) does not apply since $\dot{g}_i$ and $\dot{g}_j$ are not isomorphic if $i \neq j$. However, consider the $\mathcal{L}$-graphs $g'_i, \dot{g}'_i$ which contain the same nodes and edges as g_i and $\dot{g}_i$ respectively, but with roots (ρ_2, ρ_3, ρ_1). It is clear that $g'_2 \equiv g_1$ and $g'_3 \equiv g_2$, so that $\dot{g}_1 \approx g_2 \models \dot{g}'_2 \approx g'_3$. However, $\dot{g}'_2 \leq^g \dot{g}_2$ and $\dot{g}_2\{\dot{g}'_2 \leftarrow g'_3\} = g_3$, thus $\dot{g}_1 \approx g_2 \models \dot{g}_2 \approx g_3$. By a similar reasoning, we may show that $\dot{g}_2 \approx g_3 \models \dot{g}_3 \approx g_1$ and $\dot{g}_3 \approx g_1 \models \dot{g}_1 \approx g_2$, so that the equations $\dot{g}_1 \approx g_2$, $\dot{g}_2 \approx g_3$, and $\dot{g}_3 \approx g_1$, are actually pairwise equivalent, which entails that Γ is unsatisfiable. However, $\square$ cannot be derived from Γ if the clauses containing complementary literals are discarded.

Thus, the conditions that ensure that a clause is redundant must be stronger than those of the usual superposition calculus. The definition proposed below covers usual deletion rules such as subsumption. Actually, two different criteria will be used, namely non-strict and strict redundancy, depending on whether the considered clauses are Horn or not. Indeed, in the former case a slightly less restrictive definition can be used, which permits the deletion of (some) tautological clauses.

Definition 23. *Let C, D be two clauses and let Γ be a set of clauses. We say that C is subsumed by D and write $C \geq^{sub} D$ if $C = D \vee C'$, up to associativity and commutativity of $\vee$ and isomorphism. We write $C \rightarrow_\Gamma D$ (C demodulates to D w.r.t. Γ) if C is of the form $g \bowtie h \vee E$ (with $\bowtie \in \{\approx, \not\approx\}$), $D = g\{i \leftarrow j\} \bowtie h \vee E$, and there exists a clause $F \in \Gamma$ such that $F = (i \approx j) \vee F'$, with $F' \leq^{sub} E$, $i > j$, $F' < (i \approx j)$ and $(i \approx j) < (g \bowtie h)$.*

The set of clauses that are redundant w.r.t. a set of clauses Γ is defined inductively as follows. A clause C is redundant w.r.t. Γ iff one of the following conditions holds: (1) C contains two literals $g_1 \approx g_2$ and $g'_1 \not\approx g'_2$, with $g_i \equiv g'_i$ for $i = 1, 2$; (2) C contains a literal of the form $g \approx h$ with $g \equiv h$; (3) $C \geq^{sub} D$, for some $D \in \Gamma$; (4) $C \rightarrow_\Gamma D$ and D is redundant. The set of strictly redundant ground clauses is defined in a similar way, except that Item 1 is removed.

Intuitively, the conditions ensuring that C demodulates to D in Definition 23 are meant to ensure that D may be deduced from C by applying the rule Sp^+ or Sp^- using the clause F (with $D < C$ and $F < C$) and that $\{D\} \cup \Gamma$ is equivalent to $\{C\} \cup \Gamma$. In particular, the condition $F' \leq^{sub} E$ ensures that all the literals added by the inference already occur in C.

Definition 24. *A set of clauses Γ is saturated (resp. strictly saturated) if every clause that can be deduced from premises in Γ using one of the rules of SC (in one step) is redundant (resp. strictly redundant) w.r.t. Γ.*

We prove that SC is refutationally complete. We actually establish two completeness results, the first one for general clauses and the second one for Horn clauses. The latter is stronger since it uses the weaker non-strict saturatedness criterion instead of strict saturatedness.

Theorem 25. *Let Γ be a set of clauses. If $\square \notin \Gamma$ and Γ is strictly saturated or both Horn and saturated then Γ is satisfiable.*

5   A Constrained Graph Superposition Calculus

We now lift the calculus SC defined in Section 4 into a constrained calculus. The goal is to handle graphs labeled by terms interpreted in some arbitrary theory, and possibly containing variables. To this aim, we attach constraints to the clauses, which are formulas interpreted in the considered theory, asserting conditions on the labels. Such constraints will be updated when inference rules will be applied, by asserting the conditions that are required by the rule applications.

5.1   Constrained Clauses

Let $\mathcal{V}$ be a countably infinite set of *variables* and let Σ be a set of *function symbols*[1]. Each symbol f in Σ is associated with a unique *arity* $\#(f)$. We denote by $\mathcal{T}$ the set of *terms* built inductively as usual on $\mathcal{V}$ and Σ, and by $\mathcal{C}$ the set of first-order formulas, called *constraints*, built inductively as usual on atoms of the form $t \doteq s$, where $t, s \in \mathcal{T}$ using the logical connectives $\vee, \wedge, \neg, \Rightarrow, \Leftrightarrow$, the quantifiers $\exists, \forall$ and two logical constants $\bot$ and $\top$.

A *substitution* σ is a function mapping all variables x to a term $x\sigma$. The *domain* $dom(\sigma)$ of σ is the set of variables x such that $x\sigma \neq x$. For every term or formula e, we denote by $e\sigma$ the term or formula obtained from e by replacing every (free) variable x by $x\sigma$. A term is *ground* if it contains no variables, and a substitution σ is *ground* if $x\sigma$ is ground for all $x \in dom(\sigma)$.

$\mathcal{T}$-*graphs* are $\mathcal{L}$-graphs with labels in $\mathcal{T}$. A $\mathcal{T}$-*clause* is a clause defined on $\mathcal{T}$-graphs. Substitutions are extended to $\mathcal{T}$-graphs and $\mathcal{T}$-clauses as follows. For every $\mathcal{T}$-graph $\mathfrak{g}$, we denote by $\mathfrak{g}\sigma$ the $\mathcal{T}$-graph such that: $F_{\mathfrak{g}\sigma} = F_{\mathfrak{g}}$ for all $F \in \{N, E, R\}$ and $L_{\mathfrak{g}\sigma}(\alpha) = L_{\mathfrak{g}}(\alpha)\sigma$, for all $\alpha \in \widehat{N}_{\mathfrak{g}}$. Then: $(\mathfrak{g} \approx \mathfrak{h})\sigma \stackrel{def}{=} \mathfrak{g}\sigma \approx \mathfrak{h}\sigma$, $(\mathfrak{g} \not\approx \mathfrak{h})\sigma \stackrel{def}{=} \mathfrak{g}\sigma \not\approx \mathfrak{h}\sigma$ and $(C \vee D)\sigma \stackrel{def}{=} C\sigma \vee D\sigma$. A $\mathcal{T}$-graph $\mathfrak{g}$ is *ground* if for all $\alpha \in \widehat{N}_{\mathfrak{g}}$, $L_{\mathfrak{g}}(\alpha)$ is ground. A $\mathcal{T}$-clause is *ground* if all the $\mathcal{T}$-graphs occurring in it are ground. For every expression (term, $\mathcal{T}$-graph, constraint or $\mathcal{T}$-clause) E, we denote by $\mathcal{V}(E)$ the set of variables (freely) occurring in E.

Definition 26. *A constrained clause (or c-clause) is a pair $[C \mid \phi]$, where C is a $\mathcal{T}$-clause and $\phi \in \mathcal{C}$.*

Let $\mathcal{I}$ be some fixed set of first-order interpretations on the signature Σ. For all $I \in \mathcal{I}$, we denote by $dom(I)$ the domain of I and by f^I the interpretation of the function f (with $f \in \Sigma$). For every ground term t and for all $I \in \mathcal{I}$, we denote by $[t]^I$ the value of t in I, inductively defined as usual. To simplify

---

[1] As usual, predicates may be encoded as functions.

notations, we assume that for every $I \in \mathcal{I}$ and for every $e \in dom(I)$, there exists a ground term t such that $[t]^I = e$.

The satisfiability relation $\models$ relating interpretations in $\mathcal{I}$ and constraints in $\mathcal{C}$ is defined as usual, where $\doteq$ is interpreted as the identity, and $\bot$ and $\top$ are interpreted as false and true, respectively. We write $\phi \models_{\mathcal{I}} \psi$ if the implication $I \models \phi\sigma \implies I \models \psi\sigma$ holds for all $I \in \mathcal{I}$ and for all ground substitutions of domain $\mathcal{V}(\phi) \cup \mathcal{V}(\psi)$; and $\phi \equiv_{\mathcal{I}} \psi$ iff $\phi \models_{\mathcal{I}} \psi$ and $\psi \models_{\mathcal{I}} \phi$. For any set of constraints, we write $I \models S$ iff $I \models \phi$ for all $\phi \in S$. For any constraint (or set of constraints) ϕ, if there exists a ground substitution σ with domain $\mathcal{V}(\phi)$ and an interpretation $I \in \mathcal{I}$ such that $I \models \phi\sigma$, then ϕ is $\mathcal{I}$-satisfiable (and $\mathcal{I}$-unsatisfiable otherwise). For instance, the fixed set of first-order interpretations may be the set $\mathcal{I}_1$ of first-order interpretations on Σ that satisfy the above condition on the domain (this is not restrictive provided there are infinitely many ground terms), in which case $\mathcal{I}$-satisfiability is simply the standard satisfiability in first-order clausal logic, or the set $\mathcal{I}_\mathbb{N}$ of interpretations of domain $\mathbb{N}$ interpreting the functions $0, 1, +$ as usual. We say that $\mathcal{I}$ is *compact* if for every $\mathcal{I}$-unsatisfiable set of constraints S there exists a finite set $S' \subseteq S$ such that S' is $\mathcal{I}$-unsatisfiable. It is well-known that $\mathcal{I}_1$ is compact [21] and that $\mathcal{I}_\mathbb{N}$ is not compact[2].

Any ground $\mathcal{T}$-graph may be transformed into a $dom(I)$-graph by replacing the labels by their interpretations in I. More formally:

Definition 27. *For all $I \in \mathcal{I}$ and for all ground $\mathcal{T}$-graphs $\mathfrak{g}$ we denote by $[\mathfrak{g}]^I$ the graph such that $F_{[\mathfrak{g}]^I} = F_{\mathfrak{g}}$ for all $F \in \{N, E, R\}$ and $L_{[\mathfrak{g}]^I}(\alpha) = [L_{\mathfrak{g}}(\alpha)]^I$, for all $\alpha \in \widehat{N}_{\mathfrak{g}}$. For every ground $\mathcal{T}$-clause C, we denote by $[C]^I$ the clause obtained from C by replacing every $\mathcal{T}$-graph $\mathfrak{g}$ by $[\mathfrak{g}]^I$. For all sets of c-clauses Γ, we denote by $[\Gamma]^I$ the set of clauses of the form $[C\sigma]^I$, where $C \in \Gamma$ and σ is a substitution mapping every variable in C to a ground term.*

Note that by definition, all the labels of $[\mathfrak{g}]^I$ are elements of the domain of I. Proposition 28 follows immediately from Definition 27.

Proposition 28. *Let $\mathfrak{g}, \mathfrak{h}$ be $\mathcal{T}$-graphs, let $I \in \mathcal{I}$ and let σ be a ground substitution with domain $\mathcal{V}(\mathfrak{g}) \cup \mathcal{V}(\mathfrak{h})$. If $\mathfrak{g} \equiv \mathfrak{h}$ then $[\mathfrak{g}\sigma]^I \equiv [\mathfrak{h}\sigma]^I$.*

Definition 29. *An $\mathcal{I}$-interpretation is a pair $(I, \sim)$, where $I \in \mathcal{I}$ and $\sim$ is a congruence on $dom(I)$-graphs. An $\mathcal{I}$-interpretation $(I, \sim)$ validates a set of c-clauses Γ (written $(I, \sim) \models \Gamma$) if $\sim \models [\Gamma]^I$.*

5.2 Lifting the Calculus

In the constrained calculus, the equality of labels will not be checked when an inference rule is applied. Instead, the corresponding conditions will be extracted from the considered graphs and added to the constraints of the conclusion. We first introduce a relation stating that two $\mathcal{T}$-graphs are identical up to their

---

[2] For instance, the set $\{n \doteq i \mid i \in \mathbb{N}\}$ is unsatisfiable if n is interpreted as a natural number, but admits no finite unsatisfiable subset.

labels. This relation is parameterized by a constraint that asserts conditions on the labels ensuring that the graphs are identical (modulo $\mathcal{I}$).

Definition 30. *Let* $\mathfrak{g}, \mathfrak{h}$ *be two* $\mathcal{T}$*-graphs and let* $\phi \in \mathcal{C}$*. We write* $\mathfrak{g} =_\phi \mathfrak{h}$ *if* $N_\mathfrak{g} = N_\mathfrak{h}$*,* $E_\mathfrak{g} = E_\mathfrak{h}$*,* $R_\mathfrak{g} = R_\mathfrak{h}$*, and* $\phi = \bigwedge_{\alpha \in \widehat{N}_\mathfrak{g}} (L_\mathfrak{g}(\alpha) \doteq L_\mathfrak{h}(\alpha))$ *(up to associativity and commutativity of* $\wedge$*).*

Example 31. Consider the $\mathcal{T}$-graphs $\mathfrak{g}$ and $\mathfrak{h}$ below, of root (ρ_1). We have $\mathfrak{g} =_\phi \mathfrak{h}$, with $\phi = (x \doteq 0 \wedge 0 \doteq y)$.

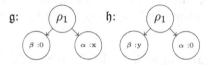

Every relation between $\mathcal{T}$-graphs or $\mathcal{T}$-clauses may be adapted in a similar way, keeping the conditions on the nodes, edges and roots, and asserting conditions ensuring that the label of every given node is unique (up to equality modulo $\mathcal{I}$). Definitions 32 and 33 lift the subgraph and subsumption relations, respectively:

Definition 32. *We write* $\mathfrak{h} \leq_\phi^\mathfrak{g} \mathfrak{g}$ *if* $N_\mathfrak{h} \subseteq N_\mathfrak{g}$*;* $E_\mathfrak{h} \sqsubseteq E_\mathfrak{g}$*; every node* $\alpha \in N_\mathfrak{h}$ *occurring in* $R_\mathfrak{g}$ *also occurs in* $R_\mathfrak{h}$*; if* $\alpha \in N_\mathfrak{h}$ *occurs in an edge in* $E_\mathfrak{g} \setminus E_\mathfrak{h}$ *then* $\alpha \in R_\mathfrak{h}$*, and* $\phi = \bigwedge_{\alpha \in \widehat{N}_\mathfrak{h}} L_\mathfrak{h}(\alpha) \doteq L_\mathfrak{g}(\alpha)$*. The notation* $\mathfrak{g}\{\mathfrak{h} \leftarrow \mathfrak{i}\}$ *may be extended to the case where* $\mathfrak{h} \leq_\phi^\mathfrak{g} \mathfrak{g}$ *(following Definition 6). Orthogonality is extended accordingly (as it does not depend on labels).*

Definition 33. *We write* $C \leq_\phi^{sub} D$ *if* C *and* D *are respectively of the form (up to associativity and commutativity of* $\vee$ *and isomorphism):* $\bigvee_{i=1}^n \mathfrak{g}_i \bowtie_i \mathfrak{h}_i$*, and* $\bigvee_{i=1}^n \mathfrak{g}_i' \bowtie_i \mathfrak{h}_i' \vee D'$*, with* $\mathfrak{g}_i =_{\phi_i} \mathfrak{g}_i'$*,* $\mathfrak{h}_i =_{\psi_i} \mathfrak{h}_i'$ *(for all* $i = 1, \ldots, n$*) and* $\phi = \bigwedge_{i=1}^n (\phi_i \wedge \psi_i)$*.*

The notion of a merge is extended analogously:

Definition 34. *A* ϕ*-merge of two* $\mathcal{T}$*-graphs* $\mathfrak{g}_1$ *and* $\mathfrak{g}_2$ *is a* $\mathcal{T}$*-graph* $\mathfrak{h}$ *such that:*
- $N_\mathfrak{h} = N_{\mathfrak{g}_1} \cup N_{\mathfrak{g}_2}$*,* $E_\mathfrak{h} = E_{\mathfrak{g}_1} \sqcup E_{\mathfrak{g}_2}$*, and* $\widehat{N}_\mathfrak{h} = \widehat{N}_{\mathfrak{g}_1} \cup \widehat{N}_{\mathfrak{g}_2}$*.*
- *For every node* $\alpha \in \widehat{N}_\mathfrak{h}$*, we have* $L_\mathfrak{h}(\alpha) = L_{\mathfrak{g}_i}(\alpha)$*, for some (arbitrarily chosen)* $i = 1, 2$ *such that* $L_{\mathfrak{g}_i}(\alpha)$ *is defined.*
- $\phi = \bigwedge_{\alpha \in \widehat{N}_{\mathfrak{g}_1} \cap \widehat{N}_{\mathfrak{g}_2}} L_{\mathfrak{g}_1}(\alpha) \doteq L_{\mathfrak{g}_2}(\alpha)$*.*

We now lift the order relation. Let $\leq_I$ (for $I \in \mathcal{I}$) be a family of well-founded preorders on $dom(I)$-$\mathcal{T}$-graphs that are closed under isomorphisms and embeddings and contain $\leq^\mathfrak{g}$. Let $\leq_\phi$ (for $\phi \in \mathcal{C}$) be a family of pre-orders on $\mathcal{T}$-graphs satisfying the following conditions: $\mathfrak{g} >_\phi \mathfrak{h} \implies \mathfrak{g} >_\psi \mathfrak{h}$, for all constraints ϕ, ψ such that $\psi \models_\mathcal{I} \phi$, and $(I \models \phi \wedge \mathfrak{g} >_\phi \mathfrak{h}) \implies [\mathfrak{g}]^I >_I [\mathfrak{h}]^I$. The simplest solution in practice is to order $\mathcal{T}$-graphs according to their number of nodes, in which case the order does not depend on I or ϕ: $\mathfrak{g} \leq_I \mathfrak{h} \iff \mathfrak{g} \leq_\phi$

$\mathfrak{h} \iff card(N_{\mathfrak{g}}) \leq card(N_{\mathfrak{h}})$. However, our framework is meant to be general enough to cope with orders that take labels into account.

A literal L is *maximal* in a c-clause $[C \mid \phi]$ if there is no literal $L' \in C$ such that $L' >_\phi L$. It is *eligible* in a c-clause $[C \mid \phi]$ if L is a $>_\phi$-maximal literal in C.

We are now in the position to define the constrained inference rules. As for the rules in Section 4.1, they apply modulo isomorphism. We assume as for the standard resolution or superposition calculus that the premises share no variables. In every rule, the conclusion inherits the constraints of the premises together with additional conditions on the labels which makes the inference valid. In all rules, the eligibility condition is tested after adding all the constraints enabling the inference, as this yields the most restrictive condition, thus reducing the branching factor.

$$\text{Sp}^+ : \frac{[\mathfrak{g}_1 \approx \mathfrak{h}_1 \vee C_1 \mid \phi_1] \quad [\mathfrak{g}_2 \approx \mathfrak{h}_2 \vee C_2 \mid \phi_2]}{[\mathfrak{i}\{\mathfrak{g}_1 \leftarrow \mathfrak{h}_1\} \approx \mathfrak{i}\{\mathfrak{g}_2 \leftarrow \mathfrak{h}_2\} \vee C_1 \vee C_2 \mid \phi_1 \wedge \phi_2 \wedge \psi]}$$

where:

1. $\mathfrak{i}$ is a ψ-merge of $\mathfrak{g}_1$ and $\mathfrak{g}_2$ and $\mathfrak{g}_1$ and $\mathfrak{g}_2$ are not orthogonal;
2. $\mathfrak{g}_i \approx \mathfrak{h}_i$ is eligible in $[\mathfrak{g}_i \approx \mathfrak{h}_i \vee C_i \mid \phi_1 \wedge \phi_2 \wedge \psi]$ (for all $i = 1, 2$);
3. $\mathfrak{g}_i \not<_{\phi_1 \wedge \phi_2 \wedge \psi} \mathfrak{h}_i$ (for all $i = 1, 2$).

$$\text{Sp}^- : \frac{[\mathfrak{g} \approx \mathfrak{h} \vee C \mid \phi] \quad [\mathfrak{i} \not\approx \mathfrak{j} \vee D \mid \psi]}{[\mathfrak{i}\{\mathfrak{g} \leftarrow \mathfrak{h}\} \not\approx \mathfrak{j} \vee C \vee D \mid \phi \wedge \psi \wedge \xi]}$$

where:

1. $\mathfrak{g} \leq^g_\xi \mathfrak{i}$ (note that ξ is uniquely defined by Definition 32);
2. $\mathfrak{g} \approx \mathfrak{h}$ and $\mathfrak{i} \not\approx \mathfrak{j}$ are eligible in $[\mathfrak{g} \approx \mathfrak{h} \vee C \mid \phi \wedge \psi \wedge \xi]$ and $[\mathfrak{i} \not\approx \mathfrak{j} \vee D \mid \phi \wedge \psi \wedge \xi]$, respectively;
3. $\mathfrak{g} \not<_{\phi \wedge \psi \wedge \xi} \mathfrak{h}$ and $\mathfrak{i} \not<_{\phi \wedge \psi \wedge \xi} \mathfrak{j}$.

$$\text{F} : \frac{[\mathfrak{g} \approx \mathfrak{h} \vee \mathfrak{g}' \approx \mathfrak{h}' \vee C \mid \phi]}{[\mathfrak{g} \approx \mathfrak{h} \vee C \mid \phi \wedge \psi \wedge \psi']}$$

where $\mathfrak{g} \approx \mathfrak{h}$ is eligible in $[\mathfrak{g} \approx \mathfrak{h} \vee \mathfrak{g}' \approx \mathfrak{h}' \vee C \mid \phi \wedge \psi \wedge \psi']$, $\mathfrak{g} =_\psi \mathfrak{g}'$, and $\mathfrak{h} =_{\psi'} \mathfrak{h}'$.

$$\text{R} : \frac{[\mathfrak{g} \not\approx \mathfrak{h} \vee C \mid \phi]}{[C \mid \phi \wedge \psi]}$$

where $\mathfrak{g} \not\approx \mathfrak{h}$ is eligible in $[\mathfrak{g} \not\approx \mathfrak{h} \vee C \mid \phi \wedge \psi]$ and $\mathfrak{g} =_\psi \mathfrak{h}$.

5.3   Soundness and Refutational Completeness

We establish the soundness and completeness of the constrained calculus, by lifting the corresponding properties for the base calculus. Note that semi decidability holds only if the base theory is semi-decidable[3] and compact (otherwise it is easy to see that unsatisfiability is not semi-decidable in general).

---

[3] in the sense that there exists a semi-decision procedure to check whether a formula in $\mathcal{C}$ is unsatisfiable.

Lemma 35. *The rules* Sp^+, Sp^-, F *and* R *(applied on c-clauses) are sound, i.e., for all* $\mathcal{I}$-*interpretations* $(I, \sim)$ *and for all c-clauses* $[C \mid \phi]$ *deducible for a set of premises* Γ, *we have* $(I, \sim) \models \Gamma \implies (I, \sim) \models [C \mid \phi]$.

The redundancy criterion may be lifted as follows:

Definition 36. *A c-clause* $[C \mid \phi]$ *is (strictly)* $\mathcal{I}$-*redundant in a set of c-clauses* Γ *if for all ground substitutions* σ *of domain* $\mathcal{V}(C) \cup \mathcal{V}(\phi)$ *and for all* $I \in \mathcal{I}$ *such that* $I \models \phi\sigma$, *the clause* $[C\sigma]^I$ *is (strictly) redundant in* $[\Gamma]^I$.

A set of c-clauses Γ *is (strictly) saturated if every c-clause that is deducible from* Γ *by the rules above is (strictly)* $\mathcal{I}$-*redundant in* Γ.

Theorem 37. *Let* Γ *be a set of c-clauses. If* Γ *is unsatisfiable and strictly saturated or Horn and saturated, then* Γ *contains a set of c-clauses* $\{[\square \mid \phi_I] \mid I \in \mathcal{I}\}$ *such that for every* $I \in \mathcal{I}$, $I \models \exists \boldsymbol{x}_I.\phi_i$, *with* $\boldsymbol{x}_I = \mathcal{V}(\phi_I)$. *If, moreover,* $\mathcal{I}$ *is compact, then* Γ *contains a finite set of c-clauses* $\{[\square \mid \phi_i] \mid i = 1, \dots, n\}$ *such that* $\bigwedge_{i=1}^{n} \neg(\exists \boldsymbol{x}.\phi_i)$ *is* $\mathcal{I}$-*unsatisfiable, with* $\boldsymbol{x}_i = \mathcal{V}(\phi_i)$.

5.4 Redundancy Testing

The redundancy criterion in Definition 36 is very general, but it may be difficult to test in practice. We thus introduce a second notion of redundancy, defined directly on constrained clauses, that is stronger and easier to decide.

Definition 38. *Let* $[C \mid \phi], [D \mid \psi]$ *be two clauses and let* Γ *be a set of clauses. Let* $\boldsymbol{x}$ *and* $\boldsymbol{y}$ *be the vectors of variables occurring in* $[C \mid \phi]$ *and* $[D \mid \psi]$, *respectively (we assume by renaming that* $\boldsymbol{x}$ *and* $\boldsymbol{y}$ *share no variable).*

We say that $[C \mid \phi]$ *is subsumed by* $[D \mid \psi]$ *and we write* $[C \mid \phi] \geq^{sub} [D \mid \psi]$ *if there exists* $\xi \in \mathcal{C}$ *such that* $D \leq^{sub}_{\xi} C$ *and* $\phi \models_{\mathcal{I}} \exists \boldsymbol{y}.(\psi \wedge \xi)$.

We write $[C \mid \phi] \rightarrow_{\Gamma} [D \mid \psi]$ *(*$[C \mid \phi]$ *demodulates to* $[D \mid \psi]$ *w.r.t.* Γ*) if* C *is of the form* $\mathfrak{g} \bowtie \mathfrak{h} \vee E$, $D = \mathfrak{g}\{\mathfrak{i} \leftarrow \mathfrak{j}\} \bowtie \mathfrak{h} \vee E$, *and there exists a c-clause* $[F \mid \xi] \in \Gamma$ *(with free variables* $\boldsymbol{z}$*) such that* $F = (\mathfrak{i} \approx \mathfrak{j}) \vee F'$, $\mathfrak{i} \leq^{\mathfrak{g}}_{\xi'} \mathfrak{g}$, $F' \leq^{sub}_{\xi''} E$, $\phi \models_{\mathcal{I}} \exists \boldsymbol{y}.\exists \boldsymbol{z}.(\psi \wedge \xi \wedge \xi' \wedge \xi'')$, $\mathfrak{i} >_{\xi} \mathfrak{j}$, $F' <_{\xi} (\mathfrak{i} \approx \mathfrak{j})$ *and* $(\mathfrak{i} \approx \mathfrak{j}) <_{\xi} (\mathfrak{g} \bowtie \mathfrak{h})$.

A c-clause $[C \mid \phi]$ *is redundant w.r.t.* Γ *iff one of the following conditions holds: (1)* $\exists \boldsymbol{x}.\phi$ *is* $\mathcal{I}$-*unsatisfiable, with* $\boldsymbol{x} = \mathcal{V}(\phi)$. *(2)* C *contains two literals* $\mathfrak{g}_1 \approx \mathfrak{g}_2$ *and* $\mathfrak{g}'_1 \not\approx \mathfrak{g}'_2$, *with* $\mathfrak{g}_i =_{\phi_i} \mathfrak{g}'_i$, *and* $\phi \models_{\mathcal{I}} \phi_i$ *(for all* $i = 1, 2$*); (3)* C *contains a literal of the form* $\mathfrak{g} \approx \mathfrak{h}$ *with* $\mathfrak{g} =_{\psi} \mathfrak{h}$ *and* $\phi \models_{\mathcal{I}} \psi$; *(4)* $[C \mid \phi] \geq^{sub} [D \mid \psi]$, *for some* $[D \mid \psi] \in \Gamma$; *(5)* $[C \mid \phi] \rightarrow_{\Gamma} [D \mid \psi]$ *and* $[D \mid \psi]$ *is redundant.*

The notion of strictly redundant c-clause is defined in a similar way, removing Item 2.

Example 39. Consider the following $\mathcal{T}$-graphs, of root ():

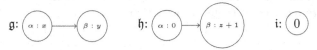

We have $\mathfrak{g} \approx \mathfrak{i} \leq^{sub}_{\phi} \mathfrak{h} \approx \mathfrak{i}$, with $\phi = (x \doteq 0 \wedge y \doteq z + 1 \wedge 0 \doteq 0)$. Thus, if $\mathcal{I}$ only contains the standard model of Presburger arithmetic, then $[\mathfrak{g} \approx \mathfrak{i} \mid y \not\approx 0]$ subsumes $[\mathfrak{h} \approx \mathfrak{i} \mid \top]$.

The following lemma states the relation between the new notion of redundancy and $\mathcal{I}$-redundancy (as defined in Definition 36).

Lemma 40. *Let Γ be a set of c-clauses. If $[C \mid \phi]$ is (strictly) redundant w.r.t. Γ then it is (strictly) $\mathcal{I}$-redundant w.r.t. Γ.*

Remark 41. By the previous definitions, checking whether a given c-clause is (strictly) redundant involves testing the validity of entailments of the form $\phi \models_{\mathcal{I}} \exists \boldsymbol{y}.\psi$, which may be infeasible in practice (for instance the problem is undecidable if $\mathcal{I}$ contains all interpretations). Stronger conditions may be used instead, e.g., one may check whether there exists a substitution σ such that ϕ is of the form $\psi\sigma \wedge \psi$, which is decidable.

6   Conclusion

We devised a constrained superposition calculus to test the satisfiability of sets of clauses defined over graphs. Its soundness and refutational completeness was established, modulo a redundancy criterion that captures the usual deletion and simplification rules: subsumption, demodulation, deletion of clauses with trivial equations and – in the case of Horn clauses only – deletion of clauses containing complementary literals. The considered structures are rooted directed labeled graphs, which are general enough to capture most existing equational graph theories, such as those developed for quantum circuits. In contrast to [14], the calculus is able to handle disjunctions as well as interpreted labels, and in contrast to [22], our solution avoids any encoding of graphs into terms, by defining inference rules operating directly on graphs.

From a practical point of view, it would be interesting to get more general redundancy criteria, to reduce the branching factor and improve the efficiency of the procedure. In particular, is it possible to define a version of the calculus in which tautology deletion is allowed, even for non Horn clauses? As evidenced by Example 22, this would require to define a new equational factorization rule, allowing for non trivial superposition inferences within a single clause.

Another interesting issue is to add variables denoting not only labels, but also graphs. This would allow for instance to synthesize graphs satisfying some properties. As graphs can be viewed as functions with multiple inputs and outputs (denoted by the roots) such an addition would yield a second order logic.

Finally, it would be interesting to identify fragments for which the calculus terminates, ensuring decidability of the satisfiability problem. In contrast to terms, the calculus does not terminate (and the satisfiability problem is undecidable) for ground unit clauses [14], hence strong restrictions on the shape of the graphs are required to ensure termination.

References

1. L. Bachmair and H. Ganzinger. Rewrite-based equational theorem proving with selection and simplification. *Journal of Logic and Computation*, 3(4):217–247, 1994.

2. L. Bachmair and H. Ganzinger. Strict basic superposition. In C. Kirchner and H. Kirchner, editors, *Automated Deduction - CADE-15, 15th International Conference on Automated Deduction, Lindau, Germany, July 5-10, 1998, Proceedings,* volume 1421 of *Lecture Notes in Computer Science,* pages 160–174. Springer, 1998.
3. M. Backens and A. Kissinger. ZH: A complete graphical calculus for quantum computations involving classical non-linearity. *arXiv preprint arXiv:1805.02175,* 2018.
4. F. Bonchi, F. Gadducci, A. Kissinger, P. Sobocinski, and F. Zanasi. Confluence of graph rewriting with interfaces. In *26th European Symposium on Programming (21/04/17 - 28/04/17),* February 2017.
5. F. Bonchi, F. Gadducci, A. Kissinger, P. Sobocinski, and F. Zanasi. String diagram rewrite theory I: rewriting with frobenius structure. *J. ACM,* 69(2):14:1–14:58, 2022.
6. J. H. Brenas, R. Echahed, and M. Strecker. Verifying graph transformation systems with description logics. In *Graph Transformation - 11th International Conference, ICGT 2018, Held as Part of STAF 2018, Toulouse, France, June 25-26, 2018, Proceedings,* volume 10887 of *Lecture Notes in Computer Science,* pages 155–170. Springer, 2018.
7. R. Caferra, R. Echahed, and N. Peltier. A term-graph clausal logic: Completeness and incompleteness results. *Journal of Applied Non-classical Logics,* 18(4):373–411, 2008.
8. C. Chareton, S. Bardin, F. Bobot, V. Perrelle, and B. Valiron. An automated deductive verification framework for circuit-building quantum programs. In N. Yoshida, editor, *Programming Languages and Systems - 30th European Symposium on Programming, ESOP 2021, Held as Part of the European Joint Conferences on Theory and Practice of Software, ETAPS 2021, Luxembourg City, Luxembourg, March 27 - April 1, 2021, Proceedings,* volume 12648 of *Lecture Notes in Computer Science,* pages 148–177. Springer, 2021.
9. A. Clément, N. Heurtel, S. Mansfield, S. Perdrix, and B. Valiron. Lo_v-calculus: A graphical language for linear optical quantum circuits. In S. Szeider, R. Ganian, and A. Silva, editors, *47th International Symposium on Mathematical Foundations of Computer Science, MFCS 2022, August 22-26, 2022, Vienna, Austria,* volume 241 of *LIPIcs,* pages 35:1–35:16. Schloss Dagstuhl - Leibniz-Zentrum für Informatik, 2022.
10. A. Clément and S. Perdrix. PBS-calculus: A graphical language for quantum-controlled computations. *arXiv preprint arXiv:2002.09387,* 2020.
11. B. Coecke and R. Duncan. Tutorial: Graphical calculus for quantum circuits. In *International Workshop on Reversible Computation,* pages 1–13. Springer, 2012.
12. A. Corradini, D. Duval, R. Echahed, F. Prost, and L. Ribeiro. The PBPO graph transformation approach. *J. Log. Algebraic Methods Program.,* 103:213–231, 2019.
13. R. Echahed. Inductively sequential term-graph rewrite systems. In H. Ehrig, R. Heckel, G. Rozenberg, and G. Taentzer, editors, *Graph Transformations, 4th International Conference, ICGT 2008, Leicester, United Kingdom, September 7-13, 2008. Proceedings,* volume 5214 of *Lecture Notes in Computer Science,* pages 84–98. Springer, 2008.
14. R. Echahed, M. Echenim, M. Mhalla, and N. Peltier. A superposition-based calculus for diagrammatic reasoning. In N. Veltri, N. Benton, and S. Ghilezan, editors, *PPDP 2021: 23rd International Symposium on Principles and Practice of Declarative Programming, Tallinn, Estonia, September 6-8, 2021,* pages 10:1–10:13. ACM, 2021.

15. H. Ehrig, K. Ehrig, U. Prange, and G. Taentzer. *Fundamentals of Algebraic Graph Transformation*. Monographs in Theoretical Computer Science. An EATCS Series. Springer, 2006.

16. H. Ehrig, G. Engels, H.-J. Kreowski, and G. Rozenberg, editors. *Handbook of Graph Grammars and Computing by Graph Transformations, Volume 2: Applications, Languages and Tools*. World Scientific, 1999.

17. H. Ehrig and B. König. Deriving bisimulation congruences in the DPO approach to graph rewriting. In I. Walukiewicz, editor, *Foundations of Software Science and Computation Structures, 7th International Conference, FOSSACS 2004, Held as Part of the Joint European Conferences on Theory and Practice of Software, ETAPS 2004, Barcelona, Spain, March 29 - April 2, 2004, Proceedings*, volume 2987 of *Lecture Notes in Computer Science*, pages 151–166. Springer, 2004.

18. H. Ehrig, H.-J. Kreowski, U. Montanari, and G. Rozenberg, editors. *Handbook of Graph Grammars and Computing by Graph Transformations, Volume 3: Concurrency, Parallelism and Distribution*. World Scientific, 1999.

19. H. Ehrig, M. Pfender, and H. J. Schneider. Graph-grammars: An algebraic approach. In *14th Annual Symposium on Switching and Automata Theory, Iowa City, Iowa, USA, October 15-17, 1973*, pages 167–180, 1973.

20. J. Engelfriet and G. Rozenberg. Node replacement graph grammars. In G. Rozenberg, editor, *Handbook of Graph Grammars and Computing by Graph Transformations, Volume 1: Foundations*, pages 1–94. World Scientific, 1997.

21. M. Fitting. *First-Order Logic and Automated Theorem Proving*. Texts and Monographs in Computer Science. Springer-Verlag, 1990.

22. J. Gorard, M. Namuduri, and X. D. Arsiwalla. Zx-calculus and extended wolfram model systems II: fast diagrammatic reasoning with an application to quantum circuit simplification. *CoRR*, abs/2103.15820, 2021.

23. A. Habel and K. Pennemann. Correctness of high-level transformation systems relative to nested conditions. *Math. Struct. Comput. Sci.*, 19(2):245–296, 2009.

24. A. Hadzihasanovic. The algebra of entanglement and the geometry of composition. *arXiv preprint arXiv:1709.08086*, 2017.

25. A. Kissinger and V. Zamdzhiev. Quantomatic: A proof assistant for diagrammatic reasoning. In *International Conference on Automated Deduction*, pages 326–336. Springer, 2015.

26. C. M. Poskitt and D. Plump. A hoare calculus for graph programs. In H. Ehrig, A. Rensink, G. Rozenberg, and A. Schürr, editors, *Graph Transformations - 5th International Conference, ICGT 2010, Enschede, The Netherlands, September 27 - - October 2, 2010. Proceedings*, volume 6372 of *Lecture Notes in Computer Science*, pages 139–154. Springer, 2010.

27. A. Rensink. The GROOVE simulator: A tool for state space generation. In *Second International Workshop on Applications of Graph Transformations with Industrial Relevance, AGTIVE 2003*, volume 3062 of *LNCS*, pages 479–485. Springer, 2003.

28. A. Riazanov and A. Voronkov. Vampire 1.1 (system description). In R. Goré, A. Leitsch, and T. Nipkow, editors, *Automated Reasoning, First International Joint Conference, IJCAR 2001, Siena, Italy, June 18-23, 2001, Proceedings*, volume 2083 of *Lecture Notes in Computer Science*, pages 376–380. Springer, 2001.

29. G. Rozenberg, editor. *Handbook of Graph Grammars and Computing by Graph Transformations, Volume 1: Foundations*. World Scientific, 1997.

30. S. Schulz, S. Cruanes, and P. Vukmirovic. Faster, higher, stronger: E 2.3. In P. Fontaine, editor, *Automated Deduction - CADE 27 - 27th International Conference on Automated Deduction, Natal, Brazil, August 27-30, 2019, Proceedings*,

volume 11716 of *Lecture Notes in Computer Science*, pages 495–507. Springer, 2019.

31. D. Varró. Automated formal verification of visual modeling languages by model checking. *Journal of Software and Systems Modeling*, 3(2):85–113, May 2004.

32. C. Weidenbach, D. Dimova, A. Fietzke, R. Kumar, M. Suda, and P. Wischnewski. SPASS version 3.5. In R. A. Schmidt, editor, *Automated Deduction - CADE-22, 22nd International Conference on Automated Deduction, Montreal, Canada, August 2-7, 2009. Proceedings*, volume 5663 of *Lecture Notes in Computer Science*, pages 140–145. Springer, 2009.

A Programming Language Characterizing Quantum Polynomial Time

Emmanuel Hainry⬤, Romain Péchoux⬤, and Mário Silva$^{(\boxtimes)}$⬤

Université de Lorraine, CNRS, Inria, LORIA, 54000 Nancy, France
{hainry,pechoux,mmachado}@loria.fr

Abstract. We introduce a first-order quantum programming language, named FOQ, whose terminating programs are reversible. We restrict FOQ to a strict and tractable subset, named PFOQ, of terminating programs with bounded width, that provides a first programming language-based characterization of the quantum complexity class FBQP. We finally present a tractable semantics-preserving algorithm compiling a PFOQ program to a quantum circuit of size polynomial in the number of input qubits.

1 Introduction

Motivations. Quantum computing is an emerging and promising computational model that has been in the scientific limelight for several decades. This phenomenon is mainly due to the advantage of quantum computers over their classical competitors, based on the use of purely quantum properties such as superposition and entanglement. The most notable example being Shor's algorithm for finding the prime factors of an integer [15], which is exponentially faster than the most efficient known classical factoring algorithm and which is expected to have implications in cryptography (RSA encryption, etc.).

Whether due to the fragility of quantum systems, namely the engineering problem of maintaining a large number of qubits in a coherent state, or by lack of reliable technological alternatives, quantum computing is typically described at a level close to hardware. Without any hope of being exhaustive, one can think to quantum circuits [9,11], to measurement-based quantum computers [4,7] or to circuit description languages [13]. This low-level machinery restricts drastically the abstraction and programming ease offered by these models and quantum programs currently suffer from the comparison with their classical competitors, which have many high-level tools and formalisms based on more than 50 years of scientific research, engineering development, and practical and industrial applications.

In order to solve these issues, a major effort is made to realize the promise of a quantum computer, which requires the development of different layers of hardware and software, together referred to as the *quantum stack*. Our paper is part of this line of research. We focus on the highest layers of the quantum stack: quantum programming languages and quantum algorithms. We seek to better understand what can be done efficiently on a quantum computer and we are

O. Kupferman and P. Sobocinski (Eds.): FoSSaCS 2023, LNCS 13992, pp. 156–175, 2023.
https://doi.org/10.1007/978-3-031-30829-1_8

particularly interested in the development of quantum programming languages where program complexity can be certified automatically by some static analysis technique.

Contribution. Towards this end, we take the notion of polynomial time computation as our main object of study. Our contributions are the following.

- We introduce a quantum programming language, named FOQ, that includes first-order recursive procedures. The input of a FOQ program consist in a sorted set of qubits, a list of pairwise distinct qubit indexes. A FOQ program can apply to each of its qubits basic operators corresponding to unary unitary operators. The considered set of operators has been chosen in accordance with [16] to form a universal set of gates.
- After showing that terminating FOQ programs are reversible (Theorem 1), we restrict programs to a strict subset, named PFOQ, for *polynomial time* FOQ. The restrictions put on a PFOQ programs are tractable (*i.e.*, can be decided in polynomial time, see Theorem 2), ensure that programs terminate on any input (Lemma 1), and prevent programs from having any exponential blow up (Lemma 2).
- We show that the class of functions computed by PFOQ programs is *sound* and *complete* for the quantum complexity class FBQP. FBQP is the functional extension of *bounded-error quantum polynomial time*, known as BQP [2], the class of decision problems solvable by a quantum computer in polynomial time with an error probability of at most $\frac{1}{3}$ for all instances. Hence the language PFOQ is, to our knowledge, the first programming language characterizing quantum polynomial time functions. Soundness (Theorem 3) is proved by showing that any PFOQ program can be simulated by a quantum Turing machine running in polynomial time [2]. The completeness of our characterization (Theorem 6) is demonstrated by showing that PFOQ programs strictly encompass Yamakami's function algebra, known to be FBQP-complete [16].
- We also describe a polynomial-time deterministic algorithm **compile** (based on the subroutines described in Algorithms 1 and 2), that takes in a PFOQ program P and an integer n and outputs a quantum circuit of size polynomial in n that simulates P on an input size of n qubits. The existence of such circuits is not surprising, as a direct consequence of Yao's characterization of the class BQP in terms of uniform families of circuits of polynomial size [17]. However, a constructive generation based on Yao's algorithm is not satisfactory because of the use of quantum Turing machines which makes the circuits complex and not optimal (in size). We show that, in our setting, circuits can be effectively computed and that the **compile** algorithm is tractable (Theorem 9).

Our programming language FOQ and the restriction to PFOQ are illustrated throughout the paper, using the Quantum Fourier Transform QFT as a leading algorithm (Example 1).

Related work. This paper belongs to a long standing line of works trying to specify, understand, and analyze the semantics of quantum programming languages, starting with the cornerstone work of Selinger [14]. The motivations in restricting the considered programs to PFOQ were inspired by the works on *implicit computational complexity*, that seek to characterize complexity classes by putting restrictions (type systems or others) on standard programming languages and paradigms [1,5,12]. These restrictions have to be implicit (*i.e.*, not provided by the programmer) and tractable. Among all these works, we are aware of two results [16] and [6] studying polynomial time computations on quantum programming languages, works from which our paper was greatly inspired. [6] provides a characterization of BQP based on a quantum lambda-calculus. Our work is an extension to FBQP with a restriction to first-order procedures. Last but not least, [6] is based on Yao's simulation of quantum Turing machines [17] while we provide an explicit algorithm for generating circuits of polynomial size. Our work is also inspired by the function algebra of [16], that characterizes FBQP: our completeness proof shows that any function in [16] can be simulated by a PFOQ program (Theorem 6). However, we claim that FOQ is a more general language for FBQP in so far that it is much less constraining (in terms of expressive power) than the function algebra of [16]: any function of [16] can be, by design, transformed into a PFOQ program, whereas the converse is not true. We can take as example the quantum Fourier transform (QFT) which, as noted in [16], cannot be exactly computed by the function algebra without an additional initial quantum function. Furthermore, the *multi-qubit recursion* construction described in [16] is more restrictive than what we allow in PFOQ, since we may only call the same recursive function in each branch.

2   First-order quantum programming language

Syntax and well-formedness. We consider a quantum programming language, called FOQ for First-Order Quantum programming language, that includes basic data types such as Integers, Booleans, Qubits, Operators, and Sorted Sets of qubits, lists of finite length where all elements are different. A FOQ program has the ability to call first-order (recursive) procedures taking a sorted set of qubits as a parameter. Its syntax is provided in Figure 1.

Let x denote an integer variable and $\bar{p}$, $\bar{q}$ denote sorted sets variables. The size of the sorted set stored in $\bar{q}$ will be denoted by $|\bar{q}|$. We can refer to the i-th qubit in $\bar{q}$ as $\bar{q}[i]$, with $1 \leq i \leq |\bar{q}|$. Hence, each non-empty sorted set variable $\bar{q}$ can be viewed as a list $[\bar{q}[1], \ldots, \bar{q}[|\bar{q}|]]$. The empty sorted set, of size 0, will be denoted by nil and $\bar{q} \ominus [i]$ will denote the sorted set obtained by removing the qubit of index i in $\bar{q}$. For notational convenience, we extend this notation by $\bar{q} \ominus [i_1, \ldots, i_k]$, for the list obtained by removing the qubits of indexes $i_1, \ldots, i_k$ in the sorted set $\bar{q}$.

The language also includes some constructs U^f to represent (unary) unitary operators, for some total function $f \in \mathbb{Z} \to [0, 2\pi) \cap \tilde{\mathbb{R}}$. The function f is required to be polynomial-time approximable: its output is restricted to $\tilde{\mathbb{R}}$, the set of real numbers that can be approximated by a Turing machine for any precision 2^{-k} in time polynomial in k.

(Integers)	i	$\triangleq n \mid x \mid i+n \mid i-n \mid \lvert s \rvert$, with $n \in \mathbb{N}$
(Booleans)	b	$\triangleq i > i \mid i \geq i \mid i = i \mid b \wedge b \mid b \vee b \mid \neg b$
(Sorted Sets)	s	$\triangleq \text{nil} \mid \bar{q} \mid s \ominus [i]$
(Qubits)	q	$\triangleq s[i]$
(Operators)	$U^f(i)$	$\triangleq \text{NOT} \mid R_Y^f(i) \mid \text{Ph}^f(i)$, with $f \in \mathbb{Z} \to [0, 2\pi) \cap \tilde{\mathbb{R}}$
(Statements)	S	$\triangleq \textbf{skip}; \mid q \mathrel{*=} U^f(i); \mid S\,S \mid \textbf{if } b \textbf{ then } S \textbf{ else } S$
		$\mid \textbf{qcase } q \textbf{ of } \{0 \to S, 1 \to S\} \mid \textbf{call } \text{proc}[i](s);$
(Procedure declarations) D		$\triangleq \varepsilon \mid \textbf{decl } \text{proc}[x](\bar{p})\{S\}, D$
(Programs)	$P(\bar{q})$	$\triangleq D :: S$

Fig. 1: Syntax of FOQ programs

A FOQ *program* $P(\bar{q})$ consists of a sequence of *procedure declarations* D followed by a *program statement* S, ε denoting the empty sequence. In what follows, we will sometimes refer to program $P(\bar{q})$ simply as P. Let $var(S)$ be the set of variables appearing in the statement S. Let $|P|$ be the size of program P, that is the total number of symbols in P.

A procedure declaration **decl** $\text{proc}[x](\bar{p})\{S\}$ takes a sorted set parameter $\bar{p}$ and some optional integer parameter x as inputs. S is called the *procedure statement*, proc is the *procedure name* and belongs to a countable set Procedures. We will write S^{proc} to refer to S and proc $\in$ P holds if proc is declared in D.

Statements include a no-op instruction, applications of a unitary operator to a qubit ($q \mathrel{*=} U^f(i);$), sequences, (classical) conditionals, *quantum cases*, and *procedure calls* (**call** $\text{proc}[i](s);$). A quantum case **qcase** q **of** $\{0 \to S_0, 1 \to S_1\}$ provides a quantum control feature that will execute statements S_0 and S_1 in superposition. For example, the $CNOT$ gate on qubits $\bar{q}[i]$ and $\bar{q}[j]$, for $i, j \in \mathbb{N}$, $i \neq j$, can be simulated by the following statement:

$$\text{CNOT}(\bar{q}[i], \bar{q}[j]) \triangleq \textbf{qcase } \bar{q}[i] \textbf{ of } \{0 \to \ \textbf{skip};, 1 \to \bar{q}[j] \mathrel{*=} \text{NOT};\}.$$

Throughout the paper, we restrict our study to *well-formed* programs, that is, programs $P = D :: S$ satisfying the following properties: $var(S) \subseteq \{\bar{q}\}$; $\forall \text{proc} \in P$, $var(S^{\text{proc}}) \subseteq \{x, \bar{p}\}$; procedure names declared in D are pairwise distinct; for each procedure call, the procedure name is declared in D.

Semantics. Let $\mathcal{H}_{2^n}$ be the *Hilbert space* $\mathbb{C}^{2^n}$ of n qubits. We use Dirac notation to denote a quantum state $|\psi\rangle \in \mathcal{H}_{2^n}$. Each $|\psi\rangle \in \mathcal{H}_{2^n}$ can be written as a superposition of bitstrings of size n: $|\psi\rangle = \sum_{w \in \{0,1\}^n} \alpha_w |w\rangle$, with $\alpha_w \in \mathbb{C}$ and $\sum_w |\alpha_w|^2 = 1$. The *length* $\ell(|\psi\rangle)$ of the state $|\psi\rangle$ is n. Given two matrices M, N, we denote by $M^\dagger$ the transpose conjugate of M and by $M \otimes N$ the tensor product of M by N. $\langle\psi|$ is equal to $|\psi\rangle^\dagger$ and $|\psi\rangle\langle\phi|$ and $\langle\psi|\phi\rangle$ are respectively the inner product and outer product of $|\psi\rangle$ and $|\phi\rangle$. Let I_n be the identity matrix in $\mathbb{C}^{n\times n}$. Given $m \le n$ and $i \in \{0,1\}$, define $|i\rangle_m \triangleq I_{2^{m-1}} \otimes |i\rangle \otimes I_{2^{n-m}}$ and $\langle i|_m \triangleq (|i\rangle_m)^\dagger$.

A function $[\![U^f]\!] \in \mathbb{Z} \to \tilde{\mathbb{C}}^{2\times 2}$ is associated to each U^f as follows:

$$[\![\text{NOT}]\!](n) \triangleq \begin{pmatrix} 0 & 1 \\ 1 & 0 \end{pmatrix}, \quad [\![R_Y^f]\!](n) \triangleq \begin{pmatrix} \cos(f(n)) & -\sin(f(n)) \\ \sin(f(n)) & \cos(f(n)) \end{pmatrix}, \quad [\![\text{Ph}^f]\!](n) \triangleq \begin{pmatrix} 1 & 0 \\ 0 & e^{if(n)} \end{pmatrix},$$

where $\tilde{\mathbb{C}}$ is the set of complex numbers whose both real and imaginary parts are in $\tilde{\mathbb{R}}$. One can check easily that each matrix $M \triangleq [\![U^f]\!](n) \in \tilde{\mathbb{C}}^{2\times 2}$ is unitary, *i.e.*, it satisfies $M^\dagger M = M M^\dagger = I_2$.

Let $\mathbb{B}$ to be the set of Boolean values $b \in \{\textbf{false}, \textbf{true}\}$. For a given set X, let $\mathcal{L}(X)$ be the set of lists of elements in X. Let $l = [x_1, \dots, x_m]$, with $x_1, \dots, x_m \in X$, denote a list of m-elements in $\mathcal{L}(X)$ and $[]$ be the empty list (when $m = 0$). For $l, l' \in \mathcal{L}(X)$, $l@l'$ denotes the concatenation of l and l'. $hd(l)$ and $tl(l)$ represent the tail and the head of l, respectively. Lists of integers will be used to represent Sorted Sets. They contain pointers to qubits (*i.e.*, indexes) in the global memory.

We interpret each basic data type τ as follows: $[\![\text{Integers}]\!] \triangleq \mathbb{Z}$, $[\![\text{Booleans}]\!] \triangleq \mathbb{B}$, $[\![\text{SortedSets}]\!] \triangleq \mathcal{L}(\mathbb{N})$, $[\![\text{Qubits}]\!] \triangleq \mathbb{N}$, and $[\![\text{Operators}]\!] \triangleq \tilde{\mathbb{C}}^{2\times 2}$. Each basic operation op $\in \{+, -, >, \ge, =, \wedge, \vee, \neg\}$ of arity n, with $1 \le n \le 2$, has a type signature $\tau_1 \times \dots \times \tau_n \to \tau$ fixed by the program syntax. For example, the operation $+$ has signature Integers $\times$ Integers $\to$ Integers. A total function $[\![\text{op}]\!] \in [\![\tau_1]\!] \times \dots \times [\![\tau_n]\!] \to [\![\tau]\!]$ is associated to each op.

For each basic type τ, the reduction $\Downarrow_{[\![\tau]\!]}$ is a map in $\tau \times \mathcal{L}(\mathbb{N}) \to [\![\tau]\!]$. Intuitively, it maps an expression of type τ to its value in $[\![\tau]\!]$ for a given list l of pointers in memory. These reductions are defined in Figure 2, where e and d denote either an integer expression i or a boolean expression b.

Note that in rule $(\text{Rm}_{\notin})$, if we try to delete an undefined index then we return the empty list, and in rule $(\text{Qu}_{\notin})$, if we try to access an undefined qubit index then we return the value 0 (defined indexes will always be positive). The standard gates $R_Y(\pi/4)$, $P(\pi/4)$, and $CNOT$, form a universal set of gates [3], which justifies the choice of NOT, $R_Y^f(i)$, and $\text{Ph}^f(i)$ as basic operators. For instance, we can simulate the application of an Hadamard gate H on q by the following statement q *= $R_Y^f(0)$; q *= NOT;, with the function f defined by $\forall n, f(n) = \pi/4 \in [0, 2\pi) \cap \tilde{\mathbb{R}}$. By abuse of notation, we will sometimes use q *= H; to denote this statement. Using CNOT, we can also define the SWAP operation swapping the state between two qubits $\bar{q}[i]$ and $\bar{q}[j]$, with $i, j \in \mathbb{N}$, $i \ne j$:

$$\text{SWAP}(\bar{q}[i], \bar{q}[j]) \triangleq \text{CNOT}(\bar{q}[i], \bar{q}[j])\, \text{CNOT}(\bar{q}[j], \bar{q}[i])\, \text{CNOT}(\bar{q}[i], \bar{q}[j]).$$

Let $\top$ and $\bot$ be two special symbols for termination and error, respectively, and let $\diamond$ stand for a symbol in $\{\top, \bot\}$. The set of *configurations* of dimension 2^n, denoted Conf_n, is defined by

$$\text{Conf}_n \triangleq (\text{Statements} \cup \{\top, \bot\}) \times \mathcal{H}_{2^n} \times \mathcal{P}(\mathbb{N}) \times \mathcal{L}(\mathbb{N}),$$

with $\mathcal{P}(\mathbb{N})$ being the powerset over $\mathbb{N}$. A configuration $c = (S, |\psi\rangle, A, l) \in \text{Conf}_n$ contains a statement S to be executed (provided that S $\notin \{\top, \bot\}$), a quantum

$$\frac{(e,l) \Downarrow_{[\![\tau_1]\!]} m \quad (d,l) \Downarrow_{[\![\tau_2]\!]} n}{(e \text{ op } d,l) \Downarrow_{[\![op]\!]([\![\tau_1]\!],[\![\tau_2]\!])} [\![op]\!](m,n)} \text{ (Op)} \qquad \frac{(i,l) \Downarrow_{\mathbb{Z}} n}{(U^f(i),l) \Downarrow_{\mathbb{C}^{2\times 2}} [\![U^f]\!](n)} \text{ (Unit)}$$

$$\frac{}{(n,l) \Downarrow_{\mathbb{Z}} n} \text{ (Cst)} \qquad \frac{(s,l) \Downarrow_{\mathcal{L}(\mathbb{N})} [x_1,\dots,x_m] \quad (i,l) \Downarrow_{\mathbb{Z}} k \in [1,m]}{(s \ominus [i],l) \Downarrow_{\mathcal{L}(\mathbb{N})} [x_1,\dots,x_{k-1},x_{k+1},\dots,x_m]} \text{ (Rm}_\in)$$

$$\frac{(s,l) \Downarrow_{\mathcal{L}(\mathbb{N})} [x_1,\dots,x_n]}{(|s|,l) \Downarrow_{\mathbb{Z}} n} \text{ (Size)} \qquad \frac{(s,l) \Downarrow_{\mathcal{L}(\mathbb{N})} [x_1,\dots,x_m] \quad (i,l) \Downarrow_{\mathbb{Z}} k \notin [1,m]}{(s \ominus [i],l) \Downarrow_{\mathcal{L}(\mathbb{N})} []} \text{ (Rm}_\notin)$$

$$\frac{}{(\text{nil},l) \Downarrow_{\mathcal{L}(\mathbb{N})} []} \text{ (Nil)} \qquad \frac{(s,l) \Downarrow_{\mathcal{L}(\mathbb{N})} [x_1,\dots,x_m] \quad (i,l) \Downarrow_{\mathbb{Z}} k \in [1,m]}{(s[i],l) \Downarrow_{\mathbb{N}} x_k} \text{ (Qu}_\in)$$

$$\frac{}{(\bar{q},l) \Downarrow_{\mathcal{L}(\mathbb{N})} l} \text{ (Var)} \qquad \frac{(s,l) \Downarrow_{\mathcal{L}(\mathbb{N})} [x_1,\dots,x_m] \quad (i,l) \Downarrow_{\mathbb{Z}} k \notin [1,m]}{(s[i],l) \Downarrow_{\mathbb{N}} 0} \text{ (Qu}_\notin)$$

Fig. 2: Semantics of expressions

state $|\psi\rangle$ of length n, a set A containing the indexes of qubits that are allowed to be accessed by statement S, and a list l of qubit pointers.

The program big-step semantics $\longrightarrow$, described in Figure 3, is defined as a relation in $\bigcup_{n\in\mathbb{N}} \text{Conf}_n \times \text{Conf}_n$. In the rules of Figure 3, $\longrightarrow$ is annotated by an integer, called *level*. For example, the level of the conclusion in the (Call$_{[]}$) rule is 1. The level is used to count the total number of procedure calls that are not in superposition (*i.e.*, in distinct branches of a quantum case).

We now give a brief intuition on the rules of Figure 3. Rules (Asg$_\perp$) and (Asg$_\top$) evaluate the application of a unitary operator, corresponding to $U^f(j)$, to a qubit s[i]. For that purpose, they evaluate the index n of s[i] in the global memory. Rule (Asg$_\perp$) deals with the error case, where the corresponding qubit is not allowed to be accessed. Rule (Asg$_\top$) deals with the success case: the new quantum state is obtained by applying the result of tensoring the evaluation of $U^f(j)$ to the right index. Rules (Seq$_\diamond$) and (Seq$_\perp$) evaluate the sequence of statements, depending on whether an error occurs or not. The (If) rule deals with classical conditionals in a standard way. The three rules (Case$_\top$), (Case$_\perp$), and (Case$_\notin$) evaluate the qubit index n of the control qubit s[i]. Then they check whether this index belongs to the set of accessible qubits (is n in A?). If so, the two statements S_0 and S_1 are intuitively evaluated in superposition, on the projected state $\langle 0|_n|\psi\rangle$ and $\langle 1|_n|\psi\rangle$, respectively. During these evaluations, the index n cannot be accessed anymore. The rule (Call$_{[]}$) treats the base case of a procedure call when the sorted set parameter is empty. In the non-empty case, rule (Call$_\diamond$) evaluates the sorted set parameter s to l' and the integer parameter

$$\frac{}{(\mathbf{skip}, |\psi\rangle, A, l) \xrightarrow{0} (\top, |\psi\rangle, A, l)} \text{ (Skip)}$$

$$\frac{(s[i], l) \Downarrow_{\mathbb{N}} n \notin A}{(s[i] \mathrel{*}= \mathrm{U}^f(j);, |\psi\rangle, A, l) \xrightarrow{0} (\bot, |\psi\rangle, A, l)} \text{ (Asg}_\bot)$$

$$\frac{(s[i], l) \Downarrow_{\mathbb{N}} n \in A \quad (\mathrm{U}^f(j), l) \Downarrow_{\mathbb{C}^{2\times 2}} M}{(s[i] \mathrel{*}= \mathrm{U}^f(j);, |\psi\rangle, A, l) \xrightarrow{0} (\top, I_{2^{n-1}} \otimes M \otimes I_{2^{l(|\psi\rangle)-n}} |\psi\rangle, A, l)} \text{ (Asg}_\top)$$

$$\frac{(S_1, |\psi\rangle, A, l) \xrightarrow{m_1} (\top, |\psi'\rangle, A, l) \quad (S_2, |\psi'\rangle, A, l) \xrightarrow{m_2} (\diamond, |\psi''\rangle, A, l)}{(S_1\ S_2, |\psi\rangle, A, l) \xrightarrow{m_1+m_2} (\diamond, |\psi''\rangle, A, l)} \text{ (Seq}_\diamond)$$

$$\frac{(S_1, |\psi\rangle, A, l) \xrightarrow{m} (\bot, |\psi\rangle, A, l)}{(S_1\ S_2, |\psi\rangle, A, l) \xrightarrow{m} (\bot, |\psi\rangle, A, l)} \text{ (Seq}_\bot)$$

$$\frac{(b, l) \Downarrow_{\mathbb{B}} b \in \mathbb{B} \quad (S_b, |\psi\rangle, A, l) \xrightarrow{m_b} (\diamond, |\psi'\rangle, A, l)}{(\mathbf{if}\ b\ \mathbf{then}\ S_{\mathbf{true}}\ \mathbf{else}\ S_{\mathbf{false}}, |\psi\rangle, A, l) \xrightarrow{m_b} (\diamond, |\psi'\rangle, A, l)} \text{ (If)}$$

$$\frac{(s[i], l) \Downarrow_{\mathbb{N}} n \in A \quad (S_k, |\psi\rangle, A\backslash\{n\}, l) \xrightarrow{m_k} (\top, |\psi_k\rangle, A\backslash\{n\}, l)}{(\mathbf{qcase}\ s[i]\ \mathbf{of}\ \{0 \to S_0, 1 \to S_1\}, |\psi\rangle, A, l) \xrightarrow{\max_k m_k} (\top, \sum_k |k\rangle_n\langle k|_n |\psi_k\rangle, A, l)} \text{ (Case}_\top)$$

$$\frac{(s[i], l) \Downarrow_{\mathbb{N}} n \in A \quad (S_k, |\psi\rangle, A\backslash\{n\}, l) \xrightarrow{m_k} (\diamond_k, |\psi_k\rangle, A\backslash\{n\}, l) \quad \bot \in \{\diamond_0, \diamond_1\}}{(\mathbf{qcase}\ s[i]\ \mathbf{of}\ \{0 \to S_0, 1 \to S_1\}, |\psi\rangle, A, l) \xrightarrow{\max_k m_k} (\bot, |\psi\rangle, A, l)} \text{ (Case}_\bot)$$

$$\frac{(s[i], l) \Downarrow_{\mathbb{N}} n \notin A}{(\mathbf{qcase}\ s[i]\ \mathbf{of}\ \{0 \to S_0, 1 \to S_1\}, |\psi\rangle, A, l) \xrightarrow{0} (\bot, |\psi\rangle, A, l)} \text{ (Case}_\notin)$$

$$\frac{(s, l) \Downarrow_{\mathcal{L}(\mathbb{N})} l' \neq [] \quad (i, l) \Downarrow_{\mathbb{Z}} n \quad (S^{\mathrm{proc}}\{n/x\}, |\psi\rangle, A, l') \xrightarrow{m} (\diamond, |\psi'\rangle, A, l')}{(\mathbf{call}\ proc[i](s);, |\psi\rangle, A, l) \xrightarrow{m+1} (\diamond, |\psi'\rangle, A, l)} \text{ (Call}_\diamond)$$

$$\frac{(s, l) \Downarrow_{\mathcal{L}(\mathbb{N})} []}{(\mathbf{call}\ proc[i](s);, |\psi\rangle, A, l) \xrightarrow{1} (\top, |\psi\rangle, A, l)} \text{ (Call}_{[]})$$

Fig. 3: Semantics of statements

x to n. It returns the result of evaluating the procedure statement $S^{\mathrm{proc}}\{n/x\}$, where n has been substituted to x, w.r.t. the updated qubit pointers list l'.

For a given program $P = D :: S$ and a given quantum state $|\psi\rangle \in \mathcal{H}_{2^n}$, the *initial configuration* for input $|\psi\rangle$ is $c_{init}(|\psi\rangle) \triangleq (S, |\psi\rangle, \{1, \ldots, n\}, [1, \ldots, n]) \in$

Conf_n. A program is *error-free* if there is no initial configuration $c_{init}(|\psi\rangle)$ such that $c_{init}(|\psi\rangle) \longrightarrow (\bot, |\psi'\rangle, A, l)$. We write $[\![P]\!](|\psi\rangle) = |\psi'\rangle$, whenever $c_{init}(|\psi\rangle) \xrightarrow{m} (\top, |\psi'\rangle, A, l)$ holds for some m. $(\top, |\psi'\rangle, A, l)$ is called a *terminal configuration*. Let $\mathcal{H} = \bigcup_n \mathcal{H}_{2^n}$, a program *terminates* if $[\![P]\!]$ is a total function in $\mathcal{H} \to \mathcal{H}$. Note that if a program terminates then it is obviously error-free but the converse property does not hold. Every program P can be efficiently transformed into an error-free program $P_{\neg\bot}$ such that $\forall|\psi\rangle$, if $[\![P]\!](|\psi\rangle)$ is defined then $[\![P]\!](|\psi\rangle) = [\![P_{\neg\bot}]\!](|\psi\rangle)$. For example, an assignment s[i] *= U^f(j); can be transformed into the conditional statement **if** $((0 < i) \wedge (i \leq |s|))$ **then** s[i] *= U^f(j); **else skip**;.

Example 1. A notable example of quantum algorithm is the Quantum Fourier Transform (QFT), used as a subroutine in Shor's algorithm [15], and whose quantum circuit is provided below, with $R_n \triangleq [\![\mathrm{Ph}^{\lambda x.\pi/2^{x-1}}]\!](n)$, for $n \geq 2$. After applying Hadamard and controlled R_n gates, the circuit performs a permutation of qubits using swap gates.

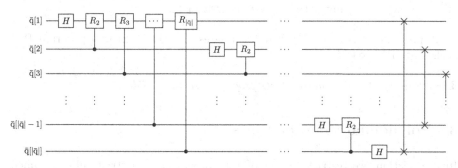

Note that $\lambda x.\pi/2^{x-1}$ is a total function in $\mathbb{Z} \to [0, 2\pi) \cap \tilde{\mathbb{R}}$. Hence, it is polynomial time approximable. The above circuit can be simulated for any number of qubits |q| by the following FOQ program QFT.

```
decl rec(p̄){                decl rot[x](p̄){                    decl inv(p̄){
  p̄[1] *= H;                  if |p̄| > 1 then                    if |p̄| > 1 then
  call rot[2](p̄);              qcase p̄[2] of {                     SWAP(p̄[1], p̄[|p̄|]);
  call rec(p̄ ⊖ [1]); },        0 → skip;                          call inv(p̄ ⊖ [1, |p̄|]);
                              1 → p̄[1] *= Ph^{λx.π/2^{x-1}}(x);   else skip; } ::
                              }
                              call rot[x + 1](p̄ ⊖ [2]);
                              else skip; },

call rec(q̄); call inv(q̄);
```

Derivation tree and level. Given a configuration c wrt a fixed program P, $\pi_P \rhd c$ denotes the *derivation tree* of P, the tree of root c whose children are obtained by applying the rules of Figures 2 and 3 on configuration c with respect to P. We write π instead of $\pi_P \rhd c$ when P and c are clear from the context. Note that a derivation tree π can be infinite in the particular case of a non-terminating computation. When π' is finite, $\pi \trianglelefteq \pi'$ denotes that π is a subtree of π'.

In the case of a terminating computation $\pi \rhd c$, there exists a terminal configuration c' and a level $m \in \mathbb{N}$ such that $c \xrightarrow{m} c'$ holds. In this case, the level of π is defined as $\mathrm{lv}_\pi \triangleq m$. Given a FOQ program P that terminates, levelp is a total function in $\mathbb{N} \to \mathbb{N}$ defined as $\mathrm{level}_P(n) \triangleq \max_{|\psi\rangle \in \mathcal{H}_{2^n}} \mathrm{lv}_{\pi_P \rhd c_{init}(|\psi\rangle)}$.

Intuitively, $\mathrm{level}_P(n)$ corresponds to the maximal number of non-superposed procedure calls in any program execution on an input of length n.

Example 2. Consider the program QFT of example 1. Assume temporarily that QFT terminates (this will be shown in Example 3). For all $n \in \mathbb{N}$, $\mathrm{level}_{\mathrm{QFT}}(n) = \frac{(n+1)(n+2)}{2} + \lfloor \frac{n}{2} \rfloor + 1$. Indeed, on sorted sets of size n, procedure rec is called recursively $n + 1$ times and makes $n + 1$ calls to procedure rot on sorted sets of size n, $n - 1$, ..., and 1. On sorted sets of size n, rot performs n recursive calls. Hence the total number of calls to rot is equal to $\sum_{i=1}^{n} i$. Finally, on a sorted set of size n, procedure inv does $\lfloor \frac{n}{2} \rfloor + 1$ recursive call.

A program P is reversible if it terminates and there exists a program P^{-1} such that $[\![P^{-1}]\!] \circ [\![P]\!] = Id$.

Theorem 1. *All terminating* FOQ *programs are reversible.*

3   Polynomial time soundness

In this section, we restrict the set of FOQ programs to a strict subset, named PFOQ, that is sound for the quantum complexity class FBQP. For this, we define two criteria: a criterion ensuring that a program terminates and a criterion preventing a terminating program from having an exponential runtime.

Polynomial-time FOQ. Given two statements S, S', we write $S \in S'$ to mean that S is a substatement of S' and proc $\in S$ holds if there are i and s such that **call** proc[i](s); $\in S$. Given a program $P = D :: S$, we define the relation $>_P \subseteq$ Procedures $\times$ Procedures by $\mathrm{proc}_1 >_P \mathrm{proc}_2$ if $\mathrm{proc}_2 \in S^{\mathrm{proc}_1}$, for any two procedures $\mathrm{proc}_1, \mathrm{proc}_2 \in S$. Let the partial order $\succeq_P$ be the transitive and reflexive closure of $>_P$ and define the equivalence relation $\sim_P$ by $\mathrm{proc}_1 \sim_P \mathrm{proc}_2$ if $\mathrm{proc}_1 \succeq_P \mathrm{proc}_2$ and $\mathrm{proc}_2 \succeq_P \mathrm{proc}_1$ both hold. Define also the strict order $\succ_P$ by $\mathrm{proc}_1 \succ_P \mathrm{proc}_2$ if $\mathrm{proc}_1 \succeq_P \mathrm{proc}_2$ and $\mathrm{proc}_1 \nsucceq_P \mathrm{proc}_2$ both hold.

Definition 1. *Let* WF *be the set of* FOQ *programs* P *that are error-free and satisfy the well-foundedness constraint:* $\forall \mathrm{proc} \in P$, $\forall \textbf{call}\ \mathrm{proc}'[i](s); \in S^{\mathrm{proc}}$,

$$\mathrm{proc} \sim_P \mathrm{proc}' \Rightarrow \exists k > 0, \exists i_1, \ldots, i_k,\ s = \bar{p} \ominus [i_1, \ldots, i_k].$$

Lemma 1 *If* $P \in$ WF, *then* P *terminates.*

Example 3. Consider the program QFT of Example 1. The statements of the procedure declarations define the following relation: rec $>_{\text{QFT}}$ rec, rec $>_{\text{QFT}}$ rot, rot $>_{\text{QFT}}$ rot, and inv $>_{\text{QFT}}$ inv. Consequently, rec $\sim_{\text{QFT}}$ rec, rot $\sim_{\text{QFT}}$ rot, inv $\sim_{\text{QFT}}$ inv, and rec $\succ_{\text{QFT}}$ rot hold. For each call to an equivalent procedure, we check that the argument decreases: $\bar{p} \ominus [1]$ in rec, $\bar{p} \ominus [2]$ in rot, and $\bar{p} \ominus [1, |\bar{p}|]$ in inv. Consequently, QFT $\in$ WF. We deduce from Theorem 1 that QFT terminates.

We now add a further restriction on mutually recursive procedure calls for guaranteeing polynomial time using a notion of width.

Definition 2. *Given a program* P *and a procedure* proc $\in$ P, *the* width *of* proc *in* P, *noted* $\text{width}_P(\text{proc})$, *and the* width *of* proc *in* P *relatively to statement* S, *noted* $w_P^{\text{proc}}(S)$, *are two positive integers in* $\mathbb{N}$. *They are defined inductively by:*

$$\text{width}_P(\text{proc}) \triangleq w_P^{\text{proc}}(S^{\text{proc}}),$$

$$w_P^{\text{proc}}(\textbf{skip;}) \triangleq 0,$$

$$w_P^{\text{proc}}(\texttt{q *= } U^f(i);) \triangleq 0,$$

$$w_P^{\text{proc}}(S_1\ S_2) \triangleq w_P^{\text{proc}}(S_1) + w_P^{\text{proc}}(S_2),$$

$$w_P^{\text{proc}}(\textbf{if } b \textbf{ then } S_{\text{true}} \textbf{ else } S_{\text{false}}) \triangleq \max(w_P^{\text{proc}}(S_{\text{true}}), w_P^{\text{proc}}(S_{\text{false}})),$$

$$w_P^{\text{proc}}(\textbf{qcase } q \textbf{ of } \{0 \rightarrow S_0, 1 \rightarrow S_1\}) \triangleq \max(w_P^{\text{proc}}(S_0), w_P^{\text{proc}}(S_1)),$$

$$w_P^{\text{proc}}(\textbf{call } \text{proc}'[i](s);) \triangleq \begin{cases} 1 & \textit{if } \text{proc} \sim_P \text{proc}', \\ 0 & \textit{otherwise.} \end{cases}$$

Definition 3 (PFOQ). *Let* PFOQ *be the set of programs* P *in* WF *that satisfy the following constraint:* $\forall \text{proc} \in P, \text{width}_P(\text{proc}) \leq 1$.

Example 4. In the program of Example 1, $\text{width}_{\text{QFT}}(\text{rec}) = \text{width}_{\text{QFT}}(\text{rot}) = \text{width}_{\text{QFT}}(\text{inv}) = 1$, since rec $\succ_{\text{QFT}}$ rot holds. Since QFT $\in$ WF, by Example 3, we conclude that QFT is a PFOQ program.

We now show that the level of a PFOQ program is bounded by a polynomial in the length of its input.

Lemma 2 *For each* PFOQ *program* P, *there exists a polynomial* $Q \in \mathbb{N}[X]$ *such that* $\forall n \in \mathbb{N}$, $\text{level}_P(n) \leq Q(n)$.

Moreover, checking whether a program is PFOQ is tractable.

Theorem 2. *For each* FOQ *program* P, *it can be decided in time* $O(|P|^2)$ *whether* $P_{\neg\perp} \in$ PFOQ.

Quantum Turing machines and FBQP. Following Bernstein and Vazirani [2], a k-tape *Quantum Turing Machine* (QTM), with $k \geq 1$, is defined by a triplet (Σ, Q, δ) where Σ is a finite alphabet including a blank symbol #, Q is a finite set of states with an initial state s_0 and a final state $s_T \neq s_0$, and δ is the quantum transition function in $Q \times \Sigma^k \to \tilde{C}^{Q \times \Sigma^k \times \{L,N,R\}^k}$; $\{L, N, R\}$ being the set of possible movements of a head on a tape. Each tape of the QTM is two-way infinite and contains cells indexed by $\mathbb{Z}$. A QTM successfully terminates if it reaches a superposition of only the final state $s_\top$. A QTM is said to be *well-formed* if the transition function δ preserves the norm of the superposition (or, equivalently, if the time evolution of the machine is unitary). The starting position of the tape heads is the *start cell*, the cell indexed by 0. If the machine terminates with all of its tape heads back on the start cells, it is called *stationary*. We will use *stationary* in the case where the machine terminates with its input tape head in the first cell, and all other tape heads in the last non-blank cell. We will further refer to a QTM as being *in normal form* if the only transitions from the final state $s_\top$ are towards the initial state s_0. These will be important conditions for the composition and branching constructions of QTMs. If a QTM is well-formed, stationary, and in normal form, we will call it *conservative* [16] (N.B.: our notion of stationary QTM differs but can be shown to be equivalent to the definition of stationary QTM in [16]).

A configuration γ of a k-tape QTM is a tuple $(s, \overline{w}, \overline{n})$, where s is a state in Q, $\overline{w}$ is a k-tuple of words in Σ^*, and $\overline{n}$ is a k-tuple of indexes (head positions) in $\mathbb{Z}$. An initial (final) configuration γ_{init} (resp. γ_{fin}) is a configuration of the shape $(s_0, \overline{w}, \overline{0})$ (resp. $(s_\top, \overline{w}, \overline{0})$). We use $\gamma(w)$ to denote a configuration γ where the word w is written on the input/output tape. Following [2], we write $\mathcal{S}$ to represent the inner-product space of finite complex linear combinations of configurations of the QTM M with the Euclidean norm. A QTM M defines a linear time operator $U_M : \mathcal{S} \to \mathcal{S}$, that outputs a superposition of configurations $\sum_i \alpha_i |\gamma_i\rangle$ obtained by applying a single-step transition of M to a configuration $|\gamma\rangle$ (*i.e.*, $U_M |\gamma\rangle = \sum_i \alpha_i |\gamma_i\rangle$). Let U_M^t, for $t \geq 1$, be the t-steps transition obtained from U_M as follows: $U_M^1 \triangleq U_M$ and $U_M^{t+1} \triangleq U_M \circ U_M^t$. Given a quantum state $|\psi\rangle = \sum_{w \in \{0,1\}^n} \alpha_w |w\rangle$ and a configuration γ, let $\gamma(|\psi\rangle) \in \mathcal{S}$ be the quantum configuration defined by $\gamma(|\psi\rangle) \triangleq \sum_{w \in \{0,1\}^n} \alpha_w \gamma(w)$.

A quantum function $f : \mathcal{H} \to \mathcal{H}$ is computed by the QTM M in time t if for any $|\psi\rangle \in \mathcal{H}$, $U_M^t(\gamma_{init}(|\psi\rangle)) = \gamma_{fin}(f(|\psi'\rangle))$. Given $T : \mathbb{N} \to \mathbb{N}$ and a quantum function f, we say that the QTM M computes f in time T if for inputs of length n, M computes f in time $T(n)$.

Definition 4. *Given two functions $f : \{0,1\}^* \to \{0,1\}^*$, $F : \mathcal{H} \to \mathcal{H}$, and a value $p \in [0,1]$, we say that f is computed by F with probability p if $\forall x \in \{0,1\}^*$, $|\langle f(x)|F(|x\rangle)\rangle|^2 \geq p$.*

The class FBQP is the functional extension of the complexity class BQP.

Definition 5 ([2]). *A function $f \in \{0,1\}^* \to \{0,1\}^*$ is in FBQP iff there exist a QTM M and a polynomial $P \in \mathbb{N}[X]$ s.t. M computes f in time P with probability $\frac{2}{3}$.*

A function $f \in \{0,1\}^* \to \{0,1\}^*$ has a *polynomial bound* $P \in \mathbb{N}[X]$ if $\forall n \in \mathbb{N}, \forall x \in \{0,1\}^n, \exists k \leq P(n), f(x) \in \{0,1\}^k$. Functions in FBQP have a polynomial bound as the size of their output is smaller than the polynomial time bound.

Soundness. We show that QTMs can simulate the function computed by any terminating FOQ program. The time complexity of this simulation depends on the length of the input quantum state and on the level of the considered program.

Lemma 3 *For any terminating* FOQ *program* P, *there exists a conservative QTM M that computes* $\llbracket P \rrbracket$ *in time* $O(n + n \times \text{level}_P(n))$.

Now we show that any PFOQ program computes a FBQP function.

Theorem 3. *Given a* PFOQ *program* P, *a function* $f : \{0,1\}^* \to \{0,1\}^*$, *and a value* $p \in (\frac{1}{2}, 1]$. *If* f *is computed by* $\llbracket P \rrbracket$ *with probability* p *then* $f \in$ FBQP.

Proof. Using Lemma 2 and Lemma 3. □

4 FBQP completeness

In this section we show that any function in FBQP can be faithfully approximated by a PFOQ program. Toward this end, we show that Yamakami's [16] FBQP-complete function algebra can be exactly simulated in PFOQ.

Yamakami's function algebra. A characterization of FBQP was provided in [16] using a function algebra, named $\widehat{\square_1^{\text{QP}}}$. Given a quantum state $|\psi\rangle$ and a word $w \in \{0,1\}^n$, with $n \leq l(|\psi\rangle)$. $|\psi\rangle$ can be written as $|\psi\rangle = \sum_i \alpha_i |w_i z_i\rangle$, with $w_i \in \{0,1\}^n$ and $z_i \in \{0,1\}^{l(|\psi\rangle)-n}$. We write $\langle w|\psi\rangle$ as an abuse of notation for the quantum state defined by $\langle w|\psi\rangle \triangleq \sum_i \alpha_i \langle w|w_i\rangle |z_i\rangle$.

Definition 6. $\widehat{\square_1^{\text{QP}}}$ *is the smallest class of functions including the basic initial functions* $\{I, Ph_\theta, Rot_\theta, NOT, SWAP\}$, *with* $\theta \in [0, 2\pi] \cap \tilde{\mathbb{C}}$,

- $I(|\psi\rangle) \triangleq |\psi\rangle$
- $Ph_\theta(|\psi\rangle) \triangleq |0\rangle\langle 0|\psi\rangle + e^{i\theta}|1\rangle\langle 1|\psi\rangle$
- $Rot_\theta(|\psi\rangle) \triangleq \cos\theta|\psi\rangle + \sin\theta(|1\rangle\langle 0|\psi\rangle - |0\rangle\langle 1|\psi\rangle)$
- $NOT(|\psi\rangle) \triangleq |0\rangle\langle 1|\psi\rangle + |1\rangle\langle 0|\psi\rangle$
- $SWAP(|\psi\rangle) \triangleq \begin{cases} |\psi\rangle & \text{if } l(|\psi\rangle) \leq 1 \\ \sum_{a,b \in \{0,1\}} |ba\rangle\langle ab|\psi\rangle & \text{otherwise} \end{cases}$

and closed under schemes Comp, Branch, and $kQRec_t$, *for* $k, t \in \mathbb{N}$,

- $Comp[F, G](|\psi\rangle) \triangleq F(G(|\psi\rangle))$
- $Branch[F, G](|\psi\rangle) \triangleq \begin{cases} |\psi\rangle & \text{if } l(|\psi\rangle) \leq 1 \\ |0\rangle \otimes F(\langle 0|\psi\rangle) + |1\rangle \otimes G(\langle 1|\psi\rangle) & \text{otherwise} \end{cases}$
- $kQRec_t[F, G, H](|\psi\rangle) \triangleq \begin{cases} F(|\psi\rangle) & \text{if } l(|\psi\rangle) \leq t \\ G\left(\sum_{w \in \{0,1\}^k} |w\rangle \otimes F_w(\langle w|H(|\psi\rangle))\right) & \text{otherwise} \end{cases}$

where each $F_w \in \{kQRec_t[F, G, H], I\}$.

To handle general FBQP functions, [16] defines the extended encoding of an input $x \in \{0,1\}^*$ as $\phi_P(|x\rangle) \triangleq |0^{l(|x\rangle)}1\rangle|0^{P(l(|x\rangle))}10^{11P(l(|x\rangle))+6}1\rangle|x\rangle$, for some polynomial $P \in \mathbb{N}[X]$ that is an upper bound on the output size of the desired FBQP function. ϕ_P simply consists in the quantum state $|x\rangle$ preceded by a polynomial number of ancilla qubits. These ancilla provide space for internal computations and account for the polynomial bound associated to polynomial time QTMs.

Theorem 4 ([16]). *Given* $f : \{0,1\}^* \to \{0,1\}^*$ *with polynomial bound* $P \in \mathbb{N}[X]$, *the following statements are equivalent.*

1. *The function* f *is in* FBQP.
2. *There exists* $F \in \widehat{\square_1^{\text{QP}}}$ *such that* $F \circ \phi_P$ *computes* f *with probability* $\frac{2}{3}$.

We show the following result by structural induction on a function in $\widehat{\square_1^{\text{QP}}}$.

Theorem 5. *Let* F *be a function in* $\widehat{\square_1^{\text{QP}}}$. *Then there exists a* PFOQ *program* P *such that* $[\![P]\!] = F$.

We are now ready to state the completeness result.

Theorem 6. *For every function* f *in* FBQP *with polynomial bound* $Q \in \mathbb{N}[X]$, *there is a* PFOQ *program* P *such that* $[\![P]\!] \circ \phi_Q$ *computes* f *with probability* $\frac{2}{3}$.

Proof. By Theorem 4 and Theorem 5. $\square$

5   Compilation to polynomial-size quantum circuits

In this section, we provide an algorithm that compiles a PFOQ program on a given input length $n \in \mathbb{N}$ into a quantum circuit of size polynomial in n.

Quantum circuits [8] are a well-known graphical computational model for describing quantum computations. Qubits are represented by wires. Each unitary transformation U acting on n qubits can be represented as a gate U with n inputs and n outputs. A circuit C is an element of a PROP category ([10], a symmetric strict monoidal category whose morphisms are generated by gates G and wires. Let $\mathbb{1}$ be the identity circuit (for any length) and $\circ$ and $\otimes$ be the composition and product, respectively. By abuse of notation, given k circuits $C^1, \ldots, C^k$, $\circ_{i=1}^k C^i$ will denote the circuit $\tilde{C}^1 \circ \cdots \circ \tilde{C}^k$, where each circuit $\tilde{C}^i$ is obtained by tensoring C^i appropriately with identities so that the output of C^i matches the input of C^{i+1}. By construction, a circuit is acyclic. Each circuit C_n can be indexed by its number $n \in \mathbb{N}$ of input wires (i.e., non ancilla qubits) and computes a function $[\![C_n]\!] \in \mathcal{H}_{2^n} \to \mathcal{H}_{2^n}$. To deal with functions in $\mathcal{H} \to \mathcal{H}$, we consider families of circuits $(C_n)_{n \in \mathbb{N}}$, that are sequences of circuits such that each C_n encodes computation on quantum states of length n. Hence each circuit has n input qubits plus some extra ancilla qubits. These ancillas can be used to perform intermediate computations but also to represent functions whose output size is strictly greater than their input size. To avoid the consideration of families encoding undecidable properties, we put a uniformity restriction.

Definition 7. *A family of circuits* $(C_n)_{n\in\mathbb{N}}$ *is said to be* uniform *if there exists a polynomial time Turing machine that takes n as input and outputs a representation of C_n, for all $n \in \mathbb{N}$.*

In quantifying the complexity of a circuit, it is necessary to specify the considered elementary gates, and define the complexity of an operation as the number of elementary gates needed to perform it. In our setting, we consider the following set of universal elementary gates $\{R_Y(\pi/4), P(\pi/4), CNOT\}$. The size $\#C$ of a circuit C is equal to the number of its gates and wires.

Definition 8. *A family of circuits* $(C_n)_{n\in\mathbb{N}}$ *is said to be* polynomial-size *with $\alpha \in \mathbb{N} \to \mathbb{N}$ ancilla qubits if there exists a polynomial $P \in \mathbb{N}[X]$ such that, for each $n \in \mathbb{N}$, $\#C_n \leq P(n)$ and the number of ancilla qubits in C_n is exactly $\alpha(n)$.*

Let $\chi_m : \mathcal{H}_{2^n} \to \mathcal{H}_{2^{n+m}}$ be defined by $\chi_m(|\psi\rangle) \triangleq |\psi\rangle \otimes |0^m\rangle$, for a state $|\psi\rangle$ of size n. Let $\xi_m : \mathcal{H}_{2^n} \to \mathcal{H}_{2^m}$, with $m \leq n$, be defined by $\xi_m(|\psi\rangle) \triangleq \sum_{w\in\{0,1\}^m} \sum_{z\in\{0,1\}^{n-m}} \langle wz|\psi\rangle |w\rangle$. Finally, let $|w|$, for $w \in \{0,1\}^\star$, be the size of the word w.

Theorem 7. (Adapted from [17] and [11]) *A function $f : \{0,1\}^\star \to \{0,1\}^\star$ is in* FBQP *iff there exists a uniform polynomial-size family of circuits* $(C_n)_{n\in\mathbb{N}}$ *with α ancilla qubits s.t. $\forall x \in \{0,1\}^\star$, $\left|\langle f(x)|\xi_{|f(x)|} \circ [\![C_{|x|}]\!] \circ \chi_{\alpha(|x|)}(|x\rangle)\rangle\right|^2 \geq \frac{2}{3}$.*

In Theorem 7, $[\![C_{|x|}]\!]$ is a function in $\mathcal{H}_{2^{|x|+\alpha(|x|)}} \to \mathcal{H}_{2^{|x|+\alpha(|x|)}}$ The function $\chi_{\alpha(|x|)}$ pads the input with ancilla in state $|0\rangle$ to match the circuit dimension. The function $\xi_{|f(x)|}$ projects the output of the circuit to match the length of the function output $|f(x)|$. Hence, for $|x\rangle \in \mathcal{H}_{2^{|x|}}$, $\xi_{|f(x)|} \circ [\![C_{|x|}]\!] \circ \chi_{\alpha(|x|)}(|x\rangle) \in \mathcal{H}_{2^{|f(x)|}}$.

Compilation to circuits. For each PFOQ program P, the existence of a polynomial-size uniform family of circuits $(C_n)_{n\in\mathbb{N}}$ that computes $[\![P]\!]$ is entailed by the combination of Lemma 2 and Theorem 7. However, due to the complex machinery of QTM, the constructions of both proofs cannot be used in practice to generate a circuit. In this section, we exhibit an algorithm that compiles directly a PFOQ program to a polynomial-size circuit. Note that this compilation process requires some care since recursive procedure calls in quantum cases may yield an exponential number of calls. The remainder of this section will be devoted to presenting an algorithm, named **compile**, which, for a given PFOQ program P and a given integer n produces a circuit C_n such that $\forall|\psi\rangle \in \mathcal{H}_{2^n}$, $[\![P]\!](|\psi\rangle) = \xi_n \circ [\![C_n]\!] \circ \chi_{\alpha(n)}(|\psi\rangle)$.

The **compile** algorithm uses two subroutines, named **compr** and **optimize**, and is defined by $\mathbf{compile}(P, n) \triangleq \mathbf{compr}(P, [1, \ldots, n], \cdot)$.

The subroutine **compr** (Algorithm 1) generates the circuit inductively on the program statement. It takes as inputs: a program P, a list of qubit pointers l, and a control structure cs. A *control structure* cs is a partial function in $\mathbb{N} \to \{0,1\}$, mapping a qubit pointer to a control value (of a quantum case). Let $\cdot$ be the control structure of empty domain. For $n \in \mathbb{N}$ and $k \in \{0,1\}$, $cs[n := k]$ is the control structure obtained from cs by setting $cs(n) \triangleq k$. For a given $x \in \{0,1\}^{\star}$, we say that state $|x\rangle$ *satisfies* cs if, $\forall n \in dom(cs)$, $cs(n) = k \Rightarrow |\langle k|_n |x\rangle|^2 = 1$. Two control structures cs and cs' are *orthogonal* if there does not exist a state $|x\rangle$ that satisfies cs and cs'. Note that if $\exists i \in dom(cs) \cap dom(cs')$, $cs(i) + cs'(i) = 1$ then cs and cs' are orthogonal.

Algorithm 1 (compr)

Input: $(P, l, cs) \in \text{Programs} \times \mathcal{L}(\mathbb{N}) \times (\mathbb{N} \to \{0,1\})$

Let $D :: S = P$ **in**
if $S = $ **skip;** **then**
   $C \leftarrow \mathbb{1}$ ▷ Identity circuit

else if $S = s[i]$ ***=** $U^f(j)$; **and** $(s[i], l) \Downarrow_{\mathbb{N}} n$ **and** $(U^f(j), l) \Downarrow_{\mathbb{C}^2 \times 2} M$ **then**
   $C \leftarrow M(cs, [n])$ ▷ Controlled gate

else if $S = S_1 S_2$ **then**
   $C \leftarrow \textbf{compr}(D :: S_1, l, cs) \circ \textbf{compr}(D :: S_2, l, cs)$ ▷ Composition

else if $S = $ **if** b **then** S_{true} **else** S_{false} **and** $(b, l) \Downarrow_{\mathbb{B}} b$ **then**
   $C \leftarrow \textbf{compr}(D :: S_b, l, cs)$ ▷ Conditional

else if $S = $ **qcase** s[i] **of** $\{0 \to S_0, 1 \to S_1\}$ **and** $(s[i], l) \Downarrow_{\mathbb{N}} n$ **then**
   $C \leftarrow \textbf{compr}(D :: S_0, l, cs[n := 0]) \circ \textbf{compr}(D :: S_1, l, cs[n := 1])$ ▷ Quantum case

else if $S = $ **call** proc[i](s) **and** $(s, l) \Downarrow_{\mathcal{L}(\mathbb{N})} []$ **then**
   $C \leftarrow \mathbb{1}$ ▷ Nil call

else if $S = $ **call** proc[i](s) **and** $(s, l) \Downarrow_{\mathcal{L}(\mathbb{N})} l' \neq []$ **and** $(i, l) \Downarrow_{\mathbb{Z}} n$ **then**
   if $\text{width}_P(\text{proc}) = 0$ **then**
      $C \leftarrow \textbf{compr}(D :: S^{\text{proc}}\{n/x\}, l', cs)$ ▷ Non-recursive call
   else if $\text{width}_P(\text{proc}) = 1$ **then**
      $C \leftarrow \textbf{optimize}(D, [(cs, S^{\text{proc}}\{n/x\})], \text{proc}, l', \{\})$ ▷ Recursive call
   end if
end if
return C

Given a control structure cs and a statement S, a *controlled statement* is a pair $(cs, S) \in \text{Cst} \triangleq (\mathbb{N} \to \{0,1\}) \times \text{Statements}$. Intuitively, a controlled statement (cs, S) denotes a statement controlled by the qubits whose indices are in $dom(cs)$. For a unitary gate $U \in \mathcal{H}_{2^n} \to \mathcal{H}_{2^n}$, a control structure cs, and a list of pointers $l = [x_1, \ldots, x_n] \in \mathcal{L}(\mathbb{N})$ such that $\{x_1, \ldots, x_n\} \cap dom(cs) = \emptyset$, $U(cs, l)$ denotes the circuit applying gate U on qubits $\bar{q}[x_1], \ldots, \bar{q}[x_n]$, whenever $\forall m \in dom(cs)$, $\bar{q}[m]$ is in state $|cs(m)\rangle$. As demonstrated in [11], this circuit can be built with $O(card(dom(cs)))$ elementary gates and ancillas, and a single controlled-U gate.

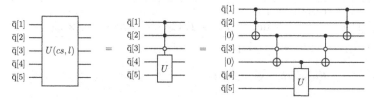

Fig. 4: Example of circuit $U(cs, l)$

Example 5. As an illustrative example, consider a binary gate U and a control structure cs such that $dom(cs) = \{1, 2, 3\}$, $cs(1) = cs(2) = 1$, and $cs(3) = 0$. Also consider a list $l = [4, 5] \in \mathcal{L}(\mathbb{N})$. The circuit $U(cs, l)$ is provided in Figure 4.

Similarly, we can define a generalized Toffoli gate as a circuit of the shape $NOT(cs, n)$. Since $card(dom(cs))$ will not scale with the size of the input, such a circuit has a constant cost in gates and ancillas and can thus be considered as an elementary gate. We will also be interested in rearranging wires under a given control structure. For two lists of qubit pointers $l_1 = [x_1, \ldots, x_n]$, $l_2 = [x'_1, \ldots, x'_n] \in \mathcal{L}(\mathbb{N})$, define $SWAP(cs, l_1, l_2)$ as the circuit that swaps the wires in l_1 with wires in l_2, controlled on cs. This circuit needs in the worst case one ancilla and $O(n)$ controlled $SWAP$ gates (also known as Fredkin gates).

Let $\mathcal{D} \triangleq \mathcal{D}(\text{Procedures} \times \mathbb{Z} \times \mathbb{N} \to \mathbb{N} \times \mathcal{L}(\mathbb{N}))$ be the set of dictionaries mapping keys of the shape $(proc, i, j)$ to pairs of the shape (a, l), where i is the value of a classical parameter, j is the size of a sorted set, and a is a qubit index. We will denote the empty dictionary by $\{\}$. Let also $a \leftarrow \textbf{new } ancilla()$ be an instruction that sets a to a fresh qubit index.

The subroutine **optimize** (Algorithm 2) treats the complex cases where circuit optimizations (merging) are needed, that is for recursive procedure calls. It takes as input a sequence of procedure declarations D, a list of controlled statements l_{Cst}, a procedure name proc, a list of qubit pointers l, and a dictionary Anc. The subroutine iterates on list l_{Cst} of controlled statements, indicating the statements left to be treated together with their control qubits. When recursive procedure calls appear in distinct branches of a quantum case, the algorithm merges these calls together. For that purpose, it uses new ancilla qubits as control qubits. Given procedure calls of shape **call** proc[i](s);, with respect to a given list $l \in \mathcal{L}(\mathbb{N})$, such that $(i, l) \Downarrow_{\mathbb{Z}} i$, $(s, l) \Downarrow_{\mathcal{L}(\mathbb{N})} l'$, and $(|s|, l) \Downarrow_{\mathbb{N}} j$. If the key $(proc, i, j)$ already exists in the dictionary Anc, the associated ancilla is re-used, otherwise, Anc[$proc, i, j$] is set to (a, l'). We can assume w.l.o.g. that the statement controlled on the ancilla can be treated only after all the re-uses of the ancilla. This can be done without increasing the total complexity of **optimize**.

Some extra ancillas e are also created for swapping wires and are not explicitly indexed since they are not revisited by the subroutine, and are just considered unique. Ancillas a and e are indexed and treated as input qubits, therefore they can be part of the domain of control structures.

Algorithm 2 (optimize) Build circuit for recursive procedure proc
Inputs: $(D, l_{Cst}, proc, l, Anc) \in Decl \times \mathcal{L}(Cst) \times Procedures \times \mathcal{L}(\mathbb{N}) \times \mathcal{D}$

$C_L \leftarrow \mathbb{1}; C_R \leftarrow \mathbb{1}; P \leftarrow D :: \textbf{skip};$
while $l_{Cst} \neq [\,]$ **do**
$\quad (cs, S) \leftarrow hd(l_{Cst}); \; l_{Cst} \leftarrow tl(l_{Cst})$

$\quad$ **if** $S = S_1 S_2$ **then**
$\qquad$ **if** $w_P^{proc}(S_1) = 1$ **then**
$\qquad\quad l_{Cst} \leftarrow l_{Cst}@[(cs, S_1)]; \; C_R \leftarrow \textbf{compr}(D :: S_2, l, cs) \circ C_R$
$\qquad$ **else**
$\qquad\quad l_{Cst} \leftarrow l_{Cst}@[(cs, S_2)]; \; C_L \leftarrow C_L \circ \textbf{compr}(D :: S_1, l, cs)$
$\qquad$ **end if**
$\quad$ **end if**

$\quad$ **if** $S = $ **if** b **then** $S_{\textbf{true}}$ **else** $S_{\textbf{false}}$ **and** $(b, l) \Downarrow_{\mathbb{B}} b$ **then**
$\qquad$ **if** $w_P^{proc}(S_b) = 1$ **then**
$\qquad\quad l_{Cst} \leftarrow l_{Cst}@[(cs, S_b)]$
$\qquad$ **else**
$\qquad\quad C_L \leftarrow C_L \circ \textbf{compr}(D :: S_b, l, cs)$
$\qquad$ **end if**
$\quad$ **end if**

$\quad$ **if** $S = $ **qcase** $s[i]$ **of** $\{0 \rightarrow S_0, 1 \rightarrow S_1\}$ **and** $(s[i], l) \Downarrow_{\mathbb{N}} n$ **then**
$\qquad$ **if** $w_P^{proc}(S_0) = 1$ **and** $w_P^{proc}(S_1) = 1$ **then**
$\qquad\quad l_{Cst} \leftarrow l_{Cst}@[(cs[n := 0], S_0), (cs[n := 1], S_1)]$
$\qquad$ **else if** $w_P^{proc}(S_1) = 0$ **then**
$\qquad\quad l_{Cst} \leftarrow l_{Cst}@[(cs[n := 0], S_0)];$
$\qquad\quad C_R \leftarrow \textbf{compr}(D :: S_1, l, cs[n := 1]) \circ C_R$
$\qquad$ **else if** $w_P^{proc}(S_0) = 0$ **then**
$\qquad\quad l_{Cst} \leftarrow l_{Cst}@[(cs[n := 1], S_1)];$
$\qquad\quad C_R \leftarrow \textbf{compr}(D :: S_0, l, cs[n := 0]) \circ C_R$
$\qquad$ **end if**
$\quad$ **end if**

$\quad$ **if** $S = $ **call** $proc'[i](s)$ **and** $(s, l) \Downarrow_{\mathcal{L}(\mathbb{N})} l' \neq [\,]$ **and** $(i, l) \Downarrow_{\mathbb{Z}} n$ **then**
$\qquad$ **if** $(proc', n, |l'|) \in Anc$ **then**
$\qquad\quad$ **Let** $(a, l'') = Anc[proc', n, |l'|]$ **in**
$\qquad\quad e \leftarrow \textbf{new } ancilla();$
$\qquad\quad C_L \leftarrow C_L \circ NOT(cs, e) \circ NOT(\cdot[e = 1], a) \circ SWAP(\cdot[e = 1], l', l'');$
$\qquad\quad C_R \leftarrow SWAP(\cdot[e = 1], l'', l') \circ NOT(\cdot[e = 1], a) \circ NOT(cs, e) \circ C_R$
$\qquad$ **else**
$\qquad\quad a \leftarrow \textbf{new } ancilla()$
$\qquad\quad Anc[proc', n, |l'|] \leftarrow (a, l');$
$\qquad\quad C_L \leftarrow C_L \circ NOT(cs, a); \; C_R \leftarrow NOT(cs, a) \circ C_R;$
$\qquad\quad l_{Cst} \leftarrow l_{Cst}@[(\cdot[a = 1], S^{proc'}\{n/x\})]$
$\qquad$ **end if**
$\quad$ **end if**
end while
return $C_L \circ C_R$

Theorem 8. *For any* P *in* PFOQ, *there is* $Q \in \mathbb{N}[X]$, $\forall n \in \mathbb{N}$, $\forall |\psi\rangle \in \mathcal{H}_{2^n}$, $[\![P]\!](|\psi\rangle) = \xi_n \circ [\![\mathbf{compile}(P, n)]\!] \circ \chi_{\alpha(n)}(|\psi\rangle)$ *and* $\#\mathbf{compile}(P, n) \le Q(n)$.

Example 6. **compile**(QFT, n) outputs the circuit provided in Example 1. Notice that there is no extra ancilla as no procedure call appears in the branch of a quantum case.

Polynomial-size circuits. We show Theorem 8 by exhibiting that any exponential growth of the circuit can be avoided by the **compile** algorithm using an argument based on orthogonal control structures. With a linear number of gates and a constant number of extra ancillas, we can merge calls referring to the same procedure, on different branches of a quantum case, when they are applied to sorted sets of equal size. An example of the construction is given in Figure 5 where two instances of a gate U are merged into one using $SWAP$ gates and gates controlled by orthogonal control structures.

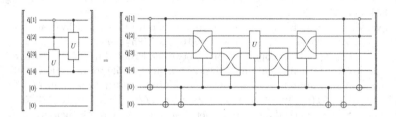

Fig. 5: Example of circuit optimization.

The following proposition shows that multiple uses of a gate can be merged in one provided they are applied to orthogonal control structures.

Lemma 4 *For any circuit* $C_n \triangleq \circ_{i=1}^k U(cs_i, l_i)$, *with a unitary gate* U, *pairwise orthogonal* $cs_1, \dots, cs_k \in \mathrm{Cst}$, *and* $l_1, \dots l_k \in \mathcal{L}(\mathbb{N})$, *there exists a circuit* C *using one controlled gate* U, $O(kn)$ *gates, and* $O(k)$ *ancillas, and such that* $[\![C]\!] = [\![C_n]\!]$.

Now we show that orthogonality is an invariant property of **compile**.

Lemma 5 *Orthogonality is an invariant property of the control structures in* l_{Cst} *of the subroutine* **optimize**. *In other words, for any two distinct pairs* (cs, S), (cs', S') *in* l_{Cst}, *cs and cs' are orthogonal.*

Theorem 9. *For any* P *in* PFOQ, **compile**(P, n) *runs in time* $O(n^{2|P|+1})$.

Proof. Using Lemma 4 and Lemma 5.   □

As there is no circuit duplication in the assignments of **compile**, we can deduce from Theorem 9 that the compiled circuit is of polynomial size.

Corollary 1. *For any* P *in* PFOQ, *there exists a polynomial* $Q \in \mathbb{N}[X]$ *such that* $\#\mathbf{compile}(P, n) \le Q(n)$.

References

1. Bellantoni, S., Cook, S.: A new recursion-theoretic characterization of the polytime functions. computational complexity **2**(2), 97–110 (Jun 1992). https://doi.org/10.1007/BF01201998
2. Bernstein, E., Vazirani, U.: Quantum complexity theory. SIAM Journal on Computing **26**(5), 1411–1473 (1997). https://doi.org/10.1137/S0097539796300921
3. Boykin, P.O., Mor, T., Pulver, M., Roychowdhury, V., Vatan, F.: On universal and fault-tolerant quantum computing (1999). https://doi.org/10.48550/ARXIV.QUANT-PH/9906054
4. Briegel, H.J., Browne, D.E., Dür, W., Raussendorf, R., Van den Nest, M.: Measurement-based quantum computation. Nature Physics **5**(1), 19–26 (2009). https://doi.org/10.1038/nphys1157
5. Dal Lago, U.: A short introduction to implicit computational complexity. In: ESSLLI 2010. pp. 89–109 (2011). https://doi.org/10.1007/978-3-642-31485-8_3
6. Dal Lago, U., Masini, A., Zorzi, M.: Quantum implicit computational complexity. Theoretical Computer Science **411**(2), 377–409 (2010). https://doi.org/10.1016/j.tcs.2009.07.045
7. Danos, V., Kashefi, E.: Determinism in the one-way model. Physical Review A **74**(5), 052310 (2006). https://doi.org/10.1103/PhysRevA.74.052310
8. Deutsch, D.E.: Quantum computational networks. Proceedings of the Royal Society of London. A. Mathematical and Physical Sciences **425**(1868), 73–90 (1989)
9. Feynman, R.P.: Simulating physics with computers. International Journal of Theoretical Physics **21**(6), 467–488 (Jun 1982). https://doi.org/10.1007/BF02650179
10. MacLane, S.: Categorical algebra. Bulletin of the American Mathematical Society **71**(1), 40–106 (1965). https://doi.org/10.1090/S0002-9904-1965-11234-4
11. Nielsen, M.A., Chuang, I.L.: Quantum Computation and Quantum Information: 10th Anniversary Edition. Cambridge University Press (2011)
12. Péchoux, R.: Implicit computational complexity: past and future. Mémoire d'habilitation à diriger des recherches (2020), https://tel.archives-ouvertes.fr/tel-02978986, université de Lorraine
13. Ross, N.J.: Algebraic and logical methods in quantum computation. PhD thesis (2015). https://doi.org/10.48550/ARXIV.1510.02198
14. Selinger, P.: Towards a quantum programming language. Mathematical Structures in Computer Science **14**(4), 527–586 (2004). https://doi.org/10.1017/S0960129504004256
15. Shor, P.W.: Algorithms for quantum computation: discrete logarithms and factoring. In: Proceedings 35th Annual Symposium on Foundations of Computer Science. pp. 124–134 (1994). https://doi.org/10.1109/SFCS.1994.365700
16. Yamakami, T.: A schematic definition of quantum polynomial time computability. J. Symb. Log. **85**(4), 1546–1587 (2020). https://doi.org/10.1017/jsl.2020.45
17. Yao, A.C.C.: Quantum circuit complexity. In: Proceedings of 1993 IEEE 34th Annual Foundations of Computer Science. pp. 352–361 (1993). https://doi.org/10.1109/SFCS.1993.366852

On the Existential Arithmetics with Addition and Bitwise Minimum

Mikhail R. Starchak$^{(\boxtimes)}$ (iD)

St. Petersburg State University, St. Petersburg, Russia
m.starchak@spbu.ru

Abstract. This paper presents a similar approach for existential first-order characterizations of the languages recognizable by finite automata, by Parikh automata, and by multi-counter machines over the alphabet $\{0, 1, ..., k-1\}^n$ for some $k \geq 2$. The set of k-FA-recognizable relations coincides with the set of relations, which are existentially definable in the structure $\langle \mathbb{N}; 0, 1, +, \&_k, = \rangle$, where $\&_k$ corresponds to the bitwise minimum of base k. In order to obtain an existential first-order description of k-Parikh automata languages, we extend this structure with the predicate $EqNZB_k(x, y)$ which is true if and only if x and y have the same number of non-zero bits in k-ary encoding. Using essentially the same ideas, we encode computations of k-multi-counter machines and thus show that every recursively enumerable relation over the natural numbers is existentially definable in the aforementioned structure supplemented with concatenation $z = x \frown_k y \rightleftharpoons z = x + k^{l_k(x)}y$, where $l_k(x)$ is the bit-length of x in base k. This result gives us another proof of DPR-theorem.

Keywords: Bitwise minimum · Büchi arithmetic · Parikh automata · Existential definability · Recursively enumerable sets · DPR-theorem · Concatenation

1   Introduction

In a recent paper [11], Haase and Różycki considered definability problems in k-Büchi arithmetic, an extension of Presburger arithmetic with a relation V_k such that $V_k(x, y)$ if and only if x is the largest power of k that divides y. They proved that there are relations which are definable in k-Büchi arithmetic (k-definable) and not definable by any existential formula of the corresponding language. By a slight modification of a theorem of Villemaire [24, Corollary 2.4], they show that every k-definable relation can actually be expressed via some $\exists\forall$-formula, whereas Villemaire constructs a $\exists\forall\exists$-formula.

Büchi arithmetic of base $k \geq 2$ can be considered as a first-order characterization of the languages, recognizable by finite-state automata over the alphabet $\{0, 1, ..., k-1\}^n$ (called k-FA-recognizable). Interpreting the words of this language as tuples $(x_1, ..., x_n)$ of natural numbers in base k encoding, we obtain the Büchi-Bruyère theorem [3,5], which states that every relation $R \subseteq \mathbb{N}^n$ is k-FA-recognizable if and only if it is k-definable. A second-order version of this theorem

O. Kupferman and P. Sobocinski (Eds.): FoSSaCS 2023, LNCS 13992, pp. 176–195, 2023.
https://doi.org/10.1007/978-3-031-30829-1_9

(which was proved independently by Büchi [5], Elgot [9], and Trakhtenbrot [22]) says that every relation is 2-FA-recognizable iff it is weak monadic second-order (WMSO-)definable in the structure $\langle \mathbb{N}; S \rangle$, where S is a unary function symbol for the successor function over the natural numbers. The WMSO-theory of $\langle \mathbb{N}; S \rangle$ is usually denoted by WS1S.

Coming back to the Villemaire's result, we see that his encoding of k-FA via $\exists\forall\exists$-formulas of the language of k-Büchi arithmetic uses a unique bounded universal quantifier. A similar construction often appears in logical descriptions of abstract machines. For example, Klaedtke and Rueß considered in [16] various definability and decidability properties for WMSO-formulas with successor S and cardinality constraints of the form $|X_1| + ... + |X_r| < |Y_1| + ... + |Y_s|$; the corresponding WMSO-theory of $\mathbb{N}$ was denoted by WS1S^{card}. They introduced Parikh automata, an extension of finite automata, and obtained an analogue of Büchi's Theorem, namely every relation recognizable by a Parikh automaton over the alphabet $\{0, 1\}^n$ is existentially WMSO-definable in $\mathbb{N}$ with S and cardinality constraints, and vice versa. Here, only second-order variables are existentially quantified, while the formula, which describes a computation of a given Parikh automaton, still contains a universally quantified first-order variable (see [16, Theorem 10], where the universal quantifier $\forall x$ can be bounded by the maximal element of the existentially quantified second-order variable U).

Note that while WS1S is decidable, WS1S^{card} is already undecidable, and its decidable fragments [16, Theorem 16] were obtained as a consequence of decidability of the emptiness problem for Parikh automata. Translating these undecidability results into first-order context, Bès showed [2, Proposition 3.8] in particular that the graph of multiplication function is definable in the structure $\langle \mathbb{N}; 0, 1, +, V_2, EqNonZeroBits, = \rangle$, where $EqNonZeroBits(x, y)$ is true iff x and y have the same number of non-zero bits in their binary representations. This implies undecidability of the first-order theory of this structure, but it is not known, for example, whether the existential first-order theory is decidable. In the concluding section [2], Bès remarks that *"it would be interesting to study the expressive power of fragments of FO arithmetic which include predicates like EqNonZeroBits"*. We will further shorten the name of this predicate to *EqNZB*.

The Davis-Putnam-Robinson theorem (DPR-theorem) [8] was a milestone in the undecidability proof of the Hilbert's Tenth Problem. This theorem states that every relation $R \subseteq \mathbb{N}^n$ is recursively enumerable (r.e.) if and only if it is existentially first-order definable in the structure $\langle \mathbb{N}; 0, 1, +, \cdot, exp, = \rangle$ (these relations are also called *exponential diophantine*). As the starting point, the proof uses the result of Davis [7], which states that every r.e. set is $\exists\forall\exists$-definable in the structure $\langle \mathbb{N}; 0, 1, +, \cdot, = \rangle$ with one bounded universal quantifier. It is important for us that elimination of this quantifier in the proof of DPR-theorem involves multiplication, factorial, binomial coefficients, and does not seem useful when we try to eliminate bounded universal quantifier in weaker structures. However in 1976, Matiyasevich presented an alternative proof of DPR-theorem [19] by purely existential encoding of computations of Turing machines, which thus gives us another approach for eliminating bounded universal quantifier [20, Section 6.1].

It is easy to modify the final steps of Matiyasevich's proof in order to obtain an existential formula of the language with 0, 1, addition, bitwise minimum &, and concatenation $\frown$, where $t = x \frown y \rightleftharpoons t = x + 2^{l(x)}y$ and $l(x)$ is the bit-length of x. Kummer's lemma [18] then plays a crucial role, since it gives an exponential diophantine representation of bitwise minimum (see also an exponential diophantine representation of *masking* relation $\preccurlyeq$ in [14]). Note that it is not difficult to define & in the structure $\langle \mathbb{N}; 0, 1, +, V_2, = \rangle$ by a formula with one bounded universal quantifier, whereas there is an existential formula that defines V_2 in $\langle \mathbb{N}; 0, 1, +, \&, = \rangle$. This suggests the question whether every 2-FA-recognizable relation is existentially first-order definable in $\langle \mathbb{N}; 0, 1, +, \&, = \rangle$.

In Theorem 1, we show that every relation is actually k-FA-recognizable if and only if it is existentially definable in the structure $\langle \mathbb{N}; 0, 1, +, \&_k, = \rangle$, where $\&_k$ corresponds to the binary bitwise minimum operation of base k. The same approach is applied in Theorem 2 to obtain an existential first-order characterization of the languages, recognizable by Parikh automata over the alphabet $\{0, 1, ..., k-1\}^n$. In this case, the structure must be extended by the binary predicate $EqNZB_k$, which is true for those pairs of natural numbers (x, y) such that x and y have the same number of non-zero bits of base k.

Applying essentially the same ideas as in Theorem 1, we are able to show in Theorem 3 that every relation $R \subseteq \mathbb{N}^n$ is recognizable by multi-counter machines over the alphabet $\{0, 1, ..., k-1\}^n$ if and only if it is existentially definable in the structure $\langle \mathbb{N}; 0, 1, +, \&_k, \frown_k, = \rangle$, where $z = x \frown_k y \rightleftharpoons z = x + k^{l_k(x)}y$ and $l_k(x)$ is the bit-length of x in base k. Since such machines recognize exactly r.e. sets, this provides yet another [14,19,20] proof of DPR-theorem by purely existential arithmetization of abstract machines.

2   Definitions and the main example

This section recalls some basic definitions from logic and automata theory, which will be used in the sequel. Then we illustrate the main idea of the existential characterisations constructed in Sections 3 and 4.

2.1   Definability and automata

First-order definability. The domain of all the structures considered in this paper will be the set of natural numbers $\mathbb{N} = \{0, 1, 2, ...\}$, and we will consider existential definability in some extensions of $\langle \mathbb{N}; 0, 1, +, = \rangle$.

Denote by L_σ the first-order language of some signature σ. An L_σ-formula φ is existential if it has the form $\exists \overline{x} \psi(\overline{x}, \overline{y})$, where $\psi(\overline{x}, \overline{y})$ is a quantifier-free L_σ-formula. Here, $\overline{x}$ denotes a list of variables $x_1, ..., x_n$. We say that an n-ary relation R over $\mathbb{N}$ is *first-order (FO-)definable in the structure* $\langle \mathbb{N}; \sigma \rangle$ if there exists an L_σ-formula $\varphi(\overline{x})$ such that for every $\overline{a} \in \mathbb{N}^n$ we have $R(\overline{a})$ if and only if $\varphi(\overline{a})$. When the formula $\varphi(\overline{x})$ is existential, the corresponding relation is called *existentially first-order ($\exists$FO-)definable*, and similarly for the case of quantifier-free formulas, universal formulas and other quantifier prefixes. We will subsequently write the prefix "FO" in the cases where we also discuss second-order definability, and in general it will be omitted.

In this paragraph, we focus on definability in the structure $\langle \mathbb{N}; 0, 1, +, V_k, = \rangle$, where $k \geq 2$ is an integer, and V_k is a binary relation such that $V_k(x, y)$ if and only if x is the largest power of k dividing y. Büchi arithmetic of base k is the first-order theory of this structure. The relations definable in this structure are called k-*definable*. Recall that for every multiplicatively independent integer $l \geq 2$ (i.e., $k^a \neq l^b$ for every positive integers a, b), V_l is not definable in $\langle \mathbb{N}; 0, 1, +, V_k, = \rangle$ [23,24] (see also a generalization of this result by Bès [1]). In the following, we consider some fixed base k. Let $\&_k$ be the binary bitwise minimum operation of base k, where we assume that the natural number of smaller bit-length is supplemented with a sufficient number of leading zeros. For example, we have $120202 \&_3 21201201 = 100201$. It is not difficult to prove the following lemma.

Lemma 1. *Every relation is k-definable if and only if it is definable in the structure $\langle \mathbb{N}; 0, 1, +, \&_k, = \rangle$.*

Proof. In order to define bitwise minimum, for every $j \in [0..k - 1]$ we use the relation $X_{k,j}(x, y)$, which is defined as "x is a power of k and the coefficient of this power of k in the representation of y in base k equals j". There is a simple existential formula for this relation in [4,11,24]:

$$X_{k,j}(x, y) \rightleftharpoons V_k(x, x) \wedge \exists z \exists t \exists u (y = z + jx + t \wedge z < x \wedge (t = 0 \vee (V_k(u, t) \wedge x < u))),$$

where $x < y \rightleftharpoons \exists z (y = x + z + 1)$. Therefore, the graph of bitwise minimum can be expressed by a formula with a universal quantifier

$$z = x \&_k y \rightleftharpoons \forall t \bigwedge_{(i,j) \in [0..k-1]^2} \left(X_{k,i}(t, x) \wedge X_{k,j}(t, y) \Leftrightarrow X_{k,\min(i,j)}(t, z) \right).$$

For the converse, by using monus $z = x - y \rightleftharpoons (z = 0 \wedge x < y) \vee (x = z + y)$, define the set of powers of k by the formula $P_k(x) \Leftrightarrow (kx - 1) \&_k x = x \wedge \neg x = 0$. Finally, we have $V_k(x, y) \Leftrightarrow P_k(x) \wedge \bigvee_{j \in [1..k-1]} (kx - 1) \&_k y = jx$. □

We see that $X_{k,j}(x, y)$ can be defined in $\langle \mathbb{N}; 0, 1, +, \&_k, = \rangle$ by the quantifier-free formula $P_k(x) \wedge y \&_k x = jx$. Let $\lambda_k(x)$ be the greatest power of k less or equal to x when $x > 0$, and $\lambda_k(0) = 1$. Formally, we have the definition $y = \lambda_k(x) \Leftrightarrow (x = 0 \wedge y = 1) \vee (P_k(y) \wedge y \leq x \wedge x < y)$. Now an analogue of bitwise negation can be defined as follows: $\sim_k (y, x) = (k\lambda_k(y) - 1) - x \&_k (k\lambda_k(y) - 1)$. Here, $\sim_k (y, x)$ has the same bit-length as y, and we assume that $\&_k$ has a higher precedence than $+$ or monus. For our purposes, it is useful to include in the signature a binary function symbol for bitwise maximum

$$z = x |_k y \Leftrightarrow (x < y \wedge z = \sim_k (y, \sim_k (y, x) \&_k \sim_k (y, y)) \vee$$
$$(y \leq x \wedge z = \sim_k (x, \sim_k (x, x) \&_k \sim_k (x, y)).$$

We will write $\frac{x}{k^n}$ with some fixed natural number n for the function whose graph is quantifier-free definable by the formula $y = \frac{x}{k^n} \Leftrightarrow k^n y \le x \wedge x < k^n(y+1)$. The function $\mathbf{1}_k(y)$ gives a natural number of the same bit-length with y, but with all k-ary digits equal to one: $x = \mathbf{1}_k(y) \Leftrightarrow (k-1)x = k\lambda_k(y) - 1$. For notational convenience, let us introduce a binary predicate symbol $\preccurlyeq_k$ such that $x \preccurlyeq_k y \rightleftharpoons x \&_k y = x$. The following lemma summarizes these definability results and will be implicitly used in the next sections.

Lemma 2. *The predicates P_k, V_k, $X_{k,j}$, $<$, $\le$ and the graphs of functions $-$, λ_k, $\sim_k$, $\mathbf{1}_k$, $|_k$, and $\frac{\cdot}{k^n}$ for every fixed $n \ge 1$ are $\exists$-definable in the structure $\langle \mathbb{N}; 0, 1, +, \&_k, = \rangle$.*

The existential encoding of k-automata in Subsection 2.2 uses a $\exists$-definable function, which echoes a construction that was applied by Matiyasevich [19] in his arithmetization of Turing machines. For every $a \in [1..k-1]$ the function $\Theta_{k,a}(x)$ substitutes 1 for every digit of x equal to a, and 0 otherwise. Then, the graph of this function is defined as follows:

$$y = \Theta_{k,a}(x) \Leftrightarrow \exists x_1...\exists x_{k-1} \Big(\bigwedge_{1 \le i < j \le k-1} x_i \&_k x_j = 0 \wedge$$
$$(x_1 + ... + x_{k-1}) \preccurlyeq_k \mathbf{1}_k(x) \wedge \tag{1}$$
$$x_1 + 2x_2 + ... + (k-1)x_{k-1} = x \wedge y = x_a \Big).$$

Note that each digit in the k-ary representation of every quantified variable in (1) is either 0 or 1. Moreover, if we denote $\bar{\mathbf{1}}_k(x) \rightleftharpoons x \&_k \mathbf{1}_k(x)$ then the sum $x_1 + ... + x_{k-1}$ is exactly $\bar{\mathbf{1}}_k(x)$. In the case of digit zero, the function $\Theta_{k,0}$ has an extra parameter that specifies the number of leading zeros, which must be replaced by ones:

$$y = \Theta_{k,0}(t, x) \Leftrightarrow y = \mathbf{1}_k(t) - \bar{\mathbf{1}}_k(x). \tag{2}$$

In particular, when $\lambda_k(t) < \lambda_k(x)$, we always have $\Theta_{k,0}(t, x) = 0$ and otherwise we obtain, for example, $\Theta_{3,0}(100000, 1020) = 110101$.

Remark 1. In Subsection 2.2 and Section 3 it is convenient to write $\Theta_{k,a}(t, x)$ instead of $\Theta_{k,a}(x)$ when $a \in \{1, ..., k-1\}$. In Section 4 there is no need to consider auxiliary zeros, and we use $\Theta_{k,a}$ with a single parameter assuming that $\Theta_{k,0}(x) \rightleftharpoons \Theta_{k,0}(x, x)$.

We conclude this paragraph by defining a set of natural numbers $\bar{\mathbf{1}}_k(\mathbb{N}) = \{\bar{\mathbf{1}}_k(x) \mid x \in \mathbb{N}\}$. This definition will be useful in the next paragraph.

Second-order definability. Similarly to Bès [2], let us denote by $\mathcal{F}$ the set of *finite* subsets of $\mathbb{N}$ and also define a function $cod_k : \mathcal{F}^n \to \mathbb{N}^n$ which maps every tuple $(X_1, ..., X_n) \in \mathcal{F}^n$ to the tuple of non-negative integers $cod_k(\overline{X}) = (\sum_{i \in X_1} k^i, ..., \sum_{i \in X_n} k^i)$. We see that the image of cod_k is $\bar{\mathbf{1}}_k(\mathbb{N})$. This function establishes a connection between first-order definability and weak monadic second-order (WMSO-)definability in $\langle \mathbb{N}; S \rangle$ in the following way.

Recall that WMSO-language L_σ^{WMSO} allows to quantify over finite subsets of the domain, and its signature σ has auxiliary binary predicate symbol $\in$ for the membership relation $x \in X$. Again, let the domain of our structures be the set of natural numbers $\mathbb{N}$. Then a relation $R \subseteq \mathcal{F}^n$ is *WMSO-definable in the structure* $\langle \mathbb{N}; \sigma \rangle$ if there exists a L_σ^{WMSO}-formula $\varphi(X_1, ..., X_n)$ such that $R(\overline{A}) \Leftrightarrow \varphi(\overline{A})$ for every $\overline{A} \in \mathcal{F}^n$. As was explicitly shown by Villemaire [23, Theorem 3.3], every relation $R \subseteq \mathcal{F}^n$ is WMSO-definable in the structure $\langle \mathbb{N}; S \rangle$ if and only if $cod_2(R)$ is FO-definable in $\langle \mathbb{N}; 0, 1, +, V_2, = \rangle$.

Note that cod_k is bijective only in the case $k = 2$ when we have $\overline{1}_2(\mathbb{N}) = \mathbb{N}$. In the case when $k > 2$, we can transfer FO-definability results for extensions of k-Büchi arithmetic to their WMSO-definability analogues using the function $\overline{cod}_k : \mathbb{N} \to \mathcal{F}^{k-1}$ which maps every $x \in \mathbb{N}$ to the tuple $\overline{cod}_k(x) = (cod_k^{-1}(\Theta_{k,1}(x)), ..., cod_k^{-1}(\Theta_{k,k-1}(x)))$. This function can obviously be extended such that $\overline{cod}_k : \mathbb{N}^n \to (\mathcal{F}^{k-1})^n$. We use $\overline{cod}_k$ to establish a relationship between $\exists$FO-definability in $\langle \mathbb{N}; 0, 1, +, \&_k, EqNZB_k, = \rangle$ and $\exists$WMSO-definability in $\langle \mathbb{N}; S \rangle$ extended with cardinality constraints of the form $|X_1| + ... + |X_r| < |Y_1| + ... + |Y_s|$. Section 3 focuses on the existential definability in these structures and recognizability by Parikh automata [16]. We say that $R \subseteq \mathcal{F}^n$ is *existentially ($\exists$)WMSO-definable in the structure* $\langle \mathbb{N}; \sigma \rangle$ if there exists an L_σ^{WMSO}-formula $\exists \overline{Y} \varphi(\overline{X}, \overline{Y})$, where $\varphi(\overline{X}, \overline{Y})$ may include arbitrary first-order quantifiers, such that for every $\overline{A} \in \mathcal{F}^n$ we have $R(\overline{A})$ if and only if $\exists \overline{Y} \varphi(\overline{A}, \overline{Y})$.

The following lemma shows that it is sufficient to extend $\langle \mathbb{N}; S \rangle$ with the relation $EqCard(X, Y) \rightleftharpoons |X| = |Y|$ to reason about $\exists$WMSO-definability in $\mathbb{N}$ with successor S and cardinality constraints.

Lemma 3. *Every cardinality constraint* $|X_1| + ... + |X_r| < |Y_1| + ... + |Y_s|$ *is existentially WMSO-definable in the structure* $\langle \mathbb{N}; S, EqCard \rangle$.

Proof. Let us first define the graph of $\cap$ using a formula with one universal first-order quantifier $\forall x (x \in Z \Leftrightarrow x \in X \wedge x \in Y)$ (and analogously, the graphs of union $Z = X \cup Y$ and difference $Z = X \setminus Y$ and the empty set $X = \emptyset \Leftrightarrow \forall x (\neg x \in X)$).

Now it is not difficult to see that

$$|X_1| + ... + |X_r| < |Y_1| + ... + |Y_s| \Leftrightarrow \exists U \exists V \exists X_1' ... \exists X_r' \exists Y_1' ... \exists Y_s' \Big($$

$$\bigwedge_{1 \le i < j \le r} X_i' \cap X_j' = \emptyset \wedge \bigwedge_{1 \le i \le r} EqCard(X_i, X_i') \wedge$$

$$\bigwedge_{1 \le i < j \le s} Y_i' \cap Y_j' = \emptyset \wedge \bigwedge_{1 \le i \le s} EqCard(Y_i, Y_i') \wedge \qquad (3)$$

$$\bigcup_{1 \le i \le r} X_i' = U \wedge \bigcup_{1 \le i \le s} Y_i' = V \wedge U \cap V = U \wedge \neg(V \setminus U = \emptyset)\Big).$$

$\square$

The following fact is an analogue of Villemaire's theorem [23]. Note that when $k = 2$ the function $\overline{cod}_2$ is exactly cod_2^{-1}.

Proposition 1. (i) *If a relation $R \subseteq \mathcal{F}^n$ is existentially WMSO-definable in the structure $\langle \mathbb{N}; S, EqCard \rangle$ then $cod_k(R)$ is existentially FO-definable in $\langle \mathbb{N}; 0, 1, +, \&_k, EqNZB_k, = \rangle$.*
(ii) *If a relation $R \subseteq \mathbb{N}^n$ is $\exists FO$-definable in $\langle \mathbb{N}; 0, 1, +, \&_k, EqNZB_k, = \rangle$ then $\overline{cod}_k(R)$ is $\exists WMSO$-definable in $\langle \mathbb{N}; S, EqCard \rangle$.*

The proof of this proposition is rather straightforward and follows along similar lines as the proof of Villemaire's theorem. Only notice that in order to deal with universal FO-quantifiers in *(i)*, we apply Corollary 1 from Subsection 2.2.

Klaedtke and Rueß show in [16] that every relation $R \subseteq \mathcal{F}^n$ is existentially WMSO-definable in the structure $\langle \mathbb{N}; S, EqCard \rangle$ if and only if it is recognizable by some Parikh automaton over the alphabet $\{0, 1\}$. By reduction to the emptiness problem for Parikh automata, they show that satisfiability of existential WMSO-formulas in the structure $\langle \mathbb{N}; S, EqCard \rangle$ is decidable. The next paragraph gives the necessary definitions.

Automata languages. Büchi-Bruyère's theorem [4,5] states that every relation is first-order definable in the structure $\langle \mathbb{N}; 0, 1, +, V_k, = \rangle$ if and only if it is recognizable by a finite k-automaton. Haase and Różycki [11] prove that this statement is however not true if we consider *existential* first-order definability in $\langle \mathbb{N}; 0, 1, +, V_k, = \rangle$. We first recall some automata-theoretic definitions and then show that substituting $\&_k$ for V_k yields the desired existential description of k-recognizable sets.

Let Σ be some alphabet and Σ^* denote the set of words of finite length over Σ with a unique empty word ϵ of length 0. Then a *(non-deterministic) finite Σ-automaton (Σ-FA)* is a 4-tuple $\mathcal{A} = (Q, q_0, F, \delta)$, where $Q = \{q_0, ..., q_s\}$ is a finite set of states with initial state q_0 and the set $F \subseteq Q$ of finial states; $\delta : Q \times \Sigma \to 2^Q$ is the transition function, where 2^Q is the power set of Q. A configuration of $\mathcal{A}$ is a pair (q, x), where $q \in Q$ is a current state and $x \in \Sigma^*$ is an unused part of an input word. A transition relation $\to$ over configurations of $\mathcal{A}$ is defined such that $(q, ax) \to (q', x)$ if and only if $q' \in \delta(q, a)$. A sequence of transitions between configurations is called a *computation of $\mathcal{A}$*. We say that $x = x_0 x_1 \cdots x_t \in \Sigma^{t+1}$ is accepted by a given Σ-FA $\mathcal{A}$ if there is an accepting computation of $\mathcal{A}$ for x, that is, a sequence $(q_0, x_0 x_1 ... x_t) \to (q', x_1 ... x_t) \to \cdots \to (q'', x_t) \to (q_f, \epsilon)$ for some $q_f \in F$. The set of all words $x \in \Sigma^*$ accepted by Σ-FA $\mathcal{A}$ defines the language recognizable by this automaton. This language is denoted by $L(\mathcal{A})$.

A *finite k-automaton (k-FA)* is defined as a Σ_k^n-FA, where every letter from Σ_k^n is an n-tuple of digits from $\Sigma_k = \{0, 1, ..., k-1\}$. To each language $L \subseteq (\Sigma_k^n)^*$ there corresponds a relation R_L over $\mathbb{N}^n$ in the following way: $R_L = \{\sum_{i=0}^{t} x_i k^i \mid x_0 \cdots x_t \in L\}$. An n-ary relation R over $\mathbb{N}$ is called *k-FA-recognizable* if there exists a k-FA $\mathcal{A}$ such that for every $\bar{a} \in \mathbb{N}^n$ we have $R(\bar{a}) \Leftrightarrow R_{L(\mathcal{A})}(\bar{a})$. For technical convenience, the notion of k-recognizability is commonly defined [4,23,24] for deterministic k-FA (k-DFA), where for every state q and letter $a \in \Sigma_k^n$ it holds that $|\delta(q, a)| \leq 1$. Since Σ-FA and Σ-DFA recognize the same class of languages [17], i.e. the class of regular languages over the alphabet Σ, this restriction does not change the class of recognizable relations. In our logical characterization of k-FA-recognizable relations we will not benefit from such restrictions on the transition function.

The definition of Σ-FA can be extended by adjoining to every letter of Σ a vector $v \in D$, where D is a finite subset of $\mathbb{N}^m$, and imposing certain restrictions on the accepting sequences of transitions to obtain *Parikh finite automata* (Σ-*PFA*). That is, for some $m > 0$ and a finite set $D \subseteq \mathbb{N}^m$, a Σ-PFA is a pair $(\mathcal{A}, \varphi)$, denoted by $\mathcal{A}_\varphi$, where $\mathcal{A}$ is a $(\Sigma \times D)$-FA and $\varphi(x_1, ..., x_m)$ is an existential $L_{\langle 0,1,+,=\rangle}$-formula. It is convenient to think of a configuration of Σ-PFA as an $(m+2)$-tuple $(q, x, y_1, ..., y_m)$ where the pair (q, x) is the same as in the definition of configurations of Σ-FA, and $(y_1, ..., y_m)$ is a vector from $\mathbb{N}^m$. A transition relation between two configurations of Σ-PFA $\mathcal{A}_\varphi$ is now defined as follows: $(q, ax, y_1, ..., y_m) \to (q', x, y_1+d_1, ..., y_m+d_m)$ if and only if $q' \in \delta(q, a, d_1, ..., d_m)$. A word $x = x_0 x_1 \cdots x_t \in \Sigma^{t+1}$ is accepted by $\mathcal{A}_\varphi$ if there is a computation $(q_0, x_0 x_1 \cdots x_t, 0, ..., 0) \to (q', x_1 \cdots x_t, y_1', ..., y_m') \to \cdots \to (q'', x_t, y_1'', ..., y_m'') \to (q_f, \epsilon, y_1, ..., y_m)$ for some $q_f \in F$ and the formula $\varphi(y_1, ..., y_m)$ is true. We denote by $L(\mathcal{A}_\varphi)$ the language recognizable by Σ-PFA $\mathcal{A}_\varphi$.

In order to deal with definability over the natural numbers, we again consider Σ_k^n-PFA, which we call a k-*Parikh finite automata* (k-*PFA*). The k-PFA-recognizable relations $R \in \mathbb{N}^n$ are defined analogously. The prefixes Σ- and k- will be sometimes omitted when the exact alphabet Σ or value of k is not significant.

The original definition of Parikh automata [16] uses semi-linear sets $C \subseteq \mathbb{N}^t$ instead of existential formulas of Presburger arithmetic, but it is well-known [10] that these definitions of PFA are equivalent. The main result by Klaedtke and Rueß [15, Theorems 12 and 15] states that every relation $R \subseteq \mathcal{F}^n$ is $\exists$WMSO-definable in the structure $\langle \mathbb{N}; S, EqCard \rangle$ if and only if the relation $cod_2^{-1}(R)$ is 2-PFA-recognizable. The "only if" part of this WMSO-characterization follows from the fact that the class of languages recognizable by PFA is closed under union, intersection, left and right quotients [15, Property 4] and that $EqCard$ with its negation are recognizable by 2-PFA. Since it is easy to construct k-PFA for the predicate $EqNZB_k$ and for its negation, the following proposition can be proved in a similar way.

Proposition 2. *If some relation $R \subseteq \mathbb{N}^n$ is existentially FO-definable in the structure $\langle \mathbb{N}; 0, 1, +, \&_k, EqNZB_k, = \rangle$ then it is k-PFA-recognizable.*

Based on Parikh's theorem [21], Klaedtke and Rueß proved decidability of the emptiness problem for PFA, and thus decidability of the existential WMSO-theory of $\langle \mathbb{N}; S, EqCard \rangle$. They also proved that the universality problem for Parikh automata is undecidable. In contrast to finite automata, *deterministic* Parikh automata, where for every $(q, a) \in Q \times \Sigma_k^n$ there exists at most one pair $(q', \bar{d}) \in Q \times D$ such that $q' \in \delta(q, (a, \bar{d}))$, are less powerful than PFA. The paper by Cadilhac, Finkel and McKenzie [6] provides some explicit examples of languages recognizable by PFA but not by any deterministic PFA. These authors continued the study of other properties of PFA and, in particular, proved undecidability of the regularity property for PFA. This result will be used in Section 3.

2.2   Existential characterization of k-FA-recognizable languages

In this section we illustrate the main idea of the existential characterisation from Section 3. Our aim now is to prove the following theorem.

Theorem 1. *For an integer $k \geq 2$ every relation is k-FA-recognizable if and only if it is existentially definable in the structure $\langle \mathbb{N}; 0, 1, +, \&_k, = \rangle$.*

Proof. Let $\mathcal{A} = (Q, q_0, F, \delta)$ be a k-FA. We are going to prove existential definability of the relation $R_{L(\mathcal{A})}$ in the structure $\langle \mathbb{N}; 0, 1, +, \&_k, = \rangle$ by encoding the existence of an accepting computation of $\mathcal{A}$ when the input word is the k-ary representation of $\bar{x} = x_1, ..., x_n$. To this end, let us first introduce new variables $\bar{q} = q_0, ..., q_s$ for every state $q_i \in Q$; for a state $p \in Q$, we denote by $\nu(p)$ its number from $[0..s]$. The following restriction on $\bar{q}$ expresses the fact that at each step of a computation the automaton $\mathcal{A}$ has a unique state from Q:

$$K_k(t, \bar{q}) \rightleftharpoons \bigwedge_{0 \leq i < j \leq s} q_i \&_k q_j = 0 \land q_0 + ... + q_s = \mathbf{1}_k(t) \land 1 \preccurlyeq_k q_0 \land \bigvee_{p \in F} t \preccurlyeq_k q_{\nu(p)}. \quad (4)$$

Here t will be another existentially quantified variable that will be a power of k. This variable corresponds to a configuration (p, ϵ) for some $p \in F$, and formula (4) also requires that the computation starts in the state q_0. It is obvious that t must be greater than x_i for every $i \in [1..n]$; this restriction will appear in the resulting formula below.

In order to express the fact that each step of a computation is performed in accordance with the transition function $\delta : Q \times \Sigma_k^n \to 2^Q$, we introduce a predicate $\Delta_{(p, \bar{a})}$. For every pair $(p, \bar{a}) \in Q \times \Sigma_k^n$, we have

$$\Delta_{(p, \bar{a})}(t, \bar{q}, \bar{x}) \rightleftharpoons \left(q_{\nu(p)} \&_k \underset{i \in [1..n]}{\&_k} \Theta_{k, a_i}(t, x_i) \right) \preccurlyeq_k \left(\Big|_{\bar{p} \in \delta(p, \bar{a})}^k \frac{q_{\nu(\bar{p})}}{k} \right), \quad (5)$$

where, by definition, $\Big|_{y \in \emptyset}^k y = 0$. From this formula we see that at each step of an accepting computation there are either no configurations with the state p and a word starting with the letter $\bar{a} = (a_1, ..., a_n)$, or in the next configuration the state will be from $\delta(p, \bar{a})$. By combining formulas (4) and (5), we conclude that

$$R_{L(\mathcal{A})}(\bar{x}) \Leftrightarrow \exists t \exists \bar{q} \Big(P_k(t) \land \bigwedge_{i \in [1..n]} x_i < t \land K_k(t, \bar{q}) \land \bigwedge_{(p, \bar{a}) \in Q \times \Sigma_k^n} \Delta_{(p, \bar{a})}(t, \bar{q}, \bar{x}) \Big). \quad (6)$$

It remains to use formulas (1) and (2), Büchi-Bruyère's theorem and Lemmas 1 and 2. $\qquad \square$

Corollary 1. *If a relation is definable in the structure $\langle \mathbb{N}; 0, 1, +, \&_k, = \rangle$ then it is existentially definable in this structure.*

This result for $k = 2$ can be transferred to the second-order case similarly to Proposition 1. Thus, we obtain a corollary, which was essentially proved by Elgot [9, Theorem 5.3 (b)].

Corollary 2. *If a relation $R \in \mathcal{F}^n$ is WMSO-definable in the structure $\langle \mathbb{N}; S \rangle$ then it is existentially WMSO-definable in this structure.*

3   First-order characterization of Parikh automata

The aim of this section is to prove the converse statement to Proposition 2 and thus obtain an existential first-order characterization of Parikh automata languages. Parikh map over the natural numbers can be defined as a function $\Phi_k : \mathbb{N} \to \mathbb{N}^k$ such that $\Phi_k(x) = (\#_{k,0}(x), ..., \#_{k,k-1}(x))$, where every function $\#_{k,i}$ counts the number of occurrences of the digit i in k-ary representation of x. For such counting functions we have the following lemma.

Lemma 4. Let $R(x_1, ..., x_n)$ be a relation that is existentially definable in the structure $\langle \mathbb{N}; 0, 1, +, = \rangle$, and let $\bar{a}$ be some vector from $\{0, ..., k-1\}^n$. Then the relation $R(\#_{k,a_1}(x_1), ..., \#_{k,a_n}(x_n))$ is $\exists$-definable in $\langle \mathbb{N}; 0, 1, +, \&_k, EqNZB_k, = \rangle$.

Proof. It is sufficient to define the relations $\#_{k,a}(x) = d$ for integers $d \geq 0$ and $\#_{k,a}(x) + \#_{k,b}(y) = \#_{k,c}(z)$ by some existential formulas. For the first relation we have the formula $EqNZB_k(\Theta_{k,a}(x), k^d - 1)$, and for the second one there is the following first-order analogue to formula (3):

$$\#_{k,a}(x) + \#_{k,b}(y) = \#_{k,c}(z) \Leftrightarrow \exists x' \exists y' (EqNZB_k(x' + y', \Theta_{k,c}(z)) \wedge$$
$$x' \&_k y' = 0 \wedge EqNZB_k(\Theta_{k,a}(x), x') \wedge EqNZB_k(\Theta_{k,b}(y), y')).$$

It remains to use existential definability of the graph of $\Theta_{k,i}$ in the structure $\langle \mathbb{N}; 0, 1, +, \&_k, = \rangle$.

Note that every function $\#_{k,i}$ can be represented in terms of Subsection 2.1 as $\#_{k,i}(x) = |cod_k^{-1}(\Theta_{k,i}(x))|$, and thus this lemma can also be proved using Lemma 3 and the first part of Proposition 1.   □

Let D be some finite subset of $\mathbb{N}^m$, and let $M(D)$ be the maximum integer occurring in D. The same as Klaedtke and Rueß [16], we encode vectors from D of a given k-Parikh automaton by introducing $M(D) + 1$ new variables $y_{i,0}, ..., y_{i,M(D)}$ for each coordinate y_i. For every $i \in [1..m]$, these variables will be pairwise *disjoint* (i.e. $y_{i,j_1} \&_k y_{i,j_2} = 0$ for $j_1 \neq j_2$) and their representation in base k will contain only zeros and ones. For this reason, we use only $\#_{k,1}$ in our encoding and denote $\#_k \rightleftharpoons \#_{k,1}$.

Theorem 2. For every integer $k \geq 2$ a relation $R \subseteq \mathbb{N}^n$ is k-PFA-recognizable if and only if it is $\exists$-definable in the structure $\langle \mathbb{N}; 0, 1, +, \&_k, EqNZB_k, = \rangle$.

Proof. The "if" direction of this theorem is Proposition 2. In the proof of the "only if" direction, suppose we are given a k-Parikh automaton $\mathcal{A}_\varphi$ for some finite set $D \in \mathbb{N}^m$, where $\mathcal{A} = (Q, q_0, F, \delta)$ is a FA over the language $\Sigma_k^n \times D$ and φ is an existential $L_{\langle 0,1,+,= \rangle}$-formula. We are going to construct an existential $L_{\langle 0,1,+,\&_k,EqNZB_k,= \rangle}$-formula ψ such that $R_{L(\mathcal{A}_\varphi)}(\bar{a})$ if and only if $\psi(\bar{a})$ for every $\bar{a} \in \mathbb{N}^n$. Again, $\psi(\bar{x})$ will encode the existence of an accepting computation of $\mathcal{A}_\varphi$ when the input word is the k-ary representation of $\bar{x}$.

The sequence of states from an accepting computation of $\mathcal{A}$ can be encoded using the predicate $K_k(t, \bar{q})$, defined by the existential $L_{\langle 0,1,+,\&_k,= \rangle}$-formula (4).

We modify formula (5) so that it works with the alphabet $\Sigma_k^n \times D$. To this end, let us introduce $m(M(D) + 1)$ variables $\overline{y} = y_{1,0},...,y_{1,M(D)},...,y_{m,0},...,y_{m,M(D)}$ such that for every $i \in [1..m]$ it holds that $\theta_k(t, y_{i,0}, ..., y_{i,M(D)})$, where

$$\theta_k(t, y_0, ..., y_M) \rightleftharpoons \bigwedge_{0 \leq i < j \leq M} y_i \&_k y_j = 0 \wedge y_0 + ... + y_M = \mathbf{1}_k(t).$$

Now for every $(p, \overline{a}, \overline{d}) \in Q \times \Sigma_k^n \times D$ we have:

$$\Delta_{(p,\overline{a},\overline{d})}(t, \overline{q}, \overline{x}, \overline{y}) \rightleftharpoons \left(q_{\nu(p)} \&_k \underset{i \in [1..n]}{\&_k} \Theta_{k,a_i}(t, x_i) \&_k \underset{j \in [1..m]}{\&_k} y_{j,d_j} \right) \preccurlyeq_k$$

$$\left(\Big|_k \underset{\widetilde{p} \in \delta(p,\overline{a},\overline{d})}{\frac{q_{\nu(\widetilde{p})}}{k}} \right).$$

Recall that the expression with bitwise maximums $\Big|_k$ evaluates to zero when $\delta(p, \overline{a}, \overline{d}) = \emptyset$.

By combining all the parts of the existential definition of $R_{L(\mathcal{A}_\varphi)}$, we get the following analogue to formula (6):

$$R_{L(\mathcal{A}_\varphi)}(\overline{x}) \Leftrightarrow \exists t \exists \overline{q} \exists \overline{y} \left(P_k(t) \wedge \bigwedge_{i \in [1..n]} x_i < t \wedge K_k(t, \overline{q}) \wedge \right.$$

$$\bigwedge_{i \in [1..m]} \theta_k(t, y_{i,0}, ..., y_{i,M(D)}) \wedge \bigwedge_{(p,\overline{a},\overline{d}) \in Q \times \Sigma_k^n \times D} \Delta_{(p,\overline{a},\overline{d})}(t, \overline{q}, \overline{x}, \overline{y}) \wedge$$

$$\left. \varphi \left(\sum_{c \in [1..M(D)]} c \#_k(y_{1,c}), ..., \sum_{c \in [1..M(D)]} c \#_k(y_{m,c}) \right) \right).$$

It remains to apply Lemma 4 to obtain the desired existential formula.   □

This result gives us the following statement concerning decidability of fragments of the first-order theory of the structure $\langle \mathbb{N}; 0, 1, +, \&_k, EqNZB_k, = \rangle$.

Corollary 3. *The existential theory of $\langle \mathbb{N}; 0, 1, +, \&_k, EqNZB_k, = \rangle$ is decidable and the $\forall\exists$-theory of this structure is undecidable.*

Proof. The first part of the corollary is just a variation on the automata-theoretic techniques that were formalized by Hodgson [12]. It follows from the decidability of the emptiness problem for PFA. Undecidability of the universality problem, combined with Theorem 2, imply undecidability already for the problem of deciding $\forall\exists$-formulas with a single universal quantifier.   □

Haase and Różycki [11, Conclusion] ask whether the property of $\exists$-definability is decidable for the relations definable in the structure $\langle \mathbb{N}; 0, 1, +, V_k, = \rangle$. Using Theorem 1, this problem can be reformulated so that we consider only existentially definable sets, but now the signatures are different. Namely, the question is whether we can decide if a set $\exists$-definable in the structure $\langle \mathbb{N}; 0, 1, +, V_k, \&_k, = \rangle$ is $\exists$-definable in $\langle \mathbb{N}; 0, 1, +, V_k, = \rangle$. A similar question can be answered in the negative for the structure with $\&_k$ and $EqNZB_k$.

Proposition 3. *The problem of deciding whether a set existentially definable in the structure* $\langle \mathbb{N}; 0, 1, +, \&_k, EqNZB_k, = \rangle$ *is* $\exists$*-definable in* $\langle \mathbb{N}; 0, 1, +, \&_k, = \rangle$ *is undecidable.*

This follows from Theorems 1 and 2, and from undecidability of the regularity property for Parikh automata, which was proved by Cadilhac, Finkel and McKenzie [6, Proposition 7].

Parikh automata are closely related to multi-counter machines (MCM): they recognize exactly the same languages as reversal-bounded MCM [15, Section A.3] (see also [6, Subsection 3.3]). Recall that a MCM is *reversal-bounded* (the notion was introduced by Ibarra [13]) if there exists a pair of integers (r, s) such that in every accepting computation the value of each counter increases and decreases at most r times and the input head reverses at most s times. Theorem 2 now gives an existential first-order characterization of this restricted version of MCM. It is clear that the model of PFA is more suitable for our logical descriptions. However, as we will see in the next section, the behaviour of MCM can be described in a similar way when the structure is extended with concatenation.

4   Multi-counter machines and DPR-theorem

4.1   Two-way multi-counter machines

Same as Ibarra [13], we define a *two-way multi-counter machine* $\mathcal{M}$ over an alphabet Σ (Σ-*MCM*) with two special symbols $\vdash, \dashv$ as a tuple (m, Q, q_0, F, δ). Here, $m \geq 0$ is the number of the counters of $\mathcal{M}$, the triple (Q, q_0, F) has its standard meaning, and δ is a function from $Q \times (\Sigma \cup \{\vdash, \dashv\}) \times \{0, 1\}^m$ to $2^{Q \times \{-1, 0, 1\}^{m+1}}$. Every computation of $\mathcal{M}$ starts with an input $x \in \Sigma^*$ written on the tape between the delimiters: $\vdash x \dashv$, and the input head of $\mathcal{M}$ reading the left delimiter $\vdash$. A configuration of $\mathcal{M}$ on an input $\vdash x \dashv$ is given by an $(m+3)$-tuple $(q, \vdash x \dashv, i, y_1, ..., y_m)$ denoting the fact that $\mathcal{M}$ is in state q, the read-only input head scans the i-th symbol of the input, and $y_1, ..., y_m$ are some non-negative integer values of the counters. The relation $\rightarrow$ over configurations is defined such that $(q, \vdash x \dashv, i, y_1, ..., y_m) \rightarrow (q', \vdash x \dashv, i + \Delta, y_1 + d_1, ..., y_m + d_m)$ if and only if $(q', \Delta, d_1, ..., d_m) \in \delta(q, a, [y_1 > 0], ..., [y_m > 0])$, where a is the i-th symbol of the input and $[y > 0]$ returns 1 if $y > 0$, and 0 otherwise. A natural restriction on δ prevents the cases when: (1) $[y_j > 0] = 0$ and $d_j = -1$; (2) $i = 0$ and $\Delta = -1$; (3) the i-th symbol of the input is $\dashv$ and $\Delta = 1$.

We say that $x \in \Sigma^*$ is accepted by a given Σ-MCM if for the input word $\vdash x \dashv$ there is a computation $(q_0, \vdash x \dashv, 0, 0, ..., 0) \rightarrow ... \rightarrow (q_f, \vdash x \dashv, 0, 0, ..., 0)$ for some $q_f \in F$. The set of all the words $x \in \Sigma^*$ accepted by a Σ-MCM $\mathcal{M}$ defines the language recognized by this machine, which we denote by $L(\mathcal{M})$. In order to properly relate Σ-MCM with definability over $\mathbb{N}$, we again assume that $\Sigma = \Sigma_k^n$ for $k \geq 2$. Every $x \in \Sigma^*$ is now an element of $\mathbb{N}^n$ in the inverse base k representation. An n-ary relation R over $\mathbb{N}$ is called k-*MCM-recognizable* if there exists a Σ_k^n-MCM $\mathcal{M}$ such that for every $\bar{a} \in \mathbb{N}^n$ we have $R(\bar{a}) \Leftrightarrow R_{L(\mathcal{M})}(\bar{a})$.

Two-way multi-counter machines can simulate Turing machines (see e.g. [17]), and thus every relation R over $\mathbb{N}^n$ is r.e. iff it is k-MCM-recognizable. The aim of this section is to use the same arguments as in the cases of k-FA and k-PFA in order to obtain an existential characterization of r.e. relations, and Theorem 3 gives us the desired result. The proof will be in some sense intermediate between the arithmetization of Turing machines by Matiyasevich [19] and the encoding of register machines by Jones and Matiyasevich in [14], but here we emphasize the role of concatenation in existential characterizations of multi-counter languages.

4.2   The role of concatenation in DPR-theorem

Matiyasevich's proof [19] implicitly gives us a description of every r.e. set via $\exists$-formulas of the first-order language with 0, 1, addition, bitwise multiplication $\&_2$, concatenation $\frown_2$, and equality. Here, $t = x \frown_k y \rightleftharpoons t = x + k^{l_k(x)}y = x + k\lambda_k(x)y$, where $l_k(x)$ is the length of x in k-ary notation. This section aims to prove this theorem using the ideas from Subsection 2.2. Informally speaking, the main difference between the case of k-MCM and k-FA is that we now consider *byte*wise multiplication instead of *bit*wise from Theorem 1. Suppose a given k-MCM accepts $\overline{x} \in \Sigma_k^n$ and let M be the maximum value of all the counters of some accepting computation for $\overline{x}$. If u is a power of k which is greater than the maximum of k^M and all the x_i, then $l_k(u)$ will be the size of the byte in our encoding. Every non-negative integer can be represented as a sequence of bytes of size $l_k(u)$, which will be called u-*bytes*.

First, we introduce some auxiliary devices, which are required in our construction. Define the predicate $\Delta_k(u,t,x)$, which is true when u is a power of k greater than k^2, the variable x has the same u-byte-length as t and has the following form

$$x = \underbrace{1000...0}_{l_k(u)} * *...\underbrace{0..010..0}_{l_k(u)}...\underbrace{000...001}_{l_k(u)},$$

where $**$ is either 10 or 01, and for every two consecutive u-bytes b_1, b_2 in x the only 1 in b_2 is either in the same place or one bit left/right of its position in b_1. Moreover, the two most significant bits in every u-byte are equal to zero. We will use this predicate to describe a position of the input head and values of the counters in configurations of a given k-MCM. Before we proceed with the existential definition of this relation, we need to introduce some auxiliary functions. The first one performs the right shift by $l_k(z)$ bits and can be defined via the formula $y = \frac{x}{z} \Leftrightarrow \exists v \exists u (\lambda_k(z) = u \wedge \lambda_k(v) \leq u \wedge x = u \frown_k y - u + v)$. The second function is $\widehat{Copy}_k(u,t,x)$ which maps to zero when $\lambda_k(u) < \lambda_k(x)$, and otherwise gives us the sequence of u-bytes of the same u-byte-length as t such that each u-byte is equal to x. The following lemma gives the desired definition, and then we immediately prove existential definability of $\Delta_k(u,t,x)$.

Lemma 5. *The function* $Copy_k$ *is* $\exists$-*definable in* $\langle \mathbb{N}; 0, 1, +, \&_k, \frown_k, = \rangle$.

Proof. We start with the predicate $Cpy_k(x,y)$ which is true whenever y has the form $x \frown_k ... \frown_k x$. Its definition is rather standard:

$$Cpy_k(x,y) \Leftrightarrow y = x \vee \exists z(y = x \frown_k z \wedge y = z \frown_k x).$$

The predicate $I_k(u, x) \Leftrightarrow x = 1 \vee \exists y (Cpy_k(\lambda_k(u), y) \wedge x = ky+1)$ is an another special case of $Copy_k$ which is true when x is a sequence of u-bytes, each of which is equal to 1. Then, the minimum power of k of the same u-byte-length as x can be expressed as $y = \Lambda_k(u, x) \Leftrightarrow \exists v (I_k(u, v) \wedge v \leq x \wedge v \frown_k u > x \wedge y = \lambda_k(v))$.

It is now clear that

$$y = Copy_k(u, t, x) \Leftrightarrow \lambda_k(u) < \lambda_k(x) \wedge y = 0 \vee \Lambda_k(u, y) = \Lambda_k(u, t) \wedge$$

$$\left(\lambda_k(u) = \lambda_k(x) \wedge Cpy_k(x, y) \vee \lambda_k(u) > \lambda_k(x) \wedge \exists y' \exists y'' \left(\right. \right.$$

$$\left. \left. Cpy_k(x + \lambda_k(u), y') \wedge Cpy_k(\lambda_k(u), y'') \wedge \lambda_k(y') = \lambda_k(y'') \wedge y = y' - y'' \right) \right).$$

In this formula, the variables y' and y'' are introduced in order to supplement every u-byte with a sufficient number of leading zeros. $\qquad\square$

Lemma 6. *The relation* Δ_k *is* $\exists$-*definable in* $\langle \mathbb{N}; 0, 1, +, \&_k, \frown_k, = \rangle$.

Proof. We are going to prove the correctness of the following definition:

$$\Delta_k(u, t, x) \Leftrightarrow \exists z_1 \exists z_2 \exists x_1 \exists x_2 \exists x_3 \left(P_k(u) \wedge k^3 \leq u \wedge \right.$$

$$z_1 = Copy_k(u, t, 1) \wedge \lambda_k(z_1) = \lambda_k(x) \wedge x \&_k (ku - 1) = 1 \wedge x \preccurlyeq_k \mathbf{1}_k(z_1) \wedge \quad (7)$$

$$x_1 = \frac{(kx)}{u} \wedge x_2 = \frac{x}{u} \wedge x_3 = \frac{x}{ku} \wedge x = \lambda_k(x) + x \&_k x_1 + x \&_k x_2 + x \&_k x_3 \wedge \quad (8)$$

$$x_1 \&_k x_2 = 0 \wedge x_2 \&_k x_3 = 0 \wedge x_2 \&_k x_3 = 0 \wedge \quad (9)$$

$$z_2 = Copy_k(u, t, u) \wedge x \&_k (z_2 + \frac{z_2}{k}) = 0 \Big). \quad (10)$$

Conjunction (7) expresses that x is a sequence of the same number of u-bytes as t that starts and ends with the u-byte $000...01$, and in every u-byte there can only be zeros and ones. Condition (10) specifies that the two most significant bits in every u-byte of x are equal to zero. Next, the variables x_1, x_2, x_3 correspond to the right shifts of x one u-byte plus $D \in \{-1, 0, +1\}$. Let us prove that in every u-byte there is a unique 1 and that it has the same position plus $D \in \{-1, 0, +1\}$ compared to the previous u-byte.

From (8), we see that in every u-byte of x there is at least one 1. Indeed, if $x \neq u$ then the first u-byte of x_1, or x_2, or x_3 must contain 1 (the least significant bit); thus, the second u-byte of x is also non-zero, etc. This 1 in every u-byte is in the desired position since the values $x \&_k x_1$, $x \&_k x_2$, $x \&_k x_3$ describe the three cases in which the position in the next u-byte is the same plus -1, 0, $+1$, respectively.

Now we prove that there are no other non-zero bits in every u-byte of x. Assume for a contradiction that there is a u-byte in x with more than one 1. Then, there are two consecutive u-bytes (which are depicted on the next page) such that the left u-byte has the only 1, and the right one has at least two 1. This pair exists because the most significant u-byte of x equals 1. From the representation of x in (8), we see that the bits a, b, f, g are all equal to zero.

Next, since by (9) x_1, x_2 and x_3 are pairwise disjoint, among c, d and e there is only one 1. This contradicts our assumption.

$$x = \quad ...0..000..\underbrace{\boxed{010}..000..00..*a*..*b\boxed{cde}}_{l_k(u)}f*..*g*..*...$$

$$x_1 = \quad ...0..0\,0\,0..\quad 0\underbrace{\boxed{100}}_{l_k(u)}0\quad ..0\,0\,0..00..0c\underbrace{\boxed{de0}}_{l_k(u)}00..0...$$

$$x_2 = \quad ...0..0\,0\,0..\quad 0\underbrace{\boxed{010}}_{l_k(u)}0\quad ..0\,0\,0..00..00\underbrace{\boxed{cde}}_{l_k(u)}00..0...$$

$$x_3 = \quad ...0..0\,0\,0..\quad 0\underbrace{\boxed{001}}_{l_k(u)}0\quad ..0\,0\,0..00..00\underbrace{\boxed{0cd}}_{l_k(u)}e0..0...$$

It remains to prove that for every u and x such that $\Delta_k(u,t,x)$ there exist non-negative integers from the definition above. This is obvious for z_1 and z_2; the existence of x_1, x_2, x_3 follows from the fact that there are at least two zeros between every pair of 1 in x. □

In our proof we check whether or not the u-bytewise minimum of two natural numbers equals zero. In order to express this property, let us introduce a function U_k which modifies x as follows. If x can be split into consecutive u-bytes where the most significant bit is equal to zero, then $U_k(u,x)$ replaces every non-zero u-byte by 1. Otherwise, this function maps to zero. For example, when $x = 10\,000\,011\,000\,010$ we have $U_2(100,x) = 1\,000\,001\,000\,001$ and $U_2(1000,x) = 0$.

Lemma 7. *The function U_k is $\exists$-definable in $\langle \mathbb{N}; 0, 1, +, \&_k, \frown_k, = \rangle$.*

Proof. Let us first define a predicate $\overline{U_k}$, which (in comparison with the function U_k) is also true for the cases when y has u-bytes equal 1 while the corresponding u-bytes of x are equal to zero. In $\overline{U_k}$ there are also no restrictions on the most significant bits of u-bytes. We have the definition

$$\overline{U_k}(u,x,y) \Leftrightarrow \exists t \exists t' \exists v \left(Cpy_k(\lambda_k(u),t) \wedge t' \preccurlyeq_k t \wedge v = kt' - \frac{(kt')}{u} \wedge x \preccurlyeq_k v \wedge \right.$$
$$\left. y = v \&_k Copy_k(u,x,1) \right).$$

The k-ary representation of v is a sequence of u-bytes which are either zero or equal to $ku - 1$; moreover, for every unit in x there is $(k-1)$ in v. Then we select the desired 1 in y via a bitwise multiplication of v by a sequence of u-bytes of the same u-byte-length as x, where all bytes are equal to 1.

In order to exclude extra non-zero u-bytes from y, we consider the difference $kx - y$. Recall that the definition of U_k requires zeroness of the most significant bit in every u-byte. Thus, we have

$$y = U_k(u,x) \Leftrightarrow x \&_k Copy_k(u,x,u) > 0 \wedge y = 0 \vee$$
$$x \&_k Copy_k(u,x,u) = 0 \wedge \overline{U_k}(u,x,y) \wedge (k-1)y \preccurlyeq_k (kx - y). \tag{11}$$

Consider the case when the most significant bits in u-bytes of x are all zero. The least significant bit in every u-byte of kx now equals 0, and the fact that there is a unique y that satisfies the definition can be illustrated as follows:

$$
\begin{array}{ccccccccc}
\ldots*\ldots*1 & \underbrace{0\ldots}_{l_k(u)} & 0 & \underbrace{0\ldots*\ldots*}_{l_k(u)} & 0 & \bar{0} & \underbrace{0\ldots}_{l_k(u)} & 0 & 0\ldots \\[2mm]
\ldots\underbrace{0\ldots00}_{l_k(u)} & 0\ldots & 0 & \underbrace{1\ldots0\ldots0}_{l_k(u)} & 1 & \bar{0} & \underbrace{0\ldots}_{l_k(u)} & 0 & 1\ldots \\[2mm]
\ldots\underbrace{*\ldots*0(k-1)\ldots(k-1)(k-1)}_{l_k(u)} & \underbrace{\ldots*\ldots*(k-2)}_{l_k(u)} & & \overline{(k-1)} & \underbrace{(k-1)\ldots(k-1)(k-1)\ldots}_{l_k(u)} & & &
\end{array}
$$

These three lines represent the numbers kx, y, and $(kx - y)$, respectively. The left column demonstrates the general "correct" case. The middle and the right columns show why the existence of an extra non-zero u-byte in y contradicts definition (11). □

We are now able to prove the main result of this section.

Theorem 3. *For every integer $k \geq 2$ a relation is k-MCM-recognizable if and only if it is $\exists$-definable in the structure $\langle \mathbb{N}; 0, 1, +, \&_k, \smallfrown_k, = \rangle$. Therefore, every relation $R \subseteq \mathbb{N}^n$ is r.e. iff it is $\exists$-definable in this structure.*

Proof. For a given k-MCM $\mathcal{M} = (m, Q, q_0, F, \delta)$ and an input vector $\bar{x} \in \mathbb{N}^n$ in k-ary notation, we are going to encode the existence of an accepting sequence of transitions between configurations of $\mathcal{M}$. First choose a variable u such that $P_k(u) \wedge \bigwedge_{i \in [1..n]} k^4 x_i \leq u$; this choice specifies the size of bytes in our encoding. We multiply by k^4 since in u-byte there must be two bits for delimiters $\vdash, \dashv$ and at least two auxiliary zeros from the definition of Δ_k.

A sequence of states is encoded similarly to formula (4), that is,

$$
K_k(u, t, \bar{q}) \rightleftharpoons \bigwedge_{0 \leq i < j \leq s} q_i \&_k q_j = 0 \wedge q_0 + \ldots + q_s = Copy_k(u, t, 1) \wedge
$$

$$
1 \preccurlyeq_k q_0 \wedge \bigvee_{p \in F} \Lambda_k(u, t) \preccurlyeq_k q_{\nu(p)},
$$

where $\bar{q} = q_0, \ldots, q_s$ and t corresponds to the number of steps of an accepting computation of $\mathcal{M}$. Here we also require q_0 to be the initial state and the most significant u-byte of t corresponds to a final configuration.

We now define a predicate $C_{\mathcal{M}}$ that encodes a sequence of configurations of $\mathcal{M}$. Similar to Matiyasevich [19], in this definition for every $x_i \in \bar{x}$ a sequence of copies of x_i is decomposed into disjoint variables $\theta_{i,0}, \ldots, \theta_{i,k-1}$ such that every u-byte of $\theta_{i,a}$ equals $\Theta_{k,a}(x_i)$. Let $\bar{\theta}$ denote the list of variables $\theta_{1,0}, \ldots, \theta_{1,k-1}, \theta_{2,0}, \ldots, \theta_{n,k-1}, \theta_{\vdash}, \theta_{\dashv}$, where the extra variables $\theta_{\vdash}, \theta_{\dashv}$ encode the positions of the delimiters. The variable h stores the positions of the input head of $\mathcal{M}$, and the list of variables $\bar{y} = y_1, \ldots, y_m$ corresponds to the values of the counters at each step of computation.

It is convenient to introduce a function b_k, which gives the smallest power of k greater than every $x_i \in \bar{x}$. The graph of this function can be defined as

$$y = b_k(\bar{x}) \Leftrightarrow \bigvee_{i \in [1..n]} y = k\lambda_k(x_i) \wedge \bigwedge_{i \in [1..n]} y \geq k\lambda_k(x_i).$$

This function will be applied to encode the positions of the right delimiter $\dashv$. The following formula describes a sequence of configurations of $\mathcal{M}$.

$$C_{\mathcal{M}}(u, t, \bar{q}, \bar{x}, \bar{\theta}, h, \bar{y}) \rightleftharpoons P_k(u) \wedge \bigwedge_{i \in [1..n]} k^4 x_i \leq u \wedge u \leq t \wedge K_k(u, t, \bar{q}) \wedge$$

$$\theta_\vdash = Copy_k(u, t, 1) \wedge \bigwedge_{i \in [1..n]} \left(\theta_{i,0} = Copy_k(u, t, k\Theta_{k,0}(x_i + b_k(\bar{x})) \wedge \right.$$

$$\left. \bigwedge_{a \in [1..k-1]} \theta_{i,a} = Copy_k(u, t, k\Theta_{k,a}(x_i)) \right) \wedge \theta_\dashv = Copy_k(u, t, kb_k(\bar{x})) \wedge$$

$$\Delta_k(u, t, h) \wedge \bigwedge_{i \in [1..m]} \Delta_k(u, t, y_i).$$

It is easy to see that $\theta_\vdash$, $\theta_\dashv$ are disjoint with the other variables from $\bar{\theta}$. For notational convenience, we subsequently assume that $\theta_{i,\vdash} \rightleftharpoons \theta_\vdash$ and $\theta_{i,\dashv} \rightleftharpoons \theta_\dashv$ for every $i \in [1..n]$, and the letters for the delimiters be the vectors $(\vdash, ..., \vdash)$ and $(\dashv, ..., \dashv)$ of length n.

We now proceed to the encoding of the fact that a given sequence of configurations is actually a sequence of transitions in $\mathcal{M}$. For a letter $(a_1, ..., a_n) \in \Sigma_k^n \cup \{\vdash, \dashv\}$, a state $p \in Q$, and a tuple $\bar{c} \in \{0, 1\}^m$ such that the values of the counters from $Y_{\bar{c}} = \{i \in [1..m] \mid c_i = 0\}$ are equal to zero and from $[1..m] \setminus Y_{\bar{c}}$ are non-zero, the following formula is an analogue to definition (5):

$$\Delta_{(p,\bar{a},\bar{c})}(u, t, \bar{q}, \bar{\theta}, h, \bar{y}) \rightleftharpoons \left(q_{\nu(p)} \&_k \underset{i \in [1..n]}{\&_k} U_k(u, (\theta_{i,a_i} \&_k h)) \&_k \right.$$

$$\left. \underset{i \in Y_{\bar{c}}}{\&_k} y_i \&_k \underset{i \in [1..m] \setminus Y_{\bar{c}}}{\&_k} U_k(u, y_i - Copy_k(u, t, 1) \&_k y_i) \right) \preccurlyeq_k$$

$$\Big|_k \underset{(\tilde{p}, d, \bar{d}) \in \delta(p, \bar{a}, \bar{c})}{} \left(\frac{q_{\nu(\tilde{p})}}{u} \&_k U_k(u, h \&_k \frac{(k^d h)}{u}) \&_k \underset{i \in [1..m]}{\&_k} U_k(u, y_i \&_k \frac{(k^{d_i} y_i)}{u}) \right).$$

The key difference with (5) is that now in order to compare two consecutive configurations we shift by one u-byte instead of one bit. It is obvious that the predicate $\Delta_{(p,\bar{a},\bar{c})}$ makes sense when it is complemented with $C_{\mathcal{M}}$. In this case, for example, $U_k(u, h \&_k \frac{(k^d h)}{u})$ highlights the configurations for which in the following configuration the position of the input head shifts by d. Indeed, we obtain a sequence of u-bytes, each of which is equal to one if and only if the position of the unique 1 in the next u-byte is the same plus d, otherwise this u-byte is equal to zero.

It remains to define the relation $R_{L(\mathcal{M})}$ that corresponds to the language recognizable by $\mathcal{M}$. To this end, we have to consider every tuple $(p, \bar{a}, \bar{c})$ in $Q \times (\Sigma_k^n \cup \{\vdash, \dashv\}) \times \{0,1\}^m$ and apply already defined predicates $C_{\mathcal{M}}$ and $\Delta_{(p,\bar{a},\bar{c})}$.

$$R_{L(\mathcal{M})}(\bar{x}) \Leftrightarrow \exists u \exists t \exists \bar{q} \exists \bar{\theta} \exists h \exists \bar{y} \Big(C_{\mathcal{M}}(u, t, \bar{q}, \bar{x}, \bar{\theta}, h, \bar{y}) \wedge$$

$$\bigwedge_{(p,\bar{a},\bar{c}) \in Q \times (\Sigma_k^n \cup \{\vdash, \dashv\}) \times \{0,1\}^m} \Delta_{(p,\bar{a},\bar{c})}(u, t, \bar{q}, \bar{\theta}, h, \bar{y}) \Big).$$

This completes the proof.   □

Since by [14,19] the bitwise minimum operation $\&_2$ is existentially definable in $\langle \mathbb{N}; 0, 1, +, \cdot, exp, = \rangle$, we obtain DPR-theorem as a corollary.

Corollary 4 (DPR-theorem). *Every relation $R \subseteq \mathbb{N}^n$ is r.e. if and only if it is $\exists$-definable in the structure $\langle \mathbb{N}; 0, 1, +, \cdot, exp, = \rangle$.*

Let us fix $k = 2$ and omit mentioning k in $\frown_k$ and $EqNZB_k$. Since we have $z = x \&_2 y \Leftrightarrow z \preccurlyeq y \wedge y \preccurlyeq x + y - z$ (see [14]), bitwise minimum is $\exists$-definable in $\langle \mathbb{N}; 0, 1, +, \preccurlyeq, \frown, = \rangle$. Next, exponential diophantiness of $\preccurlyeq$ follows from the fact that $x \preccurlyeq y$ iff $\binom{y}{x} \equiv 1 \pmod 2$, where $\binom{y}{x}$ is a binomial coefficient. Factorial representation of binomial coefficients and Legendre's formula imply that

$$x \preccurlyeq y \Leftrightarrow s_2(y) = s_2(x) + s_2(y - x),$$

where $s_2(x)$ is the number of 1's in base 2 expansion of x. Therefore, the masking relation is definable by the formula $x \preccurlyeq y \Leftrightarrow EqNZB(y, x \frown (y - x))$ and we have the following result.

Corollary 5. *Every relation $R \subseteq \mathbb{N}^n$ is r.e. if and only if it is $\exists$-definable in the structure $\langle \mathbb{N}; 0, 1, +, EqNZB, \frown, = \rangle$.*

5   Conclusion

The purpose of this paper is to emphasize similarities in existential first-order characterizations of the languages recognizable by various abstract machines. Such descriptions in Sections 3 and 4 allowed us (in some sense) to answer the question of Bès [2, Open Problems] concerning the expressive power of fragments of FO-arithmetic with the predicate $EqNZB$.

Let us mention one natural question which is related to Theorems 1 and 3. Villemaire proves [23,24] that multiplication is definable in $\langle \mathbb{N}; 0, 1, +, V_k, V_l, = \rangle$ when k and l are multiplicatively independent. Bès strengthens this result [1] by showing that the same is true when V_l is replaced by any l-recognizable relation R_l that is not definable in $\langle \mathbb{N}; 0, 1, +, = \rangle$. It would be interesting to see whether multiplication is *existentially* definable in $\langle \mathbb{N}; 0, 1, +, \&_k, \&_l, = \rangle$, and more generally, to study $\exists$-definability in the structures $\langle \mathbb{N}; 0, 1, +, \&_k, R_l, = \rangle$.

Acknowledgements. The author is grateful to the anonymous reviewers for their useful suggestions and comments.

References

1. Bès, A.: Undecidable extensions of Büchi arithmetic and Cobham-Semënov theorem. Journal of Symbolic Logic **62**(4), 1280–1296 (1997). https://doi.org/10.2307/2275643
2. Bès, A.: Expansions of MSO by cardinality relations. Logical Methods in Computer Science **9**(4) (2013). https://doi.org/10.2168/lmcs-9(4:18)2013
3. Bruyère V.: Entiers et automates finis. Mémoire de fin d'études, University of Mons, Belgium (1985)
4. Bruyère V., Hansel G., Michaux C., Villemaire R.: Logic and p-recognizable sets of integers. Bulletin of the Belgian Mathematical Society - Simon Stevin **1**(2), 191–238 (1994). https://doi.org/10.36045/bbms/1103408547
5. Büchi R.J.: Weak second-order arithmetic and finite automata. Mathematical Logic Quarterly **6**(1-6), 66–92 (1960). https://doi.org/10.1002/malq.19600060105
6. Cadilhac M., Finkel A., McKenzie P.: On the expressiveness of Parikh automata and related models. In: Proceedings of the Third Workshop on Non-Classical Models for Automata and Applications - NCMA 2011, pp. 103-119. Milan, Italy (2011)
7. Davis M.: Arithmetical problems and recursively enumerable predicates. Journal of Symbolic Logic **18**(1), 33–41 (1953). https://doi.org/10.2307/2266325
8. Davis M., Putnam H., Robinson J.: The decision problem for exponential diophantine equations. Annals of Mathematics **74**(3), 425–436 (1961). https://doi.org/10.2307/1970289
9. Elgot C.C.: Decision problems of finite automata design and related arithmetics. Transactions of the American Mathematical Society **98**(1), 21–51 (1961). https://doi.org/10.1090/s0002-9947-1961-0139530-9
10. Ginsburg S., Spanier E.: Semigroups, Presburger formulas, and languages. Pacific Journal of Mathematics **16**(2), 285–296 (1966). https://doi.org/10.2140/pjm.1966.16.285
11. Haase C., Różycki J.: On the expressiveness of Büchi arithmetic. In: Kiefer, S., Tasson, C. (eds) FOSSACS 2021, Lecture Notes in Computer Science, vol. 12650, pp. 310–323. Springer International Publishing (2021). https://doi.org/10.1007/978-3-030-71995-1_16
12. Hodgson B.R.: Décidabilité par automate fini. Annales des sciences mathématiques du Québec, **7**(1), 39–57 (1983).
13. Ibarra O.H.: Reversal-bounded multicounter machines and their decision problems. Journal of the ACM **25**(1), 116–133 (1978). https://doi.org/10.1145/322047.322058
14. Jones J.P., Matijasevič Yu.V.: Register machine proof of the theorem on exponential diophantine representation of enumerable sets. Journal of Symbolic Logic **49**(3), 818–829 (1984). https://doi.org/10.2307/2274135
15. Klaedtke F., Rueß H.: Parikh automata and monadic second-order logics with linear cardinality constraints. Tech. rep. 177, Universität Freiburg (2002)
16. Klaedtke F., Rueß H.: Monadic second-order logics with cardinalities. In: Baeten, J.C.M., Lenstra, J.K., Parrow, J., Woeginger, G.J. (eds) ICALP 2003, Lecture Notes in Computer Science, vol. 2719, pp. 681–696. Springer, Heidelberg (2003). https://doi.org/10.1007/3-540-45061-0_54
17. Kozen D.C.: Automata and Computability. Springer, New York (1997). https://doi.org/10.1007/978-1-4612-1844-9
18. Kummer E.E.: Über die Ergänzungssätze zu den allgemeinen Reciprocitätsgesetzen. Journal für die reine und angewandte Mathematik, **44**, 93–146 (1852). https://doi.org/10.1515/crll.1852.44.93

19. Matiyasevich Yu.V.: A new proof of the theorem on exponential diophantine representation of enumerable sets (in Russian). Zapiski Nauchnykh Seminarov LOMI **60**, 75–92 (1976). (English translation: Journal of Soviet Mathematics **14**(5), 1475–1486 (1980) https://doi.org/doi:10.1007/BF01693980)
20. Matiyasevich Yu.V.: Hilbert's tenth problem. MIT Press, Massachusetts (1993)
21. Parikh R.J.: On context-free languages. Journal of the ACM **13**(4) 570–581 (1966). https://doi.org/10.1145/321356.321364
22. Trakhtenbrot B.A.: Finite automata and the logic of one-place predicates (in Russian). Sibirskiĭ Matematicheskiĭ Zhurnal **3**, 103–131 (1962).
23. Villemaire R.: Joining k- and l-recognizable sets of natural numbers. In: Finkel, A., Jantzen, M. (eds) STACS 1992, Lecture Notes in Computer Science, vol. 577, pp. 83–94. Springer, Heidelberg (1992). https://doi.org/10.1007/3-540-55210-3_175
24. Villemaire R.: The theory of $\langle \mathbb{N}; +, V_k, V_l \rangle$ is undecidable. Theoretical Computer Science **106**(2), 337–349 (1992). https://doi.org/10.1016/0304-3975(92)90256-f

Coverability in 2-VASS with One Unary Counter is in NP *

Filip Mazowiecki[1] , Henry Sinclair-Banks[2] (✉) , and Karol Węgrzycki[3]

[1] University of Warsaw, Warsaw, Poland
f.mazowiecki@mimuw.edu.pl
[2] Centre for Discrete Mathematics and its Applications (DIMAP) & Department
of Computer Science, University of Warwick, Coventry, UK
h.sinclair-banks@warwick.ac.uk
[3] Saarland University and Max Planck Institute for Informatics, Saarbrücken,
Germany
wegrzycki@cs.uni-saarland.de

Abstract. Coverability in Petri nets finds applications in verification
of safety properties of reactive systems. We study coverability in the
equivalent model: Vector Addition Systems with States (VASS).

A k-VASS can be seen as k counters and a finite automaton whose transitions are labelled with k integers. Counter values are updated by adding
the respective transition labels. A configuration in this system consists
of a state and k counter values. Importantly, the counters are never allowed to take negative values. The coverability problem asks whether one
can traverse the k-VASS from the initial configuration to a configuration
with at least the counter values of the target.

In a well-established line of work on k-VASS, coverability in 2-VASS is
already **PSPACE**-hard when the integer updates are encoded in binary.
This lower bound limits the practicality of applications, so it is natural
to focus on restrictions. In this paper we initiate the study of 2-VASS
with one unary counter. Here, one counter receives binary encoded updates and the other receives unary encoded updates. Our main result
is that coverability in 2-VASS with one unary counter is in **NP**. This
improves upon the inherited state-of-the-art **PSPACE** upper bound. Our
main technical contribution is that one only needs to consider runs in a
certain compressed linear form.

Keywords: Vector Addition Systems · Coverability Problem · Linear
Path Schemes

1 Introduction

Vector Addition Systems with States (VASS) are a well-studied class of infinite-
state systems (see the survey [37]). These are finite automata with counters that

* Filip Mazowiecki is supported by the ERC grant INFSYS, agreement no. 950398.
Henry Sinclair-Banks is supported by EPSRC Standard Research Studentship
(DTP), grant EP/T5179X/1. Karol Węgrzycki is supported by the ERC grant TI-
PEA agreement no. 850979.

O. Kupferman and P. Sobocinski (Eds.): FoSSaCS 2023, LNCS 13992, pp. 196–217, 2023.
https://doi.org/10.1007/978-3-031-30829-1_10

can be updated, but are never allowed to take negative values. Thus, a configuration consists of a state and a vector over the natural numbers. The central decision problems are the reachability and coverability problems. The reachability problem asks whether from a given start configuration one can reach the target configuration. The coverability problem is the same except that the target configuration need not be reached exactly, counter values are allowed to be greater. Both problems are not only mathematically elegant, but they have interesting theoretical applications [7] and implementations [6]. Coverability is provably a simpler problem that is better suited for applications; reachability tools are mostly applied to coverability benchmarks [14]. Yet coverability has applications in the verification of safety conditions in reactive systems [17,21]. Such systems may require additional data structures to be accurately represented, like counters for example. Safety conditions often boil down to whether a particular state can be reached as opposed to a particular configuration [8].

Coverability and reachability have been studied for decades. The equivalent model of Petri nets was introduced already in the sixties [34]. For general VASS, Lipton proved in 1976 an EXPSPACE lower bound that applies to both coverability and reachability [31]. Two years later, Rackoff proved a matching EXPSPACE upper bound for coverability [35]. Later in 1981, Mayr proved that reachability is decidable [32] without providing an upper bound for the algorithm. The construction was simplified by Kosaraju [24] and Lambert [25], and a recent series of papers by Leroux and Schmitz ended in 2019 by proving an Ackermann upper bound [27]. A matching Ackermann lower bound was published in 2021 by two independent groups [12,26].

Plenty of attention has been given to VASS with fixed dimension, that is when the number of counters k is invariable, denoted k-VASS. For fixed dimension VASS it matters much whether the counter updates are encoded in unary or binary. Already, Rackoff gives NL and PSPACE upper bounds for coverability in unary encoded and binary encoded k-VASS, respectively [35]. The coverability problem where there are no counters is just directed graph reachability that is NL-complete [3]. Thus, coverability in unary encoded k-VASS is NL-complete, for every fixed k. Coverability in binary encoded 1-VASS is in NC^2 [2], it can therefore be decided in deterministic polynomial time. If there are two or more binary counters, coverability is PSPACE-hard [5] via a reduction from reachability in bounded one-counter automata that is PSPACE-complete [18]. Therefore, coverability in binary encoded k-VASS is PSPACE-complete for every $k \geq 2$. See Figure 1 for the complexities of coverability in VASS with a fixed number of unary and binary encoded counters. This is all in striking contrast to the reachability problem in fixed dimension VASS, since reachability in 8-VASS is already known to be nonelementary [13].

There is a prominent line of work on 2-VASS with various encodings. The seminal paper in 1979 of Hopcroft and Pansiot [23] shows reachability in 2-VASS is decidable, proving that the reachability set is effectively semi-linear. Moreover, in the same paper the authors show, by an example, that the 3-VASS reachability set need not be semi-linear. Later, this was improved as it was shown that for

Number of unary counters

		0	1	≥ 2
Number of binary counters	0	NL-complete [3]	NL-complete [38]	NL-complete [35]
	1	in NC^2 ⊆ P [2]	**in NP** [*this paper*]	Open
	≥ 2	PSPACE-complete [5]	PSPACE-complete	PSPACE-complete [35]

Fig. 1. The complexities of coverability in VASS with a fixed number of unary and binary encoded counters. All NL lower bounds arise from the zero counters case, here coverability is directed graph reachability and that is well known to be NL-complete [3]. In the case of one binary counter, regardless of the number of unary counters, we are aware only of this trivial NL lower bound. Furthermore, with one binary counter and at least two unary counters, we are not aware of a non-trivial upper bound (denoted "Open" in the table). When there are at least two binary counters and any number of unary counters, coverability is PSPACE-complete. The lower bound holds for 2-VASS with two binary counters [5] and the upper bound is given by Rackoff for any fixed dimension [35]. Recall that coverability in general VASS, where the number of counters is not fixed, is EXPSPACE-complete [35].

2-VASS the reachability relation is effectively semi-linear [28]. This proof shows that every 2-VASS can be characterised by a *flat model*, i.e. where the underlying finite automaton does not contain nested cycles. A more careful analysis of that paper, resulted in a PSPACE upper bound result for reachability in binary encoded 2-VASS [5]. Since coverability in binary encoded 2-VASS is PSPACE-hard [5], the authors were able to conclude that both coverability and reachability are PSPACE-complete. Just as coverability demonstrated the difference encoding makes to complexity, so does reachability; later it was proved that reachability in unary encoded 2-VASS is NL-complete [16].

Our Results and Techniques. We consider the coverability problem for 2-VASS with one unary counter. Here, updates of one counter are encoded in binary and the updates of the other are encoded in unary, see Figure 2 for an example. Notice that the unary counter need not be limited to polynomially bounded values. Otherwise, the value of the unary counter could be encoded into the states for an instance of coverability in binary encoded 1-VASS. Furthermore, we do not impose any restrictions on the initial and the target configurations, i.e. both coordinates of these vectors are encoded in binary. Our main result is that coverability in 2-VASS with one unary counter is in NP.

Coverability in binary encoded k-VASS is PSPACE-complete, for $k \geq 2$. The lower bound limits the practicality of applications. Therefore, it is sensible to consider restricted variations and quantify their complexity. We remark that coverability in fixed dimension VASS had widely-open complexity if there was exactly one binary counter and at least one unary counter. See Figure 1 for a summary of the known results.

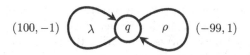

Fig. 2. Example 2-VASS with one unary counter V. Consider the instance of coverability consisting of V, the initial configuration $q(0,1)$, and the target configuration $q(0,10)$. Consider the path $\pi = \lambda\rho\,\lambda\rho\cdots\lambda\rho\,\rho\cdots\rho$ which induces a run in V from the initial configuration $q(0,1)$. There are 990 repetitions of the pair of cycles $\lambda\rho$ to witness the configuration $q(990,1)$. The cycles alternate so both counters remain non-negative throughout the run. This is followed by 10 iterations of the cycle ρ so the configuration $q(0,11)$ is witnessed, achieving coverability of the target configuration $q(0,10)$.

The natural starting point is the characterisation of runs via *linear path schemes* [4]. Intuitively, the authors prove that if coverability or reachability holds then there is a witnessing path of a specific shape. Namely, all paths can be characterised by a bounded language defined by a regular expression of the form $\tau_0\gamma_1^*\tau_1\ldots\tau_{k-1}\gamma_k^*\tau_k$. Here $\tau_0,\ldots,\tau_k$ are paths that connect disjoint cycles $\gamma_1,\ldots,\gamma_k$. Since the language is bounded, checking if there is a path for a given expression essentially amounts to an instance of integer linear programming. In particular, the authors argue that both k and $|\tau_0|+|\gamma_1|+|\tau_1|+\ldots+|\tau_{k-1}|+|\gamma_k|+|\tau_k|$ are pseudo-polynomially bounded [4]. However, a polynomial bound would immediately yield an NP upper bound as such a regular expression can be guessed. Given that coverability in 2-VASS with two binary counters is PSPACE-hard [5], we cannot simply directly apply the known results when dealing with 2-VASS with one binary and one unary counter. In Section 3, we provide a detailed discussion and a difficult yet motivating example in Figure 3.

To overcome this problem, we show that coverability can be witnessed by paths in *compressed linear form*. We relax the condition of the bounded language, by allowing to nest linear forms, provided that the exponents are fixed. Intuitively, an expression of the form $(\tau\gamma^*\tau')^*$ is still forbidden, but we allow for $(\tau\gamma^e\tau')^*$, where e is fixed but can be exponentially large (encoded using polynomially many bits). Such a form easily provides an NP upper bound.

We rely on two crucial observations to prove that we can focus on paths in compressed linear form. First, notice that the $*$ operation in a linear path scheme corresponds to iterating some cycle in the VASS. Since $\gamma_1,\ldots,\gamma_k$ need to be short, one naturally focuses on short cycles. The issue is that there are exponentially many cycles of polynomial size. In Section 4 we prove that for coverability there are only polynomially many 'optimal' cycles. In Section 5 we deal with the problem when some cycle γ occurs many times in a linear path scheme witnessing coverability, resulting in a polynomial bound on k, the width of the linear path scheme. Then we prove that, either we can merge some γ_i and γ_j thus reducing the width, or that there is a cycle that has positive effect on one counter and non-negative effect on the other counter. Intuitively, in the latter case, we can reduce the problem to coverability in 1-VASS by pumping such a cycle that forces one counter to take an arbitrarily large value. Moreover, such a cycle is witnessed by a linear path scheme. Since we need to pump this cycle, we require compressed linear forms to describe the repetitions of the cycle.

We highlight that both our crucial observations rely on that we work with coverability, not reachability. We further highlight that we address these crucial observations through our technical contributions that often depend on the fact there is one unary counter.

Further Related Work. Asymmetric treatment of the counters has been already considered for VASS. Recall that Minsky machines can be seen as VASS with the additional ability of zero-testing. For this model coverability is undecidable [33], even with two counters. This raised natural questions of what happens where only one of the counters is able to be reset or tested for zero. This, and more generally, reachability in VASS with hierarchical zero-tests are known to be decidable [36]. There is a further investigation into VASS with one zero-test [20]. Recently, work has appeared containing detailed analysis about 2-VASS where counters have different powers [19,29]. Finally, one of the most famous open problems in the community is whether reachability is decidable for 1-VASS with a pushdown stack. For these systems, coverability is known to be decidable [30]. The best known lower bound is that coverability, thus reachability also, is PSPACE-hard [15]. Our model, 2-VASS with one unary counter, can be seen as 1-VASS with a singleton alphabet pushdown stack.

The complexity of reachability in binary encoded 3-VASS remains an intriguing open problem. It is PSPACE-hard, like in dimension two, and the only known upper bound is primitive recursive, but not even elementary [27]. Recent works on reachability in fixed dimension VASS [11,9,13] provide new examples and a better understanding of the VASS model. Interestingly, many techniques applied to fixed dimension VASS are very closely related to recent progress on the nonelementary and Ackermann lower bounds for general VASS [10,12,26]. We finally and additionally motivate coverability in VASS with one binary counter and (at least) one unary counter as an avenue for finding new techniques to approach VASS problems with.

2   Preliminaries

Given an integer $z \in \mathbb{Z}$ we denote $\text{bitsize}(z) = \log_2(|z| + 1) + 1$. For a vector $\mathbf{v} := (v_1, v_2)$ we use $(\mathbf{v})_1 := v_1$ and $(\mathbf{v})_2 := v_2$ to be the projections to the first and second coordinates, respectively. We use $|\mathbf{v}|_{\max} := \max\{|v_1|, |v_2|\} + 1$ to denote the size of vector $\mathbf{v}$. We write $\mathbf{v} \leq \mathbf{w}$ if the inequalities hold on each coordinate. We write $\mathbf{v} < \mathbf{w}$ if at least one of the inequalities is strict.

A *2-VASS with one unary counter* $V = (Q, T)$ consists of a finite set of control *states* Q and a set of *transitions* $T \subseteq Q \times \mathbb{Z} \times \{-1, 0, 1\} \times Q$. We shall refer to the first counter as the *binary counter* and the second counter as the *unary counter*. The size of V is $|V| = |Q| + \sum_{(p,b,u,q) \in T} \text{bitsize}(b)$. With

$|V|_{\max} := |Q| + |T| \cdot |T|_{\max}$ we denote the total 'pseudo-polynomial size' of the automaton, where $|T|_{\max}$ denotes the maximum absolute value that occurs in the transitions. Note that in a standard 2-VASS both counters are in binary, i.e. the domain of updates for the second counter is also $\mathbb{Z}$.

A *path* π in V is a, possibly empty, sequence of transitions $\pi = (t_i)_{i=1}^m$ such that $t_i = (q_{i-1}, b_i, u_i, q_i) \in T$. A path is *simple* if $q_0, \ldots, q_m$ are distinct. A path is a *cycle* if $q_0 = q_m$ and $m > 0$ (thus empty cycles are forbidden). We call it a q_0-cycle to emphasise the first and last state of the cycle. A cycle is *simple* if $q_1, \ldots, q_m$ are distinct. A cycle is *short* if $m \leq |Q|$. The *length* of a path is the number of transitions in the path, denoted $\mathrm{len}(\pi) = m$. We write $\pi[i..j]$ to denote the path that is the subsequence of transitions $(t_i, \ldots, t_j)$ in π.

A *configuration* $(p, \mathbf{u}) \in Q \times \mathbb{N}^2$, denoted $p(\mathbf{u})$, is a state paired with the current binary and unary counter values. A *run* is a sequence of configurations $(q_i(\mathbf{v}_i))_{i=0}^m$ such that $(q_{i-1}, (\mathbf{v}_i)_1 - (\mathbf{v}_{i-1})_1, (\mathbf{v}_i)_2 - (\mathbf{v}_{i-1})_2, q_i) \in T$. A run can equivalently be defined by the sequence of configurations induced by following a path π starting from an initial configuration $q_0(\mathbf{v}_0)$. We denote this run $q_0(\mathbf{v}_0) \xrightarrow{\pi} q_m(\mathbf{v}_m)$. We also write $q_0(\mathbf{v}_0) \xrightarrow{*} q_m(\mathbf{v}_m)$ to indicate the existence of a run between two configurations.

In this paper we study the *coverability* problem for VASS.

VASS COVERABILITY

INPUT: A VASS $V = (Q, T)$ and two configurations $p(\mathbf{u})$ and $q(\mathbf{v})$.

QUESTION: Does $p(\mathbf{u}) \xrightarrow{*} q(\mathbf{v}')$ hold, for some $\mathbf{v}' \geq \mathbf{v}$?

Do note that the initial configuration $p(\mathbf{u})$ and the target configuration $q(\mathbf{v})$ have both the binary and unary components encoded as binary integers. The *reachability problem* for VASS—which we will not study in this paper—requires $\mathbf{v}' = \mathbf{v}$.

Consider a path $\pi = (t_i)_{i=1}^m$, where $t_i = (q_{i-1}, b_i, u_i, q_i)$. The *effect* of π is the sum of the counter updates, i.e. the vector $\mathrm{eff}(\pi) := \sum_{i=1}^m (b_i, u_i)$. We often focus on the two projections: the *binary effect* $\mathrm{eff}_b(\pi) := \sum_{i=1}^m b_i$, and the *unary effect* $\mathrm{eff}_u(\pi) := \sum_{i=1}^m u_i$.

We say that a cycle γ is *monotone* if $\mathrm{eff}(\gamma) \geq \mathbf{0}$ or $\mathrm{eff}(\gamma) \leq \mathbf{0}$. Otherwise, we say that γ is *non-monotone*. Note the two variants of a non-monotone cycle: a *positive-negative* cycle $\mathrm{eff}_b(\gamma) > 0$ and $\mathrm{eff}_u(\gamma) < 0$, and a *negative-positive* cycle $\mathrm{eff}_b(\gamma) < 0$ and $\mathrm{eff}_u(\gamma) > 0$.

Let γ be a cycle. Given $e \in \mathbb{N}$ we write γ^e for the path obtained by e repetitions of γ. We refer to e as the *exponent*. A linear path scheme is a regular expression of the form $\tau_0 \gamma_1^* \tau_1 \cdots \tau_{k-1} \gamma_k^* \tau_k$, where the paths $\tau_0, \tau_1, \ldots, \tau_k$ connect disjoint cycles $\gamma_1, \ldots, \gamma_k$. Note that a collection of cycles is disjoint if no two cycles have a common state. Given $\ell = (\tau_0, \gamma_1, \tau_1, \ldots, \tau_{k-1}, \gamma_k, \tau_k)$, we say the a a path π is in linear form ℓ if $\pi = \pi_\ell = \tau_0 \gamma_1^{e_1} \tau_1 \cdots \tau_{k-1} \gamma_k^{e_k} \tau_k$ for some exponents $e_1, \ldots, e_k$. Note that in this definition every path has a linear form, e.g. $\tau_0 = \pi$ is valid. To leverage the definition, we will ask whether paths are in a linear form of certain size. The size of a linear form ℓ is $\sum_{i=0}^k \mathrm{len}(\tau_i) + \sum_{i=1}^k \mathrm{len}(\gamma_i)$. The size of π_ℓ is $\sum_{i=0}^k \mathrm{len}(\tau_i) + \sum_{i=1}^k \mathrm{len}(\gamma_i) + \sum_{i=1}^k \mathrm{bitsize}(e_i)$, i.e. includes the exponents. We refer to k as the *width* of the linear form.

3 Coverability in 2-VASS with One Unary Counter

In this section we briefly discuss why the state-of-the-art techniques are not enough to prove that coverability in 2-VASS with one unary counter is in NP. Blondin et al. [4] show that for a given 2-VASS V there exists a set of linear path schemes S such that if $p(\mathbf{u}) \xrightarrow{*} q(\mathbf{v})$ in V, then there exists a path π in a linear path scheme $\rho \in S$ such that $p(\mathbf{u}) \xrightarrow{\pi} q(\mathbf{v})$. For every linear path scheme $\rho \in S$ the width of ρ, and therefore the width of every path, is bounded above by $\mathsf{poly}(|Q|, |T|_{\max})$ [4, Theorem 3.1]. Such a path π is not necessarily a polynomial size witness, as the width depends on $|T|_{\max}$ polynomially. We provide an example of a 2-VASS with one unary counter where the width of every linear form ℓ for a path is exponential in the input size. This demonstrates that the combinatorial structure of linear path schemes is not self-sufficient to show that there always exists a polynomial size witness of coverability.

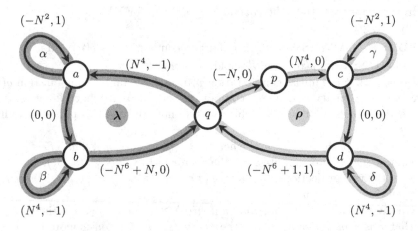

Fig. 3. Example 2-VASS with one unary counter V, where $N = 2^n$, where n is an input parameter (thus making N exponentially large). Consider the coverability instance with the initial configuration $q(0, 1)$, and the target configuration $q(N, 1)$. Let $\lambda = t_{qa}\alpha^{N^2}t_{ab}\beta^{N^2}t_{bq}$ and $\rho = t_{qp}t_{pc}\gamma^{N^2}t_{cd}\delta^{N^2}t_{dq}$, where t_{xy} is the transition from state x to state y. Observe that $\mathrm{eff}(\lambda) = (N, -1)$ and $\mathrm{eff}(\rho) = (-N+1, 1)$, thus $\mathrm{eff}(\lambda\rho) = (1, 0)$. It is easy to then see that $q(0, 1) \xrightarrow{(\lambda\rho)^N} q(N, 1)$. Intuitively the cycles λ and ρ alternate so both counters remain non-negative throughout the run. In the appendix, we prove that there does not exist a linear form of polynomial size for a path that induces a coverability run.

Paths in Compressed Linear Form. Nevertheless, there is a natural way to succinctly describe the path presented in Figure 3. Let $\sigma = \lambda\rho$, and note that

$$\sigma^N = \left(t_{qa} \, \alpha^{N^2} \, t_{ab} \, \beta^{N^2} \, t_{bq} t_{qp} t_{pc} \, \gamma^{N^2} \, t_{cd} \, \delta^{N^2} \, t_{dq} \right)^N .$$

All paths and cycles are 'small', and the bitsize of N and N^2 are polynomial in n, so σ itself is a path in linear form. We introduce the following generalisation of linear form paths that encapsulates the idea behind paths of this kind of arrangement.

Definition 1 (Compressed linear form path). *A path π is in* compressed linear form *if $\pi = \rho_0 \sigma_1^{f_1} \rho_1 \cdots \rho_{k-1} \sigma_k^{f_k} \rho_k$ for some connected paths in linear form $\rho_0, \rho_1, \ldots, \rho_k$; cycles in linear form $\sigma_1, \ldots, \sigma_k$; and exponents $f_1, \ldots, f_k$. The size of a compressed linear form path is the sum of the sizes of all ρ_i and σ_i (including the bitsize of their exponents) plus the bitsize of the exponents f_i.*

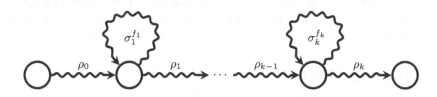

Fig. 4. A compressed linear form path.

The following theorem is our main contribution.

Theorem 1. *Let V be a 2-VASS with one unary counter and fix two configurations $p(\mathbf{u})$ and $q(\mathbf{v})$. If $p(\mathbf{u}) \xrightarrow{*} q(\mathbf{v})$, then there exists a path in compressed linear form π such that $p(\mathbf{u}) \xrightarrow{\pi} q(\mathbf{v}')$ and $\mathbf{v}' \geq \mathbf{v}$. The size of the compressed linear form path is polynomial in $|V| + \text{bitsize}(\mathbf{u}) + \text{bitsize}(\mathbf{v})$.*

Corollary 1. *Coverability in 2-VASS with one unary counter is in NP.*

Proof. By Theorem 1 it suffices to consider paths in compressed linear form of polynomial size, that can be guessed in NP. It suffices to observe that a coverability instance on a given compressed linear form amounts to an instance of integer linear programming. Intuitively, this is because the nested cycles are fixed. Thus to check whether a run drops below zero it suffices to check before applying a cycle and after applying it for the last time (see e.g. [5, Section V, Lemma 14]). □

We highlight that it is rather unexpected that only one extra 'level' of linear form paths is enough to obtain polynomial size witnesses of coverability in a 2-VASS with one unary counter, since the problem is PSPACE-complete for general

2-VASS. Roughly speaking, the example given in Figure 3 observes the most complex behaviour possible and this instance of coverability is witnessed by a compressed linear form path. More specifically, compressed linear form paths containing only one linear form cycle suffice as witnesses for coverability in 2-VASS with one unary counter. Therefore, all witnesses can be represented by a compressed linear form path $\rho \sigma^N \tau$ where ρ and τ are linear form paths to and from the single linear form cycle σ which is iterated N times.

The rest of the paper is dedicated to proving Theorem 1. We heavily exploit both distinguishing features of the problem: the fact that one counter receives unary encoded updates (as opposed to both counters in binary) and the fact that we aim to assert coverability (as opposed to reachability). Our approach is as presented in the introduction. In 4 we observe that we can polynomially bound the total number of distinct short cycles. We formalise this and show that there are only polynomially many 'irreplaceable' short cycles. In 5 we provide a 'reshuffling procedure'. If some short cycle γ repeats exponentially many times we aim to modify the path π by moving the cycles γ close to each other. Then either every short cycle γ will appear only in polynomially many 'bundles' γ^e, or we find a cycle σ such that $\text{eff}(\sigma) > \mathbf{0}$. In the latter case, by pumping σ we are essentially left with one counter. Finally, in Section 6 we conclude the proof of Theorem 1.

4   Replacing Short Cycles

In this section, we show that there are only polynomially many short cycles that need occur in a run witnessing coverability. Fix a path $\pi = (q_{i-1}, b_i, u_i, q_i)_{i=1}^k$. Let $0 \leq i_b, i_u \leq k$ be the first indices such that $g_b = \sum_{i=1}^{i_b} b_i$ and $g_u = \sum_{i=1}^{i_u} u_i$ are at their lowest, respectively. Note that $g_b, g_u \leq 0$ since by convention if we consider $i_b, i_u = 0$ then the sum evaluates to 0. We call and denote these two numbers the *binary guard* $\text{grd}_b(\pi) = g_b$ and the *unary guard* $\text{grd}_u(\pi) = g_u$. The following claim immediately follows from these definitions.

Claim 1. Both $\text{grd}_b(\pi[i_b + 1..k]) = 0$ and $\text{grd}_u(\pi[i_u + 1..k]) = 0$.

Much like the *nadir* of a cycle in a one-counter net, defined in [1], we define the *binary-nadir state* as q_{i_b}, i.e. the first state in which the binary counter first attains the lowest value when executing π. We call the *binary-nadir decomposition* $\pi = \pi_1^b \pi_2^b$, for $\pi_1^b = \pi[1..i_b]$ and $\pi_2^b = \pi[i_b + 1..k]$, as intimated in Claim 1. Notice that this decomposition necessitates the binary guard of the path π is equal to the binary effect of the prefix π_1^b, $\text{grd}_b(\pi) = \text{eff}_b(\pi_1^b) = \text{grd}_b(\pi_1^b)$. Furthermore, the suffix of the binary-nadir decomposition has zero binary guard $\text{grd}_b(\pi_2^b) = 0$. We primarily utilise binary-nadir states and binary-nadir decompositions, hence the omission of matching unary-nadir states and unary-nadir-decompositions.

Definition 2 (Replaceable cycles). *Let γ be a q-cycle and let p be the binary-nadir state of γ. We say that γ is replaceable if there exists a q-cycle γ' with the same binary-nadir state p, such that*

(a) $\mathrm{eff}_b(\gamma') \geq \mathrm{eff}_b(\gamma)$ and $\mathrm{eff}_u(\gamma') \geq \mathrm{eff}_u(\gamma)$,
(b) $\mathrm{grd}_b(\gamma') \geq \mathrm{grd}_b(\gamma)$ and $\mathrm{grd}_u(\gamma') \geq \mathrm{grd}_u(\gamma)$, and
(c) $\mathrm{len}(\gamma') \leq \mathrm{len}(\gamma)$.

Additionally, at least one inequality is strict and we write $\gamma \prec \gamma'$.

We say a cycle is *irreplaceable* if it is not replaceable. We also say that an irreplaceable q-cycle γ with the binary-nadir state p is *characterised* by the five values: $\mathrm{eff}_b(\gamma)$, $\mathrm{eff}_u(\gamma)$, $\mathrm{grd}_b(\gamma)$, $\mathrm{grd}_u(\gamma)$, and $\mathrm{len}(\gamma)$.

Lemma 1 (Replacing cycles). *Let $\pi = \pi_1\gamma\pi_2$, where γ is a q-cycle. Suppose $p(\mathbf{u}) \xrightarrow{\pi} q(\mathbf{v})$ then the following hold.*

- *If γ is replaceable, then there exists an irreplaceable q-cycle $\gamma \prec \gamma'$ such that*
  $$p(\mathbf{u}) \xrightarrow{\pi_1\gamma'\pi_2} q(\mathbf{v}').$$
- *If γ is irreplaceable, then for every irreplaceable q-cycle γ' that has the same characterisation as γ, $p(\mathbf{u}) \xrightarrow{\pi_1\gamma'\pi_2} q(\mathbf{v}')$.*

In both cases $\mathbf{v}' \geq \mathbf{v}$ and $\mathrm{len}(\pi) \geq \mathrm{len}(\pi_1\gamma'\pi_2)$.

For convenience, we define the polynomial $R(|Q|) := |Q|^4(|Q|+1)(2|Q|+1)^2$.

Lemma 2. *There exists at most $R(|Q|)$ many irreplaceable short cycles with different characterisations.*

Proof. We fix two states q and p and consider only q-cycles γ with the binary-nadir state p. Thus in the final argument one must multiply everything by $|Q|^2$. Since we consider short cycles, the unary effect and the unary guard are small, i.e. $-|Q| \leq \mathrm{eff}_u(\gamma) \leq |Q|$ and $-|Q| \leq \mathrm{grd}_u(\gamma) \leq 0$.

Towards a contradiction, suppose there exists more than $|Q|^2(|Q|+1)(2|Q|+1)^2$ many such irreplaceable q-cycles with different characterisations. By the pigeonhole principle there must exist two cycles, denoted in binary-nadir decomposition $\gamma = \gamma_1\gamma_2$ and $\gamma' = \gamma_1'\gamma_2'$, that have the same values $\mathrm{eff}_u(\gamma_1) = \mathrm{eff}_u(\gamma_1')$, $\mathrm{eff}_u(\gamma_2) = \mathrm{eff}_u(\gamma_2')$, $\mathrm{grd}_u(\gamma) = \mathrm{grd}_u(\gamma')$, $\mathrm{len}(\gamma_1) = \mathrm{len}(\gamma_1')$, and $\mathrm{len}(\gamma_2) = \mathrm{len}(\gamma_2')$.

We know that the irreplaceable q-cycles γ and γ' have different characterisations, so it must be the case that their binary effects differ $\mathrm{eff}_b(\gamma) \neq \mathrm{eff}_b(\gamma')$. Otherwise, the cycle with the lesser binary guard is replaceable, because the unary effect, unary guard, and length do not differ. Without loss of generality, suppose $\mathrm{eff}_b(\gamma) > \mathrm{eff}_b(\gamma')$, then $\mathrm{grd}_b(\gamma) < \mathrm{grd}_b(\gamma')$. Otherwise, γ' would be replaceable as $\gamma \prec \gamma'$.

Now consider the q-cycle $\sigma = \gamma_1'\gamma_2$, also with the binary-nadir state p. We will show that $\gamma \prec \sigma$ contradicting the fact that γ is an irreplaceable q-cycle. First, observe that σ has greater binary effect than γ as

$$\mathrm{eff}_b(\sigma) = \mathrm{eff}_b(\gamma_1') + \mathrm{eff}_b(\gamma_2) > \mathrm{eff}_b(\gamma_1) + \mathrm{eff}_b(\gamma_2) = \mathrm{eff}_b(\gamma),$$

where the inequality holds because $\mathrm{grd}_b(\gamma) < \mathrm{grd}_b(\gamma')$. Second, σ and γ have equal unary effect because $\mathrm{eff}_u(\gamma_1') = \mathrm{eff}_u(\gamma_1)$. Third, we show that σ has a greater binary guard than γ. Since γ_2 is the suffix of the binary-nadir decomposition of γ, it must be true that $\mathrm{grd}_b(\gamma_2) = 0$. By Claim 1 $\mathrm{grd}_b(\sigma) = \mathrm{grd}_b(\gamma_1')$. Combining these facts, $\mathrm{grd}_b(\sigma) = \mathrm{grd}_b(\gamma') > \mathrm{grd}_b(\gamma)$. Fourth, σ has at least the unary guard of γ because, in particular, the unary guard of the prefix of a path is at most the unary guard of the entire path.

$$\begin{aligned}
\mathrm{grd}_u(\sigma) &= \min\{\mathrm{grd}_u(\gamma_1'), \mathrm{eff}_u(\gamma_1') + \mathrm{grd}_u(\gamma_2)\} \\
&\geq \min\{\mathrm{grd}_u(\gamma'), \mathrm{eff}_u(\gamma_1') + \mathrm{grd}_u(\gamma_2)\} \\
&= \min\{\mathrm{grd}_u(\gamma), \mathrm{eff}_u(\gamma_1) + \mathrm{grd}_u(\gamma_2)\} = \mathrm{grd}_u(\gamma).
\end{aligned}$$

Fifth and finally, σ and γ have equal length because $\mathrm{len}(\gamma_1') = \mathrm{len}(\gamma_1)$. We have at least one strict inequality. Thus, we have reached the desired contradiction. $\square$

5   Reshuffling Linear Form Paths

5.1   Reshuffling Procedure

There can be many linear forms for a path π. We will try to find an 'optimal' one, so we introduce a cost function to quantify linear forms. Recall that a linear form ℓ is a sequence of paths $\tau_0, \tau_1, \ldots, \tau_k$ and a sequence of cycles $\gamma_1, \ldots, \gamma_k$. If π is in the linear form $\ell = (\tau_0, \gamma_1, \tau_1, \ldots, \tau_{k-1}, \gamma_k, \tau_k)$ then we write $\pi_\ell = \tau_0 \gamma_1^{e_1} \tau_1 \cdots \tau_{k-1} \gamma_k^{e_k} \tau_k$, where $\pi = \pi_\ell$ (the index is here to stress the exact linear form). For this section, we will consider linear forms only containing short cycles γ, they will play a key role in the following arguments.

We define a cost function that assigns, to a linear form ℓ, the following pair of naturals $C(\ell) := \left(\sum_{i=0}^{k} \mathrm{len}(\tau_i), k\right)$. For convenience, we define the polynomial $P(|Q|) := 2(|Q|^2 + 1)(|Q|^2 + 2) \cdot R(|Q|)$, where R is the polynomial defined for Lemma 2. We say that a linear form ℓ is *narrow* if $C(\ell) \leq (|Q|(P(|Q|) + 1), P(|Q|))$, otherwise we say that ℓ is *wide*. We say that the triple (π', σ, π'') is a monotone cycle decomposition of a path π if σ is a monotone cycle, $\pi = \pi'\sigma\pi''$, and $\mathrm{len}(\sigma) < \mathrm{len}(\pi)$.

Lemma 3 (Reshuffling). *Let π be a path such that $p(\mathbf{u}) \xrightarrow{\pi} q(\mathbf{v})$. Then there exists a path ρ such that $p(\mathbf{u}) \xrightarrow{\rho} q(\mathbf{w})$ where $\mathbf{w} \geq \mathbf{v}$, $\mathrm{len}(\rho) \leq \mathrm{len}(\pi)$, and either*

(i) there exists a narrow linear form for ρ, or
(ii) there exists a monotone cycle decomposition of ρ.

Proof. We start with a series of preparations. In the early part of this proof, we provide simple observations to ascertain some auspicious properties of our path. In the later part of this proof, we present the 'reshuffling procedure' and conclude with one of the cases in the statement of this lemma. In this proof we will compare linear forms using the lexicographic order $\prec_{lex}$, that is known to be a linear-order and a well-order. Formally,

$$\begin{aligned}
C(\ell') \prec_{lex} C(\ell) \iff &(C(\ell'))_1 < (C(\ell))_1 \text{ or,} \\
&(C(\ell'))_1 = (C(\ell))_1 \text{ and } (C(\ell'))_2 < (C(\ell))_2.
\end{aligned}$$

We start with a path π' such that $p(\mathbf{u}) \xrightarrow{\pi'} q(\mathbf{v}')$ where $\mathbf{v}' \geq \mathbf{v}$, $\text{len}(\pi') \leq \text{len}(\pi)$, and π' has a linear form ℓ' that has the least cost among all linear forms for all like-paths. That means there does not exist another path π'' such that $p(\mathbf{u}) \xrightarrow{\pi''} q(\mathbf{v}'')$ where $\mathbf{v}'' \geq \mathbf{v}$, $\text{len}(\pi'') \leq \text{len}(\pi)$, and π'' has a linear form ℓ'' such that $C(\ell'') \prec_{lex} C(\ell')$.

For the first observation, suppose there exists $0 \leq i \leq k$ such that $\text{len}(\tau_i) > |Q|$. Then the path τ_i can be written as $\tau_i = \tau'\gamma\tau''$, where γ is a short cycle. We can define the linear form ℓ'' by modifying ℓ' where τ_i is swapped for $\tau'\gamma\tau''$. Although this increments the number of cycles k, we decrease the total length of the paths as $\text{len}(\tau') + \text{len}(\tau'') < \text{len}(\tau_i)$ (recall that empty cycles are forbidden). Thus $C(\ell'') \prec_{lex} C(\ell')$ contradicting the assumption that ℓ has minimum cost. Therefore, we assume that $\text{len}(\tau_i) \leq |Q|$ for all $0 \leq i \leq k$.

For the second observation, we define $U := \{0 \leq i \leq m : (\mathbf{v}_i)_2 < |Q|\}$ to be the set of indices of configurations in the run that have unary counter value less than $|Q|$. Observe that if $|U| > |Q|^2 + 1$ then there are two indices $0 < i < j \leq m$ such that the two corresponding configurations in the run have matching states $q_i = q_j$ and equal unary counter values $(\mathbf{v}_i)_2 = (\mathbf{v}_j)_2$. Then, regardless of sign of its binary effect, $\pi'[i..j]$ is a monotone cycle. Here, case (ii) immediately holds by decomposing π' itself using the monotone cycle $\pi'[i..j]$, given that $i > 0$ and $j \leq m$ implies $\text{len}(\pi'[i..j]) = j - i < m = \text{len}(\pi')$. Therefore, we assume $|U| \leq |Q|^2 + 1$. We continue with the aim of satisfying the conditions of case (ii) by finding a monotone cycle decomposition.

Let $d = |\{\gamma_1, \ldots, \gamma_k\}|$ be the number of distinct cycles in the linear form ℓ'. By Lemma 1 and Lemma 2, we can assume that $d \leq R(|Q|)$. Otherwise, we can exchange replaceable q-cycles for irreplaceable q-cycles using the first point in Lemma 1. It is possible that for a particular characterisation, we can observe more than one irreplaceable q-cycle. Then using the second point in Lemma 1, we can arbitrarily select one of these irreplaceable q-cycles with equal characterisations to exchange all others with. By applying these cycle replacements to π', we obtain a different path ρ. Definition 2 ensures that we do so without decreasing the effect (a), without allowing the counters to take a negative value (b), and without increasing the length of the path (c). Therefore $p(\mathbf{u}) \xrightarrow{\rho} q(\mathbf{w})$ and $\mathbf{w} \geq \mathbf{v}' \geq \mathbf{v}$, and $\text{len}(\rho) \leq \text{len}(\pi') \leq \text{len}(\pi)$. We remark since cycles have been exchanged one-for-one, then ρ takes a linear form ℓ with the same path segments as ℓ'. Therefore, it is clear that neither the number of cycles k, nor the sum of the lengths of the paths between cycles, have changed. We also know that ℓ is a linear form for ρ with minimum cost $C(\ell) = C(\ell')$, as per the initialisation in this proof.

Suppose $\rho = \rho_\ell = \tau_0\gamma_1^{e_1}\tau_1 \cdots \tau_{k-1}\gamma_k^{e_k}\tau_k$. Let $(q_j(\mathbf{v}_j))_{j=0}^m$ be the run obtained by following the path ρ_ℓ from the initial configuration $q_0(\mathbf{v}_0) = p(\mathbf{u})$ to the final configuration $q_m(\mathbf{v}_m) = q(\mathbf{w})$. We may assume that ℓ is wide. Otherwise, case (i) is immediately satisfied. We also know that $\text{len}(\rho_\ell) \geq \max\{(C(\ell))_1, (C(\ell))_2\} > P(|Q|)$. We may also assume that each cycle $\gamma_1, \ldots, \gamma_k$ is non-monotone, i.e. it is positive-negative or negative-positive. Otherwise, case (ii) immediately holds by decomposing ρ itself using some monotone cycle γ_i, given that $\text{len}(\gamma_i) \leq |Q| <$

$P(|Q|) < \text{len}(\rho_\ell)$. Notice this is valid since each $e_i > 0$ by the minimality of $C(\ell)$, otherwise you can write $\cdots \tau_{i-1} \gamma_i^0 \tau_i \cdots$ with one less cycle, decreasing $(C(\ell))_2$.

From the first observation, we get $\sum_{i=0}^k \text{len}(\tau_i) \leq (k+1)|Q|$. Given that ℓ is wide, either $|Q|(P(|Q|)+1) < (C(\ell'))_1 = \sum_{i=0}^k \text{len}(\tau_i) \leq (k+1)|Q|$ that implies $P(|Q|) < k$, or $P(|Q|) < (C(\ell'))_2 = k$. Regardless, $P(|Q|) < k$ holds. Recall that $|U| \leq |Q|^2 + 1$ from the second observation. Since there are relatively 'few' configurations indexed by U, there must exist a relatively 'distant' pair of consecutive configurations indexed by U. More formally, there are i and j such that $0 \leq i < j \leq k$ and $j - i \geq 2(|Q|^2 + 2)R(|Q|)$ and all configurations that occur in the run over the path segment $\tau_i \gamma_{i+1}^{e_{i+1}} \cdots \gamma_j^{e_j} \tau_j$ have unary counter value at least $|Q|$. Notice that $j - i$ is the number of cycles in this path segment. Since $j - i \geq 2(|Q|^2 + 2)R(|Q|)$ and by pigeonhole principle on the number of irreplaceable cycles, there is a common irreplaceable cycle γ repeated at least $x = 2(|Q|^2 + 2)$ many times. We will focus on the first x such occurrences of this cycle. Let $s_1, \ldots, s_x$ be the indices of this cycle γ, i.e. $\gamma = \gamma_{s_1} = \ldots = \gamma_{s_x}$. To highlight these cycles, we decompose this path segment into

$$\tau_i \gamma_{i+1}^{e_{i+1}} \cdots \gamma_j^{e_j} \tau_j = \Lambda_0 \gamma^{f_1} \Lambda_1 \cdots \Lambda_{x-1} \gamma^{f_x} \Lambda_x,$$

where $f_j := e_{s_j}$ and Λ_j are the concatenated paths (and cycles) in between iterations of γ, see Figure 5. To reiterate, we know that all configurations that occur in the run over this path segment have at least $|Q|$ unary counter value and γ is a short cycle.

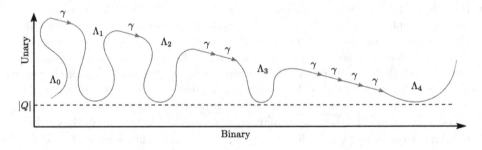

Fig. 5. The decomposition of the path segment into $\Lambda_0 \gamma^{f_1} \Lambda_1 \cdots \Lambda_{x-1} \gamma^{f_x} \Lambda_x$, as above. Notice that the unary counter is always at least $|Q|$ as no configurations indexed by U are present.

Reshuffling Procedure. In the rest of the proof we will modify the path segment (above) of the path ρ_ℓ with a procedure that we call *reshuffling*. At the end of this procedure we will find a monotone cycle and satisfy case (ii) of this lemma. We either find this cycle directly, or we obtain a linear form ℓ'' such that $C(\ell'') \prec_{lex} C(\ell)$ contradicting the assumption that ℓ has minimal cost.

Note that $x = 2(|Q|^2 + 2)$ is even, and for every pair of consecutive cycles γ_{2j-1} and γ_{2j} (for $1 < 2j \leq x$), consider the subsegment $\gamma^{f_{2j-1}} \Lambda_{2j-1} \gamma^{f_{2j}}$. There are two scenarios depending on the variant of the non-monotone cycle γ. In the scenario where γ is positive-negative, we move an iteration of γ from right to left obtaining $\gamma^{f_{2j-1}+1}\Lambda_{2j-1}\gamma^{f_{2j}-1}$. In the scenario where γ is negative-positive, we move an iteration of γ in the opposite direction obtaining $\gamma^{f_{2j-1}-1}\Lambda_{2j-1}\gamma^{f_{2j}+1}$.

We repeat this procedure until one of two conditions are met. The first is when there are no iterations of γ on one side, so either f_{2j-1} or f_{2j} becomes 0. The second is when there appears a configuration, in the run over the path subsegment after reshuffling, with unary counter value less than $|Q|$. See Figure 6 for a pictorial presentation of reshuffling in the scenario where γ is positive-negative.

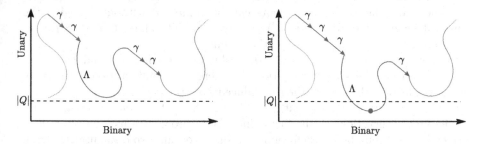

Fig. 6. Reshuffling around a path Λ (blue) where γ (red) is positive-negative. Before reshuffling, the path subsegment $\cdots\gamma\Lambda\gamma\cdots$ all configurations have unary counter value at least $|Q|$ in the run (left). After reshuffling, the path subsegment $\cdots\gamma\gamma\Lambda\cdots$, there is a configuration with unary counter value less than $|Q|$ in the run (right).

We claim that after each reshuffling step, the corresponding run remains executable, so we must check that both counters remain non-negative. Notice that by only moving a cycle, the total effect of the path subsegment remains the same. Therefore, if the run was executable before reshuffling, we can safely assume that the prefix before the path subsegment and the suffix after the path subsegment are still executable. For that reason, consider the counter values of configurations occurring in the run over the reshuffled path subsegment. We focus on a single step of the reshuffling procedure that concerns the subsegment $\gamma^{f_{2j-1}}\Lambda_{2j-1}\gamma^{f_{2j}}$.

Suppose γ is a positive-negative cycle. Then the reshuffling procedure moves γ from right to left. We claim that since $f_{2j-1} > 0$ and $\Lambda_0\gamma^{f_1}\Lambda_1\cdots\Lambda_{2j-1}\gamma^{f_{2j-1}}$ is executable, the subsegment $\Lambda_0\gamma^{f_1}\Lambda_1\cdots\Lambda_{2j-1}\gamma^{f_{2j-1}+1}$ is executable from the initial configuration. This is because one prerequisite of the reshuffling procedure is that all configurations occurring in the run over the path subsegment have at least $|Q|$ unary counter value. Moreover, the cycle γ has length at most $|Q|$ so $\mathrm{grd}_u(\gamma) \geq -|Q|$ means the unary counter value remains non-negative. As for the binary counter value, since a single execution of γ increases the binary counter and an iteration of γ was already executed before reshuffling, $\Lambda_0\gamma^{f_1}\Lambda_1\cdots\Lambda_{2j-1}\gamma^{f_{2j-1}+1}$ is executable. In the same way, from the initial configuration, $\Lambda_0\gamma^{f_1}\Lambda_1\cdots\Lambda_{2j-1}\gamma^{f_{2j-1}+1}\Lambda_{2j}\gamma_{2j}^{f_{2j}-1}$ is executable. This is because $\mathrm{eff}_u(\gamma) \geq -|Q|$, and again, all configurations occurring in the run over the path subsegment have at least $|Q|$ unary counter value, and also because of the monotonicity on the binary counter.

The argument when γ is a negative-positive cycle is analogous. This concludes the correctness analysis of the reshuffling procedure.

Finishing Reshuffling. We analyse what happens when reshuffling is finished. Suppose that there exists a pair $2j-1$ and $2j$ such that the reshuffling finishes under the first condition where all iterations of γ have been moved to one side of Λ_{2j-1}. In this case we obtain a new linear form ℓ'' for ρ, where one collection of the cycle γ has been removed (decrementing k). So $(C(\ell''))_2 = k - 1 < (C(\ell))_2$ and the two adjacent path segments can be combined without changing the summed length of paths so $(C(\ell''))_1 = (C(\ell))_1$. Therefore, $C(\ell'') \prec_{lex} C(\ell)$ contradicting the assumption ℓ has the minimal cost.

Otherwise, for every $1 \leq j \leq x/2$ the reshuffling of pair $2j-1$ and $2j$ finishes under condition the second condition. So there is a configuration with unary counter value less than $|Q|$ in the run induced from the path ρ for each pair $2j-1$ and $2j$ (see Figure 7). Recall that $\frac{x}{2} = |Q|^2 + 2$, that is the number of pairs. Akin to the first observation (in the beginning of this proof), we use the pigeonhole principle on the number of such configurations to obtain two configurations with matching states and equal unary counter values. The path segment inducing the part of the run between these two configurations is a monotone cycle, regardless of the binary effect. Again, it must be true that the length of this cycle is less than the length of the whole path, so we obtain a monotone cycle decomposition of ρ. Thus case (ii) of the lemma holds.   □

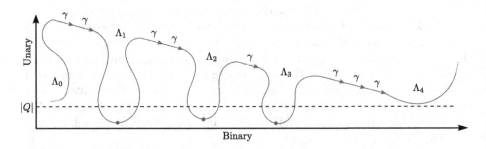

Fig. 7. After reshuffling is finished under condition the second condition, we can find a zero unary effect cycle using the (sufficiently many) configurations with unary counter less $|Q|$.

5.2   Applying Reshuffling

Lemma 3 does not necessarily return a narrow linear form for a path π witnessing coverability. Instead it may return a monotone cycle decomposition (ρ, σ, τ) of π.

Our next goal is to show that there exists polynomial size certificates for ρ and σ (Lemma 4), and then to show that there exists a polynomial size certificate for τ (Lemma 5). Like linear forms, there can be many monotone cycle decompositions for a path. Following, we will use the cost function assigning monotone cycle decompositions to pairs of natural numbers $D((\rho, \sigma, \tau)) := (\text{len}(\rho\sigma), \text{len}(\sigma))$. Note that we can compare two decompositions using their cost, even if they are for two different paths.

Lemma 4. *Suppose $p(\mathbf{u}) \xrightarrow{*} q(\mathbf{v})$ yet there is no narrow linear form ℓ for any path π such that $p(\mathbf{u}) \xrightarrow{\pi} q(\mathbf{w})$ and $\mathbf{w} \geq \mathbf{v}$, then there exists a path π' such that*

(a) $p(\mathbf{u}) \xrightarrow{\pi'} q(\mathbf{w}')$ where $\mathbf{w}' \geq \mathbf{v}$,
(b) there is a monotone cycle decomposition (ρ, σ, τ) of π' where $\text{eff}(\sigma) > \mathbf{0}$, and
(c) there are narrow linear forms for both ρ and σ.

Proof. We will again use the lexicographical order $\prec_{lex}$ to compare the cost of monotone cycle decompositions. Let π be a path of minimum length such that $p(\mathbf{u}) \xrightarrow{\pi} q(\mathbf{w})$ where $\mathbf{w} \geq \mathbf{v}$. Let $c = (\rho, \sigma, \tau)$ be the monotone cycle decomposition of π that minimizes the cost $D(c)$ under the $\prec_{lex}$ order. Such a decomposition must exist, otherwise applying Lemma 3 would return a narrow linear form ℓ' for ρ such that $p(\mathbf{u}) \xrightarrow{*} q(\mathbf{w}')$ and $\mathbf{w}' \geq \mathbf{w} \geq \mathbf{v}$, contradicting an assumption of this lemma. Observe that $\text{eff}(\sigma) > \mathbf{0}$, otherwise one can remove σ and consider the shorter path $\rho\tau$, contradicting the minimal length of π. Next, we argue that ρ and σ do not have monotone cycle decompositions, we then leverage Lemma 3 to obtain the narrow linear forms required.

Path ρ cannot be decomposed further. Towards a contradiction, assume that there is a monotone cycle decomposition $c' = (\rho', \sigma', \tau')$ of ρ. Observe that the following monotone cycle decomposition $c' = (\rho', \sigma', \tau'\sigma\tau)$ of π has lower cost $D(c') \prec_{lex} D(c)$ as $(D(c'))_1 = \text{len}(\rho') + \text{len}(\sigma') < \text{len}(\rho) + \text{len}(\sigma) = (D(c))_1$. This contradicts the assumption that (ρ, σ, τ) has minimum cost.
    Suppose $p(\mathbf{u}) \xrightarrow{\rho} p'(\mathbf{x})$. Since there is no monotone cycle decomposition, applying Lemma 3 to ρ returns a path ρ' with a narrow linear form such that $p(\mathbf{u}) \xrightarrow{\rho'} p'(\mathbf{x}')$ where $\mathbf{x}' \geq \mathbf{x}$ and $\text{len}(\rho') \leq \text{len}(\rho)$.

Cycle σ cannot be decomposed further. Towards a contradiction, assume that there is a monotone cycle decomposition (ρ', σ', τ') of σ. Observe that the following monotone cycle decomposition $c' = (\rho\rho', \sigma', \tau'\tau)$ of π has lower cost $D(c') \prec_{lex} D(c)$ as $(D(c))_1 = \text{len}(\rho) + \text{len}(\rho') + \text{len}(\sigma') \leq \text{len}(\rho) + \text{len}(\sigma) = (D(c))_1$ and $(D(c'))_2 = \text{len}(\sigma') < \text{len}(\sigma) = (D(c))_2$. This contradicts the assumption that (ρ, σ, τ) has minimum cost.
    Suppose $p'(\mathbf{x}) \xrightarrow{\sigma} p'(\mathbf{y})$. Since there is no monotone cycle decomposition, applying Lemma 3 to σ returns a path σ' with a narrow linear form such that $p'(\mathbf{x}) \xrightarrow{\sigma'} p'(\mathbf{y}')$ where $\mathbf{y}' \geq \mathbf{y}$ and $\text{len}(\sigma') \leq \text{len}(\sigma)$. In particular, it is also true that $\text{eff}(\sigma') \geq \text{eff}(\sigma) > \mathbf{0}$.

Replacing ρ' for ρ and σ' for σ in π yields a path π'. Clearly if $p(\mathbf{u}) \xrightarrow{\pi} q(\mathbf{w})$ where $\mathbf{w} \geq \mathbf{v}$, then $p(\mathbf{u}) \xrightarrow{\pi'} q(\mathbf{w}')$ where $\mathbf{w}' \geq \mathbf{w} \geq \mathbf{v}$. Finally, (ρ', σ', τ) is monotone cycle decomposition of π' such that $\text{eff}(\sigma') > \mathbf{0}$ and ρ' and σ' have narrow linear forms, as required.   □

We now aim to obtain a narrow linear form for τ. Note that Lemma 4 gives us a monotone cycle σ with positive effect on at least one counter, i.e. $\text{eff}(\sigma) > \mathbf{0}$. By pumping σ we can force one of the counters to take an arbitrarily large value (following, the vector $\mathbf{x}$ reflects this large value for Lemma 5). Then, loosely speaking, the problem reduces to coverability in 1-VASS. However, proving the existence of a polynomial size compressed linear form path in Theorem 1 requires more care. Note that Lemma 5 is stated for 2-VASS (not necessarily with one unary counter). First we need to recall the following bound on counter values observed throughout runs. Recall that $|V|_{\max} := |Q| + |T| \cdot |T|_{\max}$ is the pseudo-polynomial size of the input.

Theorem 2 (Corollary from Theorem 3.2 in [4]). *Consider a 2-VASS (with both counters in binary) $V = (Q, T)$ and let $p(\mathbf{u}) \xrightarrow{*} q(\mathbf{v})$, then there exists a run $p(\mathbf{u}) = q_0(\mathbf{v}_0), q_1(\mathbf{v}_1), \ldots, q_m(\mathbf{v}_m) = q(\mathbf{v})$ such that $|\mathbf{v}_0|_{\max}, |\mathbf{v}_1|_{\max}, \ldots, |\mathbf{v}_m|_{\max} \leq (|V|_{\max} + |\mathbf{u}|_{\max} + |\mathbf{v}|_{\max})^{\mathcal{O}(1)}$.*

In the following lemma, that is proved in the appendix, given a 2-VASS V, the initial configuration $p(\mathbf{u})$, and target configuration $q(\mathbf{v})$, we write B in place of $(|V|_{\max} + |\mathbf{u}|_{\max} + |\mathbf{v}|_{\max})^{\mathcal{O}(1)}$ from Theorem 2 and we fix $\mathbf{x} = (4B|Q|^2|V|_{\max}^2, 0)$.

Lemma 5. *Consider a 2-VASS (with both counters in binary) $V = (Q, T)$ and let $p(\mathbf{u}) \xrightarrow{*} q(\mathbf{v})$, then there exists a narrow linear form path π' such that $p(\mathbf{u} + \mathbf{x}) \xrightarrow{\pi'} q(\mathbf{v}')$ for some $\mathbf{v}' \geq \mathbf{v}$.*

6   Proof of Theorem 1

Before proving Theorem 1, we employ the fact that for a general 2-VASS, not necessarily with one unary counter, the exponents of cycles in linear forms can be pseudo-polynomially bounded.

Lemma 6 (Corollary from Lemma 18 in [5]). *Let π be path in a 2-VASS with a linear form $\pi = \tau_0 \gamma_1^{f_1} \tau_1 \ldots \gamma_k^{f_k} \tau_k$ such that $p(\mathbf{u}) \xrightarrow{\pi} q(\mathbf{v})$. Then there exist a path $\pi' = \tau_0 \gamma_1^{e_1} \tau_1 \cdots \tau_{k-1} \gamma_k^{e_k} \tau_k$ such that $p(\mathbf{u}) \xrightarrow{\pi'} q(\mathbf{v}')$ where $\mathbf{v}' \geq \mathbf{v}$ and $\text{bitsize}(e_1), \ldots, \text{bitsize}(e_k)$ are all bounded by a polynomial in $|V| + \text{bitsize}(\mathbf{u}) + \text{bitsize}(\mathbf{v})$.*

Proof of Theorem 1. Let $p(\mathbf{u}) \xrightarrow{\pi} q(\mathbf{v})$ for some path π. If there is a narrow linear form ℓ for π then by Lemma 6 we obtain $\pi' = \tau_0 \gamma_1^{e_1} \tau_1 \cdots \tau_{k-1} \gamma_k^{e_k} \tau_k$ such that $p(\mathbf{u}) \xrightarrow{\pi'} q(\mathbf{v}')$ where $\mathbf{v}' \geq \mathbf{v}$ and $\text{bitsize}(e_1), \ldots, \text{bitsize}(e_k)$ are all bounded above by a polynomial in $|V| + \text{bitsize}(\mathbf{u}) + \text{bitsize}(\mathbf{v})$. Since ℓ is a narrow linear form, we know that $k \leq P(|Q|)$ so $\sum_{i=1}^{k} \text{len}(\gamma_i) \leq k|Q| \leq |Q|P(|Q|)$ and we also know that $\sum_{i=0}^{k} \text{len}(\tau_i) \leq |Q|(P(|Q|)+1)$. Together, this implies the linear form path π' is of polynomial size.

It remains to consider the case when there is no narrow linear form ℓ for π. By Lemma 4 (via Lemma 3) there exists a path π' such that $p(\mathbf{u}) \xrightarrow{\pi'} q(\mathbf{v'})$ and $\mathbf{v'} \geq \mathbf{v}$. Moreover, there is a monotone cycle decomposition (ρ, σ, τ) of π' such that $\text{eff}(\sigma) > \mathbf{0}$ and there are narrow linear forms for both ρ and σ.

Assume that $(\text{eff}(\sigma))_1 > 0$. This is without loss of generality because if $(\text{eff}(\sigma))_1 = 0$ then one can flip the coordinates in V, $\mathbf{u}$ and $\mathbf{v}$ (for the remainder of the proof it will not matter that one counter is unary). Let $p'(\mathbf{m})$ be the configuration such that $p(\mathbf{u}) \xrightarrow{\rho} p'(\mathbf{m}) \xrightarrow{\sigma\tau} q(\mathbf{v'})$. Observe that since $\text{eff}(\sigma) > \mathbf{0}$ for every $i \in \mathbb{N}$ the path $\rho\sigma^i$ induces the run $p(\mathbf{u}) \xrightarrow{\rho\sigma^i} p'(\mathbf{m} + i \cdot \text{eff}(\sigma))$. Consider $x = (\mathbf{x})_1 = 4B|Q|^2|V|^2_{\max}$ (for Lemma 5), clearly x is large enough so that $p(\mathbf{u}) \xrightarrow{\rho\sigma^x} p'(\mathbf{m'})$ and $\mathbf{m'} \geq \mathbf{m} + \mathbf{x}$. By Lemma 5 there exists a narrow linear form for a path τ' such that $p'(\mathbf{m'}) \xrightarrow{\tau'} q(\mathbf{v''})$ and $\mathbf{v''} \geq \mathbf{v'}$.

We conclude by considering the compressed linear form path $\rho\sigma^x\tau'$ such that $p(\mathbf{u}) \xrightarrow{\rho\sigma^x\tau'} q(\mathbf{v''})$ and $\mathbf{v''} \geq \mathbf{v'} \geq \mathbf{v}$. Since ρ, σ, and τ' have narrow linear forms, we can also bound the exponents using Lemma 6 as in the beginning of this proof. Finally, $\text{bitsize}(x)$ is polynomial in $|V| + \text{bitsize}(\mathbf{u}) + \text{bitsize}(\mathbf{v})$ much like the exponents of the cycles in the linear forms. Therefore, the size of the compressed linear form $\rho\sigma^x\tau'$ is polynomial in $|V| + \text{bitsize}(\mathbf{u}) + \text{bitsize}(\mathbf{v})$. $\square$

7 Conclusion and Future Work

In this paper we proved that coverability in 2-VASS with one unary counter is in NP, a drop in complexity from PSPACE for general 2-VASS. We achieve this by using our new techniques. Most notably, we polynomially bounded the number of short cycles that need to be used (Section 4). Then, we attempt to find a polynomial linear form path by replacing short cycles and reshuffling the path (Section 5).

A natural extension is to consider whether coverability in 3-VASS with one binary counter and two unary counters is also in NP. More generally, there is the problem of determining the complexity of coverability in k-VASS with one binary counter and $k - 1$ unary counters. The technique for polynomially bounding the number of short cycles that need be used can easily be generalised to these higher dimension VASS with only one binary counter. However, it is not clear how to modify and use our reshuffling technique. Another open problem is whether reachability in 2-VASS with one unary counter is also in NP. Note that completeness would immediately follow from the fact that reachability in binary encoded 1-VASS is NP-hard [22].

References

1. Shaull Almagor, Udi Boker, Piotr Hofman, and Patrick Totzke. Parametrized Universality Problems for One-Counter Nets. In Igor Konnov and Laura Kovács, editors, *31st International Conference on Concurrency Theory, CONCUR 2020, September 1-4, 2020, Vienna, Austria (Virtual Conference)*, volume 171 of *LIPIcs*, pages 47:1–47:16. Schloss Dagstuhl - Leibniz-Zentrum für Informatik, 2020. doi: 10.4230/LIPIcs.CONCUR.2020.47.

2. Shaull Almagor, Nathann Cohen, Guillermo A. Pérez, Mahsa Shirmohammadi, and James Worrell. Coverability in 1-VASS with Disequality Tests. In Igor Konnov and Laura Kovács, editors, *31st International Conference on Concurrency Theory, CONCUR 2020, September 1-4, 2020, Vienna, Austria (Virtual Conference)*, volume 171 of *LIPIcs*, pages 38:1–38:20. Schloss Dagstuhl - Leibniz-Zentrum für Informatik, 2020. doi:10.4230/LIPIcs.CONCUR.2020.38.

3. Sanjeev Arora and Boaz Barak. *Computational complexity: a modern approach.* Cambridge University Press, 2009.

4. Michael Blondin, Matthias Englert, Alain Finkel, Stefan Göller, Christoph Haase, Ranko Lazić, Pierre McKenzie, and Patrick Totzke. The Reachability Problem for Two-Dimensional Vector Addition Systems with States. *J. ACM*, 68(5):34:1–34:43, 2021. doi:10.1145/3464794.

5. Michael Blondin, Alain Finkel, Stefan Göller, Christoph Haase, and Pierre McKenzie. Reachability in Two-Dimensional Vector Addition Systems with States Is PSPACE-Complete. In *30th Annual ACM/IEEE Symposium on Logic in Computer Science, LICS 2015, Kyoto, Japan, July 6-10, 2015*, pages 32–43. IEEE Computer Society, 2015. doi:10.1109/LICS.2015.14.

6. Michael Blondin, Christoph Haase, and Philip Offtermatt. Directed reachability for infinite-state systems. In Jan Friso Groote and Kim Guldstrand Larsen, editors, *Tools and Algorithms for the Construction and Analysis of Systems - 27th International Conference, TACAS 2021, Held as Part of the European Joint Conferences on Theory and Practice of Software, ETAPS 2021, Luxembourg City, Luxembourg, March 27 - April 1, 2021, Proceedings, Part II*, volume 12652 of *Lecture Notes in Computer Science*, pages 3–23. Springer, 2021. doi:10.1007/978-3-030-72013-1_1.

7. Mikołaj Bojańczyk, Claire David, Anca Muscholl, Thomas Schwentick, and Luc Segoufin. Two-variable logic on data words. *ACM Trans. Comput. Log.*, 12(4):27:1–27:26, 2011. doi:10.1145/1970398.1970403.

8. Hubert Comon and Yan Jurski. Multiple counters automata, safety analysis and presburger arithmetic. In Alan J. Hu and Moshe Y. Vardi, editors, *Computer Aided Verification, 10th International Conference, CAV '98, Vancouver, BC, Canada, June 28 - July 2, 1998, Proceedings*, volume 1427 of *Lecture Notes in Computer Science*, pages 268–279. Springer, 1998. doi:10.1007/BFb0028751.

9. Wojciech Czerwiński, Slawomir Lasota, Ranko Lazic, Jérôme Leroux, and Filip Mazowiecki. Reachability in Fixed Dimension Vector Addition Systems with States. In Igor Konnov and Laura Kovács, editors, *31st International Conference on Concurrency Theory, CONCUR 2020, September 1-4, 2020, Vienna, Austria (Virtual Conference)*, volume 171 of *LIPIcs*, pages 48:1–48:21. Schloss Dagstuhl - Leibniz-Zentrum für Informatik, 2020. doi:10.4230/LIPIcs.CONCUR.2020.48.

10. Wojciech Czerwiński, Sławomir Lasota, Ranko Lazic, Jérôme Leroux, and Filip Mazowiecki. The Reachability Problem for Petri Nets Is Not Elementary. *J. ACM*, 68(1):7:1–7:28, 2021. doi:10.1145/3422822.

11. Wojciech Czerwiński, Sławomir Lasota, Christof Löding, and Radoslaw Piórkowski. New Pumping Technique for 2-Dimensional VASS. In Peter Rossmanith, Pinar Heggernes, and Joost-Pieter Katoen, editors, *44th International Symposium on Mathematical Foundations of Computer Science, MFCS 2019, August 26-30, 2019, Aachen, Germany*, volume 138 of *LIPIcs*, pages 62:1–62:14. Schloss Dagstuhl - Leibniz-Zentrum für Informatik, 2019. doi:10.4230/LIPIcs.MFCS.2019.62.

12. Wojciech Czerwiński and Łukasz Orlikowski. Reachability in Vector Addition Systems is Ackermann-complete. In *62nd IEEE Annual Symposium on Foundations of Computer Science, FOCS 2021, Denver, CO, USA, February 7-10, 2022*, pages 1229–1240. IEEE, 2021. doi:10.1109/FOCS52979.2021.00120.

13. Wojciech Czerwiński and Łukasz Orlikowski. Lower Bounds for the Reachability Problem in Fixed Dimensional VASSes. In Christel Baier and Dana Fisman, editors, *LICS '22: 37th Annual ACM/IEEE Symposium on Logic in Computer Science, Haifa, Israel, August 2 - 5, 2022*, pages 40:1–40:12. ACM, 2022. doi:10.1145/3531130.3533357.

14. Alex Dixon and Ranko Lazic. KReach: A Tool for Reachability in Petri Nets. In Armin Biere and David Parker, editors, *Tools and Algorithms for the Construction and Analysis of Systems - 26th International Conference, TACAS 2020, Held as Part of the European Joint Conferences on Theory and Practice of Software, ETAPS 2020, Dublin, Ireland, April 25-30, 2020, Proceedings, Part I*, volume 12078 of *Lecture Notes in Computer Science*, pages 405–412. Springer, 2020. doi:10.1007/978-3-030-45190-5_22.

15. Matthias Englert, Piotr Hofman, Sławomir Lasota, Ranko Lazić, Jérôme Leroux, and Juliusz Straszyński. A lower bound for the coverability problem in acyclic pushdown VAS. *Inf. Process. Lett.*, 167:106079, 2021. doi:10.1016/j.ipl.2020.106079.

16. Matthias Englert, Ranko Lazić, and Patrick Totzke. Reachability in Two-Dimensional Unary Vector Addition Systems with States is NL-complete. In Martin Grohe, Eric Koskinen, and Natarajan Shankar, editors, *Proceedings of the 31st Annual ACM/IEEE Symposium on Logic in Computer Science, LICS '16, New York, NY, USA, July 5-8, 2016*, pages 477–484. ACM, 2016. doi:10.1145/2933575.2933577.

17. Javier Esparza, Ruslán Ledesma-Garza, Rupak Majumdar, Philipp J. Meyer, and Filip Niksic. An SMT-Based Approach to Coverability Analysis. In Armin Biere and Roderick Bloem, editors, *Computer Aided Verification - 26th International Conference, CAV 2014, Held as Part of the Vienna Summer of Logic, VSL 2014, Vienna, Austria, July 18-22, 2014. Proceedings*, volume 8559 of *Lecture Notes in Computer Science*, pages 603–619. Springer, 2014. doi:10.1007/978-3-319-08867-9_40.

18. John Fearnley and Marcin Jurdzinski. Reachability in two-clock timed automata is pspace-complete. In Fedor V. Fomin, Rusins Freivalds, Marta Z. Kwiatkowska, and David Peleg, editors, *Automata, Languages, and Programming - 40th International Colloquium, ICALP 2013, Riga, Latvia, July 8-12, 2013, Proceedings, Part II*, volume 7966 of *Lecture Notes in Computer Science*, pages 212–223. Springer, 2013. doi:10.1007/978-3-642-39212-2_21.

19. Alain Finkel, Jérôme Leroux, and Grégoire Sutre. Reachability for Two-Counter Machines with One Test and One Reset. In Sumit Ganguly and Paritosh K. Pandya, editors, *38th IARCS Annual Conference on Foundations of Software Technology and Theoretical Computer Science, FSTTCS 2018, December 11-13, 2018,*

Ahmedabad, India, volume 122 of *LIPIcs*, pages 31:1–31:14. Schloss Dagstuhl - Leibniz-Zentrum für Informatik, 2018. doi:10.4230/LIPIcs.FSTTCS.2018.31.

20. Alain Finkel and Arnaud Sangnier. Mixing coverability and reachability to analyze VASS with one zero-test. In Jan van Leeuwen, Anca Muscholl, David Peleg, Jaroslav Pokorný, and Bernhard Rumpe, editors, *SOFSEM 2010: Theory and Practice of Computer Science, 36th Conference on Current Trends in Theory and Practice of Computer Science, Spindleruv Mlýn, Czech Republic, January 23-29, 2010. Proceedings*, volume 5901 of *Lecture Notes in Computer Science*, pages 394–406. Springer, 2010. doi:10.1007/978-3-642-11266-9_33.

21. Pierre Ganty and Rupak Majumdar. Algorithmic verification of asynchronous programs. *ACM Trans. Program. Lang. Syst.*, 34(1):6:1–6:48, 2012. doi:10.1145/2160910.2160915.

22. Christoph Haase, Stephan Kreutzer, Joël Ouaknine, and James Worrell. Reachability in Succinct and Parametric One-Counter Automata. In Mario Bravetti and Gianluigi Zavattaro, editors, *CONCUR 2009 - Concurrency Theory, 20th International Conference, CONCUR 2009, Bologna, Italy, September 1-4, 2009. Proceedings*, volume 5710 of *Lecture Notes in Computer Science*, pages 369–383. Springer, 2009. doi:10.1007/978-3-642-04081-8_25.

23. John E. Hopcroft and Jean-Jacques Pansiot. On the Reachability Problem for 5-Dimensional Vector Addition Systems. *Theor. Comput. Sci.*, 8:135–159, 1979. doi:10.1016/0304-3975(79)90041-0.

24. S. Rao Kosaraju. Decidability of Reachability in Vector Addition Systems (Preliminary Version). In Harry R. Lewis, Barbara B. Simons, Walter A. Burkhard, and Lawrence H. Landweber, editors, *Proceedings of the 14th Annual ACM Symposium on Theory of Computing, May 5-7, 1982, San Francisco, California, USA*, pages 267–281. ACM, 1982. doi:10.1145/800070.802201.

25. Jean-Luc Lambert. A Structure to Decide Reachability in Petri Nets. *Theor. Comput. Sci.*, 99(1):79–104, 1992. doi:10.1016/0304-3975(92)90173-D.

26. Jérôme Leroux. The Reachability Problem for Petri Nets is Not Primitive Recursive. In *62nd IEEE Annual Symposium on Foundations of Computer Science, FOCS 2021, Denver, CO, USA, February 7-10, 2022*, pages 1241–1252. IEEE, 2021. doi:10.1109/FOCS52979.2021.00121.

27. Jérôme Leroux and Sylvain Schmitz. Reachability in Vector Addition Systems is Primitive-Recursive in Fixed Dimension. In *34th Annual ACM/IEEE Symposium on Logic in Computer Science, LICS 2019, Vancouver, BC, Canada, June 24-27, 2019*, pages 1–13. IEEE, 2019. doi:10.1109/LICS.2019.8785796.

28. Jérôme Leroux and Grégoire Sutre. On Flatness for 2-Dimensional Vector Addition Systems with States. In Philippa Gardner and Nobuko Yoshida, editors, *CONCUR 2004 - Concurrency Theory, 15th International Conference, London, UK, August 31 - September 3, 2004, Proceedings*, volume 3170 of *Lecture Notes in Computer Science*, pages 402–416. Springer, 2004. doi:10.1007/978-3-540-28644-8_26.

29. Jérôme Leroux and Grégoire Sutre. Reachability in Two-Dimensional Vector Addition Systems with States: One Test Is for Free. In Igor Konnov and Laura Kovács, editors, *31st International Conference on Concurrency Theory, CONCUR 2020, September 1-4, 2020, Vienna, Austria (Virtual Conference)*, volume 171 of *LIPIcs*, pages 37:1–37:17. Schloss Dagstuhl - Leibniz-Zentrum für Informatik, 2020. doi:10.4230/LIPIcs.CONCUR.2020.37.

30. Jérôme Leroux, Grégoire Sutre, and Patrick Totzke. On the Coverability Problem for Pushdown Vector Addition Systems in One Dimension. In Magnús M. Halldórsson, Kazuo Iwama, Naoki Kobayashi, and Bettina Speckmann, editors,

Automata, Languages, and Programming - 42nd International Colloquium, ICALP 2015, Kyoto, Japan, July 6-10, 2015, Proceedings, Part II, volume 9135 of *Lecture Notes in Computer Science*, pages 324–336. Springer, 2015. doi:10.1007/978-3-662-47666-6_26.

31. Richard Lipton. The Reachability Problem Requires Exponential Space. *Department of Computer Science. Yale University*, 62, 1976.

32. Ernst W. Mayr. An Algorithm for the General Petri Net Reachability Problem. *SIAM J. Comput.*, 13(3):441–460, 1984. doi:10.1137/0213029.

33. Marvin L. Minsky. *Computation: Finite and Infinite Machines*. Prentice-Hall, Inc., 1967.

34. C. Petri. Kommunikation mit Automaten, Ph. D. dissertation. *University of Bonn*, 1962.

35. Charles Rackoff. The Covering and Boundedness Problems for Vector Addition Systems. *Theor. Comput. Sci.*, 6:223–231, 1978. doi:10.1016/0304-3975(78)90036-1.

36. Klaus Reinhardt. Reachability in Petri Nets with Inhibitor Arcs. *Electron. Notes Theor. Comput. Sci.*, 223:239–264, 2008. doi:10.1016/j.entcs.2008.12.042.

37. Sylvain Schmitz. The Complexity of Reachability in Vector Addition Systems. *ACM SIGLOG News*, 3(1):4–21, 2016. URL: https://dl.acm.org/citation.cfm?id=2893585.

38. Leslie G. Valiant and Mike Paterson. Deterministic One-Counter Automata. *J. Comput. Syst. Sci.*, 10(3):340–350, 1975. doi:10.1016/S0022-0000(75)80005-5.

On History-Deterministic One-Counter Nets

Aditya Prakash[ORCID] and K. S. Thejaswini[✉][ORCID]

Department of Computer Science, University of Warwick, Coventry, UK
{aditya.prakash,thejaswini.raghavan.1}@warwick.ac.uk

Abstract. We consider the model of history-deterministic one-counter nets (OCNs). History-determinism is a property of transition systems that allows for a limited kind of non-determinism which can be resolved 'on-the-fly'. Token games, which have been used to characterise history-determinism over various models, also characterise history-determinism over OCNs. By reducing 1-token games to simulation games, we are able to show that checking for history-determinism of OCNs is decidable. Moreover, we prove that this problem is **PSPACE**-complete for a unary encoding of transitions, and **EXPSPACE**-complete for a binary encoding and undecidable for one-counter automata (OCA), which are OCNs that can test for zeroes.

We then study the language properties of history-deterministic OCNs. We show that the resolvers of non-determinism for history-deterministic OCNs are eventually periodic. As a consequence, for a given history-deterministic OCN, we construct a language equivalent deterministic OCA. We also show the decidability of comparing languages of history-deterministic OCNs, such as language inclusion and language universality.

Keywords: History-determinism · Token games · One-counter nets · One-counter automaton.

1 Introduction

While deterministic automata are algorithmically efficient for problems such as synthesis or for solving games, they are often much less succinct, or less expressive than their non-deterministic counterparts. As such, many intermediate models between determinism and non-determinism have been studied [1,2,3,4,5], with history-determinism being one such well-studied notion over the recent years. History-deterministic automata over infinite words with parity acceptance condition was introduced by Henzinger and Piterman as a tool to solve verification games, although dubbed good-for-games in their work [6]. Such automata are known to be exponentially more succinct than their deterministic counterpart [7], and are known to form a robust class of automata that is both algorithmically and conceptually interesting [6,8,9,7,10,11,12,13,14].

The notion of history-determinism emerged independently in the setting of cost automata that can capture all regular cost functions as opposed to their

O. Kupferman and P. Sobocinski (Eds.): FoSSaCS 2023, LNCS 13992, pp. 218–239, 2023.
https://doi.org/10.1007/978-3-031-30829-1_11

deterministic version [15]. Recently, history-determinism has been studied in quantitative settings [16,17], as well as infinite-state systems such as pushdown automata [18,19], Parikh automata [20], and timed automata [21,22], where they are often more succinct and expressive than their deterministic counter part.

One-counter nets are finite-state systems along with a counter that stores a non-negative integer value which can never be explicitly tested for zero. They correspond to 1-dimensional VASS, Petri nets with exactly one unbounded place, and are a subclass of one-counter automata which do not have zero tests, and hence are also a subclass of pushdown automata. They are one of the simplest infinite-state systems, and hence many problems pertaining to one-counter nets are easier than models that subsume them.

The structure of the resolvers that resolve non-determinism on-the-fly are crucial to understand history-determinism in various models. While for automata over infinite words with parity conditions, these resolvers take the shape of deterministic parity automata [6], the situation for resolvers in history-deterministic infinite-state systems is not as well understood. Indeed, the computability of such a resolver for a given history-deterministic pushdown automaton is left as an open problem in the works of Guha, Jecker, Lehtinen and Zimmermann [18]. For history-deterministic Parikh automata, it is still an open problem if the resolver can be given by a deterministic Parikh transducer [20]. Moreover, many other problems such as deciding history-determinism or even language inclusion among history-deterministic automata are undecidable for pushdown automata and Parikh automata [18,19,20]. We consider history-determinism over one-counter nets, where we are able to answer positively to all of the above questions.

To answer several of these questions, we use results and techniques from the simulation problem over one-counter nets [23,24]. This is not surprising, since simulation of various models has close ties with history-determinism [6,21].

Our Contribution We study history-deterministic OCNs and establish them as a class of infinite-state systems where many problems pertaining to history-determinism are decidable. This is unlike many other classes of history-deterministic infinite-state systems that have been studied so far.

Firstly, we show that checking for history-determinism of a given one-counter net is **PSPACE**-complete when the transitions are encoded in unary, and is **EXPSPACE**-complete for a more succinct encoding (Theorem 4, Theorem 26). We achieve the upper bound by giving a novel reduction from the one-token game [11] to the simulation problem over OCNs. One-token games characterise history-determinism over OCNs, and thus our reduction further extends the link between history-determinism and simulation. This decidability result is in contrast to one-counter automata (OCA), where checking for history-determinism becomes undecidable by just adding zero-tests to OCNs (Theorem 27).

Secondly, we show that resolvers for non-determinism in history-deterministic OCNs can be expressed as an eventually periodic set. Using this, we are able to determinise history-deterministic OCNs to give a language equivalent deterministic OCA.

Finally, we show the problems of language inclusion and language universality for history-deterministic OCNs to be in **PSPACE** and **P** respectively. This is in unlike non-deterministic OCNs, where these problems are known to be undecidable and Ackermann-complete respectively. Even for the class of deterministic OCA—which we show history-deterministic OCNs can be converted to—the inclusion problem is known to be undecidable.

Good-for-Gameness A notion closely related to history-determinism (HD) is that of good-for-gameness. An automaton is said to be *good-for-games* (GFG) if its composition with a game whose acceptance condition is given by the language of the automaton yields an equivalent game. For parity automata over infinite words, these two notions are known to be equivalent [6,25], but they do not coincide on all models [16]. For the purposes of our paper, we deal with history-deterministic OCNs, as in our setting the notion of history-determinism is equivalent to good-for-gameness when composition with infinitely branching games is considered [26]. We note however, that this is not true when compositionality is restricted to only finitely branching games [26].

2 Preliminaries

We use $\mathbb{N}$ to denote the set of positive integers and $\mathbb{N}_0$ to denote non-negative integers. An *alphabet*, denoted by Σ, is any finite non-empty set of *letters*, and the set of all finite words over Σ is denoted by Σ^*. The empty word over Σ is denoted by ϵ, and we use Σ_ϵ to denote the set $\Sigma \cup \{\epsilon\}$. A *language* $\mathcal{L}$ over Σ is a subset of Σ^*.

Labelled Transition System A *labelled transition system* (LTS) is a tuple $\mathcal{S}$ consisting of $\mathcal{S} = (Q, \Sigma, \rightarrow, q_0, F)$. In this paper, we assume that Q is a (countable) set of states, $q_0 \in Q$ is the initial state, $F \subseteq Q$ is the set of final states, Σ is a finite alphabet, $\rightarrow \subseteq Q \times \Sigma_\epsilon \times Q$ is the set of transitions.

If a transition (q_1, a, q_2) belongs to $\rightarrow$, we instead represent it as $q_1 \xrightarrow{a} q_2$ as well. On a finite word w, a ρ is said to be a *run* of the labelled transition system $\mathcal{S}$ if it is a finite alternating sequence of states and letters of Σ: $\rho = q_0 \xrightarrow{a_0} q_1 \xrightarrow{a_1} \ldots q_{k-1} \xrightarrow{a_k} q_k$, where each i, $q_i \xrightarrow{a_i} q_{i+1} \in \rightarrow$ and $a_i \in \Sigma_\epsilon$ such that $w = a_0 \cdot a_1 \ldots a_k$. A run ρ described above is accepting if the state $q_k \in F$.

An LTS that has no ϵ-transitions is said to be a *realtime LTS*. For an LTS $\mathcal{S} = (Q, \Sigma, \rightarrow, q_0, F)$ being realtime, we have $\rightarrow \subseteq Q \times \Sigma \times Q$. Unless mentioned otherwise, we mostly deal with realtime LTS for the sake of a simpler presentation. An LTS $\mathcal{S} = (Q, \Sigma, \rightarrow, q_0, F)$ is *deterministic* if $\rightarrow$ is a function from $Q \times \Sigma$ to Q and not just a relation.

Two player games Throughout the paper, we will be using two player games on countably sized arenas, between the players Adam and Eve, denoted by $\forall$ and $\exists$ respectively. The winning condition will be a reachability condition for one of the players, often $\forall$. These can be interpreted as a Gale-Stewart games [27] and we know that such games are determined, that is they have a winner, which is either ∀ or ∃. Moreover, each of the players have a positional strategy, where their current strategy depends on their positions in the current arena. We say that two games are *equivalent*, if they have the same winner.

One-Counter Automata A *one-counter automaton* (OCA) $\mathcal{A}$ is given by a tuple $\mathcal{A} = (Q, \Sigma, \Delta, q_0, F)$, where Q is a finite set of states, $q_0 \in Q$ is the initial state, $F \subseteq Q$ is the set of final states, Σ is a finite alphabet, and Δ is the set of transitions, given as a relation $\Delta \subseteq Q \times \{\text{zero}, \neg\text{zero}\} \times \Sigma \times \{-1, 0, 1\} \times Q$.

Here, the symbols zero and ¬zero are used to distinguish between transitions that can happen when the counter value is 0, and when the counter value is positive respectively. One can think of the counter as a stack, where the stack has a distinguished bottom-of-the-stack symbol, which cannot be popped. The configurations in the automaton are given by pairs (q, m), where q denotes the current state, and $m \in \mathbb{N}_0$ denotes the counter value. We use $\mathcal{C}(\mathcal{A})$ to denote the set of configurations of $\mathcal{A}$.

A one-counter automaton generates an infinite-state LTS over the set of configurations $Q \times \mathbb{N}$, such that the transitions are as defined below. For each configuration (q, m), upon reading $a \in \Sigma_\epsilon$,

- if $m > 0$, takes a transition of the form $(q, \neg\text{zero}, a, d, q')$, where $d \in \{-1, 0, 1\}$ to $(q', m + d)$;
- if $m = 0$, takes a transition of the form $(q, \text{zero}, a, d, q')$, where $d \in \{0, 1\}$ to $(q', m + d)$.

For two configurations $c, c' \in \mathcal{C}(A) = Q \times \mathbb{N}_0$, we use the notation $c \xrightarrow{a,d} c'$ to denote the fact that c' can be reached from c upon taking some transition $\delta \in \Delta$ upon reading a, with a change of counter value d. We shall also say that $c \xrightarrow{a,d} c'$ is a transition in $\mathcal{A}$, as $c \xrightarrow{a,d} c'$ is a transition in the infinite LTS of $\mathcal{A}$. We thus view $\mathcal{A}$ as both an automaton and a LTS (generated by $\mathcal{A}$), and switch between these two notions interchangeably. A run of $\mathcal{A}$ over a word w is a finite sequence of alternating configurations and transitions : $\rho = c_0 \xrightarrow{a_0,d_0} c_1 \cdots c_n \xrightarrow{a_n,d_n} c_{n+1}$ such that $a_0 a_1 \cdots a_n = w$, and $c_0 = (q_0, 0)$. The run ρ is an *accepting run* if its last configuration $c_{n+1} = (q_{n+1}, k_{n+1})$ is accepting, i.e. $q_{n+1} \in F$. We say a word w is an *accepting word* in $\mathcal{A}$ if it has an accepting run in $\mathcal{A}$. Finally, we define the language of $\mathcal{A}$, denoted by $\mathcal{L}(\mathcal{A})$ to be the set of all accepting words in $\mathcal{A}$. We say that $\mathcal{A}$ is a *deterministic one-counter automaton*, if Δ is a (partial) function from $Q \times \{\text{zero}, \neg\text{zero}\} \times \Sigma$ to $\{-1, 0, 1\} \times Q$.

One-counter nets The model of *one-counter nets* (OCNs) can be interpreted as a restriction added to one-counter automaton that do not have the ability to test for zero. Alternatively, one can view this as a finite-state automaton that has access to a stack which can store only one symbol and no bottom-of-the-stack element. Any feasible run cannot pop an empty stack. More formally, a one-counter net $\mathcal{N}$ is a tuple $(Q, \Sigma, \Delta, q_0, F)$ where Q is the set of finite states, Σ is a finite alphabet, $q_0 \in Q$ is the initial state and $F \subseteq Q$ is the set of final or accepting states. The set $\Delta \subseteq Q \times \Sigma \times \{-1, 0, 1\} \times Q$ are the transitions in the net $\mathcal{N}$.

The configurations of an OCN are similar to that of an OCA. It consists of a pair $(q, n) \in Q \times \mathbb{N}_0$. We shall use the notation $\mathcal{C}(\mathcal{N}) = Q \times \mathbb{N}_0$ to denote the set of configurations of $\mathcal{N}$. From a configuration (q, n), we reach a configuration $(p, n + d)$ in one step, if there is a transition $\delta = (q, a, d, p)$, for some $a \in \Sigma$ and $d \in \{-1, 0, +1\}$ and $n + d \geq 0$. We can define a run on an OCN, an accepting run and an accepting word similar to an OCA. We say an OCN $\mathcal{N}$ is *complete* if for every configuration $c \in \mathcal{C}(\mathcal{N})$ and every letter $a \in \Sigma$, there exists a transition $c \xrightarrow{a,d} c'$.

Remark 1. For the most of the paper we talk about one-counter nets (automata) with unary transitions, i.e. transitions that increment or decrement the counter by at most 1. However, they are as expressive as succinct models where the one-counter net has a *binary encoding*, i.e. when the transitions allow the counter to be incremented or decremented by positive integers represented in binary. This can be observed, for instance, by giving a construction similar to that of Valiant's for deterministic pushdown automata ([28], Section 1.7).

History-Deterministic One-Counter Nets We define history-determinism in the setting of one-counter net. Informally, an OCN $\mathcal{N}$ is *history-deterministic*, if the non-deterministic choices required to accept a word w which is in $\mathcal{L}(\mathcal{N})$ can be made on-the-fly. These choices depend only on the word read so far, and do not require the knowledge of the future of the word to construct an accepting run for a word in $\mathcal{L}(\mathcal{N})$ (hence the term history-determinism). Formally, we say an OCN $\mathcal{N}$ is history-deterministic, if $\exists$ wins the letter game on $\mathcal{N}$ defined below.

Definition 2 (Letter game for OCN). *Given an OCN* $\mathcal{N} = (Q, \Sigma, \Delta, q_0, F)$, *the letter game on $\mathcal{N}$ is defined between the players $\forall$ and $\exists$ as follows: the positions of the game are* $\mathcal{C}(\mathcal{N}) \times \Sigma^*$, *with the initial position* $((q_0, 0), \epsilon)$. *At round i of the play, where the position is* (c_i, w_i):

- $\forall$ *selects* $a_i \in \Sigma$
- $\exists$ *selects a transition δ which can be taken at the configuration c_i on reading* a_i, *i.e.* $c_i \xrightarrow{a_i, d_i} c_{i+1}$

If $\exists$ is unable to choose a transition (i.e. there is no a_i transition at the configuration c_i in the LTS generated by the net $\mathcal{N}$), and $w_{i+1} = w_i a_i$ is the prefix of an accepting word, $\exists$ loses immediately. The player $\forall$ wins immediately when the word w_{i+1} is accepting but the configuration c_{i+1} is not at an accepting state, and the game terminates. The game continues from (c_{i+1}, w_{i+1}) *otherwise. Player $\exists$ wins any infinite play.*

We say a strategy for $\exists$ in the letter game of $\mathcal{N}$ is a *resolver* for $\mathcal{N}$, if it is a winning strategy for $\exists$ in the letter game.

Our characterization of history-deterministic one-counter nets by the above letter game is slightly different from the one presented in the work of Guha,

Jecker, Lehtinen, and Zimmermann [18] for pushdown automata. In their work, they define history-determinism as having a consistent strategy based on the transitions taken so far. It is easy to argue that these two definitions are equivalent.

The letter game can be formulated as a reachability game over countably many vertices, where the player ∀ is trying to reach a position of the form $(c, w) \in \mathcal{C}(\mathcal{N}) \times \Sigma^*$, where c is at a rejecting state, while w is accepting. As such games are determined [27], the notion of history-determinism formulated as ∃ winning the letter game is well-defined.

Letter games have been used extensively to characterise history-determinism for other models as well, such as parity automata [6] and for various kinds of quantitative and timed automata on both finite and infinite words [12,16,21].

To aid our understanding of history-determinism as well as the above definition, we provide an example of a game where ∃ wins the letter game on this automaton but the strategy is based on her counter configuration.

Example 3. Consider the language

$$\mathcal{L} = \left\{ a^n \$b^{n_1} \$b^{n_2} \$ \ldots \$b^{n_k} \$ \mid \sum_{i=1}^{k} n_i \leq n \text{ or } n_k = 2, \sum_{i=1}^{k-1} n_i = n - 1 \right\}$$

which can be accepted by a history-deterministic OCN as shown in Figure 1. The initial state is indicated with an arrow pointing to it, and the final states are double-circled. Missing transitions are assumed to go to a rejecting sink state. In the corresponding letter game, ∀ plays the letter a several times, say n-many times followed by a $. The corresponding transitions so far are deterministic. Later, ∀ reads some series of bs and $s, such that the word continues to be in the language. Note that the non-determinism occurs in only one state, which is marked with an X, upon reading the letter b. A winning strategy of ∃ which proves that this net is history-deterministic is the following: she takes the 'down' transition if the counter value is strictly larger than 1, but the 'right' transition on b otherwise. This non-determinism can't be resolved by removing transitions, because removing either of the 'down' b-transition or the 'right' b-transition changes the language accepted. We note that an equivalent deterministic OCN exists nevertheless, where on reading a b after any $ does not change the value of the counter, but reduces the counter by two for the second b after a $ and reduces the counter by 1 for any b after that, until a $ is seen again.

3   Deciding History-Determinism

The main result of this section is that deciding history-determinism for a given OCN is decidable and is **PSPACE**-complete as stated in the theorem below.

Theorem 4. *Given a one-counter net $\mathcal{N}$, checking if $\mathcal{N}$ is history-deterministic is* **PSPACE**-*complete.*

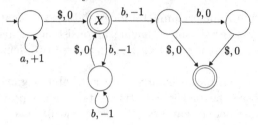

Fig. 1. A history-deterministic OCN accepting $\mathcal{L}$

The rest of this section is dedicated to the proof of the above statement.

The proof of showing the upper bound proceeds by a series of polynomial time reductions as below.

Deciding history-determinism

$\Updownarrow$

Deciding if $\exists$ wins letter game

$\Updownarrow$

Deciding if $\exists$ wins 1-token game

$\Downarrow$

Deciding if $\exists$ wins simulation game

We shall define these games rigorously and prove these reductions in Subsection 3.1. Finally, since the winner of the simulation game over one-counter nets is in **PSPACE** [24], this gives us the upper bound.

For the lower bound, we reduce from the problem of emptiness checking for alternating finite-state automata over a unary alphabet to deciding if $\exists$ wins the letter game.

3.1 Token Games

Deciding history-determinism efficiently for finite-state parity automata over infinite words has been a major area of study over the recent years. Bagnol and Kupergerg [11], gave a polynomial time procedure for deciding history-determinism when the finite automata accepts with a Büchi condition. Their underlying technique is a two-player game, called G_2 or 2-token games, which they proved to be equivalent to the letter game when the automaton is Büchi. Boker, Kuperberg, Lehtinen, and Skrzypczak [12] extended this to show that the game G_2 is equivalent to the letter game when the automaton is co-Büchi as well. Deciding the winner in G_2 for an automaton of a fixed parity index takes polynomial time [12], and hence deciding history-determinism for the cases of when the parity automata accepts words based on Büchi or co-Büchi condition is polynomial.

It is conjectured that winning G_2 is equivalent to the letter game for higher parity indices as well, and this is known as the G_2 conjecture [12]. Token games have also been instrumental in deciding history-determinism for quantitative automata, in the works of Boker and Lehtinen [17]. In their paper, they show that for finite words on a finite-state boolean automaton, history-determinism is characterised by G_1. This was later adapted to labelled transition systems with safety acceptance condition, in the works of Henzinger, Lehtinen, and Totzke [21]. Thus, the 1-token games also characterise history-determinism for OCNs over finite words. We include a proof nonetheless, for the sake of completeness.

In a play of the letter game, $\forall$ picks the letters while $\exists$ picks the transitions, and the winning condition for $\exists$ is to produce an accepting run for any word that is in the language. Token games work similarly, but they impose more constraints on $\forall$. This is done by asking him to also display a valid run during the game with the help of some number of tokens. Here, we concentrate on the 1-token game G_1. The player $\forall$ wins the game G_1 if and only if he produces an accepting run, whilst $\exists$ produces a rejecting run. We make this more formal in the definition below.

Definition 5 (One token game G_1). *Let $\mathcal{N} = (Q, \Sigma, \Delta, q_0, F)$ be a one-counter net. The positions of the game G_1 on $\mathcal{N}$ are a pair of configurations, $\mathcal{C}(\mathcal{N}) \times \mathcal{C}(\mathcal{N})$, where the first configuration in the pair denotes the position of $\exists$'s token, and the second $\forall$'s token. The game starts with the initial position $(c_0^{\exists}, c_0^{\forall}) = ((q_0, 0), (q_0, 0))$. At the ith iteration of the play, where the position is $(c_i^{\exists}, c_i^{\forall})$:*

1. *$\forall$ selects $a \in \Sigma$*
2. *$\exists$ selects a transition for her token, $c_i^{\exists} \xrightarrow{a,d} c_{i+1}^{\exists}$*
3. *$\forall$ selects a transition for his token, $c_i^{\forall} \xrightarrow{a,d'} c_{i+1}^{\forall}$*

If $\exists$ is unable to choose a transition for her token whereas $\forall$ can choose a transition and extend the run on his token to an accepting run, then the game terminates and $\exists$ loses the game. However, irrespective of $\exists$'s ability to extend her run, if $\forall$ is unable to choose a transition for his token, then the game again terminates but $\forall$ loses the game.

If both the players can extend their runs by picking a transition then and if $\forall$'s state in $c_{i+1}^{\forall}$ is accepting, but $\exists$'s state in $c_{i+1}^{\exists}$ is rejecting then again the game terminates and $\exists$ loses the game. Else, the game goes to (c_{i+1}, c_{i+1}') for another round of the play. We add that $\exists$ wins any infinite play.

Letter games can be seen as a version of token games where $\forall$ plays with infinitely many tokens. We show in the following lemma that one-token games—even with this limited power of $\forall$—can capture letter games.

Lemma 6. *For an OCN $\mathcal{N}$, if $\exists$ wins the game G_1 on $\mathcal{N}$, then $\exists$ has a winning strategy in the letter game.*

To prove the above lemma, we need to understand better the structure of the resolvers for OCNs. Consider the definition given below of *residual transitions*. Intuitively, these are transitions such that if there was an accepting word from a configuration with the first letter as a, then upon taking a residual transition on a, there is still an extension of the run on the word from the new configuration that is accepting. More formally, we say that a transition $(q, k) \xrightarrow{a,d} (q', k')$ is *residual* if $\mathcal{L}(q', k') = a^{-1}\mathcal{L}(q, k)$, where $\mathcal{L}(q, k)$ (and $\mathcal{L}(q', k')$) is the set of words that are accepted in $\mathcal{N}$ when the initial configuration is (q, k) $((q', k'))$, instead of $(q_0, 0)$. The proposition below shows any winning strategy of $\exists$ can be characterised by these residual transitions.

Proposition 7. *For an OCN $\mathcal{N}$, an $\exists$ strategy σ in the letter game is winning for $\exists$ if and only if σ takes only residual transitions.*

Note that in the letter game, each player winning the game has a positional winning strategy, as it is a reachability game. Suppose that $\exists$ wins the letter game, then $\exists$ has a winning strategy which can be given by a (partial) function $\sigma : (Q \times \mathbb{N}) \times \Sigma^* \times \Sigma \to \Delta$. Using Proposition 7, we can show that $\exists$'s strategy only depends on the configuration, and is independent of the word read so far.

Proposition 8. *If $\exists$ wins the letter game, then $\exists$ has a winning strategy σ that only depends on the current configuration of the play, i.e σ is a partial function $\sigma : (Q \times \mathbb{N}) \times \Sigma \to \Delta$*

Having shown that G_1 is equivalent to the letter game, we show that deciding the winner in the game G_1 is in **PSPACE**. This implies deciding history-determinism is also decidable, and in **PSPACE**. We do so by reducing G_1 to the simulation problem between two one-counter nets, which is known to be **PSPACE**-complete ([24], Theorem 7).

Given two OCNs $\mathcal{N}$ and $\mathcal{N}'$ at configurations (q, n) and (q', n'), we say $\mathcal{N}'$ simulates $\mathcal{N}$ (or $\mathcal{N}$ is simulated by $\mathcal{N}'$) from their corresponding configurations if for any sequence of transitions from (q, n), there is also a sequence of transitions from (q', n') which is built 'on-the-fly'. This alternation between existential and universal quantifiers in the above statement renders this definition perfect to be captured by the following game between the players $\forall$ and $\exists$.

Definition 9 (Simulation Game). *Given two OCNs $\mathcal{N} = (Q, \Sigma, \Delta, q_I, F)$ and $\mathcal{N}' = (Q', q_0', \Sigma, \Delta', q_I', F')$ and two configurations $c = (p, k)$ and $c' = (p', k')$ in $\mathcal{C}(\mathcal{N})$ and $\mathcal{C}(\mathcal{N}')$ respectively where $k, k' \in \mathbb{N}$. The simulation game between the OCNs $\mathcal{N}$ and $\mathcal{N}'$ at a position (c, c'), denoted by $\mathcal{G}((\mathcal{N}, c) \longleftrightarrow (\mathcal{N}', c'))$, is a two player game between $\forall$ and $\exists$, with positions in $\mathcal{C}(\mathcal{N}) \times \mathcal{C}(\mathcal{N}')$ where the initial position is $(c_0, c_0') = (c, c')$. At round i of the play, where the position is (c_i, c_i'):*

- *$\forall$ selects a letter $a \in \Sigma$, and a transition $c_i \xrightarrow{a,d} c_{i+1}$ in $\mathcal{N}$*
- *$\exists$ selects an a-transition $c_i' \xrightarrow{a,d'} c_{i+1}'$ in $\mathcal{N}'$*

If ∀ *is unable to choose a transition, then* ∀ *loses the game immediately. If* ∃ *is unable to choose a transition but* ∀ *can select a transition and extend the run in* $\mathcal{N}$ *to an accepting run, then* ∃ *loses the game.*

Otherwise, if ∀*'s state in* c_{i+1} *is accepting but* ∃*'s state in* c'_{i+1} *is rejecting, then* ∃ *loses the game, and the game terminates. Else, the game goes to* (c_{i+1}, c'_{i+1}) *for another round of the play. The player* ∃ *wins any infinite play.*

If ∃ wins the above game, we say $(\mathcal{N}', (p', k'))$ simulates $(\mathcal{N}, (p, k))$, and we denote it by $(\mathcal{N}, (p, k)) \longrightarrow (\mathcal{N}', (p', k'))$. Furthermore, we say $\mathcal{N}'$ simulates $\mathcal{N}$ or $\mathcal{N} \hookrightarrow \mathcal{N}'$ if $(\mathcal{N}, (q_I, 0)) \longrightarrow (\mathcal{N}', (q'_I, 0))$.

As the simulation game is a reachability game over a countably sized arena, it is determined, and the winning player has a positional strategy. Thus, if ∃ wins the above simulation game $\mathcal{G}((\mathcal{N}, (p, k)) \longrightarrow (\mathcal{N}', (p', k')))$, then ∃ has a positional winning strategy $\sigma_\exists : \mathcal{C}(\mathcal{N}) \times \mathcal{C}(\mathcal{N}') \times \Sigma \to \Delta'$.

Remark 10. In the literature over one-counter nets [29,24,30], the winning condition for the players on the simulation game is expressed differently, via the inability of the players to choose transitions, rather than accepting states. The player ∀ (∃) loses the game if ∀ (∃) is unable to choose a transition. It can however, be shown that the two versions of the simulation games are log-space reducible to each other.

Note the similarities (and differences) in G_1 and the simulation game. In both, the winning condition for ∀ would like ∀'s run to be accepting, while ∃'s to be rejecting. In G_1 however, ∃ is picking the transition first, while in the simulation game, ∀ is picking the transition first.

With some modifications to the structure of the underlying net in G_1, we can ensure that the simulation game between the modified net and the original net captures G_1. The intuition is that, in the simulation game, the net which is simulated is modified so that ∀ is forced to delay choosing his transition. This is formalized in the proof of the following lemma, and explained with a diagram in Figure 2.

Lemma 11. *Given a one-counter net* $\mathcal{N}$, *there are one-counter nets* $\mathcal{M}$ *and* $\mathcal{M}'$, *which have size at most polynomial in size of* $\mathcal{N}$ *such that* ∃ *wins* G_1 *on* $\mathcal{N}$ *if and only if* ∃ *wins* $\mathcal{M} \hookrightarrow \mathcal{M}'$.

Proof. (Sketch) For each run in $\mathcal{N}$, we have a run in $\mathcal{M}$ that lags behind one transition. The one-counter net $\mathcal{M}'$ on the other hand is relatively similar to $\mathcal{N}$. We impose this "one-transition lag" in $\mathcal{M}$ by construction where each transition chosen by ∀ in $\mathcal{M}$ corresponds to a letter along with a transition of $\mathcal{N}$. But this transition of $\mathcal{N}$ is over the letter that ∀ had chosen last turn. The alternation produced between ∀ and ∃ in a play of the simulation game between $\mathcal{M}$ and $\mathcal{M}'$ of the nets constructed corresponds exactly the alternation produced between ∀ and ∃ in G_1 over $\mathcal{N}$. Figure 2 captures the intuition behind this construction discussed.

The net $\mathcal{M}'$ is linear in the size of $\mathcal{N}$ whereas $\mathcal{M}$ has size approximately $\mathcal{N} \times |\Sigma|$, where $|\Sigma|$ is the size of the alphabet. This factor of $|\Sigma|$ arises due to remembering the previous letter read in the state space to create this lag for ∀'s decisions.

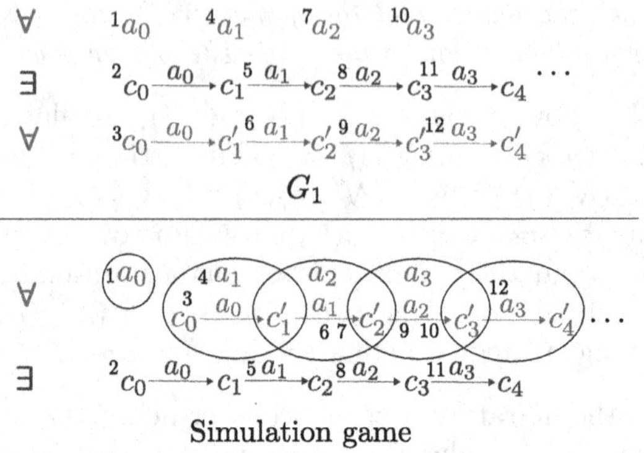

Fig. 2. An illustration of a play of G_1, seen as a play of the simulation game

Finally, we see that the following theorem from the work of Hofman, Lasota, Mayr, and Totzke [24] shows that the winner of a simulation game can be solved in **PSPACE**. We recall their results to fit our notation below.

Theorem 12 ([24], Theorem 7). *Given two one-counter nets $\mathcal{N}$ and $\mathcal{N}'$, with configurations (p, k) and (p', k') in $\mathcal{C}(\mathcal{N})$ and $\mathcal{C}(\mathcal{N}')$ respectively, with k and k' represented in binary, deciding whether $(\mathcal{N}', (p', k'))$ simulates $(\mathcal{N}, (p, k))$ is in* **PSPACE**. *Moreover, the set of (k, k') for which $(\mathcal{N}, (p, k)) \longrightarrow (\mathcal{N}', (p', k'))$ is semilinear, and can be computed in* **EXPSPACE**.

We get the following lemma as a corollary of Lemmas 6 and 11 and Theorem 12.

Lemma 13. *Given a one-counter net $\mathcal{N}$, we can decide in* **PSPACE** *if $\mathcal{N}$ is history-deterministic.*

3.2   Lower Bounds

Although solving the simulation game turns out to be **PSPACE**-complete itself from the work of Srba [29], this lower bound result does not work for our reduction to simulation games. The reduction we give from G_1 to simulation games produces only a restricted class of simulation games which solve G_1.

Nevertheless, we show that deciding history-determinism is still **PSPACE**-hard, showing that even this restriction of the simulation problem is enough to induce **PSPACE**-hardness.

Lemma 14. *Given a one-counter net $\mathcal{N}$, it is* **PSPACE**-*hard to decide if $\mathcal{N}$ is history-deterministic.*

Proof (Sketch). We reduce from the problem of checking non-emptiness of an alternating finite-state automaton over a unary alphabet. This problem was proven to be **PSPACE** complete by Holzer [31], with its proof simplified by Jančar and Sawa [32]. The intuition behind the reduction is to recreate a run of the alternating automaton in the letter game of a constructed OCN. In the letter game, a "fair" play of $\forall$ corresponds to a branch of a run-tree in the automaton, with $\exists$ resolving universal transitions and $\forall$ resolving existential ones. The player $\forall$ can ensure that he wins the letter game if and only if the alternating automaton has some word that he can demonstrate is in the language. If $\forall$ plays "unfairly", then there are gadgets to ensure that $\exists$ automatically wins.

4   Languages and History-Determinism in OCNs

We dedicate this section to tackling different questions about languages accepted by history-deterministic one-counter nets and decision problems on such languages.

4.1   Languages Accepted by History-Deterministic OCNs

While in history-deterministic models we are able to resolve the non-determinism on-the-fly, it is not well-understood how these resolvers might look like in general. In fact, Guha, Jecker, Lehtinen, and Zimmermann showed that there are history-deterministic pushdown automata whose resolvers cannot be given by a pushdown automata [18], and whether such a resolver can be computed is an open problem.

In this sub-section, our goal is to understand better the languages of history-deterministic OCNs. As a first-step towards this goal, we already have some intuition from the previous section on the eventually periodic nature of the transitions that are residual (as a corollary of Lemma 11 and Theorem 12). Here, we solidify this intuition by defining what it means to have *semilinear-strategy property* for a resolver and to then show that all nets have this property. For the case of history-deterministic nets, using this semi-linearity of the resolvers, we show the existence of a language-equivalent deterministic OCA.

We first show a sufficient characterisation which we call the *semilinear-strategy property*, for if a given history-deterministic one-counter net can be determinised.

We say a transition $\delta = (p, a, d, p')$ in an one-counter net $\mathcal{N}$ is a good transition at (p, k), if $((p, k), (p, k))$ is in the winning region of G_1, and the transition $\delta = (p, k) \xrightarrow{a,d} (p', k+d)$ is a winning move for $\exists$ in G_1 when $\forall$ chooses the letter a. We also write this sometimes as $(p, k) \xrightarrow{a,d} (p', k + d)$ is a good transition in $\mathcal{N}$. The following lemma can be seen as a weakening of Proposition 7.

Lemma 15. *Let $\mathcal{N} = (Q, \Sigma, \Delta, q_0, F)$ be a history-deterministic one-counter net. An $\exists$ strategy σ in the letter game is winning for $\exists$ if and only if the strategy σ only takes good transitions $\delta = (p, k) \xrightarrow{a,d} (p', k')$.*

Given a one-counter net $\mathcal{N}$, we say $\mathcal{N}$ satisfies *semilinear-strategy property* if for each transition $\delta = (q, a, d, q')$, the set of $k \in \mathbb{N}$ such that δ is a good transition at (q, k) is semilinear. That is, for each transition $\delta = (q, a, d, q') \in \Delta$, we have that the following set is eventually periodic

$$ \mathcal{S}_\delta = \left\{ k : (q, k) \xrightarrow{a, d} (q', k') \text{ is a good transition at } (q, k) \right\}. $$

Lemma 16. *If a history-deterministic OCN $\mathcal{N} = (Q, \Sigma, q_0, \Delta, F)$ satisfies the semilinear-strategy property, then there is a language-equivalent deterministic OCA $\mathcal{D}$.*

Proof (Sketch). We assume the history-deterministic OCN $\mathcal{N}$ is such that it satisfies semilinear-strategy property. We shall first construct a non-deterministic one-counter automata $\mathcal{B}$, which can be determinised easily by removing a minimal set of transitions to get rid of non-determinism while still preserving the language. The non-deterministic one-counter automata $\mathcal{B}$ would essentially be designed so that the transitions in $\mathcal{B}$ correspond to the good transitions in $\mathcal{N}$, from any configuration. The eventual periodicity of the sets $\mathcal{S}_\delta$ allows us to express this as a one-counter automaton, rather than as a labelled transition system with countably many states.

Intuitively, the automaton $\mathcal{B}$ is constructed such that the state space of the automaton stores in its memory the period and the initial block of the semilinear sets. The idea is that this automaton's runs would be in bijection with those runs that take only good transitions in the OCN $\mathcal{N}$. We know that such a run exists in $\mathcal{N}$ by Lemma 15, as $\mathcal{N}$ is history-deterministic. However, the counter values in $\mathcal{B}$ are 'scaled down' to only remember how many periods have passed, while counter value 0 indicates that the counter value in the original run would have been at most I. The exact value of the counter in a run of $\mathcal{N}$ can be inferred as a function of the state space and the counter value of $\mathcal{B}$.

Having shown that every history-deterministic one-counter net that satisfies semilinear-strategy property has a language equivalent DOCA, we proceed to show that every one-counter net satisfies semilinear-strategy property. We first display an example which solidifies an intuition of the above statement.

Example 17. Consider the net $\mathcal{N}_7$, as shown in Figure 3, where all states labelled q_F are accepting. This automaton is not history-deterministic. However, if the counter value at q_1 is not a multiple of 7, then $\exists$ can resolve the non-determinism from q_1. Observe that the automaton accepts words of the form $a^n \$ b^k \$ \cdot (\heartsuit, \clubsuit)$ such that $k \leq n$. Consider the following play of $\forall$ in the letter game from q_0: For $7n$ steps he reads a, after which he reads a $\$$. So far, all transitions are deterministic. After that, assume he again reads, $7n$ many times, the letter b. This ensures that the transition ends at the state q_1 with counter value 0. If he reads $\$$ here, this is the only position where $\exists$ has a choice. Note that she has to choose between transitions leading to $q_\heartsuit$ and $q_\clubsuit$. However, since both the suffixes $\heartsuit$ and $\clubsuit$ are accepting and only one of $\heartsuit$ or $\clubsuit$ is accepting from either states, $\forall$ can ensure $\exists$ loses no matter what she picks. However, if $\forall$ had read a

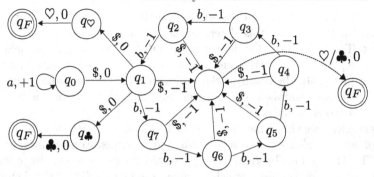

Fig. 3. The one-counter net $\mathcal{N}_7$ from Example 17

number of 'b's that was not a multiple of 7, the play of an accepting word would end at $q_\$$ which is accepting.

Lemma 18. *Every one-counter net $\mathcal{N}$ satisfies semilinear-strategy property.*

The proof of the above lemma follows from Theorem 12 on using a construction similar to the proof of Lemma 11 along wit. As an easy corollary of the above two lemmas, we get the following theorem.

Theorem 19. *Every history-deterministic OCN can be determinised to produce an equivalent deterministic OCA.*

An easy analysis of our proof combined with the results on the representation of simulation preorder ([24], Lemma 28) shows a doubly exponential upper bound on the size of the equivalent deterministic OCA constructed from the proof of the theorem above.

Remark 20. On the topic of expressivity of history-determinism, we conclude this subsection with a remark that history-deterministic OCNs are strictly less expressive than non-deterministic OCNs. This can be demonstrated with the language $\mathcal{L} = \{a^i \$ b^j \$ b^k \mid j \leq i \text{ or } k \leq i\}$. It is routine to verify that such a language is not accepted by any history-deterministic OCN, but this language can be accepted by a non-deterministic OCN. Note that history-determinism itself is not the limiting factor in accepting this language, as this language is accepted by a history-deterministic pushdown automaton [18].

4.2 Complexity of comparing languages of history-deterministic OCNs

Comparisons between languages of non-deterministic OCNs are undecidable [23], and even the restricted question of universality, is Ackermann-complete [33]. In this section, we show that for history-deterministic nets, these problems are no longer undecidable and have a significantly lower complexity when compared to non-deterministic nets.

Although we show that history-deterministic OCNs can be converted to a deterministic automaton, this determinisation does not help us answer these questions. This is because for deterministic OCAs, the problem of inclusion is undecidable [28]. Even though equality and universality for a deterministic OCA is **NL**-complete [34], the resulting deterministic OCA we get from determinisation of history-deterministic OCNs could be much larger than our input net, leading to a larger complexity.

Nevertheless, we show that checking for language inclusion, and hence checking language equivalence between two history-deterministic one-counter nets is in **PSPACE**. This is done by giving a polynomial-time reduction to the problem of deciding history-determinism, which we showed to be in **PSPACE** in Lemma 13. Moreover, combining our techniques with results of Kucera [35] gives us decidability in **P** for checking language universality of HD-OCNs.

Lemma 21. *Deciding language inclusion and language equivalence between two history-deterministic one-counter nets is in* **PSPACE***.*

We can show that the problem of checking language inclusion between two history-deterministic OCNs reduces to checking if a larger OCN (linear in the sum of the size of the two OCNs) is history-deterministic. Since language equivalence is essentially checking language inclusion both ways, we have the above results.

Lemma 22. *Deciding language universality for a given history-deterministic one-counter net is in* **P***.*

The problem of universality reduces to checking if the input net $\mathcal{M}$ simulates a finite state automata. This problem was shown to be **P** by Kucera ([35], Lemma 2), showing that universality is in **P**.

We therefore have the following theorem.

Theorem 23. *For nets $\mathcal{H}$ and $\mathcal{H}'$ that are history-deterministic, the problem of checking if $\mathcal{L}(\mathcal{H}) \subseteq \mathcal{L}(\mathcal{H}')$ as well as checking if $\mathcal{L}(\mathcal{H}) = \mathcal{L}(\mathcal{H}')$ can be done in* **PSPACE***. If $\mathcal{H}$ is instead a deterministic finite-state automaton, this problem can be solved in* **P***.*

We summarise known results and complexity of relevant results for comparison with other automata models in Table 1.

5   Extensions and Variations of OCN

We revisit the question of deciding history-determinism in this section for one-counter nets and its variants. In the first subsection, we tackle the question of how the complexity changes if the nets are encoded succinctly. We show that as expected, this increases the complexity of the problem from **PSPACE**-complete to **EXPSPACE**-complete. We then answer affirmatively to the question of whether adding zero-tests add too much power to one-counter nets by showing that the problem of deciding history-determinism becomes undecidable.

	$\mathcal{L} \subseteq \mathcal{L}'$	$\mathcal{L} = \mathcal{L}'$	$\mathcal{L} = \Sigma^*$
DOCN	**NL**-complete [33]	**NL**-complete [33]	**NL**-complete [33]
HOCN	In **PSPACE**	In **PSPACE**	In **P**
OCN	Undecidable [28]	Undecidable [23]	Ackermann-complete [33]
DOCA	Undecidable [28]	**NL**-complete [36]	**NL**-complete [36]

Table 1. Complexities for the problems of deciding language inclusion, equivalence and universality over deterministic OCN, HD-OCN, non-deterministic OCN and deterministic OCA.

5.1 Succinct Encoding of Counters

We consider a succinct representation of the input nets or a succinct one-counter net, where the transitions can allow for increments or decrements by integers (potentially greater than 1) that are represented in binary. Unsurprisingly, we show that checking for history-determinism becomes **EXPSPACE**-complete in this case. The upper bound follows from the previous proof of the **PSPACE** upper bound from Lemma 13 of deciding history-determinism for one-counter nets, where counter values are in unary. Any succinct one-counter net can be converted with only an exponential blow-up into another language equivalent net with unary encoding, preserving history-determinism thereby giving us an **EXPSPACE** upper bound.

Proposition 24. *Given a succinct one-counter net $\mathcal{N}$, deciding if $\mathcal{N}$ is history-deterministic is in* **EXPSPACE**.

However, much more work is needed to show a matching lower bound, which we do by giving a reduction from reachability games on succinct one-counter nets (SOCN). Intuitively, these games are played on the configuration graphs of a succinct OCN whose alphabet is a singleton. The states of this SOCN are partitioned among two players, denoted by $\wedge$ and $\vee$ who are responsible for choosing the transition from that state. The goal of $\vee$ is to take the play to a designated winning state with value 0. This problem of deciding the winner in the SOCN-reachability game was shown to be **EXPSPACE**-complete by Hunter [37] and later, several of its variants were also shown to have the same complexity [30]. A polynomial reduction from checking for history-determinism in a SOCN gives us **EXPSPACE**-hardness.

Lemma 25. *Given a SOCN $\mathcal{N}$, deciding if $\mathcal{N}$ is history-deterministic is* **EXPSPACE**-*hard*.

Proof (Sketch). Given an instance of a SOCN-reachability game on $\mathcal{N}$, We construct a SOCN $\mathcal{M}$ such that $\vee$ wins in the SOCN-reachability game on $\mathcal{N}$ if and only if $\forall$ wins in the letter game on $\mathcal{M}$.

The high-level idea of the construction is such that in a play of the letter game on $\mathcal{M}$, the players $\forall$ and $\exists$ create a transcript of a run of $\mathcal{N}$. This is done by $\forall$ ensuring that picking the letters in $\mathcal{M}$ corresponds to picking a transition out of $\vee$ states in $\mathcal{N}$. Since $\exists$ resolves the non-determinism in the letter game on $\mathcal{M}$, her choice of transitions correspond to transitions out of a $\wedge$ state in the SOCN-reachability game.

However, there are some subtleties in the construction as we need to ensure a few important aspects while constructing $\mathcal{M}$. Firstly, any sequence of letters chosen by $\forall$ in $\mathcal{M}$'s letter game so far must correspond to a run in $\mathcal{N}$ and secondly, the interplay between $\exists$'s and $\forall$'s choices in the letter game of $\mathcal{M}$ must correspond to the choices of the player $\wedge$ and $\vee$ respectively in the SOCN-reachability game of $\mathcal{N}$. These are the main challenges while constructing such an OCN $\mathcal{N}$ and they are resolved by the use of a few gadgets.

We conclude this subsection by combining Proposition 24 and Lemma 25 to obtain the following theorem.

Theorem 26.   *Given a SOCN $\mathcal{N}$, deciding if $\mathcal{N}$ is history-deterministic is* **EXPSPACE**-*complete.*

5.2   Deciding History-Determinsm for OCA

We show that, given a one-counter automaton $\mathcal{A}$, deciding if $\mathcal{A}$ is history-deterministic is undecidable. It was shown by Guha, Jecker, Lehtinen, and Zimmermann [18] that deciding if a given non-deterministic pushdown automaton is history-deterministic is undecidable. This extends their result to OCAs, which follows via a reduction from checking for language inclusion for deterministic one-counter automata (DOCA), which is known to be undecidable [28].

Theorem 27.   *Given an OCA $\mathcal{A}$, deciding if $\mathcal{A}$ is history-deterministic is undecidable.*

Proof (Sketch).   Consider the following problem :

DOCA Inclusion: Given two DOCAs $\mathcal{A}$ and $\mathcal{B}$, is $\mathcal{L}(\mathcal{A}) \subseteq \mathcal{L}(\mathcal{B})$?

The above problem was shown to be undecidable in Section 5.1 of Valiant's thesis [28]. We show that the problem of deciding if a given one-counter automaton is history-deterministic is also undecidable, by giving a reduction from the DOCA inclusion problem to checking for history-determinism of a given OCA.

6   Discussion

We showed several decision problems related to history-determinism to be decidable over OCNs. This is unlike other classes of infinite-state systems that subsume them, where either some or all of these problems are undecidable.

We note that we only deal with realtime nets with no ϵ-transitions, but our results hold without too much modification when ϵ-transitions are present, as weak simulation over OCNs can be decided in **PSPACE** (and **EXPSPACE** for a succinct encoding), and the weak simulation pre-order is semilinear as well [24].

We also showed that testing the counter for zero made checking for history-determinism undecidable. Along these lines, one could ask about models like reversal bounded one-counter automata [38], or automata with bounded number of zero-tests, to gauge the frontier between decidability and undecidability on these systems.

Although not obvious from the main part of the paper, we are confident that our results could easily be extended to safety acceptance conditions. One could also ask, for instance, to look at reachability or Büchi and co-Büchi acceptance conditions and understand how history-determinism works in these models.

There are several questions about the expressivity of history-deterministic OCNs which we believe need further study. Overloading the notation and assuming DOCN, DOCA, OCN, HD-OCN and HD-OCA to denote the class of languages that are accepted by the corresponding models, we have shown that

$$\text{DOCN} \subseteq \text{HD-OCN} \subseteq \text{OCN} \cap \text{DOCA}.$$

An interesting problem would be to prove or disprove if any of these inclusions are strict. In fact, we don't have an example of a language that is accepted by a history-deterministic OCN which is not accepted by a deterministic OCN.

One could ask similar questions about expressivity of history-determinism in OCAs, i.e. if HD-OCA = DOCA. Although deciding history-determinism is undecidable, it might be possible for one to show that the language accepted by a history-deterministic OCA is as expressive as deterministic OCA. We remark that the 1-token game G_1 characterises history-determinisation for OCAs as well. Moreover, we can again show with similar techniques that if history-deterministic OCAs satisfy the semilinear-strategy property, then these languages can also be expressed by a deterministic OCA. The key part that we need to prove for determinisation of history-deterministic OCA would be the semilinear-strategy property. It would be interesting to see how such a proof would look like, given that checking for history-determinism is undecidable for OCAs.

Acknowledgements We would like to thank Dmitry Chistikov for listening to our conjectures and pointing us to important references. We are also grateful for his comments on our introduction. We are thankful to Neha Rino for carefully proofreading our paper, and suggesting improvements in our presentation. We also thank Sougata Bose, Piotrek Hofman, Filip Mazowiecki, David Purser, and Patrick Totzke for their insightful remarks on our draft, and for telling us about weak simulation. We are grateful to Shaull Almagor and Asaf Yeshurun for a fun talk about OCNs. Finally, we thank Marcin Jurdziński for his support, and for bringing us homemade rhubarb crumble.

References

1. Thomas Colcombet. Unambiguity in automata theory. In Jeffrey O. Shallit and Alexander Okhotin, editors, *Descriptional Complexity of Formal Systems - 17th In-*

ternational Workshop, DCFS 2015, Waterloo, ON, Canada, June 25-27, 2015. Proceedings, volume 9118 of *Lecture Notes in Computer Science*, pages 3–18. Springer, 2015.

2. Denis Kuperberg and Anirban Majumdar. Width of non-deterministic automata. In Rolf Niedermeier and Brigitte Vallée, editors, *35th Symposium on Theoretical Aspects of Computer Science, STACS 2018, February 28 to March 3, 2018, Caen, France*, volume 96 of *LIPIcs*, pages 47:1–47:14. Schloss Dagstuhl - Leibniz-Zentrum für Informatik, 2018.

3. Ernst Moritz Hahn, Mateo Perez, Sven Schewe, Fabio Somenzi, Ashutosh Trivedi, and Dominik Wojtczak. Good-for-MDPs automata for probabilistic analysis and reinforcement learning. In Armin Biere and David Parker, editors, *Tools and Algorithms for the Construction and Analysis of Systems - 26th International Conference, TACAS 2020, Held as Part of the European Joint Conferences on Theory and Practice of Software, ETAPS 2020, Dublin, Ireland, April 25-30, 2020, Proceedings, Part I*, volume 12078 of *Lecture Notes in Computer Science*, pages 306–323. Springer, 2020.

4. Bader Abu Radi, Orna Kupferman, and Ofer Leshkowitz. A hierarchy of nondeterminism. In Filippo Bonchi and Simon J. Puglisi, editors, *46th International Symposium on Mathematical Foundations of Computer Science, MFCS 2021, August 23-27, 2021, Tallinn, Estonia*, volume 202 of *LIPIcs*, pages 85:1–85:21. Schloss Dagstuhl - Leibniz-Zentrum für Informatik, 2021.

5. Emile Hazard and Denis Kuperberg. Explorable automata, May 2022. working paper or preprint.

6. Thomas A. Henzinger and Nir Piterman. Solving games without determinization. In Zoltán Ésik, editor, *Computer Science Logic, 20th International Workshop, CSL 2006, 15th Annual Conference of the EACSL, Szeged, Hungary, September 25-29, 2006, Proceedings*, volume 4207 of *Lecture Notes in Computer Science*, pages 395–410. Springer, 2006.

7. Denis Kuperberg and Michal Skrzypczak. On determinisation of good-for-games automata. In Magnús M. Halldórsson, Kazuo Iwama, Naoki Kobayashi, and Bettina Speckmann, editors, *Automata, Languages, and Programming - 42nd International Colloquium, ICALP 2015, Kyoto, Japan, July 6-10, 2015, Proceedings, Part II*, volume 9135 of *Lecture Notes in Computer Science*, pages 299–310. Springer, 2015.

8. Thomas Colcombet. Forms of Determinism for Automata (Invited Talk). In Christoph Dürr and Thomas Wilke, editors, *29th International Symposium on Theoretical Aspects of Computer Science (STACS 2012)*, volume 14 of *Leibniz International Proceedings in Informatics (LIPIcs)*, pages 1–23, Dagstuhl, Germany, 2012. Schloss Dagstuhl–Leibniz-Zentrum fuer Informatik.

9. Udi Boker, Denis Kuperberg, Orna Kupferman, and Michał Skrzypczak. Nondeterminism in the presence of a diverse or unknown future. In *Proceedings of the 40th International Conference on Automata, Languages, and Programming - Volume Part II*, ICALP'13, page 89–100, Berlin, Heidelberg, 2013. Springer-Verlag.

10. Udi Boker, Orna Kupferman, and Michal Skrzypczak. How Deterministic are Good-For-Games Automatal. In Satya Lokam and R. Ramanujam, editors, *37th IARCS Annual Conference on Foundations of Software Technology and Theoretical Computer Science (FSTTCS 2017)*, volume 93 of *Leibniz International Proceedings in Informatics (LIPIcs)*, pages 18:1–18:14, Dagstuhl, Germany, 2018. Schloss Dagstuhl–Leibniz-Zentrum fuer Informatik.

11. Marc Bagnol and Denis Kuperberg. Büchi Good-for-Games Automata Are Efficiently Recognizable. In Sumit Ganguly and Paritosh Pandya, editors, *38th IARCS Annual Conference on Foundations of Software Technology and Theoretical Computer Science (FSTTCS 2018)*, volume 122 of *Leibniz International Proceedings in Informatics (LIPIcs)*, pages 16:1–16:14, Dagstuhl, Germany, 2018. Schloss Dagstuhl–Leibniz-Zentrum fuer Informatik.

12. Udi Boker, Denis Kuperberg, Karoliina Lehtinen, and Michał Skrzypczak. On the Succinctness of Alternating Parity Good-For-Games Automata. In Nitin Saxena and Sunil Simon, editors, *40th IARCS Annual Conference on Foundations of Software Technology and Theoretical Computer Science (FSTTCS 2020)*, volume 182 of *Leibniz International Proceedings in Informatics (LIPIcs)*, pages 41:1–41:13, Dagstuhl, Germany, 2020. Schloss Dagstuhl–Leibniz-Zentrum für Informatik.

13. Antonio Casares, Thomas Colcombet, and Karoliina Lehtinen. On the size of good-for-games rabin automata and its link with the memory in muller games. In Mikolaj Bojanczyk, Emanuela Merelli, and David P. Woodruff, editors, *49th International Colloquium on Automata, Languages, and Programming, ICALP 2022, July 4-8, 2022, Paris, France*, volume 229 of *LIPIcs*, pages 117:1–117:20. Schloss Dagstuhl - Leibniz-Zentrum für Informatik, 2022.

14. Bader Abu Radi and Orna Kupferman. Minimization and canonization of GFG transition-based automata. *Log. Methods Comput. Sci.*, 18(3), 2022.

15. Thomas Colcombet. The theory of stabilisation monoids and regular cost functions. In Susanne Albers, Alberto Marchetti-Spaccamela, Yossi Matias, Sotiris E. Nikoletseas, and Wolfgang Thomas, editors, *Automata, Languages and Programming, 36th Internatilonal Colloquium, ICALP 2009, Rhodes, Greece, July 5-12, 2009, Proceedings, Part II*, volume 5556 of *Lecture Notes in Computer Science*, pages 139–150. Springer, 2009.

16. Udi Boker and Karoliina Lehtinen. History determinism vs. good for gameness in quantitative automata. In Mikolaj Bojanczyk and Chandra Chekuri, editors, *41st IARCS Annual Conference on Foundations of Software Technology and Theoretical Computer Science, FSTTCS 2021, December 15-17, 2021, Virtual Conference*, volume 213 of *LIPIcs*, pages 38:1–38:20. Schloss Dagstuhl - Leibniz-Zentrum für Informatik, 2021.

17. Udi Boker and Karoliina Lehtinen. Token games and history-deterministic quantitative automata. In Patricia Bouyer and Lutz Schröder, editors, *Foundations of Software Science and Computation Structures - 25th International Conference, FOSSACS 2022, Held as Part of the European Joint Conferences on Theory and Practice of Software, ETAPS 2022, Munich, Germany, April 2-7, 2022, Proceedings*, volume 13242 of *Lecture Notes in Computer Science*, pages 120–139. Springer, 2022.

18. Shibashis Guha, Ismaël Jecker, Karoliina Lehtinen, and Martin Zimmermann. A Bit of Nondeterminism Makes Pushdown Automata Expressive and Succinct. In Filippo Bonchi and Simon J. Puglisi, editors, *46th International Symposium on Mathematical Foundations of Computer Science (MFCS 2021)*, volume 202 of *Leibniz International Proceedings in Informatics (LIPIcs)*, pages 53:1–53:20, Dagstuhl, Germany, 2021. Schloss Dagstuhl – Leibniz-Zentrum für Informatik.

19. Karoliina Lehtinen and Martin Zimmermann. Good-for-games ω-pushdown automata. *Log. Methods Comput. Sci.*, 18(1), 2022.

20. Enzo Erlich, Shibashis Guha, Ismaël Jecker, Karoliina Lehtinen, and Martin Zimmermann. History-deterministic parikh automata. *CoRR*, abs/2209.07745, 2022.

21. Thomas A. Henzinger, Karoliina Lehtinen, and Patrick Totzke. History-deterministic timed automata. In Bartek Klin, Slawomir Lasota, and Anca Muscholl, editors, *33rd International Conference on Concurrency Theory, CONCUR 2022, September 12-16, 2022, Warsaw, Poland*, volume 243 of *LIPIcs*, pages 14:1–14:21. Schloss Dagstuhl - Leibniz-Zentrum für Informatik, 2022.

22. Sougata Bose, Thomas A. Henzinger, Karoliina Lehtinen, Sven Schewe, and Patrick Totzke. History-deterministic timed automata are not determinizable. In Anthony W. Lin, Georg Zetzsche, and Igor Potapov, editors, *Reachability Problems - 16th International Conference, RP 2022, Kaiserslautern, Germany, October 17-21, 2022, Proceedings*, volume 13608 of *Lecture Notes in Computer Science*, pages 67–76. Springer, 2022.

23. Piotr Hofman, Richard Mayr, and Patrick Totzke. Decidability of weak simulation on one-counter nets. In *28th Annual ACM/IEEE Symposium on Logic in Computer Science, LICS 2013, New Orleans, LA, USA, June 25-28, 2013*, pages 203–212. IEEE Computer Society, 2013.

24. Piotr Hofman, Slawomir Lasota, Richard Mayr, and Patrick Totzke. Simulation problems over one-counter nets. *Log. Methods Comput. Sci.*, 12(1), 2016.

25. Udi Boker and Karoliina Lehtinen. Good for games automata: From nondeterminism to alternation. In Wan J. Fokkink and Rob van Glabbeek, editors, *30th International Conference on Concurrency Theory, CONCUR 2019, August 27-30, 2019, Amsterdam, the Netherlands*, volume 140 of *LIPIcs*, pages 19:1–19:16. Schloss Dagstuhl - Leibniz-Zentrum für Informatik, 2019.

26. Shibashis Guha, Ismaël Jecker, Karoliina Lehtinen, and Martin Zimmermann. Parikh automata over infinite words, 2022.

27. David Gale and Frank M Stewart. Infinite games with perfect information. *Contributions to the Theory of Games*, 2(245-266):2–16, 1953.

28. Leslie G. Valiant. *Decision procedures for families of deterministic pushdown automata*. PhD thesis, University of Warwick, Coventry, UK, 1973.

29. Jirí Srba. Visibly pushdown automata: From language equivalence to simulation and bisimulation. In Zoltán Ésik, editor, *Computer Science Logic, 20th International Workshop, CSL 2006, 15th Annual Conference of the EACSL, Szeged, Hungary, September 25-29, 2006, Proceedings*, volume 4207 of *Lecture Notes in Computer Science*, pages 89–103. Springer, 2006.

30. Petr Jancar, Petr Osicka, and Zdenek Sawa. EXPSPACE-hardness of behavioural equivalences of succinct one-counter nets. *CoRR*, abs/1801.01073, 2018.

31. Markus Holzer. On emptiness and counting for alternating finite automata. In Jürgen Dassow, Grzegorz Rozenberg, and Arto Salomaa, editors, *Developments in Language Theory II, At the Crossroads of Mathematics, Computer Science and Biology, Magdeburg, Germany, 17-21 July 1995*, pages 88–97. World Scientific, Singapore, 1995.

32. Petr Jancar and Zdenek Sawa. A note on emptiness for alternating finite automata with a one-letter alphabet. *Inf. Process. Lett.*, 104(5):164–167, 2007.

33. Piotr Hofman and Patrick Totzke. Trace inclusion for one-counter nets revisited. In Joël Ouaknine, Igor Potapov, and James Worrell, editors, *Reachability Problems - 8th International Workshop, RP 2014, Oxford, UK, September 22-24, 2014. Proceedings*, volume 8762 of *Lecture Notes in Computer Science*, pages 151–162. Springer, 2014.

34. Stanislav Böhm, Stefan Göller, and Petr Jancar. Equivalence of deterministic one-counter automata is NL-complete. In Dan Boneh, Tim Roughgarden, and Joan Feigenbaum, editors, *Symposium on Theory of Computing Conference, STOC'13, Palo Alto, CA, USA, June 1-4, 2013*, pages 131–140. ACM, 2013.

35. Antonín Kucera. On simulation-checking with sequential systems. In Jifeng He and Masahiko Sato, editors, *Advances in Computing Science - ASIAN 2000, 6th Asian Computing Science Conference, Penang, Malaysia, November 25-27, 2000, Proceedings*, volume 1961 of *Lecture Notes in Computer Science*, pages 133–148. Springer, 2000.

36. Stanislav Böhm and Stefan Göller. Language equivalence of deterministic real-time one-counter automata is nl-complete. In Filip Murlak and Piotr Sankowski, editors, *Mathematical Foundations of Computer Science 2011 - 36th International Symposium, MFCS 2011, Warsaw, Poland, August 22-26, 2011. Proceedings*, volume 6907 of *Lecture Notes in Computer Science*, pages 194–205. Springer, 2011.

37. Paul Hunter. Reachability in succinct one-counter games. In Mikolaj Bojanczyk, Slawomir Lasota, and Igor Potapov, editors, *Reachability Problems - 9th International Workshop, RP 2015, Warsaw, Poland, September 21-23, 2015, Proceedings*, volume 9328 of *Lecture Notes in Computer Science*, pages 37–49. Springer, 2015.

38. Oscar H. Ibarra. Automata with reversal-bounded counters: A survey. In Helmut Jürgensen, Juhani Karhumäki, and Alexander Okhotin, editors, *Descriptional Complexity of Formal Systems - 16th International Workshop, DCFS 2014, Turku, Finland, August 5-8, 2014. Proceedings*, volume 8614 of *Lecture Notes in Computer Science*, pages 5–22. Springer, 2014.

Unboundedness Problems for Machines with Reversal-Bounded Counters

Pascal Baumann[1]([✉])[iD], Flavio D'Alessandro[2], Moses Ganardi[1][iD],
Oscar Ibarra[3], Ian McQuillan[4], Lia Schütze[1]([✉]) [iD], and Georg Zetzsche[1][iD]

[1] Max Planck Institute for Software Systems (MPI-SWS), Kaiserslautern and
Saarbrücken, Germany
[2] Dept. of Mathematics G. Castelnuovo, Sapienza University of Rome, Rome, Italy
[3] Dept. of Computer Science, University of California, Santa Barbara, CA, USA
[4] Dept. of Computer Science, University of Saskatchewan, Saskatoon, Canada

Abstract. We consider a general class of decision problems concerning
formal languages, called "(one-dimensional) unboundedness predicates",
for automata that feature reversal-bounded counters (RBCA). We show
that each problem in this class reduces—non-deterministically in polynomial time—to the same problem for just finite automata. We also show
an analogous reduction for automata that have access to both a pushdown stack and reversal-bounded counters (PRBCA).

This allows us to answer several open questions: For example, we show
that it is coNP-complete to decide whether a given (P)RBCA language
L is bounded, meaning whether there exist words $w_1, \ldots, w_n$ with $L \subseteq$
$w_1^* \cdots w_n^*$. For PRBCA, even decidability was open. Our methods also
show that there is no language of a (P)RBCA of intermediate growth.
This means, the number of words of each length grows either polynomially or exponentially. Part of our proof is likely of independent interest:
We show that one can translate an RBCA into a machine with $\mathbb{Z}$-counters
in logarithmic space, while preserving the accepted language.

Keywords: Formal languages · Decidability · Complexity · Counter
automata · Reversal-bounded · Pushdown · Boundedness · Unboundedness

1 Introduction

A classic idea in the theory of formal languages is the concept of boundedness
of a language. A language L over an alphabet Σ is called *bounded* if there ex-
ists a number $n \in \mathbb{N}$ and words $w_1, \ldots, w_n \in \Sigma^*$ such that $L \subseteq w_1^* \cdots w_n^*$.
What makes boundedness important is that a rich variety of algorithmic prob-
lems become decidable for bounded languages. For example, when Ginsburg and
Spanier [25] introduced boundedness in 1964, they already showed that given
two context-free languages, one of them bounded, one can decide inclusion [25,
Theorem 6.3]. This is because if $L \subseteq w_1^* \cdots w_n^*$ for a context-free language, then
the set $\{(x_1, \ldots, x_n) \in \mathbb{N}^n \mid w_1^{x_1} \cdots w_n^{x_n} \in L\}$ is effectively semilinear, which

© The Author(s) 2023
O. Kupferman and P. Sobocinski (Eds.): FoSSaCS 2023, LNCS 13992, pp. 240–264, 2023.
https://doi.org/10.1007/978-3-031-30829-1_12

permits expressing inclusion in Presburger arithmetic. Here, boundedness is a crucial assumption: Hopcroft has shown that if $L_0 \subseteq \Sigma^*$ is context-free, then the problem of deciding $L_0 \subseteq L$ for a given context-free language L is decidable if and only if L_0 is bounded [35, Theorem 3.3].

The idea of translating questions about bounded languages into Presburger arithmetic has been applied in several other contexts. For example, Esparza, Ganty, and Majumdar [20] have shown that many classes of infinite-state systems are *perfect modulo bounded languages*, meaning that the bounded languages form a subclass that is amenable to many algorithmic problems. As another example, the subword ordering has a decidable first-order theory on bounded context-free languages [45], whereas on languages Σ^*, even the existential theory is undecidable [33]. This, in turn, implies that initial limit Datalog is decidable for the subword ordering on bounded context-free languages [7]. Finally, bounded context-free languages can be closely approximated by regular ones [16].

This raises the question of how one can decide whether a given language is bounded. For context-free languages this problem is decidable [25, Theorem 5.2(a)] in polynomial time [24, Theorem 19].

Boundedness for RBCA. Despite the importance of boundedness, it had been open for many years [9, 17][1] whether boundedness is decidable for one of the most well-studied types of infinite-state systems: *reversal-bounded (multi-)counter automata* (RBCA). These are machines with counters that can be incremented, decremented, and even tested for zero. However, in order to achieve decidability of basic questions, there is a bound on the number of times each counter can *reverse*, that is, switch between *incrementing* and *decrementing phases*. They were first studied in the 1970s [2, 36] and have received a lot of attention since [8–13, 18, 23, 28, 32, 33, 39–41, 58]. The desirable properties mentioned above for bounded context-free languages also apply to bounded RBCA. Furthermore, any bounded language accepted by an RBCA (even one augmented with a stack) can be effectively determinized [38] (see also [9, 11]), opening up even more avenues to algorithmic analysis. This makes it surprising that decidability of boundedness remained open for many years.

Decidability of boundedness for RBCA was settled in [15], which proves boundedness decidable even for the larger class of vector addition systems with states (VASS), with acceptance by configuration. However, the results from [15] leave several aspects unclarified, which we investigate here:

Q1: What is the complexity of deciding boundedness for RBCA? The algorithm in [15] employs the KLMST decomposition for VASS [43, 46, 48, 50, 54], which is well-known to incur Ackermannian complexity [49].

Q2: Is boundedness decidable for *pushdown RBCA* (PRBCA) [36]? These are automata which, in addition to reversal-bounded counters, feature a stack. They can model recursive programs with numeric data types [32]. Whether boundedness is decidable was stated as open in [17, 18].

---

[1] Note that [9] is about Parikh automata, which are equivalent to RBCA.

Q3: Are there languages of RBCA of intermediate growth? As far as we know, this is a long-standing open question in itself [37]. The *growth* of a language $L \subseteq \Sigma^*$ is the *counting function* $g_L \colon \mathbb{N} \to \mathbb{N}$, where $g_L(n)$ is the number of words of length n in L. This concept is closely tied to boundedness: For regular and context-free languages, it is known that a language has polynomial growth if and only if it is bounded (and it has exponential growth otherwise). A language is said to have *intermediate growth* if it has neither polynomial nor exponential growth.

Contribution I: We prove versions of one of the main results in [15], one for RBCA and one for PRBCA. Specifically, the paper [15] not only shows that boundedness is decidable for VASS, but it introduces a general class of *unboundedness predicates* for formal languages. It is then shown in [15] that any unboundedness predicate is decidable for VASS if and only if it is decidable for regular languages. Our first two main results are:

MR1: Deciding any unboundedness predicate for RBCA reduces in NP to deciding the same predicate for regular languages.

MR2: Deciding any unboundedness predicate for PRBCA reduces in NP to deciding the same predicate for context-free languages.

However, it should be noted that our results only apply to those unboundedness predicates from [15] that are *one-dimensional*. Fortunately, these are enough for our applications. These results allow us to settle questions (Q1)–(Q3) above and derive the exact complexity of several other problems. It follows that boundedness for both RBCA and PRBCA is coNP-complete, thus answering (Q1) and (Q2). Furthermore, the proof shows that if boundedness of a PRBCA does not hold, then its language has exponential growth. This implies that there are no RBCA languages of intermediate growth (thus settling (Q3)), and even that the same holds for PRBCA. In particular, deciding polynomial growth of (P)RBCA is coNP-complete and deciding exponential growth of (P)RBCA is NP-complete. We can also derive from our result that deciding whether a (P)RBCA language is infinite is NP-complete (but this also follows easily from [32], see Section 2). Finally, our results imply that it is PSPACE-complete to decide if an RBCA language $L \subseteq \Sigma^*$ is *factor universal*, meaning it contains every word of Σ^* as a factor (i.e. as an infix). Whether this problem is decidable for RBCA was also left as an open problem in [17, 18] (under the name *infix density*).

We prove our results (MR1) and (MR2) by first translating (P)RBCA into models that have $\mathbb{Z}$-counters instead of reversal-bounded counters. A $\mathbb{Z}$-*counter* is one that can be incremented and decremented, but cannot be tested for zero. Moreover, it can assume negative values. With these counters, acceptance is defined by reaching a configuration where all counters are zero (in particular, the acceptance condition permits a single zero-test on each counter). Here, finite automata with $\mathbb{Z}$-counters are called $\mathbb{Z}$-*VASS* [29]. $\mathbb{Z}$-counters are also known as *blind counters* [26] and it is a standard fact that RBCA are equivalent (in terms of accepted languages) to $\mathbb{Z}$-VASS [26, Theorem 2].

Problem	$\mathbb{Z}$-VASS/RBCA	$\mathbb{Z}$-grammars/PRBCA
Boundedness	coNP-complete	coNP-complete
Finiteness	coNP-complete	coNP-complete
Factor universality	PSPACE-complete	undecidable

Table 1. Complexity results. The completeness statements are meant with respect to deterministic logspace reductions.

Despite the equivalence between RBCA and $\mathbb{Z}$-VASS being so well-known, there was apparently no known translation from RBCA to $\mathbb{Z}$-VASS in polynomial time. Here, the difficulty stems from simulating zero-tests (which can occur an unbounded number of times in an RBCA): To simulate these, the $\mathbb{Z}$-VASS needs to keep track of which counter has completed which incrementing/decrementing phase, using only polynomially many control states. It is also not obvious how to employ the $\mathbb{Z}$-counters for this, as they are only checked in the end.

Contribution II: As the first step of showing (MR1), we show that

MR3: RBCA can be translated (preserving the language) into $\mathbb{Z}$-VASS in logarithmic space.

This also implies that translations to and from another equivalent model, Parikh automata [41], are possible in polynomial time: It was recently shown that Parikh automata (which have received much attention in recent years [6, 8–10, 13, 22]) can be translated in polynomial time into $\mathbb{Z}$-VASS [30]. Together with our new result, this implies that one can translate among RBCA, $\mathbb{Z}$-VASS, and Parikh automata in polynomial time. Furthermore, our result yields a logspace translation of PRBCA into $\mathbb{Z}$-grammars, an extension of context-free grammars with $\mathbb{Z}$-counters. The latter is the first step for (MR2).

2   Main Results: Unboundedness and (P)RBCA

Reversal-bounded counter automata and pushdowns. A *pushdown automaton with k counters* is a tuple $\mathcal{A} = (Q, \Sigma, \Gamma, q_0, T, F)$ where Q is a finite set of states, Σ is an input alphabet, Γ is a stack alphabet, $q_0 \in Q$ is an initial state, T is a finite set of transitions $(p, w, \text{op}, q) \in Q \times \Sigma^* \times \text{Op} \times Q$, and $F \subseteq Q$ is a set of final states. Here Op is defined as

$$\text{Op} = \{\text{inc}_i, \text{dec}_i, \text{zero}_i, \text{nz}_i \mid 1 \leq i \leq k\} \cup \Gamma \cup \bar{\Gamma} \cup \{\varepsilon\},$$

containing counter and stack operations. Here $\bar{\Gamma} = \{\bar{\gamma} \mid \gamma \in \Gamma\}$ is a disjoint copy of Γ. A *configuration* is a tuple $(p, \alpha, \boldsymbol{v}) \in Q \times \Gamma^* \times \mathbb{N}^k$. We write $(p, \alpha, \boldsymbol{u}) \xrightarrow{w}$ $(p', \alpha', \boldsymbol{u}')$ if there is a $(p, w, \text{op}, p') \in T$ such that one of the following holds:

- op $= \text{inc}_i$, $\boldsymbol{u}' = \boldsymbol{u} + \boldsymbol{e}_i$, and $\alpha' = \alpha$ where $\boldsymbol{e}_i \in \mathbb{N}^k$ is the i-th unit vector,

- op = dec_i, $\boldsymbol{u}' = \boldsymbol{u} - \boldsymbol{e}_i$, and $\alpha' = \alpha$,
- op = zero_i, $\boldsymbol{u}[i] = 0$, $\boldsymbol{u}' = \boldsymbol{u}$, and $\alpha' = \alpha$
- op = nz_i, $\boldsymbol{u}[i] \neq 0$, $\boldsymbol{u}' = \boldsymbol{u}$, and $\alpha' = \alpha$,
- op = $\gamma \in \Gamma$, $\boldsymbol{u}' = \boldsymbol{u}$, and $\alpha' = \alpha\gamma$,
- op = $\bar{\gamma} \in \bar{\Gamma}$, $\boldsymbol{u}' = \boldsymbol{u}$, and $\alpha'\gamma = \alpha$,
- op = ε, $\boldsymbol{u}' = \boldsymbol{u}$, and $\alpha' = \alpha$.

We extend this notation to longer runs in the natural way.

A (k, r)-*PRBCA* (pushdown reversal-bounded counter automaton) $(\mathcal{A}, r)$ consists of a pushdown automaton with k counters $\mathcal{A}$ and a number $r \in \mathbb{N}$, encoded in unary. A counter c_i *reverses* if the last (non-test) operation affecting it was inc_i and the next operation is dec_i, or vice versa. A run is r-*reversal bounded* if every counter reverses at most r times. The *language* of $(\mathcal{A}, r)$ is

$$L(\mathcal{A}, r) = \{w \in \Sigma^* \mid \exists q \in F, \; r\text{-reversal bounded run } (q_0, \varepsilon, \mathbf{0}) \xrightarrow{w} (q, \varepsilon, \mathbf{0})\}.$$

A (k, r)-*RBCA* (reversal-bounded counter automaton) is a (k, r)-PRBCA where $\mathcal{A}$ only uses counter operations. We denote by RBCA and PRBCA the class of (P)RBCA languages.

Notice that we impose the reversal bound *externally* (following [32]) whereas in alternative definitions found in the literature the automaton has to ensure *internally* that the number of reversals on every (accepting) run does not exceed r, e.g. [36]. Clearly, our definition subsumes the latter one; in particular, Theorem 1 also holds for (P)RBCAs with an internally checked reversal bound.

A d-dimensional $\mathbb{Z}$-*VASS* ($\mathbb{Z}$-*vector addition system with states*) is a tuple $\mathcal{V} = (Q, \Sigma, q_0, T, F)$, where Q is a finite set of states, Σ is an alphabet, $q_0 \in Q$ is an initial state, T is a finite set of transitions $(p, w, \boldsymbol{v}, p') \in Q \times \Sigma^* \times \mathbb{Z}^d \times Q$, and $F \subseteq Q$ is a set of final states. A *configuration* of a $\mathbb{Z}$-VASS is a tuple $(p, \boldsymbol{v}) \in Q \times \mathbb{Z}^d$. We write $(p, \boldsymbol{u}) \xrightarrow{w} (p', \boldsymbol{u}')$ if there is a transition $(p, w, \boldsymbol{v}, p')$ such that $\boldsymbol{u}' = \boldsymbol{u} + \boldsymbol{v}$. We extend this notation to longer runs in the natural way. The *language* of the $\mathbb{Z}$-VASS is defined as

$$L(\mathcal{V}) = \{w \in \Sigma^* \mid \exists q \in F \colon (q_0, \mathbf{0}) \xrightarrow{w} (q, \mathbf{0})\}.$$

A *(d-dimensional) $\mathbb{Z}$-grammar* is a tuple $G = (N, \Sigma, S, P)$ with disjoint finite sets N and Σ of nonterminal and terminal symbols, a start nonterminal $S \in N$, and a finite set of productions P of the form $(A, u, \boldsymbol{v}) \in N \times (N \cup \Sigma)^* \times \mathbb{Z}^d$. We also write $(A \to u, \boldsymbol{v})$ instead of $(A, u, \boldsymbol{v})$. We call $\boldsymbol{v}$ the *(counter) effect* of the production $(A \to u, \boldsymbol{v})$. For words $x, y \in (N \cup \Sigma)^*$, we write $x \Rightarrow^{\boldsymbol{v}} y$ if there is a production $(A \to u, \boldsymbol{v})$ such that $x = rAs$ and $y = rus$. Moreover, we write $x \overset{*}{\Rightarrow}{}^{\boldsymbol{v}} y$ if there are words $x_1, \ldots, x_n \in (N \cup \Sigma)^*$ and $\boldsymbol{v}_1, \ldots, \boldsymbol{v}_n \in \mathbb{Z}^d$ with $x \Rightarrow^{\boldsymbol{v}_1} x_1 \Rightarrow^{\boldsymbol{v}_2} \cdots \Rightarrow^{\boldsymbol{v}_n} x_n = y$ and $\boldsymbol{v} = \boldsymbol{v}_1 + \cdots + \boldsymbol{v}_n$. We use the notation $\Rightarrow$ if the counter effects do not matter: We have $x \Rightarrow y$ if there exists $\boldsymbol{v}$ such that $x \Rightarrow_{\boldsymbol{v}} y$; and similarly for $\overset{*}{\Rightarrow}$. If derivations are restricted to a subset $Q \subseteq P$ of productions, we write $\Rightarrow_Q$ (resp. $\overset{*}{\Rightarrow}_Q$).

The *language* of the $\mathbb{Z}$-grammar G is the set of all words $w \in \Sigma^*$ such that $S \overset{*}{\Rightarrow}{}^{\mathbf{0}} w$. In other words, if there exists a derivation $S \overset{*}{\Rightarrow} w$ where the effects of all occurring productions sum to the zero vector $\mathbf{0}$. $\mathbb{Z}$-grammars of dimension d are also known as *valence grammars over* $\mathbb{Z}^d$ [21].

For our purposes it suffices to assume a unary encoding of the $\mathbb{Z}^d$-vectors (effects) occurring in $\mathbb{Z}$-VASS and $\mathbb{Z}$-grammars. However, this is not a restriction: Counter updates with n-bit binary encoded numbers can be easily simulated with unary encodings at the expense of dn many fresh counters (see the full version [5]).

Conversion results. The following is our first main theorem:

Theorem 1. *RBCA can be converted into* $\mathbb{Z}$-*VASS in logarithmic space. PRBCA can be converted into* $\mathbb{Z}$-*grammars in logarithmic space.*

By *convert*, we mean a translation that preserves the accepted (resp. generated) language. There are several machine models that are equivalent (in terms of accepted languages) to RBCA. With Theorem 1, we provide the last missing translation:

Corollary 1. *The following models can be converted into each other in logarithmic space: (i) RBCA, (ii)* $\mathbb{Z}$-*VASS, (iii) Parikh automata with* $\exists PA$ *acceptance, and (iv) Parikh automata with semilinear acceptance.*

Roughly speaking, a Parikh automaton is a machine with counters that can only be incremented. Then, a run is accepting if the final counter values belong to some semilinear set. Parikh automata were introduced by Klaedtke and Rueß [41], where the acceptance condition is specified using a semilinear representation (with base and period vectors), yielding (iv) above. As done, e.g., in [33], one could also specify it using an existential Presburger formula (briefly $\exists PA$), yielding the model in (iii) above. Theorem 1 proves (i)$\Rightarrow$(ii), whereas (ii)$\Rightarrow$(i) is easy (a clever and very efficient translation is given in [40, Theorem 4.5]). Moreover, (ii)$\Rightarrow$(iii) and (ii)$\Rightarrow$(iv) are clear as well. For (iii)$\Rightarrow$(ii), one can proceed as in [30, Prop. V.1], and (iv)$\Rightarrow$(ii) is also simple.

Unboundedness predicates. We shall use Theorem 1 to prove our second main theorem, which involves unboundedness predicates as introduced in [15]. In [15], unboundedness predicates can be one-dimensional or multi-dimensional, but in this work, we only consider one-dimensional unboundedness predicates.

Let Σ be an alphabet. A *(language) predicate* is a set of languages over Σ. If $\mathfrak{p}$ is a predicate and $L \subseteq \Sigma^*$ is a language, then we write $\mathfrak{p}(L)$ to denote that $\mathfrak{p}$ holds for the language L (i.e. $L \in \mathfrak{p}$). A predicate $\mathfrak{p}$ is called a *(one-dimensional) unboundedness predicate* if the following conditions are met for all $K, L \subseteq \Sigma^*$:

(U1) If $\mathfrak{p}(K)$ and $K \subseteq L$, then $\mathfrak{p}(L)$.   (U3) If $\mathfrak{p}(K \cdot L)$, then $\mathfrak{p}(K)$ or $\mathfrak{p}(L)$.
(U2) If $\mathfrak{p}(K \cup L)$, then $\mathfrak{p}(K)$ or $\mathfrak{p}(L)$.   (U4) $\mathfrak{p}(L)$ if and only if $\mathfrak{p}(F(L))$.

Here $F(L) = \{v \in \Sigma^* \mid \exists u, w \in \Sigma^* : uvw \in L\}$ is the set of *factors* of L (sometimes also called *infixes*). In particular, the last condition says that $\mathfrak{p}$ only depends on the set of factors occurring in a language.

For an unboundedness predicate $\mathfrak{p}$ and a class $\mathcal{C}$ of finitely represented languages (such as automata or grammars), let $\mathfrak{p}(\mathcal{C})$ denote the problem of deciding $\mathfrak{p}$ for a given language L from $\mathcal{C}$. Formally, $\mathfrak{p}(\mathcal{C})$ is the following decision problem:

Given A language L from $\mathcal{C}$.
Question Does $\mathfrak{p}(L)$ hold?

For example, $\mathfrak{p}(\mathsf{RBCA})$ is the problem of deciding $\mathfrak{p}$ for reversal-bounded multi-counter automata and $\mathfrak{p}(\mathsf{NFA})$ is the problem of deciding $\mathfrak{p}$ for NFAs. We mention that the axioms (U1)–(U4) are slightly stronger than the axioms used in [15], but the resulting set of decision problems is the same with either definition (since in [15], one always decides whether $\mathfrak{p}(F(L))$ holds). Thus, the statement of Theorem 2 is unaffected by which definition is used. See the full version [5] for details.

The following examples of (one-dimensional) unboundedness predicates for languages $L \subseteq \Sigma^*$ have already been established in [15]. We mention them here to give an intuition for the range of applications of our results:

Not being bounded Let $\mathfrak{p}_{\mathsf{notb}}(L)$ if and only if L is *not* a bounded language.
Non-emptiness Let $\mathfrak{p}_{\neq\emptyset}(L)$ if and only if $L \neq \emptyset$.
Infinity Let $\mathfrak{p}_\infty(L)$ if and only if L is infinite.
Factor-universality Let $\mathfrak{p}_{\mathsf{funi}}(L)$ if and only if $\Sigma^* \subseteq F(L)$.

It is not difficult to prove that these are unboundedness predicates, but proofs can be found in [15]. The following is our second main theorem:

Theorem 2. *Let $\mathfrak{p}$ be a one-dimensional unboundedness predicate. There is an* NP *reduction from* $\mathfrak{p}(\mathsf{PRBCA})$ *to* $\mathfrak{p}(\mathsf{PDA})$. *Moreover, there is an* NP *reduction from* $\mathfrak{p}(\mathsf{RBCA})$ *to* $\mathfrak{p}(\mathsf{NFA})$.

Here, an NP *reduction* from problem $A \subseteq \Sigma^*$ to $B \subseteq \Sigma^*$ is a non-deterministic polynomial-time Turing machine such that for every input word $w \in \Sigma^*$, we have $w \in A$ iff there exists a run of the Turing machine producing a word in B.

Let us now see some applications of Theorem 2, see also Table 1. The following completeness results are all meant w.r.t. deterministic logspace reductions.

Corollary 2. *Boundedness for* PRBCA *and for* RBCA *is* coNP-*complete.*

For Corollary 2, we argue that deciding *non-boundedness* is NP-complete. To this end, we apply Theorem 2 to the predicate $\mathfrak{p}_{\mathsf{notb}}$ and obtain an NP upper bound, because boundedness for context-free languages is decidable in polynomial time [24]. The NP lower bound follows easily from NP-hardness of the non-emptiness problem for RBCA [28, Theorem 3] and thus PRBCA.

Corollary 3. *Finiteness for* PRBCA *and for* RBCA *is* coNP-*complete.*

We show Corollary 3 by proving that checking *infinity* is NP-complete. The upper bound follows from Theorem 2 via the predicate $\mathfrak{p}_\infty$. As above, NP-hardness is inherited from the non-emptiness problem for RBCA and PRBCA.

The results in Corollary 3 are, however, not new. They follow directly from the fact that for a given PRBCA (or RBCA), one can construct in polynomial time a formula in existential Presburger arithmetic (∃PA) for its Parikh image, as shown in [36] for RBCA and in [32] for PRBCA. It is a standard result about ∃PA that for each formula φ, there exists a bound B such that (i) B is at most exponential in the size of φ and (ii) φ defines an infinite set if and only if φ is satisfied for some vector with some entry above B. For example, this can be deduced from [53]. Therefore, one can easily construct a second ∃PA formula φ' such that φ defines an infinite set if and only if φ' is satisfiable.

Corollary 4. *Factor universality for* RBCA *is* PSPACE-*complete.*

Whether factor universality is decidable for RBCA was left as an open problem in [17, 18] (there under the term *infix density*). Corollary 4 follows from Theorem 2 using $\mathfrak{p}_{\mathsf{funi}}$, because factor universality for NFAs is PSPACE-complete: To decide if $\Sigma^* \subseteq F(R)$, for a regular language R, we can just compute an automaton for $F(R)$ and check inclusion in PSPACE. For the lower bound, one can reduce the PSPACE-complete universality problem for NFAs, since for $R \subseteq \Sigma^*$, the language $(R\#)^* \subseteq (\Sigma \cup \{\#\})^*$ is factor universal if only if $R = \Sigma^*$. Note that factor universality is known to be undecidable already for one-counter languages [18], and thus in particular for PRBCA. However, it is decidable for pushdown automata with a bounded number of reversals of the stack [18].

Beyond pushdowns. Theorem 2 raises the question of whether for any class $\mathcal{M}$ of machines, one can reduce any unboundedness predicates for $\mathcal{M}$ extended with reversal-bounded counters to the same predicate for just $\mathcal{M}$. This is not the case: For example, consider second-order pushdown automata, short 2-PDA. If we extend these by adding reversal-bounded counters, then we obtain 2-PRBCA. Then, the infinity problem is decidable for 2-PDA [34] (see [3, 4, 14, 31, 52, 56] for stronger results). However, the class of 2-PRBCA does not even have decidable emptiness, let alone decidable infinity. This is shown in [57, Proposition 7] (see [42, Theorem 4] for an alternative proof). Thus, infinity for 2-PRBCA cannot be reduced to infinity for 2-PDA.

Growth. Finally, we employ the methods of the proof of Theorem 2 to show a dichotomy of the growth behavior of languages accepted by RBCA. For an alphabet Σ, we denote by $\Sigma^{\leq m}$ the set of all words over Σ of length at most m. We say that a language $L \subseteq \Sigma^*$ has *polynomial growth*[2] if there is a polynomial $p(x)$ such that $|L \cap \Sigma^{\leq m}| \leq p(m)$ for all $m \geq 0$. Languages of polynomial growth are also called *sparse* or *poly-slender*. We say that L has *exponential growth* if there is a real number $r > 1$ such hat $|L \cap \Sigma^{\leq m}| \geq r^m$ for infinitely many m. Since a language of the form $w_1^* \cdots w_n^*$ clearly has polynomial growth, it is well-known that bounded languages have polynomial growth. We show that (a) within the PRBCA languages (and in particular within the RBCA languages), the converse

---

[2] In [24], polynomial and exponential growth are defined with Σ^m in place of $\Sigma^{\leq m}$, but this leads to equivalent notions, see the full version [5].

is true as well and (b) all other languages have exponential growth (in contrast to some models, such as 2-PDA [27], where this dichotomy does not hold):

Theorem 3. *Let L be a language accepted by a PRBCA. Then L has polynomial growth if and only if L is bounded. If L is not bounded, it has exponential growth.*

3   Translating reversal-bounded counters into $\mathbb{Z}$-counters

Reducing the number of reversals to one. In this section we prove Theorem 1, the conversion from RBCA to $\mathbb{Z}$-VASS. In [28, Lemma 1], it is claimed that given a (k,r)-RBCA, one can construct in time polynomial in k and r a $(k\lceil(r+1)/2\rceil,1)$-RBCA that accepts the same language. The reference [2] that they provide does include such a construction [2, proof of Theorem 5]. The construction in [2] is only a rough sketch and makes no claims about complexity, but by our reading of the construction, it keeps track of the reversals of each counter in the state, which would result in an exponential blow-up.

Instead, we proceed as follows. Consider a (k,r)-RBCA with counters $c_1, \ldots, c_k$. Without loss of generality, assume $r = 2m - 1$. We will construct an equivalent $(2k(r+1),1)$-RBCA. Looking at the behavior of a single counter c_i, we can decompose every r-reversal bounded run into subruns without reversals. We call these subruns *phases* and number them from 1 to at most $2m$. The odd (even) numbered phases are *positive* (*negative*), where c_i is only incremented (decremented). We replace c_i by m one-reversal counters $c_{i,1}, \ldots, c_{i,m}$, where $c_{i,j}$ records the increments on c_i during the positive phase $2j - 1$.

However, our machine needs to keep track of which counters are in which phase, in order to know which of the counters $c_{i,j}$ it currently has to use. We achieve this as follows: For each of the k counters c_i, we also have an additional set of $2m = r+1$ "phase counters" $p_{i,1}, \ldots, p_{i,2m}$ to store which phase we are in. This gives $km + k(r+1) \leq 2k(r+1)$ counters in total. We encode that counter c_i is in phase j by setting $p_{i,j}$ to 1 and setting $p_{i,j'}$ to 0 for each $j' \neq j$. Since we only ever increase the phase, the phase counters are one-reversal as well.

Using non-zero-tests, at any point, the automaton can nondeterministically guess and verify the current phase of each counter. This allows it to pick the correct counter $c_{i,j}$ for each instruction. When counter c_i is in a positive phase $2j - 1$, then increments and decrements on c_i are simulated as follows:

increment increment $c_{i,j}$

decrement go into the next (negative) phase $2j$; then non-deterministically pick some $\ell \in [1,j]$ and decrement $c_{i,\ell}$. We cannot simply decrement $c_{i,j}$ as we might have switched to phase j while c_i had a non-zero value and hence it is possible that c_i could be decremented further than just $c_{i,j}$ allows.

When counter c_i is in a negative phase $2j$, then we simulate increments and decrements as follows:

increment go into the next phase $2j + 1$ (unless $j = m$; then the machine blocks) and increment $c_{i,j+1}$.

decrement non-deterministically pick some $\ell \in [1, j]$ and decrement $c_{i,\ell}$.

Finally, to simulate a zero-test on c_i, we test all counters $c_{i,1}, \ldots, c_{i,m}$ for zero, while for the simulation of a non-zero-test on c_i we non-deterministically pick one of the counters $c_{i,1}, \ldots, c_{i,m}$ to test for non-zero.

Correctness can be easily verified by the following properties. If at some point c_i is in phase $2j - 1$ or $2j$ then (i) $\sum_{\ell=1}^{j} c_{i,\ell} = c_i$, (ii) the counters $c_{i,1}, \ldots, c_{i,j}$ have made at most one reversal, and (iii) the counters $c_{i,j+1}, \ldots, c_{i,m}$ have not been touched (in particular, they are zero). Furthermore, if c_i is in a positive phase $2j - 1$ then $c_{i,j}$ has made no reversal yet.

Note that this construction replaces every transition of the original system with $\mathcal{O}(r)$ new transitions (and states). Our construction therefore yields only a linear blowup in the size of the system (constant if r is fixed). See the full version [5] for the details of the construction.

From 1-reversal to $\mathbb{Z}$-counters. We now turn the $(k, 1)$-RBCA into a $\mathbb{Z}$-VASS. The difference between a 1-reversal-bounded counter and a $\mathbb{Z}$-counter is that (i) a non-negative counter should block if it is decremented on counter value 0, and (ii) a 1-reversal-bounded counter allows (non-)zero-tests. Observe that all zero-tests occur before the first increment or after the last decrement. All non-zero-tests occur between the first increment and the last decrement.

If the number k of counters is bounded, then the following simple solution works. The $\mathbb{Z}$-VASS stores the information which of the counters has not been incremented yet and which counters will not be incremented again in the future. This information suffices to simulate the counters faithfully (in terms of the properties (i) and (ii) above) and increases the state space by a factor of $2^k \cdot 2^k$. The latter information needs to be guessed (by the automaton) and is verified by means that all counters are zero in the end.

In the general case we introduce a variant of $\mathbb{Z}$-VASS that can guess polynomially many bits in the beginning and read them throughout the run. A d-dimensional $\mathbb{Z}$-VASS with guessing ($\mathbb{Z}$-VASSG) has almost the same format as a d-dimensional $\mathbb{Z}$-VASS, except that each transition additionally carries a propositional formula over some finite set of variables X. A word $w \in \Sigma^*$ is accepted by the $\mathbb{Z}$-VASSG if there exists an assignment $\nu \colon X \to \{0, 1\}$ and an accepting run $(q_0, \mathbf{0}) \xrightarrow{w} (q, \mathbf{0})$ for some $q \in F$ such that all formulas appearing throughout the run are satisfied by ν.

We have to eliminate zero- and non-zero-tests of the $(k, 1)$-RBCA. Whether a (non-)zero-test is successful depends on which phase a counter is currently in (and whether in the end, every counter is zero; but we assume that our acceptance condition ensures this). Each counter goes through at most 4 phases:

1. before the first increment,
2. the "increment phase",
3. the "decrement phase", and
4. after the last decrement.

Hence, every run can be decomposed into $4k$ (possibly empty) segments, in which no counter changes its phase. The idea is to guess the phase of each counter in each segment. Hence, we have propositional variables $\mathbf{p}_{i,j,\ell}$ for $i \in [1, 4k]$, $j \in [1, k]$, and $\ell \in [1, 4]$. Then $\mathbf{p}_{i,j,\ell}$ is true iff in segment i, counter j is in phase ℓ. We will have to check that the assignment is *admissible* for each counter, meaning that the sequence of phases for each counter adheres to the order described above.

We modify the machine as follows. In its state, it keeps a number $i \in [1, 4k]$ which holds the current segment. At the beginning of the run, the machine checks that the assignment ν is admissible using a propositional formula: It checks that (i) for each segment i and each counter j there exists exactly one phase ℓ so that $\mathbf{p}_{i,j,\ell}$ is true, and (ii) the order of phases above is obeyed. Then, for every operation on a counter, the machine checks that the operation is consistent with the current segment. Moreover, if the current operation warrants a change of the segment, then the segment counter i is incremented. For example, if a counter in phase 1 is incremented, it switches to phase 2 and the segment counter is incremented; or, if a counter in phase 3 is tested for zero, it switches to phase 4 and the segment counter is incremented.

With these modifications, we can zero-test by checking variables corresponding to the current segment: A zero-test can only succeed in phase 1 and 4. Similarly, for a non-zero-test, we can check if the counter is in phase 2 or 3.

Turning a $\mathbb{Z}$-VASSG into a $\mathbb{Z}$-VASS. To handle the general case mentioned above, we need to show how to convert $\mathbb{Z}$-VASSG into ordinary $\mathbb{Z}$-VASS. In a preparatory step, we ensure that each formula is a literal. A transition labeled by a formula φ is replaced by a series-parallel graph: After bringing φ in negation normal form by pushing negations inwards, we can replace conjunctions by a series composition and disjunctions by a parallel composition (non-determinism).

The $\mathbb{Z}$-VASS works as follows. In addition to the original counters of the $\mathbb{Z}$-VASSG, it has for each variable $\mathbf{x} \in X$ two additional counters: $\mathbf{x}^+$ and $\mathbf{x}^-$. Here, $\mathbf{x}^+$ ($\mathbf{x}^-$) counts how many times $\mathbf{x}$ is read with a positive (negative) assignment. By making sure that either $\mathbf{x}^+ = 0$ or $\mathbf{x}^- = 0$ in the end, we guarantee that we always read the same value of $\mathbf{x}$.

Thus, in order to check a literal, our $\mathbb{Z}$-VASS increments the corresponding counter. In the end, before reaching a final state, it goes through each variable $\mathbf{x} \in X$ and either enters a loop decrementing $\mathbf{x}^+$ or a loop decrementing $\mathbf{x}^-$. Then, it can reach the zero vector only if all variable checks had been consistent.

From PRBCA to $\mathbb{Z}$-grammars. It remains to convert in logspace an (r, k)-PRBCA into an equivalent $\mathbb{Z}$-grammar. Just as for converting an RBCA into a $\mathbb{Z}$-VASS, one can convert a PRBCA into an equivalent $\mathbb{Z}$-*PVASS* (pushdown vector addition system with $\mathbb{Z}$-counters). Afterwards, one applies the classical transformation from pushdown automata to context-free grammars (a.k.a. triple construction), cf. [1, Lemma 2.26]: We introduce for every state pair (p, q) a nonterminal $X_{p,q}$, deriving all words which are read between p to q (starting and ending with empty stacks). For example, we introduce productions $X_{p,q} \rightarrow a X_{p',q'} b$ for all push transitions (p, a, γ, p') and pop transitions $(q', b, \bar{\gamma}, q)$. The counter effects of transitions in the $\mathbb{Z}$-PVASS (vectors in $\mathbb{Z}^k$) are translated into effects of the productions, e.g. the effect of the production $X_{p,q} \to aX_{p',q'}b$ above is the sum of the effects of the corresponding push- and pop-transition.

4   Deciding unboundedness predicates

Proof overview. In this section, we prove Theorem 2. Let us begin with a sketch. Our task is to take a PRBCA $\mathcal{A}$ and non-deterministically compute a PDA $\mathcal{A}'$ so that $L(\mathcal{A})$ satisfies $\mathfrak{p}$ if and only if some of the outcomes for $\mathcal{A}'$ satisfy $\mathfrak{p}$. It will be clear from the construction that if the input was an RBCA, then the resulting PDA will be an NFA. Using Theorem 1 we will phrase the main part of the reduction in terms of $\mathbb{Z}$-grammars, meaning we take a $\mathbb{Z}$-grammar G as input and non-deterministically compute context-free grammars G'.

The idea of the reduction is to identify a set of productions in G that, in some appropriate sense, can be canceled (regarding the integer counter values) by a collection of other productions. Then, G' is obtained by only using a set of productions that can be canceled. Moreover, these productions are used regardless of what counter updates they perform. Then, to show the correctness, we argue in two directions: First, we show that any word derivable by G' occurs as a factor of $L(G)$. Essentially, this is because each production used in G' can be canceled by adding more productions in G, thus yielding a complete derivation of G. Thus, we have that $L(G') \subseteq F(L(G))$, which by the axioms of unboundedness predicates means that $\mathfrak{p}(L(G'))$ implies $\mathfrak{p}(L(G))$. Second, we show that $L(G)$ is a finite union of products (i.e. concatenations) $P_i = L_1 \cdot L_2 \cdots L_k$ such that each L_i is either finite or included in $L(G')$ for some G' among all non-deterministic outcomes. Again, by the axioms of unboundedness predicates, this means that if $\mathfrak{p}(L(G))$, then $\mathfrak{p}(L(G'))$ must hold for some G'.

Unboundedness predicates and finite languages. Before we start with the proof, let us observe that we may assume that our unboundedness predicate is only satisfied for infinite sets. First, suppose $\mathfrak{p}$ is satisfied for $\{\varepsilon\}$. This implies that $\mathfrak{p} = \mathfrak{p}_{\neq\emptyset}$ and hence we can just decide whether $\mathfrak{p}(L)$ by deciding whether $L \neq \emptyset$, which can be done in NP [32]. From now on, suppose that $\mathfrak{p}$ is not satisfied for $\{\varepsilon\}$. Consider the alphabet $\Sigma_1 := \{a \in \Sigma \mid \mathfrak{p}(\{a\})\}$. Now observe that if $K \subseteq \Sigma^*$ is finite, then by the axioms of unboundedness predicates, we have $\mathfrak{p}(K)$ if and only if some letter from Σ_1 appears in K. Thus, if $L \subseteq (\Sigma \backslash \Sigma_1)^*$, then $\mathfrak{p}(L)$ can only hold if L is infinite. This motivates the following definition. Given a language $L \subseteq \Sigma^*$, we define

$$L_0 = L \cap (\Sigma \backslash \Sigma_1)^*, \quad L_1 = L \cap \Sigma^* \Sigma_1 \Sigma^*.$$

Then, $\mathfrak{p}(L)$ if and only if $\mathfrak{p}(L_0)$ or $\mathfrak{p}(L_1)$. Moreover, $\mathfrak{p}(L_1)$ is equivalent to $L_1 \neq \emptyset$.

Therefore, our reduction proceeds as follows. We construct (P)RBCA for L_0 and for L_1. This can be done in logspace, because intersections with regular languages can be done with a simple product construction. Then, we check in NP whether $L_1 \neq \emptyset$. If yes, then we return "unbounded". If no, we regard $\mathfrak{p}$ as an unboundedness predicate on languages over $\Sigma \setminus \Sigma_1$ with the additional property that $\mathfrak{p}$ is only satisfied for infinite languages. Thus, it suffices to prove Theorem 2 in the case that $\mathfrak{p}$ is only satisfied for infinite sets.

Pumps and cancelation. In order to define our notion of cancelable productions, we need some terminology. We will need to argue about derivation trees for $\mathbb{Z}$-grammars. For any alphabet Γ and $d \in \mathbb{N}$, let $\mathcal{T}_{\Gamma,d}$ be the set of all finite trees where every node is labeled by both (i) a letter from Γ and (ii) a vector from $\mathbb{Z}^d$. Suppose $G = (N, \Sigma, P, S)$ is a d-dimensional $\mathbb{Z}$-grammar. For a production $p = (A \rightarrow u, \boldsymbol{v})$, we write $\varphi(p) := \boldsymbol{v}$ for its associated counter effect. To each derivation in G, we associate a derivation tree from $\mathcal{T}_{N \cup \Sigma, d}$ as for context-free grammars. The only difference is that whenever we apply a production $(A \rightarrow u, \boldsymbol{v})$, then the node corresponding to the rewritten A is also labeled with $\boldsymbol{v}$. As in context-free grammars, the leaf nodes carry terminal letters; their vector label is just $\boldsymbol{0} \in \mathbb{Z}^d$.

We extend the map φ to both vectors in $\mathbb{N}^P$ and to derivation trees. If $\boldsymbol{u} \in \mathbb{N}^P$, then $\varphi(\boldsymbol{u}) = \sum_{p \in P} \varphi(p) \cdot \boldsymbol{u}[p]$. Similarly, if τ is a derivation tree, then $\varphi(\tau) \in \mathbb{Z}^d$ is the sum of all labels from $\mathbb{Z}^d$. A derivation tree τ for a derivation $A \stackrel{*}{\Rightarrow} u$ is called *complete* if $A = S$, $u \in \Sigma^*$ and $\varphi(\tau) = \boldsymbol{0}$. In other words, τ derives a terminal word and the total counter effect of the derivation is zero. For such a complete derivation, we also write $\mathsf{yield}(\tau)$ for the word u. A derivation tree τ is called a *pump* if it is the derivation tree of a derivation of the form $A \stackrel{*}{\Rightarrow} uAv$ for some $u, v \in \Sigma^*$ and $A \in N$. A subset $M \subseteq N$ of the non-terminals is called *realizable* if there exists a complete derivation of G that contains all non-terminals in M and no non-terminals outside of M.

A production p in P is called M-*cancelable* if there exist pumps $\tau_1, \ldots, \tau_k$ (for some $k \in \mathbb{N}$) such that (i) p occurs in some τ_i and (ii) $\varphi(\tau_1) + \cdots + \varphi(\tau_k) = \boldsymbol{0}$, i.e. the total counter effect of $\tau_1, \ldots, \tau_k$ is zero and (iii) all productions in $\tau_1, \ldots, \tau_k$ only use non-terminals from M. We say that a subset $Q \subseteq P$ is M-*cancelable* if all productions in Q are M-cancelable.

The reduction. Using the notions of M-cancelable productions, we are ready to describe how the context-free grammars are constructed. Suppose that M is realizable, that $Q \subseteq P$ is M-cancelable, and that $A \in M$. Consider the language

$$L_{A,Q} = \{u, v \in \Sigma^* \mid \exists \text{ derivation } A \stackrel{*}{\Rightarrow}_Q uAv\}.$$

Thus $L_{A,Q}$ consists of all words u and v appearing in derivations (whose counter values are not necessarily zero) of the form $A \stackrel{*}{\Rightarrow} uAv$, if we only use M-cancelable productions. The $L_{A,Q}$ will be the languages $L(G')$ mentioned above.

It is an easy observation that we can, given G and a subset $Q \subseteq P$, construct a context-free grammar for $L_{A,Q}$:

Lemma 1. *Given a $\mathbb{Z}$-grammar G, a non-terminal A, and a subset $Q \subseteq P$, we can construct in logspace a context-free grammar for $L_{A,Q}$. Moreover, if G is left-linear, then the construction yields an NFA for $L_{A,Q}$.*

We provide details in the full version [5]. Now, our reduction works as follows:

1. Guess a subset $M \subseteq N$ and an $A \in M$; verify that M is realizable.
2. Guess a subset $Q \subseteq P$; verify that Q is M-cancelable.
3. Compute a context-free grammar for $L_{A,Q}$.

Here, we need to show that steps 1 and 2 can be done in NP:

Lemma 2. *Given a subset $M \subseteq N$, we can check in* NP *whether M is realizable. Moreover, given $M \subseteq N$ and $p \in P$, we can check in* NP *if p is M-cancelable.*

Both can be done using the fact that for a given context-free grammar, one can construct a Parikh-equivalent existential Presburger formula [55] and the fact that satisfiability of existential Presburger formulas is in NP. See the full version [5] for details. This completes the description of our reduction. Therefore, it remains to show correctness of the reduction. In other words, to prove:

Proposition 1. *We have $\mathfrak{p}(L(G))$ if and only if $\mathfrak{p}(L_{A,Q})$ for some subset $Q \subseteq P$ such that there is a realizable $M \subseteq N$ with $A \in M$ and Q being M-cancelable.*

Proposition 1 will be shown in two lemmas:

Lemma 3. *If M is realizable and Q is M-cancelable, then $L_{A,Q} \subseteq F(L(G))$ for every $A \in M$.*

Lemma 4. *$L(G)$ is included in a finite union of sets of the form $K_1 \cdot K_2 \cdots K_m$, where each K_i is either finite or a set $L_{A,Q}$, where Q is M-cancelable for some realizable $M \subseteq N$, and $A \in M$.*

Let us see why Proposition 1 follows from Lemmas 3 and 4.

Proof (Proposition 1). We begin with the "if" direction. Thus, suppose $\mathfrak{p}(L_{A,Q})$ for A and Q as described. Then by Lemma 3 and the first and fourth axioms of unboundedness predicates, this implies $\mathfrak{p}(L(G))$.

For the "only if" direction, suppose $\mathfrak{p}(L(G))$. By the first axiom of unboundedness predicates, $\mathfrak{p}$ must hold for the finite union provided by Lemma 4. By the second axiom, this implies that $\mathfrak{p}(K_1 \cdots K_m)$ for a finite product $K_1 \cdots K_m$ as in Lemma 4. Moreover, by the third axiom, this implies that $\mathfrak{p}(K_i)$ for some $i \in \{1, \ldots, m\}$. If K_i is finite, then by assumption, $\mathfrak{p}(K_i)$ does not hold. Therefore, we must have $\mathfrak{p}(K_i)$ for some $K_i = L_{A,Q}$, as required.   □

Flows. It remains to prove Lemmas 3 and 4. We begin with Lemma 3 and for this we need some more terminology. Let Σ be an alphabet. By $\Psi \colon \Sigma^* \to \mathbb{N}^\Sigma$, we denote the *Parikh map*, which is defined as $\Psi(w)(a) = |w|_a$ for $w \in \Sigma^*$ and $a \in \Sigma$. In other words, $\Psi(w)(a)$ is the number of occurrences of a in $w \in \Sigma^*$. If $\Gamma \subseteq \Sigma$ is a subset, then $\pi_\Gamma \colon \Sigma^* \to \Gamma^*$ is the homomorphism with $\pi_\Gamma(a) = \varepsilon$ for $a \in \Sigma \setminus \Gamma$ and $\pi_\Gamma(a) = a$ for $a \in \Gamma$. We also call π_Γ the *projection to Γ*.

Suppose we have a $\mathbb{Z}$-grammar $G = (N, \Sigma, P, S)$ with non-terminals N and productions P. For a derivation tree τ, we write $\Psi(\tau)$ for the vector in $\mathbb{N}^P$ that counts how many times each production appears in τ. We introduce a map ∂, which counts how many non-terminals each production consumes and produces. Formally, $\partial\colon \mathbb{N}^P \to \mathbb{Z}^N$ is the monoid homomorphism that sends the production $p = A \to w$ to the vector $\partial(p) = -A + \Psi(\pi_N(w))$. Here, $-A \in \mathbb{Z}^N$ denotes the vector with -1 at the position of A and 0 everywhere else. A vector $\boldsymbol{u} \in \mathbb{N}^P$ is a *flow* if $\partial(\boldsymbol{u}) = \boldsymbol{0}$. Observe that a derivation tree τ is a pump if and only if $\Psi(\tau)$ is a flow. In this case, we also call the vector $\boldsymbol{u} \in \mathbb{N}^P$ with $\boldsymbol{u} = \Psi(\tau)$ a *pump*.

The following lemma will provide an easy way to construct derivations. It is a well-known result by Esparza [19, Theorem 3.1], and has since been exploited in several results on context-free grammars. Our formulation is slightly weaker than Esparza's. However, it is enough for our purposes and admits a simple proof, which is inspired by a proof of Kufleitner [44].

Lemma 5. *Let $\boldsymbol{f} \in \mathbb{N}^P$. Then $\boldsymbol{f}$ is a flow if and only if it is a sum of pumps.*

Proof. The "if" direction is trivial, because every pump is clearly a flow. Conversely, suppose $\boldsymbol{f} \in \mathbb{N}^P$ is a flow. We can clearly write $\boldsymbol{f} = \Psi(\tau_1) + \cdots + \Psi(\tau_n)$, where $\tau_1, \ldots, \tau_n$ are derivation trees: We can just view each production in $\boldsymbol{f}$ as its own derivation tree. Now suppose that we have $\boldsymbol{f} = \Psi(\tau_1) + \cdots + \Psi(\tau_n)$ so that n is minimal. We claim that then, each τ_i is a pump, proving the lemma.

Suppose not, then without loss of generality, τ_1 is not a pump. Since τ_1 is a derivation, this means $\Psi(\tau_1)$ cannot be a flow and thus there must be a non-terminal A with $\partial(\tau_1)(A) \neq 0$.

Let us first assume that $\partial(\tau_1)(A) > 0$. This means there is a non-terminal A occurring at a leaf of τ_1 such that A is not the start symbol of τ_1. Since $\boldsymbol{f} = \Psi(\tau_1) + \cdots + \Psi(\tau_n)$ is a flow, we must have $\partial(\Psi(\tau_2) + \cdots + \Psi(\tau_n))(A) < 0$. This, in turn, is only possible if some τ_j has A as its start symbol. We can therefore merge τ_1 and τ_j by replacing τ_1's A-labelled leaf by the new subtree τ_j. We obtain a new collection of $n - 1$ trees whose Parikh image is $\boldsymbol{f}$, in contradiction to the choice of n. If $\partial(\tau_1)(A) < 0$, then there must be a τ_j with $\partial(\tau_j)(A) > 0$ and thus we can insert τ_1 below τ_j, reaching a similar contradiction. □

Constructing derivations. Using flows, we can now prove Lemma 3.

Proof. Suppose there is a derivation $\tau\colon A \Rightarrow_Q uAv$ with $A \in M$ and $u, v \in \Sigma^*$. We have to show that both u and v occur in some word $w \in L(G)$. Furthermore, if G is in Chomsky normal form, we can choose w such that $|w|$ is linear in $|u|$ and $|v|$. Our goal is to construct a derivation of G in which we find u and v as factors. We could obtain a derivation tree by inserting τ into some derivation tree for G (at some occurrence of A), but this might yield non-zero counter values. Therefore, we will use the fact that Q is M-cancelable to find other pumps that can be inserted as well in order to bring the counter back to zero.

Since $M \subseteq N$ is realizable, there exists a complete derivation τ_0 that derives some word $w_0 \in L(G)$ and uses precisely the non-terminals in M. Since $Q \subseteq P$ is M-cancelable, we know that for each production $p \in Q$, there exist pumps $\tau_1, \ldots, \tau_k$ such that (i) p occurs in some τ_i, (ii) $\varphi(\tau_1) + \cdots + \varphi(\tau_k) = \boldsymbol{0}$ and

(iii) all productions in $\tau_1, \ldots, \tau_k$ only use non-terminals in M. This allows us to define $f_p := \Psi(\tau_1) + \cdots + \Psi(\tau_k)$. Observe that f_p contains only productions with non-terminals from M, we have $f_p[p] > 0$, and $\varphi(f_p) = 0$. We can use the flows f_p to find the desired canceling pumps. Since by Lemma 5, every flow can be decomposed into a sum of pumps, it suffices to construct a particular flow. Specifically, we look for a flow $f_\tau \in \mathbb{N}^P$ such that:

1. any production p with $f_\tau[p] > 0$ uses only non-terminals from M, and
2. $\varphi(f_\tau + \Psi(\tau)) = 0$.

The first condition ensures that all the resulting pumps can be inserted into τ_0. The second condition ensures that the resulting total counter values will be zero. We claim that with

$$f_\tau = \left(\sum_{p \in Q} \Psi(\tau)[p] \cdot f_p \right) - \Psi(\tau), \tag{1}$$

we achieve these conditions. First, observe that $f_\tau \in \mathbb{N}^P$: We have

$$f_\tau[q] \;\geq\; \Psi(\tau)[q] \cdot f_q[q] - \Psi(\tau)[q] \;=\; \Psi(\tau)[q] \cdot (f_q[q] - 1)$$

which is at least zero as $f_q[q]$ must be non-zero by definition. Second, note that f_τ is indeed a flow, because it is a $\mathbb{Z}$-linear combination of flows. Moreover, all productions appearing in f_τ also appear in f_p for some $p \in Q$ or in τ, meaning that all non-terminals must belong to M. Finally, the total counter effect of $f_\tau + \Psi(\tau)$ is zero as $f_\tau + \Psi(\tau) = \sum_{p \in Q} \Psi(\tau)[p] \cdot f_p$ is a sum of flows each with total counter effect zero.

Now, since f_τ is a flow, Lemma 5 tells us that there are pumps $\tau_1', \ldots, \tau_m'$ such that $f_\tau = \Psi(\tau_1') + \cdots + \Psi(\tau_m')$. Therefore, inserting τ and $\tau_1', \ldots, \tau_m'$ into τ_0 must yield a derivation of a word that has both u and v as factors and also has counter value

$$\underbrace{\varphi(\tau_0)}_{=0} + \underbrace{\varphi(\tau) + \varphi(\tau_1') + \cdots \varphi(\tau_m')}_{=\varphi(\tau) + \varphi(f_\tau) = 0} = 0.$$

Thus, we have a complete derivation of G. Hence $L_{A,Q} \subseteq F(L(G))$. □

Decomposition into finite union. It remains to prove Lemma 4. For the decomposition, we show that there exists a finite set D_0 of complete derivations such that all complete derivations of G can be obtained from some derivation in D_0 and then inserting pumps that produce words in $L_{A,Q}$, for some appropriate A and Q. Here, it is key that the set D_0 of "base derivations" is finite. Showing this for context-free grammars would just require a simple "unpumping" argument based on the pigeonhole principle as in Parikh's theorem [51]. However, in the case of $\mathbb{Z}$-grammars, where D_0 should only contain derivations that have counter value zero, this is not obvious. To achieve this, we employ a well-quasi ordering on (labeled) trees. Recall that a *quasi ordering* is a reflexive and transitive ordering. For a quasi ordering $(X, \leq)$ and a subset $Y \subseteq X$, we write $Y \uparrow$ for the set $\{x \in X \mid \exists y \in Y : y \leq x\}$. We say that $(X, \leq)$ is a *well-quasi ordering* (WQO) if every non-empty subset $Y \subseteq X$ has a finite subset $Y_0 \subseteq Y$ such that $Y \subseteq Y_0 \uparrow$.

We define an ordering on all trees in $\mathcal{T}_{N \cup \Sigma, d}$. A tree s is a *subtree* of t if there exists a node x in t such that s consists of all nodes of t that are descendants of x. If $\tau_1, \ldots, \tau_n$ are trees, then we denote by $r[\tau_1, \ldots, \tau_n]$ the tree with a root node r and the subtrees $\tau_1, \ldots, \tau_n$ directly under the root. Now let $\tau = (A, \boldsymbol{u})[\tau_1, \ldots, \tau_n]$ and $\tau' = (B, \boldsymbol{v})[\sigma_1, \ldots, \sigma_m]$ be trees in $\mathcal{T}_{N \cup \Sigma, d}$. We define the ordering $\preceq$ as follows. If $n = 0$ (i.e. τ consists of only one node), then we have $\tau \preceq \tau'$ if and only if $A = B$ and $m = 0$. If $n \geq 1$, then we define inductively:

$$\tau \preceq \tau' \quad \Longleftrightarrow \quad A = B \text{ and } \exists \text{ subtree } \tau'' = (A, \boldsymbol{u}')[\tau_1', \ldots, \tau_n'] \text{ of } \tau'$$
$$\text{with } \tau_i \preceq \tau_i' \text{ for } i = 1, \ldots, n$$

Based on $\preceq$, we define as slight refinement: We write $\tau \sqsubseteq \tau'$ if and only if $\tau \preceq \tau'$ and the set of non-terminals appearing in τ is the same as in τ'.

Lemma 6. $(\mathcal{T}_{N \cup \Sigma, d}, \sqsubseteq)$ *is a WQO.*

Proof. In [47, Lemma 3.3], it was shown that $\preceq$ is a WQO. Then $\sqsubseteq$ is the product of equality on a finite set, which is a WQO, and the WQO $\preceq$. $\square$

Lemma 6 allows us to decompose $L(G)$ into a finite union: For each complete derivation τ of G, we define

$$L_\tau(G) = \{w \in \Sigma^* \mid \exists \text{ complete derivation } \tau' \text{ with } \tau \sqsubseteq \tau' \text{ and yield}(\tau') = w\}.$$

Lemma 7. *There exists a finite set $D_0 \subseteq \mathcal{T}_{N \cup \Sigma, d}$ of complete derivations of G such that $L(G) = \bigcup_{\tau \in D_0} L_\tau(G)$.*

Proof. Since $(\mathcal{T}_{N \cup \Sigma, d}, \sqsubseteq)$ is a WQO, the set $D \subseteq \mathcal{T}_{N \cup T, d}$ of all complete derivations of G has a finite subset D_0 with $D \subseteq D_0 \uparrow$. This implies the lemma. $\square$

Decomposition into finite product. In light of Lemma 7, it remains to be shown that for each tree τ, we can find a product $K_1 \cdot K_2 \cdots K_m$ of languages such that $L_\tau(G) \subseteq K_1 \cdot K_2 \cdots K_m$ and each K_i is either finite or is of the form $L_{A,Q}$. We construct the overapproximation of $L_\tau(G)$ inductively as follows. Let $M \subseteq N$ and $Q \subseteq P$ be subsets of the non-terminals and the productions, respectively. If τ has one node, labeled by $a \in \Sigma$, then we set $\text{App}_Q(\tau) := \{a\}$. Moreover, if $\tau = (A, \boldsymbol{u})[\tau_1, \ldots, \tau_n]$ for $A \in N$ and trees $\tau_1, \ldots, \tau_n$, then we set

$$\text{App}_Q(\tau) := L_{A,Q} \cdot \text{App}_Q(\tau_1) \cdot \text{App}_Q(\tau_2) \cdots \text{App}_Q(\tau_n) \cdot L_{A,Q}.$$

Finally, we set $\text{App}(\tau) := \text{App}_Q(\tau)$, where $Q \subseteq P$ is the set of all M-cancelable productions, where M is the set of all non-terminals appearing in τ. Now clearly, each $\text{App}(\tau)$ is a finite product $K_1 \cdot K_2 \cdots K_m$ as desired: This follows by induction on the size of τ. Thus, to prove Lemma 4, the following suffices:

Lemma 8. *For every complete derivation tree τ of G, we have $L_\tau(G) \subseteq \mathrm{App}(\tau)$.*

Proof. Suppose $w \in L_\tau(G)$ is derived using a complete derivation tree τ' with $\tau \sqsubseteq \tau'$. Then, the set of non-terminals appearing in τ must be the same as in τ'; we denote it by M. Let $Q \subseteq P$ be the set of all M-cancelable productions. Moreover, since $\tau \preceq \tau'$, we can observe that there exist pumps $\tau_1, \ldots, \tau_n$ with root non-terminals $A_1, \ldots, A_n$ and nodes $x_1, \ldots, x_n$ in τ such that τ' can be obtained from τ by replacing each node x_i by the pump τ_i.

Since both τ and τ' are complete derivations of G, each must have counter effect $\mathbf{0}$. Thus, $\varphi(\tau_1) + \cdots + \varphi(\tau_n) = \varphi(\tau') - \varphi(\tau) = \mathbf{0}$. Hence, the pumps $\tau_1, \ldots, \tau_n$ witness that the productions appearing in $\tau_1, \ldots, \tau_n$ are M-cancelable. Thus, the derivation corresponding to τ_i uses only productions in Q and thus τ_i corresponds to $A_i \overset{*}{\Rightarrow}_Q u_i A v_i$ for some u_i, v_i and we have $u_i, v_i \in L_{A,Q}$.   □

5   Growth

In this section, we prove Theorem 3. Since clearly, a bounded language has polynomial growth, it remains to be shown that if L is accepted by a PRBCA and L is not bounded, then it has exponential growth. For two languages $L_1, L_2 \subseteq \Sigma^*$, we write $L_1 \hookrightarrow_{\mathrm{lin}} L_2$ if there exists a constant $c \in \mathbb{N}$ such that for every word $w_1 \in L_1$, there exists $w_2 \in L_2$ with $|w_2| \leq c \cdot |w_1|$ and w_1 is a factor of w_2. It is not difficult to observe that for two languages $L_1, L_2 \subseteq \Sigma^*$, if $L_1 \hookrightarrow_{\mathrm{lin}} L_2$ and L_1 has exponential growth, then so does L_2.

In order to show Theorem 3, we need an adapted version of Lemma 3. A $\mathbb{Z}$-grammar is in *Chomsky normal form* if all productions are of the form $(A \to BC, \boldsymbol{v})$ or $(A \to a, \boldsymbol{v})$ with $A, B, C \in N$, $a \in \Sigma$, and $\boldsymbol{u}, \boldsymbol{v} \in \mathbb{Z}^k$. In other words, the context-free grammar obtained by forgetting all counter vectors is in Chomsky normal form. Fernau and Stiebe [21, Proposition 5.12] have shown that every $\mathbb{Z}$-grammar has an equivalent $\mathbb{Z}$-grammar in Chomsky normal form.

Lemma 9. *If $G = (N, \Sigma, P, S)$ is a $\mathbb{Z}$-grammar in Chomsky normal form, $M \subseteq N$ is realizable, $Q \subseteq P$ is M-cancelable, and $A \in M$, then $L_{A,Q} \hookrightarrow_{\mathrm{lin}} L(G)$.*

This is shown essentially the same way as Lemma 3. Let us now show that if a language L accepted by a PRBCA is not bounded, then it must have exponential growth. We have seen above that as a PRBCA language, L is generated by some $\mathbb{Z}$-grammar. As shown by Fernau and Stiebe [21, Proposition 5.12], this implies that $L = L(G)$ for some $\mathbb{Z}$-grammar G in Chomsky normal form. Since L is not bounded, Lemma 4 yields A and Q such that $L_{A,Q}$ is not a bounded language. It is well-known that any context-free language that is not bounded has exponential growth (this fact has apparently been independently discovered at least six times, see [24] for references). Thus, $L_{A,Q}$ has exponential growth. By Lemma 9, we have $L_{A,Q} \hookrightarrow_{\mathrm{lin}} L$ and thus L has exponential growth.

Acknowledgments We are grateful to Manfred Kufleitner for sharing the manuscript [44] before it was publicly available. It provides an alternative proof for constructing an existential Presburger formula for the Parikh image of a context-free grammar. The latter was also shown in [55], based on [19]. We use it in Lemma 5, which could also be derived from [19, Theorem 3.1]. However, we provide a simple direct proof of Lemma 5 inspired by Kufleitner's proof.

This work is funded by the European Union (ERC, FINABIS, 101077902). Views and opinions expressed are however those of the author(s) only and do not necessarily reflect those of the European Union or the European Research Council Executive Agency. Neither the European Union nor the granting authority can be held responsible for them.

References

[1] Alfred V. Aho and Jeffrey D. Ullman. *The theory of parsing, translation, and compiling. 1: Parsing.* Prentice-Hall, 1972. ISBN: 0139145567. URL: https://www.worldcat.org/oclc/310805937.

[2] Brenda S Baker and Ronald V Book. "Reversal-bounded multipushdown machines". In: *Journal of Computer and System Sciences* 8.3 (1974), pp. 315–332. DOI: 10.1016/S0022-0000(74)80027-9.

[3] David Barozzini, Lorenzo Clemente, Thomas Colcombet, and Pawel Parys. "Cost Automata, Safe Schemes, and Downward Closures". In: *47th International Colloquium on Automata, Languages, and Programming, ICALP 2020, July 8-11, 2020, Saarbrücken, Germany (Virtual Conference).* Ed. by Artur Czumaj, Anuj Dawar, and Emanuela Merelli. Vol. 168. LIPIcs. Schloss Dagstuhl - Leibniz-Zentrum für Informatik, 2020, 109:1–109:18. DOI: 10.4230/LIPIcs.ICALP.2020.109.

[4] David Barozzini, Pawel Parys, and Jan Wroblewski. "Unboundedness for Recursion Schemes: A Simpler Type System". In: *49th International Colloquium on Automata, Languages, and Programming, ICALP 2022, July 4-8, 2022, Paris, France.* Ed. by Mikolaj Bojanczyk, Emanuela Merelli, and David P. Woodruff. Vol. 229. LIPIcs. Schloss Dagstuhl - Leibniz-Zentrum für Informatik, 2022, 112:1–112:19. DOI: 10.4230/LIPIcs.ICALP.2022.112.

[5] Pascal Baumann, Flavio D'Alessandro, Moses Ganardi, Oscar Ibarra, Ian McQuillan, Lia Schütze, and Georg Zetzsche. *Unboundedness problems for machines with reversal-bounded counters.* 2023. DOI: 10.48550/ARXIV. 2301.10198. URL: https://arxiv.org/abs/2301.10198.

[6] Alin Bostan, Arnaud Carayol, Florent Koechlin, and Cyril Nicaud. "Weakly-Unambiguous Parikh Automata and Their Link to Holonomic Series". In: *47th International Colloquium on Automata, Languages, and Programming, ICALP 2020, July 8-11, 2020, Saarbrücken, Germany (Virtual Conference).* Vol. 168. LIPIcs. Schloss Dagstuhl - Leibniz-Zentrum für Informatik, 2020, 114:1–114:16. DOI: 10.4230/LIPIcs.ICALP.2020.114.

[7] Toby Cathcart Burn, Luke Ong, Steven J. Ramsay, and Dominik Wagner. "Initial Limit Datalog: a New Extensible Class of Decidable Constrained Horn Clauses". In: *36th Annual ACM/IEEE Symposium on Logic in Com-*

puter Science, LICS 2021, Rome, Italy, June 29 - July 2, 2021. IEEE, 2021, pp. 1–13. DOI: 10.1109/LICS52264.2021.9470527.

[8] Michaël Cadilhac, Alain Finkel, and Pierre McKenzie. "Affine Parikh automata". In: *RAIRO Theor. Informatics Appl.* 46.4 (2012), pp. 511–545. DOI: 10.1051/ita/2012013.

[9] Michaël Cadilhac, Alain Finkel, and Pierre McKenzie. "Bounded Parikh Automata". In: *Int. J. Found. Comput. Sci.* 23.8 (2012), pp. 1691–1710. DOI: 10.1142/S0129054112400709.

[10] Michaël Cadilhac, Andreas Krebs, and Pierre McKenzie. "The Algebraic Theory of Parikh Automata". In: *Theory Comput. Syst.* 62.5 (2018), pp. 1241–1268. DOI: 10.1007/s00224-017-9817-2.

[11] Arturo Carpi, Flavio D'Alessandro, Oscar H Ibarra, and Ian McQuillan. "Relationships between bounded languages, counter machines, finite-index grammars, ambiguity, and commutative regularity". In: *Theoretical Computer Science* 862 (2021), pp. 97–118. DOI: 10.1016/j.tcs.2020.10.006.

[12] Tat-hung Chan. "Pushdown Automata with Reversal-Bounded Counters". In: *J. Comput. Syst. Sci.* 37.3 (1988), pp. 269–291. DOI: 10.1016/0022-0000(88)90008-6.

[13] Lorenzo Clemente, Wojciech Czerwinski, Slawomir Lasota, and Charles Paperman. "Regular Separability of Parikh Automata". In: *44th International Colloquium on Automata, Languages, and Programming, ICALP 2017, July 10-14, 2017, Warsaw, Poland.* Vol. 80. LIPIcs. Schloss Dagstuhl - Leibniz-Zentrum für Informatik, 2017, 117:1–117:13. DOI: 10.4230/LIPIcs.ICALP.2017.117.

[14] Lorenzo Clemente, Pawel Parys, Sylvain Salvati, and Igor Walukiewicz. "The Diagonal Problem for Higher-Order Recursion Schemes is Decidable". In: *Proceedings of the 31st Annual ACM/IEEE Symposium on Logic in Computer Science, LICS '16, New York, NY, USA, July 5-8, 2016.* Ed. by Martin Grohe, Eric Koskinen, and Natarajan Shankar. ACM, 2016, pp. 96–105. DOI: 10.1145/2933575.2934527.

[15] Wojciech Czerwinski, Piotr Hofman, and Georg Zetzsche. "Unboundedness Problems for Languages of Vector Addition Systems". In: *45th International Colloquium on Automata, Languages, and Programming, ICALP 2018, July 9-13, 2018, Prague, Czech Republic.* Ed. by Ioannis Chatzigiannakis, Christos Kaklamanis, Dániel Marx, and Donald Sannella. Vol. 107. LIPIcs. Schloss Dagstuhl - Leibniz-Zentrum für Informatik, 2018, 119:1–119:15. DOI: 10.4230/LIPIcs.ICALP.2018.119.

[16] Flavio D'Alessandro and Benedetto Intrigila. "On the commutative equivalence of bounded context-free and regular languages: The semi-linear case". In: *Theor. Comput. Sci.* 572 (2015), pp. 1–24. DOI: 10.1016/j.tcs.2015.01.008. URL: https://doi.org/10.1016/j.tcs.2015.01.008.

[17] Joey Eremondi, Oscar H. Ibarra, and Ian McQuillan. "On the Density of Context-Free and Counter Languages". In: *Developments in Language Theory - 19th International Conference, DLT 2015, Liverpool, UK, July 27-30, 2015, Proceedings.* Ed. by Igor Potapov. Vol. 9168. Lecture Notes

in Computer Science. Springer, 2015, pp. 228–239. DOI: 10.1007/978-3-319-21500-6_18.

[18] Joey Eremondi, Oscar H. Ibarra, and Ian McQuillan. "On the Density of Context-Free and Counter Languages". In: *Int. J. Found. Comput. Sci.* 29.2 (2018), pp. 233–250. DOI: 10.1142/S0129054118400051.

[19] Javier Esparza. "Petri nets, commutative context-free grammars, and basic parallel processes". In: *Fundamenta Informaticae* 31.1 (1997), pp. 13–25.

[20] Javier Esparza, Pierre Ganty, and Rupak Majumdar. "A Perfect Model for Bounded Verification". In: *Proceedings of the 27th Annual IEEE Symposium on Logic in Computer Science, LICS 2012, Dubrovnik, Croatia, June 25-28, 2012.* IEEE Computer Society, 2012, pp. 285–294. DOI: 10.1109/LICS.2012.39.

[21] Henning Fernau and Ralf Stiebe. "Sequential grammars and automata with valences". In: *Theor. Comput. Sci.* 276.1-2 (2002), pp. 377–405. DOI: 10.1016/S0304-3975(01)00282-1.

[22] Emmanuel Filiot, Shibashis Guha, and Nicolas Mazzocchi. "Two-Way Parikh Automata". In: *39th IARCS Annual Conference on Foundations of Software Technology and Theoretical Computer Science, FSTTCS 2019, December 11-13, 2019, Bombay, India.* Vol. 150. LIPIcs. Schloss Dagstuhl - Leibniz-Zentrum für Informatik, 2019, 40:1–40:14. DOI: 10.4230/LIPIcs.FSTTCS.2019.40.

[23] Alain Finkel and Arnaud Sangnier. "Reversal-Bounded Counter Machines Revisited". In: *Mathematical Foundations of Computer Science 2008, 33rd International Symposium, MFCS 2008, Torun, Poland, August 25-29, 2008, Proceedings.* Ed. by Edward Ochmanski and Jerzy Tyszkiewicz. Vol. 5162. Lecture Notes in Computer Science. Springer, 2008, pp. 323–334. DOI: 10.1007/978-3-540-85238-4_26.

[24] Pawel Gawrychowski, Dalia Krieger, Narad Rampersad, and Jeffrey O. Shallit. "Finding the Growth Rate of a Regular or Context-Free Language in Polynomial Time". In: *Int. J. Found. Comput. Sci.* 21.4 (2010), pp. 597–618. DOI: 10.1142/S0129054110007441.

[25] Seymour Ginsburg and Edwin H Spanier. "Bounded ALGOL-like languages". In: *Transactions of the American Mathematical Society* 113.2 (1964), pp. 333–368.

[26] Sheila A. Greibach. "Remarks on Blind and Partially Blind One-Way Multicounter Machines". In: *Theor. Comput. Sci.* 7 (1978), pp. 311–324. DOI: 10.1016/0304-3975(78)90020-8.

[27] Rostislav Grigorchuk and A. Machì. "An example of an indexed language of intermediate growth". In: *Theoretical computer science* 215.1-2 (1999), pp. 325–327.

[28] Eitan M. Gurari and Oscar H. Ibarra. "The complexity of decision problems for finite-turn multicounter machines". In: *Journal of Computer and System Sciences* 22.2 (1981), pp. 220–229. ISSN: 0022-0000. DOI: https://doi.org/10.1016/0022-0000(81)90028-3.

[29]   Christoph Haase and Simon Halfon. "Integer Vector Addition Systems with States". In: *Reachability Problems - 8th International Workshop, RP 2014, Oxford, UK, September 22-24, 2014. Proceedings*. Ed. by Joël Ouaknine, Igor Potapov, and James Worrell. Vol. 8762. Lecture Notes in Computer Science. Springer, 2014, pp. 112–124. DOI: 10.1007/978-3-319-11439-2_9.

[30]   Christoph Haase and Georg Zetzsche. "Presburger arithmetic with stars, rational subsets of graph groups, and nested zero tests". In: *34th Annual ACM/IEEE Symposium on Logic in Computer Science, LICS 2019, Vancouver, BC, Canada, June 24-27, 2019*. IEEE, 2019, pp. 1–14. DOI: 10.1109/LICS.2019.8785850. URL: https://doi.org/10.1109/LICS.2019.8785850.

[31]   Matthew Hague, Jonathan Kochems, and C.-H. Luke Ong. "Unboundedness and downward closures of higher-order pushdown automata". In: *Proceedings of the 43rd Annual ACM SIGPLAN-SIGACT Symposium on Principles of Programming Languages, POPL 2016, St. Petersburg, FL, USA, January 20 - 22, 2016*. ACM, 2016, pp. 151–163. DOI: 10.1145/2837614.2837627.

[32]   Matthew Hague and Anthony Widjaja Lin. "Model Checking Recursive Programs with Numeric Data Types". In: *Computer Aided Verification - 23rd International Conference, CAV 2011, Snowbird, UT, USA, July 14-20, 2011. Proceedings*. Ed. by Ganesh Gopalakrishnan and Shaz Qadeer. Vol. 6806. Lecture Notes in Computer Science. Springer, 2011, pp. 743–759. DOI: 10.1007/978-3-642-22110-1_60.

[33]   Simon Halfon, Philippe Schnoebelen, and Georg Zetzsche. "Decidability, complexity, and expressiveness of first-order logic over the subword ordering". In: *32nd Annual ACM/IEEE Symposium on Logic in Computer Science, LICS 2017, Reykjavik, Iceland, June 20-23, 2017*. IEEE Computer Society, 2017, pp. 1–12. DOI: 10.1109/LICS.2017.8005141.

[34]   Takeshi Hayashi. "On Derivation Trees of Indexed Grammars—An Extension of the uvwxy-Theorem". In: *Publications of the Research Institute for Mathematical Sciences* 9.1 (1973), pp. 61–92. DOI: 10.2977/prims/1195192738.

[35]   John E. Hopcroft. "On the equivalence and containment problems for context-free languages". In: *Mathematical systems theory* 3.2 (1969), pp. 119–124.

[36]   Oscar H. Ibarra. "Reversal-Bounded Multicounter Machines and Their Decision Problems". In: *J. ACM* 25.1 (1978), pp. 116–133. DOI: 10.1145/322047.322058.

[37]   Oscar H. Ibarra and Bala Ravikumar. "On Sparseness, Ambiguity and other Decision Problems for Acceptors and Transducers". In: *STACS 86, 3rd Annual Symposium on Theoretical Aspects of Computer Science, Orsay, France, January 16-18, 1986, Proceedings*. Ed. by Burkhard Monien and Guy Vidal-Naquet. Vol. 210. Lecture Notes in Computer Science. Springer, 1986, pp. 171–179. DOI: 10.1007/3-540-16078-7_74.

[38] Oscar H. Ibarra and Shinnosuke Seki. "Characterizations of Bounded semi-linear Languages by One-Way and Two-Way Deterministic Machines". In: *Int. J. Found. Comput. Sci.* 23.6 (2012), pp. 1291–1306. DOI: 10.1142/S0129054112400539.

[39] Oscar H. Ibarra, Jianwen Su, Zhe Dang, Tevfik Bultan, and Richard A. Kemmerer. "Counter Machines and Verification Problems". In: *Theor. Comput. Sci.* 289.1 (2002), pp. 165–189. DOI: 10.1016/S0304-3975(01)00268-7.

[40] Matthias Jantzen and Alexy Kurganskyy. "Refining the hierarchy of blind multicounter languages and twist-closed trios". In: *Inf. Comput.* 185.2 (2003), pp. 159–181. DOI: 10.1016/S0890-5401(03)00087-7.

[41] Felix Klaedtke and Harald Rueß. "Monadic Second-Order Logics with Cardinalities". In: *Proceedings of ICALP 2003*. Ed. by Jos C. M. Baeten, Jan Karel Lenstra, Joachim Parrow, and Gerhard J. Woeginger. Berlin, Heidelberg: Springer, 2003, pp. 681–696.

[42] Naoki Kobayashi. "Inclusion between the frontier language of a non-deterministic recursive program scheme and the Dyck language is undecidable". In: *Theor. Comput. Sci.* 777 (2019), pp. 409–416. DOI: 10.1016/j.tcs.2018.09.035.

[43] S. Rao Kosaraju. "Decidability of Reachability in Vector Addition Systems (Preliminary Version)". In: *STOC 1982, May 5-7, 1982, San Francisco, California, USA*. 1982, pp. 267–281.

[44] Manfred Kufleitner. *Yet another proof of Parikh's Theorem.* Oct. 6, 2022. arXiv: 2210.02925.

[45] Dietrich Kuske and Georg Zetzsche. "Languages Ordered by the Subword Order". In: *Foundations of Software Science and Computation Structures - 22nd International Conference, FOSSACS 2019, Held as Part of the European Joint Conferences on Theory and Practice of Software, ETAPS 2019, Prague, Czech Republic, April 6-11, 2019, Proceedings*. Ed. by Mikolaj Bojanczyk and Alex Simpson. Vol. 11425. Lecture Notes in Computer Science. Springer, 2019, pp. 348–364. DOI: 10.1007/978-3-030-17127-8_20.

[46] Jean-Luc Lambert. "A Structure to Decide Reachability in Petri Nets". In: *Theor. Comput. Sci.* 99.1 (1992), pp. 79–104.

[47] Jérôme Leroux, M. Praveen, Philippe Schnoebelen, and Grégoire Sutre. "On Functions Weakly Computable by Pushdown Petri Nets and Related Systems". In: *CoRR* abs/1904.04090 (2019). arXiv: 1904.04090.

[48] Jérôme Leroux and Sylvain Schmitz. "Demystifying Reachability in Vector Addition Systems". In: *30th Annual ACM/IEEE Symposium on Logic in Computer Science, LICS 2015, Kyoto, Japan, July 6-10, 2015*. IEEE Computer Society, 2015, pp. 56–67. DOI: 10.1109/LICS.2015.16.

[49] Jérôme Leroux and Sylvain Schmitz. "Reachability in Vector Addition Systems is Primitive-Recursive in Fixed Dimension". In: *34th Annual ACM/IEEE Symposium on Logic in Computer Science, LICS 2019, Vancouver, BC, Canada, June 24-27, 2019*. IEEE, 2019, pp. 1–13. DOI: 10.1109/LICS.2019.8785796.

[50]   Ernst W. Mayr. "An Algorithm for the General Petri Net Reachability Problem". In: *STOC 1981, May 11-13, 1981, Milwaukee, Wisconsin, USA*. 1981, pp. 238–246.

[51]   Rohit J Parikh. "On context-free languages". In: *Journal of the ACM (JACM)* 13.4 (1966), pp. 570–581.

[52]   Pawel Parys. "The Complexity of the Diagonal Problem for Recursion Schemes". In: *37th IARCS Annual Conference on Foundations of Software Technology and Theoretical Computer Science, FSTTCS 2017, December 11-15, 2017, Kanpur, India*. Ed. by Satya V. Lokam and R. Ramanujam. Vol. 93. LIPIcs. Schloss Dagstuhl - Leibniz-Zentrum für Informatik, 2017, 45:1–45:14. DOI: 10.4230/LIPIcs.FSTTCS.2017.45.

[53]   Loic Pottier. "Minimal Solutions of Linear Diophantine Systems: Bounds and Algorithms". In: *Rewriting Techniques and Applications, 4th International Conference, RTA-91, Como, Italy, April 10-12, 1991, Proceedings*. Ed. by Ronald V. Book. Vol. 488. Lecture Notes in Computer Science. Springer, 1991, pp. 162–173. DOI: 10.1007/3-540-53904-2_94.

[54]   George S. Sacerdote and Richard L. Tenney. "The decidability of the reachability problem for vector addition systems (preliminary version)". In: *STOC 1977*. ACM. 1977, pp. 61–76.

[55]   Kumar Neeraj Verma, Helmut Seidl, and Thomas Schwentick. "On the Complexity of Equational Horn Clauses". In: *Automated Deduction - CADE-20, 20th International Conference on Automated Deduction, Tallinn, Estonia, July 22-27, 2005, Proceedings*. Ed. by Robert Nieuwenhuis. Vol. 3632. Lecture Notes in Computer Science. Springer, 2005, pp. 337–352. DOI: 10.1007/11532231_25.

[56]   Georg Zetzsche. "An Approach to Computing Downward Closures". In: *Automata, Languages, and Programming - 42nd International Colloquium, ICALP 2015, Kyoto, Japan, July 6-10, 2015, Proceedings, Part II*. Ed. by Magnús M. Halldórsson, Kazuo Iwama, Naoki Kobayashi, and Bettina Speckmann. Vol. 9135. Lecture Notes in Computer Science. Springer, 2015, pp. 440–451. DOI: 10.1007/978-3-662-47666-6_35.

[57]   Georg Zetzsche. "An approach to computing downward closures". In: *CoRR* abs/1503.01068 (2015). arXiv: 1503.01068.

[58]   Georg Zetzsche. "The Complexity of Downward Closure Comparisons". In: *43rd International Colloquium on Automata, Languages, and Programming, ICALP 2016, July 11-15, 2016, Rome, Italy*. Ed. by Ioannis Chatzigiannakis, Michael Mitzenmacher, Yuval Rabani, and Davide Sangiorgi. Vol. 55. LIPIcs. Schloss Dagstuhl - Leibniz-Zentrum für Informatik, 2016, 123:1–123:14. DOI: 10.4230/LIPIcs.ICALP.2016.123.

Reverse Bisimilarity vs. Forward Bisimilarity

Marco Bernardo[1]([⊠]) and Sabina Rossi[2]

[1] Università di Urbino, Urbino, Italy
marco.bernardo@uniurb.it
[2] Università Ca' Foscari di Venezia, Venice, Italy

Abstract. Reversibility is the capability of a system of undoing its own actions starting from the last performed one, in such a way that a past consistent state is reached. This is not trivial for concurrent systems, as the last performed action may not be uniquely identifiable. There are several approaches to address causality-consistent reversibility, some including a notion of forward-reverse bisimilarity. We introduce a minimal process calculus for reversible systems to investigate compositionality properties and equational characterizations of forward-reverse bisimilarity as well as of its two components, i.e., forward bisimilarity and reverse bisimilarity, so as to highlight their differences. The study is conducted not only in a nondeterministic setting, but also in a stochastic one where time reversibility and lumpability for Markov chains are exploited.

1 Introduction

Reversibility started to receive attention in computing several decades ago [15,3]. Landauer's principle states that any irreversible manipulation of information, such as bit erasure or computation path merging, must be accompanied by a corresponding entropy increase. Therefore, any reversible computation, in which no information is lost, may be potentially carried out without releasing any heat. Nowadays, *reversible computing* has many applications ranging from biochemical reaction modeling and parallel discrete-event simulation to robotics, control theory, fault tolerant systems, and concurrent program debugging.

In a reversible system, we can observe two directions of computation: a *forward* one, coinciding with the normal way of computing, and a *backward* one, along which the effects of the forward one are undone when needed in a *causally consistent* way, i.e., by returning to a past consistent state. The latter task is not easy to accomplish in a concurrent system, because the undo procedure necessarily starts from the last performed action and this may not be unique. The usually adopted strategy is that an action can be undone provided that all of its consequences, if any, have been undone beforehand.

In the process algebra literature, two approaches have been developed to reverse a computation based on keeping track of past actions: the dynamic one of [7] and the static one of [24]. The former yields RCCS, a variant of CCS [20] that uses stack-based memories attached to processes to record all the actions executed by those processes. In contrast, the latter proposes a general method, of which CCSK is a result, to reverse calculi, relying on the idea of retaining within the process syntax all executed actions and dynamic operators.

O. Kupferman and P. Sobocinski (Eds.): FoSSaCS 2023, LNCS 13992, pp. 265–284, 2023.
https://doi.org/10.1007/978-3-031-30829-1_13

In [24] *forward-reverse bisimilarity* is introduced too. Unlike standard bisimilarity [22,20], it is truly concurrent as it does not satisfy the expansion law of parallel composition into a choice among all possible action sequencings. The interleaving view can be restored by employing *back-and-forth bisimilarity* [8]. This is defined on computation paths instead of states, thus preserving not only causality but also history as backward moves have to occur along the path followed when going forward even in the presence of concurrency.

In this paper, we investigate compositionality properties and equational characterizations of forward-reverse bisimilarity as well as of its two components, i.e., forward bisimilarity and reverse bisimilarity, so as to highlight their differences. To this purpose, we introduce a minimal calculus including only the terminated process $\underline{0}$, the unary action prefix operator $a \,.\, \_$ where a stands for an action, and the binary alternative composition operator $\_ + \_$ also called choice. These operators are enough to compare the essential features of the three equivalences, in a neutral way with respect to interleaving view vs. true concurrency.

The paper is divided into two parts. In Section 2, we conduct our study on *nondeterministic* reversible processes, with the operational semantic rules defined in the style of [24] generating only forward transitions that are viewed as bidirectional, in lieu of a forward transition relation separated from a backward transition relation. In Section 3, we repeat our study on *stochastic* reversible processes, whose operational semantic rules in the style of [24] generate a single transition relation encompassing both forward transitions and backward transitions, by exploiting time reversibility [13] and lumpability [14] for Markov chains. In Section 4, we recap the differences between forward and reverse bisimilarities.

2   The Nondeterministic Case

In this section, we investigate forward bisimilarity, reverse bisimilarity, and forward-reverse bisimilarity over nondeterministic reversible processes. We start by introducing the syntax (Section 2.1) and the semantics (Section 2.2) for these processes through a minimal calculus, then we provide the definitions of the three equivalences (Section 2.3) and we study their congruence properties (Section 2.4) and equational characterizations (Section 2.5).

2.1   Syntax of Nondeterministic Reversible Processes

In the formalization of a process, we usually describe only its future behavior, hence the following syntax for sequential processes where $a \in A$:
$$P ::= \underline{0} \mid a \,.\, P \mid P + P$$
However, in order to support the definition of the semantics in the style of [24], we need to enrich the syntax above with information about the past, i.e., the actions that have already been executed. Due to the absence of a parallel composition operator, unlike [24] there is no need to add communication keys to executed actions. It thus suffices to mark them with some symbol, which we choose to be †. This yields the following syntax extended with information about the past:
$$P ::= \underline{0} \mid a \,.\, P \mid a^\dagger .\, P \mid P + P$$

We can syntactically characterize several classes of processes generated by the grammar above through suitable predicates. Firstly, we have *initial* processes, i.e., processes in which all the actions are unexecuted:

$$initial(\underline{0})$$
$$initial(a \,.\, P) \Longleftarrow initial(P)$$
$$initial(P_1 + P_2) \Longleftarrow initial(P_1) \wedge initial(P_2)$$

Secondly, we have *final* processes, i.e., processes in which all the actions along a single path have been executed:

$$final(\underline{0})$$
$$final(a^\dagger.\, P) \Longleftarrow final(P)$$
$$final(P_1 + P_2) \Longleftarrow (final(P_1) \wedge initial(P_2)) \vee$$
$$(initial(P_1) \wedge final(P_2))$$

Multiple paths arise only in the presence of alternative compositions. At each occurrence of +, only the subprocess chosen for execution advances, while the other one, although not selected, is kept as an initial subprocess within the overall process to support the definition of the semantics in the style of [24].

Thirdly, we have the processes that are *reachable* from an initial one, whose set we denote by $\mathbb{P}$:

$$reachable(\underline{0})$$
$$reachable(a \,.\, P) \Longleftarrow initial(P)$$
$$reachable(a^\dagger.\, P) \Longleftarrow reachable(P)$$
$$reachable(P_1 + P_2) \Longleftarrow (reachable(P_1) \wedge initial(P_2)) \vee$$
$$(initial(P_1) \wedge reachable(P_2))$$

It is worth noting that:

- $\underline{0}$ is the only process that is both initial and final as well as reachable.
- Any initial or final process is reachable too.
- $\mathbb{P}$ also contains processes that are neither initial nor final, like e.g. $a^\dagger.\, P$ with $initial(P)$ and $P \neq \underline{0}$.
- The relative positions of already executed actions and actions to be executed matter; in particular, an action of the former kind can never follow one of the latter kind. For instance, $a^\dagger.\, b \,.\, P \in \mathbb{P}$ if $initial(P)$ whereas $b \,.\, a^\dagger.\, P \notin \mathbb{P}$.

2.2   Semantics of Nondeterministic Reversible Processes

According to the approach of [24], dynamic operators such as action prefix and alternative composition have to be made static by the semantics, so as to retain within the syntax all the information needed to enable reversibility. For the sake of minimality, unlike [24] we do not generate two distinct transition relations – a forward one $\longrightarrow$ and a backward one $\rightsquigarrow$ – but a single transition relation, which we implicitly regard as being symmetric like in [8] to enforce the *loop property*: any executed action can be undone and any undone action can be redone.

In our setting, a backward transition from P' to P ($P' \overset{a}{\rightsquigarrow} P$) is subsumed by the corresponding forward transition t from P to P' ($P \overset{a}{\longrightarrow} P'$). As will become clear with the definition of behavioral equivalences in Section 2.3, like in [8] when going forward we view t as an *outgoing* transition of P, while when

$$\text{ACT}_f \ \frac{initial(P)}{a \,.\, P \xrightarrow{a} a^\dagger .\, P} \qquad\qquad \text{ACT}_p \ \frac{P \xrightarrow{b} P'}{a^\dagger .\, P \xrightarrow{b} a^\dagger .\, P'}$$

$$\text{CHO}_l \ \frac{P_1 \xrightarrow{a} P_1' \quad initial(P_2)}{P_1 + P_2 \xrightarrow{a} P_1' + P_2} \qquad \text{CHO}_r \ \frac{P_2 \xrightarrow{a} P_2' \quad initial(P_1)}{P_1 + P_2 \xrightarrow{a} P_1 + P_2'}$$

Table 1. Operational semantic rules for nondeterministic reversible processes

going backward we view t as an *incoming* transition of P'. The semantic rules in Table 1 generate the labeled transition system $(\mathbb{P}, A, \longrightarrow)$ where $\longrightarrow \, \subseteq \mathbb{P} \times A \times \mathbb{P}$.

The first rule for action prefix (ACT_f where f stands for forward) applies only if P is initial and retains the executed action in the target process of the generated forward transition by decorating the action itself with $\dagger$. The second rule for action prefix (ACT_p where p stands for propagation) propagates actions executed by inner initial subprocesses.

In both rules for alternative composition (CHO_l and CHO_r where l stands for left and r stands for right), the subprocess that has not been selected for execution is retained as an initial subprocess in the target process of the generated transition. When both subprocesses are initial, both rules for alternative composition are applicable, otherwise only one of them can be applied and in that case it is the non-initial subprocess that can move, because the other one has been discarded at the moment of the selection.

Any state corresponding to a process different from $\underline{0}$ has at least one outgoing transition and exactly one incoming transition due to the decoration of executed actions. The labeled transition system underlying an initial process turns out to be a tree, whose branching points correspond to occurrences of $+$.

Example 1. The labeled transition systems generated by the rules in Table 1 for the two initial processes $a \,.\, \underline{0} + a \,.\, \underline{0}$ and $a \,.\, \underline{0}$ are depicted below:

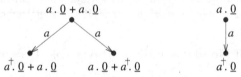

As far as the one on the left is concerned, we observe that, in the case of a standard process calculus, a single a-transition from $a \,.\, \underline{0} + a \,.\, \underline{0}$ to $\underline{0}$ would have been generated due to the absence of action decorations within processes. ∎

2.3   Bisimilarities for Nondeterministic Reversible Processes

The asymmetry between the relative positions of already executed actions and actions to be executed within reachable processes, as well as the asymmetry between the use of predicates *initial* and *final* in the operational semantic rules, determine a number of asymmetries between forward and reverse bisimilarity defined below that will become evident in Sections 2.4 and 2.5.

The difference between the definitions of forward bisimilarity and reverse bisimilarity is that the former considers only *outgoing* transitions [22,20] whereas the latter considers only *incoming* transitions. We also address forward-reverse bisimilarity [24], which considers both outgoing transitions and incoming ones. All the equivalences are strong, i.e., they do not abstract from invisible actions.

Definition 1. *We say that $P_1, P_2 \in \mathbb{P}$ are* forward bisimilar, *written $P_1 \sim_{FB} P_2$, iff $(P_1, P_2) \in \mathcal{B}$ for some forward bisimulation $\mathcal{B}$. A symmetric relation $\mathcal{B}$ over $\mathbb{P}$ is a* forward bisimulation *iff for all $(P_1, P_2) \in \mathcal{B}$ and $a \in A$:*

- *Whenever $P_1 \xrightarrow{a} P_1'$, then $P_2 \xrightarrow{a} P_2'$ with $(P_1', P_2') \in \mathcal{B}$.* ∎

Definition 2. *We say that $P_1, P_2 \in \mathbb{P}$ are* reverse bisimilar, *written $P_1 \sim_{RB} P_2$, iff $(P_1, P_2) \in \mathcal{B}$ for some reverse bisimulation $\mathcal{B}$. A symmetric relation $\mathcal{B}$ over $\mathbb{P}$ is a* reverse bisimulation *iff for all $(P_1, P_2) \in \mathcal{B}$ and $a \in A$:*

- *Whenever $P_1' \xrightarrow{a} P_1$, then $P_2' \xrightarrow{a} P_2$ with $(P_1', P_2') \in \mathcal{B}$.* ∎

Definition 3. *We say that $P_1, P_2 \in \mathbb{P}$ are* forward-reverse bisimilar, *written $P_1 \sim_{FRB} P_2$, iff $(P_1, P_2) \in \mathcal{B}$ for some forward-reverse bisimulation $\mathcal{B}$. A symmetric relation $\mathcal{B}$ over $\mathbb{P}$ is a* forward-reverse bisimulation *iff for all $(P_1, P_2) \in \mathcal{B}$ and $a \in A$:*

- *Whenever $P_1 \xrightarrow{a} P_1'$, then $P_2 \xrightarrow{a} P_2'$ with $(P_1', P_2') \in \mathcal{B}$.*
- *Whenever $P_1' \xrightarrow{a} P_1$, then $P_2' \xrightarrow{a} P_2$ with $(P_1', P_2') \in \mathcal{B}$.* ∎

It holds that $\sim_{FRB} \subsetneq \sim_{FB} \cap \sim_{RB}$. The inclusion is strict because for example the two final processes $a^\dagger . \underline{0}$ and $a^\dagger . \underline{0} + c . \underline{0}$ are identified by $\sim_{FB}$ and by $\sim_{RB}$, but distinguished by $\sim_{FRB}$ as in the latter process action c is enabled again after undoing a. Moreover, $\sim_{FB}$ and $\sim_{RB}$ are incomparable because for instance:

$$a^\dagger . \underline{0} \sim_{FB} \underline{0} \quad \text{but} \quad a^\dagger . \underline{0} \not\sim_{RB} \underline{0}$$
$$a . \underline{0} \sim_{RB} \underline{0} \quad \text{but} \quad a . \underline{0} \not\sim_{FB} \underline{0}$$

The *first asymmetry* is that $\sim_{FRB} = \sim_{FB}$ over initial processes, with $\sim_{RB}$ strictly coarser, whilst $\sim_{FRB} \neq \sim_{RB}$ over final processes because, after going backward, previously discarded subprocesses come into play again in the forward direction.

Example 2. The two processes shown in Example 1 are identified by all the three equivalences. This is witnessed by any bisimulation that contains the pairs $(a . \underline{0} + a . \underline{0}, a . \underline{0})$, $(a^\dagger . \underline{0} + a . \underline{0}, a^\dagger . \underline{0})$, and $(a . \underline{0} + a^\dagger . \underline{0}, a^\dagger . \underline{0})$. ∎

2.4 Congruence Properties

In principle, it makes sense that $\sim_{FB}$ identifies processes with a different past and that $\sim_{RB}$ identifies processes with a different future, in particular with $\underline{0}$ that has neither past nor future. However, for $\sim_{FB}$ this results in a compositionality violation with respect to alternative composition. As an example:

$$a^\dagger . b . \underline{0} \sim_{FB} b . \underline{0}$$
$$a^\dagger . b . \underline{0} + c . \underline{0} \not\sim_{FB} b . \underline{0} + c . \underline{0}$$

because in $a^\dagger . b . \underline{0} + c . \underline{0}$ action c is disabled due to the presence of the already executed action $a^\dagger$, while in $b . \underline{0} + c . \underline{0}$ action c is enabled as there are no past actions preventing it from occurring. Note that a similar phenomenon does not happen with $\sim_{\mathrm{RB}}$ as $a^\dagger . b . \underline{0} \not\sim_{\mathrm{RB}} b . \underline{0}$ due to the incoming a-transition of $a^\dagger . b . \underline{0}$, thus yielding the *second asymmetry* between forward and reverse bisimilarity.

This problem, which does not show up for $\sim_{\mathrm{RB}}$ and $\sim_{\mathrm{FRB}}$ because these two equivalences cannot identify an initial process with a non-initial one, leads to the following variant of $\sim_{\mathrm{FB}}$ that is sensitive to the presence of the past.

Definition 4. *We say that $P_1, P_2 \in \mathbb{P}$ are* past-sensitive forward bisimilar, *written $P_1 \sim_{\mathrm{FB,ps}} P_2$, iff $(P_1, P_2) \in \mathcal{B}$ for some past-sensitive forward bisimulation $\mathcal{B}$. A symmetric relation $\mathcal{B}$ over $\mathbb{P}$ is a* past-sensitive forward bisimulation *iff for all $(P_1, P_2) \in \mathcal{B}$:*

- *$initial(P_1) \iff initial(P_2)$.*
- *For all $a \in A$, whenever $P_1 \xrightarrow{a} P_1'$, then $P_2 \xrightarrow{a} P_2'$ with $(P_1', P_2') \in \mathcal{B}$.*   ∎

Now $\sim_{\mathrm{FB,ps}}$ is sensitive to the presence of the past:
$$a^\dagger . b . \underline{0} \not\sim_{\mathrm{FB,ps}} b . \underline{0}$$
but can still identify non-initial processes having a different past:
$$a_1^\dagger . P \sim_{\mathrm{FB,ps}} a_2^\dagger . P$$
It holds that $\sim_{\mathrm{FRB}} \subsetneq \sim_{\mathrm{FB,ps}} \cap \sim_{\mathrm{RB}}$, with $\sim_{\mathrm{FRB}} = \sim_{\mathrm{FB,ps}}$ over initial processes as well as $\sim_{\mathrm{FB,ps}}$ and $\sim_{\mathrm{RB}}$ being incomparable because e.g. for $a_1 \neq a_2$:
$$a_1^\dagger . P \sim_{\mathrm{FB,ps}} a_2^\dagger . P \text{ but } a_1^\dagger . P \not\sim_{\mathrm{RB}} a_2^\dagger . P$$
$$a_1 . P \sim_{\mathrm{RB}} a_2 . P \text{ but } a_1 . P \not\sim_{\mathrm{FB,ps}} a_2 . P$$
We conclude by formalizing the congruence properties of all the considered equivalences. When present in the results below, side conditions just ensure that the overall processes are reachable.

Theorem 1. *Let $\sim \in \{\sim_{\mathrm{FB}}, \sim_{\mathrm{FB,ps}}, \sim_{\mathrm{RB}}, \sim_{\mathrm{FRB}}\}$, $\sim' \in \{\sim_{\mathrm{FB,ps}}, \sim_{\mathrm{RB}}, \sim_{\mathrm{FRB}}\}$, and $P_1, P_2 \in \mathbb{P}$:*

- *If $P_1 \sim P_2$ then for all $a \in A$:*
  - *$a . P_1 \sim a . P_2$ provided that $initial(P_1) \wedge initial(P_2)$.*
  - *$a^\dagger . P_1 \sim a^\dagger . P_2$.*
- *If $P_1 \sim' P_2$ then for all $P \in \mathbb{P}$:*
  - *$P_1 + P \sim' P_2 + P$ and $P + P_1 \sim' P + P_2$ provided that $initial(P) \vee (initial(P_1) \wedge initial(P_2))$.*
- *$\sim_{\mathrm{FB,ps}}$ is the coarsest congruence with respect to $+$ contained in $\sim_{\mathrm{FB}}$.*   ∎

2.5 Equational Characterizations

We now investigate the equational characterizations of $\sim_{\mathrm{FB,ps}}$, $\sim_{\mathrm{RB}}$, and $\sim_{\mathrm{FRB}}$ so as to highlight the fundamental laws of these behavioral equivalences. In the following, by deduction system we mean a set comprising the following axioms and inference rules on $\mathbb{P}$ – possibly enriched by a set of additional axioms $\mathcal{A}$ – corresponding to the fact that $\sim_{\mathrm{FB,ps}}$, $\sim_{\mathrm{RB}}$, and $\sim_{\mathrm{FRB}}$ are equivalence relations as well as congruences with respect to action prefix and alternative composition:

$(\mathcal{A}_1)$		$(P_1 + P_2) + P_3 = P_1 + (P_2 + P_3)$	
$(\mathcal{A}_2)$		$P_1 + P_2 = P_2 + P_1$	
$(\mathcal{A}_3)$		$P + \underline{0} = P$	
$(\mathcal{A}_4)$	$[\sim_{\mathrm{FB,ps}}]$	$a^\dagger . P = P$	if $\neg initial(P)$
$(\mathcal{A}_5)$	$[\sim_{\mathrm{FB,ps}}]$	$a_1^\dagger . P = a_2^\dagger . P$	if $initial(P)$
$(\mathcal{A}_6)$	$[\sim_{\mathrm{FB,ps}}]$	$P + Q = P$	if $\neg initial(P)$, where $initial(Q)$
$(\mathcal{A}_7)$	$[\sim_{\mathrm{RB}}]$	$a . P = P$	where $initial(P)$
$(\mathcal{A}_8)$	$[\sim_{\mathrm{RB}}]$	$P + Q = P$	if $initial(Q)$
$(\mathcal{A}_9)$	$[\sim_{\mathrm{FB,ps}}]$	$P + P = P$	where $initial(P)$
$(\mathcal{A}_{10})$	$[\sim_{\mathrm{FRB}}]$	$P + Q = P$	if $initial(Q) \wedge to\_initial(P) = Q$

Table 2. Axioms characterizing bisimilarity over nondeterministic reversible processes

- Reflexivity, symmetry, transitivity: $P = P$, $\dfrac{P_1 = P_2}{P_2 = P_1}$, $\dfrac{P_1 = P_2 \quad P_2 = P_3}{P_1 = P_3}$.

- .-Substitutivity: $\dfrac{P_1 = P_2 \quad initial(P_1) \wedge initial(P_2)}{a . P_1 = a . P_2}$, $\dfrac{P_1 = P_2}{a^\dagger . P_1 = a^\dagger . P_2}$.

- +-Substitutivity: $\dfrac{P_1 = P_2 \quad initial(P) \vee (initial(P_1) \wedge initial(P_2))}{P_1 + P = P_2 + P \quad P + P_1 = P + P_2}$.

It is well known that, in the case of bisimilarity over standard nondeterministic processes, alternative composition turns out to be associative and commutative and to admit $\underline{0}$ as neutral element [11]. The same holds true for $\sim_{\mathrm{FB,ps}}$, $\sim_{\mathrm{RB}}$, and $\sim_{\mathrm{FRB}}$ because the two operational semantic rules for alternative composition are symmetric and $\underline{0}$ has no outgoing or incoming transitions. This is formalized by axioms $\mathcal{A}_1$ to $\mathcal{A}_3$ in Table 2.

Then, we have axioms specific to $\sim_{\mathrm{FB,ps}}$. Axioms $\mathcal{A}_4$ and $\mathcal{A}_5$ together establish that the past can be neglected when moving only forward, but the presence of the past cannot be ignored. Axiom $\mathcal{A}_6$ states that a previously non-selected alternative can be discarded after starting moving only forward.

Likewise, we have axioms specific to $\sim_{\mathrm{RB}}$. Axiom $\mathcal{A}_7$ means that the future can be completely canceled when moving only backward. Axiom $\mathcal{A}_8$ states that a previously non-selected alternative can be discarded when moving only backward. Since there are no constraints on P, axiom $\mathcal{A}_8$ subsumes axiom $\mathcal{A}_3$.

Finally, the idempotency of alternative composition in the case of bisimilarity over standard nondeterministic processes, i.e., $P + P = P$ [11], changes depending on the considered equivalence:

- For $\sim_{\mathrm{FB,ps}}$, idempotency is explicitly formalized by axiom $\mathcal{A}_9$, which we note to be disjoint from axiom $\mathcal{A}_6$ where P cannot be initial.
- For $\sim_{\mathrm{RB}}$, an additional axiom is not needed as idempotency follows from axiom $\mathcal{A}_8$ by taking Q equal to P. Thus, the *third asymmetry* between forward and reverse bisimilarity has to do with idempotency.

- For $\sim_{\mathrm{FRB}}$, idempotency is formalized by axiom $\mathcal{A}_{10}$, where function $to\_initial$ brings a process back to its initial version by removing all action decorations:

$$to\_initial(\underline{0}) = \underline{0}$$
$$to\_initial(a \, . \, P) = a \, . \, P$$
$$to\_initial(a^\dagger . \, P) = a \, . \, to\_initial(P)$$
$$to\_initial(P_1 + P_2) = to\_initial(P_1) + to\_initial(P_2)$$

This axiom appeared for the first time in [16] and subsumes axioms $\mathcal{A}_9$ and $\mathcal{A}_6$ for $\sim_{\mathrm{FB,ps}}$ as well as axiom $\mathcal{A}_8$ for $\sim_{\mathrm{RB}}$.

To prove the ground completeness of the equational characterizations of the three considered bisimilarities, as usual we introduce equivalence-specific normal forms to which every process is shown to be reducible, then we work with normal forms only. All the three normal forms rely on the fact that alternative composition is associative and commutative, hence the binary $+$ can be generalized to the n-ary $\sum_{i \in I}$ for a finite nonempty index set I. In the following, we denote by $\vdash$ the deduction relation and we examine the sets of additional axioms below:

- $\mathcal{A}_{\mathrm{FB,ps}} = \{\mathcal{A}_1, \mathcal{A}_2, \mathcal{A}_3, \mathcal{A}_4, \mathcal{A}_5, \mathcal{A}_6, \mathcal{A}_9\}$.
- $\mathcal{A}_{\mathrm{RB}} = \{\mathcal{A}_1, \mathcal{A}_2, \mathcal{A}_7, \mathcal{A}_8\}$.
- $\mathcal{A}_{\mathrm{FRB}} = \{\mathcal{A}_1, \mathcal{A}_2, \mathcal{A}_3, \mathcal{A}_{10}\}$.

Definition 5. *We say that $P \in \mathbb{P}$ is in $\sim_{\mathrm{FB,ps}}$-normal form, written $\sim_{\mathrm{FB,ps}}$-nf, iff it is equal to one of the following:*

- $\underline{0}$.
- $\sum_{i \in I} a_i \, . \, P_i$, *where each P_i is initial and in $\sim_{\mathrm{FB,ps}}$-nf.*
- $a^\dagger . \, P$, *where P is initial and in $\sim_{\mathrm{FB,ps}}$-nf.* ∎

All initial processes without $\underline{0}$ summands are in $\sim_{\mathrm{FB,ps}}$-nf. We observe that, in the second case, $a_1 \, . \, P_1 \sim_{\mathrm{FB,ps}} a_2 \, . \, P_2$ trivially implies $a_1 = a_2$ and $P_1 \sim_{\mathrm{FB,ps}} P_2$. Likewise, in the third case, $a_1^\dagger . \, P_1 \sim_{\mathrm{FB,ps}} a_2^\dagger . \, P_2$ trivially implies $P_1 \sim_{\mathrm{FB,ps}} P_2$. These facts will be exploited in the proof of the forthcoming Theorem 2.

Lemma 1. *For all $P \in \mathbb{P}$ there is $Q \in \mathbb{P}$ in $\sim_{\mathrm{FB,ps}}$-nf such that $\mathcal{A}_{\mathrm{FB,ps}} \vdash P = Q$.* ∎

Theorem 2. *Let $P_1, P_2 \in \mathbb{P}$. Then $P_1 \sim_{\mathrm{FB,ps}} P_2$ iff $\mathcal{A}_{\mathrm{FB,ps}} \vdash P_1 = P_2$.* ∎

Definition 6. *We say that $P \in \mathbb{P}$ is in $\sim_{\mathrm{RB}}$-normal form, written $\sim_{\mathrm{RB}}$-nf, iff it is equal to one of the following:*

- $\underline{0}$.
- $a^\dagger . \, P$, *where P is in $\sim_{\mathrm{RB}}$-nf.* ∎

The normal form above boils down to a final process consisting of a possibly empty, finite sequence of already executed actions terminated by $\underline{0}$. As a consequence, $a_1^\dagger . \, P_1 \sim_{\mathrm{RB}} a_2^\dagger . \, P_2$ with P_1 and P_2 in $\sim_{\mathrm{RB}}$-nf implies $a_1 = a_2$ and $P_1 \sim_{\mathrm{RB}} P_2$, because $a_1^\dagger . \, P_1$ and $a_2^\dagger . \, P_2$ must feature the same sequence of already executed actions and the last executed action of P_1 (resp. P_2), when the process is different from $\underline{0}$, is the same as the last executed action of $a_1^\dagger . \, P_1$ (resp. $a_2^\dagger . \, P_2$). This fact will be exploited in the proof of the forthcoming Theorem 3.

Lemma 2. *For all $P \in \mathbb{P}$ there is $Q \in \mathbb{P}$ in $\sim_{RB}$-nf such that $\mathcal{A}_{RB} \vdash P = Q$.* ■

Theorem 3. *Let $P_1, P_2 \in \mathbb{P}$. Then $P_1 \sim_{RB} P_2$ iff $\mathcal{A}_{RB} \vdash P_1 = P_2$.* ■

Definition 7. *We say that $P \in \mathbb{P}$ is in $\sim_{FRB}$-normal form, written $\sim_{FRB}$-nf, iff it is equal to one of the following:*

- $\underline{0}$.
- $\sum_{i \in I} a_i . P_i$, *where each P_i is initial and in $\sim_{FRB}$-nf.*
- $a^\dagger . P$, *where P is in $\sim_{FRB}$-nf.*
- $a^\dagger . P + \sum_{i \in I} a_i . P_i$, *where P is in $\sim_{FRB}$-nf and each P_i is initial and in $\sim_{FRB}$-nf.* ■

As for the second case above, which is concerned with initial processes, we observe that $a_1 . P_1 \sim_{FRB} a_2 . P_2$ trivially implies $a_1 = a_2$ and $P_1 \sim_{FRB} P_2$. The last two cases together, which are concerned with non-initial processes, yield a process consisting of a finite sequence of already executed actions terminated by an initial process, such that every action in the sequence may have an initial process as an alternative. As a consequence, $a_1^\dagger . P_1 + P_1' \sim_{FRB} a_2^\dagger . P_2 + P_2'$ with P_1, P_2, P_1', P_2' in $\sim_{FRB}$-nf, P_1' and P_2' initial, and P_1' and P_2' moving only when going back to $to\_initial(a_1^\dagger . P_1)$ and $to\_initial(a_2^\dagger . P_2)$, implies $a_1 = a_2$, $P_1 \sim_{FRB} P_2$, and $P_1' \sim_{FRB} P_2'$. These facts will be exploited in the proof of the forthcoming Theorem 4.

Lemma 3. *For all $P \in \mathbb{P}$ there is $Q \in \mathbb{P}$ in $\sim_{FRB}$-nf such that $\mathcal{A}_{FRB} \vdash P = Q$.*
■

Theorem 4. *Let $P_1, P_2 \in \mathbb{P}$. Then $P_1 \sim_{FRB} P_2$ iff $\mathcal{A}_{FRB} \vdash P_1 = P_2$.* ■

3   The Markovian Case

In this section, we repeat the investigation over Markovian reversible processes. We start by recalling the theory of continuous-time Markov chains (Section 3.1) including time reversibility (Section 3.2) and lumpability (Section 3.3), then we introduce syntax and semantics for these processes (Section 3.4), we provide the definitions of the three equivalences (Section 3.5), and we study their congruence properties and equational characterizations (Section 3.6).

3.1   Markov Chains: Definition, Representation, Terminology

A Markov chain is a discrete-state stochastic process characterized by the *memoryless property* [14]. More precisely, a stochastic process $X(t)$, $t \in \mathbb{R}_{\geq 0}$, over a discrete state space $\mathcal{S}$ is a *continuous-time Markov chain (CTMC)* iff for all $n \in \mathbb{N}$, time instants $t_0 < t_1 < \cdots < t_n < t_{n+1} \in \mathbb{R}_{\geq 0}$, and states $s_0, s_1, \ldots, s_n, s_{n+1} \in \mathcal{S}$ it holds that $\Pr\{X(t_{n+1}) = s_{n+1} \mid X(t_i) = s_i, 0 \leq i \leq n\} = \Pr\{X(t_{n+1}) = s_{n+1} \mid X(t_n) = s_n\}$, i.e., the probability of moving from one state to another does not depend on the particular path that has been followed in the past to reach the current state, hence that path can be forgotten.

A CTMC is representable as a labeled transition system or as a state-indexed matrix. In the first case, each transition is labeled with some probabilistic information describing the evolution from the source state to the target state of the transition. In the second case, the same information is stored into an entry, indexed by those two states, of a matrix. The value of this probabilistic information is a function of the time at which the state change takes place.

For the sake of simplicity, we restrict ourselves to *time-homogeneous* CTMCs, in which conditional probabilities of the form $\Pr\{X(t + t') = s' \mid X(t) = s\}$ do not depend on t, so that the considered information is simply a positive real number given by $\lim_{t' \to 0} \frac{\Pr\{X(t+t')=s'|X(t)=s\}}{t'}$. This is called the *rate* at which the CTMC moves from state s to state s' and uniquely characterizes the exponentially distributed time taken by the considered move.

A CTMC is *irreducible* iff each of its states is reachable from every other state with probability greater than 0. A state $s \in \mathcal{S}$ is *recurrent* iff the CTMC will eventually return to s with probability 1, in which case s is *positive recurrent* iff the expected number of steps until the CTMC returns to it is finite. A CTMC is *ergodic* iff it is irreducible and all of its states are positive recurrent; ergodicity coincides with irreducibility in the case that the CTMC has finitely many states.

Every time-homogeneous and ergodic CTMC $X(t)$ is *stationary*, which means that $(X(t_i + t'))_{1 \leq i \leq n}$ has the same joint distribution as $(X(t_i))_{1 \leq i \leq n}$ for all $n \in \mathbb{N}_{\geq 1}$ and $t_1 < \cdots < t_n, t' \in \mathbb{R}_{\geq 0}$. In this case, $X(t)$ has a unique *steady-state probability distribution* $\boldsymbol{\pi}$ that for all $s \in \mathcal{S}$ fulfills $\pi(s) = \lim_{t \to \infty} \Pr\{X(t) = s \mid X(0) = s'\}$ for any $s' \in \mathcal{S}$. These probabilities can be computed by solving the linear system of *global balance equations* $\boldsymbol{\pi} \cdot \mathbf{Q} = \mathbf{0}$ subject to $\sum_{s \in \mathcal{S}} \pi(s) = 1$ and $\pi(s) \in \mathbb{R}_{>0}$ for all $s \in \mathcal{S}$. The *infinitesimal generator matrix* $\mathbf{Q}$ contains for each pair of distinct states the rate of the corresponding move, which is 0 in the absence of a direct move between them, while $q_{s,s} = -\sum_{s' \neq s} q_{s,s'}$ for all $s \in \mathcal{S}$, i.e., every diagonal element contains the opposite of the total exit rate of the corresponding state, so that each row of $\mathbf{Q}$ sums up to 0.

3.2 Time Reversibility of Continuous-Time Markov Chains

Due to state space explosion and numerical stability problems [27], the calculation of the solution of the global balance equation system is not always feasible. However, it can be tackled in the case that the behavior of the considered CTMC remains the same when the direction of time is reversed. A CTMC $X(t)$ is *time reversible* iff $(X(t_i))_{1 \leq i \leq n}$ has the same joint distribution as $(X(t' - t_i))_{1 \leq i \leq n}$ for all $n \in \mathbb{N}_{\geq 1}$ and $t_1 < \cdots < t_n, t' \in \mathbb{R}_{\geq 0}$. In this case, $X(t)$ and its time-reversed version $X^{\mathrm{r}}(t) = X(t' - t)$ are stochastically identical, in particular they are stationary and share the same steady-state probability distribution $\boldsymbol{\pi}$. In order for a stationary CTMC $X(t)$ to be time reversible, it is necessary and sufficient that the *partial balance equations* $\pi(s) \cdot q_{s,s'} = \pi(s') \cdot q_{s',s}$ are satisfied for all $s, s' \in \mathcal{S}$ such that $s \neq s'$ or, equivalently, that $q_{s_1,s_2} \cdot \cdots \cdot q_{s_{n-1},s_n} \cdot q_{s_n,s_1} = q_{s_1,s_n} \cdot q_{s_n,s_{n-1}} \cdot \cdots \cdot q_{s_2,s_1}$ for all $n \in \mathbb{N}_{\geq 2}$ and distinct $s_1, \ldots, s_n \in \mathcal{S}$ [13].

The time-reversed version $X^{\mathrm{r}}(t)$ of a stationary CTMC $X(t)$ can be defined even when $X(t)$ is not reversible. As shown in [13,10], this is accomplished by using the steady-state probability distribution π of $X(t)$, with $X^{\mathrm{r}}(t)$ turning out to be a CTMC too and having the same steady-state probability distribution π. More precisely, $q^{\mathrm{r}}_{s_j,s_i} = q_{s_i,s_j} \cdot \pi(s_i)/\pi(s_j)$ for all $s_i \neq s_j$, i.e., the rate from state s_j to state s_i in the time-reversed CTMC is proportional to the rate from state s_i to state s_j in the original CTMC, where the coefficient is given by the ratio of $\pi(s_i)$ to $\pi(s_j)$. Note that the time-reversed version of $X^{\mathrm{r}}(t)$ is $X(t)$.

3.3 Lumpability of Continuous-Time Markov Chains

A different approach to the state space explosion problem consists of aggregating states and transitions in a suitable way. In particular, the focus is on *exact aggregations*, i.e., partitions of the state space such that the probability of being in any of the aggregated states is equal to the sum of the probabilities of the original states it contains. In the following, we consider a time-homogeneous CTMC $X(t)$ with state space $\mathcal{S}$ and infinitesimal generator matrix $\mathbf{Q}$; the formulas for the elements of the matrix of the resulting aggregations are taken from [2].

The first notion of exact aggregation that we address is strong lumpability [14]. It was later renamed ordinary lumpability in [28,5], which we prefer to adopt so as not to generate confusion with the use of strong and weak for behavioral equivalences in concurrency theory.

Definition 8. *The partition $\mathcal{P}$ induced by an equivalence relation $\mathcal{L}$ over $\mathcal{S}$ is an ordinary lumping iff for all $(s_1, s_2) \in \mathcal{L}$ and $C \in \mathcal{P}$ such that $s_1, s_2 \notin C$:*
$$\sum_{s' \in C} q_{s_1,s'} = \sum_{s' \in C} q_{s_2,s'}$$
The resulting CTMC with state space $\mathcal{P}$ has infinitesimal generator matrix $\mathbf{Q}'$ defined as follows for all $C_1, C_2 \in \mathcal{P}$ such that $C_1 \neq C_2$:
$$q'_{C_1,C_2} = \sum_{s' \in C_2} q_{s,s'}$$
where $s \in C_1$. ∎

The second notion of exact aggregation is exact lumpability [25,28,5], which further enjoys the property that all the original states contained in the same aggregated state have the same probability. While ordinary lumpability considers the rates of outgoing transitions and does not check for rate equality within any class, exact lumpability considers the rates of incoming transitions and applies the rate equality check inside each class too.

Definition 9. *The partition $\mathcal{P}$ induced by an equivalence relation $\mathcal{L}$ over $\mathcal{S}$ is an exact lumping iff for all $(s_1, s_2) \in \mathcal{L}$ and $C \in \mathcal{P}$:*
$$\sum_{s' \in C} q_{s',s_1} = \sum_{s' \in C} q_{s',s_2}$$
The resulting CTMC with state space $\mathcal{P}$ has infinitesimal generator matrix $\mathbf{Q}'$ defined as follows for all $C_1, C_2 \in \mathcal{P}$ such that $C_1 \neq C_2$:
$$q'_{C_1,C_2} = \sum_{s' \in C_1} q_{s',s} \cdot (|C_2|/|C_1|)$$
where $s \in C_2$. ∎

The third notion of exact aggregation is strict lumpability [5], which is a combination of the previous two.

Definition 10. *The partition $\mathcal{P}$ induced by an equivalence relation $\mathcal{L}$ over $\mathcal{S}$ is a* strict lumping *iff it is both an ordinary lumping and an exact lumping.* ∎

The relationships between lumpability and time reversibility for CTMCs have been investigated in [18,19]:

- An exact lumping of a CTMC corresponds to an ordinary lumping on the time-reversed CTMC.
- An aggregation of a CTMC is a strict lumping iff it is a strict lumping for the time-reversed CTMC too.
- An exact lumping of a CTMC is also an ordinary lumping whenever the CTMC is time reversible, while the vice versa does not hold in general.

Example 3. Consider the three time-reversible, ergodic CTMCs depicted below:

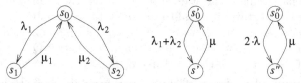

When solving the global balance equations for the first CTMC from the left, we obtain:

$$\pi(s_0) = \frac{\mu_1 \cdot \mu_2}{\mu_1 \cdot \mu_2 + \lambda_1 \cdot \mu_2 + \lambda_2 \cdot \mu_1}$$
$$\pi(s_1) = \frac{\lambda_1 \cdot \mu_2}{\mu_1 \cdot \mu_2 + \lambda_1 \cdot \mu_2 + \lambda_2 \cdot \mu_1}$$
$$\pi(s_2) = \frac{\lambda_2 \cdot \mu_1}{\mu_1 \cdot \mu_2 + \lambda_1 \cdot \mu_2 + \lambda_2 \cdot \mu_1}$$

If $\lambda_1 = \lambda_2$ but $\mu_1 \neq \mu_2$, then no exact aggregation exists for that CTMC.

If $\mu_1 = \mu_2 \triangleq \mu$ but $\lambda_1 \neq \lambda_2$, then the second CTMC from the left is an ordinary lumping of the first one, where the aggregated state s' contains the two original states s_1 and s_2 and the solution of the global balance equations is the following:

$$\pi(s_0') = \frac{\mu}{\mu + \lambda_1 + \lambda_2} = \pi(s_0)$$
$$\pi(s') = \frac{\lambda_1 + \lambda_2}{\mu + \lambda_1 + \lambda_2} = \pi(s_1) + \pi(s_2)$$

with $\pi(s_1) \neq \pi(s_2)$.

If $\lambda_1 = \lambda_2 \triangleq \lambda$ and $\mu_1 = \mu_2 \triangleq \mu$, then the third CTMC from the left is a strict – i.e., ordinary and exact – lumping of the first one, where the aggregated state s'' contains the two original states s_1 and s_2 and the solution of the global balance equations is the following:

$$\pi(s_0'') = \frac{\mu}{\mu + 2 \cdot \lambda} = \pi(s_0)$$
$$\pi(s'') = \frac{2 \cdot \lambda}{\mu + 2 \cdot \lambda} = \pi(s_1) + \pi(s_2)$$

with $\pi(s_1) = \pi(s_2)$. ∎

Example 4. The considered notions of lumpability are distinct from each other. On the one hand, in the previous example the second CTMC from the left is an ordinary lumping of the first one, but not an exact lumping as $\pi(s_1) \neq \pi(s_2)$ when $\mu_1 = \mu_2$ and $\lambda_1 \neq \lambda_2$. On the other hand, the CTMC on the right depicted below is an exact lumping of the CTMC on the left – where the aggregated state s' contains the two original states s_1 and s_2 – when $\mu' + \mu'' = \nu' + \nu''$ – corresponding to $q_{s_1,s_1} + q_{s_2,s_1} = q_{s_1,s_2} + q_{s_2,s_2}$, i.e., $-(\mu' + \mu'') + 0 = 0 - (\nu' + \nu'')$

– but it is not an ordinary lumping if $\mu' \neq \nu'$ and $\mu'' \neq \nu''$:

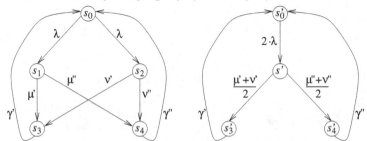

Note that the two CTMCs above are ergodic, but not time reversible. ∎

3.4   Syntax and Semantics of Markovian Reversible Processes

We have seen in Section 2 that a single forward transition relation is enough for nondeterministic processes in a reversible setting. This is due to the fact that $P \xrightarrow{a} P'$ iff $P' \overset{a}{\dashrightarrow} P$, where according to [24] the backward transition relation $\dashrightarrow$ should be used in the second clause of the definition of $\sim_{\mathrm{FRB}}$ and hence in the definition of $\sim_{\mathrm{RB}}$ as well.

A transition relation in a single direction is no longer sufficient in the case of Markovian reversible processes. The reason is that every transition of these processes is also labeled with its rate, a positive real number that uniquely identifies the exponentially distributed duration of the action associated with the transition. In general, the rate may be different depending on whether the transition goes forward or backward, without necessarily affecting time reversibility.

When moving from nondeterministic reversible processes to Markovian ones, in the syntax we thus need to replace a and $a^\dagger$ with $<a, \lambda, \mu>$ and $<a^\dagger, \lambda, \mu>$ respectively, where $\lambda \in \mathbb{R}_{>0}$ is the rate of the forward a-transition whilst $\mu \in \mathbb{R}_{>0}$ is the rate of the backward a-transition. Predicates *initial*, *final*, and *reachable* are extended accordingly and the set of reachable processes is denoted by $\mathbb{P}_M$.

In order for the semantics to be consistent with the CTMC theory recalled in Sections 3.1 to 3.3, we cannot use a transition relation $\longrightarrow$ with forward rates separated from a transition relation $\dashrightarrow$ with backward rates, as would be the case if we applied the approach of [24]. For instance, the two Markovian processes depicted below would be identified by a Markovian variant of $\sim_{\mathrm{FRB}}$ relying on $\longrightarrow$ and $\dashrightarrow$, but the CTMC underlying the labeled transition system of the process on the right is not an exact lumping of the CTMC underlying the labeled transition system of the process on the left if $\lambda_1 \neq \lambda_2$, i.e., this Markovian variant of $\sim_{\mathrm{FRB}}$ would not induce strict lumping:

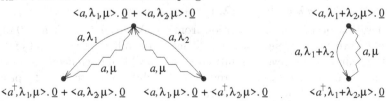

$$\text{ACT}_f \; \frac{initial(P)}{<a,\lambda,\mu>.P \xrightarrow{a,\lambda}_M <a^\dagger,\lambda,\mu>.P} \qquad \text{ACT}_r \; \frac{initial(P)}{<a^\dagger,\lambda,\mu>.P \xrightarrow{a,\mu}_M <a,\lambda,\mu>.P}$$

$$\text{ACT}_p \; \frac{P \xrightarrow{b,\xi}_M P'}{<a^\dagger,\lambda,\mu>.P \xrightarrow{b,\xi}_M <a^\dagger,\lambda,\mu>.P'}$$

$$\text{CHO}_l \; \frac{P_1 \xrightarrow{a,\xi}_M P_1' \quad initial(P_2)}{P_1 + P_2 \xrightarrow{a,\xi}_M P_1' + P_2} \qquad \text{CHO}_r \; \frac{P_2 \xrightarrow{a,\xi}_M P_2' \quad initial(P_1)}{P_1 + P_2 \xrightarrow{a,\xi}_M P_1 + P_2'}$$

Table 3. Operational semantic rules for Markovian reversible processes

We thus keep using a single transition relation, which is $\longrightarrow_M \subseteq \mathbb{P}_M \times (A \times \mathbb{R}_{>0}) \times \mathbb{P}_M$ defined in Table 3. Unlike the one in Section 2.2, it embodies both transitions with forward rates and transitions with backward rates. This has been accomplished not only by extending all the rules in Table 1 according to the new richer syntax, but also by adding a rule for action prefix (ACT_r where r stands for reverse) that generates transitions with backward rates.

Any state corresponding to a process different from $\underline{0}$ can now have several incoming transitions too. The labeled transition system underlying an initial process turns out to be a tree-like extension of a birth-death process [23,21], with branching points corresponding to occurrences of +. The reason is that between any pair of connected states there can only be a transition from the former state to the latter and a transition from the latter state back to the former, with the two transitions sharing the same name as they are generated by the same action $<a,\lambda,\mu>$. The underlying CTMC, obtained by removing actions from transitions, turns out to be not only ergodic, but also time reversible due to its tree-like birth-death structure [13]. The considered calculus thus combines causality-consistent reversibility with time reversibility like in [4].

Example 5. The labeled transition systems generated by the rules in Table 3 for the two Markovian processes $<a,\lambda,\mu>.\underline{0} + <a,\lambda,\mu>.\underline{0}$ and $<a,\lambda,\mu>.\underline{0}$ are shown below:

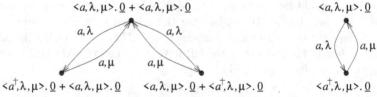

The generation of a single a-transition from $<a,\lambda,\mu>.\underline{0} + <a,\lambda,\mu>.\underline{0}$ on the left would have been wrong, as it would have not reflected the total exit rate $2 \cdot \lambda$ of the source state. Several solutions to this problem have been proposed for Markovian process calculi without reversibility, while in our setting the problem is naturally prevented by action decorations within processes. ∎

3.5   Bisimilarities for Markovian Reversible Processes

We now define the Markovian variants of forward bisimilarity, reverse bisimilarity, and forward-reverse bisimilarity based on the CTMC theory recalled in Sections 3.1 to 3.3.

In the forward case, it is known that the (discrete-time) probabilistic bisimilarity of [17] and the (continuous-time) Markovian bisimilarity of [12] induce an ordinary lumping on the Markov chains underlying the considered processes, hence so does $\sim_{\mathrm{MFB}}$ below. Unlike Definition 8, in Definition 11 the rate equality check is applied inside each class too and hence not all ordinary lumpings can be induced by $\sim_{\mathrm{MFB}}$, in particular not the one identifying every pair of processes.

The reason is that while in Markov chain theory one is interested in state probabilities, in concurrency theory one experiments with processes by observing the labels of the transitions that are executed [9,1,17]. In particular, two processes with different total exit rates cannot be identified by $\sim_{\mathrm{MFB}}$ below, which is perfectly justifiable from an observational viewpoint. As an example, consider a state with a self-looping λ-transition and a state with a self-looping μ-transition. The two states would be deemed ordinarily lumpable according to Definition 8, although the more λ and μ are different, the easier it is for an observer to tell those two states apart.

In the following, $\{\!|$ and $|\!\}$ denote multiset parentheses, while $\mathbb{P}_{\mathrm{M}}/\mathcal{B}$ is the set of equivalence classes induced by the equivalence relation $\mathcal{B}$ over $\mathbb{P}_{\mathrm{M}}$.

Definition 11. *We say that $P_1, P_2 \in \mathbb{P}_{\mathrm{M}}$ are Markovian forward bisimilar, written $P_1 \sim_{\mathrm{MFB}} P_2$, iff $(P_1, P_2) \in \mathcal{B}$ for some Markovian forward bisimulation $\mathcal{B}$. An equivalence relation $\mathcal{B}$ over $\mathbb{P}_{\mathrm{M}}$ is a Markovian forward bisimulation iff for all $(P_1, P_2) \in \mathcal{B}$, $a \in A$, and $C \in \mathbb{P}_{\mathrm{M}}/\mathcal{B}$:*

$$rate_{\mathrm{out}}(P_1, a, C) = rate_{\mathrm{out}}(P_2, a, C)$$

where $rate_{\mathrm{out}}(P, a, C) = \sum\{\!| \xi \in \mathbb{R}_{>0} \mid \exists P' \in C.\ P \xrightarrow{a,\xi}_{\mathrm{M}} P' |\!\}$.   ∎

In the reverse case, incoming transitions are considered instead of outgoing ones. As in [6,26], in the definition of $\sim_{\mathrm{MRB}}$ below an additional condition about total exit rate equality is needed, which in Definition 9 is naturally handled through the diagonal elements of the infinitesimal generator matrix. It is easily seen that $\sim_{\mathrm{MRB}}$ induces an exact lumping on the Markov chains underlying the considered processes, but not all exact lumpings can be induced.

Definition 12. *We say that $P_1, P_2 \in \mathbb{P}_{\mathrm{M}}$ are Markovian reverse bisimilar, written $P_1 \sim_{\mathrm{MRB}} P_2$, iff $(P_1, P_2) \in \mathcal{B}$ for some Markovian reverse bisimulation $\mathcal{B}$. An equivalence relation $\mathcal{B}$ over $\mathbb{P}_{\mathrm{M}}$ is a Markovian reverse bisimulation iff for all $(P_1, P_2) \in \mathcal{B}$ and $a \in A$:*

$$rate_{\mathrm{out}}(P_1, a, \mathbb{P}_{\mathrm{M}}) = rate_{\mathrm{out}}(P_2, a, \mathbb{P}_{\mathrm{M}})$$

and for all $C \in \mathbb{P}_{\mathrm{M}}/\mathcal{B}$:

$$rate_{\mathrm{in}}(P_1, a, C) = rate_{\mathrm{in}}(P_2, a, C)$$

where $rate_{\mathrm{in}}(P, a, C) = \sum\{\!| \xi \in \mathbb{R}_{>0} \mid \exists P' \in C.\ P' \xrightarrow{a,\xi}_{\mathrm{M}} P |\!\}$.   ∎

In the forward-reverse case, $\sim_{\mathrm{MFRB}}$ below induces a strict lumping on the Markov chains underlying the considered processes.

Definition 13. *We say that* $P_1, P_2 \in \mathbb{P}_M$ *are* Markovian forward-reverse bisimilar, *written* $P_1 \sim_{MFRB} P_2$, *iff* $(P_1, P_2) \in \mathcal{B}$ *for some Markovian forward-reverse bisimulation* $\mathcal{B}$. *An equivalence relation* $\mathcal{B}$ *over* $\mathbb{P}_M$ *is a* Markovian forward-reverse bisimulation *iff for all* $(P_1, P_2) \in \mathcal{B}$, $a \in A$, *and* $C \in \mathbb{P}_M/\mathcal{B}$:

$$rate_{out}(P_1, a, C) = rate_{out}(P_2, a, C)$$
$$rate_{in}(P_1, a, C) = rate_{in}(P_2, a, C) \qquad \blacksquare$$

It is worth noting that any aggregated state resulting from an ordinary lumping is $\sim_{MFB}$-equivalent to each of the original states it contains, while this is not necessarily the case for exact lumping and $\sim_{MRB}$, where $\sim_{MRB}$-equivalence certainly holds only among the original states contained in an aggregated state. This is the *fourth asymmetry* between forward and reverse bisimilarity.

Example 6. The three CTMCs of Example 3 can be viewed as underlying the labeled transition systems of the following three initial processes:

$$<a, \lambda_1, \mu_1> . \underline{0} + <a, \lambda_2, \mu_2> . \underline{0} \quad \text{corresponding to } s_0$$
$$<a, \lambda_1 + \lambda_2, \mu> . \underline{0} \qquad\qquad\qquad \text{corresponding to } s_0'$$
$$<a, 2 \cdot \lambda, \mu> . \underline{0} \qquad\qquad\qquad\quad \text{corresponding to } s_0''$$

with:

$$<a^\dagger, \lambda_1, \mu_1> . \underline{0} + <a, \lambda_2, \mu_2> . \underline{0} \quad \text{corresponding to } s_1$$
$$<a, \lambda_1, \mu_1> . \underline{0} + <a^\dagger, \lambda_2, \mu_2> . \underline{0} \quad \text{corresponding to } s_2$$
$$<a^\dagger, \lambda_1 + \lambda_2, \mu> . \underline{0} \qquad\qquad\quad \text{corresponding to } s'$$
$$<a^\dagger, 2 \cdot \lambda, \mu> . \underline{0} \qquad\qquad\qquad \text{corresponding to } s''$$

If $\mu_1 = \mu_2 \triangleq \mu$ but $\lambda_1 \neq \lambda_2$, then:

$$<a, \lambda_1, \mu> . \underline{0} + <a, \lambda_2, \mu> . \underline{0} \sim_{MFB} <a, \lambda_1 + \lambda_2, \mu> . \underline{0}$$
$$<a^\dagger, \lambda_1, \mu> . \underline{0} + <a, \lambda_2, \mu> . \underline{0} \sim_{MFB} <a^\dagger, \lambda_1 + \lambda_2, \mu> . \underline{0}$$
$$<a, \lambda_1, \mu> . \underline{0} + <a^\dagger, \lambda_2, \mu> . \underline{0} \sim_{MFB} <a^\dagger, \lambda_1 + \lambda_2, \mu> . \underline{0}$$

If $\lambda_1 = \lambda_2 \triangleq \lambda$ and $\mu_1 = \mu_2 \triangleq \mu$, then:

$$<a, \lambda, \mu> . \underline{0} + <a, \lambda, \mu> . \underline{0} \sim_{MFB} <a, 2 \cdot \lambda, \mu> . \underline{0}$$
$$<a^\dagger, \lambda, \mu> . \underline{0} + <a, \lambda, \mu> . \underline{0} \sim_{MFB} <a^\dagger, 2 \cdot \lambda, \mu> . \underline{0}$$
$$<a, \lambda, \mu> . \underline{0} + <a^\dagger, \lambda, \mu> . \underline{0} \sim_{MFB} <a^\dagger, 2 \cdot \lambda, \mu> . \underline{0}$$

but:

$$<a, \lambda, \mu> . \underline{0} + <a, \lambda, \mu> . \underline{0} \not\sim_{MRB} <a, 2 \cdot \lambda, \mu> . \underline{0}$$
$$<a^\dagger, \lambda, \mu> . \underline{0} + <a, \lambda, \mu> . \underline{0} \not\sim_{MRB} <a^\dagger, 2 \cdot \lambda, \mu> . \underline{0}$$
$$<a, \lambda, \mu> . \underline{0} + <a^\dagger, \lambda, \mu> . \underline{0} \not\sim_{MRB} <a^\dagger, 2 \cdot \lambda, \mu> . \underline{0}$$

with the only exception of the following two contained in the same aggregate:

$$<a^\dagger, \lambda, \mu> . \underline{0} + <a, \lambda, \mu> . \underline{0} \sim_{MRB} <a, \lambda, \mu> . \underline{0} + <a^\dagger, \lambda, \mu> . \underline{0} \qquad \blacksquare$$

Unlike $\sim_{FB}$, it holds that $\sim_{MFB}$ is sensitive to the presence of the past, so that in Definition 11 it is not necessary to require $initial(P_1) \iff initial(P_2)$ to gain compositionality with respect to alternative composition. For example:

$$<a^\dagger, \lambda, \mu> . <b, \delta, \gamma> . \underline{0} \not\sim_{MFB} <b, \delta, \gamma> . \underline{0}$$

because the process on the left has an outgoing a-transition with rate μ that cannot be matched by the process on the right.

Furthermore, unlike $\sim_{FB,ps}$, it holds that $\sim_{MFB}$ cannot identify processes with a different past. For instance:

$$<a^\dagger, \lambda, \mu> . \underline{0} \not\sim_{MFB} <b^\dagger, \delta, \gamma> . \underline{0}$$

whenever $a \neq b$ or $\mu \neq \gamma$, as in that case the outgoing a-transition on the left cannot be matched by the outgoing b-transition on the right.

Similarly, unlike $\sim_{RB}$, we have that $\sim_{MRB}$ is sensitive to the presence of the future and cannot identify processes with a different future. As an example:

$$<a, \lambda, \mu>.\underline{0} \not\sim_{MRB} \underline{0}$$

because the process on the left has an incoming a-transition with rate μ that cannot be matched by the process on the right. As another example:

$$<a, \lambda, \mu>.\underline{0} \not\sim_{MRB} <b, \delta, \gamma>.\underline{0}$$

whenever $a \neq b$ or $\mu \neq \gamma$, as in that case the incoming a-transition on the left cannot be matched by the incoming b-transition on the right.

We conclude by showing that $\sim_{MFRB}$ coincides with $\sim_{MRB}$ (whilst $\sim_{MFB}$ is strictly coarser) thus *extending the first asymmetry* between forward and reverse bisimilarities (see page 5). This result stems from the definition of the operational semantics and the consequent time reversibility of the underlying CTMCs.

Theorem 5. *Let $P_1, P_2 \in \mathbb{P}_M$. Then $P_1 \sim_{MFRB} P_2$ iff $P_1 \sim_{MRB} P_2$.* ∎

3.6 Congruence Properties and Equational Characterizations

We start by observing that $\sim_{MFB}$ is not totally sensitive to the past, in the same way as $\sim_{MRB}$ is not totally sensitive to the future. For both equivalences this results in a compositionality violation with respect to $+$. As an example:

$$<a, \lambda, \lambda>.\underline{0} \sim_{MFRB} <a^\dagger, \lambda, \lambda>.\underline{0}$$
$$<a, \lambda, \lambda>.\underline{0} + <c, \kappa_1, \kappa_2>.\underline{0} \not\sim_{MFRB} <a^\dagger, \lambda, \lambda>.\underline{0} + <c, \kappa_1, \kappa_2>.\underline{0}$$

because in $<a^\dagger, \lambda, \lambda>.\underline{0} + <c, \kappa_1, \kappa_2>.\underline{0}$ action c is disabled due to the presence of the already executed action $a^\dagger$, while in $<a, \lambda, \lambda>.\underline{0} + <c, \kappa_1, \kappa_2>.\underline{0}$ action c is enabled as there are no past actions preventing it from occurring.

Note that $\sim_{MFRB}$ would not equate the first two processes if their two rates were λ_1 and λ_2 with $\lambda_1 \neq \lambda_2$ or there were any other process in place of $\underline{0}$. Therefore, when investigating congruence with respect to alternative composition, we will consider the set of processes $\mathbb{P}'_M = \mathbb{P}_M \setminus \{<a, \lambda, \lambda>.\underline{0} \mid a \in A, \lambda \in \mathbb{R}_{>0}\}$.

Theorem 6. *Let $\sim_M \in \{\sim_{MFB}, \sim_{MRB}\}$ and $P_1, P_2 \in \mathbb{P}_M$:*

- *If $P_1 \sim_M P_2$ then for all $a \in A$ and $\lambda, \mu \in \mathbb{R}_{>0}$:*
  - *$<a, \lambda, \mu>.P_1 \sim_M <a, \lambda, \mu>.P_2$ provided that $initial(P_1) \wedge initial(P_2)$.*
  - *$<a^\dagger, \lambda, \mu>.P_1 \sim_M <a^\dagger, \lambda, \mu>.P_2$.*
- *If $P_1 \sim_M P_2$ with $P_1, P_2 \in \mathbb{P}'_M$ then for all $P \in \mathbb{P}'_M$:*
  - *$P_1 + P \sim_M P_2 + P$ and $P + P_1 \sim_M P + P_2$ provided that $initial(P) \vee (initial(P_1) \wedge initial(P_2))$.* ∎

With regard to equational characterizations, as expected $\sim_{MFB}$ and $\sim_{MRB}$ are such that alternative composition is associative and commutative and admits $\underline{0}$ as neutral element. This is formalized by axioms $\mathcal{A}_{M,1}$ to $\mathcal{A}_{M,3}$ in Table 4.

Markovian variants of axioms $\mathcal{A}_4$ to $\mathcal{A}_6$ in Table 2 are not valid for $\sim_{MFB}$ because this behavioral equivalence is sensitive to the presence of the past, cannot identify processes with a different past, and views all the transitions as outgoing.

$(\mathcal{A}_{M,1})$	$(P_1 + P_2) + P_3 \;=\; P_1 + (P_2 + P_3)$
$(\mathcal{A}_{M,2})$	$P_1 + P_2 \;=\; P_2 + P_1$
$(\mathcal{A}_{M,3})$	$P + \underline{0} \;=\; P$

$(\mathcal{A}_{M,4})\;[\sim_{\mathrm{MFB}}]\quad {<}a,\lambda_1,\mu{>}.P + {<}a,\lambda_2,\mu{>}.P \;=\; {<}a,\lambda_1 + \lambda_2,\mu{>}.P$
$\qquad\qquad\qquad\qquad\qquad\qquad\qquad\qquad\qquad\qquad\qquad\text{where } \mathit{initial}(P)$

$(\mathcal{A}_{M,5})\;[\sim_{\mathrm{MFB}}]\quad {<}a^{\dagger},\lambda_1,\mu{>}.P + {<}a,\lambda_2,\mu{>}.Q \;=\; {<}a^{\dagger},\lambda_1 + \lambda_2,\mu{>}.P$
$\qquad\qquad\qquad\qquad\qquad\qquad\qquad\qquad\qquad\qquad\qquad\text{if } \mathit{to\_initial}(P) = Q,$
$\qquad\qquad\qquad\qquad\qquad\qquad\qquad\qquad\qquad\qquad\qquad\text{where } \mathit{initial}(Q)$

Table 4. Axioms characterizing bisimilarity over Markovian reversible processes

Likewise, Markovian variants of axioms $\mathcal{A}_7$ and $\mathcal{A}_8$ in Table 2 are not valid for $\sim_{\mathrm{MRB}}$ because this behavioral equivalence is sensitive to the presence of the future, cannot identify processes with a different future, and views all the transitions as incoming.

As for idempotency, Markovian variants of axioms $\mathcal{A}_9$ and $\mathcal{A}_{10}$ in Table 2, which are formalized by axioms $\mathcal{A}_{M,4}$ and $\mathcal{A}_{M,5}$ in Table 4, are valid only for $\sim_{\mathrm{MFB}}$ as shown in Example 6. We further observe that in the considered example:
$${<}a^{\dagger},\lambda,\mu{>}.\underline{0} + {<}a,\lambda,\mu{>}.\underline{0} \;\sim_{\mathrm{MRB}}\; {<}a,\lambda,\mu{>}.\underline{0} + {<}a^{\dagger},\lambda,\mu{>}.\underline{0}$$
can be proved via axiom $\mathcal{A}_{M,2}$.

Theorem 7. *Let* $\mathcal{A}_{\mathrm{MFB}} = \{\mathcal{A}_{M,1}, \mathcal{A}_{M,2}, \mathcal{A}_{M,3}, \mathcal{A}_{M,4}, \mathcal{A}_{M,5}\}$ *and* $P_1, P_2 \in \mathbb{P}'_M$. *Then* $P_1 \sim_{\mathrm{MFB}} P_2$ *iff* $\mathcal{A}_{\mathrm{MFB}} \vdash P_1 = P_2$. ∎

Theorem 8. *Let* $\mathcal{A}_{\mathrm{MRB}} = \{\mathcal{A}_{M,1}, \mathcal{A}_{M,2}, \mathcal{A}_{M,3}\}$ *and* $P_1, P_2 \in \mathbb{P}'_M$. *Then* $P_1 \sim_{\mathrm{MRB}} P_2$ *iff* $\mathcal{A}_{\mathrm{MRB}} \vdash P_1 = P_2$. ∎

4   Conclusions

In this paper, we have discovered the following asymmetries that shed light on forward bisimilarity, reverse bisimilarity, and forward-reverse bisimilarity:

1. In the nondeterministic case $\sim_{\mathrm{FRB}} = \sim_{\mathrm{FB}}$ over initial processes only, while in the Markovian case $\sim_{\mathrm{MFRB}} = \sim_{\mathrm{MRB}}$ over all reachable processes.
2. The insensitivity to the presence of the past breaks the compositionality of $\sim_{\mathrm{FB}}$, while the insensitivity to the presence of the future does not violate the compositionality of $\sim_{\mathrm{RB}}$. This does not happen in the Markovian case.
3. Forward bisimilarity needs explicit idempotency axioms, while reverse bisimilarity does not, especially in the nondeterministic case.
4. Any aggregated state resulting from an ordinary lumping is $\sim_{\mathrm{MFB}}$-equivalent to each of the original states it contains, while this is not necessarily the case for exact lumping and $\sim_{\mathrm{MRB}}$, where $\sim_{\mathrm{MRB}}$-equivalence certainly holds only among the original states contained in an aggregated state.

As future work, we plan to investigate logical characterizations of the same equivalences, along with what changes when admitting irreversible actions.

Acknowledgments. This research has been supported by the PRIN project *NiRvAna – Noninterference and Reversibility Analysis in Private Blockchains* as well as the INdAM-GNCS project *Proprietà Qualitative e Quantitative di Sistemi Reversibili.*

References

1. Abramsky, S.: Observational equivalence as a testing equivalence. Theoretical Computer Science **53**, 225–241 (1987)
2. Baarir, S., Beccuti, M., Dutheillet, C., Franceschinis, G., Haddad, S.: Lumping partially symmetric stochastic models. Performance Evaluation **68**, 21–44 (2011)
3. Bennett, C.H.: Logical reversibility of computations. IBM Journal of Research and Development **17**, 525–532 (1973)
4. Bernardo, M., Mezzina, C.A.: Towards bridging time and causal reversibility. In: Proc. of the 40th Int. Conf. on Formal Techniques for Distributed Objects, Components, and Systems (FORTE 2020). LNCS, vol. 12136, pp. 22–38. Springer (2020)
5. Buchholz, P.: Exact and ordinary lumpability in finite Markov chains. Journal of Applied Probability **31**, 59–75 (1994)
6. Buchholz, P.: Exact performance equivalence: An equivalence relation for stochastic automata. Theoretical Computer Science **215**, 263–287 (1999)
7. Danos, V., Krivine, J.: Reversible communicating systems. In: Proc. of the 15th Int. Conf. on Concurrency Theory (CONCUR 2004). LNCS, vol. 3170, pp. 292–307. Springer (2004)
8. De Nicola, R., Montanari, U., Vaandrager, F.: Back and forth bisimulations. In: Proc. of the 1st Int. Conf. on Concurrency Theory (CONCUR 1990). LNCS, vol. 458, pp. 152–165. Springer (1990)
9. van Glabbeek, R.J.: The linear time – branching time spectrum I. In: Handbook of Process Algebra. pp. 3–99. Elsevier (2001)
10. Harrison, P.: Turning back time in Markovian process algebra. Theoretical Computer Science **290**, 1947–1986 (2003)
11. Hennessy, M., Milner, R.: Algebraic laws for nondeterminism and concurrency. Journal of the ACM **32**, 137–162 (1985)
12. Hillston, J.: A Compositional Approach to Performance Modelling. Cambridge University Press (1996)
13. Kelly, F.: Reversibility and Stochastic Networks. John Wiley & Sons (1979)
14. Kemeny, J.G., Snell, J.L.: Finite Markov Chains. Van Nostrand (1960)
15. Landauer, R.: Irreversibility and heat generated in the computing process. IBM Journal of Research and Development **5**, 183–191 (1961)
16. Lanese, I., Phillips, I.: Forward-reverse observational equivalences in CCSK. In: Proc. of the 13th Int. Conf. on Reversible Computation (RC 2021). LNCS, vol. 12805, pp. 126–143. Springer (2021)
17. Larsen, K.G., Skou, A.: Bisimulation through probabilistic testing. Information and Computation **94**, 1–28 (1991)
18. Marin, A., Rossi, S.: On the relations between lumpability and reversibility. In: Proc. of the 22nd IEEE Int. Symp. on Modeling, Analysis and Simulation of Computer and Telecommunication Systems (MASCOTS 2014). pp. 427–432. IEEE-CS Press (2014)
19. Marin, A., Rossi, S.: On the relations between Markov chain lumpability and reversibility. Acta Informatica **54**, 447–485 (2017)

20. Milner, R.: Communication and Concurrency. Prentice Hall (1989)
21. Palacios, J.L., Quiroz, D.: Birth and death chains on finite trees: Computing their stationary distribution and hitting times. Methodology and Computing in Applied Probability **18**, 487–498 (2016)
22. Park, D.: Concurrency and automata on infinite sequences. In: Proc. of the 5th GI Conf. on Theoretical Computer Science. LNCS, vol. 104, pp. 167–183. Springer (1981)
23. Pearce, L.H.: Random walks on trees. Discrete Mathematics **30**, 269–276 (1980)
24. Phillips, I., Ulidowski, I.: Reversing algebraic process calculi. Journal of Logic and Algebraic Programming **73**, 70–96 (2007)
25. Schweitzer, P.J.: Aggregation methods for large Markov chains. In: Proc. of the Int. Workshop on Computer Performance and Reliability. pp. 275–286. North Holland (1984)
26. Sproston, J., Donatelli, S.: Backward bisimulation in Markov chain model checking. IEEE Trans. on Software Engineering **32**, 531–546 (2006)
27. Stewart, W.: Introduction to the Numerical Solution of Markov Chains. Princeton University Press (1994)
28. Sumita, U., Rieders, M.: Lumpability and time reversibility in the aggregation-disaggregation method for large Markov chains. Communications in Statistics - Stochastic Models **5**, 63–81 (1989)

Explainability of Probabilistic Bisimilarity Distances for Labelled Markov Chains[*]

Amgad Rady and Franck van Breugel[✉]

DisCoVeri Group, Department of Electrical Engineering and Computer Science
York University, Toronto, Canada
franck@yorku.ca

Abstract. Probabilistic bisimilarity distances measure the similarity of behaviour of states of a labelled Markov chain. The smaller the distance between two states, the more alike they behave. Their distance is zero if and only if they are probabilistic bisimilar. Recently, algorithms have been developed that can compute probabilistic bisimilarity distances for labelled Markov chains with thousands of states within seconds. However, say we compute that the distance of two states is 0.125. How does one explain that 0.125 captures the similarity of their behaviour?

In this paper, we address this question by returning to the definition of probabilistic bisimilarity distances proposed by Desharnais, Gupta, Jagadeesan, and Panangaden more than two decades ago. We use a slight variation of their logic to construct for each pair of states a sequence of formulas that explains the probabilistic bisimilarity distance of the states. Furthermore, we present an algorithm that computes those formulas and we show that each formula can be computed in polynomial time.

We also prove that our logic is minimal. That is, if we leave out any operator from the logic, then the resulting logic no longer provides a logical characterization of the probabilistic bisimilarity distances.

1 Introduction

The behavioural equivalence *bisimilarity*, due to Milner [41] and Park [44], is one of the cornerstones of concurrency theory. It captures which states of a labelled transition system, a simple yet widely used model of concurrent systems, behave the same. Hennessy and Milner [29] provided a *logical characterization* of bisimilarity by introducing a logic, known as Hennessy-Milner logic, and proving that states are bisimilar if and only if they satisfy the same formulas of the logic. If the labelled transition system has finitely many states then for two states that are not bisimilar there exists a formula, often referred to as a *distinguishing formula*, such that one state satisfies the formula whereas the other state does not. This formula explains why the two states are not bisimilar. Cleaveland [12] presented a polynomial time algorithm that computes a distinguishing formula for states that are not bisimilar. Consider the following labelled transition system.

---

[*] Supported by the Natural Sciences and Engineering Research Council of Canada.

O. Kupferman and P. Sobocinski (Eds.): FoSSaCS 2023, LNCS 13992, pp. 285–307, 2023.
https://doi.org/10.1007/978-3-031-30829-1_14

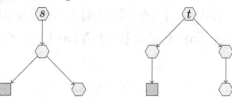

The states s and t are not bisimilar. This can be explained by a formula that expresses that a state can transition to a state that can subsequently transition to a purple (square) state as well as a green (hexagon) state. State s satisfies this formula but state t does not.

To model randomness in systems, *labelled Markov chains* are often used. Larsen and Skou [39] introduced *probabilistic bisimilarity* to capture which states of a labelled Markov chain behave the same. They also introduced a logic that characterizes probabilistic bisimilarity. Desharnais, Edalat, and Panangaden [19] simplified that logic and presented a polynomial time algorithm that produces a formula that distinguishes two states which are not probabilistic bisimilar. Consider the following labelled Markov chain.

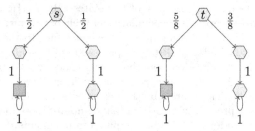

The states s and t are not probabilistic bisimilar. State t can transition with more than probability $\frac{1}{2}$ to a green state that can transition to a purple state, whereas state s cannot. This property can be expressed in the logic, giving rise to a formula that distinguishes the states s and t.

Giacalone, Jou, and Smolka [27] observed that probabilistic bisimilarity is not robust. Miniscule changes to the probabilities may alter which states are probabilistic bisimilar. Instead of an equivalence relation, they suggested exploiting a *pseudometric* to capture the behavioural similarity of states. That is, each pair of states is assigned a distance, a real number in the interval $[0, 1]$, which measures how similar the states behave. The smaller the distance, the more alike the states behave. Distance zero captures that the states are behaviourally equivalent.

Desharnais, Gupta, Jagadeesan, and Panangaden [20] presented such a pseudometric. They showed that distance zero captures probabilistic bisimilarity. Therefore, those distances are known as *probabilistic bisimilarity distances*. These distances can be computed in polynomial time, as has been shown by Chen et al. [11]. Tang [48] developed and implemented algorithms that can compute the probabilistic bisimilarity distances for labelled Markov chains with thousands of states within seconds. The states s and t in the above labelled Markov chain have distance 0.125. How does one explain that 0.125 captures the similarity of their behaviour? That is the main question that we address in this paper.

To define their probabilistic bisimilarity distances, Desharnais et al. introduce a logic. The labelled Markov chains that they consider differ slightly from the ones we study in this paper: they label transitions whereas we label states (by colours/shapes), and where we require that the probabilities of the outgoing transitions of a state add up to one, they allow them to sum to less than one as well. State-labelled Markov chains have become the norm in probabilistic model checking. Probabilistic model checkers such as PRISM [38] and Storm [14] consider state-labelled Markov chains. Since each transition-labelled Markov chain can be encoded as a state-labelled one [46], this difference does not substantially impact any of the results. If the probabilities do not sum to one, one can add an additional state and transition to that state with the remaining probability. Also this difference does not significantly change the results. Adjusted to our setting, slightly simplified, and using a different syntax, the logic can be captured by the following grammar:

$$\varphi ::= a \mid \neg\varphi \mid \varphi \wedge \varphi \mid \bigcirc\varphi \mid \varphi \ominus q$$

where a is a label of a state and q is a rational in the interval $[0, 1]$. This logic characterizes the probabilistic bisimilarity distances (see, for example, [20,6]). Roughly speaking, the distance of two states is determined by a formula of the logic that distinguishes them the most. Such a formula explains their probabilistic bisimilarity distance. Consider, for example, the states s and t in the above labelled Markov chain. As we already mentioned, their distance is 0.125. This distance can be explained by the formula $\bigcirc(\lozenge \wedge \bigcirc \blacksquare)$. This formula captures the probability of reaching a green state in one transition and subsequently reaching a purple state after the second transition. For state s that probability is 0.5 and it is 0.625 for state t. Note that the $\bigcirc$ operator is similar to the next operator of linear temporal logic. Roughly, the interpretation of the formula $\bigcirc\varphi$ in state s is the probability that φ holds in the successors of s.

As is common, we provide the above logic with a real-valued interpretation. For a formula of the logic, its interpretation maps each state of the labelled Markov chain to a real value in the interval $[0, 1]$. For example, for the formula $\bigcirc(\lozenge \wedge \bigcirc \blacksquare)$, its interpretation in state s is denoted by $[\![\bigcirc(\lozenge \wedge \bigcirc \blacksquare)]\!](s)$ and has the value 0.5. The value of $[\![\bigcirc(\lozenge \wedge \bigcirc \blacksquare)]\!](t)$ is 0.625. Their difference, which is 0.125, is the distance of the states s and t. The distinguishing formula for the states s and t is fairly simple. As we will discuss next, we need all the operators of the logic to explain the probabilistic bisimilarity distances and a single formula may not suffice.

1.1 Main Results

As we will show, the above logic is a *minimal* logic that characterizes the probabilistic bisimilarity distances. That is, if we remove any operator from the logic then the resulting logic does not characterize the probabilistic bisimilarity distances anymore. Furthermore, we will demonstrate that there exist finite labelled Markov chains for which the distances of some states cannot be explained by a single formula. However, as we will prove, we can explain the probabilistic bisimilarity distances by means of a sequence of formulas. Given two states, say u and v, we will construct a sequence of formulas φ_{uv}^0, φ_{uv}^1, φ_{uv}^2, ... such that the sequence $[\![\varphi_{uv}^0]\!](u) - [\![\varphi_{uv}^0]\!](v)$, $[\![\varphi_{uv}^1]\!](u) - [\![\varphi_{uv}^1]\!](v)$, $[\![\varphi_{uv}^2]\!](u) - [\![\varphi_{uv}^2]\!](v)$, ... converges to the probabilistic bisimilarity distance of u and v. We will also present an algorithm that computes those formulas and we will show that each formula can be computed in polynomial time.

1.2   Related Work

In addition to the references to the literature mentioned above, next we will discuss some other related work. Many of the behavioural equivalences have been characterized logically. For example, Feng and Zhang [25] provide a logical characterization of probabilistic bisimilarity for probabilistic automata. Bernardo and Miculan [4] present an algorithm that builds a distinguishing formula for states of a probabilistic automaton that are not probabilistic bisimilar. König, Mika-Michalski, and Schröder [37] propose a general method to construct a distinguishing formula for a variety of systems, including probabilistic automata.

Behavioural pseudometrics have been introduced for a large variety of systems that model randomness. For example, Ferns, Panangaden, and Precup [26] study probabilistic bisimilarity distances for Markov decision processes, Deng, Chothia, Palamidessi, and Pang [15] introduce them for probabilistic automata, and De Alfaro, Majumdar, Raman, and Stoelinga [1] present them for games.

Also many behavioural pseudometrics have been characterized logically. For example, Desharnais, Laviolette, and Tracol [23] present a logical characterization of ε-bisimilarity, a notion closely related to distances, for probabilistic automata. Du, Deng, and Gebler [24] logically characterize probabilistic bisimilarity distances for probabilistic automata. Pantelic and Lawford [43] provide a logical characterization of a behavioural pseudometric for probabilistic discrete event structures. Komorida et al. [35], König and Mika-Michalski [36], Wild and Schröder [51], as well as Wißmann, Milius, and Schröder [52], present general frameworks to obtain logical characterizations of behavioural pseudometrics.

Whereas many logics for systems with randomness have a real-valued interpretation, Castiglione, Gebler, and Tini [9,10] introduce a logic for probabilistic automata with a boolean-valued interpretation. Their logic contains an operator with which we can express properties such as "a state can transition with probability a half to a purple state and with probability a half to a green state." It is this operator that allows them to define a mimicking formula of a state. As the name suggests, this formula mimics the behaviour of the state. Furthermore, they endow the formulas with a pseudometric and show that the probabilistic bisimilarity distance of two states is the distance of their mimicking formulas. Hence, the distance of two states can be explained by means of the mimicking formulas of those states.

2   Labelled Markov Chains and Probabilistic Bisimilarity Distances

In this section, we introduce several key notions that play a central role in the remainder of the paper. We define the model of interest, namely a labelled Markov chain. Furthermore, we introduce probabilistic bisimilarity, an equivalence relation that captures which states of a labelled Markov chain behave the same, and probabilistic bisimilarity distances, which measure the similarity of behaviour of those states.

First, we recall some notions from probability theory. Given a finite set X, a function $\mu : X \to [0,1]$ is a *probability distribution* on X if $\sum_{x \in X} \mu(x) = 1$. We denote the set of probability distributions on X by $\mathcal{D}_\mathbb{R}(X)$. For $\mu \in \mathcal{D}_\mathbb{R}(X)$ and $A \subseteq X$, we often write $\mu(A)$ for $\sum_{x \in A} \mu(x)$. Similarly, for $\omega \in \mathcal{D}_\mathbb{R}(X \times X)$, $a \in X$, and $A \subseteq X$, we usually write $\omega(a, A)$ for $\sum_{x \in A} \omega(a, x)$. For $\mu \in \mathcal{D}_\mathbb{R}(X)$, we define the *support* of μ by $\mathrm{support}(\mu) = \{\, x \in X \mid \mu(x) > 0 \,\}$. A probability distribution $\mu \in \mathcal{D}_\mathbb{R}(X)$ is *rational* if $\mu(x) \in \mathbb{Q}$ for all $x \in X$. We denote the set of rational probability distributions on X by $\mathcal{D}_\mathbb{Q}(X)$. Obviously, $\mathcal{D}_\mathbb{Q} \subseteq \mathcal{D}_\mathbb{R}$.

Definition 1. *A labelled Markov chain is a tuple $\langle S, L, \tau, \ell \rangle$ consisting of*

- *a finite set S of states,*
- *a finite set L of labels,*
- *a transition probability function $\tau : S \to \mathcal{D}_\mathbb{Q}(S)$, and*
- *a labelling function $\ell : S \to L$.*

We restrict the transition probabilities to rationals as we will compute with them in Section 6 and 7. For the remainder, we fix a labelled Markov chain $\langle S, L, \tau, \ell \rangle$. We define probabilistic bisimlarity by means of the set $\Omega_\mathbb{R}(\mu, \nu)$ which is known as the *transportation polytope* [33] of the probability distributions μ and ν.

Definition 2. *For all $\mu, \nu \in \mathcal{D}_\mathbb{R}(S)$, the set $\Omega_\mathbb{R}(\mu, \nu)$ is defined by*

$$\Omega_\mathbb{R}(\mu, \nu) = \{\, \omega \in \mathcal{D}_\mathbb{R}(S \times S) \mid \forall s \in S : \omega(s, S) = \mu(s) \land \omega(S, s) = \nu(s) \,\}.$$

Definition 3. *A relation $R \subseteq S \times S$ is a probabilistic bisimulation if for all $(s, t) \in R$, $\ell(s) = \ell(t)$ and there exists $\omega \in \Omega_\mathbb{R}(\tau(s), \tau(t))$ with $\mathrm{support}(\omega) \subseteq R$. States s and t are probabilistic bisimilar, denoted $s \sim t$, if $(s, t) \in R$ for some probabilistic bisimulation R.*

To define the probabilistic bisimilarity distances, it is convenient to partition the set of state pairs into the following three sets.

Definition 4. *The sets S_0^2, S_1^2 and $S_?^2$ are defined by*

$$S_0^2 = \{\, (s, t) \in S \times S \mid s \sim t \,\}$$
$$S_1^2 = \{\, (s, t) \in S \times S \mid \ell(s) \neq \ell(t) \,\}$$
$$S_?^2 = (S \times S) \setminus (S_0^2 \cup S_1^2)$$

The set S_0^2 contains those state pairs that have distance zero (cf. Theorem 6). The set S_1^2 contains those state pairs that have a different label and, therefore, have distance one (cf. Definition 5). The set $S_?^2$ contains the remaining state pairs. Note that some of these state pairs may have distance one, but cannot have distance zero. The probabilistic bisimilarity distances are defined in terms of the following function.

Definition 5. *The function* $\Delta : (S \times S \to [0,1]) \to (S \times S \to [0,1])$ *is defined by*

$$
\Delta(d)(s,t) = \begin{cases} 0 & \text{if } (s,t) \in S_0^2 \\ 1 & \text{if } (s,t) \in S_1^2 \\ \inf_{\omega \in \Omega_{\mathbb{R}}(\tau(s),\tau(t))} \sum_{u,v \in S} \omega(u,v)\, d(u,v) & \text{if } (s,t) \in S_?^2 \end{cases}
$$

Let $d \in S \times S \to [0,1]$ and $\omega \in \mathcal{D}_{\mathbb{R}}(S \times S)$. Instead of $\sum_{u,v \in S} \omega(u,v)\, d(u,v)$ we write $\omega \cdot d$ in the remainder to avoid clutter. Similarly, for $f \in S \to [0,1]$ and $\mu \in \mathcal{D}_{\mathbb{R}}(S)$ we write $f \cdot \mu$ instead of $\sum_{s \in S} f(s)\, \mu(s)$.

For $d, e \in S \times S \to [0,1]$, we define $d \sqsubseteq e$ if for all $s, t \in S$, $d(s,t) \le e(s,t)$. According to, for example, [22, Lemma 3.2], $\langle S \times S \to [0,1], \sqsubseteq \rangle$ is a complete lattice. Since the function Δ is a monotone function from a complete lattice to itself, we can conclude from the Knaster-Tarski fixed point theorem (see, for example, [13, Theorem 2.35]) that Δ has a least fixed point. We denote this least fixed point by δ. This least fixed point maps each pair of states to a real number in the interval $[0,1]$: the *probabilistic bisimilarity distance* of the states. Distance zero captures probabilistic bisimilarity.

Theorem 6 ([21, Theorem 4.10]). *For all* $s, t \in S$, $\delta(s,t) = 0$ *if and only if* $s \sim t$.

The probabilistic bisimilarity distance function δ is the limit of the distance functions δ_n which only consider the first n transitions when comparing the similarity of the behaviour of states. This result can be seen as an instance of the Kleene fixed point theorem [34].

Definition 7. *For each* $n \ge 0$, *the function* $\delta_n : S \times S \to [0,1]$ *is defined by*

$$
\delta_n(s,t) = \begin{cases} 0 & \text{if } n = 0 \\ \Delta(\delta_{n-1})(s,t) & \text{otherwise.} \end{cases}
$$

Proposition 8. $\lim_{n \to \infty} \delta_n = \delta$.

3   A Logical Characterization

Below, we present a logical characterization of the probabilistic bisimilarity distances. We start with a logic very similar to the one introduced by Desharnais et al. [20].

Definition 9. *The logic* $\mathcal{L}_{\neg}$ *is defined by*

$$\varphi ::= a \mid \bigcirc\varphi \mid \neg\varphi \mid \varphi \ominus q \mid \varphi \vee \varphi$$

where $a \in L$ *and* $q \in \mathbb{Q} \cap [0,1]$.

The above logic is slightly different from the one presented in [20] as we consider Markov chains with labelled states, whereas Desharnais et al. studied Markov chains with labelled transitions. In particular, a and $\bigcirc\varphi$ were combined as $\langle a \rangle \varphi$. Since we restrict our attention to finite state systems, we can restrict ourselves to finite disjunctions. In our setting, the constants true and false can be expressed as $\bigvee_{a \in L} a$ (recall that we assume that the set L is finite as well) and $\neg$true, respectively. The logic of Desharnais et al. also contains the operator $\lceil\varphi\rceil^q$ which is redundant, as observed in [21, page 336]. The logic considered by Desharnais [18] lacks negation, but does include $\lceil\varphi\rceil^q$ and conjunction. The real-valued interpretation of the logic of Desharnais et al., which considers labelled transitions, is adjusted to our setting of labelled states as follows.

Definition 10. *The function* $[\![\cdot]\!] : \mathcal{L}_{\neg} \to S \to [0,1]$ *is defined by*

$$[\![a]\!](s) = \begin{cases} 1 \text{ if } \ell(s) = a \\ 0 \text{ otherwise} \end{cases}$$
$$[\![\bigcirc\varphi]\!](s) = [\![\varphi]\!] \cdot \tau(s)$$
$$[\![\neg\varphi]\!](s) = 1 - [\![\varphi]\!](s)$$
$$[\![\varphi \ominus q]\!](s) = \max([\![\varphi]\!](s) - q, 0)$$
$$[\![\varphi \vee \psi]\!](s) = \max([\![\varphi]\!](s), [\![\psi]\!](s))$$

Note that $[\![$false$]\!]$ and $[\![$true$]\!]$ are the constant zero and constant one functions, respectively. The probabilistic bisimilarity distances can be characterized in terms of the logic.

Theorem 11 ([5, Theorem 40 and 44]). *For all* $s, t \in S$,

$$\delta(s,t) = \sup_{\varphi \in \mathcal{L}_{\neg}} [\![\varphi]\!](s) - [\![\varphi]\!](t).$$

In the remainder of this paper, we consider the following logic. This logic also characterizes probabilistic bisimilarity distances. As we will show later, this logic can explain the probabilistic bisimilarity distances more concisely than the logic presented above.

Definition 12. *The logic* $\mathcal{L}$ *is defined by*

$$\varphi ::= a \mid \bigcirc\varphi \mid \varphi \ominus q \mid \varphi \oplus q \mid \varphi \vee \varphi \mid \varphi \wedge \varphi$$

where $a \in L$ *and* $q \in \mathbb{Q} \cap [0,1]$.

Note that negation has been removed and conjunction has been added. Also the operator $\oplus q$, which is dual to $\ominus q$, has been added. This logic is very similar to the one considered by Desharnais [18].

Definition 13. *The function* $[\![\cdot]\!]: \mathcal{L} \to S \to [0,1]$ *of Definition 10 is modified by*

$$[\![\varphi \oplus q]\!](s) = \min\{[\![\varphi]\!](s) + q, 1\}$$
$$[\![\varphi \wedge \psi]\!](s) = \min\{[\![\varphi]\!](s), [\![\psi]\!](s)\}$$

As already mentioned above, also this logic characterizes the probabilistic bisimilarity distances.

Theorem 14. *For all* $s, t \in S$, $\delta(s,t) = \sup_{\varphi \in \mathcal{L}} [\![\varphi]\!](s) - [\![\varphi]\!](t)$.

Proof sketch. Each formula of $\mathcal{L}$ can be rewritten to an equivalent formula of $\mathcal{L}_\neg$. For example, if φ is rewritten to ψ then $\varphi \oplus q$ is rewritten to $\neg(\neg\psi \ominus q)$. Each formula of $\mathcal{L}$ has a dual: if $[\![\varphi]\!] = 1 - [\![\psi]\!]$ then φ is a dual of ψ. For example, if φ is a dual of ψ then $\varphi \ominus q$ is a dual of $\psi \oplus q$. Each formula $\mathcal{L}_\neg$ can be rewritten to an equivalent formula of $\mathcal{L}$. For example, if φ is rewritten to ψ then $\neg\varphi$ is rewritten to a dual of ψ. The result now follows from Theorem 11.   □

4   All Operators are Necessary

The logic $\mathcal{L}$ is a minimal logic that characterizes the probabilistic bisimilarity distances. That is, if we remove any operator from the logic then the resulting logic does not characterizes the probabilistic bisimilarity distances anymore. Due to lack of space, we only consider the logic $\mathcal{L}_{\backslash \ominus}$, which does not have the $\ominus q$ operator.

Definition 15. *The logic* $\mathcal{L}_{\backslash \ominus}$ *is defined by*

$$\varphi ::= a \mid \bigcirc\varphi \mid \varphi \oplus q \mid \varphi \vee \varphi \mid \varphi \wedge \varphi$$

where $a \in L$ *and* $q \in \mathbb{Q} \cap [0,1]$.

Theorem 16. *There exists a labelled Markov chain* $\langle S, L, \tau, \ell \rangle$ *and* $s, t \in S$ *such that*

$$\delta(s,t) > \sup_{\varphi \in \mathcal{L}_{\backslash \ominus}} [\![\varphi]\!](s) - [\![\varphi]\!](t).$$

Proof sketch. Consider the following labelled Markov chain.

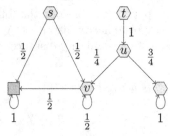

It can be shown that $\delta(s,t) = \frac{7}{8}$. Furthermore, we can prove that for all $\varphi \in \mathcal{L}_{\backslash \ominus}$ and $q \in \mathbb{Q} \cap [0,1]$, if $[\![\varphi]\!](u) < \frac{1}{8} - \frac{q}{2}$ then $[\![\varphi]\!](v) < \frac{3}{4} - q$ by structural induction on φ. Using this result and Theorem 14, we can also show that for all $\varphi \in \mathcal{L}_{\backslash \ominus}$, $[\![\varphi]\!](s) - [\![\varphi]\!](t) \leq \frac{27}{32}$ by structural induction on φ.   □

5 Explainability

In general, the probabilistic bisimilarity distance of two states cannot be explained by a single formula, as we will show next. That is, generally there does not exist a distinguishing formula for every pair of states of a labelled Markov chain. But, as we will prove below, for every pair of states there exists a sequence of formulas that explains their distance.

Theorem 17. *There exists a labelled Markov chain $\langle S, L, \tau, \ell \rangle$ and s, $t \in S$ such that for all $\varphi \in \mathcal{L}$, $\delta(s,t) > [\![\varphi]\!](s) - [\![\varphi]\!](t)$.*

Proof sketch. Consider the following labelled Markov chain.

It can be shown that $\delta(s,t) = 1$. We can also prove that for all $\varphi \in \mathcal{L}$, $[\![\varphi]\!](s) - [\![\varphi]\!](t) < 1$ by structural induction on φ. ☐

As we will show next, for every pair of states (s,t) there exists a sequence of formulas $(\xi_n)_n$ such that $\delta(s,t) = \lim_{n \to \infty} [\![\xi_n]\!](s) - [\![\xi_n]\!](t)$. This sequence $(\xi_n)_n$ explains the distance $\delta(s,t)$.

Proposition 18. *For all s, $t \in S$ there exists $(\xi_n)_n$ such that*

$$\delta(s,t) = \lim_{n \to \infty} [\![\xi_n]\!](s) - [\![\xi_n]\!](t).$$

Proof sketch. This can be concluded from Theorem 14 and the following. Let X be a nonempty subset of $\mathbb{R}$ that is bounded above. Then there exists a sequence $(x_n)_n$ in X that converges to $\sup X$ [8, page 4]. ☐

The proof of the above proposition is *not* constructive. Below, we will construct a sequence of formulas $(\varphi_{st}^n)_n$ that explains the distance of the states s and t. In particular, φ_{st}^n is constructed so that

$$[\![\varphi_{st}^n]\!](s) = \delta_n(s,t) \text{ and } [\![\varphi_{st}^n]\!](t) = 0$$

and, hence, $[\![\varphi_{st}^n]\!](s) - [\![\varphi_{st}^n]\!](t) = \delta_n(s,t)$. That is, the formula φ_{st}^n explains the distance $\delta_n(s,t)$.

If $n = 0$ then $\delta_n(s,t) = 0$. We choose the formula false since

$$[\![\text{false}]\!](s) = 0 = \delta_0(s,t) \text{ and } [\![\text{false}]\!](t) = 0.$$

Let $n > 0$. For $(s,t) \in S_0^2$, also $\delta_n(s,t) = 0$. Again we choose the formula false to explain the distance. For $(s,t) \in S_1^2$, we have that $\delta_n(s,t) = 1$. In this case the formula $\ell(s)$ explains $\delta_n(s,t)$ since $\ell(s) \neq \ell(t)$ and, therefore,

$$[\![\ell(s)]\!](s) = 1 = \delta_n(s,t) \text{ and } [\![\ell(s)]\!](t) = 0.$$

To construct a formula that explains distance $\delta_n(s,t)$ for $(s,t) \in S_?^2$, we rely on the following result about distances and nonexpansive functions. A function $f \in S \to [0,1]$ is *nonexpansive* if for all $s, t \in S$, $|f(s) - f(t)| \leq \delta_n(s,t)$. The set of nonexpansive functions is denoted by $(S, \delta_n) \twoheadrightarrow [0,1]$. This set forms a convex polytope and is known as the *Lipschitz polytope*. We denote its *vertices* by $V((S, \delta_n) \twoheadrightarrow [0,1])$.

Proposition 19. *For all* $(s,t) \in S_?^2$ *and* $n \geq 0$, *there exists* $f_{st}^n \in (S, \delta_n) \twoheadrightarrow (\mathbb{Q} \cap [0,1])$ *such that* $\delta_{n+1}(s,t) = f_{st}^n \cdot (\tau(s) - \tau(t))$.

Proof sketch. Let $(s,t) \in S_?^2$ and $n \geq 0$. Then

$$\delta_{n+1}(s,t) = \inf_{\omega \in \Omega_\mathbb{R}(\tau(s),\tau(t))} \omega \cdot \delta_n.$$

We can view $\delta_{n+1}(s,t)$ as the minimal cost of a transportation problem, where $\tau(s)(u)$ represents the amount transported from the origin u, $\tau(t)(v)$ captures the amount received at the destination v, $\delta_n(u,v)$ represents the transportation cost from u to v, and each ω captures a transportation plan, that is, $\omega(u,v)$ is the amount transported from u to v (see, for example, [40, page 15]).

From the Kantorovich-Rubinstein duality theorem [31] we can conclude that

$$\inf_{\omega \in \Omega_\mathbb{R}(\tau(s),\tau(t))} \omega \cdot \delta_n = \sup_{f \in (S,\delta_n) \twoheadrightarrow [0,1]} f \cdot (\tau(s) - \tau(t)).$$

In this dual to the above transportation problem, each f represents a price function (see, for example, [40, page 81]). Since a linear function on a convex polytope attains its maximum at a vertex (see, for example, [49, Theorem 2 of Chapter 1]), we can conclude that

$$\sup_{f \in (S,\delta_n) \twoheadrightarrow [0,1]} f \cdot (\tau(s) - \tau(t)) = \max_{f \in V((S,\delta_n) \twoheadrightarrow [0,1])} f \cdot (\tau(s) - \tau(t)).$$

Since we can prove that $V((S, \delta_n) \twoheadrightarrow [0,1]) \subseteq (S, \delta_n) \twoheadrightarrow (\mathbb{Q} \cap [0,1])$, there exists $f_{st}^n \in (S, \delta_n) \twoheadrightarrow (\mathbb{Q} \cap [0,1])$ such that $\delta_{n+1}(s,t) = f_{st}^n \cdot (\tau(s) - \tau(t))$. $\square$

The function f_{st}^n plays a key role in the formula explaining $\delta_n(s,t)$. However, f_{st}^n is not necessarily unique. Consider the following labelled Markov chain.

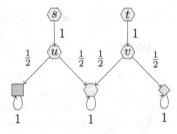

For this example, the sequence $(\delta_n)_n$ converges in three steps, that is, $\delta = \delta_3$. We have that $\delta_2(u,v) = \frac{1}{2}$ and $\delta_3(s,t) = \frac{1}{2}$. So we need the function f_{st}^2 to satisfy $\delta_3(s,t) = f_{st}^2(u) - f_{st}^2(v)$ and $|f_{st}^2(u) - f_{st}^2(v)| \leq \frac{1}{2}$. For each $0 \leq q \leq \frac{1}{2}$, $f_{st}^2(u) = \frac{1}{2} + q$ and $f_{st}^2(v) = q$ satisfies these properties. As we will see, any f_{st}^n that satisfies these properties can be used to construct φ_{st}^n. How to compute these functions f_{st}^n is the topic of the next section.

As we will show in Theorem 22, we can construct a formula ψ_{st}^n that captures the function f_{st}^n, that is, $[\![\psi_{st}^n]\!] = f_{st}^n$. More about this soon. By means of ψ_{st}^{n-1} we can explain the distance $\delta_n(s,t)$ by the formula $(\bigcirc \psi_{st}^{n-1}) \ominus (f_{st}^{n-1} \cdot \tau(t))$ since we have that

$$[\![(\bigcirc \psi_{st}^{n-1}) \ominus (f_{st}^{n-1} \cdot \tau(t))]\!](s) = \max\{([\![\psi_{st}^{n-1}]\!] \cdot \tau(s)) - (f_{st}^{n-1} \cdot \tau(t)), 0\}$$
$$= \max\{(f_{st}^{n-1} \cdot \tau(s)) - (f_{st}^{n-1} \cdot \tau(t)), 0\}$$
$$= \max\{f_{st}^{n-1} \cdot (\tau(s) - \tau(t)), 0\}$$
$$= \max\{\delta_n(s,t), 0\}$$
$$= \delta_n(s,t)$$

and, similarly, we can deduce that

$$[\![(\bigcirc \psi_{st}^{n-1}) \ominus (f_{st}^{n-1} \cdot \tau(t))]\!](t) = \max\{f_{st}^{n-1} \cdot (\tau(t) - \tau(t)), 0\} = 0.$$

Let us return to the formula ψ_{st}^n that captures the function f_{st}^n. To construct ψ_{st}^n we use the following result.

Lemma 20 ([2, Lemma A7.2]). *Let* $f \in S \to [0,1]$. *If for all* u, $v \in S$, *there exists* $g_{uv} \in S \to [0,1]$ *such that* $g_{uv}(u) = f(u)$ *and* $g_{uv}(v) = f(v)$, *then*

$$f = \min_{u \in S} \max_{v \in S} g_{uv} = \max_{u \in S} \min_{v \in S} g_{uv}.$$

To apply the above lemma, we need to construct for all u, $v \in S$ a formula ψ_{stuv}^n such that

$$[\![\psi_{stuv}^n]\!](u) = f_{st}^n(u) \text{ and } [\![\psi_{stuv}^n]\!](v) = f_{st}^n(v).$$

The details are provided in Definition 21 and Theorem 22. From Lemma 20 we can then conclude that

$$\left[\!\!\left[\bigwedge_{u \in S} \bigvee_{v \in S} \psi_{stuv}^n \right]\!\!\right] = \left[\!\!\left[\bigvee_{u \in S} \bigwedge_{v \in S} \psi_{stuv}^n \right]\!\!\right] = f_{st}^n.$$

The above can be summarized as follows.

Definition 21. *For all* s, $t \in S$,

$$\varphi_{st}^0 = \text{false}$$

and

$$\varphi_{st}^1 = \begin{cases} \text{false } if \ (s,t) \in S_0^2 \cup S_?^2 \\ \ell(s) \ if \ (s,t) \in S_1^2 \end{cases}$$

For all $s, t \in S$ and $n \geq 2$,

$$\varphi_{st}^n = \begin{cases} \text{false} & \text{if } (s,t) \in S_0^2 \\ \ell(s) & \text{if } (s,t) \in S_1^2 \\ (\bigcirc \psi_{st}^{n-1}) \ominus (f_{st}^{n-1} \cdot \tau(t)) & \text{if } (s,t) \in S_?^2 \end{cases}$$

For all $(s,t) \in S_?^2$ and $n \geq 1$,

$$\psi_{st}^n = \bigwedge_{u \in S} \bigvee_{v \in S} \psi_{stuv}^n$$

For all $(s,t) \in S_?^2$, $u, v \in S$, and $n \geq 1$,

$$\psi_{stuv}^n = \begin{cases} \text{false} \oplus f_{st}^n(u) & \text{if } f_{st}^n(u) = f_{st}^n(v) \\ (\varphi_{uv}^n \ominus (\delta_n(u,v) - (f_{st}^n(u) - f_{st}^n(v)))) \oplus f_{st}^n(v) & \text{if } f_{st}^n(u) > f_{st}^n(v) \\ (\varphi_{vu}^n \ominus (\delta_n(u,v) - (f_{st}^n(v) - f_{st}^n(u)))) \oplus f_{st}^n(u) & \text{otherwise.} \end{cases}$$

Note that, for $(s,t) \in S_?^2$ and $n \geq 2$, the formula φ_{st}^n contains $|S|^2$ subformulas of the form φ_{uv}^{n-1}. As a consequence, the size of φ_{st}^n grows exponentially in n. As we will see in Section 7, we can compute φ_{st}^n in polynomial time by sharing subformulas.

The above definition shows some similarities with the sequence of formulas introduced in [43, Definition 8]. Their setting is different: the transitions are labelled (as in [20]), the transition function is deterministic, and the labelling of the transitions is probabilistic. Their logic is simpler than the one introduced in [20] since the systems they consider are simpler. The sequence of formulas that they introduce is syntactically simpler than the one we define above. Their formulas are only used to prove a logical characterization, although those formulas can also be used for explainability.

Consider the states s and t of the following labelled Markov chain.

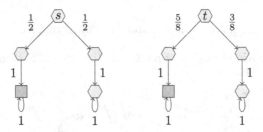

By definition, $\varphi_{st}^0 = \text{false}$ and $\varphi_{st}^1 = \text{false}$. For φ_{st}^2 we get

$$\overbrace{\phantom{(\bigcirc(((\text{false} \oplus 0) \vee (\text{false} \oplus 0) \vee \cdots \vee (\text{false} \oplus 0))\wedge}}^{\text{ten times}}$$

$$\left.\begin{array}{l} (\bigcirc(((\text{false} \oplus 0) \vee (\text{false} \oplus 0) \vee \cdots \vee (\text{false} \oplus 0))\wedge \\ ((\text{false} \oplus 0) \vee (\text{false} \oplus 0) \vee \cdots \vee (\text{false} \oplus 0))\wedge \\ \quad \vdots \\ ((\text{false} \oplus 0) \vee (\text{false} \oplus 0) \vee \cdots \vee (\text{false} \oplus 0)))) \end{array}\right\} \text{ten times}$$

$$\ominus 0$$

This formula can be simplified to false. In the logic of Desharnais et al., which lacks $\wedge$ and $\oplus$, one would need 111 additional $\neg$, making it less concise.

The formula φ^3_{st} fills more than a page, but can be simplified to the formula $(\bigcirc(\langle\diamondsuit\rangle \wedge \bigcirc\langle\diamondsuit\rangle)) \ominus 0.375$. Although generally there does not exist a distinguishing formula for each pair of states (Theorem 17), in this case the formula φ^3_{st} explains the distance of states s and t, since $\delta(s,t) = 0.125$, $[\![\varphi^3_{st}]\!](s) = 0.125$ and $[\![\varphi^3_{st}]\!](t) = 0$. The formula captures the probability of reaching a green state in one transition and subsequently reaching another green state.

The formula φ^3_{ts} can be simplified to $(\bigcirc(\langle\diamondsuit\rangle \wedge \bigcirc\blacksquare)) \ominus 0.5$. Since we have that $[\![\varphi^3_{ts}]\!](t) = 0.125$ and $[\![\varphi^3_{ts}]\!](s) = 0$, the formula φ^3_{ts} explains the distance $\delta(t,s) = 0.125$. The formula represents the probability of reaching a green state in one transition and subsequently reaching a purple state.

The outermost test can be removed from the explanation. Hence, the formulas $\bigcirc(\langle\diamondsuit\rangle \wedge \bigcirc\langle\diamondsuit\rangle)$ and $\bigcirc(\langle\diamondsuit\rangle \wedge \bigcirc\blacksquare)$ explain the distance of states s and t as well.

Theorem 22.

(a) For all s, $t \in S$ and $n \geq 0$, $[\![\varphi^n_{st}]\!](s) = \delta_n(s,t)$ and $[\![\varphi^n_{st}]\!](t) = 0$.
(b) For all $(s,t) \in S^2_?$ and $n \geq 1$, $[\![\psi^n_{st}]\!] = f^n_{st}$.
(c) For all $(s,t) \in S^2_?$, u, $v \in S$, and $n \geq 1$, $[\![\psi^n_{stuv}]\!](u) = f^n_{st}(u)$ and $[\![\psi^n_{stuv}]\!](v) = f^n_{st}(v)$.

Proof sketch. This theorem can be proved by induction on n. Most steps of the proof have already been discussed above. To prove (c), let $(s,t) \in S^2_?$, u, $v \in S$ and $n \geq 1$. We need to distinguish three cases. Here we only consider the case that $f^n_{st}(u) > f^n_{st}(v)$. Then

$$
\begin{aligned}
[\![\psi^n_{stuv}]\!](u) &= [\![(\varphi^n_{uv} \ominus (\delta_n(u,v) - (f^n_{st}(u) - f^n_{st}(v)))) \oplus f^n_{st}(v)]\!](u) \\
&= \min\{\max\{[\![\varphi^n_{uv}]\!](u) - (\delta_n(u,v) - (f^n_{st}(u) - f^n_{st}(v))), 0\} + f^n_{st}(v), 1\} \\
&= \min\{\max\{\delta_n(u,v) - (\delta_n(u,v) - (f^n_{st}(u) - f^n_{st}(v))), 0\} + f^n_{st}(v), 1\} \\
&\quad \text{[induction hypothesis of (a)]} \\
&= \min\{\max\{f^n_{st}(u) - f^n_{st}(v)), 0\} + f^n_{st}(v), 1\} \\
&= \min\{(f^n_{st}(u) - f^n_{st}(v)) + f^n_{st}(v), 1\} \qquad [f^n_{st}(u) > f^n_{st}(v)] \\
&= \min\{f^n_{st}(u), 1\} \\
&= f^n_{st}(u) \\
[\![\psi^n_{stuv}]\!](v) &= [\![(\varphi^n_{uv} \ominus (\delta_n(u,v) - (f^n_{st}(u) - f^n_{st}(v)))) \oplus f^n_{st}(v)]\!](v) \\
&= \min\{\max\{[\![\varphi^n_{uv}]\!](v) - (\delta_n(u,v) - (f^n_{st}(u) - f^n_{st}(v))), 0\} + f^n_{st}(v), 1\} \\
&= \min\{\max\{0 - (\delta_n(u,v) - (f^n_{st}(u) - f^n_{st}(v))), 0\} + f^n_{st}(v), 1\} \\
&\quad \text{[induction hypothesis of (a)]} \\
&= \min\{0 + f^n_{st}(v), 1\} \\
&\quad [f^n_{st}(u) - f^n_{st}(v) \leq \delta_n(u,v) \text{ since } f^n_{st} \text{ is nonexpansive}] \\
&= f^n_{st}(v)
\end{aligned}
$$

$\square$

Combining Proposition 8 and Theorem 22, we obtain the following explainability result.

Corollary 23. *For all s, $t \in S$, $\lim_{n \to \infty} [\![\varphi_{st}^n]\!](s) - [\![\varphi_{st}^n]\!](t) = \delta(s,t)$.*

6   Computing f_{st}^n

Proposition 19 states that the functions f_{st}^n exist. Below, we will show that these functions can be computed in polynomial time.

Let $(s,t) \in S_?^2$. The function $f_{st}^0 \in S \to (\mathbb{Q} \cap [0,1])$ is defined as the constant zero function satisfies $\delta_1(s,t) = f_{st}^0 \cdot (\tau(s) - \tau(t))$ and can be computed in polynomial time. To prove that the remaining functions f_{st}^n, with $n \geq 1$, can be computed in polynomial time as well, we use the primal network simplex algorithm to solve minimum-cost flow problems due to Orlin [42] and the ellipsoid method to solve linear programming problems due to Khachiyan [32]. As we will show below, f_{st}^n can be computed as $\text{FINDVERTEX}(\delta_n, \tau(s), \tau(t))$.

1 $\text{FINDVERTEX}(d, \mu, \nu)$
2      $input : d \in S \times S \to (\mathbb{Q} \cap [0,1])$ with $d(s,s) = 0$ for all $s \in S$, $\mu, \nu \in \mathcal{D}_{\mathbb{Q}}(S)$
3      $output : \quad \underset{f \in (S,d) \to (\mathbb{Q} \cap [0,1])}{\arg\max} \quad f \cdot (\mu - \nu)$
4 $d_{\mu\nu} = \underset{\omega \in \Omega_{\mathbb{R}}(\mu,\nu)}{\inf} \omega \cdot d$
5 $f_{\mu\nu} = \text{vertex of } \{f \in (S,d) \to [0,1] \mid f \cdot (\mu - \nu) = d_{\mu\nu}\}$
6 $\text{return } f_{\mu\nu}$

In line 4 we use Orlin's primal network simplex algorithm to compute the minimum cost for the following network (N, E). The nodes of the network consist of two copies of each $u \in S$, denoted u_0 and u_1. The supply of node u_0 is $\mu(u)$ and the demand of node u_1 is $\nu(u)$. Each edge (u_0, v_1) has cost $d(u,v)$.

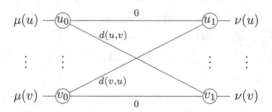

Each $\omega \in \Omega_{\mathbb{R}}(\mu, \nu)$ corresponds to a feasible flow, where $\omega(u,v)$ captures the flow from u_0 to v_1. The constraints $\omega(u, S) = \mu(u)$ and $\omega(S, u) = \nu(u)$, defining $\Omega_{\mathbb{R}}(\mu, \nu)$, capture that the supply of u_0 flows from u_0 and the demand of u_1 flows to u_1. For a feasible flow ω, its cost is $\omega \cdot d$. Hence, $d_{\mu\nu}$ captures the minimum cost.

Note that, by definition, the supplies and demands are rational. We can prove that $d_{\mu\nu} = \omega \cdot d$ for some $\omega \in \Omega_{\mathbb{Q}}(\mu, \nu)$. Since d is rational as well, we can conclude that $d_{\mu\nu}$ is also rational. Orlin's primal network simplex algorithm can compute the minimum cost and, hence, can be used to compute $d_{\mu\nu}$. Orlin's algorithm is strongly polynomial: $O(|N|^2|E|^2 \log |N|)$. Since there are $2|S|$ nodes and $|S|^2$ edges, $d_{\mu\nu}$ can be computed in $O(|S|^6 \log |S|)$.

In line 5 we use Khachiyan's ellipsoid method to find a feasible solution of a linear programming problem with the variables x_s, for $s \in S$, and the constraints

$$\forall s,t \in S : x_s - x_t \leq d(s,t)$$
$$\forall s \in S : x_s \geq 0$$
$$\forall s \in S : x_s \leq 1$$
$$\sum_{s \in S} x_s (\mu(s) - \nu(s)) = d_{\mu\nu}$$

By means of the ellipsoid method we can find a vertex of the convex polytope defined by the above constraints. This method is polynomial in the size of the constraints, in this case, the size of d, μ, ν, and $d_{\mu\nu}$.

Let $n \geq 1$ and $(s,t) \in S_?^2$. Since we can show that δ_n is rational and $\delta_n(s,s) = 0$ for all $s \in S$, we can apply FINDVERTEX to δ_n, $\tau(s)$ and $\tau(t)$. In this case, line 4 computes $\inf_{\omega \in \Omega_{\mathbb{R}}(\tau(s),\tau(t))} \omega \cdot \delta_n$, which equals $\delta_{n+1}(s,t)$. As a consequence, FINDVERTEX$(\delta_n, \tau(s), \tau(t))$ returns $f_{st}^n : (S, \delta_n) \nrightarrow (\mathbb{Q} \cap [0,1])$ such that $f_{st}^n \cdot (\tau(s) - \tau(t)) = \delta_{n+1}(s,t)$.

As we already observed above, line 4 can be computed in polynomial time in the size of the labelled Markov chain and line 5 can be computed in polynomial time in the size of δ_n, $\tau(s)$, $\tau(t)$, and $\delta_{n+1}(s,t)$, which we can show to be polynomial time in the size of the labelled Markov chain and n. Hence, the running time of FINDVERTEX$(\delta_n, \tau(s), \tau(t))$ is polynomial in the size of the labelled Markov chain and n.

7   The Algorithm

Given a labelled Markov chain $\langle S, L, \tau, \ell \rangle$ and $N \in \mathbb{N}$, we can explain the distances $\delta(s,t)$ for $s, t \in S$ by computing the formulas φ_{st}^n for $0 \leq n \leq N$. To obtain this sequence of formulas, we implement Definition 21 as follows. Below, for s, t, $u \in S$, we use the array cells distance$[s][t]$, function$[s][t][u]$, and formula$[s][t][n]$ to represent the distance $\delta_{n-1}(s,t)$, the function value $f_{st}^{n-1}(u)$, and the formula φ_{st}^n, respectively. In line 5-17, we compute δ_0, f_{st}^0, φ_{st}^0, and φ_{st}^1. The loop of line 20–50, first computes the distances δ_n (line 21–27), then determines the function f_{st}^n (line 30), and finally computes formulas φ_{st}^{n+1} (line 31–49).

```
1   EXPLAINDISTANCES(τ, ℓ, N):
2       input : τ ∈ S → D_Q(S), ℓ ∈ S → L, N ≥ 1
3       output : (φ_st^n)_{n=0}^N for all s, t ∈ S
```

```
 4   ~ = DecideProbabilisticBisimilarity(τ, ℓ) for s ∈ S and t ∈ S
 5       formula[s][t][0] = false
 6       distance[s][t] = 0
 7       if  s ∼ t
 8           for  1 ≤ n ≤ N
 9               formula[s][t][N] = false
10       else  if  ℓ(s) ≠ ℓ(t)
11           for  1 ≤ n ≤ N
12               formula[s][t][N] = ℓ(s)
13       else
14           formula[s][t][1] = false
15           for  u ∈ S
16               function[s][t][u] = 0
17
18   n = 1
19   while n < N
20       for  s ∈ S and t ∈ S
21           if  ℓ(s) ≠ ℓ(t)
22               distance[s][t] = 1
23           if  s ≁ t ∧ ℓ(s) = ℓ(t)
24               distance[s][t] = 0
25               for  u ∈ S
26                   distance[s][t] += function[s][t][u] * (τ(s)(u) − τ(t)(u))
27       for  s ∈ S and t ∈ S
28           if  s ≁ t ∧ ℓ(s) = ℓ(t)
29               function[s][t] = FindVertex(distance, τ(s), τ(t))
30               disjunction = false
31               for  u ∈ S
32                   conjunction = true
33                   for  v ∈ S
34                       if  function[s][t][u] = function[s][t][v]
35                           subformula = false ⊕ function[s][t][u]
36                       else
37                           minusShift = distance[u][v] − |function[s][t][u] − function[s][t][v]|
38                           plusShift  = min {function[s][t][u], function[s][t][v]}
39                           if  function[s][t][u] > function[s][t][v]
40                               subformula = (formula[u][v][n] ⊖ minusShift) ⊕ plusShift
41                           else
42                               subformula = (formula[v][u][n] ⊖ minusShift) ⊕ plusShift
43                       disjunction ∨= subformula
44                   conjunction ∧= disjunction
45                   shift  = 0;
46                   for  u ∈ S
47                       shift += function[s][t][u] * τ(t)(u)
48                   formula[s][t][n + 1] = (○ disjunction) ⊖ shift
49       n = n + 1
```

Let us first discuss the correctness of the above algorithm. In line 4, ∼ is computed by deciding probabilistic bisimilarity. The loop spanning line 20–50 has the following invariant.

$$\forall s, t \in S : \text{distance}[s][t] = \delta_{n-1}(s, t) \tag{1}$$

$$\forall (s, t) \in S_?^2 : \forall u \in S : \text{function}[s][t][u] = f_{st}^{n-1}(u) \tag{2}$$

$$\forall s, t \in S : \forall 0 \leq i \leq n : \text{formula}[s][t][i] = \varphi_{st}^i \tag{3}$$

Let us check that the above loop invariant holds when we reach line 21 for the first time. In line 7 we set distance to zero. Hence, (1) is satisfied when we reach line 21. In line 17 we set function to zero. Hence, (2) is also satisfied when we reach line 21. In line 6, 10, 13, and 15 we set formula such that (3) is satisfied when we reach line 21.

Next, we check that the loop maintains the above invariant, that is, if the invariant holds at line 21 then it also holds at line 50. Assume that the invariant holds at line 21. From (2) and line 22–27 we can conclude that

$$\text{distance}[s][t] = \begin{cases} 0 & \text{if } (s, t) \in S_0^2 \\ 1 & \text{if } (s, t) \in S_1^2 \\ f_{st}^{n-1} \cdot (\tau(s) - \tau(t)) & \text{otherwise} \end{cases}$$

once we arrive at line 28. Hence, from Proposition 19 we can conclude that distance$[s][t] = \delta_n(s, t)$ for all $s, t \in S$. Therefore, (1) holds at line 50.

Since distance $= \delta_n$ at line 30 and, as we have seen in Section 6, FINDVERTEX($\delta_n, \tau(s), \tau(t)$) returns f_{st}^n, we assign f_{st}^n to function$[s][t]$ in line 30. Hence, (2) holds at line 50. We can also verify that line 31–49 ensure that (3) is maintained by the loop.

Finally, we will argue that the running time of the above algorithm is polynomial in the size of the labelled Markov chain and N. Probabilistic bisimilarity can be decided in polynomial time as was first shown by Baier [3]. More efficient algorithms have been proposed by Buchholz [7], Derisavi, Hermanns, and Sanders [17] and Valmari and Franceschinis [50]. Hence, line 4 is polynomial time.

Each line of 6–17 can be implemented in constant time. Since each line of this part is executed at most $N|S|^3$ times, the running time of line 5–17 is polynomial in the size of the labelled Markov chain and N.

The loop consisting of line 20–50 is executed $N - 1$ times. As we already discussed in Section 6, the running time of FINDVERTEX($\delta_n, \tau(s), \tau(t)$) is polynomial in the size of the labelled Markov chain and n. When we arrive at line 30, distance equals δ_n and, hence, this line is polynomial in the size of the labelled Markov chain and n. All other lines of the loop can be implemented in constant time. Each line is executed at most $|S|^4$ times. Therefore, the running time of line 20–50 is polynomial in the size of the labelled Markov chain and N.

8   Conclusion

In this paper, we study a minor variation of the logic introduced by Desharnais et al. in [20]. In particular, we show that

1. the logic is a minimal one that characterizes the probabilistic bisimilarity distances,
2. in general, there does not exist a distinguishing formula φ_{st} for states s and t such that $[\![\varphi_{st}]\!](s) - [\![\varphi_{st}]\!](t) = \delta(s,t)$,
3. there exists a sequence $(\varphi_{st}^n)_n$ of formulas that explains distance $\delta(s,t)$ as $\lim_{n\to\infty} [\![\varphi_{st}^n]\!](s) - [\![\varphi_{st}^n]\!](t) = \delta(s,t)$, and
4. each formula φ_{st}^n can be computed in polynomial time.

As pointed out by Hillerström in [30], an early paper on computing distinguishing formulas, to explain why states are not bisimilar "arguments must be *concise* in the sense that an argument must not contain redundant or irrelevant information." This applies to our setting as well. The distinguishing formulas introduced in Definition 21 are in many cases far from concise. We leave the simplification of these formulas for future research.

One may wonder whether adding *fixed points* to the logic, in the form variables X and either operators μX and νX or equations of the form $X = \varphi$, would allow us to explain the probabilistic bisimilarity distance of two states by means of a single formula. A logic similar to the one studied in this paper that contains fixed points has been studied by De Alfaro et al. [1]. Whether simply adding fixed points to the logic suffices is not immediately clear as the $\ominus p_n$ and $\oplus q_n$ in the formula ψ_{uvst}^n vary as n varies. Extending the logic so that the probabilistic bisimilarity distance of two states can be explained by means of a single formula is another potential topic for future research.

Graf and Sifakis [28] introduce the notion of a *characteristic formula* for a state s: a state satisfies this formula if and only if it is behaviourally equivalent to s. Characteristic formulas have been developed for probabilistic bisimilarity. For example, Deng and van Glabbeek [16] present characteristic formulas for probabilistic automata. Sack and Zhang [47] introduce a general framework to construct characteristic formulas for probabilistic automata. In the setting of probabilistic bisimilarity distances, a characteristic formula for a state s of a labelled Markov chain can be formalized in the following ways. The formula φ_s is a characteristic formula for the state s if

$$\text{for all states } t, \ [\![\varphi_s]\!](s) - [\![\varphi_s]\!](t) = \delta(s,t) \tag{4}$$

or

$$\text{for all states } t, \ [\![\varphi_s]\!](t) = \delta(s,t). \tag{5}$$

It can be shown that (4) and (5) are equivalent: if there exists a formula that satisfies (4) then there also exists a (different) formula that satisfies (5). Whether such a formula or a sequence of such formulas exists for the logic studied in this paper is an open question that may be tackled in future research.

A preliminary implementation of the algorithm in Java is available [45]. Improving the code is another avenue for further research.

Acknowledgements The authors thank the referees for their very detailed and constructive feedback. The second author thanks the Department of Computer Science of the University of Oxford for hosting him for his sabbatical during which part of this research was carried out.

References

1. Luca de Alfaro, Rupak Majumdar, Vishwanath Raman, and Mariëlle Stoelinga. Game relations and metrics. In *Proceedings of the 22nd Annual IEEE Symposium on Logic in Computer Science*, pages 99–108, Wroclaw, Poland, July 2007. IEEE.
2. Robert Ash. *Real Analysis and Probability*. Academic Press, New York, NY, USA, 1972.
3. Christel Baier. Polynomial time algorithms for testing probabilistic bisimulation and simulation. In Rajeev Alur and Thomas Henzinger, editors, *Proceedings of the 8th International Conference on Computer Aided Verification*, volume 1102 of *Lecture Notes in Computer Science*, pages 50–61, New Brunswick, NJ, USA, July/August 1996. Springer-Verlag.
4. Marco Bernardo and Marino Miculan. Constructive logical characterizations of bisimilarity for reactive probabilistic systems. *Theoretical Computer Science*, 764(11):80–99, April 2019.
5. Franck van Breugel, Claudio Hermida, Michael Makkai, and James Worrell. Recursively defined metric spaces without contraction. *Theoretical Computer Science*, 380(1/2):143–163, June 2007.
6. Franck van Breugel and James Worrell. Towards quantitative verification of probabilistic systems. In Fernando Orejas, Paul Spirakis, and Jan van Leeuwen, editors, *Proceedings of the 28th International Colloquium on Automata, Languages and Programming*, volume 2076 of *Lecture Notes in Computer Science*, pages 421–432, Crete, Greece, July 2001. Springer-Verlag.
7. Peter Buchholz. Efficient computation of equivalent and reduced representations for stochastic automata. *Computer Systems Science and Engineering*, 15(2):93–103, 2000.
8. Neil Carothers. *Real analysis*. Cambridge University Press, Cambridge, United Kingdom, 2000.
9. Valentina Castiglioni, Daniel Gebler, and Simone Tini. Logical characterization of bisimulation metrics. In Mirco Tribastone and Herbert Wiklicky, editors, *Proceedings 14th International Workshop Quantitative Aspects of Programming Languages and Systems*, volume 227 of *Electronic Proceedings in Theoretical Computer Science*, pages 44–62, Eindhoven, The Netherlands, April 2016.
10. Valentina Castiglioni and Simone Tini. Logical characterization of branching metrics for nondeterministic probabilistic transition systems. *Information and Computation*, 268, October 2019.
11. Di Chen, Franck van Breugel, and James Worrell. On the complexity of computing probabilistic bisimilarity. In Lars Birkedal, editor, *Proceedings of the 15th International Conference on Foundations of Software Science and Computational Structures*, volume 7213 of *Lecture Notes in Computer Science*, pages 437–451, Tallinn, Estonia, March/April 2012. Springer-Verlag.
12. Rance Cleaveland. On automatically distinguishing inequivalent processes. In Edmund Clarke and Robert Kurshan, editors, *Proceedings of a DIMACS Workshop on Computer Aided Verification*, volume 3 of *DIMACS Series in Discrete Mathematics and Theoretical Computer Science*, pages 463–476, New Brunswick, NJ, USA, June 1990. DIMACS/AMS.
13. Brian Davey and Hilary Priestley. *Introduction to lattices and order*. Cambridge University Press, Cambridge, United Kingdom, 2002.
14. Christian Dehnert, Sebastian Junges, Joost-Pieter Katoen, and Matthias Volk. A Storm is coming: A modern probabilistic model checker. In Rupak Majumdar

and Viktor Kuncak, editors, *Proceedings of the 29th International Conference on Computer Aided Verification*, volume 10427 of *Lecture Notes in Computer Science*, pages 592–600, Heidelberg, Germany, July 2017. Springer-Verlag.

15. Yuxin Deng, Tom Chothia, Catuscia Palamidessi, and Jun Pang. Metrics for action-labelled quantitative transition systems. In Antonio Cerone and Herbert Wiklicky, editors, *Proceedings of 3rd Workshop on Quantitative Aspects of Programming Languages*, volume 153(2) of *Electronic Notes in Theoretical Computer Science*, pages 79–96, Edinburgh, UK, April 2005. Elsevier.

16. Yuxin Deng and Rob van Glabbeek. Characterising probabilistic processes logically. In Christian G. Fermüller and Andrei Voronkov, editors, *Proceedings of the 17th International Conference on Logic for Programming, Artificial Intelligence, and Reasoning*, volume 6397 of *Lecture Notes in Computer Science*, pages 278–293, Yogyakarta, Indonesia, October 2010. Springer-Verlag.

17. Salem Derisavi, Holger Hermanns, and William Sanders. Optimal state-space lumping in Markov chains. *Information Processing Letters*, 87(6):309–315, September 2003.

18. Josée Desharnais. *Labelled Markov Processes*. PhD thesis, McGill University, Montreal, November 1999.

19. Josée Desharnais, Abbas Edalat, and Prakash Panangaden. A logical characterization of bisimulation for labeled Markov processes. In *Proceedings of the 13th Annual IEEE Symposium on Logic in Computer Science*, pages 478–487, Indianapolis, IN, USA, June 1998. IEEE.

20. Josée Desharnais, Vineet Gupta, Radha Jagadeesan, and Prakash Panangaden. Metrics for labeled Markov systems. In Jos Baeten and Sjouke Mauw, editors, *Proceedings of the 10th International Conference on Concurrency Theory*, volume 1664 of *Lecture Notes in Computer Science*, pages 258–273, Eindhoven, The Netherlands, August 1999. Springer-Verlag.

21. Josée Desharnais, Vineet Gupta, Radha Jagadeesan, and Prakash Panangaden. Metrics for labelled Markov processes. *Theoretical Computer Science*, 318(3):323–354, June 2004.

22. Josée Desharnais, Radha Jagadeesan, Vineet Gupta, and Prakash Panangaden. The metric analogue of weak bisimulation for probabilistic processes. In *Proceedings of the 17th Annual IEEE Symposium on Logic in Computer Science*, pages 413–422, Copenhagen, Denmark, July 2002. IEEE.

23. Josée Desharnais, François Laviolette, and Mathieu Tracol. Approximate analysis of probabilistic processes: logic, simulation and games. In *Proceedings of the 5th International Conference on the Quantitative Evaluation of Systems*, pages 264–273, Saint-Malo, France, September 2008. IEEE.

24. Wenjie Du, Yuxin Deng, and Daniel Gebler. Behavioural pseudometrics for nondeterministic probabilistic systems. In Martin Fränzle, Deepak Kapur, and Naijun Zhan, editors, *Proceedings of the 2nd International Symposium on Dependable Software Engineering: Theories, Tools, and Applications*, volume 9984 of *Lecture Notes in Computer Science*, pages 67–84, Beijing, China, November 2016. Springer-Verlag.

25. Yuan Feng and Lijun Zhang. When equivalence and bisimulation join forces in probabilistic automata. In Cliff Jones, Pekka Pihlajasaari, and Jun Sun, editors, *Proceedings of the 19th International Symposium on Formal Methods*, volume 8442 of *Lecture Notes in Computer Science*, pages 247–262, Singapore, May 2014. Springer-Verlag.

26. Norm Ferns, Prakash Panangaden, and Doina Precup. Metrics for finite Markov decision processes. In *Proceedings of the 20th Annual Conference on Uncertainty in Artificial Intelligence*, pages 162–169, Banff, Canada, July 2004. AUAI Press.

27. Alessandro Giacalone, Chi-Chang Jou, and Scott Smolka. Algebraic reasoning for probabilistic concurrent systems. In *Proceedings of the IFIP WG 2.2/2.3 Working Conference on Programming Concepts and Methods*, pages 443–458, Sea of Gallilee, Israel, April 1990. North-Holland.

28. Susanne Graf and Joseph Sifakis. A modal characterization of observational congruence on finite terms of CCS. In Jan Paredaens, editor, *Proceedings of the 11th Colloquium on Automata, Languages and Programming*, volume 172 of *Lecture Notes in Computer Science*, pages 222–234, Antwerp, Belgium, July 1984. Springer-Verlag.

29. Matthew Hennessy and Robin Milner. On observing nondeterminism and concurrency. In Jaco de Bakker and Jan van Leeuwen, editors, *Proceedings of the 7th Colloquium on Automata, Languages and Programming*, volume 85 of *Lecture Notes in Computer Science*, pages 299–309, Noordwijkerhout, The Netherlands, July 1980. Springer-Verlag.

30. Michael Hillerström. Verification of CSS-processes. Master's thesis, Aalborg University, Aalborg, Denmark, January 1987.

31. Leonid Kantorovich and Gennadi Rubinstein. On the space of completely additive functions (in Russian). *Vestnik Leningradskogo Universiteta*, 3(2):52–59, 1958.

32. Leonid Khachiyan. A polynomial algorithm in linear programming (in Russian). *Doklady Akademii Nauk SSSR*, 244(5):1093–1096, 1979. English translation in *Soviet Mathematics Doklady*, 20:191–194, 1979.

33. Viktor Klee and Christoph Witzgall. Facets and vertices of transportation polytopes. In George Dantzig and Arthur Veinott, editors, *Proceedings of 5th Summer Seminar on the Mathematics of the Decision Sciences*, volume 11 of *Lectures in Applied Mathematics*, pages 257–282, Stanford, CA, USA, June/July 1967. AMS.

34. Stephen Kleene. *Introduction to Metamathematics*. Van Nostrand, New York, NY, USA, 1952.

35. Yuichi Komorida, Shin-ya Katsumata, Clemens Kupke, Jurriaan Rot, and Ichiro Hasuo. Expressivity of quantitative modal logics : Categorical foundations via codensity and approximation. In *Proceedings of the 36th Annual ACM/IEEE Symposium on Logic in Computer Science*, pages 1–14, Rome, Italy, June/July 2021.

36. Barbara König and Christina Mika-Michalski. (Metric) bisimulation games and real-valued modal logics for coalgebras. In Sven Schewe and Lijun Zhang, editors, *Proceedings of the 29th International Conference on Concurrency Theory*, volume 118 of *Leibniz International Proceedings in Informatics*, pages 37:1–37:17, Beijing, China, September 2018. Schloss Dagstuhl - Leibniz-Zentrum für Informatik.

37. Barbara König, Christina Mika-Michalski, and Lutz Schröder. Explaining nonbisimilarity in a coalgebraic approach: Games and distinguishing formulas. In Daniela Petrisan and Jurriaan Rot, editors, *Proceedings of 15th IFIP WG 1.3 International Workshop on Coalgebraic Methods in Computer Science*, volume 12094 of *Lecture Notes in Computer Science*, pages 133–154, Dublin, Ireland, April 2020. Springer-Verlag.

38. Marta Kwiatkowska, Gethin Norman, and David Parker. PRISM 4.0: Verification of probabilistic real-time systems. In Ganesh Gopalakrishnan and Shaz Qadeer, editors, *Proceedings of the 23rd International Conference on Computer Aided Verification*, volume 6806 of *Lecture Notes in Computer Science*, pages 585–591, Snowbird, UT, USA, July 2011. Springer-Verlag.

39. Kim Larsen and Arne Skou. Bisimulation through probabilistic testing. In *Proceedings of the 16th Annual ACM Symposium on Principles of Programming Languages*, pages 344–352, Austin, TX, USA, January 1989. ACM.

40. David Luenberger and Yinyu Ye. *Linear and nonlinear programming*. Springer-Verlag, New York, NY, USA, 2008.

41. Robin Milner. *A Calculus of Communicating Systems*, volume 92 of *Lecture Notes in Computer Science*. Springer-Verlag, Berlin, Germany, 1980.

42. James Orlin. A polynomial time primal network simplex algorithm for minimum cost flows. *Mathematical Programming*, 78(2):109–129, August 1997.

43. Vera Pantelic and Mark Lawford. A pseudometric in supervisory control of probabilistic discrete event systems. *Discrete Event Dynamic Systems*, 22(4):479–510, December 2012.

44. David Park. Concurrency and automata on infinite sequences. In Peter Deussen, editor, *Proceedings of 5th GI-Conference on Theoretical Computer Science*, volume 104 of *Lecture Notes in Computer Science*, pages 167–183, Karlsruhe, Germany, March 1981. Springer-Verlag.

45. Amgad Rady and Franck van Breugel. Java code to explain probabilistic bisimilarity distances for labelled Markov chains, February 2023. https://doi.org/10.5281/zenodo.7626542.

46. Michel Reniers, Rob Schoren, and Tim Willemse. Results on embeddings between state-based and event-based systems. *The Computer Journal*, 57(1):73–92, 2014.

47. Joshua Sack and Lijun Zhang. A general framework for probabilistic characterizing formulae. In Viktor Kuncak and Andrey Rybalchenko, editors, *Proceedings of the 13th International Conference on Verification, Model Checking, and Abstract Interpretation*, volume 7148 of *Lecture Notes in Computeer Science*, pages 396–411, Philadelphia, PA, USA, January 2012. Springer-Verlag.

48. Qiyi Tang. *Computing probabilistic bisimilarity distances*. PhD thesis, York University, Toronto, Canada, August 2018.

49. Kathleen Trustrum. *Linear programming*. Routledge & Kegan Paul, London, UK, 1971.

50. Antti Valmari and Giuliana Franceschinis. Simple $O(m \log n)$ time Markov chain lumping. In Javier Esparza and Rupak Majumdar, editors, *Proceedings of the 16th International Conference on Tools and Algorithms for the Construction and Analysis of Systems*, volume 6015 of *Lecture Notes in Computer Science*, pages 38–52, Paphos, Cyprus, March 2010. Springer-Verlag.

51. Paul Wild and Lutz Schröder. Characteristic logics for behavioural metrics via fuzzy lax extensions. In Igor Konnov and Laura Kovács, editors, *Proceedings of the 31st International Conference on Concurrency Theory*, volume 171 of *Leibniz International Proceedings in Informatics*, pages 27:1–27:23, Vienna, Austria, September 2020. Schloss Dagstuhl - Leibniz-Zentrum für Informatik.

52. Thorsten Wißmann, Stefan Milius, and Lutz Schröder. Explaining behavioural inequivalence generically in quasilinear time. In Serge Haddad and Daniele Varacca, editors, *Proceedings of the 32nd International Conference on Concurrency Theory*, volume 203 of *Leibniz International Proceedings in Informatics*, pages 32:1–32:18, Paris, France, April 2021. Schloss Dagstuhl - Leibniz-Zentrum für Informatik.

Weighted and Branching Bisimilarities from Generalized Open Maps

Jérémy Dubut[1]([✉])[ⓘ] and Thorsten Wißmann[2,3][ⓘ][*]

[1] National Institute of Advanced Industrial Science and Technology, Tokyo, Japan
jeremy.dubut@aist.go.jp
[2] Radboud University, Nijmegen, the Netherlands
t.wissmann@cs.ru.nl
[3] Friedrich-Alexander-Universität Erlangen-Nürnberg, Erlangen, Germany

Abstract. In the open map approach to bisimilarity, the paths and their runs in a given state-based system are the first-class citizens, and bisimilarity becomes a derived notion. While open maps were successfully used to model bisimilarity in non-deterministic systems, the approach fails to describe quantitative system equivalences such as probabilistic bisimilarity. In the present work, we see that this is indeed impossible and we thus generalize the notion of open maps to also accommodate weighted and probabilistic bisimilarity. Also, extending the notions of strong path and path bisimulations into this new framework, we show that branching bisimilarity can be captured by this extended theory and that it can be viewed as the history preserving restriction of weak bisimilarity.

Keywords: Open maps · Weighted Bisimilarity · Probabilistic Bisimilarity · Branching Bisimilarity · Weak Bisimilarity

1 Introduction

The theory of open maps is a categorical framework to reason about systems and their bisimilarities [16]. Given a category of systems and a description of the shape of the executions and how to extend them, open maps are morphisms with lifting properties with respect to those extensions. Intuitively, open maps are morphisms which preserve and reflect transitions of systems, that is, they are morphisms whose graphs are bisimulations. The theory covers various classical notions of bisimilarity. For example, two LTSs are strongly bisimilar if and only if there is a span of open maps between them. Varying the category of models and the execution shapes allows describing weak bisimilarity, timed bisimilarity, probabilistic Larsen and Skou bisimilarity, and history-preserving bisimilarity of event structures (see [16,3,12] for examples).

Another categorical framework for bisimilarity is coalgebra [22]. This time, given a category and an endofunctor describing respectively the type of state spaces and the type of transitions, a 'system' is understood as a coalgebra for this

---

[*] Supported by the NWO TOP project 612.001.852.

O. Kupferman and P. Sobocinski (Eds.): FoSSaCS 2023, LNCS 13992, pp. 308–327, 2023.
https://doi.org/10.1007/978-3-031-30829-1_15

functor. Coalgebra homomorphisms are then very similar to open maps in spirit: they also are morphisms that preserve and reflect transitions. This intuition has been made formal by transformations between the categorical frameworks in both ways; from open maps to coalgebra [19], and conversely [25]. However, the latter suggests that open maps are only adapted to modeling non-deterministic systems and would struggle with other types of branchings, such as probabilistic.

In coalgebra, there are no particular difficulties in modeling weighted systems, and by extension, discrete probabilistic systems [17]. There is also some work for continuous probabilities, although the theory is much more complicated [5,4]. As we will explain more precisely later, there have been some attempts to do so with open maps in [3,5], but the result is somewhat disappointing.

Conversely, coalgebra is not adapted to bisimilarities for systems where transitions are not history-preserving, that is, for which the behavioral equivalence does not just depend on the transitions at a given state, but on the whole history of the execution that led to this state. That is the case for example for branching bisimilarity [23]. Branching bisimilarity arose precisely to make weak bisimilarity history-preserving. In [3], weak bisimilarity has been described using open maps by carefully choosing the underlying category, with a general theory developed in [9] using presheaf models. Branching bisimilarity has also been studied using open maps in [1,2], but indirectly, through a translation into presheaves.

To resume, the goal of this paper is to capture weighted and branching bisimilarities using a generalization of open maps. Concretely, the contributions are:

1. a proof that it is impossible to appropriately model probabilistic system using standard open maps (Section 3.2),
2. a faithful extension of the theory of open maps and (strong) path bisimulations (Section 4),
3. a generalized open map situation capturing weighted and probabilistic bisimilarities (Section 5),
4. a generalized open map situation where strong path bisimulations correspond to stuttering branching bisimulations, open map bisimilarity to branching bisimilarity, and path bisimulations to weak bisimulations (Section 6).

Full proofs can be found in the appendix: http://arxiv.org/abs/2301.07004

2   From Path Categories to Bisimilarity

Before discussing weighted bisimilarity, let us first recall the main ideas of modeling bisimilarity via open maps, as introduced by Joyal et al. [16]. The definition is parametric in a functor $J \colon \mathbb{P} \to \mathbb{M}$, from a category $\mathbb{P}$ of paths to a category $\mathbb{M}$ of models or systems of interest. In the prime example, $\mathbb{M}$ is the category of labelled transition systems LTS as defined next:

Definition 2.1. *For a fixed set A of labels, the category* LTS *contains:*

1. *Objects: a labelled transition system $(X, \to, x_0)$ is a set X of states, a transition relation $\to \, \subseteq X \times A \times X$ and a distinguished initial state $x_0 \in X$. We*

write $x \xrightarrow{a} x'$ to denote that $(x, a, x') \in \ \to$ and simply refer to the LTS as X if $\to$ and x_0 are clear from the context. For disambiguation, we use $\to$ for morphisms and $\to$ for transitions.

2. *Morphisms:* a functional simulation $f : (X, \to, x_0) \to (Y, \to, y_0)$ is a function $f : X \to Y$ with $f(x_0) = y_0$ and for all $x \xrightarrow{a} x'$ in X, we have $f(x) \xrightarrow{a} f(x')$.

A functional simulation $f : X \to Y$ intuitively means that the system Y has at least the transitions of X, but possibly more. A special case of a functional simulation is the *run* of a word in a system:

Definition 2.2. *For the label set A, let $(A^*, \leqslant)$ be the partially ordered set of words, ordered by the prefix ordering. The functor $J : (A^*, \leqslant) \to$ LTS sends a word $w \in A^*$ to the LTS $Jw = (\{v \mid v \leqslant w\}, \to, \varepsilon)$ of all prefixes of w with $v \xrightarrow{a} va$ for all $a \in A$, $va \leqslant w$.*

This functor J (or more precisely, its image) is often called *path category* of LTS: the possible runs of a word $w \in A^*$ in $(X, \to, x_0)$ correspond precisely to the functional simulations $Jw \to (X, \to, x_0)$ in LTS.

On the abstract level, for a general functor $J : \mathbb{P} \to \mathbb{M}$, we understand the set of morphisms $r : Jw \to X$ for $w \in \mathbb{P}$ and $X \in \mathbb{M}$ as the runs of the path w in the model X. We can already make the trivial observation that all morphisms $f : X \to Y$ in $\mathbb{M}$ preserve runs: given a run $r : Jw \to X$ of some path $w \in \mathbb{P}$ in X, there is a run $f \cdot r : Jw \to Y$ of w in Y.

The converse does not hold for a general $f : X \to Y$ in $\mathbb{M}$: given a run of w in Y, there is not necessarily a run of w in X. If f reflects runs, it is called *open:*

Definition 2.3. *For a functor $J : \mathbb{P} \to \mathbb{M}$, a morphism $f : X \to Y$ in $\mathbb{M}$ is called* open *if f satisfies the following lifting property for all $e : v \to w$ in $\mathbb{P}$:*

$$
\begin{array}{ccc}
Jv \ -r\to\ X & & Jv \ -r\to\ X \\
\downarrow_{Je} \quad \circlearrowleft \quad \downarrow^{f} & \quad \text{there is } d : Jw \to X \text{ with} \quad & \downarrow_{Je} \ \overset{\circlearrowleft}{\underset{d}{\nearrow}} \ \downarrow^{f} \\
Jw \ -s\to\ Y & & Jw \ -s\to\ Y
\end{array}
$$

That is, for all commutative squares $(s \cdot Je = f \cdot r)$, there is $d : Jw \to X$ in $\mathbb{M}$ that makes both triangles on the right commute $(f \cdot d = s$ and $d \cdot Je = r)$.

By construction, we can only make statements about states that are reachable via some run. Thus, one often restricts $\mathbb{M}$ beforehand to contain only models in which all states are reachable from the initial state.

For LTSs in which all states are reachable from the initial state, open maps are related to strong bisimulations [20]: open maps are precisely functions whose graph relation $\{(x, fx) \mid x \in X\}$ is a strong bisimulation. Reformulated in the context of allegories [10], open maps are precisely the maps in the allegory of relations that are strong bisimulations. It is then natural to recover bisimulations as tabulations of open maps, that is:

Definition 2.4. *For a functor $J : \mathbb{P} \to \mathbb{M}$, we say that two models X and Y are* J-bisimilar, *if there exist another model Z and two J-open maps $f : Z \to X$ and $g : Z \to Y$, that is, if there is a span of J-open maps between them.*

Of course, J-bisimilarity is a reflexive (identities are open maps) and symmetric (by permuting f and g in the definition) relation on models, but it is not transitive in general. It is when the category $\mathbb{M}$ has pullbacks [16].

Given a functor $J\colon \mathbb{P} \to \mathbb{M}$, there are more classical ways of defining bisimilarities given in [16]. The first one is *(strong) path bisimulations*, which are relations on runs (similar to history-preserving bisimulations) satisfying the usual bisimilarity conditions. The second one is by using a modal logic similar to the Hennessy-Milner theorem. In the case of LTSs with strong bisimilarity, all those notions describe the same notion of bisimilarity, but that is not true for general $J\colon \mathbb{P} \to \mathbb{M}$: it can only be proved that J-bisimilarity implies the existence of a (strong) path bisimulation, which itself implies that the two models satisfy the same formulas of the modal logic. In [6], some mild sufficient conditions in terms of trees (i.e., colimits of paths in $\mathbb{M}$) are given for those three notions to coincide. In particular, all the examples of bisimilarities covered by open maps cited earlier satisfy these conditions.

We use coalgebra for uniform statements about state-based systems of different branching type (including non-deterministic and probabilistic branching):

Definition 2.5. *For an object* 1 *of a category* C *and an endofunctor* $F\colon C \to C$, *a pointed coalgebra is a pair of morphisms of* C *of the form* $1 \xrightarrow{\ i\ } X \xrightarrow{\ \xi\ } FX$.

For example, LTSs can be modeled as pointed coalgebras with $C = $ Set, 1 any singleton, and $F = \mathcal{P}(A \times \_)$, where $\mathcal{P}$ is the power set functor. The usual notion of morphisms of coalgebras can be spelt out as follows:

Definition 2.6. *A (proper) homomorphism of pointed coalgebras from* (X, ξ, i) *to* (Y, ζ, j) *is a morphism* $f\colon X \to Y$ *of* C *such that the diagram on the right commutes.*

$$
\begin{array}{ccccc}
1 & \xrightarrow{\ i\ } & X & \xrightarrow{\ \xi\ } & FX \\
& \searrow & \downarrow{\scriptstyle f} & & \downarrow{\scriptstyle Ff} \\
& {\scriptstyle j} & Y & \xrightarrow{\ \zeta\ } & FY
\end{array}
$$

Pointed coalgebras and proper homomorphisms always form a category, but in the case of LTSs as described above, this category is not equivalent to the category LTS. Indeed, proper homomorphisms are not just morphisms that preserve transitions, but similarly to open maps, they also reflect them. In [25], the authors proved that for a large class of endofunctors, whose coalgebras basically are non-deterministic, proper homomorphisms precisely correspond to J-open maps for a certain functor J. To model morphisms that are only required to preserve transitions, homomorphisms have to be made lax as follows (see [25]):

Definition 2.7. *Assume a relation* $\sqsubseteq$ *on every Hom-set* $C(X, FY)$. *A lax homomorphism of pointed coalgebras from* (X, ξ, i) *to* (Y, ζ, j) *is a morphism* $f\colon X \to Y$ *of* C *such that the diagram on the right laxly commutes, that is,* $f \cdot i = j$ *and* $Ff \cdot \xi \sqsubseteq \zeta \cdot f$ *in* $C(X, FY)$.

$$
\begin{array}{ccccc}
1 & \xrightarrow{\ i\ } & X & \xrightarrow{\ \xi\ } & FX \\
& \searrow & \downarrow{\scriptstyle f} & \sqsubseteq & \downarrow{\scriptstyle Ff} \\
& {\scriptstyle j} & Y & \xrightarrow{\ \zeta\ } & FY
\end{array}
$$

In the case of the functor $\mathcal{P}(A \times \_)$, we can consider the pointwise inclusion on every Hom-set $\mathrm{Set}(X, \mathcal{P}(A \times Y))$. With this, pointed coalgebras and lax homomorphisms form a category which is isomorphic to the category LTS. However, it is not true in general that they form a category, as a compatibility of $\sqsubseteq$ with the composition is needed as follows:

Definition 2.8. *A partial order on F is a collection of partial orders $\sqsubseteq$, one for each Hom-set of the form $\mathcal{C}(X, FY)$ such that*

$$\forall X \xrightarrow{f_1, f_2} FY,\ X' \xrightarrow{g} X,\ Y \xrightarrow{h} Y': \quad f_1 \sqsubseteq f_2 \ \Rightarrow \ Fh \cdot f_1 \cdot g \sqsubseteq Fh \cdot f_2 \cdot g.$$

This is equivalent to the requirement that the Hom-functor $\mathcal{C}(\_, F\_)$ factors through partially ordered sets: $\mathcal{C}(\_, F\_) \colon \mathcal{C}^{\mathrm{op}} \times \mathcal{C} \to \mathsf{Pos}$.

Remark 2.9. The present definition subsumes the definition of order on a Set-functor established by Hughes and Jacobs [11, Def 2.1] (details in the appendix).

Lemma 2.10 [25]. *When $\sqsubseteq$ is a partial order on F, pointed coalgebras and lax homomorphisms form a category, which we denote by $\mathsf{LCoalg}(1, F)$.*

Much as with open maps, many flavors of bisimilarity can be recovered using spans of proper homomorphisms:

Definition 2.11. *We say that two pointed coalgebras are coalgebraically bisimilar if there is a span of proper homomorphisms between them.*

There are many ways of defining bisimilarities in coalgebra (see [13] for an overview), but they coincide for the purpose of the present paper.

3 Weighted Bisimilarity and Open Maps

In this section, we describe known attempts to model weighted systems, and particularly probabilistic ones, using open maps. They all work with some variations of the (discrete) distribution functor on Set. We will denote this functor, which maps a set X to the set

$$\mathcal{D}X = \{f \colon X \to [0, 1] \mid f^{-1}\big((0, 1]\big) \text{ is finite and } \sum_{x \in X} f(x) = 1\},$$

by $\mathcal{D}$ and the variation where the condition $= 1$ is replaced by $\leqslant 1$ by $\mathcal{D}_{\leqslant 1}$ (i.e. $\mathcal{D}_{\leqslant 1}X := \mathcal{D}(X + 1)$). We will prove that, even though Larsen-Skou bisimulations for reactive systems can be modeled with open maps, that is impossible for bisimulations for generative systems.

3.1 Larsen-Skou Bisimilarity Using Open Maps

In [3], Cheng et al. describe an open map situation for Probabilistic Transition Systems (PTSs), which corresponds to coalgebras for the functor $(\mathcal{D}(\_) + 1)^A$. In this setting, they consider Partial PTSs (PPTS) which are coalgebras for $(\mathcal{D}_{\leqslant 1}^{\varepsilon}(\_) + 1)^A$ where the sub-probability distributions can have values in hyper-reals, allowing infinitesimals ε. The category of PTSs embeds in that of PPTSs, and the path category is the full subcategory of PPTSs consisting of finite linear systems whose probabilities of transitions are infinitesimals. It is then proved that J-bisimilarity, restricted to PTSs, for this path category corresponds to Larsen-Skou's probabilistic bisimilarity [18].

This open map situation has been reformulated in [7] in terms of coreflections: the obvious functor from PPTSs to TSs is a coreflection whose left-adjoint maps a LTS T to the PPTS whose underlying LTS is T and where all transitions have infinitesimal probabilities. In general, given a coreflection $F : \mathcal{C} \to \mathcal{D}$ with left-adjoint G and a path category J on $\mathcal{D}$, one automatically has the path category $G \circ J$ on $\mathcal{C}$, and this construction preserves good properties of J. In particular, one has that two systems A and B are $(G \circ J)$-bisimilar if and only if FA and FB are J-bisimilar. Cheng et al.'s path category is obtained in this manner with the coreflection above and the standard path category on LTSs. In particular, it means that two PPTSs are bisimilar if and only if their underlying TSs are strongly bisimilar.

3.2 Impossibility Result for Generative Systems

In [5], Desharnais et al. describe several bisimilarities for generative probabilistic systems, that is, coalgebras for the functor $\mathcal{D}_{\leqslant 1}(A \times \_)$, in a coalgebraic way. They pointed out that their efforts to model those bisimilarities using open maps failed [5, p. 188]. In the following, we see that it is in fact not possible. We will show that for generative probabilistic systems modeled by the category $M :=$ LCoalg$(1, \mathcal{D}_{\leqslant 1}(A \times \_))$, there is no open map characterization of the coalgebraic bisimilarity. Actually, the argument here is valid for many other types of weights and is not limited to reals.

Here, for two functions $f, g \colon X \to \mathcal{D}_{\leqslant 1}(Y)$, $f \sqsubseteq g$ means that for all $x \in X$, for all $y \in Y$, $f(x)(y) \leqslant g(x)(y)$, where $\leqslant$ is the usual ordering on $[0, 1]$.

In this situation:

Theorem 3.1. *For* $M :=$ LCoalg$(1, \mathcal{D}_{\leqslant 1}(A \times \_))$ *there is no category* $\mathbb{P}$ *and no functor* $J \colon \mathbb{P} \to M$ *such that for every* $h \colon X \to Y$ *with reachable* X *the following equivalence holds:*

$$h \text{ is } J\text{-open} \quad \Longleftrightarrow \quad h \text{ is a proper homomorphism}$$

and there is no $\mathbb{P}$ *and no functor* J *such that for every* X *and* Y*:*

$$X \text{ and } Y \text{ are } J\text{-bisimilar} \quad \Longleftrightarrow \quad X \text{ and } Y \text{ are coalgebraically bisimilar.}$$

Proof (Sketch). By contradiction, assume that there is such a J. We prove that there is a proper homomorphism of the form:

which cannot be J-open. Consider first the unique lax homomorphism $0_M \to Y$ where 0_M consists in one state and no transition. This is not a proper homomorphism, so it is not open by assumption. That is there is a square:

$$
\begin{array}{ccc}
JP & \xrightarrow{\;p\;} & 0_M \\
\downarrow{\scriptstyle J\phi} & & \downarrow{\scriptstyle !_Y} \\
JQ & \xrightarrow{\;q\;} & Y
\end{array}
$$

with no lifting. It is mechanical to check that $JP \simeq 0_M$ and JQ has at least one transition from its initial state to another state $r \xrightarrow{w,a} z$ with $w \neq 0$. With $n = 2 \cdot \lceil \frac{1}{w} \rceil$, the proper homomorphism h above is not open: there cannot be a morphism from JQ to X because $w > \frac{1}{n}$. $\qquad\square$

4 Generalized Open Maps

The main argument of the proof of impossibility is the fact that sometimes, a transition with some probability w in the codomain comes from probabilities $w_1, \ldots, w_n$ with $\sum_i w_i = w$ in the domain, which makes a lifting morphism impossible with the current framework of open maps.

In this section, we will extend the open map framework with the main intuition that the lifting morphism *splits* the probability w into smaller parts $w_1, \ldots, w_n$. After defining these generalized open maps, we show some basic properties of the bisimilarity generated by them.

4.1 Generalized Open Maps Situation

Here, we describe our extension of the open maps framework. The data is similar: we start with a category of models M, but we need more than just a functor $J : \mathbb{P} \to M$. Assume:

- a set V together with a function $J : V \to ob(M)$,
- two small categories $\mathbb{E}$ and $\mathbb{S}$ whose sets of objects are V,
- two functors $J_{\mathbb{E}} : \mathbb{E} \to M$ and $J_{\mathbb{S}} : \mathbb{S} \to M$ coinciding with J on objects.

The classical open maps situation $J : \mathbb{P} \to M$ fits in this extension as follows. The category $\mathbb{E}$ is given by $\mathbb{P}$ with the intention that they model path shapes and their *extensions*. The functor $J_{\mathbb{E}}$ is given by J. The category $\mathbb{S}$ is given by the discrete category $|\mathbb{P}|$, that is, the category whose objects are those of $\mathbb{P}$ and whose morphisms are only identities. The functor $J_{\mathbb{S}}$ is the only possible one respecting the conditions of the definition above.

In the general context of this extension, the interpretation is a bit different. Now V is meant to be a set of trees labelled by alphabets and weights. $\mathbb{E}$ still consists in extensions, extending trees into trees with longer branches. $\mathbb{S}$ then consists in *merging morphisms*, similar to the description above: for the example of weighted systems, those morphisms are allowed to merge states into one, as long as they sum up the weights of the in-going branches. Generally, those morphisms are allowed to perform some merges that are harmless for bisimilarity.

With this data, we can define generalized open maps:

Definition 4.1. *A morphism $f: X \to Y$ in $\mathbb{M}$ is called $(\mathbb{E}, \mathbb{S})$-open if it satisfies the following lifting property for all $e: v \to w$ in $\mathbb{E}$:*

$$
\text{for all} \quad
\begin{array}{ccc}
Jv & \xrightarrow{\ x\ } & X \\
\scriptstyle{J_{\mathbb{E}}e} \downarrow & \circlearrowleft & \downarrow \scriptstyle{f} \\
Jw & \xrightarrow{\ y\ } & Y
\end{array}
\qquad \text{there is} \qquad
\begin{array}{ccc}
Jv & \xrightarrow{\qquad x \qquad} & X \\
\scriptstyle{J_{\mathbb{E}}e} \downarrow \; {\scriptstyle J_{\mathbb{E}}e'} & \circlearrowleft \quad {\scriptstyle x'} & \downarrow \scriptstyle{f} \\
J_{\mathbb{E}}e \downarrow \quad Ju & \circlearrowleft & \\
\downarrow \; {\scriptstyle J_{\mathbb{S}}s} & & \\
Jw & \xrightarrow{\qquad y \qquad} & Y
\end{array}
$$

The interpretation starts the same as in usual open maps. Assume that we have a tree y in Y extending the image by f of the tree x in X. If f is open, there should be a tree x' extending x and whose image by f is y. However, x' may have a different shape than y, since it might be necessary to split transitions. That is what u and s are modeling: w is obtained from u by merging some states.

The connection with the classical open maps can be formulated as follows

Proposition 4.2. *Given a functor $J: \mathbb{P} \to \mathbb{M}$ and a morphism $f: X \to Y$,*

$$f \text{ is } J\text{-open if and only if } f \text{ is } (\mathbb{P}, |\mathbb{P}|)\text{-open.}$$

Again, bisimilarity can be defined as the existence of a span of open maps

Definition 4.3. *We say that X and Y are $(\mathbb{E}, \mathbb{S})$-bisimilar if there is a span of $(\mathbb{E}, \mathbb{S})$-open maps between them.*

4.2   Basic Properties

In this section, we will prove general properties of $(\mathbb{E}, \mathbb{S})$-bisimilarity similar to the classical case. First, we show that if $\mathbb{M}$ has pullbacks, then $(\mathbb{E}, \mathbb{S})$-bisimilarity is an equivalence relation. Secondly, we describe two notions of path bisimulations, both implied by $(\mathbb{E}, \mathbb{S})$-bisimilarity. Finally, we prove that it is enough to check openness on some generators of $\mathbb{E}$.

In order to see when $(\mathbb{E}, \mathbb{S})$-bisimilarity is an equivalence relation, we need to check symmetry, reflexivity, and transitivity. *Symmetry* always holds because we can always swap the legs of the span. For *reflexivity*, it is enough to prove that identities are open which is valid because $\mathbb{S}$ is a category and $J_{\mathbb{S}}$ is a functor, as shown in the diagram on the right. The proof of *transitivity* relies on composition and pullbacks:

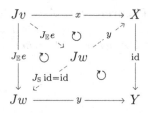

Lemma 4.4. $(\mathbb{E}, \mathbb{S})$-*open maps are closed under composition and pullbacks.*

Theorem 4.5. *If $\mathbb{M}$ has pullbacks, then $(\mathbb{E}, \mathbb{S})$-bisimilarity is a transitive relation, and thus is an equivalence relation.*

Generalized Path Bisimulations. In the classical open map setup [16], another notion of bisimilarity can be defined by using path extensions directly: so-called strong path and path bisimulations, which can be generalized as follows. Like originally [16], we assume that there is an element $0 \in V$, such that $J0$ is an initial object of $\mathbb{M}$ (note that 0 is not required to be initial in $\mathbb{E}$ or $\mathbb{S}$). The intuition is that the unique morphism $!_X : J0 \to X$ points to the initial state of X. For example, $J0$ can be given by $(1, \mathrm{id}_1, \bot)$ in a category of pointed coalgebras if 1 is the final object of $\mathcal{C}$ and if $\mathcal{C}(1, F1)$ has the least element $\bot : 1 \to F1$ (those conditions hold in the cases of interest).

Definition 4.6. *A path simulation* from A to B in $\mathbb{M}$ *is a set R of spans of the form $A \xleftarrow{a} Jv \xrightarrow{b} B$ (for $v \in V$) satisfying the following two properties*

- **initial condition:** *the span $A \xleftarrow{!_A} J0 \xrightarrow{!_B} B$ belongs to R.*
- **forward closure:** *for all spans $A \xleftarrow{a} Jv \xrightarrow{b} B$ in R, all $e: v \to w \in \mathbb{E}$ and all $a': Jw \to A \in \mathbb{M}$ such that $a = a' \cdot J_{\mathbb{E}}e$, there are $e': v \to u \in \mathbb{E}$, $s: u \to w \in \mathbb{S}$, and $b': Ju \to B \in \mathbb{M}$ such that $J_{\mathbb{E}}e = J_{\mathbb{S}}s \cdot J_{\mathbb{E}}e'$, $b = b' \cdot J_{\mathbb{E}}e'$, and the span $A \xleftarrow{a' \cdot J_{\mathbb{S}}s} Ju \xrightarrow{b'} B$ belongs to R.*

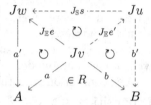

We say that R is a strong path simulation if it additionally satisfies the following:

- **backward closure:** *for all spans $A \xleftarrow{a} Jv \xrightarrow{b} B$ in R and all $e: w \to v \in \mathbb{E}$, we have that the span $A \xleftarrow{a \cdot J_{\mathbb{E}}e} Jw \xrightarrow{b \cdot J_{\mathbb{E}}e} B$ belongs to R.*

$$Jv \xleftarrow{J_{\mathbb{E}}e} Jw \xrightarrow{J_{\mathbb{E}}e} Jv$$

We say that R is a (strong) path bisimulation from A to B *if R and $R^\dagger = \{ B \xleftarrow{b} Jv \xrightarrow{a} A \mid A \xleftarrow{a} Jv \xrightarrow{b} B \in R \}$ are (strong) path simulations.*

Remark that this version of (strong) path bisimulations has the same type as the one by Joyal et al. [16], but satisfies more general conditions. In particular, when $\mathbb{S}$ is a discrete category, the formulation above is exactly the one from [16]. Obviously, a strong path bisimulation is a path bisimulation.

The main result of this section is the following.

Theorem 4.7. *Assume two models A and B in $\mathbb{M}$. If there is a span $A \xleftarrow{f} C \xrightarrow{g} B$ where g is a morphism of $\mathbb{M}$ and f is an $(\mathbb{E}, \mathbb{S})$-open map, then the following set is a strong path simulation:*

$$R_{f,g} := \{ A \xleftarrow{a} Jv \xrightarrow{b} B \mid \exists c: Jv \to C \text{ with } a = f \cdot c \text{ and } b = g \cdot c \}$$

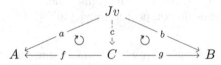

Consequently, if A and B are $(\mathbb{E}, \mathbb{S})$-bisimilar, then there is strong path bisimulation between them.

As in the classical case of [16], there is no reason for the converse to be true in general: there might be a strong path bisimulation between two models, but no span of generalized open maps. However, conditions from [6] could be accommodated to describe a general framework in which the converse holds. Since this is not the main focus of this paper, we will not do it here, but will show a particular case in Section 6.

Generators of the Category of Extensions. In the first example of open maps for LTSs introduced in Section 2, the path category was described as the poset of words with the prefix order. Consequently, to prove that a functional simulation is J-open, we have to prove the lifting property of Definition 4.1 with respect to all pairs $w \leqslant w'$. However, it is sufficient to check the lifting property for extensions by one letter: $w' = w.a$ for some $a \in A$. The general reason is that, as a category, $(A^*, \leqslant)$ is generated by the morphisms $w \leqslant w.a$, and verifying the lifting property with respect to generators of the category $\mathbb{P}$ is enough to obtain J-openness. This can be extended to generalized open maps, with additional care.

Proposition 4.8. *Assume a subgraph $\mathbb{E}'$ of $\mathbb{E}$ that generates $\mathbb{E}$, that is, every morphism of $\mathbb{E}$ is a finite composition of morphisms of $\mathbb{E}'$. Assume additionally, that for every $e \in \mathbb{E}'$ and $s \in \mathbb{S}$ for which $J_\mathbb{E}e \cdot J_\mathbb{S}s$ is well-defined, there are $s' \in \mathbb{S}$ and $e' \in \mathbb{E}'$ such that $J_\mathbb{E}e \cdot J_\mathbb{S}s = J_\mathbb{S}s' \cdot J_\mathbb{E}e'$.*

In that case, if a morphism of $\mathbb{M}$ satisfies the lifting property of Definition 4.1 for all morphisms in $\mathbb{E}'$, then it is $(\mathbb{E}, \mathbb{S})$-open. Also, if a set of spans satisfies the conditions of Definition 4.6, where $\mathbb{E}$ is replaced by $\mathbb{E}'$, then it is a (strong) path bisimulation.

The first condition is satisfied when $\mathbb{E}$ is a free category and $\mathbb{E}'$ is its class of generators. The second condition is satisfied for e.g. $\mathbb{E} = \mathbb{P}$ and $\mathbb{S} = |\mathbb{P}|$.

5   Open Maps for Weighted Systems

In this section, we will prove that weighted systems can be captured by this generalized open map theory for a large variety of weights, including those needed to capture probabilistic systems.

5.1   Category of Coalgebras for Weighted Systems

In this section, we will consider weighted functors as follows.

Definition 5.1. *Given a commutative monoid $(K, +, e)$, the K-weighted functor $(K, +, e)^{(-)} \colon \mathsf{Set} \to \mathsf{Set}$ is defined as follows on sets and maps:*

sets: $X \mapsto (K, +, e)^{(X)} = \{\mu \colon X \to K \mid \mu^{-1}(K \backslash \{e\})\ is\ finite\}$

maps: $f \colon X \to Y \mapsto (K, +, e)^{(f)}(\mu) = \big(y \in Y \mapsto \sum \{\mu(x) \mid x \in X, f(x) = y\}\big)$

An element μ of $(K,+,e)^{(X)}$ is a finite distributions sending each $x \in X$ to a weight in K. Whenever a map $f \colon X \to Y$ identifies elements $f(x_1) = f(x_2) = \cdots$, then the functor action turns μ into a distribution on Y by adding up the weights $\mu(x_1) + \mu(x_2) + \cdots$ as elements of X are sent to the same element in Y. Since μ is finite and K is commutative, this addition is well-defined.

Given a commutative monoid $(K,+,e)$ and an alphabet A, we want to consider weighted systems as coalgebras for the functor $(K,+,e)^{(A \times -)}$. As described in Section 2, we want to be able to talk about lax homomorphisms, so we need an order on $(K,+,e)^{(A \times -)}$ as in Definition 2.8. For that, we need to assume an ordered commutative monoid $(K,+,e,\sqsubseteq)$, that is, a monoid $(K,+,e)$ with a partial order $\sqsubseteq$ such that $+$ is monotone in both its arguments.

Lemma 5.2. *Given an ordered commutative monoid* $(K,+,e,\sqsubseteq)$*, then for all sets* X *and* Y*, the relation on the hom-set* $\mathsf{Set}\big(X,(K,+,e)^{(A \times Y)}\big)$ *defined by*

$$f_1 \sqsubseteq f_2 \iff \forall x \in X,\ \forall y \in Y,\ \forall a \in A,\ f_1(x)(a,y) \sqsubseteq f_2(x)(a,y)$$

is an order on $(K,+,e)^{(A \times -)}$.

So, we have a category $\mathsf{LCoalg}\big(1,(K,+,e)^{(A \times -)}\big)$ of pointed coalgebras and lax homomorphisms. The goal of this section is to design a generalized open maps situation for which $(\mathbb{E},\mathbb{S})$-bisimilarity characterizes coalgebraic bisimilarity and more precisely for which $(\mathbb{E},\mathbb{S})$-openness characterizes proper homomorphisms.

In the course of the constructions and proofs, we will need additional assumptions that we list here.

Definition 5.3. *We call an ordered commutative monoid* $(K,+,e,\sqsubseteq)$ *a rearrangement monoid if it satisfies the additional requirement that if* $n,m \geqslant 1$ *and*

$$\sum_{i=1}^{n} x_i \sqsubseteq \sum_{j=1}^{m} y_j,$$

then there exists a family $(u_{i,j})_{1 \leqslant i \leqslant n, 1 \leqslant j \leqslant m}$ *such that*

$$\text{for all } j,\ \sum_{i=1}^{n} u_{i,j} \sqsubseteq y_j \quad \text{and} \quad \text{for all } i,\ \sum_{j=1}^{m} u_{i,j} = x_i.$$

In addition, we say that a rearrangement monoid is strict *if the condition above holds also when replacing* $\sqsubseteq$ *with* $=$.

The intuition is as follows. We have some weights arranged as $x_1, \ldots, x_n$. We want to be able to decompose those weights into smaller weights, the $u_{i,j}$s, and by rearranging those small weights obtaining weights smaller than the y_j. This condition states that this is possible when there is enough weight in total. The special case of strictness is called the *row-column property* in [17].

Lemma 5.4. *For any subgroup G of the real numbers $(\mathbb{R}^n, +, -, 0)$ such that for all x, y in G $(\min(x_1, y_1), \ldots, \min(x_n, y_n)) \in G$, the monoids $(G, +, 0, \leqslant)$ and $(G_{\geqslant 0}, +, 0, \leqslant)$, where $\leqslant$ is the usual order on $\mathbb{R}^n$, are strict rearrangement monoids.*

For any lattice with bottom element $(L, \leqslant, \sqcup, \sqcap, \bot)$, $(L, \sqcup, \bot, \leqslant)$ is a rearrangement monoid if and only if $(L, \leqslant, \sqcup, \sqcap)$ is distributive. Furthermore, in that case, it is always strict.

Another property is a form of positivity: we say that an ordered monoid is *positively ordered* if e is the bottom element for $\sqsubseteq$, that is, for all $k \in K$, $e \sqsubseteq k$.

Example 5.5. The positive real line $(\mathbb{R}_+, +, 0, \leqslant)$ is a positively ordered strict rearrangement monoid and it is necessary to define probabilistic systems. Another example is the monoid of natural numbers $(\mathbb{N}, +, 0, \leqslant)$, which defines the bag functor. Finally, any distributive lattice with bottom element $(L, \sqcup, \bot, \leqslant)$, typically powerset lattices $(\mathcal{P}(X), \cup, \varnothing, \subseteq)$, is too. On the contrary, $(\mathbb{R}, +, 0, \leqslant)$ and $(\mathbb{Z}, +, 0, \leqslant)$ are strict rearrangement monoids but are not positively ordered. Conversely $(\mathbb{N}_{\geqslant 1}, \times, 1, \leqslant)$ is positively ordered but not a rearrangement monoid. Indeed, it is impossible to rearrange the inequality $2 \times 5 \leqslant 3 \times 4$.

5.2 Generalized Open Maps Situation for Weighted Systems

Let $(K, +, e, \sqsubseteq)$ be a commutative ordered monoid. Elements of V_K are

- either words on $A \times (K \backslash \{e\})$, $w = (a_1, k_1), \ldots, (a_n, k_n)$,
- or triples (w_1, b, w_2) of a word w_1 on $A \times (K \backslash \{e\})$, a letter $b \in A$, and a non-empty word w_2 on $(K \backslash \{e\})$.

The function J_K maps

- a word $w = (a_1, k_1), \ldots, (a_n, k_n)$ to the system

$$Jw = \boxed{\begin{array}{ccccc} \rightarrow 0 & \xrightarrow{(a_1, k_1)} & 1 & \xrightarrow{(a_2, k_2)} & \cdots & \xrightarrow{(a_n, k_n)} n \end{array}}$$

  that is, to the coalgebra $Jw: \{0, \ldots, n\} \to K^{(A \times \{0, \ldots, n\})}$ such that if $b = a_{i+1}$ and $j = i + 1$ then $Jw(i)(b, j) = k_{i+1}$, else $= e$.
- a triple (w_1, b, w_2) with $w_1 = (a_1, k_1), \ldots, (a_n, k_n)$ and $w_2 = l_1, \ldots, l_m$ is mapped to the system

$$J(w_1, b, w_2) = \boxed{\begin{array}{c} \rightarrow 0 \xrightarrow{(a_1, k_1)} 1 \xrightarrow{(a_2, k_2)} \cdots \xrightarrow{(a_n, k_n)} n \overset{(b, l_1)}{\underset{(b, l_m)}{\rightrightarrows}} \begin{array}{c} (n+1, 1) \\ \vdots \\ (n+1, m) \end{array} \end{array}}$$

  that is, $J(w_1, b, w_2)(n)(n+1, i) = (b, l_i)$.

The category $\mathbb{E}_K$ is defined as follows. For every w_1, b, and w_2, there is a unique edge e from w_1 to (w_1, b, w_2). The functor then maps this edge e to $J_{\mathbb{E}} e$, the obvious injection.

The category $\mathbb{S}_K$ has two types of morphisms:

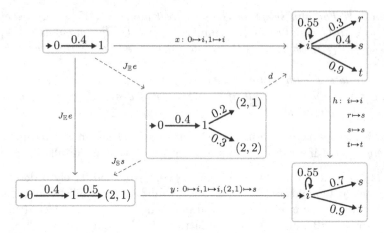

Fig. 1. Example of a lifting of a path extension in $\mathbb{R}_+$-weighted systems and for a singleton label alphabet $|A| = 1$, thus omitting action labels.

- identities on words w_1,
- morphisms from (w_1, b, w_2') to (w_1, b, w_2), with $w_2' = l_1', \ldots, l_{m'}'$ and $m \leqslant m'$, which are given by surjective monotone functions $s \colon \{1, \ldots, m'\} \to \{1, \ldots, m\}$ such that for all $i \leqslant m$, $l_i = \sum_{\{j|s(j)=i\}} l_j'$.

The functor $J_{\mathbb{S}}$ then maps s of the second type to the proper homomorphism $J_{\mathbb{S}}s$ which maps i to i and $(n+1, j)$ to $(n+1, s(j))$.

As a piece of notation, for a morphism $x \colon Jw_1 \to X$, with w_1 of length n we denote $x(n) \in X$ by $\mathrm{end}(x)$. We then say that a state p of X is reachable if there is a morphism of type $x \colon Jw_1 \to X$ with $\mathrm{end}(x) = p$. By extension, we say that X is reachable if all its states are reachable.

5.3   Equivalence between Open Maps and Proper Homomorphisms

An example of an $(\mathbb{E}, \mathbb{S})$-open map h is provided in Figure 1, together with a path extension that is lifted. Like it is often the case in the non-deterministic systems, the lifting map d is not unique. Hence, only existence (and no uniqueness) is required in the lifting property. Since h is a proper homomorphism, it provides a lifting for all extensions, as we show in general:

Theorem 5.6. *Assume a lax homomorphism $f \colon X \to Y$. If f is $(\mathbb{E}_K, \mathbb{S}_K)$-open, X is reachable, and K is positively ordered, then f is a proper homomorphism. Conversely, if f is a proper homomorphism and K is a rearrangement monoid, then f is $(\mathbb{E}_K, \mathbb{S}_K)$-open. In particular, if K is a positively ordered rearrangement monoid, two weighted systems X and Y are $(\mathbb{E}_K, \mathbb{S}_K)$-bisimilar if and only if they are coalgebraically bisimilar.*

For an endofunctor on Set, to prove that coalgebraic bisimilarity is an equivalence relation it is enough to show that the functor preserves weak-pullbacks. In the case of the weighted functor, this is given by strictness (see also [17]):

Corollary 5.7. *If K is a positively ordered strict rearrangement monoid, then $(\mathbb{E}_K, \mathbb{S}_K)$-bisimilarity is an equivalence relation.*

5.4 About Sub-distribution Functor

Until now, we have not dealt with probabilistic systems, that is, coalgebras for the sub-distribution functor $\mathcal{D}_{\leqslant 1}$. Those coalgebras are particular cases of coalgebras for the weighted functor $X \mapsto (\mathbb{R}_+, +)^{(X)}$. We want to show in this section that it is equivalent to consider coalgebras for $X \mapsto \mathcal{D}_{\leqslant 1}(A \times X)$ as coalgebras for $X \mapsto (\mathbb{R}_+, +)^{(A \times X)}$, in the sense that, two coalgebras for the former are bisimilar if and only if they are bisimilar when seen as coalgebras for the latter. The main ingredient is the following remark.

Lemma 5.8. *Assume a pointed coalgebra $1 \xrightarrow{i} X \xrightarrow{c} \mathcal{D}_{\leqslant 1}(A \times X)$ and assume given a lax (resp. proper) homomorphism f from $1 \xrightarrow{j} Y \xrightarrow{d} (\mathbb{R}_+, +)^{(A \times Y)}$ to $1 \xrightarrow{i} X \xrightarrow{c} \mathcal{D}_{\leqslant 1}(A \times X) \subseteq (\mathbb{R}_+, +)^{(A \times X)}$. Then $Y \xrightarrow{d} \mathcal{D}_{\leqslant 1}(A \times Y)$ and f is a lax (resp. proper) homomorphism from $1 \xrightarrow{j} Y \xrightarrow{d} \mathcal{D}_{\leqslant 1}(A \times Y)$ to $1 \xrightarrow{i} X \xrightarrow{c} \mathcal{D}_{\leqslant 1}(A \times X)$.*

Remark that this property is not true for the proper distribution functor $\mathcal{D}$. This suggests that we can define a generalized open maps situation $\mathbb{E}_{\mathcal{D}}, \mathbb{S}_{\mathcal{D}}$ for coalgebras for the functor $X \mapsto \mathcal{D}_{\leqslant 1}(A \times X)$ by considering $\mathbb{E}_{(\mathbb{R}_+, +)}, \mathbb{S}_{(\mathbb{R}_+, +)}$ as defined in Section 5.2, and restricting it to those v such that Jv is a coalgebra for $X \mapsto \mathcal{D}_{\leqslant 1}(A \times X)$.

Corollary 5.9. *A lax homomorphism from $1 \xrightarrow{j} Y \xrightarrow{d} \mathcal{D}_{\leqslant 1}(A \times Y)$ to $1 \xrightarrow{i} X \xrightarrow{c} \mathcal{D}_{\leqslant 1}(A \times X)$ is $(\mathbb{E}_{\mathcal{D}}, \mathbb{S}_{\mathcal{D}})$-open if and only if it is $(\mathbb{E}_{(\mathbb{R}_+, +)}, \mathbb{S}_{(\mathbb{R}_+, +)})$-open. Furthermore, two $\mathcal{D}_{\leqslant 1}(A \times \_)$-coalgebras are $(\mathbb{E}_{\mathcal{D}}, \mathbb{S}_{\mathcal{D}})$-bisimilar if and only if they are $(\mathbb{E}_{(\mathbb{R}_+, +)}, \mathbb{S}_{(\mathbb{R}_+, +)})$-bisimilar.*

Finally, the main result of this section:

Theorem 5.10. *Let $f: X \to Y$ be a lax homomorphism between $\mathcal{D}_{\leqslant 1}(A \times \_)$-coalgebras (X, c, i) and (Y, d, j). If (X, c, i) is reachable and f is $(\mathbb{E}_{\mathcal{D}}, \mathbb{S}_{\mathcal{D}})$-open, then f is a proper homomorphism. Conversely, if f is a proper homomorphism, then it is $(\mathbb{E}_{\mathcal{D}}, \mathbb{S}_{\mathcal{D}})$-open. Moreover, two $\mathcal{D}_{\leqslant 1}(A \times \_)$-coalgebras (X, c, i) and (Y, d, j) are $(\mathbb{E}_{\mathcal{D}}, \mathbb{S}_{\mathcal{D}})$-bisimilar if and only if they are coalgebraically bisimilar.*

6 Open Maps for Branching Bisimilarity

In this section, we present a new way of modeling branching and weak bisimulations using our generalized framework of open maps. Using this additional flexibility, we do not need to rely on weak morphisms anymore, but on a slight modification of the morphism described in Definition 2.1. Concretely, we build a generalized open map situation such that stuttering branching bisimulations coincide with strong path bisimulations, and that in this case, they precisely characterize $(\mathbb{E}, \mathbb{S})$-bisimilarity. In addition, in this framework, path bisimulations precisely correspond to weak bisimulations, witnessing branching bisimilarity as the history-preserving analogue to weak bisimilarity.

6.1   LTSs with Internal Moves, Category and Bisimilarities

Definition 6.1. *For a fixed set A of labels with a particular element τ (called internal move), the category* WLTS *contains the same objects as* LTS*, and its morphisms $f\colon (X, \to, x_0) \to (Y, \to, y_0)$ are functions $f\colon X \to Y$ such that $f(x_0) = y_0$ and for all $x \xrightarrow{a} x'$ in X, we have $f(x) \xrightarrow{a} f(x')$, or $a = \tau$ and $f(x) = f(x')$.*

LTS is a (non-full) subcategory of WLTS, and in fact the LTS-morphisms will be used later in the paper. For easier distinction, we use the terminology *strong morphisms* for WLTS-morphisms that are also in LTS (alluding to *strong bisimulations* which were the bisimulation notion in LTS). Another notion of morphisms are so-called *weak morphisms* [3]:

- if $x \xrightarrow{a} x'$ in X, then $f(x) \xrightarrow{\tau}{}^\star \xrightarrow{a} \xrightarrow{\tau}{}^\star f(x')$ in Y,
- if $x \xrightarrow{\tau} x'$ in X, then $f(x) \xrightarrow{\tau}{}^\star f(x')$ in Y.

Though we do not use weak morphisms in the following development of the paper, it is worth mentioning the WLTS-morphisms form a proper subclass of the weak morphisms.

Definition 6.2. *A branching bisimulation from $(X, \to_X, i_X)$ to $(Y, \to_Y, i_Y)$ is a relation $R \subseteq X \times Y$ such that $(i_X, i_Y) \in R$, and for $(x, y) \in R$:*

- *if $x \xrightarrow{a} x'$ then*
  - *$a = \tau$ and $(x', y) \in R$, or*
  - *$y \xrightarrow{\tau} y_1 \xrightarrow{\tau} \ldots \xrightarrow{\tau} y_n \xrightarrow{a} z_1 \xrightarrow{\tau} \ldots \xrightarrow{\tau} z_m$ such that (x, y_n), (x', z_1), and $(x', z_m) \in R$.*
- *symmetrically when $y \xrightarrow{a} y'$.*

If furthermore in the second condition (x, y_i), $(x', z_i) \in R$ for all i (and symmetrically in the third condition), then R is said to be stuttering.

It is known from [23] that the largest branching bisimulation is stuttering, so that both notions generate the same bisimilarity. In the following, we will prove that strong path bisimulations are more naturally related to stuttering branching bisimulations thanks to their backward closure.

Definition 6.3. *A weak bisimulation from $(X, \to_X, i_X)$ to $(Y, \to_Y, i_Y)$ is a relation $R \subseteq X \times Y$ such that $(i_X, i_Y) \in R$, and for $(x, y) \in R$:*

- *if $x \xrightarrow{\tau} x'$, then there is y' such that $(x', y') \in R$ and $y \xrightarrow{\tau}{}^\star y'$,*
- *if $x \xrightarrow{a} x'$ with $a \neq \tau$, then there is y' such that $(x', y') \in R$ and $y \xrightarrow{\tau}{}^\star \xrightarrow{a} \xrightarrow{\tau}{}^\star y'$.*
- *symmetrically when $y \xrightarrow{\tau} y'$ or $y \xrightarrow{a} y'$.*

It is clear that a (stuttering) branching bisimulation is a weak bisimulation.

6.2 Generalized Open Maps for Branching Bisimulations

In this section, we describe the generalized open maps situation that captures branching bisimulation. Like for plain LTSs (Def. 2.2), elements of V will be words on A, representing a finite linear LTS labelled by this word. However, to emphasize the particularity of the internal move τ, we will provide another presentation here.

Here, V is the set of sequences of the form: $v = n_1, a_1, n_2, \ldots, n_k, a_k, n_{k+1}$ such that $a_i \in A\backslash\{\tau\}$ and $n_i \in \mathbb{N}$, e.g. $\tau\tau a\tau b c\tau \stackrel{\wedge}{=} 2, a, 1, b, 0, c, 1$. The natural numbers $n_i \in \mathbb{N} \cong \{\tau\}^*$ represent the number of internal moves between two observable moves. Then, J maps this sequence to the usual linear LTS:

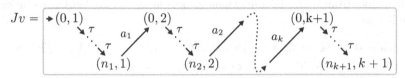

Elements of $\mathbb{E}$ append *at most* one observable (i.e. non-τ) move:

- **Only internal moves:** for sequences $v = n_1, a_1, \ldots, a_k, n_{k+1}$ and $w = n_1, a_1, \ldots, a_k, n'_{k+1}$ with $n_{k+1} \leqslant n'_{k+1}$ there is a unique edge $e_\tau \colon v \to w$ in $\mathbb{E}$, e.g. $e_\tau \colon 2, a, 1, b, 0, c, 1 \to 2, a, 1, b, 0, c, 3$
- **One observable move:** for sequences $v = n_1, a_1, \ldots, a_k, n_{k+1}$ and $w = n_1, a_1, \ldots, a_k, n'_{k+1}, a, n_{k+2}$ with $n_{k+1} \leqslant n'_{k+1}$ there is a unique edge $e_a \colon v \to w$ in $\mathbb{E}$.

The graph morphism $J_{\mathbb{E}} \colon \mathbb{E} \to \mathbb{M}$ maps those edges to the obvious inclusion, mapping state (i, j) of Jv to the same state in Jw.

Strictly speaking, $\mathbb{E}$ is not a category, but just a graph, because we have $a \xrightarrow{e_b} ab$ and $ab \xrightarrow{e_c} abc$, but there is no morphism from a to abc. To fit in the framework of Section 4, we take the free category Free($\mathbb{E}$) generated by this graph and the unique functor extending the graph homomorphism $J_{\mathbb{E}}$. By Proposition 4.8, it is equivalent to consider Free($\mathbb{E}$) and $\mathbb{E}$ for openness and path bisimulations, so we will talk of $(\mathbb{E}, \mathbb{S})$-openness, when we mean (Free($\mathbb{E}$), $\mathbb{S}$)-openness, and all the statements and proofs will be done using $\mathbb{E}$ only.

Elements of $\mathbb{S}$ are trickier to describe. The intuition is that they are morphisms that merge states. In the context of LTSs with internal moves, merging happens when the source and the target of a τ-transition are mapped to the same state. This is crucial for the open maps we want to describe: to lift one τ-transition, it might be necessary to use several τ-transitions. With this knowledge, elements of $\mathbb{S}$ are as follows.

- **Merging internal moves:** morphisms in $\mathbb{S}$ from $v = n_1, a_1, \ldots, a_k, n_{k+1}$ to $w = n'_1, a_1, \ldots, a_k, n'_{k+1}$ with $n_i \geqslant n'_i$ are $(k+1)$-tuples $s = (s_1, \ldots, s_{k+1})$ of monotone surjective functions $s_i \colon \{0 < 1 < \ldots < n_i\} \to \{0 < 1 < \ldots < n'_i\}$.

For example, there are two morphisms from $a\tau\tau b \stackrel{\wedge}{=} 0, a, 2, b, 0$ to $a\tau b \stackrel{\wedge}{=} 0, a, 1, b, 0$, one for each τ that can be dropped. The functor $J_{\mathbb{S}}$ then maps s to the morphism from Jv to Jw defined by $J_{\mathbb{S}}(s)(i, j) = (s_j(i), j)$.

As a piece of notation, for a morphism $x\colon J(n_1, a_1, \ldots, a_k, n_{k+1}) \to X$, we denote $x(n_{k+1}, k+1) \in X$ by $\mathrm{end}(x)$.

6.3   Equivalence of Bisimilarities

In this section, we prove that $(\mathbb{E}, \mathbb{S})$-bisimilarity indeed coincides with branching bisimilarity. To do so, we prove first that for the present instance of $\mathbb{E}$ and $\mathbb{S}$ (Sec. 6.2), $(\mathbb{E}, \mathbb{S})$-bisimilarity coincides with strong path bisimilarity. In general, $(\mathbb{E}, \mathbb{S})$-bisimilarity implies strong path bisimilarity (Theorem 4.7), so it remains to show the converse direction for the present instance. To this end, we start by internalizing strong path bisimulations into objects of LTS/WLTS, in order to relate it them to open maps:

Definition 6.4. *For a strong path bisimulation R from X to Y, define the LTS $\tilde{R} = (R, \to_R, (X \xleftarrow{!} J0 \xrightarrow{!} Y))$ to have transitions*

$$(X \xleftarrow{x} Jv \xrightarrow{y} Y) \xrightarrow{a}_R (X \xleftarrow{x'} Jw \xrightarrow{y'} Y)$$

- *for $a \neq \tau$ with $v = (n_1, a_1, \ldots, a_k, n_{k+1})$, $w = (n_0, a_1, \ldots, a_k, n_{k+1}, a, 0)$, $x' = x \cdot J_{\mathbb{E}} e_a$, and $y' = y \cdot J_{\mathbb{E}} e_a$ (for the unique $e_a\colon v \to w$);*
- *for $a = \tau$ with $v = (n_1, a_1, \ldots, a_k, n_{k+1})$, $w = (n_1, a_1, \ldots, a_k, n_{k+1} + 1)$, $x' = x \cdot J_{\mathbb{E}} e_\tau$, and $y' = y \cdot J_{\mathbb{E}} e_\tau$ (for the unique $e_\tau\colon v \to w$).*

As a first observation, we describe runs in $\tilde{R}$ in terms of projection maps:

Lemma 6.5. *In WLTS, we have projection maps $X \xleftarrow{\pi_X} \tilde{R} \xrightarrow{\pi_Y} Y$ given by $\pi_X\colon (X \xleftarrow{x} Jv \xrightarrow{y} Y) \mapsto \mathrm{end}(x)$ and $\pi_Y\colon (X \xleftarrow{x} Jv \xrightarrow{y} Y) \mapsto \mathrm{end}(y)$. For every strong morphism $r\colon Jv \to \tilde{R}$ (i.e. $r \in$ LTS),*

$$\mathrm{end}(r) \text{ is of the form } (X \xleftarrow{\pi_X \cdot r} Jv \xrightarrow{\pi_Y \cdot r} Y).$$

Remark that in this statement, we require r to be strong and not just a morphism of WLTS. With a morphism of WLTS, the statement would become that there is $s\colon v' \to v \in \mathbb{S}$ such that $\pi_X \cdot r = x \cdot J_{\mathbb{S}} s$ instead. For the characterization of open maps in WLTS, it suffices for our needs to restrict to strong morphisms:

Lemma 6.6. *For $f\colon X \to Y$ in WLTS to be $(\mathbb{E}, \mathbb{S})$-open, it is sufficient to verify the lifting in Definition 4.1 in the special case of x being a strong morphism.*

We use this simplification to prove that the projection maps π_X, π_Y are open:

Proposition 6.7. *For a strong path bisimulation R from X to Y, the projections $X \xleftarrow{\pi_X} \tilde{R} \xrightarrow{\pi_Y} Y$ are both $(\mathbb{E}, \mathbb{S})$-open.*

The next step is to prove the equivalence between strong path and stuttering branching bisimulations.

Table 1. Equivalences of bisimilarity notions in LTSs with τ-actions $X, Y \in \mathsf{WLTS}$

branching bisimilarity $\iff$	strong path bisimilarity	(Theorem 6.8)
$\iff$	$(\mathbb{E}, \mathbb{S})$-bisimilarity	(Proposition 6.7 & Theorem 4.7)
weak bisimilarity $\iff$	path bisimilarity	(Theorem 6.9)

Theorem 6.8. *If R is a stuttering branching bisimulation from X to Y, then*

$$\overline{R} = \{X \xleftarrow{x} Jv \xrightarrow{y} Y \mid v = (n_1, a_1, \ldots, n_{k+1}) \wedge \forall i, j. \, (x(i,j), y(i,j)) \in R\}$$

is a strong path bisimulation. Conversely, if R is a strong path bisimulation, then

$$\check{R} = \{(end(x), end(y)) \mid (X \xleftarrow{x} Jv \xrightarrow{y} Y) \in R\}$$

is a stuttering branching bisimulation.

The same reasoning can be made for weak and path bisimulations:

Theorem 6.9. *If R is a weak bisimulation from X to Y, then*

$$\widehat{R} = \{X \xleftarrow{x} Jv \xrightarrow{y} Y \mid (end(x), end(y)) \in R\}$$

is a path bisimulation. If R is a path bisimulation, then $\check{R}$ is a weak bisimulation.

In total, we can describe branching and weak bisimilarity by categorical bisimilarity notions, as summarized in Table 1.

7   Conclusions and Future Work

In this paper, we investigate bisimilarities of weighted and probabilistic systems through the theory of open maps. After showing that the usual theory cannot capture weights, we provide a faithful extension of the theory by the notion of mergings. The new theory has similar properties (equivalence relation, characterization as sets of spans, restriction to generators) as classical open maps but also captures bisimilarity of weighted systems and even branching bisimilarity.

The new instances come at the cost of more parameters to the theory. It remains for future work whether the parameters $\mathbb{E}$, $\mathbb{S}$ can be combined in a single path category with two morphism classes and morphism factorizations. It would also be illuminating to know whether this new theory satisfies the axioms of a *class of open maps* from [15], in particular for toposes of coalgebras [14].

For the framework as presented, we would like to formally relate it to coalgebra – as this has been done for non-deterministic systems [19,25]. Furthermore, we would like to investigate how system semantics of true concurrency, such as Higher Dimensional Automata [21] can be integrated. Designing open maps for them turned out to be complicated (see [8]), but a hope would be that the addition of mergings would allow modeling homotopy more naturally.

Finally, it would be interesting to see whether our theory capture quantitative extensions of systems classically modeled by open maps, such as probabilistic and quantum extensions of petri nets and event structures (see [24] for example).

References

1. Beohar, H., Cuijpers, P.J.L.: Open Maps in Concrete Categories and Branching Bisimulation for Prefix Orders. Electronic Notes in Theoretical Computer Science **319**, 51–66 (2015). https://doi.org/10.1016/j.entcs.2015.12.005
2. Beohar, H., Küpper, S.: Bisimulation Maps in Presheaf Categories. Electronic Notes in Theoretical Computer Science **347**, 5–24 (2019). https://doi.org/10.1016/j.entcs.2019.09.002
3. Cheng, A., Nielsen, M.: Open Maps (at) Work. B R I C S Report Series (RS-95-23) (1995)
4. Danos, V., Desharnais, J., Laviolette, F., Panangaden, P.: Bisimulation and cocongruence for probabilistic systems. Information and Computation **204**(4), 503–523 (2006). https://doi.org/10.1016/j.ic.2005.02.004
5. Desharnais, J., Edalat, A., Panangaden, P.: Bisimulation for Labelled Markov Processes. Information and Computation **179**(2), 163–193 (2003). https://doi.org/10.1006/inco.2001.2962
6. Dubut, J., Goubault, E., Goubault-Larrecq, J.: Bisimulations and unfolding in P-accessible categorical models. In: Desharnais, J., Jagadeesan, R. (eds.) 27th International Conference on Concurrency Theory, CONCUR 2016. LIPIcs, vol. 59, pp. 25:1–25:14. Schloss Dagstuhl - Leibniz-Zentrum für Informatik (2016). https://doi.org/10.4230/LIPIcs.CONCUR.2016.25
7. Dubut, J., Hasuo, I., Katsumata, S., Sprunger, D.: Quantitative bisimulations using coreflections and open morphisms (2018), arXiv:1809.09278
8. Fahrenberg, U., Legay, A.: History-Preserving Bisimilarity for Higher-Dimensional Automata via Open Maps. Electronic Notes in Theoretical Computer Science **298**, 165–178 (2013). https://doi.org/10.1016/j.entcs.2013.09.012
9. Fiore, M., Cattani, G.L., Winskel, G.: Weak bisimulation and open maps. In: Proceedings. 14th Symposium on Logic in Computer Science. pp. 67–76 (1999). https://doi.org/10.1109/LICS.1999.782590
10. Freyd, P., Scedrov, A.: Categories, Allegories, Mathematical Library, vol. 39. North-Holland (1990)
11. Hughes, J., Jacobs, B.: Simulations in coalgebra. Theor. Comput. Sci. **327**(1-2), 71–108 (2004). https://doi.org/10.1016/j.tcs.2004.07.022
12. Hune, T., Nielsen, M.: Timed bisimulations and open maps. In: Brim, L., Gruska, J., Zlatuška, J. (eds) Mathematical Foundations of Computer Science 1998. MFCS 1998. Lecture Notes in Computer Science, vol. 1450. Springer, Berlin, Heidelberg (1998). https://doi.org/10.1007/BFb0055787
13. Jacobs, B.: Introduction to Coalgebra: Towards Mathematics of States and Observation, Cambridge Tracts in Theoretical Computer Science, vol. 59. Cambridge University Press (2016)
14. Johnstone, P., Power, J., Tsujishita, T., Watanabe, H., Worrell, J.: On the structure of categories of coalgebras. Theoretical Computer Science **260**, 87–117 (2001). https://doi.org/10.1016/S0304-3975(00)00124-9
15. Joyal, A., Moerdijk, I.: A completeness theorem for open maps. Annals of Pure and Applied Logic **70**, 51–86 (1994). https://doi.org/10.1016/0168-0072(94)90069-8
16. Joyal, A., Nielsen, M., Winskel, G.: Bisimulation from Open Maps. Information and Computation **127**, 164–185 (1996). https://doi.org/10.1006/inco.1996.0057
17. Klin, B.: Semantics and Algebraic Specification, Lecture Notes in Computer Science, vol. 5700, chap. Structural Operational Semantics for Weighted Transition Systems, pp. 121–139. Springer, Berlin, Heidelberg (2009)

18. Larsen, K.G., Skou, A.: Bisimulations through Probabilistic Testing. Information and Computation **94**, 1–28 (1991). https://doi.org/10.1016/0890-5401(91)90030-6

19. Lasota, S.: Coalgebra morphisms subsume open maps. Theoretical Computer Science **280**(1), 123 – 135 (2002). https://doi.org/10.1016/S0304-3975(01)00023-8

20. Park, D.: Concurrency and automata on infinite sequences. In: Proceedings of the 5th GI-Conference on Theoretical Computer Science. Lecture Notes in Computer Science, vol. 104, pp. 167–183. Springer (1981). https://doi.org/10.1007/BFb0017309

21. Pratt, V.: Higher dimensional automata revisited. Mathematical Structures in Computer Science **10**(4), 525–548 (2000). https://doi.org/10.1017/S0960129500003169

22. Rutten, J.: Universal coalgebra: a theory of systems. Theoretical Computer Science **249**(1), 3 – 80 (2000). https://doi.org/10.1016/S0304-3975(00)00056-6

23. van Glabbeek, R.J., Weijland, W.P.: Branching Time and Abstraction in Bisimulation Semantics. Journal of the ACM **43**(3), 555–600 (1996). https://doi.org/10.1145/233551.233556

24. Winskel, G.: Distributed probabilistic and quantum strategies. Electronic Notes in Theoretical Computer Science **298**, 403–425 (2013). https://doi.org/10.1016/j.entcs.2013.09.024

25. Wißmann, T., Dubut, J., Katsumata, S., Hasuo, I.: Path category for free. In: Bojańczyk, M., Simpson, A. (eds.) Foundations of Software Science and Computation Structures (FoSSaCS 2019). pp. 523–540. Springer International Publishing, Cham (04 2019). https://doi.org/10.1007/978-3-030-17127-8_30

Preservation and Reflection of Bisimilarity
via Invertible Steps

Ruben Turkenburg$^{(\boxtimes)1}$, Clemens Kupke[2], Jurriaan Rot[1], and
Ezra Schoen[2]

[1] Institute for Computing and Information Sciences (iCIS), Radboud University,
Nijmegen, The Netherlands
ruben.turkenburg@ru.nl
[2] Department of Computer and Information Sciences, Strathclyde University,
Glasgow, UK

Abstract. In the theory of coalgebras, distributive laws give a general
perspective on determinisation and other automata constructions. This
perspective has recently been extended to include so-called weak distributive laws, covering several constructions on state-based systems that are
not captured by regular distributive laws, such as the construction of a
belief-state transformer from a probabilistic automaton, and ultrafilter
extensions of Kripke frames.

In this paper we first observe that weak distributive laws give rise to the
more general notion of what we call an invertible step: a pair of natural
transformations that allows to move coalgebras along an adjunction. Our
main result is that part of the construction induced by an invertible
step preserves and reflects bisimilarity. This covers results that have
previously been shown by hand for the instances of ultrafilter extensions
and belief-state transformers.

Keywords: Coalgebra · Bisimulations · Weak distributive laws

1 Introduction

Distributive laws between a monad T and a functor B are ubiquitous in the
theory of coalgebras. They capture various forms of interaction between algebras
and coalgebras, including structural operational semantics [45,33], efficient proof
techniques [9] and a general coalgebraic determinisation procedure which applies
to a wide range of automata and other state-based systems [43,15,29].

The central idea of this general determinisation procedure is to interpret
coalgebras in the Eilenberg-Moore category $\mathcal{EM}(T)$, as coalgebras for a lifting of
B that arises from the distributive law. Behavioural equivalence in $\mathcal{EM}(T)$ then
amounts to desired notions of equivalence. For instance: language equivalence of
non-deterministic automata; weighted automata [7]; Mealy and Moore machines
with side-effects [43]; or various types of trace equivalence of transition systems [8].

An illustrative *non-example* of this general determinisation procedure is in
a natural construction of belief-state transformers from probabilistic automata,
which feature both non-determinism and probabilities. From a categorical perspective, the problem is related to the classical result that there is no suitable
distributive law of the probability distribution monad $\mathcal{D}$ over the powerset monad

O. Kupferman and P. Sobocinski (Eds.): FoSSaCS 2023, LNCS 13992, pp. 328–348, 2023.
https://doi.org/10.1007/978-3-031-30829-1_16

$\mathcal{P}$ [46] (also see [47,34] for other non-existence results of distributive laws). Hence, general determinisation via distributive laws seems not applicable here.

Nevertheless, in [12] a concrete coalgebraic account of the construction of belief-state transformers is given, in terms of a two-stage process:

1. from probabilistic automata to coalgebras in $\mathcal{EM}(\mathcal{D})$, which are a type of labelled transition systems over convex algebras;
2. from these coalgebras in $\mathcal{EM}(\mathcal{D})$ back to plain transition systems in Set, yielding the belief-state transformer.

A key result in *op. cit.* is that the second stage preserves and reflects behavioural equivalence. This shows that behavioural equivalence of coalgebras in $\mathcal{EM}(\mathcal{D})$ coincides with distribution bisimilarity on the belief-state transformer.

In [12,21] it was shown that this construction, in fact, arises from a canonical *weak distributive law* of $\mathcal{D}$ over $\mathcal{P}$ [22]. Weak distributive laws correspond to so-called weak liftings [19], and—as shown in [22]—these yield a new generalised determinisation procedure which covers the above example, and precisely instantiates to the two stages above. Further examples are the treatment of alternating automata via weak distributive laws in [23], and weak distributive laws for combining non-determinism with semimodules in [10].

However, the result for probabilistic automata that the second stage above preserves and reflects behavioural equivalence has not yet been accounted for in the abstract theory of determinisation via weak distributive laws.

In this paper we provide such an account, starting from a more general setting than weak distributive laws: what we call *invertible steps*. These basically replace the Eilenberg-Moore adjunction inherent in the weak liftings approach by a general adjunction. In this context, a *step* allows one to lift the left adjoint to coalgebras—this is a widely occurring phenomenon, for instance in the semantics of coalgebraic modal logic, testing semantics and trace semantics (see [41] for an overview). The key idea here is to assume a right inverse, allowing the lifting of the right adjoint, such that we generalise the two-stage construction above.

We show that, in this setting of an invertible step, the second stage of the two-stage construction preserves and reflects bisimilarity, under mild conditions. As a consequence, we recover the above-mentioned results on preservation and reflection of behavioural equivalence for probabilistic automata [12] for free from the abstract theory.[3] Another motivating example is that of coalgebras for the Vietoris functor on the category of Stone spaces: we obtain that bisimilarity is preserved and reflected by the forgetful functor, recovering the main result in [5].

In fact, the latter example is related to a coalgebraic presentation [36] of ultrafilter extensions, a standard construction in modal logic [6]. It fits within the general setting of invertible steps, but not directly in weak liftings, as it involves the category of Stone spaces (for the duality with Boolean algebras). However, if we move from Stone spaces to compact Hausdorff spaces, then the relevant weak lifting (or invertible step) arises precisely from the weak distributive law

---

[3] We focus on bisimilarity, but our setting allows for an easy argument that this coincides with behavioural equivalence in this and many related examples.

constructed by Garner [19]. The weak distributive law in *loc. cit.* thus gives rise to ultrafilter extensions in modal logic.

Finally, we include an example of an invertible step involving $\mathsf{Set}^{\mathsf{op}}$ instead of an Eilenberg-Moore category. Steps for adjunctions with opposite categories are a standard way of presenting the semantics of coalgebraic modal logic [40,32]. The included example shows the generality of the approach.

Outline. Section 2 presents (invertible) steps, the relation to weak liftings and distributive laws, and a range of examples. In Section 3 we recall the standard notion of coalgebraic bisimilarity, defined via relation lifting. Section 4 contains the main results on preservation and reflection of bisimilarity. In Section 5 we discuss applications and instances of these results. We discuss other notions of bisimulation, and future work, in Section 6.

2   Forward and Backward Steps

We briefly present the required theory of steps, first termed as such in [41]. This structure occurs already in work on coalgebraic modal logic [35,14,40,32,17,38] where a step gives the one-step semantics of a logic. In existing work, only what we call a *forward* step is considered. Here, we also speak of *backward* steps, being arrows in the opposite direction. In the sequel, such forward and backward steps will usually be each other's (one-sided) inverses, referred to as *invertible steps*.

Next, we recall how such steps give rise to liftings of functors between categories of coalgebras and further, when the adjunction underlying the steps can also be lifted to coalgebras [27]. Finally, we present examples of invertible steps from the literature, which we return to in later sections.

For a functor $B\colon \mathcal{C} \to \mathcal{C}$, a *coalgebra* is a pair (X, f) consisting of an object X and an arrow $f\colon X \to BX$. A homomorphism from (X, f) to (Y, g) is an arrow $h\colon X \to Y$ such that $g \circ h = Bh \circ f$. Coalgebras and homomorphisms between them form a category, denoted by $\mathsf{Coalg}(B)$, or $\mathsf{Coalg}_{\mathcal{C}}(B)$ if we wish to make the underlying category explicit.

The category of sets and functions is denoted by Set. For a monad T, we write $\mathcal{EM}(T)$ for the category of Eilenberg-Moore algebras. The powerset monad is denoted by $\mathcal{P}\colon \mathsf{Set} \to \mathsf{Set}$, given on objects by $\mathcal{P}(X) = \{S \mid S \subseteq X\}$, and the finitely-supported distribution monad by $\mathcal{D}\colon \mathsf{Set} \to \mathsf{Set}$, given by $\mathcal{D}(X) = \{\varphi\colon X \to [0,1] \mid \sum_{x \in X} \varphi(x) = 1,\ \mathrm{supp}(\varphi)\ \text{finite}\}$ (see also [12]).

2.1   Invertible Steps

The basic setting of interest in this work consists of the following:

Definition 2.1. *Given an adjunction $P \dashv Q\colon \mathcal{D} \to \mathcal{C}$ and endofunctors $B\colon \mathcal{C} \to \mathcal{C}$ and $L\colon \mathcal{D} \to \mathcal{D}$ as in the diagram*

$$B \,\substack{\curvearrowright}\, \mathcal{C} \underset{Q}{\overset{P}{\rightleftarrows}} \mathcal{D} \,\substack{\curvearrowright}\, L, \tag{1}$$

a (forward) step *is a natural transformation* $\delta: BQ \to QL$. *A backward step is simply a natural transformation* $\iota: QL \to BQ$ *going the other way. If, moreover,* $\delta \circ \iota = \mathrm{id}$ *then we call* δ *an* invertible step *(with right inverse* ι*). Finally, if* δ *witnesses an isomorphism then we call it an* isomorphic step.

Notice the asymmetry in the definition of invertible step: ι is always assumed to be a *right* inverse of δ. These invertible steps are the main focus of this paper. Examples are given below in Section 2.2.

Step-induced liftings There is a bijective correspondence between a step and its *mate* $\hat{\delta}: PB \to LP$ given by $PB \xrightarrow{PB\eta} PBQP \xrightarrow{P\delta P} PQLP \xrightarrow{\varepsilon LP} LP$ (see [37,31]). This mate and the backward step allow us to define liftings of P and Q to the categories of coalgebras for B and L.

Definition 2.2. *Given steps* $\delta: BQ \to QL$ *and* $\iota: QL \to BQ$, *the step-induced coalgebra liftings* $\overline{P}: \mathsf{Coalg}(B) \to \mathsf{Coalg}(L)$ *and* $\overline{Q}: \mathsf{Coalg}(L) \to \mathsf{Coalg}(B)$ *of* P *and* Q *are defined by*

$$f: X \to BX \quad \mapsto \quad \hat{\delta}_X \circ Pf: PX \to LPX \tag{2}$$

$$g: Y \to LY \quad \mapsto \quad \iota_Y \circ Qg: QY \to BQY \tag{3}$$

on objects and act as P *and* Q *on arrows. This is well-defined due to functoriality of* P *and* Q *and naturality of* $\hat{\delta}$ *and* ι.

It is shown in [27, Theorem 2.14] that, when δ and ι form an isomorphism, the adjunction $P \dashv Q$ lifts to an adjunction $\overline{P} \dashv \overline{Q}$ between the step-induced liftings. For our purposes it will be useful to split the isomorphism condition into the cases where ι is the left or right inverse of δ.

Lemma 2.3. *If* $\delta \circ \iota = \mathrm{id}$, *then the counit* $\varepsilon: PQ \to \mathsf{Id}$ *of the adjunction* $P \dashv Q$ *lifts to a natural transformation* $\overline{\varepsilon}: \overline{P}\,\overline{Q} \to \mathsf{Id}$. *If* $\iota \circ \delta = \mathrm{id}$, *then the unit* $\eta: \mathsf{Id} \to QP$ *of the adjunction lifts to a natural transformation* $\overline{\eta}: \mathsf{Id} \to \overline{Q}\,\overline{P}$.

The combination of these two liftings gives us the lifting of the adjunction.

Corollary 2.4. *If* δ *and* ι *form an isomorphism, then* $\overline{P} \dashv \overline{Q}$.

In such a situation, $\overline{Q}$ (being a right adjoint) preserves the final coalgebra for L (the limit of the empty diagram) when this exists. However, there are a number of known examples where the step is not an isomorphism; instead we only have a one-sided inverse. We consider, in particular, these invertible steps, and in the next subsection give a number of examples of this setting.

2.2   Steps from weak liftings, and other examples

Example 2.5. Our first example arises from the work of Garner, who shows that the Vietoris monad $\mathcal{V}$ on the category CHaus of compact Hausdorff spaces arises as a so-called *weak lifting* of the powerset monad [19] (we discuss weak liftings in general after this example). For the definition of the Vietoris monad the reader is referred to [19, Sec. 2.3]. The category CHaus is equivalent to the Eilenberg-Moore category $\mathcal{EM}(\beta)$ of the ultrafilter monad β [39]. The weak lifting provided by Garner consists of natural transformations ι, δ, satisfying $\delta \circ \iota = \mathrm{id}$:

$$\mathcal{P} \hookleftarrow \mathsf{Set} \underset{U}{\overset{\mathcal{F}}{\rightleftarrows}} \mathcal{EM}(\beta) \hookleftarrow \mathcal{V} \qquad U\mathcal{V} \overset{\iota}{\longrightarrow} \mathcal{P}U \overset{\delta}{\longrightarrow} U\mathcal{V} \qquad (4)$$

where $\mathcal{F} \dashv U$ is the Eilenberg-Moore adjunction of β. Notice that δ is an invertible step, with right inverse ι. As shown by Garner, a component $\delta_X \colon \mathcal{P}UX \to U\mathcal{V}X$, sends each subset $S \in \mathcal{P}UX$ to its topological closure. The components of ι simply include the closed subsets into the powerset.

It turns out that this invertible step gives rise to ultrafilter extensions of Kripke frames. In modal logic, ultrafilter extensions [6,20,4] are a construction taking a Kripke frame (which we can see as a coalgebra for the powerset functor $\mathcal{P}$) with state space W and forming a new Kripke frame with states being ultrafilters over W. The central motivation for this is in "bisimilarity-somewhere-else" results: two states are modally equivalent iff they are bisimilar in the ultrafilter extension.

Now, the composition of the step-induced coalgebra liftings $\overline{\mathcal{F}} \colon \mathsf{Coalg}(\mathcal{P}) \to \mathsf{Coalg}(\mathcal{V})$ and $\overline{U} \colon \mathsf{Coalg}(\mathcal{V}) \to \mathsf{Coalg}(\mathcal{P})$, precisely yields the ultrafilter extension of a Kripke frame. The first stage $\overline{\beta}$ is the actual extension, which turns the Kripke frame into a $\mathcal{V}$-coalgebra. The second stage $\overline{U}$ turns this back into a Kripke frame, i.e., a powerset coalgebra in Set.

In [36], ultrafilter extensions are developed more generally for coalgebras for a functor $B \colon \mathsf{Set} \to \mathsf{Set}$, via the duality between Boolean algebras and Stone spaces. In fact, since both $\mathcal{V}$ and the left adjoint $\mathcal{F}$ restrict to the category Stone of Stone spaces, the invertible step δ, ι restricts to an invertible step in the restriction of the above adjunction to Stone.

In general, for monads S, T on a category $\mathcal{C}$, Garner [19] defines $\tilde{S} \colon \mathcal{EM}(T) \to \mathcal{EM}(T)$ to be a weak lifting of S if there are natural transformations

$$U\tilde{S} \overset{\iota}{\longrightarrow} SU \overset{\delta}{\longrightarrow} U\tilde{S} \qquad (5)$$

with $\delta \circ \iota = \mathrm{id}$ and satisfying further axioms, where U denotes the forgetful functor from $\mathcal{EM}(T)$ to $\mathcal{C}$. They show that there is a bijective correspondence between weak distributive laws of T over S, and weak liftings of S to $\mathcal{EM}(T)$, in case idempotents in $\mathcal{C}$ split (which holds for Set). Here, we do not assume a monad structure on S (which is why the additional axioms are not relevant). In this case, a weak lifting is precisely an invertible step, where the underlying adjunction is an Eilenberg-Moore adjunction.

Example 2.6. In [11,12], a procedure is given for "determinising" probabilistic automata (PAs), which model systems with both non-determinism and probabilities, into belief state transformers. It was shown in [22] that this is an instance of a more general determinisation procedure induced by a weak lifting, which in turn corresponds to a canonical weak distributive law.

Stated for a general monad T with the usual Eilenberg-Moore adjunction $\mathcal{F} \dashv U \colon \mathcal{EM}(T) \to \mathcal{C}$, this general determinisation procedure thus starts from an invertible step (weak lifting) $\delta \colon BU \to U\overline{B}$. This gives rise to a two-step process:

$$\mathsf{Coalg}_{\mathcal{C}}(BT) \xrightarrow{\ \overline{\mathcal{F}}\ } \mathsf{Coalg}_{\mathcal{EM}(T)}(\overline{B}) \xrightarrow{\ \overline{U}\ } \mathsf{Coalg}_{\mathcal{C}}(B) \tag{6}$$

where the second functor $\overline{U}$ is simply the step-induced lifting of U. The first is a variation of a step-induced lifting (notice that it takes BT-coalgebras rather than B-coalgebras as input), mapping a coalgebra $f \colon X \to BTX$ to

$\mathcal{F}X \xrightarrow{\mathcal{F}f} \mathcal{F}BU\mathcal{F}X \xrightarrow{\hat{\delta}_{U\mathcal{F}X}} \overline{B}\mathcal{F}U\mathcal{F}X \xrightarrow{\overline{B}\varepsilon_{\mathcal{F}X}} \overline{B}\mathcal{F}X$, where ε is the counit of the Eilenberg-Moore adjunction. In fact, this can be viewed as a step-induced lifting for BT which arises by composing δ and the counit, see [41].

We instantiate this to the Eilenberg-Moore adjunction of the distribution monad $\mathcal{D}$, where $\mathcal{P}_c$ is the convex powerset monad:

$$\mathcal{P} \overset{\curvearrowright}{\mathsf{Set}} \underset{U}{\overset{\mathcal{F}}{\rightleftarrows}} \mathcal{EM}(\mathcal{D}) \overset{\curvearrowleft}{\supset} \mathcal{P}_c \tag{7}$$

We take $\mathcal{P}_c(X)$ to have as underlying set $\{S \subseteq X \mid S \text{ convex}\}$ following [22]. This matches the usage of $\mathcal{P}_{ne} + 1$ and $\mathcal{P}_c + 1$ in [12], where $\mathcal{P}_{ne}$ and $\mathcal{P}_c$ are defined to exclude the empty set. A subset is convex if it is closed under convex combinations (see [12] for details). Further, the category $\mathcal{EM}(\mathcal{D})$ is equivalent to the category of convex algebras and convex maps.

It is explained in [22, Sec. 5] that we have an invertible step in the setting of Eq. (7), which sends a subset X to its convex hull (the smallest convex set containing X) and that the lifting $\overline{\mathcal{F}}$ of (6) then gives the transformation of a probabilistic automaton into a belief state transformer in the category $\mathcal{EM}(\mathcal{D})$. The second step is then to transfer the obtained belief state transformer back to Set with the step-induced lifting of U. As shown in [12] and later recovered from our abstract theory (Section 5), this yields a system with the same behaviour. In fact, this is done for automata with labels, i.e., for the functors $\mathcal{P}^L$ and $\mathcal{P}_c^L$ with L a set of labels. The weak lifting we will require in this context is given in [21].

Example 2.7. The following example from automata and languages considers a dual adjunction $P \dashv Q \colon \mathcal{D}^{op} \to \mathcal{C}$. One motivation to discuss this kind of example stems from coalgebraic modal logic where $\mathcal{C}$ commonly is some category of 'spaces' and $\mathcal{D}$ commonly is a category of 'algebras' [32]. The setup is as follows:

$$B \overset{\curvearrowright}{\mathsf{Set}} \underset{2^-}{\overset{2^-}{\rightleftarrows}} \mathsf{Set}^{op} \overset{\curvearrowleft}{\supset} L \qquad 2^L \xrightarrow{\ \iota\ } B(2^-) \xrightarrow{\ \delta\ } 2^L \tag{8}$$

Here, we have $BX = 2 \times (\mathcal{P}X)^{\Sigma}$ and $LX = 1 + \Sigma \times X$ for a fixed alphabet Σ. The step δ is given by

$$\delta(i, \xi) = \{\mathsf{inl}(*) \mid i = 1\} \cup \{\mathsf{inr}(a, x) \mid a \in \Sigma, x \in \bigcup \xi(a)\} \tag{9}$$

This step δ is invertible, e.g., by ι as in Eq. (10).

$$\iota(u) = (1 \text{ iff } \mathsf{inl}(*) \in u, a \mapsto \{v \mid \{(a,x) \mid x \in v\} \subseteq u\}) \tag{10}$$

A B-coalgebra is a non-deterministic automaton. An L-coalgebra in $\mathsf{Set}^{\mathsf{op}}$ is an algebra $X \leftarrow 1 + \Sigma \times X$ in Set, which can be seen as specifying the initial state and transition structure of a deterministic automaton. From this point of view, the coalgebra lifting $\overline{Q} \colon \mathsf{Coalg}(L) \to \mathsf{Coalg}(B)$ can be seen as first reversing, and then performing a powerset construction. The specific powerset construction might depend on the chosen right inverse ι, as it is not unique. For ι as in (10), for example, $u \xrightarrow{a} v$ in $\overline{Q}(\mathcal{A})$ if and only if each state in v is reachable from a state in u via an a-transition in the reverse of $\mathcal{A}$.

In Section 5 we return to these examples and show how we can apply the techniques from Section 4 to obtain preservation and reflection of bisimilarity.

3   Relations, Liftings and Coalgebraic Bisimulations

We recall the standard notion of coalgebraic bisimulation defined via relation lifting, broadly following [30,28]. Note, we will use some terminology from the theory of fibrations to allow us to be more concise and many of the coming results can be generalised to a larger class of fibrations, but knowledge of fibrations is not required as we give a self-contained presentation of the fibration of relations.

We make the following assumptions for the remainder of the paper:

Assumption 3.1. *We assume categories $\mathcal{C}, \mathcal{D}$ with all finite limits, and factorisation systems $(\mathcal{E}_1, \mathcal{M}_1)$, $(\mathcal{E}_2, \mathcal{M}_2)$ respectively for which $\mathcal{M}_1 = \mathsf{Mono}_\mathcal{C}, \mathcal{M}_2 = \mathsf{Mono}_\mathcal{D}$ and for any left adjoint functor $P \colon \mathcal{C} \to \mathcal{D}$ we have $P(\mathcal{E}_1) \subseteq \mathcal{E}_2$.*

We assume finite limits mainly for binary products and pullbacks to allow the definitions of relations and inverse images. The assumptions that maps in $\mathcal{M}$ are mono means that pullbacks of abstract monos and factorisation both yield monos, which represent subobjects. The final condition specifies that left adjoints preserve abstract epis. This is required in Section 4.2 and holds, e.g., when the involved categories possess a $(\mathsf{RegEpi}, \mathsf{Mono})$-factorisation system [16,2], as in all our examples from Sections 2.2 and 5.

For a category $\mathcal{C}$ satisfying the above, the category $\mathsf{Rel}(\mathcal{C})$ consists of:

- Objects of $\mathsf{Rel}(\mathcal{C})$ are subobjects $R \rightarrowtail X \times X$ of the binary product of the object X with itself;
- A map $R \rightarrowtail X \times X \to S \rightarrowtail Y \times Y$ in $\mathsf{Rel}(\mathcal{C})$ consists of a map $u \colon X \to Y$ in $\mathcal{C}$ such that there is the following commutative diagram

$$\begin{array}{ccc} R & \dashrightarrow & S \\ \downarrow & & \downarrow \\ X \times X & \xrightarrow{u \times u} & Y \times Y \end{array} \tag{11}$$

In Set, these are subsets of the binary product of underlying sets as usual, and maps between relations constitute maps between the products sending R to S, i.e., $x\,R\,y$ implies $u(x)\,S\,u(y)$. Objects of Rel(Stone) are closed relations, as the image of a mono representing a subobject is homeomorphic to its domain, and images of continuous functions are compact and thus closed. In the case of an Eilenberg-Moore category for a monad T, objects of $\mathsf{Rel}(\mathcal{EM}(T))$ are congruences, as the map into the product is an algebra morphism.

Remark 3.2. A note on notation: we use $\twoheadrightarrow$ for epis and $\rightarrowtail$ for monos and the subobjects they represent. We use $\dashrightarrow$ for abstract epis and $\mapsto$ for abstract monos, i.e., maps in $\mathcal{E}$ and $\mathcal{M}$ respectively.

Using the factorisation system on $\mathcal{D}$, we lift a functor $F\colon \mathcal{C} \to \mathcal{D}$ to a functor $\mathsf{Rel}(F)\colon \mathsf{Rel}(\mathcal{C}) \to \mathsf{Rel}(\mathcal{D})$. The action on objects is given by the factorisation

$$
\begin{array}{ccccc}
FR & \xrightarrow{\;Fr\;} & F(X\times X) & \xrightarrow{\langle F\pi_1, F\pi_2\rangle} & FX\times FX \\
& \searrow_{e} & \mathsf{Rel}(F)(R) & \xrightarrow{\;m\;} &
\end{array}
\tag{12}
$$

The action on arrows is defined by orthogonality. The resulting functor $\mathsf{Rel}(F)$ is a lifting in the sense that the following diagram commutes

$$
\begin{array}{ccc}
\mathsf{Rel}(\mathcal{C}) & \xrightarrow{\mathsf{Rel}(F)} & \mathsf{Rel}(\mathcal{D}) \\
{\scriptstyle p}\downarrow & & \downarrow{\scriptstyle q} \\
\mathcal{C} & \xrightarrow{\;F\;} & \mathcal{D}
\end{array}
\tag{13}
$$

where $p\colon \mathsf{Rel}(\mathcal{C}) \to \mathcal{C}$ sends a relation $R \rightarrowtail X\times X$ to the object X, and similarly for q. We say (following the terminology of fibrations) that the relation R is above the object X and a map between relations is above the map u from Eq. (11). Note that commutativity of diagram (13) expresses that $\mathsf{Rel}(F)$, applied to a relation $R \rightarrowtail X\times X$ on X, yields a relation on FX.

Given a category of relations $\mathsf{Rel}(\mathcal{C})$, called the total category, the subcategory (also called a fibre) Rel_X consists of objects $R \rightarrowtail X\times X$ and maps above the identity on X. For relations in Set, such maps are inclusions of relations. In general, these maps are unique, and writing $R \leq S$ iff there is an arrow from R to S turns the fibre into a poset. A relation lifting $\mathsf{Rel}(F)$ can be restricted to the fibres to give a functor $\mathsf{Rel}(F)_X\colon \mathsf{Rel}_X \to \mathsf{Rel}_{FX}$. Since Rel_X and Rel_{FX} are posetal categories, $\mathsf{Rel}(F)_X$ can be viewed as a monotone map.

For a map $f\colon X \to Y$ in $\mathcal{C}$, we have the direct image and inverse image functors $\coprod_f\colon \mathsf{Rel}_X \to \mathsf{Rel}_Y$ and $f^*\colon \mathsf{Rel}_Y \to \mathsf{Rel}_X$. For relations on sets, we have $\coprod_f(R \subseteq X\times X) = \{(f(x), f(y)) \mid (x,y) \in R\}$ and $f^*(S \subseteq Y\times Y) = \{(x,y) \in X\times X \mid (f(x), f(y)) \in S\}$. More generally, they are obtained as the factorisation and pullback in the left and right diagram below respectively

$$
\begin{array}{ccc}
R & \dashrightarrow & \coprod_f(R) \\
{\scriptstyle r}\downarrow & & \downarrow{\scriptstyle \coprod_f(r)} \\
X\times X & \xrightarrow{f\times f} & Y\times Y
\end{array}
\qquad\qquad
\begin{array}{ccc}
f^*(S) & \dashrightarrow & S \\
{\scriptstyle f^*(s)}\downarrow & \lrcorner & \downarrow{\scriptstyle s} \\
X\times X & \xrightarrow{f\times f} & Y\times Y
\end{array}
\tag{14}
$$

It can further be shown that $\coprod_f \dashv f^*$. We say that $\mathsf{Rel}(F)\colon \mathsf{Rel}(\mathcal{C}) \to \mathsf{Rel}(\mathcal{D})$ preserves inverse images if $\mathsf{Rel}(F)_X \circ f^* = (Ff)^* \circ \mathsf{Rel}(F)_Y$.

In this context, *a bisimulation for a B-coalgebra* $f\colon X \to BX$ is a post-fixed point of the endofunctor $f^* \circ \mathsf{Rel}(B)_X\colon \mathsf{Rel}_X \to \mathsf{Rel}_X$, i.e., a relation $R \rightarrowtail X \times X$ such that $R \leq f^* \circ \mathsf{Rel}(B)_X(R)$. Bisimilarity is then obtained as the greatest fixed point $\nu(f^* \circ \mathsf{Rel}(B)_X)$, if it exists. In Set a bisimulation is a relation R such that $R \subseteq (f \times f)^{-1}(\mathsf{Rel}(B)(R))$, i.e., if $x\,R\,y$ then $f(x)\,\mathsf{Rel}(B)(R)\,f(y)$.

4 Preserving and Reflecting Bisimilarity

In this section we show that, in the presence of an invertible step, bisimilarity is preserved and reflected by the step-induced lifting of the right adjoint, given some further mild conditions. This allows us to recover a number of existing results for concrete instances (Section 5).

Our approach is as follows:

- In Section 4.1, we make precise what it means for a monotone map to preserve and reflect bisimulations;
- In Section 4.2, we obtain conditions which ensure that the step-induced lifting of the right adjoint to bisimulations preserves and reflects bisimulations/bisimilarity.

Throughout this section we assume categories $\mathcal{C}$ and $\mathcal{D}$ as in Assumption 3.1, and an invertible step $\delta\colon BQ \to QL$ with right inverse $\iota\colon QL \to BQ$ (and P, Q, B, L as in Definition 2.1).

4.1 Preservation and reflection

We now make precise what it means for a monotone map h to preserve and reflect bisimulations. This will be instantiated to bisimulations, captured abstractly as post-fixed points of a monotone map $f\colon \Gamma \to \Gamma$ on a poset Γ, which typically consists of relations (Section 3). These are compared against a second type of bisimulations, modelled as post-fixed points of another monotone map $g\colon \Delta \to \Delta$. This motivates the following definition.

Definition 4.1. *Let* Γ *and* Δ *be posets, and* $f\colon \Gamma \to \Gamma$, $g\colon \Delta \to \Delta$ *monotone maps. A monotone map* $h\colon \Gamma \to \Delta$ *preserves post-fixed points if* $x \leq f(x)$ *implies* $h(x) \leq g(h(x))$. *It reflects post-fixed points if the converse implication holds.*

In the step setting of Eq. (1), bisimulations for B- and L-coalgebras can be represented as post-fixed points of monotone maps on posets of relations as in Section 3. More concretely:

- Bisimulations for an L-coalgebra $f\colon X \to LX$ are post-fixed points of the monotone map $f^* \circ \mathsf{Rel}(L)_X\colon \mathsf{Rel}_X \to \mathsf{Rel}_X$;
- Bisimulations for the B-coalgebra $\iota_X \circ Qf\colon QX \to BQX$ resulting from the application of the step-induced lifting of Q are post-fixed points of $(\iota_X \circ Qf)^* \circ \mathsf{Rel}(B)_{QX}\colon \mathsf{Rel}_{QX} \to \mathsf{Rel}_{QX}$.

The two can be compared via the restriction $\mathsf{Rel}(Q)_X \colon \mathsf{Rel}_X \to \mathsf{Rel}_{QX}$ of the functor $\mathsf{Rel}(Q)$. Indeed, our main objective is to show that in the presence of an invertible step, $\mathsf{Rel}(Q)_X$ preserves and reflects post-fixed points representing bisimulations, and that it maps the greatest fixed point in Rel_X (bisimilarity on f) to the greatest fixed point in Rel_{QX} (bisimilarity on $\iota_X \circ Qf$). In this context we speak about *preservation and reflection of bisimulations/bisimilarity*.

4.2   Proof of preservation and reflection

We are now ready to prove preservation and reflection of bisimilarity, in the sense described in the previous subsection. First, the following basic lemma provides a method of showing preservation and reflection of post-fixed points, which will be useful for our purposes.

Lemma 4.2. *Let Γ and Δ be posets, and $f \colon \Gamma \to \Gamma$, $g \colon \Delta \to \Delta$ and $h \colon \Gamma \to \Delta$ monotone maps. Suppose that h has a left (lower) adjoint $k \colon \Delta \to \Gamma$, and the equality $gh = hf$ holds. Then h maps the greatest fixed point of f to the greatest fixed point of g, when these exist; h preserves post-fixed points; and if h is order-reflecting, then h reflects post-fixed points.*

Categorically speaking, the equality $gh = hf$ is an isomorphic step. Instantiated to our setting of interest, Lemma 4.2 gives us a method for proving preservation and reflection of bisimilarity: it suffices to show each of the following.

1. A left adjoint for $\mathsf{Rel}(Q)_X$ (Lemma 4.7).
2. The equality $(\iota_X \circ Qf)^* \circ \mathsf{Rel}(B)_{QX} \circ \mathsf{Rel}(Q)_X = \mathsf{Rel}(Q)_X \circ f^* \circ \mathsf{Rel}(L)_X$ (Theorem 4.9).
3. Order-reflection of $\mathsf{Rel}(Q)_X$ (assumption; discussed at the end of this section).

To obtain the required adjunction between the fibres Rel_X and Rel_{QX}, we first establish the adjunction $\mathsf{Rel}(P) \dashv \mathsf{Rel}(Q)$ between the total relation categories. Given Theorem 3.1, we can lift the unit and counit of the adjunction $P \dashv Q$, using the transformations constructed in the following lemma.

Lemma 4.3. *Let $F \colon \mathcal{C} \to \mathcal{D}$ and $G \colon \mathcal{D} \to \mathcal{E}$ be functors, with $\mathsf{Rel}(F) \colon \mathsf{Rel}(\mathcal{C}) \to \mathsf{Rel}(\mathcal{D})$ and $\mathsf{Rel}(G) \colon \mathsf{Rel}(\mathcal{D}) \to \mathsf{Rel}(\mathcal{E})$ the corresponding relation liftings. Then we have a natural transformation $\mathsf{Rel}(GF) \to \mathsf{Rel}(G)\,\mathsf{Rel}(F)$. Further, if G preserves abstract epis, then there is also a natural transformation $\mathsf{Rel}(G)\,\mathsf{Rel}(F) \to \mathsf{Rel}(GF)$. Also, the constructed transformations are above the identity.*

We note that the first part is in [28, Exercise 4.4.6] and the result is proved for Set endofunctors in [9, Lemma 14.1]. This allows the lifting of the adjunction, which we note may also be obtainable from results on fibred adjunctions in [30,26], but a direct proof is quite straightforward; the main idea is to use Lemma 4.3 together with preservation of abstract epis by P.

Lemma 4.4. *The adjunction* $P \dashv Q \colon \mathcal{D} \to \mathcal{C}$ *lifts to relations, i.e., the following diagram is commutative, and the unit and counit of the upper adjunction are above the unit and counit of* $P \dashv Q$.

$$\begin{array}{c} \mathsf{Rel}(P) \\ \mathsf{Rel}(\mathcal{C}) \underset{\mathsf{Rel}(Q)}{\overset{\perp}{\rightleftarrows}} \mathsf{Rel}(\mathcal{D}) \\ {\scriptstyle p} \Big\downarrow \qquad\quad \Big\downarrow {\scriptstyle q} \\ \mathcal{C} \underset{Q}{\overset{P}{\rightleftarrows}} \mathcal{D} \end{array} \qquad (15)$$

The relation lifting defined in Section 3 allows us to define endofunctors $\mathsf{Rel}(B)$, $\mathsf{Rel}(L)$ in the context of the above adjunction:

$$\mathsf{Rel}(B) \overset{\curvearrowright}{} \mathsf{Rel}(\mathcal{C}) \underset{\mathsf{Rel}(Q)}{\overset{\mathsf{Rel}(P)}{\rightleftarrows}} \mathsf{Rel}(\mathcal{D}) \overset{\curvearrowleft}{} \mathsf{Rel}(L) \qquad (16)$$

In this setting, we may try to lift the step δ or its converse ι to this adjunction. It turns out that δ always lifts. For ι, there is a sufficient condition which is independent of ι itself: that Q preserves abstract epis. In both cases, this result follows essentially from Lemma 4.3.

Proposition 4.5. *For a forward step δ and backward step ι, we have:*

1. *δ lifts to relations, i.e., there exists a natural transformation $\overline{\delta} \colon \mathsf{Rel}(B) \circ \mathsf{Rel}(Q) \to \mathsf{Rel}(Q) \circ \mathsf{Rel}(L)$ above δ.*
2. *If Q preserves abstract epis, then ι lifts to relations, i.e., there exists a natural transformation $\overline{\iota} \colon \mathsf{Rel}(Q) \circ \mathsf{Rel}(L) \to \mathsf{Rel}(B) \circ \mathsf{Rel}(Q)$ above ι.*

The condition that Q preserves abstract epis holds, e.g., in case it is the forgetful functor in an adjunction monadic over Set. This is because Eilenberg-Moore categories of monads on Set have (RegEpi, Mono)-factorisation systems, and the forgetful functor sends regular epis to epis in Set as discussed in [13, Example 2.3]. It also holds in the Stone-Set case, as Stone is a reflective subcategory of CHaus (which is equivalent to the category of algebras for the ultrafilter monad).

The lifted steps $\overline{\delta}$ and $\overline{\iota}$ give step-induced liftings of $\mathsf{Rel}(P)$ and $\mathsf{Rel}(Q)$ between $\mathsf{Coalg}(\mathsf{Rel}(B))$ and $\mathsf{Coalg}(\mathsf{Rel}(L))$. Since bisimulations can be equivalently presented as coalgebras for $\mathsf{Rel}(B)$ and $\mathsf{Rel}(L)$, these liftings can be used to capture preservation of bisimulations. But it is less obvious what reflection means in this context and how to prove it. For reflection of bisimulations by $\mathsf{Rel}(Q)$, we turn our attention to the fibres, as described in the beginning of this section.

As a consequence of Proposition 4.5 and of $\delta \circ \iota = \mathrm{id}$, we obtain the following result, which will later be used in the construction of a step on the fibres.

Lemma 4.6. *Let δ be an invertible step with right inverse ι, and suppose Q preserves abstract epis. Then $\mathsf{Rel}(Q)_{LX} \circ \mathsf{Rel}(L)_X = \iota_X^* \circ \mathsf{Rel}(B)_{QX} \circ \mathsf{Rel}(Q)_X$.*

Adjoining the fibres Next, we construct an adjunction between the fibres Rel_X and Rel_{QX}. The usual restriction $\mathsf{Rel}(Q)_X$ of $\mathsf{Rel}(Q)$ to the fibre Rel_X will be the right adjoint, similarly to the adjunction obtained earlier. To map back into the fibre Rel_X, we post-compose $\mathsf{Rel}(P)_{QX}$ with $\coprod_\varepsilon$, the direct image functor obtained from the counit of the adjunction $\mathsf{Rel}(P) \dashv \mathsf{Rel}(Q)$. We note the similarity with results on fibred adjunctions in [30], where only adjunctions over a single base category are considered.

Lemma 4.7. *We have an adjunction* $\coprod_\varepsilon \circ \mathsf{Rel}(P)_{QX} \dashv \mathsf{Rel}(Q)_X \colon \mathsf{Rel}_X \to \mathsf{Rel}_{QX}$.

The above lemma fulfils the first proof obligation stated in the beginning of Section 4.2. It now remains to show the second proof obligation, i.e., that we have an isomorphic step in the following setting:

$$(\iota_X \circ Qf)^* \circ \mathsf{Rel}(B)_{QX} \; \substack{\coprod_\varepsilon \, \circ \, \mathsf{Rel}(P)_{QX} \\ \curvearrowright \\ \mathsf{Rel}_{QX} \substack{\overset{\longrightarrow}{\perp} \\ \longleftarrow} \mathsf{Rel}_X \\ \mathsf{Rel}(Q)_X} \; f^* \circ \mathsf{Rel}(L)_X \qquad (17)$$

To this end, we first show that $\mathsf{Rel}(Q)$ preserves inverse images, using the fact that we can obtain inverse images as pullbacks inside the category of relations. Since $\mathsf{Rel}(Q)$ is a right adjoint, it preserves these pullbacks.

Lemma 4.8. $\mathsf{Rel}(Q)$ *preserves inverse images.*

We are now ready to show the existence of the required isomorphic step.

Theorem 4.9. *If Q preserves abstract epis, then for any L-coalgebra (X, f):*

$$(\iota_X \circ Qf)^* \circ \mathsf{Rel}(B)_{QX} \circ \mathsf{Rel}(Q)_X = \mathsf{Rel}(Q)_X \circ f^* \circ \mathsf{Rel}(L)_X \qquad (18)$$

Proof. We have

$$(\iota_X \circ Qf)^* \circ \mathsf{Rel}(B)_{QX} \circ \mathsf{Rel}(Q)_X = (Qf)^* \circ \iota_X^* \circ \mathsf{Rel}(B)_{QX} \circ \mathsf{Rel}(Q)_X \qquad (19)$$
$$= (Qf)^* \circ \mathsf{Rel}(Q)_{LX} \circ \mathsf{Rel}(L)_X \qquad (20)$$
$$= \mathsf{Rel}(Q)_X \circ f^* \circ \mathsf{Rel}(L)_X \qquad (21)$$

where Eq. (19) is an application of a basic fact on inverse images (technically, that the poset fibration of relations is split), Eq. (20) holds by Lemma 4.6, and Eq. (21) holds by Lemma 4.8. $\qquad\square$

We now reach our main result on preservation and reflection of bisimulations and bisimilarity by $\mathsf{Rel}(Q)_X$.

Theorem 4.10. *Let (X, f) be an L-coalgebra. Suppose that Q preserves abstract epis. Then $\overline{\mathsf{Rel}(Q)_X}$ maps bisimilarity on (X, f) (when it exists) to bisimilarity on $\overline{Q}(X, f)$. Further, $\mathsf{Rel}(Q)_X$ preserves bisimulations and, if it is order-reflecting, also reflects bisimulations.*

Proof. We have seen in Lemma 4.7, that $\mathsf{Rel}(Q)_X$ has a left adjoint, and in Theorem 4.9, that in this setting we have an isomorphic step. The result now follows from Lemma 4.2. □

While this result is formulated in terms of $\mathsf{Rel}(Q)_X$, we will also speak of simply $\overline{Q}$ preserving and reflecting both bisimulations and bisimilarity.

As a special case of Theorem 4.10, we recover (a version of) the following existing result found in [42,3,11,12].

Lemma 4.11. *Assume functors* $B, L \colon \mathcal{C} \to \mathcal{C}$, *and a natural transformation* $\iota \colon L \to B$. *Then the functor* $\overline{\mathsf{Id}} \colon \mathsf{Coalg}(L) \to \mathsf{Coalg}(B)$ *defined by* $(X, f) \mapsto (X, \sigma_X \circ f)$ *on objects and identity on morphisms, preserves bisimulations. If additionally* ι *has a left inverse,* $\overline{\mathsf{Id}}$ *reflects bisimulations.*

We briefly turn to the condition of order-reflectingness. As we are often interested in cases where the right adjoint is a forgetful functor in the context of an Eilenberg-Moore adjunction, it is useful to state the following.

Lemma 4.12. *For a monad* T *with forgetful functor* $U \colon \mathcal{EM}(\mathcal{T}) \to \mathcal{C}$, *the (restricted) lifting* $\mathsf{Rel}(U)_X$ *is an order-reflecting map.*

If $\mathcal{C} = \mathsf{Set}$ in the above lemma, then $\mathsf{Rel}(U)_X$ is just the inclusion of the poset of congruences Rel_X on an algebra X into the poset of all relations on its carrier.

In that case, we can also use the above to show preservation and reflection of *behavioural equivalence*. Two states of a coalgebra (in Set) are behaviourally equivalent if they can be identified by some coalgebra homomorphism. This can be captured more abstractly using kernel bisimulations (see, e.g., [44]). Since U is assumed to be a forgetful functor to Set, we simply define preservation and reflection of behavioural equivalence by $\overline{U}$ to mean that for any two states x, y of an L-coalgebra (X, f), x and y are behaviourally equivalent (for (X, f)) if and only if they are behaviourally equivalent for $\overline{U}(X, f)$.

It turns out that, in our setting, coincidence of bisimilarity and behavioural equivalence for L-coalgebras reduces to coincidence for B-coalgebras. This is stated in the following lemma; the essence is that $\overline{U}$ is easily shown to preserve behavioural equivalence.

Lemma 4.13. *For a monad* T, *consider the Eilenberg-Moore adjunction* $\mathcal{F} \dashv U \colon \mathcal{EM}(T) \to \mathsf{Set}$ *with functors* $L \colon \mathcal{EM}(T) \to \mathcal{EM}(T)$ *and* $B \colon \mathsf{Set} \to \mathsf{Set}$, *and an invertible step* $\delta \colon BU \to UL$. *Further suppose that* $\overline{U}$ *preserves and reflects bisimilarity, and that* B *preserves weak pullbacks. Then bisimilarity and behavioural equivalence for* L-*coalgebras coincide (and hence,* $\overline{U}$ *preserves and reflects behavioural equivalence).*

Remark 4.14. We conclude with a brief exploration of preservation and reflection by the restriction of the *left* adjoint $\mathsf{Rel}(P)_X$, in the setting of

$$f^* \circ \mathsf{Rel}(B)_X \hookrightarrow \mathsf{Rel}_X \xrightarrow{\mathsf{Rel}(P)_X} \mathsf{Rel}_{PX} \circlearrowright (\hat{\delta}_X \circ Pf)^* \circ \mathsf{Rel}(L)_{PX} \qquad (22)$$

with $f\colon X \to BX$ a B-coalgebra in this case. Here, we can obtain a backward step $\mathsf{Rel}(P)_X \circ f^* \circ \mathsf{Rel}(B)_X \leq (\hat{\delta}_X \circ Pf)^* \circ \mathsf{Rel}(L)_{PX} \circ \mathsf{Rel}(P)_X$ which means that we can lift $\mathsf{Rel}(P)_X$ to bisimulations, so that these are preserved. However, we cannot obtain a forward step in this context, thus reflection will not hold. This is illustrated, e.g., by the example of ultrafilter extensions, where the ultrafilter monad β certainly does not reflect bisimulations: in general, in the ultrafilter extension more states will be bisimilar.

5   Applications

Now that we have obtained conditions for the preservation and reflection of bisimilarity, we return to the examples of Section 2.2. We will show how a number of existing non-trivial results can be recovered in a concise way. Further, the Set-Stone adjunction used in the first example is known to not be monadic, and so outside the scope of weak liftings, which indicates the generality of our results.

Ultrafilter Extensions and Vietoris bisimulations In Example 2.5, we have seen how the construction of ultrafilter extensions can be obtained from an invertible step, which arises from a weak lifting described by Garner. In the current treatment of reflection and preservation of bisimilarity, we focus on the restriction of this invertible step to the category Stone.

This brings us in line with [5], where a comparison is made between bisimilarity for the Vietoris functor $\mathcal{V}\colon \mathsf{Stone} \to \mathsf{Stone}$ and bisimilarity for the powerset functor $\mathcal{P}\colon \mathsf{Set} \to \mathsf{Set}$, called Vietoris-bisimilarity and Kripke-bisimilarity respectively in *op. cit.* More precisely, for a $\mathcal{V}$-coalgebra (X, f), Kripke bisimilarity is bisimilarity on $\overline{U}(X, f)$, where $\overline{U}$ is the step-induced lifting of the forgetful functor $U\colon \mathsf{Stone} \to \mathsf{Set}$. Vietoris bisimilarity is simply bisimilarity on the coalgebra (X, f) itself.

We consider the following results from [5]:

1. The relation liftings of $\mathcal{P}$ and $\mathcal{V}$ coincide for closed subsets [5, Prop 3.4]
2. Vietoris bisimulations are equivalently closed Kripke bisimulations [5, Thm 3.6]
3. The closure of a Kripke bisimulation is a Vietoris bisimulation [5, Thm 5.2]
4. Vietoris- and Kripke-bisimilarity are equivalent [5, Cor 3.10]

From the above discussion, we see that these results fit into the setting of Section 4, so that they can be recovered using our results on the preservation and reflection of bisimilarity as follows:

1. This follows from the equality of Lemma 4.6, as the action of ι^* is exactly the restriction to closed subsets. We can apply this lemma as U preserves abstract epis, due to the same argument as for adjunctions monadic over Set (see the discussion after Proposition 4.5), as Stone is also a regular category.
2. For this, we use preservation and reflection of bisimulations by the (restricted) relation lifting $\mathsf{Rel}(U)_X\colon \mathsf{Rel}_X \to \mathsf{Rel}_{UX}$ of the forgetful functor, which is simply the inclusion of the poset of closed relations on a Stone space X to that of all relations on the underlying set.

Indeed, preservation and reflection by $\mathsf{Rel}(U)_X$ follows from Theorem 4.10. We have seen that $U\colon \mathsf{Stone} \to \mathsf{Set}$ preserves abstract epis, so it only remains to check that $\mathsf{Rel}(U)_X$ is order-reflecting. This holds because Stone is a reflective (i.e. full) subcategory of CHaus, which is monadic over Set.

3. The left adjoint $\coprod_\varepsilon \circ \mathsf{Rel}(\beta)_{UX}$ of Lemma 4.7 gives the closure of a relation. Its lifting to bisimulations (cf. Remark 4.14) yields the desired result.

4. This holds since $\mathsf{Rel}(U)_X$ maps the greatest fixed point of $(\iota_X \circ Uf)^* \circ \mathsf{Rel}(\mathcal{P})_{UX}$ to that of $f^* \circ \mathsf{Rel}(\mathcal{V})_X$, i.e., it preserves and reflects bisimilarity.

PAs and Belief State Transformers As discussed in Example 2.6, we can determinise a PA to a coalgebra for the convex powerset functor $\mathcal{P}_c\colon \mathcal{EM}(\mathcal{D}) \to \mathcal{EM}(\mathcal{D})$ using a lifting of $\mathcal{F}\colon \mathsf{Set} \to \mathcal{EM}(\mathcal{D})$. The step-induced lifting of the corresponding forgetful functor $U\colon \mathcal{EM}(\mathcal{D}) \to \mathsf{Set}$ maps the $\mathcal{P}_c$-coalgebra back into Set, but we must take care that this does not change its behaviour. What we can do now, is show that bisimilarity is preserved and reflected.

Once we know this, we can apply Lemma 4.13 to show the coincidence of bisimilarity and behavioural equivalence in the case of the convex powerset functor on $\mathcal{EM}(\mathcal{D})$ and the powerset functor on Set as this preserves weak pullbacks. This coincidence is relevant for the generalisation of the corresponding results of [12] (restricted to the convex powerset functor), which are formulated in terms of behavioural equivalence. As mentioned in Example 2.6, the weak lifting we require to cover automata with labels can be found in [21]. Consider the following:

1. The lifting of the forgetful functor $U\colon \mathcal{EM}(\mathcal{D}) \to \mathsf{Set}$ preserves and reflects behavioural equivalence on $\mathcal{P}_c^L$-coalgebras [12, Proposition 6.6].
2. A relation R is a kernel bisimulation for a $\mathcal{P}_c^L$-coalgebra $(\mathbb{S}, c)$ in $\mathcal{EM}(\mathcal{D})$ iff it is a kernel bisimulation for $\overline{U}(\mathbb{S}, c)$ and also a congruence.

Again, we can apply the results of Section 4 to recover these results. In fact, in [12, Proposition 6.5], the second result is proved more generally, namely for settings where a so-called *lax lifting* exists rather than the weak lifting we require.

1. We have seen that U preserves abstract epis as the adjunction in question is monadic over Set. This allows us to apply Theorem 4.10 so that $\overline{U}$ indeed preserves and reflects bisimulations, and the relevant lifting preserves and reflects bisimilarity. From Lemma 4.13, it follows that $\overline{U}$ also preserves and reflects behavioural equivalence.
2. Assuming $(\mathbb{S}, c)$ is a $\mathcal{P}_c^L$-coalgebra, this follows from Lemma 4.13 together with the previous item, and the fact that bisimulations in Eilenberg-Moore categories are congruences.

Automata For a different instance, we revisit Example 2.7 and consider the basic adjunction $P \dashv Q\colon \mathcal{D}^{\mathrm{op}} \to \mathcal{C}$. As a general remark, we note that if $\mathcal{D}$ admits a factorization system $(\mathcal{E}, \mathcal{M})$ with $\mathcal{E}$ a class of epis, and $\mathcal{M}$ a class of monos, then $(\mathcal{M}, \mathcal{E})$ forms a factorization system for $\mathcal{D}^{\mathrm{op}}$, with $\mathcal{M}$ a class of epis *in* $\mathcal{D}^{\mathrm{op}}$, and $\mathcal{E}$ a class of monos *in* $\mathcal{D}^{\mathrm{op}}$. We can explicitly describe $\mathsf{Rel}(\mathcal{D}^{\mathrm{op}})$ as follows:

- Objects of $\mathsf{Rel}(\mathcal{D}^{\mathsf{op}})$ are quotients $X + X \twoheadrightarrow E$ of $X + X$;
- A map $X + X \twoheadrightarrow E \to Y + Y \twoheadrightarrow F$ consists of a map $u \colon Y \to X$ in $\mathcal{D}$ such that there is the following commutative diagram

$$
\begin{array}{ccc}
E & \longleftarrow\!- - - - - - - - & F \\
\uparrow & & \uparrow \\
X + X & \xleftarrow{\;\;u+u\;\;} & Y + Y
\end{array}
\tag{23}
$$

In the case $\mathcal{D} = \mathsf{Set}$, $\mathcal{E} = \mathsf{Epi}$ and $\mathcal{M} = \mathsf{Mono}$. Further, every epi $e \colon X + X \twoheadrightarrow E$ is isomorphic to an epi of the form $X + X \twoheadrightarrow (X + X)/\!\!\sim$ with $\sim$ an equivalence relation on $X + X$. This gives us an equivalent description of $\mathsf{Rel}(\mathsf{Set}^{\mathsf{op}})$:

- Objects of $\mathsf{Rel}(\mathsf{Set}^{\mathsf{op}})$ are equivalence relations $\sim$ on $X + X$ for a set X;
- A map $\sim\, \subseteq (X + X)^2 \to\, \approx\, \subseteq (Y + Y)^2$ consists of a map $u \colon Y \to X$ such that if $j(y) \approx j'(y')$, then $j(u(y)) \sim j'(u(y'))$, with j, j' arbitrary coproduct inclusions.

In particular, we see that the fibre over a set X consists of all equivalence relations on $X + X$, ordered by *reverse* inclusion. Reindexing along a map $u \colon X \leftarrow Y$ maps an equivalence relation $\approx$ on $Y + Y$ to the least equivalence relation $\sim$ on $X + X$, such that $j(u(y)) \sim j'(u(y'))$ for all $j(y) \approx j'(y')$.

Focusing on the setting of (8) in Example 2.7, the lifting $\mathsf{Rel}(L)$ is given by

$$
\mathsf{inl}(*) \ \mathsf{Rel}(L)(\sim) \ \mathsf{inr}(*)
\tag{24}
$$

$$
j((a, x)) \ \mathsf{Rel}(L)(\sim) \ j'((b, x)) \iff a = b \text{ and } j(x) \sim j'(y)
\tag{25}
$$

If $f \colon X \leftarrow 1 + \Sigma \times X$ is an L-coalgebra, we see that $f^* \circ \mathsf{Rel}(L)_X$ maps an equivalence relation $\sim$ on $X + X$ to the least equivalence relation $\approx$ satisfying

$$
\mathsf{inl}(f(*)) \approx \mathsf{inr}(f(*))
\tag{26}
$$

$$
j(f(a, x)) \approx j'(f(a, y)) \text{ whenever } j(x) \sim j'(y)
\tag{27}
$$

A post-fixed point of this map is an equivalence relation $\sim$ which relates $\mathsf{inl}(f(*))$ and $\mathsf{inr}(f(*))$ and is closed under the action of Σ on $X + X$. The greatest post-fixed point is the *least* such relation, as relations in Rel_X are ordered by reverse inclusion. It is easy to see that this is exactly the relation which identifies $\mathsf{inl}(x)$ and $\mathsf{inr}(x)$ for those x reachable from $f(*)$.

$\mathsf{Rel}(Q)$, meanwhile, maps an equivalence relation $\sim$ on $X + X$ to the relation R on 2^X given by

$$
uRv \iff \mathsf{inl}[u] \cup \mathsf{inr}[v] \text{ is } \sim\text{-closed}
\tag{28}
$$

If X' is the set of reachable states, we conclude that $\mathsf{Rel}(Q)$ maps the greatest bisimulation $\sim$ to the relation

$$
uRv \iff u \cap X' = v \cap X'
\tag{29}
$$

The functor Q preserves (abstract) epis, as all epis in $\mathsf{Set}^{\mathsf{op}}$ are regular. Now, Theorem 4.10 tells us that the relation (29) coincides with bisimilarity on the automaton $\overline{Q}(X, f)$ from Example 2.7. It follows that the subautomaton on $2^{X'}$ is minimal, and is the minimal automaton equivalent to $\overline{Q}(X, f)$.

6   Discussion and Future Work

We studied the notion of an *invertible step*, which provides several constructions on coalgebras via functor liftings. We showed that the lifting of the right adjoint, induced by such an invertible step, preserves and reflects bisimilarity. This abstract result instantiates to several concrete results from the literature, in examples related to ultrafilter extensions and weak distributive laws.

We have focused on preservation and reflection of bisimilarity, defined in terms of relation lifting. There are several other coalgebraic notions of behavioural equivalence and bisimilarity [44]—we discuss these in the next subsection. Finally, in Section 6.2 we list directions for future work.

6.1   Remarks on other notions of bisimulation

Aczel-Mendler bisimulations For a coalgebra $f\colon X \to LX$, an Aczel-Mendler bisimulation $R \rightarrowtail X \times X$ is defined by the existence of an L-coalgebra structure $R \to LR$ on R such that the projection maps are coalgebra homomorphisms [1].

In the invertible step setting, applying a lifting $\overline{Q}$ to such a bisimulation, yields a structure $QR \to BQR$. However, this is not immediately a bisimulation, as QR may not be a relation. We can obtain a relation by taking the image of $\langle Q\pi_1, Q\pi_2 \rangle$ as we do to define relation lifting, but in general this is a Hermida-Jacobs bisimulation [28, Exercise 4.5.2], rather than an Aczel-Mendler one.

On the other hand, if we wish to speak of reflection of Aczel-Mendler bisimulations, we start with a span $QX \leftarrow R \to QX$ and try to construct a relation on X. Using the adjunction of the step setting, we can transpose the projections to obtain a span $X \leftarrow PR \to X$. Again PR is not immediately a relation in general, and taking the image yields a $\mathsf{Rel}(L)$-coalgebra (not an L-coalgebra) as the projections and the counit ε are coalgebra homomorphisms (see also [28, Exercise 4.5.4]). This in fact comes down to the same as the left adjoint $\coprod_\varepsilon \circ \mathsf{Rel}(P)_{QX}$ constructed earlier. There we factorise to obtain the relation lifting and factorise again for the direct image of ε, instead of factorising the paired transposes defined using ε. We also do not explicitly use that ε is a coalgebra homomorphism (although this follows from the step with right inverse and Lemma 2.3); instead we lift the adjunction at the level of relations to give a map between bisimulations. This is part of the motivation for the use of relation liftings and the corresponding notion of bisimulations.

Going further, it is shown in [5] that there exists a Vietoris bisimulation which is not an Aczel-Mendler bisimulation and, stronger, that there exist Vietoris coalgebras with states which can be related by a Vietoris but not an Aczel-Mendler bisimulation. Thus, the correspondences between bisimulations on Set and Stone we have discussed in the previous sections are not obtainable when we consider Aczel-Mendler bisimulations.

Kernel bisimulations/behavioural equivalence In applying our results to the preservation and reflection of behavioural equivalence, we currently work concretely; considering sets of states and identification of elements.

We prefer to work more abstractly, as we have done for bisimilarity. To this end, we may consider kernel bisimulations. A relation $R \rightarrowtail X \times X$ is a kernel bisimulation on a coalgebra $(X, f \colon X \to LX)$ in a category $\mathcal{D}$, if it is the pullback of morphisms $X \to Z \leftarrow X$ in $\mathcal{D}$ forming a cospan of coalgebra homomorphisms $(X, f) \to (Z, z) \leftarrow (X, f)$ in $\mathsf{Coalg}_{\mathcal{D}}(L)$. In a concrete setting this coincides with behavioural equivalence, as such a pullback contains exactly the pairs of elements of X which are identified in Z by the morphisms forming the cospan. We can thus view this as a generalisation of behavioural equivalence as defined earlier.

Assuming an invertible step $\delta \colon BQ \to QL$, we would like to relate R to a kernel bisimulation on the coalgebra $\overline{Q}(X, f)$ obtained by applying the step-induced lifting of Q. Applying Q to the pullback square for R yields a pullback square as Q is a right adjoint. However, as in our discussion of Aczel-Mendler bisimulations, this may not be a relation. We may try to also use relation liftings here, and take $\mathsf{Rel}(Q)(R)$ instead of $Q(R)$, however this may no longer be a pullback. It is not currently clear to us how to resolve these problems in general.

6.2   Future work

There are several further directions for future work. First, in this paper we focused primarily on fibrations of *relations*, which suffice for our purposes of studying bisimilarity. However, we expect that some of our results can be generalised to arbitrary (posetal) fibrations. Such a generalisation could be the basis to study preservation and reflection of other coinductive predicates and relations than bisimilarity, which can be formulated in terms of fibrations and liftings (e.g., [25]).

Secondly, while we have shown in Section 5 how our results can be used to recover the central results from [5], the latter have been generalised in two directions: the recent [24] considers bisimulations for Vietoris coalgebras on the category of *arbitrary* topological spaces, while [18] develops a notion of neighbourhood bisimulation for coalgebras that allows to generalise the results from [5] to a large variety of functors on the category of Stone spaces and their corresponding functors on Set. We would like to understand whether or not our framework is able to recover these generalisations.

Finally, the examples that we have studied in this paper do not yet exploit the full generality of invertible steps: our main motivating examples are based on an Eilenberg-Moore adjunction (or close, as in the example based on Stone spaces). In [41] it is shown that steps are relevant in a much wider setting, for instance when based on a Kleisli adjunction or on contravariant adjunctions and dualities. The latter type of steps are relevant for coalgebraic modal logics—we have studied a first instance in our example of deterministic and non-deterministic automata. Investigating the meaning of invertible steps in these other types of adjunctions is left for future work.

Acknowledgements This research has been partially funded by the NWO grant OCENW.M20.053 and by Leverhulme Trust Research Project Grant RPG-2020-232.

References

1. Aczel, P., Mendler, N.P.: A final coalgebra theorem. In: Category Theory and Computer Science. Lecture Notes in Computer Science, vol. 389, pp. 357–365. Springer (1989)
2. Adámek, J., Herrlich, H., Strecker, G.E.: Abstract and Concrete Categories - The Joy of Cats. Dover Publications (2009)
3. Bartels, F., Sokolova, A., de Vink, E.P.: A hierarchy of probabilistic system types. Theor. Comput. Sci. **327**(1-2), 3–22 (2004)
4. van Benthem, J.: Canonical modal logics and ultrafilter extensions. The Journal of Symbolic Logic **44**(1), 1–8 (1979), publisher: Cambridge University Press
5. Bezhanishvili, N., Fontaine, G., Venema, Y.: Vietoris bisimulations. J. Log. Comput. **20**(5), 1017–1040 (2010)
6. Blackburn, P., de Rijke, M., Venema, Y.: Modal Logic, Cambridge Tracts in Theoretical Computer Science, vol. 53. Cambridge University Press (2001)
7. Bonchi, F., Bonsangue, M.M., Boreale, M., Rutten, J.J.M.M., Silva, A.: A coalgebraic perspective on linear weighted automata. Inf. Comput. **211**, 77–105 (2012)
8. Bonchi, F., Bonsangue, M.M., Caltais, G., Rutten, J., Silva, A.: A coalgebraic view on decorated traces. Math. Struct. Comput. Sci. **26**(7), 1234–1268 (2016)
9. Bonchi, F., Petrisan, D., Pous, D., Rot, J.: A general account of coinduction up-to. Acta Informatica **54**(2), 127–190 (2017)
10. Bonchi, F., Santamaria, A.: Combining semilattices and semimodules. In: FoSSaCS. Lecture Notes in Computer Science, vol. 12650, pp. 102–123. Springer (2021)
11. Bonchi, F., Silva, A., Sokolova, A.: The power of convex algebras. In: CONCUR. LIPIcs, vol. 85, pp. 23:1–23:18. Schloss Dagstuhl - Leibniz-Zentrum für Informatik (2017)
12. Bonchi, F., Silva, A., Sokolova, A.: Distribution bisimilarity via the power of convex algebras. Log. Methods Comput. Sci. **17**(3) (2021)
13. Bonsangue, M.M., Hansen, H.H., Kurz, A., Rot, J.: Presenting distributive laws. Log. Methods Comput. Sci. **11**(3) (2015)
14. Bonsangue, M.M., Kurz, A.: Duality for logics of transition systems. In: FoSSaCS. Lecture Notes in Computer Science, vol. 3441, pp. 455–469. Springer (2005)
15. Bonsangue, M.M., Milius, S., Silva, A.: Sound and complete axiomatizations of coalgebraic language equivalence. ACM Trans. Comput. Log. **14**(1), 7:1–7:52 (2013)
16. Borceux, F.: Handbook of categorical algebra: volume 1, Basic category theory, vol. 1. Cambridge University Press (1994)
17. Chen, L., Jung, A.: On a categorical framework for coalgebraic modal logic. In: MFPS. Electronic Notes in Theoretical Computer Science, vol. 308, pp. 109–128. Elsevier (2014)
18. Enqvist, S., Sourabh, S.: Bisimulations for coalgebras on Stone spaces. J. Log. Comput. **28**(6), 991–1010 (2018)
19. Garner, R.: The Vietoris monad and weak distributive laws. Appl. Categorical Struct. **28**(2), 339–354 (2020)
20. Goldblatt, R.I.: Metamathematics of modal logic. Bulletin of the Australian Mathematical Society **10**(3), 479–480 (1974), publisher: Cambridge University Press
21. Goy, A.: On the compositionality of monads via weak distributive laws. (Compositionnalité des monades par lois de distributivité faibles). Ph.D. thesis, University of Paris-Saclay, France (2021)
22. Goy, A., Petrisan, D.: Combining probabilistic and non-deterministic choice via weak distributive laws. In: LICS. pp. 454–464. ACM (2020)

23. Goy, A., Petrisan, D., Aiguier, M.: Powerset-like monads weakly distribute over themselves in toposes and compact Hausdorff spaces. In: ICALP. LIPIcs, vol. 198, pp. 132:1–132:14. Schloss Dagstuhl - Leibniz-Zentrum für Informatik (2021)
24. Gumm, H.P., Taheri, M.: Saturated Kripke structures as Vietoris coalgebras. In: CMCS. Lecture Notes in Computer Science, vol. 13225, pp. 88–109. Springer (2022)
25. Hasuo, I., Kataoka, T., Cho, K.: Coinductive predicates and final sequences in a fibration. Math. Struct. Comput. Sci. **28**(4), 562–611 (2018)
26. Hermida, C.: On fibred adjunctions and completeness for fibred categories. In: COMPASS/ADT. Lecture Notes in Computer Science, vol. 785, pp. 235–251. Springer (1992)
27. Hermida, C., Jacobs, B.: Structural induction and coinduction in a fibrational setting. Inf. Comput. **145**(2), 107–152 (1998)
28. Jacobs, B.: Introduction to Coalgebra: Towards Mathematics of States and Observation, Cambridge Tracts in Theoretical Computer Science, vol. 59. Cambridge University Press (2016)
29. Jacobs, B., Silva, A., Sokolova, A.: Trace semantics via determinization. J. Comput. Syst. Sci. **81**(5), 859–879 (2015)
30. Jacobs, B.P.F.: Categorical Logic and Type Theory, Studies in logic and the foundations of mathematics, vol. 141. North-Holland (2001)
31. Kelly, G.M., Street, R.: Review of the elements of 2-categories. In: Kelly, G.M. (ed.) Category Seminar: Proceedings Sydney Category Seminar 1972/1973. No. 420 in Lecture Notes in Mathematics, Springer-Verlag (1974)
32. Klin, B.: Coalgebraic modal logic beyond sets. In: MFPS. Electronic Notes in Theoretical Computer Science, vol. 173, pp. 177–201. Elsevier (2007)
33. Klin, B.: Bialgebras for structural operational semantics: An introduction. Theor. Comput. Sci. **412**(38), 5043–5069 (2011)
34. Klin, B., Salamanca, J.: Iterated covariant powerset is not a monad. In: MFPS. Electronic Notes in Theoretical Computer Science, vol. 341, pp. 261–276. Elsevier (2018)
35. Kupke, C., Kurz, A., Pattinson, D.: Algebraic semantics for coalgebraic logics. In: CMCS. Electronic Notes in Theoretical Computer Science, vol. 106, pp. 219–241. Elsevier (2004)
36. Kupke, C., Kurz, A., Pattinson, D.: Ultrafilter extensions for coalgebras. In: CALCO. Lecture Notes in Computer Science, vol. 3629, pp. 263–277. Springer (2005)
37. Leinster, T.: Higher Operads, Higher Categories, London Mathematical Society Lecture Notes, vol. 298. Cambridge University Press (2004)
38. Levy, P.B.: Final coalgebras from corecursive algebras. In: CALCO. LIPIcs, vol. 35, pp. 221–237. Schloss Dagstuhl - Leibniz-Zentrum für Informatik (2015)
39. Manes, E.: A triple theoretic construction of compact algebras. In: Seminar on triples and categorical homology theory. pp. 91–118. Springer (1969)
40. Pavlovic, D., Mislove, M.W., Worrell, J.: Testing semantics: Connecting processes and process logics. In: AMAST. Lecture Notes in Computer Science, vol. 4019, pp. 308–322. Springer (2006)
41. Rot, J., Jacobs, B., Levy, P.B.: Steps and traces. J. Log. Comput. **31**(6), 1482–1525 (2021)
42. Rutten, J.J.M.M.: Universal coalgebra: a theory of systems. Theor. Comput. Sci. **249**(1), 3–80 (2000)
43. Silva, A., Bonchi, F., Bonsangue, M.M., Rutten, J.J.M.M.: Generalizing determinization from automata to coalgebras. Log. Methods Comput. Sci. **9**(1) (2013)
44. Staton, S.: Relating coalgebraic notions of bisimulation. Log. Methods Comput. Sci. **7**(1) (2011)

45. Turi, D., Plotkin, G.D.: Towards a mathematical operational semantics. In: LICS. pp. 280–291. IEEE Computer Society (1997)
46. Varacca, D.: Probability, Nondeterminism and Concurrency: Two Denotational Models for Probabilistic Computation. Ph.D. thesis, University of Aarhus (2003)
47. Zwart, M., Marsden, D.: No-go theorems for distributive laws. Log. Methods Comput. Sci. **18**(1) (2022)

Quantitative Safety and Liveness

Thomas A. Henzinger, Nicolas Mazzocchi, and N. Ege Saraç[✉]

Institute of Science and Technology Austria (ISTA), Klosterneuburg, Austria
{tah,nmazzocc,esarac}@ist.ac.at

Abstract. Safety and liveness are elementary concepts of computation, and the foundation of many verification paradigms. The safety-liveness classification of boolean properties characterizes whether a given property can be falsified by observing a finite prefix of an infinite computation trace (always for safety, never for liveness). In quantitative specification and verification, properties assign not truth values, but quantitative values to infinite traces (e.g., a cost, or the distance to a boolean property). We introduce quantitative safety and liveness, and we prove that our definitions induce conservative quantitative generalizations of both (1) the safety-progress hierarchy of boolean properties and (2) the safety-liveness decomposition of boolean properties. In particular, we show that every quantitative property can be written as the pointwise minimum of a quantitative safety property and a quantitative liveness property. Consequently, like boolean properties, also quantitative properties can be min-decomposed into safety and liveness parts, or alternatively, max-decomposed into co-safety and co-liveness parts. Moreover, quantitative properties can be approximated naturally. We prove that every quantitative property that has both safe and co-safe approximations can be monitored arbitrarily precisely by a monitor that uses only a finite number of states.

1 Introduction

Safety and liveness are elementary concepts in the semantics of computation [39]. They can be explained through the thought experiment of a *ghost monitor*—an imaginary device that watches an infinite computation trace at runtime, one observation at a time, and always maintains the set of *possible prediction values* to reflect the satisfaction of a given property. Let Φ be a boolean property, meaning that Φ divides all infinite traces into those that satisfy Φ, and those that violate Φ. After any finite number of observations, True is a possible prediction value for Φ if the observations seen so far are consistent with an infinite trace that satisfies Φ, and False is a possible prediction value for Φ if the observations seen so far are consistent with an infinite trace that violates Φ. When True is no possible prediction value, the ghost monitor can reject the hypothesis that Φ is satisfied. The property Φ is *safe* if and only if the ghost monitor can always reject the hypothesis Φ after a finite number of observations: if the infinite trace that is being monitored violates Φ, then after some finite number of observations, True is no possible prediction value for Φ. Orthogonally, the property Φ is *live* if and only if the ghost monitor can never reject the hypothesis Φ after a finite number of

© The Author(s) 2023
O. Kupferman and P. Sobocinski (Eds.): FoSSaCS 2023, LNCS 13992, pp. 349–370, 2023.
https://doi.org/10.1007/978-3-031-30829-1_17

observations: for all infinite traces, after every finite number of observations, True remains a possible prediction value for Φ.

The safety-liveness classification of properties is fundamental in verification. In the natural topology on infinite traces—the "Cantor topology"—the safety properties are the closed sets, and the liveness properties are the dense sets [4]. For every property Φ, the location of Φ within the Borel hierarchy that is induced by the Cantor topology—the so-called "safety-progress hierarchy" [17]—indicates the level of difficulty encountered when verifying Φ. On the first level, we find the safety and co-safety properties, the latter being the complements of safety properties, i.e., the properties whose falsehood (rather than truth) can always be rejected after a finite number of observations by the ghost monitor. More sophisticated verification techniques are needed for second-level properties, which are the countable boolean combinations of first-level properties—the so-called "response" and "persistence" properties [17]. Moreover, the orthogonality of safety and liveness leads to the following celebrated fact: *every* property can be written as the intersection of a safety property and a liveness property [4]. This means that every property Φ can be decomposed into two parts: a safety part—which is amenable to simple verification techniques, such as invariants—and a liveness part—which requires heavier verification paradigms, such as ranking functions. Dually, there is always a disjunctive decomposition of Φ into co-safety and co-liveness.

So far, we have retold the well-known story of safety and liveness for *boolean* properties. A boolean property Φ is formalized mathematically as the *set* of infinite computation traces that satisfy Φ, or equivalently, the characteristic *function* that maps each infinite trace to a truth value. Quantitative generalizations of the boolean setting allow us to capture not only correctness properties, but also performance properties [31]. In this paper we reveal the story of safety and liveness for such *quantitative* properties, which are functions from infinite traces to an arbitrary set $\mathbb{D}$ of *values*. In order to compare values, we equip the value domain $\mathbb{D}$ with a partial order $<$, and we require $(\mathbb{D}, <)$ to be a complete lattice. The membership problem [18] for an infinite trace f and a quantitative property Φ asks whether $\Phi(f) \geq v$ for a given threshold value $v \in \mathbb{D}$. Correspondingly, in our thought experiment, the ghost monitor attempts to reject hypotheses of the form $\Phi(f) \geq v$, which cannot be rejected as long as all observations seen so far are consistent with an infinite trace f with $\Phi(f) \geq v$. We will define Φ to be a *quantitative safety* property if and only if every hypothesis of the form $\Phi(f) \geq v$ can always be rejected by the ghost monitor after a finite number of observations, and we will define Φ to be a *quantitative liveness* property if and only if some hypothesis of the form $\Phi(f) \geq v$ can never be rejected by the ghost monitor after any finite number of observations. We note that in the quantitative case, after every finite number of observations, the set of possible prediction values for Φ maintained by the ghost monitor may be finite or infinite, and in the latter case, it may not contain a minimal or maximal element.

Let us give a few examples. Suppose we have four observations: observation rq for "request a resource," observation gr for "grant the resource," observation tk for "clock tick," and observation oo for "other." The boolean property

Resp requires that every occurrence of rq in an infinite trace is followed eventually by an occurrence of gr. The boolean property NoDoubleReq requires that no occurrence of rq is followed by another rq without some gr in between. The quantitative property MinRespTime maps every infinite trace to the largest number k such that there are at least k occurrences of tk between each rq and the closest subsequent gr. The quantitative property MaxRespTime maps every infinite trace to the smallest number k such that there are at most k occurrences of tk between each rq and the closest subsequent gr. The quantitative property AvgRespTime maps every infinite trace to the lower limit value lim inf of the infinite sequence $(v_i)_{i \geq 1}$, where v_i is, for the first i occurrences of tk, the average number of occurrences of tk between rq and the closest subsequent gr. Note that the values of AvgRespTime can be ∞ for some computations, including those for which the value of Resp is True. This highlights that boolean properties are not embedded in the limit behavior of quantitative properties.

The boolean property Resp is live because every finite observation sequence can be extended with an occurrence of gr. In fact, Resp is a second-level liveness property (namely, a response property), because it can be written as a countable intersection of co-safety properties. The boolean property NoDoubleReq is safe because if it is violated, it will be rejected by the ghost monitor after a finite number of observations, namely, as soon as the ghost monitor sees a rq followed by another occurrence of rq without an intervening gr. According to our quantitative generalization of safety, MinRespTime is a safety property. The ghost monitor always maintains the minimal number k of occurrences of tk between any past rq and the closest subsequent gr seen so far; the set of possible prediction values for MinRespTime is always $\{0, 1, \ldots, k\}$. Every hypothesis of the form "the MinRespTime-value is at least v" is rejected by the ghost monitor as soon as $k < v$; if such a hypothesis is violated, this will happen after some finite number of observations. Symmetrically, the quantitative property MaxRespTime is co-safe, because every wrong hypothesis of the form "the MaxRespTime-value is at most v" will be rejected by the ghost monitor as soon as the smallest possible prediction value for MaxRespTime, which is the maximal number of occurrences of tk between any past rq and the closest subsequent gr seen so far, goes above v. By contrast, the quantitative property AvgRespTime is both live and co-live because no hypothesis of the form "the AvgRespTime-value is at least v," nor of the form "the AvgRespTime-value is at most v," can ever be rejected by the ghost monitor after a finite number of observations. All nonnegative real numbers and ∞ always remain possible prediction values for AvgRespTime. Note that a ghost monitor that attempts to reject hypotheses of the form $\Phi(f) \geq v$ does not need to maintain the entire set of possible prediction values, but only the sup of the set of possible prediction values, and whether or not the sup is contained in the set. Dually, updating inf (and whether it is contained) suffices to reject hypotheses of the form $\Phi(f) \leq v$.

By defining quantitative safety and liveness via ghost monitors, we not only obtain a conservative and quantitative generalization of the boolean story, but also open up attractive frontiers for quantitative semantics, monitoring, and verification. For example, while the approximation of boolean properties reduces to adding and removing traces to and from a set, the approximation of quantitative properties offers a rich landscape of possibilities. In fact, we can approximate the notion of safety itself. Given an error bound α, the quantitative property Φ is α-*safe* if and only if for every value v and every infinite trace f whose value $\Phi(f)$ is less than v, all possible prediction values for Φ are less than $v + \alpha$ after some finite prefix of f. This means that, for an α-safe property Φ, the ghost monitor may not reject wrong hypotheses of the form $\Phi(f) \geq v$ after a finite number of observations, once the violation is below the error bound. We show that every quantitative property that is both α-safe and β-co-safe, for any finite α and β, can be monitored arbitrarily precisely by a monitor that uses only a finite number of states.

We are not the first to define quantitative (or multi-valued) definitions of safety and liveness [41,27]. While the previously proposed quantitative generalizations of safety share strong similarities with our definition (without coinciding completely), our quantitative generalization of liveness is entirely new. The definitions of [27] do not support any safety-liveness decomposition, because their notion of safety is too permissive, and their liveness too restrictive. While the definitions of [41] admit a safety-liveness decomposition, our definition of liveness captures strictly fewer properties. Consequently, our definitions offer a stronger safety-liveness decomposition theorem. Our definitions also fit naturally with the definitions of emptiness, equivalence, and inclusion for quantitative languages [18].

Overview. In Section 2, we introduce quantitative properties. In Section 3, we define quantitative safety as well as safety closure, namely, the property that increases the value of each trace as little as possible to achieve safety. Then, we prove that our definitions preserve classical boolean facts. In particular, we show that a quantitative property Φ is safe if and only if Φ equals its safety closure if and only if Φ is upper semicontinuous. In Section 4, we generalize the safety-progress hierarchy to quantitative properties. We first define limit properties. For $\ell \in \{\inf, \sup, \lim\inf, \lim\sup\}$, the class of ℓ-properties captures those for which the value of each infinite trace can be derived by applying the limit function ℓ to the infinite sequence of values of finite prefixes. We prove that inf-properties coincide with safety, sup-properties with co-safety, lim inf-properties are suprema of countably many safety properties, and lim sup-properties infima of countably many co-safety properties. The lim inf-properties generalize the boolean persistence properties of [17]; the lim sup-properties generalize their response properties. For example, AvgRespTime is a lim inf-property. In Section 5, we introduce quantitative liveness and co-liveness. We prove that our definitions preserve the classical boolean facts, and show that there is a unique property which is both safe and live. As main result, we provide a safety-liveness decomposition that holds for every quantitative property. In Section 6, we define approximate safety and co-safety. We generalize the well-known unfolding approximation of discounted properties for approximate safety and co-safety properties over the extended reals. This allows us to provide a finite-state approximate monitor for these properties. In Section 7, we conclude with future research directions. For complete proofs of all results, we refer the reader to the full version of the paper.

Related Work. The notions of safety and liveness for boolean properties appeared first in [39] and were later formalized in [4], where safety properties were characterized as closed sets of the Cantor topology on infinite traces, and liveness properties as dense sets. As a consequence, the seminal decomposition theorem followed: every boolean property is an intersection of a safety property and a liveness property. A benefit of such a decomposition lies in the difference between the mathematical arguments used in their verification. While safety properties enable simpler methods such as invariants, liveness properties require more complex approaches such as well-foundedness [42,5]. These classes were characterized in terms of Büchi automata in [5] and in terms of linear temporal logic in [46].

The safety-progress classification of boolean properties [17] proposes an orthogonal view: rather than partitioning the set of properties, it provides a hierarchy of properties starting from safety. This yields a more fine-grained view of nonsafety properties which distinguishes whether a "good thing" happens at least once (co-safety or "guarantee"), infinitely many times (response), or eventually always (persistence). This classification follows the Borel hierarchy that is induced by the Cantor topology on infinite traces, and has corresponding projections within properties that are definable by finite automata and by formulas of linear temporal logic.

Runtime verification, or monitoring, is a lightweight, dynamic verification technique [6], where a monitor watches a system during its execution and tries to decide, after each finite sequence of observations, whether the observed finite computation trace or its unknown infinite extension satisfies a desired property. The safety-liveness dichotomy has profound implications for runtime verification as well: safety is easy to monitor [28], while liveness is not. An early definition of boolean monitorability was equivalent to safety with recursively enumerable sets of bad prefixes [35]. The monitoring of infinite-state boolean safety properties was later studied in [26]. A more popular definition of boolean monitorability [44,8] accounts for both truth and falsehood, establishing the set of monitorable properties as a strict superset of finite boolean combinations of safety and co-safety [23]. Boolean monitors that use the set possible prediction values can be found in [7]. The notion of boolean monitorability was investigated through the safety-liveness lens in [43] and through the safety-progress lens in [23].

Quantitative properties (a.k.a. "quantitative languages") [18] extend their boolean counterparts by moving from the two-valued truth domain to richer domains such as real numbers. Such properties have been extensively studied from a static verification perspective in the past decade, e.g., in the context of model-checking probabilistic properties [38,37], games with quantitative objectives [10,15], specifying quantitative properties [11,1], measuring distances between systems [2,16,22,29], best-effort synthesis and repair [9,20], and quantitative analysis of transition systems [47,14,21,19]. More recently, quantitative properties have been also studied from a runtime verification perspective, e.g., for limit monitoring of statistical indicators of infinite traces [25] and for analyzing resource-precision trade-offs in the design of quantitative monitors [33,30].

To the best of our knowledge, previous definitions of (approximate) safety and liveness in nonboolean domains make implicit assumptions about the specification language [48,34,24,45]. We identify two notable exceptions. In [27], the authors generalize the framework of [43] to nonboolean value domains. They provide neither a safety-liveness decomposition of quantitative properties, nor a fine-grained classification of nonsafety properties. In [41], the authors present a safety-liveness decomposition and some levels of the safety-progress hierarchy on multi-valued truth domains, which are bounded distributive lattices. Their motivation is to provide algorithms for model-checking properties on multi-valued truth domains. We present the relationships between their definitions and ours in the relevant sections below.

2   Quantitative Properties

Let $\Sigma = \{a, b, \ldots\}$ be a finite alphabet of observations. A *trace* is an infinite sequence of observations, denoted by $f, g, h \in \Sigma^\omega$, and a *finite trace* is a finite sequence of observations, denoted by $s, r, t \in \Sigma^*$. Given $s \in \Sigma^*$ and $w \in \Sigma^* \cup \Sigma^\omega$, we denote by $s \prec w$ (resp. $s \preceq w$) that s is a strict (resp. nonstrict) prefix of w. Furthermore, we denote by $|w|$ the length of w and, given $a \in \Sigma$, by $|w|_a$ the number of occurrences of a in w.

A *value domain* $\mathbb{D}$ is a poset. Unless otherwise stated, we assume that $\mathbb{D}$ is a nontrivial (i.e., $\bot \neq \top$) complete lattice and, whenever appropriate, we write $0, 1, -\infty, \infty$ instead of $\bot$ and $\top$ for the least and the greatest elements. We respectively use the terms minimum and maximum for the greatest lower bound and the least upper bound of finitely many elements.

Definition 1 (Property). *A* quantitative property *(or simply* property*) is a function* $\Phi : \Sigma^\omega \to \mathbb{D}$ *from the set of all traces to a value domain.*

A boolean property $P \subseteq \Sigma^\omega$ is defined as a set of traces. We use the boolean domain $\mathbb{B} = \{0, 1\}$ with $0 < 1$ and, in place of P, its *characteristic property* $\Phi_P : \Sigma^\omega \to \mathbb{B}$, which is defined by $\Phi_P(f) = 1$ if $f \in P$, and $\Phi_P(f) = 0$ if $f \notin P$.

For all properties Φ_1, Φ_2 on a domain $\mathbb{D}$ and all traces $f \in \Sigma^\omega$, we let $\min(\Phi_1, \Phi_2)(f) = \min(\Phi_1(f), \Phi_2(f))$ and $\max(\Phi_1, \Phi_2)(f) = \max(\Phi_1(f), \Phi_2(f))$. For a domain $\mathbb{D}$, the *inverse* of $\mathbb{D}$ is the domain $\overline{\mathbb{D}}$ that contains the same elements as $\mathbb{D}$ but with the ordering reversed. For a property Φ, we define its *complement* $\overline{\Phi} : \Sigma^\omega \to \overline{\mathbb{D}}$ by $\overline{\Phi}(f) = \Phi(f)$ for all $f \in \Sigma^\omega$.

Some properties can be defined as limits of value sequences. A *finitary property* $\pi : \Sigma^* \to \mathbb{D}$ associates a value with each finite trace. A *value function* $\ell : \mathbb{D}^\omega \to \mathbb{D}$ condenses an infinite sequence of values to a single value. Given a finitary property π, a value function ℓ, and a trace $f \in \Sigma^\omega$, we write $\ell_{s \prec f} \pi(s)$ instead of $\ell(\pi(s_0)\pi(s_1)\ldots)$, where each s_i fulfills $s_i \prec f$ and $|s_i| = i$.

3   Quantitative Safety

Given a property $\Phi : \Sigma^\omega \to \mathbb{D}$, a trace $f \in \Sigma^\omega$, and a value $v \in \mathbb{D}$, the quantitative membership problem [18] asks whether $\Phi(f) \geq v$. We define quantitative safety as follows: the property Φ is safe iff every wrong hypothesis of the form $\Phi(f) \geq v$ has a finite witness $s \prec f$.

Definition 2 (Safety). *A property* $\Phi : \Sigma^\omega \to \mathbb{D}$ *is safe iff for every* $f \in \Sigma^\omega$ *and value* $v \in \mathbb{D}$ *with* $\Phi(f) \not\geq v$, *there is a prefix* $s \prec f$ *such that* $\sup_{g \in \Sigma^\omega} \Phi(sg) \not\geq v$.

Let us illustrate this definition with the *minimal response-time* property.

Example 3. Let $\Sigma = \{\text{rq}, \text{gr}, \text{tk}, \text{oo}\}$ and $\mathbb{D} = \mathbb{N} \cup \{\infty\}$. We define the minimal response-time property $\Phi_{\min}$ through an auxiliary finitary property $\pi_{\min}$ that computes the minimum response time so far. In a finite or infinite trace, an occurrence of rq is *granted* if it is followed, later, by a gr, and otherwise it is *pending*. Let $\pi_{\text{last}}(s) = \infty$ if the finite trace s contains a pending rq, or no rq, and $\pi_{\text{last}}(s) = |r|_{\text{tk}} - |t|_{\text{tk}}$ otherwise, where $r \prec s$ is the longest prefix of s with a pending rq, and $t \prec r$ is the longest prefix of r without pending rq. Intuitively, π_{last} provides the response time for the last request when all requests are granted, and ∞ when there is a pending request or no request. Given $s \in \Sigma^*$, taking the minimum of the values of π_{last} over the prefixes $r \preceq s$ gives us the minimum response time so far. Let $\pi_{\min}(s) = \min_{r \preceq s} \pi_{\text{last}}(r)$ for all $s \in \Sigma^*$, and $\Phi_{\min}(f) = \lim_{s \prec f} \pi_{\min}(s)$ for all $f \in \Sigma^\omega$. The limit always exists because the minimum is monotonically decreasing.

The minimal response-time property is safe. Let $f \in \Sigma^\omega$ and $v \in \mathbb{D}$ such that $\Phi_{\min}(f) < v$. Then, some prefix $s \prec f$ contains a rq that is granted after $u < v$ ticks, in which case, no matter what happens in the future, the minimal response time is guaranteed to be at most u; that is, $\sup_{g \in \Sigma^\omega} \Phi_{\min}(sg) \leq u < v$. If you recall from the introduction the ghost monitor that maintains the sup of possible prediction values for the minimal response-time property, that value is always $\pi_{\min}$; that is, $\sup_{g \in \Sigma^\omega} \Phi_{\min}(sg) = \pi_{\min}(s)$ for all $s \in \Sigma^*$. Note that in the case of minimal response time, the sup of possible prediction values is always realizable; that is, for all $s \in \Sigma^*$, there exists an $f \in \Sigma^\omega$ such that $\sup_{g \in \Sigma^\omega} \Phi_{\min}(sg) = \Phi_{\min}(sf)$. □

Remark 4. Quantitative safety generalizes boolean safety. For every boolean property $P \subseteq \Sigma^\omega$, the following statements are equivalent: (i) P is safe according to the classical definition [4], (ii) its characteristic property Φ_P is safe, and (iii) for every $f \in \Sigma^\omega$ and $v \in \mathbb{B}$ with $\Phi_P(f) < v$, there exists a prefix $s \prec f$ such that for all $g \in \Sigma^\omega$, we have $\Phi_P(sg) < v$.

We now generalize the notion of safety closure and present an operation that makes a property safe by increasing the value of each trace as little as possible.

Definition 5 (Safety closure). *The* safety closure *of a property* Φ *is the property* Φ^* *defined by* $\Phi^*(f) = \inf_{s \prec f} \sup_{g \in \Sigma^\omega} \Phi(sg)$ *for all* $f \in \Sigma^\omega$.

We can say the following about the safety closure operation.

Proposition 6. *For every property* $\Phi : \Sigma^\omega \to \mathbb{D}$, *the following statements hold.*

1. Φ^* *is safe.*
2. $\Phi^*(f) \geq \Phi(f)$ *for all* $f \in \Sigma^\omega$.
3. $\Phi^*(f) = \Phi^{**}(f)$ *for all* $f \in \Sigma^\omega$.
4. *For every safety property* $\Psi : \Sigma^\omega \to \mathbb{D}$, *if* $\Phi(f) \leq \Psi(f)$ *for all* $f \in \Sigma^\omega$, *then* $\Psi(g) \not< \Phi^*(g)$ *for all* $g \in \Sigma^\omega$.

3.1   Alternative Characterizations of Quantitative Safety

Consider a trace and its prefixes of increasing length. For a given property, the ghost monitor from the introduction maintains, for each prefix, the sup of possible prediction values, i.e., the least upper bound of the property values for all possible infinite continuations. The resulting sequence of monotonically decreasing suprema provides an upper bound on the eventual property value. Moreover, for some properties, this sequence always converges to the property value. If this is the case, then the ghost monitor can always dismiss wrong lower-bound hypotheses after finite prefixes, and vice versa. This gives us an alternative definition for the safety of quantitative properties which, inspired by the notion of Scott continuity, was called *continuity* [33]. We now believe that *upper semicontinuity* is a more appropriate term, as becomes clear when we consider the Cantor topology on Σ^ω and the value domain $\mathbb{R} \cup \{-\infty, +\infty\}$.

Definition 7 (Upper semicontinuity [33]). *A property Φ is upper semicontinuous iff $\Phi(f) = \lim_{s \prec f} \sup_{g \in \Sigma^\omega} \Phi(sg)$ for all $f \in \Sigma^\omega$.*

We note that the minimal response-time property is upper semicontinuous.

Example 8. Recall the minimal response-time property $\Phi_{\min}$ from Example 3. For every trace $f \in \Sigma^\omega$, the $\Phi_{\min}$ value is the limit of the $\pi_{\min}$ values for the prefixes of f. Therefore, $\Phi_{\min}$ is upper semicontinuous.   □

In general, a property is safe iff it maps every trace to the limit of the suprema of possible prediction values. Moreover, we can also characterize safety properties as the properties that are equal to their safety closure.

Theorem 9. *For every property Φ, the following statements are equivalent:*
1. Φ is safe. 2. Φ is upper semicontinuous. 3. $\Phi(f) = \Phi^*(f)$ for all $f \in \Sigma^\omega$.

3.2   Related Definitions of Quantitative Safety

In [41], the authors consider the model-checking problem for properties on multi-valued truth domains. They introduce the notion of multi-safety through a closure operation that coincides with our safety closure. Formally, a property Φ is *multi-safe* iff $\Phi(f) = \Phi^*(f)$ for every $f \in \Sigma^\omega$. It is easy to see the following.

Proposition 10. *For every property Φ, we have Φ is multi-safe iff Φ is safe.*

Although the two definitions of safety are equivalent, our definition is consistent with the membership problem for quantitative automata and motivated by the monitoring of quantitative properties.

In [27], the authors extend a refinement of the safety-liveness classification for monitoring [43] to richer domains. They introduce the notion of verdict-safety through dismissibility of values not less than or equal to the property value. Formally, a property Φ is *verdict-safe* iff for every $f \in \Sigma^\omega$ and $v \not\leq \Phi(f)$, there exists a prefix $s \prec f$ such that for all $g \in \Sigma^\omega$, we have $\Phi(sg) \neq v$.

We demonstrate that verdict-safety is weaker than safety. Moreover, we provide a condition under which the two definitions coincide. To achieve this, we reason about sets of possible prediction values: for a property Φ and $s \in \Sigma^*$, let $P_{\Phi,s} = \{\Phi(sf) \mid f \in \Sigma^\omega\}$.

Lemma 11. *A property Φ is verdict-safe iff $\Phi(f) = \sup(\lim_{s \prec f} P_{\Phi,s})$ for all $f \in \Sigma^\omega$.*

Notice that Φ is safe iff $\Phi(f) = \lim_{s \prec f}(\sup P_{\Phi,s})$ for all $f \in \Sigma^\omega$. Below we describe a property that is verdict-safe but not safe.

Example 12. Let $\Sigma = \{a, b\}$. Define Φ by $\Phi(f) = 0$ if $f = a^\omega$, and $\Phi(f) = |s|$ otherwise, where $s \prec f$ is the shortest prefix in which b occurs. The property Φ is verdict-safe. First, observe that $\mathbb{D} = \mathbb{N} \cup \{\infty\}$. Let $f \in \Sigma^\omega$ and $v \in \mathbb{D}$ with $v > \Phi(f)$. If $\Phi(f) > 0$, then f contains b, and $\Phi(f) = |s|$ for some $s \prec f$ in which b occurs for the first time. After the prefix s, all $g \in \Sigma^\omega$ yield $\Phi(sg) = |s|$, thus all values above $|s|$ are rejected. If $\Phi(f) = 0$, then $f = a^\omega$. Let $v \in \mathbb{D}$ with $v > 0$, and consider the prefix $a^v \prec f$. Observe that the set of possible prediction values after reading a^v is $\{0, v + 1, v + 2, \ldots\}$, therefore a^v allows the ghost monitor to reject the value v. However, Φ is not safe because, although $\Phi(a^\omega) = 0$, for every $s \prec a^\omega$, we have $\sup_{g \in \Sigma^\omega} \Phi(sg) = \infty$. □

The separation is due to the fact that, for some finite traces, the sup of possible prediction values cannot be realized by any future. Below, we present a condition that prevents such cases.

Definition 13 (Supremum closedness). *A property Φ is sup-closed iff for every $s \in \Sigma^*$ we have $\sup P_{\Phi,s} \in P_{\Phi,s}$.*

We remark that the minimal response-time property is sup-closed.

Example 14. The safety property minimal response-time $\Phi_{\min}$ from Example 3 is sup-closed. This is because, for every $s \in \Sigma^*$, the continuation $\mathbf{gr}^\omega$ realizes the value $\sup_{g \in \Sigma^\omega} \Phi(sg)$. □

Recall from the introduction the ghost monitor that maintains the sup of possible prediction values. For monitoring sup-closed properties this suffices; otherwise the ghost monitor also needs to maintain whether or not the supremum of the possible prediction values is realizable by some future continuation. In general, we have the following for every sup-closed property.

Lemma 15. *For every sup-closed property Φ and for all $f \in \Sigma^\omega$, we have $\lim_{s \prec f}(\sup P_{\Phi,s}) = \sup(\lim_{s \prec f} P_{\Phi,s})$.*

As a consequence of the lemmas above, we get the following.

Theorem 16. *A sup-closed property Φ is safe iff Φ is verdict-safe.*

4   The Quantitative Safety-Progress Hierarchy

Our quantitative extension of safety closure allows us to build a Borel hierarchy, which is a quantitative extension of the boolean safety-progress hierarchy [17]. First, we show that safety properties are closed under pairwise min and max.

Proposition 17. *For every value domain $\mathbb{D}$, the set of safety properties over $\mathbb{D}$ is closed under min and max.*

The boolean safety-progress classification of properties is a Borel hierarchy built from the Cantor topology of traces. Safety and co-safety properties lie on the first level, respectively corresponding to the closed sets and open sets of the topology. The second level is obtained through countable unions and intersections of properties from the first level: persistence properties are countable unions of closed sets, while response properties are countable intersections of open sets. We generalize this construction to the quantitative setting.

In the boolean case, each property class is defined through an operation that takes a set $S \subseteq \Sigma^*$ of finite traces and produces a set $P \subseteq \Sigma^\omega$ of infinite traces. For example, to obtain a co-safety property from $S \subseteq \Sigma^*$, the corresponding operation yields $S\Sigma^\omega$. Similarly, we formalize each property class by a value function. For this, we define the notion of *limit property*.

Definition 18 (Limit property). *A property $\Phi : \Sigma^\omega \to \mathbb{D}$ is a limit property iff there exists a finitary property $\pi : \Sigma^* \to \mathbb{D}$ and a value function $\ell : \mathbb{D}^\omega \to \mathbb{D}$ such that $\Phi(f) = \ell_{s \prec f}\pi(s)$ for all $f \in \Sigma^\omega$. We denote this by $\Phi = (\pi, \ell)$, and write $\Phi(s)$ instead of $\pi(s)$. In particular, if $\Phi = (\pi, \ell)$, where $\ell \in \{\inf, \sup, \liminf, \limsup\}$, then Φ is an ℓ-property.*

To account for the value functions that construct the first two levels of the safety-progress hierarchy, we start our investigation with inf- and sup-properties and later focus on lim inf- and lim sup- properties [18].

4.1   Infimum and Supremum Properties

Let us start with an example by demonstrating that the minimal response-time property is an inf-property.

Example 19. Recall the safety property $\Phi_{\min}$ of minimal response time from Example 3. We can equivalently define $\Phi_{\min}$ as a limit property by taking the finitary property π_{last} and the value function inf. As discussed in Example 3, the function π_{last} outputs the response time for the last request when all requests are granted, and ∞ when there is a pending request or no request. Then $\inf_{s \prec f} \pi_{\text{last}}(s) = \Phi_{\min}(f)$ for all $f \in \Sigma^\omega$, and therefore $\Phi_{\min} = (\pi_{\text{last}}, \inf)$.   □

In fact, the safety properties coincide with inf-properties.

Theorem 20. *A property Φ is safe iff Φ is an inf-property.*

Defining the minimal response-time property as a limit property, we observe the following relation between its behavior on finite traces and infinite traces.

Example 21. Consider the property $\Phi_{\min} = (\pi_{\text{last}}, \inf)$ from Example 19. Let $f \in \Sigma^\omega$ and $v \in \mathbb{D}$. Observe that if the minimal response time of f is at least v, then the last response time for each prefix $s \prec f$ is also at least v. Conversely, if the minimal response time of f is below v, then there is a prefix $s \prec f$ for which the last response time is also below v.   □

In light of this observation, we provide another characterization of safety properties, explicitly relating the specified behavior of the limit property on finite and infinite traces.

Theorem 22. *A property $\Phi : \Sigma^\omega \to \mathbb{D}$ is safe iff Φ is a limit property such that for every $f \in \Sigma^\omega$ and value $v \in \mathbb{D}$, we have $\Phi(f) \geq v$ iff $\Phi(s) \geq v$ for all $s \prec f$.*

Recall that a safety property allows rejecting wrong lower-bound hypotheses with a finite witness, by assigning a tight upper bound to each trace. We define co-safety properties symmetrically: a property Φ is co-safe iff every wrong hypothesis of the form $\Phi(f) \leq v$ has a finite witness $s \prec f$.

Definition 23 (Co-safety). *A property $\Phi : \Sigma^\omega \to \mathbb{D}$ is co-safe iff for every $f \in \Sigma^\omega$ and value $v \in \mathbb{D}$ with $\Phi(f) \not\leq v$, there exists a prefix $s \prec f$ such that $\inf_{g \in \Sigma^\omega} \Phi(sg) \not\leq v$.*

We note that our definition generalizes boolean co-safety, and thus a dual of Remark 4 holds also for co-safety. Moreover, we analogously define the notions of co-safety closure and lower semicontinuity.

Definition 24 (Co-safety closure). *The co-safety closure of a property Φ is the property $\Phi_*(f)$ defined by $\Phi_*(f) = \sup_{s \prec f} \inf_{g \in \Sigma^\omega} \Phi(sg)$ for all $f \in \Sigma^\omega$.*

Definition 25 (Lower semicontinuity [33]). *A property Φ is lower semicontinuous iff $\Phi(f) = \lim_{s \prec f} \inf_{g \in \Sigma^\omega} \Phi(sg)$ for all $f \in \Sigma^\omega$.*

Now, we define and investigate the *maximal response-time* property. In particular, we show that it is a sup-property that is co-safe and lower semicontinuous.

Example 26. Let $\Sigma = \{\mathtt{rq}, \mathtt{gr}, \mathtt{tk}, \mathtt{oo}\}$ and $\mathbb{D} = \mathbb{N} \cup \{\infty\}$. We define the maximal response-time property $\Phi_{\max}$ through a finitary property that computes the current response time for each finite trace and the value function sup. In particular, for all $s \in \Sigma^*$, let $\pi_{\mathrm{curr}}(s) = |s|_{\mathtt{tk}} - |r|_{\mathtt{tk}}$, where $r \preceq s$ is the longest prefix of s without pending $\mathtt{rq}$; then $\Phi_{\max} = (\pi_{\mathrm{curr}}, \sup)$. Note the contrast between π_{curr} and π_{last} from Example 3. While π_{curr} takes an optimistic view of the future and assumes the $\mathtt{gr}$ will follow immediately, π_{last} takes a pessimistic view and assumes the $\mathtt{gr}$ will never follow. Let $f \in \Sigma^\omega$ and $v \in \mathbb{D}$. If the maximal response time of f is greater than v, then for some prefix $s \prec f$ the current response time is greater than v also, which means that, no matter what happens in the future, the maximal response time is greater than v after observing s. Therefore, $\Phi_{\max}$ is co-safe. By a similar reasoning, the sequence of greatest lower bounds of possible prediction values over the prefixes converges to the property value. In other words, we have $\lim_{s \prec f} \inf_{g \in \Sigma^\omega} \Phi_{\max}(sg) = \Phi_{\max}(f)$ for all $f \in \Sigma^\omega$. Thus $\Phi_{\max}$ is also lower semicontinuous, and it equals its co-safety closure. Now, consider the complementary property $\overline{\Phi_{\max}}$, which maps every trace to the same value as $\Phi_{\max}$ on a domain where the order is reversed. It is easy to see that $\overline{\Phi_{\max}}$ is safe. Finally, recall the ghost monitor from the introduction, which maintains the infimum of possible prediction values for the maximal response-time property. Since the maximal response-time property is inf-closed, the output of the ghost monitor after every prefix is realizable by some future continuation, and that output is $\pi_{\max}(s) = \max_{r \preceq s} \pi_{\mathrm{curr}}(r)$ for all $s \in \Sigma^*$. $\square$

Generalizing the observations in the example above, we obtain the following characterizations due to the duality between safety and co-safety.

Theorem 27. *For every property* $\Phi : \Sigma^\omega \to \mathbb{D}$, *the following are equivalent.*

1. *Φ is co-safe.*
2. *Φ is lower semicontinuous.*
3. *$\Phi(f) = \Phi_*(f)$ for every $f \in \Sigma^\omega$.*
4. *Φ is a* sup-*property.*
5. *Φ is a limit property such that for every $f \in \Sigma^\omega$ and value $v \in \mathbb{D}$, we have*
   $\underline{\Phi}(f) \leq v$ *iff* $\Phi(s) \leq v$ *for all* $s \prec f$.
6. *$\overline{\Phi}$ is safe.*

4.2   Limit Inferior and Limit Superior Properties

Let us start with an observation on the minimal response-time property.

Example 28. Recall once again the minimal response-time property $\Phi_{\min}$ from Example 3. In the previous subsection, we presented an alternative definition of $\Phi_{\min}$ to establish that it is an inf-property. Observe that there is yet another equivalent definition of $\Phi_{\min}$ which takes the monotonically decreasing finitary property $\pi_{\min}$ from Example 3 and pairs it with either the value function lim inf, or with lim sup. Hence $\Phi_{\min}$ is both a lim inf- and a lim sup-property.   □

Before moving on to investigating lim inf- and lim sup-properties more closely, we show that the above observation can be generalized.

Theorem 29. *Every ℓ-property Φ, for $\ell \in \{\inf, \sup\}$, is both a* lim inf- *and a* lim sup-*property.*

An interesting response-time property beyond safety and co-safety arises when we remove extreme values: instead of minimal response time, consider the property that maps every trace to a value that bounds from below, not all response times, but all of them from a point onward (i.e., all but finitely many). We call this property *tail-minimal response time*.

Example 30. Let $\Sigma = \{\mathtt{rq}, \mathtt{gr}, \mathtt{tk}, \mathtt{oo}\}$ and π_{last} be the finitary property from Example 3 that computes the last response time. We define the tail-minimal response-time property as $\Phi_{\text{tmin}} = (\pi_{\text{last}}, \lim\inf)$. Intuitively, it maps each trace to the least response time over all but finitely many requests. This property is interesting as a performance measure, because it focuses on the long-term performance by ignoring finitely many outliers. Consider $f \in \Sigma^\omega$ and $v \in \mathbb{D}$. Observe that, if the tail-minimal response time of f is at least v, then there is a prefix $s \prec f$ such that for all longer prefixes $s \preceq r \prec f$, the last response time in r is at least v, and vice versa.   □

Similarly as for inf-properties, we characterize lim inf-properties through a relation between property behaviors on finite and infinite traces.

Theorem 31. *A property $\Phi : \Sigma^\omega \to \mathbb{D}$ is a* lim inf-*property iff Φ is a limit property such that for every $f \in \Sigma^\omega$ and value $v \in \mathbb{D}$, we have $\Phi(f) \geq v$ iff there exists $s \prec f$ such that for all $s \preceq r \prec f$, we have $\Phi(r) \geq v$.*

Now, we show that the tail-minimal response-time property can be expressed as a countable supremum of inf-properties.

Example 32. Let $i \in \mathbb{N}$ and define $\pi_{i,\text{last}}$ as a finitary property that imitates π_{last} from Example 3, but ignores the first i observations of every finite trace. Formally, for $s \in \Sigma^*$, we define $\pi_{i,\text{last}}(s) = \pi_{\text{last}}(r)$ for $s = s_i r$ where $s_i \preceq s$ with $|s_i| = i$, and $r \in \Sigma^*$. Observe that an equivalent way to define Φ_{tmin} from Example 30 is $\sup_{i \in \mathbb{N}}(\inf_{s \prec f}(\pi_{i,\text{last}}(s)))$ for all $f \in \Sigma^\omega$. Intuitively, for each $i \in \mathbb{N}$, we obtain an inf-property that computes the minimal response time of the suffixes of a given trace. Taking the supremum over these, we obtain the greatest lower bound on all but finitely many response times.   □

We generalize this observation and show that every lim inf-property is a countable supremum of inf-properties.

Theorem 33. *Every* lim inf*-property is a countable supremum of* inf*-properties.*

We would also like to have the converse of Theorem 33, i.e., that every countable supremum of inf-properties is a lim inf-property. Currently, we are able to show only the following.

Theorem 34. *For every infinite sequence* $(\Phi_i)_{i \in \mathbb{N}}$ *of* inf*-properties, there is a* lim inf*-property* Φ *such that* $\sup_{i \in \mathbb{N}} \Phi_i(f) \leq \Phi(f)$.

We conjecture that some lim inf-property that satisfies Theorem 34 is also a lower bound on the countable supremum that occurs in the theorem. This, together with Theorem 34, would imply the converse of Theorem 33. Proving the converse of Theorem 33 would give us, thanks to the following duality, that the lim inf- and lim sup-properties characterize the second level of the Borel hierarchy of the topology induced by the safety closure operator.

Proposition 35. *A property* Φ *is a* lim inf*-property iff its complement* $\overline{\Phi}$ *is a* lim sup*-property.*

5   Quantitative Liveness

Similarly as for safety, we take the perspective of the quantitative membership problem to define liveness: a property Φ is live iff, whenever a property value is less than $\top$, there exists a value v for which the wrong hypothesis $\Phi(f) \geq v$ can never be dismissed by any finite witness $s \prec f$.

Definition 36 (Liveness). *A property* $\Phi : \Sigma^\omega \to \mathbb{D}$ *is live iff for all* $f \in \Sigma^\omega$, *if* $\Phi(f) < \top$, *then there exists a value* $v \in \mathbb{D}$ *such that* $\Phi(f) \not\geq v$ *and for all prefixes* $s \prec f$, *we have* $\sup_{g \in \Sigma^\omega} \Phi(sg) \geq v$.

An equivalent definition can be given through the safety closure.

Theorem 37. *A property* Φ *is live iff* $\Phi^*(f) > \Phi(f)$ *for every* $f \in \Sigma^\omega$ *with* $\Phi(f) < \top$.

Our definition generalizes boolean liveness. A boolean property $P \subseteq \Sigma^\omega$ is live according to the classical definition [4] iff its characteristic property Φ_P is live according to our definition. Moreover, the intersection of safety and liveness contains only the single degenerate property that always outputs $\top$.

Proposition 38. *A property Φ is safe and live iff $\Phi(f) = \top$ for all $f \in \Sigma^\omega$.*

We define co-liveness symmetrically, and note that the duals of the observations above also hold for co-liveness.

Definition 39 (Co-liveness). *A property $\Phi : \Sigma^\omega \to \mathbb{D}$ is co-live iff for all $f \in \Sigma^\omega$, if $\Phi(f) > \bot$, then there exists a value $v \in \mathbb{D}$ such that $\Phi(f) \not\leq v$ and for all prefixes $s \prec f$, we have $\inf_{g \in \Sigma^\omega} \Phi(sg) \leq v$.*

Next, we present some examples of liveness and co-liveness properties. We start by showing that lim inf- and lim sup-properties can be live and co-live.

Example 40. Let $\Sigma = \{a, b\}$ be an alphabet, and let $P = \Box \Diamond a$ and $Q = \Diamond \Box b$ be boolean properties defined in linear temporal logic. Consider their characteristic properties Φ_P and Φ_Q. As we pointed out earlier, our definitions generalize their boolean counterparts, therefore Φ_P and Φ_Q are both live and co-live. Moreover, Φ_P is a lim sup-property: define $\pi_P(s) = 1$ if $s \in \Sigma^* a$, and $\pi_P(s) = 0$ otherwise, and observe that $\Phi_P(f) = \limsup_{s \prec f} \pi_P(s)$ for all $f \in \Sigma^\omega$. Similarly, Φ_Q is a lim inf-property. $\qquad \Box$

Now, we show that the maximal response-time property is live, and the minimal response time is co-live.

Example 41. Recall the co-safety property $\Phi_{\max}$ of maximal response time from Example 26. Let $f \in \Sigma^\omega$ such that $\Phi_{\max}(f) < \infty$. We can extend every prefix $s \prec f$ with $g = \text{rq tk}^\omega$, which gives us $\Phi_{\max}(sg) = \infty > \Phi(f)$. Equivalently, for every $f \in \Sigma^\omega$, we have $\Phi^*_{\max}(f) = \infty > \Phi_{\max}(f)$. Hence $\Phi_{\max}$ is live and, analogously, the safety property $\Phi_{\min}$ from Example 3 is co-live. $\qquad \Box$

Finally, we show that the *average response-time* property is live and co-live.

Example 42. Let $\Sigma = \{\text{rq}, \text{gr}, \text{tk}, \text{oo}\}$. For all $s \in \Sigma^*$, let $p(s) = 1$ if there is no pending rq in s, and $p(s) = 0$ otherwise. Define $\pi_{\text{valid}}(s) = |\{r \preceq s \mid \exists t \in \Sigma^* : r = t \, \text{rq} \wedge p(t) = 1\}|$ as the number of valid requests in s, and define $\pi_{\text{time}}(s)$ as the number of tk observations that occur after a valid rq and before the matching gr. Then, $\Phi_{\text{avg}} = (\pi_{\text{avg}}, \lim\inf)$, where $\pi_{\text{avg}}(s) = \frac{\pi_{\text{time}}(s)}{\pi_{\text{valid}}(s)}$ for all $s \in \Sigma^*$ with $\pi_{\text{valid}}(s) > 0$, and $\pi_{\text{avg}}(s) = \infty$ otherwise. For example, $\pi_{\text{avg}}(s) = \frac{3}{2}$ for $s = \text{rq tk gr tk rq tk rq tk}$. Note that Φ_{avg} is a lim inf-property.

The property Φ_{avg} is defined on the value domain $[0, \infty]$ and is both live and co-live. To see this, let $f \in \Sigma^\omega$ such that $0 < \Phi_{\text{avg}}(f) < \infty$ and, for every prefix $s \prec f$, consider $g = \text{rq tk}^\omega$ and $h = \text{gr} \, (\text{rq gr})^\omega$. Since sg has a pending request followed by infinitely many clock ticks, we have $\Phi_{\text{avg}}(sg) = \infty$. Similarly, since sh eventually has all new requests immediately granted, we get $\Phi_{\text{avg}}(sh) = 0$. $\qquad \Box$

5.1   The Quantitative Safety-Liveness Decomposition

A celebrated theorem states that every boolean property can be expressed as an intersection of a safety property and a liveness property [4]. In this section, we prove the analogous result for the quantitative setting.

Example 43. Let $\Sigma = \{\mathtt{rq}, \mathtt{gr}, \mathtt{tk}, \mathtt{oo}\}$. Recall the maximal response-time property $\Phi_{\max}$ from Example 26, and the average response-time property Φ_{avg} from Example 42. Let $n > 0$ be an integer and define a new property Φ by $\Phi(f) = \Phi_{\mathrm{avg}}(f)$ if $\Phi_{\max}(f) \leq n$, and $\Phi(f) = 0$ otherwise. For the safety closure of Φ, we have $\Phi^*(f) = n$ if $\Phi_{\max}(f) \leq n$, and $\Phi^*(f) = 0$ otherwise. Now, we further define $\Psi(f) = \Phi_{\mathrm{avg}}(f)$ if $\Phi_{\max}(f) \leq n$, and $\Psi(f) = n$ otherwise. Observe that Ψ is live, because every prefix of a trace whose value is less than n can be extended to a greater value. Finally, note that for all $f \in \Sigma^\omega$, we can express $\Phi(f)$ as the pointwise minimum of $\Phi^*(f)$ and $\Psi(f)$. Intuitively, the safety part Φ^* of this decomposition checks whether the maximal response time stays below the permitted bound, and the liveness part Ψ keeps track of the average response time as long as the bound is satisfied.   □

Following a similar construction, we show that a safety-liveness decomposition exists for every property.

Theorem 44. *For every property Φ, there exists a liveness property Ψ such that $\Phi(f) = \min(\Phi^*(f), \Psi(f))$ for all $f \in \Sigma^\omega$.*

In particular, if the given property is safe or live, the decomposition is trivial.

Remark 45. Let Φ be a property. If Φ is safe (resp. live), then the safety (resp. liveness) part of the decomposition is Φ itself, and the liveness (resp. safety) part is the constant property that maps every trace to $\top$.

For co-safety and co-liveness, the duals of Theorem 44 and Remark 45 hold. In particular, every property is the pointwise maximum of its co-safety closure and a co-liveness property.

5.2   Related Definitions of Quantitative Liveness

In [41], the authors define a property Φ as *multi-live* iff $\Phi^*(f) > \bot$ for all $f \in \Sigma^\omega$. We show that our definition is more restrictive, resulting in fewer liveness properties while still allowing a safety-liveness decomposition.

Proposition 46. *Every live property is multi-live, and the inclusion is strict.*

We provide a separating example on a totally ordered domain below.

Example 47. Let $\Sigma = \{a, b, c\}$, and consider the following property: $\Phi(f) = 0$ if $f \models \Box a$, and $\Phi(f) = 1$ if $f \models \Diamond c$, and $\Phi(f) = 2$ otherwise (i.e., if $f \models \Diamond b \wedge \Box \neg c$). For all $f \in \Sigma^\omega$ and prefixes $s \prec f$, we have $\Phi(sc^\omega) = 1$. Thus $\Phi^*(f) \neq \bot$, which implies that Φ is multi-live. However, Φ is not live. Indeed, for every $f \in \Sigma^\omega$ such that $f \models \Diamond c$, we have $\Phi(f) = 1 < \top$. Moreover, f admits some prefix s that contains an occurrence of c, thus satisfying $\sup_{g \in \Sigma^\omega} \Phi(sg) = 1$.   □

In [27], the authors define a property Φ as *verdict-live* iff for every $f \in \Sigma^\omega$ and value $v \not\leq \Phi(f)$, every prefix $s \prec f$ satisfies $\Phi(sg) = v$ for some $g \in \Sigma^\omega$. We show that our definition is more liberal.

Proposition 48. *Every verdict-live property is live, and the inclusion is strict.*

We provide a separating example below, concluding that our definition is strictly more general even for totally ordered domains.

Example 49. Let $\Sigma = \{a, b\}$, and consider the following property: $\Phi(f) = 0$ if $f \not\models \Diamond b$, and $\Phi(f) = 1$ if $f \models \Diamond(b \wedge \bigcirc \Diamond b)$, and $\Phi(f) = 2^{-|s|}$ otherwise, where $s \prec f$ is the shortest prefix in which b occurs. Consider an arbitrary $f \in \Sigma^\omega$. If $\Phi(f) = 1$, then the liveness condition is vacuously satisfied. If $\Phi(f) = 0$, then $f = a^\omega$, and every prefix $s \prec f$ can be extended with $g = ba^\omega$ or $h = b^\omega$ to obtain $\Phi(sg) = 2^{-(|s|+1)}$ and $\Phi(sh) = 1$. If $0 < \Phi(f) < 1$, then f satisfies $\Diamond b$ but not $\Diamond(b \wedge \bigcirc \Diamond b)$, and every prefix $s \prec f$ can be extended with b^ω to obtain $\Phi(sb^\omega) = 1$. Hence Φ is live. However, Φ is not verdict-live. To see this, consider the trace $f = a^k b a^\omega$ for some integer $k \geq 1$ and note that $\Phi(f) = 2^{-(k+1)}$. Although all prefixes of f can be extended to reach the value 1, the value domain contains elements between $\Phi(f)$ and 1, namely the values 2^{-m} for $1 \leq m \leq k$. Each of these values can be rejected after reading a finite prefix of f, because for $n \geq m$ it is not possible to extend a^n to reach the value 2^{-m}.   □

6   Approximate Monitoring through Approximate Safety

In this section, we consider properties on extended reals $\mathbb{R}^{\pm\infty} = \mathbb{R} \cup \{-\infty, +\infty\}$. We denote by $\mathbb{R}_{\geq 0}$ the set of nonnegative real numbers.

Definition 50 (Approximate safety and co-safety). *Let $\alpha \in \mathbb{R}_{\geq 0}$. A property Φ is α-safe iff for every $f \in \Sigma^\omega$ and value $v \in \mathbb{R}^{\pm\infty}$ with $\Phi(f) < v$, there exists a prefix $s \prec f$ such that $\sup_{g \in \Sigma^\omega} \Phi(sg) < v + \alpha$. Similarly, Φ is α-co-safe iff for every $f \in \Sigma^\omega$ and $v \in \mathbb{R}^{\pm\infty}$ with $\Phi(f) > v$, there exists $s \prec f$ such that $\inf_{g \in \Sigma^\omega} \Phi(sg) > v - \alpha$. When Φ is α-safe (resp. α-co-safe) for some $\alpha \in \mathbb{R}_{\geq 0}$, we say that Φ is* approximately safe *(resp.* approximately co-safe).

Approximate safety can be characterized through the following relation with the safety closure.

Proposition 51. *For every error bound $\alpha \in \mathbb{R}_{\geq 0}$, a property Φ is α-safe iff $\Phi^*(f) - \Phi(f) \leq \alpha$ for all $f \in \Sigma^\omega$.*

An analogue of Proposition 51 holds for approximate co-safety and the co-safety closure. Moreover, approximate safety and approximate co-safety are dual notions that are connected by the complement operation, similarly to their precise counterparts (Theorem 27).

6.1   The Intersection of Approximate Safety and Co-safety

Recall the ghost monitor from the introduction. If, after a finite number of observations, all the possible prediction values are close enough, then we can simply freeze the current value and achieve a sufficiently small error. This happens for properties that are both approximately safe and approximately co-safe, generalizing the unfolding approximation of discounted properties [13].

Proposition 52. *For every limit property Φ and all error bounds $\alpha, \beta \in \mathbb{R}_{\geq 0}$, if Φ is α-safe and β-co-safe, then the set $S_\delta = \{s \in \Sigma^* \mid \sup_{r_1 \in \Sigma^*} \Phi(sr_1) - \inf_{r_2 \in \Sigma^*} \Phi(sr_2) \geq \delta\}$ is finite for all reals $\delta > \alpha + \beta$.*

Based on this proposition, we show that, for limit properties that are both approximately safe and approximately co-safe, the influence of the suffix on the property value is eventually negligible.

Theorem 53. *For every limit property Φ such that $\Phi(f) \in \mathbb{R}$ for all $f \in \Sigma^\omega$, and for all error bounds $\alpha, \beta \in \mathbb{R}_{\geq 0}$, if Φ is α-safe and β-co-safe, then for every real $\delta > \alpha + \beta$ and trace $f \in \Sigma^\omega$, there is a prefix $s \prec f$ such that for all continuations $w \in \Sigma^* \cup \Sigma^\omega$, we have $|\Phi(sw) - \Phi(s)| < \delta$.*

We illustrate this theorem with a *discounted safety* property.

Example 54. Let $P \subseteq \Sigma^\omega$ be a boolean safety property. We define the finitary property $\pi_P : \Sigma^* \to [0,1]$ as follows: $\pi_P(s) = 1$ if $sf \in P$ for some $f \in \Sigma^\omega$, and $\pi_P(s) = 1 - 2^{-|r|}$ otherwise, where $r \preceq s$ is the shortest prefix with $rf \notin P$ for all $f \in \Sigma^\omega$. The limit property $\Phi = (\pi_P, \inf)$ is called *discounted safety* [3]. Because Φ is an inf-property, it is safe by Theorem 20. Now consider the finitary property π'_P defined by $\pi'_P(s) = 1 - 2^{-|s|}$ if $sf \in P$ for some $f \in \Sigma^\omega$, and $\pi'_P(s) = 1 - 2^{-|r|}$ otherwise, where $r \preceq s$ is the shortest prefix with $rf \notin P$ for all $f \in \Sigma^\omega$. Let $\Phi' = (\pi'_P, \sup)$, and note that $\Phi(f) = \Phi'(f)$ for all $f \in \Sigma^\omega$. Hence Φ is also co-safe, because it is a sup-property.

Let $f \in \Sigma^\omega$ and $\delta > 0$. For every prefix $s \prec f$, the set of possible prediction values is either the range $[1 - 2^{-|s|}, 1]$ or the singleton $\{1 - 2^{-|r|}\}$, where $r \preceq s$ is chosen as above. In the latter case, we have $|\Phi(sw) - \Phi(s)| = 0 < \delta$ for all $w \in \Sigma^* \cup \Sigma^\omega$. In the former case, since the range becomes smaller as the prefix grows, there is a prefix $s' \prec f$ with $2^{-|s'|} < \delta$, which yields $|\Phi(s'w) - \Phi(s')| < \delta$ for all $w \in \Sigma^* \cup \Sigma^\omega$.   □

6.2   Finite-state Approximate Monitoring

Monitors with finite state spaces are particularly desirable, because finite automata enjoy a plethora of desirable closure and decidability properties. Here, we prove that properties that are both approximately safe and approximately co-safe can be monitored approximately by a finite-state monitor. First, we recall the notion of abstract quantitative monitor from [30].

A binary relation $\sim$ over Σ^* is an *equivalence relation* iff it is reflexive, symmetric, and transitive. Such a relation is *right-monotonic* iff $s_1 \sim s_2$ implies $s_1 r \sim s_2 r$ for all $s_1, s_2, r \in \Sigma^*$. For an equivalence relation $\sim$ over Σ^* and a finite trace $s \in \Sigma^*$, we write $[s]_\sim$ for the equivalence class of $\sim$ to which s belongs. When $\sim$ is clear from the context, we write $[s]$ instead. We denote by $\Sigma^*/\sim$ the quotient of the relation $\sim$.

Definition 55 (Abstract monitor [30]). *An abstract monitor $\mathcal{M} = (\sim, \gamma)$ is a pair consisting of a right-monotonic equivalence relation $\sim$ on Σ^* and a function $\gamma \colon (\Sigma^* / \sim) \to \mathbb{R}^{\pm\infty}$. The monitor $\mathcal{M}$ is finite-state iff the relation*

$\sim$ *has finitely many equivalence classes. Let* $\delta_{\mathrm{fin}}, \delta_{\mathrm{lim}} \in \mathbb{R}^{\pm\infty}$ *be error bounds. We say that* $\mathcal{M}$ *is a* $(\delta_{\mathrm{fin}}, \delta_{\mathrm{lim}})$*-monitor for a given limit property* $\Phi = (\pi, \ell)$ *iff for all* $s \in \Sigma^*$ *and* $f \in \Sigma^\omega$, *we have* $|\pi(s) - \gamma([s])| \leq \delta_{\mathrm{fin}}$ *and* $|\ell_{s \prec f}(\pi(s)) - \ell_{s \prec f}(\gamma([s]))| \leq \delta_{\mathrm{lim}}$.

Building on Theorem 53, we identify a sufficient condition to guarantee the existence of an abstract monitor with finitely many equivalence classes.

Theorem 56. *For every limit property* Φ *such that* $\Phi(f) \in \mathbb{R}$ *for all* $f \in \Sigma^\omega$, *and for all error bounds* $\alpha, \beta \in \mathbb{R}_{\geq 0}$, *if* Φ *is* α*-safe and* β*-co-safe, then for every real* $\delta > \alpha + \beta$, *there exists a finite-state* (δ, δ)*-monitor for* Φ.

Due to Theorem 56, the discounted safety property of Example 54 has a finite-state monitor for every positive error bound. We remark that Theorem 56 is proved by a construction that generalizes the unfolding approach for the approximate determinization of discounted automata [12], which unfolds an automaton until the distance constraint is satisfied.

7   Conclusion

We presented a generalization of safety and liveness that lifts the safety-progress hierarchy to the quantitative setting of [18] while preserving major desirable features of the boolean setting, such as the safety-liveness decomposition.

Monitorability identifies a boundary separating properties that can be verified or falsified from a finite number of observations, from those that cannot. Safety-liveness and co-safety-co-liveness decompositions allow us separate, for an individual property, monitorable parts from nonmonitorable parts. The larger the monitorable parts of the given property, the stronger the decomposition. We provided the strongest known safety-liveness decomposition, which consists of a pointwise minimum between a safe part defined by a quantitative safety closure, and a live part which corrects for the difference. We then defined approximate safety as the relaxation of safety by a parametric error bound. This further increases the monitorability of properties and offers monitorability at a parametric cost. In fact, we showed that every property that is both approximately safe and approximately co-safe can be monitored arbitrarily precisely by a finite-state monitor. A future direction is to extend our decomposition to approximate safety together with a support for quantitative assumptions [32].

The literature contains efficient model-checking procedures that leverage the boolean safety hypothesis [36,40]. We thus expect that also quantitative safety and co-safety, and their approximations, enable efficient verification algorithms for quantitative properties.

Acknowledgments. We thank the anonymous reviewers for their helpful comments. This work was supported in part by the ERC-2020-AdG 101020093.

References

1. de Alfaro, L., Faella, M., Henzinger, T.A., Majumdar, R., Stoelinga, M.: Model checking discounted temporal properties. Theor. Comput. Sci. **345**(1), 139–170 (2005). https://doi.org/10.1016/j.tcs.2005.07.033
2. de Alfaro, L., Faella, M., Stoelinga, M.: Linear and branching metrics for quantitative transition systems. In: Díaz, J., Karhumäki, J., Lepistö, A., Sannella, D. (eds.) Automata, Languages and Programming: 31st International Colloquium, ICALP 2004, Turku, Finland, July 12-16, 2004. Proceedings. Lecture Notes in Computer Science, vol. 3142, pp. 97–109. Springer (2004). https://doi.org/10.1007/978-3-540-27836-8_11
3. de Alfaro, L., Henzinger, T.A., Majumdar, R.: Discounting the future in systems theory. In: Baeten, J.C.M., Lenstra, J.K., Parrow, J., Woeginger, G.J. (eds.) Automata, Languages and Programming, 30th International Colloquium, ICALP 2003, Eindhoven, The Netherlands, June 30 - July 4, 2003. Proceedings. Lecture Notes in Computer Science, vol. 2719, pp. 1022–1037. Springer (2003). https://doi.org/10.1007/3-540-45061-0_79
4. Alpern, B., Schneider, F.B.: Defining liveness. Inf. Process. Lett. **21**(4), 181–185 (1985). https://doi.org/10.1016/0020-0190(85)90056-0
5. Alpern, B., Schneider, F.B.: Recognizing safety and liveness. Distributed Comput. **2**(3), 117–126 (1987). https://doi.org/10.1007/BF01782772
6. Bartocci, E., Falcone, Y., Francalanza, A., Reger, G.: Introduction to runtime verification. In: Bartocci, E., Falcone, Y. (eds.) Lectures on Runtime Verification - Introductory and Advanced Topics, Lecture Notes in Computer Science, vol. 10457, pp. 1–33. Springer (2018). https://doi.org/10.1007/978-3-319-75632-5_1
7. Bauer, A., Leucker, M., Schallhart, C.: Comparing LTL semantics for runtime verification. J. Log. Comput. **20**(3), 651–674 (2010). https://doi.org/10.1093/logcom/exn075
8. Bauer, A., Leucker, M., Schallhart, C.: Runtime verification for LTL and TLTL. ACM Trans. Softw. Eng. Methodol. **20**(4), 14:1–14:64 (2011). https://doi.org/10.1145/2000799.2000800
9. Bloem, R., Chatterjee, K., Henzinger, T.A., Jobstmann, B.: Better quality in synthesis through quantitative objectives. In: Bouajjani, A., Maler, O. (eds.) Computer Aided Verification, 21st International Conference, CAV 2009, Grenoble, France, June 26 - July 2, 2009. Proceedings. Lecture Notes in Computer Science, vol. 5643, pp. 140–156. Springer (2009). https://doi.org/10.1007/978-3-642-02658-4_14
10. Bloem, R., Chatterjee, K., Jobstmann, B.: Graph games and reactive synthesis. In: Clarke, E.M., Henzinger, T.A., Veith, H., Bloem, R. (eds.) Handbook of Model Checking, pp. 921–962. Springer (2018). https://doi.org/10.1007/978-3-319-10575-8_27
11. Boker, U., Chatterjee, K., Henzinger, T.A., Kupferman, O.: Temporal specifications with accumulative values. ACM Trans. Comput. Log. **15**(4), 27:1–27:25 (2014). https://doi.org/10.1145/2629686
12. Boker, U., Henzinger, T.A.: Approximate determinization of quantitative automata. In: D'Souza, D., Kavitha, T., Radhakrishnan, J. (eds.) IARCS Annual Conference on Foundations of Software Technology and Theoretical Computer Science, FSTTCS 2012, December 15-17, 2012, Hyderabad, India. LIPIcs, vol. 18, pp. 362–373. Schloss Dagstuhl - Leibniz-Zentrum für Informatik (2012). https://doi.org/10.4230/LIPIcs.FSTTCS.2012.362
13. Boker, U., Henzinger, T.A.: Exact and approximate determinization of discounted-sum automata. Log. Methods Comput. Sci. **10**(1) (2014). https://doi.org/10.2168/LMCS-10(1:10)2014

14. Bouyer, P., Fahrenberg, U., Larsen, K.G., Markey, N.: Quantitative analysis of real-time systems using priced timed automata. Commun. ACM **54**(9), 78–87 (2011). https://doi.org/10.1145/1995376.1995396

15. Bouyer, P., Markey, N., Randour, M., Larsen, K.G., Laursen, S.: Average-energy games. Acta Informatica **55**(2), 91–127 (2018). https://doi.org/10.1007/s00236-016-0274-1

16. Cerný, P., Henzinger, T.A., Radhakrishna, A.: Simulation distances. Theor. Comput. Sci. **413**(1), 21–35 (2012). https://doi.org/10.1016/j.tcs.2011.08.002

17. Chang, E., Manna, Z., Pnueli, A.: The safety-progress classification. In: Bauer, F.L., Brauer, W., Schwichtenberg, H. (eds.) Logic and Algebra of Specification. pp. 143–202. Springer Berlin Heidelberg, Berlin, Heidelberg (1993). https://doi.org/10.1007/978-3-642-58041-3_5

18. Chatterjee, K., Doyen, L., Henzinger, T.A.: Quantitative languages. ACM Trans. Comput. Log. **11**(4), 23:1–23:38 (2010). https://doi.org/10.1145/1805950.1805953

19. Chatterjee, K., Henzinger, T.A., Otop, J.: Nested weighted automata. ACM Trans. Comput. Log. **18**(4), 31:1–31:44 (2017). https://doi.org/10.1145/3152769

20. D'Antoni, L., Samanta, R., Singh, R.: Qlose: Program repair with quantitative objectives. In: Chaudhuri, S., Farzan, A. (eds.) Computer Aided Verification - 28th International Conference, CAV 2016, Toronto, ON, Canada, July 17-23, 2016, Proceedings, Part II. Lecture Notes in Computer Science, vol. 9780, pp. 383–401. Springer (2016). https://doi.org/10.1007/978-3-319-41540-6_21

21. Fahrenberg, U., Legay, A.: Generalized quantitative analysis of metric transition systems. In: Shan, C. (ed.) Programming Languages and Systems - 11th Asian Symposium, APLAS 2013, Melbourne, VIC, Australia, December 9-11, 2013. Proceedings. Lecture Notes in Computer Science, vol. 8301, pp. 192–208. Springer (2013). https://doi.org/10.1007/978-3-319-03542-0_14

22. Fahrenberg, U., Legay, A.: The quantitative linear-time-branching-time spectrum. Theor. Comput. Sci. **538**, 54–69 (2014). https://doi.org/10.1016/j.tcs.2013.07.030

23. Falcone, Y., Fernandez, J., Mounier, L.: What can you verify and enforce at runtime? Int. J. Softw. Tools Technol. Transf. **14**(3), 349–382 (2012). https://doi.org/10.1007/s10009-011-0196-8

24. Faran, R., Kupferman, O.: Spanning the spectrum from safety to liveness. Acta Informatica **55**(8), 703–732 (2018). https://doi.org/10.1007/s00236-017-0307-4

25. Ferrère, T., Henzinger, T.A., Kragl, B.: Monitoring event frequencies. In: Fernández, M., Muscholl, A. (eds.) 28th EACSL Annual Conference on Computer Science Logic, CSL 2020, January 13-16, 2020, Barcelona, Spain. LIPIcs, vol. 152, pp. 20:1–20:16. Schloss Dagstuhl - Leibniz-Zentrum für Informatik (2020). https://doi.org/10.4230/LIPIcs.CSL.2020.20

26. Ferrère, T., Henzinger, T.A., Saraç, N.E.: A theory of register monitors. In: Dawar, A., Grädel, E. (eds.) Proceedings of the 33rd Annual ACM/IEEE Symposium on Logic in Computer Science, LICS 2018, Oxford, UK, July 09-12, 2018. pp. 394–403. ACM (2018). https://doi.org/10.1145/3209108.3209194

27. Gorostiaga, F., Sánchez, C.: Monitorability of expressive verdicts. In: Deshmukh, J.V., Havelund, K., Perez, I. (eds.) NASA Formal Methods - 14th International Symposium, NFM 2022, Pasadena, CA, USA, May 24-27, 2022, Proceedings. Lecture Notes in Computer Science, vol. 13260, pp. 693–712. Springer (2022). https://doi.org/10.1007/978-3-031-06773-0_37

28. Havelund, K., Rosu, G.: Synthesizing monitors for safety properties. In: Katoen, J., Stevens, P. (eds.) Tools and Algorithms for the Construction and Analysis of Systems, 8th International Conference, TACAS 2002, Held as Part of

the Joint European Conference on Theory and Practice of Software, ETAPS 2002, Grenoble, France, April 8-12, 2002, Proceedings. Lecture Notes in Computer Science, vol. 2280, pp. 342–356. Springer (2002). https://doi.org/10.1007/3-540-46002-0_24

29. Henzinger, T.A.: Quantitative reactive modeling and verification. Comput. Sci. Res. Dev. **28**(4), 331–344 (2013). https://doi.org/10.1007/s00450-013-0251-7

30. Henzinger, T.A., Mazzocchi, N., Saraç, N.E.: Abstract monitors for quantitative specifications. In: Dang, T., Stolz, V. (eds.) Runtime Verification - 22nd International Conference, RV 2022, Tbilisi, Georgia, September 28-30, 2022, Proceedings. Lecture Notes in Computer Science, vol. 13498, pp. 200–220. Springer (2022). https://doi.org/10.1007/978-3-031-17196-3_11

31. Henzinger, T.A., Otop, J.: From model checking to model measuring. In: D'Argenio, P.R., Melgratti, H.C. (eds.) CONCUR 2013 - Concurrency Theory - 24th International Conference, CONCUR 2013, Buenos Aires, Argentina, August 27-30, 2013. Proceedings. Lecture Notes in Computer Science, vol. 8052, pp. 273–287. Springer (2013). https://doi.org/10.1007/978-3-642-40184-8_20

32. Henzinger, T.A., Saraç, N.E.: Monitorability under assumptions. In: Deshmukh, J., Nickovic, D. (eds.) Runtime Verification - 20th International Conference, RV 2020, Los Angeles, CA, USA, October 6-9, 2020, Proceedings. Lecture Notes in Computer Science, vol. 12399, pp. 3–18. Springer (2020). https://doi.org/10.1007/978-3-030-60508-7_1

33. Henzinger, T.A., Saraç, N.E.: Quantitative and approximate monitoring. In: 36th Annual ACM/IEEE Symposium on Logic in Computer Science, LICS 2021, Rome, Italy, June 29 - July 2, 2021. pp. 1–14. IEEE (2021). https://doi.org/10.1109/LICS52264.2021.9470547

34. Katoen, J., Song, L., Zhang, L.: Probably safe or live. In: Henzinger, T.A., Miller, D. (eds.) Joint Meeting of the Twenty-Third EACSL Annual Conference on Computer Science Logic (CSL) and the Twenty-Ninth Annual ACM/IEEE Symposium on Logic in Computer Science (LICS), CSL-LICS '14, Vienna, Austria, July 14 - 18, 2014. pp. 55:1–55:10. ACM (2014). https://doi.org/10.1145/2603088.2603147

35. Kim, M., Kannan, S., Lee, I., Sokolsky, O., Viswanathan, M.: Computational analysis of run-time monitoring - fundamentals of java-mac. In: Havelund, K., Rosu, G. (eds.) Runtime Verification 2002, RV 2002, FLoC Satellite Event, Copenhagen, Denmark, July 26, 2002. Electronic Notes in Theoretical Computer Science, vol. 70, pp. 80–94. Elsevier (2002). https://doi.org/10.1016/S1571-0661(04)80578-4

36. Kupferman, O., Vardi, M.Y.: Model checking of safety properties. Formal Methods Syst. Des. **19**(3), 291–314 (2001). https://doi.org/10.1023/A:1011254632723

37. Kwiatkowska, M., Norman, G., Parker, D.: Probabilistic Model Checking: Advances and Applications, pp. 73–121. Springer International Publishing, Cham (2018). https://doi.org/10.1007/978-3-319-57685-5_3

38. Kwiatkowska, M.Z.: Quantitative verification: models techniques and tools. In: Crnkovic, I., Bertolino, A. (eds.) Proceedings of the 6th joint meeting of the European Software Engineering Conference and the ACM SIGSOFT International Symposium on Foundations of Software Engineering, 2007, Dubrovnik, Croatia, September 3-7, 2007. pp. 449–458. ACM (2007). https://doi.org/10.1145/1287624.1287688

39. Lamport, L.: Proving the correctness of multiprocess programs. IEEE Trans. Software Eng. **3**(2), 125–143 (1977). https://doi.org/10.1109/TSE.1977.229904

40. Latvala, T.: Efficient model checking of safety properties. In: Ball, T., Rajamani, S.K. (eds.) Model Checking Software, 10th International SPIN Workshop. Portland, OR, USA, May 9-10, 2003, Proceedings. Lecture Notes in Computer Science,

vol. 2648, pp. 74–88. Springer (2003). https://doi.org/10.1007/3-540-44829-2_5

41. Li, Y., Droste, M., Lei, L.: Model checking of linear-time properties in multi-valued systems. Inf. Sci. **377**, 51–74 (2017). https://doi.org/10.1016/j.ins.2016.10.030

42. Manna, Z., Pnueli, A.: Adequate proof principles for invariance and liveness properties of concurrent programs. Sci. Comput. Program. **4**(3), 257–289 (1984). https://doi.org/10.1016/0167-6423(84)90003-0

43. Peled, D., Havelund, K.: Refining the safety-liveness classification of temporal properties according to monitorability. In: Margaria, T., Graf, S., Larsen, K.G. (eds.) Models, Mindsets, Meta: The What, the How, and the Why Not? - Essays Dedicated to Bernhard Steffen on the Occasion of His 60th Birthday. Lecture Notes in Computer Science, vol. 11200, pp. 218–234. Springer (2018). https://doi.org/10.1007/978-3-030-22348-9_14

44. Pnueli, A., Zaks, A.: PSL model checking and run-time verification via testers. In: Misra, J., Nipkow, T., Sekerinski, E. (eds.) FM 2006: Formal Methods, 14th International Symposium on Formal Methods, Hamilton, Canada, August 21-27, 2006, Proceedings. Lecture Notes in Computer Science, vol. 4085, pp. 573–586. Springer (2006). https://doi.org/10.1007/11813040_38

45. Qian, J., Shi, F., Cai, Y., Pan, H.: Approximate safety properties in metric transition systems. IEEE Trans. Reliab. **71**(1), 221–234 (2022). https://doi.org/10.1109/TR.2021.3139616

46. Sistla, A.P.: Safety, liveness and fairness in temporal logic. Formal Aspects Comput. **6**(5), 495–512 (1994). https://doi.org/10.1007/BF01211865

47. Thrane, C.R., Fahrenberg, U., Larsen, K.G.: Quantitative analysis of weighted transition systems. J. Log. Algebraic Methods Program. **79**(7), 689–703 (2010). https://doi.org/10.1016/j.jlap.2010.07.010

48. Weiner, S., Hasson, M., Kupferman, O., Pery, E., Shevach, Z.: Weighted safety. In: Hung, D.V., Ogawa, M. (eds.) Automated Technology for Verification and Analysis - 11th International Symposium, ATVA 2013, Hanoi, Vietnam, October 15-18, 2013. Proceedings. Lecture Notes in Computer Science, vol. 8172, pp. 133–147. Springer (2013). https://doi.org/10.1007/978-3-319-02444-8_11

On the Comparison of Discounted-Sum Automata with Multiple Discount Factors

Udi Boker*[iD] and Guy Hefetz[(✉)][iD]

Reichman University, Herzliya, Israel
`udiboker@runi.ac.il, ghefetz@gmail.com`

Abstract. We look into the problems of comparing nondeterministic discounted-sum automata on finite and infinite words. That is, the problems of checking for automata $\mathcal{A}$ and $\mathcal{B}$ whether or not it holds that for all words w, $\mathcal{A}(w) = \mathcal{B}(w)$, $\mathcal{A}(w) \leq \mathcal{B}(w)$, or $\mathcal{A}(w) < \mathcal{B}(w)$.

These problems are known to be decidable when both automata have the same single integral discount factor, while decidability is open in all other settings: when the single discount factor is a non-integral rational; when each automaton can have multiple discount factors; and even when each has a single integral discount factor, but the two are different.

We show that it is undecidable to compare discounted-sum automata with multiple discount factors, even if all are integrals, while it is decidable to compare them if each has a single, possibly different, integral discount factor. To this end, we also provide algorithms to check for given nondeterministic automaton $\mathcal{N}$ and deterministic automaton $\mathcal{D}$, each with a single, possibly different, rational discount factor, whether or not $\mathcal{N}(w) = \mathcal{D}(w)$, $\mathcal{N}(w) \geq \mathcal{D}(w)$, or $\mathcal{N}(w) > \mathcal{D}(w)$ for all words w.

Keywords: Discounted-sum Automata · Comparison · Containment

1 Introduction

Equivalence and containment checks of Boolean automata, namely the checks of whether $L(\mathcal{A}) = L(\mathcal{B})$, $L(\mathcal{A}) \subseteq L(\mathcal{B})$, or $L(\mathcal{A}) \subset L(\mathcal{B})$, where $L(\mathcal{A})$ and $L(\mathcal{B})$ are the languages that $\mathcal{A}$ and $\mathcal{B}$ recognize, are central in the usage of automata theory in diverse areas, and in particular in formal verification (e.g, [34,26,17,33,35,28]). Likewise, comparison of quantitative automata, which extends the equivalence and containment checks by asking whether $\mathcal{A}(w) = \mathcal{B}(w)$, whether $\mathcal{A}(w) \leq \mathcal{B}(w)$, or whether $\mathcal{A}(w) < \mathcal{B}(w)$ for all words w, are essential for harnessing quantitative-automata theory to the service of diverse fields and in particular to the service of quantitative formal verification (e.g, [15,14,21,11,27,3,5,22]).

Discounted summation is a common valuation function in quantitative automata theory (e.g, [19,12,14,15]), as well as in various other computational models, such as games (e.g, [37,4,1]), Markov decision processes (e.g, [23,29,16]), and reinforcement learning (e.g, [32,36]), as it formalizes the concept that an immediate reward is better than a potential one in the far future, as well as that a

---

* Research supported by the Israel Science Foundation grant 2410/22.

O. Kupferman and P. Sobocinski (Eds.): FoSSaCS 2023, LNCS 13992, pp. 371–391, 2023.
https://doi.org/10.1007/978-3-031-30829-1_18

potential problem (such as a bug in a reactive system) in the far future is less troubling than a current one.

A nondeterministic discounted-sum automaton (NDA) has rational weights on the transitions, and a fixed rational discount factor $\lambda > 1$. The value of a (finite or infinite) run is the discounted summation of the weights on the transitions, such that the weight in the ith transition of the run is divided by λ^i. The value of a (finite or infinite) word is the infimum value of the automaton runs on it. An NDA thus realizes a function from words to real numbers.

NDAs cannot always be determinized [15], they are not closed under basic algebraic operations [8], and their comparison is not known to be decidable, relating to various longstanding open problems [9]. However, restricting NDAs to have an integral discount factor $\lambda \in \mathbb{N} \setminus \{0,1\}$ provides a robust class of automata that is closed under determinization and under algebraic operations, and for which comparison is decidable [8].

Various variants of NDAs are studied in the literature, among which are *functional, k-valued, probabilistic*, and more [21,20,13]. Yet, until recently, all of these models were restricted to have a single discount factor. This is a significant restriction of the general discounted-summation paradigm, in which multiple discount factors are considered. For example, Markov decision processes and discounted-sum games allow multiple discount factors within the same entity [23,4]. In [6], NDAs were extended to NMDAs, allowing for multiple discount factors, where each transition can have a different one. Special attention was given to integral NMDAs, namely to those with only integral discount factors, analyzing whether they preserve the good properties of integral NDAs. It was shown that they are generally not closed under determinization and under algebraic operations, while a restricted class of them, named tidy-NMDAs, in which the choice of discount factors depends on the prefix of the word read so far, does preserve the good properties of integral NDAs.

While comparison of tidy-NMDAs with the same choice function is decidable in PSPACE [6], it was left open whether comparison of general integral NMDAs $\mathcal{A}$ and $\mathcal{B}$ is decidable. It is even open whether comparison of two integral NDAs with different (single) discount factors is decidable.

We show that it is undecidable to resolve for given NMDA $\mathcal{N}$ and deterministic NMDA (DMDA) $\mathcal{D}$, even if both have only integral discount factors, on both finite and infinite words, whether $\mathcal{N} \equiv \mathcal{D}$ and whether $\mathcal{N} \leq \mathcal{D}$, and on finite words also whether $\mathcal{N} < \mathcal{D}$. We prove the undecidability result by reduction from the halting problem of two-counter machines. The general scheme follows similar reductions, such as in [18,2], yet the crux is in simulating a counter by integral NMDAs. Upfront, discounted summation is not suitable for simulating counters, since a current increment has, in the discounted setting, a much higher influence than of a far-away decrement. However, we show that multiple discount factors allow in a sense to eliminate the influence of time, having automata in which no matter where a letter appears in the word, it will have the same influence on the automaton value. (See Lemma 1 and Fig. 3). Another main part of the proof is in showing how to nondeterministically adjust the automaton weights and discount factors in order to "detect" whether a counter is at a current value 0. (See Figs. 5, 6, 8 and 9.)

On the positive side, we provide algorithms to decide for given NDA $\mathcal{N}$ and deterministic NDA (DDA) $\mathcal{D}$, with arbitrary, possibly different, rational discount factors, whether $\mathcal{N} \equiv \mathcal{D}$, $\mathcal{N} \geq \mathcal{D}$, or $\mathcal{N} > \mathcal{D}$ (Theorem 4). Our algorithms work on both finite and infinite words, and run in PSPACE when the automata weights are represented in binary and their discount factors in unary. Since integral NDAs can always be determinized [8], our method also provides an algorithm to compare two integral NDAs, though not necessarily in PSPACE, since determinization might exponentially increase the number of states. (Even though determinization of NDAs is in PSPACE [8,6], the exponential number of states might require an exponential space in our algorithms of comparing NDAs with different discount factors.)

The challenge with comparing automata with different discount factors comes from the combination of their different accumulations, which tends to be intractable, resulting in the undecidability of comparing integral NMDAs, and in the open problems of comparing rational NDAs and of analyzing the representation of numbers in a non-integral basis [30,24,25,9]. Yet, the main observation underlying our algorithm is that when each automaton has a single discount factor, we may unfold the combination of their computation trees only up to some level k, after which we can analyze their continuation separately, first handling the automaton with the lower (slower decreasing) discount factor and then the other one. The idea is that after level k, since the accumulated discounting of the second automaton is already much more significant, even a single non-optimal transition of the first automaton cannot be compensated by a continuation that is better with respect to the second automaton. We thus compute the optimal suffix words and runs of the first automaton from level k, on top which we compute the optimal runs of the second automaton.

2   Preliminaries

Words. An *alphabet* Σ is an arbitrary finite set, and a *word* over Σ is a finite or infinite sequence of letters in Σ, with ε for the empty word. We denote the concatenation of a finite word u and a finite or infinite word w by $u \cdot w$, or simply by uw. We define Σ^+ to be the set of all finite words except the empty word, i.e., $\Sigma^+ = \Sigma^* \backslash \{\varepsilon\}$. For a word $w = \sigma_0\sigma_1\sigma_2 \cdots$ and indexes $i \leq j$, we denote the *letter at index i* as $w[i] = \sigma_i$, and the *sub-word from i to j* as $w[i..j] = \sigma_i\sigma_{i+1} \cdots \sigma_j$.

For a finite word w and letter $\sigma \in \Sigma$, we denote the number of occurrences of σ in w by $\#(\sigma, w)$, and for a set $S \subseteq \Sigma$, we denote $\sum_{\sigma \in S} \#(\sigma, w)$ by $\#(S, w)$.

For a finite or infinite word w and a letter $\sigma \in \Sigma$, we define the *prefix of w up to σ*, $\text{PREF}_\sigma(w)$, as the minimal prefix of w that contains a σ letter if there is a σ letter in w or w itself if it does not contain any σ letters. Formally,

$$\text{PREF}_\sigma(w) = \begin{cases} w[0..\min\{i \mid w[i] = \sigma\}] & \exists i \mid w[i] = \sigma \\ w & \text{otherwise} \end{cases}$$

Automata. A nondeterministic discounted-sum automaton (NDA) [15] is an automaton with rational weights on the transitions, and a fixed rational discount factor $\lambda > 1$. A nondeterministic discounted-sum automaton with multiple discount factors (NMDA) [6] is similar to an NDA, but with possibly a different discount factor on each of its transitions. They are formally defined as follows:

Definition 1 ([6]). *A nondeterministic discounted-sum automaton with multiple discount factors (NMDA), on finite or infinite words, is a tuple $\mathcal{A} = \langle \Sigma, Q, \iota, \delta, \gamma, \rho \rangle$ over an alphabet Σ, with a finite set of states Q, an initial set of states $\iota \subseteq Q$, a transition function $\delta \subseteq Q \times \Sigma \times Q$, a weight function $\gamma : \delta \to \mathbb{Q}$, and a discount-factor function $\rho : \delta \to \mathbb{Q} \cap (1, \infty)$, assigning to each transition its discount factor, which is a rational greater than one.* [1]

- *A run of $\mathcal{A}$ is a sequence of states and alphabet letters, $p_0, \sigma_0, p_1, \sigma_1, p_2, \cdots$, such that $p_0 \in \iota$ is an initial state, and for every i, $(p_i, \sigma_i, p_{i+1}) \in \delta$.*
- *The length of a run r, denoted by $|r|$, is n for a finite run $r = p_0, \sigma_0, p_1, \cdots, \sigma_{n-1}, p_n$, and ∞ for an infinite run.*
- *For an index $i < |r|$, we define the i-th transition of r as $r[i] = (p_i, \sigma_i, p_{i+1})$, and the prefix run with i transitions as $r[0..i] = p_0, \sigma_0, p_1, \cdots, \sigma_i, p_{i+1}$.*
- *The value of a finite/infinite run r is $\mathcal{A}(r) = \sum_{i=0}^{|r|-1} \left(\gamma(r[i]) \cdot \prod_{j=0}^{i-1} \frac{1}{\rho(r[j])} \right)$. For example, the value of the run $r_1 = q_0, a, q_0, a, q_1, b, q_2$ of $\mathcal{A}$ from Fig. 1 is $\mathcal{A}(r_1) = 1 + \frac{1}{2} \cdot \frac{1}{3} + 2 \cdot \frac{1}{2 \cdot 3} = \frac{3}{2}$.*
- *The value of $\mathcal{A}$ on a finite or infinite word w is $\mathcal{A}(w) = \inf\{\mathcal{A}(r) \mid r \text{ is a run of } \mathcal{A} \text{ on } w\}$.*
- *For every finite run $r = p_0, \sigma_0, p_1, \cdots, \sigma_{n-1}, p_n$, we define the target state as $\delta(r) = p_n$ and the accumulated discount factor as $\rho(r) = \prod_{i=0}^{n-1} \rho(r[i])$.*
- *When all discount factors are integers, we say that $\mathcal{A}$ is an integral NMDA.*
- *In the case where $|\iota| = 1$ and for every $q \in Q$ and $\sigma \in \Sigma$, we have $|\{q' \mid (q, \sigma, q') \in \delta\}| \leq 1$, we say that $\mathcal{A}$ is deterministic, denoted by DMDA, and view δ as a function from words to states.*
- *When the discount factor function ρ is constant, $\rho \equiv \lambda \in \mathbb{Q} \cap (1, \infty)$, we say that $\mathcal{A}$ is a nondeterministic discounted-sum automaton (NDA) [15] with discount factor λ (a λ-NDA). If $\mathcal{A}$ is deterministic, it is a λ-DDA.*
- *For a state $q \in Q$, we write $\mathcal{A}^q$ for the NMDA $\mathcal{A}^q = \langle \Sigma, Q, \{q\}, \delta, \gamma, \rho \rangle$.*

Counter machines. A two-counter machine [31] $\mathcal{M}$ is a sequence $(l_1, \ldots, l_n)$ of commands, for some $n \in \mathbb{N}$, involving two counters x and y. We refer to $\{1, \ldots, n\}$ as the *locations* of the machine. For every $i \in \{1, \ldots, n\}$ we refer to l_i as the *command in location* i. There are five possible forms of commands:

$$\text{INC}(c), \quad \text{DEC}(c), \quad \text{GOTO } l_k, \quad \text{IF } c=0 \text{ GOTO } l_k \text{ ELSE GOTO } l_{k'}, \quad \text{HALT},$$

where $c \in \{x, y\}$ is a counter and $1 \leq k, k' \leq n$ are locations. For not decreasing a zero-valued counter $c \in \{x, y\}$, every $\text{DEC}(c)$ command is preceded by the

---

[1] Discount factors are sometimes defined as numbers between 0 and 1, under which setting weights are multiplied by these factors rather than divided by them.

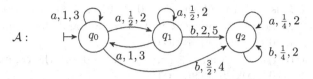

Fig. 1. An NMDA $\mathcal{A}$. The labeling on the transitions indicate the alphabet letter, the weight of the transition, and its discount factor.

command IF $c{=}0$ GOTO <CURRENT_LINE> ELSE GOTO <NEXT_LINE>, and there are no other direct goto-commands to it. The counters are initially set to 0. An example of a two-counter machine is given in Fig. 2.

$l_1.$ INC(x)
$l_2.$ INC(x)
$l_3.$ IF $x{=}0$ GOTO l_3 ELSE GOTO l_4
$l_4.$ DEC(x)
$l_5.$ IF $x{=}0$ GOTO l_6 ELSE GOTO l_3
$l_6.$ HALT

Fig. 2. An example of a two-counter machine.

Let L be the set of possible commands in $\mathcal{M}$, then a *run* of $\mathcal{M}$ is a sequence $\psi = \psi_1, \ldots, \psi_m \in (L \times \mathbb{N} \times \mathbb{N})^*$ such that the following hold:

1. $\psi_1 = \langle l_1, 0, 0 \rangle$.
2. For all $1 < i \leq m$, let $\psi_{i-1} = (l_j, \alpha_x, \alpha_y)$ and $\psi_i = (l', \alpha'_x, \alpha'_y)$. Then, the following hold.
   - If l_j is an INC(x) command (resp. INC(y)), then $\alpha'_x = \alpha_x + 1$, $\alpha'_y = \alpha_y$ (resp. $\alpha_y = \alpha_y + 1$, $\alpha'_x = \alpha_x$), and $l' = l_{j+1}$.
   - If l_j is DEC(x) (resp. DEC(y)) then $\alpha'_x = \alpha_x - 1$, $\alpha'_y = \alpha_y$ (resp. $\alpha_y = \alpha_y - 1$, $\alpha'_x = \alpha_x$), and $l' = l_{j+1}$.
   - If l_j is GOTO l_k then $\alpha'_x = \alpha_x$, $\alpha'_y = \alpha_y$, and $l' = l_k$.
   - If l_j is IF $x{=}0$ GOTO l_k ELSE GOTO $l_{k'}$ then $\alpha'_x = \alpha_x$, $\alpha'_y = \alpha_y$, and $l' = l_k$ if $\alpha_x = 0$, and $l' = l_{k'}$ otherwise.
   - If l_j is IF $y{=}0$ GOTO l_k ELSE GOTO $l_{k'}$ then $\alpha'_x = \alpha_x$, $\alpha'_y = \alpha_y$, and $l' = l_k$ if $\alpha_y = 0$, and $l' = l_{k'}$ otherwise.
   - If l' is HALT then $i = m$, namely a run does not continue after HALT.

If, in addition, we have that $\psi_m = \langle l_j, \alpha_x, \alpha_y \rangle$ such that l_j is a HALT command, we say that ψ is a *halting run*. We say that a machine $\mathcal{M}$ 0-halts if its run is halting and ends in $\langle l, 0, 0 \rangle$. We say that a sequence of commands $\tau \in L^*$ *fits* a run ψ, if τ is the projection of ψ on its first component.

The *command trace* $\pi = \sigma_1, \ldots, \sigma_m$ of a halting run $\psi = \psi_1, \ldots, \psi_m$ describes the flow of the run, including a description of whether a counter c was equal to 0 or larger than 0 in each occurrence of an IF $c{=}0$ GOTO l_k ELSE GOTO $l_{k'}$ command. It is formally defined as follows. $\sigma_m =$ HALT and for every $1 < i \leq m$, we define σ_{i-1} according to $\psi_{i-1} = (l_j, \alpha_x, \alpha_y)$ in the following manner:

- $\sigma_{i-1} = l_j$ if l_j is not of the form IF c=0 GOTO l_k ELSE GOTO $l_{k'}$.
- $\sigma_{i-1} = (\text{GOTO } l_k, c = 0)$ for $c \in \{x, y\}$, if $\alpha_c = 0$ and the command l_j is of the form IF c=0 GOTO l_k ELSE GOTO $l_{k'}$.
- $\sigma_{i-1} = (\text{GOTO } l_{k'}, c > 0)$ for $c \in \{x, y\}$, if $\alpha_c > 0$ and the command l_j is of the form IF c=0 GOTO l_k ELSE GOTO $l_{k'}$.

For example, the command trace of the halting run of the machine in Fig. 2 is INC(x), INC(x), (GOTO $l_4, x > 0$), DEC(x), (GOTO $l_3, x > 0$), (GOTO $l_4, x > 0$), DEC(x), (GOTO $l_6, x = 0$), HALT.

Deciding whether a given counter machine $\mathcal{M}$ halts is known to be undecidable [31]. Deciding whether $\mathcal{M}$ halts with both counters having value 0, termed the 0-*halting problem*, is also undecidable. Indeed, the halting problem can be reduced to the latter by adding some commands that clear the counters, before every HALT command.

3   Comparison of NMDAs

We show that comparison of (integral) NMDAs is undecidable by reduction from the halting problem of two-counter machines. Notice that our NMDAs only use integral discount factors, while they do have non-integral weights. Yet, weights can be easily changed to integers as well, by multiplying them all by a common denominator and making the corresponding adjustments in the calculations.

We start with a lemma on the accumulated value of certain series of discount factors and weights. Observe that by the lemma, no matter where the pair of discount-factor $\lambda \in \mathbb{N} \setminus \{0, 1\}$ and weight $w = \frac{\lambda - 1}{\lambda}$ appear along the run, they will have the same effect on the accumulated value. This property will play a key role in simulating counting by NMDAs.

Lemma 1. *For every sequence $\lambda_1, \cdots, \lambda_m$ of integers larger than 1 and weights $w_1, \cdots, w_m$ such that $w_i = \frac{\lambda_i - 1}{\lambda_i}$, we have $\sum_{i=1}^{m} \left(w_i \cdot \prod_{j=1}^{i-1} \frac{1}{\lambda_j} \right) = 1 - \frac{1}{\prod_{j=1}^{m} \lambda_j}$.*

The proof is by induction on m and appears in [7].

3.1   The Reduction

We turn to our reduction from the halting problem of two-counter machines to the problem of NMDA containment. We provide the construction and the correctness lemma with respect to automata on finite words, and then show in Section 3.2 how to use the same construction also for automata on infinite words.

Given a two-counter machine $\mathcal{M}$ with the commands $(l_1, \ldots, l_n)$, we construct an integral DMDA $\mathcal{A}$ and an integral NMDA $\mathcal{B}$ on finite words, such that $\mathcal{M}$ 0-halts iff there exists a word $w \in \Sigma^+$ such that $\mathcal{B}(w) \geq \mathcal{A}(w)$ iff there exists a word $w \in \Sigma^+$ such that $\mathcal{B}(w) > \mathcal{A}(w)$.

The automata $\mathcal{A}$ and $\mathcal{B}$ operate over the following alphabet Σ, which consists of $5n + 5$ letters, standing for the possible elements in a command trace of $\mathcal{M}$:

$$\Sigma^{\text{INCDEC}} = \{\,\text{INC}(x), \text{DEC}(x), \text{INC}(y), \text{DEC}(y)\,\}$$

$$\Sigma^{\text{GOTO}} = \{\text{GOTO}\ \ l_k : k \in \{1,\ldots,n\}\}\cup$$

$$\{(\text{GOTO}\ \ l_k, c = 0) : k \in \{1,\ldots,n\}, c \in \{x,y\}\}\cup$$

$$\{(\text{GOTO}\ \ l_{k'}, c > 0) : k' \in \{1,\ldots,n\}, c \in \{x,y\}\}$$

$$\Sigma^{\text{NOHALT}} = \Sigma^{\text{INCDEC}} \cup \Sigma^{\text{GOTO}}$$

$$\Sigma = \Sigma^{\text{NOHALT}} \cup \{\text{HALT}\}$$

When $\mathcal{A}$ and $\mathcal{B}$ read a word $w \in \Sigma^+$, they intuitively simulate a sequence of commands τ_u that induces the command trace $u = \text{PREF}_{\text{HALT}}(w)$. If τ_u fits the actual run of $\mathcal{M}$, and this run 0-halts, then the minimal run of $\mathcal{B}$ on w has a value strictly larger than $\mathcal{A}(w)$. If, however, τ_u does not fit the actual run of $\mathcal{M}$, or it does fit the actual run but it does not 0-halt, then the violation is detected by $\mathcal{B}$, which has a run on w with value strictly smaller than $\mathcal{A}(w)$.

In the construction, we use the following partial discount-factor functions $\rho_p, \rho_d : \Sigma^{\text{NOHALT}} \to \mathbb{N}$ and partial weight functions $\gamma_p, \gamma_d : \Sigma^{\text{NOHALT}} \to \mathbb{Q}$.

$$\rho_p(\sigma) = \begin{cases} 5 & \sigma = \text{INC}(x) \\ 4 & \sigma = \text{DEC}(x) \\ 7 & \sigma = \text{INC}(y) \\ 6 & \sigma = \text{DEC}(y) \\ 15 & \text{otherwise} \end{cases} \qquad \rho_d(\sigma) = \begin{cases} 4 & \sigma = \text{INC}(x) \\ 5 & \sigma = \text{DEC}(x) \\ 6 & \sigma = \text{INC}(y) \\ 7 & \sigma = \text{DEC}(y) \\ 15 & \text{otherwise} \end{cases}$$

$\gamma_p(\sigma) = \frac{\rho_p(\sigma)-1}{\rho_p(\sigma)}$, and $\gamma_d(\sigma) = \frac{\rho_d(\sigma)-1}{\rho_d(\sigma)}$. We say that ρ_p and γ_p are the *primal* discount-factor and weight functions, while ρ_d and γ_d are the *dual* functions. Observe that for every $c \in \{x,y\}$ we have that

$$\rho_p(\text{INC}(c)) = \rho_d(\text{DEC}(c)) > \rho_p(\text{DEC}(c)) = \rho_d(\text{INC}(c)) \qquad (1)$$

Intuitively, we will use the primal functions for $\mathcal{A}$'s discount factors and weights, and the dual functions for identifying violations. Notice that if changing the primal functions to the dual ones in more occurrences of $\text{INC}(c)$ letters than of $\text{DEC}(c)$ letters along some run, then by Lemma 1 the run will get a value lower than the original one.

We continue with their formal definitions. $\mathcal{A} = \langle \Sigma, \{q_{\mathcal{A}}, q_{\mathcal{A}}^h\}, \{q_{\mathcal{A}}\}, \delta_{\mathcal{A}}, \gamma_{\mathcal{A}}, \rho_{\mathcal{A}} \rangle$ is an integral DMDA consisting of two states, as depicted in Fig. 3. Observe that the initial state $q_{\mathcal{A}}$ has self loops for every alphabet letter in Σ^{NOHALT} with weights and discount factors according to the primal functions, and a transition $(q_{\mathcal{A}}, \text{HALT}, q_{\mathcal{A}}^h)$ with weight of $\frac{14}{15}$ and a discount factor of 15.

The integral NMDA $\mathcal{B} = \langle \Sigma, Q_{\mathcal{B}}, \iota_{\mathcal{B}}, \delta_{\mathcal{B}}, \gamma_{\mathcal{B}}, \rho_{\mathcal{B}} \rangle$ is the union of the following eight gadgets (checkers), each responsible for checking a certain type of violation in the description of a 0-halting run of $\mathcal{M}$. It also has the states $q_{\text{freeze}}, q_{\text{halt}} \in Q_{\mathcal{B}}$

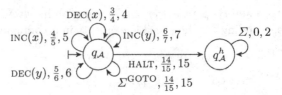

Fig. 3. The DMDA $\mathcal{A}$ constructed for the proof of Lemma 2.

such that for all $\sigma \in \Sigma$, there are 0-weighted transitions $(q_{\text{freeze}}, \sigma, q_{\text{freeze}}) \in \delta_{\mathcal{B}}$ and $(q_{\text{halt}}, \sigma, q_{\text{halt}}) \in \delta_{\mathcal{B}}$ with an arbitrary discount factor. Observer that in all of $\mathcal{B}$'s gadgets, the transition over the letter HALT to q_{halt} has a weight higher than the weight of the corresponding transition in $\mathcal{A}$, so that when no violation is detected, the value of $\mathcal{B}$ on a word is higher than the value of $\mathcal{A}$ on it.

1. Halt Checker. This gadget, depicted in Fig. 4, checks for violations of non-halting runs. Observe that its initial state q_{HC} has self loops identical to those of $\mathcal{A}$'s initial state, a transition to q_{halt} over HALT with a weight higher than the corresponding weight in $\mathcal{A}$, and a transition to the state q_{last} over every letter that is not HALT, "guessing" that the run ends without a HALT command.

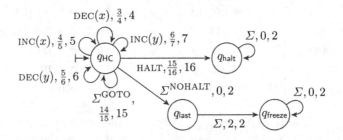

Fig. 4. The Halt Checker in the NMDA $\mathcal{B}$.

2. Negative-Counters Checker. The second gadget, depicted in Fig. 5, checks that the input prefix u has no more DEC(c) than INC(c) commands for each counter $c \in \{x, y\}$. It is similar to $\mathcal{A}$, however having self loops in its initial states that favor DEC(c) commands when compared to $\mathcal{A}$.

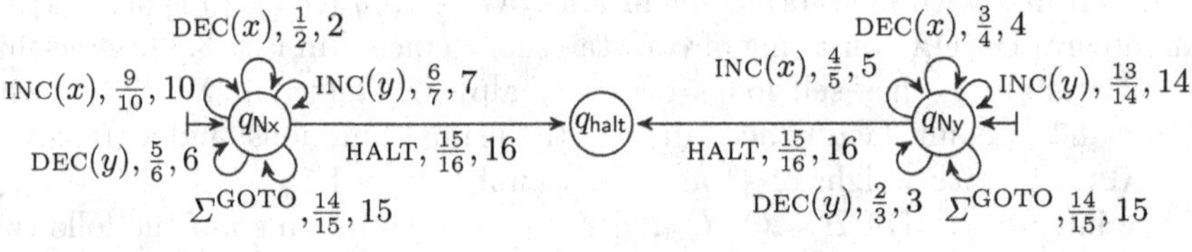

Fig. 5. The negative-counters checker, on the left for x and on the right for y, in the NMDA $\mathcal{B}$.

3. Positive-Counters Checker. The third gadget, depicted in Fig. 6, checks that for every $c \in \{x, y\}$, the input prefix u has no more INC(c) than DEC(c) commands. It is similar to $\mathcal{A}$, while having self loops in its initial state according to the dual functions rather than the primal ones.

$$\text{DEC}(x), \tfrac{4}{5}, 5$$

$$\text{INC}(x), \tfrac{3}{4}, 4 \qquad \text{INC}(y), \tfrac{5}{6}, 6$$

$$\text{DEC}(y), \tfrac{6}{7}, 7 \qquad q_{BC} \qquad q_{halt}$$

$$\text{HALT}, \tfrac{15}{16}, 16$$

$$\Sigma^{\text{GOTO}}, \tfrac{14}{15}, 15$$

Fig. 6. The Positive-Counters Checker in the NMDA $\mathcal{B}$.

4. Command Checker. The next gadget checks for local violations of successive commands. That is, it makes sure that the letter w_i represents a command that can follow the command represented by w_{i-1} in $\mathcal{M}$, ignoring the counter values. For example, if the command in location l_2 is INC(x), then from state q_2, which is associated with l_2, we move with the letter INC(x) to q_3, which is associated with l_3. The test is local, as this gadget does not check for violations involving illegal jumps due to the values of the counters. An example of the command checker for the counter machine in Fig. 2 is given in Fig. 7.

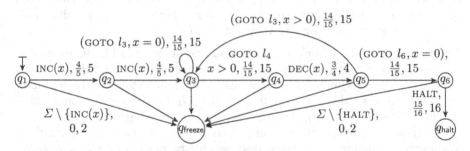

Fig. 7. The command checker that corresponds to the counter machine in Fig. 2.

The command checker, which is a DMDA, consists of states $q_1, \ldots, q_n$ that correspond to the commands $l_1, \ldots, l_n$, and the states q_{halt} and q_{freeze}. For two locations j and k, there is a transition from q_j to q_k on the letter σ iff l_k can *locally follow* l_j in a run of $\mathcal{M}$ that has σ in the corresponding location of the command trace. That is, either l_j is a GOTO l_k command (meaning $l_j = \sigma = $ GOTO l_k), k is the next location after j and l_j is an INC or a DEC command (meaning $k = j+1$ and $l_j = \sigma \in \Sigma^{\text{INCDEC}}$), l_j is an IF c=0 GOTO l_k ELSE GOTO $l_{k'}$ command with $\sigma = $ (GOTO $l_k, c = 0$), or l_j is an IF c=0 GOTO l_s ELSE GOTO l_k command with $\sigma = $ (GOTO $l_k, c > 0$). The weights and discount factors of the Σ^{NOHALT} transitions mentioned above are according to the primal functions γ_p and ρ_p respectively. For every location j such that $l_j = $ HALT, there is a transition from q_j to q_{halt} labeled by the letter HALT with a weight of $\tfrac{15}{16}$ and a discount factor of 16. Every other transition that was not specified above leads to q_{freeze} with weight 0 and some discount factor.

5,6. Zero-Jump Checkers. The next gadgets, depicted in Fig. 8, check for violations in conditional jumps. In this case, we use a different checker instance for each counter $c \in \{x, y\}$, ensuring that for every IF $c{=}0$ GOTO l_k ELSE GOTO $l_{k'}$ command, if the jump GOTO l_k is taken, then the value of c is indeed 0.

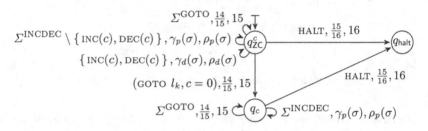

Fig. 8. The Zero-Jump Checker (for a counter $c \in \{x, y\}$) in the NMDA $\mathcal{B}$.

Intuitively, q^c_{ZC} profits from words that have more INC(c) than DEC(c) letters, while q_c continues like $\mathcal{A}$. If the move to q_c occurred after a balanced number of INC(c) and DEC(c), as it should be in a real command trace, neither the prefix word before the move to q_c, nor the suffix word after it result in a profit. Otherwise, provided that the counter is 0 at the end of the run (as guaranteed by the negative- and positive-counters checkers), both prefix and suffix words get profits, resulting in a smaller value for the run.

7,8. Positive-Jump Checkers. These gadgets, depicted in Fig. 9, are dual to the zero-jump checkers, checking for the dual violations in conditional jumps. Similarly to the zero-jump checkers, we have a different instance for each counter $c \in \{x, y\}$, ensuring that for every IF $c{=}0$ GOTO l_k ELSE GOTO $l_{k'}$ command, if the jump GOTO $l_{k'}$ is taken, then the value of c is indeed greater than 0.

Intuitively, if the counter is 0 on a (GOTO $l_{k'}, c > 0$) command when there was no INC(c) command yet, the gadget benefits by moving from q^c_{PC0} to q_{freeze}. If there was an INC(c) command, it benefits by having the dual functions on the move from q^c_{PC0} to q^c_{PC1} over INC(c) and the primal functions on one additional self loop of q^c_{PC1} over DEC(c).

Lemma 2. *Given a two-counter machine $\mathcal{M}$, we can compute an integral DMDA $\mathcal{A}$ and an integral NMDA $\mathcal{B}$ on finite words, such that $\mathcal{M}$ 0-halts iff there exists a word $w \in \Sigma^+$ such that $\mathcal{B}(w) \geq \mathcal{A}(w)$ iff there exists a word $w \in \Sigma^+$ such that $\mathcal{B}(w) > \mathcal{A}(w)$.*

The proof uses the construction presented above, and can be found in [7].

3.2   Undecidability of Comparison

For finite words, the undecidability result directly follows from Lemma 2 and the undecidability of the 0-halting problem of counter machines [31].

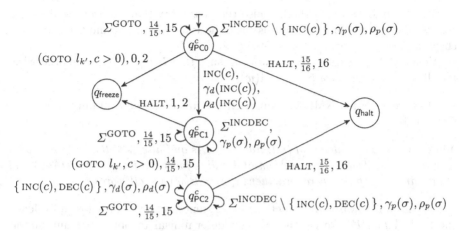

Fig. 9. The Positive-Jump Checker (for a counter c) in the NMDA $\mathcal{B}$.

Theorem 1. *Strict and non-strict containment of (integral) NMDAs on finite words are undecidable. More precisely, the problems of deciding for given integral NMDA $\mathcal{N}$ and integral DMDA $\mathcal{D}$ whether $\mathcal{N}(w) \leq \mathcal{D}(w)$ for all finite words w and whether $\mathcal{N}(w) < \mathcal{D}(w)$ for all finite words w.*

For infinite words, undecidability of non-strict containment also follows from the reduction given in Section 3.1, as the reduction considers prefixes of the word until the first HALT command. We leave open the question of whether strict containment is also undecidable for infinite words. The problem with the latter is that a HALT command might never appear in an infinite word w that incorrectly describes a halting run of the two-counter machine, in which case both automata $\mathcal{A}$ and $\mathcal{B}$ of the reduction will have the same value on w. On words w that have a HALT command but do not correctly describe a halting run of the two-counter machine we have $\mathcal{B}(w) < \mathcal{A}(w)$, and on a word w that does correctly describe a halting run we have $\mathcal{B}(w) > \mathcal{A}(w)$. Hence, the reduction only relates to whether $\mathcal{B}(w) \leq \mathcal{A}(w)$ for all words w, but not to whether $\mathcal{B}(w) < \mathcal{A}(w)$ for all words w.

Theorem 2. *Non-strict containment of (integral) NMDAs on infinite words is undecidable. More precisely, the problem of deciding for given integral NMDA $\mathcal{N}$ and integral DMDA $\mathcal{D}$ whether $\mathcal{N}(w) \leq \mathcal{D}(w)$ for all infinite words w.*

Proof. The automata $\mathcal{A}$ and $\mathcal{B}$ in the reduction given in Section 3.1 can operate as is on infinite words, ignoring the Halt-Checker gadget of $\mathcal{B}$ which is only relevant to finite words.

Since the values of both $\mathcal{A}$ and $\mathcal{B}$ on an input word w only relate to the prefix $u = \text{PREF}_{\text{HALT}(w)}$ of w until the first HALT command, we still have that $\mathcal{B}(w) > \mathcal{A}(w)$ if u correctly describes a halting run of the two-counter machine $\mathcal{M}$ and that $\mathcal{B}(w) < \mathcal{A}(w)$ if u is finite and does not correctly describe a halting run of $\mathcal{M}$.

Yet, for infinite words there is also the possibility that the word w does not contain the HALT command. In this case, the value of both $\mathcal{A}$ and the command checker of $\mathcal{B}$ will converge to 1, getting $\mathcal{A}(w) = \mathcal{B}(w)$.

Hence, if $\mathcal{M}$ 0-halts, there is a word w, such that $\mathcal{B}(w) > \mathcal{A}(w)$ and otherwise, for all words w, we have $\mathcal{B}(w) \leq \mathcal{A}(w)$. $\qquad\qquad$ □

Observe that for NMDAs, equivalence and non-strict containment are interreducible.

Theorem 3. *Equivalence of (integral) NMDAs on finite as well as infinite words is undecidable. That is, the problem of deciding for given integral NMDAs $\mathcal{A}$ and $\mathcal{B}$ on finite or infinite words whether $\mathcal{A}(w) = \mathcal{B}(w)$ for all words w.*

Proof. Assume toward contradiction the existence of a procedure for equivalence check of $\mathcal{A}$ and $\mathcal{B}$. We can use the nondeterminism to obtain an automaton $\mathcal{C} = \mathcal{A} \cup \mathcal{B}$, having $\mathcal{C}(w) \leq \mathcal{A}(w)$ for all words w. We can then check whether $\mathcal{C}$ is equivalent to $\mathcal{A}$, which holds if and only if $\mathcal{A}(w) \leq \mathcal{B}(w)$ for all words w. Indeed, if $\mathcal{A}(w) \leq \mathcal{B}(w)$ then $\mathcal{A}(w) \leq \min(\mathcal{A}(w), \mathcal{B}(w)) = \mathcal{C}(w)$, while if there exists a word w, such that $\mathcal{B}(w) < \mathcal{A}(w)$, we have $\mathcal{C}(w) = \min(\mathcal{A}(w), \mathcal{B}(w)) < \mathcal{A}(w)$, implying that $\mathcal{C}$ and $\mathcal{A}$ are not equivalent. Thus, such a procedure contradicts the undecidability of non-strict containment, shown in Theorems 1 and 2. $\qquad$ □

4   Comparison of NDAs with Different Discount Factors

We present below our algorithm for the comparison of NDAs with different discount factors. We start with automata on infinite words, and then show how to solve the case of finite words by reduction to the case of infinite words.

The algorithm is based on our main observation that, due to the difference between the discount factors, we only need to consider the combination of the automata computation trees up to some level k, after which we can consider first the best/worst continuation of the automaton with the smaller discount factor, and on top of it the worst/best continuation of the second automaton.

For an NDA $\mathcal{A}$, we define its *lowest* (resp. *highest*) *infinite run value* by LOWRUN($\mathcal{A}$) (resp. HIGHRUN($\mathcal{A}$)) = min (resp. max) $\{\mathcal{A}(r) \mid r$ is an infinite run of $\mathcal{A}$ (on some word $w \in \Sigma^\omega$)$\}$.

Observe that we can use min and max (rather than inf and sup) since the infimum and supremum values are indeed attainable by specific infinite runs of the NDA (cf. [10, Proof of Theorem 9]). Notice that LOWRUN($\mathcal{A}$) and HIGHRUN($\mathcal{A}$) can be calculated in PTIME by a simple reduction to one-player discounted-payoff games [4].

Considering word values, we also refer to the *lowest* (resp. *highest*) *word value* of $\mathcal{A}$, defined by LOWWORD($\mathcal{A}$) (resp. HIGHWORD($\mathcal{A}$))= min (resp. max) $\{\mathcal{A}(w) \mid w \in \Sigma^\omega\}$. Observe that LOWWORD($\mathcal{A}$) = LOWRUN($\mathcal{A}$), HIGHWORD($\mathcal{A}$) $\leq$ HIGHRUN($\mathcal{A}$), and for deterministic automaton, HIGHWORD($\mathcal{A}$) = HIGHRUN($\mathcal{A}$).

For an NMDA $\mathcal{A}$ with states Q, we define the *maximal difference between suffix runs* of $\mathcal{A}$ as MAXDIFF($\mathcal{A}$) = max $\{$ HIGHRUN($\mathcal{A}^q$) − LOWRUN($\mathcal{A}^q$) $\mid q \in Q \}$.

Notice that MAXDIFF($\mathcal{A}$) ≥ 0 and that $\mathcal{A}^q(w)$ is bounded as follows.

$$\text{LOWRUN}(\mathcal{A}^q) \leq \mathcal{A}^q(w) \leq \text{LOWRUN}(\mathcal{A}^q) + \text{MAXDIFF}(\mathcal{A}) \tag{2}$$

Lemma 3. *There is an algorithm that computes for every input discount factors* $\lambda_A, \lambda_D \in \mathbb{Q} \cap (1, \infty)$, λ_A-*NDA* $\mathcal{A}$ *and* λ_D-*DDA* $\mathcal{D}$ *on infinite words the value of* $\min\{\mathcal{A}(w) - \mathcal{D}(w) \mid w \in \Sigma^\omega\}$.

Proof. Consider an alphabet Σ, discount factors $\lambda_A, \lambda_D \in \mathbb{Q} \cap (1, \infty)$, a λ_A-NDA $\mathcal{A} = \langle \Sigma, Q_A, \iota_A, \delta_A, \gamma_A \rangle$ and a λ_D-DDA $\mathcal{D} = \langle \Sigma, Q_D, \iota_D, \delta_D, \gamma_D \rangle$. When $\lambda_A = \lambda_D$, we can generate a λ_A-NDA $\mathcal{C} \equiv \mathcal{A} - \mathcal{D}$ over the product of $\mathcal{A}$ and $\mathcal{D}$ and compute LOWWORD($\mathcal{C}$).

When $\lambda_A \neq \lambda_D$, **we consider first the case that** $\lambda_A < \lambda_D$.

Our algorithm unfolds the computation trees of $\mathcal{A}$ and $\mathcal{D}$, up to a level in which only the minimal-valued suffix words of $\mathcal{A}$ remain relevant – Due to the massive difference between the accumulated discount factor in $\mathcal{A}$ compared to the one in $\mathcal{D}$, any "penalty" of not continuing with a minimal-valued suffix word in $\mathcal{A}$, defined below as m_A, cannot be compensated even by the maximal-valued word of $\mathcal{D}$, which "profit" is at most as high as MAXDIFF($\mathcal{D}$). Hence, at that level, it is enough to look among the minimal-valued suffixes of $\mathcal{A}$ for the one that implies the highest value in $\mathcal{D}$.

For every transition $t = (q, \sigma, q') \in \delta_A$, let MINVAL$(q, \sigma, q') = \gamma_A(q, \sigma, q') + \frac{1}{\lambda_A} \cdot$ LOWWORD($\mathcal{A}^{q'}$) be the best (minimal) value that $\mathcal{A}^q$ can get by taking t as the first transition. We say that t is *preferred* if it starts a minimal-valued infinite run of $\mathcal{A}^q$, namely $\delta_{pr} = \{ t = (q, \sigma, q') \in \delta_A \mid \text{MINVAL}(t) = \text{LOWWORD}(\mathcal{A}^q) \}$ is the set of preferred transitions of $\mathcal{A}$. Observe that an infinite run of $\mathcal{A}^q$ that takes only transitions from δ_{pr}, has a value equal to LOWRUN($\mathcal{A}^q$) (cf. [10, Proof of Theorem 9]).

If all the transitions of $\mathcal{A}$ are preferred, $\mathcal{A}$ has the same value on all words, and then $\min\{\mathcal{A}(w) - \mathcal{D}(w) \mid w \in \Sigma^\omega\} = \text{LOWRUN}(\mathcal{A}) - \text{HIGHWORD}(\mathcal{D})$. (Recall that since $\mathcal{D}$ is deterministic, we can easily compute HIGHWORD($\mathcal{D}$).) Otherwise, let m_A be the minimal penalty for not taking a preferred transition in $\mathcal{A}$, meaning

$$m_A = \min \left\{ \text{MINVAL}(t') - \text{MINVAL}(t'') \;\middle|\; \begin{array}{l} t' = (q, \sigma', q') \in \delta_A \setminus \delta_{pr}, \\ t'' = (q, \sigma'', q'') \in \delta_{pr} \end{array} \right\}. \text{ Observe that}$$

$m_A > 0$.

Considering the connection between m_A and MAXDIFF($\mathcal{D}$), notice first that if MAXDIFF($\mathcal{D}$) $= 0$, $\mathcal{D}$ has the same value on all words, and then we have $\min\{\mathcal{A}(w) - \mathcal{D}(w) \mid w \in \Sigma^\omega\} = \text{LOWRUN}(\mathcal{A}) - \text{LOWRUN}(\mathcal{D})$. Otherwise, meaning MAXDIFF($\mathcal{D}$) > 0, we unfold the computation trees of $\mathcal{A}$ and $\mathcal{D}$ for the first k levels, until the maximal difference between suffix runs in $\mathcal{D}$, divided by the accumulated discount factor of $\mathcal{D}$, is smaller than the minimal penalty for not taking a preferred transition in $\mathcal{A}$, divided by the accumulated discount factor of $\mathcal{A}$. Meaning, k is the minimal integer such that

$$\frac{\text{MAXDIFF}(\mathcal{D})}{\lambda_D{}^k} < \frac{m_A}{\lambda_A{}^k} \tag{3}$$

Starting at level k, the penalty gained by taking a non-preferred transition of $\mathcal{A}$ cannot be compensated by a higher-valued word of $\mathcal{D}$.

At level k, we consider separately every run ψ of $\mathcal{A}$ on some prefix word u. We should look for a suffix word w, that minimizes

$$\mathcal{A}(uw) - \mathcal{D}(uw) = \mathcal{A}(\psi) + \frac{1}{\lambda_A{}^k} \cdot \mathcal{A}^{\delta_A(\psi)}(w) - \mathcal{D}(u) - \frac{1}{\lambda_D{}^k} \cdot \mathcal{D}^{\delta_D(u)}(w) \quad (4)$$

A central point of the algorithm is that every word that minimizes $\mathcal{A} - \mathcal{D}$ must take only preferred transitions of $\mathcal{A}$ starting at level k (full proof in [7]). As all possible remaining continuations after level k yield the same value in $\mathcal{A}$, we can choose among them the continuation that yields the highest value in $\mathcal{D}$.

Let $\mathcal{B}$ be the partial automaton with the states of $\mathcal{A}$, but only its preferred transitions δ_{pr}. (We ignore words on which $\mathcal{B}$ has no runs.) We shall use the automata product $\mathcal{B}^{\delta_A(\psi)} \times \mathcal{D}^{\delta_D(u)}$ to force suffix words that only take preferred transitions of $\mathcal{A}$, while calculating among them the highest value in $\mathcal{D}$.

Let $\mathcal{C}^{(\delta_A(\psi),\delta_D(u))} = \langle \Sigma, Q_A \times Q_D, \{(\delta_A(\psi), \delta_D(u))\}, \delta_{pr} \times \delta_D, \gamma_C \rangle$ be the partial λ_D-NDA that is generated by the product of $\mathcal{B}^{\delta_A(\psi)}$ and $\mathcal{D}^{\delta_D(u)}$, while only considering the weights (and discount factor) of $\mathcal{D}$, meaning $\gamma_C((q,p),\sigma,(q',p')) = \gamma_D(p,\sigma,p')$.

A word w has a run in $\mathcal{A}^{\delta_A(\psi)}$ that uses only preferred transitions iff w has a run in $\mathcal{C}^{(\delta_A(\psi),\delta_D(u))}$. Also, observe that the nondeterminism in $\mathcal{C}$ is only related to the nondeterminism in $\mathcal{A}$, and the weight function of $\mathcal{C}$ only depends on the weights of $\mathcal{D}$, hence all the runs of $\mathcal{C}^{(\delta_A(\psi),\delta_D(u))}$ on the same word result in the same value, which is the value of that word in $\mathcal{D}$. Combining both observations, we get that a word w has a run in $\mathcal{A}^{\delta_A(\psi)}$ that uses only preferred transitions iff w has a run r in $\mathcal{C}^{(\delta_A(\psi),\delta_D(u))}$ such that $\mathcal{C}^{(\delta_A(\psi),\delta_D(u))}(r) = \mathcal{D}^{\delta_D(u)}(w)$. Hence, after taking the k-sized run ψ of $\mathcal{A}$, and under the notations defined in Eq. (4), a suffix word w that can take only preferred transitions of $\mathcal{A}$, and maximizes $\mathcal{D}^{\delta_D(u)}(w)$, has a value of $\mathcal{D}^{\delta_D(u)}(w) = \text{HIGHRUN}(\mathcal{C}^{(\delta_A(\psi),\delta_D(u))})$. This leads to

$$\min\{\mathcal{A}(v) - \mathcal{D}(v) \mid v \in \Sigma^\omega\} =$$

$$\min\left\{\mathcal{A}(\psi) + \frac{\mathcal{A}^{\delta_A(\psi)}(w)}{\lambda_A{}^k} - \mathcal{D}(u) - \frac{\mathcal{D}^{\delta_D(u)}(w)}{\lambda_D{}^k} \,\middle|\, \begin{array}{l} u \in \Sigma^k, w \in \Sigma^\omega, \\ \psi \text{ is a run of } \mathcal{A} \text{ on } u \end{array}\right\} =$$

$$\min_\psi\left\{\mathcal{A}(\psi) + \frac{\text{LOWRUN}(\mathcal{A}^{\delta_A(\psi)})}{\lambda_A{}^k} - \mathcal{D}(u) - \frac{\text{HIGHRUN}(\mathcal{C}^{(\delta_A(\psi),\delta_D(u))})}{\lambda_D{}^k} \,\middle|\, \begin{array}{l} u \in \Sigma^k, \\ \psi \text{ is a run} \\ \text{of } \mathcal{A} \text{ on } u \end{array}\right\}$$

and it is only left to calculate this value for every k-sized run of $\mathcal{A}$, meaning for every leaf in the computation tree of $\mathcal{A}$.

The case of $\lambda_A > \lambda_D$ is analogous, with the following changes:

- For every transition of $\mathcal{D}$, we compute $\text{MAXVAL}(p,\sigma,p') = \gamma_D(p,\sigma,p') + \frac{1}{\lambda_D} \cdot$ $\text{HIGHWORD}(\mathcal{D}^{p'})$, instead of $\text{MINVAL}(q,\sigma,q')$.
- The preferred transitions of $\mathcal{D}$ are the ones that start a maximal-valued infinite run, that is $\delta_{pr} = \{t = (p,\sigma',p') \in \delta_D \mid \text{MAXVAL}(t) = \text{HIGHRUN}(\mathcal{D}^p)\}$,

and the minimal penalty $m_{\mathcal{D}}$ is

$$m_{\mathcal{D}} = \min \left\{ \text{MAXVAL}(t'') - \text{MAXVAL}(t') \;\middle|\; \begin{array}{l} t'' = (p, \sigma'', p'') \in \delta_{pr}, \\ t' = (p, \sigma', p') \in \delta_{\mathcal{D}} \setminus \delta_{pr} \end{array} \right\}$$

- k should be the minimal integer such that $\frac{\text{MAXDIFF}(\mathcal{A})}{\lambda_A{}^k} < \frac{m_{\mathcal{D}}}{\lambda_D{}^k}$.
- We define $\mathcal{B}$ to be the restriction of $\mathcal{D}$ to its preferred transitions, and $\mathcal{C}^{(\delta_A(\psi), \delta_{\mathcal{D}}(u))}$ as a partial λ_A-NDA on the product of $\mathcal{A}^{\delta_A(\psi)}$ and $\mathcal{B}^{\delta_{\mathcal{D}}(u)}$ while considering the weights of $\mathcal{A}$. We then calculate $\text{LOWRUN}(\mathcal{C}^{(\delta_A(\psi), \delta_{\mathcal{D}}(u))})$ for every k-sized run of $\mathcal{A}$, ψ, and conclude that $\min \{ \mathcal{A} - \mathcal{D} \}$ is equal to

$$\min_\psi \left\{ \mathcal{A}(\psi) + \frac{\text{LOWRUN}(\mathcal{C}^{(\delta_A(\psi), \delta_{\mathcal{D}}(u))})}{\lambda_A{}^k} - \mathcal{D}(u) - \frac{\text{HIGHRUN}(\mathcal{D}_{\delta_{\mathcal{D}}(u)})}{\lambda_D{}^k} \right\}.$$

Observe that in this case, it might not hold that all runs of $\mathcal{C}^{(\delta_A(\psi), \delta_{\mathcal{D}}(u))}$ on the same word have the same value, but such property is not required, since we look for the minimal run value (which is the minimal word value).

$\square$

Notice that the algorithm of Lemma 3 does not work if switching the direction of containment, namely if considering a deterministic $\mathcal{A}$ and a nondeterministic $\mathcal{D}$. The determinism of $\mathcal{D}$ is required for finding the maximal value of a valid word in $\mathcal{B}^{\delta_A(\psi)} \times \mathcal{D}^{\delta_{\mathcal{D}}(u)}$. If $\mathcal{D}$ is not deterministic, the maximal-valued run of $\mathcal{B}^{\delta_A(\psi)} \times \mathcal{D}^{\delta_{\mathcal{D}}(u)}$ on some word w equals the value of some run of $\mathcal{D}$ on w, but not necessarily the value of $\mathcal{D}$ on w. We also need $\mathcal{D}$ to be deterministic for computing $\text{HIGHWORD}(\mathcal{D}^p)$ in the case that $\lambda_A > \lambda_D$.

Moving to automata on finite words, we reduce the problem to the corresponding problem handled in Lemma 3, by adding to the alphabet a new letter that represents the end of the word, and making some required adjustments.

Lemma 4. *There is an algorithm that computes for every input discount factors $\lambda_A, \lambda_D \in \mathbb{Q} \cap (1, \infty)$, λ_A-NDA $\mathcal{A}$ and λ_D-DDA $\mathcal{D}$ on finite words the value of $\inf \{ \mathcal{A}(u) - \mathcal{D}(u) \mid u \in \Sigma^+ \}$, and determines if there exists a finite word u for which $\mathcal{A}(u) - \mathcal{D}(u)$ equals that value.*

Proof. Without loss of generality, we assume that initial states of automata have no incoming transitions. (Every automaton can be changed in linear time to an equivalent automaton with this property.)

We convert, as described below, an NDA $\mathcal{N}$ on finite words to an NDA $\hat{\mathcal{N}}$ on infinite words, such that $\hat{\mathcal{N}}$ intuitively simulates the finite runs of $\mathcal{N}$. For an alphabet Σ, a discount factor $\lambda \in \mathbb{Q} \cap (1, \infty)$, and a λ-NDA (DDA) $\mathcal{N} = \langle \Sigma, Q_{\mathcal{N}}, \iota_{\mathcal{N}}, \delta_{\mathcal{N}}, \gamma_{\mathcal{N}} \rangle$ on finite words, we define the λ-NDA (DDA) $\hat{\mathcal{N}} = \langle \hat{\Sigma}, Q_{\mathcal{N}} \cup \{ q_\tau \}, \iota_{\mathcal{N}}, \delta_{\hat{\mathcal{N}}}, \gamma_{\hat{\mathcal{N}}} \rangle$ on infinite words. The new alphabet $\hat{\Sigma} = \Sigma \cup \{ \tau \}$ contains a new letter $\tau \notin \Sigma$ that indicates the end of a finite word. The new state q_τ has 0-valued self loops on every letter in the alphabet, and there are 0-valued transitions from every non-initial state to q_τ on the new letter τ. Formally, $\delta_{\hat{\mathcal{N}}} = \delta_{\mathcal{N}} \cup \{ (q_\tau, \sigma, q_\tau \mid \sigma \in \hat{\Sigma}) \} \cup \{ (q, \tau, q_\tau \mid q \in Q_{\mathcal{N}} \setminus \iota_{\mathcal{N}}) \}$, and

$$\gamma_{\hat{\mathcal{N}}}(t) = \begin{cases} \gamma_{\mathcal{N}}(t) & t \in \delta_{\mathcal{N}} \\ 0 & \text{otherwise} \end{cases}$$

Observe that for every state $q \in Q_{\mathcal{N}}$, the following hold.

1. For every finite run $r_\mathcal{N}$ of $\mathcal{N}^q$, there is an infinite run $r_{\hat{\mathcal{N}}}$ of $\hat{\mathcal{N}}^q$, such that $\hat{\mathcal{N}}^q(r_{\hat{\mathcal{N}}}) = \mathcal{N}^q(r_\mathcal{N})$, and $r_{\hat{\mathcal{N}}}$ takes some τ transitions. ($r_{\hat{\mathcal{N}}}$ can start as $r_\mathcal{N}$ and then continue with only τ transitions.)

2. For every infinite run $r_{\hat{\mathcal{N}}}$ of $\hat{\mathcal{N}}^q$ that has a τ transition, there is a finite run $r_\mathcal{N}$ of $\mathcal{N}^q$, such that $\hat{\mathcal{N}}^q(r_{\hat{\mathcal{N}}}) = \mathcal{N}^q(r_\mathcal{N})$. ($r_\mathcal{N}$ can be the longest prefix of $r_{\hat{\mathcal{N}}}$ up to the first τ transition).

3. For every infinite run $r_{\hat{\mathcal{N}}}$ of $\hat{\mathcal{N}}^q$ that has no τ transition, there is a series of finite runs of $\mathcal{N}^q$, such that the values of the runs in $\mathcal{N}^q$ converge to $\hat{\mathcal{N}}^q(r_{\hat{\mathcal{N}}})$. (For example, the series of all prefixes of $r_{\hat{\mathcal{N}}}$).

Hence, for every $q \in Q_\mathcal{N}$ we have $\inf \{ \mathcal{N}^q(r) \mid r \text{ is a run of } \mathcal{N}^q \} = \text{LOWRUN}(\hat{\mathcal{N}}^q)$ and $\sup \{ \mathcal{N}^q(r) \mid r \text{ is a run of } \mathcal{N}^q \} = \text{HIGHRUN}(\hat{\mathcal{N}}^q)$. (For a non-initial state q, we also consider the "run" of $\mathcal{N}^q$ on the empty word, and define its value to be 0.) Notice that the infimum (supremum) run value of $\mathcal{N}^q$ is attained by an actual run of $\mathcal{N}^q$ iff there is an infinite run of $\hat{\mathcal{N}}^q$ that gets this value and takes a τ transition.

For every state $q \in Q_{\hat{\mathcal{N}}}$, we can determine, as follows, whether $\text{LOWRUN}(\hat{\mathcal{N}}^q)$ is attained by an infinite run taking a τ transition. We calculate $\text{LOWRUN}(\hat{\mathcal{N}}^q)$ for all states, and then start a process that iteratively marks the states of $\hat{\mathcal{N}}$, such that at the end, $q \in Q_{\hat{\mathcal{N}}}$ is marked iff $\text{LOWRUN}(\hat{\mathcal{N}}^q)$ can be achieved by a run with a τ transition. We start with q_τ as the only marked state. In each iteration we further mark every state q from which there exists a preferred transition $t = (q, \sigma, q') \in \delta_{pr}$ to some marked state q'. The process terminates when an iteration has no new states to mark. Analogously, we can determine whether $\text{HIGHRUN}(\hat{\mathcal{N}}^q)$ is attained by a run that goes to q_τ.

Consider discount factors $\lambda_A, \lambda_D \in \mathbb{Q} \cap (1, \infty)$, a λ_A-NDA $\mathcal{A}$ and a λ_D-DDA $\mathcal{D}$ on finite words. When $\lambda_A = \lambda_D$, similarly to Lemma 3, the algorithm finds the infimum value of $\mathcal{C} \equiv \mathcal{A} - \mathcal{D}$ using $\hat{\mathcal{C}}$, and determines if an actual finite word attains this value using the process described above.

Otherwise, the algorithm converts $\mathcal{A}$ and $\mathcal{D}$ to $\hat{\mathcal{A}}$ and $\hat{\mathcal{D}}$, and proceeds as in Lemma 3 over $\hat{\mathcal{A}}$ and $\hat{\mathcal{D}}$. According to the above observations, we have that $\inf \{ \mathcal{A}(u) - \mathcal{D}(u) \mid u \in \Sigma^+ \} = \min\{\hat{\mathcal{A}}(w) - \hat{\mathcal{D}}(w) \mid w \in \Sigma^\omega\}$, and that $\inf \{ \mathcal{A}(u) - \mathcal{D}(u) \}$ is attainable iff $\min\{\hat{\mathcal{A}}(w) - \hat{\mathcal{D}}(w)\}$ is attainable by some word that has a τ transition. Hence, whenever computing LOWRUN or HIGHRUN, we also perform the process described above, to determine whether this value is attainable by a run that has a τ transition. We determine that $\inf \{ \mathcal{A}(u) - \mathcal{D}(u) \}$ is attainable iff exists a leaf of the computation tree that leads to it, for which the relevant values LOWRUN and HIGHRUN are attainable.   □

Complexity analysis We show below that the algorithm of Lemmas 3 and 4 only needs a polynomial space, with respect to the size of the input automata, implying a PSPACE algorithm for the corresponding decision problems. We define the size of an NDA $\mathcal{N}$, denoted by $|\mathcal{N}|$, as the maximum between the number of its transitions, the maximal binary representation of any weight in it, and the maximal unary representation of the discount factor. (Binary representation of the discount factors might cause our algorithm to use an exponential space, in case that the two factors are very close to each other.) The input NDAs may have rational weights, yet it will be more convenient to consider equivalent NDAs with integral weights that are obtained by multiplying all the weights by their common denominator [6]. (Observe that it causes the values of all words to be multiplied by this same ratio, and it keeps the same input size, up to a polynomial change.)

Before proceeding to the complexity analysis, we provide an auxiliary lemma (proof appears in [7]).

Lemma 5. *For every integers $p > q \in \mathbb{N}\setminus\{0\}$, a $\frac{p}{q}$-NDA A with integral weights, and a lasso run $r = t_0, t_1, \ldots, t_{x-1}, (t_x, t_{x+1}, \ldots, t_{x+y-1})^\omega$ of A, there exists an integer b, such that $A(r) = \frac{b}{p^x(p^y - q^y)}$.*

Proceeding to the complexity analysis, let the input size be $S = |A| + |D|$, the reduced forms of λ_A and λ_D be $\frac{p}{q}$ and $\frac{p_D}{q_D}$ respectively, the number of states in A be n, and the maximal difference between transition weights in D be M. Observe that $n \leq S, p \leq S, M \leq 2 \cdot 2^S$, $\frac{\lambda_D}{\lambda_D - 1} \leq \frac{p_D}{p_D - q_D} \leq p_D \leq S$, and for $\lambda_D > \lambda_A > 1$, we also have $\frac{\lambda_D}{\lambda_A} = \frac{p \cdot q_D}{q \cdot p_D} \geq 1 + \frac{1}{S^2}$.

Observe that A has a best infinite run (and D has a worst infinite run), in a lasso form as in Lemma 5, with $x, y \in [1..n]$. Indeed, following preferred transitions, a run must complete a lasso, and then may forever repeat its choices of preferred transitions. Hence, m_A, being the difference between two lasso runs, is in the form of

$$m_A = \frac{b_1}{p^{x_1}(p^{y_1} - q^{y_1})} - \frac{b_2}{p^{x_2}(p^{y_2} - q^{y_2})} = \frac{b_3}{p^n(p^{y_1} - q^{y_1})(p^{y_2} - q^{y_2})} > \frac{b_3}{p^n p^{y_1} p^{y_2}}$$

$$\geq \frac{1}{p^{3n}} \geq \frac{1}{S^{3S}} \stackrel{\text{for } S \geq 1}{>} \frac{1}{(2^S)^{3S}} = \frac{1}{2^{3S^2}}$$

for some $x_1, x_2, y_1, y_2 \leq n$ and some integers b_1, b_2, b_3. (Similarly, we can show that $m_D > \frac{1}{2^{3S^2}}$.) We have MAXDIFF$(D) \leq M \cdot \frac{\lambda_D}{\lambda_D - 1}$, hence

$$\frac{\text{MAXDIFF}(D)}{m_A} \leq \frac{M \cdot \frac{\lambda_D}{\lambda_D - 1}}{m_A} \leq \frac{2^{1+S} \cdot S}{m_A} \stackrel{\text{(for } S \geq 1)}{<} \frac{2^{3S}}{m_A} < 2^{3S + 3S^2}$$

Recall that we unfold the computation tree until level k, which is the minimal integer such that $(\frac{\lambda_D}{\lambda_A})^k > \frac{\text{MAXDIFF}(D)}{m_A}$. Observe that for $S \geq 1$ we have $(\frac{\lambda_D}{\lambda_A})^{S^2} \geq (1 + \frac{1}{S^2})^{S^2} \geq 2$, hence for $k' = S^2 \cdot (3S + 3S^2)$, we have

$$(\frac{\lambda_D}{\lambda_A})^{k'} = ((\frac{\lambda_D}{\lambda_A})^{S^2})^{3S + 3S^2} \geq 2^{3S + 3S^2} > \frac{\text{MAXDIFF}(D)}{m_A}$$

meaning that k is polynomial in S. Similar analysis shows that k is polynomial in S also for $\lambda_D < \lambda_A$.

Considering decision problems that use our algorithm, due to the equivalence of NPSPACE and PSPACE, the algorithm can nondeterministically guess an optimal prefix word u of size k, letter by letter, as well as a run ψ of $\mathcal{A}$ on u, transition by transition, and then compute the value of $\mathcal{A}(\psi) + \frac{\text{LOWRUN}(\mathcal{A}^{\delta_{\mathcal{A}}(\psi)})}{\lambda_{\mathcal{A}}{}^k} - \mathcal{D}(u) - \frac{\text{HIGHRUN}(\mathcal{C}^{(\delta_{\mathcal{A}}(\psi),\delta_{\mathcal{D}}(u))})}{\lambda_{\mathcal{D}}{}^k}$.

Observe that along the run of the algorithm, we need to save the following information, which can be done in polynomial space:

- The automaton $\mathcal{C} \equiv \mathcal{B} \times \mathcal{D}$ (or $\mathcal{A} \times \mathcal{B}$), which requires polynomial space.
- $\lambda_{\mathcal{A}}{}^k$ (for $\mathcal{A}(\psi)$) and $\lambda_{\mathcal{D}}{}^k$ (for $\mathcal{D}(u)$). Since we save them in binary representation, we have $\log_2(\lambda^k) \leq k \log_2(S)$, requiring polynomial space.

We thus get the following complexity result.

Theorem 4. *For input discount factors $\lambda_A, \lambda_D \in \mathbb{Q} \cap (1, \infty)$, λ_A-NDA $\mathcal{A}$ and λ_D-DDA $\mathcal{D}$ on finite or infinite words, it is decidable in PSPACE whether $\mathcal{A}(w) \geq \mathcal{D}(w)$ and whether $\mathcal{A}(w) > \mathcal{D}(w)$ for all words w.*

Proof. We use Lemma 3 in the case of infinite words and Lemma 4 in the case of finite words, checking whether $\min\{\mathcal{A}(w) - \mathcal{D}(w)\} < 0$ and whether $\min\{\mathcal{A}(w) - \mathcal{D}(w)\} \leq 0$. In the case of finite words, we also use the information of whether there is an actual word that gets the desired value. □

Since integral NDAs can always be determinized [8], we get as a corollary that there is an algorithm to decide equivalence and strict and non-strict containment of integral NDAs with different (or the same) discount factors. Note, however, that it might not be in PSPACE, since determinization exponentially increases the number of states, resulting in k that is exponential in S, and storing in binary representation values in the order of λ^k might require exponential space.

Corollary 1. *There are algorithms to decide for input integral discount factors $\lambda_A, \lambda_B \in \mathbb{N}$, λ_A-NDA $\mathcal{A}$ and λ_B-NDA $\mathcal{B}$ on finite or infinite words whether or not $\mathcal{A}(w) > \mathcal{B}(w)$, $\mathcal{A}(w) \geq \mathcal{B}(w)$, or $\mathcal{A}(w) = \mathcal{B}(w)$ for all words w.*

5   Conclusions

The new decidability result, providing an algorithm for comparing discounted-sum automata with different integral discount factors, may allow to extend the usage of discounted-sum automata in formal verification, while the undecidability result strengthen the justification of restricting discounted-sum automata with multiple integral discount factors to tidy NMDAs. The new algorithm also extends the possible, more limited, usage of discounted-sum automata with rational discount factors, while further research should be put into this direction.

Acknowledgements We thank Guillermo A. Perez for stimulating discussions on the comparison of integral NDAs with different discount factors.

References

1. de Alfaro, L., Henzinger, T.A., Majumdar, R.: Discounting the future in systems theory. In: proceedings of ICALP. vol. 2719, pp. 1022–1037 (2003). https://doi.org/10.1007/3-540-45061-0_79

2. Almagor, S., Boker, U., Kupferman, O.: What's decidable about weighted automata? Information and Computatio **282** (2022). https://doi.org/10.1016/j.ic.2020.104651

3. Almagor, S., Kupferman, O., Ringert, J.O., Velner, Y.: Quantitative assume guarantee synthesis. In: proceedings of CAV. pp. 353–374. Springer (2017). https://doi.org/10.1007/978-3-319-63390-9_19

4. Andersson, D.: An improved algorithm for discounted payoff games. In: proceedings of ESSLLI Student Session. pp. 91–98 (2006)

5. Bansal, S., Chaudhuri, S., Vardi, M.Y.: Comparator automata in quantitative verification. In: proceedings of FoSSaCS. LNCS, vol. 10803, pp. 420–437 (2018). https://doi.org/10.1007/978-3-319-89366-2_23

6. Boker, U., Hefetz, G.: Discounted-sum automata with multiple discount factors. In: proceedings of CSL. LIPIcs, vol. 183, pp. 12:1–12:23. Schloss Dagstuhl - Leibniz-Zentrum für Informatik (2021). https://doi.org/10.4230/LIPIcs.CSL.2021.12

7. Boker, U., Hefetz, G.: On the comparison of discounted-sum automata with multiple discount factors (2023). https://doi.org/10.48550/ARXIV.2301.04086

8. Boker, U., Henzinger, T.A.: Exact and approximate determinization of discounted-sum automata. Log. Methods Comput. Sci. **10**(1) (2014). https://doi.org/10.2168/LMCS-10(1:10)2014

9. Boker, U., Henzinger, T.A., Otop, J.: The target discounted-sum problem. In: proceedings of LICS. pp. 750–761 (2015). https://doi.org/10.1109/LICS.2015.74

10. Boker, U., Lehtinen, K.: History determinism vs. good for gameness in quantitative automata. In: proceedings of FSTTCS. pp. 38:1–38:20 (2021). https://doi.org/10.4230/LIPIcs.FSTTCS.2021.38

11. Brenguier, R., Clemente, L., Hunter, P., Pérez, G.A., Randour, M., Raskin, J.F., Sankur, O., Sassolas, M.: Non-zero sum games for reactive synthesis. In: Language and Automata Theory and Applications. pp. 3–23. Springer (2016)

12. Chatterjee, K., Doyen, L., Henzinger, T.A.: Alternating weighted automata. In: proceedings of FCT. LNCS, vol. 5699, pp. 3–13 (2009). https://doi.org/10.1007/978-3-642-03409-1_2

13. Chatterjee, K., Doyen, L., Henzinger, T.A.: Probabilistic weighted automata. In: proceedings of CONCUR. LNCS, vol. 5710, pp. 244–258 (2009). https://doi.org/10.1007/978-3-642-04081-8_17

14. Chatterjee, K., Doyen, L., Henzinger, T.A.: Expressiveness and closure properties for quantitative languages. Log. Methods Comput. Sci. **6**(3) (2010), http://arxiv.org/abs/1007.4018

15. Chatterjee, K., Doyen, L., Henzinger, T.A.: Quantitative languages. ACM Trans. Comput. Log. **11**(4), 23:1–23:38 (2010). https://doi.org/10.1145/1805950.1805953

16. Chatterjee, K., Forejt, V., Wojtczak, D.: Multi-objective discounted reward verification in graphs and MDPs. In: proceedings of LPAR. LNCS, vol. 8312, pp. 228–242 (2013). https://doi.org/10.1007/978-3-642-45221-5_17

17. Clarke, E.M., Draghicescu, I.A., Kurshan, R.P.: A unified approach for showing language containment and equivalence between various types of ω-automata. Information Processing Letters **46**, 301–308 (1993)

18. Degorre, A., Doyen, L., Gentilini, R., Raskin, J., Toruńczyk, S.: Energy and mean-payoff games with imperfect information. In: proceedings of CSL. LNCS, vol. 6247, pp. 260–274 (2010). https://doi.org/10.1007/978-3-642-15205-4_22

19. Droste, M., Kuske, D.: Skew and infinitary formal power series. Theor. Comput. Sci. **366**(3), 199–227 (2006). https://doi.org/10.1016/j.tcs.2006.08.024

20. Filiot, E., Gentilini, R., Raskin, J.: Finite-valued weighted automata. In: proceedings of FSTTCS. LIPIcs, vol. 29, pp. 133–145 (2014). https://doi.org/10.4230/LIPIcs.FSTTCS.2014.133

21. Filiot, E., Gentilini, R., Raskin, J.: Quantitative languages defined by functional automata. Log. Methods Comput. Sci. **11**(3) (2015). https://doi.org/10.2168/LMCS-11(3:14)2015

22. Filiot, E., Löding, C., Winter, S.: Synthesis from weighted specifications with partial domains over finite words. In: proceedings of FSTTCS. pp. 46:1–46:16 (2020). https://doi.org/10.4230/LIPIcs.FSTTCS.2020.46

23. Gimbert, H., Zielonka, W.: Limits of multi-discounted markov decision processes. In: proceedings of LICS. pp. 89–98 (2007). https://doi.org/10.1109/LICS.2007.28

24. Glendinning, P., Sidorov, N.: Unique representations of real numbers in non-integer bases. Mathematical Research Letters **8**(4), 535–543 (2001)

25. Hare, K.: Beta-expansions of pisot and salem numbers. In: Waterloo Workshop in Computer Algebra (2006)

26. Hojati, R., Touati, H., Kurshan, R., Brayton, R.: Efficient ω-regular language containment. In: proceedings of CAV. LNCS, vol. 663. springer (1992)

27. Hunter, P., Pérez, G.A., Raskin, J.: Reactive synthesis without regret. Acta Informatica **54**(1), 3–39 (2017). https://doi.org/10.1007/s00236-016-0268-z

28. Kupferman, O., Vardi, M., Wolper, P.: An automata-theoretic approach to branching-time model checking. Journal of the ACM **47**(2), 312–360 (2000)

29. Madani, O., Thorup, M., Zwick, U.: Discounted deterministic markov decision processes and discounted all-pairs shortest paths. ACM Trans. Algorithms **6**(2), 33:1–33:25 (2010). https://doi.org/10.1145/1721837.1721849

30. Mahler, K.: An unsolved problem on the powers of $\frac{3}{2}$. The journal of the Australian mathematical society **8**(2), 313–321 (1968)

31. Minsky, M.L.: Computation: Finite and Infinite Machines. Prentice-Hall Series in Automatic Computation, Prentice-Hall (1967)

32. Sutton, R.S., G.Barto, A.: Introduction to Reinforcement Learning. MIT Press (1998), http://dl.acm.org/doi/book/10.5555/551283

33. Tasiran, S., Hojati, R., Brayton, R.: Language containment using non-deterministic omega-automata. In: proceedings of CHARME. LNCS, vol. 987, pp. 261–277. springer (1995)

34. Vardi, M.Y.: Verification of concurrent programs: The automata-theoretic framework. In: proceedings of LICS. pp. 167–176 (1987)

35. Vardi, M.Y.: An automata-theoretic approach to linear temporal logic. In: Moller, F., Birtwistle, G. (eds.) Logics for Concurrency: Structure versus Automata. LNCS, vol. 1043, pp. 238–266 (1996)

36. Wang, Y., Ye, Q., Liu, T.: Beyond exponentially discounted sum: Automatic learning of return function. CoRR (2019), http://arxiv.org/abs/1905.11591

37. Zwick, U., Paterson, M.: The complexity of mean payoff games on graphs. Theor. Comput. Sci. **158**, 343–359 (1996). https://doi.org/10.1016/0304-3975(95)00188-3

Fast Matching of Regular Patterns
with Synchronizing Counting

Lukáš Holík[ID], Juraj Síč[✉][ID], Lenka Turoňová[ID], and Tomáš Vojnar[ID]

Brno University of Technology, Brno, Czech Republic
{holik,sicjuraj,ituronova,vojnar}@fit.vut.cz

Abstract. Fast matching of regular expressions with *bounded repetition*, aka *counting*, such as (ab){50,100}, i.e., matching linear in the length of the text and independent of the repetition bounds, has been an open problem for at least two decades. We show that, for a wide class of regular expressions with counting, which we call *synchronizing*, fast matching is possible. We empirically show that the class covers nearly all counting used in usual applications of regex matching. This complexity result is based on an improvement and analysis of a recent matching algorithm that compiles regexes to deterministic counting-set automata (automata with registers that hold sets of numbers).

1   Introduction

Fast matching of regular expressions with *bounded repetition*, aka *counting*, has been an open problem for at least two decades (cf., e.g., [33]). The time complexity of the standard matching algorithms run on a regex such as .*a.{100} is, at best, dominated by the *length of the text multiplied by the repetition bounds*. This makes matching prone to unacceptable slowdowns since the length of the text as well as the repetition bounds are often large. In this paper, we provide a theoretical basis for matching of bounded repetition with a much more reliable performance. We show that a large and practical class of regexes with counting theoretically allows **fast matching**—in time **independent of the counter bounds** and **linear in the length of the text**.

The problem also has a strong practical motivation. Regex matching is used for searching, data validation, detection of information leakage, parsing, replacing, data scraping, syntax highlighting, etc. It is natively supported in most programming languages [6], and ubiquitous (used in 30–40 % of Java, JavaScript, and Python software [7,39,8,5]). Efficiency and predictability of regex matching is important. An extreme run-time of matching can have serious consequences, such as a failed input validation against injection attacks [41] and events like the outage of Cloudflare services [18]. Regexes vulnerabilities are also a doorway for the *ReDoS (regular expression denial of service) attack*, in which the attacker crafts a text to overwhelm a matcher (as, e.g., in the case of the outage of StackOverflow [13] or the websites exposed due to their use of the popular Express.js framework [3]). ReDoS has been widely recognized as a common and serious threat [7,9,11], with counting in regexes begin especially dangerous [37].

© The Author(s) 2023
O. Kupferman and P. Sobocinski (Eds.): FoSSaCS 2023, LNCS 13992, pp. 392–412, 2023.
https://doi.org/10.1007/978-3-031-30829-1_19

Matching algorithms and complexity. The potential instability of the pattern matchers is in line with the worst-case complexity of the matching algorithms. The most widely used approach to matching is backtracking (used, e.g., in standard matchers of .NET, Python, Perl, PHP, Java, JavaScript, Ruby) for its simplicity and ease of implementation of advanced features such as back-references or look-arounds. It is, however, at worst exponential to the length of the matched text and prone to ReDoS. Even though this can be improved, for instance by memoization [11], the fastest matchers used in performance critical applications all use automata-based algorithms instead of backtracking. The basis of these approaches is Thompson's algorithm [35] (also referred to as *online NFA-simulation*). Together with many optimizations, it is implemented in Intel's Hyperscan [40]. When combined with caching, it becomes the on-the-fly subset construction of a DFA, also called *online DFA-simulation* (implemented in RE2 from Google, GNU grep, SRM, or the standard matcher of Rust [17,19,30,12]). Without counting, the major factor in the worst-case complexity is $O(nm^2)$, with n being the length of the text and m the size of the number of character occurrences in the regex (m is smaller than size of the regex, the length of string defining it). We say that the *character cost*, i.e., the cost of extending the text with one character, is m^2. This is the cost of iterating through transitions of an NFA with $O(m)$ states and $O(m^2)$ transitions compiled from the regex by some classical construction [2,16,24].

Extending the syntax of regexes with *bounded quantifiers* (or *counters*), such as (ab)$\{50,100\}$, increases the character complexity dramatically. Given k counters with the maximum bound ℓ, the number of NFA states rises to $O(m\ell^k)$, the number of transitions as well as the character cost to $O((m\ell^k)^2)$. For instance, the minimal DFA for .*a.$\{k\}$ (i.e., a appears k characters from the end) has more than 2^k states. Moreover, note that, since k is written as a decadic numeral, its value is exponential in the size of the regex. This makes matching with already moderately high k prone to significant slowdowns and ReDoS vulnerabilities with virtually every mainstream matcher (see [36,37]). At the same time, repetition bounds easily reach thousands, in extreme tens of millions (in real-life XML [4]). Writing a dangerous counting expression is easy and it is hard to identify. Security-critical solutions may be vulnerable to counting-related ReDoS [37] despite an extra effort spent in regex design and testing, hence developers sometimes avoid counting, use workarounds and restrict functionality.

The problem of matching with bounded repetition has been addressed from the theoretical as well as from the practical perspective by a number of authors [15,4,22,26,31,20,25,36]. From these, the recent work [36] is the only one offering fast matching for a practically significant class of regexes. The algorithm of [36] compiles a regex with counting to a non-deterministic *counting automaton (CA)*, an automaton with counters that can be incremented, reset, and compared with a constant. The crux of the problem is then to convert the CA to a succinct deterministic machine that could be simulated fast in matching. The work [36] achieves this by determinizing the CA into a *counting-set automaton (CSA)*, an automaton with registers that hold *sets* of numbers. Its size is independent of the counter bounds and it updates the sets by a handful of operations that are all constant time, regardless the size of the sets. However, regexes outside the supported class do appear, the class has no syntactic characterization, and it is hard to recognize (as demonstrated also by an incorrect proposal of a syntactic class in [36] itself). For instance, `.*a{5}` or `(ab){5}` are handled, but `.*(aa){5}` or `.*(ab){5}` are not (the requirement is technical, see Section 4).

Our contribution. In this paper, we

1. **generalize the algorithm of [36] to extend the class of handled regexes and**
2. **derive a useful syntactic characterization of the extended class.**

The derived class is characterized by *flat counting* (counting operators are not nested) where repetitions of each counted expression R are *synchronizing* (a word from R^n cannot have a prefix from R^{n+1}). It is the first clearly delimited practical class of regexes with counting that allows fast matching. It includes the easily recognizable and frequent case where every word in R has exactly one occurrence of a *marker*, a letter or a word from a finite set of markers that unambiguously identifies each occurrence of R (note that even this simple class was not handled by any previous fast algorithms, including [36]). In a our experiment with a large set of regexes from various sources, 99.6 % of non-trivial flat counting was synchronizing and 99.2 % was letter-marked.

To obtain the results (1) and (2) above, **we first modify the determinization of [36] to include the entire class of regexes with flat counting**. In a nutshell, this is achieved by two changes: (i) We allow copying and uniting of sets stored in registers, and (ii) in the determinization, we index counters of the CA by its states to handle CA in which nondeterministic runs that reach different states reach different counter values.

These modifications come with the main technical challenge that we solve in this paper: copying and uniting sets is not constant-time but linear to the size of the sets. This would make the character cost linear in the counter bound ℓ again. To remove the dependency on the counter bounds, we augment the determinization by optimizations that avoid the copying and uniting. First, to alleviate the cost of uniting, we store intersections of sets stored in registers in new shared registers, so that the intersection does not contribute to the cost of uniting the registers. Then, to increase the impact of intersection sharing, we synchronize register updates in order to make their intersections larger. We then show that if the CSA *does not replicate registers*, i.e, each register can in a transition appear on the right-hand side of only one register assignment, then it never copies registers and the cost of unions can be amortised. Finally, **we define the class of regexes with *synchronizing counting* for which the optimized CsA do not replicate counters so their simulation in matching is fast.**

Related work. In the context of regex matching, counting automata were used in several forms under several names (e.g. [20,36,4,15,31,32,33,14,23]). Besides [36] discussed above, other solutions to matching of counting regexes [15,4,22,26,31,20,25] handle small classes of regexes or do not allow matching linear in the text size and independent of counter bounds. The work [20] proposes a CA-to-CA determinization producing smaller automata than the explicit CA determinization for the limited class of monadic regexes, covered by letter-marked counting, and the size of their deterministic automata is still dependent on the counter bounds. The work [4] uses a notion of automata with counters of [15]. It focuses mostly on deterministic regexes, a class much smaller than regexes with synchronizing counting, and proposes a matching algorithm still dependent on the counter bounds. The paper [25] proposes an algorithm that takes time at worst quadratic to the length of the text. Extended FA (XFA) of [31,32] augment NFA with a scratch memory of bits that can represent counters, and their determinization is exponential in counter bounds already for regexes such as `.*a.{k}`. The *counter-1-unambiguous* regexes of [22,23] can be directly compiled into deterministic automata called FACs, similar to our CA, independent of counter bounds, but the class is limited, excluding e.g., `.*a.{k}`.

2 Preliminaries

We use $\mathbb{N}$ to denote the natural numbers including 0. For a set S, $\mathcal{P}(S)$ denotes its powerset and $\mathcal{P}_{\text{fin}}(S)$ is the set of all *finite* subsets of S.

A *first order language (f.o.l.)* $\Gamma = (F,P)$ consists of a set of *function symbols* F and a set of *predicate symbols* P. An *interpretation* $\mathbb{I}$ of Γ with a *domain* $D_{\mathbb{I}}$ assigns a function $f^{\mathbb{I}} : D_{\mathbb{I}}^n \to D_{\mathbb{I}}$ to each n-ary $f \in F$ and a function $p^{\mathbb{I}} : D_{\mathbb{I}}^n \to \{0,1\}$ to each n-ary $p \in P$. An *assignment* of a set of variables X in $\mathbb{I}$ is a total function $v : X \to D_{\mathbb{I}}$. The set of *terms* $\mathsf{Terms}_{\Gamma,X}$ and the set $\mathsf{QFF}_{\Gamma,X}$ of *quantifier free formulae* (boolean combinations of atomic formulae) over Γ and X, as well as the interpretation of a term, $t^{\mathbb{I}}(v)$, and a formula, $\varphi^{\mathbb{I}}(v)$, are defined as usual. We denote by $v \models_{\mathbb{I}} \varphi$ that the formula φ is *satisfied* (interpreted as true) by the assignment v. It is then *satisfiable*. We drop the sub/superscript $\mathbb{I}$ when it is clear from the context. We write $\varphi[x]$ and $t[x]$ to denote a unary formula φ or term t, respectively, with the free variable x, and we may also abuse this notation to denote the term/formula with its only free variable replaced by x. We write $t^{\mathbb{I}}(k)$ and $\varphi^{\mathbb{I}}(k)$ to denote the values $t^{\mathbb{I}}(\{x \mapsto k\})$ and $\varphi^{\mathbb{I}}(\{x \mapsto k\})$. For a set of formulae $\Psi = \{\psi_1, \ldots, \psi_n\}$, the set $\mathit{Minterms}(\Psi)$ consists of all *minterms* of Ψ, satisfiable conjunctions $\varphi_1 \wedge \cdots \wedge \varphi_n$ where for each $i : 1 \le i \le n$, φ_i is ψ_i or $\neg\psi_i$.

We fix a finite *alphabet* Σ of *symbols/letters* for the rest of the paper. Words are sequences of letters, with the *empty word* ε. The *concatenation* of words u and v is denoted $u \cdot v$, uv for short. A set of words over Σ is a *language*, the concatenation of languages is $L \cdot L' = \{u \cdot v \mid u \in L \wedge v \in L'\}$, LL' for short. *Bounded iteration* x^i, $i \in \mathbb{N}$, of a word or a language x is defined by $x^0 = \varepsilon$ for a word, $x^0 = \{\varepsilon\}$ for a language, and $x^{i+1} = x^i \cdot x$. Then $x^* = \bigcup_{i \in \mathbb{N}} x^i$. We consider a usual basic syntax of *regular expressions (regexes)*, generated by the grammar $R ::= \varepsilon \mid \mathsf{a} \mid (R) \mid RR \mid R|R \mid R* \mid R\{m,n\}$ where $m \in \mathbb{N}$, $n \in \mathbb{N} \cup \infty$, $0 \le m$, $0 < n$, $m \le n$, and $\mathsf{a} \in \Sigma$. We use $R\{m\}$ for $R\{m,m\}$. Regexes containing a sub-expression with the *counter* $R\{m,n\}$ or $R\{m\}$ are called *counting regexes* and m,n are *counter bounds*. We denote by $\max_R$ the maximum integer occurring in the counter bounds of regex R and we denote the number of counters by cnt_R. A regex with *flat counting* does not have nested counting, that is, in a sub-regex $S\{m,n\}$, S cannot contain counting. The *language* of a regex R is constructed inductively to the structure: $L(\varepsilon) = \{\varepsilon\}$, $L(\mathsf{a}) = \{a\}$ for $a \in \Sigma$, $L(RR') = L(R) \cdot L(R')$, $L(R*) = L(R)^*$, $L(R|R') = L(R) \cup L(R')$, and $L(R\{m,n\}) = \bigcup_{m \le i \le n} L(R)^i$. We understand $|R|$ simply as the length of the defining string, e.g. $|(\mathsf{ab})\{10\}| = 8$. We define $\sharp R$ as the number of character occurrences in R, formally, $\sharp a = 1$ for $a \in \Sigma$, $\sharp \varepsilon = 0$, $\sharp(R) = \sharp R\{m,n\} = \sharp R$, and $\sharp R \cdot S = \sharp R \mid S = \sharp R + \sharp S$.

A *(nondeterministic) automaton (NA)* is a tuple $A = (Q, \Delta, I, F)$ where Q is a set of *states*, Δ is a set of *transitions* of the form $q \text{-}\{a\}\text{→} r$ with $q, r \in Q$ and $a \in \Sigma$, $I \subseteq Q$ is the set of *initial states*, and $F \subseteq Q$ is the set of *final states*. A run of A over a word $w = a_1 \ldots a_n$ from state p_0 to p_n, $n \geq 0$ is a sequence of transitions $p_0 \text{-}\{a_1\} \mapsto p_1$, $p_1 \text{-}\{a_2\} \mapsto p_2$, $\ldots$, $p_{n-1} \text{-}\{a_n\} \mapsto p_n$ from Δ. The empty sequence is a run with $p_0 = p_n$ over ε. The run is *accepting* if $p_0 \in I$ and $p_n \in F$, and the language $L(A)$ of A is the set of all words for which A has an accepting run. A state q is *reachable* if there is a run from I to it. The *size* of the NA, $|A|$, is defined as the number of its states plus the number of its transitions. The automaton is *deterministic (DA)* iff $|I| = 1$ and for every state q and symbol a, Δ has at most one transition $q \text{-}\{a\} \mapsto r$. The *subset construction* transforms the NA to the DA with the same language $\mathrm{DA}(A) = (Q^\circ, \Delta^\circ, I^\circ, F^\circ)$ where $Q^\circ \subseteq \mathcal{P}(Q)$ and Δ° are the smallest sets of states and transitions satisfying $I^\circ = \{I\}$, Δ° has for each $a \in \Sigma$ and each $S \in Q^\circ$ the transition $S \text{-}\{a\} \mapsto \{s' \mid s \in S \land s \text{-}\{a\} \mapsto s' \in \Delta\}$, and $F^\circ = \{S \in Q^\circ \mid S \cap F \neq \emptyset\}$. When the set of states Q is finite, we talk about (deterministic) *finite state* automata (NFA, DFA).[1]

This paper is concerned with the problem of fast *pattern matching*, basically a membership test: given a regex R and a text w, decide whether $w \in L(R)$. While w may be very long, R is normally small, hence the dependence on $|w|$ is the major factor in the complexity. The offline DFA simulation takes time linear in $|w|$. It (1) compiles R into an NFA $\mathrm{NFA}(R)$ (2) determinizes it, and (3) follows the DFA run over w (aka *simulates* the DFA on w), all in time and space $\Theta(2^{|\mathrm{NFA}(R)|} + |w|)$. The cost of determinization, exponential in $|\mathrm{NFA}(R)|$, is however too impractical. Modern matchers such as Grep or RE2 [19,17] therefore use the techniques of online DFA simulation, where only the part of the DFA used for processing w is constructed. It reduces the complexity to $O(\min(2^{|\mathrm{NFA}(R)|} + |w|, |w| \cdot |\mathrm{NFA}(R)|))$ (the first operand of min is the explicit determinization in case the entire DFA is constructed, plus the cost of DFA-simulation; the second operand is the cost of the online-DFA simulation, coming from that every step may incur construction of a new DFA state and transition in time $O(|\mathrm{NFA}(R)|)$). For counting regexes, the factor $|\mathrm{NFA}(R)|$ depends linearly (or more if counting is nested) on $\max_R$ and thus exponentially on $|R|$. This makes counting very problematic in practice [36,37,33]. We will present a matching algorithm which is *fast* for a specific class of regexes, meaning that its run-time is still linear in $|w|$ but is independent of $\max_R$.

3   Counting Automata

We use a rephrased definition of counting automata and counting-set automata of [36]. We will present them as a special case of a generic notion of automata with registers.

Definition 1 (Automata with registers). *An* automaton with registers *(RA) operated through an f.o.l.* Γ *under an interpretation* $\mathbb{I}$ *is a tuple* $A = (X, Q, \Delta, I, F)$ *where X is a set of variables called* registers; *Q is a finite set of* states; *Δ is a finite set of* transitions *of the form* $q \text{-}\{a, \varphi, u\} \mapsto p$ *where* $p, q \in Q$, $a \in \Sigma$, $u : X \to \mathrm{Terms}_{\Gamma, X}$ *is an* update, *and* $\varphi \in \mathrm{QFF}_{\Gamma, X}$ *is a* guard; *I is a set of* initial configurations, *where a* configuration *is a pair of the form* $(q, \mathfrak{m})$ *where* $q \in Q$ *and* $\mathfrak{m} : X \to D_{\mathbb{I}}$ *is a register assignment called a* memory; *and* $F : Q \to \mathrm{QFF}_{\Gamma, X}$ *is a* final condition assignment.

---

[1] We do not require finiteness in the basic definition in order to avoid artificial restrictions of the notions of automata with registers/counters/counting sets defined later.

The language of A, L(A), is defined as the language of its configuration automaton $\mathtt{Conf}(A)$. *States of* $\mathtt{Conf}(A)$ *are* configurations *of A that are reachable. I is the set of initial states of* $\mathtt{Conf}(A)$. *It has a transition* $(q,\mathfrak{m})\text{-}\{a\}\!\!\rightarrow(q',\mathfrak{m}')$ *iff* $(q,\mathfrak{m})$ *is reachable and A has a transition* $\delta = q\text{-}\{a,\phi,u\}\!\!\rightarrow q' \in \Delta$ *such that* $(q',\mathfrak{m}')$ *is the image of* $(q,\mathfrak{m})$ *under* δ, *denoted* $(q',\mathfrak{m}') = \delta(q,\mathfrak{m})$, *meaning that (1)* δ *is enabled in* $(q,\mathfrak{m})$, $\mathfrak{m} \models \phi$, *and (2)* $\mathfrak{m}' = u(\mathfrak{m})$, *i.e.* $\mathfrak{m}'(x) = u(x)^{\mathbb{I}}(\mathfrak{m})$ *for each* $x \in X$. *We let* $\delta(C) = \{\delta(c) \mid c \in C\}$ *for a set of configurations C. A configuration* $(q,\mathfrak{m})$ *is a final if* $\mathfrak{m} \models F(q)$. *By* runs of A *we mean runs of* $\mathtt{Conf}(A)$. *The RA A is* deterministic *if* $\mathtt{Conf}(A)$ *is deterministic. The* size *of the RA is* $|A| = |Q| + \sum_{\delta \in \Delta} |\delta|$ *where* $|\delta|$ *is the sum of the sizes of the update and the guard.*

Definition 2 (Counting automata). *A* counting automaton *(CA) is an automaton with* registers, *called* counters, *operated through the* counting language Γ_{cnt} *that contains the unary increment function, denoted* $x+1$, *constants 0 and 1, and predicates* $x > k$ *and* $x \leq k$, $k \in \mathbb{N}$, *with the standard interpretation over natural numbers, that we denote* $\mathbb{I}_{\text{cnt}}$.

Regexes with counting may be translated to CA by several methods ([36,33,14,23]). We use a slightly adapted version of [14]—an extension of Glushkov's algorithm [16] to counting. For a regex R, it produces a CA $\mathtt{CA}(R) = (X,Q,\Delta,\{\alpha_0\},F)$. Figure 1 shows an example of such CA. The construction is discussed in detail in [21], here we only overview the important properties needed in Sections 4-6:

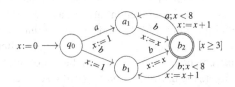

Fig. 1: $\mathtt{CA}(R)$ for $R = ((a\,|\,b)\,b)\,\{3,8\}$. The accepting condition of all states is $\perp$ except for b_2 whose accepting condition is written in the square brackets.

1. Every occurrence S of a counted sub-expression $T\{\min_S, \max_S\}$ of R corresponds to a unique counter x_S and a substructure A_S of $\mathtt{CA}(R)$. Outside A_S, x_S is inactive (a dead variable) and its value is 0, it is assigned 1 on entering A_S, and every iteration through A_S increments the value of x_S while reading a word from $L(T)$. Our minor modification of [14] is related to the fact that the original assigns 1 to inactive counters while we need 0.
2. $\mathtt{CA}(R)$ has at most $\sharp R + 1$ states, $cnt_R.\sharp R^2$ transitions, cnt_R counters. It has at most $\sharp R^2$ transitions if R is flat.
3. $\mathtt{CA}(R)$ has a single initial configuration $\alpha_0 = (q_0, \mathfrak{s}_0)$ s.t. $\mathfrak{s}_0(x_S) = 0$ for each $x_S \in X$.
4. Guards and final conditions are conjunctions consisting of at most one conjunct of the form $\min_S \leq x_S$ or $\max_S > x_S$ per counter $x_S \in X$. A transition update may assign to $x_S \in X$ only one of the terms $0, 1, x_S$, and $x_S + 1$. It has no guard on x_S if it is assigned x_S, i.e. kept unchanged, it has the guard $x_S \geq \min_S$ iff x_S is reset to 0 or 1 (a counter cannot be reset before reaching its lower bound), and it has the guard $x_S < \max_S$ iff x_S is assigned $x_S + 1$ (counter can never exceed its maximum value $\max_S$). Hence, a counter can never exceed $\max_R$.
5. Flatness of R translates to the fact that configurations of $\mathtt{CA}(R)$ assign a non-zero value to at most one counter. This implies that $\mathtt{Conf}(\mathtt{CA}(R))$ has at most $|Q|.\max_R$ states and also that $\mathtt{CA}(R)$ is *Cartesian*, a property that will be defined in Section 4 and is crucial for correctness of our CA determinization (Theorem 3 in Section 6.)

A DFA can be obtained by the subset construction in the form $\mathrm{DA}(\mathrm{Conf}(\mathrm{CA}(R)))$, called *explicit determinization*. Due to the factor $\max_R$ in the size of $\mathrm{Conf}(\mathrm{CA}(R))$, the explicit determinization is exponential to $\max_R$ even if R is flat, meaning doubly exponential to $|R|$ (R has $\max_R$ written as a decadic numeral). If R is not flat, then the factor $\max_R$ is replaced by $(\max_R)^{cnt_R}$.

4   Counter-subset Construction

In this section, we formulate a modified version of determinization of CA from [36] that constructs a machine of a size independent of $\max_R$. Our version handles the entire class of Cartesian CA (defined below) and in turn also all regexes with flat counting.

The main idea of the determinization remains the same as in [36]. The standard subset construction is augmented with registers, we call them *counting sets*, that can store sets of counter values that would be generated by non-deterministic runs of the CA. The automata with counting-sets as registers are called *counting-set automata*. Our first modification of [36] is indexing of counters by states. In intuitively, this allows to handle cases such as $\mathrm{a}*(\mathrm{ba}\,|\,\mathrm{ab})\{5\}$, where, after reading the first ab, the counter is either incremented or not (b is the first letter of the counted sub-expression or not). This would violate the uniformity property of CA necessary in [36]—the set of values generated by the non-deterministic CA runs must be the same for every CA state. In our modified version, values at distinct states are stored separately in registers indexed by those states and may differ. Then, in order to handle the indexed counters, we have to introduce a general assignment of counters, allowing to assign the *union* of other counters.[2] Intuitively, when a run non-deterministically branches into several states, each branch needs to continue with its *own copy* of the set, stored in a counter indexed by the state. The union of sets is used when the branches join again. This brings a technical challenge that we solve in this work: how to simulate the counting-set automata fast when the set union and copy are used? The solution is presented in Sections 5 and 6.

Definition 3 (Counting-set automata). *A counting-set automaton (CSA) is an automaton with registers operated through the* counting-set language Γ_{set} *under the number-set interpretation* $\mathbb{I}_{\mathrm{cnt}}^{\emptyset}$ *where the language* Γ_{set} *extends the counting language* Γ_{cnt} *with the constant* $\emptyset$, *binary union* $\cup$, *and set-filter functions* ∇_p *where p is a predicate symbol of* Γ_{cnt}. *For simplicity, we restrict terms assigned to counters by transition updates to the form* $t = t_1 \cup \cdots \cup t_n$ *where each t_i is either (a) a term of* Γ_{cnt} *or* $\emptyset$, *(b) of the form* $\nabla_{p(t')}$ *where t' is a term of* Γ_{cnt}. *Each t_i is called an r-term of t.*

The domain of $\mathbb{I}_{\mathrm{set}}$ *is sets of natural numbers,* $\mathcal{P}(\mathbb{N})$. *The interpretation of the predicates and functions of* Γ_{cnt} *under* $\mathbb{I}_{\mathrm{set}}$ *is derived from the base number interpretation of the same predicates and functions: A function returns the image of the set in the argument under the base semantics,* $f^{\mathbb{I}_{\mathrm{set}}}(S) = \{f^{\mathbb{I}_{\mathrm{cnt}}}(n) \mid n \in S\}$. *A set satisfies a predicate if some of its elements satisfy the base semantics of that predicate,* $p^{\mathbb{I}_{\mathrm{set}}}(S) \iff \exists e \in S : p^{\mathbb{I}_{\mathrm{cnt}}}(e)$. *Filters then filter out values that do not satisfy the base semantics of their predicate,* $\nabla_p^{\mathbb{I}_{\mathrm{set}}}(S) = \{e \in S \mid p^{\mathbb{I}_{\mathrm{cnt}}}(e)\}$. *Finally,* $\emptyset$ *is interpreted as*

---

[2] [36] could assign to a counter x only a constant or function of the current value of x.

the empty set and $\cup$ as the union of sets. We denote memories of the CSA by $\mathfrak{s}$ to distinguish them from memories of CA. We write DCSA to abbreviate deterministic CSA.

Less formally, registers of CSA hold sets of numbers and are manipulated by the increment $x + 1$ of all values, assignment of constant sets $\{0\}$, $\{1\}$, and $\emptyset$, denoted by 0, 1, and $\emptyset$, filtering out values smaller or larger than a constant, denoted $\nabla_{x \leq k}(x)$ and $\nabla_{x < k}(x)$, and testing on a presence of a value x satisfying $x \leq k$ or $x < k$, $k \in \mathbb{N}$.

We will present an algorithm that determinizes a CA $A = (X, Q, \Delta, I, F)$, fixed for the rest of the section, into a DCSA $\text{DCSA}(A) = (X^{\circ}, Q^{\circ}, \Delta^{\circ}, I^{\circ}, F^{\circ})$. We assume that guards of transitions in Δ and final conditions are of the form $\bigwedge_{x \in Y} p_x[x], Y \subseteq X$, i.e. conjunctions with a at most a single atomic predicate per counter. This is satisfied by all $\text{CA}(R)$, for any regex R (see the list of properties of $\text{CA}(R)$ in Section 3).[3]

Runs of $\text{DCSA}(A)$ will *encode* runs of $\text{DA}(\text{Conf}(A))$ obtained from the explicit determinization of A. Recall that the states $\text{DA}(\text{Conf}(A))$ are sets of configurations of A, pairs $(q, \mathfrak{m})$ of a state and a counter assignment. $\text{DCSA}(A)$ will represent the sets of counter values within a DA state as run-time values of its registers.

Particularly, for every state q and a counter x of the CA, $\text{DCSA}(A)$ has a register x_q in which it remembers, after reading a word w, the set of all values that x reaches in runs of the base CA on w ending in q. Hence, we have $X^{\circ} = \{x_q \mid x \in X \wedge q \in Q\}$

Definition 4 (Encoding of sets of CA configurations). *A state* $S = \{(q_i, \mathfrak{m}_i)\}_{i=1}^{n}$ *of* $\text{DA}(\text{Conf}(A))$ *is encoded as the* $\text{DCSA}(A)$ *configuration* $enc(S) = (\{q_i\}_{i=1}^{n}, \mathfrak{s})$ *where* $\mathfrak{s}(x_q) = \{\mathfrak{m}_i(x) \mid q_i = q\}_{i=1}^{n}$.

Since a set of assignments appearing with the state q is broken down to sets of values of the individual counters, it disregards relations between values of different counters. For instance, in the DA state $S_1 = \{(q, \{x \mapsto 0, y \mapsto 0\}), (q, \{x \mapsto 1, y \mapsto 1\})\}$, the values of x and y are either both 0 or both 1, but $enc(S_1) = (q, \{x_q \mapsto \{0, 1\}, y_q \mapsto \{0, 1\}\})$ does not retain this information. It is identical to the encoding of another DA state $S_2 = \{(q, \{x \mapsto 1, y \mapsto 0\}), (q, \{x \mapsto 0, y \mapsto 1\})\}$. This is the same loss of information as in the so-called Cartesian abstraction. The encoding is hence precise and unambiguous only when we assume that inside the states of $\text{DA}(A)$, the relations between counters are always unrestricted—there is no information to be lost. We then call the CA *Cartesian*, as defined below. The encoding function is then unambiguous, and we call the inverse function *decoding*, denoted *dec*.

Definition 5 (Cartesian CA). *Assuming the set of counters of A is* $X = \{x_i\}_{i=1}^{m}$, *then a set C of configurations of A is Cartesian iff, for every state q of A, there exist sets* $N_1, \ldots, N_m \subseteq \mathbb{N}$ *such that* $(q, \{x_i \mapsto n_i\}_{i=1}^{m}) \in C$ *iff* $(n_1, \ldots, n_m) \in N_1 \times \cdots \times N_m$. *The CA A is Cartesian iff all states of* $\text{DA}(\text{Conf}(A))$ *are Cartesian.*

For instance, the DA states S_1 and S_2 above are not Cartesian, while $S_1 \cup S_2$ is.

Similarly as the regex to CA construction of [36], our regex to CA construction discussed in Section 3 returns a Cartesian CA when called on a flat regex.

---

[3] Every CA can be transformed to this form by transforming the formulae to DNF and creating clones of transitions/states for individual clauses.

Subset construction for Cartesian CA. The algorithm below is a generalization of the subset construction. Let us denote by $\text{index}_q(t)$ the term that arises from t by replacing every variable $x \in X$ by x_q, analogously $\text{index}_q(\varphi)$ for formulas. We have $Q^\circ \subseteq \mathcal{P}(Q)$, the initial configuration $I^\circ = \{enc(I)\}$, and the final conditions assign to $R \in Q^\circ$ the disjunction of the final conditions of its elements, $F^\circ(R) = \bigvee_{q \in R} \text{index}_q(F(q))$.

We will construct $\text{DCSA}(A)$ which is deterministic and its runs encode the runs of DA $\text{DA}(\text{Conf}(A))$. $\text{Conf}(\text{DCSA}(A))$ will be isomorphic to $\text{DA}(\text{Conf}(A))$. For that, we need for each transition δ of $\text{DA}(\text{Conf}(A))$ one unique transition of $\text{DCSA}(A)$ over the same letter enabled in the encoding of the source of δ and generating the encoding of the target of δ. In other words, we need for each transition $dec(R,\mathfrak{s})\text{-}\{a\}\text{-}dec(R',\mathfrak{s}')$ of $\text{DA}(\text{Conf}(A))$ one unique transition $\delta' = R\text{-}\{a,\varphi,u\}\text{-}R' \in \Delta^\circ$ with $(R',\mathfrak{s}') = \delta'(R,\mathfrak{s})$. That transition δ' will be built by summarizing the effect of all base CA a-transitions enabled in the CA configurations of $dec(R,\mathfrak{s})$.

To construct the transition δ', we first translate each base transition $\delta = q\text{-}\{a,\varphi_\delta,u_\delta\}\text{-}r \in \Delta$ into its set-version δ°, supposed to transform an encoding of a (Cartesian) set C of configurations, $enc(C)$, into the encoding of the set of their images under δ, $enc(\delta(C))$, and enabled if δ is enabled for at least one configuration in C. To that end, assuming $\varphi_\delta = \bigwedge_{x \in X} p_x[x]$, we (1) construct the update u_δ^∇ from u_δ by substituting in every $u_\delta(x), x \in X$ variables $y \in X$ by their filtered versions $\nabla_{p_y}(y)$, (2) add indices to registers that mark the current state, resulting in the transition $\delta^\circ = q\text{-}\{a,\varphi_\delta^\circ,u_\delta^\circ\}\text{-}r$ where $\varphi_\delta^\circ = \text{index}_q(\varphi_\delta)$ and u_δ° assigns to every $x_r, x \in X$ the term $\text{index}_q(u_\delta^\nabla(x))$.

The states Q° and the transitions Δ° are then constructed as the smallest sets satisfying that $enc(I) \in Q^\circ$ and every $R \in Q^\circ$ has for every $a \in \Sigma$ the outgoing transitions constructed as follows. Let $\{q_j\text{-}\{a,\varphi_j,u_j\}\text{-}r_j\}_{j \in J}$ for some index set J be the set of *constituent a-transitions* for R, all a-transitions δ° where $\delta \in \Delta$ originates in R. To achieve determinism, Δ° has the transition $R\text{-}\{a,\psi,u\}\text{-}R'$ for every minterm $\psi \in \text{Minterms}(\{\varphi_j\}_{j \in J})$. The update u and target R' are constructed from the set $\{q_j\text{-}\{a,\varphi_j,u_j\}\text{-}r_j\}_{j \in K}, K \subseteq J$, of constituent transitions with guards φ_j compatible with the minterm ψ, i.e., with satisfiable $\psi \wedge \varphi_j$. R' is the set of their target states, $R' = \{r_j\}_{j \in K}$, and $u(x)$ unites all their update terms $u_j(x)$, i.e. $u(x) = \bigcup_{j \in K} u_j(x)$, for each $x \in X^\circ$.

Example 1. When showing examples of transition updates, we write $x := t$ to denote that $u(x) = t$ and we omit the assignments $x := \emptyset$ in CSA.

Let $R = \{p,q\}$ and let the a-transitions originating at R be $q\text{-}\{a,\top,x:=x\}\text{-}s$, $p\text{-}\{a,x<n,x:=x+1\}\text{-}r$, and $p\text{-}\{a,x\geq m,x:=1\}\text{-}s$. They induce three constituent transitions for R and a, $q\text{-}\{a,\top,x_s:=x_q\}\text{-}s$, $p\text{-}\{a,x_p<n,x_r:=\nabla_{x<n}(x_p)+1\}\text{-}r$, and $p\text{-}\{a,x_p\geq m,x_s:=1\}\text{-}s$. A transition $R\text{-}\{a,\psi,u'\}\text{-}R'$ is constructed for each of the following minterms ψ: $x_p<n \wedge x_p\geq m$, $\neg x_p<n \wedge x_p\geq m$, $x_p<n \wedge \neg x_p\geq m$, $\neg x_p<n \wedge \neg x_p\geq m$. For the first one, all three constituent transitions are compatible and so the update u' is $x_r := \nabla_{x<n}(x_p)+1; x_s := x_q \cup 1$ (update of x_r is taken from the first constituent transitions leading to r, update of x_s is the union of the updates of the second two transitions leading to s) and the target state is $R' = \{r,s\}$.   □

$\text{DCSA}(A)$ is deterministic since it has a single initial configuration and the guards of transitions originating in the same state are minterms. The size of $\text{DCSA}(A)$ obviously depends only on the size of A and not on the interpretation of the language. Especially, when A is $\mathtt{CA}(R)$ for some regex R, the size does not depend on $\max_R$. The theorem below is proved in [21].[4]

Theorem 1. $\mathtt{DCSA}(A)$ *is deterministic,* $|\mathtt{DCSA}(A)| \in O(2^{|A|})$, *and if A is Cartesian, then* $L(A) = L(\mathtt{DCSA}(A))$.

Since for regexes with flat counting, our regex to CA algorithm always returns a Cartesian CA, we can transform them into DCSA.

5 Fast Simulation of Counting-set Automata

In this section, we discuss how a run of a DCSA on a given word can be *simulated* efficiently to achieve fast matching. Let us fix a word $w = a_1 \cdots a_n$ together with the DCSA $A = (X, Q, \Delta, \{\alpha_0\}, F)$. We wish to construct the run of the DCSA on w and test whether the reached configuration is accepting. We aim at a running time linear to $|w|$ and independent of the sizes of the sets stored in A's registers at run-time.

We will assume that the initial configuration α_0 of A assigns to every register a singleton or the empty set. The assumption is satisfied by CSA constructed from $\mathtt{CA}(R)$, R being any regex, by the algorithms of Section 4 and also Section 6.[5]

Technically, the simulation maintains a configuration $\alpha = (q, \mathfrak{s})$, initialized with α_0, and for every i from 1 to n, it constructs the transition $\alpha\text{-}\{a_i\}\!\mapsto\!\alpha'$ of $\mathtt{Conf}(A)$ and replaces α by the successor configuration $\alpha' = (q', \mathfrak{s}')$. We use the key ingredient of fast simulation from [36], the *offset-list data structure* for sets of numbers with constant time addition of 0/1, comparison of the maximum to a constant, reset, and increment of all values. The problem is that the newly added union and copy of sets are still linear to the size of the sets, and hence linear to the maximum counter bounds. We show how, under a condition introduced below, set copy can be avoided entirely and the cost of union can be amortized by the cost of incrementing the sets. This will again allow a CSA-simulation in time independent of $\max_A$ and falling into $O(|A| \cdot |w|)$.

First, we define a property of CSA sufficient for fast simulation—that the updates on its transitions do not *replicate counters*.

Definition 6 (Counter replication). *We say that a CSA replicates counters if for some transition* $q\text{-}\{a,\varphi,u\}\!\mapsto\!r$, *some counter appears in the image of u twice, that is, it appears in two r-terms of some $u(x)$ or it appears in $u(x)$ as well as in $u(y)$ for $x \neq y$. A non-replicating CSA does not replicate counters.*

For instance, $\{x \mapsto x; y \mapsto x+1\}$ and $\{x \mapsto x \cup x+1, y \mapsto y\}$ are updates where x is replicated, $\{x \mapsto x+1, y \mapsto y\}$ is not a replicating update.

---

[4] It may be interesting to note that, as follows from our formulation of the determinization, the construction is independent of the particular f.o.l. used to manipulate registers and of its interpretation. The determinization could be applied to any kind of automata that fits the definition of automata with registers. The numbers could be manipulated by other functions and tests, natural numbers could be replaced by reals etc. The counting-set automata are themselves an instance of automata with registers. One could also think about push-down automata or, with small modifications, variants of data-word automata with registers.

[5] This is a technical assumption important in order for unions of the initial sets not to influence the overall complexity of the simulation.

Offset-list data structure. The *offset-list* data structure of [36] allows constant time implementation of the set operations of increment of all elements, reset to $\emptyset$ or $\{0\}$ or $\{1\}$, addition of 0 or 1, and comparison of the maximum with a constant.

It assigns to every counter $x \in X$ a pointer $ol(x)$ to an *offset-list pair* (o_x, l_x) with the *offset* $o_x \in \mathbb{N}$ and a sorted list $l_x = m_1, \ldots, m_k$ of integers. The data structure implementing the list needs constant access to the first and the last element, forward and backward iteration of a pointer, and insertion/deletion at/before a pointer to an element. This is satisfied for instance by a doubly-linked list that maintains pointers to the first and the last element. The offset-list pair represents the set $s(x) = \{m_1 + o_x, \ldots, m_k + o_x\}$. Union of two such sets is still linear in their size, but we will show that if the CSA does not replicate counters, the cost of set unions can be amortized by the cost of increments.

Finding the CSA transition and evaluating the update. The first step of computing α' from α is finding the transition $q \text{-}\{a_i, \varphi, u\} \!\!\mapsto\! q' \in \Delta$, the only a_i-transition from q that is enabled, i.e. where $s \models \varphi$. The simplest algorithm iterates through the transitions of Δ and, for each of them, tests whether s satisfies its guard. The cost of evaluating an atomic counter predicate p, i.e., deciding whether $s \models p$, is constant: since the lists l_x are sorted, we only need to access the first or the last element and the offset to decide $x < n$ or $x \geq n$, respectively. With that, the cost of evaluating φ is linear to the size of φ. The cost of the iteration through the transitions of Δ is then linear in the sum of their sizes, which is within $O(|\Delta|)$.

Having found $q \text{-}\{a_i, \varphi, u\} \!\!\mapsto\! q'$, we evaluate its update to compute s' and compute α' as (q', s'). We will explain the algorithm and argue that the amortized cost of computing s' is in $O(|X|)$. The update is evaluated by, for each $x \in X$, evaluating all r-terms in $u(x)$, uniting the results, and assigning the union to $ol(x)$.

First, we argue that evaluating an r-term t of $u(x)$, i.e. computing $t(s)$, is amortized constant time. Since the counters are non-replicating, we can compute the value of each r-term $t[y]$ in situ. That is, we modify the offset-list pair (o_y, l_y) and return the pointer $ol(y)$. The original value of y can be discarded after evaluating $t[y]$ since y does not appear in any other r-term. There are 5 cases: (1) If t is 0 or 1, then we return a pointer to a fresh offset-list pair with the offset 0 and the list containing only 0 or 1, respectively. This is done in constant time.

(2) If t is $y \in Y$, then we return $ol(y)$.

(3) If t is $y + 1$, then o_y is incremented by one. This constant time implementation of the increment is the reason for pairing the lists with the offsets.

(4) If t is $\nabla_p[y]$, then l_y is filtered by the atomic predicate p. Filtering with the predicate $x \geq n$ uses the invariant of sortedness of l_y. It is done by iterating the following steps: i) test whether the list head is smaller than $n - o_y$ and ii) if yes, remove the head, if not, terminate the iteration. Every iteration is constant time: The cost of the iterations which remove an element is amortized by the cost of additions of the element to the list. What remains is only the constant cost of the last iteration which detects an element greater or equal to $n - o_y$, or that the list is empty. Filtering with $x < n$ is analogous (the iterations test and remove the last element instead of the head).

(5) If t is $\nabla_p(y) + 1$, then the construction for the constant increment is applied after the constant filter discussed above.

Next, we argue that computing the union of values of the r-terms in $u(x)$ may be amortized by the cost of evaluating the increment terms. Let $l_1,\ldots,l_n$ be the offset-list representations of the values of the terms in $u(x)$ computed by the algorithm above. The offset-list representation of their union is computed by a sequence of merging, as $merge(l_1, merge(l_2,\ldots merge(l_{n-1},l_n)\ldots))$. Particularly, given two pointers to offset-lists l,l', $merge(l,l')$ implements their union: it chooses the offset-list that represents a set with the larger maximum, assume that it is l, and inserts the elements represented by the other list, l', to it. We say that l' *is merged into* l. This is done by the standard sorted-list merging in time $O(|l'|)$ where $|l'|$ is the length of l'. Since l' is without duplicities and with minimum 0, $O(|l'|) \subseteq O(\max(l'))$ where $\max(l')$ is the maximal element.

The $O(\max(l'))$ cost is amortized by the cost of evaluating increments. The offset-list pair at l' has seen at least $\max(l') - 1$ increments since the only elements inserted into it are 0, 1, or, during merge, elements from other sets smaller than $\max(l')$. These increments of l' are the budget used to pay for the mergeing of l' into l. After the merge, the offset-list pair of l' is discarded (as the CSA is non-replicating, it is no longer needed) hence the budget is used only once. Last, the assignment of the union to c is done by a constant time assignment of a pointer to the offset-list returned by the merge.

Overall complexity of the simulation. Let us define the cost $cost(x)$ of manipulations with the counter $x \in X$ during one step of the simulation as the sum of the costs of: (1) evaluating all r-terms containing c, (2) merging their offset-list into other ones, (3) creating offset-lists for terms 0 or 1 in $u(x)$ and merging them into other offset-lists, (4) the assignment of the result of $u(x)$ to x. The cost of processing a single letter a_i is then the sum $\sum_{x \in X} cost(x)$ and $|w| \cdot \sum_{x \in X} cost(x)$ is the cost of the entire simulation. Since the CSA is non-replicating and evaluating a single r-term is amortized constant time, the cost of (1) is in amortized constant time. The cost of (2) is amortized by increments from step (1). The creation and insertion of singletons in (3), at most two in $u(x)$, is constant time. The pointer assignment in (4) is constant time. The $cost(x)$ is therefore amortized constant time, the amortized time of evaluating the update u is in $O(|X|)$, and the cost of the updates through the simulation is in $O(|X| \cdot |w|)$. The cost of choosing the transitions, by evaluating their guards, is in $O(|A| \cdot |w|)$ by the above analysis. Analogously, the cost of testing the accepting condition at the reached configuration is in $O(|A|)$.

Theorem 2. *If A is non-replicating, then its simulation on w takes $O(|A| \cdot |w|)$ time.*

6   Augmented Determinization

In this section, we augment the subset construction from Section 4 with optimizations that prevent counter replication and hence extend the class of regexes that can be matched fast by simulation of the CSA. It optimizations are tailored to CA with the special properties of $CA(R)$, for a regex R, listed in Section 3.

Intuition for the optimizations. The emergence of counter replication and means of its elimination in the augmented construction, by techniques of *counter sharing* and *increment postponing*, are illustrated on simplified fragments of CA in Figure 2.

Fig. 2: Sub-structures of CA that are sources of counter replication.

In a), $\mathrm{DCSA}(\mathrm{CA}(R))$ has transitions $\{q\}\text{-}\{a,x_r:=x_q+1,x_s:=x_q+1\}\mapsto\{r,s\}\text{-}\{b,x_q:=x_r\cup x_s\}\mapsto\{q\}$. The first transition replicates the entire content of the x_q, the second one unites the two sets. Both transitions are expensive. The can be optimized by detecting that the values of x_s and x_r are the same, being generated by *syntactically identical* updates, and storing the values in a *shared counter* $x_{\{s,r\}}$. This would result in transitions $\{q\}\text{-}\{a,x_{\{r,s\}}:=x_{\{q\}}+1\}\mapsto\{s,t\}\text{-}\{b,x_{\{q\}}:=x_{\{r,s\}}\}\mapsto\{q\}$, with the replication and union eliminated.

Figure b) then illustrates why a counter x_P, $P \subseteq Q$, represents the set of values shared between the original counters x_p, $p \in P$. That is, x_P does not always hold the entire sets stored in the counters $x_p, p \in P$. If their values are not the same, it stores only their intersection. The value of each x_p is then partitioned among several shared counters x_S with $p \in S$. In b), $\mathrm{DCSA}(\mathrm{CA}(R))$ has transitions $q\text{-}\{a,x_q:=x_q;x_r:=1\}\mapsto\{q,r\}\text{-}\{a,x_q:=x_q\cup x_r+1;x_r:=1\cup x_r+1\}\mapsto\{q,r\}$, replicating the counter x_r. Counter sharing would then generate transitions $q\text{-}\{a,x_{\{q\}}:=x_{\{q\}};x_{\{r\}}:=1\}\mapsto\{q,r\}\text{-}\{a,x_{\{q\}}:=x_{\{q\}};x_{\{r\}}:=1;x_{\{q,r\}}:=x_{\{r\}}+1\}\mapsto\{q,r\}$ with counters $x_{\{q\}}$, $x_{\{r\}}$ for the subsets exclusive to x_q and x_r, respectively, and $x_{\{q,r\}}$ for the intersection.

Last, in c), we illustrate the technique of *increment postponing*. $\mathrm{DCSA}(\mathrm{CA}(R))$ would have transitions $\{q\}\text{-}\{a,x_r:=x_q+1,x_s:=x_q\}\mapsto\{s,t\}\text{-}\{b,x_q:=x_r\cup x_s+1\}\mapsto\{q\}$. Since the increments on the two branches happen in different moments, the values of x_r and x_s differ until the last increment of x_s synchronizes them. We avoid replication by storing the non-incremented value, obtained from x_q, in a counter shared by x_r and x_s and remembering that an increment of x_r has been postponed. This is marked with $+$ in the name of the shared counter $x_{\{r^+,s\}}$. When the values of x_r and x_s synchronize (the increment is applied to x_s too), the postponed increment is evaluated and the $+$-mark is removed. We would create transitions $\{q\}\text{-}\{a,x_{\{r^+,s\}}:=x_{\{q\}}\}\mapsto\{s,t\}\text{-}\{b,x_{\{q\}}:=x_{\{r^+,s\}}+1\}\mapsto\{q\}$. If, before the synchronization, the value of the marked counter is either tested or incremented for the second time, we declare an *irresolvable replication* and abort the entire construction (we allow postponing of only one increment). To prevent this situation from arising needlessly, we let states remember the counters that must have the empty value and we ignore these counters.

Augmented Determinization Algorithm. The augmented determinization produces from $\mathrm{CA}(R) = (X,Q,\Delta,\{\alpha_0\},F)$ the CSA $\mathrm{DCSA}^{\mathrm{a}}(\mathrm{CA}(R)) = (X^{\mathrm{a}},Q^{\mathrm{a}},\Delta^{\mathrm{a}},\{\alpha_0^{\mathrm{a}}\},F^{\mathrm{a}})$. Its counters in X^{a} are of the form x_S where $x \in X$ and $S \subseteq Q^+$ and $Q^+ = Q\cup\{q^+ \mid q \in Q\}$. The guiding principle of the algorithm is that an assignment $\mathfrak{s}^{\mathrm{a}}$ of X^{a} represents an assignment $\mathfrak{s}$ of the counters in $X^{\emptyset}$ of $\mathrm{DCSA}(\mathrm{CA}(R))$, namely, for each $x_q \in X^{\emptyset}$,

$$\mathfrak{s}(x_q) = \bigcup_{q\in S, S\subseteq Q^+} \mathfrak{s}^{\mathrm{a}}(x_S)\cup\bigcup_{q^+\in S, S\subseteq Q^+}\{n+1 \mid n \in \mathfrak{s}^{\mathrm{a}}(x_S)\}. \qquad (1)$$

We will use some simplifying notation. As discussed in Section 3, by the construction of $\mathrm{CA}(R)$, the increment of c and the guard $x < \mathrm{max}_x$ always appear on its transitions together, without any other guard on x. Hence, in $\mathrm{DCSA}(\mathrm{CA}(R))$, all terms with an increment or filtering are of the form $\nabla_{x<\max_x}(x_{q^\circ}) + 1$. We will denote them by the shorthand $x_{q^\circ} \oplus 1$ (we are using q° to denote an element from the set Q^+, either q or q^+, for $q \in Q$).

The states of $\mathrm{DCSA}^{\mathrm{a}}(\mathrm{CA}(R))$ will additionally be distinguished according to which of the counters of X^{a} are *active*, i.e., could have a non-empty value. Counters always valued by 0 can be ignored, which simplifies transitions and decreases the chance of an irresolvable counter replication. The states of $\mathrm{DCSA}^{\mathrm{a}}(\mathrm{CA}(R))$ are thus of the form (R, Act) where $R \subseteq Q$ and $Act \subseteq X^{\mathrm{a}}$ is a set of active counters.

The initial configuration is $\alpha_0^{\mathrm{a}} = ((\{q_0\}, \{x_{\{q_0\}} \mid x \in X\}), \mathfrak{s}_0^{\mathrm{a}})$ where $\mathfrak{s}_0^{\mathrm{a}}$ assigns $\{0\}$ to every $x_{\{q_0\}}, x \in X$ and $\emptyset$ to every other counter in X^{a}. The final condition assignment $F^{\mathrm{a}}((R, Act))$ is, for each $(R, Act) \in Q^{\mathrm{a}}$, constructed from $F^0(R)$ by replacing every predicate $p[x_q]$ by the disjunction $p[x_q]^{Act} = \bigvee_{x_S \in Act, q \in S} p[x_S]$ that encodes $p[x_q]$ using the counters of Act in the sense of (1).

The transitions in Δ^{a} are constructed from transitions in Δ^0. For source state $(R, Act) \in Q^{\mathrm{a}}$, an original transition $R\text{-}\{a, \varphi, u\}\!\!\to\! R' \in \Delta^0$, and set of active counters $Act \subseteq X^{\mathrm{a}}$, Δ^{a} has the transition $(R, Act)\text{-}\{a, \varphi^{\mathrm{a}}, u^{\mathrm{a}}\}\!\!\to\!(R', Act')$, constructed as follows:

The guard φ^{a} is made from φ by replacing every predicate $p[x_q]$ by the equivalent version with shared counters $p[x_q]^{Act}$ (as when constructing F^{a} above).

The update u^{a} is constructed in three steps. First, the update u^{sh} is made from u by expressing the r-terms of u using the shared counters X^{a}. Each $t[x_q]$ is replaced by

$$t^{\mathrm{a}} = \bigcup \left(\{t[x_S] \mid x_S \in Act, q \in S\} \cup \{t[x_S] \oplus 1 \mid x_S \in Act, q^+ \in S\} \right) .$$

Notice that all postponed increments are *evaluated* in u^{sh}, transformed to normal increments. If u^{sh} has an r-term $t \oplus 1 \oplus 1$, i.e., a double increment, then the whole construction aborts and declares an *irresolvable counter replication*. We allow postponing only one increment.[6] Otherwise, we proceed to resolve counter replication. First, we make sure that every counter appears in the image of the update only in one kind of r-term. We collect the set *Conflict* of all r-terms $x_S \oplus 1$ of u^{sh} with *conflicting increments*, i.e. such that also x_S is an r-term of u^{sh}. In update u^+, conflicting increments are *postponed*. For $x \in X$, $q \in Q$, and $u^{\mathrm{sh}}(x_q) = \bigcup T$,

$$u^+(x_q) = \bigcup (T \setminus \mathit{Conflict}) \quad \text{and} \quad u^+(x_{q^+}) = \bigcup \{x_S \mid x_S \oplus 1 \in T \cap \mathit{Conflict}\} .$$

The final update u^{a} then resolves counter replication, by grouping r-terms replicated in u^+ under a common l-value (we call z an *l-value* of r-terms of $u^+(z)$). For an r-term t of u^+, let $\mathrm{lval}(t)$ be the set of its l-values. Note that $\mathrm{lval}(t)$ is always of the form $\{x_{q^\circ}\}_{x \in S}$ for some fixed $x \in X$ (see property 4 of $\mathrm{CA}(R)$ in Section 3). We let Act' be the set of counters x_S with $\mathrm{lval}(t) = \{x_{q^\circ}\}_{x \in S}$ for some r-term of u^+. For all $x_S \in X^{\mathrm{a}}$, if $x_S \notin Act'$ then $u^{\mathrm{a}}(x_S) = \emptyset$ else

$$u^{\mathrm{a}}(x_S) = \bigcup \{t \mid t \text{ is an r-term of } u^+ \text{ and } \mathrm{lval}(t) = \{x_{q^\circ}\}_{q^\circ \in S}\} .$$

---

[6] Also transition guards and final conditions of $\mathrm{DCSA}^{\mathrm{a}}(\mathrm{CA}(R))$ must not contain the +-mark since evaluating them regardless the postponed increments would return incorrect results. However, declaring counter replication on seeing a double increment here covers these cases due to the structural properties of $\mathrm{CA}(R)$.

Example 2. Let us have $R \dashrightarrow_{\{a,\varphi,u\}} R' \in \Delta^0$ created in Example 1 with $R = \{p,q\}$, $R' = \{r,s\}$, $\varphi = x_p < n \wedge x_p \geq m$, and $u = \{x_r := x_p \oplus 1, x_s := x_q \cup 1\}$. Let $Act = \{x_{\{p,q\}}, x_{\{p,q^+\}}\}$. Then $u^{sh} = \{x_r := x_{\{p,q^+\}} \oplus 1 \cup x_{\{p,q\}} \oplus 1, x_s := x_{\{p,q^+\}} \oplus 1 \cup x_{\{p,q\}} \cup 1\}$. Note that the x_q in $u(x_s)$ becomes $x_{\{p,q^+\}} \oplus 1$, corresponding to the right part of the definition of t^a (the postponed increment x_{q^+} is evaluated in u^{sh}). Note that the r-term $x_{\{p,q\}} \oplus 1$ is in *Conflict* as $x_{\{p,q\}}$ is an r-term of u^{sh} too. Therefore it is postponed in u^+, i.e. $u^{sh}(x_r) = x_{\{p,q\}} \oplus 1 \cup \cdots$ becomes $u^+(x_{r^+}) = x_{\{p,q\}}$. We get $u^+ = \{x_r := x_{\{p,q^+\}} \oplus 1, x_s := x_{\{p,q^+\}} \oplus 1 \cup x_{\{p,q\}} \cup 1, x_{r^+} := x_{\{p,q\}}\}$. Finally, u^a groups r-terms replicated in u^+ under a common l-value: $u^a = \{x_{\{r,s\}} := x_{\{p,q^+\}} \oplus 1, x_{\{s\}} := 1, x_{\{s,r^+\}} := x_{\{p,q\}}\}$. The next active counters are $Act' = \{x_{\{r,s\}}, x_{\{s\}}, x_{\{s,r^+\}}\}$. Note that, for $x_{\{p,q^+\}}$, the postponed increment at p^+ was synchronized on this transition, while the conflict at $x_{\{p,q\}}$ was solved by postponing increment and marking r with $^+$. $\qquad\square$

The algorithm either returns the CSA $\text{DCSA}^a(\text{CA}(A))$, or detects an irresolvable counter replication, in which case $\text{DCSA}^a(\text{CA}(A))$ does not exist.[7] Let $m = \sharp R$ and recall that n denotes the length of the matched text, $|w|$. Since $\text{CA}(R)$ has at most m states and m^2 transitions, a basic analysis of the algorithm's data structures reveals that the resulting CSA has at most 2^{2^m} states, each with at most 2^{m^2} outgoing transitions, each transition of the size in $O(m2^m)$. Because $\text{DCSA}^a(\text{CA}(A))$ encodes $\text{DCSA}(\text{CA}(A))$, it has the same language, and it also inherits its determinism. Since it does not replicate counters, it can be simulated in pattern matching fast, in time linear to the text and independent of the counter bounds. The following theorem is proved in [21].

Theorem 3. *For R with flat counting, if $\text{DCSA}^a(\text{CA}(R))$ exists, then it does not replicate counters, its size is in $O(2^{2^m} m)$, $L(\text{CA}(R)) = L(\text{DCSA}^a(\text{CA}(R)))$, and it can be simulated on a word w of the length n in time $O(2^{2^m} mn)$.*

Matching can be done in time of constructing the CSA plus its simulation, which in the sum is indeed fast, not dependent on k and linear in n. It can also be noted that the m in the exponents above is not the size of the entire regex, but only the size of the counted sub-regexes.

7   Regexes with Synchronizing Counting

Finally, in this section we define the class of regexes with synchronizing counting, which precisely captures when the CSA created by our construction in Section 6 does not replicate counters and hence allow fast matching (in the sense of Theorem 3).

Definition 7 (Regexes with synchronizing counting). *A regex has* synchronizing counting *iff it has no sub-expression $S\{n,m\}$ where for some $k \in \mathbb{N}$, a word from $L(S)^k$ has a prefix from $L(S)^{k+1}$.*

For instance, $(\texttt{ac}\star)\{1,4\}(\texttt{ab}|\texttt{ba})\{3,5\}(\texttt{a}(\texttt{ab})\star)\{2,8\}$ is a regex with synchronizing counting as each word from $L(\texttt{ac}\star)^k$ must contain the symbol a exactly k times,

---

[7] Aborting the construction here simplifies the description, but it would also be possible to continue the construction and return a DCSA that does not guarantee fast simulation.

words from $L(\text{ab} \mid \text{ba})^k$ must have exactly $2k$ symbols, and words from $L(\text{a}(\text{ab})\,^*)^k$ can be uniquely split at the first a in the $\text{a}(\text{ab})\,^*$. In comparison, $(\text{a} \mid \text{aa})\{2,5\}$ does not have synchronizing counting as $a \cdot a \cdot a$ is a prefix of $aa \cdot aa$.

Intuitively, there is no pair of paths through $\text{CA}(S\{\text{m},\text{n}\})$ starting at the same state, over the same word, ending in the same state, where the number of increments differs by two. In such case, $\text{DCSA}^{\text{a}}(\text{CA}(S\{\text{m},\text{n}\}))$ would have to delay two increments, which our construction does not allow. The theorem below is proved in [21].

Theorem 4. *Given a regex R with flat counting, the algorithm of Section 6 returns* $\text{DCSA}^{\text{a}}(\text{CA}(R))$ *if and only if R has synchronizing counting.*

Corollary 1. *Regexes with flat synchronizing counting have a fast matching algorithm.*

Proof. From Theorems 3 and 4.

Counting with Markers. Even though designing and recognizing synchronizing counting is usually intuitive, it may also be tricky. For instance, $(\backslash\backslash\backslash\backslash\text{d}+\backslash\backslash\backslash\backslash\,.)\{3\}$, from the database of real-world regexes we use in our experiment, has synchronizing counting, while $\text{ICE\_Dims}.\{92\}((\_?(\text{X} \mid \backslash\text{d}+))\{13\})$ does not.[8] A vast majority of real-world regexes we examined fortunately belong to very easily recognizable subclasses of synchronizing counting. The most wide-spread and easy to recognize are regexes with *letter-marked counting*, where every sub-expression $S\{\text{m},\text{n}\}$ has a set of marker letters such that every word from $L(S)$ has exactly one occurrence of a marker letter. [9]

Marker letters may be generalized to *marker words*, though, markers that can arise by concatenation of several words from $L(S)$ cannot be used. The condition that has to be satisfied is that any word from $L(S)^k$, $k \in \mathbb{N}$, has exactly k non-overlapping occurrences of marker words as infixes. Another sufficient property of S is that it has words of a *uniform length*. The idea of markers may be generalized further until the point when the set of marker words is specified by general regexes, when we get precisely the synchronizing counting. The regexes with letter-marked counting are easily human as well as machine recognizable (see a simple $O(|R|^2)$-time algorithm in [21]).

8 Practical Considerations

Although the main point of this work is the theoretical feasibility of fast matching with synchronizing counting, we will also argue that the results are of practical relevance. To this end, we show experimentally that synchronizing counting and marked counting cover a majority of practical regexes. We also give arguments that matching with the CSA constructed in Section 6 can be done efficiently.

---

[8] An automated way of identifying synchronizing counting would be running the CSA-to-DCSA determinization from Section 6, but this is exponential to $|R|$.

[9] That letter-marked counting is a strict superset of the class that is in [36] conjectured as handled by the algorithm of [36]. The conjecture of [36] is also not correct, as shown in [21].

8.1 Occurrence of Synchronizing Counting in Practice

To substantiate the practical relevance of synchronizing counting regexes, we examined a large sample of practical regexes using a simple checker of letter-marked counting. The benchmark consists of over 540 000 regexes collected from (1) a large scale analysis of software projects [10]; (2) regexes used by network intrusion detection systems Snort [27], Bro [29], Sagan [34], and the academic papers [42,38]; (4) the RegExLib database of regexes [28].

From the regexes that we could parse[10], 31 975 contained counting. We selected those with flat counting and with the sum of upper bounds of counters larger than 20 (as was done in [36] to filter out counting with small bounds that can be handled through counter unfolding and traditional methods)[11]. This left us with 5 751 regexes. From these, only 46 regexes (0.8 %) have counting that is not letter-marked. Furthermore, we manually checked these regexes and we identified that 22 of them have synchronizing counting. We have therefore found only 24 regexes with non-synchronizing counting, i.e., 0.4 % of the examined set of regexes with flat counting.

The 24 non-synchronizing regexes are listed in [21]. Some of them may clearly be rewritten with synchronizing counting, such as `(.+){25}(.*)`, which can be rewritten as `.{25,}(.*)`. We speculate that some of them might in fact represent a mistake, such as `(.*){1,32000}[bc]` where the counter matches the empty word, or `(\n\s+)(criterion .*\n)(\s.+){1,99}` where the `\s.+` might have been intended as `\s\S+` (`\s` are white spaces, `\S` are all the other characters). Synchronizing counting seems to capture the intuition with which counting is often written, hence reporting non-synchronizing counting might help identifying bugs.

By the same methodology and from a nearly identical benchmark, [36] arrived to a sample of 5 000 regexes with flat counting with the sum of bounds larger than 20. The algorithm of [36] did not cover 571 regexes from the 5 000, which is 11 % of the examined set of regexes with flat counting (in contrast to the 0.4 % with non-synchronizing counting and the 0.8 % with counting that is not letter-marked, measured on a slightly larger set of regexes). The two sets of regexes with flat counting, the 5 751 of ours and the 5 000 of [36], are not perfectly identical, however. Differences are to a small degree caused by differences in the base database ([36] uses about 18 more regexes that are proprietary and excludes 26 regexes with counter bounds larger than 1 000), and to a larger degree by small differences in the parsers.

8.2 Practical Efficiency of Matching with Synchronizing Counting

The size and the worst-case time of simulation of $DCSA^a(CA(R))$ are still exponential to the number of states of $CA(R)$ (namely, $O(2^{2^m} m)$ and $O(2^{2m}mn)$ where $m = \sharp R$ equals the number of states of $CA(R)$, cf. Theorem 3). The potential problem is that the algorithm may generate at most 2^m counters, and this potentially threatens practicality of our matching algorithm.

---

[10] We did not parse 38 558 regexes since their syntax was broken or contained some advanced features we do not support.

[11] 926 regexes contain nested counting and 25297 regexes contain small upper bounds.

First, it should be noted that the m in the exponent can be decreased from the size of the entire regex to the size of the counted sub-expression, which is usually very small. Then, although an efficient implementation is beyond the scope of this paper and we are leaving it as a future work, we give some indirect arguments for practicality of the CA-to-CSA algorithm.[12]

By the standard techniques of register allocation [1], it is possible to decrease the number of counters and counter assignments other than identity dramatically. In fact, simply eliminating needless renaming of counters and reusing the same name whenever possible, our algorithm creates CSA isomorphic to those of [36] when run on regexes handled by [36]. The work [36] already shows that simulating these CSA may be done efficiently and that it brings dramatic improvements over best matchers on counting-intensive examples.

In our experience with hand-simulating the algorithm on practical examples, cases not handled by [36] do not behave much differently, and the numbers of CSA counters do not have a strong tendency to explode.

9   Conclusions

We have extended the regex matching algorithm of [36] and shown that the extended version allows fast pattern matching of so-called synchronising regexes, a class of regexes that we have newly introduced. The class of synchronising regexes significantly extends all previously known classes of regexes that allow fast matching and covers a majority of regexes appearing in practice (wrt. our empirical study).

In the future, we plan to study extensions of the presented techniques to regexes with nested counting (non-flat). This will probably require a more sophisticated alternative of the offset-list data structure for sets, capable of storing relations of numbers. An interesting question is also how and when regexes can be rewritten to a synchronizing form and for what cost.

Acknowledgment

This work has been supported by the Czech Ministry of Education, Youth and Sports project LL1908 of the ERC.CZ programme, the Czech Science Foundation project 23-06506S, and the FIT BUT internal project FIT-S-23-8151.

References

1. Aho, A.V., Lam, M.S., Sethi, R., Ullman, J.D.: Compilers: Principles, Techniques, and Tools (2nd Edition). Addison Wesley (August 2006), http://www.amazon.ca/exec/obidos/redirect?tag=citeulike09-20&path=ASIN/0321486811

---

[12] A competitive matcher that runs on real-world regexes requires an extensive infrastructure, optimized data structures for the shared registers, and ideally an on-the-fly version of the CA-to-CSA determinization (similar to the online DFA simulation).

2. Antimirov, V.: Partial derivatives of regular expressions and finite automaton constructions. Theoretical Computer Science **155**(2), 291 – 319 (1996). https://doi.org/10.1016/0304-3975(95)00182-4, https://doi.org/10.1016/0304-3975(95)00182-4

3. Baldwin, A.: Regular expression denial of service affecting express.js. https://medium.com/node-security/regular- expression-denial-of-service-affecting-express-js-9c397c164c43 (2016)

4. Björklund, H., Martens, W., Timm, T.: Efficient incremental evaluation of succinct regular expressions. In: CIKM'15. ACM (2015). https://doi.org/10.1145/2806416.2806434

5. Chapman, C., Stolee, K.T.: Exploring regular expression usage and context in python. In: Zeller, A., Roychoudhury, A. (eds.) Proceedings of the 25th International Symposium on Software Testing and Analysis, ISSTA 2016, Saarbrücken, Germany, July 18-20, 2016. pp. 282–293. ACM (2016). https://doi.org/10.1145/2931037.2931073, https://doi.org/10.1145/2931037.2931073

6. contributors, W.: Regular expression—wikipedia (2019), https://en.wikipedia.org/w/index.php?title=Regular_expression&%20oldid=852858998

7. Davis, J.C.: Rethinking regex engines to address ReDoS. In: ESEC/FSE'19. pp. 1256–1258. ACM (2019)

8. Davis, J.C., Coghlan, C.A., Servant, F., Lee, D.: The impact of regular expression denial of service (redos) in practice: an empirical study at the ecosystem scale. In: Leavens, G.T., Garcia, A., Pasareanu, C.S. (eds.) Proceedings of the 2018 ACM Joint Meeting on European Software Engineering Conference and Symposium on the Foundations of Software Engineering, ESEC/SIGSOFT FSE 2018, Lake Buena Vista, FL, USA, November 04-09, 2018. pp. 246–256. ACM (2018). https://doi.org/10.1145/3236024.3236027, https://doi.org/10.1145/3236024.3236027

9. Davis, J.C., Coghlan, C.A., Servant, F., Lee, D.: The impact of regular expression denial of service (ReDoS) in practice: An empirical study at the ecosystem scale. In: ESEC/FSE'18. pp. 246–256. ACM (2018)

10. Davis, J.C., Michael IV, L.G., Coghlan, C.A., Servant, F., Lee, D.: Why aren't regular expressions a lingua franca? An empirical study on the re-use and portability of regular expressions. In: ESEC/FSE'19. pp. 1256–1258. ACM (2019)

11. Davis, J.C., Servant, F., Lee, D.: Using selective memoization to defeat regular expression denial of service (ReDoS). In: 42nd IEEE Symposium on Security and Privacy, SP 2021, San Francisco, CA, USA, 24-27 May 2021. pp. 1–17. IEEE (2021). https://doi.org/10.1109/SP40001.2021.00032, https://doi.org/10.1109/SP40001.2021.00032

12. docs.rs: regex - rust. https://docs.rs/regex/1.5.4/regex/ (2021)

13. Exchange, S.: Outage postmortem. http://stackstatus.net/post/147710624694/outage-postmortem-july-20-2016 (2016)

14. Gelade, W., Gyssens, M., Martens, W.: Regular expressions with counting: Weak versus strong determinism. In: Mathematical Foundations of Computer Science 2009. pp. 369–381. Springer Berlin Heidelberg, Berlin, Heidelberg (2009). https://doi.org/10.1007/978-3-642-03816-7_32

15. Gelade, W., Gyssens, M., Martens, W.: Regular expressions with counting: Weak versus strong determinism. SIAM J. Comput. **41**(1), 160–190 (2012). https://doi.org/10.1137/100814196, extended version of paper in MFCS'09

16. Glushkov, V.M.: The abstract theory of automata. Russian Math. Surveys **16**, 1–53 (1961). https://doi.org/10.1070/RM1961v016n05ABEH004112

17. Google: RE2. https://github.com/google/re2

18. Graham-Cumming, J.: Details of the Cloudflare outage on july 2, 2019. https://blog.cloudflare.com/details-of-the-cloudflare-outage-on-july-2-2019/ (2019)

19. Haertel, M., et al.: GNU grep. https://www.gnu.org/software/grep/

20. Holík, L., Lengál, O., Saarikivi, O., Turoňová, L., Veanes, M., Vojnar, T.: Succinct determin-isation of counting automata via sphere construction. In: Proc. of APLAS'19. LNCS, vol. 11893, pp. 468–489. Springer (2019). https://doi.org/10.1007/978-3-030-34175-6_24

21. Holík, L., Síč, J., Turoňová, L., Vojnar, T.: Fast matching of regular patterns with syn-chronizing counting (technical report). Tech. rep., Brno University of Technology (2023), https://doi.org/10.48550/arXiv.2301.12851

22. Hovland, D.: Regular expressions with numerical constraints and automata with counters. In: ICTAC. LNCS, vol. 5684, pp. 231–245. Springer (2009). https://doi.org/10.1007/978-3-642-03466-4_15

23. Hovland, D.: The membership problem for regular expressions with unordered concatenation and numerical constraints. In: Language and Automata Theory and Applications. pp. 313–324. Springer Berlin Heidelberg, Berlin, Heidelberg (2012). https://doi.org/10.1007/978-3-642-28332-1_27

24. Hromkovič, J., Seibert, S., Wilke, T.: Translating regular expressions into small ε-free non-deterministic finite automata. In: Reischuk, R., Morvan, M. (eds.) STACS 97. pp. 55–66. Springer Berlin Heidelberg, Berlin, Heidelberg (1997)

25. Kilpeläinen, P., Tuhkanen, R.: Regular expressions with numerical occurrence indicators -preliminary results. In: SPLST'03. pp. 163–173. University of Kuopio, Department of Com-puter Science (2003)

26. Kilpeläinen, P., Tuhkanen, R.: One-unambiguity of regular expressions with numeric oc-currence indicators. Information and Computation 205(6), 890–916 (2007). https://doi.org/10.1016/j.ic.2006.12.003

27. M. Roesch et al.: Snort: A Network Intrusion Detection and Prevention System,. http://www.snort.org

28. RegExLib.com: The Internet's first Regular Expression Library. http://regexlib.com/

29. Robin Sommer et al.: The Bro Network Security Monitor, http://www.bro.org

30. Saarikivi, O., Veanes, M., Wan, T., Xu, E.: Symbolic regex matcher. In: Vojnar, T., Zhang, L. (eds.) TACAS'2019. LNCS, vol. 11427, pp. 372–378. Springer (2019). https://doi.org/10.1007/978-3-030-17462-0_24, https://doi.org/10.1007/978-3-030-17462-0_24

31. Smith, R., Estan, C., Jha, S.: XFA: faster signature matching with extended automata. In: IEEE Symposium on Security and Privacy. IEEE (2008). https://doi.org/10.1109/SP.2008.14

32. Smith, R., Estan, C., Jha, S., Siahaan, I.: Fast signature matching using extended finite au-tomaton (XFA). In: ICISS'08. LNCS, vol. 5352, pp. 158–172. Springer (2008). https://doi.org/10.1007/978-3-540-89862-7_15

33. Sperberg-McQueen, M.: Notes on finite state automata with counters. https://www.w3.org/XML/2004/05/msm-cfa.html, https://www.w3.org/XML/2004/05/msm-cfa.html, accessed: 2018-08-08

34. The Sagan team: The Sagan Log Analysis Engine, https://quadrantsec.com/sagan_log_analysis_engine/

35. Thompson, K.: Programming techniques: Regular expression search algorithm. Commun. ACM 11(6), 419–422 (1968)

36. Turoňová, L., Holík, L., Lengál, O., Saarikivi, O., Veanes, M., Vojnar, T.: Regex matching with counting-set automata. Proc. ACM Program. Lang. 4(OOPSLA), 218:1–218:30 (2020)

37. Turoňová, L., Holík, L., Lengál, O., Veanes, M., Vojnar, T.: Counting in regexes considered harmful (2022)

38. Češka, M., Havlena, V., Holík, L., Lengál, O., Vojnar, T.: Approximate reduction of finite automata for high-speed network intrusion detection. In: Proc. of TACAS'18. LNCS, vol. 10806. Springer (2018). https://doi.org/10.1007/978-3-319-89963-3_9

39. Wang, P., Stolee, K.T.: How well are regular expressions tested in the wild? In: Leavens, G.T., Garcia, A., Pasareanu, C.S. (eds.) Proceedings of the 2018 ACM Joint Meeting on European Software Engineering Conference and Symposium on the Foundations of Software Engineering, ESEC/SIGSOFT FSE 2018, Lake Buena Vista, FL, USA, November 04-09, 2018. pp. 668–678. ACM (2018). https://doi.org/10.1145/3236024.3236072, https://doi.org/10.1145/3236024.3236072
40. Wang, X., Hong, Y., Chang, H., Park, K., Langdale, G., Hu, J., Zhu, H.: Hyperscan: A fast multi-pattern regex matcher for modern CPUs. In: 16th USENIX Symposium on Networked Systems Design and Implementation (NSDI 19). pp. 631–648. USENIX Association, Boston, MA (Feb 2019), https://www.usenix.org/conference/nsdi19/presentation/wang-xiang
41. Wübbeling, M.: Regular expression security. ADMIN 55 (2020)
42. Yang, L., Karim, R., Ganapathy, V., Smith, R.: Improving NFA-based signature matching using ordered binary decision diagrams. In: Recent Advances in Intrusion Detection. pp. 58–78. Springer Berlin Heidelberg (2010)

Compositional Learning for Interleaving Parallel Automata

Faezeh Labbaf[1]([✉])(iD), Jan Friso Groote[2](iD),
Hossein Hojjat[1,3](iD), and Mohammad Reza Mousavi[4](iD)

[1] Tehran Institute for Advanced Studies (TeIAS), Khatam University, Tehran, Iran
`f.labaf@khatam.ac.ir`
[2] Eindhoven University of Technology, Eindhoven, The Netherlands
`j.f.Groote@tue.nl`
[3] University of Tehran, Tehran, Iran
`hojjat@ut.ac.ir`
[4] King's College London, London, UK
`mohammad.mousavi@kcl.ac.uk`

Abstract. Active automata learning has been a successful technique
to learn the behaviour of state-based systems by interacting with them
through queries. In this paper, we develop a compositional algorithm
for active automata learning in which systems comprising interleaving
parallel components are learned compositionally. Our algorithm automatically learns the structure of systems while learning the behaviour
of the components. We prove that our approach is sound and that it
learns a maximal set of interleaving parallel components. We empirically
evaluate the effectiveness of our approach and show that our approach
requires significantly fewer numbers of input symbols and resets while
learning systems. Our empirical evaluation is based on a large number of
subject systems obtained from a case study in the automotive domain.

1 Introduction

Active automata learning has been successfully used to learn models of complex
industrial systems such as communication- and security protocols [11], biometric
passports [2], smart cards [1], large-scale printing machines [33], and lithogra-
phy machines for integrated circuits [32,15]; we refer to the recent survey by
Howar and Steffen on the practical applications of active automata learning
[16]. Throughout these applications of automata learning, scalability issues have
been pointed out [32,15]. It has also been suggested that compositional learning,
i.e., learning a system through learning its components, is a promising approach
to tame the complexity of learning [10,12].

Some early attempts have been recently made in learning structured models
of systems [27,10] (we refer to the Related Work for an in-depth analysis). For
example, the approach proposed by al-Duhaiby and Groote [10] decomposes
the learning process into learning its parallel components; however, it relies on
a deep knowledge of the system under learning, and the intricate interaction

© The Author(s) 2023
O. Kupferman and P. Sobociński (Eds.): FoSSaCS 2023, LNCS 13992, pp. 413–435, 2023.
https://doi.org/10.1007/978-3-031-30829-1_20

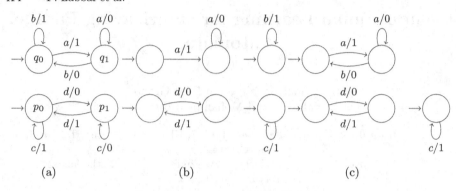

Fig. 1: (a) Initial system with two concurrent FSMs (b) Partition the input alphabet to 4 elements and learn each component individually (c) Use the counter-example ab to merge two components

of the various actions being learned. In this paper, we propose an approach based on Dana Angluin's celebrated L* algorithm [6], to learn the components of a system featuring an interleaving parallel composition. Our approach, called CL*, does not assume any pre-knowledge of the structure and the alphabet of these components; instead, we learn this information automatically and on-the-fly, while providing a rigorous guarantee of the learned information. This is particularly relevant in the context of legacy and black-box systems where architectural discovery is challenging [8,22].

The gist of our approach is to learn the System Under Learning (SUL) in separate components with disjoint alphabets. We start with a partition comprising only singleton sets. The interleaving parallel composition of the components gives us the total behavior of the system. We pass the result to the teacher, and by exploiting the counter-examples returned, we iteratively merge the alphabet of the individual components.

Example. Figure 1(a) shows an example of two parallel Finite State Machines (FSMs) over the input alphabet $\{a, b, c, d\}$ and output alphabet $\{0, 1\}$. We start by partitioning the alphabet into disjoint singleton sets of elements. The parallel composition of the 4 learned FSMs of Figure 1(b) does not comply with the original system, and the teacher may return the counter-example ab. The string ab generates the output sequence 10 in (a) but the output sequence in (b) is 11. The counter-example suggests to merge the sets $\{a\}$ and $\{b\}$ and restart the learning process which leads to the FSMs in Figure 1(c). One further merging step results in learning the original system. We provide a theoretical proof of correctness of this compositional construction, meaning that it is guaranteed to construct a correct system.

To study the effectiveness of our approach in practice, we designed an empirical experiment to investigate the following two research questions:

RQ1 Does CL* require fewer resets, compared to L*?
RQ2 Does CL* require fewer input symbols, compared to L*?

Our research questions are motivated by the following facts: 1) Resets are a major contributing factor in learning practical systems as they are immensely time- and resource consuming [31]. Hence, reducing the number of resets can have a significant impact in the learning process. 2) The total number of symbols used in interacting with the system under learning provides us with a total measure of cost for the learning process and hence, reducing the total cost is a fair indicator of improved efficiency [36,9].

To answer these questions, we use a benchmark based an industrial automotive system. We design a number of experiments on learning various combinations of components in this system, gather empirical data, and analyse them through statistical hypothesis testing. Our results indicate that our compositional approach significantly improves the efficiency of learning compared to the monolithic L* learning algorithm. The implementation of the algorithm, experiments, and their results can be found on-line in our lab package [23] (https://github.com/faezeh-lbf/CL-Star).

The remainder of this paper is organised as follows. In Section 2, we review the related work and position our research with respect to the state of the art. In Section 3, we present the preliminary definitions that are used throughout the rest of the paper. In Section 4, we present our algorithm and its proof of correctness and termination. We evaluate our algorithm on a benchmark from the automotive domain in Section 5. We conclude the paper and present the directions of our ongoing and future research in Section 6.

2   Related Work

Active automata learning is a technique used to find the underlying model of a black box system by posing queries and building a hypothesis in an iterative manner. There is substantial early work in this domain, e.g., under the name system identification or grammar inference; we refer to the accessible introduction by Vaandrager [36] for more information. A seminal work in this domain is the L* algorithm by Dana Angluin [6], which comes with theoretical complexity bounds for the learning process using a representation called the "Minimally Adequate Teacher" (MAT).

MAT hypothesises a teacher that is capable of responding to membership queries (MQs) and equivalence queries (EQs); the former checks the outcome of a sequence of inputs (e.g., with their respective outputs, or with their membership in the language of the automaton) and the latter checks whether a hypothesised automaton is equivalent to the system under learning. Our work replaces a single MAT with multiple MATs that can potentially run in parallel and learn different components of the black-box system automatically.

Learning structured systems and in particular, compositional learning of parallel systems has been studied recently in the literature. Moerman [27] proposes an algorithm to learn parallel interleaving Moore machines. Our algorithm differs from Moerman's algorithm in that in the parallel composition of Moore machines, the output of each individual component is explicitly specified, because the output of the system is specified as a tuple of the outputs of its components. In other words, the underlying structure is immediately exposed by considering the type of outputs produced by the system under learning. However, in our approach, we need to identify the components and assign outputs to them on-the-fly since the decomposition is not explicit in parallel composition. Al-Duhaiby and Groote [10] learn parallel labelled transitions systems with the possibility of synchronisation among them. In order to develop their algorithm, they assume a priori knowledge of mutual dependencies among actions in terms of a confluence relation. This type of information is difficult to obtain and the domain knowledge in this regard may be error prone. Particularly for legacy and large black-box systems (e.g., binary code), architectural discovery has proven challenging [8,22]. We address this challenge and go beyond the existing approaches by learning about confluence of actions on-the-fly through observing the minimal counter-examples generated by the MAT(s).

Frohme and Steffen [12] introduce a compositional learning approach for Systems of Procedural Automata [13]; these are collections of DFAs that may "call" each, akin to the way non-terminals may be used in defining other non-terminals in a grammar. Their approach is essentially different from ours in that the calls across automata are assumed to be observable and hence the general structure is assumed to be known; in our approach, we learn the structure by observing implicit dependencies among the learned automata through analysing counter-examples. Also their approach is aimed at a richer and more expressive type of systems, namely pushdown systems, which justifies the requirement for additional information.

L^* has been improved significantly in the past few years; the major improvements upon L^* can be broadly categorised into three categories: 1) improving the data structures used to store and retrieve the learned information [21,31,19,37]; 2) improving the way counter-examples are processed in refining the hypothesis [31,28,3,17]; 3) learning more expressive models, such as register- [18,14] and timed automata [34,5]. This third category of improvements is orthogonal to our contribution and extension of our approach can be considered in those contexts as well.

Two notable recent improvements, in the first two categories, are $L^\#$ [37] and L^λ [17], respectively. $L^\#$ uses the notion of *apartness* to organise and maintain a tree-shaped data-structure about the learned automaton. L^λ uses a search-based method to incorporate the information about the counter-example into the learned hypothesis. The improvements brought about by L^λ can be readily incorporated into our approach, particularly since our approach relies on finding minimal counter-examples. Integrating our approach into $L^\#$ requires a more careful consideration of maintaining and composing tree-shaped data structures when detecting dependencies. We expect that both of these combinations will further improve the efficiency of our proposed method.

3   Preliminaries

In this section, we review the basic notions used throughout the remainder of the paper. We start by formalising the notion of a finite state machine, which is the underlying model of the system under learning and move on to parallel composition and decomposition (called projection) as well as the concept of (in)dependent actions, which are essential in identifying the parallel components. Finally, we conclude this section by recalling the basic concepts of active automata learning and the L* algorithm.

3.1   Finite State Machines (FSMs)

Finite state machines (also called Mealy machines), defined below, are straightforward generalisations of finite automata in which the transitions produce outputs (rather than only indicating acceptance or non-acceptance):

Definition 1. *(Finite State Machine) A Finite State Machine (FSM) M is a sixtuple $(S, s_0, I, O, \delta, \lambda)$ where :*

- *S is a finite set of internal states,*
- *$s_0 \in S$ is the initial state,*
- *I is a set of actions, representing the input alphabet,*
- *O is the set of outputs,*
- *$\delta : S \times I \to S$ is a total state transition function,*
- *$\lambda : S \times I \to O$ is a total output function.*

An FSM starts in the initial state s_0 and accepts a word (a sequence of actions of its input alphabet) in order to produce an equally-sized sequence of outputs. State transition- δ and output function λ determine the next state and the output of an FSM upon receiving a single input. For each $s, s' \in S$, $i \in I$, and $o \in O$, we write $s \xrightarrow{i/o} s'$ when $\delta(s, i) = s'$ and $\lambda(s, i) = o$.

State transitions are extended inductively from a single input $i \in I$, to a sequence of inputs $w \in I^*$, i.e., we define $\delta(s, \epsilon) = s$ and $\lambda(s, \epsilon) = \epsilon$ where ϵ is the empty sequence; and for $s \in S, w \in I^*$, and $a \in I$, we have $\delta(s, wa) = \delta(\delta(s, wa), a)$ and $\lambda(s, wa) = \lambda(s, w)\lambda(\delta(s, w), a)$, where juxtaposition of sequences denotes concatenation. For the sake of conciseness, we write $\delta(w)$ and $\lambda(w)$ instead of $\delta(s_0, w)$ and $\lambda(s_0, w)$.

In much of the literature in active learning, the system under learning is assumed to be complete and deterministic and we follow this common assumption in Definition 1 by requiring the state transition and output relations to be total functions. While the determinism assumption is essential for our forthcoming results to hold, we expect that the existing recipes for learning non-deterministic state machines can be made compositional using a similar approach as ours.

3.2   (De)Composing FSMs

Our aim is to produce a compositional learning algorithm for systems composed of interleaving parallel components, defined below. Due to the interleaving nature of parallel composition and determinism of the system under learning, the alphabets of these components are assumed to be disjoint.

Definition 2. *(Interleaving Parallel Composition) For two FSMs $M_i = (S_i, s_{0_i}, I_i, O_i, \delta_i, \lambda_i)$, with $i \in \{0, 1\}$, where $I_0 \cap I_1 = \emptyset$, the interleaving parallel composition of M_0 and M_1, denoted by $M_0 \parallel M_1$, is an FSM defined as*

$$(S_0 \times S_1, (s_{0_0}, s_{0_1}), I_0 \cup I_1, O_0 \cup O_1, \delta, \lambda)$$

where δ and λ are defined by

$$\delta((s_0, s_1), a) = \begin{cases} (\delta_0(s_0, a), s_1) & \textit{if } a \in I_0, \\ (s_0, \delta_1(s_1, a)) & \textit{otherwise, and} \end{cases} \qquad \lambda((s_0, s_1), a) = \begin{cases} \lambda_0(s_0, a) & \textit{if } a \in I_0, \\ \lambda_1(s_1, a) & \textit{otherwise.} \end{cases}$$

For $s_0 \in S_0$, $s_1 \in S_1$, and $a \in I_0 \cup I_1$

Next, we define the notions of projections for FSMs and for words; these notions are further used in the notion of (in)dependence and eventually in our proof of correctness to establish that the composed system has the same behaviour as the composition of the learned components.

Definition 3. *(Projection of an FSM) The projection of an FSM $M = (S, s_0, I, O, \delta, \lambda)$ on a set of inputs $I' \subseteq I$ denoted by $P(M, I')$, is an FSM $(S, s_0, I', O', \delta', \lambda')$, where*

- *$\delta'(s, a) = \delta(s, a)$ for $a \in I'$,*
- *$\lambda'(s, a) = \lambda(s, a)$ for $a \in I'$, and*
- *$O' = \{o \in O \mid \exists a \in I'. \exists s \in S. \lambda(s, a) = o\}$.*

Definition 4. *(Projection of a word) The projection of a word $w \in I^*$ on a set of inputs $I' \subseteq I$, denoted by $P_{I'}(w)$, is inductively defined as follows:*

$$P_{I'}(\epsilon) := \epsilon,$$
$$P_{I'}(au) := \begin{cases} aP_{I'}(u) & \textit{if } a \in I', \\ P_{I'}(u) & \textit{otherwise.} \end{cases}$$

Definition 5. *(Projection of an output sequence) The projection of the output sequence $w = o_1 \ldots o_n$ with respect to an equally-sized sequence of inputs $v = i_1, \ldots, i_n \in I^*$ and a subset of inputs $I' \subseteq I$, denoted by $P_{I'}(w, v)$, is defined as follows:*

$$P_{I'}(\epsilon, \epsilon) := \epsilon,$$
$$P_{I'}(ow, av) := \begin{cases} oP_{I'}(w, v) & \textit{if } a \in I', \\ P_{I'}(w, v) & \textit{otherwise.} \end{cases}$$

Definition 6. _((In)Dependent Actions) Consider an FSM M with a set of inputs I. The subsets $I_0, \ldots, I_n \subseteq I$ form an independent partition of I when for any $u \in I^*$, $\lambda_{P(M,I_0)||\ldots||P(M,I_n)}(u) = \lambda_M(u)$. Two inputs $i_0, i_1 \in I$ are independent when they belong to two distinct subsets of an independent partition. Two input actions are dependent, when they are not independent._

Example. The partition $\{\{a\}, \{b\}, \{c,d\}\}$ in Figure 1(a) is not an independent partition because $\lambda_M(ab) = 10$ but $\lambda_{P(M,\{a\})||P(M,\{b\})||P(M,\{c,d\})}(ab) = 11$.

It immediately follows from Definition 6 and associativity of parallel composition (with respect to trace equivalence) that any coarser partitioning based on an independent partition is also an independent partitioning; this is formalised in the following corollary.

Corollary 1. _By combining two or more sets of an independent partition, the resulting partition remains independent._

Moreover, it holds that any smaller subset of an independent partitioning is also an independent partitioning of the original state machine projected on the alphabet of the smaller subset, as specified and proven below.

Lemma 1. _Consider an independent partition $I_0, \ldots, I_n$ of inputs I for an FSM M; then for $K \subseteq \{0, \ldots, n\}$, $\{I_i \mid i \in K\}$ is an independent partition for $P(M, \bigcup_{i \in K}(I_i))$._

Proof. Consider any subset $K \subseteq \{0, \ldots, n\}$ and $\{I_i \mid i \in K\}$ and consider any input sequence $u \in (\bigcup_{i \in K} I_i)^*$. Since u does not contain a symbol that is in any I_j for $j \notin K$, we have that $\lambda_{||_{i \in K} P(M,I_i)}(u) = \lambda_{P(M,I_0)||\ldots||P(M,I_n)}(u)$. Since $I_0, \ldots, I_n$ are independent, it follows likewise that $\lambda_{P(M,I_0)||\ldots||P(M,I_n)}(u) = \lambda_M(u)$. Using again that u has no symbol in any I_j for $j \notin K$, we know that $\lambda_M(u) = \lambda_{P(M,\bigcup_{i \in K}(I_i))}(u)$. Hence, $\lambda_{||_{i \in K} P(M,I_i)}(u) = \lambda_{P(M,\bigcup_{i \in K}(I_i))}(u)$, which was to be shown. ∎

Lemma 2. _For any independent partition $I_0, \ldots, I_n \subseteq I$, $w \in I^*$ and $0 \leq i \leq n$, and state s it holds that $P_{I_i}(\lambda_M(s, w), w) = \lambda_{P(M,I_i)}(s, P_{I_i}(w))$._

Proof. The proof uses induction on the length of w. Instead of proving the thesis, we prove the following stronger statement, which is possible because M can be viewed as the parallel construction of independent components.

$$P_{I_i}(\lambda_M((s_0, \ldots s_n), w), w) = \lambda_{P(M,I_i)}((s_0', \ldots, s_n'), P_{I_i}(w)) \text{ with } s_i = s_i'.$$

Note that the lemma directly follows from this. Below we write s for $s_0, \ldots, s_n$, and likewise for s' and s''.

The base case ($|w| = 0$) holds trivially as $w = \epsilon$. For the induction step we assume that the induction hypothesis holds for $|w| = k$ and we show that it holds for $w' = aw$ for arbitrary $a \in I$.

We first consider the case where $a \notin I_i$. We derive

$$
\begin{aligned}
P_{I_i}(\lambda_M(s, aw), aw) &= P_{I_i}(\lambda_M(s, a)\lambda_M(\delta(s, a), w), aw) && \text{Definition 1} \\
&= P_{I_i}(\lambda_M(\delta(s, a), w), w) && \text{Definition 5.} \\
&= \lambda_{P(M, I_i)}(s', P_{I_i}(w)) && \text{Induction hypothesis.} \\
&= \lambda_{P(M, I_i)}(s'', P_{I_i}(aw)) && \text{Definition 4.}
\end{aligned}
$$

By construction the i-th state in $\delta(s, a)$ is equal to s_i as $a \notin I_i$. Hence, using the induction hypothesis, $s'_i = s_i$. By definition $s' = \delta(s'', a)$ and hence, $s''_i = s'_i = s_i$ as we had to show.

The other case we must consider is $a \in I_i$. Again the derivation is straightforward.

$$
\begin{aligned}
P_{I_i}(\lambda_M(s, aw), aw) &= P_{I_i}(\lambda_M(s, a)\lambda_M(\delta(s, a), w), aw) && \text{Definition 1} \\
&= \lambda_M(s, a)P_{I_i}(\lambda_M(\delta(s, a), w), w) && \text{Definition 5.} \\
&= \lambda_M(s', a)\lambda_{P(M, I_i)}(\delta(s', a), P_{I_i}(w)) && \text{Induction hypothesis.} \\
&= \lambda_{P(M, I_i)}(s, P_{I_i}(aw)) && \text{Definition 4.}
\end{aligned}
$$

Using the induction hypothesis it follows that $s_i = s'_i$, which concludes the proof. ∎

3.3 Model Learning

Active model learning, introduced by Dana Angluin, was originally designed to formulate a hypothesis $\mathcal{H}$ about the behavior of a System Under Learning (SUL) as an FSM. Model learning is often described in terms of the Minimally Adequate Teacher (MAT). In the MAT framework, there are two phases: (i) hypothesis construction, where a learning algorithm poses Membership Queries (MQ) to gain knowledge about the SUL using reset operations and input sequences; and (ii) hypothesis validation, where based on the model learned so far, the learner proposes a hypothesis $\mathcal{H}$ about the "language" of the SUL and asks Equivalence Queries (EQ) to test it. The results of the queries are organised in an observation table. The table is iteratively refined and is used to formulate $\mathcal{H}$.

Definition 7. *(Observation Table) An observation table is a triple (S, E, T), where $S \subseteq I^*$ is a prefix-closed set of input strings (i.e., prefixes); $E \subseteq I^+$ is a suffix-closed set of input strings (i.e., suffixes); and T is a table where rows are labeled by elements from $S \cup (S.I)$, columns are labeled by elements from E, such that for all $pre \in S \cup (S.I)$ and $suf \in E$, $T(pre, suf)$ is the SUL's output suffix of size $|suf|$ for the input sequence $pre.suf$.*

The L^* algorithm initially starts with S only containing the empty word ϵ, and E equals set of inputs alphabet I. Two crucial properties of the observation table, closedness and consistency, defined below, allow for the construction of a hypothesis.

Definition 8. *(Closedness Property) An observation table is closed iff for all* $w \in S.I$ *there is a* $w' \in S$ *that for all* $suf \in E$, $T(w, suf) = T(w', suf)$ *holds.*

Definition 9. *(Consistency Property) An observation table is consistent iff for all* $pre_1, pre_2 \in S$, *if for all* $suf \in E$, $T(pre_1, suf) = T(pre_2, suf)$, *it holds that* $T(pre_1.\alpha, suf) = T(pre_2.\alpha, suf)$ *for all* $\alpha \in I, suf \in E$.

MQs are posed until these two properties hold, and once they do, a hypothesis $\mathcal{H}$ is formulated. After formulating $\mathcal{H}$, L^* works under the assumption that an EQ can return either a counter-example (CE) exposing the non-conformance, or yes, if $\mathcal{H}$ is indeed equivalent to the SUL. When a CE is found, a CE processing method adds prefixes and/or suffixes to the observation table and hence refines $\mathcal{H}$. The aforementioned steps are repeated until EQ confirms that $\mathcal{H}$ and SUL are the same. In between MQs, we often need to bring the FSM back to a known state; this is done through reset operations, which are one of our metrics for measuring the efficiency of the algorithm. EQs are posed by running a large number of test-cases and hence they are (two- to three) orders of magnitude larger than MQs. These test cases are generated through a random-walk of the graph or through a deterministic algorithm that tests all states and transitions for a given fault model. Two examples of deterministic test-case generation algorithms are the W- and WP-method [7]. It appears from recent empirical evaluations that for realistic systems deterministic equivalence queries are not efficient [4].

Since we are going to be learning the system in terms of components with disjoint alphabets, we define the following projection operator that removes all the transitions that are not in the projected alphabet. Our compositional learning algorithm basically learns a black-box with respect to its projection on the actions available in each purported component.

Definition 10. *(L^* with projected alphabet) Given an SUL* $M = (S, s_0, I, O, \delta, \lambda)$ *and* $I' \subset I$, $L^*(M, I')$ *returns* $P(M, I')$ *by running algorithm* L^* *with projected alphabet* I' *on* M.

4   Compositional Active Learning

In this section, we present an algorithm that learns the SUL in separate components and uses the interleaving parallel composition of the learned components to reach the total behavior of the system. Each component has an input alphabet I_i, which is disjoint from the alphabet of all the other components. The set of the input alphabets of components $I^F = \{I_1, \ldots, I_n\}$ is a partition of the total system's input alphabet. The main idea is to find an independent partitioning I^F. To reach such a partitioning, we start with a partition with singleton sets and iteratively merge those sets that are found to be dependent on each other. Then for $I_i \in I^F$, we learn the SUL with the projected alphabet I_i, and compute the product of the obtained components with interleaving parallel composition. The result is equivalent to the SUL if I^F is an independent partition.

Algorithm 1: Compositional Learning Algorithm (CL*)

Result: $\mathscr{H}$
1 **Input:** $I^F = \{I_1, \ldots, I_n\}$, M
2 $\mathscr{H} \leftarrow LearnInParts(M, I^F)$
3 $eq \leftarrow$ EQUIVALENCE-QUERY$(\mathscr{H}, M)$
4 **while** $eq \neq yes$ **do**
5 | CE $\leftarrow eq$
6 | $D \leftarrow InvolvedSets(\text{CE}, I^F)$
7 | $I^F \leftarrow Composition(I^F, D)$
8 | $\mathscr{H} \leftarrow LearnInParts(M, I^F)$
9 | $eq \leftarrow$ EQUIVALENCE-QUERY$(\mathscr{H}, M)$
10 **end**
11 **return** $\mathscr{H}, I^F$

Definition 11. *(LearnInParts) The LearnInParts function gets* $M = (S, s_0, I, O, \delta, \lambda)$ *and the partition* $I^F = \{I_1, \ldots, I_n\}$ *of* I *and returns the interleaving parallel composition of the learned components.*

$$LearnInParts(M, I^F) = L^*(M, I_1) \parallel \ldots \parallel L^*(M, I_n).$$

Definition 12. *(Composition) Given a partition* $I^F = \{I_1, \ldots, I_n\}$ *and* $D \subseteq \{1, \ldots, n\}$, *the Composition of* I^F *over* D *merges all the* I_i $(i \in D)$ *in* I^F.

$$Composition(I^F, D) = (I^F \setminus \{I_i | i \in D\}) \cup \Big\{ \bigcup_{i \in D} I_i \Big\}.$$

Example. If $I^F = \{\{a\}, \{b\}, \{c\}, \{d\}\}$ and $D = \{1, 3, 4\}$, then $Composition(I^F, D) = \{\{a, c, d\}, \{b\}\}$.

Definition 13. *(InvolvedSets) The function InvolvedSets gets a counter-example* CE *and a partition* $I^F = \{I_1, \ldots, I_n\}$ *and returns indices of the sets in* I^F *that contains at least one character of* CE:

$$InvolvedSets(\text{CE}, I^F) = \{j \mid I_j \in I^F, \exists i \; \text{CE}[i] \in I_j\},$$

where the ith character of CE is denoted by by CE$[i]$.

The function *InvolvedSets* allows us to detect some dependent sets by using a minimal counter-example since all actions in the counter-example are dependent, as we prove in Theorem 2.

Algorithm 1 shows the pseudo-code of the compositional learning algorithm. Initially the algorithm is called with the singleton partitioning I^F of the alphabet I and the SUL M, i.e., if the input alphabet is $I = \{a_1, a_2, \ldots, a_n\}$, then the initial partition of the alphabet will be $I^F = \{\{a_1\}, \{a_2\}, \ldots, \{a_n\}\}$. The *LearnInParts* method on line 2 learns each of the components given the corresponding alphabet set using the algorithm L* and returns the interleaving parallel composition of the learned components. If the oracle (MAT) returns yes for the equivalence query regarding hypothesis $\mathscr{H}$, the algorithm terminates and returns $\mathscr{H}$. Otherwise an(other) iteration of the loop is performed. The *InvolvedSets* method in line 6 extracts the dependent sets from the counter-example returned by the oracle; subsequently, *Composition* merges those sets into one. The *LearnInParts* method in line 8 is run again and the loop continues until the correct hypothesis is learned. We assume that the oracle always returns a minimal counter-example; this assumption is used in the proof of soundness (Theorem 2).

4.1   Termination Analysis

To prove the termination of our algorithm, we start with the following lemma which indicates how the counter-example is used to merge the partitions.

Lemma 3. *Let $I^F = \{I_1, \ldots, I_m\}$ be a partition of the system's input alphabet. If the teacher responds with a counter-example* CE*, then there are at least two actions $u \in I_i, v \in I_j$ in* CE *such that $I_i \neq I_j \ \wedge \ I_i, I_j \in I^F$.*

Proof. We prove this by contradiction. Suppose CE consists of actions that all belong to I_i. Let $C_i = L^*(M, I_i)$ with output function λ_{C_i}. Since the output of L^* is always the correctly learned FSM of the SUL, $\lambda_M(\text{CE}) = \lambda_{C_i}(\text{CE})$. Also, since C_i is a component of $\mathscr{H}$ produced by *LearnInParts*, $\lambda_{\mathscr{H}}(\text{CE}) = \lambda_{C_i}(\text{CE})$ based on Definition 2. This means CE can not be a counter-example.   ∎

The next lemma uses Lemma 3 to show how counter-examples will ensure progress in the algorithm, eventually guaranteeing termination.

Lemma 4. *At each round of the algorithm CL^*, $|I^F|$ decreases by at least 1.*

Proof. By Lemma 3, at each round of the algorithm, at least two dependent sets are found by InvolvedSets, and the algorithm merges these dependent sets into a single set. Thus the size of the partition decrements by at least one; hence, the lemma follows.   ∎

Now we have the necessary ingredients to prove termination below.

Theorem 1. *The Compositional Learning Algorithm terminates.*

Proof. Assume, towards contradiction, that the algorithm does not terminate. Let I be the alphabet, an I_k^F be the partition of I after the kth round of the algorithm. By Lemma 4, after at least $k = |I| - 1$ rounds, $|I_k^F| = 1$. Also by the assumption, the algorithm has not terminated at round k. Since $I_k^F = I$, the algorithm reduces to algorithm L^* which terminates. Hence, the contradiction.   ∎

We prove next that every time we merge two partitions, there is a sound reason (i.e., dependency of actions) for it.

Theorem 2. *Let* CE *be the minimal counter-example returned by the oracle at round k of the algorithm and $I^F = \{I_1, \ldots, I_n\}$ the partition of the alphabet at the same round. Then, all actions in* CE *are dependent.*

Proof. Let $CE = wa$, $w \in I^*$ and $a \in I$, and $d = \{d_1, \ldots, d_m\}$ be an independent partition for the SUL M. Assume some actions in w are independent from a (proof by contradiction). Let d_k be the set in d that includes a. The set $I \setminus d_k$ contains all the independent actions from a. For M, we define $O_M = P_{d_k}(\lambda_M(wa))$; according to Lemma 2, $O_M = \lambda_{P(M,d_k)}(P_{d_k}(wa))$. The algorithm makes the hypothesis $\mathcal{H} = P(M, I_1) || \ldots || P(M, I_n)$ at the current round k. Since d_k is the union of a subset of I^F (algorithm has not terminated yet), $O_{\mathcal{H}} = P_{d_k}(\lambda_{\mathcal{H}}(wa)) = \lambda_{P(\mathcal{H},d_k)}(P_{d_k}(wa))$. If $O_{\mathcal{H}} \neq O_M$, then $P_{d_k}(wa)$ is a smaller counter-example than wa, which is a contradiction. Otherwise if $O_{\mathcal{H}} = O_M$, given that wa is a counter-example, $P_{I \setminus d_k}(\lambda_M(wa)) \neq P_{I \setminus d_k}(\lambda_{\mathcal{H}}(wa))$; if so, $P_{I \setminus d_k}(wa)$ is a smaller counter-example, hence the contradiction. ∎

By Theorems 2 and 1, we have shown that the algorithm detects the independent action sets and eventually terminates. The next theorem is formulated to show that it terminates as soon as all dependent action sets have been detected.

Theorem 3. *Let $I^F = \{I_1, \ldots, I_n\}$ be an independent partition of the alphabet at round k. The algorithm terminates in this round.*

Proof. We prove this by contradiction. Assume that the algorithm does not terminate, and CE is the minimal counter-example returned by the oracle. By theorem 2, *InvolvedSets* returns two or more dependent sets from I^F. Since all the elements in I^F are pairwise independent, we confront the contradiction. ∎

4.2   Processing Counter-examples

As mentioned in Theorem 2, we require all the actions in a minimal counter-example returned by the oracle to be dependent. However, most equivalence checking methods do not find the minimal counter-example. For a non-minimal counter-example, we define a process called "distillation", which asks a number of extra queries to find the dependent actions. It iteratively gets a subset of *InvolvedSets*(CE, I^F) in the order of their sizes and merges its members together, producing a set M. The algorithm introduces $P_M(CE)$ as output if it is a counter-example.

Suppose CE is the counter-example returned by the oracle at round k of the algorithm, and I^F is the alphabet partition at that round. To distill two or more dependent sets from CE, we follow Algorithm 2. The function *CutCE* on line 2 takes a counter-example CE and returns the smallest prefix of CE, which is also a counter-example (i.e., the SUL and the hypothesis model produce different outputs for it). Then, iteratively, it gets a subset of *InvolvedSets*(CE, I^F) in the order of their sizes and merges its members together, producing set M. The algorithm returns $P_M(CE)$ as output if it is a counter-example.

The cost of CE-distillation algorithms is exponential in terms of the size of CE in the worst case. However, in the results section, we show that in practice, the cost of this part is not very significant compared to the total cost of learning.

Theorem 4. *All actions in the output of the CE distillation algorithm are dependent.*

The proof is omitted as it is similar to the proof of Theorem 2.

Algorithm 2: CE distillation

Result: CE_M
1 **Input:** $I^F = \{I_1, \ldots, I_n\}$, CE, M, $\mathscr{H}$
2 $CE \leftarrow CutCE(CE)$
3 $D \leftarrow InvolvedSets(CE, I^F)$
4 **for** $k \in \{2, \ldots, size(D)\}$ **do**
5      $C \leftarrow$ all k combinations(D)
6   **while** C is not empty **do**
7          $I \leftarrow C.pop$
8          $A \leftarrow \bigcup_{i \in I} I_i$
9          $CE_A \leftarrow P_A(CE)$
10   **if** CE_A is a counter-example **then**
11   **Return** CE_A
12   **end**
13   **end**
14 **end**

---

5 Empirical Evaluation

In this section, we present the design and the results of the experiments carried out to evaluate our approach, in order to answer the following research questions:

RQ1 Does CL* require fewer resets, compared to L*?
RQ2 Does CL* require fewer input symbols, compared to L*?

As stated in Section 1, these two research questions measure the efficiency of a learning method in a machine-independent manner: the number of input symbols summarises the total cost of a learning campaign, while the number of resets summarises one of its most costly parts. Note that although active learning processes are structured in terms of queries, the queries used in the processes have vastly different lengths and it has been observed earlier that the total number of input symbols is a more accurate metric for comparison of learning algorithms than the number queries [36].

5.1 Subject Systems

A meaningful benchmark for our method should feature systems of various state sizes and various numbers of parallel components and with a non-trivial structure that may require multiple learning rounds. Also, we would like to have realistic systems, so that our comparisons have meaningful practical implications.

To this end, we choose the Body Comfort System (BCS) [25], which is an automotive software product line (SPL) of a Volkswagen Golf model. This SPL has 27 components, each representing a feature that provides specific functionality. The transition system of each component is provided in a detailed technical report [24]. We use the finite state machines of the components constructed from the transition system representations in [35] and compose several random samples utilising the interleaving parallel composition (Definition 2) to build the product FSMs. We automatically constructed 100 FSMs consisting of a minimum of two and a maximum of nine components in this case study. The maximum number is chosen due the performance limits of L^*; beyond this limit, our learning campaign for L^* could take more than four hours. All experiments were conducted on a computer with an Intel® Core™ M-5Y10c CPU and and 8GB of physical memory running Ubuntu version 20 and LearnLib version 0.16.0. Our subject systems have a minimum of 300 states and a maximum of 3840 states, and their average number of states is 1278.2 with a standard deviation of 847. We started the calculation of the metrics for subject systems of at least 300 states, since for small subject systems, the advantage of compositional learning is not significant.

5.2   Experiment Design

To answer the research questions, we implemented the compositional learning algorithm on top of the LearnLib framework [30]. This implementation uses the equivalence oracle in two places; to learn projections in the *LearnInParts* function and to check the hypothesis/SUL equivalence. The performance of the algorithm significantly relies on the type of equivalence queries used by the underlying L^* algorithm. We experimented with a number of equivalence methods and settled upon using random walks; when using deterministic algorithms such as the WP- and the WP-method, for large systems, the cost of equivalence queries becomes prohibitively high and obscures any gain obtained from compositionality. To ensure that our results are sound, we have carried out similar experiments by using an additional deterministic equivalence query at the end of the learning campaign, when the last random equivalence query does not return any counter-example. This additional step verifies our comparisons when an assurance about the accuracy of the learning process is required. More details about these additional experiments can be found in our public lab package [23] (https://github.com/faezeh-lbf/CL-Star).

We enabled caching, since caching significantly reduces repetitive queries. We repeat each learning process three times, comparing the number of resets and input symbols for L^* and CL^*.

In addition to reporting the median metrics, their standard deviations, and the relative percentage of improvements, we use the statistical T-test to answer the research questions with statistical confidence and report the p-values. We analyse the distribution of the results and establish their normality using K-tests. We use the SciPy [20] library of Python to perform statistical analysis and Seaborn [38] for visualising the results.

5.3   Results

In this section, we first present the results of our experiments and use them to answer our research questions. Then we show how the number of components in an FSM affects the efficiency of our algorithm. Finally, we discuss threats to the validity of our empirical results.

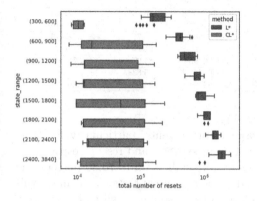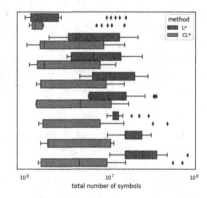

Fig. 2: The total number of input symbols and resets in the CL* and L* methods

We cluster the benchmark into eight categories based on the FSM's number of states and illustrate the distribution of input symbols and resets for each cluster in Figure 2. In this figure, the CL* and L* methods are compared based on the metrics mentioned. The scale of the x-axis (the value of metrics) is logarithmic.

Tables 1 and 2 summarise the results of our experiments. For each category, we calculate the median and standard deviation of our metrics (the number of input symbols and resets) both for L* and CL*. The metric "progress percentage" is defined to measure the improvement brought about by compositional learning (compared to L*). For each metric, the progress percentage is calculated as $(1 - \frac{p}{q}) * 100$, where p and q are the value of that metric in CL* and L*, respectively. A positive progress percentage in a metric shows that the CL* is more efficient in terms of that metric. To measure the statistical significance, we used the one-sided paired sample T-test to check if there was a significant difference ($p < 0.05$) between the metrics in the two algorithms.

Table 1: Comparing the total number of input symbols in the CL* and L* methods

#States	L* method		CL* method		Progress	p-value
	Median	Standard deviation	Median	Standard deviation	percentage	(one-sided paired T-test)
(300, 600]	1443710	2834380.581	1329818	2382620.467	14.47	7.43e-3
(600, 900]	4013396	6262292.443	1716878.5	4408369.926	36.44	1.54e-8
(900, 1200]	6387472	6663334.645	1714934.5	3757307.024	52.37	8.36e-7
(1200, 1500]	6259466	9311767.302	1576494	4798094.639	57.28	6.49e-4
(1500, 1800]	9700935	10726103.24	4498072	5576873.639	54.58	4.30e-4
(1800, 2100]	11070428	5310108.013	1649557	13958718.62	37.51	2.96e-2
(2100, 2400]	15348181	6287714.182	1888226	4215184.514	70.80	1.80e-10
(2400, 3840]	24700222.5	14837416.08	4385086	13817389.06	68.42	2.66e-12

Table 2: Comparing the total number of resets in the CL* and L* methods

#States	L* method		CL* method		Progress	p-value
	Median	Standard deviation	Median	Standard deviation	percentage	(one-sided paired T-test)
(300, 600]	157971	65257.85738	10433	28259.60196	90.46	1.05e-33
(600, 900]	425260.5	77944.01883	16808	56274.51558	86.33	1.07e-43
(900, 1200]	501347.5	147915.8363	13109	50224.87222	90.87	3.80e-16
(1200, 1500]	712999	136904.04	12811	60125.8884	91.77	4.18e-13
(1500, 1800]	823482	275862.8299	48344	80507.59837	91.73	4.97e-13
(1800, 2100]	1262025	188390.1181	12412	369932.964	84.07	2.18e-06
(2100, 2400]	1412237	220211.8459	15042	53006.08784	95.83	2.44e-14
(2400, 3840]	1900234	427883.9888	46624.5	201052.8807	94.67	2.20e-23

Both Tables 1 and 2 indicate major improvements, particularly for large systems, in terms of the total number of input symbols and resets, respectively. Compositional learning reduces the number of symbols up to 70.80 percent and the number of resets up to 95.83 percent. The statistical tests also confirm this observations and the p-values obtained from the tests are in all cases very low; in case of the number of input symbols the p-values range from 10^{-2} to 10^{-12}, while for resets they range from 10^{-6} to 10^{-43}, which are well-below the usual statistical p-values (0.05) and represent a very high statistical significance.

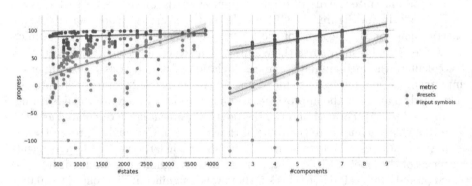

Fig. 3: The diagrams of improvement brought about by compositional learning vs. size of the SUL in terms of number states (left) and components (right).

The plots in Figure 3 visualise the improvements brought about by compositional learning. This plot demonstrates that the saving due to compositional learning increases as the number of components in SULs increases. We further analysed the trends of our measured metrics in terms of the number of states and the number of parallel components. These trends are depicted for the total number of input symbols in Figure 4 and for the number of resets in Figure 5, respectively. These figures indicate that the increase of both metrics with the number of states is more moderate for the compositional learning approach, i.e., compositional learning is more scalable. More importantly, the right-hand-side

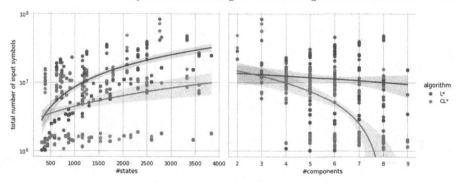

Fig. 4: The effect of FSM sizes in terms of the number of components and states on the total number of input symbols.

of both figures signifies the effect of compositional learning when the number of parallel components increases while the number of states remains fixed.

Figure 6 shows the effect of the number of components on the total number of input symbols for a fixed state-space size for algorithms L* and CL*. In this plot, as the number of components increases, the corresponding dot will become darker and larger. According to this figure, the learning cost is lower for SULs with more components in both L* and CL*. Still, for CL* (the right side), the cost of learning SULs with more components is significantly lower because we structurally learn these components essentially independently.

As mentioned in Section 4.2, the cost of the CE distillation process can increase exponentially in the size of the counter-example. However, in practice, it seems to be much more tractable. To evaluate this, we count the number of input symbols required by the CE distillation process to learn each SUL. The median value of this metric is 1961 input symbols, which is insignificant compared the total cost of learning. In fact, the cost of CE distillation process for each group in Table 1 is between 0.037 and 0.12 percent of the total learning cost; the reported total learning cost (total number of input symbols) includes the cost of CE distillation.

5.4 Threats to Validity

In this section, we summarise the major threats to the validity of our empirical conclusions. First, we analyse the threats to conclusion validity, i.e., whether the empirical conclusions necessarily follow from the experiments carried out. Then, we discuss the threats to external validity concerning the generalisation of our results to other systems.

We mitigated conclusion validity threats by using statistical tests to ensure that our observations (both in terms of improvement percentages in Tables 1 and 2 and the visual observations in Figures 2) do represent a statistically significant improvement. We opt for one-sided paired sample T-tests in order to minimise

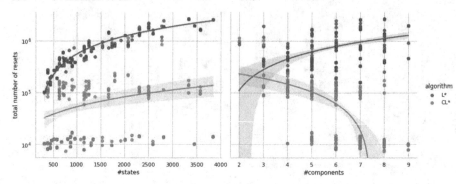

Fig. 5: The effect of the size of FSMs in terms of the number of components and states on the total number of required input resets.

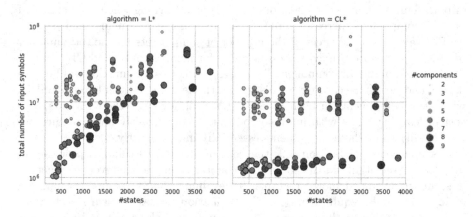

Fig. 6: The relation between the total number of symbols and the number of states and components for the algorithms L* (left) and CL* (right).

the threats to conclusion validity. We only conclude that the CL* is more efficient than the L* when there is a meaningful difference ($p < 0.05$) between the results of L* and CL*. To make sure that the chosen statistical test is applicable, we analysed the distribution of the data first.

We mitigated the risk of conclusion validity by using subject systems that are based on practical systems rather than using randomly generated FSMs. However, further research is needed to analyse the performance of our approach based on other benchmarks from other domains. We also mitigated the effect of using random equivalence queries by repeating the experiments with a final deterministic query.

6   Conclusions

In this paper, we presented a compositional learning method based on Angluin's algorithm L* that detects and independently learns interleaving parallel components of the system under learning. We proved that our algorithm, called CL*, is correct and we empirically showed that it causes significant gains in the number of input symbols and the number of resets in a learning campaign. The gain is significantly increased with the number of parallel components.

Our algorithm is naturally amenable to parallelisation and developing a parallel implementation is a natural next step. A more thorough investigation of counter-example processing in order to efficiently find a minimal counter-example is an area of further research, particularly, in the light of the recent results in this area [13]. Finding a trade-off between using deterministic and random (or mutation-based) equivalence queries is another area of future research. We would also like to investigate the possibility of developing equivalence queries that take the structure of the systems into account: we have observed that much of the effort in the final equivalence query (on the composed system) is redundant and the final equivalence query can be made much more efficient by only considering the dependencies among purportedly independent partitions. Finally, extending our notion of parallel composition to allow for a possible synchronisation of components is another direction of future work; we believe inspirations from concurrency theory and in particular, Milner and Moller's prime decomposition theorem [26] may prove effective in this regard. Independently from our work, Neele and Sammartino [29] proposed an approach to learn synchronous parallel composition, under the assumption of knowing the alphabets of the components. This is a promising approach to incorporate synchronous parallel composition into our framework.

Acknowledgments

We would like to thank Rasta Tadayon and Amin Asadi Sarijalou for their contributions to the early stages of this work. The work of Mohammad Reza Mousavi was supported by the UKRI Trustworthy Autonomous Systems Node in Verifiability, Grant Award Reference EP/V026801/2. We thank the reviewers of FOSSACS for their insightful and constructive comments, which, in our view, led to improvements in our final paper. We thank the Artifact Evaluation committee at ESOP/FOSSACS for their careful review of our lab package.

References

1. Aarts, F., de Ruiter, J., Poll, E.: Formal models of bank cards for free. In: Sixth IEEE International Conference on Software Testing, Verification and Validation, ICST 2013 Workshops Proceedings, Luxembourg, Luxembourg, March 18-22, 2013. pp. 461–468. IEEE Computer Society (2013). https://doi.org/10.1109/ICSTW.2013.60

2. Aarts, F., Schmaltz, J., Vaandrager, F.W.: Inference and abstraction of the biometric passport. In: Margaria, T., Steffen, B. (eds.) Leveraging Applications of Formal Methods, Verification, and Validation - 4th International Symposium on Leveraging Applications, ISoLA 2010, Heraklion, Crete, Greece, October 18-21, 2010, Proceedings, Part I. Lecture Notes in Computer Science, vol. 6415, pp. 673–686. Springer (2010). https://doi.org/10.1007/978-3-642-16558-0_54

3. Aichernig, B.K., Tappler, M.: Efficient active automata learning via mutation testing. Journal of Automated Reasoning **63**(4), 1103–1134 (2019). https://doi.org/10.1007/s10817-018-9486-0

4. Aichernig, B.K., Tappler, M., Wallner, F.: Benchmarking combinations of learning and testing algorithms for active automata learning. In: Ahrendt, W., Wehrheim, H. (eds.) Tests and Proofs - 14th International Conference, TAP@STAF 2020, Bergen, Norway, June 22-23, 2020, Proceedings [postponed]. Lecture Notes in Computer Science, vol. 12165, pp. 3–22. Springer (2020). https://doi.org/10.1007/978-3-030-50995-8_1

5. An, J., Chen, M., Zhan, B., Zhan, N., Zhang, M.: Learning one-clock timed automata. In: Biere, A., Parker, D. (eds.) Tools and Algorithms for the Construction and Analysis of Systems. pp. 444–462. Springer International Publishing, Cham (2020). https://doi.org/10.1007/978-3-030-45190-5_25

6. Angluin, D.: Learning regular sets from queries and counterexamples. Inf. Comput. **75**(2), 87–106 (1987). https://doi.org/10.1016/0890-5401(87)90052-6

7. Broy, M., Jonsson, B., Katoen, J., Leucker, M., Pretschner, A. (eds.): Model-Based Testing of Reactive Systems, Advanced Lectures [The volume is the outcome of a research seminar that was held in Schloss Dagstuhl in January 2004], Lecture Notes in Computer Science, vol. 3472. Springer (2005). https://doi.org/10.1007/b137241

8. Cifuentes, C., Simon, D.: Procedure abstraction recovery from binary code. In: Proceedings of the Fourth European Conference on Software Maintenance and Reengineering. pp. 55–64. IEEE (2000). https://doi.org/10.1109/CSMR.2000.827306

9. Damasceno, C.D.N., Mousavi, M.R., da Silva Simão, A.: Learning by sampling: learning behavioral family models from software product lines. Empir. Softw. Eng. **26**(1), 4 (2021). https://doi.org/10.1007/s10664-020-09912-w

10. al Duhaiby, O., Groote, J.F.: Active learning of decomposable systems. In: Bae, K., Bianculli, D., Gnesi, S., Plat, N. (eds.) FormaliSE@ICSE 2020: 8th International Conference on Formal Methods in Software Engineering, Seoul, Republic of Korea, July 13, 2020. pp. 1–10. ACM (2020). https://doi.org/10.1145/3372020.3391560

11. Fiterau-Brostean, P., Lenaerts, T., Poll, E., de Ruiter, J., Vaandrager, F.W., Verleg, P.: Model learning and model checking of SSH implementations. In: Erdogmus, H., Havelund, K. (eds.) Proceedings of the 24th ACM SIGSOFT International SPIN Symposium on Model Checking of Software, Santa Barbara, CA, USA, July 10-14, 2017. pp. 142–151. ACM (2017). https://doi.org/10.1145/3092282.3092289

12. Frohme, M., Steffen, B.: Compositional learning of mutually recursive procedural systems. Int. J. Softw. Tools Technol. Transf. **23**(4), 521–543 (2021). https://doi.org/10.1007/s10009-021-00634-y

13. Frohme, M., Steffen, B.: From languages to behaviors and back. In: Jansen, N., Stoelinga, M., van den Bos, P. (eds.) A Journey from Process Algebra via Timed Automata to Model Learning - Essays Dedicated to Frits Vaandrager on the Occasion of His 60th Birthday. Lecture Notes in Computer Science, vol. 13560, pp. 180–200. Springer (2022). https://doi.org/10.1007/978-3-031-15629-8_11

14. Garhewal, B., Vaandrager, F.W., Howar, F., Schrijvers, T., Lenaerts, T., Smits, R.: Grey-box learning of register automata. In: Dongol, B., Troubitsyna, E. (eds.)

Integrated Formal Methods - 16th International Conference, IFM 2020, Lugano, Switzerland, November 16-20, 2020, Proceedings. Lecture Notes in Computer Science, vol. 12546, pp. 22–40. Springer (2020). https://doi.org/10.1007/978-3-030-63461-2_2

15. Hooimeijer, B., Geilen, M., Groote, J.F., Hendriks, D., Schiffelers, R.R.H.: Constructive model inference: Model learning for component-based software architectures. In: Fill, H., van Sinderen, M., Maciaszek, L.A. (eds.) Proceedings of the 17th International Conference on Software Technologies, ICSOFT 2022, Lisbon, Portugal, July 11-13, 2022. pp. 146–158. SCITEPRESS (2022). https://doi.org/10.5220/0011145700003266

16. Howar, F., Steffen, B.: Active automata learning in practice - an annotated bibliography of the years 2011 to 2016. In: Bennaceur, A., Hähnle, R., Meinke, K. (eds.) Machine Learning for Dynamic Software Analysis: Potentials and Limits - International Dagstuhl Seminar 16172, Dagstuhl Castle, Germany, April 24-27, 2016, Revised Papers. Lecture Notes in Computer Science, vol. 11026, pp. 123–148. Springer (2018). https://doi.org/10.1007/978-3-319-96562-8_5

17. Howar, F., Steffen, B.: Active automata learning as black-box search and lazy partition refinement. In: Jansen, N., Stoelinga, M., van den Bos, P. (eds.) A Journey from Process Algebra via Timed Automata to Model Learning : Essays Dedicated to Frits Vaandrager on the Occasion of His 60th Birthday, pp. 321–338. Springer Nature Switzerland, Cham (2022). https://doi.org/10.1007/978-3-031-15629-8_17

18. Isberner, M., Howar, F., Steffen, B.: Learning register automata: from languages to program structures. Machine Learning 96(1), 65–98 (2014). https://doi.org/10.1007/s10994-013-5419-7

19. Isberner, M., Howar, F., Steffen, B.: The TTT algorithm: A redundancy-free approach to active automata learning. In: Bonakdarpour, B., Smolka, S.A. (eds.) Runtime Verification - 5th International Conference, RV 2014, Toronto, ON, Canada, September 22-25, 2014. Proceedings. Lecture Notes in Computer Science, vol. 8734, pp. 307–322. Springer (2014). https://doi.org/10.1007/978-3-319-11164-3_26

20. Jones, E., Oliphant, T., Peterson, P.: Scipy: Open source scientific tools for python (01 2001). https://doi.org/10.1038/s41592-019-0686-2

21. Kearns, M.J., Vazirani, U.: An Introduction to Computational Learning Theory. MIT Press (1994). https://doi.org/10.7551/mitpress/3897.001.0001

22. Koschke, R.: Architecture Reconstruction, p. 140–173. Springer-Verlag, Berlin, Heidelberg (2009). https://doi.org/10.1007/978-3-540-95888-8_6

23. Labbaf, F., Groot, J.F., Hojjat, H., Mousavi, M.R.: Compositional Learning for Interleaving Parallel Automata (CL-Star) (Apr 2023). https://doi.org/10.5281/zenodo.7624699, https://doi.org/10.5281/zenodo.7624699

24. Lachmann, R., Lity, S., Lischke, S., Beddig, S., Schulze, S., Schaefer, I.: Delta-oriented test case prioritization for integration testing of software product lines. In: Proceedings of the 19th International Conference on Software Product Line. p. 81–90. SPLC '15, ACM, New York, NY, USA (2015). https://doi.org/10.1145/2791060.2791073

25. Lity, S., Lachmann, R., Lochau, M., Schaefer, I.: Delta-oriented software product line test models-the body comfort system case study. Tech. Rep. 2012-07, TU Braunschweig (2012)

26. Milner, R., Moller, F.: Unique decomposition of processes. Theoretical Computer Science 107(2), 357–363 (1993). https://doi.org/10.1016/0304-3975(93)90176-T, https://www.sciencedirect.com/science/article/pii/030439759390176T

27. Moerman, J.: Learning product automata. In: Unold, O., Dyrka, W., Wieczorek, W. (eds.) Proceedings of The 14th International Conference on Grammatical Inference 2018. Proceedings of Machine Learning Research, vol. 93, pp. 54–66. PMLR (feb 2019), https://proceedings.mlr.press/v93/moerman19a.html

28. Naeem Irfan, M., Oriat, C., Groz, R.: Model inference and testing. Advances in Computers, vol. 89, pp. 89–139. Elsevier (2013). https://doi.org/10.1016/B978-0-12-408094-2.00003-5, https://www.sciencedirect.com/science/article/pii/B9780124080942000035

29. Neele, T., Sammartino, M.: Compositional Automata Learning of Synchronous Systems. In: Lambers, L., Uchitel, S. (eds.) FASE 2023. Lecture Notes in Computer Science, Springer (2023)

30. Raffelt, H., Steffen, B.: Learnlib: A library for automata learning and experimentation. In: Baresi, L., Heckel, R. (eds.) Fundamental Approaches to Software Engineering. pp. 377–380. Springer Berlin Heidelberg, Berlin, Heidelberg (2006). https://doi.org/10.1145/1081180.1081189

31. Rivest, R., Schapire, R.: Inference of finite automata using homing sequences. Information and Computation **103**(2), 299–347 (1993). https://doi.org/10.1006/inco.1993.1021

32. Sanchez, L., Groote, J.F., Schiffelers, R.R.H.: Active learning of industrial software with data. In: Hojjat, H., Massink, M. (eds.) Fundamentals of Software Engineering - 8th International Conference, FSEN 2019, Tehran, Iran, May 1-3, 2019, Revised Selected Papers. Lecture Notes in Computer Science, vol. 11761, pp. 95–110. Springer (2019). https://doi.org/10.1007/978-3-030-31517-7_7

33. Smeenk, W., Moerman, J., Vaandrager, F.W., Jansen, D.N.: Applying automata learning to embedded control software. In: Butler, M.J., Conchon, S., Zaïdi, F. (eds.) Formal Methods and Software Engineering - 17th International Conference on Formal Engineering Methods, ICFEM 2015, Paris, France, November 3-5, 2015, Proceedings. Lecture Notes in Computer Science, vol. 9407, pp. 67–83. Springer (2015). https://doi.org/10.1007/978-3-319-25423-4_5

34. Tappler, M., Aichernig, B.K., Larsen, K.G., Lorber, F.: Time to learn – learning timed automata from tests. In: Formal Modeling and Analysis of Timed Systems: 17th International Conference, FORMATS 2019, Amsterdam, The Netherlands, August 27–29, 2019, Proceedings. p. 216–235. Springer-Verlag, Berlin, Heidelberg (2019). https://doi.org/10.1007/978-3-030-29662-9_13

35. Tavassoli, S., Damasceno, C.D.N., Khosravi, R., Mousavi, M.R.: Adaptive behavioral model learning for software product lines. In: Felfernig, A., Fuentes, L., Cleland-Huang, J., Assunção, W.K.G., Falkner, A.A., Azanza, M., Luaces, M.Á.R., Bhushan, M., Semini, L., Devroey, X., Werner, C.M.L., Seidl, C., Le, V., Horcas, J.M. (eds.) SPLC '22: 26th ACM International Systems and Software Product Line Conference, Graz, Austria, September 12 - 16, 2022, Volume A. pp. 142–153. ACM (2022). https://doi.org/10.1145/3546932.3546991

36. Vaandrager, F.: Model learning. Commun. ACM **60**(2), 86–95 (jan 2017). https://doi.org/10.1145/2967606

37. Vaandrager, F.W., Garhewal, B., Rot, J., Wißmann, T.: A new approach for active automata learning based on apartness. In: Fisman, D., Rosu, G. (eds.) Proceedings of the 28th International Conference on Tools and Algorithms for the Construction and Analysis of Systems TACAS 2022. Lecture Notes in Computer Science, vol. 13243, pp. 223–243. Springer (2022). https://doi.org/10.1007/978-3-030-99524-9_12

38. Waskom, M.L.: seaborn: statistical data visualization. Journal of Open Source Software **6**(60), 3021 (2021). https://doi.org/10.21105/joss.03021

Pebble minimization: the last theorems

Gaëtan Douéneau-Tabot[✉]

1 Université Paris Cité, CNRS, IRIF, F-75013, Paris, France
2 Direction générale de l'armement - Ingénierie des projets, Paris, France
doueneau@irif.fr

Abstract Pebble transducers are nested two-way transducers which can drop marks (named "pebbles") on their input word. Such machines can compute functions whose output size is polynomial in the size of their input. They can be seen as simple recursive programs whose recursion height is bounded. A natural problem is, given a pebble transducer, to compute an equivalent pebble transducer with minimal recursion height. This problem has been open since the introduction of the model.

In this paper, we study two restrictions of pebble transducers, that cannot see the marks ("blind pebble transducers" introduced by Nguyên et al.), or that can only see the last mark dropped ("last pebble transducers" introduced by Engelfriet et al.). For both models, we provide an effective algorithm for minimizing the recursion height. The key property used in both cases is that a function whose output size is linear (resp. quadratic, cubic, etc.) can always be computed by a machine whose recursion height is 1 (resp. 2, 3, etc.). We finally show that this key property fails as soon as we consider machines that can see more than one mark.

Keywords: Pebble transducers · Polyregular functions · Blind pebble transducers · Last pebble transducers · Factorization forests.

1 Introduction

Transducers are finite-state machines obtained by adding outputs to finite automata. They are very useful in a lot of areas like coding, computer arithmetic, language processing or program analysis, and more generally in data stream processing. In this paper, we consider deterministic transducers which compute functions from finite words to finite words. In particular, a **deterministic two-way transducer** is a two-way automaton with outputs. This model describes the class of **regular functions**, which is often considered as one of the functional counterparts of regular languages. It has been intensively studied for its properties such as closure under composition [5], equivalence with logical transductions [12] or regular expressions [7], decidable equivalence problem [14], etc.

Pebble transducers and polyregular functions. Two-way transducers can only describe functions whose output size is at most linear in the input size. A possible solution to overcome this limitation is to consider nested two-way

O. Kupferman and P. Sobocinski (Eds.): FoSSaCS 2023, LNCS 13992, pp. 436–455, 2023.
https://doi.org/10.1007/978-3-031-30829-1_21

transducers. In particular, the model of k-**pebble transducer** has been studied for a long time [13]. For $k = 1$, a 1-pebble transducer is just a two-way transducer. For $k \geqslant 2$, a k-pebble transducer is a two-way transducer that, when on any position i of its input word, can call a $(k-1)$-pebble transducer. The latter takes as input the original input where position i is marked by a "pebble". The main two-way transducer then outputs the concatenation of all the outputs produced along its calls. The intuitive behavior of a 3-pebble transducer is depicted in fig. 1. It can be seen as a recursive program whose recursion stack has height 3. The class of functions computed by pebble transducers is known as **polyregular functions**. It has been intensively studied due to its properties such as closure under composition [11], equivalence with logical interpretations [4], etc.

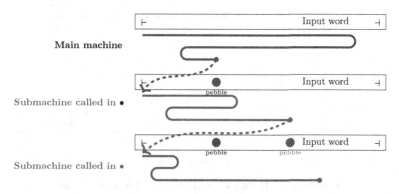

Figure 1: Behavior of a 3-pebble transducer.

Optimization of pebble transducers. Given a k-pebble transducer computing a function f, a very natural problem is to compute the least possible $1 \leqslant \ell \leqslant k$ such that f can be computed by an ℓ-pebble transducer. Furthermore, we can be interested in effectively building an ℓ-pebble transducer for f. Both questions are open, but they are meaningful since they ask whether we can optimize the recursion height (i.e. the running time) of a program.

It is easy to observe that if f is computed by a k-pebble transducer, then $|f(u)| = \mathcal{O}(|u|^k)$. It was first claimed in a LICS 2020 paper that the minimal recursion height ℓ of f (i.e. the least possible ℓ such that f can be computed by an ℓ-pebble transducer) was exactly the least possible ℓ such that $|f(u)| = \mathcal{O}(|u|^\ell)$. However, Bojańczyk recently disproved this statement in [3, Theorem 6.3]: the function inner-squaring : $u_1 \# \cdots \# u_n \mapsto (u_1\#)^n \cdots (u_n\#)^n$ can be computed by a 3-pebble transducer and is such that $|\text{inner-squaring}(u)| = \mathcal{O}(|u|^2)$, but it cannot be computed by a 2-pebble transducer. Other counterexamples were given in [16] using different proof techniques. Therefore, computing the minimal recursion height of f is believed to be hard, since this value not only depends on the output size of f, but also on the word combinatorics of this output.

Optimization of blind pebble transducers. A subclass of pebble transducers, named **blind pebble transducers**, was recently introduced in [17]. A blind k-pebble transducer is somehow a k-pebble transducer, with the difference that the positions are no longer marked when making recursive calls. The behavior of a blind 3-pebble transducer is depicted in fig. 2. The class of functions computed by blind pebble transducers is strictly included in polyregular functions [10,17]. The main result of [17] shows that for blind pebble transducers, the minimal recursion height for computing a function only depends on the growth of its output. More precisely, if f is computed by a blind k-pebble transducer, then the least possible $1 \leqslant \ell \leqslant k$ such that f can be computed by an blind ℓ-pebble transducer is the least possible ℓ such that $|f(u)| = \mathcal{O}(|u|^\ell)$.

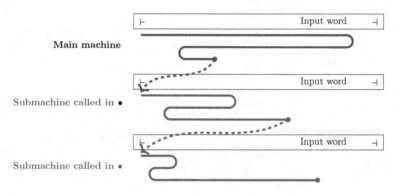

Figure 2: Behavior of a blind 3-pebble transducer.

Contributions. In this paper, we first give a new proof of the connection between minimal recursion height and growth of the output for blind pebble transducers. Furthermore, our proof provides an algorithm that, given a function computed by a blind k-pebble transducer, builds a blind ℓ-pebble transducer which computes it, for the least possible $1 \leqslant \ell \leqslant k$. This effective result is not claimed in [17], and our proof techniques significantly differ from theirs. Indeed, we make a heavy use of **factorization forests**, which have already been used as a powerful tool in the study of pebble transducers [2,8,10].

Secondly, the main contribution of this paper is to show that the (effective) connection between minimal recursion height and growth of the output also holds for the class of **last pebble transducers** (introduced in [13]). Intuitively, a last k-pebble transducer is a k-pebble transducer where a called submachine can only see the position of its call, but not the full stack of the former positions. The behavior of a last 3-pebble transducer is depicted in fig. 3. Observe that a blind k-pebble transducer is a restricted version of a last k-pebble transducer. Formally, we show that if f is computed by a last k-pebble transducer, then the least possible ℓ such that f can be computed by a last ℓ-pebble transducer is the least possible ℓ such that $|f(u)| = \mathcal{O}(|u|^\ell)$. Furthermore, our proof gives an algorithm that effectively builds a last ℓ-pebble transducer computing f.

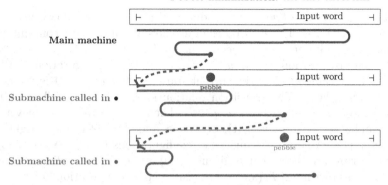

Figure 3: Behavior of a last 3-pebble transducer.

As a third theorem, we show that our result for last pebble transducers is tight, in the sense that the connection between minimal recursion height and growth of the output does not hold for more powerful models. More precisely, we define the model of **last-last k-pebble transducers**, which extends last k-pebble transducers by allowing them to see the two last positions of the calls (and not only the last one). We show that for all $k \geqslant 1$, there exists a function f such that $|f(u)| = \mathcal{O}(|u|^2)$ and that is computed by a last-last $(2k+1)$-pebble transducer, but cannot be computed by a last-last $2k$-pebble transducer. The proof of this result relies on a counterexample presented by Bojańczyk in [2].

Outline. We introduce two-way transducers in section 2. In section 3 we describe blind pebble transducers and last pebble transducers. We also state our main results that connect the minimal recursion height of a function to the growth of its output. Their proof goes over sections 4 to 6. In section 7, we finally show that these results cannot be extended to two visible marks.

2   Preliminaries on two-way transducers

Capital letters A, B denote alphabets, i.e. finite sets of letters. The empty word is denoted by ε. If $u \in A^*$, let $|u| \in \mathbb{N}$ be its length, and for $1 \leqslant i \leqslant |u|$ let $u[i]$ be its i-th letter. If $i \leqslant j$, we let $u[i{:}j]$ be $u[i]u[i+1]\cdots u[j]$ (empty if $j < i$). If $a \in A$, let $|u|_a$ be the number of letters a occurring in u. We assume that the reader is familiar with the basics of automata theory, in particular two-way automata and monoid morphisms. The type of total (resp. partial, i.e. possibly undefined on some inputs) functions is denoted $S \to T$ (resp. $S \rightharpoonup T$).

The machines described in this paper are always **deterministic**.

Definition 2.1. A **two-way transducer** $\mathscr{T} = (A, B, Q, q_0, F, \delta, \lambda)$ consists of:
- an input alphabet A and an output alphabet B;
- a finite set of states Q with $q_0 \in Q$ initial and $F \subseteq Q$ final;
- a transition function $\delta : Q \times (A \uplus \{\vdash, \dashv\}) \rightharpoonup Q \times \{\triangleleft, \triangleright\}$;
- an output function $\lambda : Q \times (A \uplus \{\vdash, \dashv\}) \rightharpoonup B^*$ with same domain as δ.

The semantics of a two-way transducer $\mathscr{T}$ is defined as follows. When given as input a word $u \in A^*$, $\mathscr{T}$ disposes of a read-only input tape containing $\vdash u \dashv$. The marks $\vdash$ and $\dashv$ are used to detect the borders of the tape, by convention we denote them by positions 0 and $|u|+1$ of u. Formally, a configuration over $\vdash u \dashv$ is a tuple (q, i) where $q \in Q$ is the current state and $0 \leqslant i \leqslant |u|+1$ is the position of the reading head. The transition relation $\to$ is defined as follows. Given a configuration (q, i), let $(q', \star) := \delta(q, u[i])$. Then $(q, i) \to (q', i')$ whenever either $\star = \triangleleft$ and $i' = i-1$ (move left), or $\star = \triangleright$ and $i' = i+1$ (move right), with $0 \leqslant i' \leqslant |u|+1$. A run is a sequence of configurations $(q_1, i_1) \to \cdots \to (q_n, i_n)$. Accepting runs are those that begin in $(q_0, 0)$ and end in a configuration of the form $(q, |u|+1)$ with $q \in F$ (and never visit such a configuration before).

The partial function $f : A^* \rightharpoonup B^*$ computed by the two-way transducer $\mathscr{T}$ is defined as follows: for $u \in A^*$, if there exists an accepting run on $\vdash u \dashv$, then it is unique, and $f(u)$ is defined as $\lambda(q_1, (\vdash u \dashv)[i_1]) \cdots \lambda(q_n, (\vdash u \dashv)[i_n]) \in B^*$. The class of functions computed by two-way transducers is called **regular functions**.

Example 2.2. Let $\widetilde{u}$ be the mirror image of $u \in A^*$. Let $\# \notin A$ be a fresh symbol. The function map-reverse : $u_1 \# \cdots \# u_n \mapsto \widetilde{u_1} \# \cdots \# \widetilde{u_n}$ can be computed by a two-way transducer, that reads each factor u_j from right to left.

It is well-known that the domain of a regular function is always a **regular language** (see e.g. [18]). From now on, we assume without losing generalities that our two-way transducers only compute total functions (in other words, they have exactly one accepting run on each $\vdash u \dashv$). Furthermore, we assume that $\lambda(q, \vdash) = \lambda(q, \dashv) = \varepsilon$ for all $q \in Q$ (we only lose generality for the image of ε).

In the rest of this section, $\mathscr{T}$ denotes a two-way transducer with input alphabet A, output alphabet B and output function λ. Now, we define the **crossing sequence** in a position $1 \leqslant i \leqslant |u|$ of input $\vdash u \dashv$. Intuitively, it regroups the states of the accepting run which are visited in this position.

Definition 2.3. *Let $u \in A^*$ and $1 \leqslant i \leqslant |u|$. Let $(q_1, i_1) \to \cdots \to (q_n, i_n)$ be the accepting run of $\mathscr{T}$ on $\vdash u \dashv$. The **crossing sequence** of $\mathscr{T}$ in i, denoted $\mathsf{cross}_{\mathscr{T}}^u(i)$, is defined as the sequence $(q_j)_{1 \leqslant j \leqslant n}$ and $i_j = i$.*

If $\mu : A^* \to \mathbb{M}$ is a monoid morphism, we say that any $m, m' \in \mathbb{M}$ and $a \in A$ define a μ-**context** that we denote by $m[\![a]\!]m'$. It is well-known that the crossing sequence in a position of the input only depends on the context of this position, for a well-chosen monoid, as claimed in proposition 2.4 (see e.g. [7]).

Proposition 2.4. *One can build a finite monoid $\mathbb{T}$ and a monoid morphism $\mu : A^* \to \mathbb{T}$, called the **transition morphism** of $\mathscr{T}$, such that for all $u \in A^*$ and $1 \leqslant i \leqslant |u|$, $\mathsf{cross}_{\mathscr{T}}^u(i)$ only depends on $\mu(u[1{:}i{-}1])$, $u[i]$ and $\mu(u[i{+}1{:}|u|])$. Thus we denote it $\mathsf{cross}_{\mathscr{T}}(\mu(u[1{:}i{-}1])[\![u[i]]\!]\mu(u[i{+}1{:}|u|]))$.*

Finally, let us define "the output produced below position i".

Definition 2.5. *Let $u \in A^*$ and $1 \leqslant i \leqslant |u|$ and $q_1 \cdots q_n := \mathsf{cross}_{\mathscr{T}}^u(i)$. We define the **production** of $\mathscr{T}$ in i, denoted $\mathsf{prod}_{\mathscr{T}}^u(i)$, as $\lambda(q_1, u[i]) \cdots \lambda(q_n, u[i])$.*

By proposition 2.4, it also makes sense to define $\mathsf{prod}_{\mathscr{T}}(m[\![a]\!]m') \in B^*$ to be $\mathsf{prod}^u_{\mathscr{T}}(i)$ whenever $m = \mu(u[1{:}i{-}1])$, $m' = \mu(u[i{+}1{:}|u|])$ and $a = u[i]$.

3   Blind and last pebble transducers

Now, we are ready to define formally the models of blind pebble transducers and last pebble transducers. Intuitively, they correspond to two-way transducers which make a tree of recursive calls to other two-way transducers.

Definition 3.1 (Blind pebble transducer [17]). *For $k \geqslant 1$, a **blind k-pebble transducer** with input alphabet A and output alphabet B is:*
- *if $k = 1$, a two-way transducer with input alphabet A and output B;*
- *if $k \geqslant 2$, a tree $\mathscr{T}\langle \mathscr{B}_1, \cdots, \mathscr{B}_p \rangle$ where the subtrees $\mathscr{B}_1, \ldots, \mathscr{B}_p$ are blind $(k{-}1)$-pebble transducers with input A and output B; and the root label $\mathscr{T}$ is a two-way transducer with input A and output alphabet $\{\mathscr{B}_1, \ldots, \mathscr{B}_p\}$.*

The (total) function $f : A^* \to B^*$ computed by the blind k-pebble transducer of definition 3.1 is built in a recursive fashion, as follows:
- for $k = 1$, f is the function computed by the two-way transducer;
- for $k \geqslant 2$, let $u \in A^*$ and $(q_1, i_1) \to \cdots \to (q_n, i_n)$ be the accepting run of $\mathscr{T} = (A, B, Q, q_0, F, \delta, \lambda)$ on $\vdash u \dashv$. For all $1 \leqslant j \leqslant n$, let $f_j : A^* \to B^*$ be the concatenation of the functions recursively computed by the sequence $\lambda(q_j, (\vdash u \dashv)[i_j]) \in \{\mathscr{B}_1, \ldots, \mathscr{B}_p\}^*$. Then $f(u) := f_1(u) \cdots f_n(u)$.

The behavior of a blind 3-pebble transducer is depicted in fig. 2.

Example 3.2. The function $\mathsf{unmarked\text{-}square} : A^* \to A^* \uplus \{\#\}, u \mapsto (u\#)^{|u|}$ can be computed by a blind 2-pebble transducer. This machine has shape $\mathscr{T}\langle \mathscr{T}' \rangle$: $\mathscr{T}$ calls $\mathscr{T}'$ on each position $1 \leqslant i \leqslant |u|$ of its input u, and $\mathscr{T}'$ outputs $u\#$.

The class of functions computed by a blind k-pebble transducer for some $k \geqslant 1$ is called **polyblind functions** [10]. They form a strict subclass of polyregular functions [8,10,17] which is closed under composition [17, Theorem 6.1].

Now, let us define last pebble transducers. They corresponds to blind pebble transducers enhanced with the ability to mark the current position of the input when doing a recursive call. Formally, this position is underlined and we define $u \bullet i := u[1] \cdots u[i{-}1]\underline{u[i]}u[i{+}1] \cdots u[|u|]$ for $u \in A^*$ and $1 \leqslant i \leqslant |u|$.

Definition 3.3 (Last pebble transducer [13]). *For $k \geqslant 1$, a **last k-pebble transducer** with input alphabet A and output alphabet B is:*
- *if $k = 1$, a two-way transducer with input alphabet $A \uplus \underline{A}$ and output B;*
- *if $k \geqslant 2$, a tree $\mathscr{T}\langle \mathscr{L}_1, \cdots, \mathscr{L}_p \rangle$ where the subtrees $\mathscr{L}_1, \ldots, \mathscr{L}_p$ are last $(k{-}1)$-pebble transducers with input A and output B; and the root label $\mathscr{T}$ is a two-way transducer with input $A \uplus \underline{A}$ and output alphabet $\{\mathscr{L}_1, \ldots, \mathscr{L}_p\}$.*

The (total) function $f : (A \uplus \underline{A})^* \to B^*$ computed by the last k-pebble transducer of definition 3.3 is defined in a recursive fashion, as follows:
- for $k = 1$, f is the function computed by the two-way transducer;

– for $k \geqslant 2$, let $u \in A^*$ and $(q_1, i_1) \to \cdots \to (q_n, i_n)$ be the accepting run of $\mathscr{T} = (A \uplus \underline{A}, B, Q, q_0, F, \delta, \lambda)$ on $\vdash u \dashv$. For all $1 \leqslant j \leqslant n$, let $f_j : A^* \to B^*$ be the concatenation of the functions recursively computed by $\lambda(q_j, (\vdash u \dashv)[i_j]) \in \{\mathscr{L}_1, \ldots, \mathscr{L}_p\}^*$. Let $\tau : (A \uplus \underline{A})^* \to A^*$ be the morphism which erases the underlining (i.e. $\tau(\underline{a}) = a$), then $f(u) := f_1(\tau(u) \bullet i_1) \cdots f_n(\tau(u) \bullet i_n)$.

The behavior of a last 3-pebble transducer is depicted in fig. 3. Observe that our definition builds a function of type $(A \uplus \underline{A})^* \to B^*$, but we shall in fact consider its restriction to A^* (the marks are only used within the induction step).

Example 3.4 ([1]). The function $\mathsf{square} : u \mapsto (u \bullet 1) \# \cdots (u \bullet |u|) \#$ can be computed by a last 2-pebble transducer, which successively marks and makes recursive calls in positions $1, 2$, etc. However this function is not polyblind [17].

We are ready to state our main result. Its proof goes over sections 4 to 6.

Theorem 3.5 (Minimization of the recursion height). *Let $1 \leqslant \ell \leqslant k$. Let $f : A^* \to B^*$ be computed by a blind k-pebble transducer (resp. by a last k-pebble transducer). Then f can be computed by a blind ℓ-pebble transducer (resp. by a last ℓ-pebble transducer) if and only if $|f(u)| = \mathcal{O}(|u|^\ell)$. This property is decidable and the construction is effective.*

As an easy consequence, the class of functions computed by last pebble transducers form a strict subclass of the polyregular functions (because theorem 3.5 does not hold for the full model of pebble transducers [3, Theorem 6.3]) and therefore it is not closed under composition (because any polyregular function can be obtained as a composition of regular functions and $\mathsf{squares}$ [1]).

Even if a (non-effective) theorem 3.5 was already known for blind pebble transducers [17, Theorem 7.1], we shall first present our proof of this case. Indeed, it is a new proof (relying on factorization forests) which is simpler than the original one. Furthermore, understanding the techniques used is a key step for understanding the proof for last pebble transducers presented afterwards.

4 Factorization forests

In this section, we introduce the key tool of factorization forests. Given a monoid morphism $\mu : A^* \to \mathbb{M}$ and $u \in A^*$, a μ-factorization forest of u is an unranked tree structure defined as follows. We use the brackets $\langle \cdots \rangle$ to build a tree.

Definition 4.1 (Factorization forest [19]). *Given a morphism $\mu : A^* \to \mathbb{M}$ and $u \in A^*$, we say that $\mathcal{F}$ is a μ-forest of u if:*
- *either $u = \varepsilon$ and $\mathcal{F} = \varepsilon$; or $u = \langle a \rangle \in A$ and $\mathcal{F} = a$;*
- *or $\mathcal{F} = \langle \mathcal{F}_1, \cdots, \mathcal{F}_n \rangle$, $u = u_1 \cdots u_n$, for all $1 \leqslant i \leqslant n$, $\mathcal{F}_i$ is a μ-forest of $u_i \in A^+$, and if $n \geqslant 3$ then $\mu(u) = \mu(u_1) = \cdots = \mu(u_n)$ is idempotent.*

We use the standard tree vocabulary of height, child, sibling, descendant and ancestor (a node being itself one of its ancestors/descendants), etc. We denote by $\mathsf{Nodes}^{\mathcal{F}}$ the set of nodes of $\mathcal{F}$. In order to simplify the statements, we identify a node $t \in \mathsf{Nodes}^{\mathcal{F}}$ with the subtree rooted in this node. Thus $\mathsf{Nodes}^{\mathcal{F}}$ can also be seen as the set of subtrees of $\mathcal{F}$, and $\mathcal{F} \in \mathsf{Nodes}^{\mathcal{F}}$. We say that a node is **idempotent** if it has at least 3 children. We denote by $\mathsf{Forests}_{\mu}(u)$ (resp. $\mathsf{Forests}_{\mu}^{d}(u)$) the set of μ-forests of $u \in A^*$ (resp. μ-forests of $u \in A^*$ of height at most d). We write $\mathsf{Forests}_{\mu}$ and $\mathsf{Forests}_{\mu}^{d}$ of all forests (of any word).

A μ-forest of $u \in A^*$ can also be seen as "the word u with brackets" in definition 4.1. Therefore $\mathsf{Forests}_{\mu}$ can be seen as a language over $\widehat{A} := A \uplus \{\langle, \rangle\}$. In this setting, it is well-known that μ-forests of bounded height can effectively be computed by a **rational function**, i.e. a particular case of regular function that can be computed by a non-deterministic one-way transducer (see e.g. [8]).

Theorem 4.2 (Simon [19,6]). *Given a morphism* $\mu : A^* \to \mathbb{M}$ *into a finite monoid* $\mathbb{M}$, *one can effectively build a rational function* $\mathsf{forest}_{\mu} : A^* \to (\widehat{A})^*$ *such that for all* $u \in A^*$, $\mathsf{forest}_{\mu}(u) \in \mathsf{Forests}_{\mu}^{3|\mathbb{M}|}(u)$.

Building μ-forests of bounded height is especially useful for us, since it enables to decompose any word in a somehow bounded way. This decomposition will be guided by the following definitions, that have been introduced in [8,10]. First, we define iterable nodes as the middle children of idempotent nodes.

Definition 4.3. *Let* $\mathcal{F} \in \mathsf{Forests}_{\mu}(u)$. *Its **iterable nodes**, denoted* $\mathsf{Iter}^{\mathcal{F}}$, *are:*
- *if* $\mathcal{F} = \langle a \rangle \in A$ *or* $\mathcal{F} = \varepsilon$, *then* $\mathsf{Iter}^{\mathcal{F}} := \varnothing$;
- *otherwise if* $\mathcal{F} = \langle \mathcal{F}_1, \cdots, \mathcal{F}_n \rangle$, *then:*

$$\mathsf{Iter}^{\mathcal{F}} := \{\mathcal{F}_i : 2 \leqslant i \leqslant n{-}1\} \cup \bigcup_{1 \leqslant i \leqslant n} \mathsf{Iter}^{\mathcal{F}_i}.$$

Now, we define the notion of skeleton of a node t, which contains all the descendants of t except those which are iterable.

Definition 4.4 (Skeleton, frontier). *Let* $\mathcal{F} \in \mathsf{Forests}_{\mu}(u)$, $t \in \mathsf{Nodes}^{\mathcal{F}}$, *we define the **skeleton** of* t, *denoted* $\mathsf{Skel}^{\mathcal{F}}(t)$, *by:*
- *if* $t = \langle a \rangle \in A$ *is a leaf, then* $\mathsf{Skel}^{\mathcal{F}}(t) := \{t\}$;
- *otherwise if* $t = \langle \mathcal{F}_1, \cdots, \mathcal{F}_n \rangle$, *then* $\mathsf{Skel}^{\mathcal{F}}(t) := \{t\} \cup \mathsf{Skel}^{\mathcal{F}}(\mathcal{F}_1) \cup \mathsf{Skel}^{\mathcal{F}}(\mathcal{F}_n)$.

*The **frontier** of* t *is the set* $\mathsf{Fr}^{\mathcal{F}}(t) \subseteq [1{:}|u|]$ *containing the positions of* u *which belong to* $\mathsf{Skel}^{\mathcal{F}}(t)$ *(when seen as leaves of the* μ-*forest* $\mathcal{F}$ *over* u).

Example 4.5. Let $\mathbb{M} := (\{-1, 1, 0\}, \times)$ and $\mu : \mathbb{M}^* \to \mathbb{M}$ the product. A μ-forest $\mathcal{F}$ of the word $(-1)(-1)0(-1)000000$ is depicted in Figure 4. Double lines denote idempotent nodes. The set of blue nodes is the skeleton of the topmost blue node.

It is easy to observe that for $\mathcal{F} \in \mathsf{Forests}_{\mu}^{d}(u)$, the size of a skeleton, or of a frontier, is bounded independently from $\mathcal{F}$. Furthermore, the set of skeletons $\{\mathsf{Skel}^{\mathcal{F}}(t) : t \in \mathsf{Iter}^{\mathcal{F}} \cup \{\mathcal{F}\}\}$ is a partition of $\mathsf{Nodes}^{\mathcal{F}}$ [8, Lemma 33]. As a consequence, the set of frontiers $\{\mathsf{Fr}^{\mathcal{F}}(t) : t \in \mathsf{Iter}^{\mathcal{F}} \cup \{\mathcal{F}\}\}$ is a partition of $[1{:}|u|]$. Given a position $1 \leqslant i \leqslant |u|$, we can thus define the **origin** of i in $\mathcal{F}$, denoted $\mathsf{origin}^{\mathcal{F}}(i)$, as the unique $t \in \mathsf{Iter}^{\mathcal{F}} \cup \{\mathcal{F}\}$ such that $i \in \mathsf{Fr}^{\mathcal{F}}(t)$.

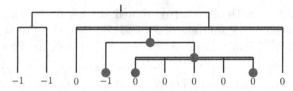

Figure 4: $\mathcal{F} \in \mathsf{Forests}_\mu((-1)(-1)0(-1)000000)$ and a skeleton.

Definition 4.6 (Observation). *Let* $\mathcal{F} \in \mathsf{Forests}_\mu$ *and* $\mathsf{t}, \mathsf{t}' \in \mathsf{Nodes}^{\mathcal{F}}$. *We say that* $\mathsf{t} \in \mathsf{Nodes}^{\mathcal{F}}$ ***observes*** $\mathsf{t}' \in \mathsf{Nodes}^{\mathcal{F}}$ *if either* t' *is an ancestor of* t, *or* t' *is the immediate right or left sibling of an ancestor of* t.

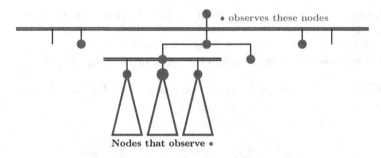

Figure 5: Nodes that observe • and that • observes

The intuition behind the notion of observation (which is *not* symmetrical) is depicted in fig. 5. Note that in a forest of bounded height, the number of nodes that some t observes is bounded. This will be a key argument in the following. We say that t and t' are **dependent** if either t observes t' or the converse. Given $\mathcal{F}$, we can translate these notions to the positions of u: we say that i **observes** (resp. **depends on**) i' if $\mathsf{origin}^{\mathcal{F}}(i)$ observes (resp. depends on) $\mathsf{origin}^{\mathcal{F}}(i')$.

5   Height minimization of blind pebble transducers

In this section, we show theorem 3.5 for blind pebble transducers. We say that a two-way transducer $\mathcal{T}$ is a **submachine** of a blind pebble transducer $\mathcal{B}$ if $\mathcal{T}$ labels a node in the tree description of $\mathcal{B}$. If $\mathcal{B} = \mathcal{T}\langle \mathcal{B}_1, \ldots, \mathcal{B}_n \rangle$, we say that the submachine $\mathcal{T}$ is the **head** of $\mathcal{B}$. We let the **transition morphism** of $\mathcal{B}$ be the cartesian product of all the transition morphisms of all the submachines of $\mathcal{B}$. Observe that it makes sense to consider the production of a submachine $\mathcal{T}$ in a context defined using the transition morphism of $\mathcal{B}$.

5.1   Pumpability

We first give a sufficient condition, named pumpability, for a blind k-pebble transducer to compute a function f such that $|f(u)| \neq \mathcal{O}(|u|^{k-1})$. The behavior of a pumpable blind 2-pebble transducer is depicted in fig. 6 over a well-chosen input: it has a factor in which the head $\mathscr{T}_1$ calls a submachine $\mathscr{T}_2$, and a factor in which $\mathscr{T}_2$ produces a non-empty output. Furthermore both factors can be iterated without destroying the runs of these machines (due to idempotents).

Definition 5.1. Let $\mathscr{B}$ be a blind k-pebble transducer whose transition morphism is $\mu : A^* \to \mathbb{T}$. We say that the transducer $\mathscr{B}$ is **pumpable** if there exists:
- submachines $\mathscr{T}_1, \ldots, \mathscr{T}_k$ of $\mathscr{B}$, such that $\mathscr{T}_1$ is the head of $\mathscr{B}$;
- $m_0, \ldots, m_k, \ell_1, \ldots, \ell_k, r_1, \ldots, r_k \in \mu(A^*)$;
- $a_1, \ldots, a_k \in A$ such that for all $1 \leqslant j \leqslant k$, $e_j := \ell_j \mu(a_j) r_j$ is an idempotent;
- a permutation $\sigma : [1{:}k] \to [1{:}k]$;

such that if $\mathcal{M}_i^j := m_i e_{i+1} m_{i+1} \cdots e_j m_j$ for all $0 \leqslant i \leqslant j \leqslant k$, and if we define the following context for all $1 \leqslant j \leqslant k$:

$$C_j := \mathcal{M}_0^{\sigma(j)-1} e_{\sigma(j)} \ell_{\sigma(j)} [\![a_{\sigma(j)}]\!] r_{\sigma(j)} e_{\sigma(j)} \mathcal{M}_{\sigma(j)}^k$$

then for all $1 \leqslant j \leqslant k-1$, $|\mathsf{prod}_{\mathscr{T}_j}(C_j)|_{\mathscr{T}_{j+1}} \neq 0$, and $\mathsf{prod}_{\mathscr{T}_k}(C_k) \neq \varepsilon$.

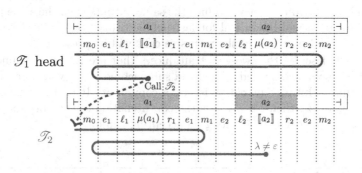

Figure 6:   Pumpability in a blind 2-pebble transducer.

Lemma 5.2 follows by choosing inverse images in A^* for the m_i, ℓ_i and r_i.

Lemma 5.2. Let f be computed by a pumpable blind k-pebble transducer. There exists words $v_0, \ldots, v_k, u_1, \ldots, u_k$ such that $|f(v_0 u_1^X \cdots u_k^X v_k)| = \Theta(X^k)$.

Now, we use pumpability as a key ingredient for showing theorem 3.5, which directly follows by induction from the more precise theorem 5.3.

Theorem 5.3 (Removing one layer).   Let $k \geqslant 2$ and $f : A^* \to B^*$ be computed by a blind k-pebble transducer $\mathscr{B}$. The following are equivalent:
1. $|f(u)| = \mathcal{O}(|u|^{k-1})$;

2. $\mathscr{B}$ *is not pumpable;*

3. f *can be computed by a blind* $(k{-}1)$*-pebble transducer.*

Furthermore, this property is decidable and the construction is effective.

Proof. Item 3 $\Rightarrow$ item 1 is obvious. Item 1 $\Rightarrow$ item 2 is lemma 5.2. Furthermore, pumpability can be tested by an enumeration of $\mu(A^*)$ and A. It remains to show item 2 $\Rightarrow$ item 3 (in an effective fashion): this is the purpose of section 5.2.

5.2   Algorithm for removing a recursion layer

Let $k \geqslant 2$ and $\mathscr{U}$ be a blind k-pebble transducer that is not pumpable, and that computes $f : A^* \to B^*$. We build a blind $(k{-}1)$-pebble transducer $\overline{\mathscr{U}}$ for f.

Let $\mu : A^* \to \mathbb{T}$ be the transition morphism of $\mathscr{U}$. We shall consider that, on input $u \in A^*$, the submachines of $\overline{\mathscr{U}}$ can in fact use $\mathsf{forest}_\mu(u) \subseteq (\widehat{A})^*$ as input. Indeed forest_μ is a rational function (by theorem 4.2), hence its information can be recovered by using a **lookaround**. Informally, the lookaround feature enables a two-way transducer to chose its transitions not only depending on its current state and current letter $u[i]$ in position $1 \leqslant i \leqslant |u|$, but also on a regular property of the prefix $u[1{:}i{-}1]$ and the suffix $u[i{+}1{:}|u|]$. It is well-known that given a two-way transducer $\mathscr{T}$ with lookarounds, one can build an equivalent $\mathscr{T}'$ that does not have this feature (see e.g. [15,12]). Furthermore, even if the accepting runs of $\mathscr{T}$ and $\mathscr{T}'$ may differ, they produce the same outputs from the same positions (this observation will be critical for last pebble transducers, in order to ensure that the marked positions of the recursive calls will be preserved).

Now, we describe the two-way transducers that are the submachines of $\overline{\mathscr{U}}$. First, it has submachines old-$\mathscr{T}$ for $\mathscr{T}$ a submachine of $\mathscr{U}$, which are described in algorithm 1. Intuitively, old-$\mathscr{T}$ is just a copy of $\mathscr{T}$. It is clear that if $\mathscr{T}$ is a submachine of $\mathscr{U}$, then old-$\mathscr{T}(u)$ is the concatenation of the outputs produced by (the recursive calls of) $\mathscr{T}$ along its accepting run on $\vdash u \dashv$.

Algorithm 1: Submachines that behave as the original ones

---

 1 **Submachine** old-$\mathscr{T}(u)$

 2     $\rho :=$ accepting run of $\mathscr{T}$ over $\vdash u \dashv$; $\lambda :=$ output function of $\mathscr{T}$;

 3   **for** $(q, i) \in \rho$ **do**

 4   **if** $\mathscr{T}$ is a leaf of $\mathscr{U}$ **then**

 5   **Output** $\lambda(q, (\vdash u \dashv)[i])$; /* $\mathscr{T}$ has output in B^*;   */

 6   **else**

 7   **for** $\mathscr{B}' \in \lambda(q, (\vdash u \dashv)[i])$ **do**

 8                 $\mathscr{T}' :=$ head of $\mathscr{B}'$;

 9   Call old-$\mathscr{T}'(u)$; /* $\mathscr{T}$ makes recursive calls;   */

10   **end**

11   **end**

12   **end**

$\overline{\mathcal{U}}$ also has submachines accelerate-$\mathcal{T}$ for $\mathcal{T}$ a submachine of $\mathcal{U}$, which are described in algorithm 2. Intuitively, accelerate-$\mathcal{T}$ simulates $\mathcal{T}$ while trying to inline recursive calls in its own run. More precisely, let $u \in A^*$ be the input and $\mathcal{F} := \text{forest}_\mu(u)$. If $\mathcal{T}$ calls $\mathcal{B}'$ in $1 \leqslant i \leqslant |u|$ that belongs to the frontier of the root node F of $\mathcal{F}$, then accelerate-$\mathcal{T}$ inlines the behavior of the head of $\mathcal{B}'$. Otherwise it makes a recursive call, except if $\mathcal{B}'$ is a leaf of $\mathcal{U}$. Hence if $\mathcal{T}$ is a submachine of $\mathcal{U}$ which is not a leaf, accelerate-$\mathcal{T}(u)$ is the concatenation of the outputs produced by the calls of $\mathcal{T}$ along its accepting run.

Algorithm 2: Submachines that try to simulate their recursive calls

---

```
1  Submachine accelerate-𝒯 (u)
2      /* 𝒯 is not a leaf of 𝒰 (i.e. it makes calls);              */
3      ρ := accepting run of 𝒯 over ⊢u⊣; ℱ := forestμ(u); λ := output fun. of 𝒯;
4      for (q, i) ∈ ρ do
5          for 𝓑' ∈ λ(q, (⊢u⊣)[i]) do
6              𝒯' := head of 𝓑';
7              if i ∈ Frᶠ(ℱ) then
8                  /* We can inline the call since |Frᶠ(ℱ)| is bounded;  */
9                  Inline the code of old-𝒯' (u) /* (see explanations); */
10             else if 𝓑' is a leaf of 𝒰 then
11                 /* Then 𝓑' = 𝒯' and we can inline the call because the
                      output of 𝒯' on input u is bounded;              */
12                 Inline the code of old-𝒯' (u) /* (see explanations); */
13             else
14                 /* It is not possible to inline the call to 𝓑', so we
                      make a recursive call;                           */
15                 Call accelerate-𝒯' (u);
16             end
17         end
18  end
```

Finally, the transducer $\overline{\mathcal{U}}$ is obtained by defining accelerate-$\mathcal{T}$ to be its head, where $\mathcal{T}$ is the head of $\mathcal{U}$. Furthermore, we remove the submachines old-$\mathcal{T}$ or accelerate-$\mathcal{T}$ which are never called. Observe that $\overline{\mathcal{U}}$ indeed computes the function f. Furthermore, we observe that $\overline{\mathcal{U}}$ has recursion height (i.e. the number of nested **Call** instructions, plus 1 for the head) $k-1$, since each inlining of lines 9, 10 and 12 in algorithm 2 removes exactly one recursion layer of $\mathcal{U}$.

It remains to justify that each accelerate-$\mathcal{T}$ can be implemented by a two-way transducer (i.e. with lookarounds but a bounded memory). We represent variable i by the current position of the transducer. Since it has access to $\mathcal{F}$, the lookaround can be used to check whether $i \in \text{Fr}^{\mathcal{F}}(\mathcal{F})$ or not (since the size of $\text{Fr}^{\mathcal{F}}(\mathcal{F})$ is bounded). It remains to explain how the inlinings are performed:

- if $i \in \text{Fr}^{\mathcal{F}}(\mathcal{F})$, the two-way transducer inlines old-$\mathcal{T}'$ by executing the same moves and calls as $\mathcal{T}'$ does. Once its computation is ended, it has to go back

to position i. This is indeed possible since belonging to $\mathsf{Fr}^{\mathcal{F}}(\mathcal{F})$ is a property that can be detected by using the lookaround, hence the machine only needs to remember that i was the ℓ-th position of $\mathsf{Fr}^{\mathcal{F}}(\mathcal{F})$ (ℓ being bounded);
 - else if $\mathscr{B}' = \mathscr{T}'$ is a blind 1-pebble transducer, we produce the output of $\mathscr{T}'$ without moving. This is possible since for all $i' \notin \mathsf{Fr}^{\mathcal{F}}(\mathcal{F})$, $\mathsf{prod}^u_{\mathscr{T}'}(i') = \varepsilon$ (hence the output of $\mathscr{T}'$ on u is bounded, and its value can be determined without moving, just by using the lookaround). Indeed, if $\mathsf{prod}^u_{\mathscr{T}'}(i') \neq \varepsilon$ for such an $i' \notin \mathsf{Fr}^{\mathcal{F}}(\mathcal{F})$ when reaching line 12 of algorithm 2, then the conditions of lemma 5.4 hold, which yields a contradiction. This lemma is the key argument of this proof, relying on the non-pumpability of $\mathscr{U}$.

Lemma 5.4 (Key lemma). *Let $u \in A^*$ and $\mathcal{F} \in \mathsf{Forests}_\mu(u)$. Assume that there exists a sequence $\mathscr{T}_1, \ldots, \mathscr{T}_k$ of submachines of $\mathscr{U}$ and a sequence of positions $1 \leqslant i_1, \ldots, i_k \leqslant |u|$ such that:*
 - *$\mathscr{T}_1$ is the head of $\mathscr{U}$;*
 - *for all $1 \leqslant j \leqslant k-1$, $|\mathsf{prod}^u_{\mathscr{T}_j}(i_j)|_{\mathscr{T}_{j+1}} \neq 0$ and $\mathsf{prod}^u_{\mathscr{T}_k}(i_k) \neq \varepsilon$;*
 - *for all $1 \leqslant j \leqslant k$, $i_j \notin \mathsf{Fr}^{\mathcal{F}}(\mathcal{F})$ (i.e. $\mathsf{origin}^{\mathcal{F}}(i_j) \in \mathsf{Iter}^{\mathcal{F}}$).*
Then $\mathscr{B}$ is pumpable.

Proof (idea). We first observe that pumpability follows as soon as the nodes $\mathsf{origin}^{\mathcal{F}}(i_j)$ are pairwise independent. We then show that this independence condition can always be obtained, up to duplicating some iterable subtrees of $\mathcal{F}$ (and some factors of u), because the behavior of a submachine in a blind pebble transducer does not depend on the positions of the above recursive calls.

6   Height minimization of last pebble transducers

In this section, we show theorem 3.5 for last pebble transducers. The notions of **submachine**, **head** and **transition morphism** for a last pebble transducer are defined as in section 5. The transition morphism is now defined over $(A \uplus \underline{A})^*$.

6.1   Pumpability

The sketch of the proof is similar to section 5. We first give an equivalent of pumpability for last pebble transducers. The intuition behind this notion is depicted in fig. 7. The formal definition is however more cumbersome, since we need to keep track of the fact that the calling position is marked.

Definition 6.1. *Let $\mathscr{L}$ be a last k-pebble transducer whose transition morphism is $\mu : (A \cup \underline{A})^* \to \mathbb{T}$. We say that the transducer $\mathscr{L}$ is **pumpable** if there exists:*
 - *submachines $\mathscr{T}_1, \ldots, \mathscr{T}_k$ of $\mathscr{L}$, such that $\mathscr{T}_1$ is the head of $\mathscr{L}$;*
 - *$m_0, \ldots, m_k, \ell_1, \ldots, \ell_k, r_1, \ldots, r_k \in \mu(A^*)$;*
 - *$a_1, \ldots, a_k \in A$ such that for all $1 \leqslant j \leqslant k$, $e_j := \ell_j \mu(a_j) r_j$ is idempotent;*
 - *a permutation $\sigma : [1{:}k] \to [1{:}k]$;*

such that if we let $\mathcal{M}_i^j := m_i e_{i+1} m_{i+1} \cdots e_j m_j$ *for all* $0 \leqslant i \leqslant j \leqslant k$, *and if we define the following context:*

$$\mathcal{C}_1 := \mathcal{M}_0^{\sigma(1)-1} e_{\sigma(1)} \ell_{\sigma(1)} [\![a_{\sigma(1)}]\!] r_{\sigma(1)} e_{\sigma(1)} \mathcal{M}_{\sigma(1)}^k$$

and for all $1 \leqslant j \leqslant k-1$ *the context:*

$$\mathcal{C}_{j+1} := \mathcal{M}_0^{\sigma(j)-1} e_{\sigma(j)} \ell_{\sigma(j)} \mu(\underline{a_{\sigma(j)}}) r_{\sigma(j)} e_{\sigma(j)} \mathcal{M}_{\sigma(j)}^{\sigma(j+1)-1}$$
$$e_{\sigma(j+1)} \ell_{\sigma(j+1)} [\![a_{\sigma(j+1)}]\!] r_{\sigma(j+1)} e_{\sigma(j+1)} \mathcal{M}_{\sigma(j+1)}^k \qquad \text{if } \sigma(j) < \sigma(j+1);$$
$$\mathcal{C}_{j+1} := \mathcal{M}_0^{\sigma(j)-1} e_{\sigma(j+1)} \ell_{\sigma(j+1)} [\![a_{\sigma(j+1)}]\!] r_{\sigma(j+1)} e_{\sigma(j+1)}$$
$$\mathcal{M}_{\sigma(j+1)}^{\sigma(j)-1} e_{\sigma(j)} \ell_{\sigma(j)} \mu(\underline{a_{\sigma(j)}}) r_{\sigma(j)} e_{\sigma(j)} \mathcal{M}_{\sigma(j)}^k \qquad \text{otherwise;}$$

then for all $1 \leqslant j \leqslant k-1$, $|\mathrm{prod}_{\mathcal{T}_j}(\mathcal{C}_j)|_{\mathcal{T}_{j+1}} \neq 0$, *and* $\mathrm{prod}_{\mathcal{T}_k}(\mathcal{C}_k) \neq \varepsilon$.

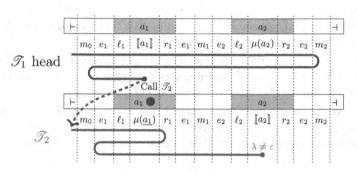

Figure 7: Pumpability in a last 2-pebble transducer.

We obtain lemma 6.2 by a proof which is similar to that of lemma 5.2.

Lemma 6.2. *Let* f *be computed by a pumpable last* k-*pebble transducer. There exists words* $v_0, \ldots, v_k, u_1, \ldots, u_k$ *such that* $|f(v_0 u_1^X \cdots u_k^X v_k)| = \Theta(X^k)$.

Theorem 6.3 (Removing one layer). *Let* $k \geqslant 2$ *and* $f : A^* \to B^*$ *be computed by a last* k-*pebble transducer* $\mathcal{L}$. *The following are equivalent:*
1. $|f(u)| = \mathcal{O}(|u|^{k-1})$;
2. $\mathcal{L}$ *is not pumpable;*
3. f *can be computed by a last* $(k-1)$-*pebble transducer.*
Furthermore, this property is decidable and the construction is effective.

Proof. Item 3 ⇒ item 1 is obvious. Item 1 ⇒ item 2 is lemma 6.2. Furthermore, pumpability can be tested by an enumeration of $\mu(A^*)$ and A. It remains to show item 2 ⇒ item 3 (in an effective fashion): this is the purpose of section 6.2.

6.2 Algorithm for removing a recursion layer

Let $k \geqslant 2$ and $\mathscr{U}$ be a last k-pebble transducer that is not pumpable, and that computes $f : A^* \to B^*$. We build a last $(k-1)$-pebble transducer $\overline{\mathscr{U}}$ for f. Let $\mu : (A \uplus \underline{A})^* \to \mathbb{T}$ be the transition morphism of $\mathscr{U}$. As before (using a lookaround), the submachines of $\overline{\mathscr{U}}$ have access to $\mathsf{forest}_\mu(u)$ on input $u \in A^*$.

Now, we describe the submachines of $\overline{\mathscr{U}}$. It has submachines old-$\mathscr{T}$-along-ρ for $\mathscr{T}$ a submachine of $\mathscr{U}$ and ρ a run of $\mathscr{T}$, which are described in algorithm 1. Intuitively, these machines mimics the behavior of $\mathscr{T}$ along the run ρ (which is not necessarily accepting) of $\mathscr{T}$ over $\vdash v \dashv$ with $v \in (A \uplus \underline{A})^*$.

Since they are indexed by a run ρ, it may seem that we create an infinite number of submachines, but it will not be the case. Indeed, a run ρ will be represented by its first configuration (q_1, i_1) and last configuration (q_n, i_n). This information is sufficient to simulate exactly the two-way moves of ρ, but there is still an unbounded information: the positions i_1 and i_n. In fact, the input will be of the form $v = u \bullet i$ and we shall guarantee that the i_1 and i_n can be detected by the lookaround if i is marked. Hence the run ρ will be represented in a bounded way, independently from the input v, and so that its first and last configurations can be detected by the lookaround of the submachine.

It follows from algorithm 3 that if $\mathscr{T}$ is a submachine of $\mathscr{U}$, then for all $v \in (A \cup \underline{A})^*$ and ρ run of $\mathscr{T}$ on $\vdash v \dashv$, old-$\mathscr{T}$-along-ρ (v) is the concatenation of the outputs produced by (the recursive calls of) $\mathscr{T}$ along ρ.

We also define a submachine normal-$\mathscr{T}$-along-ρ-pebble-i that is similar to old-$\mathscr{T}$-along-ρ, except that it ignores the mark of its input and acts as if it was in position i (as above for ρ, i will be encoded by a bounded information).

Algorithm 3: Submachines that behave like the original ones

```
1  Submachine old-𝒯-along-ρ(v)
2  │   /* v ∈ (A ⊎ A)*; ρ is a run of 𝒯 over ⊢v⊣;                    */
3  │   λ := output function of 𝒯;
4  │   for (q,i) ∈ ρ do
5  │   │   if 𝒯 is a leaf of 𝒰 then
6  │   │   │   Output λ(q,(⊢v⊣)[i]); /* 𝒯 has output in B*;          */
7  │   │   else
8  │   │   │   for ℒ' ∈ λ(q,(⊢v⊣)[i]) do
9  │   │   │   │   𝒯' := head of ℒ'; ρ' := accepting run of 𝒯' on ⊢τ(v)•i⊣;
10 │   │   │   │   Call old-𝒯'-along-ρ'(τ(v)•i); /* Recursive call;  */
11 │   │   │   end
12 │   │   end
13 │   end
14 Submachine normal-𝒯-along-ρ-pebble-i(v)
15 │   /* v ∈ (A ⊎ A)*; ρ is a run of 𝒯 over ⊢τ(v)•i⊣;               */
16 │   Simulate old-𝒯-along-ρ (τ(v)•i);
```

$\overline{\mathcal{U}}$ also has submachines accelerate-$\mathcal{T}$-along-ρ for $\mathcal{T}$ a submachine of $\mathcal{U}$, which are described in algorithm 4. Intuitively, accelerate-$\mathcal{T}$-along-ρ simulates $\mathcal{T}$ along ρ while trying to inline some recursive calls. Whenever it is in position i and needs to call recursively $\mathcal{L}'$ whose head is $\mathcal{T}'$, it first slices the accepting run ρ' of $\mathcal{T}'$ on $\vdash u\bullet i \dashv$, with respect to $\text{forest}_\mu(u)$ and i, as explained in definition 6.4 and depicted in fig. 8. Intuitively, this operation splits ρ' into a bounded number of runs whose positions either all observe i, or i observes all of them, or none of these cases occur (the positions are either 0, $|u|+1$ or independent of i).

Definition 6.4 (Slicing). *Let $u \in A^*$, $\mathcal{F} \in \text{Forests}_\mu(u)$ and $1 \leqslant i \leqslant |u|$. We let $\uparrow i$ (resp. $\downarrow i$) be the set of positions that i observes (resp. that observe i). Let $\rho = (q_1, i_1) \to \cdots \to (q_n, i_n)$ be a run of a two-way transducer $\mathcal{T}$ on $\vdash u\bullet i \dashv$. We build by induction a sequence $\ell_1, \ldots, \ell_{N+1}$ with $\ell_1 := 1$ and:*

– if $\ell_j = n+1$ then $j := N$ and the process ends;
– else if $i_{\ell_j} \in \uparrow i$ (resp. $i_{\ell_j} \in \downarrow i \smallsetminus \uparrow i$, resp. $i_{\ell_j} \in [0:|u|+1] \smallsetminus (\uparrow i \cup \downarrow i))$, then ℓ_{j+1} is the largest index such that for all $\ell_j \leqslant \ell \leqslant \ell_{j+1}-1$, $i_\ell \in \uparrow i$ (resp. $i_\ell \in \downarrow i \smallsetminus \uparrow i$, resp. $i_\ell \in [0:|u|+1] \smallsetminus (\uparrow i \cup \downarrow i))$.

*Finally the **slicing** of ρ, with respect to $\mathcal{F}$ and i, is the sequence of runs $\rho_1, \ldots, \rho_N$ where $\rho_j := (q_{\ell_j}, i_{\ell_j}) \to (q_{\ell_j+1}, i_{\ell_j+1}) \to \cdots \to (q_{\ell_{j+1}-1}, i_{\ell_{j+1}-1})$.*

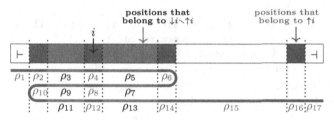

Figure 8: Slicing of a run ρ with respect to i and $\mathcal{F}$.

Now, let $\rho'_1, \ldots, \rho'_N$ be slicing of the run ρ' of $\mathcal{T}'$ on the input $u\bullet i$. For all $1 \leqslant j \leqslant N$, there are mainly two cases. Either the positions of ρ'_j all are in $\uparrow i$ or $\downarrow i$. In this case, accelerate-$\mathcal{T}$-along-ρ directly inlines old-$\mathcal{T}'$-along-ρ'_j within its own run (i.e. without making a recursive call). Otherwise, it makes a recursive call to accelerate-$\mathcal{T}'$-along-ρ'_j, except if $\mathcal{L}'$ is a leaf of $\mathcal{U}$ (thus $\mathcal{L}' = \mathcal{T}'$).

Finally, $\overline{\mathcal{U}}$ is described as follows: on input $u \in A^*$, its head is the submachine accelerate-$\mathcal{T}$-along-ρ (u), where $\mathcal{T}$ is the head of $\mathcal{U}$ and ρ is the accepting run of $\mathcal{T}$ on $\vdash u \dashv$ (represented by the bounded information that it is both initial and final). As before, we remove the submachines which are never called in $\overline{\mathcal{U}}$. Observe that we have created a machine with recursion height $k-1$ (because line 17 in algorithm 4 prevents from calling a k-th layer).

Let us justify that each accelerate-$\mathcal{T}$-along-ρ can indeed be implemented by a two-way transducer. First, let us observe that since $\mathcal{F}$ has bounded height, the number N of slices given in line 7 of algorithm 4 is bounded. Furthermore, we claim that the first and last positions of each ρ'_j belong to a given set of bounded size, which can be detected by a lookaround which has access to i. For the ρ'_j

---

Algorithm 4: Submachines that try to simulate their recursive calls

```
1  Submachine accelerate-𝒯-along-ρ (v)
2  |   /* 𝒯 is not a leaf of 𝒰 (i.e. it makes calls);              */
3  |   /* v ∈ (A ⊎ A)*; ρ is a run of 𝒯 over ⊢v⊣;                 */
4  |   u := τ(v); ℱ := forestμ(u); λ := output function of 𝒯;
5  |   for (q,i) ∈ ρ do
6  |   |   for ℒ' ∈ λ(q, (⊢v⊣)[i]) do
7  |   |   |   𝒯' := head of ℒ'; ρ' := accepting run of 𝒯' over ⊢u•i⊣;
8  |   |   |   ρ'₁,···,ρ'_N := slicing of ρ' with respect to ℱ and i;
9  |   |   |   for j = 1 to N do
10 |   |   |   |   (q₁,i₁) → ··· (qₙ,iₙ) := ρ'_j;
11 |   |   |   |   if i₁,…,iₙ ∈ ↑ i then
12 |   |   |   |   |   /* We inline the call because n is bounded;      */
13 |   |   |   |   |   Inline the code of old-𝒯'-along-ρ'_j (u•i);
14 |   |   |   |   else if i₁,…,iₙ ∈ ↓ i then
15 |   |   |   |   |   /* We can inline the call because the positions
                         i₁,…,iₙ are "below" i in ℱ;                  */
16 |   |   |   |   |   Inline the code of old-𝒯'-along-ρ'_j (u•i);
17 |   |   |   |   else if ℒ' is a leaf of 𝒰 then
18 |   |   |   |   |   /* The output of ℒ' = 𝒯' along ρ'_j is empty;   */
19 |   |   |   |   else
20 |   |   |   |   |   /* It is not possible to inline the call to ℒ', so
                         we make a recursive call;                     */
21 |   |   |   |   |   Call accelerate-𝒯'-along-ρ'_j (u•i);
22 |   |   |   |   end
23 |   |   |   end
24 |   |   end
25 |   end
```

---

whose positions are in $\uparrow i$, this is clear since $|\uparrow i|$ is bounded (because the frontier of any node is bounded). For $\downarrow i \smallsetminus \uparrow i$ we use lemma 6.5, which implies that this set is a bounded union of intervals. The last case is very similar.

Lemma 6.5. *Let* $1 \leqslant i \leqslant |u|$, $\mathsf{t} := \mathsf{origin}^{\mathcal{F}}(i)$ *and* t_1 *(resp.* t_2*) be its immediate left (resp. right) sibling (they exist whenever* $\mathsf{t} \in \mathsf{Iter}^{\mathcal{F}}$, *i.e. here* $\mathsf{t} \neq \mathcal{F}$*). Then:*

$$\downarrow i \smallsetminus \uparrow i = [\min(\mathsf{Fr}^{\mathcal{F}}(\mathsf{t}_1)) : \max(\mathsf{Fr}^{\mathcal{F}}(\mathsf{t}_2))] \smallsetminus \{\mathsf{Fr}^{\mathcal{F}}(\mathsf{t}_1), \mathsf{Fr}^{\mathcal{F}}(\mathsf{t}), \mathsf{Fr}^{\mathcal{F}}(\mathsf{t}_2)\}.$$

This analysis justifies why each ρ'_j can be encoded in a bounded way. Now, we show how to implement the inlinings while using i as the current position:

- if $i_1, \ldots, i_n \in \uparrow i$, then n is bounded (because $|\uparrow i|$ is bounded). We can thus inline old-$\mathcal{T}'$-along-ρ'_j $(u \bullet i)$ while staying in position i. However, when $\mathcal{T}'$ calls some $\mathcal{L}''$ (of head $\mathcal{T}''$) on position i_ℓ, we would need to call old-$\mathcal{T}''$-along-$\rho''(u \bullet i_\ell)$ (where ρ'' is the accepting run of $\mathcal{T}''$ along $\vdash u \bullet i_\ell \dashv$). But we cannot do this operation, since we are in position i and not in i_ℓ. The solution is that the inlined code calls normal-$\mathcal{T}''$-along-ρ''-pebble-$i_\ell(u \bullet i)$

instead, which simulates an accepting run ρ'' of $\mathscr{T}$ on $u\bullet i_\ell$, even if its input is $u\bullet i$. Note that i_ℓ can be represented as a bounded information and recovered by a lookaround given $u\bullet i$ as input, since i observes i_ℓ;

- if $i_1, \ldots, i_n \in {\downarrow} i \smallsetminus {\uparrow} i$, then the nodes $\mathrm{origin}^{\mathcal{F}}(i_1), \ldots, \mathrm{origin}^{\mathcal{F}}(i_n)$ are roughly below $\mathrm{origin}^{\mathcal{F}}(i)$ in $\mathcal{F}$ (see fig. 5). We inline old-$\mathscr{T}'$-along-ρ'_j $(u\bullet i)$, by moving along $i_1, \ldots, i_n$ as ρ'_j does. We can keep track of the height of $\mathrm{origin}^{\mathcal{F}}(i)$ above the current $\mathrm{origin}^{\mathcal{F}}(i_\ell)$ (it is a bounded information). With the lookaround, we can detect the end of ρ'_j, and go back to position i.

It remains to justify that $\overline{\mathscr{U}}$ is correct. For this, we only need to show that when it reaches line 18 in algorithm 4, the output of $\mathscr{T}'$ along ρ'_j is indeed empty. Otherwise, the conditions of lemma 6.6 would hold (since we never execute two successive recursive calls in dependent positions). It provides a contradiction.

Lemma 6.6 (Key lemma). *Let $u \in A^*$ and $\mathcal{F} \in \mathsf{Forests}_\mu(u)$. Assume that there exists a sequence $\mathscr{T}_1, \ldots, \mathscr{T}_k$ of submachines of $\mathscr{U}$ and a sequence of positions $1 \leqslant i_1, \ldots, i_k \leqslant |u|$ such that:*

- *$\mathscr{T}_1$ is the head of $\mathscr{U}$;*
- *$|\mathrm{prod}^u_{\mathscr{T}_1}(i_1)|_{\mathscr{T}_2} \neq 0$ and $\mathrm{prod}^{u\bullet i_{k-1}}_{\mathscr{T}_k}(i_k) \neq \varepsilon$;*
- *for all $2 \leqslant j \leqslant k-1$, $|\mathrm{prod}^{u\bullet i_{j-1}}_{\mathscr{T}_j}(i_j)|_{\mathscr{T}_{j+1}} \neq 0$;*
- *for all $1 \leqslant j \leqslant k-1$, $\mathrm{origin}^{\mathcal{F}}(i_j)$ and $\mathrm{origin}^{\mathcal{F}}(i_{j+1})$ are independent;*

Then $\mathscr{U}$ is pumpable.

Proof (idea). As for lemma 5.4, the key observation is that pumpability follows as soon as the nodes $\mathrm{origin}^{\mathcal{F}}(i_j)$ are pairwise independent. Furthermore, this condition can be obtained by duplicating some nodes in $\mathcal{F}$.

7 Making the two last pebbles visible

We can define a similar model to that of last k-pebble transducer, which sees the two last calling positions instead of only the previous one. Let us name this model a **last-last k-pebble transducer**. A very natural question is to know whether we can show an analog of theorem 3.5 for these machines.

Note that for $k = 1, 2$ and 3, a last-last k-pebble transducer is exactly the same as a k-pebble transducer. Hence the function inner-squaring of page 2 is such that $|\mathsf{inner\text{-}squaring}(u)| = \mathcal{O}(|u|^2)$ and can be computed by a last-last 3-pebble transducer, but it cannot be computed by a last-last 2-pebble transducer. It follows that the connection between minimal recursion height and growth of the output fails. However, this result is somehow artificial. Indeed, a last-last 2-pebble transducer is a degenerate case, since it can only see one last pebble. More interestingly, we show that the connection fails for arbitrary heights.

Theorem 7.1. *For all $k \geqslant 2$, there exists a function $f : A^* \to B^*$ such that $|f(u)| = \mathcal{O}(|u|^2)$ and that can be computed by a last-last $(2k+1)$-pebble transducer, but not by a last-last $2k$-pebble transducer.*

Proof (idea). We re-use a counterexample introduced by Bojańczyk in [2] to show a similar failure result for the model of k-pebble transducers.

8   Outlook

This paper somehow settles the discussion concerning the variants of pebble transducers for which the minimal recursion height only depends on the growth of the output. As soon as two marks are visible, the combinatorics of the output also has to be taken into account, hence minimizing the recursion height in this case (e.g. for last-last pebble transducers) seems hard with the current tools.

As observed in [13], one can extend last pebble transducers by allowing the recursion height to be unbounded (in the spirit of **marble transducers** [9]). This model enables to produce outputs whose size grows exponentially in the size of the input. A natural question is to know whether a function computed by this model, but whose output size is polynomial, can in fact be computed with a recursion stack of bounded height (i.e. by a last k-pebble transducer).

Acknowledgements. The author is grateful to Tito Nguyên for suggesting the study of the recursion height for last pebble transducers.

References

1. Bojańczyk, M.: Polyregular functions. arXiv preprint arXiv:1810.08760 (2018)
2. Bojańczyk, M.: The growth rate of polyregular functions. arXiv preprint arXiv:2212.11631 (2022)
3. Bojańczyk, M.: Transducers of polynomial growth. In: Proceedings of the 37th Annual ACM/IEEE Symposium on Logic in Computer Science. pp. 1–27 (2022)
4. Bojańczyk, M., Kiefer, S., Lhote, N.: String-to-string interpretations with polynomial-size output. In: 46th International Colloquium on Automata, Languages, and Programming, ICALP 2019 (2019)
5. Chytil, M.P., Jákl, V.: Serial composition of 2-way finite-state transducers and simple programs on strings. In: 4th International Colloquium on Automata, Languages, and Programming, ICALP 1977. pp. 135–147. Springer (1977)
6. Colcombet, T.: Green's relations and their use in automata theory. In: International Conference on Language and Automata Theory and Applications. pp. 1–21. Springer (2011)
7. Dave, V., Gastin, P., Krishna, S.N.: Regular transducer expressions for regular transformations. In: Proceedings of the 33rd Annual ACM/IEEE Symposium on Logic in Computer Science. pp. 315–324. ACM (2018)
8. Douéneau-Tabot, G.: Pebble transducers with unary output. In: 46th International Symposium on Mathematical Foundations of Computer Science, MFCS 2021 (2021)
9. Douéneau-Tabot, G., Filiot, E., Gastin, P.: Register transducers are marble transducers. In: 45th International Symposium on Mathematical Foundations of Computer Science, MFCS 2020 (2020)
10. Douéneau-Tabot, G.: Hiding pebbles when the output alphabet is unary. In: 49th International Colloquium on Automata, Languages, and Programming, ICALP 2022 (2022)
11. Engelfriet, J.: Two-way pebble transducers for partial functions and their composition. Acta Informatica **52**(7-8), 559–571 (2015)

12. Engelfriet, J., Hoogeboom, H.J.: MSO definable string transductions and two-way finite-state transducers. ACM Transactions on Computational Logic (TOCL) **2**(2), 216–254 (2001)
13. Engelfriet, J., Hoogeboom, H.J., Samwel, B.: Xml transformation by tree-walking transducers with invisible pebbles. In: Proceedings of the twenty-sixth ACM SIGMOD-SIGACT-SIGART symposium on Principles of database systems. pp. 63–72. ACM (2007)
14. Gurari, E.M.: The equivalence problem for deterministic two-way sequential transducers is decidable. SIAM Journal on Computing **11**(3), 448–452 (1982)
15. Hopcroft, J.E., Ullman, J.D.: An approach to a unified theory of automata. The Bell System Technical Journal **46**(8), 1793–1829 (1967)
16. Kiefer, S., Nguyên, L.T.D., Pradic, C.: Revisiting the growth of polyregular functions: output languages, weighted automata and unary inputs. arXiv preprint arXiv:2301.09234 (2023)
17. Nguyên, L.T.D., Noûs, C., Pradic, C.: Comparison-free polyregular functions. In: 48th International Colloquium on Automata, Languages, and Programming, ICALP 2021 (2021)
18. Shepherdson, J.C.: The reduction of two-way automata to one-way automata. IBM Journal of Research and Development **3**(2), 198–200 (1959)
19. Simon, I.: Factorization forests of finite height. Theor. Comput. Sci. **72**(1), 65–94 (1990)

Fixed Points and Noetherian Topologies

Aliaume Lopez[1,2]

[1] Université Paris Cité, CNRS, IRIF, F-75013, Paris, France
alopez@irif.fr
[2] Université Paris-Saclay, CNRS, ENS Paris-Saclay, Laboratoire Méthodes Formelles, 91190, Gif-sur-Yvette, France.

Abstract. Noetherian spaces are a generalisation of well-quasi-orderings to topologies, that can be used to prove termination of programs. They find applications in the verification of transition systems, some of which are better described using topology. The goal of this paper is to allow the systematic description of computations using inductively defined datatypes via Noetherian spaces. This is achieved through a fixed point theorem based on a topological minimal bad sequence argument.

Keywords: Noetherian spaces · topology · well-quasi-orderings · initial algebras · Kruskal's Theorem · Higman's Lemma.

1 Introduction

Let $(\mathcal{E}, \leq)$ be a set endowed with a quasi-order. A sequence $(x_n)_n \in \mathcal{E}^{\mathbb{N}}$ is *good* whenever there exists $i < j$ such that $x_i \leq x_j$. A quasi-ordered set $(\mathcal{E}, \leq)$ is a *well-quasi-ordered* — abbreviated as wqo — if every sequence is good. By calling a sequence *bad* whenever it is not good, well-quasi-orderings are equivalently defined as having no infinite bad sequences. This generalisation of well-founded total orderings can be used as a basis for proving program termination. For instance, algorithms alike Example 1.1 can be studied via well-quasi-orderings and the length of their bad sequences [5]. More generally, one can map the states of a run to a wqo via a so-called quasi-ranking function to both prove the termination of the program and gain information about its runtime [27, Chapter 2]. Let us provide a concrete example of this proof scheme.

Example 1.1. Let Alg be the algorithm with three integer variables a, b, c that non-deterministically performs one of the following operations until a, b or c becomes negative: (l) $\langle a, b, c \rangle \leftarrow \langle a-1, b, 2c \rangle$ or (r) $\langle a, b, c \rangle \leftarrow \langle 2c, b-1, 1 \rangle$.

Lemma 1.2. *For every choice of $a, b, c \in \mathbb{N}^3$, the algorithm Alg terminates.*

Proof. Let us prove that Alg builds a bad sequence of triples when ordering $\mathbb{N}^3$ with $(a_1, b_1, c_1) \leq (a_2, b_2, c_2)$ whenever $a_1 \leq a_2$, $b_1 \leq b_2$, and $c_1 \leq c_2$. If (a_i, b_i, c_i) and (a_j, b_j, c_j) represent two configurations in a run of Alg, either only rule (l) was fired and $a_j < a_i$, or rule (r) was fired as least once, and $b_j < b_i$.

Because $(\mathbb{N}^3, \leq)$ is a well-quasi-ordering (see Dickson's Lemma in [28]), Alg terminates for every choice of initial triple $(a, b, c) \in \mathbb{N}^3$.

O. Kupferman and P. Sobocinski (Eds.): FoSSaCS 2023, LNCS 13992, pp. 456–476, 2023.
https://doi.org/10.1007/978-3-031-30829-1_22

As a combinatorial tool, well-quasi-orderings appear frequently in varying fields of computer science, ranging from graph theory to number theory [18, 22, 21, 3]. Well-quasi-orderings have also been highly successful in proving the termination of verification algorithms. One critical application of well-quasi-orderings is to the verification of infinite state transition systems, via the study of so-called Well-Structured Transition Systems (WSTS) [1, 2, 16, 7].

Noetherian spaces. A major roadblock arises when using well-quasi-orders: the powerset of a well-quasi-order may fail to be one itself [26]. This is particularly problematic in the study of WSTS, where the powerset construction appears frequently [19, 29, 1]. To tackle this issue, one can justify that the quasi-orders of interest are not pathological, and are actually better quasi-orders [25, 23]. Another approach is offered by the topological notion of *Noetherian space*, which as pointed out by Goubault-Larrecq, can act as a suitable generalisation of well-quasi-orderings that is preserved under the powerset construction [10].

The topological analogues to WSTS enjoy similar decidability properties, and there even exists an analogue to Karp and Miller's forward analysis for Petri nets [11]. Moreover, their topological nature allows to verify systems beyond the reach of quasi-orderings, such as lossy concurrent polynomial programs [11]. This is possible because the polynomials are handled via results from algebraic geometry, through the notion of the *Zariski topology* over $\mathbb{C}^n$ [12, Exercise 9.7.53].

One drawback of the topological approach is that many topologies correspond to a single quasi-ordering. Hence, when the problem is better described via an ordering, one has to choose a specific topology, and there usually does not exist a finest one that is Noetherian.

Inductively defined datatypes. As for well-quasi-orders, Noetherian spaces are stable under finite products and finite sums [28, 12]. While this can be enough to describe the set of configurations of a Petri net using $\mathbb{N}^k$, it does not allow to talk about more complex data structures, that are typically defined inductively, such as lists and trees. To make the above statement precise, let **1** be the singleton set, $A + B$ be the disjoint union of A and B, and $A \times B$ their cartesian product. Then, the set of finite words over an alphabet Σ is precisely the least fixed point of $F\colon X \mapsto \mathbf{1} + \Sigma \times X$. Similarly, the set of finite trees over Σ equals $\mathsf{lfp}_X.\Sigma \times X^*$, where $\mathsf{lfp}_X.F(X)$ denotes the least fixed point of F.

In the realm of well-quasi-orderings, the specific cases of finite words and finite trees are handled respectively via Higman's Lemma [18] and Kruskal's Tree Theorem [22]. Let us recall that a word u *embeds* into a word w (written $u \leq_* v$) whenever whenever there exists a strictly increasing map $h\colon |w| \to |w'|$ such that $w_i \leq w_{h(i)}$ for $1 \leq i \leq |w|$. Similarly, a tree t *embeds* into a tree t' (written $t \leq_{\mathsf{tree}} t'$) whenever there exists a map from nodes of t to nodes of t' respecting the least common ancestor relation, and increasing the colours of the nodes. Proofs that finite words and finite trees preserve well-quasi-orderings typically rely on a so-called *minimal bad sequence argument* due to Nash-Williams [24]. However, the argument is quite subtle, and needs to be handled with care [9, 30].

In addition, the argument is not compositional and has to be slightly modified whenever a new inductive construction is desired [as in, e.g., 4, 3].

This picture has been adapted by Goubault-Larrecq to the topological setting by proposing analogues of the word embedding and tree embedding, together with a proof that they preserve Noetherian spaces [12, Section 9.7]. However, both the definitions and the proofs have an increased complexity, as they rely on an adapted "topological minimal bad sequence argument" that appears to be even more subtle [14, errata n. 26]. Moreover, the newly introduced topologies have involved definitions often relying on ad-hoc constructions.

In the case of well-quasi-orderings, two generic fixed point constructions have been proposed to handle inductively defined datatypes [17, 8]. In these frameworks, $\mathsf{lfp}_X.F(X)$ is guaranteed to be a well-quasi-ordering provided that F is a "well-behaved functor" of quasi-orders. Both proposals, while relying on different categorical notions, successfully recover Higman's word embedding and Kruskal's tree embedding through their respective definitions as least fixed points. As a side effect, they reinforce the idea that these two quasi-orders are somehow canonical.

In the case of Noetherian spaces, no equivalent framework exists to build inductive datatypes, and the notions of "well-behaved" constructors from [17, 8] rule out the use of important Noetherian spaces, as they require that an element $a \in F(X)$ has been built using *finitely many* elements of X: while this is the case for finite words and finite trees, it does not hold for the arbitrary powerset. Moreover, there have been recent advances in placing Noetherian topologies over spaces that are not straightforwardly obtained through "well-behaved" definitions, such as infinite words [13], or even ordinal length words [15].

1.1   Contributions of this paper

In this paper, we propose a least fixed point theorem for Noetherian topologies. This is done in a way that greatly differs from the categorical frameworks introduced in the study of well-quasi-orders, as the construction of the space is entirely *decoupled* from the construction of the topology. In particular, the carrier set X itself need not be inductively defined.

In this setting, we consider a fixed set X and a map R from topologies τ over X to topologies $R(\tau)$ over X. Because the set of topologies over X is a complete lattice, it suffices to ask for R to be monotone to guarantee that it has a least fixed point, that we write $\mathsf{lfp}_\tau.R(\tau)$. In general, this least fixed point will not be Noetherian, but we show that a simple sufficient condition on R guarantees that it is. This main theorem (Theorem 3.21), encapsulates all the complexity of the topological adaptations of the minimal bad sequences arguments [12, Section 9.7], and we believe that it has its own interest.

The necessity to separate the construction of the set of points from the construction of the topology might be perceived as a weakness of the theory, when it is in fact a strength of our approach. We illustrate this by giving a shorter proof that the words of ordinal length are Noetherian [15], without providing an inductive definition of the space. As an illustration of the versatility of our framework, we introduce a reasonable topology over ordinal branching trees (with finite depth), and prove that it is Noetherian using the same technique.

In the specific cases where the space of interest can be obtained as a least fixed point of a "well-behaved" functor, we show how Theorem 3.21 can be used to generalise the categorical framework of Hasegawa [17] to a topological setting. As well as adding inductively defined topologies (hence, inductively defined datatypes) to the theory of Noetherian spaces, this provide a reasonable answer to the canonicity issue previously mentioned.

Outline. In Section 2 we recall some of the main results in the theory of Noetherian spaces. In Section 3 we prove our main result (Theorem 3.21). In Section 4 we explore how this result covers existing topological results in the literature, and provide a new non-trivial Noetherian space (Definition 4.7). In Section 5, we leverage our main result to devise a Noetherian topology over inductively defined datatypes (Theorem 5.13), and prove that this generalises the work of Hasegawa over well-quasi-orders (Theorem 5.15).

2   A Quick Primer on Noetherian Topologies

A *topological space* is a pair $(\mathcal{X}, \tau)$ where $\tau \subseteq \mathbb{P}(\mathcal{X})$, τ is stable under finite intersections, and τ is stable under arbitrary unions. A subset $U \subseteq \mathcal{X}$ is an *open subset* when $U \in \tau$, and a *closed subset* when $\mathcal{X} \setminus U \in \tau$. As an order-theoretic counterpart to open and closed subsets, we say that a subset U of a quasi-ordered set $(\mathcal{E}, \leq)$ is *upwards-closed* whenever for all $x \in U$, $x \leq y$ implies $y \in U$. Similarly, a subset is *downwards-closed* whenever its complement is upwards-closed. One can convert back and forth between the two as follows:

Notation 2.1. Let $(\mathcal{E}, \leq)$ be a quasi-order and $(\mathcal{X}, \tau)$ be a topological space. The *Alexandroff topology* $\mathsf{alex}(\leq)$ over $\mathcal{E}$ is the collection of upwards-closed subsets of $\mathcal{E}$. The *specialisation preorder* $\leq_\tau$ is defined via $x \leq_\tau y$ whenever for every open subset $U \in \tau$, if $x \in U$ then $y \in U$.

It is an easy check that the specialisation pre-order of the Alexandroff topology of a quasi-order $\leq$ is the quasi-order itself. Beware that several topologies can share the same specialisation pre-order $\leq$, and among those, the Alexandroff topology is the finest.

We can now build the topological analogue to wqos through the notion of compactness: a subset K of $\mathcal{X}$ is defined as *compact* whenever from every family $(U_i)_{i \in I}$ of open sets such that $K \subseteq \bigcup_{i \in I} U_i$, one can extract a finite subset $J \subseteq I$ such that $K \subseteq \bigcup_{i \in J} U_i$. A quasi-order $(\mathcal{E}, \leq)$ is wqo if and only if every subset K of $\mathcal{E}$ is compact for $\mathsf{alex}(\leq)$. Generalising this property to arbitrary topological spaces $(\mathcal{X}, \tau)$, a topological space $(\mathcal{X}, \tau)$ is said to be a *Noetherian space* whenever every subset of $\mathcal{X}$ is compact.

Table 1. An *algebra* of Noetherian spaces [see 10, 12, 15].

Constructor	Syntax	Topology
Well-quasi-orders	$\mathcal{E}$	Alexandroff topology
Complex vectors	$\mathbb{C}^k$	Zariski topology
Disjoint sum	$\mathcal{X}_1 + \mathcal{X}_2$	co-product topology
Product	$\mathcal{X}_1 \times \mathcal{X}_2$	product topology
Finite words	$\mathcal{X}^*$	subword topology
Finite trees	$\mathsf{T}(\mathcal{X})$	tree topology
Finite multisets	$\mathcal{X}^\circledast$	multiset topology
Transfinite words	$\mathcal{X}^{<\alpha}$	transfinite subword topology
Powerset	$\mathsf{P}(\mathcal{X})$	Lower-Vietoris

Remark 2.2. A space $(\mathcal{X}, \tau)$ is Noetherian if and only if for every increasing sequence of open subsets $(U_i)_{i \in \mathbb{N}}$, there exists $j \in \mathbb{N}$ such that $\bigcup_{i \in \mathbb{N}} U_i = \bigcup_{i \leq j} U_i$.

In order to inductively define Noetherian spaces, we will often rely on basic constructors such as the disjoint sum and the finite product. For completeness, we recall in Table 1 usual constructors that preserve Noetherian spaces. This table also illustrate the versatility of the concept, that encompasses both the algebraic properties of $\mathbb{C}^k$ and the order properties of well-quasi-orders.

3   Refinements of Noetherian topologies

Let us fix a set $\mathcal{X}$. The collection of topologies over $\mathcal{X}$ is itself a set, and forms a complete lattice for inclusion. In this lattice, the least element is the *trivial topology* $\tau_{\mathrm{triv}} := \{\emptyset, \mathcal{X}\}$, and the greatest element is the *discrete topology* $\mathbb{P}(\mathcal{X})$. Thanks to Tarski's fixed point theorem, every monotone function R mapping topologies over $\mathcal{X}$ to topologies over $\mathcal{X}$ has a least fixed point, which can be obtained by transfinitely iterating R from the trivial topology. Writing $\mathsf{lfp}_\tau.R(\tau)$ for the least fixed point of R, our goal is to provide sufficient conditions for $(\mathcal{X}, \mathsf{lfp}_\tau.R(\tau))$ to be Noetherian.

Definition 3.1. *A* refinement function *over a set* $\mathcal{X}$ *is a function* R *mapping topologies over* $\mathcal{X}$ *to topologies over* $\mathcal{X}$. *Moreover, we assume that* $\mathsf{R}(\tau)$ *is Noetherian whenever* τ *is, and that* $\mathsf{R}(\tau) \subseteq \mathsf{R}(\tau')$ *when* $\tau \subseteq \tau'$.

As $(\mathcal{X}, \tau_{\mathrm{triv}})$ is always Noetherian, $(\mathcal{X}, \mathsf{R}^n(\tau_{\mathrm{triv}}))$ is Noetherian for all $n \in \mathbb{N}$ and refinement function R. However, it remains unclear whether the transfinite iterations needed to reach a fixed point preserve Noetherian spaces.

We demonstrate in Example 3.2 how to obtain the topology $\mathsf{alex}(\leq)$ over $\mathbb{N}$ as a least fixed point of some simple refinement function. Before that, let us define the notion of upwards-closure: given a quasi-order $(\mathcal{E}, \leq)$ and a set $E \subseteq \mathcal{E}$, let us define the *upwards-closure* of E, written $\uparrow_{\leq} E$, as the set of elements that are greater or equal than some element of E in $\mathcal{E}$.

Example 3.2 (Natural Numbers). Over $X := \mathbb{N}$, one can define $\mathsf{Div}(\tau)$ as the collection of the sets $\uparrow_{\leq} (U + 1)$ for $U \in \tau$, plus $\mathbb{N}$ itself. Then $\mathsf{Div}(\tau_{\mathrm{triv}}) = \{\emptyset, \uparrow_{\leq} 1, \mathbb{N}\}$, $\mathsf{Div}^2(\tau_{\mathrm{triv}}) = \{\emptyset, \uparrow_{\leq} 1, \uparrow_{\leq} 2, \mathbb{N}\}$. More generally, for every $k \geq 0$, $\mathsf{Div}^k(\tau_{\mathrm{triv}}) = \{\emptyset, \uparrow_{\leq} 1, \ldots, \uparrow_{\leq} k, \mathbb{N}\}$. It is an easy check that $\mathsf{lfp}_{\tau}.\mathsf{Div}(\tau)$ is precisely $\mathsf{alex}(\leq)$, which is Noetherian because $(\mathbb{N}, \leq)$ is a well-quasi-ordering.

3.1   An ill-behaved refinement function

Not all refinement functions behave as nicely as in Example 3.2, and one can obtain non-Noetherian topologies via their least fixed points.

Let us consider for this section $\Sigma := \{a, b\}$ with the discrete topology, i.e., $\{\emptyset, \{a\}, \{b\}, \Sigma\}$. Let us now build the set Σ^* of finite words over Σ. Whenever U and V are subsets of Σ^*, let us write UV for their concatenation, defined as $\{uv \colon u \in U, v \in V\}$. To construct an ill-behaved refinement function, we will associate to a topology τ the set $\{UV \colon U \in \{\emptyset, \{a\}, \{b\}, \Sigma\}, V \in \tau\}$. However, the latter fails to be a topology in general. This problem frequently appears in this paper, and is solved by considering the so-called generated topology.

Let us briefly recall that for every set $\mathcal{X}$ and collection of subsets $B \subseteq \mathbb{P}(\mathcal{X})$, one can construct the topology generated from B as the least topology on $\mathcal{X}$ containing B. This topology coincides with the one containing arbitrary unions of finite intersections of subsets in B. We say that B is a *subbasis* of τ when τ is the topology generated by B. Alexanders's Subbase Lemma allows to study Noetherian spaces in this setting [12, Thm. 4.4.29]: it states that checking whether a subset K of $\mathcal{X}$ is compact in τ can be done by considering only open subsets in B, i.e., that for every family $(U_i)_{i \in I}$ of a subbasis B of τ such that $K \subseteq \bigcup_{i \in I} U_i$, one can extract a finite subset $J \subseteq I$ such that $K \subseteq \bigcup_{j \in J} U_j$.

Definition 3.3. *Let $\mathsf{R}_{\mathrm{pref}}$ be the function mapping a topology τ over Σ^* to the topology generated by the sets UV where $U \subseteq \Sigma$ and $V \in \tau$,*

We refer to Figure 1 for a graphical presentation of the first two iterations of the refinement function $\mathsf{R}_{\mathrm{pref}}$. For the sake of completeness, let us compute $\mathsf{lfp}_{\tau}.\mathsf{R}_{\mathrm{pref}}(\tau)$, which is the Alexandroff topology of the prefix ordering on words.

Definition 3.4. *The prefix topology[3] τ_{pref^*}, over Σ^* is generated by the following open sets: $U_1 \ldots U_n \Sigma^*$, where $n \geq 0$ and $U_i \subseteq \Sigma$.*

Lemma 3.5. *The prefix topology over Σ^* is the least fixed point of $\mathsf{R}_{\mathrm{pref}}$.*

Lemma 3.6. *The function $\mathsf{R}_{\mathrm{pref}}$ is a refinement function.*

Proof. It is an easy check that whenever $\tau \subseteq \tau'$, $\mathsf{R}_{\mathrm{pref}}(\tau) \subseteq \mathsf{R}_{\mathrm{pref}}(\tau')$. Now, assume that τ is Noetherian, it remains to prove that $\mathsf{R}_{\mathrm{pref}}(\tau)$ remains Noetherian. Consider a subset $E \subseteq \Sigma^*$ and let us prove that E is compact in $\mathsf{R}_{\mathrm{pref}}(\tau)$.

---

[3] This definition differs from what is called the "prefix topology" in the literature [see 6, 12, resp. Section 8 and Exercise 9.7.36].

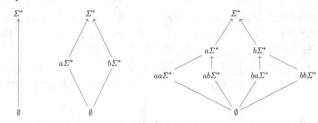

Fig. 1. Iterating R_{pref} over Σ^*. On the left the trivial topology τ_{triv}, followed by R_{pref}, and on the right R_{pref}^2.

For that, we consider an open cover $E \subseteq \bigcup_{i \in I} W_i$, where $W_i \in R_{pref}(\tau)$. Thanks to Alexander's subbase lemma, we can assume without loss of generality that W_i is a subbasic open set of $R_{pref}(\tau)$, that is, $W_i = U_i V_i$ with $U_i \subseteq \Sigma$ and $V_i \in \tau$.

Since $(\Sigma^*, \tau) \times (\Sigma^*, \tau)$ is Noetherian (see Table 1), there exists a finite set $J \subseteq I$ such that $\bigcup_{i \in J} U_i \times V_i = \bigcup_{i \in I} U_i \times V_i$. This implies that $E \subseteq \bigcup_{i \in J} U_i V_i$, and provides a finite subcover of E. □

The sequence $\bigcup_{0 \le i \le k} a^i b \Sigma^*$, for $k \in \mathbb{N}$, is a strictly increasing sequence of opens. Therefore, the prefix topology is not Noetherian. The terms $a^i b \Sigma^*$ can be observed in Figure 1 as a diagonal of incomparable open sets.

Corollary 3.7. *The topology* $lfp_\tau.R_{pref}(\tau)$ *is not Noetherian.*

The prefix topology is not Noetherian, even when starting from a finite alphabet. However, we claimed in Section 1 that there is a natural generalisation of the subword embedding to topological spaces which is Noetherian. Before introducing this topology, let us write $[U_1, \ldots, U_n]$ as a shorthand notation for the set $\Sigma^* U_1 \Sigma^* \ldots \Sigma^* U_n \Sigma^*$.

Definition 3.8 (Subword topology [12, Definition 9.7.26]). *Given a topological space* (Σ, τ), *the space* Σ^* *of finite words over* Σ *can be endowed with the subword topology, generated by the open sets* $[U_1, \ldots, U_n]$ *when* $U_i \in \tau$.

The *topological Higman lemma* [12, Theorem 9.7.33] states that the subword topology over Σ^* is Noetherian if and only if Σ is Noetherian. Although the subword topology might seem ad-hoc, it can be validated as a generalisation of the subword embedding because the subword topology of $\mathsf{alex}(\le)$ equals the Alexandroff topology of the subword ordering of $\le$, for every quasi-order $\le$ over Σ [12, Exercise 9.7.30]. Let us now reverse engineer a refinement function whose least fixed point is the subword topology.

Definition 3.9. *Let* (Σ, θ) *be a topological space. Let* E^θ_{words} *be defined as mapping a topology* τ *over* Σ^* *to the topology generated by the following sets:* $\uparrow_{\le_*} UV$ *for* $U, V \in \tau$; *and* $\uparrow_{\le_*} W$, *for* $W \in \theta$.

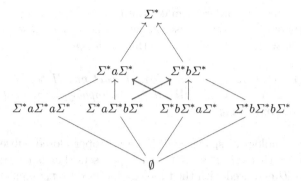

Fig. 2. The topology $E_{\text{words}}^{\theta}{}^{2}(\tau_{\text{triv}})$, with bold red arrows for the inclusions that were not present between the "analogous sets" in $R_{\text{pref}}^{2}(\tau_{\text{triv}})$. We have taken θ to be the discrete topology over Σ.

Lemma 3.10. *Let (Σ, θ) be a topological space. The subword topology over Σ^* is the least fixed point of $E_{\text{words}}^{\theta}$.*

In order to show that $E_{\text{words}}^{\theta}$ is a refinement function, we first claim that the two parts of the topology can be dealt with separately.

Lemma 3.11 ([12, Proposition 9.7.18]). *If $(\mathcal{X}, \tau)$ and $(\mathcal{X}, \tau')$ are Noetherian, then $\mathcal{X}$ endowed with the topology generated by $\tau \cup \tau'$ is Noetherian.*

Lemma 3.12. *Let (Σ, θ) be a Noetherian topological space. The map $E_{\text{words}}^{\theta}$ is a refinement function over Σ.*

Proof. We leave the monotonicity of $E_{\text{words}}^{\theta}$ as an exercice and focus on the proof that $E_{\text{words}}^{\theta}(\tau)$ is Noetherian, whenever τ is. Thanks to Lemma 3.11, it suffices to prove that the topology generated by the sets $\uparrow_{\leq_*} UV$ (U, V open in τ), and the topology generated by the sets $\uparrow_{\leq_*} W$ (W open in θ) are Noetherian.

Let $(\uparrow_{\leq_*} U_i V_i)_{i \in \mathbb{N}}$ be a sequence of open sets. Because Noetherian topologies are closed under products (see Table 1), there exists k such that $\bigcup_{i \leq k} U_i \times V_i = \bigcup_{i \in \mathbb{N}} U_i \times V_i$. Hence, $\bigcup_{i \leq k} \uparrow_{\leq_*} U_i V_i = \bigcup_{i \in \mathbb{N}} \uparrow_{\leq_*} U_i V_i$

Let $\uparrow_{\leq_*} W_i$ be a sequence of open sets. Because θ is Noetherian, there exists k such that $\bigcup_{i \leq k} W_i = \bigcup_{i \in \mathbb{N}} W_i$, hence $\bigcup_{i \leq k} \uparrow_{\leq_*} W_i = \bigcup_{i \in \mathbb{N}} \uparrow_{\leq_*} W_i$. □

We have designed two refinement functions R_{pref} and $E_{\text{words}}^{\theta}$ over Σ^*. Fixing θ to be the discrete topology over Σ, the least fixed point of R_{pref} is not Noetherian while the least fixed point of $E_{\text{words}}^{\theta}$ is. We have depicted the result of iterating $E_{\text{words}}^{\theta}$ twice over the trivial topology in Figure 2. As opposed to R_{pref}, the "diagonal" elements are comparable for inclusion.

3.2   Well-behaved refinement functions

In this section, we will show how the behaviour of refinement function with respect to subsets will act as a sufficient condition to separate the well-behaved ones from the others. In order to make the idea of computing the refinement function directly over a subset precise, we will replace a subset with the induced topology by a "restricted" topology over the whole space.

Definition 3.13. *Let $(\mathcal{X}, \tau)$ be a topological space and H be a closed subset of $\mathcal{X}$. Define the* subset restriction $\tau | H$ *to be the topology generated by the open subsets $U \cap H$ where U ranges over τ.*

Let $\mathcal{X}$ be a topological space, and H be a proper closed subset of $\mathcal{X}$. The space $\mathcal{X}$ endowed with $\tau | H$ has a lattice of open sets that is isomorphic to the one of the space H endowed with the topology induced by τ, except for the entire space $\mathcal{X}$ itself. As witnessed by Example 3.14, the two spaces are in general not homeomorphic.

Example 3.14. Let $\mathbb{R}$ be endowed with the usual metric topology. The set $\{a\}$ is a closed set when $a \in \mathbb{R}$. The induced topology over $\{a\}$ is $\{\emptyset, \{a\}\}$. The subset restriction of the topology to $\{a\}$ is $\tau_a := \{\emptyset, \{a\}, \mathbb{R}\}$. Clearly, $(\mathbb{R}, \tau_a)$ and $(\{a\}, \tau_{\text{triv}})$ are not homeomorphic.

In order to build intuition, let us consider the special case of an Alexandroff topology over $\mathcal{X}$ and compute the specialisation preorder of $\tau | H$, where H is a downwards closed set.

Lemma 3.15. *Let $\tau = \mathsf{alex}(\leq)$ over a set $\mathcal{X}$, and $x, y \in X$. Then, $x \leq_{\tau|H} y$ if and only if $x \leq_\tau y \wedge y \in H$ or $x \notin H$. In other words, H^c is collapsed to an equivalence class below H itself.*

Definition 3.16. *A* topology expander *is a refinement function E that satisfies the following extra property: for every Noetherian topology τ satisfying $\tau \subseteq \mathsf{E}(\tau)$, for all closed set H in τ, $\mathsf{E}(\tau)|H \subseteq \mathsf{E}(\tau|H)|H$.*

Lemma 3.17. *The refinement function R_{pref} is not a topology expander.*

Proof. Let us consider $\tau := \{\emptyset, a\Sigma^*, b\Sigma^*, \Sigma^*\}$. Remark that $H := a\Sigma^* \cup \{\varepsilon\}$ is a closed subset because $\Sigma = \{a, b\}$. It is an easy check that $\mathsf{R}_{\text{pref}}(\tau)|H = \{\emptyset, aa\Sigma^*, ab\Sigma^*, a\Sigma^*, \Sigma^*\} \neq \{\emptyset, aa\Sigma^*, a\Sigma^*, \Sigma^*\} = \mathsf{R}_{\text{pref}}(\tau|H)|H$.

Lemma 3.18. *When θ is Noetherian, $\mathsf{E}^\theta_{\text{words}}$ is a topology expander.*

Proof. We have proven in Lemma 3.12 that $\mathsf{E}^\theta_{\text{words}}$ is a refinement function. Let us now prove that it is a topology expander.

Let τ be a Noetherian topology over Σ^*, such that $\tau \subseteq \mathsf{E}^\theta_{\text{words}}(\tau)$. Let H be a closed subset of (Σ^*, τ). Notice that as H is closed in τ, and since $\tau \subseteq \mathsf{E}^\theta_{\text{words}}(\tau)$, H is downwards closed for $\leq_*$. As a consequence, $(\uparrow_{\leq_*} UV) \cap H = (\uparrow_{\leq_*} (U \cap H)(V \cap H)) \cap H$. Hence, $\mathsf{E}^\theta_{\text{words}}(\tau)|H \subseteq \mathsf{E}^\theta_{\text{words}}(\tau|H)|H$. □

3.3   Iterating Expanders

Our goal is now to prove that topology expanders are refinement functions that can be safely iterated. For that, let us first define precisely what "iterating transfinitely" a refinement function means.

Definition 3.19. *Let $(\mathcal{X}, \tau)$ be a topological space, and E be a topology expander. The limit topology $\mathsf{E}^\alpha(\tau)$ is defined as: τ when $\alpha = 0$, $\mathsf{E}(\mathsf{E}^\beta(\tau))$ when $\alpha = \beta + 1$, and as the join of the topologies $\mathsf{E}^\beta(\tau)$ for all $\beta < \alpha$, when α is a limit ordinal.*

We devote the rest of this section to proving our main theorem, which immediately implies that least fixed points of topology expanders are Noetherian. Notice that the theorem is trivial whenever α is a successor ordinal.

Proposition 3.20. *Let α be an ordinal, τ be a topology, and E be a topology expander. If $\mathsf{E}^\beta(\tau)$ is Noetherian for all $\beta < \alpha$, and $\tau \subseteq \mathsf{E}(\tau)$, then $\mathsf{E}^\alpha(\tau)$ is Noetherian.*

Theorem 3.21 (Main Result). *Let $\mathcal{X}$ be a set and E be a topology expander. The least fixed point of E is a Noetherian topology over $\mathcal{X}$.*

The topological minimal bad sequence argument. In order to prove Theorem 3.21, we will use a topological minimal bad sequence argument. To that end, let us first introduce a well-founded partial ordering over the elements of $\mathsf{E}^\alpha(\tau)$. With an open set $U \in \mathsf{E}^\alpha(\tau)$, we associate a depth $\mathsf{depth}(U)$, defined as the smallest ordinal $\beta \leq \alpha$ such that $U \in \mathsf{E}^\beta(\tau)$. We then define $U \trianglelefteq V$ to hold whenever $\mathsf{depth}(U) \leq \mathsf{depth}(V)$, and $U \triangleleft V$ whenever $\mathsf{depth}(U) < \mathsf{depth}(V)$. It is an easy check that this is a well-founded total quasi-order over $\mathsf{E}^\alpha(\tau)$.

As a first step towards proving that $\mathsf{E}^\alpha(\tau)$ is Noetherian for a limit ordinal α, we first reduce the problem to open subsets of depth strictly less than α itself.

Lemma 3.22. *Let α be a limit ordinal, and E be a topology expander. The topology $\mathsf{E}^\alpha(\tau)$ has a subbasis of elements of depth strictly below α.*

Let us recall the notion of topological bad sequence designed by Goubault-Larrecq [12, Lemma 9.7.31] in the proof of the Topological Kruskal Theorem, adapted to our ordering of subbasic open sets.

Definition 3.23. *Let $(\mathcal{X}, \tau)$ be a topological space. A sequence $\mathcal{U} = (U_i)_{i \in \mathbb{N}}$ of open subsets is good if there exists $i \in \mathbb{N}$ such that $U_i \subseteq \bigcup_{j<i} U_j$. A sequence that is not good is called bad.*

Lemma 3.24. *Let α be a limit ordinal, and E be a topology expander such that $\mathsf{E}^\alpha(\tau)$ is not Noetherian. Then, there exists a bad sequence $\mathcal{U}$ of open subsets in $\mathsf{E}^\alpha(\tau)$ of depth less than α that is lexicographically minimal for $\trianglelefteq$. Such a sequence is called minimal bad.*

We deduce that in a limit topology, minimal bad sequences are not allowed to use open subsets of arbitrary depth. This will then be leveraged via Lemma 3.27 to decrease the depth by one.

Lemma 3.25. *Let α be a limit ordinal, τ be a topology and E be a topology expander such that $\mathsf{E}^\beta(\tau)$ is Noetherian for all $\beta < \alpha$. Assume that $\mathcal{U} = (U_i)_{i \in \mathbb{N}}$ is a minimal bad sequence of $\mathsf{E}^\alpha(\tau)$. Then, for every $i \in \mathbb{N}$, $\mathsf{depth}(U_i)$ is either 0 or a successor ordinal.*

Definition 3.26. *Let α be an ordinal, τ be a topology, E be a topology expander such that $\tau \subseteq \mathsf{E}(\tau)$, and let $U \in \mathsf{E}^\alpha(\tau)$. The topology $\mathsf{Down}(U)$ is generated by the open sets V such that $V \lhd U$, where V ranges over $\mathsf{E}^\alpha(\tau)$.*

Lemma 3.27. *Let α be an ordinal, E be a topology expander and $U \in \mathsf{E}^\alpha(\tau)$. If $\mathsf{depth}(U)$ is a successor ordinal, then $U \in \mathsf{E}(\mathsf{Down}(U))$.*

If $\mathcal{U}$ is a minimal bad sequence in $(X, \mathsf{E}^\alpha(\tau))$, then $U_i \not\subseteq \bigcup_{j<i} U_j := V_i$, i.e., $U_i \cap V_i^c \neq \emptyset$. We can now use our subset restriction operator to devise a topology associated to this minimal bad sequence. Noticing that $H_i := V_i^c$ is a closed set in $\mathsf{E}^\alpha(\tau)$, hence we can build the subset restriction $\mathsf{Down}(U_i)|H_i$.

Definition 3.28. *Let α be an ordinal, τ be a topology, E be a topology expander such that $\tau \subseteq \mathsf{E}(\tau)$, and let $\mathcal{U} = (U_i)_{i \in \mathbb{N}}$ be a minimal bad sequence in $\mathsf{E}^\alpha(\tau)$. Then, the minimal topology $\mathcal{U}(\mathsf{E}^\alpha(\tau))$ is generated by $\bigcup_{i \in \mathbb{N}} \mathsf{Down}(U_i)|H_i$, where $H_i := (\bigcup_{j<i} U_j)^c$.*

Lemma 3.29. *Let α be an ordinal, τ be a topology, E be a topology expander such that $\tau \subseteq \mathsf{E}(\tau)$, and let $\mathcal{U} = (U_i)_{i \in \mathbb{N}}$ be a minimal bad sequence in $\mathsf{E}^\alpha(\tau)$. Then, the minimal topology $\mathcal{U}(\mathsf{E}^\alpha(\tau))$ is Noetherian.*

Proof. Assume by contradiction that $\mathcal{U}(\mathsf{E}^\alpha(\tau))$ is not Noetherian. Let us define V_i as $\bigcup_{j<i} U_j$, and H_i as V_i^c.

Thanks to [12, Lemma 9.7.15] there exists a bad sequence $\mathcal{W} := (W_i)_{i \in \mathbb{N}}$ of subbasic elements of $\mathcal{U}(\mathsf{E}^\alpha(\tau))$. By definition, W_i is in some $\mathsf{Down}(U_j)|H_j$. Let us select a mapping $\rho \colon \mathbb{N} \to \mathbb{N}$, such that $W_i \in \mathsf{Down}(U_{\rho(i)})|H_{\rho(i)}$. This amounts to the existence of an open $T_{\rho(i)}$, such that $T_{\rho(i)} \lhd U_{\rho(i)}$, and $W_i = T_{\rho(i)} \setminus V_{\rho(i)}$. Without loss of generality we assume that ρ is monotonic.

Let us build the sequence $\mathcal{Y}$ defined by $Y_i := U_i$ if $i < \rho(0)$ and $Y_i := T_{\rho(i)}$ otherwise. This is a sequence of open sets in $\mathsf{E}^\alpha(\tau)$ that is lexicographically smaller than $\mathcal{U}$, hence $\mathcal{Y}$ is a good sequence: there exists $i \in \mathbb{N}$ such that $Y_i \subseteq \bigcup_{j<i} Y_j$.

- If $i < \rho(0)$, then $U_i \subseteq \bigcup_{j<i} U_j$ contradicting that $\mathcal{U}$ is *bad*.
- If $i \geq \rho(0)$, let us write $Y_i = T_{\rho(i)} \subseteq \bigcup_{j<\rho(0)} U_j \cup \bigcup_{j<i} T_{\rho(j)}$. By taking the intersection with $H_{\rho(i)}$, we obtain $W_i \subseteq \bigcup_{j<i} W_j$, contradicting the fact that $\mathcal{W}$ is a bad sequence. □

We are now ready to leverage our knowledge of minimal topologies associated with minimal bad sequences to carry on the proof of our main theorem.

Proposition 3.20. *Let α be an ordinal, τ be a topology, and E be a topology expander. If $\mathsf{E}^\beta(\tau)$ is Noetherian for all $\beta < \alpha$, and $\tau \subseteq \mathsf{E}(\tau)$, then $\mathsf{E}^\alpha(\tau)$ is Noetherian.*

Proof. If α is a successor ordinal, then $\alpha = \beta + 1$ and $\mathsf{E}^\alpha(\tau) = \mathsf{E}(\mathsf{E}^\beta(\tau))$. Because E respects Noetherian topologies, we immediately conclude that $\mathsf{E}^\alpha(\tau)$ is Noetherian. We are therefore only interested in the case where α is a limit ordinal.

Assume by contradiction that $\mathsf{E}^\alpha(\tau)$ is not Noetherian, using Lemma 3.24 there exists a minimal bad sequence $\mathcal{U} := (U_i)_{i \in \mathbb{N}}$. Let us write $d_i := \mathsf{depth}(U_i) < \alpha$. Thanks to Lemma 3.25, d_i is either 0 or a successor ordinal.

Because $\mathsf{E}^\beta(\tau)$ is Noetherian for $\beta < \alpha$, there are finitely many open subsets U_i at depth β for every ordinal $\beta < \alpha$. Indeed, if they were infinitely many, one would extract an infinite bad sequence of opens in $\mathsf{E}^\beta(\tau)$, which is absurd.

Furthermore, the sequence $(d_i)_{i \in \mathbb{N}}$ must be monotonic, otherwise $\mathcal{U}$ would not be lexicographically minimal. We can therefore construct a strictly increasing map $\rho \colon \mathbb{N} \to \mathbb{N}$ such that $0 < \mathsf{depth}(U_{\rho(j)})$ and $\mathsf{depth}(U_i) < \mathsf{depth}(U_{\rho(j)})$ whenever $0 \le i < \rho(j)$.

Let us consider some $i = \rho(n)$ for some $n \in \mathbb{N}$. Let us write $V_i := \bigcup_{j<i} U_j$, and $H_i := X \setminus V_i$. The set V_i is open in $\mathsf{Down}(U_i)$ by construction of ρ, hence H_i is closed in $\mathsf{Down}(U_i)$. As E is a topology expander, we derive the following inclusions:

$$\mathsf{E}(\mathsf{Down}(U_i))|H_i \subseteq \mathsf{E}(\mathsf{Down}(U_i)|H_i)|H_i$$
$$\subseteq \mathsf{E}(\mathcal{U}(\mathsf{E}^\alpha(\tau)))|H_i$$

Recall that $U_i \in \mathsf{E}(\mathsf{Down}(U_i))$ thanks to Lemma 3.27. As a consequence, $U_i \setminus V_i = W_i \setminus V_i$ for some open set W_i in $\mathsf{E}(\mathcal{U}(\mathsf{E}^\alpha(\tau)))$. Thanks to Lemma 3.29, and preservation of Noetherian topologies through topology expanders, the latter is a Noetherian topology. Therefore, $(W_{\rho(i)})_{i \in \mathbb{N}}$ is a good sequence. This provides an $i \in \mathbb{N}$ such that $W_{\rho(i)} \subseteq \bigcup_{\rho(j) < \rho(i)} W_{\rho(j)}$. In particular,

$$U_{\rho(i)} \setminus V_{\rho(i)} = W_{\rho(i)} \setminus V_{\rho(i)} \subseteq \bigcup_{\rho(j)<\rho(i)} W_{\rho(j)} \setminus V_{\rho(i)} \subseteq \bigcup_{\rho(j)<\rho(i)} W_{\rho(j)} \setminus V_{\rho(j)}$$
$$\subseteq \bigcup_{\rho(j)<\rho(i)} U_{\rho(j)} \setminus V_{\rho(j)} \subseteq \bigcup_{j<\rho(i)} U_j = V_{\rho(i)}$$

This proves that $U_{\rho(i)} \subseteq V_{\rho(i)}$, i.e. that $U_{\rho(i)} \subseteq \bigcup_{j<\rho(i)} U_j$. Finally, this contradicts the fact that $\mathcal{U}$ is bad. $\square$

We have effectively proven that being well-behaved with respect to closed subspaces is enough to consider least fixed points of refinement functions. This behaviour should become clearer in the upcoming sections, where we illustrate how this property can be ensured both in the case of Noetherian spaces and well-quasi-orderings.

4   Applications of Topology Expanders

We now briefly explore topologies that can be proven to be Noetherian using Theorem 3.21. It should not be surprising that both the topological Higman lemma and the topological Kruskal theorem fit in the framework of topology expanders, as both were already proven using a minimal bad sequence argument. However, we will proceed to extend the use of topology expander to spaces for which the original proof did not use a minimal bad sequence argument, and illustrate how they can easily be used to define new Noetherian topologies.

Finite words and finite trees. As a first example, we can easily recover the *topological Higman lemma* [12, Theorem 9.7.33] because the subword topology is the least fixed point of $\mathsf{E}^{\theta}_{\text{words}}$, which is a topology expander (see Lemmas 3.10 and 3.18).

It does not require much effort to generalise this proof scheme to the case of the *topological Kruskal theorem* [12, Theorem 9.7.46]. As a shorthand notation, let us write $t \in \diamond U \langle V \rangle$ whenever there exists a subtree t' of t whose root is labelled by an element of U and whose list of children belongs to V. Recall that we write $u \leq_* v$ when u is a scattered subword of v, and $t \leq_{\text{tree}} t'$ when t embeds in t' as a tree (see page 2). As for the subword topology, the definition is ad-hoc but correctly generalises the tree embedding relation because the tree topology of $\text{alex}(\leq)$ is the Alexandroff topology of $\leq_{\text{tree}}$, for every ordering $\leq$ over Σ [12, Exercise 9.7.48].

Definition 4.1 ([12, Definition 9.7.39]). *Let (Σ, θ) be a topological space. The space $\mathsf{T}(\Sigma)$ of finite trees over Σ can be endowed with the tree topology, the coarsest topology such that $\diamond U \langle V \rangle$ is open whenever U is an open set of Σ, and V is an open set of $\mathsf{T}(\Sigma)^*$ in its subword topology.*

Definition 4.2. *Let (Σ, θ) be a topological space. Let $\mathsf{E}_{\text{tree}}{}^{\theta}$ be the function that maps a topology τ to the topology generated by the sets $\uparrow_{\leq_{\text{tree}}} U \langle V \rangle$, for U open in θ, V open in $\mathsf{T}(\Sigma)^*$ with the subword topology of τ.*

Lemma 4.3. *The tree topology is the least fixed point of $\mathsf{E}_{\text{tree}}{}^{\theta}$, which is a topology expander. Hence, the tree topology is Noetherian when θ is.*

Ordinal words. Let us now demonstrate how Theorem 3.21 can be applied over spaces which are proved to be Noetherian without using a minimal bad sequence argument. For that, let us consider $\Sigma^{<\alpha}$ the set of words of ordinal length less than α, where α is a fixed ordinal. Since $\leq_*$ is in general not a wqo on $\Sigma^{<\alpha}$ when $\leq$ is wqo on Σ, this also provides an example of a topological minimal bad sequence argument that has no counterpart in the realm of wqos.

Definition 4.4 ([15]). *Let (Σ, θ) be a topological space. The ordinal subword topology over $\Sigma^{<\alpha}$ is the topology generated by the closed sets $F_1^{<\beta_1} \cdots F_n^{<\beta_n}$, for $n \in \mathbb{N}$, F_i closed in θ, $\beta_i < \alpha$, and where $F^{<\beta}$ is the set of words of length less than β with all of their letters in F.*

The ordinal subword topology is Noetherian [15], but the proof is quite technical and relies on the in-depth study of the possible inclusions between the subbasic closed sets. Before defining a suitable topology expander, given an ordinal β and a set $U \subseteq \Sigma^{<\alpha}$, let us write $w \in \beta \triangleright U$ if and only if $w_{>\gamma} \in U$ for all $0 \le \gamma < \beta$.

Definition 4.5. *Let (Σ, θ) be a topological space, and α be an ordinal. The function $\mathsf{E}^\theta_{\alpha\text{-words}}$ maps a topology τ to the topology generated by the following sets: $\uparrow_{\le_*} UV$ for U, V opens in τ; $\uparrow_{\le_*} \beta \triangleright U$, for U open in τ, $\beta \le \alpha$; $\uparrow_{\le_*} W$, for W open in θ.*

Lemma 4.6. *Given a Noetherian space (Σ, θ), and an ordinal α. The map $\mathsf{E}^\theta_{\alpha\text{-words}}$ is a topology expander, whose least fixed point contains the ordinal subword topology. Therefore, the ordinal subword topology is Noetherian.*

Remark that Definitions 4.2, 4.5 and 3.9 all follow the same blueprint: new open sets are built as upwards closure for the corresponding quasi-order of the natural constructors associated to the space. We argue that this blueprint mitigates the canonicity issue and the complexity of Definitions 4.1, 4.4 and 3.8.

Ordinal branching trees. As an example of a new Noetherian topology derived using Theorem 3.21, we will consider α-*branching trees* $\mathsf{T}^{<\alpha}(\Sigma)$, i.e., the least fixed point of the constructor $X \mapsto 1 + \Sigma \times X^{<\alpha}$ where α is a given ordinal. This example was not known to be Noetherian, and fails to be a well-quasi-order, and illustrates how Theorem 3.21 easily applies on inductively defined spaces.

Definition 4.7. *Let (Σ, θ) be a Noetherian space. The ordinal tree topology over α-branching trees is the least fixed point of $\mathsf{E}^\theta_{\alpha\text{-trees}}$, mapping a topology τ to the topology generated by the sets $\uparrow_{\le_{\text{tree}}} U\langle V \rangle$, where $U \in \theta$, V is open in $(\mathsf{T}^{<\alpha}(\Sigma))^{<\alpha}$ with the ordinal subword topology, and $U\langle V \rangle$ is the set of trees whose root is labelled by an element of U and list of children belongs to V.*

Theorem 4.8. *The α-branching trees endowed with the ordinal tree topology forms a Noetherian space.*

Proof. It suffices to prove that $\mathsf{E}^\theta_{\alpha\text{-trees}}$ is a topology expander. It is clear that $\mathsf{E}^\theta_{\alpha\text{-trees}}$ is monotone, and a closed set of $\mathsf{E}^\theta_{\alpha\text{-trees}}(\tau)$ is always downwards closed for $\le_{\text{tree}}$. As a consequence, if $\tau \subseteq \mathsf{E}^\theta_{\alpha\text{-trees}}(\tau)$ and H is closed in τ, $t \in V :=$ $(\uparrow_{\le_{\text{tree}}} U\langle V \rangle) \cap H$ if and only if $t \in H$ and every children of t belongs to H. Therefore, $(\uparrow_{\le_{\text{tree}}} U\langle V \rangle) \cap H = (\uparrow_{\le_{\text{tree}}} U\langle V \cap H^{<\alpha} \rangle) \cap H$. Notice that $H^{<\alpha} \cap V$ is an open of the ordinal subword topology over $\tau | H$. As a consequence, $V \cap H \in \mathsf{E}^\theta_{\alpha\text{-trees}}(\tau | H) | H$.

Let us now check that $\mathsf{E}^\theta_{\alpha\text{-trees}}$ preserves Noetherian topologies. Let $W_i := \uparrow_{\le_{\text{tree}}} U_i\langle V_i \rangle$ be a $\mathbb{N}$-indexed sequence of open sets in $\mathsf{E}^\theta_{\alpha\text{-trees}}(\tau)$ where τ is Noetherian. The product of the topology θ and the ordinal subword topology over τ is Noetherian thanks to Table 1 and Lemma 4.6. Hence, there exists a $i \in \mathbb{N}$ such that $U_i \times V_i \subseteq \bigcup_{j<i} U_j \times V_j$. As a consequence, $W_i \subseteq \bigcup_{j<i} W_j$. We have proven that $\mathsf{E}^\theta_{\alpha\text{-trees}}(\tau)$ is Noetherian. $\qquad\square$

At this point, we have proven that the framework of topology expanders allows to build non-trivial Noetherian spaces. We argue that this bears several advantages over ad-hoc proofs: (i) the ad-hoc proofs are often tedious and error prone [12, 13, 15] (ii) the verification that E is a topology expander on the other hand is quite simple (iii) reduces the canonicity issue of topologies to the choice of a suitable topology expander.

5   Consequences on inductive definitions

So far, the process of constructing Noetherian spaces has been the following: first build a set of points, then compute a topology that is Noetherian as a least fixed point. In the case where the set of points itself is inductively defined (such as finite words or finite trees), the second step might seem redundant, and getting rid of it provides a satisfactory answer to the canonicity concerns about Noetherian topologies.

Before studying inductive definition of topological spaces, the notion of least fixed-point in this setting has to be made precise. To that purpose, let us now introduce ome basic notions of category theory. In this paper only three categories will appear, the category Set of sets and functions, the category Top of topological spaces and continuous maps, and the category Ord of quasi-ordered spaces and monotone maps. Using this language, a unary constructor G in the algebra of wqos defines an *endofunctor* from objects of the category Ord to objects of the category Ord preserving well-quasi-orderings.

Notation 5.1. Recall that in a category $\mathcal{C}$, $\text{Hom}(A, B)$ is used to denote the collection of morphisms from the object A to the object B in $\mathcal{C}$. Moreover, $\text{Aut}(A)$ denotes the set of *automorphisms* of A, i.e., invertible elements of $(\text{Hom}(A, A), \circ)$.

In our study of Noetherian spaces (resp. well-quasi-orderings), we will often see constructors G' as first building a new set of structures, and then adapting the topology (resp. ordering) to this new set. In categorical terms, we are interested in endofunctors G' that are U-lifts of endofunctors on Set, where U is the forgetful functor from Top (resp. Ord) to Set.

5.1   Divisibility Topologies of Analytic Functors

The goal of this section is to introduce the categorical framework needed to formalise the automatic definition of a topology over an inductively defined datatype, and to compare this definition with the work that exists on well-quasi-orders by Hasegawa [17] and Freund [8]. We will avoid as much as possible the use of complex machinery related to analytic functors, and use as a definition an equivalent characterisation given by Hasegawa [17, Theorem 1.6]. For an introduction to analytic functors and combinatorial species, we redirect the reader to Joyal [20].

Notation 5.2. Given G an endofunctor of Set, the *category of elements* el(G) has as objects pairs (E, a) with $a \in G(E)$, and as morphisms between (E, a) and (E', a') maps $f \colon E \to E'$ such that $G_f(a) = a'$.

As an intuition to the unfamiliar reader, an element (E, a) in el(G) is a witness that a can be produced through G by using elements of E. Morphisms of elements are witnessing how relations between elements of $G(E)$ and $G(E')$ arise from relations between E and E'. As a way to define a "smallest" set of elements E such that a can be found in $G(E)$, we rely on transitive objects. We recall that in a category $\mathcal{C}$, if X, A are two objects, the action of $\mathrm{Aut}(X)$ on $\mathrm{Hom}(X, A)$ is transitive when for every pair $f, g \in \mathrm{Hom}(X, A)$, there exists a $h \in \mathrm{Aut}(X)$ such that $f \circ h = g$.

Notation 5.3. A *transitive object* in a category $\mathcal{C}$ is an object X satisfying the following two conditions for every object A of $\mathcal{C}$: (a) the set $\mathrm{Hom}(X, A)$ in $\mathcal{C}$ is non-empty; (b) the right action of $\mathrm{Aut}(X)$ on $\mathrm{Hom}(X, A)$ by composition is transitive.

Notation 5.4. Given an object A in a category $\mathcal{C}$, one can build the *slice category* $\mathcal{C}/A$ whose objects are elements of $\mathrm{Hom}(B, A)$ when B ranges over objects of $\mathcal{C}$ and morphisms between $c_1 \in \mathrm{Hom}(B_1, A)$ and $c_2 \in \mathrm{Hom}(B_2, A)$ are maps $f \colon B_1 \to B_2$ such that $c_2 \circ f = c_1$.

This notion of slice category can be combined with the one of transitive object to build so-called "weak normal forms".

Notation 5.5. A *weak normal form* of an object A in a category $\mathcal{C}$ is a transitive object in $\mathcal{C}/A$.

A category $\mathcal{C}$ has the *weak normal form property* whenever every object A has a weak normal form. We are now ready to formulate a definition of analytic functors through the existence of weak normal forms for objects in their category of elements.

Notation 5.6. An endofunctor G of Set is an *analytic functor* whenever its category of elements el(G) has the weak normal form property. Moreover; X is a finite set for every weak normal form $f \in \mathrm{Hom}((X, x), (Y, y))$ in el(G)$/(Y, y)$.

Example 5.7. The functor mapping X to X^* is analytic, and the weak normal form of a word (X^*, w) is (letters$(w), w$) together with the canonical injection from letters(w) to X. In this specific case, the weak normal forms are in fact initial objects.

Example 5.8. The functor mapping X to $X^{<\alpha}$ is not analytic when $\alpha \geq \omega$, because of the restriction that weak normal forms are defined using finite sets.

Let us now explain how these weak normal forms can be used to define a support associated to the analytic functor, which in turns allows us to build a notion of substructure ordering over initial algebras of analytic functors.

Definition 5.9. *Let* G *be an analytic functor,* (X, x) *be an element in* el(G) *and* $f \in \mathrm{Hom}((Y, y), (X, x))$ *be a weak normal form in the slice category* el(G)$/(X, x)$. *We define* $f(Y)$ *as the support of* x *in* X, *written* $\mathrm{supp}_X(x)$.

Definition 5.10. *Let* G *be an analytic functor and* $(\mu G, \delta)$ *be an initial algebra of* G. *We say that* $a \in \mu G$ *is a child of* $b \in \mu G$ *whenever* $a = b$ *or* $a \in \mathrm{supp}_{\mu G}(\delta^{-1}(b))$. *The transitive closure of the children relation is called the* substructure ordering *of* μG *and written* $\sqsubseteq$.

Example 5.11. The substructure ordering on μG for $G(X) := 1 + \Sigma \times X$ is the suffix ordering of words.

We leverage the notion of substructure ordering to define a suitable topology expander over initial algebras of analytic functors. Note that this ordering appears implicitly in the construction of Hasegawa [17, Definition 2.7].

Definition 5.12. *Let* $G' \colon \mathrm{Top} \to \mathrm{Top}$ *be a lifting of an analytic functor* G, *and* $(\mu G, \delta)$ *an initial algebra of* G. *We define* $\mathsf{E}_\Diamond^{G'}$ *that maps* τ *to the topology generated by* $\uparrow_\sqsubseteq \delta(U)$ *where* $U \in G'(\mu G, \tau)$.

We say that $\mathrm{lfp}_\tau . \mathsf{E}_\Diamond^{G'}$ *is the* divisibility topology *over* μG.

Theorem 5.13. *Let* $G' \colon \mathrm{Top} \to \mathrm{Top}$ *be a lifting of an analytic functor* G, *and* $(\mu G, \delta)$ *an initial algebra of* G. *Moreover, we suppose that* G' *preserves inclusions. The map* $\mathsf{E}_\Diamond^{G'}$ *is a topology expander, hence the divisibility topology is Noetherian.*

As a sanity check, we can apply Theorem 5.13 to the sets of finite words and finite trees, and recover the subword topology and the tree topology that were obtained in an ad-hoc fashion in Section 4. In addition to validating the usefulness of Theorem 5.13, we believe that these are strong indicators that the topologies introduced prior to this work were the right generalisations of Higman's word embedding and Kruskal's tree embedding in a topological setting, and addresses the canonicity issue of the aforementioned topologies.

Lemma 5.14. *The subword topology over* Σ^*, *(resp. the tree topology over* $\mathsf{T}(\Sigma)$*) is the divisibility topology associated to the inductive construction of finite words (resp. finite trees).*

5.2 Divisibility Preorders

We are now going to prove that the divisibility topology correctly generalises the corresponding notions on quasi-orderings. In the case of finite words, this translates to the equation $\mathsf{alex}(\leq)^* = \mathsf{alex}(\leq^*)$ [12, Exercise 9.7.30]. We relate the divisibility topology to the divisibility preorder introduced by Hasegawa [17, Definition 2.7].

Theorem 5.15. *Let* G' *the be the lift of an analytic functor respecting Alexandroff topologies, Noetherian spaces, and embeddings. Then, the divisibility topology of* μG *is the Alexandroff topology of the divisibility preorder of* μG, *which is a well-quasi-ordering.*

6   Outlook

We have provided a systematic way to place a Noetherian topology over an inductively defined datatype, which is correct with respect to its wqo counterpart whenever it exists. As a byproduct, we obtained a uniform framework that simplifies existing proofs, and serves as an indicator that the pre-existing topologies were the "right generalisations" of their quasi-order counterparts. Let us now briefly highlight some interesting properties of the underlying theory.

Differences with the existing categorical frameworks. The existing categorical frameworks are built around a specific kind of functors [17, 8], while the notion of topology expander only requires talking about one specific set. This allows proving that the ordinal subword topology and the α-branching trees are Noetherian, while these escape both the realm of wqos, and of "well-behaved functors" having finite support functions.

Quasi-analytic functors. In fact, the proof of Theorem 5.13, never relies on the finiteness of the support of an element. This means that the definition of analytic functors can be loosened to allow non finite weak normal forms. We do not know whether this notion of "quasi-analytic functor" already exists in the literature.

Transfinite iterations. As the reader might have noticed, all of the least fixed points considered in this paper are obtained using at most ω steps. This is because the topology expanders that are presented in the paper are all Scott-continuous, i.e., they satisfy the equation $\mathsf{E}(\sup_i \tau_i) = \sup_i \mathsf{E}(\tau_i)$. While Theorem 3.21 does apply to non Scott-continuous topology expanders, we do not know any reasonable example of such expander.

Lack of ordinal invariants. Even though our proof that the ordinal subword topology is Noetherian is shorter than the original one, it actually provides less information. In particular, it does not provide a bound for ordinal rank of the lattice of closed sets (called the *stature* of $\Sigma^{<\alpha}$), whereas a clear bound is provided by the previous approach Goubault-Larrecq et al. [15, Proposition 33]. This limitation already appears in the existing categorical frameworks [17, 8], and we believe that this is inherent to the use of minimal bad sequence arguments.

Acknowledgements. I thank the anonymous reviewers for their helpful suggestions. I thank Jean Goubault-Larrecq and Sylvain Schmitz for their help and support in writing this paper, together with Simon Halfon for his insight on transfinite words.

References

1. Abdulla, P.A., Čerāns, K., Jonsson, B., Tsay, Y.K.: General decidability theorems for infinite-state systems. Proceedings of LICS'96. pp. 313–321. IEEE (1996). https://doi.org/10.1109/LICS.1996.561359

2. Abdulla, P.A., Jonsson, B.: Verifying networks of timed processes. Proceedings of TACAS'98. Lecture Notes in Computer Science, vol. 1384, pp. 298–312. Springer (1998). https://doi.org/10.1007/BFb0054179

3. Daligault, J., Rao, M., Thomassé, S.: Well-Quasi-Order of Relabel Functions. Order 27(3), 301–315 (2010). https://doi.org/10.1007/s11083-010-9174-0

4. Dershowitz, N., Tzameret, I.: Gap Embedding for Well-Quasi-Orderings. Proceedings of WoLLIC'03. Electronic Notes in Theoretical Computer Science, vol. 84, pp. 80–90. Elsevier (2003). https://doi.org/10.1016/S1571-0661(04)80846-6

5. Figueira, D., Figueira, S., Schmitz, S., Schnoebelen, P.: Ackermannian and Primitive-Recursive Bounds with Dickson's Lemma. Proceedings of LICS'11. pp. 269–278. IEEE (2011). https://doi.org/10.1109/LICS.2011.39

6. Finkel, A., Goubault-Larrecq, J.: Forward analysis for WSTS, part I: completions. Mathematical Structures in Computer Science 30(7), 752–832 (2020). https://doi.org/10.1017/S0960129520000195

7. Finkel, A., Schnoebelen, P.: Well-structured transition systems everywhere! Theoretical Computer Science 256(1), 63–92 (2001). https://doi.org/10.1016/S0304-3975(00)00102-X

8. Freund, A.: From Kruskal's Theorem to Friedman's gap condition. Mathematical Structures in Computer Science 30(8), 952–975 (2020). https://doi.org/10.1017/S0960129520000298

9. Gallier, J.H.: Ann. Pure Appl. Logic: Erratum to "What's so special about Kruskal's Theorem and the ordinal γ_0? A survey of some results in proof theory" [53 (1991) 199–260]. Annals of Pure and Applied Logic 89(2), 275 (1997). https://doi.org/10.1016/S0168-0072(97)00043-2

10. Goubault-Larrecq, J.: On Noetherian spaces. Proceedings of LICS'07. pp. 453–462. IEEE (2007). https://doi.org/10.1109/LICS.2007.34

11. Goubault-Larrecq, J.: Noetherian Spaces in Verification. Proceedings of ICALP'10. Lecture Notes in Computer Science, vol. 6199, pp. 2–21. Springer (2010). https://doi.org/10.1007/978-3-642-14162-1_2

12. Goubault-Larrecq, J.: Non-Hausdorff Topology and Domain Theory, New Mathematical Monographs, vol. 22. Cambridge University Press (2013). https://doi.org/10.1017/CBO9781139524438

13. Goubault-Larrecq, J.: Infinitary Noetherian Constructions I. Infinite Words. Colloquium Mathematicum (168), 257–286 (2022). https://doi.org/10.4064/cm8077-4-2021

14. Goubault-Larrecq, J.: Non-Hausdorff Topology and Domain Theory. Electronic supplements to the book – errata. https://projects.lsv.ens-cachan.fr/topology/?page_id=12 (2022)

15. Goubault-Larrecq, J., Halfon, S., Lopez, A.: Infinitary Noetherian Constructions II. Transfinite Words and the Regular Subword Topology (2022), https://doi.org/10.48550/arXiv.2202.05047

16. Goubault-Larrecq, J., Seisenberger, M., Selivanov, V.L., Weiermann, A.: Well Quasi-Orders in Computer Science (Dagstuhl Seminar 16031). Dagstuhl Reports 6(1), 69–98 (2016). https://doi.org/10.4230/DagRep.6.1.69

17. Hasegawa, R.: Two applications of analytic functors. Theoretical Computer Science 272(1), 113–175 (2002). https://doi.org/10.1016/S0304-3975(00)00349-2

18. Higman, G.: Ordering by divisibility in abstract algebras. Proceedings of the London Mathematical Society 3(1), 326–336 (1952). https://doi.org/10.1112/plms/s3-2.1.326

19. Jančar, P.: A note on well quasi-orderings for powersets. Information Processing Letters 72(5), 155–160 (Dec 1999). https://doi.org/10.1016/S0020-0190(99)00149-0

20. Joyal, A.: Foncteurs analytiques et espèces de structures. Combinatoire énumérative. Lecture Notes in Mathematics, vol. 1234, pp. 126–159. Springer (1986). https://doi.org/10.1007/BFb0072514

21. Kříž, I., Thomas, R.: On well-quasi-ordering finite structures with labels. Graphs and Combinatorics 6(1), 41–49 (1990). https://doi.org/10.1007/BF01787479

22. Kruskal, J.B.: The theory of well-quasi-ordering: A frequently discovered concept. Journal of Combinatorial Theory, Series A 13(3), 297–305 (1972). https://doi.org/10.1016/0097-3165(72)90063-5

23. Milner, E.C.: Basic wqo-and bqo-theory. Graphs and order, pp. 487–502. Springer (1985). https://doi.org/10.1007/978-94-009-5315-4_14

24. Nash-Williams, C.St.J.A.: On well-quasi-ordering transfinite sequences. Mathematical Proceedings of the Cambridge Philosophical Society 61(1), 33–39 (1965)

25. Pouzet, M.: Un bel ordre d'abritement et ses rapports avec les bornes d'une multirelation. CR Acad. Sci. Paris Sér. AB 274, A1677–A1680 (1972)

26. Rado, R.: Partial well-ordering of sets of vectors. Mathematika 1(2), 89–95 (1954). https://doi.org/10.1112/S0025579300000565

27. Schmitz, S.: Algorithmic Complexity of Well-Quasi-Orders. Habilitation à diriger des recherches, École normale supérieure Paris-Saclay (2017), https://tel.archives-ouvertes.fr/tel-01663266

28. Schmitz, S., Schnoebelen, P.: Algorithmic Aspects of WQO Theory (2012), https://cel.archives-ouvertes.fr/cel-00727025

29. Segoufin, L., Figueira, D.: Bottom-up automata on data trees and vertical XPath. Logical Methods in Computer Science 13 (2017). https://doi.org/10.23638/LMCS-13(4:5)2017

30. Singh, D., Shuaibu, A.M., Ndayawo: Simplified proof of Kruskal's Tree Theorem. Mathematical Theory and Modeling 3, 93–100 (2013). https://doi.org/10.13140/RG.2.2.12298.39363

An Efficient Cyclic Entailment Procedure in a Fragment of Separation Logic

Quang Loc Le[1]($\boxtimes$) and Xuan-Bach D. Le[2]

[1] Department of Computer Science, University College London, London, UK
`loc.le@ucl.ac.uk`
[2] School of Computing and Information Systems, University of Melbourne, Melbourne, Australia
`bach.le@unimelb.edu.au`

Abstract. An efficient entailment proof system is essential to compositional verification using separation logic. Unfortunately, existing decision procedures are either inexpressive or inefficient. For example, Smallfoot is an efficient procedure but only works with hardwired lists and trees. Other procedures that can support general inductive predicates run exponentially in time as their proof search requires back-tracking to deal with a disjunction in the consequent.
This paper presents a decision procedure to derive cyclic entailment proofs for general inductive predicates in polynomial time. Our procedure is efficient and does not require back-tracking; it uses normalisation rules that help avoid the introduction of disjunction in the consequent. Moreover, our decidable fragment is sufficiently expressive: It is based on compositional predicates and can capture a wide range of data structures, including sorted and nested list segments, skip lists with fast-forward pointers, and binary search trees. We implemented the proposal in a prototype tool, called S2S$_{\text{Lin}}$, and evaluated it over challenging problems from a recent separation logic competition. The experimental results confirm the efficiency of the proposed system.

Keywords: Cyclic Proofs, Entailment Procedure, Separation Logic.

1 Introduction

Separation logic [20,37] has successfully reasoned about programs manipulating pointer structures. It empowers reusability and scalability through compositional reasoning [6,7]. A compositional verification system relies on bi-abduction technology which is, in turn, based on entailment proof systems. Entailment is defined: Given an antecedent A and a consequent C where A and C are formulas in separation logic, the entailment problem checks whether $A \models C$ is valid. Thus, an efficient decision procedure for entailments is the vital ingredient of an automatic verification system in separation logic.

To enhance the expressiveness of the assertion language, for example, to specify unbounded heaps and interesting pure properties (e.g., sortedness, parent pointers), separation logic is typically combined with user-defined inductive predicates [9,31,35]. In this setting, one key challenge of an entailment procedure is the ability to support induction reasoning over the combination of heaps and data content. The problem of

© The Author(s) 2023
O. Kupferman and P. Sobocinski (Eds.): FoSSaCS 2023, LNCS 13992, pp. 477–497, 2023.
https://doi.org/10.1007/978-3-031-30829-1_23

induction is challenging, especially for an automated inductive theorem prover, where the induction rules are not explicitly stated. Indeed, this problem is undecidable [1].

Developing a sound and complete entailment procedure that could be used for compositional reasoning is not trivial. It is unknown how model-based systems, e.g. [14,15,17,18,22,23], could support compositional reasoning. In contrast, there was evidence that proof-based decision procedures, e.g., Smallfoot [2] and the variant [12], and Cycomp [42], can be extended to solve the bi-abduction problem, which enables compositional reasoning and scalability [7,25]. Smallfoot was the centre of the biabductive procedure deployed in Infer [7], which which greatly impacted academia and industry [13]. Furthermore, Smallfoot is very efficient due to its use of the "exclude-the-middle" rule, which can avoid the proof search over the disjunction in the consequent. However, Smallfoot works for hardwired lists and binary trees only. In contrast, Cycomp, a recent complete entailment procedure, is a cyclic proof system without "exclude-the-middle" and can support general inductive predicates but has double exponential time complexity due to the proof search (and back-tracking) in the consequent.

This paper introduces a cyclic proof system with an "exclude-the-middle"-styled decision procedure for decidable yet expressive inductive predicates. We especially show that our procedure runs in polynomial time when the maximum number of fields of data structures is bounded by a constant. The decidable fragment, SHLIDe, contains inductive definitions of compositional predicates and pure properties. These predicates can capture nested list segments, skip lists and trees. The pure properties of small models can model a wide range of common data structures, e.g. a list with fast-forward pointers, sorted nested lists, and binary search trees [22,32]. This fragment is much more expressive than Smallfoot's and is incomparable to Cycomp's [42]: there exist some entailments our system can handle, but Cyccomp could not, and vice versa.

Our procedure is a variant of the cyclic proof system introduced by Brotherston [3,5] and has become one of the leading solutions to induction reasoning in separation logic. Intuitively, a cyclic proof is naturally represented as a tree of statements (entailments in this paper). The leaves are either axioms or nodes linked back to inner nodes; the tree's root is the theorem to be proven, and nodes are connected to one or more children by proof rules. Alternatively, a cyclic proof can be viewed as a tree possibly containing some back-links (a.k.a. cycles, e.g., "C, if B, if C") such that the proof satisfies some global soundness condition. This condition ensures that the proof can be viewed as a proof of *infinite descent*. For instance, for a cyclic entailment proof with inductive definitions, if every cycle contains an unfolding of some inductive predicate, then that predicate is infinitely often reduced into a strictly "smaller" predicate. This infinity is impossible as the semantics of inductive definitions only allows finite steps of unfolding. Hence, that proof path with the cycle can be disregarded.

The proposed system advances Brotherston's system in three ways. First, the proposed proof search algorithm is specialized to SHLIDe, which includes "exclude-the-middle" rules and excludes any back-tracking. The existing proof procedures typically search for proof (and back-track) over disjunctive cases generated from unfolding inductive predicates in the RHS of an entailment. To avoid such costly searches, we propose "exclude-the-middle"-styled normalised rules in which the unfolding of inductive predicates in the RHS always produces one disjunct. Therefore, our system is much more efficient than existing systems. Second, while a standard Brotherston system is incomplete, our proof search is complete in SHLIDe: If it is stuck (i.e., it can not apply any inference rules), then the root entailment is invalid.

Lastly, while the global soundness in [5] must be checked globally and explicitly, every back-link generated in SHLIDe is sound by design. We note that Cycomp, introduced in [42], was the first work to show the completeness of a cyclic proof system. However, in contrast to ours, it did not discuss the global soundness condition, which is the crucial idea attributing to the soundness of cyclic proofs.

Contributions Our primary contributions are summarized as follows.

- We present a novel decision procedure, S2S$_{\text{Lin}}$, for the entailment problem in separation logic with inductive definitions of compositional predicates.
- We provide a complexity analysis of the procedure.
- We have implemented the proposal in a prototype tool and tested it with the SL-COMP benchmarks [38,39]. The experimental results show that S2S$_{\text{Lin}}$ is effective and efficient compared to state-of-the-art solvers.

Organization The remainder of the paper is organised as follows. Sect. 2 describes the syntax of formulas in fragment SHLIDe. Sect. 3 presents the basics of an "exclude-the-middle" proof system and cyclic proofs. Sect. 4 elaborates on the result, the novel cyclic proof system, including an illustrative example. Sect. 5 discusses soundness and completeness. Sect. 6 presents the implementation and evaluation. Sect. 7 discusses related work. Finally, Sect. 8 concludes the work.

2   Decidable Fragment SHLIDe

Subsection 2.1 presents syntax of separation logic formulae and recursive definitions of linear predicates and local properties. Subsection 2.2 shows semantics.

2.1   Separation Logic Formulas

Concrete heap models assume a fixed finite collection of data structures *Node*, a fixed finite collection of field names *Fields*, a set *Loc* of locations (heap addresses), a set of non-addressable values *Val*, with the requirement that $Val \cap Loc = \emptyset$ (i.e., no pointer arithmetic). null is a special element of *Val*. $\mathbb{Z}$ denotes the set of integers ($\mathbb{Z} \subseteq Val$) and k denotes integer numbers. *Var* an infinite set of variables, $\bar{v}$ a sequence of variables.

Syntax Disjunctive formula Φ, symbolic heaps Δ, spatial formula κ, pure formula π, pointer (dis)equality ϕ, and (in)equality formula α are as follows.

$$\Phi ::= \Delta \mid \Phi \vee \Phi \qquad \Delta ::= \kappa \wedge \pi \mid \exists v.\ \kappa \wedge \pi \qquad \pi ::= \text{true} \mid \alpha \mid \neg \pi \mid \pi \wedge \pi$$
$$\kappa ::= \text{emp} \mid x \mapsto c(f{:}v, .., f{:}v) \mid \text{P}(\bar{v}) \mid \kappa * \kappa \qquad \alpha ::= a{=}a \mid a{\leq}a \qquad a ::= k \mid v$$

where $v \in Var$, $c \in Node$ and $f \in Fields$. Note that we often discard field names f of points-to predicates $x \mapsto c(f{:}v, .., f{:}v)$ and use the short form as $x \mapsto c(\bar{v})$. $v_1 \neq v_2$ is the short form of $\neg(v_1 {=} v_2)$. E denotes for either a variable or null. $\Delta[E/v]$ denotes the formula obtained from Δ by substituting v by E. *A symbolic heap is referred as a base, denoted as Δ^b, if it does not contain any occurrence of inductive predicates.*

Inductive Definitions We write $\mathcal{P}$ to denote a set of n defined predicates $\mathcal{P}=\{P_1, ..., P_n\}$ in our system. Each inductive predicate has following types of parameters: a pair of root and segment defining segment-based linked points-to heaps, reference parameters (e.g., parent pointers, fast-forwarding pointers), transitivity parameters (e.g., singly-linked lists where every heap cell contains the same value a) and pairs of ordering parameters (e.g., trees being binary search trees). An inductive predicate is defined as

$$\texttt{pred P}(r,F,\bar{B},u,sc,tg) \equiv \texttt{emp}\wedge r{=}F\wedge sc{=}tg$$
$$\vee\ \exists X_{tl}, \bar{Z}, sc'.r{\mapsto}c(X_{tl},\bar{p},u,sc') * \kappa' * \texttt{P}(X_{tl},F,\bar{B},u,sc',tg) \wedge r{\neq}F \wedge sc \diamond sc'$$

where r is the root, F the segment, $\bar{B}$ the borders, u the parameter for a transitivity property, sc and tg source and target, respectively, parameters of an order property, $r{\mapsto}c(X_{tl},\bar{p},u,sc') * \kappa'$ the matrix of the heaps, and $\diamond \in \{=,\geq,\leq\}$. (The extension for multiple local properties is straightforward.) Moreover, this definition is constrained by the following three conditions on heap connectivity, establishment, and termination.

Condition C1. In the recursive rule, $\bar{p} = \{\texttt{null}\}\cup\bar{Z}$. This condition implies that If two variables points to the same heap, their content must be the same. For instance, the following definition of singly-linked lists of even length does not satisfy this condition.

$$\texttt{pred ell}(r,F) \equiv \texttt{emp}\wedge r{=}F \vee \exists x_1,X.r{\mapsto}c_1(x_1)*x_1{\mapsto}c_1(X)*\texttt{ell}(X,F)\wedge r{\neq}F$$

as n_3 and X are not field variables of the node pointed-to by r.

Condition C2. The matrix heap defines nested and connected list segments as:

$$\kappa':=\texttt{Q}(Z,\bar{U}) \mid \kappa'{*}\kappa' \mid \texttt{emp}$$

where $Z{\in}\bar{p}$ and $(\bar{U} \setminus \bar{p}) \cap Z = \emptyset$. This condition ensures connectivity (i.e. all allocated heaps are connected to the root) and establishment (i.e. every existential quantifier either is allocated or equals to a parameter).

Condition C3. There is no mutual recursion. We define an order $\prec_{\mathcal{P}}$ on inductive predicates as: $P \prec_{\mathcal{P}} Q$ if at least one occurrence of predicate Q appears in the definition of P and Q is called a direct sub-term of P. We use $\prec_{\mathcal{P}}^*$ to denote the transitive closure of $\prec_{\mathcal{P}}$.

Several definition examples are shown as follows.

$$\texttt{pred ll}(r,F) \equiv \texttt{emp}\wedge r{=}F \vee \exists X_{tl}.r{\mapsto}c_1(X_{tl})*\texttt{ll}(X_{tl}, F)\wedge r{\neq}F$$
$$\texttt{pred nll}(r,F,B) \equiv \texttt{emp}\wedge r{=}F$$
$$\vee \exists X_{tl},Z.r{\mapsto}c_3(X_{tl},Z)*\texttt{ll}(Z, B)*\texttt{nll}(X_{tl},F,B)\wedge r{\neq}F$$
$$\texttt{pred skl1}(r,F) \equiv \texttt{emp}\wedge r{=}F \vee \exists X_{tl}.r{\mapsto}c_4(X_{tl},\texttt{null},\texttt{null})*\texttt{skl1}(X_{tl}, F)\wedge r{\neq}F$$
$$\texttt{pred skl2}(r,F) \equiv \texttt{emp}\wedge r{=}F$$
$$\vee \exists X_{tl}, Z_1.r{\mapsto}c_4(Z_1,X_{tl},\texttt{null})*\texttt{skl1}(Z_1,X_{tl})*\texttt{skl2}(X_{tl}, F)\wedge r{\neq}F$$
$$\texttt{pred skl3}(r,F) \equiv \texttt{emp}\wedge r{=}F$$
$$\vee \exists X_{tl},Z_1,Z_2.r{\mapsto}c_4(Z_1,Z_2,X_{tl})*\texttt{skl1}(Z_1,Z_2)*\texttt{skl2}(Z_2,X_{tl})*\texttt{skl3}(X_{tl},F)\wedge r{\neq}F$$
$$\texttt{pred tree}(r,B) \equiv \texttt{emp}\wedge r{=}B$$
$$\vee \exists r_l,r_r.r{\mapsto}c_t(r_l,r_r)*\texttt{tree}(r_l,B)*\texttt{tree}(r_r,B) \wedge r{\neq}B$$

`ll` defines singly-linked lists, `nll` defines lists of acyclic lists, `slk1`, `slk2` and `slk3` define skip-lists. Finally, `tree` defines binary trees. We extend predicate `ll` with transitivity and order parameters to obtain predicate $\texttt{lla}$ and $\texttt{lls}$, respectively, as follows.

$$\texttt{pred } \texttt{lla}(r,F,a) \equiv \texttt{emp} \wedge r=F \ \vee \ \exists X_{tl}.r \mapsto c_2(X_{tl},a) * \texttt{lla}(X_{tl},F,a) \wedge r \neq F$$
$$\texttt{pred } \texttt{lls}(r,F,mi,ma) \equiv \texttt{emp} \wedge r=F \wedge ma=mi$$
$$\vee \ \exists X_{tl},mi_1.r \mapsto c_4(X_{tl},mi_1) * \texttt{lls}(X_{tl},F,mi_1,ma) \wedge r \neq F \wedge mi \leq mi_1$$

Unfolding Given $\texttt{pred } P(\bar{t}) \equiv \Phi$ and a formula $P(\bar{v})*\Delta$, then unfolding $P(\bar{v})$ means replacing $P(\bar{v})$ by $\Phi[\bar{v}/\bar{t}]$. We annotate a number, called unfolding number, for each occurrence of inductive predicates. Suppose $\exists \bar{w}.r \mapsto c(\bar{p}) * Q_1(\bar{v}_1)*...*Q_m(\bar{v}_m) * P(\bar{v}_0) \wedge \pi$ be the recursive rule, then in the unfolded formula, if $P(\bar{v}_0[\bar{v}/\bar{t}])^{k_1}$ and $Q_i(...)^{k_2}$ are direct sub-terms of $P(\bar{v})^k$ like above, then $k_1=k+1$ and $k_2 = 0$. When it is unambiguous, we discard the annotation of the unfolding number for simplicity.

2.2 Semantics

The program state is interpreted by a pair (s,h) where $s \in Stacks$, $h \in Heaps$ and stack *Stacks* and heap *Heaps* are defined as:

$$Heaps \stackrel{\text{def}}{=} Loc \rightharpoonup_{fin}(Node \rightarrow (Fields \rightarrow Val \cup Loc)^m)$$
$$Stacks \stackrel{\text{def}}{=} Var \rightarrow Val \cup Loc$$

Note that we assume that every data structure contains at most m fields. Given a formula Φ, its semantics is given by a relation: $s,h \models \Phi$ in which the stack s and the heap h satisfy the constraint Φ. The semantics is shown below

$$
\begin{array}{lll}
s,h \models \texttt{emp} & \texttt{iff} & dom(h)=\emptyset \\
s,h \models v \mapsto c(f_i : v_i) & \texttt{iff} & dom(h)=\{s(v)\}, h(s(v))=g, g(c, f_i)=s(v_i) \\
s,h \models P(\bar{v}) & \texttt{iff} & (h, s(\bar{v}_1), .., s(\bar{v}_k)) \in \llbracket P \rrbracket \\
s,h \models \kappa_1 * \kappa_2 & \texttt{iff} & \exists h_1, h_2 \ s.t \ h_1 \# h_2, \ h=h_1 \cdot h_2,, \ s, h_1 \models \kappa_1 \ \text{and} \ s, h_2 \models \kappa_2 \\
s,h \models \texttt{true} & \texttt{iff} & \text{always} \\
s,h \models \kappa \wedge \pi & \texttt{iff} & s, h \models \kappa \ \text{and} \ s \models \pi \\
s,h \models \exists v.\Delta & \texttt{iff} & \exists \alpha.s[v \mapsto \alpha], h \models \Delta \\
s,h \models \Phi_1 \vee \Phi_2 & \texttt{iff} & s, h \models \Phi_1 \ \text{or} \ s, h \models \Phi_2
\end{array}
$$

$dom(g)$ is the domain of g, $h_1 \# h_2$ denotes disjoint heaps h_1 and h_2 i.e., $dom(h_1) \cap dom(h_2)=\emptyset$, and $h_1 \cdot h_2$ denotes the union of two disjoint heaps. If s is a stack, $v \in Var$, and $\alpha \in Val \cup Loc$, we write $s[v \mapsto \alpha] = s$ if $v \in dom(s)$, otherwise $s[v \mapsto \alpha] = s \cup \{(v, \alpha)\}$. Semantics of non-heap (pure) formulas is omitted for simplicity. The interpretation of an inductive predicate $P(\bar{t})$ is based on the least fixed point semantics $\llbracket P \rrbracket$.

Entailment $\Delta \models \Delta'$ holds iff for all s and h, if $s, h \models \Delta$ then $s, h \models \Delta'$.

3 Entailment Problem & Overview

Throughout this work, we consider the following problem.

PROBLEM: QF_ENT−SL$_{\text{LIN}}$.
INPUT: $\Delta_a \equiv \kappa_a \wedge \pi_a$ and $\Delta_c \equiv \kappa_c \wedge \pi_c$ where $FV(\Delta_c) \subseteq FV(\Delta_a) \cup \{\texttt{null}\}$.
QUESTION: Does $\Delta_a \models \Delta_c$ hold?

An entailment, denoted as e, is syntactically formalized as: $\Delta_a \vdash \Delta_c$ where Δ_a and Δ_c are quantifier-free formulas whose syntax are defined in the preceding section.

In Sect. 3.1, we present the basis of an exclude-the-middle proof system and our approach to $\texttt{QF\_ENT}-\texttt{SL}_{\texttt{LIN}}$. In Sect. 3.2, we describe the foundation of cyclic proofs.

3.1 Exclude-the-Middle Proof System

Given a goal $\Delta_a \vdash \Delta_c$, an entailment proof system might derive entailments with a disjunction in the right-hand side (RHS). Such an entailment can be obtained by a proof rule that replaces an inductive predicate by its definition rules. Authors of Smallfoot [2] introduced a normal form and proof rules to prevent such entailments when the predicate are lists or trees. Smallfoot considers the following two scenarios.

- **Case 1** (Exclude-the-middle and Frame): The inductive predicate matches with a points-to predicate in the left-hand side (LHS). For instance, let us consider an entailment which is of the form $e_1 : x \mapsto c(z) * \Delta \vdash \texttt{ll}(x, y) * \Delta'$, where $\texttt{ll}$ is singly-linked lists and $\texttt{ll}(x, y)$ matches with $x \mapsto c(z)$ as they have the same root x. A typical proof system might search for proof through two definition rules of predicate $\texttt{ll}$ (i.e., by unfolding $\texttt{ll}(x, y)$ into two disjuncts): One includes the base case with $x = y$, and another contains the recursive case with $x \neq y$. Smallfoot prevents such unfolding by excluding the middle in the LHS: It reduces the entailment into two premises: $x \mapsto c(z) * \Delta \wedge x = y \vdash \texttt{ll}(x, y) * \Delta'$ and $x \mapsto c(z) * \Delta \wedge x \neq y \vdash \texttt{ll}(x, y) * \Delta'$. The first one considers the base case of the list (that is, $\texttt{ll}(x, x)$) and is equivalent to $x \mapsto c(z) * \Delta \wedge x = y \vdash \Delta'$. Furthermore, the second premise checks the inductive case of the list and is equivalent to $\Delta \wedge x \neq y \vdash \texttt{ll}(x, z) * \Delta'$.
- **Case 2** (Induction proving via hard-wired Lemma). The inductive predicate matches other inductive predicates in the LHS. For example, consider the entailment $e_2 :$ $\texttt{ll}(x, z) * \Delta \vdash \texttt{ll}(x, \texttt{null}) * \Delta'$. Smallfoot handle e_2 by using a proof rule as the consequence of applying the following hard-wired lemma $\texttt{ll}(x, z) * \texttt{ll}(z, \texttt{null}) \models$ $\texttt{ll}(x, \texttt{null})$ and reduces the entailment to $\Delta \vdash \texttt{ll}(z, \texttt{null}) * \Delta'$.

In doing so, Smallfoot does not introduce a disjunction in the RHS. However, as it uses specific lemmas in the induction reasoning, it only works for the hardwired lists.

This paper proposes $\texttt{S2S}_{\texttt{Lin}}$ as an exclude-the-middle system for user-defined predicates, those in $\texttt{SHLIDe}$. Instead of using hardwired lemmas, we apply cyclic proofs for induction reasoning. For instance, to discharge the entailment e_2 above, $\texttt{S2S}_{\texttt{Lin}}$ first unfolds $\texttt{ll}(x, z)$ in the LHS and obtains two premises:

- $e_{21} : (\texttt{emp} \wedge x = z) * \Delta \vdash \texttt{ll}(x, \texttt{null}) * \Delta'$; and
- $e_{22} : (x \mapsto c(y) * \texttt{ll}(y, z) \wedge x \neq z) * \Delta \vdash \texttt{ll}(x, \texttt{null}) * \Delta'$

While it reduces e_{21} to $\Delta[z/x] \vdash \texttt{ll}(z, \texttt{null}) * \Delta'[z/x]$, for e_{22}, it further applies the frame rule as in **Case 1** above and obtains $\texttt{ll}(y, z) * \Delta \wedge x \neq z \vdash \texttt{ll}(y, \texttt{null}) * \Delta'$. Then, it makes a backlink between the latter and e_2 and closes this path. Doing so does not introduce disjunctions in the RHS and can handle user-defined predicates.

3.2   Cyclic Proofs

Central to our work is a procedure that constructs a cyclic proof for an entailment. Given an entailment $\Delta \vdash \Delta'$, if our system can derive a cyclic proof, then $\Delta \models \Delta'$. If instead, it is stuck without proof, then $\Delta \not\models \Delta'$ is not valid.

The procedure includes proof rules, each of which is of the form:

$$\text{PR}_0 \;\frac{e_1 \quad \cdots \quad e_n}{e} \; \text{cond}$$

where entailment e (called the conclusion) is reduced to entailments $e_1, .., e_n$ (called the premises) through inference rule PR_0 given that the *side condition* cond holds.

A cyclic proof is a proof tree $\mathcal{T}_i$ which is a tuple (V, E, C) where

- V is a finite set of nodes representing entailments derived during the proof search;
- A directed edge $(e, \text{PR}, e') \in E$ (where e' is a child of e) means that the premise e' is derived from the conclusion e via inference rule PR. For instance, suppose that the rule PR_0 above has been applied, then the following n edges are generated: $(e, \text{PR}_0, e_1), .., (e, \text{PR}_0, e_n)$;
- and C is a partial relation which captures back-links in the proof tree. If $C(e_c {\rightarrow} e_b, \sigma)$ holds, then e_b is linked back to its ancestor e_c through the substitution σ (where e_b is referred to as a *bud* and e_c is referred to as a *companion*). In particular, e_c is of the form: $\Delta \vdash \Delta'$ and e_b is of the form: $\Delta_1 \wedge \pi \vdash \Delta'_1$ where $\Delta \equiv \Delta_1 \sigma$ and $\Delta' \equiv \Delta'_1 \sigma$.

A leaf node is marked as closed if it is evaluated as valid (i.e. the node is applied with an axiom), invalid (i.e. no rule can apply), or linked back. Otherwise, it is marked as open. A proof tree is *invalid* if it contains at least one invalid leaf node. It is *pre-proof* if all its leaf nodes are either valid or linked back. Furthermore, a pre-proof is a cyclic proof if a global soundness condition is established in the tree. Intuitively, this condition requires that for every $C(e_c {\rightarrow} e_b, \sigma)$, there exist inductive predicates $P(\bar{t}_1)$ in e_c and $Q(\bar{t}_2)$ in e_b such that $Q(\bar{t}_2)$ is a subterm of $P(\bar{t}_1)$.

Definition 1 (Trace) *Let $\mathcal{T}_i$ be a pre-proof of $\Delta_a \vdash \Delta_c$ and $(\Delta_{a_i} \vdash \Delta_{c_i})_{i \geq 0}$ be a path of $\mathcal{T}_i$. A trace following $(\Delta_{a_i} \vdash \Delta_{c_i})_{i \geq 0}$ is a sequence $(\alpha_i)_{i \geq 0}$ such that each α_i (for all $i \geq 0$) is a subformula of Δ_{a_i} containing predicate $P(\bar{t})^u$, and either:*

- *α_{i+1} is the subformula occurrence in $\Delta_{a_{i+1}}$ corresponding to α_i in Δ_{a_i}.*
- *or $\Delta_{a_i} \vdash \Delta_{c_i}$ is the conclusion of a left-unfolding rule, $\alpha_i \equiv P(\bar{t})^u$ is unfolded, and α_{i+1} is a subformula in $\Delta_{a_{i+1}}$ and is the definition rule of $P(\bar{x})^u[\bar{t}/\bar{x}]$. In this case, i is said to be a progressing point of the trace.*

Definition 2 (Cyclic proof) *A pre-proof $\mathcal{T}_i$ of $\Delta_a \vdash \Delta_c$ is a cyclic proof if, for every infinite path $(\Delta_{a_i} \vdash \Delta_{c_i})_{i \geq 0}$ of $\mathcal{T}_i$, there is a tail of the path $p = (\Delta_{a_i} \vdash \Delta_{c_i})_{i \geq n}$ such that there is a trace following p which has infinitely progressing points.*

Suppose that all proof rules are (locally) sound (i.e., if the premises are valid, then the conclusion is valid). The following Theorem shows *global soundness*.

Theorem 1 (Soundness [5]). *If there is a cyclic proof of $\Delta_a \vdash \Delta_c$, then $\Delta_a \models \Delta_c$.*

The proof is by contraction (c.f. [5]). Intuitively, if we can derive a cyclic proof for $\Delta_a \vdash \Delta_c$ and $\Delta_a \not\models \Delta_c$, then the inductive predicates at the progress points are unfolded infinitely often. This infinity contradicts the least semantics of the predicates.

4   Cyclic Entailment Procedure

This section presents our main proposal, the entailment procedure ω-ENT with the proposed inference rules (subsection 4.1), and an illustrative example (subsection 4.2).

4.1   Proof Search

The proof search algorithm ω-ENT is presented in Fig. 1. ω-ENT takes e_0 as input, produces cyclic proofs, and based on that, decides whether the input is valid or invalid. The idea of ω-ENT is to iteratively reduce $\mathcal{T}_0$ into a sequence of cyclic proof trees $\mathcal{T}_i$, $i \geq 0$. Initially, for every $P(\bar{v})^k \in e_0$, k is reset to 0, and $\mathcal{T}_0$ only has e_0 as an open leaf, the root. On line 3, through the procedure is_closed($\mathcal{T}_i$), ω-ENT chooses an *open* leaf node e_i, and a proof

---

ω−ENT

input: e_0 output: valid *or* invalid
1: $i \leftarrow 0$; $\mathcal{T}_i \leftarrow e_0$;
2: **while true do**
3:     $(\text{res}, e_i, PR_i) \leftarrow$ is_closed($\mathcal{T}_i$);
4:     **if** res=valid **then return** valid;
5:     **if** res=invalid **then return** invalid;
6:     **if** link_back$_e$($\mathcal{T}_i$, e_i) = false **then**
7:         $\mathcal{T}_{i+1} \leftarrow$ apply($\mathcal{T}_i$, e_i, PR_i);
8:         $i \leftarrow i+1$;
9: **end**

Fig. 1: Proof tree construction procedure

rule PR_i to apply. If is_closed($\mathcal{T}_i$) returns valid (that is, every leaf is applied to an axiom rule or involved in a back-link), ω-ENT returns valid on line 4. If it returns invalid, then ω-ENT returns invalid (one line 5). Otherwise, it tries to link e_i back to an internal node (on line 6). If this attempt fails, it applies the rule (line 7).

Note that at each leaf, is_closed attempts rules in the following order: normalization rules, axiom rules, and reduction rules. A rule PR_i is chosen if its conclusion can be unified with the leaf through some substitution σ. Then, on line 7, for each premise of PR_i, procedure apply creates a new open node and connects the node to e_i via a new edge. If PR_i is an axiom, procedure apply marks e_i as closed and returns.

Procedure is_closed($\mathcal{T}_i$)   This procedure examines the following three cases.

1. First, if all leaf nodes are marked closed, and none is invalid, then is_closed returns valid.
2. Secondly, is_closed returns invalid if there exists an open leaf node e_i : $\Delta \vdash \Delta'$ in NF such that one of the four following conditions hold:
   (a) e_i could not be applied by any inference rule.
   (b) there exists a predicate $op_1(E) \in \Delta$ such that $op_2(E) \notin \Delta'$ and one of the following conditions holds:
       – either $P(E',E,...)$ or $E' \mapsto c(E,..)$ are on both sides
       – both $P(E',E,...) \notin \Delta$ and $E' \mapsto c(E,..) \notin \Delta$
   (c) there exists a predicate $op_1(E) \in \Delta'$ such that $G(op_1(E)) \in \Delta$ and $op_2(E) \notin \Delta$.
   (d) there exist $x \mapsto c_1(\bar{v}_1) \in \Delta$, $x \mapsto c_2(\bar{v}_2) \in \Delta'$ such that $c_1 \not\equiv c_2$ or $\bar{v}_1 \not\equiv \bar{v}_2$.
3. Lastly, an open leaf node e_i could be applied by an inference rule (e.g. PR_i), is_closed returns the triple (unknown, e_i, PR_i).

In the rest, we discuss the proof rules and the auxiliary procedures in detail.

Normalisation An entailment is in the normal form (NF) if its LHS is in NF. We write $op(E)$ to denote for either $E \mapsto c(\bar{v})$ or $P(E,F,\bar{B},\bar{v})$. Furthermore, the guard $G(op(E))$ is defined by: $G(E \mapsto c(\bar{v})) \stackrel{\text{def}}{=} \text{true}$ and $G(P(E,F,\bar{B},\bar{v})) \stackrel{\text{def}}{=} E \neq F$.

Definition 3 (Normal Form) *A formula $\kappa \wedge \phi \wedge a$ is in normal form if:*

1. $op(E) \in \kappa$ *implies* $G(op(E)) \in \phi$
2. $op(E) \in \kappa$ *implies* $E \neq \text{null} \in \phi$
3. $op_1(E_1) * op_2(E_2) \in \kappa$ *implies* $E_1 \neq E_2 \in \phi$
4. $E_1 = E_2 \notin \phi$
5. $E \neq E \notin \phi$
6. *a is satisfiable*

If Δ is in NF and for any $s, h \models \Delta$, then $dom(h)$ is uniquely defined by s.

The normalisation rules are presented in Fig. 2. Basically, ω-ENT applies these rules to a leaf exhaustively and transforms it into NF before others. Given an inductive predicate $P(E, F, ...)$, rule ExM excludes the middle by doing case analysis for the predicate between base-case (i.e., $E = F$) and recursive-case (i.e., $E \neq F$). The normalisation rule $\neq \text{null}$ follows the following facts: $E \mapsto c(\_) \Rightarrow E \neq \text{null}$ and $P(E,F,\_) \wedge E \neq F \Rightarrow E \neq \text{null}$. Similarly, rule $\neq *$ follows the following facts: $x \mapsto \_ * P(y,F,\_) \wedge y \neq F \Rightarrow x \neq y$, $x \mapsto \_ * y \mapsto \_ \Rightarrow x \neq y$, and $P_i(x,F_1,\_) * P_j(y,F_2,\_) \wedge x \neq F_1 \wedge y \neq F_2 \Rightarrow x \neq y$.

Axiom and Reduction Axiom rules include Emp, Inconsistency and Id, presented in Fig. 3. If each of these rules is applied to a leaf node, the node is evaluated as valid and marked as closed. The remaining ones in Fig. 3 are reduction rules.

For simplicity, the unfoldings in rules Frame, RInd, and LInd are applied with the following definition of inductive predicates:

$$P(x,F,\bar{B},u,sc,tg) \equiv emp \wedge x = F \wedge sc = tg$$
$$\vee \exists X, sc', d_1, d_2. x \mapsto c(X, d_1, d_2, u, sc) * Q_1(d_1, B) * Q_2(d_2, X) * P(X, F, \bar{B}, u, sc', tg) \wedge \pi_0$$

where $B \in \bar{B}$, the matrix κ' contains two nested predicates Q_1 and Q_2, and the heap cell $c \in Node$ is defined as data $c\{c\ next; c_1\ down_1; c_2\ down_2; \tau_s\ scdata; \tau_u\ udata\}$ where $c_1, c_2 \in Node$, $down_1$ and $down_2$ fields are for the nested predicates in the matrix

$$\text{Subst} \frac{\Delta[E/x] \vdash \Delta'[E/x]}{\Delta \wedge x = E \vdash \Delta'} \qquad \text{ExM} \frac{\Delta \wedge E_1 = E_2 \vdash \Delta' \quad \Delta \wedge E_1 \neq E_2 \vdash \Delta'}{\Delta \vdash \Delta'} \quad \begin{array}{l} E_1 = E_2, E_1 \neq E_2 \notin \pi \ \& \\ FV(E_1, E_2) \subseteq (FV(\Delta) \cup FV(\Delta'))^S \end{array}$$

$$=\text{L} \frac{\Delta \vdash \Delta'}{\Delta \wedge E = E \vdash \Delta'} \qquad \text{LBase} \frac{(\kappa \wedge \pi)[tg/sc] \vdash \Delta'[tg/sc]}{P(E,E,\bar{B},u,sc,tg) * \kappa \wedge \pi \vdash \Delta'}$$

$$\neq \text{null} \frac{op(E) * \kappa \wedge \pi \wedge G(op(E)) \wedge E \neq \text{null} \vdash \Delta'}{op(E) * \kappa \wedge \pi \wedge G(op(E)) \vdash \Delta'} \qquad E \neq \text{null} \notin \pi$$

$$\neq * \frac{op_1(E_1) * op_2(E_2) * \kappa \wedge \pi \wedge E_1 \neq E_2 \vdash \Delta'}{op_1(E_1) * op_2(E_2) * \kappa \wedge \pi \vdash \Delta'} \qquad E_1 \neq E_2 \notin \pi \text{ and } G(op_1(E_1)), G(op_2(E_2)) \in \pi$$

Fig. 2: Normalization rules

$$\text{Id } \frac{}{\Delta \wedge \pi \vdash \Delta} \qquad \text{Emp } \frac{}{\text{emp} \wedge \pi \vdash \text{emp} \wedge \text{true}} \qquad \text{Inconsistency } \frac{}{\kappa \wedge \pi \vdash \Delta} \ \pi \models \text{false}$$

$$=\!\!R \ \frac{\Delta \vdash \Delta'}{\Delta \vdash \Delta' \wedge E = E} \qquad \text{Hypothesis } \frac{\Delta \wedge \pi \vdash \Delta'}{\Delta \wedge \pi \vdash \Delta' \wedge \pi'} \ \pi \models \pi' \qquad \text{RBase } \frac{\Delta \vdash \Delta' \wedge tg = sc}{\Delta \vdash P(E,E,\bar{B},u,sc,tg) * \Delta'}$$

$$* \ \frac{\kappa_1 \wedge \pi \vdash \kappa_2 \quad \kappa \wedge \pi \vdash \kappa' \wedge \pi'}{\kappa_1 * \kappa \wedge \pi \vdash \kappa_2 * \kappa' \wedge \pi'} \ \frac{\text{roots}(\kappa_1) \cap \text{roots}(\kappa) = \emptyset \ \& \ FV(\kappa_2) \subseteq FV(\kappa_1 \wedge \pi) \cup \{\text{null}\}}{\& \ FV(\kappa') \subseteq FV(\kappa \wedge \pi) \cup \{\text{null}\}}$$

$$\text{Frame } \frac{\begin{array}{c} Q_1(E_1,B)^0 * Q_2(E_2,X)^0 * P(X,F,\bar{B},u,sc',tg)^k * \Delta_1 \wedge x \neq F_3 \wedge \pi_0 \\ \vdash Q(x,F_3,\bar{B},u,sc,tg_2) * \kappa_2 \wedge \pi_2 \end{array}}{P(x,F,\bar{B},u,sc,tg)^k * \Delta_1 \wedge x \neq F_3 \vdash x \mapsto c(X,E_1,E_2,u,sc') * \kappa_2 \wedge \pi_2} \ x \mapsto c(\_) \notin \kappa_2$$

$$\text{RInd } \frac{\begin{array}{c} x \mapsto c(X,E_1,E_2,u,sc') * \kappa_1 \wedge \pi_1 \wedge x \neq F \\ \vdash x \mapsto c(X,E_1,E_2,u,sc') * Q_1(E_1,B) * Q_2(E_2,X) * P(X,F,\bar{B},u,sc',tg) * \kappa_2 \wedge \pi_2 \wedge \pi_0 \end{array}}{x \mapsto c(X,E_1,E_2,u,sc') * \kappa_1 \wedge \pi_1 \wedge x \neq F \vdash P(x,F,\bar{B},u,sc,tg) * \kappa_2 \wedge \pi_2} \ \dagger$$

$$\text{LInd } \frac{\begin{array}{c} x \mapsto c(X,E_1,E_2,u,sc') * Q_1(E_1,B)^0 * Q_2(E_2,X)^0 * P(X,F,\bar{B},u,sc',tg)^{k+1} * \Delta_1 \wedge x \neq F_3 \wedge \pi_0 \\ \vdash Q(x,F_3,\bar{B},u,sc,tg_2) * \kappa_2 \wedge \pi_2 \end{array}}{P(x,F,\bar{B},u,sc,tg)^k * \Delta_1 \wedge x \neq F_3 \vdash Q(x,F_3,\bar{B},u,sc,tg_2) * \kappa_2 \wedge \pi_2} \ \sharp$$

Fig. 3: Reduction rules (where $\sharp$: $P(x,F,\bar{B},u,sc,tg) \notin \kappa_2$, $\dagger$: $x \mapsto c(X,E_1,E_2,u,sc') \notin \kappa_2$)

heaps, the *udata* field is for the transitivity data, and the *scdata* field is for ordering data. The rules for the general form of the matrix heaps κ' are presented in [28].

$=\!R$ and Hypothesis eliminate pure constraints in the RHS. In rule $*$, $\text{roots}(\kappa)$ is defined inductively as: $\underline{\text{roots}}(\text{emp}) \equiv \{\}$, $\text{roots}(r \mapsto \_) \equiv \{r\}$, $\text{roots}(P(r,F,..)) \equiv \{r\}$ and $\text{roots}(\kappa_1 * \kappa_2) \equiv \text{roots}(\kappa_1) \cup \text{roots}(\kappa_2)$. This rule is applied in three ways. First, it is applied into an entailment which is of the form $\kappa \wedge \pi \vdash \kappa \wedge \pi'$. It matches and discards the identified heap predicates between the two sides to generate a premise with empty heaps. As a result, this premise may be applied with the axiom rule EMP. Secondly, it is applied to an entailment of the form $x_i \mapsto c_i(\bar{v}_i) * ... * x_n \mapsto c_n(\bar{v}_n) \wedge \pi \vdash \kappa' \wedge \pi'$. For each points-to predicate $x_i \mapsto c_i(\bar{v}_i) \in \kappa'$, ω-ENT searches for one points-to predicate $x_j \mapsto c_j(\bar{v}_j)$ in the LHS such that $x_j \mapsto c_j(\bar{v}_j) \equiv x_i \mapsto c_i(\bar{v}_i)$. Lastly, it is applied into an entailment that is of the form $\Delta_1 * \Delta \vdash \Delta_2 * \Delta'$ where either $\Delta_1 \vdash \Delta_2$ or $\Delta \vdash \Delta'$ could be linked back into an internal node.

In RInd, for each occurrence of inductive predicates $P(r,F,\bar{B},u,sc,tg)$ in κ', ω-ENT searches for a points-to predicate $r \mapsto \_$. If any of these searches fail, ω-ENT decides the conclusion as invalid. Rule LInd unfolds the inductive predicates in the LHS. Every LHS of entailments in this rule also captures the unfolding numbers for the subterm relationship and generates the progressing point in the cyclic proofs afterwards. These numbers are essential for our system to construct cyclic proofs. This rule is applied in a *depth-first* manner, i.e., if there are more than one occurrences of inductive predicates in the LHS that could be applied by this rule, the one with the greatest unfolding number is chosen. We emphasise that the last five rules still work well when the predicate in the RHS contains only a subset of the local properties wrt. the predicate in the LHS.

Back-Link Generation Procedure $\texttt{link\_back}_e$ generates a back-link as follows. In a pre-proof, given a path containing a back-link, say $e_1, e_2, .., e_m$ where e_1 is a companion and e_m a bud, then e_1 is in NF and of the following form:

- $e_1 \equiv P(x,F,\bar{B},u,sc,tg)^k * \kappa \wedge \pi \wedge x \neq F \wedge x \neq \texttt{null} \vdash Q(x,F_2,\bar{B},u,sc,tg_2)*\kappa'\wedge\pi'$.
- e_2 is obtained from applying LInd into e_1. e_2 is of the form:

$$x \mapsto c(X,\bar{p},,u,sc)*\kappa'*P(X,F,\bar{B},u,sc',tg)^{k+1}*\kappa\wedge\pi\wedge x \neq F \wedge x \neq \texttt{null}\wedge\pi_1$$
$$\vdash Q(x,F_2,\bar{B},u,sc,tg_2)*\kappa'\wedge\pi'$$

We remark that $sc \diamond sc' \in \pi_1$, and if $k \geq 1$, then $sc_i \diamond sc \in \pi$

- $e_3, .., e_{m-4}$ are obtained from applications of normalisation rules to normalise the LHS of e_2 due to the presence of κ'. As the roots of inductive predicates in κ' are fresh variables, the applications of the normalization rules above do not affect the RHS of e_2. That means the RHS of $e_3, ..,$ and e_{m-4} are the same as that of e_2. As a result, e_{m-4} is of the form:

$$x \mapsto c(X,\bar{p},,u,sc)*\kappa''_1*P(X,F,\bar{B},u,sc',tg)^{k+1}*\kappa\wedge\pi\wedge x \neq F \wedge x \neq \texttt{null}\wedge\pi_1\wedge\pi_2$$
$$\vdash Q(x,F_2,\bar{B},u,sc,tg_2)*\kappa'\wedge\pi'$$

where κ''_1 may be emp and π_2 is a conjunction of disequalities coming from ExM.
- e_{m-3} is obtained from the application of ExM over x and F_2 and of the form:

$$x \mapsto c(X,\bar{p},,u,sc)*\kappa''_1*P(X,F,\bar{B},u,sc',tg)^{k+1}*\kappa\wedge\pi\wedge x \neq F \wedge x \neq \texttt{null}\wedge\pi_1\wedge\pi_2$$
$$\wedge x \neq F_2 \vdash Q(x,F_2,\bar{B},u,sc,tg_2)*\kappa'\wedge\pi'$$

(For the case $x = F_2$, the rule ExM is kept applying until either $F \equiv F_2$, that is, two sides are reaching the end of the same heap segment, or it is stuck.)
- e_{m-2} is obtained from the application of RInd and is of the form:

$$x \mapsto c(X,\bar{p},,u,sc)*\kappa''_1*P(X,F,\bar{B},u,sc',tg)^{k+1}*\kappa\wedge\pi\wedge x \neq F \wedge x \neq \texttt{null}\wedge\pi_1\wedge\pi_2$$
$$\wedge x \neq F_2 \vdash x \mapsto c(X,\bar{p},u,sc)*\kappa''_2*Q(X,F_2,\bar{B},u,sc',tg_2)*\kappa'\wedge\pi'\wedge\pi'_2$$

- e_{m-1} is obtained from the application of the Hypothesis to eliminate π'_2 (otherwise, it is stuck) and is of the form:

$$x \mapsto c(X,\bar{p},,u,sc)*\kappa''_1*P(X,F,\bar{B},u,sc',tg)^{k+1}*\kappa\wedge\pi\wedge x \neq F \wedge x \neq \texttt{null}\wedge\pi_1\wedge\pi_2$$
$$\wedge x \neq F_2 \vdash x \mapsto c(X,\bar{p},u,sc)*\kappa''_2*Q(X,F_2,\bar{B},u,sc',tg_2)*\kappa'\wedge\pi'$$

- e_m is obtained from the application of $*$ and is of the form:

$$P(X,F,\bar{B},u,sc',tg)^{k+1}*\kappa\wedge\pi\wedge x \neq F \wedge x \neq \texttt{null}\wedge\pi_1\wedge\pi_2\wedge x \neq F_2$$
$$\vdash Q(X,F_2,\bar{B},u,sc',tg_2)*\kappa'\wedge\pi'$$

When $k \geq 1$, it is always possible to link e_m back to e_1 through the substitution is $\sigma \equiv [x/X, sc/sc']$ after weakening some pure constraints in its LHS.

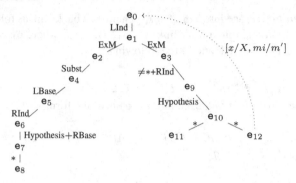

Fig. 4: Cyclic Proof of $\mathtt{lls}(x,\mathtt{null},mi,ma)^0 \wedge x{\neq}\mathtt{null} \vdash \mathtt{llb}(x,\mathtt{null},mi)$.

4.2 Illustrative Example

We illustrate our system through the following example:

$$e_0: \mathtt{lls}(x,\mathtt{null},mi,ma)^0 \wedge x{\neq}\mathtt{null} \vdash \mathtt{llb}(x,\mathtt{null},mi)$$

where the sorted linked-list $\mathtt{lls}$ (mi is the minimum value and ma is the maximum value) is defined in Sect. 2.1 and $\mathtt{llb}$ define singly-linked lists whose values are greater than or equal to a constant number. Particularly, predicate $\mathtt{llb}$ is defined as follows.

$$\mathtt{pred}\ \mathtt{llb}(r,F,b) \equiv \mathtt{emp} \wedge r{=}F$$
$$\vee\ \exists X_{tl},d.\, r{\mapsto}c_4(X_{tl},d) * \mathtt{llb}(X_{tl},F,b) \wedge r{\neq}F \wedge b{\leq}d$$

Since the LHS is stronger than the RHS, this entailment is valid. Our system could generate the cyclic proof (shown in Fig. 4) to prove the validity of e_0. In the following, we present step-by-step to show how the proof was created. Firstly, e_0, which is in NF, is applied with rule LInd to unfold predicate $\mathtt{lls}(x,\mathtt{null},mi,ma)^0$ and obtain e_1 as:

$$e_1: x{\mapsto}c_4(X, m') * \mathtt{lls}(X,\mathtt{null},m',ma)^1 \wedge x{\neq}\mathtt{null} \wedge mi{\leq}m' \vdash \mathtt{llb}(x,\mathtt{null},mi)$$

We remark that the unfolding number of the recursive predicate $\mathtt{lls}$ in the LHS is increased by 1. Next, our system normalizes e_1 by applying rule ExM into X and $\mathtt{null}$ to generate two children, e_2 and e_3, as follows.

$$e_2: x{\mapsto}c_4(X, m') * \mathtt{lls}(X,\mathtt{null},m',ma)^1 \wedge x{\neq}\mathtt{null} \wedge mi{\leq}m' \wedge X{=}\mathtt{null}$$
$$\vdash \mathtt{llb}(x,\mathtt{null},mi)$$
$$e_3: x{\mapsto}c_4(X, m') * \mathtt{lla}(X,\mathtt{null},m',ma)^1 \wedge x{\neq}\mathtt{null} \wedge mi{\leq}m' \wedge X{\neq}\mathtt{null}$$
$$\vdash \mathtt{llb}(x,\mathtt{null},mi)$$

For the left child, it applies normalization rules to obtain e_4 (substitute X by $\mathtt{null}$) and then e_5, by LBase to unfold $\mathtt{lls}(\mathtt{null},\mathtt{null},m',ma)^1$ to the base case, as:

$$e_4: x{\mapsto}c_4(\mathtt{null}, m') * \mathtt{lls}(\mathtt{null},\mathtt{null},m',ma)^1 \wedge x{\neq}\mathtt{null} \wedge mi{\leq}m' \vdash \mathtt{llb}(x,\mathtt{null},mi)$$
$$e_5: x{\mapsto}c_4(\mathtt{null}, ma) \wedge x{\neq}\mathtt{null} \wedge mi{\leq}ma \vdash \mathtt{llb}(x,\mathtt{null},mi)$$

Now, e_5 is in NF. $S2S_{Lin}$ applies RInd and then RBase to 11b in the RHS as:

e_6: $x \mapsto c_4(\text{null}, ma) \wedge x \neq \text{null} \wedge mi \leq ma$
$\vdash x \mapsto c_4(\text{null}, ma) * 11b(\text{null},\text{null},mi) \wedge mi \leq ma$
$e_{6'}$: $x \mapsto c_4(\text{null}, ma) \wedge x \neq \text{null} \wedge mi \leq ma \vdash x \mapsto c_4(\text{null}, ma) \wedge mi \leq ma$

After that, as $mi \leq ma \Rightarrow mi \leq ma$, $e_{6'}$ is applied with Hypothesis to obtain e_7.

e_7: $x \mapsto c_4(\text{null}, ma) \wedge x \neq \text{null} \wedge mi \leq ma \vdash x \mapsto c_4(\text{null}, ma)$

As the LHS of e_7 is in NF and a base formula, it is sound and complete to apply rule $*$ to have e_8 as emp $\wedge x \neq \text{null} \wedge mi \leq ma \vdash$ emp. By Emp, e_8 is decided as valid. For the right branch of the proof, e_3 is applied with rule $\neq*$ and then RInd to obtain e_9:

e_9: $x \mapsto c_4(X, m') * 11s(X,\text{null},m',ma)^1 \wedge x \neq \text{null} \wedge mi \leq m' \wedge X \neq \text{null} \wedge x \neq X$
$\vdash x \mapsto c_4(X, m') * 11b(X,\text{null},mi) \wedge mi \leq m'$

Then, e_9 is applied with Hypothesis to eliminate the pure constraint in the RHS:

e_{10}: $x \mapsto c_4(X, m') * 11s(X,\text{null},m',ma)^1 \wedge x \neq \text{null} \wedge mi \leq m' \wedge X \neq \text{null} \wedge x \neq X$
$\vdash x \mapsto c_4(X, m') * 11b(X,\text{null},mi)$

e_{10} is then applied the rule $*$ to obtain e_{11} and e_{12} as follows.

e_{11}: $x \mapsto c_4(X, m') \vdash x \mapsto c_4(X, m')$
e_{12}: $11s(X,\text{null},m',ma)^1 \wedge x \neq \text{null} \wedge mi \leq m' \wedge X \neq \text{null} \wedge x \neq X \vdash 11b(X,\text{null},mi)$

e_{11} is valid by Id. e_{12} is successfully linked back to e_0 to form a pre-proof as

$$(11s(X,\text{null},m',ma)^1 \wedge X \neq \text{null})[x/X, mi/m'] \vdash 11b(X,\text{null},mi)[x/X, mi/m']$$

is identical to e_0. Since $11s(X,\text{null},m',ma)^1$ in e_{12} is the subterm of $11s(x,\text{null},mi,ma)^0$ in e_0, our system decided that e_0 is valid with the cyclic proof presented in Fig. 4.

5   Soundness, Completeness, and Complexity

We describe the soundness, termination, and completeness of ω-ENT. First, we need to show the invariant about the quantifier-free entailments of our system.

Corollary 1. *Every entailment derived from ω-ENT is quantifier-free.*

The following lemma shows the soundness of the proof rules.

Lemma 1 (Soundness). *For each proof rule, the conclusion is valid if all premises are valid.*

As every backlink generated contains at least one pair of inductive predicate occurrences in a subterm relationship, the global soundness condition holds in our system.

Lemma 2 (Global Soundness). *A pre-proof derived is indeed a cyclic proof.*

The termination relies on the number of premises/entailments generated by $*$. As the number of inductive symbols and their arities are finite, there is a finite number of equivalence classes of these entailments in which any two entailments in the same class are equivalent under some substitution and linked back together. Therefore, the number of premises generated by the rule $*$ is finite, considering the back-links generation.

Lemma 3. ω-ENT *terminates.*

In the following, we show the complexity analysis. First, we show that every occurrence of inductive predicates in the LHS is unfolded at most two times.

Lemma 4. *Given any entailment* $P(\bar{v})^k * \Delta_a \vdash \Delta_c$, $0 \le k \le 2$.

Let n be the maximum number of predicates (both inductive predicates and points-to predicates) among the LHS of the input and the definitions in $\mathcal{P}$, and m be the maximum number of fields of data structures. Then, the complexity is defined as follows.

Proposition 1 (Complexity). QF_ENT$-$SL$_{\text{LIN}}$ *is* $\mathcal{O}(n \times 2^m + n^3)$.

If m is bounded by a constant, the complexity becomes polynomial in time.

Our completeness proofs are shown in two steps. First, we show the proofs for an entailment whose LHS is a base formula. Second, we show the correctness when the LHS contains inductive predicates. In the following, we first define the base formulas of the LHS derived by ω-ENT from occurrences of inductive predicates. Based on that, we define bad models to capture counter-models of invalid entailments.

Definition 4 (SHLIDe **Base**) *Given* κ, *define* $\bar{\kappa}$ *as follows.*

$$\overline{P(E,F,\bar{B},u,sc,tg)} \overset{def}{=} E{\mapsto}c(F,E_1,E_2,u,tg) * \overline{Q_1(E_1,B)}*\overline{Q_2(E_2,F)} \wedge \pi_0$$
$$\overline{E{\mapsto}c(\bar{v})} \overset{def}{=} E{\mapsto}c(\bar{v}) \qquad \overline{\text{emp}} \overset{def}{=} \text{emp} \qquad \overline{\kappa_1 * \kappa_2} \overset{def}{=} \overline{\kappa_1} * \overline{\kappa_2}$$

The definition for general predicates with arbitrary matrix heaps is presented in [28]. As $\mathcal{P}$ does not include mutual recursion (Condition **C3**), the definition above terminates in a finite number of steps. In a pre-proof, these SHLIDe base formulas of the LHS are obtained once every inductive predicate has been unfolded.

Lemma 5. *If* $\kappa \wedge \pi$ *is in NF, then* $\bar{\kappa} \wedge \pi$ *is in NF, and* $\bar{\kappa} \wedge \pi \vdash \kappa$ *is valid.*

In other words, $\bar{\kappa} \wedge \pi$ is an under-approximation of $\kappa \wedge \pi$; invalidity of $\bar{\kappa} \wedge \pi \vdash \Delta'$ implies invalidity of $\kappa \wedge \pi \vdash \Delta'$.

Definition 5 (Bad Model) *The bad model for* $\bar{\kappa} \wedge \phi \wedge a$ *in NF is obtained by assigning*

- *a distinct non-*null *value to each variable in* $FV(\bar{\kappa} \wedge \phi)$; *and*
- *a value to each variable in* $FV(a)$ *such that a is satisfiable.*

Lemma 6. 1. *For every proof rule except the rule* $*$, *all premises are valid only if the conclusion is valid.*
   2. *For the rule* $*$, *where the conclusion is of the form* $\Delta^b \vdash \kappa'$, *all premises are valid only if the conclusion is valid and* Δ^b *is in NF.*

The following lemma states that the correctness of the procedure is_closed for cases 2(b-d).

Lemma 7 (Stuck Invalidity). *Given* $\kappa \wedge \pi \vdash \Delta'$ *in NF, it is* invalid *if the procedure* is_closed *returns* invalid *for cases 2(b-d).*

A bad model of the $\overline{\kappa} \wedge \pi$ is a counter-model. Cases 2b) and 2c) show that the heaps of bad models are not connected, and thus accordingly to conditions **C1** and **C2**, any model of the LHS could not be a model of the RHS. Case 2d) shows that heaps of the two sides could not be matched. We next show the correctness of Case 2(a) of the procedure is_closed, and invalidity is preserved during the proof search in ω-ENT.

Proposition 2 (Invalidity Preservation). *If* ω-ENT *is stuck, the input is invalid.*

In other words, if ω-ENT returns invalid, we can construct a bad model.

Theorem 2. QF_ENT$-$SL$_{LIN}$ *is decidable.*

6   Implementation and Evaluation

We implement S2S$_{Lin}$ using OCaml. This implementation is an instantiation of a general framework for cyclic proofs. We utilize the cyclic proof systems to derive bases for inductive predicates shown in [24] to discharge satisfiability of separation logic formulas. We use the solver presented in [29,31] for those formulas beyond this fragment. We also develop a built-in solver for discharging equalities.

We evaluated S2S$_{Lin}$ to show that i) it can discharge problems in SHLIDe effectively; and ii) its performance is compatible with state-of-the-art solvers. The evaluation of S2S$_{Lin}$ is provided as a companion artifact [27].

Experiment settings We have evaluated S2S$_{Lin}$ on entailment problems taken from SL-COMP benchmarks [38], a competition of separation logic solvers. We take 356 problems (out of 983) in two divisions of the competition, *qf_shls_entl* and *qf_shlid_entl*, and one new division, *qf_shlid2_entl*. All these problems semantically belong to our decidable fragment, and their syntax is written in SMT 2.6 format [39].

- Division *qf_shls_entl* includes 296 entailment problems, 122 invalid problems and 174 valid problems, with only singly-linked lists. The authors in [33] randomly generated them
- Division *qf_shlid_entl* contains 60 entailment problems which the authors in [15] handcrafted. They include singly-linked lists, doubly-linked lists, lists of singly-linked lists, or skip lists. Furthermore, the system of inductive predicates must satisfy the following condition: For two different predicates P, Q in the system of definitions, either P $\prec_{\mathcal{P}}^*$ Q or Q $\prec_{\mathcal{P}}^*$ P.
- In the third division, we introduce new benchmarks, with 27 problems, beyond the above two divisions. In particular, every system of predicate definitions includes two predicates, P and Q, that are semantically equivalent. We have submitted this division to the Github repository of SL-COMP.

Table 1: Experimental results

Tool	qf_shls_entl			qf_shlid_entl			qf_shlid2_entl		
	invalid (122)	valid (174)	Time (296)	invalid (24)	valid (36)	Time (60)	invalid (14)	valid (13)	Time (27)
SLS	12	174	507m42s	2	35	133m28s	0	11	97m54s
Spen	122	174	10.78s	14	13	3.44s	8	2	1.69s
Cyclist$_{SL}$	0	58	1520m5s	0	24	360m38s	0	3	240m3s
Harrsh	39	116	425m19s	18	27	53m56s	8	7	156m45s
Songbird	12	174	237m25s	2	35	40m38s	0	12	47m11s
S2S$_{Lin}$	122	174	6.22s	24	36	0.96s	14	13	1.20s

To evaluate S2S$_{Lin}$'s performance, we compared it with the state-of-the-art tools such as Cyclist$_{SL}$ [5], Spen [15], Songbird [40], SLS [41] and Harrsh [23]. We omitted Cycomp [42], as these benchmarks are beyond its decidable fragment. Note that Cyclist$_{SL}$, Songbird and SLS are not complete; for non-valid problems, while Cyclist$_{SL}$ returns unknown, Songbird and SLS use some heuristic to guess the outcome. For each division, we report the number of correct outputs (invalid, valid) and the time (in minutes and seconds) taken by each tool. Note that we use the status (invalid, valid) annotated with each problem in the SL-COMP benchmark as the ground truth. If the output is the same as the status, we classify it as correct; otherwise, it is marked as incorrect. We also note that in these experiments, we used the competition pre-processing tool [39] to transform the SMT 2.6 format into the corresponding formats of the tools before running them. All experiments were performed on an Intel Core i7-6700 CPU 3.4Gh and 8GB RAM. The CPU timeout is 600 seconds.

Experiment results The experimental results are reported in Table 1. In this table, the first column presents the names of the tools. The following three columns show the results of the first division, including the number of correct invalid outputs, the number of correct valid outputs and the taken time (where *m* for minutes and *s* for seconds), respectively. The number between each pair of brackets *(...)* in the third row shows the number of problems in the corresponding column. Similarly, the following two groups of six columns describe the results of the second and third divisions, respectively.

In general, the experimental results show that S2S$_{Lin}$ is the one (and only one) that could produce all the correct results. Other solvers either produced wrong results or could discharge a fraction of the experiments. Moreover, S2S$_{Lin}$ took a short time for the experiments (8.38 seconds compared to 15.91 seconds for Spen, 324 minutes for Songbird, 635 minutes for Harrsh, 739 minutes for SLS and 2120 minutes for Cyclist$_{SL}$). While SLS returned 14 false negatives, Spen reported 20 false positives. Cyclist$_{SL}$, Songbird and Harrsh did not produce any wrong results. Of 569 tests, Cyclist$_{SL}$ could handle 85 tests (15%), Harrsh could handle 215 tests (38%), and Songbird could decide on 235 tests (41.3%). In the total of 223 valid tests, Cyclist$_{SL}$ could handle 85 problems (38%), and Songbird could decide 222 problems (99.5%).

Now we examine the results for each division in detail. For *qf_shls_entl*, Spen returned all correct, Songbird 186, Harrsh 155, and Cyclist$_{SL}$ 58. If we set the timeout to 2400 seconds, both Songbird and Harrsh produced all the correct results. Division *qf_shlid_entl* includes 24 `invalid` problems and 36 `valid` problems. While Songbird produced 37 problems correctly, Cyclist$_{SL}$ produced 24 correct results. Spen reported 27 correct results and 13 false positives (sk12−vc{01 − 04} sk13−vc01, sk13−vc{03 − 10}). The last division, *qf_shlid2_entl*, includes 14 `invalid` and 13 `valid` test problems. While Songbird decided only 12 problems correctly, Cyclist$_{SL}$ produced 3 correct outcomes. Spen reported 10 correct results. However, it produced 7 false positives (ls−mul−vc{01 − 03}, ls−mul−vc05, nll−mul−vc{01 − 03}). We believe that engineering design and effort play an essential role alongside theory development. Since our experiments provide breakdown results of the two SL-COMP competition divisions, we hope that they provide an initial understanding of the SL-COMP benchmarks and tools. Consequently, this might reduce the effort to prepare experiments over these benchmarks to evaluate new SL solvers. Finally, one might point out that S2S$_{Lin}$ performed well because the entailments in the experiments are within its scope. We do not entirely disagree with this argument but would like to emphasize that tools do not always work well on favourable benchmarks. For example, Spen introduced wrong results on *qf_shlid_entl*, and Harrsh did not handle *qf_shlid_entl* and *qf_shlid2_entl* well, although these problems are in their decidable fragments.

7   Related Work

S2S$_{Lin}$ is a variant of the cyclic proof systems [3,4,5,26] and [42]. Unlike existing cyclic proof systems, the soundness of S2S$_{Lin}$ is local, and the proof search is not backtracking. The work presented in [42] shows the completeness of the cyclic proof system. Its main contribution is introducing the rule ∗ for those entailments with a disjunction in the RHS obtained from predicate unfolding. In contrast to [42], our work includes normalization to soundly and completely avoid disjunction in the RHS during unfolding. Moreover, our decidable fragment SHLIDe is non-overlapping to the cone predicates introduced in [42]. Furthermore, due to the empty heap in the base cases, the matching rule in [42] cannot be applied to the predicates in SHLIDe. Finally, our work also presents how to obtain the global soundness condition for cyclic proofs.

Our work relates to the inductive theorem provers introduced in [10], [40] and Smallfoot [2]. While [10] is based on structural induction, [40] is based on mathematical induction. Smallfoot [2] proposed a decision procedure for linked lists and trees. It used a fixed compositional rule as a consequence of induction reasoning to handle inductive entailments. Compared with Smallfoot, our proof system replaces the compositional rule by combining rule LInd and the back-link construction. Our system could support induction reasoning on a much more expressive fragment of inductive predicates.

Our proposal also relates to works that use lemmas as consequences of induction reasoning [2,16,30,41]. These works in [16,25,30,41] automatically generate lemmas for some classes of inductive predicates. S2 [25] generated lemmas to normalize (such as split and equivalence) the shapes of the synthesized data structures. [16] proposed to generate several sets of lemmas not only for compositional predicates but also for different predicates (e.g., completion lemmas, stronger lemmas and static parameter contraction lemmas). SLS [41] aims to infer general lemmas to prove an entailment. Similarly, S2ENT [30] solves a more generic problem, frame inference, using cyclic proofs and lemma synthesis. It infers a shape-based residual frame in the LHS and then synthesizes the pure constraints over the two sides.

S2S$_{Lin}$ relates to model-based decision procedures that reduce the entailment problem in separation logic to a well-studied problem in other domains. For instance, in [8,11,17], the entailment problem, including singly-linked lists and their invariants, is reduced to the problem of inclusion checking in a graph theory. The authors in [18] reduced the entailment problem to the satisfiability problem in second-order monadic logic. This reduction could handle an expressive fragment of spatial-based predicates called bounded-tree width. Moreover, the work presented in [23] shows a model-based decision procedure for a subfragment of the bounded-tree width. Furthermore, while the work in [15,19] reduced the entailment problem to the inclusion checking problem in tree automata, [21] presented an idea to reduce the problem to the inclusion checking problem in heap automata. Moreover, while the procedure in [15] supported compositional predicates (single and double links) well, the procedure in [19] could handle predicates satisfying local properties (e.g., trees with parent pointers). Our decidable fragment subsumes the one described in [2,11,15] but is incomparable to the ones presented in [8,17,18,19]. Works in [34] and [35,36] reduced the entailment problem in separation logic into the satisfiability problem in SMT. While GRASShoper [35,36] could handle transitive closure pure properties, S2S$_{Lin}$ is capable of supporting local ones. Unlike GRASShoper, which reduces entailment into SMT problems, S2S$_{Lin}$ reduces an entailment to admissible entailments and detects repetitions via cyclic proofs.

Decidable fragments and complexity results of the entailment problem in separation logic with inductive predicates were well studied. The entailment is 2-EXPTIME in cone predicates [42], the bounded tree-width predicates and beyond [18,14], and EXPTIME in a sub-fragment of cone predicates [19]. In the other class, entailment is in polynomial time for singly-linked lists [11] and semantically linear inductive predicates [15]. Moreover, the extensions with arithmetic [17] are in polynomial but become EXPTIME when the lists are extended with double links [8]. SHLIDe (with nested lists, trees and arithmetic properties) is roughly in the "middle" of the two classes above. The entailment is EXPTIME and becomes polynomial under the upper bound restriction.

8   Conclusion

We have presented a novel decision procedure for the quantifier-free entailment problem in separation logic combined with inductive definitions of compositional predicates and pure properties. Our proposal is the first complete cyclic proof system for the problem in separation logic without back-tracking. We have implemented the proposal in S2S$_{Lin}$ and evaluated it over the set of nontrivial entailments taken from the SL-COMP competition. The experimental results show that our proposal is effective and efficient when compared to the state-of-the-art solvers. For future work, we plan to develop a bi-abductive procedure based on an extension of this work with the cyclic frame inference procedure presented in [30]. This extension is fundamental to obtaining a compositional shape analysis beyond the lists and trees. Another work is to formally prove that our system is as strong as Smallfoot in the decidable fragment with lists and trees [2]: Given an entailment, if Smallfoot can produce proof, so is S2S$_{Lin}$.

References

1. Timos Antonopoulos, Nikos Gorogiannis, Christoph Haase, Max Kanovich, and Joël Ouaknine. Foundations for decision problems in separation logic with general inductive predicates. In Anca Muscholl, editor, *Foundations of Software Science and Computation Structures*, pages 411–425, Berlin, Heidelberg, 2014. Springer Berlin Heidelberg.
2. J. Berdine, C. Calcagno, and P. W. O'Hearn. Symbolic Execution with Separation Logic. In *APLAS*, volume 3780, pages 52–68, November 2005.
3. J. Brotherston. Cyclic proofs for first-order logic with inductive definitions. In *Proceedings of TABLEAUX-14*, volume 3702 of *LNAI*, pages 78–92. Springer-Verlag, 2005.
4. J. Brotherston, N. Gorogiannis, and R. L. Petersen. A generic cyclic theorem prover. In *Proceedings of APLAS-10*, LNCS, pages 350–367. Springer, 2012.
5. James Brotherston, Dino Distefano, and Rasmus Lerchedahl Petersen. Automated cyclic entailment proofs in separation logic. In *Proceedings of the 23rd International Conference on Automated Deduction*, CADE'11, page 131–146, Berlin, Heidelberg, 2011. Springer-Verlag.
6. Cristiano Calcagno, Dino Distefano, Jeremy Dubreil, Dominik Gabi, Pieter Hooimeijer, Martino Luca, Peter O'Hearn, Irene Papakonstantinou, Jim Purbrick, and Dulma Rodriguez. Moving fast with software verification. In Klaus Havelund, Gerard Holzmann, and Rajeev Joshi, editors, *NASA Formal Methods*, pages 3–11, Cham, 2015. Springer International Publishing.
7. Cristiano Calcagno, Dino Distefano, Peter W. O'Hearn, and Hongseok Yang. Compositional shape analysis by means of bi-abduction. In *POPL*, pages 289–300, 2009.
8. Taolue Chen, Fu Song, and Zhilin Wu. Tractability of Separation Logic with Inductive Definitions: Beyond Lists. In Roland Meyer and Uwe Nestmann, editors, *28th International Conference on Concurrency Theory (CONCUR 2017)*, volume 85 of *Leibniz International Proceedings in Informatics (LIPIcs)*, pages 37:1–37:17, Dagstuhl, Germany, 2017. Schloss Dagstuhl–Leibniz-Zentrum fuer Informatik.
9. W.-N. Chin, C. Gherghina, R. Voicu, Q.-L. Le, F. Craciun, and S. Qin. A specialization calculus for pruning disjunctive predicates to support verification. In *CAV*. 2011.
10. Duc-Hiep Chu, Joxan Jaffar, and Minh-Thai Trinh. Automatic induction proofs of datastructures in imperative programs. In *Proceedings of PLDI*, PLDI '15, pages 457–466, New York, NY, USA, 2015. ACM.
11. B. Cook, C. Haase, J. Ouaknine, M. Parkinson, and J. Worrell. Tractable reasoning in a fragment of separation logic. In *CONCUR*, volume 6901, pages 235–249. 2011.
12. Christopher Curry, Quang Loc Le, and Shengchao Qin. Bi-abductive inference for shape and ordering properties. In *2019 24th International Conference on Engineering of Complex Computer Systems (ICECCS)*, pages 220–225, 2019.
13. Dino Distefano, Manuel Fähndrich, Francesco Logozzo, and Peter W. O'Hearn. Scaling static analyses at facebook. *Commun. ACM*, 62(8):62–70, jul 2019.
14. Mnacho Echenim, Radu Iosif, and Nicolas Peltier. Unifying decidable entailments in separation logic with inductive definitions. In *Automated Deduction-CADE 28-28th International Conference on Automated Deduction, Virtual Event, July 12-15, 2021, Proceedings*, pages 183–199, 2021.
15. Constantin Enea, Ondrej Lengál, Mihaela Sighireanu, and Tomás Vojnar. Compositional entailment checking for a fragment of separation logic. *Formal Methods in System Design*, 51(3):575–607, 2017.
16. Constantin Enea, Mihaela Sighireanu, and Zhilin Wu. On automated lemma generation for separation logic with inductive definitions. *ATVA*, 2015.
17. Xincai Gu, Taolue Chen, and Zhilin Wu. *A Complete Decision Procedure for Linearly Compositional Separation Logic with Data Constraints*, pages 532–549. Springer International Publishing, Cham, 2016.

18. R. Iosif, A. Rogalewicz, and J. Simácek. The tree width of separation logic with recursive definitions. In *CADE*, pages 21–38, 2013.
19. Radu Iosif, Adam Rogalewicz, and Tomás Vojnar. Deciding entailments in inductive separation logic with tree automata. *ATVA*, 2014.
20. S. Ishtiaq and P.W. O'Hearn. BI as an assertion language for mutable data structures. In *ACM POPL*, pages 14–26, London, January 2001.
21. Christina Jansen, Jens Katelaan, Christoph Matheja, Thomas Noll, and Florian Zuleger. *Unified Reasoning About Robustness Properties of Symbolic-Heap Separation Logic*, pages 611–638. Springer Berlin Heidelberg, Berlin, Heidelberg, 2017.
22. Katelaan Jens, Jovanovic Dejan, and Weissenbacher Georg. A separation logic with data: Small models and automation. In *IJCAI*, 2018.
23. Jens Katelaan, Christoph Matheja, and Florian Zuleger. Effective entailment checking for separation logic with inductive definitions. In Tomáš Vojnar and Lijun Zhang, editors, *Tools and Algorithms for the Construction and Analysis of Systems*, pages 319–336, Cham, 2019. Springer International Publishing.
24. Quang Loc Le. Compositional satisfiability solving in separation logic. In Fritz Henglein, Sharon Shoham, and Yakir Vizel, editors, *Verification, Model Checking, and Abstract Interpretation*, pages 578–602, Cham, 2021. Springer International Publishing.
25. Quang Loc Le, Cristian Gherghina, Shengchao Qin, and Wei-Ngan Chin. Shape analysis via second-order bi-abduction. In *CAV*, volume 8559, pages 52–68. 2014.
26. Quang Loc Le and Mengda He. A decision procedure for string logic with quadratic equations, regular expressions and length constraints. In Sukyoung Ryu, editor, *Programming Languages and Systems*, pages 350–372, Cham, 2018. Springer International Publishing.
27. Quang Loc Le and Xuan-Bach D. Le. Artifact for an efficient cyclic entailment procedure in a fragment of separation logic, February 2023. https://doi.org/10.5281/zenodo.7619870.
28. Quang Loc Le and Xuan-Bach D. Le. An efficient cyclic entailment procedure in a fragment of separation logic, January 2023. Technical Report.
29. Quang Loc Le, Jun Sun, and Wei-Ngan Chin. Satisfiability modulo heap-based programs. In *CAV*. 2016.
30. Quang Loc Le, Jun Sun, and Shengchao Qin. Frame inference for inductive entailment proofs in separation logic. In Dirk Beyer and Marieke Huisman, editors, *Tools and Algorithms for the Construction and Analysis of Systems*, pages 41–60, 2018.
31. Quang Loc Le, Makoto Tatsuta, Jun Sun, and Wei-Ngan Chin. A decidable fragment in separation logic with inductive predicates and arithmetic. In *CAV*, pages 495–517, 2017.
32. Scott McPeak and George C. Necula. Data structure specifications via local equality axioms. In Kousha Etessami and Sriram K. Rajamani, editors, *Computer Aided Verification*, pages 476–490, Berlin, Heidelberg, 2005. Springer Berlin Heidelberg.
33. Juan Antonio Navarro Pérez and Andrey Rybalchenko. Separation logic + superposition calculus = heap theorem prover. In *Proceedings of the 32nd ACM SIGPLAN Conference on Programming Language Design and Implementation*, PLDI '11, page 556–566, New York, NY, USA, 2011. Association for Computing Machinery.
34. JuanAntonio Navarro Pérez and Andrey Rybalchenko. Separation logic modulo theories. In *APLAS*, volume 8301, pages 90–106. 2013.
35. R. Piskac, T. Wies, and D. Zufferey. Automating separation logic using smt. In Natasha Sharygina and Helmut Veith, editors, *CAV*, volume 8044, pages 773–789. 2013.
36. Ruzica Piskac, Thomas Wies, and Damien Zufferey. Automating separation logic with trees and data. In *CAV*, volume 8559, pages 711–728. 2014.
37. J. Reynolds. Separation Logic: A Logic for Shared Mutable Data Structures. In *IEEE LICS*, pages 55–74, 2002.

38. Mihaela Sighireanu and Quang Loc Le. SL-COMP 2022. https://sl-comp.github.io/, 2022. [Online; accessed Jun-2022].

39. Mihaela Sighireanu, Juan Antonio Navarro Pérez, Andrey Rybalchenko, Nikos Gorogiannis, Radu Iosif, Andrew Reynolds, Cristina Serban, Jens Katelaan, Christoph Matheja, Thomas Noll, Florian Zuleger, Wei-Ngan Chin, Quang Loc Le, Quang-Trung Ta, Ton-Chanh Le, Thanh-Toan Nguyen, Siau-Cheng Khoo, Michal Cyprian, Adam Rogalewicz, Tomás Vojnar, Constantin Enea, Ondrej Lengál, Chong Gao, and Zhilin Wu. SL-COMP: competition of solvers for separation logic. In *Tools and Algorithms for the Construction and Analysis of Systems - 25 Years of TACAS: TOOLympics*, pages 116–132, 2019.

40. Quang-Trung Ta, Ton Chanh Le, Siau-Cheng Khoo, and Wei-Ngan Chin. Automated mutual explicit induction proof in separation logic. In John Fitzgerald, Constance Heitmeyer, Stefania Gnesi, and Anna Philippou, editors, *FM 2016: Proceedings*, pages 659–676, 2016.

41. Quang-Trung Ta, Ton Chanh Le, Siau-Cheng Khoo, and Wei-Ngan Chin. Automated lemma synthesis in symbolic-heap separation logic. *POPL*, 2018.

42. Makoto Tatsuta, Koji Nakazawa, and Daisuke Kimura. Completeness of cyclic proofs for symbolic heaps with inductive definitions. In Anthony Widjaja Lin, editor, *Programming Languages and Systems*, pages 367–387, Cham, 2019. Springer International Publishing.

Just Testing

Rob van Glabbeek[1,2]($\boxtimes$) (iD) *

[1] School of Informatics, University of Edinburgh, Edinburgh, UK
[2] School of Computer Science and Engineering, University of New South Wales,
Sydney, Australia
`rvg@cs.stanford.edu`

Abstract. The concept of must testing is naturally parametrised with
a chosen completeness criterion, defining the complete runs of a system. Here I employ justness as this completeness criterion, instead of
the traditional choice of progress. The resulting must-testing preorder is
incomparable with the default one, and can be characterised as the fair
failure preorder of Vogler. It also is the coarsest precongruence preserving
linear time properties when assuming justness.

As my system model I here employ Petri nets with read arcs. Through
their Petri net semantics, this work applies equally well to process algebras. I provide a Petri net semantics for a standard process algebra extended with signals; the read arcs are necessary to capture those signals.

1 Introduction

May- and must-testing was proposed by De Nicola & Hennessy in [9]. It yields
semantic equivalences where two processes are distinguished if and only if they
react differently on certain tests. The tests are processes that additionally feature success states. A test $\mathcal{T}$ is applied to a process N by taking the CCS
parallel composition $\mathcal{T}|N$, and implicitly applying a CCS restriction operator to
it that removes the remnants of unsuccessful communication. Applying $\mathcal{T}$ to N
is deemed successful if and only if this composition yields a process that may,
respectively must, reach a success state. It is trivial to recast this definition using
the CSP parallel composition $\|_{\mathcal{A}}$ [39] instead of the one from CCS.

It is not a priori clear how a given process *must* reach a success state. For all
we know it might stay in its initial state and never take any transition leading
to this success state. To this end one must employ an assumption saying that
under appropriate circumstances certain enabled transitions will indeed be taken.
Such an assumption is called a *completeness criterion* [18]. The theory of testing
from [9] implicitly employs a default completeness criterion that in [25] is called
progress. However, one can parameterise the notion of must testing by the choice
of any completeness criterion, such as the many notions of *fairness* classified in
[25]. Here I employ *justness*, a completeness criterion that is better justified than
either progress or fairness [25].

---

* Supported by Royal Society Wolfson Fellowship RSWF\R1\221008

O. Kupferman and P. Sobocinski (Eds.): FoSSaCS 2023, LNCS 13992, pp. 498–519, 2023.
https://doi.org/10.1007/978-3-031-30829-1_24

The resulting must-testing equivalence is incomparable to the progress-based one from [9]. On the one hand, it no longer distinguishes deadlock and livelock, i.e., the Petri nets N and N' of Ex. 3; on the other hand, it keeps recording information past a divergence. I characterise the corresponding preorder as the fair failure preorder of Vogler [43], which using my terminology ought to be called the *just failures preorder*. I show that it also is the coarsest precongruence preserving linear time properties when assuming justness. Finally I show that the same preorder originates from the timed must-testing framework explored in [43], but only if all quantitative information is removed from that approach.

I carry out this work within the model of Petri nets extended with read arcs [35,7], so that it also applies to process algebras through their standard Petri net semantics. The extension with read arcs is necessary to capture *signalling*, a process algebra operator that cannot be adequately modelled by standard Petri nets. Signalling, or read arcs, can be used to accurately model mutual exclusion without making a fairness assumption [43,8,11]. This is not possible in standard Petri nets [31,43,24], or in process algebras with a standard Petri net semantics [24]. Here I give a Petri net semantics of signalling, and illustrate its use in modelling a traffic light, interacting with passing cars.

Acknowledgement I am grateful to Weiyou Wang for valuable feedback.

2   Labelled Petri nets with read arcs

I will employ the following notations for multisets.

Definition 1 Let X be a set.
- A *multiset* over X is a function $A: X \to \mathbb{N}$, i.e. $A \in \mathbb{N}^X$.
- $x \in X$ is an *element of* A, notation $x \in A$, iff $A(x) > 0$.
- For multisets A and B over X I write $A \subseteq B$ iff $A(x) \le B(x)$ for all $x \in X$;
  $A \cup B$ denotes the multiset over X with $(A \cup B)(x) := \max(A(x), B(x))$,
  $A \cap B$ denotes the multiset over X with $(A \cap B)(x) := \min(A(x), B(x))$,
  $A + B$ denotes the multiset over X with $(A + B)(x) := A(x) + B(x)$,
  $A - B$ is given by $(A - B)(x) := \max(A(x) - B(x), 0)$, and
  for $k \in \mathbb{N}$ the multiset $k \cdot A$ is given by $(k \cdot A)(x) := k \cdot A(x)$.
- The function $\emptyset: X \to \mathbb{N}$, given by $\emptyset(x) := 0$ for all $x \in X$, is the *empty* multiset over X.
- The cardinality $|A|$ of a multiset A over X is given by $|A| := \sum_{x \in X} A(x)$.
- A multiset A over X is *finite* iff $|A| < \infty$, i.e., iff the set $\{x \mid x \in A\}$ is finite.

With $\{x, x, y\}$ I denote the multiset over $\{x, y\}$ with $A(x)=2$ and $A(y)=1$, rather than the set $\{x, y\}$ itself. A multiset A with $A(x) \le 1$ for all x is identified with the set $\{x \mid A(x) = 1\}$.

I employ general labelled place/transition systems extended with read arcs [35,7].

Definition 2 Let $\mathcal{A}$ be a set of *visible actions* and $\tau \notin \mathcal{A}$ be an *invisible action*. Let $\mathcal{A}_\tau := \mathcal{A} \,\dot\cup\, \{\tau\}$. A *(labelled) Petri net (over $\mathcal{A}_\tau$)* is a tuple (S, T, F, R, M_0, ℓ) where

- S and T are disjoint sets (of *places* and *transitions*),
- $F : ((S \times T) \cup (T \times S)) \to \mathbb{N}$ (the *flow relation* including *arc weights*),
- $R : S \times T \to \mathbb{N}$ (the *read relation*),
- $M_0 : S \to \mathbb{N}$ (the *initial marking*), and
- $\ell : T \to \mathcal{A}_\tau$ (the *labelling function*).

Petri nets are depicted by drawing the places as circles and the transitions as boxes, containing their label. Identities of places and transitions are displayed next to the net element. When $F(x, y) > 0$ for $x, y \in S \cup T$ there is an arrow (*arc*) from x to y, labelled with the *arc weight* $F(x, y)$. Weights 1 are elided. An element (s, t) of the multiset R is called a *read arc*. Read arcs are drawn as lines without arrowhead. When a Petri net represents a concurrent system, a global state of this system is given as a *marking*, a multiset M of places, depicted by placing $M(s)$ dots (*tokens*) in each place s. The initial state is M_0.

The behaviour of a Petri net is defined by the possible moves between markings M and M', which take place when a finite multiset G of transitions *fires*. In that case, each occurrence of a transition t in G consumes $F(s, t)$ tokens from each place s. Naturally, this can happen only if M makes all these tokens available in the first place. Moreover, for each $t \in G$ there need to be at least $R(s, t)$ tokens in each place s that are not consumed when firing G. Next, each t produces $F(t, s)$ tokens in each place s. Definition 4 formalises this notion of behaviour.

Definition 3 Let $N = (S, T, F, R, M_0, \ell)$ be a Petri net. The multisets $\widehat{t},\ ^\bullet t,\ t^\bullet : S \to \mathbb{N}$ are given by $\widehat{t}(s) = R(s, t)$, $^\bullet t(s) = F(s, t)$ and $t^\bullet(s) = F(t, s)$ for all $s \in S$. The elements of $\widehat{t},\ ^\bullet t$ and $t^\bullet$ are called *read-*, *pre-* and *postplaces* of t, respectively. These functions extend to finite multisets $G : T \to \mathbb{N}$ by $\widehat{G} := \bigcup_{t \in G} \widehat{t},\ ^\bullet G := \sum_{t \in T} G(t) \cdot {}^\bullet t$ and $G^\bullet := \sum_{t \in T} G(t) \cdot t^\bullet$.

Definition 4 ([7]) Let $N = (S, T, F, R, M_0, \ell)$ be a Petri net, $G \in \mathbb{N}^T$ non-empty and finite, and $M, M' \in \mathbb{N}^S$. G is a *step* from M to M', written $M\,[G\rangle_N\,M'$, iff

- $^\bullet G + \widehat{G} \subseteq M$ (G is *enabled*) and
- $M' = (M - {}^\bullet G) + G^\bullet$.

Note that steps are (finite) multisets, thus allowing self-concurrency, i.e. the same transition can occur multiple times in a single step. One writes $M\,[t\rangle_N\,M'$ for $M\,[\{t\}\rangle_N\,M'$, whereas $M[t\rangle_N$ abbreviates $\exists M'.\ M\,[t\rangle_N\,M'$. The subscript N may be omitted if clear from context.

In my Petri nets transitions are labelled with *actions* drawn from a set $\mathcal{A} \,\dot\cup\, \{\tau\}$. This makes it possible to see these nets as models of *reactive systems* that interact with their environment. A transition t can be thought of as the occurrence of the action $\ell(t)$. If $\ell(t) \in \mathcal{A}$, this occurrence can be observed and influenced by the environment, but if $\ell(t) = \tau$, it cannot and t is an *internal* or *silent* transition. Transitions whose occurrences cannot be distinguished by the environment carry the same label. In particular, since the environment cannot observe the occurrence of internal transitions at all, they are all labelled τ.

In [31,43,24] it was established that mutual exclusion protocols cannot be correctly modelled in standard Petri nets (without read arcs, i.e., satisfying $R(s,t) = 0$ for all $s \in S$ and $t \in T$), unless their correctness becomes contingent on making a fairness assumption. In [24] it was concluded from this that mutual exclusion protocols can likewise not be correctly expressed in standard process algebras such as CCS [34], CSP [6] or ACP [4], at least when sticking to their standard Petri net semantics. Yet Vogler showed that mutual exclusion can be correctly modelled in Petri nets with read arcs [43], and [8,11] demonstrate how mutual exclusion can be correctly modelled in a process algebra extended with *signalling* [3]. Thus signalling adds expressiveness to process algebra that cannot be adequately modelled in terms of standard Petri nets. This is my main reason to use Petri nets with read arcs as system model in this paper.

In many papers on Petri nets, the sets of places and transitions are required to be finite, or at least countable. Here I need a milder restriction, and will limit attention to nets that are finitary in the following sense.

Definition 5 A Petri net $N = (S, T, F, R, M_0, \ell)$ is *finitary* if M_0 is countable, $t^\bullet$ is countable for all $t \in T$, and moreover the set of transitions t with $^\bullet t = \emptyset$ is countable.

3   A Petri net semantics of CCSP with signalling

CCSP [37] is a natural mix of the process algebras CCS [34] and CSP [6], often used in connection with Petri nets. Here I will present a Petri net semantics of a version CCSPS of CCSP enriched with *signalling* [3]. This builds on work from [29,44,27,10,37,38]; the only novelty is the treatment of signalling. Petri net semantics of other process algebras, like CCS [34], CSP [6] or ACP [4], are equally well known. This Petri net semantics lifts any semantic equivalence on Petri nets to CCSPS, or to any other process algebra, so that the results of this work apply equally well to process algebras.

CCSPS is parametrised by the choice of sets $\mathcal{A}$ of visible actions and $\mathcal{K}$ of *agent identifiers*. Its syntax is given by

$$P, Q, P_i ::= \sum_{i \in I} a_i P_i \ \Big| \ a \triangleright \sum_{i \in I} a_i P_i \ \Big| \ P\|_A Q \ \Big| \ \tau_A(P) \ \Big| \ f(P) \ \Big| \ K$$

with $a, a_i \in \mathcal{A}$, $A \subseteq \mathcal{A}$, $f : \mathcal{A} \to \mathcal{A}$ and $K \in \mathcal{K}$. Here the guarded choice $\sum_{i \in I} a_i P_i$ executes one of the actions a_i, followed by the process P_i. The process $a \triangleright P$ behaves as P, except that in its initial state it it is sending the signal a.[1] [2] The process $P\|_A Q$ is the partially synchronous parallel composition of processes

---

[1] The notation $a \triangleright P$ follows [8]; in [3,11] this is denoted $P\hat{\ }a$.

[2] Here I require P to be a guarded choice in order to avoid the need for a *root condition* [13] to make the equivalences of this paper into congruences. This is also the reason my language features a guarded choice, instead of action prefixing and general choice.

P and Q, where actions from A can take place only when both P and Q can engage in such an action, while other actions of P and Q occur independently. The abstraction operator τ_A hides action from A from the environment by renaming them into τ, whereas f is a straightforward relabelling operator (leaving internal actions alone). Each agent identifier K comes with a *defining equation* $K \stackrel{def}{=} P$, with P a *guarded* CCSPS expression; it behaves exactly as the body of its defining equation. Here P is guarded if each occurrence of an agent identifier within P lays in the scope of a guarded choice $\sum_{i \in I} a_i P_i$ or $a \rhd \sum_{i \in I} a_i P_i$.

A formal Petri net semantics of CCSPS, and of each of the operators $\sum$, $\rhd$, $\|_A$, τ_A and f, appears in [22, Appendix A]. Here I give an informal summary.

Given nets N_i for $i \in I$, the net $\sum_{i \in I} a_i N_i$ is obtained by taking their disjoint union, but without their initial markings $(M_0)_i$, and adding a single marked place r, and for each $i \in I$ a fresh transition t_i, labelled a_i, with ${}^\bullet t_i = \{r\}$, $\widehat{t_i} = \emptyset$ and $(t_i^\bullet) = (M_0)_i$.

The parallel composition $N \|_A N'$ is obtained out of the disjoint union of N and N' by dropping from N and N' all transitions t with $\ell(t) \in A$, and instead adding synchronisation transitions (t, t') for each pair of transitions t and t' from N and N' with $\ell(t) = \ell(t') \in A$. One has ${}^\bullet(t, t') := {}^\bullet t + {}^\bullet t'$, and similarly for $\widehat{(t, t')}$ and $(t, t')^\bullet$, i.e., all arcs are inherited.

τ_A and f are renaming operators that only affect the labels of transitions.

The net $a \rhd N$ adds to the net N a single transition u, labelled a, that may fire arbitrary often, but is enabled in the initial state of N only. To this end, take ${}^\bullet u = u^\bullet = \emptyset$ and $\widehat{u} = M_0$, the initial marking of N. I apply this construction only to nets for which its initially marked places have no incoming arcs.

Example 1 A traffic light can be modelled by the recursive equation

$$TL \stackrel{def}{=} tr.tg.(drive \rhd ty.TL).$$

Here the actions tr, tg and ty stand for "turn red", "turn green" and "turn yellow", and $drive$ indicates a state where it is OK to drive through. A sequence of two passing cars is modelled as $Traffic \stackrel{def}{=} drive.drive.\mathbf{0}$. Here $\mathbf{0}$ stands for the empty sum $\sum_{i \in \emptyset} a_i.E_i$ and models inaction. In the parallel composition $TL \|_{\{drive\}} Traffic$ the cars only drive through when the light is green. All three processes are displayed in Fig. 1.

4   Justness and other completeness criteria

Definition 6 Let $N = (S, T, F, R, M_0, \ell)$ be a Petri net. An *execution path* π is an alternating sequence $M_0 t_1 M_1 t_2 M_2 \ldots$ of markings and transitions of N, starting with M_0, and either being infinite or ending with a marking, such that $M_i \, [t_{i+1}\rangle_N \, M_{i+1}$ for all $i < length(\pi)$. Here $length(\pi) \in \mathbb{N} \cup \{\infty\}$ is the number of transitions in π.

Let $\ell(\pi) \in \mathcal{A}_\tau^\infty$ be the string $\ell(t_1)\ell(t_2)\ldots$. Here $\mathcal{A}_\tau^\infty$ denotes the collection of finite and infinite sequences of actions. Moreover, $trace(\pi) \in \mathcal{A}^\infty$ is obtained from $\ell(\pi)$ by dropping all occurrences of τ.

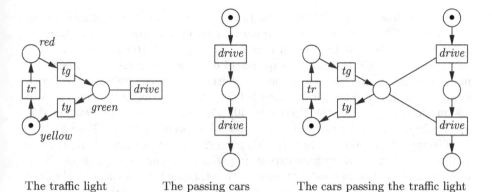

The traffic light   The passing cars   The cars passing the traffic light

Fig. 1. Traffic passing traffic light

The execution path π is said to *enable* a transition t, notation $\pi[t\rangle$, if $M_k[t\rangle$ for some $k \in \mathbb{N} \wedge k \leq length(\pi)$ and for all $k \leq j < length(\pi)$ one has $t_j \neq t$ and $(^\bullet t + \hat{t}) \cap {}^\bullet t_{j+1} = \emptyset$.

Path π is *B-just*, for some $B \subseteq \mathcal{A}$, if $\ell(t) \in B$ for all $t \in T$ with $\pi[t\rangle$.

In the definition of $\pi[t\rangle$ above one also has $M_{j+1}[t\rangle$ for all $k \leq j < length(\pi)$. Hence, a finite execution path enables a transition iff its final marking does so.

Informally, $\pi[t\rangle$ holds iff transition t is enabled in some marking on the path π, and after that state no transition of π uses any of the resources needed to fire t. Here the read- and preplaces of t count as such resources. The clause $t_j \neq t$ moreover counts the transition itself as one of its resources, in the sense that a transition is no longer enabled when it occurs. This clause is redundant for transitions t with $^\bullet t \neq \emptyset$. One could interpret this clause as saying that a transition t with $^\bullet t = \emptyset$ comes with implicit marked private preplace p_t, and arcs (p_t, t) as well as (t, p_t).

In [18] I posed that Petri nets or transition systems constitute a good model of concurrency only in combination with a *completeness criterion*: a selection of a subset of all execution paths as complete executions, modelling complete runs of the represented system. The default completeness criterion, called *progress* in [25], declares an execution path complete iff it either is infinite, or its final marking enables no transition. An alternative, called *justness* in [25], declares an execution path complete iff it enables no transition. Justness is a *stronger* completeness criterion than progress, in the sense that it deems fewer execution paths complete. The difference is illustrated by the Petri net of Fig. 2(a). There, the execution of an infinite sequence of b-transitions, not involving the a-transition,

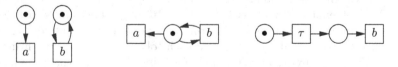

Fig. 2. (a) Progress vs. justness; (b) Justness vs. fairness; (c) $\{b\}$-progress vs. $\emptyset$-progress

is complete when assuming progress, but not when assuming justness. In the survey paper [25], 20 different completeness criteria are ordered by strength: progress, justness, and 18 kinds of fairness. Most of the latter are stronger than justness: in Fig. 2(b) the infinite sequence of b-transitions is just but unfair—i.e. incomplete according to these notions of fairness. Whereas justness was a new idea in the context of transition systems [25], it was used as an unnamed default assumption in much work on Petri nets [40]. That justness is better warranted in applications than other completeness criteria has been argued in [25,18,24,17].

The mentioned completeness criteria from [25] are all stronger than progress, in the sense that not all infinite execution paths are deemed complete; on the finite execution paths they judge the same. An orthogonal classification is obtained by varying the set $B \subseteq \mathcal{A}$ of actions that may be blocked by the environment. This fits the reactive viewpoint, in which a visible action can be regarded as a synchronisation between the modelled system and its environment. An environment that is not ready to synchronise with an action $b \in \mathcal{A}$ can be regarded as blocking b. Now B-progress is the criterion that deems a path complete iff it is either infinite, or its final marking M enables only transitions with labels from B. When the environment may block such transitions, it is possible for the system to not progress past M. In Fig. 2(c) the execution that performs only the τ-transition is complete when assuming $\{b\}$-progress, but not when assuming $\emptyset$-progress. Definition 6 defines B-justness accordingly, and [25] furthermore defines 18 different notions of B-fairness, for any choice of $B \subseteq \mathcal{A}$. The internal action $\tau \notin B$ can never be blocked by the environment. The default forms of progress and justness described above correspond with $\emptyset$-progress and $\emptyset$-justness. In [40] blocking and non-blocking transitions are called *cold* and *hot*, respectively.

Two subtly different computational interpretations of Petri nets appear in the literature [14]: in the *individual token interpretation* multiple tokens appearing in the same place are seen as different resources, whereas in the *collective token interpretation* only the number of tokens in a place is semantically relevant. The difference is illustrated in Fig. 3.

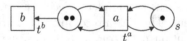

Fig. 3. Run a^∞ is just under the individual token interpretation of Petri nets

The idea underlying justness is that once a transition t is enabled, eventually either t will fire, or one of the resources necessary for firing t will be used by some other transition. The execution path π in the net of Fig. 3 that fires the action a infinitely often, but never the action b, is $\emptyset$-just by Def. 6. Namely, t^b is not enabled by π, as $(^\bullet t^b + \widehat{t^b}) \cap {}^\bullet t^a \neq \emptyset$. This fits with the individual token interpretation, as in this run it is possible to eventually consume each token that is initially present, and each token that stems from firing transition t^a. This way any resource available for firing t^b will eventually be used by some other transition.

When adhering to the collective token interpretation of nets, execution path π could be deemed $\emptyset$-unjust, since transition t^b can fire when there is at least one token in its preplace, and this state of affairs can be seen as a single resource that is never taken away. This might be formalised by adapting the definition of $\pi[t\rangle$, a path enabling a transition, namely by changing the condition $({}^\bullet t + \widehat{t}) \cap {}^\bullet t_{j+1} = \emptyset$ from Def. 6 into ${}^\bullet t + \widehat{t} + {}^\bullet t_{j+1} \subseteq M_j$. However, this formalisation doesn't capture that after dropping place s from the net of Fig. 3 there is still an infinite run in which b does not occur, namely when regularly firing two as simultaneously. This contradicts the conventional wisdom that firing multiple transitions at once can always be reduced to firing them in some order. To avoid that type of complication, I here stick to the individual token interpretation. Alternatively, one could restrict attention to 1-safe nets [40], on which there is no difference between the individual and collective token interpretations, or to the larger class of *structural conflict nets* [23,21], on which the conditions $({}^\bullet t + \widehat{t}) \cap {}^\bullet t_{j+1} = \emptyset$ and ${}^\bullet t + \widehat{t} + {}^\bullet t_{j+1} \subseteq M_j$ are equivalent [21, Section 23.1], so that Def. 6 applies equally well to the collective token interpretation.

5   Feasibility

A standard requirement on fairness assumptions, or completeness criteria in general, is *feasibility* [2], called *machine closure* in [33]. It says that any finite execution path can be extended into a complete one. The following theorem shows that B-justness is feasible indeed.

Theorem 1 For any $B \subseteq \mathcal{A}$, each finite execution path of a finitary Petri net can be extended into a B-just path.

Proof. Without loss of generality I restrict attention to nets without transitions t with ${}^\bullet t = \emptyset$. Namely, an arbitrary net can be enriched with marked private preplaces p_t for each such t, and arcs (p_t, t) and (t, p_t). In essence, this enrichment preserves the collection of execution path of the net, ordered by the relation "is an extension of", the validity of statements $\pi[t\rangle$, and the property of B-justness.

I present an algorithm extending any given path $M_0 t_1 M_1 t_2 \ldots t_{k-1} M_k$ into a B-just path $\pi = M_0 t_1 M_1 t_2 M_2 \ldots$ The extension only uses transitions t_i with $\ell(t_i) \notin B$. As data structure my algorithm employs an $\mathbb{N} \times \mathbb{N}$-matrix with columns named i, for $i \geq k$, where each column has a head and a body. The head of column k contains M_k and its body lists the places $s \in M_k$, leaving empty most slots if there are only finitely many such places. Since the given net is finitary, M_k has only countable many elements, so that they can be listed in the $\mathbb{N}$ slots of column k.

The head of each column $i > k$ with $i-1 < length(\pi)$ will contain the pair (t_i, M_i) and its body will list the places $s \in M_i$, again leaving empty most slots if there are only finitely many such places. Once more, finitariness ensures that there are enough slots in column i.

An entry in the body of the matrix is either (still) empty, filled in with a place, or crossed out. Let $f : \mathbb{N} \to \mathbb{N} \times \mathbb{N}$ be an enumeration of the entries in the body of this matrix.

At the beginning only column k is filled in; all subsequent columns of the matrix are empty. At each step $i > k$ I first cross out all entries s in the body of the matrix for which there is no transition t with $\ell(t) \notin B$, $M_{i-1}[t\rangle$ and $s \in {}^\bullet t$. In case all entries of the matrix are crossed out, the algorithm terminates, with output $M_0 t_1 M_1 t_2 \ldots M_{i-1}$. Otherwise I fill in column i as follows and cross out some more places occurring in body of the matrix.

I take n to be the smallest value such that entry $f(n) \in \mathbb{N} \times \mathbb{N}$ is already filled in, say with place r, but not yet crossed out. By the previous step of the algorithm, $M_{i-1}[t_i\rangle$ for some transition t_i with $\ell(t_i) \notin B$ and $r \in {}^\bullet t_i$. I now fill in (t_i, M_i) in the head of column i; here M_i is the unique marking such that $M_{i-1}[t_i\rangle M_i$. Subsequently I cross out all entries in the body of the matrix containing a place $r' \in {}^\bullet t_i$. This includes the entry $f(n)$. Finally, I fill in the body of column i with the places $s \in M_i$.

In case the algorithm doesn't terminate, the desired path π is the sequence $\pi = M_0 t_1 M_1 t_2 M_2 \ldots$ that is constructed in the limit. It remains to show that π is B-just.

Towards a contradiction, suppose $\pi[t\rangle$ for a transition t with $\ell(t) \notin B$. By Def. 6 there is an $m \in \mathbb{N} \wedge m \leq length(\pi)$ such that $M_m[t\rangle$ and $({}^\bullet t + \widehat{t}) \cap {}^\bullet t_{j+1} = \emptyset$ for all $m \leq j < length(\pi)$. Let h be the smallest such m with $m \geq k$. Then there is a place $r \in {}^\bullet t$ appearing in column h. Here I use that ${}^\bullet t \neq \emptyset$. This place was not yet crossed out when column h was constructed. Since $r \notin {}^\bullet t_{j+1}$ and $M_{j+1}[t\rangle$ for all $h \leq j < length(\pi)$, place r will never be crossed out. It follows that π must be infinite. The entry r in column h is enumerated as $f(n)$ for some $n \in \mathbb{N}$, and is eventually reached by the algorithm and crossed out. In this regard the matrix acts as a priority queue. This yields the required contradiction.   □

The above proof is a variant of [18, Thm. 1], which itself is a variant of [25, Thm. 6.1]. The side condition of finitariness is essential, as the below counterexample shows.

Example 2 Let $N = (S, T, F, R, M_0, \ell)$ be the net with $T = \{t_r \mid r \in \mathbb{R}\}$, $S = \{s_r \mid r \in \mathbb{R}\}$, $M_0(s_r) = 1$, $\ell(t_r) = \tau$, ${}^\bullet t_r = \{s_r\}$ and $\widehat{t}_r = t_r^\bullet = \emptyset$ for each $r \in \mathbb{R}$. It contains uncountably many action transitions, each with a marked private preplace. As each execution path π contains only countably many transitions, many transitions remain enabled by π.

6   The coarsest preorders preserving linear time properties

A *linear time property* is a predicate on system runs, and thus also on the execution paths of Petri nets. One writes $\pi \models \varphi$ if the execution path π satisfies the linear-time property φ. As the observable behaviour of an execution path π of a Petri net is deemed to be $trace(\pi)$, in this context one studies only linear time properties φ such that

$$trace(\pi) = trace(\pi') \quad \Leftrightarrow \quad (\pi \models \varphi \Leftrightarrow \pi' \models \varphi) . \tag{1}$$

For this reason, a linear time property can be defined or characterised as a subset of $\mathcal{A}^\infty$.

Linear time properties can be used to formalise correctness requirements on systems. They are deemed to hold for (or be satisfied by) a system iff they hold for all its complete runs. Following [20] I write $\mathcal{D} \models^{CC} \varphi$ iff property φ holds for all runs of the distributed system $\mathcal{D}$—and $N \models^{CC} \varphi$ iff it holds for all execution paths of the Petri net N—that are complete according to the completeness criterion CC. Prior to [20], $\models$ was a binary predicate predicate between systems—or system representations such as Petri nets—and properties; in this setting the default completeness criterion of Section 4 was used. When using a completeness criterion B-C, where C is one of the 20 completeness criteria classified in [25] and $B \subseteq \mathcal{A}$ is a modifier of C based on the set B of actions that may be blocked by the environment, $N \models^{B\text{-}C} \varphi$ is written $N \models_B^C \varphi$ [20]. In this paper I am mostly interested in the values Pr and J of C, standing for progress and justness, respectively. To be consistent with previous work on temporal logic, $N \models \varphi$ is a shorthand for $N \models_\emptyset^{Pr} \varphi$.

For each completeness criterion B-C, let $\sqsubseteq_B^C$ be the coarsest preorder that preserves linear time properties when assuming B-C. Moreover, $\sqsubseteq^C$ is the coarsest preorder that preserves linear time properties when assuming completeness criterion C in each environment, meaning regardless which set of actions B can be blocked.

Definition 7 Write $N \sqsubseteq_B^C N'$ iff $N \models_B^C \varphi \Rightarrow N' \models_B^C \varphi$ for all linear time properties φ. Write $N \sqsubseteq^C N'$ iff $N \sqsubseteq_B^C N'$ for all $B \subseteq \mathcal{A}$.

It is trivial to give a more explicit characterisation of these preorders. To preserve the analogy with the failure pairs of CSP [6], instead of sets $B \subseteq \mathcal{A}$ I will record their complements $\overline{B} := \mathcal{A} \backslash B$. As $\overline{\overline{B}} = B$, such sets carry the same information. Since B contains the actions that *may* be blocked by the environment, meaning that we consider environments that at any state may decide which actions from B to block, the set $\overline{B} \cup \{\tau\}$ contains actions that may not be blocked by the environment. This means that we only consider environments that in any state are willing to synchronise with any action in $\overline{B}$.

Definition 8 For completeness criterion C, B ranging over $\mathscr{P}(\mathcal{A})$, and Petri net N, let

$$\mathscr{F}^C(N) := \{(\sigma, \overline{B}) \mid N \text{ has a } B\text{-}C\text{-complete execution path } \pi \text{ with } \sigma = trace(\pi)\}$$
$$\mathscr{F}_B^C(N) := \{ \ \sigma \ \mid N \text{ has a } B\text{-}C\text{-complete execution path } \pi \text{ with } \sigma = trace(\pi)\}.$$

An element (σ, X) of $\mathscr{F}^C(N)$ could be called a *C-failure pair* of N, because it indicates that the system represented by N, when executing a path with visible content σ, may fail to execute additional actions from X, even when all these actions are offered by the environment, in the sense that the environment is perpetually willing to partake in those actions. Note that if $(\sigma, X) \in \mathscr{F}^C(N)$ and $Y \subseteq X$ then $(\sigma, Y) \in \mathscr{F}^C(N)$.

Proposition 1 $N \sqsubseteq_B^C N'$ iff $\mathscr{F}_B^C(N) \supseteq \mathscr{F}_B^C(N')$.
Likewise, $N \sqsubseteq^C N'$ iff $\mathscr{F}^C(N) \supseteq \mathscr{F}^C(N')$.

Proof. Suppose $N \sqsubseteq_B^C N'$ and $\sigma \notin \mathscr{F}_B^C(N)$. Let φ be the linear time property satisfying $\pi \models \varphi$ iff $trace(\pi) \neq \sigma$. Then $N \models_B^C \varphi$ and thus $N' \models_B^C \varphi$. Hence $\sigma \notin \mathscr{F}_B^C(N')$.

Suppose $N \not\sqsubseteq_B^C N'$. There there exists a linear time property φ such that $N \models_B^C \varphi$, yet $N' \not\models_B^C \varphi$. Let π' be a B-C-complete execution path of N' such that $\pi' \not\models \varphi$, and let $\sigma = trace(\pi')$. By (1) $\pi \not\models \varphi$ for any execution path π (of any net) such that $trace(\pi) = \sigma$. Hence $\sigma \in \mathscr{F}_B^C(N')$, yet $\sigma \notin \mathscr{F}_B^C(N)$. It follows that $\mathscr{F}_B^C(N) \not\supseteq \mathscr{F}_B^C(N')$.

The second statement follows as a corollary of the first, using that $\mathscr{F}^C(N) \supseteq \mathscr{F}^C(N')$ iff $\mathscr{F}_B^C(N) \supseteq \mathscr{F}_B^C(N')$ for all $B \subseteq \mathcal{A}$.   □

The preorders $\sqsubseteq_B^C$ can be classified as linear time semantics [12], as they are characterised through reverse trace inclusions. The preorders $\sqsubseteq^C$ on the other hand capture a minimal degree of branching time. This is because they should be ready for different choices of a system's environment at runtime.

Note that $\sqsubseteq^C$ is contained in $\sqsubseteq_B^C$ for each $B \subseteq \mathcal{A}$, in the sense that $N \sqsubseteq^C N'$ implies $N \sqsubseteq_B^C N'$. There is a priori no reason to assume inclusions between preorders $\sqsubseteq^C$ and $\sqsubseteq^D$ when D is a stronger completeness criterion than C.

To relate the preorders $\sqsubseteq_B^C$ and $\sqsubseteq^C$ with ones established in the literature, I consider the case $C = Pr$, i.e., taking progress as the completeness criterion C. The preorder $\sqsubseteq_\emptyset^{Pr}$ is characterised as reverse inclusion of complete traces, where completeness is w.r.t. the default completeness criterion of Section 4. These complete traces include

- the infinite traces of a system,
- its *divergence traces* (stemming from execution paths that end in infinitely many τ-transitions), and
- its *deadlock traces* (stemming from finite execution paths that end in a marking enabling no transitions).

Deadlock and divergence traces are not distinguished. This corresponds with what is called *divergence sensitive trace semantics* (T^λ) in [12]. The above concept of complete traces of a process p is the same as in [15], there denoted $CT(p)$.

The preorder $\sqsubseteq_\mathcal{A}^{Pr}$ is characterised as reverse inclusion of infinite and partial traces, i.e., the traces of *all* execution paths. This corresponds with what is called *infinitary trace semantics* (T^∞) in [12]. It is strictly coarser (making more identifications) than T^λ.

To analyse the preorder $\sqsubseteq^{Pr}$, one has $(\sigma, X) \in \mathscr{F}^{Pr}(N)$ if either

- σ is an infinite trace of N—the set X plays no rôle in that case,
- σ is a divergence trace of N, or

– σ is the trace of a finite path of N whose end-marking enables no transition t with $\ell(t) \in X$.

The resulting preorder does not occur in [12]—it can be placed strictly between *divergence sensitive failure semantics* $(F^\triangle)$ and *divergence sensitive trace semantics* (T^λ).

The entire family of preorders $\sqsubseteq_B^C$ and $\sqsubseteq^C$ proposed in this section was inspired by its most interesting family member, $\sqsubseteq^J$ (i.e., taking justness as the completeness criterion C), proposed earlier by Walter Vogler [43, Def. 5.6], also on Petri nets with read arcs. Vogler [43] uses the word *fair* for what I call *just*. I believe the choice of the word "just" is warranted to distinguish the concept from the many other kinds of fairness that appear in the literature, which are all of a very different nature. Accordingly, Vogler calls the semantics induced by $\sqsubseteq^J$ the *fair failure* semantics, whereas I call it the *just failures* semantics. My set $\mathscr{F}^J(N)$ is called $\mathscr{FF}(N)$ in [43], and Vogler addresses $\sqsupseteq^J$ simply as $\mathscr{FF}$-inclusion, thereby defining it via the right-hand side of Prop. 1.

7   Congruence properties

A preorder $\sqsubseteq$ is called a *precongruence* for an n-ary operator Op, if $N_i \sqsubseteq N_i'$ for $i = 1, \ldots, n$ implies that $Op(N_1, \ldots, N_n) \sqsubseteq Op(N_1', \ldots, N_n')$. In this case the operator Op is said to be *monotone* w.r.t. the preorder $\sqsubseteq$. Being a precongruence for important operators is known to be a valuable tool in compositional verification [41].

I write $\equiv$ for the kernel of $\sqsubseteq$, that is, $N \equiv N'$ iff $N \sqsubseteq N' \wedge N' \sqsubseteq N$. Here I also imply that $\equiv_B^C$ is the kernel of $\sqsubseteq_B^C$. If $\sqsubseteq$ is a precongruence for Op, then $\equiv$ is a *congruence* for Op, meaning that $N_i \equiv N_i'$ for $i = 1, \ldots, n$ implies that $Op(N_1, \ldots, N_n) \equiv Op(N_1', \ldots, N_n')$.

The preorder $\sqsubseteq_A^{Pr}$, characterised as reverse inclusion of infinite and partial traces, is well-known to be precongruence for the operators of CCSP. However, none of the other preorders $\sqsubseteq_B^{Pr}$, nor $\sqsubseteq^{Pr}$, is a precongruence for parallel composition.

Example 3 Let $N =$ (•) , $N' =$ (•) [with a τ loop] and $\mathcal{T} =$ (•)→w . The definition of $\|_\emptyset$ yields $\mathcal{T}\|_\emptyset N =$ (•) (•)→w and $\mathcal{T}\|_\emptyset N' =$ (•) [with τ loop] (•)→w . One has $N \equiv^{Pr} N'$, and thus also $N \equiv_B^{Pr} N'$, for each $B \subseteq \mathcal{A}$. Namely $\mathscr{F}^{Pr}(N) = \mathscr{F}^{Pr}(N') = \{(\varepsilon, X) \mid X \subseteq \mathcal{A}\}$. Here ε denotes the empty string. When fixing B such that $B \neq \mathcal{A}$ one may choose $w \notin B$. Now $\varepsilon \in \mathscr{F}_B^{Pr}(\mathcal{T}\|_\emptyset N')$, for this process has an infinite execution path that avoids the w-transition, which generates a divergence trace ε. Yet $\varepsilon \notin \mathscr{F}_B^{Pr}(\mathcal{T}\|_\emptyset N)$. Hence $\mathcal{T}\|_\emptyset N \not\sqsubseteq_B^{Pr} \mathcal{T}\|_\emptyset N'$, and thus also $\mathcal{T}\|_\emptyset N \not\sqsubseteq^{Pr} \mathcal{T}\|_\emptyset N'$. So neither $\sqsubseteq_B^{Pr}$ nor $\sqsubseteq^{Pr}$ are precongruences for $\|_\emptyset$.

A common solution to the problem of a preorder $\sqsubseteq$ not being a precongruence for certain operators is to instead consider its *congruence closure*, defined as the largest precongruence contained in $\sqsubseteq$.

In [30,15] the congruence closure of $\sqsubseteq^{Pr}$ is characterised as the so-called *NDFD* preorder $\sqsubseteq_{NDFD}$. Here $N \sqsubseteq_{NDFD} N'$ iff $N \sqsubseteq^{Pr} N'$ (characterised in the previous section) and moreover the divergence traces of N' are included in those of N. As remarked in [15], here it does not matter whether one requires congruence closure merely w.r.t. parallel composition and injective relabelling, or w.r.t. all operators of CSP (or CCSP, or anything in between).

Unlike $\sqsubseteq^{Pr}$, the preorder $\sqsubseteq^J$ is a precongruence for parallel composition. Although this has been proven already by Vogler [43], [22, in Appendix B] I provide a proof that bypasses the auxiliary notion of urgent transitions, and provides more details.

Proposition 2 ([43]) $\sqsubseteq^J$ is a precongruence for relabelling and abstraction.

Proof. This follows since $\mathscr{F}^J(f(N)) = \{(f(\sigma), X) \mid (\sigma, f^{-1}(X)) \in \mathscr{F}^J(N)\}$ and moreover $\mathscr{F}^J(\tau_I(N)) = \{(\tau_I(\sigma), X) \mid (\sigma, X \cup I) \in \mathscr{F}^J(N)\}$. Here $\tau_I(\sigma)$ is the result of pruning all I-actions from $\sigma \in \mathcal{A}^\infty$.   □

Trivially, $\sqsubseteq^J$ also is a precongruence for $\sum a_i P_i$ and $a \triangleright \sum a_i P_i$.

The preorder $\sqsubseteq_{\mathcal{A}}^J$ can be seen to coincide with $\sqsubseteq_{\mathcal{A}}^{Pr}$, characterised as reverse inclusion of infinite and partial traces, and thus is a precongruence for the operators of CCSP. Leaving open the case $|\mathcal{A}\backslash B| = 1$, the preorders $\sqsubseteq_B^J$ with $|\mathcal{A}\backslash B| \geq 2$ fail to be precongruences for parallel composition.

Example 4 Take $b, c \notin B$. Let N, N' and $\mathcal{T}$ be as shown in Fig. 4. Then

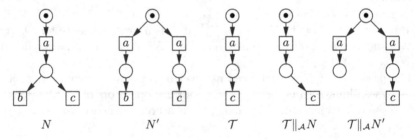

N N' $\mathcal{T}$ $\mathcal{T}\|_{\mathcal{A}}N$ $\mathcal{T}\|_{\mathcal{A}}N'$

Fig. 4. The preorders $\sqsubseteq_B^J$ with $|\mathcal{A}\backslash B| \geq 2$ fail to be precongruences for parallel comp.

$N \equiv_B^J N'$, as $\mathscr{F}_B^J(N) = \mathscr{F}_B^J(N') = \{\varepsilon, ab, ac\}$. (Whether ε is included depends on whether $a \in B$.) Yet $\mathcal{T}\|_{\mathcal{A}}N \not\equiv_B^J \mathcal{T}\|_{\mathcal{A}}N'$, as $a \in \mathscr{F}_B^J(\mathcal{T}\|_{\mathcal{A}}N')$, yet $a \notin \mathscr{F}_B^J(\mathcal{T}\|_{\mathcal{A}}N)$.

Moreover, as illustrated below, the preorders $\sqsubseteq_B^J$ with $B \neq \emptyset$ and $|\mathcal{A}\backslash B| \geq 1$ fail to be precongruences for abstraction. In the next section I will show that, for $\mathcal{A}$ infinite and $B \neq \mathcal{A}$, the congruence closure of $\sqsubseteq_B^J$ for parallel composition, abstraction and relabelling is $\sqsubseteq^J$.

Example 5 Take $b \in B$ and $c \notin B$. Let N and N' be as shown in Fig. 5. Then $N \equiv_B^J N'$, as $\mathscr{F}_B^J(N) = \mathscr{F}_B^J(N') = \{\varepsilon, bc\}$. Yet $\tau_{\{b\}}(N) \not\equiv_B^J \tau_{\{b\}}(N')$, since $\varepsilon \in \mathscr{F}_B^J(\tau_{\{b\}}(N'))$, yet $\varepsilon \notin \mathscr{F}_B^J(\tau_{\{b\}}(N))$.

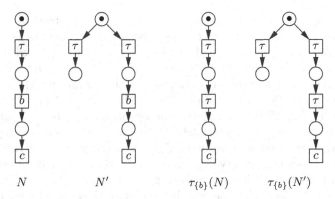

$$N \qquad N' \qquad \tau_{\{b\}}(N) \qquad \tau_{\{b\}}(N')$$

Fig. 5. The preorders $\sqsubseteq_B^J$ with $\emptyset \neq B \neq \mathcal{A}$ fail to be precongruences for abstraction

8   Must Testing

A *test* is a Petri net, but featuring a special action $w \notin \mathcal{A}_\tau$, not used elsewhere. This action is used to mark *success markings*: those in which w is enabled. If $\mathcal{T}$ is a test and N a net then $\tau_{\mathcal{A}}(\mathcal{T}\|_{\mathcal{A}}N)$ is also a test. An execution path of $\tau_{\mathcal{A}}(\mathcal{T}\|_{\mathcal{A}}N)$ is *successful* iff it contains a success marking.

Definition 9 A Petri net N *may pass* a test $\mathcal{T}$, notation N **may** $\mathcal{T}$, if $\tau_{\mathcal{A}}(\mathcal{T}\|_{\mathcal{A}}N)$ has a successful execution path. It *must pass* $\mathcal{T}$, notation N **must** $\mathcal{T}$, if each complete execution path of $\tau_{\mathcal{A}}(\mathcal{T}\|_{\mathcal{A}}N)$ is successful. It *should pass* $\mathcal{T}$, notation N **should** $\mathcal{T}$, if each finite execution path of $\tau_{\mathcal{A}}(\mathcal{T}\|_{\mathcal{A}}N)$ can be extended into a successful execution path.

Write $N \sqsubseteq_{\text{must}} N'$ if N **must** $\mathcal{T}$ implies N' **must** $\mathcal{T}$ for each test $\mathcal{T}$. The preorders $\sqsubseteq_{\text{may}}$ and $\sqsubseteq_{\text{should}}$ are defined similarly.

The may- and must-testing preorders stem from De Nicola & Hennessy [9], whereas should-testing was added independently in [5] and [36].

In the original work on testing [9] the CCS parallel composition $\mathcal{T}|N$ was used instead of the concealed CCSP parallel composition $\tau_{\mathcal{A}}(\mathcal{T}\|_{\mathcal{A}}N)$; moreover, only those execution paths consisting solely of internal actions mattered for the definitions of passing a test. The present approach is equivalent. First of all, restricting attention to execution paths of $\mathcal{T}|N$ consisting solely of internal actions is equivalent to putting $\mathcal{T}|N$ is the scope of a CCS restriction operator $\backslash \mathcal{A}$ [34], for that operator drops all transitions of its argument that are not labelled τ or w. Secondly, CCS features a complementary action $\bar{a}$ for each $a \in \mathcal{A}$, and one has $\bar{\bar{a}} = a$. For $\mathcal{T}$ a test, let $\overline{\mathcal{T}}$ denote the complementary test in which each action $a \in \mathcal{A}$ is replaced by $\bar{a}$; again $\overline{\overline{\mathcal{T}}} = \mathcal{T}$. It follows directly from the definitions of the operators involved that $\tau_{\mathcal{A}}(\mathcal{T}\|_{\mathcal{A}}N)$ is identical[3] to $(\overline{\mathcal{T}}|N)\backslash \mathcal{A}$. This proves the equivalence of the two approaches.

---

[3] The standard definition of $|$ on Petri nets [28] is given only up to isomorphism. By choosing the names of places and transitions similar to those in the defintion of $\|_{\mathcal{A}}$ from [22, Appendix A] one can obtain $\tau_{\mathcal{A}}(\mathcal{T}\|_{\mathcal{A}}N) = (\overline{\mathcal{T}}|N)\backslash \mathcal{A}$.

Unlike may- and should-testing, the concept of must-testing is naturally parametrised with a completeness criterion, deciding what counts as a complete execution. To make this choice explicit I use the notation $\sqsubseteq_{\text{must}}^C$, where C could be any of the completeness criteria surveyed in [25]. Since processes $\tau_{\mathcal{A}}(\mathcal{T}\|_{\mathcal{A}}N)$ (or $(\mathcal{T}|N)\backslash\mathcal{A}$) do not feature any actions other than τ and w, where w is used merely to point to the success states, the modifier $B \subseteq \mathcal{A}$ of a completeness criteria B-C has no effect, i.e., any two choices of this modifier are equivalent.

In the original work of [9] the default completeness criterion progress from Section 4 was employed. Interestingly, $\sqsubseteq_{\text{must}}^{Pr}$ is a congruence for the operators of CCSP that does not preserve all linear time properties. It is strictly coarser than $\sqsubseteq_{NDFD}$. In fact, it is the coarsest precongruence for the CCSP parallel composition and injective relabelling that preserves those linear time properties that express that a system will eventually reach a state in which something [good] has happened [15]. (In [15], following [32], but deviating from the standard terminology of [1], such properties are called *liveness properties*.)

In this paper I investigate the must-testing preorder when taking justness as the underlying completeness criterion, $\sqsubseteq_{\text{must}}^J$. Thm. 2 below shows that it can be characterised as the just failures preorder $\sqsubseteq^J$ of Section 6.

First note that Def. 9 can be simplified. When dealing with justness as completeness criterion, the word "complete" in Def. 9 is instantiated by "just" or "B-just", for some $B \subseteq \mathcal{A}$ (not including w). As the result is independent of B, one may take $B := \emptyset$. Since the labelling of a net has no bearing on its execution paths, or on whether such a path is $\emptyset$-just, or successful, one may now drop the operator τ_A from Def. 9 without affecting the resulting notion of must testing.

Theorem 2 $N \sqsubseteq_{\text{must}}^J N'$ iff $N \sqsubseteq^J N'$.

Proof. The "if" direction is established in [22, Appendix C].

For "only if", suppose $N \sqsubseteq_{\text{must}}^J N'$. Using Prop. 1, it suffices to show that $\mathscr{F}^J(N) \supseteq \mathscr{F}^J(N')$. Let $(\sigma, X) \in \mathscr{F}^J(N')$, where $\sigma = a_1 a_2 \ldots \in \mathcal{A}^\infty$ is a finite or infinite sequence of actions. Let $\mathcal{T}$ be the test displayed in Fig. 6. The drawing is for the case that $\sigma = a_1 a_2 \ldots a_n$ finite; in the infinite case, there is no need to display a_n separately. Now K **must** $\mathcal{T}$, for any net K, when using justness as completeness criterion, iff each $\emptyset$-just execution path of $\mathcal{T}\|_{\mathcal{A}}K$ is successful, which is the case iff $(\sigma, X) \notin \mathscr{F}^J(K)$. (In other words, $\mathcal{T}\|_{\mathcal{A}}K$ has an unsuccessful $\emptyset$-just execution path iff $(\sigma, X) \in \mathscr{F}^J(K)$. For the meaning of $(\sigma, X) \in \mathscr{F}^J(K)$ is that K has an execution path π with $trace(\pi) = \sigma$ such that $\ell_K(t) \in X \Rightarrow \neg\pi[t\rangle$.) Hence N' **must not** $\mathcal{T}$ and thus N **must not** $\mathcal{T}$, and thus $(\sigma, X) \in \mathscr{F}^J(N)$. □

Proposition 3 Let $\mathcal{A}$ be infinite and $B \neq \mathcal{A}$. Then $\sqsubseteq^J$ is the congruence closure of $\sqsubseteq_B^J$ for parallel composition, abstraction and injective relabelling.

Proof. Pick an action $w \in \mathcal{A}\backslash B$. Assume $N \not\sqsubseteq^J N'$. By applying an injective relabelling, one can assure that w does not occur in N or N'. Let $(\sigma, X) \in \mathscr{F}^J(N')$, yet $(\sigma, X) \notin \mathscr{F}^J(N)$, with $w \notin X$. Let T be the net of Fig. 6. Then, writing $A := \mathcal{A}\backslash\{w\}$, $(\sigma, \mathcal{A}) \in \mathscr{F}^J(\mathcal{T}\|_A N')$, yet $(\sigma, \mathcal{A}) \notin \mathscr{F}^J(\mathcal{T}\|_A N)$. Moreover, $(\rho, \mathcal{A}) \notin \mathscr{F}^J(\mathcal{T}\|_A N')$ and $(\rho, \mathcal{A}) \notin \mathscr{F}^J(\mathcal{T}\|_A N)$ for any $\rho \neq \sigma$ not containing the action

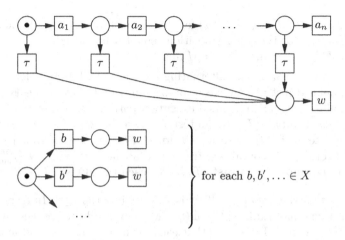

Fig. 6. Universal test for just must testing

w. Hence, applying the proof of Prop. 2, using that $A \cup \overline{B} = \mathcal{A}$, one has $(\varepsilon, \overline{B}) \in \mathcal{F}^J(\tau_A(\mathcal{T} \| _A N'))$, yet $(\varepsilon, \overline{B}) \notin \mathcal{F}^J(\tau_A(\mathcal{T} \| _A N))$. Thus $\varepsilon \in \mathcal{F}^J_B(\tau_A(\mathcal{T} \| _A N'))$, yet $\varepsilon \notin \mathcal{F}^J_B(\tau_A(\mathcal{T} \| _A N))$. It follows that $\tau_A(\mathcal{T} \| _A N) \not\sqsubseteq^J_B \tau_A(\mathcal{T} \| _A N')$.   □

9   Timed must-testing

A timed form of must-testing was proposed by Vogler in [43]. Justness says that each transition that gets enabled must fire eventually, unless one of its necessary resources will be taken away. In Vogler's framework, each transition t must fire within 1 unit of time after it becomes enabled, even though it can fire faster. The implicit timer is reset each time t becomes disabled and enabled again, by another transition taken a token and returning it to one of the replaces of t. Since there is no lower bound on the time that may elapse before a transition fires, this view encompasses the same asynchronous behaviour of nets as under the assumption of justness.

Vogler's work only pertains to *safe* nets: those with the property that no reachable marking allocates multiple tokens to the same place. Here a marking is *reachable* if it occurs in some execution path. Transitions t with $^\bullet t = \emptyset$ are excluded. Although he only considered finite nets, here I apply his work unchanged to *finitely branching* nets: those in which only finitely many transitions are enabled in each reachable marking.

Definition 10 ([43]) A *continuous(ly timed) instantaneous description (CID)* of a net N is a pair (M, ξ) consisting of a marking M of N and a function ξ mapping the transitions enabled under M to $[0, 1]$; ξ describes the residual activation time of an enabled transition.

The initial CID is $\text{CID}_0 = (M_0; \xi_0)$ with $\xi_0(t) = 1$ for all t with $M_0[t\rangle$.

One writes $(M, \xi)[\eta\rangle(M', \xi')$ if one of the following cases applies:

(1) $\eta = t \in T$, $M[t\rangle M'$, $\xi'(t) := \xi(t)$ for those transitions t enabled under $M - {}^{\bullet}t$ and $\xi'(t) := 1$ for the other transitions enabled under M'.

(2) $\eta = r \in \mathbb{R}^+$, $r \le \min(\xi)$, $M' = M$ and $\xi' = \xi - r$.

A *timed execution path* π is an alternating sequence of CIDs and elements $t \in T$ or $r \in \mathbb{R}^+$, defined just like an execution path in Def. 6. Let $\zeta(\pi) \in \mathbb{R} \cup \{\infty\}$ be the sum of all time steps in a timed execution path π, the *duration* of π.

A *timed test* is a pair $(\mathcal{T}, D)$ of a test $\mathcal{T}$ and a *duration* $D \in \mathbb{R}_0^+$. A net *must pass* a timed test $(\mathcal{T}, D)$, notation N **must** $(\mathcal{T}, D)$, if each timed execution path π with $\zeta(\pi) > D$ contains a transition labelled w. Write $N \sqsubseteq_{\mathrm{must}}^{\mathrm{timed}} N'$ if N **must** $(\mathcal{T}, D)$ implies N' **must** $(\mathcal{T}, D)$ for each timed test $(\mathcal{T}, D)$.

Vogler shows that the preorder $\sqsubseteq_{\mathrm{must}}^{\mathrm{timed}}$ is strictly finer than $\sqsubseteq^J$. In fact, although $\tau.a.\mathbf{0} \equiv^J a.\mathbf{0}$, one has $\tau.a.\mathbf{0} \not\equiv_{\mathrm{must}}^{\mathrm{timed}} a.\mathbf{0}$, since only the latter process must pass the timed test $(a.w, 2)$. Here I use that each of the actions τ, a and w may take up to 1 unit of time to occur. A statement $N \sqsubseteq_{\mathrm{must}}^{\mathrm{timed}} N'$ says that N' is *faster* than N, in the sense that composed with a test it is guaranteed to reach success states in less time than N.

Here I show that when abstracting from the quantitative dimension of timed must-testing, it exactly characterises $\sqsubseteq^J$.

Definition 11 A net *must eventually pass* a test $\mathcal{T}$ if there exists a $D \in \mathbb{R}_0^+$ such that N **must** $(\mathcal{T}, D)$. Write $N \sqsubseteq_{\mathrm{must}}^{\mathrm{ev.}} N'$ if when N must eventually pass a test $\mathcal{T}$, then so does N'.

Theorem 3 Let N, N' be finitely branching safe nets. Then $N \sqsubseteq_{\mathrm{must}}^{\mathrm{ev.}} N'$ iff $N \sqsubseteq^J N'$.

A proof can be found in [22, Appendix D].

10   Conclusion

The just failures preorder $\sqsubseteq^J$ was introduced by Walter Vogler [43] in 2002. Since then it has not received much attention in the literature, and has not been used as the underlying semantic principle justifying actual verifications. In my view this can be seen as a fault of the subsequent literature, as $\sqsubseteq^J$ captures exactly what is needed—no more and no less—for the verification of safety and liveness properties of realistic systems.

I substantiate this claim by pointing out that $\sqsubseteq^J$ is the coarsest preorder preserving safety and liveness properties when assuming justness, that is a congruence for basic process algebra operators, such as the partially synchronous parallel composition, abstraction from internal actions, and renaming. As argued in [25,18,24,17], justness is better motivated and more suitable for applications than competing completeness criteria, such as progress or the many notions of fairness surveyed in [24].

Moreover, I adapt the well-known must-testing preorder of De Nicola & Hennessy [9], by using justness as the underlying completeness criterion, instead of the traditional choice of progress. By showing that the resulting must-testing preorder $\sqsubseteq^J_{must}$ coincides with $\sqsubseteq^J$ I strengthen the case that this is a natural and fundamental preorder.

This conclusion is further strengthened by my result that it also coincides with a qualitative version $\sqsubseteq^{ev.}_{must}$ of the timed must-testing preorder $\sqsubseteq^{timed}_{must}$ of Vogler [43]. (Although $\sqsubseteq^{timed}_{must}$ and $\sqsubseteq^J$ stem from the same paper [43], this connection was not made there.)

All this was shown in the setting of Petri nets extended with read arcs, and therefore also applies to the settings of standard process algebras such as CCS, CSP or ACP. Since I cover read arcs, it also applies to process algebras enriched with signalling, an operator that extends the expressiveness of standard process algebras and is needed to accurately model mutual exclusion. I leave it for future work to explore these matters for probabilistic models of concurrency, or other useful extensions.

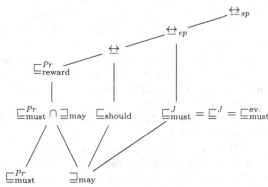

Fig. 7. A spectrum of testing preorders and bisimilarities preserving liveness properties

Fig. 7 situates $\sqsubseteq^J_{must}$ w.r.t. the some other semantic preorders from the literature. The lines indicate inclusions. Here $\sqsubseteq^{Pr}_{must}$, $\sqsubseteq_{may}$ and $\sqsubseteq_{should}$ are the classical must-, may- and should-testing preorders from [9] and [5,36]—see Def. 9—and $\sqsubseteq^{Pr}_{reward}$ is the reward-testing preorder introduced by me in [19]. The failures-divergences preorder of CSP [6,42], defined in a similar way as $\sqsubseteq^J_{must}$, coincides with $\sqsubseteq^{Pr}_{must}$ [9,19]. $\leftrightarrow$ denotes the classical notion of strong bisimilarity [34], and $\leftrightarrow_{ep}$, $\leftrightarrow_{sp}$ are essentially the only other preorders (in fact equivalences) that preserve linear time properties when assuming justness: the *enabling preserving bisimilarity* of [26] and the *structure preserving bisimilarity* of [16].

The inclusions follow directly from the definitions—see refs. —and counterexamples against further inclusions appear below.

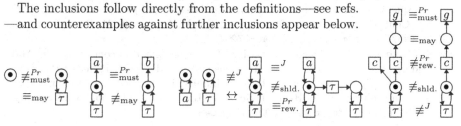

References

1. Alpern, B., Schneider, F.B.: Defining liveness. Infromation Processing Letters **21**(4), 181–185 (1985). https://doi.org/10.1016/0020-0190(85)90056-0
2. Apt, K.R., Francez, N., Katz, S.: Appraising fairness in languages for distributed programming. Distributed Computing **2**(4), 226–241 (1988). https://doi.org/10.1007/BF01872848
3. Bergstra, J.A.: ACP with signals. In: Grabowski, J., Lescanne, P., Wechler, W. (eds.) Proc. International Workshop on Algebraic and Logic Programming. LNCS, vol. 343, pp. 11–20. Springer (1988). https://doi.org/10.1007/3-540-50667-5_53
4. Bergstra, J.A., Klop, J.W.: Algebra of communicating processes with abstraction. Theor. Comput. Sci. **37**(1), 77–121 (1985). https://doi.org/10.1016/0304-3975(85)90088-X
5. Brinksma, E., Rensink, A., Vogler, W.: Fair testing. In: Lee, I., Smolka, S.A. (eds.) Proc. 6th International Conference on Concurrency Theory, CONCUR'95. LNCS, vol. 962, pp. 313–327. Springer (1995). https://doi.org/10.1007/3-540-60218-6_23
6. Brookes, S.D., Hoare, C.A.R., Roscoe, A.W.: A theory of communicating sequential processes. J. ACM **31**(3), 560–599 (1984). https://doi.org/10.1145/828.833
7. Busi, N., Pinna, G.M.: Non sequential semantics for contextual P/T nets. In: Billington, J., Reisig, W. (eds.) Proc. 17th Int. Conf. on Application and Theory of Petri Nets. LNCS, vol. 1091, pp. 113–132. Springer (1996). https://doi.org/10.1007/3-540-61363-3_7
8. Corradini, F., Di Berardini, M.R., Vogler, W.: Time and fairness in a process algebra with non-blocking reading. In: Nielsen, M., Kucera, A., Miltersen, P.B., Palamidessi, C., Tuma, P., Valencia, F.D. (eds.) Theory and Practice of Computer Science, SOFSEM'09. LNCS, vol. 5404, pp. 193–204. Springer (2009). https://doi.org/10.1007/978-3-540-95891-8_20
9. De Nicola, R., Hennessy, M.: Testing equivalences for processes. Theor. Comput. Sci. **34**, 83–133 (1984). https://doi.org/10.1016/0304-3975(84)90113-0
10. Degano, P., De Nicola, R., Montanari, U.: CCS is an (augmented) contact free C/E system. In: Venturini Zilli, M. (ed.) Advanced School on Mathematical Models for the Semantics of Parallelism, 1986. LNCS, vol. 280, pp. 144–165. Springer (1987). https://doi.org/10.1007/3-540-18419-8_13
11. Dyseryn, V., van Glabbeek, R.J., Höfner, P.: Analysing mutual exclusion using process algebra with signals. In: Peters, K., Tini, S. (eds.) Proceedings Combined 24th International Workshop on Expressiveness in Concurrency and 14th Workshop on Structural Operational Semantics. EPTCS, vol. 255, pp. 18–34 (2017). https://doi.org/10.4204/EPTCS.255.2
12. van Glabbeek, R.J.: The linear time – branching time spectrum II; the semantics of sequential systems with silent moves. In: Best, E. (ed.) Proc. CONCUR'93, 4th Int. Conf. on Concurrency Theory. LNCS, vol. 715, pp. 66–81. Springer (1993). https://doi.org/10.1007/3-540-57208-2_6
13. van Glabbeek, R.J.: A characterisation of weak bisimulation congruence. In: Middeldorp, A., van Oostrom, V., van Raamsdonk, F., de Vrijer, R. (eds.) Processes, Terms and Cycles: Steps on the Road to Infinity: Essays Dedicated to Jan Willem Klop on the Occasion of His 60th Birthday. LNCS, vol. 3838, pp. 26–39. Springer (2005). https://doi.org/10.1007/11601548_4

14. van Glabbeek, R.J.: The individual and collective token interpretations of Petri nets. In: Abadi, M., de Alfaro, L. (eds.) Proc. CONCUR'05, 16th Int. Conf. on Concurrency Theory. LNCS, vol. 3653, pp. 323–337. Springer (2005). https://doi.org/10.1007/11539452_26

15. van Glabbeek, R.J.: The coarsest precongruences respecting safety and liveness properties. In: Calude, C., Sassone, V. (eds.) Proc. 6th IFIP TC 1/WG 2.2 Int. Conf. on Theoretical Computer Science, TCS'10; held as part of the *World Computer Congress*. IFIP, vol. 323, pp. 32–52. Springer (2010). https://doi.org/10.1007/978-3-642-15240-5_3, http://arxiv.org/abs/1007.5491

16. van Glabbeek, R.J.: Structure preserving bisimilarity, supporting an operational petri net semantics of CCSP. In: Meyer, R., Platzer, A., Wehrheim, H. (eds.) Proceedings Correct System Design - Symposium in Honor of Ernst-Rüdiger Olderog on the Occasion of His 60th Birthday. LNCS, vol. 9360, pp. 99–130. Springer (2015). https://doi.org/10.1007/978-3-319-23506-6_9, http://arxiv.org/abs/1509.05842

17. van Glabbeek, R.J.: Ensuring liveness properties of distributed systems: Open problems. Journal of Logical and Algebraic Methods in Programming **109**, 100480 (2019). https://doi.org/10.1016/j.jlamp.2019.100480

18. van Glabbeek, R.J.: Justness: A completeness criterion for capturing liveness properties. In: Bojańczyk, M., Simpson, A. (eds.) Proc. 22st Int. Conf. on Foundations of Software Science and Computation Structures, FoSSaCS'19; held as part of ETAPS'19. LNCS, vol. 11425, pp. 505–522. Springer (2019). https://doi.org/10.1007/978-3-030-17127-8_29, https://arxiv.org/abs/1909.00286

19. van Glabbeek, R.J.: Reward testing equivalences for processes. In: Boreale, M., Corradini, F., Loreti, M., Pugliese, R. (eds.) Models, Languages, and Tools for Concurrent and Distributed Programming, Essays Dedicated to Rocco De Nicola on the occasion of his 65th Birthday, LNCS, vol. 11665, pp. 45–70. Springer (2019). https://doi.org/10.1007/978-3-030-21485-2_5, https://arxiv.org/abs/1907.13348

20. van Glabbeek, R.J.: Reactive temporal logic. In: Dardha, O., Rot, J. (eds.) Proc. Combined 27th Int. Workshop on Expressiveness in Concurrency and 17th Workshop on Structural Operational Semantics. EPTCS, vol. 322, pp. 51–68 (2020). https://doi.org/10.4204/EPTCS.322.6

21. van Glabbeek, R.J.: Modelling mutual exclusion in a process algebra with time-outs (2021), https://arxiv.org/abs/2106.12785

22. van Glabbeek, R.J.: Just Testing (2022), version of this paper extended with four appendices, https://arxiv.org/abs/2212.08829

23. van Glabbeek, R.J., Goltz, U., Schicke, J.W.: Abstract processes of place/transition systems. Information Processing Letters **111**(13), 626–633 (2011). https://doi.org/10.1016/j.ipl.2011.03.013, https://arxiv.org/abs/1103.5916

24. van Glabbeek, R.J., Höfner, P.: CCS: it's not fair! – fair schedulers cannot be implemented in CCS-like languages even under progress and certain fairness assumptions. Acta Informatica **52**(2-3), 175–205 (2015). https://doi.org/10.1007/s00236-015-0221-6, https://arxiv.org/abs/1505.05964

25. van Glabbeek, R.J., Höfner, P.: Progress, justness and fairness. ACM Computing Surveys **52**(4), 69 (August 2019). https://doi.org/10.1145/3329125, https://arxiv.org/abs/1810.07414

26. van Glabbeek, R.J., Höfner, P., Wang, W.: Enabling preserving bisimulation equivalence. In: Haddad, S., Varacca, D. (eds.) Proc. 32nd Int. Conference on Concurrency Theory, CONCUR'21. Leibniz International Proceedings

in Informatics (LIPIcs), vol. 203. Schloss Dagstuhl–Leibniz-Zentrum für Informatik (2021). https://doi.org/10.4230/LIPIcs.CONCUR.2021.33, https://arxiv.org/abs/2108.00142

27. van Glabbeek, R.J., Vaandrager, F.W.: Petri net models for algebraic theories of concurrency. In: Bakker, J.W.d., Nijman, A.J., Treleaven, P.C. (eds.) Proc. PARLE, Parallel Architectures and Languages Europe, Vol. II. LNCS, vol. 259, pp. 224–242. Springer (1987). https://doi.org/10.1007/3-540-17945-3_13

28. Goltz, U.: CCS and Petri nets. In: Guessarian, I. (ed.) Proc. Semantics of Systems of Concurrent Processes, LITP Spring School on Theoretical Computer Science. LNCS, vol. 469, pp. 334–357. Springer (1990). https://doi.org/10.1007/3-540-53479-2_14

29. Goltz, U., Mycroft, A.: On the relationship of CCS and Petri nets. In: Paredaens, J. (ed.) Proc. 11th Colloquium on Automata, Languages and Programming, ICALP84. LNCS, vol. 172, pp. 196–208. Springer (1984). https://doi.org/10.1007/3-540-13345-3_18

30. Kaivola, R., Valmari, A.: The weakest compositional semantic equivalence preserving nexttime-less linear temporal logic. In: Cleaveland, R. (ed.) Proc. CONCUR'92. LNCS, vol. 630, pp. 207–221. Springer (1992). https://doi.org/10.1007/BFb0084793

31. Kindler, E., Walter, R.: Mutex needs fairness. Inf. Process. Lett. **62**(1), 31–39 (1997). https://doi.org/10.1016/S0020-0190(97)00033-1

32. Lamport, L.: Proving the correctness of multiprocess programs. IEEE Transactions on Software Engineering **3**(2), 125–143 (1977). https://doi.org/10.1109/TSE.1977.229904

33. Lamport, L.: Fairness and hyperfairness. Distributed Computing **13**(4), 239–245 (2000). https://doi.org/10.1007/PL00008921

34. Milner, R.: Communication and Concurrency. Prentice-Hall (1989), alternatively see *A Calculus of Communicating Systems*, LNCS 92, Springer, 1980, https://doi.org/10.1007/3-540-10235-3

35. Montanari, U., Rossi, F.: Contextual nets. Acta Informatica **32**(6), 545–596 (1995). https://doi.org/10.1007/BF01178907

36. Natarajan, V., Cleaveland, R.: Divergence and fair testing. In: Fülöp, Z., Gécseg, F. (eds.) Proc. 22nd Int. Colloquium on Automata, Languages and Programming, ICALP'95. LNCS, vol. 944, pp. 648–659. Springer (1995). https://doi.org/10.1007/3-540-60084-1_112

37. Olderog, E.R.: Operational Petri net semantics for CCSP. In: Rozenberg, G. (ed.) Advances in Petri Nets 1987. LNCS, vol. 266, pp. 196–223. Springer (1987). https://doi.org/10.1007/3-540-18086-9_27

38. Olderog, E.R.: Nets, Terms and Formulas: Three Views of Concurrent Processes and Their Relationship. Cambridge Tracts in Theoretical Computer Science 23, Cambridge University Press (1991)

39. Olderog, E.R., Hoare, C.A.R.: Specification-oriented semantics for communicating processes. Acta Inf. **23**, 9–66 (1986). https://doi.org/10.1007/BF00268075

40. Reisig, W.: Understanding Petri Nets — Modeling Techniques, Analysis Methods, Case Studies. Springer (2013). https://doi.org/10.1007/978-3-642-33278-4

41. Roever, W.P.d., de Boer, F.S., Hannemann, U., Hooman, J., Lakhnech, Y., Poel, M., Zwiers, J.: Concurrency Verification: Introduction to Compositional and Non-compositional Methods, Cambridge Tracts in TCS, vol. 54. Cambridge University Press (2001)

42. Roscoe, A.W.: The Theory and Practice of Concurrency. Prentice-Hall (1997), http://www.comlab.ox.ac.uk/bill.roscoe/publications/68b.pdf

43. Vogler, W.: Efficiency of asynchronous systems, read arcs, and the MUTEX-problem. Theor. Comput. Sci. **275**(1-2), 589–631 (2002). https://doi.org/10.1016/S0304-3975(01)00300-0

44. Winskel, G.: A new definition of morphism on Petri nets. In: Fontet, M., Mehlhorn, K. (eds.) Proc. Symposium on Theoretical Aspects of Computer Science, STACS'84. LNCS, vol. 166, pp. 140–150. Springer (1984). https://doi.org/10.1007/3-540-12920-0_13

Model and Program Repair via Group Actions

Paul C. Attie[1] and William L. Cocke[1(✉)]

School of Computer and Cyber Sciences, Augusta University, Augusta, GA, USA
pattie@augusta.edu, wcocke@augusta.edu

Abstract. Given a textual representation of a finite-state concurrent program P, one can construct the corresponding Kripke structure $\mathcal{M}$. However, the size of $\mathcal{M}$ can be exponentially larger than the textual size of P. This state explosion can make model checking properties of P via $\mathcal{M}$ expensive or even infeasible. The action of a symmetry group G on $\mathcal{M}$ can be used to produce a smaller Kripke structure $\overline{\mathcal{M}}$. Various authors have exploited the direct correspondence between $\mathcal{M}$ and $\overline{\mathcal{M}}$ to perform model checking. When the structure $\mathcal{M}$ does not satisfy a formula, one can look for a substructure that will satisfy the formula. We call this *substructure-repair*: identifying a substructure $\mathcal{N}$ of $\mathcal{M}$ that satisfies a given temporal logic formula.

In this paper we extend previous work by showing that repairs of $\overline{\mathcal{M}}$ lift to repairs of $\mathcal{M}$. In other words, we can repair a computer program P, which exhibits a high degree of symmetry, by repairing the smaller Kripke structure $\overline{\mathcal{M}}$ and then symmetrizing the corresponding program. To do this we arrange the substructures of $\mathcal{M}$ and $\overline{\mathcal{M}}$ into substructure lattices that are ordered by substructure inclusion. We show that the substructures of $\mathcal{M}$ preserved by G form a (sub)lattice that maps to the substructure lattice of $\overline{\mathcal{M}}$. When restricted to the lattice of substructures of $\mathcal{M}$ that are "maximal" with the action of G on $\mathcal{M}$, the above map is a lattice isomorphism.

These results enable us to repair $\overline{\mathcal{M}}$ and then to lift the repair to $\mathcal{M}$. In cases where a program has a high degree of symmetry, such as in many concurrent programs, we can repair the program by repairing the small Kripke structure $\overline{\mathcal{M}}$.

Keywords: Model checking · symmetry reduction · model repair

1 Introduction

To model check a program P, one first constructs a Kripke structure $\mathcal{M}$. In general, the Kripke structure $\mathcal{M}$ is generated by all potential executions of P. The model checking problem for a program P w.r.t. a temporal logic formula φ is to verify that the Kripke structure $\mathcal{M}$ generated by the execution of P satisfies φ [8]. A major obstacle to model checking a concurrent program via its Kripke structure is *state explosion*: in general, the size of $\mathcal{M}$ is exponential in the number of processes n. As studied by Emerson and Sistla [18] and extended by others [10,14,21], the use of *symmetry reduction* to ameliorate state-explosion

© The Author(s) 2023
O. Kupferman and P. Sobocinski (Eds.): FoSSaCS 2023, LNCS 13992, pp. 520–540, 2023.
https://doi.org/10.1007/978-3-031-30829-1_25

can yield a significant reduction in the complexity of model checking $\mathcal{M} \models \varphi$ when both $\mathcal{M}$ and φ have a high degree of symmetry in the process index set $\{1, \dots, n\}$.

For a Kripke structure $\mathcal{M}$, we capture the symmetry of $\mathcal{M}$ using the group G of automorphisms of both $\mathcal{M}$ and φ. The quotient structure $\overline{\mathcal{M}} = \mathcal{M}/G$ of $\mathcal{M}$ by G often has significantly fewer states than $\mathcal{M}$. Since $\overline{\mathcal{M}}$ can be computed directly from the original P, we avoid the expensive computation of the large structure $\mathcal{M}$. Model checking $\overline{\mathcal{M}} \models \varphi$ is linear in the size of $\overline{\mathcal{M}}$ [8], so this provides significant savings if $\overline{\mathcal{M}}$ is small, i.e., if G is large.

If $\mathcal{M} \not\models f$, then we can search for a model $\mathcal{N}$ related to $\mathcal{M}$ such that $\mathcal{N} \models f$. In this paper we focus on *substructure-repair*: we require $\mathcal{N}$ to be a substructure of $\mathcal{M}$. The key idea behind substructure-repair is to remove execution paths which violate required properties, e.g., paths that lead to a violation of mutual exclusion. We give examples in Section 6 of different properties and substructure repairs with respect to these properties. Substructure-repairs can always repair $\mathcal{M}$ w.r.t. all universal properties (those expressible using universal path quantification [26]).[1]

1.1 Our Contributions

We present a theory of substructures of Kripke structures. Using this theory we establish an evaluation preserving correspondence between certain substructures of the original Kripke structure $\mathcal{M}$ and the substructures of the quotient structure $\overline{\mathcal{M}}$ (this is Theorem 2). This correspondence is a functorial form of bisimilarity between a certain lattice of substructures of $\mathcal{M}$ and the lattice of substructures of $\overline{\mathcal{M}}$. Hence for a given formula φ, substructure-repairs of $\overline{\mathcal{M}}$ with respect to φ can be lifted to substructure-repairs of $\mathcal{M}$ with respect to φ (this is Theorem 3). This correspondence of Kripke substructures lattices is of independent mathematical interest as an example of a monotone Galois connection.

We build on our theory to extend group theoretic model checking to *concurrent program repair*: given a concurrent program P that may not satisfy φ, modify P to produce a program that does satisfy φ. Given P, φ, and a group G that acts on both P and φ, our method directly computes the quotient $\mathcal{M}/G$ (following [18]), then repairs $\mathcal{M}/G$, using the algorithm of [2], and finally, extracts a correct program from the repaired structure.

The rest of the paper proceeds as follows: Section 3 contains the formal definition of Kripke structures and substructures. In Section 4, after briefly recalling group actions, we show how one can use a group to obtain a quotient $\overline{\mathcal{M}}$ of $\mathcal{M}$ and the repair correspondence between $\mathcal{M}$ and $\overline{\mathcal{M}}$. We extend our results to the repair of concurrent programs in Section 5. Section 6 presents some examples. In particular, we show that a structure $\mathcal{M}$ might have a nonempty repair even

---

[1] Existential path properties could be dealt with by first adding sufficient transitions to $\mathcal{M}$ so that the augmented structure now contains the desired paths. One can then perform substructure-repair so that universal path properties are also satisfied.

if the quotient $\overline{\mathcal{M}}$ does not. In Section 7 we examine what classes of Kripke structures and what types of formulae guarantee the existence of quotient based repairs.

2   Related Work

Our work combines model/program repair [5,25,29,32] and symmetry reductions via group actions [7,10,16,18–22]. Le Goues et al. [25] provides a modern introduction to program repair; although their results generally relate to program repair based on the textual representation of the program. Our approach repairs a Kripke structure w.r.t. a computation tree logic (CTL) formula and uses that to repair the corresponding program.

2.1   Computation Tree Logic Repair

Buccafuri et. al. [5] posed the repair problem for CTL and solved it using abductive reasoning to generate repair suggestions that are verified by model checking. Jobstmann et. al. [29] and Staber et. al. [32] used game-based repair methods for programs and circuits, although their method is complete for invariants only.

Chatzieleftheriou et. al. [6] repair abstract structures, using Kripke modal transition systems and 3-valued CTL semantics. Von Essen and Jobstmann [23] present a game-based repair method which attempts to keep the repaired program close to the original faulty program, by also specifying a set of traces that the repair must leave intact.

The work of Attie et al. [2] establishes that repair by abstraction can avoid state explosion. However, repairs of abstracted structures do not always lift to repairs of the original structure. Within networks, Namjoshi and Trefler [30] have shown that a combination of abstraction and group actions can be used to produce smaller structures.

2.2   Group theoretic model checking

Group theoretic approaches to symmetry-reduction in model checking began in 1995 with work by Emerson and a collection of coauthors [7,10,14,16,18–22] compute the quotient $\mathcal{M}/G$ and model check $\mathcal{M}/G$, instead of the original (much larger) structure $\mathcal{M}$. The group theoretic approach to model checking works because $\mathcal{M}$ and $\mathcal{M}/G$ are bisimilar with respect to certain formulae.

A requirement for group theoretic model checking or repair is calculating the group of symmetries in question. We will see that larger groups of symmetries result in smaller quotient models. Clarke et al. [7] showed that calculating the orbit of a group action, a part of model checking via symmetry, is at least as difficult as graph isomorphism. However, in many practical cases concurrent programs have a natural symmetry by swapping certain processes. Hence many concurrent programs have a small known symmetry group in advance. Donaldson and Miller [11] showed that there is a process to build a larger symmetry group for a program from a smaller symmetry group.

A related approach is the use of structural methods to express symmetric designs, e.g., parameterized systems, where processes are all instances of a common template (possibly with a distinguished controller process) [1, 9, 24], and rings of processes, where all communication is between a process and its neighbors in the ring [9, 15, 17].

3   Temporal Logic and Kripke Structures

Computation tree logic (CTL) is a propositional branching-time temporal logic used to model the possible computational branches taken by a system [12, 13]. The semantics of CTL are defined with respect to a Kripke structure.

Definition 1 (Kripke structure). *A **Kripke structure** $\mathcal{M}$ is a tuple (S, S_0, T, L, AP) where S is a finite set of states, $S_0 \subseteq S$ is a set of initial states, $T \subseteq (S \times S)$ is a transition relation, AP is a finite set of atomic propositions, and $L : S \to 2^{AP}$ is a labeling function that associates each state $s \in S$ with a subset of atomic propositions, namely those that hold in state s.*

We require that $\mathcal{M}$ be total: $\forall s \in S, \exists t \in S : (s, t) \in T$, and that $S \neq \emptyset$ implies $S_0 \neq \emptyset$. Also, different states have different labels: $s \neq t \Rightarrow L(s) \neq L(t)$. We admit the empty Kripke structure, i.e., $S = \emptyset$, due to mathematical necessity.

When referring to the constituents of $\mathcal{M} = (S, S_0, T, L, AP)$, we write $\mathcal{M}_S$, $\mathcal{M}_{S_0}$, $\mathcal{M}_T$, $\mathcal{M}_L$, and $\mathcal{M}_{AP}$ respectively. State t is a *successor* of state s in M iff $(s, t) \in T$. We will write $s \to t$ in this case. A path π in $\mathcal{M}$ is a (finite or infinite) sequence of states, $\pi = s_0, s_1, \ldots$, such that $\forall i \geq 0 : (s_i, s_{i+1}) \in T$.

To model the behavior of a concurrent program $P = P_1, \ldots, P_n$, we define a special type of Kripke structure: a *multiprocess Kripke structure* is one in which the set of atomic propositions AP is partitioned into disjoint subsets $AP_1, \ldots, AP_n$, states have the form $(s_1, \ldots, s_n)$ and transitions T are partitioned into disjoint subsets $T_1, \ldots, T_n$. The set of atomic propositions "owned" by P_i is denoted by AP_i: they can only be changed by P_i, but can be read by other processes. The local state of P_i is written as s_i, and is labelled by the subset of AP_i whose propositions are true in s_i. Then, the truth value of $p \in AP_i$ in global state $(s_1, \ldots, s_n)$ is given by its value in local state s_i. T_i gives the transitions of process P_i, which are denoted as $s \xrightarrow{i} t$. For state $s = (s_1, \ldots, s_n)$, define $s{\restriction}i = s_i$, and $s{\downarrow}i = (s_1, \ldots, s_{i-1}, s_{i+1}, \ldots, s_n)$. We then require $s{\downarrow}i = t{\downarrow}i$ for every transition $s \xrightarrow{i} t$, i.e., transitions by P_i do not change atomic propositions of other processes.

A CTL formula φ is evaluated (i.e., is true or false) in a state s of a Kripke structure $\mathcal{M}$ [13]. We write $\mathcal{M}, s \models \varphi$ when s is true in state s of structure $\mathcal{M}$, and write $\mathcal{M} \models \varphi$ to abbreviate $\forall s_0 \in S_0 : \mathcal{M}, s_0 \models \varphi$, i.e., φ holds in all initial states of $\mathcal{M}$. The formal definition of $\models$, proceeds by induction on the structure of CTL formulae [12, 13] and is omitted for space reasons.

Example 1 (Example Box) The "Box" Kripke structure in Figure 1 has 4 states and transitions as
shown. Its set of atomic propositions is empty, and
so all states have empty labels, as indicated by
"()". There is a natural group acting on this Kripke
structure, i.e., the group generated by the action
which exchanges the state **s1** with **s2**, and the state
t1 with **t2**.

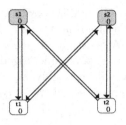

The theory of substructures presented below is
motivated by the concept of a substructure-repair
of a structure $\mathcal{M}$ with respect to a formula f, i.e.,
a substructure $\mathcal{N}$ of $\mathcal{M}$ such that $\mathcal{N} \models f$.

Fig. 1. The Box Kripke
structure.

Definition 2 (Substructure, $\leq$). *Given Kripke structures $\mathcal{M}$ and $\mathcal{N}$, we say
that $\mathcal{N}$ is a* **substructure** *of $\mathcal{M}$, denoted $\mathcal{N} \leq \mathcal{M}$, iff the following all hold:*

1. $\mathcal{N}_S \subseteq \mathcal{M}_S$.
2. $\mathcal{N}_{S_0} = \mathcal{M}_{S_0} \cap \mathcal{M}'_S$.
3. $\mathcal{N}_T \subseteq \mathcal{M}_T$.
4. $\mathcal{N}_{AP} = \mathcal{M}_{AP}$.
5. $\mathcal{N}_L = \mathcal{M}_L \upharpoonright S'$ *(where $\upharpoonright$ denotes domain restriction).*
6. *For all $s \in \mathcal{N}_S$ there is a $t \in \mathcal{N}_S$ such that $(s,t) \in \mathcal{N}_T$, i.e., $\mathcal{N}$ is total.*

For mathematical necessity in what follows, we allow for the 'empty' substructure. We do not, however, accept an empty substructure as a valid repair.
It is immediate that $\leq$ is a reflexive partial order. Lemmas 1 and 2 below imply
that the substructures of $\mathcal{M}$ can be regarded as a lattice, with join and meet
operations as follows.

Lemma 1. *Let $\mathcal{M}$ be a Kripke structure and suppose that $\mathcal{N}$ and $\mathcal{N}'$ are substructures of $\mathcal{M}$. Then*

$$\mathcal{N} \vee \mathcal{N}' = (\mathcal{N}_S \cup \mathcal{N}'_S, \mathcal{N}_{S_0} \cup \mathcal{N}'_{S_0}, \mathcal{N}_T \cup \mathcal{N}'_T, \mathcal{M}_L \upharpoonright (\mathcal{N}_S \cup \mathcal{N}'_S), \mathcal{M}_{AP})$$

is the smallest substructure of $\mathcal{M}$ containing both $\mathcal{N}$ and $\mathcal{N}'$.

Given a nonempty finite set $X = \{X_0, X_1, \ldots, X_n\}$ of substructures of $\mathcal{M}$,
we define the structure $\bigvee X = X_0 \vee X_1 \vee \cdots \vee X_n$.

Lemma 2. *Let $\mathcal{M}$ be a Kripke structure and suppose that $\mathcal{N}$ and $\mathcal{N}'$ are substructures of $\mathcal{M}$. Then there exists a largest substructure of $\mathcal{M}$ contained in both
$\mathcal{N}$ and $\mathcal{N}'$.*

Definition 3 (Join, Meet of Substructures). *Let $\mathcal{N}$ and $\mathcal{N}'$ be two substruc-
tures of $\mathcal{M}$. The* **join** *of $\mathcal{N}$ and $\mathcal{N}'$, written $\mathcal{N} \vee \mathcal{N}'$, is the smallest substructure
of $\mathcal{M}$ containing both $\mathcal{N}$ and $\mathcal{N}'$. The* **meet** *of $\mathcal{N}$ and $\mathcal{N}'$, written $\mathcal{N} \wedge \mathcal{N}'$, is
the largest substructure of $\mathcal{M}$ contained in both $\mathcal{N}$ and $\mathcal{N}'$.*

The join $\mathcal{N} \vee \mathcal{N}'$ has a simple description as given in Lemma 1. However, the meet $\mathcal{N} \wedge \mathcal{N}'$, while well-defined, does not have such a simple description. It is possible that for two substructures $\mathcal{N}$ and $\mathcal{N}'$ of a Kripke structure $\mathcal{M}$, there are no non-empty substructures contained in both $\mathcal{N}$ and $\mathcal{N}'$. Hence the largest substructure contained in both $\mathcal{N}$ and $\mathcal{N}'$ could be empty.

We can now define a lattice of substructures $\Lambda_{\mathcal{M}}$ for a given structure $\mathcal{M}$.

Definition 4 (Lattice of Substructures). *Given a Kripke structure $\mathcal{M}$ the **lattice of substructures of** $\mathcal{M}$ is $\Lambda_{\mathcal{M}} = (\{\mathcal{N} : \mathcal{N}$ is a substructure of $\mathcal{M}\}, \leq)$ where the meet and join in $\Lambda_{\mathcal{M}}$ are as given in Definition 3.*

4   Quotient Structures

We capture the symmetry in a Kripke structure $\mathcal{M}$ with the notion of *state-mapping*: a graph isomorphism on $\mathcal{M}$ which preserves initial states. State-mappings also preserve paths since they are isomorphisms. We ignore for now the labelling function $\mathcal{M}_L$, i.e., which atomic propositions hold in which states, and concern ourselves only with the graph structure of $\mathcal{M}$. Since the atomic proposition labelling obviously affects the truth of CTL formulae in states of $\mathcal{M}$, it must be accounted for. We do this below using the notion of G-invariant CTL formula. Thus, we decompose the symmetry characerization of $\mathcal{M}$ into two separate concerns: the graph structure of $\mathcal{M}$, handled using state-mapping, and the atomic proposition labelling of states of $\mathcal{M}$, handled using G-invariant CTL formulae.

A type of symmetry of particular interest is the symmetry of a multiprocess Kripke structure w.r.t. the process indices $1, \ldots, n$ of the corresponding concurrent program $P_1 \| \cdots \| P_n$, as we illustrate below. Our theory, however, applies to Kripke structures in general.

4.1   Groups Acting on Kripke Structures

Definition 5. *A state-mapping of $\mathcal{M}$ is a graph isomorphism of the state-space of $\mathcal{M}$ such that its restriction to the initial states is also an isomorphism, i.e., takes initial states to initial states. Formally, for a Kripke structure $\mathcal{M}$, a **state-mapping** of $\mathcal{M}$ is a bijection $f : \mathcal{M}_S \to \mathcal{M}_S$ such that:*

- *$f(\mathcal{M}_{S_0}) = \mathcal{M}_{S_0}$;*
- *For states $s, t \in \mathcal{M}_S$ we have that $(s, t) \in \mathcal{M}_T \iff (f(s), f(t)) \in \mathcal{M}_T$.*

The set of all state-mappings of $\mathcal{M}$ forms a group. This means that the composition of any two state-mappings is another state-mapping and for any state-mapping f on $\mathcal{M}$ there is another state-mapping g on $\mathcal{M}$ such that $f(g(s)) = s$ and $g(f(s)) = s$. We refer to the manuscripts by Issacs [27, 28], and Serre [31] for a more in-depth introduction to group theory.

Definition 6 (G-closed). *For a group G of state-mappings of a Kripke structure $\mathcal{M}$, a substructure $\mathcal{N}$ of $\mathcal{M}$ is called **G-closed** if G is a group of state-mappings of $\mathcal{N}$, i.e., for every $g \in G$ and $s \in \mathcal{N}_S$ we have $g(s) \in \mathcal{N}_S$.*

Lemma 3. *Let $\mathcal{M}$ be a Kripke structure and let G be a group of state mappings of $\mathcal{M}$. Let $\mathcal{N}$, $\mathcal{N}'$ be two G-closed substructures of $\mathcal{M}$. Then $\mathcal{N} \vee \mathcal{N}'$ and $\mathcal{N} \wedge \mathcal{N}'$ are both G-closed.*

By Lemma 3, we see that the G-closed substructures of $\mathcal{M}$ form a sublattice of $\Lambda_{\mathcal{M}}$. This is a proper sublattice in that the meet and join operations are the same as those of $\Lambda_{\mathcal{M}}$.

Definition 7 (Lattice of G-closed substructures). *Given a Kripke structure $\mathcal{M}$ and a group G of state mappings of $\mathcal{M}$, the poset of G-closed substructures of $\mathcal{M}$ forms a lattice. We call this the **lattice of G-closed substructures of $\mathcal{M}$** and write it as $\Lambda_{\mathcal{M},G}$.*

Example 1 (Example Box). Let $\mathcal{M}$ be Example Box, i.e., the Kripke structure presented in Figure 1. Let g be the map that simultaneously switches s_1 and s_2, and switches t_1 and t_2, i.e., $g(s_1) = s_2$, $g(s_2) = s_1$, $g(t_1) = t_2$, $g(t_2) = t_1$. Let G be the group consisting of g and the identity map on $\mathcal{M}_S$. We note that G is not the entire group of state-mappings of $\mathcal{M}$. The structure $\mathcal{M}$ has 10 G-closed substructures, including the empty structure. We present some of these structures in Figure 2.

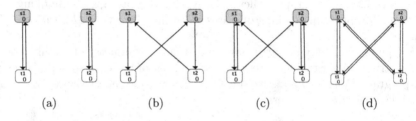

| (a) | (b) | (c) | (d) |

Fig. 2. Four G-closed substructures of Example Box. Where G is the group generated by the simultaneous swapping of indexes of both the s_i and the t_i. Note that each of the structures is a substructure of the substructure to the right. Looking ahead to Definition 10, only the entire structure (d) is G-maximal.

4.2   Constructing the Quotient structure

Given a group G of state-mappings of a structure $\mathcal{M}$, we want to construct a quotient structure $\mathcal{M}/G$. However, as noted, state-mappings do not contain any information about $\mathcal{M}_L$. To remedy this situation, we need a function that assigns a representative to each orbit of G, where for $s \in \mathcal{M}_S$ the orbit of s is $\{g(s) : g \in G\}$.

Definition 8 (Representative map). *Let $\mathcal{M}$ be a Kripke structure and suppose that G is a group of state-mappings of $\mathcal{M}$. A **representative map** of $\mathcal{M}$ with respect to G is a function $\vartheta_G : \mathcal{M}_S \to \mathcal{M}_S$ satisfying the following:*

- For all $s, s' \in \mathcal{M}_S$, if there is some $g \in G$ such that $g(s) = s'$ then $\vartheta_G(s) = \vartheta_G(s')$. (respects orbits)
- For all $s, s' \in \mathcal{M}_S$, if there is no $g \in G$ such that $g(s) = s'$ then $\vartheta_G(s) \neq \vartheta_G(s')$. (separates orbits)
- For all $s \in \mathcal{M}_S$, we have that $\vartheta_G(\vartheta_G(s)) = \vartheta_G(s)$, i.e., each orbit has a stable representative. (idempotent)

We define $\vartheta_G(S) = \{\vartheta_G(s) \mid s \in S\}$.

Definition 9 (Quotient structure). *Given a Kripke structure $\mathcal{M}$, a group G of state-mappings of $\mathcal{M}$, and a representative map ϑ_G of $\mathcal{M}$ with respect to G, we define the **quotient structure** $\overline{\mathcal{M}} = \mathcal{M}/(G, \vartheta_G)$ of $\mathcal{M}$ with respect to G and ϑ_G as follows, where we write $\bar{s}, \bar{t}$ for $\vartheta_G(s), \vartheta_G(t)$, respectively:*

- $\overline{\mathcal{M}}_S = \vartheta_G(\mathcal{M}_S)$, i.e., the states of $\overline{\mathcal{M}}$ are the image under ϑ_G of the states of $\mathcal{M}$.
- $\overline{\mathcal{M}}_T$ consists of all $(\bar{s}, \bar{t})$ such that there exist $s \in \mathcal{M}_S$ with $\vartheta_G(s) = \bar{s}$ and $t \in \mathcal{M}_S$ with $\vartheta_G(t) = \bar{t}$ such that $(s, t) \in \mathcal{M}_T$.
- $\overline{\mathcal{M}}_{S_0} = \vartheta_G(\mathcal{M}_{S_0})$, i.e., the initial states of $\overline{\mathcal{M}}$ are the image under ϑ_G of the initial states of $\mathcal{M}$.
- $\overline{\mathcal{M}}_L(\bar{s}) = \mathcal{M}_L(\bar{s})$, i.e., the label of a state in $\overline{\mathcal{M}}$ is the same as its label in $\mathcal{M}$.
- $\overline{\mathcal{M}}_{AP} = \mathcal{M}_{AP}$, i.e., $\overline{\mathcal{M}}$ has the same atomic propositions as $\mathcal{M}$.

Thus *the states of a quotient structure correspond exactly to the orbits of states of the original structure* under the group of state mappings. For transitions, we have a slightly more subtle correspondence. Consider the following examples:

Example 2. In Figure 3 we demonstrate the correspondence between Kripke structures, G-closed substructures, and their quotients. In the figure, we present a multiprocess Kripke structure $\mathcal{M}$ corresponding to two concurrent processes P_1 (atomic propositions and transitions in blue) and P_2 (atomic propositions and transitions in red). The group G of state mappings swaps the indexes of the processes. This structure has a G-closed substructure $\mathcal{N}$ constructed by removing the 'center' state $\mathbf{u_0}$. Define ϑ_G to take the 'left-most' state in the orbit, i.e., $\vartheta_G(\mathbf{t_1}) = \mathbf{t_0}$, $\vartheta_G(\mathbf{t_5}) = \mathbf{t_2}$, $\vartheta_G(\mathbf{u_0}) = \mathbf{u_0}$, $\vartheta_G(\mathbf{t_6}) = \mathbf{t_3}$, $\vartheta_G(\mathbf{t_4}) = \mathbf{t_4}$. The quotient structure $\mathcal{M}/(G, \vartheta_G)$ appears in the top right. While the quotient structure is isomorphic to a substructure of $\mathcal{M}$, this is not always the case. (See Figure 6 in Example 5 for an example where the quotient gains a new transition.) The quotient structure $\mathcal{N}/(G, \vartheta_G|\mathcal{N}_S)$ appears in the bottom right.

Example 3 (Example Box). Let $\mathcal{M}$ and G be as in Example 1. Let ϑ_G be defined by $\vartheta_G(\mathbf{s_1}) = \vartheta_G(\mathbf{s_2}) = \mathbf{s_1}$ and $\vartheta_G(\mathbf{t_1}) = \vartheta_G(\mathbf{t_2}) = \mathbf{t_1}$. Then the quotient structure $\mathcal{M}/(G, \vartheta_G)$ has exactly 2 states, $\mathbf{s_1}$ and $\mathbf{t_1}$ with transitions $(\mathbf{s_1}, \mathbf{t_1}), (\mathbf{t_1}, \mathbf{s_1})$. Also, the G-closed substructure substructures of $\mathcal{M}$ given in Figure 2 (a), (b), and (c) also map to this quotient structure via $\mathcal{N} \to \mathcal{N}/(G, \vartheta_G)$. Note that the transition $(\mathbf{t_1}, \mathbf{s_1})$ is present in the quotient, but is not present, for example, in the structure of Figure 2 (b). However, the "corresponding" transition $(\mathbf{t_2}, \mathbf{s_1})$ is present in Figure 2 (b).

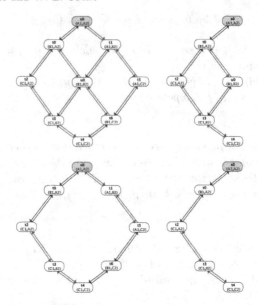

Fig. 3. As discussed in Example 2, we have a Kripke structure in the top left and a G-closed substructure in the bottom left. On the right, we have the quotients of the whole structure (top) and the G-closed substructure (bottom).

In the sequel, we fix a Kripke structure $\mathcal{M}$, a group G of state mappings of $\mathcal{M}$, and a representative map ϑ_G of $\mathcal{M}$ with respect to G.

Example 3 shows that **many G-closed substructures can have the same quotient structure**, and also that, in general, a transition in the quotient may not itself be present in the original structure. We show, however, in Theorem 1 below that a "corresponding" transition is guaranteed to be present in the original structure. These corresponding transitions can be joined into a path which corresponds state-by-state to the path in the quotient. This "path correspondence" is what allows for model checking of $\mathcal{M}$ via model checking of $\overline{\mathcal{M}}$ and is formalized in the following theorem from Emerson and Sistla [18, **3.1**].

Theorem 1 (Path Correspondence Theorem). *There is a bidirectional correspondence between paths of $\mathcal{M}$ and paths of $\overline{\mathcal{M}}$. Formally we have the following:*

1. *If $x = s_0, s_1, s_2, \ldots$ is a path in $\mathcal{M}$, then $\overline{x} = \overline{s_0}, \overline{s_1}, \overline{s_2}, \ldots$ is a path in $\overline{\mathcal{M}}$ where $\overline{s_i} = \vartheta_G(s_i)$.*
2. *If $\overline{x} = \overline{s_0}, \overline{s_1}, \overline{s_2}, \ldots$ is a path in $\overline{\mathcal{M}}$, then for every state $s'_0 \in \mathcal{M}_S$ such that $\vartheta_G(s'_0) = \overline{s_0}$ there is a path $s'_0, s'_1, s'_2, \ldots$ in $\mathcal{M}$ such that $\vartheta_G(s'_i) = \overline{s_i}$.*

We now extend the path correspondence between $\mathcal{M}$ and $\overline{\mathcal{M}}$ to a correspondence between G-closed substructures of $\mathcal{M}$ and substructures of $\overline{\mathcal{M}}$. Define $\Psi : \Lambda_{\mathcal{M},G} \to \Lambda_{\overline{\mathcal{M}}}$, by $\Psi(\mathcal{N}) = \mathcal{N}/(G, \vartheta_G)$, so that Ψ maps a G-closed substructure $\mathcal{N}$ of $\mathcal{M}$ to a corresponding substructure of $\overline{\mathcal{M}}$. We call Ψ the *quotient map*.

Ψ establishes a join-semilattice homomorphism between $\Lambda_{\mathcal{M},G}$ and $\Lambda_{\overline{\mathcal{M}}}$ as we now show in the following series of lemmas.

Lemma 4. *For every substructure $\overline{\mathcal{N}}$ of $\overline{\mathcal{M}}$, there is a G-closed substructure $\mathcal{N}$ of $\mathcal{M}$ such that $\mathcal{N}/(G, \vartheta_G) = \overline{\mathcal{N}}$.*

Lemma 4 establishes that Ψ is surjective. We note that every substructure $\overline{\mathcal{N}}$ of $\overline{\mathcal{M}}$ defines a set of states of $\overline{\mathcal{M}}$, i.e., the orbits of the states in $\overline{\mathcal{N}}$. However, in general, the transitions of $\overline{\mathcal{N}}$ do not uniquely define transitions in $\overline{\mathcal{M}}$.

The next lemma demonstrates that Ψ is a homomorphism of the join-semilattices $\Lambda_{\mathcal{M},G}$ and $\Lambda_{\overline{\mathcal{M}}}$. We note that it is not a homomorphism of the lattices themselves because the meet of two G-closed structures mapping might be empty.

Lemma 5 (Quotient map respects join). *Let $\mathcal{N}, \mathcal{N}' \in \Lambda_{\mathcal{M},G}$. Then*

$$\Psi(\mathcal{N} \vee \mathcal{N}') = \Psi(\mathcal{N}) \vee \Psi(\mathcal{N}').$$

As seen in Example 3, it is possible for multiple G-closed substructures of $\mathcal{M}$ to map to the same substructure of the quotient structure $\overline{\mathcal{M}}$. To obtain a single well-defined preimage for each substructure of the quotient structure, we introduce the concept of G-maximal. Recall that the join of G-closed substructures of $\mathcal{M}$ is G-closed.

Definition 10 (G-maximal). *A G-closed substructure $\mathcal{N}$ of $\mathcal{M}$ is G-maximal if*

$$\mathcal{N} = \bigvee_{\substack{\mathcal{N}' \in \Lambda_{\mathcal{M},G} \\ \mathcal{N}'/(G,\vartheta_G) \leq \mathcal{N}/(G,\vartheta_G)}} \mathcal{N}'.$$

That is, $\mathcal{N}$ is the join of all G-closed substructures of $\mathcal{M}$ whose quotient is a substructure of the quotient of $\mathcal{N}$ itself, namely of $\mathcal{N}/(G, \vartheta_G)$. A G-closed substructure $\mathcal{N}$ fails to be G-maximal exactly when there are states $s, t \in \mathcal{N}$, such that $(s, t) \in \mathcal{N}/(G, \vartheta_G)$, but (s, t) is not in $\mathcal{N}$.

Among all of the G-closed substructures in Figure 2 only the entire structure itself is G-maximal

Lemma 6. *Let $\mathcal{M}', \mathcal{M}''$ be two G-maximal substructures of $\mathcal{M}$. Then $\mathcal{M}' \vee \mathcal{M}''$ is G-maximal and $\mathcal{M}' \wedge \mathcal{M}''$ is G-maximal.*

Lemma 6 allows us to make the following definition.

Definition 11 (G-maximal lattice of substructures). *The set of G-maximal substructures of $\mathcal{M}$ forms a sublattice $\Lambda_{\mathcal{M},G-max}$ of $\Lambda_{\mathcal{M}}$.*

While in general the quotient map from $\Lambda_{\mathcal{M},G}$ to $\Lambda_{\overline{\mathcal{M}}}$ is always surjective, when restricted to $\Lambda_{\mathcal{M},G-max}$, the map is injective and is a lattice isomorphism.

Theorem 2 (G-Maximal Lattice Correspondence). *The restriction of the quotient map Ψ to $\Lambda_{\mathcal{M},G-max}$ is an isomorphism from $\Lambda_{\mathcal{M},G-max}$ to $\Lambda_{\overline{\mathcal{M}}}$, i.e., between the lattice of G-maximal substructures of $\mathcal{M}$ and the lattice of structures of $\overline{\mathcal{M}}$.*

At this point, we would like to remind the reader of the various lattices that we have defined and how they relate to each other:

$$\underbrace{G\text{-maximal substructures}}_{\Lambda_{\mathcal{M},G-max}} \subseteq \underbrace{G\text{-closed substructures}}_{\Lambda_{\mathcal{M},G}} \subseteq \underbrace{\text{All substructures}}_{\Lambda_{\mathcal{M}}}.$$

4.3   Semantic Relationships Between Structures and Quotient Structures

Definition 12. *Let G be a group of state mappings of $\mathcal{M}$. A CTL formula φ is G-**invariant** over $\mathcal{M}$, if for every state s, every $g \in G$, for all maximal propositional subformulae φ' of φ, we have*

$$\mathcal{M}, s \models \varphi' \iff \mathcal{M}, g(s) \models \varphi'.$$

Lemma 7. *If φ is G-invariant, then the valuation of φ in $\overline{\mathcal{M}}$ does not depend on the choice of representative map ϑ_G.*

This allows us to connect semantic statements about $\mathcal{M}$ with semantic statements about $\overline{\mathcal{M}}$ for formulae that are G-invariant. The path correspondence theorem establishes a bisimulation between $\mathcal{M}$ and $\overline{\mathcal{M}}$, in which state s of $\mathcal{M}$ and state $\bar{s}$ of $\overline{\mathcal{M}}$ are bisimilar iff s is in the orbit of $\bar{s}$, i.e., $s = g(\bar{s})$ for some $g \in G$. We call such a bisimulation a G-bisimulation. Hence, G-bisimilar states satisfy the same propositional subformulae of any G-invariant CTL formula φ. A straightforward induction over path length then shows that s and $\bar{s}$ satisfy the same G-invariant CTL formulae:

Corollary 1. *$\mathcal{M} \models \varphi$ iff $\overline{\mathcal{M}} \models \varphi$ for all G invariant CTL formulae φ.*

Lemma 8. *Let $s \in \mathcal{M}_S$, $t \in \overline{\mathcal{M}}_S$. Let φ be a G-invariant CTL formula. If $t = \vartheta_G(s)$, then $\mathcal{M}, s \models \varphi \iff \overline{\mathcal{M}}, t \models \varphi$.*

Section 3 developed the theory of substructures of a Kripke structure. This development was motivated by the following definition and theorem.

Definition 13 (Substructure-Repair). *Given a structure $\mathcal{M}$ and a CTL formula φ, we call a nonempty substructure $\mathcal{N}$ of $\mathcal{M}$ a **substructure-repair** of $\mathcal{M}$ with respect to φ if $\mathcal{N} \models \varphi$.*

If a CTL formula φ is G-invariant, then the lattice correspondence will respect the valuation of φ.

Theorem 3 (Repair Correspondence). *Let φ be a G-invariant CTL formula. Let $\mathcal{N}$ be a non-empty G-closed substructure of $\mathcal{M}$, $s \in \mathcal{N}_S$, and $\overline{\mathcal{N}} = \mathcal{N}/(G, \vartheta_G)$. Then $\mathcal{N}, s \models \varphi \iff \overline{\mathcal{N}}, \vartheta_G(s) \models \varphi$.*

5   Repair of Concurrent Programs

A concurrent program $P = P_1 \parallel \ldots \parallel P_n$ consists of n sequential processes executing in parallel. Each process P_i is a set of i-*actions* (s_i, B, t_i), where s_i, t_i are local states of P_i and B is a guard (a predicate on the global state). We say *action* when we ignore the process id. We assume a given set S_0 of initial states. The program $P_1 \parallel \cdots \parallel P_n$ generates a transition $s \xrightarrow{i} t$ iff P_i contains an action (s_i, B, t_i) such that $s{\restriction}i = s_i$, $t{\restriction}i = t_i$, and $s(B) = true$, where $s(B)$ is the value of guard B in global state s. The transition updates only atomic propositions in AP_i, and so $s{\downarrow}i = t{\downarrow}i$. The state-transition graph of P is the closure of this "transition generation" operation, starting in the initial state set S_0.

Given a concurrent program P and a CTL formula φ, we wish to modify P to produce a repaired program P^r such that $\mathcal{M}' \models \varphi$, where $\mathcal{M}'$ is the state-transition graph of P^r. The modification is "subtractive", that is, it only removes behaviors and does not add them. We assume henceforth that when $\mathcal{M}$ is a multiprocess Kripke structure over process indices $1, \ldots, n$, that the symmetry group G is a subgroup of S_n, the group of permutations on $\{1, \ldots, n\}$.

5.1   Repair of Symmetry-reduced Structures

We first generate the symmetry-reduced state transition graph $\overline{\mathcal{M}}$ of P. We use the algorithm of Emerson and Sistla [18, Figure 1]. We then apply the model repair algorithm of Attie et. al. [2] to $\overline{\mathcal{M}}$, and the specification φ of P. This algorithm is sound and complete, so that if $\overline{\mathcal{M}}$ has some substructure that satisfies φ, then the algorithm will return such a substructure $\overline{\mathcal{N}}$. If not, the algorithm will report that no repair exists. As noted, applying this algorithm to the symmetry-reduced state transition graph is only complete with respect to the symmetric repairs, see Example 6.3.

5.2   Extraction of Concurrent Programs from Symmetry-reduced Structures

We want to extract a repaired concurrent program from $\overline{\mathcal{N}}$ using the projection method of [4,13]: each transition $s \xrightarrow{i} t$ is turned into an i-action $action(s \xrightarrow{i} t) \triangleq (s{\restriction}i, B, t{\restriction}i)$, with guard $B = \{s\}$ where $\{s\} \triangleq \text{``}(\bigwedge_{Q \in \mathcal{N}_L(s)} Q) \wedge (\bigwedge_{Q \notin \mathcal{N}_L(s)} \neg Q)\text{''}$ and Q ranges over AP. When process i is in local state s_i, guard B checks that the current global state is actually s.

A key problem is that the definition of the quotient $\overline{\mathcal{M}}$ allows transitions in which the atomic propositions of more than one process are changed, since any representative of an orbit can be chosen. Hence the repaired $\overline{\mathcal{N}} \preceq \overline{\mathcal{M}}$ can also contain such transitions, e.g., the transition from **S6** to **S1** in Figure 6 below, which we write as $[C_1 \, T_2] \rightarrow [T_1 \, N_2]$. Note that the propositions of both processes 1 and 2 are changed. To generate i-actions, such transitions must be converted so that only the atomic propositions of a single process are modified.

Define a transition from s to t to be *regular* iff it modifies atomic propositions in at most one AP_i, so that $s{\downarrow}i = t{\downarrow}i$ for some process index i, and write the transition as $s \xrightarrow{i} t$. Also define a transition from s to t to be *irregular* iff it is not regular, i.e., it modifies atomic propositions in more than one AP_i, and write the transition as $s \rightarrow t$, with no process index labelling the arrow.

For each irregular transition $s \rightarrow t \in \overline{\mathcal{N}}_T$, there is $g' \in G$ such that $s \rightarrow g'(t)$ is regular. Such an element g' always exists. Let $\overline{s} \rightarrow \overline{t} \in \overline{\mathcal{M}}_T$ for arbitrary $\overline{\mathcal{M}}_T$. By Definition 9, there exists $s \rightarrow t \in \mathcal{M}_T$ such that $\overline{s} = \vartheta_G(s)$ and $\overline{t} = \vartheta_G(t)$. Hence there is some $g \in G$ such that $g(s) = \overline{s}$ since s and $\overline{s}$ are in the same orbit. Since g is a symmetry of $\mathcal{M}$, we have $g(s) \rightarrow g(t) \in \mathcal{M}_T$. Hence $\overline{s} \rightarrow g(t) \in \mathcal{M}_T$. Now $t = h(\overline{t})$ for some $h \in G$ since t and $\overline{t}$ are in the same orbit. Hence $\overline{s} \rightarrow g(h(\overline{t})) \in \mathcal{M}_T$, and so the needed g' is the product of g and h. For example, by applying the permutation of process indices 1, 2 to $[T_1 N_2]$, from the irregular transition $[C_1 T_2] \rightarrow [T_1 N_2]$ we extract the regular transition $[C_1 T_2] \xrightarrow{1} [N_1 T_2]$.

Define $Reg_i(\overline{\mathcal{N}}_T)$ to be the set of regular transitions $s \xrightarrow{i} g(t)$ such that $g \in G$ and $s \rightarrow t \in \overline{\mathcal{N}}_T$. Since g can be the identity element of G, it follows that this account for both regular and irregular transitions in $\overline{\mathcal{N}}_T$. Define $Act_i(\overline{\mathcal{N}}_T) = \{action(s \xrightarrow{i} t) \mid s \xrightarrow{i} t \in Reg_i(\overline{\mathcal{N}}_T)\}$, be the set of actions obtained from $Reg_i(\overline{\mathcal{N}}_T)$.

Define the action of $g \in G$ on syntactic elements of P_i as follows. For local state s_i: $g(s_i) = s_{g(i)}$. For atomic proposition Q_i: $g(Q_i) = Q_{g(i)}$. For guard B, by induction: $g(\neg B) = \neg g(B)$ and $g(B1 \wedge B2) = g(B1) \wedge g(B2)$, with the base case given by $g(Q_i)$ above. For i-action (s_i, B, t_i): $g(s_i, B, t_i) = (g(s_i), g(B), g(t_i))$. That is, we apply g to all process indices in the syntactic element. Now define $Act_i^G(\overline{\mathcal{N}}_T)$, the symmetrization of $Act_i(\overline{\mathcal{N}}_T)$, by $Act_i^G(\overline{\mathcal{N}}_T) = \{g(a) \mid g \in G, a \in Act_j(\overline{\mathcal{N}}_T), g(j) = i\}$. The repaired concurrent program arises from process-wise repair $\overline{P}^G = \overline{P}_1^G \| \cdots \| \overline{P}_n^G$, where $\overline{P}_i^G$ consists of the i-actions in $Act_i^G(\overline{\mathcal{N}}_T)$.

Theorem 4. *Let $\overline{P}^G$ be the concurrent program extracted from $\overline{\mathcal{N}}$ as above, let $\mathcal{N}^p$ be the state transition graph generated by the execution of $\overline{P}^G$, and let $\overline{\mathcal{N}}^p = \mathcal{N}^p/(G, \vartheta_G)$. Then $\mathcal{N}^p$ is G-closed and $\overline{\mathcal{N}}^p = \overline{\mathcal{N}}$.*

Corollary 2. *Let $\overline{P}^G$ be the repaired program and φ the CTL specification that was used to repair $\overline{\mathcal{M}}$, resulting in $\overline{\mathcal{N}}$. Then $\overline{P}^G \models \varphi$.*

6 Examples

6.1 Two process Mutual Exclusion

We consider mutual exclusion for two processes P_1, P_2. Each P_i has three local states: N_i (neutral, computing locally), T_i (trying, has requested critical section entry), and C_i (in the critical region). We start with the "trivial" program P shown in Figure 4 in which all action guards are "true" and apply the program repair algorithm of Section 5 to repair this program w.r.t. the specification $\varphi = AG\neg(C_1 \wedge C_2) \wedge AG((T_1 \vee T_2) \Rightarrow AF(C_1 \vee C_2))$. The first conjunct specifies mutual exclusion of the critical sections (safety) and the second specifies progress: if some process requests the critical section then some process will obtain it (liveness). Figure 5 (left side) shows the Kripke structure $\mathcal{M}$ generated by execution of P. Transitions of P_1, P_2 are shown in blue, red, respectively. Clearly, $\mathcal{M} \not\models \varphi$. Actually both conjuncts are violated: $\mathsf{AG}\neg(C_1 \land C_2)$ due to the reachability of state **S8** from the initial state, and $\mathsf{AG}((T_1 \lor T_2) \Rightarrow \mathsf{AF}(C_1 \lor C_2))$ due to the self loop on state **S4**.

$\mathcal{M}$ has exactly two symmetries: the identity map, and the map that swaps process indices 1 and 2. Our program repair algorithm does not generate $\mathcal{M}$ since $\mathcal{M}$ may be large, and we show $\mathcal{M}$ only for exposition. We generate $\overline{\mathcal{M}} = \mathcal{M}/(G, \vartheta_G)$ directly from P, and we show $\overline{\mathcal{M}}$ in Figure 5 (right side). $\overline{\mathcal{M}}$ has a transition (shown in black) from state **S6** to **S1**, which is the quotient of the transition from **S6** to **S2** in $\mathcal{M}$, i.e., $\vartheta_G(\mathbf{S6}) = \mathbf{S6}$ and $\vartheta_G(\mathbf{S2}) = \mathbf{S1}$ so the edge $(\vartheta_G(\mathbf{S6}), \vartheta_G(\mathbf{S2}))$ occurs in $\overline{\mathcal{M}}$.

Figure 6 shows the repair $\overline{\mathcal{N}}$ of the reduced structure $\overline{\mathcal{M}}$, and the resultant lifting of the repair to $\mathcal{M}$. The deleted transitions and states are shown dashed. Figure 7 shows the repaired concurrent program $\overline{P}^G$ that is extracted from $\overline{\mathcal{N}}$. Note that $\oplus$ means disjunction [3]. By Corollary 2, $\overline{P}^G \models \varphi$.

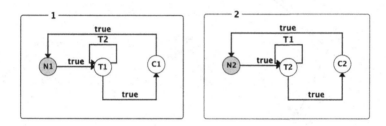

Fig. 4. Initial incorrect mutual exclusion program from Section 6.1.

6.2 n-Process Mutual Exclusion

We now consider mutual exclusion for n-processes. To reduce clutter, we remove the trying **Ti** state, and we give a concrete example for 3 processes — the generalization to n processes is straightforward. Each process can move directly from N to C with the appropriate indexes, i.e., the guards on all actions are initially "true", just like in Figure 4.

We consider the mutual exclusion specification $\bigwedge_{i \neq j} \mathsf{AG}\neg(C_i \land C_j)$. The group of state mappings G for both structure and specification is the full permutation group on the indices $\{1, \ldots, N\}$. For N-processes, we have that the quotient model by the full group of symmetries has $N+1$ states, while the original model would have 2^N states. Figure 8 shows the repair of the quotient $\overline{\mathcal{M}}$ and then

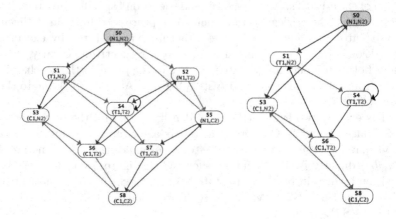

Fig. 5. The original model $\mathcal{M}$ and quotient $\overline{\mathcal{M}} = \mathcal{M}/(G, \vartheta_G)$ for the Kripke structures in Section 6.1.

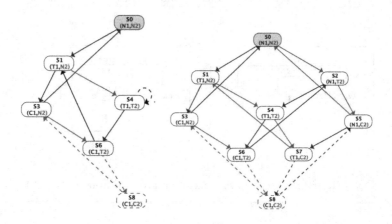

Fig. 6. The repair of $\overline{\mathcal{M}}$ and the lifting of the repair to $\mathcal{M}$ from Section 6.1.

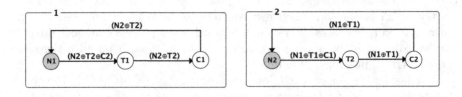

Fig. 7. The mutual exclusion concurrent program extracted from $\mathcal{M}$ in Figure 6.

the lifting of the repair to the original structure $\mathcal{M}$. Figure 9 shows the correct (repaired) program $\overline{P}^G$ that is extracted from the repaired quotient in Figure 8. For N processes, the guard on actions of $\overline{P}_i^G$ is $\bigwedge_{j \neq i} N_j$.

6.3   No G-closed Repairs

Consider the structure in Figure 10 and the formula $f = \mathsf{AXAXAX}P$. The structure $\mathcal{M}$ has a single initial state. Let G be the group consisting of the identity and the map swapping $S1$ and $S2$. In Figure 10 we see that the quotient structure $\mathcal{M}/(G, \vartheta_G)$ does not have any nonempty repairs with respect to f. But, $\mathcal{M}$ does contain a substructure $\mathcal{N}$ that satisfies f.

7   Relative Completeness of Group Theoretic Repair

By the Repair Correspondence (Theorem 3), the existence of a repair $\overline{\mathcal{N}}$ of $\overline{\mathcal{M}}$ implies the existence of a repair $\mathcal{N}$ of $\mathcal{M}$. In Example 6.3, we gave an example in which a repair $\mathcal{N}$ of $\mathcal{M}$ exists but no G-closed repair does, i.e., $\overline{\mathcal{M}}$ has no repairs. This leads us to ask: is there a fragment of CTL, and/or a class of Kripke structures, for which group theoretic repair is complete? That is, the existence of a repair (substructure $\mathcal{N}$ of $\mathcal{M}$ that satisfies φ) implies the existence of a G-closed repair (substructure $\overline{\mathcal{N}}$ of $\overline{\mathcal{M}}$ that satisfies φ).

One attempt to answer this question is to examine formulae and structures where substructures are equivalent to the smallest G-closed substructure containing them. Assume there exists $\mathcal{N} \leq \mathcal{M}$ such that $\mathcal{N} \models \varphi$. Write $\mathcal{N}^G$ for the smallest G-closed structure that contains $\mathcal{N}$. We call $\mathcal{N}^G$ the G-closure of $\mathcal{N}$ in $\mathcal{M}$. If $\mathcal{N}^G$ is bisimilar to $\mathcal{N}$, then $\mathcal{N}^G \models \varphi$ and $\overline{\mathcal{N}^G} \models \varphi$ which is a substructure of $\overline{\mathcal{M}}$.

In [14], Emerson et al., give a criteria for a structure $\mathcal{M}$ to be bisimilar to the symmetrized structure $\mathcal{M}^G$, their criteria is: for any transition $(s, t) \in (\mathcal{M}^G)_T$, there must be a $g \in G$ such that $(s, gt) \in \mathcal{M}_T$. When asking about substructures, it is not clear what criteria on $\mathcal{M}$ is needed to ensure that each substructure $\mathcal{N}$ of $\mathcal{M}$ is bisimilar to $\mathcal{N}^G$.

Definition 14 (G-Repair Complete). *Let $\mathcal{M}$ be a Kripke structure with a group of state mappings G and φ a G-invariant CTL formula. Let $\mathcal{N} \leq \mathcal{M}$ be any repair of $\mathcal{M}$ with respect to φ, and let s be any state in $\mathcal{N}_S$. Then the pair $(\mathcal{M}, \varphi)$ is G-repair complete if: $\mathcal{N}, s \models \varphi$ implies for all $g \in G$, we have $\mathcal{N}^G, g(s) \models \varphi$.*

It is clear that propositional formulae are always G-repair complete. In addition we note the following:

Theorem 5. *If φ and ψ are purely propositional formulae then for any Kripke structure $\mathcal{M}$, the pair $(\mathcal{M}, \mathsf{A}[\varphi \,\mathsf{R}\, \psi])$ is G-repair complete.*

There exists structures $\mathcal{M}$ and φ, ψ formulae such that $(\mathcal{M}, \varphi)$ G-repair complete, and $(\mathcal{M}, \psi)$ G-repair complete, but $(\mathcal{M}, \varphi \wedge \psi)$ not G-repair complete.

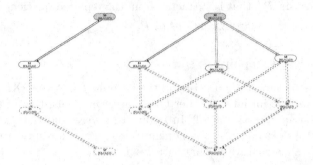

Fig. 8. The Kripke structure defined in Section 6.2. On the left is the repair of $\overline{\mathcal{M}}$ and the lifting of the repair to $\mathcal{M}$ appears on the right.

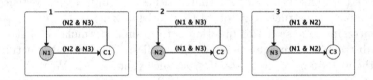

Fig. 9. The repaired program $\overline{P}^G$ for the program in Section 6.2.

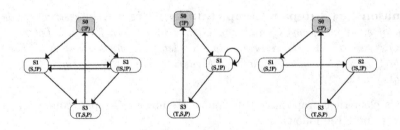

Fig. 10. The models from Section 6.3 from left to right: the model $\mathcal{M}$, the quotient of $\mathcal{M}$, a repair of $\mathcal{M}$ with respect to $f = \mathsf{AXAXAX}P$ that is not G-closed.

Example 4. Let $\mathcal{M}$ be the Kripke structure described by Figure 11. Let G be the group of state mappings generated by swapping $s1$ and $s2$. Let $\varphi = \mathsf{A}[p \, \mathsf{R} \, q]$ and $\psi = \mathsf{AF} \neq q$. The structure $\mathcal{M}$ has a nonempty G-closed repair for φ. Similarly there is a single nonempty G-closed repair for ψ. But $\mathcal{M}$ has no G-closed repairs of $\varphi \wedge \psi$.

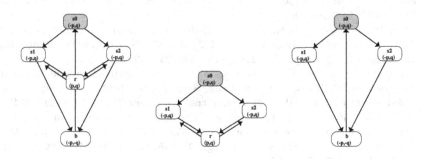

Fig. 11. The Kripke Structure from Example 4 (note that (b, s_0) is a transition, while (b, r) is not) (left), G-closed repairs of $\mathcal{M}$ with respect to the formulae $\mathsf{A}[p \, \mathsf{R} \, q]$ (center), and $\mathsf{AF} \neg q$ (right).

8   Conclusions

We present a theory of how group actions could be used to assist in the repair of a Kripke structure.

We presented a theory for the substructures of a given Kripke structure $\mathcal{M}$, their organization into lattices, and how these substructures interact with a group of state-mappings of $\mathcal{M}$. We show a lattice isomorphism between substructure-repairs of $\overline{\mathcal{M}}$ and G-maximal repairs of $\mathcal{M}$ (Theorem 3: Repair Correspondence). This monotone Galois correspondence guarantees that a repair of $\overline{\mathcal{M}}$ lifts to a repair of $\mathcal{M}$: that is to say that model repairs of $\overline{\mathcal{M}}$ with respect to a G-invariant CTL formula φ lift to model repairs of $\mathcal{M}$ with respect to φ. Using this theory we were able to devise a method for repairing concurrent programs which exploits this correspondence, thus avoiding state explosion. We construct the quotient structure $\overline{\mathcal{M}}$ directly from P without the need to construct the structure $\mathcal{M}$. By our correspondence, repairing $\overline{\mathcal{M}}$ will lift to a repair of the structure $\mathcal{M}$, which in turn corresponds to a repair of P. We show how to construct a repair of P using the repair of $\overline{\mathcal{M}}$ while circumventing the creation of the larger Kripke structure.

A Kripke structure $\mathcal{M}$ that can be repaired with respect to a formulae φ can be repaired via abstraction. However, not every repair of an abstracted structure $\mathcal{N}$ corresponds to a repair of $\mathcal{M}$. In contrast, the structure might not be repairable using the quotient structure, but any repair of the quotient structure will lift to a repair of the original structure.

References

1. Aminof, B., Jacobs, S., Khalimov, A., Rubin, S.: Parameterized model checking of token-passing systems. In: McMillan, K.L., Rival, X. (eds.) Verification, Model Checking, and Abstract Interpretation - 15th International Conference, VMCAI 2014, San Diego, CA, USA, January 19-21, 2014, Proceedings. Lecture Notes in Computer Science, vol. 8318, pp. 262–281. Springer (2014). https://doi.org/10.1007/978-3-642-54013-4_15, https://doi.org/10.1007/978-3-642-54013-4_15

2. Attie, P.C., Dak-Al-Bab, K., Sakr, M.: Model and program repair via SAT solving. ACM Trans. Embed. Comput. Syst. 17(2), 32:1–32:25 (2018). https://doi.org/10.1145/3147426, https://doi.org/10.1145/3147426

3. Attie, P.C., Emerson, E.A.: Synthesis of concurrent systems with many similar processes. ACM Trans. Program. Lang. Syst. 20(1), 51–115 (jan 1998). https://doi.org/10.1145/271510.271519, https://doi.org/10.1145/271510.271519

4. Attie, P.C., Emerson, E.A.: Synthesis of concurrent programs for an atomic read/write model of computation. ACM Trans. Program. Lang. Syst. 23(2), 187–242 (mar 2001). https://doi.org/10.1145/383043.383044, https://doi.org/10.1145/383043.383044

5. Buccafurri, F., Eiter, T., Gottlob, G., Leone, N.: Enhancing model checking in verification by AI techniques. Artif. Intell. 112, 57–104 (1999)

6. Chatzieleftheriou, G., Bonakdarpour, B., Smolka, S., Katsaros, P.: Abstract model repair. In: Goodloe, A., Person, S. (eds.) NASA Formal Methods, Lecture Notes in Computer Science, vol. 7226, pp. 341–355. Springer Berlin Heidelberg, Norfolk, VA, USA (2012)

7. Clarke, E.M., Emerson, E.A., Jha, S., Sistla, A.P.: Symmetry reductions in model checking. In: CAV. Lecture Notes in Computer Science, vol. 1427, pp. 147–158. Springer (1998)

8. Clarke, E.M., Emerson, E.A., Sistla, A.P.: Automatic verification of finite-state concurrent systems using temporal logic specifications. ACM Trans. Program. Lang. Syst. 8(2), 244–263 (1986)

9. Clarke, E.M., Grumberg, O., Jha, S.: Verifying parameterized networks. ACM Trans. Program. Lang. Syst. 19(5), 726–750 (1997). https://doi.org/10.1145/265943.265960, https://doi.org/10.1145/265943.265960

10. Clarke, E.M., Jha, S., Enders, R., Filkorn, T.: Exploiting symmetry in temporal logic model checking. Formal Methods Syst. Des. 9(1/2), 77–104 (1996). https://doi.org/10.1007/BF00625969, https://doi.org/10.1007/BF00625969

11. Donaldson, A.F., Miller, A.: Automatic symmetry detection for model checking using computational group theory. In: International Symposium on Formal Methods. pp. 481–496. Springer (2005)

12. Emerson, E.A.: Temporal and modal logic. In: Handbook of Theoretical Computer Science, Volume B: Formal Models and Sematics (B), pp. 995–1072. Elsevier and MIT Press (1990)

13. Emerson, E.A., Clarke, E.M.: Using branching time temporal logic to synthesize synchronization skeletons. Sci. Comput. Program. 2(3), 241–266 (1982)

14. Emerson, E.A., Havlicek, J., Trefler, R.J.: Virtual symmetry reduction. In: LICS. pp. 121–131. IEEE Computer Society (2000)

15. Emerson, E.A., Kahlon, V.: Parameterized model checking of ring-based message passing systems. In: CSL. Lecture Notes in Computer Science, vol. 3210, pp. 325–339. Springer (2004)

16. Emerson, E.A., Namjoshi, K.S.: Reasoning about rings. In: POPL. pp. 85–94. ACM Press (1995)

17. Emerson, E.A., Namjoshi, K.S.: On reasoning about rings. Int. J. Found. Comput. Sci. **14**(4), 527–550 (2003)

18. Emerson, E.A., Sistla, A.P.: Symmetry and model checking. Formal Methods Syst. Des. **9**(1/2), 105–131 (1996)

19. Emerson, E.A., Sistla, A.P.: Utilizing symmetry when model-checking under fairness assumptions: An automata-theoretic approach. ACM Trans. Program. Lang. Syst. **19**(4), 617–638 (1997)

20. Emerson, E.A., Trefler, R.J.: Model checking real-time properties of symmetric systems. In: MFCS. Lecture Notes in Computer Science, vol. 1450, pp. 427–436. Springer (1998)

21. Emerson, E.A., Trefler, R.J.: From asymmetry to full symmetry: New techniques for symmetry reduction in model checking. In: CHARME. Lecture Notes in Computer Science, vol. 1703, pp. 142–156. Springer (1999)

22. Emerson, E.A., Wahl, T.: Dynamic symmetry reduction. In: TACAS. Lecture Notes in Computer Science, vol. 3440, pp. 382–396. Springer (2005)

23. von Essen, C., Jobstmann, B.: Program repair without regret. Formal Methods Syst. Des. **47**(1), 26–50 (2015). https://doi.org/10.1007/s10703-015-0223-6, https://doi.org/10.1007/s10703-015-0223-6

24. German, S.M., Sistla, A.P.: Reasoning about systems with many processes. J. ACM **39**(3), 675–735 (1992). https://doi.org/10.1145/146637.146681, https://doi.org/10.1145/146637.146681

25. Goues, C.L., Pradel, M., Roychoudhury, A.: Automated program repair. Commun. ACM **62**(12), 56–65 (nov 2019). https://doi.org/10.1145/3318162, https://doi.org/10.1145/3318162

26. Grumberg, O., Long, D.E.: Model checking and modular verification. ACM Trans. Program. Lang. Syst. **16**(3), 843–871 (may 1994). https://doi.org/10.1145/177492.177725, https://doi.org/10.1145/177492.177725

27. Isaacs, I.M.: Finite group theory, vol. 92. American Mathematical Soc. (2008)

28. Isaacs, I.M.: Algebra: a graduate course, vol. 100. American Mathematical Soc. (2009)

29. Jobstmann, B., Griesmayer, A., Bloem, R.: Program repair as a game. In: CAV. pp. 226–238. Springer-Verlag, Berlin, Heidelberg (2005)

30. Namjoshi, K.S., Trefler, R.J.: Uncovering symmetries in irregular process networks. In: International Workshop on Verification, Model Checking, and Abstract Interpretation. pp. 496–514. Springer (2013)

31. Serre, J.P.: Finite groups: an introduction. International Press Somerville, MA (2016)

32. Staber, S., Jobstmann, B., Bloem, R.: Finding and fixing faults. In: CHARME '05. pp. 35–49. Springer-Verlag, Berlin, Heidelberg (2005), springer LNCS no. 3725

Subgame Optimal Strategies in Finite Concurrent Games with Prefix-Independent Objectives

Benjamin Bordais[✉], Patricia Bouyer and Stéphane Le Roux

Université Paris-Saclay, CNRS, ENS Paris-Saclay, LMF, 91190 Gif-sur-Yvette, France
bordais@lsv.fr

Abstract. We investigate concurrent two-player win/lose stochastic games on finite graphs with prefix-independent objectives. We characterize subgame optimal strategies and use this characterization to show various memory transfer results: 1) For a given (prefix-independent) objective, if every game that has a subgame *almost-surely winning* strategy also has a positional one, then every game that has a subgame *optimal* strategy also has a positional one; 2) Assume that the (prefix-independent) objective has a neutral color. If every *turn-based* game that has a subgame almost-surely winning strategy also has a positional one, then every game that has a *finite-choice* (notion to be defined) subgame optimal strategy also has a positional one.
We collect or design examples to show that our results are tight in several ways. We also apply our results to Büchi, co-Büchi, parity, mean-payoff objectives, thus yielding simpler statements.

1 Introduction

Turn-based two-player win/lose (stochastic) games on finite graphs have been intensively studied in the context of model checking in a broad sense [19,1]. These games behave well regarding optimality in various settings. Most importantly for this paper, [14] proved the following results for finite turn-based stochastic games with prefix-independent objectives: (1) every game has deterministic optimal strategies; (2) from every value-1 state, there is an optimal, i.e. almost-surely winning, strategy; (3) if from every value-1 state of every game there is an optimal strategy using some fixed amount of memory, every game has an optimal strategy using this amount of memory. These results are of either of the following generic forms:

- In all games, (from all nice states) there is a nice strategy.
- If from all *nice states* of all games there is a nice strategy, so it is from all *states*.

The concurrent version of these turn-based (stochastic) games has a higher modeling power than the turn-based version: this is really useful in practice since real-world systems are intrinsically concurrent [15]. They are played on a finite graph as follows: at each player state, the two players stochastically and independently choose one among finitely many actions. This yields a Nature state,

© The Author(s) 2023
O. Kupferman and P. Sobocinski (Eds.): FoSSaCS 2023, LNCS 13992, pp. 541–560, 2023.
https://doi.org/10.1007/978-3-031-30829-1_26

which stochastically draws a next player state, from where each player chooses one action again, and so on. Each player state is labelled by a color, and who wins depends on the infinite sequence of colors underlying the (stochastically) generated infinite sequence of player states. Unfortunately, these concurrent games do not behave well in general even for simple winning conditions and simple graph structures, like finite graphs:

- Reachability objectives: there is a game without optimal strategies [13];
- Büchi objectives: there is a game with value 1 while all finite-memory strategies have value 0 [12];
- Co-Büchi objectives: although there are always positional ε-optimal strategies [8], there is a game with optimal strategies but without finite-memory optimal strategies [4];
- Parity [12] and mean-payoff [10] objectives: there is a game with subgame almost-surely-winning strategies, but where all finite-memory strategies have value 0.

In this paper, we focus on concurrent stochastic finite games. Therefore, the generic forms of our results will be more complex, in order to take into account the above-mentioned discrepancies. They will somehow be given as generic statements as follows:

- Every game that has a *nice* strategy also has a *nicer* one.
- If all *special games* that have a nice strategy have a nicer one, so it is for all *games*.

Much of the difficulty consists in fine-tuning the strength of "nice", "nicer" and "special" above. We present below our main contributions on finite two-player win/lose concurrent stochastic games with prefix-independent objectives:

1. We provide a characterization of subgame optimal strategies, which are strategies that are optimal after every history (Theorem 1): a Player A strategy is subgame optimal iff 1) it is locally optimal and 2) for every Player B deterministic strategy, after every history, if the visited states have the same positive value, Player A wins with probability 1. This characterization is used to prove all the results below.
2. We prove memory transfer results from subgame almost-surely winning strategies to subgame optimal strategies:
   (a) Theorem 2: If every game that has a subgame *almost-surely winning* strategy also has a positional one, then every game that has a subgame *optimal* strategy also has a positional one.
   (b) Corollary 1: every Büchi or co-Büchi game that has a subgame optimal strategy has a positional one. (Whereas parity games may require infinite memory [12].)
   Note that the transfer result **2a** can be generalized from positional to finite memory.
3. We say that a strategy has finite-choice, if it uses only finitely many action distributions. Note that finite-memory (resp. deterministic) strategies clearly have finite choice.

(a) Theorem 4: In a given game, if there is a finite-choice optimal strategy, there is a finite-choice *subgame* optimal strategy.

(b) Theorem 5: Assume that the objective has a neutral color. If every *turn-based* game that has a subgame almost-surely winning strategy also has a positional one, then every game that has a *finite-choice* subgame optimal strategy also has a positional one.

(c) Corollary 2: every parity or mean-payoff game that has a finite-memory subgame optimal strategy also has a positional one.

Note that **3a** and **3b** are false if the word finite-choice is removed [4]. The proof of **3b** invokes **3a**. Flavor (and proofs) of **3b** and **2a** are similar, but both premises and conclusions are weakened in **3b**, as emphasized.

Related works. A large part of this paper is dedicated to the extension to concurrent games of the results from [14] regarding the transfer of memory from almost-surely winning strategies to optimal strategies in turn-based games. Note that the proof technique used in [14] is different and could not be adapted to our more general setting. In their proof, both players agree on a preference over Nature states and play according to this preference. In our proof, we slice the graph into value areas (that is, sets of states with the same value), and show that it is sufficient to play an almost-sure winning strategy in each slice; we then glue these (partial) strategies together to get a subgame-optimal strategy over the whole graph.

The slicing technique was already used in the context of concurrent games in [8]. The authors focus on parity objectives and establishes a memory transfer result from limit-sure winning strategies to almost-optimal strategies. As an application, they show that, for co-Büchi objectives, since positional strategies are sufficient to win limit-surely, they also are to win almost-optimally. Their construction made heavy use of the specific nature of parity objectives.

We also mention [6], where the focus is also on concurrent games with prefix-independent objectives. In particular, the authors establish a (very useful) result: if all states have positive values, then they all have value 1. (Note that a strengthening of this result is presented in this paper (Theorem 3), which also appears as an adaptation of a result proved in [14]). This result is then used in another context with non-zero-sum games.

Finally, some recent works on concurrent games have been done in [2,3,4], where the goal is the following: local interactions of the two players in the player state are given by bi-dimensional tables; those tables can be abstracted as *game forms*, where (output) variables are issues of the local interaction (possibly several issues are labelled by the same variable). The goal of this series of works is to give (intrinsic) properties of these game forms, so that, when used in a graph game, the existence of optimal strategies is ensured. For instance, in [3], a property of games forms, called RM, is given, which ensures that, if one only uses RM game forms in a graph, then for every reachability objective, Player A will always have an optimal strategy for that objective. This property is a characterization of well-behaved game forms regarding reachability objectives since every game form which is not RM can be embedded into a (small) graph game in such a way that Player A does not have an optimal strategy. This line of works really differs from the target of the current paper.

Structure of the paper. Section 2 presents notations, Section 3 recalls the notion of game forms, Section 4 introduces our formalism, Section 5 exhibits a necessary and sufficient pair of conditions for subgame optimality, Section 6 shows a memory transfer from subgame almost-surely winning to subgame optimal in concurrent games, and Section 7 adapts the results of the previous section to the case of the existence of a subgame finite-choice strategy.

Detailed proofs and additional formal definitions are available in [5].

2   Preliminaries

Consider a non-empty set Q. We denote by Q^*, Q^+ and Q^ω the set of finite sequences, non-empty finite sequences and infinite sequences of elements of Q respectively. For $n \in \mathbb{N}$, we denote by Q^n (resp. $Q^{\leq n}$) the set of sequences of (resp. at most) n elements of Q. For all $\rho = q_1 \cdots q_n \in Q^n$ and $i \leq n$, we denote by ρ_i the element $q_i \in Q$ and by $\rho_{\leq i} \in Q^i$ the finite sequence $q_1 \cdots q_i$. For a subset $S \subseteq Q$, we denote by $Q^* \cdot S^\omega \subseteq Q^\omega$ the set of infinite paths that eventually settle in S and by $(Q^* \cdot S)^\omega \subseteq Q^\omega$ the set of infinite paths visiting infinitely often the set S.

A *discrete probabilistic distribution* over a non-empty finite set Q is a function $\mu : Q \to [0,1]$ such that $\sum_{x \in Q} \mu(x) = 1$. The *support* $\mathsf{Supp}(\mu)$ of a probabilistic distribution $\mu : Q \to [0,1]$ is the set of non-zeros of the distribution: $\mathsf{Supp}(\mu) = \{q \in Q \mid \mu(q) \in (0,1]\}$. The set of all distributions over Q is denoted $\mathcal{D}(Q)$.

3   Game forms

We recall the definition of game forms – informally, bi-dimensional tables with variables – and of games in normal forms – game forms whose outcomes are values between 0 and 1.

Definition 1 (Game form and game in normal form). *A game form (GF for short) is a tuple $\mathcal{F} = \langle \mathsf{Act}_\mathsf{A}, \mathsf{Act}_\mathsf{B}, \mathsf{O}, \varrho \rangle$ where Act_A (resp. Act_B) is the non-empty finite set of actions available to Player A (resp. B), O is a non-empty set of outcomes, and $\varrho : \mathsf{Act}_\mathsf{A} \times \mathsf{Act}_\mathsf{B} \to \mathsf{O}$ is a function that associates an outcome to each pair of actions. When the set of outcomes O is equal to $[0,1]$, we say that $\mathcal{F}$ is a game in normal form. For a valuation $v \in [0,1]^\mathsf{O}$ of the outcomes, the notation $\langle \mathcal{F}, v \rangle$ refers to the game in normal form $\langle \mathsf{Act}_\mathsf{A}, \mathsf{Act}_\mathsf{B}, [0,1], v \circ \varrho \rangle$.*

We use game forms to represent interactions between two players. The strategies available to Player A (resp. B) are convex combinations of actions given as the rows (resp. columns) of the table. In a game in normal form, Player A tries to maximize the outcome, whereas Player B tries to minimize it.

Definition 2 (Outcome of a game in normal form). *Consider a game in normal form* $\mathcal{F} = \langle \mathsf{Act_A}, \mathsf{Act_B}, [0,1], \varrho \rangle$. *The set* $\mathcal{D}(\mathsf{Act_A})$ *(resp.* $\mathcal{D}(\mathsf{Act_B})$*) is the set of strategies available to Player* A *(resp.* B*). For a pair of strategies* $(\sigma_A, \sigma_B) \in \mathcal{D}(\mathsf{Act_A}) \times \mathcal{D}(\mathsf{Act_B})$, *the outcome* $\mathsf{out}_{\mathcal{F}}(\sigma_A, \sigma_B)$ *in* $\mathcal{F}$ *of the strategies* (σ_A, σ_B) *is defined as:* $\mathsf{out}_{\mathcal{F}}(\sigma_A, \sigma_B) := \sum_{a \in \mathsf{Act_A}} \sum_{b \in \mathsf{Act_B}} \sigma_A(a) \cdot \sigma_B(b) \cdot \varrho(a, b) \in [0, 1]$.

Definition 3 (Value of a game in normal form and optimal strategies). *Consider a game in normal form* $\mathcal{F} = \langle \mathsf{Act_A}, \mathsf{Act_B}, [0,1], \varrho \rangle$ *and a strategy* $\sigma_A \in \mathcal{D}(\mathsf{Act_A})$ *for Player* A. *The* value *of the strategy* σ_A, *denoted* $\mathsf{val}_{\mathcal{F}}(\sigma_A)$ *is equal to:* $\mathsf{val}_{\mathcal{F}}(\sigma_A) := \inf_{\sigma_B \in \mathcal{D}(\mathsf{Act_B})} \mathsf{out}_{\mathcal{F}}(\sigma_A, \sigma_B)$, *and analogously for Player* B, *with a* sup *instead of an* inf. *When* $\sup_{\sigma_A \in \mathcal{D}(\mathsf{Act_A})} \mathsf{val}_{\mathcal{F}}(\sigma_A) = \inf_{\sigma_B \in \mathcal{D}(\mathsf{Act_B})} \mathsf{val}_{\mathcal{F}}(\sigma_B)$, *it defines the* value *of the game* $\mathcal{F}$, *denoted* $\mathsf{val}_{\mathcal{F}}$.

A strategy $\sigma_A \in \mathcal{D}(\mathsf{Act_A})$ *ensuring* $\mathsf{val}_{\mathcal{F}} = \mathsf{val}_{\mathcal{F}}(\sigma_A)$ *is called* optimal. *The set of all optimal strategies for Player* A *is denoted* $\mathsf{Opt_A}(\mathcal{F}) \subseteq \mathcal{D}(\mathsf{Act_A})$, *and analogously for Player* B. *Von Neuman's minimax theorem [20] ensures the existence of optimal strategies (for both players).*

In the following, strategies in games in normal forms will be called GF-strategies, in order not to confuse them with strategies in concurrent (graph) games.

4 Concurrent games and optimal strategies

4.1 Concurrent arenas and strategies

We introduce the definition of concurrent arenas played on a finite graph.

Definition 4 (Finite stochastic concurrent arena). *A colored concurrent arena* $\mathcal{C}$ *is a tuple* $\langle Q, (A_q)_{q \in Q}, (B_q)_{q \in Q}, \mathsf{D}, \delta, \mathsf{dist}, \mathsf{K}, \mathsf{col} \rangle$ *where* Q *is the non-empty finite set of states, for all* $q \in Q$, A_q *(resp.* B_q*) is the non-empty finite set of actions available to Player* A *(resp.* B*) at state* q, D *is the finite set of Nature states,* $\delta : \bigcup_{q \in Q}(\{q\} \times A_q \times B_q) \to \mathsf{D}$ *is the transition function,* $\mathsf{dist} : \mathsf{D} \to \mathcal{D}(Q)$ *is the distribution function. Furthermore,* K *is the non-empty finite set of colors and* $\mathsf{col} : Q \to \mathsf{K}$ *is the coloring function.*

In the following, the arena $\mathcal{C}$ will refer to the tuple $\langle Q, (A_q)_{q \in Q}, (B_q)_{q \in Q}, \mathsf{D}, \delta, \mathsf{dist}, \mathsf{K}, \mathsf{col} \rangle$, unless otherwise stated. A concurrent game is obtained from a concurrent arena by adding a winning condition: the set of infinite paths winning for Player A (and losing for Player B).

Definition 5 (Finite stochastic concurrent game). *A* finite *concurrent game is a pair* $\langle \mathcal{C}, W \rangle$ *where* $\mathcal{C}$ *is a finite concurrent colored arena and* $W \subseteq \mathsf{K}^\omega$ *is Borel. The set* W *is called the* objective, *as it corresponds to the set of colored paths winning for Player* A.

In this paper, we only consider a specific kind of objectives: prefix-independent ones. Informally, they correspond to objectives W such that an infinite path ρ is in W if and only if any of its suffixes is in W. More formally:

Definition 6 (Prefix-independent objectives). *For a non-empty finite set of colors* K *and* $W \subseteq K^\omega$, *W is said to be* prefix-independent *(PI for short) if, for all* $\rho \in K^\omega$ *and* $i \geq 0$, $\rho \in W \Leftrightarrow \rho_{\geq i} \in W$.

In the following, we refer to concurrent games with prefix-independent objectives as PI concurrent games.

Definition 7 (Parity, Büchi, co-Büchi objectives). *Let* $K \subset \mathbb{N}$ *be a finite non-empty set of integers. Consider a concurrent arena* C *with* K *as set of colors. For an infinite path* $\rho \in Q^\omega$, *we denote by* $\mathrm{col}(\rho)_\infty \subseteq \mathbb{N}$ *the set of colors seen infinitely often in* ρ: $\mathrm{col}(\rho)_\infty := \{n \in \mathbb{N} \mid \forall i \in \mathbb{N}, \exists j \geq i, \mathrm{col}(\rho_j) = n\}$. *Then, the* parity *objective w.r.t.* col *is the set* $W^{\mathsf{Parity}}(\mathrm{col}) := \{\rho \in Q^\omega \mid \max \mathrm{col}(\rho)_\infty$ *is even* $\}$. *The* Büchi *(resp.* co-Büchi*) objective correspond to the parity objective with* $K := \{1, 2\}$ *(resp.* $K := \{0, 1\}$*).*

Strategies are then defined as functions that, given the history of the game (i.e. the sequence of states already seen) associate a distribution on the actions available to the Player.

Definition 8 (Strategies). *Consider a concurrent game* C. *A strategy for Player* A *is a function* $\mathsf{s_A} : Q^+ \to \mathcal{D}(A)$ *with* $A := \bigcup_{q \in Q} A_q$ *such that, for all* $\rho = q_0 \cdots q_n \in Q^+$, *we have* $\mathsf{s_A}(\rho) \in \mathcal{D}(A_{q_n})$. *We denote by* S_C^A *the set of all strategies in arena* C *for Player* A. *This is analogous for Player* B.

Given two strategies $\mathsf{s_A}, \mathsf{s_B}$ for both players in an arena C from a starting state q_0, we define in the usual manner the probability $\mathbb{P}_{\mathsf{s_A},\mathsf{s_B}}^{C,q_0}$ of a finite path which induces the probability of an arbitrary Borel subset of infinite paths. Values of strategies and of the game are defined below.

Definition 9 (Value of strategies and of the game). *Let* $\mathcal{G} = \langle C, W \rangle$ *be a PI concurrent game and consider a strategy* $\mathsf{s_A} \in \mathsf{S}_C^A$ *for Player* A. *The function* $\chi_\mathcal{G}[\mathsf{s_A}] : Q \to [0, 1]$ *giving the value of the strategy* $\mathsf{s_A}$ *is such that, for all* $q_0 \in Q$, *we have* $\chi_\mathcal{G}[\mathsf{s_A}](q_0) := \inf_{\mathsf{s_B} \in \mathsf{S}_C^B} \mathbb{P}_{\mathsf{s_A},\mathsf{s_B}}^{C,q_0}[W]$. *The function* $\chi_\mathcal{G}[A] : Q \to [0, 1]$ *giving the value for Player* A: *is such that, for all* $q_0 \in Q$, *we have* $\chi_\mathcal{G}[A](q_0) := \sup_{\mathsf{s_A} \in \mathsf{S}_C^A} \chi_\mathcal{G}[\mathsf{s_A}](q_0)$. *The function* $\chi_\mathcal{G}[B] : Q \to [0, 1]$ *giving the value of the game for Player* B *is defined similarly by reversing the supremum and infimum.*

By Martin's result on the determinacy of Blackwell games [17], for all concurrent games $\mathcal{G} = \langle C, W \rangle$, the value functions for both Players are equal, this defines the value function $\chi_\mathcal{G} : Q \to [0, 1]$ of the game: $\chi_\mathcal{G} := \chi_\mathcal{G}[A] = \chi_\mathcal{G}[B]$.

We define value areas: subsets of states whose values are the same.

Definition 10 (Value area). *In a PI concurrent game* $\mathcal{G}$, $V_\mathcal{G}$ *refers to the set of values appearing in the game:* $V_\mathcal{G} := \{\chi_\mathcal{G}[q] \mid q \in Q\}$. *Furthermore, for all* $u \in V_\mathcal{G}$, $Q_u \subseteq Q$ *refers to the set of states whose values are* u *w.r.t.* $\chi_\mathcal{G}$: $Q_u := \{q \in Q \mid \chi_\mathcal{G}(q) = u\}$.

In concurrent games, game forms appear at each state and describe the interactions of the players at that state. Furthermore, the valuation mapping each state to its value in the game can be lifted, via a convex combination, into a valuation of the Nature states. This, in turn, induces a natural way to define the game in normal form appearing at each state.

Definition 11 (Local interactions, Lifting valuations). *In a PI concurrent game $\mathcal{G}$ where the valuation $\chi_{\mathcal{G}} : Q \to [0,1]$ gives the values of the game, the lift $\nu_{\mathcal{G}} : \mathsf{D} \to [0,1]$ is such that, for all $d \in \mathsf{D}$, we have $\nu_{\mathcal{G}}(d) := \sum_{q \in Q} \chi_{\mathcal{G}}(q) \cdot \mathrm{dist}(d)(q)$ (recall that $\mathrm{dist} : \mathsf{D} \to \mathcal{D}(Q)$ is the distribution function).*

Let $q \in Q$. The local interaction *at state q is the game form $\mathcal{F}_q = \langle A_q, B_q, \mathsf{D}, \delta(q, \cdot, \cdot) \rangle$. The game in normal form at state q is then $\mathcal{F}_q^{\mathsf{nf}} := \langle \mathcal{F}_q, \nu_{\mathcal{G}} \rangle$.*

The values of the game in normal form $\mathcal{F}_q^{\mathsf{nf}}$ and of the state q are equal.

Proposition 1. *In a PI concurrent game $\mathcal{G}$, for all states $q \in Q$, we have $\chi_{\mathcal{G}}(q) = \mathsf{out}_{\mathcal{F}_q^{\mathsf{nf}}}$.*

4.2 More on strategies

In this subsection, we define several kinds of strategies. Let us fix a PI concurrent game $\mathcal{G}$ for the rest of this section. First, we consider optimal strategies, i.e. strategies realizing the value of the game. Strategies are positively-optimal if their values are positive from all states whose value is positive.

Definition 12 ((Positively-) optimal strategies). *A Player A strategy $\mathsf{s}_\mathsf{A} \in \mathsf{S}_\mathcal{C}^\mathsf{A}$ is (resp. positively-) optimal from a state $q \in Q$ if $\chi_{\mathcal{G}}(q) = \chi_{\mathcal{G}}[\mathsf{s}_\mathsf{A}](q)$ (resp. if $\chi_{\mathcal{G}}(q) > 0 \Rightarrow \chi_{\mathcal{G}}[\mathsf{s}_\mathsf{A}](q) > 0$). It is (resp. positively-) optimal if this holds from all states $q \in Q$.*

Note that the definition of optimal strategies we consider is sometimes referred to as uniform optimality, as it holds from every state of the game. However, it does not say anything about what happens once some sequence of states have been seen. We would like now to define a notion of strategy that is optimal from any point that can occur after any finite sequence of states has been seen. This correspond to subgame optimal strategies. To define them, we need to introduce the notion of residual strategy.

Definition 13 (Residual and Subgame Optimal Strategies). *For all finite sequences $\rho \in Q^+$, the residual strategy $\mathsf{s}_\mathsf{A}^\rho$ of a Player A strategy s_A is the strategy $\mathsf{s}_\mathsf{A}^\rho : Q^+ \to \mathcal{D}(A)$ such that, for all $\pi \in Q^+$, we have $\mathsf{s}_\mathsf{A}^\rho(\pi) := \mathsf{s}_\mathsf{A}(\rho \cdot \pi)$.*

The Player A strategy s_A is subgame optimal if, for all $\rho = \rho' \cdot q \in Q^+$, the residual strategy $\mathsf{s}_\mathsf{A}^\rho$ is optimal from q, i.e. $\chi_{\mathcal{G}}[\mathsf{s}_\mathsf{A}^\rho](q) = \chi_{\mathcal{G}}(q)$.

Note that, in particular, subgame optimal strategies are optimal strategies. When such strategies do exist, we want them to be as simple as possible, for instance we want them to be positional, that is that they only depend on the current state of the game.

As for Player B, we will consider a specific kind of strategies, namely deterministic strategies. That is because, once a Player A strategy is fixed we obtain an (infinite) MDP. In such a context, ε-optimal strategies can be chosen among deterministic strategies (see for instance the explanation in [9, Thm. 1]).

Definition 14 (Positional, Deterministic strategies). *A Player* A *strategy* s_A *is positional if, for all states* $q \in Q$ *and paths* $\rho \in Q^+$ *we have* $s_A(\rho \cdot q) = s_A(q)$.

A Player B *strategy* s_B *is deterministic if, for all finite sequences* $\rho \cdot q \in Q^+$, *there exists* $b \in B_q$ *such that* $s_B(\rho \cdot q)(b) = 1$.

5 Necessary and sufficient condition for subgame optimality

In this section, we present a necessary and sufficient pair of conditions for a Player A strategy to be subgame optimal, formally stated in Theorem 1. The arguments given here are somewhat similar to the ones given in Section 4 of [4], which deals with the same question restricted to positional strategies.

The first condition is local: it specifies how a strategy behaves in the games in normal form at each local interaction of the game. As mentioned in Proposition 1, at each state q, the value of the game in normal form $\mathcal{F}_q^{nf}$ is equal to the value of the state q (given by the valuation $\chi_{\mathcal{G}} \in [0,1]^Q$). This suggests that, for all finite sequences of states $\rho \in Q^+$ ending at that state q, the GF-strategy $s_A(\rho)$ needs to be optimal in the game in normal form $\mathcal{F}_q^{nf}$ for the residual strategy s_A^ρ to be optimal from q. Strategies with such a property are called locally optimal. This is a necessary condition for subgame optimality. (However, it is neither a necessary nor a sufficient condition for optimality, as argued in Section 6).

Definition 15 (Locally optimal strategies). *Consider a PI concurrent game* $\mathcal{G}$. *A Player* A *strategy* s_A *is locally optimal if, for all* $\rho = \rho' \cdot q \in Q^+$, *the GF-strategy* $s_A(\rho)$ *is optimal in the game in normal form* $\mathcal{F}_q^{nf}$. *That is – recalling that* $\nu_{\mathcal{G}} \in [0,1]^D$ *lifts the valuation* $\chi_{\mathcal{G}} \in [0,1]^Q$ *to the Nature states – for all* $b \in B_q$: $\chi_{\mathcal{G}}(q) \leq \sum_{a \in A} s_A(\rho)(a) \cdot \nu_{\mathcal{G}} \circ \delta(q,a,b) = \mathsf{out}_{\mathcal{F}_q^{nf}}(s_A(\rho), b)$

Lemma 1. *In a PI concurrent game, subgame optimal strategies are locally optimal.*

Note that this was already shown for positional strategies in [4].

Local optimality does not ensure subgame optimality in general. However, it does ensure that, for all Player B deterministic strategies, the game almost-surely eventually settles in a value area, i.e. in some Q_u for some $u \in V_{\mathcal{G}}$.

Lemma 2. *Consider a PI concurrent game* $\mathcal{G}$ *and a Player* A *locally optimal strategy* s_A. *For all Player* B *deterministic strategies, almost surely the states seen infinitely often have the same value. That is:* $\mathbb{P}^{s_A,s_B}[\bigcup_{u \in V_{\mathcal{G}}} Q^* \cdot (Q_u)^\omega] = 1$.

Proof (Sketch). First, if a state of value 1 is reached (i.e. a state in Q_1), then all states that can be seen with positive probability have value 1 (i.e. are in Q_1), since the strategy s_A is locally optimal. Let now $u \in V_{\mathcal{G}}$ be the highest value in $V_{\mathcal{G}}$ that is not 1 and consider the set of infinite paths such that the set Q_u is seen infinitely often but the game does not settle in it, i.e. the set $(Q^* \cdot (Q \setminus Q_u))^\omega \cap (Q^* \cdot Q_u)^\omega \subseteq Q^\omega$. Since the strategy s_A is locally optimal (and since $V_\mathcal{G}$ is finite), one can show that there is a positive probability $p > 0$ such that, the conditional probability of reaching Q_1 knowing that Q_u is left is at least p. Hence, if Q_u is left infinitely often, almost-surely the set Q_1 is seen (and never left). It follows that the probability of the event $(Q^* \cdot (Q \setminus Q_u))^\omega \cap (Q^* \cdot Q_u)^\omega$ is 0. This implies that, almost-surely, if the set Q_u is seen infinitely often, then at some point it is never left. The same arguments can then be used with the highest value in $V_\mathcal{G}$ that is less than u, etc. Overall, we obtain that, for all $u \in V_\mathcal{G}$, if a set Q_u is seen infinitely often, it is eventually never left almost-surely.

Local optimality ensures that, at each step, the expected values of the states reached does not worsen (and may even improve if Player B does not play optimally). By propagating this property, we obtain that, given a Player A locally optimal strategy and a Player B deterministic strategy, the convex combination of the values u in $V_\mathcal{G}$ weighted by the probability of settling in the value area Q_u, from a state q is at least equal to its value $\chi_\mathcal{G}(q)$. This is stated in Lemma 3 below.

Lemma 3. *For a PI concurrent game $\mathcal{G}$, a Player A locally optimal strategy s_A, a Player B deterministic strategy s_B and a state $q \in Q$: $\chi_\mathcal{G}(q) \leq \sum_{u \in V_\mathcal{G}} u \cdot \mathbb{P}_q^{s_A, s_B}[Q^* \cdot (Q_u)^\omega]$.*

Note that if Player B plays subgame optimally, then this inequality is an equality.

Proof (Sketch). First, let us denote $\mathbb{P}_q^{s_A, s_B}$ by $\mathbb{P}$. It can be shown by induction that, for all $i \in \mathbb{N}^*$, we have the property $\mathcal{P}(i) : \chi_\mathcal{G}(q) \leq \sum_{\pi \cdot q' \in q \cdot Q^i} \chi_\mathcal{G}(q') \cdot \mathbb{P}(\pi \cdot q') = \sum_{u \in V_\mathcal{G} \setminus \{0\}} u \cdot \mathbb{P}[q \cdot Q^{i-1} \cdot Q_u]$. Furthermore, since by Lemma 2, the game almost-surely settles in a value area, it can be shown that for n large enough, the probability of being in Q_u after n steps (i.e. $\mathbb{P}[q \cdot Q^{n-1} \cdot Q_u]$) is arbitrarily close to the probability of eventually settling in Q_u (i.e. $\mathbb{P}[Q^* \cdot (Q_u)^\omega]$). We can then apply $\mathcal{P}(n)$ to obtain the desired inequality.

Recall that we are considering a pair of conditions to characterize that a strategy is subgame optimal. The first condition is local optimality. To summarize, we have seen that the fact that a strategy is locally optimal ensures that, from any state q, the expected values of the value areas where the game settles is at least $\chi_\mathcal{G}(q)$. However, local optimality does not ensure anything as to the probability of W given that the game settles in a specific value area. This is where the second condition comes into play. For the explanations regarding this condition, we will need Lemma 4 below: a consequence of Levy's 0-1 Law.

Lemma 4. *Let $\mathcal{M}$ be a countable Markov chain with a PI objective. If there is a $q \in Q$ such that $\chi_\mathcal{M}(q) < 1$, then $\inf_{q' \in Q} \chi_\mathcal{M}(q') = 0$.*

Consider now a Player A subgame optimal strategy s_A and a Player B deterministic strategy. Let us consider what happens if the game eventually settles in Q_u for some $u \in V_\mathcal{G} \setminus \{0\}$. Assume towards a contradiction that there is a finite path after which the probability of W given that the play eventually settles in Q_u is less than 1. Then, there is a continuation of this path ending in Q_u for which this probability of W is less than u. Indeed, it was shown that, for a PI objective, in a countable Markov chain (which is what we obtain once strategies for both players are fixed), if there is a state with a value less than 1, then the infimum of the values in the Markov chain is 0 (this is what is stated in Lemma 4). Following our above towards-a-contradiction-assumption, there would be a finite path from which the Player A strategy s_A is not optimal. This is in contradiction with the fact that it is subgame optimal. Hence, a second necessary condition – in addition to the local optimality assumption – for subgame optimality is: from all finite paths, for all Player B deterministic strategies, for all positive values $u \in V_{\mathcal{G}} \setminus \{0\}$, the probability of W and eventually settling in Q_u is equal to the probability of eventually settling in Q_u. We obtain the theorem below.

Theorem 1. *Consider a concurrent game $\mathcal{G}$ with a PI objective W and a Player A strategy $s_A \in S_C^A$. The strategy s_A is subgame optimal if and only if:*

- *it is locally optimal;*
- *for all $\rho \in Q^+$, for all Player B deterministic strategies s_B, for all values $u \in V_{\mathcal{G}} \setminus \{0\}$, we have $\mathbb{P}_\rho^{s_A, s_B}[W \cap Q^* \cdot (Q_u)^\omega] = \mathbb{P}_\rho^{s_A, s_B}[Q^* \cdot (Q_u)^\omega]$.*

Proof (Sketch). Lemma 1 states that local optimality is necessary and we have informally argued above why the second condition is also necessary for subgame optimality. As for the fact that they are sufficient conditions, this is a direct consequence of Lemmas 2 and 3 and the fact that deterministic strategies can achieve the same values as arbitrary strategies in MDPs (which we obtain once a Player A strategy is fixed), as cited in Subsection 4.2.

One may ask what happens in the special case where the strategy s_A considered is positional. As mentioned above, such a characterization was already presented in [4][1]. Overall, we obtain a similar result except that the second condition is replaced by what happens in the game restricted to the End Components in the Markov Decision Process induced by the positional strategy s_A.

6   From subgame almost-surely winning to subgame optimality

In [14, Thm. 4.5], the authors have proved a transfer result in PI turn-based games: the amount of memory sufficient to play optimally in every state of value 1 of every game is also sufficient to play optimally in every game. This result does not hold on concurrent games as is. First, although there are always optimal strategies in PI turn-based games (as proved in the same paper [14, Thm. 4.3]), there are PI concurrent games without optimal strategies. Second, infinite memory may be required to play optimally in co-Büchi concurrent games whereas almost-surely winning strategies can be found among positional strategies in a turn-based setting. This can be seen in the game of Figure 1 with $\text{col}(q_0) = 0$ and $\text{col}(q_1) = \text{col}(q_1') = 1$. The green values in the local interaction at state q_0 are the

---

[1] The proof was only presented for a specific class of objectives.

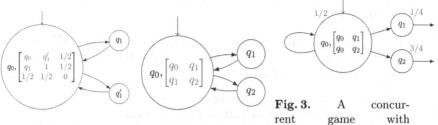

Fig. 1. A co-Büchi game.   **Fig. 2.** A parity game.   **Fig. 3.** A concurrent game with $A_{q_0} = \{a_1, a_2\}$.

values of the game if they are reached (the game ends immediately). If a green value is not reached, the objective of Player A is to see only finitely often states q_1 and q_1'. It has already been argued in [4] that the value of this game is $1/2$ and that there is an optimal strategy for Player A but it requires infinite memory. To play optimally, Player A must play the top row with probability $1 - \varepsilon_k$ and the middle row with probability ε_k for $\varepsilon_k > 0$ that goes (fast) to 0 when k goes to ∞ (where k denotes the number of steps). The ε_k must be chosen so that, if Player B always plays the left column with probability 1, then the state q_1 is seen finitely often with probability 1. Furthermore, as soon as the state q_1' is visited, Player A switches to a positional strategy playing the bottom row with probability ε_k' small enough (where k denotes the number of steps before the state q_1' was seen) and the two top rows with probability $(1 - \varepsilon_k')/2$.

Hence, the transfer of memory from almost-surely winning to optimal does not hold in concurrent games even if it is assumed that optimal strategies exist. However, one can note that although the strategy described above is optimal, it is not subgame optimal. Indeed, when the strategy switches, the value of the residual strategy is $1/2 - \varepsilon_k' < 1/2$. In fact, there is no subgame optimal strategy in that game. Actually, if we assume that, not only optimal but subgame optimal strategies exist, then the transfer of memory will hold.

The aim of this section is twofold: first, we identify a necessary and sufficient condition for the existence of subgame optimal strategies[2]. Second, we establish the above-mentioned memory transfer that relates the amount of memory to play subgame optimally and to be almost-surely winning. Before stating the main theorem of this section, let us first introduce the definition of positionally subgame almost-surely winnable objective, i.e. objectives for which subgame almost-surely winning strategies can be found among positional strategies.

Definition 16 (Positionally subgame almost-surely winnable objective).
Consider a PI objective $W \subseteq K^\omega$. It is said to be a positionally subgame almost-surely winnable objective (PSAW for short) if the following holds: in all concur-

---

[2] Note that this is different from what we did in the previous section: there, we established a necessary and sufficient condition for a specific strategy to be subgame optimal. Here, given a game, we consider necessary and sufficient conditions on the game for the existence of a subgame optimal strategy.

rent games $\mathcal{G} = \langle \mathcal{C}, W \rangle$ where there is a subgame almost-surely winning strategy, there is a positional one.

Theorem 2. *Consider a non-empty finite set of colors K and a PI objective $\emptyset \subsetneq W \subseteq K^\omega$. Consider a concurrent game $\mathcal{G}$ with objective W. Then, the three following assertions are equivalent:*

  a. *there exists a subgame optimal strategy;*
  b. *there exists an optimal strategy that is locally optimal;*
  c. *there exists a positively-optimal strategy that is locally optimal.*

Furthermore, if this holds and if the objective W is PSAW, then there exists a subgame optimal positional strategy.

First, note that the equivalence is stated in terms of existence of strategies, not on the strategies themselves. In particular, any subgame optimal strategy is both optimal and locally optimal, however, an optimal strategy that is locally optimal is not necessarily a subgame optimal strategy. Second, it is straightforward that point *a* implies point *b* (from Theorem 1) and that point *b* implies point *c* (by definition of positively-optimal strategies). In the remainder of this section, we explain informally the constructions leading to the proof of this theorem, i.e. to the proof that point *c* implies point *a*. The transfer of memory is a direct consequence of the way this theorem is proven. We fix a PI concurrent game $\mathcal{G} = \langle \mathcal{C}, W \rangle$ for the rest of the section.

The idea is as follows. As stated in Theorem 1, subgame optimal strategies are locally optimal and win the game almost-surely if the game settles in a value area Q_u for some positive $u \in V_\mathcal{G} \setminus \{0\}$. Our idea is therefore to consider subgame almost-surely winning strategies in the derived game $\mathcal{G}_u$: a "restriction" of the game $\mathcal{G}$ to Q_u (more details will be given later). We can then glue together these subgame almost-surely winning strategies – defined for all $u \in V_\mathcal{G} \setminus \{0\}$ – into a subgame optimal strategy. However, there are some issues:

  1. the state values in the game $\mathcal{G}_u$ should be all equal to 1;
  2. furthermore, there must exist a subgame almost-surely winning strategy in $\mathcal{G}_u$;
  3. this subgame almost-surely winning strategy in $\mathcal{G}_u$ should be locally optimal when considered in the whole game $\mathcal{G}$.

Note that the method we use here is different from what the authors of [14] did to prove the transfer of memory in turn-based games.

Let us first deal with issue 3. One can ensure that the almost-surely winning strategies in the game $\mathcal{G}_u$ are all locally optimal in $\mathcal{G}$ by properly defining the game $\mathcal{G}_u$. More specifically, this is done by enforcing that the only Player A possible strategies in $\mathcal{G}_u$ are locally optimal in the game $\mathcal{G}$. To do so, we construct the game $\mathcal{G}_u$ whose state space is Q_u (plus gadget states) but whose set of actions $A_{\mathcal{F}_q^{nf}}$, at a state $q \in Q_u$, is such that the set of strategies $\mathcal{D}(A_{\mathcal{F}_q^{nf}})$ corresponds exactly to the set of optimal strategies in the original game in normal form $\mathcal{F}_q^{nf}$, while keeping the set of actions $A_{\mathcal{F}_q^{nf}}$ for Player A finite. This is possible thanks

$$\begin{array}{c} a_1 \\ a_2 \end{array} \left[\begin{array}{cc} q_0 & q_1 \\ q_0 & q_2 \end{array} \right] \qquad \begin{array}{c} a_1 \\ a_2 \end{array} \left[\begin{array}{cc} \frac{1}{2} & \frac{1}{4} \\ \frac{1}{2} & \frac{3}{4} \end{array} \right] \qquad \begin{array}{c} \frac{a_1+a_2}{2} \\ a_2 \end{array} \left[\begin{array}{cc} \frac{1}{2} & \frac{1}{2} \\ \frac{1}{2} & \frac{3}{4} \end{array} \right] \qquad \begin{array}{c} \frac{a_1+a_2}{2} \\ a_2 \end{array} \left[\begin{array}{cc} q_0 & \frac{q_1+q_2}{2} \\ q_0 & q_2 \end{array} \right]$$

Fig. 4. The local **Fig. 5.** The game in **Fig. 6.** The game **Fig. 7.** The game interaction $\mathcal{F}_{q_0}$ at normal form $\mathcal{F}_{q_0}^{\mathsf{nf}}$ at $\mathcal{F}_{q_0}^{\mathsf{opt,nf}}$ with only op- form $\mathcal{F}_{q_0}^{\mathsf{opt}}$ with only state q_0. the state q_0. timal strategies. optimal strategies.

to Proposition 2 below: in every game in normal form $\mathcal{F}_q^{\mathsf{nf}}$ at state $q \in Q_u$, there exists a finite set $A_{\mathcal{F}_q^{\mathsf{nf}}}$ of optimal strategies such that the optimal strategies in $\mathcal{F}_q^{\mathsf{nf}}$ are exactly the convex combinations of strategies in $A_{\mathcal{F}_q^{\mathsf{nf}}}$. This is a well known result, argued for instance in [18].

Proposition 2. *Consider a game in normal form* $\mathcal{F}^{\mathsf{nf}} = \langle A, B, [0,1], \delta \rangle$ *with* $|A| = n$ *and* $|B| = k$. *There exists a set* $A_{\mathcal{F}^{\mathsf{nf}}} \subseteq \mathsf{Opt}_A(\mathcal{F}^{\mathsf{nf}})$ *of optimal strategies such that* $|A_{\mathcal{F}^{\mathsf{nf}}}| \leq n + k$ *and* $\mathcal{D}(A_{\mathcal{F}^{\mathsf{nf}}}) = \mathsf{Opt}_A(\mathcal{F}^{\mathsf{nf}})$.

Proof (Sketch). One can write a system of $n + k$ inequalities (with some additional equalities) whose set of solutions is exactly the set of optimal GF-strategies $\mathsf{Opt}_A(\mathcal{F}^{\mathsf{nf}})$. The result then follows from standard system of inequalities arguments as the space of solutions is in fact a polytope with at most $n + k$ vertices.

.

We illustrate this construction: a part of a concurrent game is depicted in Figure 3 and the change of the interaction of the players at state q_0 is depicted in Figures 4, 5, 6 and 7.

The game $\mathcal{G}_u$ has the same objective W as the game $\mathcal{G}$. Since we want all the states to have value 1 in $\mathcal{G}_u$ (recall issue 1), we will build the game $\mathcal{G}_u$ such that any edge leading to a state not in Q_u in $\mathcal{G}$ now leads to a PI concurrent game $\mathcal{G}_W$ (with the same objective W) where all states have value 1. The game $\mathcal{G}_W$ is (for instance) a clique with all colors in K where Player A plays alone.

An illustration of this construction can be found in Figures 8 and 9. The blue dotted arrows are the ones that need to be redirected when the game is changed. With such a definition, we have made some progress w.r.t. the issue 1 cited previously (regarding the values being equal to 1): the values of all states of the game $\mathcal{G}_u$ are positive (for positive u).

Lemma 5. *Consider the game* $\mathcal{G}_u$ *for some positive* $u \in V_{\mathcal{G}} \setminus \{0\}$ *and assume that, in* $\mathcal{G}$, *there exists a positively-optimal strategy that is locally optimal. Then, for all states* q *in* $\mathcal{G}_u$, *the value of the state* q *in* $\mathcal{G}_u$ *is positive:* $\chi_{\mathcal{G}_u}(q) > 0$.

Proof (Sketch). Consider a state $q \in Q_u$ and a Player A locally optimal strategy s_A in $\mathcal{G}$ that is positively-optimal from q. Then, the strategy s_A (restricted to Q_u^+) can be seen as a strategy in $\mathcal{G}_u$ (it has to be defined in $\mathcal{G}_W$, but this can done straightforwardly). Note that this is only possible because the strategy s_A is locally optimal (due to the definition of $\mathcal{G}_u$). For a Player B strategy s_B in $\mathcal{G}_u$, consider what happens with strategies s_A and s_B in both games $\mathcal{G}_u$ and $\mathcal{G}$. Either

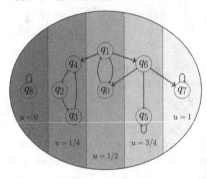 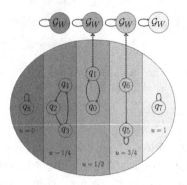

Fig. 8. The depiction of a PI concurrent game with its value areas.

Fig. 9. The PI concurrent game after the modifications described above.

the game stays indefinitely in Q_u, and what happens in $\mathcal{G}_u$ and $\mathcal{G}$ is identical. Or it eventually leaves Q_u, leading to states of value 1 in $\mathcal{G}_u$. Hence, the value of the game $\mathcal{G}_u$ from q with strategies $\mathsf{s_A}$ and $\mathsf{s_B}$ is at least the value of the game $\mathcal{G}$ from q with the same strategies. Thus, the value of the state q is positive in $\mathcal{G}_u$.

As it turns out, Lemma 5 suffices to deal with both issues 1 and 2 at the same time. Indeed, as stated in Theorem 3 below, it is a general result that in a PI concurrent game, if all states have positive values, then all states have value 1 and there is a subgame almost-surely winning strategy.

Theorem 3. *Consider a PI concurrent game $\mathcal{G}$ and assume that all state values are greater than or equal to $c > 0$, i.e. for all $q \in Q$, $\chi_{\mathcal{G}}(q) \geq c$. Then, there is a subgame almost-surely winning strategy in $\mathcal{G}$.*

Remark 1. This theorem can be seen as a strengthening of Theorem 1 from [6]. Indeed, this Theorem 1 states that if all states have positive values, then they all have value 1 (this is then generalized to games with countably-many states). Theorem 3 is stronger since it ensures the existence of (subgame) almost-surely winning strategies. Although a detailed proof is provided in the complete version of this paper [5], note that this theorem was already stated and proven in [14] in the context of PI turn-based games. Nevertheless their arguments could have been used *verbatim* for concurrent games as well. In [5], we give a proof using the same construction (namely, reset strategies) but we argue differently why the construction proves the theorem.

We can now glue together pieces of strategies $\mathsf{s_A^u}$ defined in all games $\mathcal{G}_u$ into a single strategy $\mathsf{s_A}[(\mathsf{s_A^u})_{u \in V_{\mathcal{G}} \setminus \{0\}}]$. Informally, the glued strategy mimics the strategy on Q_u^+ and switches strategy when a value area is left and another one is reached.

Definition 17 (Gluing strategies). *Consider a PI concurrent game $\mathcal{G}$ and for all values $u \in V_{\mathcal{G}} \setminus \{0\}$, a strategy $\mathsf{s_A^u}$ in the game $\mathcal{G}_u$. Then, we glue these* *strategies into the strategy* $s_A[(s_A^u)_{u \in V_{\mathcal{G}} \setminus \{0\}}] : Q^+ \to \mathcal{D}(A)$ *simply written* s_A *such that, for all* ρ *ending at state* $q \in Q$:

$$s_A(\rho) := \begin{cases} s_A^u(\pi) & \text{if } u = \chi_{\mathcal{G}}(q) > 0 \text{ for } \pi \text{ the longest suffix of } \rho \text{ in } Q_u^+ \\ \text{is arbitrary} & \text{if } \chi_{\mathcal{G}}(q) = 0 \end{cases}$$

As stated in Lemma 6 below, the construction described in Definition 17 transfers almost-surely winning strategies in $\mathcal{G}_u$ into a subgame optimal strategy in $\mathcal{G}$.

Lemma 6. *For all* $u \in V_{\mathcal{G}} \setminus \{0\}$, *let* s_A^u *be a subgame almost-surely winning strategy in* $\mathcal{G}_u$. *The glued strategy* $s_A[(s_A^u)_{u \in V_{\mathcal{G}} \setminus \{0\}}]$, *denoted* s_A, *is subgame optimal in* $\mathcal{G}$.

Proof (Sketch). We apply Theorem 1. First, the strategy s_A is locally optimal in all Q_u for $u > 0$ by the strategy restriction done to define the game $\mathcal{G}_u$ (only optimal strategies are considered at each game in normal form $\mathcal{F}_q^{nf}$ at states $q \in Q_u$). Furthermore, any strategy is optimal in a game in normal form of value 0 (which is the case of the game in normal forms of states in Q_0). Second, if the game eventually settles in a value area Q_u for some $u > 0$, from then on the strategy s_A mimics the strategy s_A^u, which is subgame almost-surely winning in $\mathcal{G}_u$. Hence, the probability of W given that the game eventually settles in Q_u is 1. This holds for all $u \in V_{\mathcal{G}} \setminus \{0\}$, so the second condition of Theorem 1 holds.

We now have all the ingredients to prove Theorem 2.

Proof (Of Theorem 2). We consider the PI concurrent game $\mathcal{G}$ and assume that there is a positively-optimal strategy that is locally optimal. Then, by Lemma 5, for all positive values $u \in V_{\mathcal{G}} \setminus \{0\}$, all states in $\mathcal{G}_u$ have positive values. It follows, by Theorem 3, that there exists a subgame almost-surely winning strategy in every game $\mathcal{G}_u$ for $u \in V_{\mathcal{G}} \setminus \{0\}$. We then obtain a subgame optimal strategy by gluing these strategies together, given by Lemma 6.

The second part of the theorem, dealing with transfer of positionality from subgame almost-surely winning to subgame optimal follows from the fact that if all strategies s_A^u are positional for all $u \in V_{\mathcal{G}} \setminus \{0\}$, then so is the glued strategy $s_A[(s_A^u)_{u \in V_{\mathcal{G}} \setminus \{0\}}]$.

We now apply the result of Theorem 2 to two specific classes of objectives: Büchi and co-Büchi objectives. Note that this result is already known for Büchi objectives, proven in [4].

Corollary 1. *Consider a concurrent game with a Büchi (resp. co-Büchi) objective and assume that there is a positively-optimal strategy that is locally optimal. Then there is a subgame optimal positional strategy.*

Note that it is also possible to prove a memory transfer from subgame almost-surely winning to subgame optimal for an arbitrary memory skeleton, instead of only positional strategies. This adds only a few minor difficulties.

Application to the turn-based setting. The aim of Section 6 was to extend an already existing result on turn-based games in the context of concurrent games. This required an adaptation of the assumptions. However, it is in fact possible to retrieve the original result on turn-based games from Theorem 2 in a fairly straightforward manner. It amounts to show that, in all finite turn-based games $\mathcal{G}$, for all values $u \in V_\mathcal{G} \setminus \{0\}$, there is a locally optimal strategy that is positively-optimal from all states in Q_u.

7   Finite-choice strategies

In this section, we introduce a new kind of strategies, namely finite-choice strategies. Let us first motivate why we consider such strategies. Consider again the co-Büchi game of Figure 1. Recall that the optimal strategy we described first plays the top row with increasing probability and the middle row with decreasing probability and then, once Player B plays the second column, switches to a positional strategy playing the bottom row with positive, yet small enough probability. Note that switching strategy is essential. Indeed, if Player A does not switch, Player B could at some point opt for the middle column and see indefinitely the state q'_1 with very high probability. In fact, what happens in that case is rather counter-intuitive: once Player B switches, there is infinitely often a positive probability to reach the outcome of value 1. However, the probability to ever reaching this outcome can be arbitrarily small, if Player B waits long enough before playing the middle row. This happens because the probability ε_k to visit that outcome goes (fast) to 0 when k goes to ∞. In fact, such an optimal strategy has "infinite choice" in the sense that it may prescribe infinitely many different probability distribution.

In this section, we consider *finite-choice strategies*, i.e. strategies that can use only finitely many GF-strategies at each state.

Definition 18 (Finite-choice strategy). *Let $\mathcal{G}$ be a concurrent game. A Player* A *strategy* $\mathsf{s_A}$ *in* $\mathcal{G}$ *has* finite choice *if, for all* $q \in Q$, *the set* $S_q^{\mathsf{s_A}} := \{\mathsf{s_A}(\rho \cdot q) \mid \rho \in Q^+\} \subseteq \mathcal{D}(A_q)$ *is finite.*

Note that positional (even finite-memory) and deterministic strategies are examples of finite-choice strategies.

Interestingly, we can link finite-choice strategies with the existence of subgame optimal strategies. In general it does not hold that if there are optimal strategies, then there exists subgame optimal strategies (as exemplified in the game of Figure 1). However, in Theorem 4 below, we state that if we additionally assume that the optimal strategy considered has finite choice, then there is a subgame optimal strategy (that has also finite choice).

Theorem 4. *Consider a PI concurrent game* $\mathcal{G}$. *If there is a finite-choice optimal strategy, then there is a finite-choice subgame optimal strategy.*

Proof (Sketch). Consider such an optimal finite-choice strategy $\mathsf{s_A}$. In particular, note that there is a constant $c > 0$ such that for all $\rho \cdot q \in Q^+$, for all $a \in A_q$ we have: $s_A(\rho \cdot q)(q) > 0 \Rightarrow s_A(\rho \cdot q)(q) \geq c$. We build a subgame optimal strategy s'_A in the following way: for all $\rho = \rho' \cdot q \in Q^+$, if the residual strategy s_A^ρ is optimal, then $s'_A(\rho) := s_A(\rho)$, otherwise $s'_A(\rho) := s_A(q)$ (i.e. we reset the strategy). Straightforwardly, the strategy s'_A has finite choice. We want to apply Theorem 1 to prove that it is subgame optimal. One can see that it is locally optimal (by the criterion chosen for resetting the strategy). Consider now some $\rho \in Q^+$ ending at state $q \in Q$ and another state $q' \in Q$. Assume that the residual strategy s_A^ρ is optimal but that the residual strategy $s_A^{\rho \cdot q'}$ is not. Then, similarly to why local optimality is necessary for subgame optimality (see Proposition 1), one can show that any Player B action b leading to q' from ρ with positive probability is such that $\chi_{\mathcal{G}}(q) < \mathrm{out}_{\mathcal{F}_q^{nf}}(s_A(\rho), b)$. Hence, there is positive probability from ρ, if Player B opts for the action b, to reach a state of value different from $u = \chi_{\mathcal{G}}(q)$. And if this happens infinitely often, a state of value different from u will be reached almost-surely[3]. In other words, if a value area is never left, almost-surely, the strategy s'_A only resets finitely often.

Consider now some $\rho \in Q^+$, a Player B deterministic strategy s_B and a value $u \in V_{\mathcal{G}} \setminus \{0\}$. From what we argued above, the probability of the event $Q^* \cdot (Q_u)^\omega$ (resp. $W \cap Q^* \cdot (Q_u)^\omega$) is the same if we intersect it with the fact that the strategy s'_A only resets finitely often. Furthermore, if the strategy does not reset anymore from some point on, and all states have the same value $u > 0$, then it follows that the probability of W is 1 (since W is PI). We can then conclude by applying Theorem 1.

Finite-choice strategies are interesting for another reason. In the previous section, we applied the memory transfer from Theorem 2 to the Büchi and co-Büchi objectives. We did not apply it to other objectives – in particular to the parity objective. Indeed, in general, contrary to the case of turn-based games, infinite-memory is necessary to be almost-surely winning in parity games. This happens in Figure 2 (already described in [12]) where the objective of Player A is to see q_1 infinitely often, while seeing q_2 only finitely often. Let us describe a Player A subgame almost-surely winning strategy. The top row is played with probability $1 - \varepsilon_k$ and the bottom row is played with probability $\varepsilon_k > 0$ with ε_k going to 0 when k goes to ∞ (the (ε_k) used in the game in Figure 1 works here as well) where k denotes the number of times the state q_0 is seen. Such a strategy is subgame almost-surely winning and does not have finite choice. In fact, it can be shown that all Player A finite-choice strategies have value 0 in that game.

Interestingly, the transfer of memory of Theorem 2 is adapted in Theorem 5 with the memory that is sufficient in turn-based games – for those PI objectives that have a "neutral color"– if we additionally assume that the subgame optimal strategy considered has finite choice. First, let us define what is meant by "neutral color", then we define the turn-based version of PSAW.

---

[3] This holds because the strategy s_A has finite choice: the probability to see a state of different value is bounded below by the product of c and the smallest positive probability among all Nature states.

Definition 19 (Objective with a neutral color). *Consider a set of colors* K *and a PI objective* $W \subseteq \mathsf{K}^\omega$. *It has a* neutral color *if there is some (neutral) color* $k \in \mathsf{K}$ *such that, for all* $\rho = \rho_0 \cdot \rho_1 \cdots \in \mathsf{K}^\omega$, *we have* $\rho \in W \Leftrightarrow \rho_0 \cdot k \cdot \rho_1 \cdot k \cdots \in W$.

Definition 20 (PASW objective in turn-based games). *Consider a PI objective* $W \subseteq \mathsf{K}^\omega$. *It is* positionally subgame almost-surely winnable in turn-based games *(PSAWT for short) if in all turn-based games* $\mathcal{G} = \langle \mathcal{C}, W \rangle$ *where there is a subgame almost-surely winning strategy, there is a positional one.*

Theorem 5. *Consider a PSAWT PI objective* $W \subseteq \mathsf{K}^\omega$ *with a neutral color and a concurrent game* $\mathcal{G}$ *with objective* W. *Assume there is a subgame optimal strategy that has finite choice. Then, there is a positional one.*

Proof (Sketch). A finite-choice strategy $\mathsf{s_A}$ plays only among a finite number of GF-strategies at each state. The idea is therefore to modify the game $\mathcal{G}_u$ of the previous subsection into a game $\mathcal{G}'_u$ by transforming it into a (finite) turn-based game. At each state, Player A chooses first her GF-strategy. She can choose among only a finite number of them: she has at her disposal, at a state q, only optimal GF-strategies in $S_q^{\mathsf{s_A}}$ (recall Definition 18). We consider the objective W in that new arena where Player B states are colored with a neutral color. The existence, in $\mathcal{G}$, of a subgame optimal strategy that has finite choice ensures that all states in $\mathcal{G}'_u$ have positive values. We can then conclude as for Theorem 2: a subgame optimal strategy can be obtained by gluing together subgame almost-surely winning strategies in the (turn-based) games $\mathcal{G}'_u$ (that can be chosen positional by assumption).

As an application, one can realize that the parity, mean-payoff and generalized Büchi objectives have a neutral color and are PSAWT ([11,16,7]). Hence, for these objectives, if there exists an optimal strategy that has finite choice, then there is one that is positional.

Corollary 2. *Consider a concurrent game* $\mathcal{G}$ *with a parity (resp. mean-payoff, resp. generalized Büchi) objective. Assume that there is an optimal strategy that has finite choice in* $\mathcal{G}$. *Then, there is a positional one.*

References

1. Roderick Bloem, Krishnendu Chatterjee, and Barbara Jobstmann. *Handbook of Model Checking*, chapter Graph games and reactive synthesis, pages 921–962. Springer, 2018.
2. Benjamin Bordais, Patricia Bouyer, and Stéphane Le Roux. From local to global determinacy in concurrent graph games. In Mikolaj Bojanczyk and Chandra Chekuri, editors, *41st IARCS Annual Conference on Foundations of Software Technology and Theoretical Computer Science, FSTTCS 2021, December 15-17, 2021, Virtual Conference*, volume 213 of *LIPIcs*, pages 41:1–41:14. Schloss Dagstuhl - Leibniz-Zentrum für Informatik, 2021.

3. Benjamin Bordais, Patricia Bouyer, and Stéphane Le Roux. Optimal strategies in concurrent reachability games. In Florin Manea and Alex Simpson, editors, *30th EACSL Annual Conference on Computer Science Logic, CSL 2022, February 14-19, 2022, Göttingen, Germany (Virtual Conference)*, volume 216 of *LIPIcs*, pages 7:1–7:17. Schloss Dagstuhl - Leibniz-Zentrum für Informatik, 2022.

4. Benjamin Bordais, Patricia Bouyer, and Stéphane Le Roux. Playing (almost-)optimally in concurrent büchi and co-büchi games. *CoRR*, abs/2203.06966, 2022.

5. Benjamin Bordais, Patricia Bouyer, and Stéphane Le Roux. Sub-game optimal strategies in concurrent games with prefix-independent objectives. *CoRR*, abs/2301.10697, 2023.

6. Krishnendu Chatterjee. Concurrent games with tail objectives. *Theor. Comput. Sci.*, 388(1-3):181–198, 2007.

7. Krishnendu Chatterjee, Luca de Alfaro, and Thomas A. Henzinger. Trading memory for randomness. In *1st International Conference on Quantitative Evaluation of Systems (QEST 2004), 27-30 September 2004, Enschede, The Netherlands*, pages 206–217. IEEE Computer Society, 2004.

8. Krishnendu Chatterjee, Luca de Alfaro, and Thomas A. Henzinger. The complexity of quantitative concurrent parity games. In *Proceedings of the Seventeenth Annual ACM-SIAM Symposium on Discrete Algorithms, SODA 2006, Miami, Florida, USA, January 22-26, 2006*, pages 678–687. ACM Press, 2006.

9. Krishnendu Chatterjee, Laurent Doyen, Hugo Gimbert, and Thomas A. Henzinger. Randomness for free. *Inf. Comput.*, 245:3–16, 2015.

10. Krishnendu Chatterjee and Rasmus Ibsen-Jensen. Qualitative analysis of concurrent mean-payoff games. *Inf. Comput.*, 242:2–24, 2015.

11. Krishnendu Chatterjee, Marcin Jurdzinski, and Thomas A. Henzinger. Quantitative stochastic parity games. In J. Ian Munro, editor, *Proceedings of the Fifteenth Annual ACM-SIAM Symposium on Discrete Algorithms, SODA 2004, New Orleans, Louisiana, USA, January 11-14, 2004*, pages 121–130. SIAM, 2004.

12. Luca de Alfaro and Thomas A. Henzinger. Concurrent omega-regular games. In *15th Annual IEEE Symposium on Logic in Computer Science, Santa Barbara, California, USA, June 26-29, 2000*, pages 141–154. IEEE Computer Society, 2000.

13. Hugh Everett. Recursive games. *Annals of Mathematics Studies – Contributions to the Theory of Games*, 3:67–78, 1957.

14. Hugo Gimbert and Florian Horn. Solving simple stochastic tail games. In Moses Charikar, editor, *Proceedings of the Twenty-First Annual ACM-SIAM Symposium on Discrete Algorithms, SODA 2010, Austin, Texas, USA, January 17-19, 2010*, pages 847–862. SIAM, 2010.

15. Marta Kwiatkowska, Gethin Norman, Dave Parker, and Gabriel Santos. Automatic verification of concurrent stochastic systems. *Formal Methods in System Design*, 58:188–250, 2021.

16. Thomas M Liggett and Steven A Lippman. Stochastic games with perfect information and time average payoff. *Siam Review*, 11(4):604–607, 1969.

17. Donald A. Martin. The determinacy of blackwell games. *The Journal of Symbolic Logic*, 63(4):1565–1581, 1998.

18. Lloyd S Shapley and RN Snow. Basic solutions of discrete games. *Contributions to the Theory of Games*, 1(24):27–27, 1950.

19. Wolfgang Thomas. Infinite games and verification. In *Proc. 14th International Conference on Computer Aided Verification (CAV'02)*, volume 2404 of *Lecture Notes in Computer Science*, pages 58–64. Springer, 2002. Invited Tutorial.

20. John von Neumann and Oskar Morgenstern. *Theory of Games and Economic Behavior*. Princeton Univ. Press, Princeton, 1944.

Author Index

Printed in the United States
by Baker & Taylor Publisher Services